THE OXFORD HANDBOOK OF

ASSESSMENT POLICY AND PRACTICE IN MUSIC EDUCATION, VOLUME 1

THE OXFORD HANDBOOK OF

ASSESSMENT POLICY AND PRACTICE IN MUSIC EDUCATION, VOLUME 1

Edited by
TIMOTHY S. BROPHY

OXFORD
UNIVERSITY PRESS

OXFORD
UNIVERSITY PRESS

Oxford University Press is a department of the University of Oxford.
It furthers the University's objective of excellence in research, scholarship,
and education by publishing worldwide. Oxford is a registered trade mark of
Oxford University Press in the UK and certain other countries.

Published in the United States of America by Oxford University Press
198 Madison Avenue, New York, NY 10016, United States of America.

Library of Congress Cataloging-in-Publication Data
Names: Brophy, Timothy S., 1952–
Title: The Oxford handbook of assessment policy and practice in music education /
edited by Timothy S. Brophy.
Description: New York, NY : Oxford University Press, [2019] |
Series: Oxford handbooks | Includes bibliographical references and index.
Identifiers: LCCN 2018020428 | ISBN 9780190248093 (vol 1 : cloth) |
ISBN 9780190248123 (Oxford Handbooks Online) | ISBN 9780190248130 (vol 2 : cloth) |
ISBN 9780190248161 (Oxford Handbooks Online)
Subjects: LCSH: Music—Instruction and study—Evaluation.
Classification: LCC MT1 .O92 2019 | DDC 780.71—dc23
LC record available at https://lccn.loc.gov/2018020428

1 3 5 7 9 8 6 4 2
Printed by Sheridan Books, Inc., United States of America

This handbook is dedicated to my wife, Frances

CONTENTS

National Perspectives

PART II MEASUREMENT

Theoretical Foundations

PART III ASSESSMENT IN HIGHER MUSIC EDUCATION

PART IV MUSIC TEACHER EVALUATION

LIST OF CONTRIBUTORS

James R. Austin, Professor of Music Education, University of Colorado, Boulder

Timothy S. Brophy, Professor of Music Education and Director of Institutional Assessment, University of Florida

Frederick Burrack, Director of Assessment, Professor of Music Education, and Chair of Graduate Studies, Kansas State University

Hsiao-Fen Chen, Professor of Piano and Music Education, National Taiwan Normal University

Jian-Jun Chen-Edmund, Assistant Professor of Music Education, University of Minnesota Duluth

Ming-Jen Chuang, Professor of Music and Music Education, National Taichung University of Education

Richard Colwell, Professor Emeritus, University of Illinois Urbana-Champaign

Dru Davison, Fine Arts Advisor, Shelby County Schools

Dario De Cicco, Professor of Music Pedagogy, Conservatory of Music of Cuneo

Luciana Del-Ben, Associate Professor of Music Education, Federal University of Rio Grande do Sul

Charles A. DePascale, Senior Associate, National Center for the Improvement of Educational Assessment

Paul F. Doerksen, Associate Professor of Music Education and Chair of Music Education and Music Therapy, Duquesne University

David C. Edmund, Associate Professor and Chair of Music Education, University of Minnesota Duluth

Martin Fautley, Professor of Education, Birmingham City University

Sergio Figueiredo, Associate Professor, State University of Santa Catarina

Ryan A. Fisher, Associate Professor of Music Education and Associate Dean of the College of Communication and Fine Arts, University of Memphis

Ana Lucía Frega, Profesora Catedrática, Fundación Universidad Argentina de la Empresa (UADE)

Laura Goe, Research Scientist, Educational Testing Service (ETS)

Dilek Göktürk-Cary, Independent Researcher, Music Education, Freelance Writer

Demaris Hansen, Professor of Music Education, The Hartt School, University of Hartford

Alena V. Holmes, Associate Professor and Coordinator of Music Education, University of Wisconsin-Whitewater

René Human, Lecturer in Music and Director of Africa Music and Choral Trust, University of Pretoria, South Africa

Suzanne Lane, Professor, University of Pittsburgh

Don Lebler, Professor, Queensland Conservatorium Griffith University

Andreas Lehmann-Wermser, Director of the Institute for Music Education Research, Hannover University of Music, Drama and Media

Wei Shin Leong, Assistant Dean of Degree and Student Life, National Institute of Education, Nanyang Technological University

Ramiro Limongi, Associate Professor of Music Analysis, National University for the Arts, Buenos Aires, Argentina

Sheau-Yuh Lin, Professor of Department of Music and Dean of College of Humanities and Arts, University of Taipei

Roger Mantie, Associate Professor, University of Toronto Scarborough

Jennifer S. McDonel, Assistant Professor of Music and Director of Music Education, Radford University

Gary E. McPherson, Ormond Professor of Music, University of Melbourne Australia

Glenn E. Nierman, Glenn Korff Professor of Music, University of Nebraska-Lincoln

Meki Nzewi, Professor of African Music, Theory and Practice, University of Port Harcourt, Nigeria

Douglas C. Orzolek, Professor of Music and Director of Graduate Programs in Music Education, University of St. Thomas

Kelly A. Parkes, Associate Professor, Teachers College, Columbia University

Gary K. Ritcher, Professor Emeritus of Music Education, James Madison University

Patrick Schmidt, Associate Professor, Western University

M. Christina Schneider, NWEA

Johanna J. Siebert, Teaching with Primary Sources Project Director, National Association for Music Education

Bret P. Smith, Associate Professor and Assessment Coordinator, Central Washington University

Julie Tan, Lecturer, Yong Siew Toh Conservatory of Music, National University of Singapore; Past President, The Singapore Music Teachers' Association

Dennis Ping-Cheng Wang, Associate Professor of Music Education and Assistant Dean for Student Affairs, University of Macau

Jeffrey Ward, Director of the School of Music, Theatre, and Dance, Kansas State University

Peter R. Webster, Scholar-in-Residence, Thornton School of Music, University of Southern California

Brian C. Wesolowski, Associate Professor of Music Education, The University of Georgia

Stefanie A. Wind, Assistant Professor of Educational Measurement, The University of Alabama

Ya Zhang, Assistant Professor of Evaluation, Measurement, and Research, Western Michigan University

PART I

ASSESSMENT POLICY IN MUSIC EDUCATION

POLICY AND PHILOSOPHY

CHAPTER 1

....

ASSESSMENT POLICY IN MUSIC EDUCATION

....

RICHARD COLWELL

EVALUATORS take pride in the perceived value and longevity of the use of tests and observations as policy tools. Many introductory texts in measurement begin by citing the use of high-stakes tests as early as the Han dynasty in China (206–220 CE) although there is no documented evidence that test scores were used as a qualification for government service until the Sui dynasty, some 800 years later. Faith that tests could identify competence and reduce political influence in appointments to government service was not just a Chinese historical fact. We are reasonably sure that China had a music examination to determine who could be appointed music master, an important post in early dynasties. Competence in music was merged with poetry, thus measuring a degree of creativity in a formal examination. Key appointees were often interviewed by the emperor, indicating that one's philosophy was part of the criteria for selection, promotion, and status within the governmental bureaucracy; so it continues today. Music was not the only "special" examination; Sun Tzu's writings (500 BC) indicate there were competency examinations for military officers.

The content of qualifying examinations for government civil service has no doubt changed along with other values in China and elsewhere, but evaluation continues to command respect as a fair indicator for measuring policies. The United States has a civil service examination (456 agencies and 15 levels) that is mandatory for government service with the exception of the FBI, diplomats, and select others. Tests are important for more than US government service; one must have high test scores worldwide for admission to select schools, universities, and study abroad; one qualifies to drive and to be eligible for multiple professions in most countries through various types of examinations.

The audition or competition (test) in music has been accepted for as long as we have records. The Eisteddfod festival, an early competition for poetry and music, dates from the 12th century; and certainly crumhorn players competed to see who could hold a note the longest. These music competitions had no relationship to schooling; music belonged to the community. Community pride in 1958 was widespread when an American, Harvey Levan "Van" Cliburn, won the Tchaikovsky competition in Moscow at the height of the cold war. The outcome (judge's rating) was important; few cared about the process Van Cliburn used to develop his competency or even whether he was homeschooled. Selection of major conductors, orchestral players, and opera singers and for fellowships and professional positions depends on fair tests of performance competence. Performance is also the primary criterion for admission to selective conservatories such as Curtis and Juilliard; being college-ready, a cliché in the reform movement, has a completely different meaning in music than in other subjects—if one wants to major in music at any institution, one certainly has to be college-ready.

Government policy has also long supported music; court musicians are only one example, as are today's military bands. In many countries governments support orchestras, opera companies, and more; communist countries have been especially lavish in their support at both the local and national levels. The United States supported more than 100 orchestras during the depression. In this chapter, the focus is on the relationship of policy and the music assessment tools (tests, portfolios, questionnaires, interviews, rating scales, observations) used by policymakers to evaluate individuals, groups, schools, teachers, teaching, curricula, extramusical outcomes, and general academic competence. Tests are also important to research, including classroom interventions of various kinds. There is a research test for self-efficacy, pertinent to Gary McPherson's research (McPherson & McCormick, 2006; McPherson & Zimmerman, 2002; TSES: Tschannen-Moran & Woolfolk Hoy, 2001). Tests such as TOEIC (Test of English for International Communication) and TOEFL (Test of English as a Foreign Language) influence how English is taught in Japan and other Asian countries. Policy, power, and politics are closely related; policy assessments change depending on the political party in power, more particularly in countries with an enforceable state curriculum. In the preface to his *Art Education: The Development of Public Policy* (2005) Charles Dorn states that it was the national and state policies driving the push for student assessment and the need for public accountability that led him to write a text on art education *and* public policy.

The rationale for the organization of this chapter is that policymakers are focused on reforming education to solve a wide variety of needs at the local and national level, both in the United States and in much of the world. Pasi Sahlberg writes about not only Finland but also the Global Educational Reform Movement (pasisahlerg.com). Music is caught up in the *backwash* of this global education reform and accompanying accountability. Policy occurs at multiple levels and usually is a course of action or set of procedures that is agreed on after serious consideration of alternatives. Policymakers have focused on accountability as the enforcement tool for their policy decisions. A snapshot is provided in this chapter of music assessment in several countries with an emphasis on the United States as a baseline. Thus, I devote space to the history of testing prior to 1945 followed by a discussion of the US educational reform movement, although the relationship between governmental policy and education is weak until after World War II or later. Most of music's assessment tools measure the elements or skills of music with limited attention to a music program although policymakers' concern is about educational programs. I focus on observation as a common assessment tool in music teacher education and in much performance evaluation. I conclude with a discussion of the importance of both program- and competency-based evaluation, two types of assessment missing in most countries.

US Policy on Testing Until World War II

Group (school) evaluation was initiated around 1840 in the United States by Horace Mann, the first state superintendent of education and a major reformer. He found there was no "objective" check on whether state money was accomplishing its intended purpose of improving teaching and learning. (Schooling was primarily a district responsibility, but then, as now, state funds were used for the disadvantaged.) His tests allowed for comparisons among students and teachers; this accountability was successful, and achievement testing was widely adopted. Mann, as he struggled to subordinate and control the district system (Cubberly, 1919), established policy credibility; he wrote brilliantly and frequently about insufficient funding and antiquated school management, discipline, and supervision. He saw the primary role of the newly created (1830s) role of school superintendents as the testing and certification of teachers, the disbursement of school money, visiting (observing) and reporting on schools. He squabbled with the clergy over separation of church and state, an early policy issue (Tyack, 1966).

Observational data indicate that Lowell Mason's 1836 introduction of music in the schools was not an immediate success; it was a quarter of a century later that music and drawing became generally recognized as subjects of study, even in the better city schools (Cubberly, 1919). The early instruction was primarily drill with little singing until 1900. Mason did not realize that children do not think along the same logical lines as adults.

An early involvement of the US federal government in education was the Smith-Hughes Act of 1917 for vocational education. It was not successful in matching graduates to jobs; nevertheless, historical research does not discourage the federal government from continuing to try (e.g., School to Work Opportunity Act of 1994). The graduates of the 1917 program seldom found jobs in the areas for which they had been trained, and most evaluations of vocational programs found that their graduates earned no more than graduates from regular courses of study (Kantor & Lowe, 2013). Around this time, Arthur Otis and Robert Yerkes developed the Alpha Army Test that measured a soldier's mental capabilities. This test was so successful in the military that the idea of testing became widespread in US schools, including the music tests of Carl Seashore and Jacob Kwalwasser. Elwood Cubberly, Lewis Terman, Edward Thorndike, and Carl Seashore were committed to a scientific approach to education in the belief that one bright child was worth more than thousands of children with low mentality (Meens & Howe, 2015). (It was Horace Mann, the reformer, who believed in equality of educational opportunity as essential to the functioning of democracy.)

We cannot ignore the 20th-century music aptitude work, most famously of Seashore but continued by Edwin Gordon. The Eastman School of Music used the Seashore tests for placements for years, an attempt at a scientific approach to musical aesthetics. The belief was that one has to assess "talent" in order to make the best investment in education. Although it may not be politically correct, most music educators today recognize the importance of talent and that it cannot be completely replaced by the best education—age, education, and experience are not the determining factors in being selected as a conductor or soloist. Many of the tasks on aptitude assessment warrant new investigation.

Educational Reform after World War II

After World War II, school policy became political—social equity, effectiveness, and democratic rights dominated policy discussions (Katz & Rose, 2013). The educational world quickly changed with integration, and also with federal support through the GI Bill. The education players from school boards to teachers' unions, state agencies, and the federal courts found themselves involved in major and minor reform issues. The launching of the Soviet satellite, Sputnik, actually forced the United States to initiate, through the National Defense Act of 1957, *curriculum* changes in an effort to raise test scores. It may seem strange to relate music teaching to competition with the Soviet Union, but federal support became available for the first and last time for multiple music curriculum research projects. Other curriculum projects included new math, physics, biology, Man a Course of Study (MACOS), and in music, Manhattanville, Reimer, and Comprehensive Musicianship. Accountability was rampant in the 1960s and 1970s with evaluations of these curricula. None of these curricula lasted very long; only the National Assessment of Educational Progress (NAEP, which included music and visual arts) begun in 1972 survived. In 1966, the National Center for Education Statistics authorized a study that became known as the *Coleman Report, Equity for Diverse Populations* (Coleman et al., 1966). Despite the importance of its findings, this report did little to influence education policy.

In 1982, the *Harvard Educational Review* published a special issue (vol. 52, no. 4) on the federal role in education based on proceedings of a conference hosted by Harvard's dean Paul Ylvisaker. This publication provided the background for the 1983 change in education policy and assessment. Secretary of Education Terrence Bell, who was conference leader, suggested that the role for the US federal government in education was limited to civil rights, leadership, advocacy and constructive criticism, educational research, and capacity building. No federal program was to be permanent, with the possible exception of limited funding for special education. He identified his leadership as secretary with his recent appointment of a national commission on excellence in education. He believed that, if the findings of this commission were persuasive, the federal government could use its leadership role to make an impact by convening meetings, stimulating debate, and increasing the awareness and concern about the status of both public and private schools (Bell, 1982, pp. 376–377). Federal help was to be used frugally. President Ronald Reagan (to whom Secretary Bell reported) believed that character and capabilities grow stronger as federal resources are withdrawn. Minter (1982) reported that initial evaluations of Title I and Head Start produced negative findings; these findings have continued to the present. Chester Finn remarked that once we move beyond basic literacy and basic numeracy, we run into big differences of what is important, suggesting that most federal efforts to improve school practice are fundamentally unrelated to what most people care about, which is improved education outcomes (Finn, 1982). The purpose of education continues to be contested, with Lawrence Cremin's definition the most cited: "Education is the deliberate systematic and sustained effort to transmit, evoke, or acquire knowledge, values, attitudes, skills, and sensibilities as well as any learning that results from that effort, direct or indirect, intended or unintended" (1988, p. x).

Without goals, policy formation is impossible. What are important education goals in the face of a competitive worldwide reform movement? Berliner and Glass (2015) argue that we cannot easily measure or identify competing school and district initiatives, classroom culture, peer influence, teacher beliefs, and principal leadership for resilience, grit, practical intelligence, social intelligence, and creativity, all necessary when making goal comparisons (p. 12). Jal Mehta (2015) suggests that the functions of schooling have traditionally included creating citizens and social cohesion; patriotic values; incorporation of immigrants; stimulation of student growth, creativity, and critical thinking; and the provision of an avenue for upward mobility (p. 23).

The remarks at the Harvard conference are among the greatest predictive *understatements* in the history of American education. In April 1983, after 18 months of work, Bell's national commission report headed by David Gardner (1983) was released and was quickly named *A Nation at Risk* (National Commission on Excellence in Education, 1983) based on Gerald Horton's eye-catching introduction to a rather traditional government report (Tomlinson, 2015). With this publication, federal education policy increasingly shifted to federal authority and away from social science research and welfare programs (Trujillo & Howe, 2015; Trujillo & Renee, 2015). The nation's economic future was declared at risk because of educational mediocrity. Within one year, 250 task forces had been formed to study education and recommend changes (Mehta, 2015). Educators resented the implication that economic problems should be laid at their feet and that the economic purposes of schooling should be elevated over its many other purposes. The low or absent relationship between education and the economy has not discouraged policymakers from relying on this argument for some 30 years; a coalition of businessmen, politicians, philanthropists, and educational policymakers has put in place their solution: multiple, untested market reforms. Obama's Race to the Top of 2009 adopted market-oriented performance benchmarks, competitive pressures, and rewards and sanctions (Kantor, 2015). The *American School Board Journal* (Gentzel, 2014) states that the most disturbing policy issue is the intrusion of market forces.

The educational reform that ensued in the late 1980s gave states additional responsibility. (State departments favor curriculum control, and their policies are usually mandates.) School districts responded in turn, asking for relief from policies and regulations in exchange for greater accountability. Districts received waivers for class size, safety, competitive bidding, and minimum graduation requirements. This was the era of site-based management (Elmore & Fuhrman, 1995). Districts found that there was a lack of appropriate outcome measures, and that specialty teachers, like those in music, preferred keeping the state policies that required students to "take" general music with little or no accountability. Policymakers wanted to make state-by-state comparisons, but any comparison required that all districts and states give the same test, like those that have recently been developed in core subjects (Smarter Balanced & PARCC, the Partnership for Assessment of Readiness for College and Careers) and for which PISA (the Program for International Student Assessment), PIRLS (the Progress in International Reading Study), and TIMSS (the Trends in International Mathematics and Science Study) are international tests used for national comparisons. Since about the year 2000 the standards movement has been stimulated by the publishing of international league tables of PISA scores; these math-focused scores made headlines and sent tremors through governments everywhere (Robinson & Aronica, 2015, p. 7), just what reformers wanted (Ercikan, Roth, & Asil, 2015; Labaree, 2014; Munch, 2014; Perry & Ercikan, 2015). Tasks on any comparison assessments should be not only instructionally sensitive but also educationally valuable, valid, reliable, and fair. Comparison assessments should be internationally benchmarked in terms of kinds of tasks as well as indicating the level of performance expected. Berliner (2015), in "The Many Facets of PISA" argues that the results must be interpreted the same way, associated with economic outcome; this has not been the case. In 2015, we have no evidence that high school graduates are more knowledgeable and skilled than they were when *Nation at Risk* was published in 1983 (Hirsch, 2015). Reformers were faced with determining the weight that should be given to student assessment results versus longer-term student outcomes. In 2014–2015, 47 states were testing high school seniors for college readiness in mathematics and language arts.

The policy literature on reform is extensive as educators vie to comply with policies from numerous sources. To encourage a pause in reform, Berliner and Glass (2015) argue that we should trust but verify. Few researchers do the high-quality work that would reveal noneffect or negative effect for some children in the hands of some teachers in some schools. The replication rate for research in education journals is under 1%, yet replicability of research is the gold standard.

Well-Known Reforms, with and Without Assessment

The major US federal education program, the Elementary and Secondary Education Act (ESEA), passed in 1965. Head Start was part of the Economic Opportunity Act (1958), followed by the Education of All Handicapped Children Act in 1975. A 1988 amendment to the 1965 Elementary and Secondary Act required states to define levels of academic achievement of students receiving Title I support. Title I, unfortunately, has not had its intended effect, which was to equate educational opportunity (Kantor & Lowe, 2006, 2013). It was at a senate hearing (1965) that Robert Kennedy asked Harold Howe, the secretary of education, about the effectiveness of ESEA, and Mr. Howe did not know. Kennedy responded "you spend billions of dollars and you don't know whether (the children) can read or not?" (Kantor & Lowe, 2006, p. 480). Should we give the responsibility for compensatory education to the very institution that creates the problem? Kennedy hoped parents would put pressure on educators, but only one in four parents presently knows whether their school is low-performing (Rogers, 2006). Today, teachers are the cause *and* the solution. David Labaree (2013) states that the mantra of the current school reform movement is that high-quality teachers produce high-achieving students. If true, we should hold teachers accountable for student outcomes and remove teachers whose students do not achieve these. It was not until the America's Schools Act in 1994 that states were required to develop content and performance standards for all children, the first time the federal government had created a policy that required setting expectations for all students. (The increasing reach of the federal government on local education matters should be apparent.) Federal mandates have traditionally been occasioned by forces outside of education, such as national defense concerns, the poor and disadvantaged, and the handicapped. In 2002, civil rights advocates promoted a reform policy that required assessment data to be disaggregated by subgroups of gender, minority, and socioeconomic status (SES). This disaggregation inspired data-driven reform policies when it was revealed that students in the lowest 5% of performing schools had a 31% gap in reading proficiency and 36% in math. (When one initially "selects" the lowest scoring schools, one is guaranteed to find gaps on required subjects). The courts have stipulated that educating all students is a critical state obligation. Opportunity to Learn (OTL) is the best policy tool available to states for such responsibility. However, OTL is conveniently missing in state and federal documents, notably in music. Policies which set standards that schools should meet (OTL) would identify the money, materials, teachers, curricula, and neighborhood needs that must be filled (Anyon, 2005). Linkages between economic growth and tax-supported public schools have, unfortunately, been present since the early 19th century and have been a permanent presence in school policy since World War II. Only at one historical period, the short progressive education movement, did the schools promote democratic principles and the practice of citizenship in classrooms.

Policy

"Amazingly, the United States has no national education policy" (Cross, 2015, July 6, p. 1). There is no understanding about responsibilities between federal government and the states. Lyndon Johnson believed that if money were given to schools to educate poor children, educators would know what to do. According to the critics Robinson and Aronica (2015), federal policymakers think their analysis is sound, and the fact that test scores in targeted disciplines have hardly improved is because standards have fallen and a lack of local accountability exists. Thus, policymakers continue to stress the importance in education of data-driven decision-making (tests) and evidence-based practice (other assessments) as essential. Lacking familiarity with assessment in their discipline, teachers cannot use data to influence state and local policy. With teachers lacking the needed assessment skills, data teams have been established in schools; these teams are encouraged to work with the Data Wise Project at Harvard for a national "reform" perspective (Bocala & Boudett, 2015; Datnow & Park, 2015). The concern is that public policies, not only those in education, have always been developed and implemented under the shadow of politics, advocacy, and support from outside public and private institutions. In 2016, education policymaking is complex, with no single thread that unifies the process (Cuban, 2012; 2015).

Policies affecting assessment usually require someone to develop and implement appropriate assessments. Understanding requires background information about the history and support of the policy. Sam Hope, retired executive secretary of the arts accrediting agencies, has long posed excellent policy questions (1992, 2002, 2004, 2005, 2008) similar to the following 12:

1. What is impacting schooling and what is the purpose of each policy?
2. Is it clear what should be done, is it a worthy goal, feasible to implement, and amenable to assessment?
3. Is the policy directed toward the value of music for the individual, will the study of music facilitate the attainment of important nonmusical goals, does it integrate competencies taught in all subjects, is the policy directed toward improving teaching and teachers, is the purpose to extend education beyond schools and classrooms, is it about administration, finance, and opportunity to learn, or is the policy directed toward curricular issues?
4. Policies are context dependent; every policy should be appropriate for the intended situation—school, community, age-level, teacher competence, and beliefs. To what extent are the policies mandated in educational reform movements pertinent (positive or negative) to the teaching and learning of music?
5. To what extent are policies focused on advocacy and program promotion rather than on learning outcomes?
6. What philosophical and/or theoretical foundations (assumptions) support the policy?

7. Will the policy be widely supported by educators, foundations, and the community, and to what extent will their support impact actions to be taken?
8. How can one avoid past mistakes?
9. To what extent will the policy correct deficiencies in the present program?
10. How might extant policies be altered to better fit a particular situation?
11. Is the policy based on providing an aesthetic experience or other outcomes that shape the human experience?
12. Is the policy primarily focused on the gifted and near-gifted or to provide remediation?

Chester Finn and Brandon Wright (2015a, b, c) have expressed concern that the United States is failing our brightest kids; we lack gifted and talented programs. These policy questions arise:

1. Are the desired behaviors dispositions?
2. Are the desired behaviors unique to music, and do these policies support a unique way of knowing?
3. What baggage will one assume?
4. Is the policy directed toward a change in pedagogy?
5. Does the policy focus primarily on present student interests or on their present inadequacies?

Decisions based on how test scores are interpreted are usually made by those in positions of power. Policy, testing, and power are closely related to most of 21st-century organized life. Defense policy (e.g., to fight two wars simultaneously) requires a specified number of troops and supporting resources that traditionally are provided without discussion of the wisdom of the policy. Health policies are implemented by bureaucrats, based on technical and cost data. Education policy (to close the achievement gap) among all school-age population subgroups requires judgments based on experience (Orland, 2015). Closing this gap may be considered unrealistic. Not only is 21st-century life complex but also the causes of gaps in education relate to multiple factors in addition to the schools (Darling-Hammond, 2015; Darling-Hammond, Amrein-Beardsley, Haertel, & Rothstein, 2012). Establishing educational priorities including music programs is a policy task, as resources are finite. Any priorities need to be hierarchical; not all goals and/or experiences are of equal importance. The importance and priority of developing assessments for music in the schools has not been substantiated, and evidence of how assessment, other than formative, will improve teaching and learning has not been established (Finn, Kahlenberg, & Kress, 2015). The situation may be, however, like that of Ronald B. Thomas, whose unwillingness to establish measurable outcomes contributed to the short life of the Manhattanville Project (Moon & Humphreys, 2010). If the reform movement was stimulated by test scores on international tests (PISA, etc.), how can these scores be improved by individual governmental policies (Hanushek, 2009)? Smaller class size was a policy tool that came at a high cost and little improvement in student achievement.

Tests and Accountability

If *A Nation at Risk* (National Commission on Excellence in Education, 1983) was a wake-up call in the United States, international testing (PISA and TIMSS) has had a similar impact across the globe (Tomlinson, 2015). Reformers have advanced few new policies. Those who link successful education programs to the national economy are thinking conceptually, in terms of curricula and programs, not about how subjects are taught. For example, reformers continue to have faith that teachers can determine sub-goals of the core language arts program and determine the weight to be given to reading and interpreting meanings from both fiction and nonfiction (Tannenbaum & Rosenfeld, 1997).

Music Assessment outside the United States

I conducted an incomplete and informal survey of assessments of students, teachers, or programs in countries impacted by educational reform and where music assessment data were available. The countries surveyed were Canada, Great Britain, Poland, Germany, Mexico and Latin America, Scandinavia, Turkey, East Asia, Japan, China, and Australia–New Zealand. I found that there was minimal assessment of students, but rigorous assessment of teachers. The survey failed to find assessments of curricula or programs. In Canada, Favaro (2000) and MacGregor, Lemerise, Potts, and Roberts (1994) found no agreement on fine arts assessment, with teachers using technical, personal, analytic/conceptual, social, and attitudinal criteria for the assessment of student learning. A movement to integrate music complicated assessment. Moreno (2014) provided the only response to program evaluation with the suggestion that assessment can shape music programs and respond to political and philosophical factors that influence curricula. Great Britain, with a national curriculum, is assessed by inspectors from the nonministerial government agency of Ofsted (Office for Standards in Education) with the results published in league tables. The music topics assessed have been influenced by the type of governance in power. As we wrote this, inspectors were focusing on impressions of student progress based on 20-minute instructional blocks, although Ofsted returned to more direct evidence in 2017.

The education system in Germany is based on the philosophy of Bildung, which allows a teacher to use any materials as long as the instruction leads to developing a mature, critical, creative, and aesthetically experienced population. German educational reform was occasioned by the shock of relatively low PISA scores, and schools have been closed due to low academic test scores (Kertz-Welzel, 2015). There is opposition to standards in music. Assessments are not common unless a student wishes to focus on music at the gymnasium and higher education, where the exams are rigorous and the student is expected to be reasonably competent on two instruments. Privately taught students are commonly assessed by the Associate Board of Royal Schools of Music (ABRSM) examinations. In Turkey, aptitude tests are given at the end of 4th and 8th grade. Although Scandinavia has a "national" curriculum, teachers are free to teach to their strengths. Traditional examinations are given for students who wish to focus on music at the secondary level and, of course, for college. East Asia, including China, has laws and regulations on hours of instruction, goals, teaching, materials, and grading of education, all dictated by the national government. The general purpose of music is the development of citizen "aesthetic ability" and some nonmusical outcomes. Government emphasis on integrating all subjects is being resisted by music teachers. Although there are competence indicators representative of artistic abilities at each learning stage, there has been little assessment. China's 13 learning outcomes are similar to the US voluntary national standards (Leong & Leung, 2013) with no accompanying assessment, although students can take the Hong Kong Diploma of Secondary Education (HKDSE) examination. A junior high school examination was piloted in Taiwan in 2012 with the hope that an assessment would elevate the public's view of the importance of music. Music is part of the humanities requiring assessment measures to give some priority to appreciation and understanding. Exploration and performance are two additional components. With an oversupply of teachers, the performance examination for university admission is critical. Hong Kong has a state curriculum and assessment guide consisting of listening, performing, and creating, with an additional elective section (Leong & Leung, 2013). The music focus in Singapore is on identifying the gifted. Barrier exams include the Cambridge General Certificate of Education (GCE) Ordinary Level Music Examination. The Australian music examinations board continues to rely on syllabi and tests based on the British Associated Schools of Music Examinations. Australia supports policies similar to America's *No Child Left Behind*, although the states and territories cite it as an undesirable model of educational practice which has led only to short-term interventions for underachieving students at the expense of broader structural changes (Dixon, Borman, & Cotner, 2009). New Zealand measures achievement and attitudes in year 4 and year 8 with a model similar to the NAEP in the United States but with a tighter focus. Most informal assessments reported in all countries are of the important constructs of music, for example, pitch, rhythm, and tonal memory, and no holistic assessment of what constitutes a musically educated individual.

Policy and Assessment in the United States

The goal of the reform movement in the United States is to use data to bring about a systemic change in teaching and learning in teacher education and in the PreK-12 schooling (Schrag, 2014, March 14). Policies set by the courts are the strongest; local policies are relatively weak. Although music is part of this educational turbulence, it is not a primary target for reform. Policies most pertinent to music educators involve teacher education, the curriculum, and the expectation that the programs of instruction will produce interesting, musically educated students. Policymakers, usually at the state level, have limited interest in the mechanics of instruction (Hirsch, 2015). Their interest is in having rich, satisfying, experiences of all types that constitute a music program. These policymakers work with state education agencies to formulate "requirements," requirements that are relatively easy to change as the state political situation changes. These requirements vary; for example, "taking" a course, passing an examination, or demonstrating proficiency. Without specifying the how, states may encourage outcomes published by education organizations. Few outcomes are uncontested. Because of the importance of talent and out-of-school culture in music teaching and learning, it is not feasible to require grade-level objectives in assessing policies; one has to think in terms of proficiencies and programs. Schools in Adams County Colorado have replaced grade structure with 14 competency levels in every subject (Adams County School District 50, 2015). New Hampshire prohibits the use of time-based credits statewide.

Music educators in the United States have been minimally involved in policy change made possible by the reform movement. Sam Hope (2004), the long-serving chief officer of several college-level arts accrediting agencies, sees policy as activity or as wisdom seeking. He has desired music policies that are not standards (assessment based) but supportive. Policies related to music curricula would involve judgments, which brings up the questions (1) Who should set such policies, how original, and to what purpose?, and (2) Are these policies beyond teacher control? Responding to activist policymakers has tended to focus on single facets of a curriculum such as knowledge and skills, which narrows one's perspective of the possibilities of music. Carla Aguilar (2011) argued in her doctoral dissertation that the audience for the 1994 national standards was not teachers but other governmental agencies. As we write, some music educators are promoting a new, more extensive set of grade level standards with accompanying assessments. This change in standards does not appear to change Aguilar's conclusion. Standards do not establish policy. Mike Schmoker (2006, 2011a, 2011b, 2012a, 2012b, 2012c, 2014) suggests that most fields are not ready for standards as the research has not been done and, more importantly, *complexity kills reform efforts.* Sam Hope (2004) argues that there is a danger in relying on curriculum standards and losing control of music's internal purpose. He cites the use of music to teach other subjects as "one of loss of control" (p. 98). Music educators must decide what program policies protect those elements essential to music's survival; one such policy might be to avoid economic-education policy thinking. There is a need to determine what the music education policy/assessment issues are. Youth cultures are a critical policy issue for music education. Presently the quantity of music is expanding, but when instructional time is not, program priorities are required. Interdisciplinary objectives are not sufficiently specific as goals, although possibly worthwhile as an experience. An excellent example of program change has occurred in visual arts with its recent focus on visual culture, where visual encounters are subject to analysis and reflection. Elliot Eisner (2001, 2002) suggested that this change of focus is influenced by critical theory, which pays less attention to culture's aesthetics than to its politics, forcing Eisner to question how unified and clear is the field's new message about its uniqueness.

A connection between policy and assessment occurs when individuals think they understand test results but misinterpret evidence because of their own unique personal knowledge and experience, and act on those misconceptions (Herman & Baker, 2009). Making an unjustified interpretation (validity) results in bad decisions whether the assessment is norm referenced, criterion referenced, or standards based (Davidson, 2014). Curriculum-embedded assessments often come with specific instructional materials and may be end-of-chapter examinations, or integrated by educational software. Embedded assessments, however, cannot be used to determine proficiency. The results of formative assessments are not neutral, they also have consequences. Assessment, formative and summative, as a policy instrument directly and/or indirectly advances education and social goals to determine the effectiveness of educational policies, practices, programs, and individuals as well as institutions. A good or adequate test result certifies that one has the required knowledge and skills, but these may or may not relate to priority program outcomes. An assessment is the policymaker's commitment to quality, a necessary commitment as curricula at public school and college level are adjusted on the basis of assessments—assuming alignment with content and performance standards. It is not easy to determine whether adequate progress is being made in any subject or whether the assessment is a reasonable tool for grades, rewards, sanctions, accreditation, or readiness. The Kahn Academy (https://www.khanacademy.org/) trumpets the importance of students moving at their own pace, which is typical of music instruction. Music educators want continuing, adult participation in music, lessening the importance of group objectives. Competency-based assessment of individuals and groups may satisfy reform-oriented policymakers, at least when music is an elective.

Two Reform Assessment Issues

Educational reform is directed at teacher education programs and at the K-12 or K-16 program outcomes of core subjects (Marzano, 2012; Sanger & Osguthorpe, 2013). Music teacher education and the assessment of preservice teachers is part of today's reform movement, with teacher certification competencies, like the preservice Educator Teacher Performance Assessment (edTPA), a joint responsibility of the state and colleges of education. This student assessment has long had the tacit support of the National Association of Schools of Music, which, like the public schools, prefers the status quo. The assessments of interest to music educators are Praxis I for program admission; Praxis II, the subject matter assessment component and often considered a summative assessment; and Praxis III, developed to assess first-year teachers. Praxis II, used in 45 states, has a uniform cut score, a requirement of all standardized measures. In establishing the cut (or passing) score, Educational Testing Service (ETS) included music. Fifteen percent of the sample were art teachers, 7% music, 5% science, and 29% math.

The Praxis competencies, general and subject specific, have been judged important for effective classroom performance and also for curriculum inclusion in teacher training and development programs. With the variety of music teacher education programs, the question arises whether item judgments and Praxis passing scores are replicable across different panels of experts. Confidence in the present cut score is evident, as 20 of the 22 statements met the 3.5 cut score. There is a direct relationship between these Praxis competencies and the popular Charlotte Danielson observation schemata (http://www.danielsongroup.org/), which is often required by colleges of education in assessing student teachers, including those in music. (A rated observation by college supervisors is presently a critical assessment in music teacher evaluation.) Two Danielson observation statements that did not meet the standard were how teachers organize physical space, and the teacher's contribution to the school and district. Charlotte Danielson's observation tool originally consisted of 22 statements describing teaching; 19 of these are used as the basis for the Praxis II and Praxis III, Classroom Performance Assessment. Tannenbaum and Rosenfeld (1997) suggest that Praxis III is good for both beginning and experienced teachers. Charlotte Danielson and Carol Dwyer (1995) outlined the development of the observation framework and how the 19 criteria matched the four Danielson and four Praxis domains (organizing content knowledge, creating a learning environment, teaching for student learning, and professionalism). Interviews, observations, written documents, and trained assessors were used, to justify that the 19 criteria correlated to a behaviorally anchored scale of teaching. Observation has been music's primary assessment tool, but one can expect to encounter a variety of suggested/required assessment tools, some more accurate than others. The National Observational Teaching Exam (NOTE, http://www.ets.org/note/), another ETS assessment, promises to evaluate a prospective teachers' ability for effective practice in the classroom. The evaluation would consist of leading a discussion, modeling and explaining content, eliciting student thinking, and communicating with a parent (Marzano & Heflebower, 2011; Wei, Pecheone, & Wilczak, 2014).

Of the 46 states that applied for Race to the Top funds (US Department of Education, 2010), 29 made policy changes creating statewide teacher evaluation systems. Forty-two states and the District of Columbia now require that student achievement data be used in annual teacher evaluations, which has so far been difficult in music (Russell, Meredith, Childs, Stein, & Prine, 2015, p. 92). In 2013 all but 10 states required teacher evaluations to include objective evidence of student learning. Presently, however, there is no consensus about which measures are valid for teacher accountability (Harris & Herrington, 2015). Even value-added data, when available, are statistically unreliable over time (Darling-Hammond, 2015). In nonmeasurable subjects, the common measures include observation and student learning objectives (SLOs) that are state or locally determined. This local and state policy power, which seems to be accepted, is a deterrent in any national assessment of music teachers. The Bill and Melinda Gates Foundation has invested at least 355 million dollars in better teacher evaluations, much focused on observation

(Labaree, 2013). Mixed-result data exist from the Bill and Melinda Gates Measures of Effective Teaching (MET) study using 500 well-trained "observers" and 2300 hours of examples.

The Danielson observation framework is based on the premise that successful teaching consists of the four domains: planning and preparation, classroom environment, instruction, and professional responsibilities, which she argues apply to all teachers irrespective of grade or subject (Danielson, 2012, 2015; Garrett & Steinberg, 2015). Other observation systems (CLASS-S, PLATO, MQI, QST, McREL)[1] have similar domains (McCaffrey, Yuan, Savitsky, Lockwood, & Edelen, 2015). Despite observation's acceptance, the nonrandom assignment of students to a classroom means that the relationship of observation to academic or music achievement is unknown. If observations are to be helpful in music, they must be subject-specific, involve content experts in the process of observation, and provide information that is both accurate and useful for teachers. Without robust criteria and focused standards, criticism and teacher evaluation becomes mere fashion. Presently high-stakes policy decisions in elementary school music are rarely made solely on the basis of student achievement on SLOs or on any state longitudinal data system. At the secondary school level, competence is a factor.

Halpin and Kieffer (2015) have devised an approach to analyzing classroom observation data. No known observation system focuses on process or on learning style; policymakers continue to believe that measurable outcomes are possible, and many in the arts agree. Halpin and Kieffer applied latent class analysis to classroom observational instruments. Latent class analysis provides diagnostic information about instructional strengths and weaknesses along with estimates of measurement error for individual teachers, thus it supports formative feedback and is useful for research. Mehta (2013a, b) argues that reformers and politicians are trying to do at the back end with external accountability what they should have done with capacity building. McCaffrey et al. (2015) looked at middle school classroom teaching using observation data from the CLASS-S protocol. They found that any two raters produce a different factor structure, suggesting that one often obtains incorrect inferences about the factor structure at the teacher level. All of the current observation instruments, rating forms, and achievement tests on SLOs provide no evidence that these data permit valid inferences about a teacher's instructional quality (Popham, 2013a). Just changing teacher evaluation will not transform the quality of teaching. Of the possible observation instruments, PLATO is based on a theory of instruction, Danielson (Framework for Teaching Practice, or FFT) on constructivism, QST on science teaching, and MQI on math knowledge. Descriptive studies have found only a small to moderate correlation with student learning, with some variation by grade and subject (Garrett & Steinberg, 2015). All observation systems are inadequate as sole measures for policy decisions on teachers and teaching. Elisabeth Soep (2004) is spot-on when she suggests that the relationship between art and assessment is best characterized as awkward, if not overtly hostile.

PreK-12 Music Assessment in
the United States

Cocco (2014) found that music teachers in the United States, like music teachers worldwide, continue to measure student growth in terms of rhythm, tone, scales, sight reading, and observation of group instruction. His findings are not unusual. State and national ratings of such constructs need to have a range of performance descriptors above and below standards. Most of the assessment reports in the International Symposium on Assessment in Music Education (ISAME) books (Brophy, 2008, 2010; Brophy, Lai, & Chen, 2014; Brophy & Lehmann-Wermser, 2013; Brophy, Marlatt, & Ritcher, 2016) are on these elements of music or on short instructional units. One report (LaCognata, 2013) described assessments used by American high school band directors, raising the question whether band constitutes a music program. Is it possible to have a music program without a band? Again, instructional priorities are necessary; all elements are not of equal importance except possibly at the lowest taxonomic levels. The evaluation tail is wagging the reform movement dog in the backwash of the reform movement when the elements of music are of more importance than large policy issues. To satisfy policymakers, an effort at curriculum evaluation is required. The music program/curriculum constitutes the student experiences in systemic educational reform (Ahmann, 1967; Scriven, 1967; Stake, 1967; Tyler, 1967).

The respected *Curriculum Studies Reader, 4th edition* (Flinders & Thornton, 2012) has a chapter on music that may reflect the present public understanding of the unassessed music curriculum. The editors, in their foreword to the music chapter, suggest that music holds a particular status in the hierarchy of secondary school curricula, affecting how music garners resources and that music differs from many subjects in its assessment strategies and traditions (p. 211). (Required general music appears to be acknowledged but not valued in curriculum discussions.) I have attempted to follow closely the language in Siskin's (2013) chapter, "Outside the Core: Accountability in Tested and Untested Subjects." She states that standards-based accountability policies entered the public schooling system at the end of the 20th century as a major reform effort, one that has the potential to dramatically change the face and function of the comprehensive high school as we know it. When policies directed at the whole school district are applied to the high school, these policies collide with the differentiated curriculum structure. In some subjects, policymakers explicitly quantify learning; this has been done in Kentucky. The Kentucky Department of Education includes music (or at least the humanities) among the tested subjects. Performance outcomes in the humanities are worth 7.13% of the school's total evaluation score. (Performance in English counts for 14.25%). Siskin did not limit her chapter to Kentucky; she sought opinions from several states, and she reports them as one might in a good qualitative research study. The following statements are taken from her chapter with minimal editing; most are quotes.

Music as a subject occupies a position that, as one Massachusetts teacher explained has pretty high status; it's somewhat elite, but also…marginalized. It is not a contender for what every high school student should know and be able to do. Yes to science and how the body works but the possibility of standards for everyone in the arts does not even enter the conversation. Music teachers contend that they do have standards, long before the terminology came into vogue. We've always been sort of standards-based without knowing it. A Vermont teacher said that standards for us were established over five hundred years ago, Bach in equal temperament and Pythagoras with the scale. There are widely shared standards about what should be taught in music and even what has been taught sequentially. One must know terminology and how to read rhythms. Music is performance based. For group performance oriented subjects such as band or orchestra, shared standards are of essential importance. Preparing students to go to regional and state level performances is one example.

Kentucky teachers reported that they didn't need to change the way they taught. They didn't have to change the curriculum. State rubrics and standards seemed pretty easy in part because they do not introduce accountability into the field. Instead, music teachers have long seen themselves as accountable to their communities for the performance of their students, not on tests, but in the public area. If one is at a basketball game and when they're playing a song and it sounds awful, everybody's going to say "well that's a bad band director." Music holds a distant relationship with other departments. Music teachers described feeling like they were in a different world—nothing against the school. Discussions of standards may be taking place but not that I'm aware of. Every principal thinks you work for him even if each school has a different music program, but each doesn't have a different music department. Music programs raise much of their departmental money. Music teachers are not just subject teachers but practitioners and performers of music; music teachers are musicians in a way that physics teachers are not physicists. It is almost impossible to image a policy system where teachers could agree that all high school students should know and be able to demonstrate the national music standards. So Kentucky adopted required standards for the humanities including music along with other arts. To be able to demonstrate on a test do we inadvertently lower performance standards, weaken existing professional accountability or lose knowledge outside the core altogether?   (Siskin, 2013, pp. 271–277).

CONNECTING POLICY AND
MUSIC ASSESSMENT

The fallout from policymakers' attempts to reform education has influenced music education; the conversation of music educators has changed. Education policies in subjects considered important (science, technology, engineering, and mathematics, or STEM) can and have diverted resources from some K-12 music programs, influencing music educators to assume a defensive stance. Some music educators have picked up on the concerns of policymakers and attempted to apply strategies to their teaching that might match these concerns, strategies related to problem-solving, critical thinking, creativity, persistence, up-to-date objectives, and even new and/or improved assessments of these student learning objectives. Although policymakers have not been critical of present teaching and learning in music, one can be proactive and continue to conduct research on the teaching of the basics of music. The basics require formative assessment and are foundational as well as leading to musical self-confidence of students, especially in performance. Traditional assessment procedures need to be modified for individual student learning objectives as the foundation is likely competency based (Kuh et al., 2015). Competency assessment is appropriate for subjects when students vary greatly in talent and experience. Grade-level competencies can provide a learning-floor with the expectation that the top level is open-ended. One might start with the Australian Music Examination Board or the "levels" of the Associated Board of Royal Schools of Music, as the board has developed standards for all instruments, including theory, singing, jazz, and even group experiences. Again, these levels are for formative assessment. Although many states and districts are developing summative assessment measures, there is limited use for summative measures or measures that have consequences for students. One might find in the literature that a valid assessment program needs to cover the full-range of standards. This is misleading. An assessment "program" should focus on a few, high-priority outcomes. What the reform-minded policymaker expects is that music educators offer a balanced music program. Programs are often confused, even by professionals, with curricula. There are similarities, though (Stake, 1967; Stake & Munson, 2008)). For example, one might have a curriculum that is sequenced to develop singing competency that avoids bad habits and is inspiring and useful. A curriculum is feasible in jazz or in song-writing and other topics. A program for the years of required and elective music would offer opportunities selected from the widest field of music experiences. A music program for today's policymakers should be the first step in justifying the resources required for students to become competent. Ensemble directors often have an unstated competency standard of a graduate musically educated in performing, improvising, harmonizing, and some degree of self-assessment. It is reasonable that the music teacher (and the district) be accountable to the community and the students for offering a rich, musical program. Policymakers have had poor experiences with core subjects and are likely to expect that music teachers know how to interpret and communicate data from formative and summative assessments. Interpretation is critical with competency-based assessment, where the teacher must consider the student's background, effort, and progress and the complexities of reasonable progress in learning. The recent Testing Action Plan of the US Department of Education is a major step forward (Superville & Klein, 2015; US Department of Education, 2015). The plan acknowledges the need for flexibility and cites the waiver given to New Hampshire to have locally developed tests in four districts (a pilot for the rest of the state) that require students to apply what they know through a series of complex, multipart tasks, and, yes, a student can establish proficiency in music based on out-of-school experiences. Competency-based education is a current topic at the collegiate level, with over 600 institutions evaluating its possibilities (Blumenstyk, 2015; Kuh et al., 2015). There is also a rapidly growing network of competency-based education, also known as differentiated instruction. Western Governor's University (https://www.wgu.edu), with about 62,000 students, is the most prominent example with success in information technology, nursing, and teaching (Brookhart, 2015). Southern New Hampshire University has also been approved to award financial aid based on progress rather than credit hours and others are expected to follow if competencies can be clearly defined and assessed. One can become musically competent without attaining competence in all of the possible valuable outcomes for music—earning badges, certificates, and other indicators (Berrett, 2015, p. A22; Chronicle of Higher Education, 2015; Finn & Wright, 2015a; Wiggins, 2011).

INFLUENCE ON MUSIC TEACHER EDUCATION

A major focus of education policymakers is the inadequacies of teacher education. Several states are publishing data by institution using criteria that do not appear to be relevant to music teachers. One can assume, based on present assessment data, that colleges of education are accepting reform measures that are generic. An assessment of this premise is called for (Altschuld & Engle, 2015). A curriculum assessment seems infeasible as the courses taken by music students vary. The college of education component may be assessed as a program. The editors of the *Journal of Teacher Education* suggest that teacher education is a distinct field with knowledge, histories, research methodologies, and practices that are recognized and recognizable (Knight et al., 2015). Four education deans suggest that teacher candidates must be able to *demonstrate* the requisite commitments, practices, and knowledge inaction before earning an entry-level teaching license (Arbaugh, Lowenberg-Ball, Grossman, Heller, & Monk, 2015). This is competency-based education (Ritterband & Heller, 2015; Rose, 2015; Sturgis, 2015). Arthur Levine (2015) of the Wilson Foundation has initiated with MIT an academy that will offer graduate degrees in education based on demonstrated expertise, not accumulated credits (Cassuto, 2015, October 25). Without data on music teachers, the possibility remains that reforming music teacher education is a major concern. An analysis of teacher education is beyond the scope of this chapter. Competency in K-12 program evaluation is, however, important for music educators. Program data are extremely limited, and early program assessments were primarily descriptions with minimal attention to quality. Accreditation data are not valid (Hanushek, 2009; Kuh et al., 2015; Stake, 1967).

Methods courses appear to define the education component in music teacher education. These college method courses are not uniform or stable and at times have been characterized as band wagons, changing with personnel. Music offerings are described, not assessed.

Policymakers and professional evaluators agree on the importance of program evaluation. There are some 34,000 professional evaluators worldwide who speak a common language and actively communicate with one another. There are subtle differences among the approaches to program evaluation, but all focus on providing data for decision-making to assess and improve programs. One major goal is promoting social betterment. In 2001, *New Directions for Evaluation* published a critique of some twenty-two "approaches" with names like "empowerment," "utilization focused," "case study," "responsive/client centered," "objectives based," "connoisseur/critic," and "outcome/value added" (Stufflebeam, 2001). Program assessment is designed for important issues—drug addiction, AIDS, genetically modified agriculture projects, school dropouts, and homeless prevention programs. In education, program evaluators assess teacher education and school curricula, including music. External professional evaluators are recommended.

The focus of program evaluation is the determination of merit or worth, with attention to identifiable strengths and weaknesses of a particular program. Programs produce outcomes or changes that are valuable and desired. In music, policymakers would be interested in curricula designed to produce a musically educated citizen and not in how those competencies are taught. Wiebe's (1941) article on music captured the attention of scholars in all disciplines when he asked to what extent the achievement in music education matched the needs of students in contemporary society. Wiebe's program assessment question was: In what ways does the music program contribute to the education of students who are not going to be professional musicians? He also stated, if education is to change the behavior patterns of people, then an assessment of programs that impact attendance at music events is of concern. Wiebe suggested that the primary curriculum purpose was the manner in which music contributed to producing the kind of human being the school proposed to produce. Wiebe argued that music should dramatize and idealize democratic values (Bildung?). Unfortunately data on audience size, student letters of appreciation, and op-ed pieces in the local paper do not address the question of merit or worth.

The focus in this chapter has been on the relationship of reform to creeping assessments, and whether rigorous music curriculum/program evaluation is at the heart of systemic education reform. An enacted music curriculum can be judged by measures of student success, and a mandated district or state curriculum can have outcomes subject to judgment by experts. A program evaluation should have a vision of the importance of the music curriculum within the school district. Partnerships are part of the music program. Policymakers do not distinguish among string, wind and percussion, vocal, and general music. These are subdivisions of a program. Colwell (1985) reviewed what was termed "music program evaluation" at that time. In 1927, Jacob Kwalwasser gave his music information test to 4,177 students, finding little consistency in music knowledge. One conclusion was that further random teaching might come at a loss of interest in learning. E. Thayer Gaston repeated the testing of students in school ensembles in 1940. Although the curriculum (probably song books) suggested that 5th grade students should be able to sight-read, he found that his ensemble students could not sight-read accurately. In 1936, Fullerton tested 3,000 adult singers, finding that 2% paid attention to the syllables. Subjects liked the songs they had been taught to sing. In 1932, McEachern surveyed music teacher education at 150 institutions, finding that music courses constituted between 19% and 87% of the total number of hours required for music certification! Seventy-five percent of the institutions gave entrance examinations, but only 26% used the results to exclude the incompetent. Learning to make lesson plans was judged to be a waste of time. Peterson's (1956) survey of teachers in the field found that teacher preparation was not realistic in terms of teaching situations. By 1972, the recommendation was that method courses should be taught by someone simultaneously teaching in the public schools. There is no evidence that the National Association of Schools of Music has conducted any summative curriculum/program evaluation.

In four evaluations over a period of 8 years, 1971–72, 1978–79, 1997, and 2008, student competence on isolated knowledge and skills was assessed by the NAEP. The focus was not on the program. There was no report on individual student or school scores. Policymakers surveyed teachers prior to constructing the tests in an effort to match instructional objectives, with the assessment, ending with a list of skills. The NAEP (2008) was based on the 1994 voluntary national goals, rather than music program outcomes (Persky, Sandene, & Askew, 1998). The 1994 "standards" were established by an expert committee, and the extent to which these standards aligned with the enacted curricula in 2008 is unknown (Coughlan, Sadovnik, & Semel, 2015). None of the NAEP assessments have been a wake-up call to revise local and state music curricula or to portray a viable "required" music curriculum. Knowledge and skills in NAEP are not aligned to any curriculum or to the common core. High school music program assessment is more complex, often focusing on skills and little on understanding. The efforts of the National Association for Music Education (NAfME) to establish benchmarks does not replace NAEP as an assessment of a program. There do not presently appear to be assessment projects based on data from previous local or national assessments. There is, however, agreement among professional policymakers that the results from promoting a student's appreciation of music may be unassessable, yet so intrinsically meritorious that it is worth the risk of some instructional investment (Popham, 2013b). Eighth grade students at the time of the 2008 assessment were receiving ample opportunity to learn, with 57% reporting music instruction three or four times a week and 77% of that instruction by a music specialist. A trustworthy assessment of the program should be feasible with curriculum alignment. The present curriculum and instructional priority of teachers is unknown. An alignment clue is provided in that 28% of the students reported singing only once a month. Playing instruments was reported to be about once a month by 33% of the students, and 33% wrote music, with some 49% indicating that they listened to music in class. One interprets the NAEP and other data knowing that 36% of 9-year-old students report taking music lessons outside of school. The degree of other influences on student competency are unknown.

Policymakers desire data that indicate student competence in all disciplines; college-or-career-ready is among the desired competencies, not course completion. Any music curriculum evaluation for 21st-century school music would be competency-based and would include more than skills and knowledge. Student talent is an important antecedent variable. Providing "deeper" experiences in music for those with talent is a moral obligation (Carr, 2013; Sternberg, 2013).

Robert Stake and Elliot Eisner are two program evaluators who specialize in the arts, although other professionals and semiprofessionals have assessed funded projects. Policy evaluation in arts education, however, is rare (Boulton, 2004; Hatfield, 2007; Hope, 2005, 2006, 2008). Both Stake and Eisner acknowledge the importance of quantitative data but believe that merit and worth of arts programs are best assessed through qualitative (observation) means. Stake (1975) suggests that a search for understanding of quality, finding quality, and representing quality are the three fundamental duties in assessment. Program evaluators focus on only two or three major questions. Qualitative data, with a bit of quantitative data, are appropriate to learn how "things work." There is no checklist of music assessment criteria comparable to that suggested for policies on teacher evaluation. Assessment of music programs requires knowledge and more importantly, experience. An important outcome is meaning, the meaning of the product as well as meaning for the process. Curriculum experiences within programs do differ; some are better than others. A rigorous and relevant school music program is an essential component of holistic education programs. The ASCD (formerly the Association for Supervision and Curriculum Development) approach is to assess school climate, social-emotional learning, character education, and pertinent skills. A holistic model allows for connections and prioritizes students' ability to learn about themselves, their social responsibility, and their compassion. A program evaluation built on a school curriculum acknowledges out-of-school experiences that are critical in improving education, whether the evaluation is of the formal, informal, enacted, or judged curriculum. The curriculum needs to be mind-expanding. Stake (2000, 2004) and Eisner (1991, 2013a, 2013b) (along with other professional evaluators) make the point that children differ genetically with respect to their intellectual and dispositional proclivities. Further, it would be difficult to have a "standardized" music curriculum when students differ greatly on critical attributes. A program, however, is possible. Even concept formation is believed to be biologically rooted in the sensory systems that humans possess. Eisner's curriculum focus is on refining perceptual skills. Stake's responsive assessment model finds the evaluator looking closely at antecedents, transactions, and outcomes. Antecedents include music aptitude, music experience, interests, and motivation, as well as much of what we know about music teaching and learning. Some curriculum evaluation insights may be inferred from the assessment of the Central Education Midwest Research Laboratory (CEMREL) music program (Madeja, 1973). The focus of the assessment, however, was on the classroom teacher, as was the music "program" developed by the Southwest Laboratory. Foundations, especially the John D. Rockefeller (JDR) 3rd Fund, have funded most of the curriculum evaluations. Stakes's editing of *Evaluating the Arts in Education* (1975) was supported by the JDR 3rd fund. Visual arts had a major evaluation (Getty funded) of Discipline-Based Arts Education (DBAE); the evaluator, however, could find no school system that used the DBAE curriculum, K-12. *Custom and Cherishing* (Stake, Bresler, & Mabry, 1991) was funded by the National Arts Research Center to conduct a national arts curriculum assessment. Their book consists of case studies of some eight elementary school programs. Their program evaluation focused on the school, the community and its customs, school and community resources and incentives, and society, its customs, its cherishing, and its curriculum. The focus was on big "issues," not an array of objectives. Intrinsic value from experiences is possible, as well as performance and attitude. Considering the "power" of having three of the most distinguished curriculum assessors on one project, it is somewhat surprising that this research is so little known. The authors had knowledge and experience that allowed them to identify prominent events. They commented on the presence or absence of expressive outcomes. Curriculum policy's purpose is to enhance a sense of what is good; thus, assessment has a focus on quality and the ability to communicate with an audience. The uniqueness of the arts and the arts teacher is stressed in arts curriculum evaluation; the perception of the arts teachers is important as is that of an experienced evaluator. These are the individuals who can judge quality. More than most subjects, the range of music goals is extensive and visible (Braskamp & Brown, 1975). Process is important primarily in the early stages of a program, probably K-3. Curriculum evaluation allows one to determine the attitude of the administration, not only in resources provided but also in belief. In assessing works of art and music curricula, standards are not appropriated; standards define goals with respect to quantity (Dewey 1934/1989, p. 307). Dewey defined teaching as moving the student in the direction of what the experts already knows (Jackson, 1998, p. 180). Arts instruction in schools is usually based on students progressing at their own pace and demonstrating competence. Fragmented pedagogical practices in music education makes assessment even more complex.

Policymakers do not ask what is 4th grade music—the larger concern is the program offered. A program question asks: are we preparing teachers and administrators to provide competent graduates of music programs? Julia Gillard (2015), a former Australian premier, is a policymaker with an understanding of education. She believes that innovations bring hope but educators must avoid expensive distractions such as the One Laptop per Child program that failed. What innovations are we chasing? "The debate in education must be informed by regular and reliable measurements of results. If we do not understand what is going wrong, we have no hope of fixing it" (Gillard, 2015, p. 2).

NOTE

1. CLASS-S—Classroom Assessment Scoring System; PLATO—Protocol for Language Arts Teaching; MQI—Mathematical Quality Of Instruction; QST—Quality Science Teaching; McREL—Mid-Continent Research for Education and Learning.

REFERENCES

Adams County School District 50. (2015, November 10). *Vision 2020: Pathway to the future.* Retrieved from http://www.westminsterpublicschools.org/cms/lib03/CO01001133/Centricity/Domain/1/Vision%202020%20Version%201%20-%2011%2010%2015.pdf

Aguilar, C. (2011). *The development and application of a conceptual model for the analysis of policy recommendations for music education in the United States.* (Unpublished doctoral dissertation). Indiana University: Bloomington, Indiana.

Ahmann, J. S. (1967). Aspects of curriculum evaluation: A synopsis. In R. Stake (Ed.), *Perspectives of curriculum evaluation* (pp. 84–89). Chicago, IL: Rand McNally.

Altschuld, J., & Engle, M. (2015). Accreditation, certification, and credentialing: Relevant concerns for U.S. evaluators. *New Directions for Evaluation, 145*, Spring. Entire.

Anyon, B. Jean. (2005). What "counts" as educational policy? Notes toward a new paradigm. *Harvard Educational Review, 75*(1), 65–88. doi: 10.17763/haer.75.1.g1q5k721220ku176

Arbaugh, F., Lowenberg-Ball, D., Grossman, P., Heller, D., & Monk, D. (2015). Dean's corner: Views on the state of teacher education in 2015. *Journal of Teacher Education, 66*, 435–445. doi: 10.1177/0022487115602314

Bell, T. H. (1982). The federal role in education. *Harvard Educational Review, 52*, 375–382.

Berliner, D. (2015). The many facets of PISA. *Teachers College Record, 117*(1), 1–20.

Berliner, D., & Glass, G. (2015). Trust but verify. *Educational Leadership, 72*(5), 10–14.

Berrett, D. (2015). How a 40-year-old idea became higher education's next big thing. *Chronicle of Higher Education, 62*(10), A22–A24.

Blumenstyk, G. (2015). Credential "Summit" will tackle proliferation of degrees, badges, and certificates. *Chronicle of Higher Education.* Retrieved from http://chronicle.com/article/Credentialing-Summit-/233623

Bocala, C., & Boudett, K. (2015). Teaching educators habits of mind for using data wisely. *Teachers College Record, 117*(4), 1–20.

Boulton, D. (2004). Assessing art learning in changing contexts: High stakes accountability, international standards and changing conceptions of artistic development. In E. Eisner & M. Day (Eds.), *Handbook of research and policy in art education* (pp. 585–605). Mahwah, NJ: Lawrence Erlbaum Associates, Publishers, and NAEA.

Braskamp, L., & Brown, R. (1975). Accountability for the arts. In R. Stake (Ed.), *Evaluating the arts in education: A responsive approach* (pp. 59–71). Columbus, OH: Merrill.

Brookhart, S. (2015). *Performance assessment: Showing what students know and can do.* West Palm Beach, FL: Learning Sciences International.

Brophy, T. S. (Ed.). (2008). *Integrating curriculum, theory, and practice: A symposium on assessment in music education.* Chicago, IL: GIA Publications.

Brophy, T. S. (Ed.). (2010). *The practice of assessment in music education: Frameworks, models, and designs.* Chicago, IL: GIA Publications.

Brophy, T. S., Lai, M.-L., & Chen, H.-F. (Eds.). (2014). *Music assessment and global diversity: Practice, measurement, and policy.* Chicago, IL: GIA Publications.

Brophy, T. S., & Lehmann-Wermser, A. (Eds.). (2013). *Music assessment across cultures and continents: The culture of shared practice.* Chicago, IL: GIA Publications.

Brophy, T. S., Marlatt, J., & Ritcher, G. K. (Eds.). (2016). *Connecting practice, measurement, and evaluation.* Chicago, IL: GIA Publications.

Carr, D. (2013). What are the implications of aesthetics for moral development and education? In H. Sockett & R. Boostrom (Eds.), *A moral critique of contemporary education: The 112th yearbook for the National Society for the Study of Education*, Part 1 (pp. 80–97). New York, NY: Teachers College Press.

Cassuto, L. (2015, October 25). How do you measure a good teacher, anyway? *Chronicle of Higher Education, 62*(21) Retrieved from http://chronicle.com/article/How-Do-You-Measure-a-Good/233904

Chronicle of Higher Education. (2015, September 14.). *Next: The credentials craze* [Special Report]. Retrieved from http://www.chronicle.com/specialreport/Next-The-Credentials-Craze/2 [print version, September 18, 2015, Section B].

Cocco, B. (2014). *How do music teachers measure student growth?* (Unpublished doctoral dissertation). Ashland University, Ashland, Ohio.

Coleman, J., Campbell, E., Hobson, C., McPartland, J., Mood, A., Weinfeld, F., & York, R. (1966). *Equality of educational opportunity.* Washington, DC: National Center for Educational Statistics.

Colwell, R. (1985). Program evaluation in music teacher education. *Council for Research in Music Education, 81,* 18–62. doi: 10.1177/87551233070250020102

Coughlan, R., Sadovnik, A., & Semel, S. (2015). A history of informal, out-of-school education. In J. Vadeboncoeur (Ed.), *Learning in and across contexts: Reimagining education, 113*(2), 359–382. New York, NY: Teachers College, Columbia University.

Cremin, L. (1988). *American education: The metropolitan experience, 1876–1980* (Vol. 3). New York, NY: Harper & Row.

Cross, C. (2015, July 6) The U.S. needs a national policy on education. *Teachers College Record.* Retrieved from https://www.tcrecord.org/Content.asp?ContentID=18014

Cuban, L. (2012). Standards vs. customization: Finding the balance. *Educational Leadership, 69*(5), 10–15.

Cuban, L. (2015). Federal education policy and democracy. *Teachers College Record, 117*(6). 1–8.

Cubberly, E. (1919). *Public education in the United States: A study and interpretation of American educational history.* Boston, MA: Houghton Mifflin.

Danielson, C. (2012). Observing classroom practice. *Educational Leadership, 70*(3), 32–37.

Danielson, C. (2015). Framing discussion about teaching. *Educational Leadership, 72*(7), 38–41.

Danielson, C., & Dwyer, C. (1995). How praxis III supports beginning teachers. *Educational Leadership, 52*(6), 66–67.

Darling-Hammond, L. (2015). Can value added add value to teacher evaluation? *Educational Researcher, 44,* 132–137. doi: 10.3102/0013189X15575346

Darling-Hammond, L., Amrein-Beardsley, A., Haertel, E., & Rothstein, J. (2012). Evaluating teacher evaluation. *Phi Delta Kappan, 93*(6), 8–15. doi: 10.1177/003172171209300603

Datnow, A. & Park, V. (2015). Data use for equity. *Educational Leadership, 72*(5), 48–54.

Davidson, E. J. (2014). How "beauty" can bring truth and justice to life. In J. C. Griffith & B. Montrosse-Moorhead (Eds.), *Revisiting truth, beauty, and justice: Evaluating with validity in the 21st century. New Directions for Evaluation, 142,* 31–43.

Dewey, J. (1934/1989). The need for a philosophy of education. In J. A. Boydston (Ed.), *John Dewey: The later works* (vol. 9, pp. 3–21). Carbondale: Southern Illinois University Press.

Dixon, M., Borman, K., & Cotner, B. (2009). Current approaches to research in anthropology and education. In G. Sykes, B. Schneider, & T. Ford (Eds), *Handbook of education policy research* (pp. 83–92). New York, NY: Routledge & AERA.

Dorn, C. (2005). *Art education: The development of public policy.* Miami, FL: Barnhardt & Ashe.

Eisner, E. (1991). *The enlightened eye: Qualitative inquiry and the enhancement of educational practice.* New York, NY: Macmillan.

Eisner, E. (2001). Should we create new aims for art education? *Art Education, 54*(5), 6–10. doi: 10.1080/00043125.2001.11653461

Eisner, E. (2002). *The arts and the creation of mind.* New Haven, CT: Yale University Press.

Eisner, E. (2013a). Educational objectives—help or hindrance? In D. Flinders & S. Thornton (Eds.), *The curriculum studies reader* (4th ed., pp. 109–115). New York, NY: Routledge.

Eisner, E. (2013b). What does it mean to say a school is doing well? *The curriculum studies reader* (4th ed.), pp. 279–287. New York, NY: Routledge.

Elmore, R. & Fuhrman, S. (1995). Ruling out rules: The evolution of deregulation in state education policy. *Teachers College Record, 97*, 279–309.

Ercikan, K., Roth, W., & Asil, M. (2015). Cautions about inferences from international assessments: The case of PISA 2009. *Teachers College Record, 117*(1), 1–28.

Favaro, E. (2000). Changing attitudes, changing practice. In B. Hanley & B. Roberts (Eds.), *Looking forward: Challenges to Canadian music education* (pp. 41–53). The Canadian Music Educators Association.

Finn, C., Jr. (1982). Responses. *Harvard Educational Review, 52*, 529–531.

Finn, C., Jr., Kahlenberg, R., & Kress, S. (2015). Rethinking the high school diploma. *Education Next, 15*(1), 49–53.

Finn, C., Jr., & Wright, B. (2015a, August 20). The bright students left behind. *Wall Street Journal*, p. A11.

Finn, C., Jr., & Wright, B. (2015b). A different kind of lesson from Finland. *Education Week 35*(12). Retrieved from http://www.edweek.org/ew/articles/2015/11/04/a-different-kind-of-lesson-from-finland.html

Finn, C., Jr., & Wright, B. (2015c). *Failing our brightest kids: The global challenge of educating high-ability students.* Cambridge, MA: Harvard Education Press.

Flinders, D. J. & Thornton, S. J. (Eds.). (2012). *The curriculum studies reader* (4th ed.). New York, NY: Routledge.

Gardner, D. (1983). *A nation at risk: The imperative for educational reform: A report to the nation and the secretary of education.* Washington, DC: The Commission on Excellence in Education.

Garrett, R., & Steinberg, M. (2015). Examining teacher effectiveness using classroom observation scores: Evidence from the randomization of teachers to students. *Educational Evaluation and Policy Analysis, 37*, 224–242.

Gentzel, T. (2014). Tom on point: Tapping the brakes on charter school expansion. *American School Board Journal, 201*(4), 6.

Gillard, J. (2015, November 5). Innovations in education—Life and Arts. *Financial Times, 39*(1), 2.

Halpin, P., & Kieffer, M. (2015). Describing profiles of instructional practice: A new approach to analyzing classroom observation data. *Educational Researcher, 44*, 263–277. doi: 10.3102/0013189X15590804

Hanushek, E. (2009). The economic value of education and cognitive skills. In G. Sykes, B. Schneider, & D. Plank (Eds.), *Handbook of education policy research* (pp. 39–56). New York, NY: Routledge & AERA.

Harris, D., & Herrington, C. (2015). Editor's introduction: The use of teacher value-added measures in schools. *Educational Researcher, 44*(2), 71–76. doi: 10.3102/0013189X15576142

Hatfield, T. (2007). Federal government: Where's the beef: A state perspective. *Arts Education Policy Review, 108*(5), 4–6. doi: 10.3200/AEPR.108.5.4-6

Herman, J., & Baker, E. (2009). Assessment policy: Making sense of the babel. In G. Sykes, B. Schneider, & D. Plank (Eds.), *Handbook of education policy research* (pp. 176–190). New York, NY: Routledge and AERA.

Hirsch, E., Jr. (2015). Introduction—The knowledge requirement: What every American needs to know. In M. Bauerlein & A. Bellow (Eds.), *The state of the American mind* (pp. 1–16). West Conshohocken, PA: Templeton Press.

Hope, S. (1992). Professional organizations and influences. In R. Colwell (Ed.), *Handbook of research on teaching and learning* (pp. 724–734). New York, NY: Schirmer Books.

Hope, S. (2002). Policy frameworks, research, and K-12 schooling. In R. Colwell & C. Richardson (Eds.), *The new handbook of research on music teaching and learning* (pp. 5–16). New York, NY: Oxford University Press.

Hope, S. (2004). Art education in a world of cross-purposes. In E. Eisner & M. Day (Eds.), *Handbook of research and policy in art education* (pp. 93–113). Mahwah, NJ: Lawrence Erlbaum Associates, Publishers, and NAEA.

Hope, S. (2005). Art education in a world of cross-purposes. *Arts Education Policy Review, 106*(6), 3–16.

Hope, S. (2006). Characteristics of a "basic" discipline in elementary and secondary education. *Arts Education Policy Review, 108*(2), 3–5.

Hope, S. (2008). Requirements, cultural development, and arts education. *Arts Education Policy Review, 110*(1), 3–5.

Jackson, P. (1998). *John Dewey and the lessons of art.* New Haven, CT: Yale University Press.

Kantor, H. (2015). Accountability, democracy, and the political economy of education. *Teachers College Record, 117*(6), 1–10.

Kantor, H., & Lowe, R. (2006). From new deal to no deal: No Child Left Behind and the devolution of responsibility for equal opportunity. *Harvard Educational Review, 76,* 474–502.

Kantor, H., & Lowe, R. (2013). The price of human capital: The illusion of equal educational opportunity. In M. Katz & M. Rose (Eds.), *Public education under siege* (pp. 75–84). Philadelphia: University of Pennsylvania Press.

Katz, M., & Rose, M. (2013). *Public education under siege.* Philadelphia: University of Pennsylvania Press.

Kertz-Welzel, A. (2015). Lessons from elsewhere? Comparative music education in times of globalization. *Philosophy of Music Education Review, 23*(1), 48–66. doi: 10.2979/philmusieducrevi.23.1.48

Knight, S., Lloyd, G., Arbaugh, F., Gamson, D., McDonald, S., Nolan, J., Jr., & Whitney, E. (2015). Five-year retrospective (Editorial). *Journal of Teacher Education, 66*(4), 410–414. doi: 10.1177/0022487115604839

Kuh, G., Ikenberry, S., Jankowski, N., Cain, T., Ewell, P., Hutchings, P., & Kinzie, J. (2015). Beyond compliance: Masking assessment matter. *Change, 47*(5), 8–16.

Labaree, D. (2013). Targeting teachers. In M. Katz & M. Rose (Eds.), *Public education under Siege* (pp. 30–39). Philadelphia: University of Pennsylvania Press.

Labaree, D. (2014). Let's measure what no one teaches: PISA, NCLB, and the shrinking aims of education. *Teachers College Record, 116*(9), 1–14.

LaCognata, J. (2013). Current student assessment practices of high school band directors in the United States. In T. Brophy & A. Lehmann-Wermser (Eds.), *Music assessment across cultures and continents: The culture of shared practice* (pp. 109–128). Chicago, IL: GIA Publications.

Leong, S., & Leung, B. (Eds.). (2013). *Creative arts in education and culture: Perspectives from greater China.* Dordrecht, Netherlands: Springer.

Levine, A. (2015). Time is right for colleges to shift from assembly-line education. *Chronicle of Higher Education, 62*(3), A26–27.

MacGregor, R., Lemerise, S., Potts, M., & Roberts, B. (1994). *Assessment in the arts: A cross-Canada study.* Vancouver, British Columbia: University of British Columbia.

Madeja, S. (1973). *All the arts for every child: Final report on the arts in general education project in the school district of University City, MO.* New York, NY: The JDR 3rd Fund.

Marzano, R. (2012). The two purposes of teacher evaluation. *Educational Leadership, 70*(3), 14–19.

Marzano, R., & Heflebower, T. (2011). Grades that show what students know. *Educational Leadership, 69*(3), 34–39.

McCaffrey, D., Yuan, K., Savitsky, T., Lockwood, J., & Edelen, M. (2015). Uncovering multivariate structure in classroom observations in the presence of rater errors. *Educational Measurement Issues and Practice, 34*(2), 34–46. doi: 10.1111/emip.12061

McPherson, G., & McCormick, J. (2006). Self-efficacy and music performance. *Psychology of Music, 34*(3), 325–339. doi: 10.1177/0305735606064841

McPherson, G., & Zimmerman, B. (2002). Self-regulation of music learning. In R. Colwell & C. Richardson (Eds.), *The new handbook of research on music teaching and learning* (pp. 327–347). New York, NY: Oxford University Press.

Meens, D., & Howe, K. (2015, June). NCLB and its wake: Bad news for democracy. *Teachers College Record, 117*(6), 1–44.

Mehta, J. (2013a). *The allure of order: High hopes, dashed expectations and the troubled quest to remake American schooling.* New York, NY: Oxford University Press.

Mehta, J. (2013b, April 13). Teachers: Will we ever learn? *New York Times,* p. A21.

Mehta, J. (2015). Escaping the shadow: A nation at risk and its far-reaching influence. *American Educator, 39*(2), 20–26, 44.

Minter, T. (1982). The importance of the federal role in improving educational practice: Lessons from a big-city school system. *Harvard Educational Review, 52,* 500–513.

Moon, K.-S., & Humphreys, J. (2010). The Manhattanville music curriculum program: 1966–1970. *Journal of Historical Research in Music Education, 31*(2), 75–98. doi: 10.1177/153660061003100202

Moreno, M. (2014). Program evaluation: A review of impact, method and emerging trends for music education. *Canadian Music Educator, 55*(3), 32–37.

Munch, R. (2014). Education under the regime of PISA & Co.: Global standards and local traditions in conflict—the case of Germany. *Teachers College Record, 116*(9), 1–16.

National Assessment of Educational Progress (NAEP). (2008). *2008 Arts education assessment framework.* Washington, DC: National Assessment Governing Board and US Department of Education.

National Commission on Excellence in Education. (1983). *A nation at risk: The imperative for educational reform.* Retrieved from http://www2.ed.gov/pubs/NatAtRisk/index.html

Orland, M. (2015). Research and policy perspectives on data-based decision-making in education. *Teachers College Record, 117*(4), 1–10.

Perry, N., & Ercikan, K. (2015). Moving beyond country rankings in international assessments: The case of PISA. *Teachers College Record, 117*(1), 1–10.

Persky, H., Sandene, B., & Askew, J. (1998). *The NAEP 1997 Arts Report Card: Eighth-grade findings from the National Assessment of Education Progress.* Washington, DC: US Department of Education.

Peterson, H. W. (1956). *Problem areas in music education.* (Unpublishd doctoral dissertation). New Haven, CT: Yale University.

Popham, W. J. (2013a). *Evaluating America's teachers: Mission possible?* Thousand Oaks, CA: Corwin.

Popham, W. J. (2013b). Objectives. In D. J. Flinders & S. J. Thornton (Eds.), *The curriculum studies reader* (4th ed., pp. 95–108). New York, NY: Routledge.

Ritterband, V., & Heller, R. (2015). Competency education offers promise and peril for students. *Phi Delta Kappan, 97*(2), 27–29. doi: 10.1177/0031721715610087

Robinson, K., & Aronica, L. (2015). *Creative schools: The grassroots revolution that's transforming education.* New York, NY: Viking.

Rogers, J. (2006). Forces of accountability? The power of poor parents. In *NCLB Harvard Educational Review, 76*(4), 611–641, 619.

Rose, B. (2015). *Program evaluation essentials for non-evaluators.* Wellesley, MA: Brad Rose Consulting.

Russell, J., Meredith, J., Childs, J., Stein, M., & Prine, D. (2015). Designing inter-organizational networks to implement education reform: An analysis of state race to the top applications. *Educational Evaluation and Policy Analysis, 37*(1), 92–112. doi: 10.3102/0162373714527341

Sanger, M., & Osguthorpe, R. (2013). The moral vacuum in teacher education research and practice. In H. Sockett & R. Boostrom (Eds.), *A moral critique of contemporary education: The 112th yearbook for the National Society for the Study of Education*, Part 1 (pp. 41–60). New York, NY: Teachers College Press.

Schmoker, M. (2006). *Results now: How we can achieve unprecedented improvement in teaching and learning.* Alexandria, VA: ASCD.

Schmoker, M. (2011a). Curriculum now. *Phi Delta Kappan, 93*(3), 70–71. doi: 10.1177/003172171109300317

Schmoker, M. (2011b). *Focus: Elevating the essentials to radically improve student learning.* Alexandria, VA: ASCD.

Schmoker, M. (2012a). The problem with English language arts standards—and the simple, powerful solution. *Phi Delta Kappan, 93*(5), 68–69. doi: 10.1177/003172171209300516

Schmoker, M. (2012b). First things first: The madness of teacher evaluation frameworks. *Phi Delta Kappan, 93*(8), 70–71. doi: 10.1177/003172171209300817

Schmoker, M. (2012c). Refocus professional development. *Phi Delta Kappan, 93*(6), 68–69. doi: 10.1177/003172171209300616

Schmoker, M. (2014). Education's crisis of complexity, *Education Week, 33*(17), 22, 28.

Schrag, F. (2014, March 14). Evidence based education policy: A conversation. *Teachers College Record, 116*(3). Retrieved from http://www.tcrecord.org ID Number: 17465.

Scriven, M. (1967). The methodology of evaluation. In R. Stake (Ed.), *Perspectives of curriculum evaluation* (pp. 39–83). Chicago, IL: Rand McNally.

Siskin, L. (2013). Outside the core: Accountability in tested and untested subjects. In D. Flinders & S. Thornton (Eds.), *The curriculum studies reader* (4th ed., pp. 269–277). New York, NY: Routledge.

Soep, E. (2004). Assessment and visual arts education. In E. Eisner & M. Day (Eds.), *Handbook of research and policy in art education* (pp. 579–583). Mahwah, NJ: Erlbaum and NAEA.

Stake, R. (1967). Toward a technology for the evaluation of educational programs. In R. Stake (Ed.), *Perspectives of curriculum evaluation* (pp. 1–12). Chicago, IL: Rand McNally.

Stake, R. (Ed.). (1975). *Evaluating the arts in education: A responsive approach.* Columbus, OH: Merrill.

Stake, R. (2000). Case studies. In N. Denzin & Y. Lincoln (Eds.), *Handbook of qualitative research* (2nd ed., pp. 435–454). Thousand Oaks, CA: Sage.

Stake, R. (2004). *Standards-based instruction and responsive evaluation.* Thousand Oaks, CA: Sage.

Stake, R., Bresler, L., & Mabry, L. (1991). *Custom and cherishing: The arts in elementary school.* Urbana-Champaign, IL: National Arts Education Research Center.

Stake, R., & Munson, A. (2008). Qualitative assessment of arts education. *Arts Education Policy Review, 109*(6), 13–21. doi: 10.1016/j.sbspro.2012.06.592

Sternberg, R. (2013). Reform education: Teach wisdom and ethics. *Phi Delta Kappan, 94*(7), 44–47. doi: 10.1177/003172171309400715

Stufflebeam, D. L. (2001). Evaluation models. *New Directions for Evaluation, 89.* San Francisco, CA: Jossey-Bass.

Sturgis, C. (2015). *Implementing competency education on K-12 systems: Insights from local leaders.* Vienna, VA: International Association for K-12 Online Learning.

Superville, D., & Klein, A. (2015, November 4). As pressure builds to rein in testing, Ed. Dept. sets path for states, districts. *Education Week, 35*(12), 15–16.

Tannenbaum, R., & Rosenfeld, M. (1997). *Evaluation criteria of teaching practices: A study of job-relatedness and training needs assessment.* Princeton, NJ: Educational Testing Service Research Report.

Tomlinson, T. (2015). A closer look at the commission's work. *American Educator, 39*(2), 24.

Trujillo, T., & Howe, K. (2015). Weighing the effects of federal educational policy on democracy: Reframing the discourse on high-stakes accountability. *Teachers College Record, 117*(6), 1–6.

Trujillo, T., & Renee, M. (2015). Irrational exuberance for market-based reform: How federal turnaround policies thwart democratic schooling. *Teachers College Record, 117*(6), 1–34.

Tschannen-Moran, M. K., & Woolfolk Hoy, A. (2001). Teacher efficacy: Capturing an elusive construct. *Teacher and Teacher Education, 17*, 783–805. doi: 10.1016/S0742-051X(01)00036-1

Tyack, D. (1966). The kingdom of God and the common school: Protestant ministers and the educational awakening in the west. *Harvard Educational Review, 36*, 447–469. doi: 10.17763/haer.36.4.y45g220927118836

Tyler, R. (1967). Changing concepts of educational evaluation. In R. Stake (Ed.), *Perspectives of curriculum evaluation* (pp. 13–18). Chicago, IL: Rand McNally.

US Department of Education. (2010, April 14). *Race to the Top fund phase II applications CFDA 84.395A.* Retrieved from https://www2.ed.gov/legislation/FedRegister/finrule/2009-4/111809a.html

US Department of Education (2015). *Competency-based learning or personalized learning.* Retrieved October 16, 2015, from https://www.ed.gov/oii-news/competency-based-learning-or-personalized-learning

Wei, R., Pecheone, R., & Wilczak, K. (2014). *Performance assessment 2.0: Lessons from large-scale policy and practice.* Palo Alto, CA: Stanford Center for Assessment, Learning, and Equity.

Wiebe, G. (1941). Music. *Review of Educational Research, 11*(4), 408–415. doi: 10.3102/00346543011004408

Wiggins, G. (2011). A diploma worth having. *Educational Leadership, 68*(6), 28–33.

CHAPTER 2

···

THE PHILOSOPHY OF ASSESSMENT IN MUSIC EDUCATION

···

ROGER MANTIE

Interestingly, philosophies of assessment are rare.
—David Elliott (2009, p. 367)

IT is a curious feeling to write on and about the philosophy of assessment. On the one hand, assessment has not previously factored as a central scholarly interest of mine. Thus I feel pressured to evince rigor without disrespecting those who have devoted their careers to the "scholarship of assessment" (Banta, 2002; see also Brophy, 2007, 2009; Brophy, Lai, & Chen, 2013; Brophy & Lehmann-Wermser, 2011). On the other hand, like other educators I have had to engage with assessment for almost all of my professional life. While my time and place teaching in school settings did not include a lot of today's high stakes testing and teacher accountability measures, I still found myself grappling with what I considered to be tensions in school practices and expectations of measurement, assessment, and grading. I am not sure I am any closer to resolving these tensions having written this chapter, but then again, philosophy is more about posing questions than answering them.

If electronic "hits" to search phrases such as "philosophy of assessment" and "philosophy of evaluation" are any indication, philosophical thinking is not overly commonplace in assessment communities. Indeed, my review of literature revealed a good deal of "how to" and not a lot of why, whether, and what if. The music education assessment literature, in my reading, is heavy on prescription and certainty, and light on theorization and provisionality. In the published proceedings of the symposia on assessment in music education, for example, the word "practical" is a repeating trope: 2007 (appearing on 20 pages), 2009 (31 pages), 2011 (41 pages), 2013 (32 pages). Given the intense scrutiny to which assessment is exposed throughout the educational enterprise, it seems surprising that questions about assessment's nature do not warrant greater philosophical attention.

My review of literature, only a fraction of which appears in this chapter, was comprehensive but far from exhaustive, something I quickly realized would be impossible when I encountered 11 shelves of books in the Library of Congress "LB" section on testing, measurement, assessment and evaluation at the Arizona State University library. Given this is a book chapter and not a book, I have confined most of my discussion to elementary/secondary school learning and teaching, omitting higher education issues such as teacher training, certification, licensure, and so on. I have focused primarily on assessment rather than evaluation, though I realize that, with the possible exception of "program evaluation," the lines between the two terms often blur, and I have, for convenience, used both terms at times.[1] I have also avoided the issue of grading, regarding it as separate from assessment and evaluation—though I note that some writers in music education seem to believe that grading is part of assessment. My perspective and examples reflect my Canadian and American knowledge and experiences, but I believe most of the issues discussed are applicable and transferable to other contexts.

I have arranged the chapter in five "movements," intended to reflect various contrasting ways of examining assessment issues. If there is a leitmotif present, it is one of encouraging caution and reflection so our well-intended professional efforts in, with, and for assessment are not undermined by unintended consequences. Let the symphony begin...

MOVEMENT I: WE MUST HAVE ASSESSMENT

The general belief of educators in the US is that *No Child Left Behind* or *Race to the Top* and voluntary national standards constitute policy for music education. If so, assessment is required and expected.

—Colwell (2013, p. 71)

How do we get teachers to carry out more assessment?

—Vaughan, Edmund, Holmes, and LaCognata (2009, p. 122)

The abstract numbers, percentiles on published tests, standard scores on college admission tests, were developed by psychometrician's who sought to translate appraisals of human behavior into terms used in measuring material objects and physical phenomena. They were not designed to help improve learning, and they have not facilitated the efforts of educators to improve education.

—Tyler (1991, p. 12)

A noted authority on assessment and evaluation in higher education, Alexander Astin, writes that if more teaching resembled that of the performing arts, there would be little need for books on assessment, "since the role of assessment and feedback is fundamental to the implicit theories that govern the activities of all teachers of the performing arts"

(Astin, 1993, p. 185). Indeed, day-to-day instruction in music involves in situ informal assessments and evaluations without which good teaching would not be possible. Offering ongoing developmental guidance to students based on in-the-moment evaluations is not just some add-on activity to music teaching; it *is* music teaching. One might therefore sympathize with the indifference if not disdain music teachers reportedly have for researchers who, for example, attempt to construct "valid and reliable" ways of assessing the abilities of students to maintain steady tempi. Assessing and assisting with the ongoing development of beat competency is what music teachers *do*. To be offered some test or measure for "steady tempo" under the guise of a valid and reliable assessment is dismissive of the professional judgment and practices of music teachers.

Jingle All the Way

> One approaches madness when one wades through the literature in arts education that relates to evaluation issues. You can find anything. A major problem is that the language used is imprecise.... Fuzzy language is important in foreign policy as public language and private meaning are both used; similarly, vagueness has been an aid to promoting the importance of the arts.... Precision is neither wanted nor valued.
>
> —Colwell (2004, p. 1)

Regina Murphy (2007) writes, "In the field of music education, assessment is fueled by ardent passion on the one hand and blithe disregard on the other" (p. 361). Richard Colwell, arguably one of music education assessment's most ardent and longest-serving advocates might agree to the extent that, in his opinion, music educators claim either that assessment is central to all music teaching *or* that, due to its "special" nature, music teaching and learning cannot be adequately assessed (Colwell, 2007). I suspect that one of the reasons assessment suffers from for/against thinking is the assumption that everyone means the same thing when deploying the word "assessment." Linguists would no doubt have a field day were they to analyze the language usages and discourses of assessment and evaluation (in music education and beyond).

This is not to say that meanings and word usages are haphazard, but that so many writers use assessment vocabulary indiscriminately, as if words speak for themselves and require no elaboration. To some people the word "assessment" refers to formal if not large-scale measurement and testing. To others it simply means sizing things up in the course of instruction in order to ascertain whether students have "got it." Personally, I like how Astin (1993) describes assessment as one of the ways "by which we try to operationalize our notions about excellence" (p. 5)—but I appreciate that this does not necessarily clarify what does and does not constitute assessment. To complicate matters, "assess," "assessment," and "assessment practices" (not to mention "evaluation," "measurement," and "grading") all mean potentially different things. One is tempted to say that assessment (evaluation, measurement, grading) is something that someone in a superior position does to someone in an inferior position, but that would seem to rule out self-assessment.

Intertextual effects inevitably color our individual readings of concepts and ideas. Among others, Jacques Derrida has argued that words have no essential meaning, because every word depends on the meaning of other words, resulting in "chains of signification." In the academic research community, confusion over terms has come to be known as "jingle-jangle fallacies." In short, the jingle fallacy refers to using the same term to describe different things ("identity" being a prime example), whereas the jangle fallacy refers to using more than one term to describe the same thing (beat and pulse being a relatively innocuous example). My invocation of jingle-jangle here is only loose, but hopefully helpful. My aim is simply to draw attention to the heterogeneity of the word "assessment." What, precisely, do we writers mean when invoking the word "assessment"? Is assessment more about improvement or accountability (see, e.g., Banta, 2002)?

Proving Learning and Teaching

From my reading of the literature, I suspect that the purported ambivalence toward assessment expressed by many music teachers is attributable to: (1) the conflation of assessments *for* learning and assessments *of* learning, (2) the perceived infringement on professional autonomy created when assessment is wrested from the control of individual teachers, and (3) the perceived unreasonableness of the demand to scientifically "prove" that learning and teaching has taken place in spite of all common sense evidence that it has occurred. "[If] you are teaching skills that cannot be evaluated, you are in the awkward position of being unable to demonstrate that you are teaching anything at all," writes Mager (1962, p. 47), no doubt to the consternation of teachers whose ears and judgment easily confirm whether or not learning has taken place.[2]

Not unlike other professionals, abilities vary among teachers. If we assume something of a normal distribution in ability, it stands to reason that most music teaching is average or better (to which the cynic might admittedly reply: average or worse). Assessment proponents argue that better assessment results in better teaching; no matter how good the level of teaching, more (and/or better) assessment will supposedly make it better. Assessment proponents also invariably claim or imply, however, that the majority of music teachers are incapable of conducting effective assessments. On one level the logic might hold: music teachers, no matter how well they are doing, can always do better if they take better advantage of good assessment practices. On the other hand, the assessment discourse is filled with implicit and explicit statements that imply deficit, incompetence, or malpractice. At this point the logic simply does not hold up because it suggests that learning and teaching are not really occurring unless proven, or that all music teaching is and always has been lacking. After thousands of years of music making (based presumably on competent learning and teaching), assessment experts of the early 21st century have suddenly discovered the secret of "improved" teaching!

Tasting the Soup

Much has been made of the distinction between formative and summative assessment, with many writers describing the former as "assessment for learning" and the latter as "assessment of learning." A closer look at Michael Scriven's original 1967 conception, however, reveals a slightly different understanding. Scriven actually describes it as a fallacy that the terms are intrinsically different. He did not propose formative and summative as two *types* of assessment (one during instruction and one at its conclusion), but as two *roles*, something he attempted to clarify in a 1991 retrospective:

> Formative evaluation is evaluation designed, done, and intended to support the process of improvement, and normally commissioned or done by, and delivered to, someone who can make improvements. Summative evaluation is the rest of evaluation: in terms of intentions, it is evaluation done for, or by, any observers or decision makers (by contrast with developers) who need evaluative conclusions for any other reasons besides development. (Scriven, 1991, p. 20)

As summed up by Robert Stake: "when the cook tastes the soup, that's formative; when the guests taste it, that's summative" (as cited in Scriven, 1991, p. 19).

Understood as roles reflective of the broader structure of the education system, the formative/summative distinction acknowledges that teaching, when placed within schooling, becomes a public, not private concern. The home piano teacher may be bound to personal, and perhaps professional, standards of instruction, but is not subject to political oversight and public expectations. The schoolteacher is. As Daniel Stufflebeam acknowledges (in a slightly different context), "The rights of teachers and administrators must be respected, but [authorities] must also protect the rights of students to be taught well and of communities to have their schools effectively administered" (Stufflebeam, 1991, p. 268). Teachers are thus bound by obligations not only to their students, but also to parents, communities, and state and national interests.

Accountability, Mandated Tests, Improvement

> There is little doubt that we have into a new era in public education. The powerful notion of accountability has affected many school programs, and its influence is being felt increasingly in school music. The demand for accountability has grown with the rising costs of public education and the concurrent dissatisfaction of students, parents, politicians and lay people with the results of this education.
>
> —Labuta (1974, p. 19)

The words above are from Joseph Labuta's *Guide to Accountability in Music Instruction*. On the surface, they appear as if they could have been written any time in the 21st century. Similar to contemporary discourses of "transparency" in education that reflect the demand for explicit assessment criteria to ensure the educational "contract" is properly fulfilled (see Havnes & McDowell, 2008), Labuta draws attention to the then-growing concern with "teacher liability," where the teaching–learning relationship is conceptualized in contractual terms reminiscent of industrial production: "the teacher will produce specified results in an agreed-upon amount of time, given needed resources" (1974, p. 23).

However, as one reads more closely the *Guide to Accountability in Music Instruction* (Labuta, 1974) one discerns subtle differences from today's notions of accountability. Whereas Labuta claims that concern with accountability "has quite literally turned things around in the schools by placing emphasis upon what students learn, not upon how they are taught" (p. 19), educational discourses in many countries today have witnessed a subtle shift from assessment of learner and learning to assessment of teacher and teaching—a phenomenon the educationalist David Berliner (n.d.) has called "the great switcharoo." Traditional concerns in formal education rested with how to improve teaching by focusing on learners and learning, a process requiring concrete attention to learning (i.e., growth, change) with respect to specific teachers, learners, and socioeducational conditions. Today, abstracted standardized test results (i.e., "achievement") are used to draw inferences about teachers, bracketing out all learners and social context. So-called failures of achievement (determined by arbitrary cut points) are then causally connected directly to teacher deficiencies rather than conditions, a phenomenon I observe mirrored in the change in discourse in the late 20th century from "program evaluation" (i.e., holistic considerations) to "assessment" (where context is bracketed out).[3]

Concurrent with this shift in focus from learner to teacher has been, in the opinion of some of the writers I examined, the co-opting of education by politicians, policymakers, and the commercial testing industry. In historical context, one recalls that schoolteachers and teaching have always been "inspected" to ensure acceptable competence. Even in music, district inspectors and supervisors were at one time entrusted with ensuring standards of instruction. Trust in the subjective judgment of educational experts, however, has arguably been eroded in favor of egalitarian voices of the people (i.e., politicians and others now empowered by the supposed democratizing effect of the Internet), human capital agendas, and faith in "science" and the objectivity of numbers (Porter, 1995).[4] As Stake lamented as early as 1991, "as student assessment rivets attention and energy, the authority of those who have studied education deeply is not held in greater respect than the authority of those who merely have been greatly disappointed by the schools" (Stake, 1991, p. 86)—to which one in the 21st century might add the government's respect for and faith in the testing industry to spur teaching innovation and improvement.

The international media company Pearson is a case in point. According to a February 2015 *Fortune* magazine story, the US education testing and assessment "market" escalated from $1.6 billion in 2010–2011 to $2.5 billion in 2012–2013. Analysts pegged Pearson's share of this market at approximately 60%. As the story points out, "it is fully in the company's interest for standardized testing to increase" (http://fortune.com/2015/01/21/everybody-hates-pearson). My intent is not to villainize Pearson—a for-profit company simply operating according to the logic of capitalism—but rather to show how teachers can unwittingly participate in a constructed reality about the perceived centrality of mandated tests to good teaching.

As publishers of *Measurement and Assessment in Teaching* (*MAT*) (Miller, Linn, & Gronlund, 2009), a widely used textbook aimed at an audience of undergraduate and graduate students taking an introductory class in educational measurement and assessment, Pearson helps to construct the professional "truth" about teaching and learning. Unapologetically, the book begins by stating, "Federal and state legislation mandate extensive use of student assessments to hold schools, districts, and educators accountable for student achievement" (p. 1). While not necessarily incorrect, *MAT* treats this premise as a justification for all that is to follow. Student tests are presented as fair and unproblematic and large-scale testing is celebrated repeatedly. In a box labeled "Factors that make tests and assessments appealing to educational policymakers," *MAT* claims that tests are relatively inexpensive, can be externally mandated, can be rapidly implemented, and have results that are visible. Throughout the first chapter the reader is left with the unmistakable impression that mandated tests are absolutely necessary for ensuring quality teaching and quality education. Compensatory Education (Title I), Minimum-Competency Testing, A Nation at Risk, Standards-Based Reform, and No Child Left Behind are all presented as examples of why mandated tests are needed. Failing, inadequate, "at risk," and "left behind" are all part of the prominent vocabulary used to ensure that the reader appreciates the need for nationwide mandated tests. Music educators may choose to disagree with such thinking, but they are still left to deal with the widespread rationality that has come to dominate educational thinking about assessment in many countries.

Some music educators in the United States have been attempting to capitalize on accountability rationality by advocating for mandated tests in order to demonstrate the legitimacy of music and the arts as "core subjects" (see Hickey, 2011; Nierman, 2011; Smith, 2011). In the words of former National Association for Music Education (NAfME) president Glenn Nierman, "[I]t seems reasonable to be held accountable for growth in [the arts]. . . . If music educators want to be perceived as teaching a basic, core subject, then we must be willing to document that growth in skills and understanding is occurring in students who are studying music and the arts" (2011, p. 101). Nierman is far from alone. Consider this from the 2009 assessment in music education proceedings: "This is where teacher leadership in music education assessment is going to shine: creating a culture that values music because music is held to accountability standards worthy of core-curricular status" (Anderson, 2009, p. 186). Such appeals may make for good lobbying tactics (the merits of which I am in no position to judge), but in the process they empower accountability rationality by suggesting that documenting growth must take the form of mandated, standardized tests.

Appealing to accountability rhetoric in the name of legitimacy risks potentially dangerous repercussions. Because certain federal education dollars in the United States are currently tied to teacher accountability measures, school districts (which, in many areas have primary educational authority) have no choice but to implement testing for all teachers. Many districts are unlikely to invest the necessary resources to assess holistically and will resort to the least expensive and easiest solution: paper and pencil tests on simple-to-score items such as note names.[5] Moreover, districts are just as likely to use "accountability" to cut music programs as to support them. *Live by the sword, die by the sword.* For further confirmation of the potentially dangerous effects of data-driven decision-making one need look no further than the concerns expressed by long-time educational measurement proponent Gene Glass, who, in a blog post titled, "Why I Am No Longer a Measurement Specialist" (http://ed2worlds.blogspot.com/2015/08/why-i-am-no-longer-measurement.html), writes, "The degrading of public education has involved impugning its effectiveness, cutting its budget, and busting its unions. Educational measurement has been the perfect tool for accomplishing all three: cheap and scientific looking."

Reasons for the change "from trust to accountability" (Hertzberg, 2008, p. 51) are extraordinarily complex, of course, and I do not presume to claim insights overlooked by others. Certainly the international "competition fetish" in education (Naidoo, 2016), fueled by human capital theory, has only intensified since Levin wrote in 1991 about the "great pressure on the schools to improve educational outcomes in order to meet the needs for producing a labor force for an increasingly competitive world economic situation" (Levin, 1991, p. 205). As well, the widespread belief in Thorndike's assertion that whatever exists can be measured has reinforced a 21st-century "regime of truth" (Foucault, Frye, & Gordon, 1980) about the preeminence of managerial thinking and "data driven" decision-making.

> The growth of scientific statistics as a dominating reasoning creates beliefs in that the more data we gather and the more comparisons we make—the more will we know. This use of comparisons and data within statistics carries a number of presuppositions: that reality can be represented in numbers, that it can be controlled and that risks can be managed.   (Pettersson, Popkewitz, & Lindblad, 2016, p. 182)

The end result is that education in many countries is now subject to what Pettersson et al. call the "audit society," a condition they attribute to changes in the nature of the relationships between individuals, the state, and society (2016, p. 197). These relationships are, I submit, much more complicated than the general sense of "shared responsibility between public and provider" (Colwell, 2006, p. 58).

MOVEMENT II: AS THE WORLD TURNS

One of Richard Colwell's long-standing concerns is that professional status is premised, in part, on value agreement. I would argue that the identity politics involved in professionalism in music education are far more complex than generally acknowledged. Does a music teacher identify according to membership and endorsement of Orff, "general music," or "band" affiliation, a school district, a state/provincial organization, a national organization, or an international organization, for example? Do (should) all music educators believe that assessment is a matter of "many paths, one destination," to borrow a phrase from the 2011 music education assessment proceedings, or do (should) music educators believe "[t]here can be no universal yardstick for assessing the creative, performative, effective or affective features of all music" (Nzewi, 2013, p. 23)? Is there one set of comprehensive philosophical beliefs that all music educators everywhere can or should endorse to guide assessment, or should philosophical commitments reflect context? To what extent should philosophical commitments be voluntary versus compelled? To what extent should music educators be able to collectively determine educative values and to what extent should others (policymakers, local communities) have a say in what should constitute valuable learning in music? To what extent should various stakeholders participate in the construction of large-scale assessments? Should students have a voice in their own learning?

These are extremely complex questions. My own concern is that these kinds of questions seem to get short shrift in many music education assessment discourses. My reading of the literature confirms Elliott's observation that the music education profession "tends to operate not in relation to serious thinking, critical debate, and long-term planning, but in relation to a crisis-style 'advocacy mindset' that packages and repackages music to fit the latest ideology" (2006, p. 48). I do not think Elliott means to imply that the profession is not serious in its efforts but, rather, that much thinking and planning in music education tends to focus on what seems "practical" and pragmatic, eschewing deeper questions of values and what it really means to be a profession. As a result, substantive thinking gets dismissed as philosophical—as *impractical*—and educational vision becomes conflated with political action.

Regulation from Within or Without?

Self-determination is one of the hallmarks of liberty: the freedom and autonomy to do as one wishes without being subject to or coerced by others. As noted by Max Weber long ago, voluntary associations arise for various reasons and exist alongside, and often in opposition to, authoritative associations. Two examples help to illustrate the workings of voluntary associations and self-determination. The National Association of Schools of Music (NASM) in the United States is a voluntary association that emerged as the result of recognition among several leaders of tertiary level music units that government regulations and legislation would be imposed unless a music unit leaders could adequately demonstrate self-regulation (Barrows, 1999). Although NASM must still operate within and under the standards and policies of government and other agencies, NASM is a self-governing body *of institutions* that sets and monitors its own standards of practice, the collection of which rightly can be considered a "program." Membership is based on a fee and compliance with NASM's stated standards, as determined by self-study and external inspection (i.e., program evaluation). Although the standards are revised regularly by the membership (i.e., members have a voice), the standards exhibit stability over time, indicative of a high degree of homogeneity of values and purpose. Importantly, NASM institutions are accountable to each other, not the public.

NAfME, on the other hand, arose out of shared interests in the practices of school music. Membership is technically open to anyone, but in practice comprises primarily *individuals*—school music teachers and music teacher educators—who pay an annual fee in exchange for tangible benefits such as receiving a journal, eligibility to pay to attend state and national conferences, and student eligibility to participate in such things as "All-State" festivals. Intangible benefits might include a feeling of professional belonging and a sense of collective advocacy for the cause of music education. Importantly, however, teachers are accountable to the public by virtue of their employment, not their NAfME membership. While it is expected that NAfME staff and officers should dutifully serve the organization, they are not accountable to the public and possess no official educational authority to determine curriculum and assessment.

Considering the differences between the two associations sheds light on the challenges of assessment in music education. NAfME can technically be considered self-determining as an organization operationally, but unlike NASM it does not possess the authority to compel or sanction standards of practice, a responsibility of administrators and government policymakers. While some school districts in the United States compel music teachers to be members of NAfME as a condition of employment, this does not mean that individuals necessarily subscribe to the value orientation of the organization. Unlike NASM, which has a clear program of study (on which to be evaluated), school music "programs" are not really programs beyond their local contexts. One school band program might look similar to another, but there is no such thing as a state or national program of band instruction.

Efforts by NAfME to help devise and advocate for "national standards" can thus be viewed as an attempt at self-determination by forging agreement on the aims, purposes, and standards of school music learning and teaching, in order to avoid having standards and assessments being imposed on them by others (see, e.g., Banta, 2002). As the testing advocate Scott Shuler explained in 2009 about efforts in Connecticut that provided the eventual basis for the subsequent national arts standards initiative: "Connecticut's Common Arts Assessment project is providing an opportunity for arts educators to maintain control over their classroom priorities in an increasingly data-driven school environment, by developing tools to measure the arts learning that they value most" (Shuler & Wells, 2009, p. 53). The reported and purported challenges and difficulties of the process of agreeing on national standards in music and the arts point to the high degree of heterogeneity in the profession. Unlike NASM, which has a clear aim and purpose—the training of musicians as defined according to a carefully prescribed standardized, codified program of study—the aims and purposes of school music have never met with widespread agreement (locally, nationally, or internationally).

We're in This Together

As Shuler astutely surmised, the political process of successfully forging agreement among parties with disparate values and interests depends on participation. Hence, Shuler, in his capacities in Connecticut and with NAfME, wisely sought to engage grass-roots involvement in the process by providing at least the perception of voice. As someone who has participated in similar exercises in a Canadian province and an American state, however, I would offer the comment that such participation is often disingenuous and deliberately avoids engaging with scholarly thought,[6] something Colwell has similarly lamented: "[P]olicymakers are not likely to seek the opinions of scholars or individuals in higher education—local interest groups are far more influential than objective reports" (2009, p. 5). The effort to achieve "democratic participation" (or at least the appearance of such) and the avoidance of the elitism of the ivory tower results in a political process where all opinions are equal: The first-year teacher has as much (or often more) to say as the lifetime researcher of educational assessment.

Regardless of the process employed to achieve large-scale professional agreement, the demand for national standards and assessments is somewhat puzzling. Shuler proudly proclaimed that the 1994 National Standards in Arts Education "provided the first truly nationwide attempt to codify the key components of what students should know and be able to do" (2007, p. 124). The demand for national standards and assessment is not confined to the United States. Bordin, Cantamessa, and DeCicco (2011) describe how membership in the European Union brought about "the need for consistency and uniformity in the development of skills," which has in turn "demanded that similar standards of assessment should be found in every type of school" (p. 176). One wonders, however, why music education and its assessment requires national codification. Do students in Concord, New Hampshire, really benefit if their music education looks exactly the same as that in Missoula, Montana, or Chattanooga, Tennessee? Do we need national comparability? Can excellence not be achieved in the absence of parallel content and assessment? Does excellence in music take only one form?

At least three observations can be made about forging collective agreement on educational matters related to assessment. First, by its nature, it will strengthen the values and priorities of those already in power. Weiss (1991) concludes, "[m]ost of the political implications of evaluation have an establishment orientation. They accept—and bolster—the status quo" (p. 224). Second, problems with equity and diversity in music education, already serious, will continue. As House (1991) remarks about large-scale assessments: "The powerless and the poor are excluded from inner bargaining processes, and typically their interests are ignored" (p. 239). The collective "we" of music education will continue to be grounded in white and middle-class values, even as it claims to speak for and on behalf of all people. Third, difference will be regarded as a threat. The dialectical reasoning of consensus depends on the elimination of difference necessary for any large-scale effort claiming to speak with one voice. *United we stand, divided we fall* can thus be viewed as a tactic that ensures the dominant values and voices that result from supposedly democratic and participatory decision-making have the appearance of consensus and representativeness.

MOVEMENT III: INTERLUDE

In a book chapter titled, "How We Think About Evaluation," the educational evaluation specialist Ernest House draws on Lakoff and Johnson's *Metaphors We Live By* to examine metaphors in assessment and evaluation (House, 1983). If, as is so often argued, assessment is vital, if not intrinsic, to good teaching, it is striking to contrast familiar metaphors in education with metaphors of assessment. Consider, for example, some metaphors of the teacher, such as gardener, trainer, coach, juggler, tour guide, artist, engineer, captain/ navigator, conductor, farmer, performer, and so on. Consider some that straddle teaching/ learning: planting, playing cards, banking, switching on a light bulb, diet/eating, being a detective, peeling an onion, a quest, sculpting, wrestling. Such lists could go on and on. (In addition to many articles and book chapters on metaphors in education, there are at least two books entitled *Metaphors We Teach By*.) Teaching/learning metaphors con-trast, often dramatically, with those in formal assessment, which, as House points out, tend to be driven by metaphors of industrial production, machines, conduits, and sport-ing events: discrete elements, operation, implementation, replication, inputs-outputs, production runs, time, costs, procedures, products, monitoring of processes, outcomes, contamination, purification, level of variables, targets, goals, and so on. Within such metaphoric paradigms, the process and function of education become understood in terms of efficiency, effectiveness, adequacy, and usefulness: "Raw materials come in one end of the assembly line, labor is performed in stages, and products come out the other end" (p. 12). One suspects that metaphors of assessment have Dewey rolling in his grave.

What Are Our Metaphors?

Lest one think such a discussion far removed from the concerns of music education, consider the following vocabulary from a recent *Music Educators Journal* article on assessment in music education: "tracking student achievement," "choosing growth targets," "setting posttest targets," "objectives-based teaching," "managing growth assessment data," "benchmark expectations." Or, to take another example, consider the metaphoric overtones of the word "tool," which shows up with abundance in the published proceed-ings of the biennial symposia on assessment in music education: 2007 (59 pages), 2009 (111 pages), 2011 (65 pages), 2013 (65 pages). Quite clearly, metaphoric thinking is deeply embedded in the DNA of music educators. This is not to imply that such thinking is wrong, however. As House points out, industrial production and sport contests meta-phors are frequently embraced "because they are pervasive experiences in our society . . . and these structural metaphors embody core values of American society" (1983, p. 19).

Metaphors, House writes, "will always be close to our core values" (p. 20), something that likely helps to explain how a national education policies called *No Child Left Behind* and *Race to the Top* could meet with such little opposition; it appears as "common sense" that teaching and learning should be conceptualized in terms of linear distance where the goal is to keep up with the pack or, better still, win.

One of the things a metaphorical analysis exercise can do is provide an opportunity for critical self-evaluation. House asks, "To what degree does metaphor characterize all evaluative thinking? How does it work? Where do these metaphors come from?...Are all metaphors equally good?" (1983, p. 19). A closer look at metaphors in music education and music education assessment reveals tensions between espoused and enacted values. This speaks in some ways to differences in the imagined and claimed purposes of assessment, as well as the desired degree of homogeneity of professional values. It is one thing to espouse creativity, collaboration, sensitivity, and participation in line with metaphors of artist, quest, or farmer/gardener, but if one's enacted assessment practices consist of note name tests and playing tests of prepared repertoire in order to measure individual growth and achievement, one's espoused values matter little.

Because it has come to appear as common sense that assessment means ascertaining *progress toward a goal*, the discourse of "objectives"—understood almost universally today as *behavioral* objectives—has become so commonplace and pervasive that many educators cannot imagine learning and assessment in any other way. I recently experienced the limits of "academic freedom" when a university official repeatedly rejected my proposed course syllabus because it did not include behavioral objectives. Ultimately, the syllabus reviewer pointed me to the official university policy requiring behavioral objectives (and sent me examples of required wording, presumably believing that my omission represented ignorance rather than an educational choice). I would like to believe that an official university policy requiring the inclusion of behavioral objectives in course syllabi is a manifestation of growing litigiousness in education (itself an outgrowth of accountability thinking where the teaching–learning relationship is conceptualized in the form of a contract) rather than a genuine belief that good teaching and learning is dependent on the explicit articulation of behavioral objectives.

"Clearly defined" objectives—so important to assessment discourses—risk foreclosing learning as adventure and exploration and risk reducing education to training. The student has no voice and no agency in a teaching–learning relationship defined by behavioral objectives because everything must be stipulated by the teacher in advance ("what students should know and be able to do," "beginning with the end in mind"); any sense of emergence that deviates from the teacher's desired path thus becomes a threat to be managed, reduced, and ideally eliminated. Moreover, it reduces the *art* of teaching to a *science*. As Havnes and McDowell describe it,

> Our new assessment culture very often sits alongside a rationalist, managerialist culture which regards assessment as a technology. From this perspective all that is required is to make explicit what the assessment requirements are and to describe in detail what standards learners need to attain.   (2008, pp. 116–117)

Codified and standardized assessment practices and expectations speak to both philosophical commitments and a collective vision for the profession. For many educators, objectives, tracking, targets, and benchmarks are the sine qua non of licensed and credentialed teaching. For others, however, it could be that normative discourses of management, control, and conformity represent an infringement on professional teaching autonomy, especially for those whose envisioned educational values diverge from imposed sets of "standards" premised on, in the present case of the United States, for example, metaphors of work and production that inevitably lead to particular assessment paradigms. Creative metaphors could be forwarded as a kind of "counter narrative," but, as House suggests, "conventional metaphors shape most of our thinking and therefore seem natural" (1983, p. 21). "Outcomes thinking" has become so pervasive in education, if not society at large, that one is hard-pressed to imagine assessment in any other way. While metaphors can be helpful (many argue that *all* thinking is metaphorical), the unconscious embrace of a given metaphor "may lead us to overlook other important features in the situation that the metaphor does not capture" (1983, p. 9). How, for example, might assessment in music education be different if we ceased thinking about it as "practical" or as a set of "tools"?

Movement IV: Truth or Consequences?

The prevalence of the term "authentic assessment" seems to have waned somewhat from its heyday in the 1980s and 1990s, but the concept behind the term is still very much present. In many cases, "valid and reliable" seems to have taken the place of "authentic," as if valid and reliable implies or subsumes authenticity. This reflects an impoverished conception of validity, however, as if "measuring what it purports to measure" is all there is to say on the matter. While there may be affinities between authentic assessment and validity, I would argue that, despite the pitfalls and landmines in the concept, authenticity holds the potential to better elucidate our understandings of assessment and validity. One could, for example, create a so-called valid and reliable assessment of children's ability to notate quarter notes and eighth notes using Western staff notation, but the authenticity of such an assessment is clearly open to scrutiny if (1) typical classroom tasks rarely if ever require such knowledge (skill), and (2) such knowledge has no use value in a child's future.

Colwell (2002) suggests authentic assessment "is seldom related to assessment in music education [because] almost all assessment in music is authentic" (p. 1129). To the extent Colwell means that good teaching practices in music incorporate assessment and feedback organically as part of instruction, one is inclined to agree. As others have pointed out, however, the question of authenticity is unequivocally subjective. Gulkers, Bastiaens, and Kirschner (2008), for example, write, "[W]hat students perceive as authentic is not necessarily the same as what teachers and assessment developers see as authentic" (p. 76). The subjective nature of authenticity holds the potential to help us think differently when we consider questions such as authentic to what and to whom. For example, despite concerns raised about the lack of evidence for documenting individual student growth/learning, ensemble evaluations would seem to be authentic insofar as ensemble performance constitutes the lion's share of what is typically done in most American secondary school music programs. The musical practice of large ensemble performance is a group, not individual activity. What would seem to be inauthentic is to have a system of individualized assessment practices far removed from the day-to-day norms and expectations of the music classroom (assessment practices based, incidentally, on assumptions so often contrary to Vygotsky and theories of social constructivism).

None of this is to suggest that individualized assessment is wrong, of course. Rather, it is to point out the tensions that exist when we consider deeper questions of authenticity. This is likely why Colwell suggests, "[w]e need an 'authentic' philosophy of music education before we can have 'authentic' evaluation" (Colwell, 2006, p. 59). If teachers' enacted values show that secondary school music is fundamentally about large ensemble performance, where the goal is to emulate the standards and practices of professional (or quasi-professional) large ensembles, claims to authenticity in evaluation will be refracted through this experience, regardless of any espoused values to the contrary. This is one reason why one-dimensional conceptions of validity are problematic. Despite elaborated views on validity in the wider literature (e.g., content, criterion-related, construct, concurrent, predictive, consequential, systemic, relational), the music education literature seems largely stuck on content validity, ignoring Colwell's (1970) caution that validity is a function of intended use, not the test or measurement instrument (see also Colwell, 2013), a caution in line with the updated view of test validity found in the latest edition of *Standards for Educational and Psychological Testing*: "Statements about validity should refer to particular interpretations for specified uses. It is incorrect to use the unqualified phrase 'the validity of the test'" (American Educational Research Association, 2014, p. 11). In the absence of some sort of clearly articulated aims for school music, content validity is inert. As Melissa Silverman asks, "if a teacher focuses on assessing a student's tonal and rhythmic accuracy, tone quality, sight-reading, and expressiveness, how do such assessments relate to anything beyond a student's success or failure in achieving these skills?" (2009, p. 382). Put differently, even if deemed "valid," assessments hold little meaning in the absence of a larger vision of why people learn music and, relatedly, reasons why music exists as part of compulsory schooling.

Assessing Assessment

As someone who has spent his entire career doing research, writing, and thinking about educational testing and assessment issues, I would like to conclude by summarizing a compelling case showing that the major uses of tests for student and school accountability during the past 50 years have improved education and student learning in dramatic ways. Unfortunately, that is not my conclusion.

—Linn (2000, p. 14)

One of the meanings of *consequential validity* refers to "intended and unintended effects of assessment on instruction or teaching" (Gulkers et al., 2008, p. 74). Along these lines, Silverman asks, "Is there a possibility that seemingly excellent models of 'rigorous' and 'reliable' assessment have the potential to damage the very things we value most about music and music education?" (2009, p. 382). I would argue that increased attention to consequential validity (rather than just "validity") holds tremendous potential to reexamine what David Elliott describes as "education-as-assessment-ism" where the "tail is now wagging, tripping, and strangling the dog" (2009, p. 368).

In his contribution to the 2009 music education assessment proceedings, Elliott draws attention to how Paul Lehman poured cold water on the idea that developing a lifelong love of music or incorporating music into one's life could or should be incorporated into the then-MENC National Standards because (1) such things are not standards, and (2) such things "cannot be readily and validly assessed" (as quoted in Elliott, 2009, p. 371). While Lehman may have been technically correct in the limited sense, such a response fails to recognize the inherent problem: assessment practices are invalid if they fail to support a comprehensive view of education. If conceptions of assessment were oriented based on consequential validity, any assessment that failed to contribute to, or worse, did harm to the aim of lifelong love and participation in music would be deemed invalid—assuming, of course, that lifelong love of and participation in music represents a desired aim for the profession. In this spirit, Elliott asks, "What good are formative and summative assessments of musical 'knowings and doings' if teachers fail to develop students' intrinsic interest and commitment to music making and listening at the same time they are being assessed?" (2009, p. 371).

Cost-benefit analysis in education is tricky business because the variables and contexts are enormously complex. The logic of mandated tests and teacher accountability is presumably based in the belief that their purported benefits outweigh associated costs. The contestability of this claim rests on what constitutes a benefit and what constitutes a cost. It would seem that, according to those who promote the value of mandated tests, such assessments provide a measure of transparency and accountability to the publicly funded education system and allow for more effective deployment of resources (financial and other) by identifying strengths and deficiencies in the system. Sometimes, however, costs and effects can be difficult to identify. Richard Ingersoll's research (Ingersoll, Merrill, & Stuckey, 2014) on teacher turnover and retention, for example, suggests that teacher attrition now costs schools billions of dollars each year. A primary reason cited for teachers leaving the profession is the lack of a say in decisions that impact on their teaching.[7] Mandated assessments remove (or reduce) teachers' abilities to determine curriculum, instruction, the nature and timing of assessments, and so on. One should not just consider consequential validity in terms of students, but in terms of teachers as well.

What Would Foucault Say?

> The examination, surrounded by all its documentary techniques, makes each individual a "case": a case which at one and the same time constitutes an object for a branch of knowledge and a hold for a branch of power.
>
> —Foucault (1995, p. 191)

> People know what they do; they frequently know why they do what they do; but what they don't know is what what they do does.
>
> —Dreyfus, Foucault, and Rabinow (1982, p. 187)

Although nominally about the emergence of the modern prison system, Michel Foucault's 1972 book *Discipline and Punish* is, at heart, a study of how "discipline" has helped to create the modern individual. The book has been popular among critical educators because of the ways it shows how the emergence of modern schooling mirrors the rise of the prison system. One of Foucault's precious lines from *Discipline and Punish* reads: "Is it surprising that prisons resemble factories, schools, barracks, hospitals, which all resemble prisons?" (1995, p. 228). Another reason Foucault's work has been popular with educators is because of the way he analyzes the relationships between knowledge and power. The ability to test or examine someone relies on and reinforces particular knowledge systems that reflect historically produced power relations. It is, for example, inconceivable (at least in the United States) that credentialed, licensed school music teachers could be community hip hop artists lacking in the ability to code and decode Western staff notation because the entire structure of music teacher training and the norms and expectations of school music practices have been built on the power-knowledge system of Western European art music. As Havnes and McDowell (2008) explain, "Assessment is always to some extent about the exercise of power in order to serve certain interests and achieve specific purposes. This is not always explicit, especially when viewed from the perspectives of teachers and learners engaged in assessment practice in their own contexts" (p. 118). The "examination," in other words, is constructed and conducted by those authorized and recognized as always already possessing the necessary knowledge and expertise. This becomes, for those part of the system at least, so natural and just that alternatives are invalidated or not recognized, something Foucault describes with the term "subjugated knowledge."

Advocates obviously have their reasons for believing in the importance of testing and assessment. In the words of Papageorgi and Hallam (2010), tests "promote motivation, enable comparisons to be made, provide a structure for learning, enable individuals to compete against their previous examination performance, and can provide some assessment of the effectiveness of teachers" (p. 151)—to say nothing of the widespread belief that assessment is the key to "raising standards." While Papageorgi and Hallam acknowledge the potential "anxiety-provoking aspects" of tests for both students and teachers, I would submit that music educators have not always sufficiently thought about the full consequences of assessment—how it helps to create one kind of musical being rather than another, and how it privileges certain ways of being musical over others, as if there is just one, or a "right" way to be musical.

Thinking about the consequences of assessment goes deeper than just worrying about test anxiety or the kind of curricular narrowing implied by aphorisms like "we measure what we treasure" or "you get what you assess"; it speaks to the heart of how education so powerfully determines the kind of people we become and the societal structures that are reproduced. Dysthe (2008) writes, "When students are assessed, whether by a teacher or by peers, the very language that is used is important for how they gradually come to view themselves as learners" (p. 21). Similarly, Tan (2011) writes about how the widespread practice of ABRSM[8] exams in Singapore "have since instilled a culture that views music lessons as synonymous to music testing" (p. 218). From a Foucaultian perspective, these observations only begin to scratch the surface. The current National Core Arts Standards in the United States, for example, reflect a belief in the "artistic process model" (creating, performing, responding—and now "connecting"), a model that, for many arts educators in the United States, has become so synonymous with music learning and teaching they cannot imagine it any other way. A close reading of the new arts standards reveals how the language of "artistic work" (the word "work" appears in 10 of the 11 standards) and "standard notation" (as if Western staff notation is standard for everyone) privileges one way of musical being over another. One can only imagine the kind of musical people and musical society that might result if the standards instead employed works like "joy," "play," "risk taking," "interaction," and "well-being." These, however, do not register as the proper concerns of music education and its assessment.

MOVEMENT V: IT'S A MAD, MAD, MAD, MAD WORLD

Lest I be misunderstood, I am in no way suggesting in this chapter that assessment is bad or that music teaching should operate devoid of standards or, to borrow one of Colwell's mantras, *excellence*. Good teachers assess their students and their own teaching. Better teachers communicate and model desired life values, offer constructive feedback that supports learning excellence, and figure out ways to satisfy stakeholder expectations that teaching is sufficiently competent to justify the expense. (Yes, everyone desires an above average teacher in spite of the statistical impossibility.) Let me be clear: *assessment is good*. However...

The folk musician Pete Seeger famously remarked that the question should not be *What music is good?*, but *What is music good for?* I would respectfully offer that the music education profession might be better served by asking *What is assessment good for?* rather than the seemingly perennial question, *What is good assessment?* Repeated prescriptions in the literature to "develop meaningful assessments" are not helpful because they fail to address the importance of *Meaningful to whom and in what ways?* Elliot Eisner reminds us, "[w]hat constitutes data and what constitutes garbage depends upon frame of reference, aim, and method" (1991, p. 183). Assessment "data" and its meanings are subjective and relative to individual and collective values and value systems. I would boldly suggest that the quest for the Holy Grail of perfect assessment methods in music education is destined to fail because it is a misguided quest. Thinking more about the intended and *unintended* consequences of our actions might be a better place to start.

Arguably, the international phenomena of assessment creep and "national monitoring" (Murphy, 2007, p. 367) has been wreaking havoc on education for some time. "We find ourselves ensnared in a global examinations pandemic in which the pursuit of standards through what can be cheaply and defensibly measured is driving out genuine engagement in learning," observes Broadfoot (2008, p. 216). My worry is that music educators will capitulate to this pandemic by adopting an attitude of *if you can't beat 'em, join 'em*. Stanley Kramer's 1963 comedy, *It's a Mad, Mad, Mad, Mad World* is about a group of strangers who, lured by the prospect of fast cash, are quick to jettison their sense of right and wrong. My fear is that music educators, lured by the tantalizing prospect of "legitimacy" through mandated testing, may be tempted to abandon what they know is good and true about music and music education, and may fail to see how the quest for the Holy Grail may be unintentionally perpetuating various forms of injustice.

To paraphrase the early 20th-century Italian intellectual, Antonio Gramsci (1971), we are all philosophers because we all think. This is not to suggest all thinking is philosophical in nature, but rather, that philosophers are not some special breed of people with a special claim on the truth or on moral principles. Thinking deeply and carefully is a choice we make, not just as academics and "intellectuals" (to borrow Gramsci's term) but also as human beings, in order to conduct ourselves ethically and responsibly. Thinking deeply and carefully about our choices in music education is how we define ourselves as professionals. Not unlike Christopher Small, who wrote, "music is too important to be left to the musicians" (1977, p. 200), I would submit that philosophical thinking about assessment is too important to be left to the philosophers.

Notes

1. I subscribe to the view that meaning is use, though I do personally regard the two terms as distinguishable. According to Colwell (2002), evaluation "is distinguished by the making of judgments based on the data derived from measurements," whereas assessment "refers to the considerable body of data that has the potential to diagnose and provide clues to causes" (p. 1129).
2. Kincheloe writes, "Numbers-crunching test advocates are convinced that rigor cannot exist without measurement driven by both politicians and fear-filled school administrators. There is an innate refusal to acknowledge that any learning can take place without strict measurement" (2006, p. vii).
3. Stake (1991) remarks, "By 1980, student assessment rather than program evaluation was the major player in the school improvement movement" (p. 75).
4. Taylor (2006) writes about "the apparent need to neutralize teachers' professional judgments, and to silence children out of their own learning" (p. xiv).
5. This is not conjecture. I know of instances where this is, in fact, happening.
6. In my first experience with government curriculum and assessment design, back when I was a school teacher, no higher education representatives were present; they were

deemed too out of touch with the classroom to really understand the classroom. After a year of regular meetings we generated a document that was then taken under advisement, to be vetted and eventually changed by official policymakers, leading me to cynically wonder whether the whole exercise was just for show (since the final version could boast that it was the result of practitioner involvement). In my second experience, operating as a higher education member, I advocated strongly (based on scholarly arguments; I was the only higher education representative for the music area) for some wording that could ensure flexibility and openness in music instruction. Our subcommittee's submission, adopted from the National Core Arts Standards, read: "With appropriate guidance, organize personal musical ideas using notation (e.g. iconic notation and/or recording technology)." While this wording exists at the kindergarten level in the official adopted version of the state standards, the wording of all other levels (grades 1–8) was changed (by government officials, one assumes) to "Use notation to document personal or collective musical ideas." I submit that the difference in wording is far from innocent, as the word "notation" alone will almost certainly be interpreted to mean Western staff notation, thus ensuring the perpetuation of a value set that equates music education with notation education, consistent with the NASM definition of a musician as someone who can read staff notation.

7. See also: http://www.npr.org/sections/ed/2015/03/30/395322012/the-hidden-costs-of-teacher-turnover.
8. Associated Board of the Royal Schools of Music.

References

American Educational Research Association, American Psychological Association, National Council on Measurement in Education, & Joint Committee on Standards for Educational and Psychological Testing (US). (2014). *Standards for educational and psychological testing.* Washington, DC: American Educational Research Association.

Anderson, A. K. (2009). Assessment in elementary music education: One district's approach to authentic assessment in the elementary classroom. In T. Brophy (Ed.), *The practice of assessment in music education: Frameworks, models, and designs* (pp. 179–204). Chicago, IL: GIA Publications.

Astin, A. W. (1993). *Assessment for excellence: The philosophy and practice of assessment and evaluation in higher education.* Phoenix, AZ: Oryx Press.

Banta, T. W. (2002). *Building a scholarship of assessment* (1st ed.). San Francisco, CA: Jossey-Bass.

Barrows, S. A. (1999). *Historical perspectives, 1924–1999: National Association of Schools of Music, seventy-fifth anniversary.* Reston, VA: National Association of Schools of Music.

Berliner, D. (n.d.). *Inequality and schooling: Why the USA is falling behind in education* [PowerPoint slides]. Retrieved from http://slideplayer.com/slide/7546124/

Bordin, A., Cantamessa, M., & DeCicco, D. (2011). Musical learning and assessment: Normatives, practices and methods in the context of the Italian education system. In T. Brophy & A. Lehmann-Wermser (Eds.), *Music assessment across cultures and continents: The culture of shared practice* (pp. 175–186). Chicago, IL: GIA Publications.

Broadfoot, P. (2008). Assessment for learners. In A. Havnes & L. McDowell (Eds.), *Balancing dilemmas in assessment and learning in contemporary education* (pp. 213–224). New York, NY: Routledge.

Brophy, T. (Ed.). (2007). *Assessment in music education: Integrating curriculum, theory, and practice*. Chicago, IL: GIA Publications.

Brophy, T. (Ed.). (2009). *The practice of assessment in music education: Frameworks, models, and designs*. Chicago, IL: GIA Publications.

Brophy, T., Lai, M.-L., & Chen, H.-F. (Eds.). (2013). *Music assessment and global diversity: Practice, measurement, and policy*. Chicago, IL: GIA Publications.

Brophy, T., & Lehmann-Wermser, A. (Eds.). (2011). *Music assessment across cultures and continents: The culture of shared practice*. Chicago, IL: GIA Publications.

Colwell, R. (1970). *The evaluation of music teaching and learning*. Englewood Cliffs, NJ: Prentice-Hall.

Colwell, R. (2002). Assessment's potential in music education. In R. Colwell & C. Richardson (Eds.), *The new handbook of research on music teaching and learning* (pp. 1128–1158). New York, NY: Oxford University Press.

Colwell, R. (2004). Evaluation in the arts is sheer madness. *Arts Praxis, 1*, 1–12.

Colwell, R. (2006). An assessment of assessment in music. In P. Taylor (Ed.), *Assessment in arts education* (pp. 57–80). Portsmouth, NH: Heinemann.

Colwell, R. (2007). Music assessment in an increasingly politicized, accountability-driven educational environment. In T. Brophy (Ed.), *Assessment in music education: Integrating curriculum, theory, and practice* (pp. 3–16). Chicago, IL: GIA Publications.

Colwell, R. (2009). Many voices, one goal: Practices of large-scale music assessment. In T. Brophy (Ed.), *The practice of assessment in music education: Frameworks, models, and designs* (pp. 3–22). Chicago, IL: GIA Publications.

Colwell, R. (2013). The black swans of summative assessment. In T. Brophy, M.-L. Lai, & H.-F. Chen (Eds.), *Music assessment and global diversity: Practice, measurement, and policy* (pp. 67–100). Chicago, IL: GIA Publications.

Dreyfus, H. L., Foucault, M., & Rabinow, P. (1982). *Michel Foucault, beyond structuralism and hermeneutics* (2nd ed.). Chicago: University of Chicago Press.

Dysthe, O. (2008). The challenges of assessment in a new learning culture. In A. Havnes & L. McDowell (Eds.), *Balancing dilemmas in assessment and learning in contemporary education* (pp. 15–28). New York, NY: Routledge.

Eisner, E. (1991). Taking a second look: Educational connoisseurship revisited. In M. W. McLaughlin & D. C. Phillips (Eds.), *Evaluation and education: At quarter century* (pp. 169–187). Chicago, IL: University of Chicago Press.

Elliott, D. (2006). Music Education and assessment: Issues and suggestions. In P. Taylor (Ed.), *Assessment in arts education* (pp. 41–56). Portsmouth, NH: Heinemann.

Elliott, D. (2009). Assessing the concept of assessment: Some philosophical perspectives. In T. Brophy (Ed.), *The practice of assessment in music education: Frameworks, models, and designs* (pp. 367–380). Chicago, IL: GIA Publications.

Foucault, M. (1995). *Discipline and punish: The birth of the prison*. New York, NY: Vintage Books.

Foucault, M., Frye, N., & Gordon, C. (1980). *Power/knowledge: Selected interviews and other writings, 1972–1977*. New York, NY: Pantheon Books.

Gramsci, A. (1971). *Selections from the prison notebooks of Antonio Gramsci*. (Hoare, Q., & Nowell-Smith, G., Trans. and Eds.). London, UK: Lawrence and Wishart.

Gulkers, J., Bastiaens, T., & Kirschner, P. (2008). Defining authentic assessment: Five dimensions of authenticity. In A. Havnes & L. McDowell (Eds.), *Balancing dilemmas in assessment and learning in contemporary education* (pp. 73–86). New York, NY: Routledge.

Havnes, A., & McDowell, L. (2008). *Balancing dilemmas in assessment and learning in contemporary education.* New York, NY: Routledge.

Hertzberg, F. (2008). Assessment of writing in Norway: A case of balancing dilemmas. In A. Havnes & L. McDowell (Eds.), *Balancing dilemmas in assessment and learning in contemporary education* (pp. 51–60). New York, NY: Routledge.

Hickey, M. (2011). Standards, assessment, and creativity in American music education: Intersection of opportunities. In T. Brophy & A. Lehmann-Wermser (Eds.), *Music assessment across cultures and continents: The culture of shared practice* (pp. 15–35). Chicago, IL: GIA Publications.

House, E. (Ed.). (1983). *Philosophy of evaluation.* San Francisco, CA: Jossey-Bass.

House, E. (1991). Evaluation and social justice: Where are we? In M. W. McLaughlin & D. C. Phillips (Eds.), *Evaluation and education: At quarter century* (pp. 233–247). Chicago, IL: University of Chicago Press.

Ingersoll, R., Merrill, L., & Stuckey, D. (2014). *Seven trends: The transformation of the teaching force.* CPRE Research Reports. Retrieved from http://repository.upenn.edu/cpre_researchreports/79.

Labuta, J. A. (1974). *Guide to accountability in music instruction.* West Nyack, NY: Parker.

Levin, H. (1991). Cost-effectiveness at quarter century. In M. W. McLaughlin & D. C. Phillips (Eds.), *Evaluation and education: At quarter century* (pp. 189–209). Chicago, IL: University of Chicago Press.

Linn, R. (2000). Assessment and accountability. *Educational Researcher, 29*(2), 4–16. doi: 10.3102/0013189X029002004

Mager, R. F. (1962). *Preparing instructional objectives.* Belmont, CA: Fearon-Pitman.

Miller, M. D., Linn, R. L., & Gronlund, N. E. (2009). *Measurement and assessment in teaching* (10th ed.). Upper Saddle River, NJ: Merrill/Pearson.

Murphy, R. (2007). Harmonizing assessment and music in the classroom. In L. Bresler (Ed.), *International handbook of research in arts education* (pp. 361–379). Dordrecht, The Netherlands: Springer.

Naidoo, R. (2016). The competition fetish in higher education: Varieties, animators and consequences. *British Journal of Sociology of Education, 37*(1), 1–10. doi: 10.1080/01425692.2015.1116209

Nierman, G. E. (2011). Making the case for high-stakes assessment in music. In T. Brophy & A. Lehmann-Wermser (Eds.), *Music assessment across cultures and continents: The culture of shared practice* (pp. 97–107). Chicago, IL: GIA Publications.

Nzewi, M. (2013). Assessing the kernel and/or the husk of music essence?—Positing sustainable humanity directions/actions. In T. Brophy (Ed.), *Music assessment and global diversity: Practice, measurement, and policy* (pp. 19–52). Chicago, IL: GIA Publications.

Papageorgi, I., & Hallam, S. (2010). Issues of assessment and performance. in S. Hallam & A. Creech (Eds.), *Music education in the 21st century in the United Kingdom: Achievements, analysis and aspirations* (pp. 141–158). London, UK: Institute of Education, University of London.

Pettersson, D., Popkewitz, T. S., & Lindblad, S. (2016). On the use of educational numbers: Comparative constructions of hierarchies by means of large-scale assessments. *Espacio, Tiempo y Educación, 3*(1), 177–202. doi: 10.14516/ete.2016.003.001.10

Porter, T. M. (1995). *Trust in numbers: The pursuit of objectivity in science and public life.* Princeton, NJ: Princeton University Press.

Scriven, M. (1991). Beyond formative and summative evaluation. In M. W. McLaughlin & D. C. Phillips (Eds.), *Evaluation and education: At quarter century* (pp. 19–64). Chicago, IL: University of Chicago Press.

Shuler, S. C. (2007). Large-scale assessment of music performance: Some whys and hows for today's data-driven educational environment. In T. Brophy (Ed.), *Assessment in music education: Integrating curriculum, theory, and practice* (pp. 123–138). Chicago, IL: GIA Publications.

Shuler, S. C., & Wells, R. (2009). Connecticut's common arts assessment initiative: Helping teachers improve music learning in a data-driven school environment. In T. Brophy (Ed.), *The practice of assessment in music education: Frameworks, models, and designs* (pp. 43–56). Chicago, IL: GIA Publications.

Silverman, M. (2009). Aims in the age of assessment: A special case. In T. Brophy (Ed.), *The practice of assessment in music education: Frameworks, models, and designs* (pp. 381–390). Chicago, IL: GIA Publications.

Small, C. (1977). *Music, society, education: A radical examination of the prophetic function of music in Western, Eastern and African cultures with its impact on society and its use in education.* London, UK: Calder.

Smith, B. P. (2011). Arts classroom-based performance assessment in Washington State: The journey continues. In T. Brophy & A. Lehmann-Wermser (Eds.), *Music assessment across cultures and continents: The culture of shared practice* (pp. 233–243). Chicago, IL: GIA Publications.

Stake, R. (1991). Retrospective on "The countenance of educational evaluation." In M. W. McLaughlin & D. C. Phillips (Eds.), *Evaluation and education: At quarter century* (pp. 67–88). Chicago, IL: University of Chicago Press.

Stufflebeam, D. (1991). Professional Standards and Ethics for Evaluators. In M. W. McLaughlin & D. C. Phillips (Eds.), *Evaluation and education: At quarter century* (pp. 249–282). Chicago, IL: University of Chicago Press.

Tan, J. J. L. (2011). Piano graded examinations, friend or foe: The relevance to piano teachers in Singapore in the 21st century. In T. Brophy (Ed.), *Music assessment across cultures and continents: The culture of shared practice* (pp. 215–232). Chicago, IL: GIA Publications.

Taylor, P. (2006). *Assessment in arts education.* Portsmouth, NH: Heinemann.

Tyler, R. (1991). General statement on program evaluation. In M. W. McLaughlin & D. C. Phillips (Eds.), *Evaluation and education: At quarter century* (pp. 3–17). Chicago, IL: University of Chicago Press.

Vaughan, C. J., Edmund, D. C., Holmes, A. V., & LaCognata, J. (2009). Frameworks, models, and designs: Key issues for assessment in music education. In T. Brophy (Ed.), *The practice of assessment in music education: Frameworks, models, and designs* (pp. 117–128). Chicago, IL: GIA Publications.

Weiss, C. (1991). Evaluation research in the political context: Sixteen years and four administrations later. In M. W. McLaughlin & D. C. Phillips (Eds.), *Evaluation and education: At quarter century* (pp. 211–231). Chicago, IL: University of Chicago Press.

CHAPTER 3

EDUCATIONAL POLICY AND ASSESSMENT IN MUSIC

PATRICK SCHMIDT

THE GROWING ROLE AND IMPACT OF EDUCATIONAL POLICY THINKING AND PRACTICE

POLICY is a contested terrain. The history of policy thought and action is the history of the tensions generated by struggles for resources and voice, and assessment writ large, has always been an integral part this history. Policy is also central to the ways in which ideas are edified into practice. Lewis and Miller (2003) argue that, at minimum, policy brings with it certain ways of thinking and acting and consequently "once we introduce notions of policy [they] assist us in excavating the structures that push cultures in certain directions" (p. 19). Going further, Deborah Stone (2011) argues that analyses of policy enterprises are "strategically crafted arguments, designed to create ambiguities and paradoxes and to resolve them in a particular direction" (p. 7). Certain, then, is the fact that policy matters and can powerfully impact the social, cultural, and personal lives of individuals; growingly so in environments where contestation is a key descriptor of public and political life. It is also certain that assessment has and continues to play a significant part in these processes.

It is important to understand that within the pendular nature of policy discourse and practice, one is bound to experience times of greater rigidity or flexibility, greater conservatism or progressivism, and greater integration or galvanization. Notions of policy analysis as a pristine and scientific environ, unaltered by contingency and politics, were built after the postwar period and counted on notions of data-driven assessment that were understood not only to be efficient but also undeniably efficacious. In the United States of the 1960s and early 1970s, enormous sums were directed toward public policy efforts intended to correct societal problems, and policy as science was the central tenet guiding them—think, for instance, of the War of Poverty policies emanating from the Johnson administration and their offshoots in housing and education. By the late 1970s the failure of such macro social engineering efforts led to the beginning of a conceptual and practical reevaluation of the nature, impact, and roles of assessment and policy. Wildavsky (1979), in his now classic text, highlights the rationale for such reevaluation, arguing, "the technical base of policy analysis is weak" and highlighting that limitations of policy work "are those of social science's innumerable discrete propositions of varying validity and uncertain applicability" (p. 45). Near 50 years ago Wildavsky cautioned that given the often-complex realities and multiple variables involved in social (and educational) realities, objective accounts are delicate and limited, and certainty often an unrealistic request. In 2013, the policy scholar and economist Charles Manski asks for the same, saying, "I hope to move policy analysis away from incredible certitude and toward honest portrayal of partial knowledge" (p. 3). We should listen.

In the last decade, technology enabled *big data*, the commodification of testing, and the persistence of competitive agendas—as those fomented by the growing impact of agencies such as the Organization for Economic Cooperation and Development (OECD) or those pushed forward by national legislation such as No Child Left Behind— have brought the pendulum back to policy decision-making that is conservative and econometric directed. As if to confirm the pendular nature of policy, however, at the time of this writing recent an ongoing analysis of the new Every Student Succeeds Act of 2015 (2015) provisions suggest a move toward local decision-making and away from the marked narrowing of the curriculum institutionalized during the 2000s (Au, 2007; Beveridge, 2009; Chapman, 2005; Gerrity, 2009). As the United States moves from struggles over major federal policies to multiple and perhaps more powerful committees at the local and state levels, states and local school districts will likely reestablish education polices on curricula, assessment, teacher education, and all of the accompanying nuts and bolts that constitute the provision of a "well-rounded" education for all students.[1] Assessment too will experience devolution, perhaps to such an extent that practices focused on local needs and constituencies might gain traction again. Naturally, an effect of localization is heightened implementation irregularity and/or dissimilarity; which on one hand might create space for autonomy and on the other might lead to diminished policy coherence.[2]

Regardless of location power and decision-making, it is difficult to deny that educational policy "has been transformed from relatively unimportant to vital in the drive for increase profitability and the renewal of society" (Adams, 2014, p. ix). We see a growth in policy thinking as a commodity—for instance, through the exponential growth in the influence of think tanks—but we are also experiencing the establishment of policy thinking and practice as a significant formational tool for those engaged in education. As Paul Adams (2014) articulates:

On education studies, related degrees, and masters level courses there has been a surge of interest and application [of policy]. Indeed, policy and politics are now often seen as another of the underpinning disciplines of education alongside philosophy, sociology, history, and psychology.   (p. 3)

Statements such as this amplify both the growing value of policy thinking as well as the need for greater understanding of its complexities. Policy capacity will be critical to our profession as future policies will determine how funds and other resources are divided at the city, school, and state levels. With decentralization, a few influential voices at the local level can make a difference in whether sound policies are adopted or loopholes are devised to reward special interests. Said capacity will also require that we consider that policy in general and assessment policies in specific are, in ways more significant than we care to acknowledge, a matter of choice and interpretation, or what Trowler (2003) has called encoding and decoding. For Trowler, policy encoding is the creation of policy out of competing interpretations and interests, and policy decoding is "the selective interpretation or mediation of policy missive into the local space" (p. 56). For us educators, understanding that we have a responsibility and the right to engage in such processes is a change in attitude that may harbor significant implications.

The Presence of Assessment in Educational Reform and Decision-Making

While it seems undeniable that the Western educational world has seen a rise of an assessment culture, it is also challenging to ascertain a balanced position in terms of the gains provided by assessment practices. This is particularly so when assessment is delivered in standardized forms, when we consider the potentially pernicious side-effects of overemphasis on assessment, or the misleading usage of limited assessment practices to deliver political aims. Regardless of the many actualized or potential positive impacts of assessment, Wyckoff (2009) reminds us "government policy is consistently oversold to citizens, to politicians, and even to academics" (p. 3), and consequently, whenever engaging with policy and assessment, or assessment policy, a sober and skeptic stance might be the most appropriate.

As a tool for social change—aimed at explaining and resolving social and educational issues—assessment has been one of the best efforts put forth by social sciences. We also know that "value-free methods for the writing and reading of policy…have attempted to give technical and scientific sophistication to the policy process in order to buttress its intellectual legitimacy" (Olssen, Codd, & O'Neill, 2004, p. 2). As an ideal and a set of practices, assessment has been central to the politics of educational policy legitimacy. At the same time, the ways in which certain assessment policies have been designed and implemented have highlighted the fact that compelling data remain only one element of decision-making, which often, if not always, also involves values, bias, and agendas.

This is important to keep in mind so that we can make clear when and how to use meaningful and ethical assessment structures to policy aims, as well as to be aware and able to identify when aims are other than truly educative or disrupted by inept networks. Daly, Finnigan, Jordan, Moolenaar, and Che (2014) provide examples of how inept "brokering" of assessment information within school administration can have deleterious effects in school reform—where the term "broker" refers to those individuals who link disconnected individuals or groups (Scott, 2000). Daly and his colleagues point out that even if/when helpful assessment data is available "for many school leaders, especially principals, seeking advice about data may be 'dangerous' and potentially a high-risk activity" (2014, p. 167). On the other hand, they also uncover that while superintendents and assistant superintendents should lead evidence-based curricular adjustment, problems often arise in that "many district leaders hold their pre-reform portfolios of managerial responsibilities, and their supervisees do not necessarily look to them as legitimate leaders in instruction" (p. 165). It is not sufficient to establish policy, it is essential that stakeholders and decision-makers understand policy thinking and be willing to engage in policy processes.

As assessment policies are widely used in a wide array of policies, either guiding or instituting educational reform, they can easily become a tool for political rationalization rather than a tool of/for policy implementation, analysis, and adjustment. Therefore, being able to distinguish ends/means politics from mindful decision-making seems the kind of capacity all in education should possess.

ASSESSMENT AND POLICY AS FORMS OF EDUCATIONAL GOVERNANCE

Wyckoff (2009) argues, "understanding the limitations of our policy tools has profound implications for the way we conduct education reform, and even has a bearing on wider social reforms" (p. 76). Educational debates since the Coleman report have challenged the notion that school resources were the only or even principal elements impacting student achievement. While schools did matter, particularly to the lives of poor and minority students, other social variables such as income and parental background had strong, if not stronger effects, they argued. Studies by Wallberg and Fowler (1987) showed a moderate standardized coefficient ($\beta = .522$) for socioeconomic status, almost five times as big as the most powerful policy variable, teacher experience. Hoxby (2001) and Hanushek (2003) critiqued investment in education as superfluous, with funds dispersed so inefficiently as to be wasted. At the same time, analyses such as those by Lafortune, Rothstein, and Schanzenbach (2015) using test score data from the National Assessment of Educational Progress (NAEP), found that financial reforms that started in the 1990s "caused gradual increases in the relative achievement of students in low-income school districts, consistent with the goal of improving educational opportunity for these students." According with their analysis, "the implied effect of school resources on educational achievement is large" (p. 1).

Considering this history, it is interesting (albeit unsurprising) that most of the conservative efforts over the last 15 years—including, unfortunately, those of the Obama administration in the United States—have focused on school input changes based on data-driven information, mostly focusing on assessment-led accountability of teachers and students (Martens, Nagel, Windzio, & Weymann, 2010). Regardless of the understanding of the limitations of policy tools, the temptation to shape educational governance and thus claim political gains is rather strong. The *Gordon Commission Report on the Future of Assessment in Education*, supported by the Educational Testing Service (ETS), exemplifies this position:

> Although assessment, broadly construed, is a central element of education and must be aligned with both teaching and learning goals, it is not the only—or even the major—tool for improving student outcomes. Indeed, for education to be effective, schools must be designed with clear and precise teaching and learning goals in mind and supported in ways that make them likely to reach those goals.   (ETS, 2013, p. 5)

While the report acknowledges the limitations of assessment—moving wisely and perhaps self-servingly away from the notion of assessment as panacea—ETS clearly places assessment as a key element in the formation of "clear and precise" tools for "effective" schools. A clear strategy in policy, stakeholders attempt to generate influence and thus steer governance by defining the terms of the conversation.

What might be worth establishing in clear terms then is that governance and discourse are constantly entwined. Kenneth Gergen (1995) suggests for example that when creating a policy about literacy, the policy itself defines our notions of literacy. That is, it solidifies and privileges what at any given time might be distinct or even contending ideas about an issue, and thus shapes future thought and action. The report above is patently aware of ETS's need not simply to engage in "assessment work" but also to play a role in establishing the terms of assessment policy and thus having a hand at defining policy discourse in this area. Consequently, by influencing assessment policies and delineating the parameters on which they will be delivered, one is also able to shape and over time define the meaning of assessment. Governance then is widely susceptible to influence, and capacity to impact governance stems from a certain sagacity, or what Booth and Ainscow (2000) have called *policy savvy*. Policy savvy is based on the idea that policy is not simply developed and applied in direct fashion—as the traditional notion of policy cycles implies—but it is actively performed. Policy therefore is as much a process as it is a set of rules or delineated outcomes—and anyone engaged in lobbying as well as in policy implementation understands this very well. As policies get established, however, they become or significantly shape modes of governance, and in that process the fundamental notions/ideas/practices behind those policies are codified, becoming more stable, and even self-evident.

Consequently, while academic discussion will persist and likely be varied, supporting multiple viewpoints on assessment, and while pendular shifts in opinion will have an impact on decision-making, governance is most directly shaped via policies and their accepted discourses. This is significant, particularly when we understand that once policy language has been established and certain meanings delineated, variability and alternative signifiers—ideas, definitions, processes, language—are likely to suffer significant suppression. Once institutionalized into governance, policies clearly represent the narrowing of pathways, the codification of certain values. In these terms policies and governance not only direct action—the most traditional understanding—but also can define worldviews.

As I pointed out earlier, assessment as analysis and assessment as a tool for feedback or evaluation are thus not simply meaningful on their own, but have played a significant role in the complex process of shaping perception and consequently directing and/or legitimizing educational policy action. For nearly 15 years (and arguably longer) conservative ideals framed educational policies that were legitimized by large-scale assessment regimes. These policies, in turn, consolidated and codified value notions that reinforced the initial ideals. Regardless of oppositional voices, the ideological trend created policy that reinforced the trend. This equilibrium seems to have been punctuated, and the pendulum started to move in a different direction creating a possible policy window for change (Kingdon, 1995).

Policy and Assessment in the Public Sphere

Understanding that policies can define worldviews and action not only might bring to our attention the value of policy thinking and action but also may help us realize that placing policy at the center of the public sphere of our disciplines or our own engagements is desirable, if not necessary, today. To place policy and assessment in the public sphere might help us see the complexity required for educational change and also understand in what ways certain constituencies behave according to overt and covert needs. Consider, for example, that educational equity in the United States would likely require a level of engagement that goes far beyond the tradition of policies directed at school inputs or outputs—possibly requiring broader changes in social welfare, health policies, labor markets, and housing policies, just to cite a few. Given that educational equity is too costly a political proposition, and given educational equity's weak presence in the public sphere,[3] the narrowing of educational governance and the focus on human capital and efficiency as key parameters for school reform is anything but surprising (Spring, 2004).

The notion of a public sphere where individuals, organizations, and communities play a role in generating participative governance, might lead us also to consider that the role and impact of the music educator in policy thinking and practice has not been significantly explored and supported by our profession. This presents an important gap, particularly considering the growing and challenging policy initiatives that place educators of all stripes, and in particular music educators, as targets of policy issues such as teacher accountability and autonomy, work intensification, curricular streamlining, and of course, assessment.

Meaningful here might be Stephen Ball's (2006) notion that policies are texts and are born out of struggle. For Ball, texts can be more "writerly" or "readerly," where for the first the scope for individual interpretation is reduced, but for the latter, interpretation can be more easily present or inserted. For Trowler (2003) this kind of position "stresses the importance of social agency, of struggle and compromise, and the importance of understanding how policy is read" (p. 131). I would suggest then that bolstering our understanding of how to engage in participative public spheres—of learning or politics, for example—can be quite valuable (Schmidt, 2012a, 2012b, 2013, 2017). The aim should be to develop a set of concepts and experiences that can lead to greater policy capacity, to help music educators uncover values behind policy propositions, and establish more dynamic and clear goal-setting capacity. I believe this matters, particularly if we also look at the role of assessment in policy formation and implementation. This kind of framing—a disposition really—can generate more successful action led by music teachers within the larger education community, but also raise the standing of music teachers as active "players" in the politics of schooling.

THE INTERSECTION BETWEEN EDUCATION POLICY AND ASSESSMENT

Rationales, Constituencies, and Codependence

The challenge of what happens as policy is encoded and decoded is exemplified by the differences we can find between positions and perceptions articulated by various constituencies. The Finnish educational policy researcher Pati Sahlberg notes that a 2015 study by the Council of the Great City Schools (CGCS) examining the amount of standardized testing in American urban schools found that students in the 66 districts were required to take an average of 112.3 tests between pre-K and grade 12. Sahlberg (2015) reminds us that this number does not include optional tests, diagnostic tests for students with disabilities or English learners, school-developed or required tests, or teacher-designed or -developed tests. He argues that data-driven policy articulations can be dangerous, particularly when assessment becomes an end in itself, or a mere tool for agenda setting. On the other side of the spectrum, OECD's education chief Andreas Schleicher, according to the Hechinger Report, stated after a 2015 education summit at the White House, that if one listened to many of the presentations, "you got this impression [that] if they would only get rid of tests, everything would improve." He goes on to say: "[Assessment] certainly isn't the bottleneck for improvement. The US is not a country of heavy testing."[4]

Critiquing Schleicher's stance, Sahlberg states that what Schleicher's—and by implication OECD's—"simple international comparisons ignore" is that "toxic and often misused accountability systems link data from standardized tests to teachers, schools, districts and, through PISA, to entire education systems." Sahlberg's point is that macro assessment systems are often homogenizing and easily manipulated politically. At the same time, Schleicher's position seems to aim at the possible contradiction that such macro regimes might also create suggesting, "there doesn't seem to be a strong culture of assessment in the U.S." and pointing out that "when it's done, [assessment] generally comes from the outside, [from standardized-test makers]." Given the plausibility of both positions, the question we are left with is: How can policy be encoded and decoded in equitable and comprehensive ways when distinct visions/interpretations are in place?

Just as in general policy, assessment policy and assessment work experience pendular realities. As mentioned previously, standardized testing might be at a turning point in the United States. Consider for example that 20% of parents and their children opted out of standardized testing during the 2015 academic year and that even conservative Texas engaged in legislative discussions about curbing testing. At the same time, it seems dangerous not to consider that the backlash against standardization might have unintended consequences and prevent serious—for example teacher-derived and contextually appropriate—assessment enterprises. Regardless, what is significant is not just that assessment has and will continue to play a significant role in educational reform and in policy decision-making. But rather, that the nature, impact, and design of assessment regimes have always been, and will likely remain, susceptible to positionality and self-interest.

What is necessary is a clear understanding of the import and impact of constituency and participation. The paired issues of contingence and constituency provide the space for agency and the possibility for constructive, if challenging, interaction between distinct segments of the public sphere. Naturally, certain contingencies such as lack of access and participation capacity create the space for undue influence. The presence of multiple constituencies is not then the "problem" of policy—that which makes it untenable and biased. The challenge is to be aware and critical of forces and established patterns of thought and action that hope to delineate and define who has a legitimate claim to policy.

The Institutionalization of Assessment as Policy Norm

One of the challenges to policy in the public sphere is the role of players with disproportionate access to speech, and consequently, influence. Participants with outsized voice have a greater chance to establish certain ideals and practices into norms. A norm is a form of truth, a representation of assumed values. As such, a normative notion might experience content variation but will retain expectation of conduct. Assessment is undoubtedly a normative element of educational policy—an expected or indisputable arena of thought and action. No educational policy today is addressed without assessment considerations. And while norms are valuable, providing a basis for ongoing work, norms can also be manipulated.

Corporations involved in large-scale assessment—who play a significant role in policy lobbying—are a clear representation of the extent to which assessment has become a normative element of educational policy; after all, the sustained and sustainable presence of assessment in education is what allows Pearson or ETS, for example, to be in business. The Gordon Commission on the Future of Assessment in Education established by Educational Testing Service in 2011, for example, acknowledges the politics of how assessment is used as a tool for social and educational engineering saying, "we are very much aware that equally determinative of the future will be the judgments and preferences of the policymakers who decide what will be required and what practitioners and the public will expect."[5] As active players in the policy field, companies represent the institutionalization of assessment. They clearly understand the pendular nature of norms, and thus the need for influence. Companies that profit from testing regimes attempt to portray their brand names as synonymous with assessment. To do so, they work to legitimize themselves within assessment communities, normalizing the notion that corporations should and must be part of said community, and establishing the idea that their vested interest in successful assessment policy work is synonymous to the general public interest. This is of course, not unlike other policy lobby work.

While assessment is indisputably integral to educational work and policy, its normative characteristics—intensified in the last two decades—are certainly worth exploration and debate. It seems imperative, for example, to consider the impact of the institutionalization of commercial testing as part of the education industry (Boulding, 1972). Specifically, further exploration seems granted on the role companies have played in heightening assessment as a key element of policy agendas, or, as problematically, their role in establishing testing and evaluation as proxy for assessment (Gifford, 2012). In other words, it would be plausible to argue that the commercialization of assessment is both the result of policy decisions and, at the same time, has also created a new and narrower educational policy norm.

If one thinks this to be too far-fetched, it is worth noting that test validity discussions are often not present in policy conception and implementation, and widely absent in the public sphere. A possible effect of the commercialization of testing, discussions about validity or bias are regularly curtailed or relegated to highly specialized circles. Hanley (2012) critiques at length:

> I think that if you're trying to ferret out the symbolic value, what is really behind people's concern about bias, it is more similar to the issue of [what the testing literature calls] group parity than to bias as psychometrically defined. Yet testing experts have retreated from considerations of group parity because they say those group parity models deal with issues of social and political values. Since we are technical experts, they say, we have no special insight into which models of group parity are most appropriate. Incredibly enough, however, people who advance such arguments pretend that the psychometric models for analyzing bias are somehow technically above the fray and do not involve implicit assumptions about social and political values.   (p. 57)

As concerning, the influence and the role of the academic public sphere or community in analyzing engagements with assessment at large and testing in specific is also rather dubious. Hanley (2012) again:

> If we look at the political history of testing, we have to conclude that the worst abuses of testing have not been curtailed by any kind of technical analysis, any kind of professional unanimity, but rather by political organization, political protest and litigations.   (p. 60)

Cui Bono?

The blatant commercialization efforts by Pearson illustrate the point that policy conception matters (as established earlier) and that policy positions are always intersecting with certain individual or institutional interests. Recently, Pearson has had to address significant drops in its stock market value, patently using language that places its corporate aims as part and parcel of its educational efforts: "When we create successful learning resources, assessments, and services which schools and students want to use, this creates value for Pearson shareholders and helps to improve educational outcomes."[6] Naturally, commercial enterprises profiting from the educational milieu tend to employ less visible and direct economic language, often deploying communication strategies that boast quality and legitimacy and thus distract from the question, *Who benefits here?* Pearson, for example, claims to have, "world-class capabilities in educational courseware, assessment, and teaching and learning services." Their work is to our benefit.

Legitimacy is linked to scientific acumen and thus contracting or employing scholars becomes paramount. Companies are only as good as their talent. Regardless of the content and quality of scholastic efforts of individuals working in such environs, however, it might be difficult to bracket the positionality of work produced under the auspices of companies whose survival and profit is dependent on the validation of the positive value and impact of assessment systems. Bennett (2015), for example, argues,

> Testing to serve [institutional] purposes is very likely to continue, if not increase, because those purposes are key to institutional, and arguably state and national, interests. For example, education policymakers need trustworthy information on which to base decisions about system effectiveness, including what system components—programs, school leaders, teachers, and students—to target for special attention.   (p. 375)

Knowing that he writes as a scholar employed by the ETS, are we to understand the language deployed here as a feature of scholastic positioning or as influenced by place of employment? Does it matter when scholarly arguments seem to positively align with possible company interests? Are we to take at face value that current testing regimes are patently beneficial to "institutional," read school districts', interests? Is data provided by testing indeed "trustworthy" given the revolving questions about limitations of assessment protocols, politics, and usage, across educational settings? And does the language of absolute dependence—of education on testing—not veil the reality that "trustworthy" information, even when reliable, can also, at the same time, be methodologically tendentious or easily manipulated?

Reordering the Nature of Learning

It is clear to many that the issue is not simply about data or policies themselves, but precisely the way data and policies are used to engage in reform or decision-making. In other words, the issue is how to systematically engage with mindful assessment policy work, and at the same time, grow awareness of the deleterious aspects of certain policy regimes. Maddock, Drummond, Koralek, and Nathan (2007) situate this question at the micro level of the classroom, explaining how a powerful principle such as accountability can generate a disturbing "source of energy in schools." Accountability, he says, takes place "in thousands of daily manifestations" and can be understood as "the pressure not just to do it right, but to be seen to be doing it right. This is the source of energy that goes into creating and sustaining a quiet class, a busy hum, a brisk pace and the satisfying completion of each orchestrated movement of the school day" (p. 53). The challenge is that these same outcomes can be the result of coordinated and mindful work, or the tragically empty gestures of behavioristic structures.

Mitch Robinson (2015) makes a similar point as he critiques assessment policy and its impact on teacher labor conditions, saying, "The result of uncoupling accountability from the improvement of instruction in the use of data has been that for perhaps the first time in our nation's educational history, we now see policies that are punitive rather than educative in nature" (p. 10). Given these and myriad other challenges, and given the overwhelming presence of assessment practices and their impact on educational policy, it would seem that significant efforts toward greater understanding of assessment as part of the public discourse are necessary (see Brophy, Lai, & Chen, 2014; Colwell, 2005; Fautley, 2017). This might mean a greater approximation between stakeholders and a critical dialogue regarding assessment practices, particularly in terms of how assessment discourses—particularly those linked to accountability and evaluation—have reordered the nature of learning today by reshaping assessment policy normative assumptions.

Can Assessment Policy Be Smart?

A first step in the establishment of new norms for thinking and practicing assessment policy from within our field is the more clear understanding of the distinction between analysis *of* policy and analysis *for* policy. Analysis *of* policy is more commonly done and has taken a significant part of the work focused on assessment policy within the music education field (Brophy, 2009; Brophy et al., 2014). Adams (2014) states that analysis *of* policy "is the study of contents, outputs, and processes" and implies the reading and interpretation of policies and policy instruments. Analysis *for* policy has a different intent and agenda, and leads us to consider different "actions and value positions so that policy might be influenced and made" (p. 45). That is policy as agenda setting.

A better balance between the production of literature and active engagement in policy analysis, particularly analysis *for* policy, can bring the field of music education to contribute to smarter educational and arts-directed policy. Smarter policies would mean those that are procedurally aware, conceptually strong, collaboratively construed, meaningful to and observant of the needs of our constituencies, and mindful of the normative (or counternormative) contributions they might make. Self-awareness—individual and in terms of a field—is then a critical element for "smarter" policies. Just as Bandura (1989) articulated in terms of motivation and setting internal standards, the development of self-awareness of educators as a critical policy constituency could be more significantly explored and critically supported. Scaffolding in practical and scholastic ways such a disposition can prove to be impactful at a time when assessment can either continue to exacerbate schisms between politics and competent and equitable policy or help to approximate educators to the constructive roles they can play as decision makers.

It is clear however that from a performative standpoint, "smart" policy is that which pushes toward ever-greater efficiency and accountability (Horsley, 2009), presenting a contrasting view of the earlier one, particularly in terms of suppression of self-awareness and agency (Ranson, 2007). Hargreaves (2000) has argued that educational policy changes have signaled toward the development of teacher professionalism, but in practice have moved teaching from autonomy to the postprofessional era. Day and Harris (2002) outline the problem at its macro level, locating the source of globally oriented efficiency policies leading school reform within five common themes:

> 1) they occur because governments believe that by intervening they can raise levels of attainment and increase economic competitiveness; 2) governments wish to stem the [perceived] decline in personal and social values; 3) governments see the need to challenge teachers' existing practices; 4) governments have, by default, increased teachers' workloads; and 5) governments do not pay attention to teacher identity in the changes they promote.   (pp. 972–974)

It is critical then, particularly in the role assessment communities can play toward the policies, norms, and ideals they can help enact, that professional and ethical practices accompany empirical ones when engaging in policy work. The pendular shift we spoke about earlier further points to this need. Consequently, becoming "smarter" about policy means finding a balance between professional and community autonomy and input and larger social and economic challenges. In terms of policy process, this means taking policy design seriously (Howlett, 2011; Fung, 2003) while constructing processes that are evidence-based but that account for contextual variance.[7] In music education, the critiques developed by Fautley (2017) point to the deleterious effects of poorly designed policy. At the same time, the literature gathered by Brophy (2009) and Brophy et al. (2014) demonstrates that thoughtful practices are widely available. What is more patently absent is the expansion of concerted policy framing (or analysis *for* policy, as mentioned earlier) so that independent and disconnected efforts can start to converge into systemic thinking that leads to cohesive, substantive (and ethical) assessment policy design in music education.

Policy, Assessment, and Ethics

In this chapter I have articulated several reasons why educators should value policy. Policy is related to inquiry and change. Policy is not simply about problem-solving but also about *problem grappling*. And at its best policy work aims to convene opinion, establish debate and directives, and facilitate how to enact proposed ideas and follow up on the outcomes of implementation. Understood in these terms, policy is akin to the most significant ideas in teaching: first, that inquiry must lead argumentation and action, and second, that opportunities for change are part of a constant struggle and constant participative adaptation, particularly because of the constant shift of the cultural, social, ideological, technological, psychological, and personal conditions in which learning takes place (Schmidt, 2015).

Policy-oriented thinking, then, should be dear to educators, for it can help teachers to push for more firm ethical spaces within the politics of education. This is not a simple proposition. Addressing the ethical and political parameters of policy work, Rosemarie Tong (1986) reminds us that "policy experts soon confront the limits of their abilities," and this is due to the changing nature of a process that is "anything but neutral, rational and efficient" (p. 4). Rather than seeing this as a constant negative, we might look at policy as being first and foremost about *constituents* and their interests. This stance implies that we should be able to see the *epistemology* of policy and policy analysis as value-laden and interpretative, and consequently avoid tendencies toward "incredible certitude" against which Manski (2013) warns us. In that sense, then, policy is a balance between art and science, it requires a willingness to be active, to participate, to understand context, to hear multiple voices, to speak creatively, to recast assumptions, to look at data ethically and critically, in sum, to be close to the process and challenge at hand.

Policy and Assessment as Critical Listening

Forester (2006) calls this viewpoint policy as critical listening. Linking critical listening and interviewing to policymaking, Forester places them as key to a day-to-day approach to policy action. His work begins from the premise that "to find out what we can do effectively in politically uncertain and fluid settings, we need to learn—and to learn we very often need to ask questions and listen carefully" (p. 124). While this seems commonsensical and even simplistic, Forester argues that when individuals really adhere to this idea and process, they act as policy planners in the widest sense of the word, "exploring what is possible and exploring what we can and cannot do" (p. 124). This sense of clarity—not to be confused with objectivity—is central to ethical behavior. The ethical commitment to critical questioning and listening might also lead us to consider how a disposition toward inquiry also implies a disposition toward active participation in the lives of our programs and work environs. This is a central premise of a commitment to *policy thought*. Having such a frame of mind might lead us to conceive that our work could/should start from an understanding that most teaching realities require some level of change and consequently, planning for change. This, in turn, requires that teachers learn their schools in "pragmatic and politically astute ways" which is the basis to approach policy as critical listening, as Forester proposes.

This has deep implications to assessment practices and assessment *for* policy, particularly if we acknowledge that appropriate assessment always starts with *calibration*, that is, an understanding the of parameters and outcome desires for an assessment instrument or assessment process. As Forester (2006) suggests,

> Understanding multiple perspectives may enhance planners' own understanding of a particular case because the planners themselves have no special access to truth, full or perfect information. Politically, understanding of being able to integrate many perspectives enables planners to address questions of visibility and power as well.   (p. 124)

Given that assessment work that aims to impact policy must be self-critical and ethical, engaging in critical listening as a tactic and practice may prove to be a valuable process with consequences to assessment action and analysis, particularly within the meso level of school or district policy.

The Struggle Between Pragmatics and Conceptualization

Charles Lindblom (1984) in a now classic book articulates at least three key reasons why analysis alone cannot provide definite answers to policy challenges. First is the idea that our analytical capacities, from conceptual to implementational, are limited. The second limitation for Lindblom is focused on the fact that the more complex the analytical enterprise the more it requires money, "man power" or human resources, time, and continued political will, and the list goes on and on (pp. 19–25). Third is the understanding that policy is based on values and interests and these always shape or cloud analysis parameters and evaluative decisions. This could be placed differently by saying as Lindblom does, that a "purely analytical" formulation of the question a policy addresses is impossible. For instance, what is the right policy regarding allowing/forcing a child to repeat a school year? There are arguments on multiple fronts, but do we, and even can we, find answers that are empirically conclusive, particularly considering variability in the child's family background, sociopsychological status, learning needs, interests, and motivational factors, among others? And even if/when we might feel confident on an empirically sound decision on one child, does that construct the sufficient parameters for the formation of a wide-ranging policy?

Consequently, when we are faced with issues such as education, social justice, urban design, child development and learning, poverty, and economic distribution, we often fail to develop a sufficiently complex analytical apparatus to "resolve" said problems. This is a dual problem of conceptualization and assessment that requires a strategic policy apparatus prepared to withstand the pressures of long-term cycles of preparation-evaluation-reconfiguration; which of course does not mean that we do not continue to attack issues in partial or multifaceted ways. Ritzen (2013) provides a similar assessment of this notion when examining large-scale assessment in educational reform, saying they "can be important change agents, provided that the assessment addresses the primary concerns of stakeholders in education" (p. 24). The key point here is that macro structures can be linked to local strategies. Particularly because "the diversity in the objectives of education and differences in the priorities that different stakeholders place on distinguishable objectives (like mathematics versus citizenship) will generally reduce the impact of large-scale assessment as a change agent to some extent," it is important to "include a variety of measures in the assessment that reflect principal components of the diversity in the missions schools have adopted" (p. 24). Imperative is that we attend to the pragmatics of implementation and policy communication and how they matter, because "If you want large-scale assessment to have an impact on schools, then you need disseminate results and discuss them with teachers, parents, school boards, and so forth on the local level" (p. 23). All this makes ethics a critical part of decision-making, particularly at the policy level, where pragmatics can easily disrupt policy conception and where policy design at times fails to forecast practical implementation challenges.

Values, Economics, and Decision-Making

Creating the support structure for the values embedded in careful and ethical consideration is another challenge, given that a focus on ethics is not necessarily commonplace, desirable, nor widely accepted as efficient in the policy world (Self, 2000). Discussions about "smart policy" (as previously described) have been entwined with economic metrics and efficiency, particularly since the 1980s and have become normalized in many policy circles. Programs/doctrines such as the New Public Management, NPM, in England, and Reinventing Government, in the United States have involved the "deployment of competition and market mechanisms, such as competitive tendering, consumer choice, or benchmarking" as key parameters for effective decision-making in policy (Martin, 1995). While some of these efforts were framed as having democratizing elements such as direct consumer access to service providers and therefore implying more attention to consumer interests, efforts to engage in "smart policy" processes were often organized in phases that combined marketizing and minimizing (Pollitt & Bouckaert, 2004), that is, personnel cuts, less consultation and rule making, shortened time frames, and so forth. In other words, doctrines such as NPM brought into governing the truisms of business, assuming the public sphere—and later, education—to be a mere extension of traditional markets.

The exploration of managerial elements migrated from economic practices onto education are, paradoxically, both abundant and widely critiqued (from Bowles & Gintis, 1976, to Sahlberg, 2011 and Ravitch, 2010). In the realm of assessment, critics point to ethical and value challenges that vary from misuse of data within educational decision-making (Robinson, 2015) to the overpredilection and overclaiming of cognitive gains and their transferability (human capital theories) onto labor and economic realities (Stone, 2011; Supovitz & Spillane, 2015). Part of the lure, as Levin (2013) reminds us, is that "a relatively small sample of test performance can be obtained at low cost and with what appears to have predictive validity for individuals, at least for further academic performance and occupational placement and earnings." And when even "real estate brokers use achievement results to suggest the desirability of a particular residential neighborhood" (p. 65), it is not surprising that assessment has gained such preeminence.

Just as significant—from a policy and ethics standpoint—is that the conjunction between internal (school progress) and external (economic development) parameters has been made on the assumption that cognitive gains in school—the basis for our current assessment regime—have positive and direct impact on the marketplace. Levin (2013) argues that this view is "countered by the fact that microeconomic studies show that such tests explain only a relatively small portion of the variance in earnings and supervisory ratings and a minor portion of the statistical relation between schooling attainments and economic outcomes" (p. 68). This is not to argue, he continues, the irrelevance of what is measured by the test scores to adult outcomes and economic results, but only that

> [cognitive testing] account[s] for much less power in molding adult outcomes than is normally assumed and should not be used exclusively as a statistical measure to evaluate the educational merit or quality of educational systems. Cognitive achievement is important and should continue to be assessed. But it is a highly incomplete category for measuring student and adult success.   (p. 69)

The response to current economically incentivized assessment policies is not the deconstruction of assessment, but as mentioned earlier, greater local autonomy, strong policy design and macro-micro balance, and stronger capacity building, among others. But even within the macro structure of assessment regimes alternatives are possible. Levin (2013) again makes the case that noncognitive assessment, regardless of its nascent status, could significantly impact the ways in which schooling and curriculum are thought, suggesting that an assessment policy that pairs cognitive efforts and dispositional ones could address *both* economic and humanistic or ethical needs channeled through education. Bandura (1989) has shown the importance of self-efficacy in educational attainment, and Cunha and Heckman (2008) have laid out a very ambitious theory of optimal investment between cognitive and noncognitive skills from birth to the labor force.

It would be curious to speculate the impact of assessment policy designs that would merge traditional content-driven and cognitive-based assessment with those based on parameters such as those Levin suggests:

1. *Openness*—inventive and curious as opposed to consistent and cautious
2. *Conscientiousness*—efficient and organized as opposed to easygoing and careless
3. *Extraversion*—outgoing and energetic as opposed to solitary and reserved
4. *Agreeableness*—friendly and compassionate as opposed to cold and unkind
5. *Neuroticism*—sensitive and nervous as opposed to secure and confident

(Levin, 2013, p.45)

Policy, Assessment, and the Creation of Quality

It seems to me that, just as with artistic work, ethical, mindful and implementable engagement with policy is mostly about *regularly renewable understandings*, which is another way to name what I have called a framing disposition (Laes & Schmidt, 2016; Schmidt, 2014). To develop one's (or an institution's) framing disposition requires awareness of the limitations of policy as science (Manski, 2013) and an acknowledgment of policy as art (Wildavsky, 1979). In other words, it requires not only our ability to identify recurring and established patterns within our context—objectively and empirically— but also our ability to critique and change interpretative assumptions, remaining open to implementation adaptability.

While this might sound abstract, it is not. If we want to change the nature of our music program, for example, we might start by understanding participation habits within our school in the last 5 to 10 years, we might also survey program participants about strengths and weaknesses, and nonparticipants for their choice reasons. Of course, we might also investigate previous hiring practices in the district, principal allocation patterns, and other district-wide incentive and disincentive practices. But new program choices and their implementation will also depend on strategic vision and tactical outlining of a feasible, sustainable, and adaptable path that is appealing to multiple constituents while also pedagogically and ethically sound. This requires a *framing disposition*, not simply in the data-gathering part of the analysis, but in the *visioning* of the rationale and implementation plan for the new program pathway. Issues of how many more students I might bring into my program if I diversify it, what the reaction and buy-in of the larger school community would be, how I might make this a win-win with my principal, how I get parents to advocate for the changes, and in what ways the proposal will positively impact learning are all entwined. They all require the kind of complex thinking about policy that a framing disposition incites. Alternatively, consider that a college wants to improve its graduations rate (as many do). The policy analysis, taken as a science, might point us to key indicators—such as previous failure rates in key courses, access to advisors, positive interactions with financial aid, or positive community spaces within the institution. But a policy analysis that might also not simply indicate statistical predictors but also validate implementation strategies, will need to *artfully* explore the many variables constantly impacting the campus and classroom environs and match it with the personal, familial, emotional, and intellectual landscapes of students.

Policies' strengths, and here is how they are linked to an *art*, "lie in the ability to make a little knowledge go a long way by combining an understanding of the constraints of the situation with the ability to explore the environment constructively" (Wildavsky, 1979, p. 15). Policy is not simply about *targets*, then, but rather (and also) about *engagements* and about *regularly renewable understanding*. Significant here is the possibility that as/if/ when we reconsider the parameters and processes through which we assess educational experiences and environs, for instance by placing ethically directed considerations, we might also re-establish our perceptions of quality.

Policy and Assessment Process: From Agenda to Implementation

The Challenges of Establishing Parameters and Tracing a Course

Establishing and implementing policy can be a haphazard affair where politics, perception, and legitimacy can play a strong role. Zeserson and Welch's (2017) explanation of the process policy funding for the "Sing Up" program in the United Kingdom, corroborates this view:

> The catalysing factors that unlocked the unprecedentedly high levels of Government investment in Sing Up were generated by a combination of targeted lobbying by high profile figures in music (e.g., composer Howard Goodall), passion from politicians with specific childhood associations with singing or music (e.g., Lord Andrew Adonis, then Minister of State for Schools and David Miliband then Secretary of State for Education), structured cross-sectoral advocacy and campaigning through the Music Manifesto, founded by David Miliband, as well as quiet cultivation of civil servants through both personal and professional networks. Very little research evidence of the benefits of high quality singing in schools was deployed in this advocacy process, which was underpinned more by vivid anecdote, authentic craft knowledge and appeal to an ethical and moral proposition about social inclusion.   (p. 68)

Wallner (2008) helps us understand the link between policy success (or failure) and legitimacy, explain that even if a policy is

> implemented and achieves its objectives in an efficient and effective fashion, the policy can fail in terms of legitimacy. Failure in policy legitimacy may subsequently compromise the long-term goals and interests of authoritative decision makers by eroding society's acceptance of their legitimate claims to govern. The substantive elements of public policies and the procedural steps taken by authoritative decision makers during the policy cycle affect the perception of policy legitimacy held by both stakeholders and the public. In substantive terms, policy content should align with the dominant attitudes of the affected stakeholders and, ideally, the broader public. Procedurally, factors such as the incubation period, the emotive appeals deployed to gain support for an initiative, and the processes of stakeholder engagement in policy development shape the legitimacy of public policies and the governments who promote them.   (p. 421)

This is significant if considering how to trace a course for assessment or any other policy, as the change of fortune (legitimacy issues) regarding the Common Core Standards efforts exemplifies. In 2010 the consensus seemed to be that

> After more than 20 years of messy thinking, mistakes, and misguided direction, policy makers have finally given teachers and students a solid set of standards in mathematics and literacy. The Common Core of Standards only begins the process of moving

academic performance in these subjects to the levels we need, but it's such a relief to have them. Now, the Race to the Top funding and the federal investments in state assessment systems have targets that make sense.   (Phillips & Wong, 2010, p. 37)

This more than enthusiastic support for the establishment of "fewer and clearer" standards would have broader implications to educational and assessment policy. The argument went:

> Having a set of common standards lays the groundwork for developing assessments aligned with those college-ready standards and for developing teaching tools that are aligned with both the standards and the assessments. It is a mountain of work, but it's work that is essential for creating a system of education that is cohesive and coherent.   (p. 38)

Policy scholars and think tanks were more skeptical, some suggesting, "states should be encouraged to carefully examine and experiment with broad-based school-evaluation systems" (Mathis, 2010, p. 16), adding that "properly measuring the higher-order skills to which the administration and the NGA/CCSSO aspire is considerably more problematic for state-wide testing programs. Scoring open-ended or constructed responses on tests measuring and problem solving represents a far more demanding set of challenges" (p. 13).

Regardless of the critique that Common Core came as just another response (albeit improved) to the challenge of "international economic competitiveness"; or the critique that it represented another high-stakes accountability system regardless of its underperforming history; or the lack of evidence of a positive relationship between high-stakes standards and NAEP scores; or the evidence that such systems have deleterious effects to underprivileged populations; or the large variation and volatility in effects for White, Black, and Hispanic students among the states (Amrein & Berliner, 2002; Braun, 2004; McCluskey, 2010), what really did the Common Core in was political backlash given its association with the "progressive" politics of President Obama—regardless of the fact that the Common Core State Standards (CCSO) was "developed at the behest of state governors and chief state school officers to explicitly avoid the fallout of charges of federal intrusion" (Supovitz & Spillane, 2015, p. xv). Regardless of the fact that President Obama's educational policies were, arguably, anything but progressive, policy legitimization weakened CCSSO's trajectory, and by 2015 the initiative had amassed enormous opposition, to the extent that detracting or at least disavowing Common Core had become a conservative rallying cry.

As Rocheford and Cobb (1994) tell us, "definition of issues or problems is crucial in the development of a conflict because the outside audience does not enter the fray randomly or in equal proportion for the competing sides. Rather, the uninterested become engaged in response to the way participants portray their struggle" (p. 5). According to them "the definition of the alternatives is the supreme instrument of power" and understanding these challenges is key to our efforts to establish parameters for action and tracing its course. Given the volatility of policy and the role of political interests in shaping policy legitimacy, it is important then that we focus on stakeholders' own capacities to think in terms of policy and consider how they might have a role to play as policy thinkers and implementers.

Learning to Follow Through

Education professionals of all types, including teachers, should consider their position in relationship to policy in general and assessment policies in particular. I suggested elsewhere (Laes & Schmidt, 2016; Schmidt & Morrow, 2016) that the development of *policy thought*—a disposition to consider educative practices in their relation to policy terms—is a clear necessity in today's educational environ. Research shows that coherent strategies that rely on a combination of both bureaucratic activities—those initiated by district administrators—and professional activities—those that rely on teachers to define and enforce standards of practice (O'Day, 2002)—are key for impactful policy implementation at the district level. At the same time, policy thought aligns with a sense of follow through (implementation) that is critical for policy success (Wallner, 2008) of any kind and aligns with what Hargreaves (1994) has called the ethic of practicality, a phrase he uses to refer to teachers' "powerful sense of what works and what doesn't; of which changes will go and which will not" (p. 12). This "simple yet deeply consequential sense of practicality among teachers," he argues, "is the distillation of complex and potent combinations of purpose, person, politics and workplace constraints" (p. 12).

All this matters then if we want assessment policies to become an integral part of instructional culture in a productive and integrated way. Particularly, when we know that "research on the impact of policy instruments has consistently shown, for example, that sanctions create adversarial relationships between actors at various levels in the implementation system" (Opfer, Henry, & Mashburn, 2008, p. 326). To engage in strategic policy follow-through, which starts by developing a capacity to envision future action and have some ownership over them, is one of those notions that should be guiding the school work of both teachers and administrators. But follow-through requires interaction and collaboration that can be accomplished only when systematic communication is in place. Existing models to this process have been in place. Networked Learning Communities, for example, are purposefully led social entities that "promote the dissemination of good practice, enhance the professional development of teachers, support capacity building in schools, mediate between centralised and decentralised structures, and assist in the process of re-structuring and re-culturing educational organisational systems" (OECD, 2003, p. 154). While establishing such organizational structures is not easy (Chapman & Fullan, 2007), at the personal level a disposition toward such work can be facilitated by a mode of thinking and acting guided by three notions: feasibility, influence, and institutional constraint.

Feasibility, Influence, and Institutional Constraint

There is important research that examines the way in which the constellation of relationships in schools and school systems may facilitate or constrain the flow of "relational resources," that is, advice, attitudes, information, and materials, among others (Daly et al., 2014). Understanding how to work tactically and strategically in terms of policy (Hope, 1992) is key, gauging both feasibility of our propositions and the level of influence we should develop. Part of this process is understanding constraint and addressing how to maneuver around impediments. Given that policy choices are always a statement of values, eliminating or softening constraints are often a manner of reframing willingness and priorities. Wildavsky (1979) said this best, noting, "a problem is a problem only if something can be done about it" (p. 42).

This is critical because only when we offer an alternative, a pathway for change, do we really create a policy problem (policies are always working for someone), and so it is imperative that this framing disposition be developed. Language, strategy, and collaboration with multiple constituencies are often key and can be aided by presenting issues in diverse and adroit ways. Consider for example these categories for problem definition: Causality—defining issues in terms of origins and culpability; Severity—delineating a need to remove constraints given the potential damage of inaction or how evidence has accumulated or the (un)ethical impact of existing directives; Incidence—framing issues by comparison, by exemplification, storying, metaphors, and overwhelming data, and so on; Novelty—positively highlighting the potential of alternative pathways; Proximity—approaching an issue by delineating direct and personal connections to individuals or organizations; or Crisis—defining the terms of a debate in which half-measures are not possible. The list can go on, but the important element here is that we have resources at hand and we can be agency-full, and thus see feasibility, influence, and constraint as both part of the reality of policy work and an area of skill exploration and professional development for educators in the 21st century (Schmidt & Robbins, 2011).

Understanding and Gaining Greater Access to Decision-Making

Notwithstanding the evidence that policy thinking and activism can shape educational leadership and directly impact the nature, extent, and impact of our programs (Fulcher, 1999), policy engagement is not widely viewed as part of teacher identity. Remarkably, research shows that even the political and policy aspects of principals' work are often overlooked in principal preparation programs (e.g., Blase & Blase, 2002b; Crow & Weindling, 2010). Further, a recent review of the literature found that only a few studies considered whether and how aspiring school leaders learn political skills (e.g., McGinn, 2005). It is unsurprising, then, that teachers are not expected to engage in leadership and not taught to think in policy terms. Part of bringing policy thinking to our learning networks is a constructive avoidance of "policy as decisionism" (Majone, 1989), which is represented not by simple resistance but by greater valuation of process and awareness.

Why Processes Matter

Regardless of the growing acceptance that "because politics and policy can happen only in communities, community must be the starting point of our polis" (Stone, 2011 p. 20), engaging in policy process and understanding its subtleties remain a concern. The ongoing devolution processes will certainly re-energize assessment policy and educational politics at the state level, but it can bring with it old concerns regarding equity and access. Consider, for example, that as a representation of social economic distribution across space—and therefore providing racial and ethnic divides as well—geography is often the real unifier in terms of arts educational presence in the United States. While urban endeavors varied, for example, one is likely to find greater proximity in the realities of schools in urban centers across the nation than between urban and suburban schools within the same state. This reality has led the Wallace Foundation leadership to ask:

> How can urban, low-income tweens and teens gain equal access to high-quality arts experiences? Is there a model of practices that could provide a blueprint for community-based organizations to emulate, so that proven approaches could be deployed in more places, more often? And how do the insights of what tweens and teens *want* align with what other experts say they *need?*
>
> (Montgomery, Rogovin, & Persaud, 2013, p. 11)

Embedded throughout these questions are underlying concerns of how to meaningfully assess educational and cultural work, and how to use said assessments to provide not simply better (and more equitable) policy but also more sustainable and just policy processes. Disconnected assessment models, curricular propositions, and research findings, while significant, as they can provide contending visions, are nevertheless constantly imperiled by the fact that they are not concerned with or have mechanisms to influence or impact policy processes.

Why Awareness Matters

Naturally, stronger engagements with policy processes require better awareness of policy practices and shifting realities. We now know that ESSA will shift authority from federal back to local (state) authority, heightening the space for local implementation to continue to be irregular, possibly failing to translate the mandate for arts presence in the "well-rounded" education of pupils as a clear directive. In this context, NAfME, the National Association for Music Educators in the United States, serves as an example of the challenges ahead, as it finds itself in a precarious position. Representing nearly 90,000 music teachers, NAfME established itself at the national level and focused all its work in Washington, DC. Devolution of policy decision to the state level means that the association will potentially lose significant influence and capacity, as local infrastructures with local action and local voice will tend to be more apt policy structures in the next decade. Given that NAfME has failed to build such a capacity—there are very recent signs of reversal—and missed opportunities to approximate its membership to policy issues, promote policy thinking and research, and establish a structure for greater grassroots engagement, the work to reverse such an unidirectional structure will require significant effort (and resources).

Policy awareness and the challenges of shaping—or at minimum engaging in talking back to policy—are understood by many on-the-ground organizations working with the arts, however. Dallas-based *Big Thought* for example, focused its 2014–2015 report on "opportunity gaps" calling them a "crisis"—making use of a language category as I described earlier. They claim to have served near 150,000 students measuring impact in terms of instructional, academic, and social-emotional aspects—attempting to measure "relationship skills competencies"—but also looking at possible impact of arts programs on parental/caregiver realities, arguing that home life conditions would be negatively impacted by the absence of afterschool programs such as those offered by the program.[8] While programs such as this are myriad, and while their contributions can and often are significant at the community level, at the assessment level we remain with an untethered policy structure where systematic appraisal is difficult, measured parameters diffused, and strategic planning of concerted effort nearly inexistent. Consulting evaluation firms such as Wolfbrow[9] fill the significant void left by governmental guidance/support/ intervention and therefore often have a powerful role to play in shaping the discourse of what counts in terms of arts programs impact and how it is to be related back to funders and policymakers. Greater policy awareness in the profession is needed.

CLOSING THOUGHTS: POLICY AND ASSESSMENT IN AN ACTIVIST CONTEXT

The Role of Networks in Establishing Better Practices

A central idea underpinning this chapter is that a policy frame-of-mind is necessary for individuals concerned with how to create meaningful and impactful assessment regimes. I suggest further that stronger focus on policy within all our practices—no matter what subdiscipline or area of study—must be constructed by networked practices and shifts on how we view leadership. The previous examples indicate both the need for and the potential in networks. Successes and challenges of policy development and implementation in multiple contexts, continuously remind us that

> participation is at the core of what makes a network different from other organizational or process forms. Who participates (issues around power, and resources), how they participate (issues about relationships, coordination, facilitation, governance) why they participate (issues around vision, values, needs, benefits, motivation, commitment), and for how long (issues around sustainability).   (Church et al., 2002, p. 14)

Following Hadfield and Chapman (2015), I suggest in turn that stronger networks can impact the establishment of better practices—irrigated by subdisciplines and coalesced by policy concerns/efforts/frameworks. The model is not new and involves: "1) *understanding context*—developing a detailed understanding of the context; 2) *defining purposes*—providing leadership to foster coherence and clarity; 3) *analysing evidence*—identifying existing expertise and gaps in knowledge; 4) *taking action*—to spread existing expertise and generate new knowledge" (p. 927). But making it happen in more structural ways within the field of music education remains a challenge. This challenge can be defined as the need for "capacity building." While this chapter delineates policy capacity for educators, according to Mitchell and Sackney (2000), capacity building is a defining element for improving schools or other learning communities, having implications at the student level as well. MacBeath, Frost, Swaffield, and Waterhouse (2006), for example, suggest that we involve students in this process, creating curricular and leadership spaces so that they can develop and implement their own learning and assessment policies—specifically they suggest that assessment regularly migrate between focus on curricular content and aims and be embedded in review and reflection practices.

More progressive and policy-oriented assessment and evaluative cultures must be a central element in building this structural capacity. An assessment policy culture interested in data as much as in process, in modeling as much as in wide-critique, in educational gains as much as in equity, can serve as a balancing space between innovation, communication, organization, and strategic development where dynamic value contentions can still vie for space, but be checked against larger public sphere aims.

Capacity building based on a policy framework thus changes the traditional directive understanding of policy and focuses on a new vision where policy thinking aids in the development of an educational culture in which self-evaluation, innovation, and improvement are valued and operationalized daily. This places policy as a process constantly working to adjust the structural conditions that facilitate schools, communities, organizations, and individuals to figure out how to adapt and improve (Lambert & McCombs, 1998). This is perhaps a humanistic view where strong assessment cultures can intersect with equally strong senses of agency.

Puzzling Current and Innovative Practice

In line with calls for preparation of young musicians beyond technical capacities and in tandem with creative economies notions that arts organizations (particularly those engaged in classical Western music) need to be more attuned to their communities and more engaged as innovating civic players, my own work has led me to engagements with the New World Symphony (NWS). New World has recently re-engaged critically with its community-oriented mission. Applications for musical fellows (as its musicians are called) require a community-engagement element; a commitment to community action is part of their 3-year contract. Entrepreneurship and community engagement are part of the work done live and virtually, with fellows running committees that chart future action and evaluate chosen pathways.[10] New World is an interesting model where innovation, supported by internal policy restructuring and participation, is leading to changes to one of the most traditionally oriented spaces in American culture, the orchestra. Furthermore, its policy participation attitude invites fellow to consider their roles beyond musicians and helps them to see alternative forms of artistic/educational work that are ethically in-tune with the limited orchestral labor market.

The multifaceted work developed by the International Contemporary Ensemble (ICE) is another example. ICE functions as a collective or a nongovernmental organization would. Its members generate employment opportunities; create artistic products; provide a platform for sharing ideas and art production; generate commissions and captivate grant funding; link their own artistic work to distinct contexts and distinct communities; and not to be outdone, engage in educational programs.[11]

All this seems to me to suggest examples of critical, if still marginal, engagements with an understanding of adaptability and an engagement with policy thinking that is conceptually innovative and strategically savvy. Their current strategies and structural policies are dependent, I argue, on the kind of progressive assessment cultural articulated previously. An interest in the interaction between data, ethics, and innovation/adaptation is at center and seems to facilitate the diverse and dynamic work developed in both cases. Assessment both institutional and informal is central here, but led by critical framing dispositions that are finding balances between external (economic) needs and internal (content-driven and community-oriented) goals. Arguably, they represent an emerging reality in arts education and cultural work where leadership is attuned to policy and political realities, and where institutional and individual parameters are less clearly delineated. In other words, these individuals and organizations have come to understand that policy matters in the arts and that policy understanding and participation are critical to facilitate change and innovation.

Understanding When the Tail Is Wagging the Dog

Supovitz and Spillane (2015) state, "policymaking is the craft of building systems that direct people's attention and behavior in certain (ideally) predictable and productive way" and argue policy is the educator's bailiwick. They remind us, "regardless of level of education system in which you operate, you are a policymaker because the decisions you make influenced activities of those around you" (p. ix). This notion and all that was presented in this chapter requires a shift in how we think about the intersection between policy and assessment and how we value both as part of our professional identities. I would argue that to have a wide spectrum impact in any field, policy assessment thinking must shift from a model of unidirectional mandates to a system of multidirectional contributions. Greater policy participation seems both desirable and needed. It is compelled, on the one hand, by the rapid and complex changes driven by creative economies (Florida, 2002), and on the other, by accountability discourses and the streamlining of one-size-fits-all administrative "solutions" to educational challenges (Abril & Gault, 2008; Gerrity, 2009).

Steven Ball (2008) argues that policies construct what is perceived to be necessary and at times inevitable. If this is so, more apt, active, and thoughtful engagement with policy is indeed needed. Educators in several fields, and those who see themselves as leaders, are becoming fully aware of the consequences of the absence of policy savvy, and are themselves articulating their impact:

> Teacher leaders are capable of far more than feedback…we are capable of even more than closing the "implementation gap" between a policy's intended outcome and its actual impact on students in the classroom. We are capable of helping to design and assess the kinds of systems our students need in order to fulfill their full potential as thinkers, scientists, writers, mathematicians and human beings.
>
> (NNSTOY, 2015, p. 10)

Mintrom and Norman (2009) call those who seek to initiate dynamic policy change "policy entrepreneurs." These individuals (or groups of individuals) identify issues, facilitate policy circles, work to shape the terms of debates, and build coalitions. That is what is at hand for us. Are we up for the challenge?

NOTES

1. For detailed information on the legislation and the definition of "well-rounded," see http://www.nafme.org/wp-content/files/2015/11/NAfME-ESSA-Comprehensive-Analysis-2015.pdf.
2. As I write this in early 2017, the potential for further deregulation and privatization of public education through the directives of Secretary DeVos might lead to greater policy inequity and misalignment.
3. It is worth watching Pasi Sahlberg's talk at Harvard, in which he places significant stock in locating the distinctions between American and Finish educational systems to a difference between allocation of values, between equity and competition; followed by according policy choices, naturally. See: https://www.youtube.com/watch?v=WeMM-hLoKFY&t=2715s.
4. Jill Barshay, *Education myth American students are over-tested.* December 7, 2015. http://hechingerreport.org/24830-2.
5. Gordon Commission on the future of assessment in education. Accessed January 2016. http://www.gordoncommission.org/rsc/pdfs/gordon_commission_public_policy_report.pdf.
6. Pearson Trading Update. January 21, 2016. https://www.pearson.com/news/announcements/2016/january/january-trading-update.html.
7. For an extended model explanation, see http://epod.cid.harvard.edu.
8. For further information, see http://www.bigthought.org/impact/.
9. For further information, see http://wolfbrown.com/insights.
10. For further information, see https://www.nws.edu/.
11. For further information, see http://iceorg.org/digitice.

REFERENCES

Abril, C., & Gault, B. (2008). The state of music in secondary schools: The principal's perspective. *Journal of Research in Music Education, 56*(1), 68–81.

Adams, P. (2014). *Policy and education: Foundations of education studies*. New York, NY: Routledge.

Amrein, A. L., & Berliner, D. C. (2002). High-stakes testing and student learning. *Education Policy Analysis Archives, 10*(18).

Au, W. (2017). High-stakes testing and curricular control: A qualitative metasynthesis *Educational Researcher 36*(5), 258–267.

Ball, S. (2006). *Education policy and social class*. London, UK: Routledge.

Ball, S. J. (2008). *The education debate*. Bristol, UK: Policy Press.

Bandura, A. (1989). Self-regulation of motivation and action through internal standards and goal systems. In L. Pervin (Ed.), *Goal concepts in personality and social psychology* (pp. 19–85). Hillsdale, NJ: Erlbaum.

Bennett, R. (2015). The changing nature of educational assessment. *Review of Research in Education, 39*, 370–407. doi: 10.3102/0091732X14554179

Beveridge, T. (2009). No Child Left Behind and fine arts classes. *Arts Education Policy Review, 111*(1), 23–38.

Booth, T., & Ainscow, M. (2000). *The index for inclusion*. Bristol: Centre for Studies on Inclusive Education.

Bowles, S., & Gintis, H. (1976). *Schooling in capitalist America: Educational reform and the contradictions of economic life*. New York, NY: Basic Books.

Braun, H. (2004). Reconsidering the impact of high-stakes testing. *Education Policy Analysis Archives, 12*(1). doi: 10.14507/epaa.v12n1.2004

Brophy, T. (2009). *The practice of assessment in music education: Frameworks, models, and designs*. Chicago, IL: GIA.

Brophy, T. S., Lai, M. L., & Chen, H. F. (2014). *Music assessment and global diversity: Practice, measurement and policy*. Chicago, IL: GIA.

Chapman, L. (2005). No child left behind in arts? *Art Education, 58*(1), 17–23.

Chapman, C., & Fullan, M. (2007). Collaboration and partnership for equitable improvement: Towards a networked learning system. *School Leadership and Management, 27*, 205–211.

Church, M., Bitel, M., Armstrong, K., Fernando, P., Gould, H., Joss, S.,...Vouhe, C. (2002). *Participation, relationships and dynamic change: New thinking on evaluating the work of international networks*. London, UK: University College London.

Colwell, R. (2005). Whiter programs and arts policy? *Arts Education Policy Review, 106*(6), 19–29. doi: 10.3200/AEPR.106.6.19-30

Crow, G. M., & Weindling, D. (2010). Learning to be political: New English headteachers' roles. *Educational Policy, 24*(1), 137–158.

Cunha, F., & Heckman, J. J. (2008). Formulating, identifying and estimating the technology of cognitive and noncognitive skill formation. *Journal of Human Resources, 42*, 738–782.

Daly, A. J., Finnigan, K. S., Jordan, S., Moolenaar, N. M., & Che, J. (2014). Misalignment and perverse incentives: Examining the politics of district leaders as brokers in the use of research evidence. *Educational Policy, 28*, 145–174.

Day, C., & Harris, A. (2002). Teacher leadership, reflective practice and school improvement. In K. Leithwood & P. Hallinger (Eds.) *Second international handbook of educational leadership and administration* (pp. 957–978). Dordrecht, The Netherlands: Kluwer Academic.

Educational Testing Service (ETS). (2013). *The Gordon Commission on the future of assessment in education*. Retrieved from http://www.gordoncommission.org/rsc/pdfs/gordon_commission_public_policy_report.pdf

Every Student Succeeds Act of 2015, Pub. L. No. 114-95 § 114 Stat. 1177 (2015).

Fautley, M. (2017). Policy and the question of assessment. In P. Schmidt & R. Colwell (Eds.), *Policy and the political life of music education: Standpoints for understanding and action.* New York, NY: Oxford University Press.

Florida, R. (2002). *The rise of the creative class: And how it's transforming work, leisure and everyday life.* New York, NY: Basic Books.

Forester, J. (2006). Policy analysis as critical listening. In M. Moran, M. Rein & R. Goodin (Eds.), *The Oxford Handbook of Public Policy.* (pp. 120–139). New York: Oxford University Press.

Fulcher, G. (1999). *Disabling policies? A comparative approach to education policy and disability.* London, UK: The Falmer Press.

Fung, A. (2003). Recipes for public sphere: Eight institutional design choices and their consequences. *Journal of Political Phlosophy, 11*, 338–367.

Gergen, K. (1995). *The saturated self: Dilemmas of identity in contemporary life.* New York: Basic Books.

Gerrity, K. (2009). No child left behind: Determining the impact of policy on music education in Ohio. *Bulletin of the Council for Research in Music Education, 179*, 79–93.

Gifford, B. (Ed). (2012). *Test policy and test performance: Education, language, and culture.* Boston, MA: Springer.

Hadfield, M., & Chapman, C. (2015). Leading school-based networks and collaborative learning: Working together for better outcomes? In T. Townsend & J. MacBeath (Eds.), *International handbook of leadership for learning.* Boston, MA: Springer International Handbooks of Education. doi: 10.1007/978-94-007-1350-5

Hanley, W. (2012). Making sense of school testing. In B. Gifford (Ed.), *Test policy and test performance: Education, language, and culture* (pp. 51–62). Boston, MA: Springer.

Hanushek, E. A. (2003). The failure of input-based schooling policies. *The Economic Journal, 113*, F64–F98.

Hargreaves, A. (1994). *Changing teachers, changing times:* Teachers' Work and Culture in the Postmodern Age. London, UK: Cassell.

Hargreaves, A. (2000). Four stages of professionalism and professional learning. *Teachers and Teaching History and Practice, 6*, 151–182.

Hope, S. (1992). Professional organization and influences. In R. Colwell (Ed.), *Handbook of research on music teaching and learning* (pp. 724–734). New York: Schirmer Books.

Horsley, S. (2009). The politics of public accountability: Implications for centralized music education policy development and implementation. *Arts Education Policy Review, 110*(4), 6–13.

Hoxby, C. (2001). All school finance equalizations are not created equal. *The Quarterly Journal of Economics, 116*(4), 1189–1231.

Howlett, M. (2011). *Designing public policies: Principles and instruments.* London, UK: Routledge.

Kingdon, John W. (1995). *Agendas, alternatives, and public policies* (2nd ed.). Boston, MA: Little, Brown & Company.

Laes, T., & Schmidt, P. (2016). Activism within music education: Working towards inclusion and policy change in the Finnish music school context. *British Journal of Music Education, 33*(1), 5–23. doi: 10.1017/S0265051715000224

Lafortune, J., Rothstein, J., & Schanzenbach, D. (2015). *School finance reform and the distribution of student achievement.* Retrieved from http://eml.berkeley.edu/~jrothst/workingpapers/LRS_schoolfinance_120215.pdf

Lambert, N. M., & McCombs, B. L. (Eds.). (1998). *How students learn.* Washington, DC: American Psychological Association.

Levin, H. M. (2013). The utility and need for incorporating noncognitive skills into large-scale educational assessments. In M. V. Davier, E. Gonzalez, I. Kirsch, & K. Yamamoto (Eds.), *The role of international large-scale assessments: Perspectives from technology, economy, and educational research*. Dordrecht, Netherlands: Springer.

Lewis, J., & Miller, T. (Eds.). (2003). *Critical cultural policy studies: A reader*. Malden, MA: Blackwell Publishing.

Lindblom, C. E. (1984). *The policy-making process, 2nd edition*, Englewood Cliffs, New Jersey: Prentice-Hall.

MacBeath, J., Frost, D., Swaffield, S., & Waterhouse, J. (2006). *Leadership for learning: Making the connections*. Cambridge, UK: University of Cambridge Faculty of Education.

Maddock, M., Drummond, M. J., Koralek, B., & Nathan, I. (2007). Doing school differently: Creative practitioners at work. *Education, 3*(13), 47–58.

Majone, G. (1989). *Evidence, argument, and persuasion in the policy process*. New Haven, CT: Yale University Press.

Manski, C. (2013). *Public policy in an uncertain world: Analysis and decisions*. Cambridge, MA: Harvard University Press.

Martens, K., Nagel, A., Windzio, M., & Weymann, A. (2010). *Transformation of education policy*. New York, NY: Palgrave Macmillan.

Martin, J. (1995). Contracting and accountability. In J. Boston (Ed.), *The state under contract*. Wellington, NZ: Bridget Williams.

Mathis, W. J. (2010). *The "Common Core" standards initiative: An effective reform tool?* Boulder, CO, and Tempe, AZ: Education and the Public Interest Center & Education Policy Research Unit. Retrieved from http://epicpolicy.org/publication/common-core-standars

McCluskey, N. (2010, February 17). *Behind the curtain: Assessing the case for national curriculum standards, policy analysis 66*.Washington, DC: CATO Institute. Retrieved April 18, 2016, from http://www.cato.org/pub_display.php?pub_id=11217

McGinn, A. (2005). The story of 10 principals whose exercise of social and political acumen contributes to their success. *International Electronic Journal for Leadership in Learning, 9*(5), 4–11.

Mintrom, M., & Norman, P. (2009). Policy entrepreneurship and policy change. *Policy Studies Journal, 37*, 649–667. doi: 10.1111/j.1541-0072.2009.00329.x

Mitchell, C., & Sackney, L. (Eds.). (2000). *Profound improvement: Building capacity for a learning community*. Dorbrecht, Netherlands: Swets & Zeitlinger.

Montgomery, D., Rogovin, P., & Persaud, N. (2013). *Something to say: Success principles for afterschool arts programs from urban youth and other experts*. New York: Wallace Foundation.

NNSTOY. (2015). *Engaged: Educators and the policy process*. National Network of Teachers of the Year.

O'Day, J. (2002). Complexity, Accountability, and School Improvement. *Harvard Educational Review, 72*(3), 293–329.

OECD. (2003). Networks of innovation: Towards new models for managing schools and systems. In *Schooling for tomorrow*. Paris, France: OECD.

OECD. (2005). *Innovation policy and performance: A cross country comparison*. Paris, France: OECD.

Olssen, M., Codd, J., & O'Neill, A. (2004). Education policy: Globalization, citizenship & democracy. London, UK: Sage.

Opfer, D., Henry, G., & Mashburn, A. (2008). The district effect: Systemic responses to high stakes accountability policies in six southern states. *American Journal of Education, 114*, 299–332.

Phillips, V., & Wong, C. (2010). Tying together the Common Core of Standards, instruction, and assessments. *Phi Delta Kappan, 91*(5), 37–42.

Pollitt, C., & Bouckaert, G. (2004). *Public management reform: A comparative analysis* (2nd ed.). Oxford, UK: Oxford University Press.

Ranson, S. (2007). *Public accountability in the age of neo-liberal governance.* New York, NY: Routledge.

Ravitch, D. (2010). *The death and life of the great American school system: How testing and choice are undermining education* New York, NY: Basic Books.

Ritzen, J. (2013). International large-scale assessments as change agents. In M. v. Davier, E. Gonzalez, I. Kirsch, & K. Yamamoto (Eds.), *The role of international large-scale assessments: Perspectives from technology, economy, and educational research* (pp. 13–27). Dordrecht, Netherlands: Springer.

Robinson, M. (2015). The inchworm and the nightingale: On the (mis)use of data in music teacher evaluation. *Arts Education Policy Review, 116*, 9–21.

Rocheford, D. A., & Cobb, R. W. (Eds). (1994). *The politics of problem definition: Shaping the policy agenda.* Lawrence: University Press of Kansas.

Sahlberg, P. (2011). *Finish lessons: What can the world learn from educational change in Finland.* New York, NY: Teachers College Press.

Sahlberg, P. (2015). *Myth of the myth about standardized testing in the U.S.* December 2015. http://pasisahlberg.com/the-myth-about-the-myth-about-standardized-testing-in-the-u-s/

Schmidt, P. (2011). Living by a simple logic: Standards and critical leadership. In P. Woodford (Ed.), *Re-thinking standards for the twenty-first century: New realities, new challenges and new propositions* (Vol. 23). London, Ontario, CA: University of Western Ontario Press.

Schmidt, P. (2012a). Music, policy and place-centered education: Finding space for adaptability. In P. Schmidt & C. Benedict (Eds.), *National Society for the Study of Education* (Vol. 111, pp. 51–73). New York, NY: Teachers College Press.

Schmidt, P. (2012b). Critical leadership and music educational practice. *Theory into Practice, 51*, 221–228.

Schmidt, P. (2013). Creativity as a complex practice: Developing a framing capacity in higher music education. In P. Burnard (Ed.), *Developing creativities in higher music education: International perspectives and practices* (pp. 23–36). London, UK: Routledge.

Schmidt, P. (2014). NGOs as a framework for an education in and through music: Is the third sector viable? *International Journal of Music Education, 32*(1), 31–52.

Schmidt, P. (2015). The ethics of policy: Why a social justice vision of music education requires a commitment to policy thought. In C. Benedict, P. Schmidt, G. Spruce, & P. Woodford (Eds.), *Oxford handbook of social justice in music education.* (pp. 47–61). New York: Oxford University Press.

Schmidt, P. (2017). Why policy matters: Developing a policy vocabulary within music education. In P. Schmidt & R. Colwell (Eds), *Policy and the political life of music education: Standpoints for understanding and action.* New York, NY: Oxford University Press.

Schmidt, P., & Morrow, S. (2016). Hoarse with no name: Chronic voice problems, policy and music teacher marginalization. *Music Education Research, 18*, 109–126.

Schmidt, P., & Robbins, J. (2011). Looking backwards to reach forward: A strategic architecture for professional development in music education. *Arts Education Policy Review, 112*(2), 95–103.

Scott, J. (2000). *Social network analysis* (2nd ed.). London, UK: SAGE.

Self, P. (2000). *Rolling back the state: Economic dogma and political choice.* New York, NY: St. Martin's Press.

Spring, J. (2004). *Education and the rise of the global economy*. Mahwah, NJ: Erlbaum.

Stone, D. (2011). *Policy paradox: The art of political decision making*. New York, NY: W.W. Norton.

Supovitz, J., & Spillane, J. (Eds). (2015). *Challenging standards: Navigating conflict and building capacity in the era of Common Core*. Boulder, CO: Rowman & Littlefield.

Trowler, P. (2003). *Education policy*. London, UK: Routledge.

Wallberg, H. J., & Fowler, W. F. (1987). Expenditure and size efficiencies of public school districts. *Educational Researcher, 16*, 5–15.

Wallner, J. (2008). Legitimacy and Public Policy: Seeing Beyond Effectiveness, Efficiency, and Performance. *The Policy Studies Journal, 36*(3), 421–443.

Wildavsky, A. (1979). *Speaking truth to power: The art and craft of policy analysis*. New Brunswick, NJ: Transaction Publishers.

Wyckoff, P. G. (2009). *Policy and evidence in a partisan age: The great disconnect*. Washington, DC: Urban Institute Press.

Zeserson, K., & Welch, G. (2017). Policy and research endeavors. In P. Schmidt & R. Colwell (Eds), *Policy and the political life of music education: Standpoints for understanding and action*. New York, NY: Oxford University Press.

INTERNATIONAL
PERSPECTIVES

CHAPTER 4

MUSIC ASSESSMENT POLICY IN AFRICA

MEKI NZEWI

PRELUDE: POSITING MUSIC ASSESSMENT POLICY THAT COMMANDS AFRICA-CONSCIOUS HERITAGE INTEGRITY

The arguments in this chapter urge the reinstatement of a heritage African music assessment policy that drives modern educational practice and addresses contemporary literacy imperatives. African heritage policies enabled musical arts education and practices that instilled an overriding spiritual disposition and godly conscience in the conduct of social systems in African culture groups, before the imposition of foreign, modern inventions that were inharmonious to these practices. In authentic African life imagination, all aspects of living were underpinned by a deep consciousness of the Supreme Deity as the omnipresent Creator of the world who apportioned defined roles for oversight of the cosmic and nature forces that affect human existence on earth and after life to interactive minor deities. Human creativity and nurture belonged to the enabling domains of the Earth Deity. Historically, Africa peoples rationalized that God endowed womanhood with the essence of earth force—gestation, giving birth, nourishment (mind, life, and disposition), and education for proper living. The woman was the modestly commanding gender. Hence in indigenous African terminology, music, a divine phenomenon, is a womanly force.

This Africa-sensed exposition on modern assessment policy strategizes the abiding educational force of allegorical narrative style; the abiding voice of the superintending Womanly Sage therefore foregrounds and concludes it through dramatic instruction on music learning, application, and assessment policy in modern Africa.

To set the stage for the allegory that follows, the Womanly Sage urges that modern society will benefit immensely from the heritage sense and meaning of musical arts as a holistic soft science of society and humanity (particularly the mind) management with this maxim:

> *Maxim: Music of life is every human's potential; every culture's historic, intellectualization has peculiar constructional logics. Grounding in such accumulative formulations is essential for proactive policies and methods that advance humanning knowledge onward.*[1]

Then: The Spiritual Saturated Worldview to Oversee Humanning Knowledge Policies and Dissemination

Music is, in essence, an applied soft science that has served as a stabilizing force in society throughout history. So, what about policies, which can reclaim and regenerate abiding old wisdoms and then apply them in advanced designs that will restrain contemporary people from irrationally unleashing brilliant inventions that destroy mind, life, amity, society, and nature? The allegory is shown in Box 4.1.

Box 4.1 The Allegory of the Child, the Adult, and the Womanly Sage

---

Child: What is the primary evidence that a person is alive?
Adult: Eating and drinking.
Child: NO!
Adult: Okay, we are able to do things.
Child: And before we are able to do?
Adult: We think.
Child: NO!! WE BREATHE AIR.
Adult: Ah, yes, of course, we breathe air to be alive, naughty child.
Child: Now, dear father, capture and show me the breath that proves you are alive.
Adult: Do not be ridiculous, child! You cannot touch or see breath.
Child: So, what is nonmaterial can then become very critical for actual living?
Adult: Hm-m-m..., Well...
Child: Now father, what intangible force enabled our great ancestors to survive over generations without self- and other-annihilation now increasingly witnessed in our modern, money-crazy wisdoms and high technology wonders?
Adult: Don't harass me, child. How do you get such precocious ideas? Maybe the supervisory Womanly Sage listening can enlighten us.

Womanly Sage: Since you evoke and solicit my counsel, reflect that the invisible, invincible force, Death, is equally mightier than the tangible inventions and acquisitions, which modern brilliance boasts. But, of course, human genius now traps or contaminates air in obsessive pursuit of monetary gains and fame. Such polluted air begins to impair life, even unto death; so also with polluting nature, and trivializing prodigious phenomena such as life-managing natural music, to which the child's question specifically alludes. Music originated as the art and science of wholesome living and relating. It is profound, an invincible force. It complements air to consummate salubrious aliveness. Then High-mind genius excised the utilitarian intentions and capabilities of music, a divine force that honed the human mind to aspire for virtuous inventions and productions; conjunctly interactively overseeing as well as proclaiming virtuous societal systems.

In old societies, musical arts science[2] was designed to induce humans to interact harmonious emotions and aspirations in all life situations and issues. Temperate ancestral civilizations that progressively evolved the current hi-modern human societies were not wantonly destroying life and nature as the hi-minds now indulge, for money grabbing and ego-aggrandizement. Stone-hearted modern societal policies, which in actuality serve the interests of the privileged elite, now sponsor the trivialization and silencing of mind-sanitizing music. So humans no longer cherish fellow-love and fellow-caring promoted by humanning music designs of old. The privileged stone hearts who command the world, and exert policies, are preoccupied with prescribing development as maximization of wealth, power, and fame for a few. The mesmerized masses, ordinary humans who flounder in abject marginalization, remain ingeniously diverted with mind-numbing techno and humanoid entertainment frivolities in homes, education, work, and leisure sites, globally. What is unmodern about sensitizing and cherishing common humanness instead of deviously indoctrinating diversity's differentness ideology? Propagating diversity-mentality implants different humanness, discriminations, and exclusions in interrelationships. What is unmodern about resourcing and advancing old meritorious but humble knowledge policies and models that inspired consciousness of common-humankind, irrespective of superficial race, creed, means, and life circumstances? The intangible force of mind-taming musical arts science types performatively instilled such basic common-humanity attitudes, which prioritize what is best for all mankind through proactive policy formulations and executions. Attainment of such heritage ideal in modern living commands conscientious interrogation and assessment of the virtue-content underpinning current conflicting governance, business, religious, educational, and relational polices, actions, and legalities globally.

Note that entertainment is not the musical arts food; just the fleshing, mere relish. The idea of entertainment, which possesses modern human imaginations and longings of good life and musicking was a functional-aesthetic in indigenous cultures—now flippant aesthetic in modern fashion. It was only a seasoning in old shrewd cultural creative intentions. It was a lure that sustained immersion in accomplishing the serious utilitarian business of virtue-based music-for-life in indigenous Africa. Modern African and other world societies urgently need to once more emphasize creative and educational policies, which should command functional musical arts science, such that would stimulate hearts as much as minds to pulse with humane emotions and aspirations in the conduct of polity systems and life aspirations. A dancing heart heals the spirit; spiritual wellness inspires fellow-humanity conscience and consciousness; sublime minds kindle policies that sustain viable, egalitarian society. Altruistic music assessment policy effectuates and oversees quality education and brilliance that conduce virtuous living.

(continued)

Box 4.1 Continued

You want a remedy? Life orientation was formed by early childhood socialization and attitude-shaping experiences at home and community interactions. Classroom education sites during school hours can adequately substitute for community socialization in modern dispensation when appropriately constituted. As such, culture-cognitive musical arts educators need to liaise with modern governance and educational bureaucracy to fashion humanning musical arts policy goals. Curricula designs and assessment policies will then reckon with the so far supplanted indigenous logics, and theory-in-practice models and methods that instill mutuality attributes and purposive creative aspirations irrespective of envisaged later disciplinary specializations. Music facilitates acquisition and memorization of knowledge points in other subjects. And old music propagation policy, at least in our African cultures, emphasized practical and explorative knowledge acquisition methodologies. Musical arts constructs were designed and assessed in effective-affective terms as paranormal life expediency. What the modern generation now needs is edu-play dissemination policy, which should advance the indigenous models to systematically but playfully instill worthy social dispositions and creative aptitudes from early school age through instructional activities. All learners are already innately musically capable. Qualitative policy interventions will enable them to withstand the mind-deforming dangers of modern flamboyant theories, control syndromes, and technological wonders that contradict sublime living. Humane mindedness is for all ages and classes to cherish.

The mind-tempering and de-stressing configurations of advanced indigenous African play-shopping drumming sessions, for instance, will socialize minds and attitudes of stiff public officers in governance, business, and law and order, particularly those who normally experience mind-stiffening training regimens and tense, control-ridden work rules. Whatever is too rigid or controlled, and inflexible, snaps easily under pressure. Assessment policy in musical arts science should foster evidence of instructive play model, mind-relaxing, in musical arts knowledge transmission and acquisition from creativity to public experiencing. Music education will again humanize aspirations and attitudes in and out of classrooms when policy eschews currently fashionable vogues of control and quantitative probing of mind, albeit illusory fabrications.

The musical arts are divine, knowledge-embedding devices. I again urge modern humans to all qualitatively interact through musical arts learning and assessment designs founded on consciousness of commonalities, which imbues mind and body wellness, promoting societal cohesion. Thus, your generation's global and national ideologists should efface the insidious promotion of differences through media and education. Instead, propagate the culture-interconnecting doctrine of common humanness, which interacting cultural musical arts stimulates. Heed my ancient but modern counsel for the survival of humanity on earth. Advance unique African wisdoms and humanizing media prototypes in imperative cultural, intercultural, international, and global interactions.

Now: The Reign of the Techno-Economy Controls and Dazzles Life, Inventing Dehumanizing Knowledge Policies and Productions

The operationalization of African assessment policy ideals that support dynamic and humane assessment policy has been the bedrock for endorsing knowledge inventions, creations, practices, and advancements over human history within the prevailing canons in any African society. The essential nature of what has to be assessed must be cognitively understood for assessment policy that is factual, beneficial, and progressive. When the disposition and stipulations of assessment policy, which guide knowledge creation and acquisition, are blemished because of ignorance or bigoted mindsets, assessment could become insidious, a disabling agency undermining virtuous knowledge delivery, acquisition, and progression at a personal or national level. Musical arts assessment policy in African modern school systems then needs to be humane, adopting a heritage policy spirit in advancing knowledge lore. This approach ensures that performance continues to accomplish its roles in a society's polity practices, particularly engendering governance integrity that is conscious of common humanity.

Indigenous assessment canons transpired procedurally as spontaneous, sincere, flexible expressions (verbal, performative, metaphoric, or gestural), applied objectively to inspire and endorse the effectiveness of the musical arts in the translation and management of ongoing, normative contextual narratives. Indigenous assessment policy cherishes applied egalitarian inputs in performance sites. Post performance reflective discourses endorse effectiveness, while knowledge experienced and mentally ingrained guides further growth of musical capabilities. Such assessment policy acknowledges that musicality is an innate, shared human characteristic that must be intuitively interacted in performative contexts within prevailing frameworks and cultural standards for musical types and styles. The *humane* orientation requires that originality and effort be commended before recommending any needed improvements or amendments. Evidence of unique effort is commended irrespective of quality or magnitude. Failure is not anticipated. Creative and performative merits are then assessed in terms of conformational appropriateness in effecting contextual intentions. Contemporary Africans need to regenerate their cultural knowledge creeds so that assessment policy in contemporary musical arts education can humanize and not intimidate original capability, or discriminate based on human and cultural origins. Indigenous musical practices, when used as a basic knowledge foundation, provide mental and cultural security for interacting with comparable other-cultural varieties of music and compatible modern inventions. The soft science of natural music sounds is configured to vibe and animate souls, and thereby engenders spiritual enrichment, which uplifts the individual when engaging in inter/multicultural connections, accommodation of others, and mutual solace.

The legacy of humanity-grounded assessment policy principles that should inspire and credit every level of capability and genius in contemporary education cautions that policy design must abjure inciting, judging, or apportioning failures and mistakes in assessing sincere, original efforts. All unique expressions outside policy stipulations deserve positive evaluation, which could spur exploration of new dimensions of the known. It thus becomes imperative to foreground indigenous African epistemological fundamentals framing purposive musical arts logic and education assessment framework. Modern policy directions, heeding the counsel of the ancient and modern Womanly Sage (the crucible of life), will be addressed accordingly.

ASSESSMENT POLICY IN INDIGENOUS AFRICAN MUSICAL ARTS AND SOFT SCIENCE EDUCATION—HUMANITY-BASED POLITY FRAMING

Delimitation

This discourse is delimited to sub-Saharan Africa, which embraces autonomous culture groups that evidentially share some common fundamental knowledge. Africans have never evoked diversity sentiments in interactions throughout a history of intermingled peculiarities of cultural commonalities. Hence the old African relational aphorism: *All humans are the same constitution irrespective of peculiar outward appearance.* This pervasive disposition accounted for hospitably welcoming initial foreign adventurers into Africa, which backfired in the eventual, easy colonial conquest of the African mind and civilization. The Africa-generic substructural knowledge philosophies and constructs resulted from various groups amicably intermingling, interchanging and fusing fundamental cultural knowledge. Hence, in music, a sound can, at the first level of perception, be identified as of African origin. Common knowledge substructures thus underpin music's peculiar superstructural manifestations, which mark various African culture groups in the musical arts and science knowledge field (Nketia, 1974). The superstructural peculiarities derive from language and cosmic/environmental factors, which furnish performance resources and stimulations that account for peculiar creative outcomes and performance aesthetics. The basic open-minded, hospitable African disposition warranted that new settlers were genetically assimilated into a host culture group through intermarriages that commanded exchange of intercultural specialties resulting in musical arts fusions. Over generations of intercultural interactions and assimilation, sub-Saharan African culture groups forged commonalities of creative intentions and constructs in the musical arts and science epistemologies and assessment ideology.

Evidences of shared creative philosophy, theory, and structural-textural rationalizations include that music sonically signifies, marshals, and validates the other African cultural institutions, knowledge practices and societal mores. Ensemble texture sonically ingrains a complementary instead of subordinate life philosophy of role delineation that reflects ideal family living. As such, ensemble members perform complementary sonic roles and functions not dependent parts (Nzewi, 1997), thus performance instructs a soundly organized humanity (Blacking, 1976). The epistemological principles and functional aesthetics (Nzewi, 1997), backed by folk terminology, which have profound consequences for contemporary societal living, and which classroom music education and assessment policy should inculcate, include: The concept of *mother musicianship*—the mother musician/instrument role is the ensemble (life) organizer/conductor responsible for event (family) management. The *phrasing reference* (baby) role is the soft science of repetition (topos-circling), which acts as the attention alert for other ensemble family members. A distinct phrasing reference topos can be migrated to different music items, types, and styles. Repetition is also applied in isolation as a medical device, a sonic anesthesia, also self-administered as sleep aid. The ensemble cohering principle of the *pulse* instrument role is perceived and discussed as the Father. A comprehensive ensemble also features the *siblings* and extended family roles that furnish interactive framework, the pedestal for creativity. Standard thematic configurations and structural relationships employed in progressing ensemble texture rationalize peculiar formats: the *internal variation* (recycling ideology of life) principle is used to develop the energy as well as affect/effect of a thematic identity. It compels mental absorption, which when applied in isolation induces calmness of mind as a soft science of concentration for managing stressful or anxiety situations. Interactional *space-sharing* is thematic structuring that stimulates and instills other-human consciousness disposition while actuating confident insertion of self (creative/expressive) presence. The indigenous African ideology of life foregrounds that the chorus (group/community) is the foundation for solo emergence/assertion. This is instilled in the principle of acting out *chorus-solo* (not solo-chorus) as microform principle of life in group musical arts sites. Harmonic ideology of *theme-matching* (compatible linear, not vertical harmonization of a theme) instructs complementary principles in life relationships. Yet independent ensemble voices, vocal or/and instrumental, must intuitively conform to normative cultural concord in music and other life situations. The *ensemble thematic cycle* (individualized yet complementary ensemble thematic identities, roles) is the crystallized sonic identity of a piece. This ensemble theme is the microform recycled to compose a full (event) performance form of a piece or a section thereof, and so forth.

Modern Assessment Policy Pointers

Mental and social-performative implantation, as well as assessing of these and other epistemological principles, are of consequence in modern African education policy design that stresses music-for-life—musical arts education that forms attitude, and social and life skills as in indigenous paradigms. Analytical/reflective discussions of practical learning experiences illuminate the essential translation and advancement of the indigenous philosophies, theoretical designs, and creative/performative principles as "foundations of social life" (Blacking, 1970) much needed for modern virtuous living in the present.

Intended Humanity/Societal Utility Outcomes

Intended humanity/societal utility outcomes factor thematic configurations, textural conformations, and expressive vocabularies as well as production logic, organization, and resources. An indigenous African sonic expression normally identifies/signifies a societal context and usage, hence *event* music (Nzewi, 1991). Generic epistemological frameworks mark creativity in styles and types. Children's autonomous creations (Campbell, 2007) are theoretically astute, being systematic, and transact life skills. Discussion and analysis must then be in the context of why, how, when, and where musical arts is used, which informs peculiar structural and formal logics. Agawu (2004) argues factoring the morphology of the archetypal molds of creative intentions already outlined in Nzewi (2003). These archetypes shape creative/performative architecture, which encrypts meanings and accomplishes assigned practical social, political, religious, and economic objectives. Other conceptual utilities that Africa-sensed assessment policy should stress expressing and analyzing in classrooms education for-life include (but are not limited to):

1. health science rationalizations of instrument technology resources and designs (for instance, robust drum tones resonate tissue-health in vibrations that mask distinctive pitches);
2. flexible performance moods, forms, and blocking that eschew stress and control tendencies;
3. obligatory delineation and inclusivity that make benefits of active participation in music, dance, and dramatic enactments available to all;
4. reasons and locations for special group or personal (solo) musicking; use of voice masking, semantics and innuendos in lyrics, intonations and vocalizations;
5. texted instrumental communications; presentation blocking that prescribes the cohering psychology of the circle; event-form or sections thereof sequenced as narratives;
6. subtleties of body energy and gestures that stage peculiar emotions (Nzewi, 1999);
7. gendered choreographic semantics such as maternity (female) and muscle destress (male) dancing;
8. dramatic features and narrative symbolism of particularly spirit-manifest drama, and the embedded life as well as morality lessons depicted;
9. functional aesthetic ideology of interactively articulating the pleasure derived when musical arts enactment accomplishes its purposive utility;
10. open, spontaneous, and post-performance assessment criteria, the vocabulary of which are occasionally euphemistic and gestural; and
11. subtle creative, performance, and evaluation terminologies, often metaphorical and instructive without being condemnatory.

Modern Assessment Policy Pointers

Creative philosophy and ideology, and performative outcomes, should be assessed in human terms of sincere effort invested and evidence of active participation and original creative individuality, irrespective of magnitude. Thereafter, there should be group or individual reflective retrospection to pinpoint benefits to self, others, and society that are generated by performances. These include emphasizing knowledge and pride of heritage regenerated as well as advancement genius, human consciousness and conscience, and creative and critical dispositions instilled by interactive music learning activities.

Performance Composition

Performance composition is mandatory in indigenous epistemology; it engenders creative individuality-in-conformity with the human ideology of mustering unique intellectual mettle, requisite for confidently coping with the exigencies of life in a society. Tradition expects every human to confidently demonstrate self-expression and peculiar capabilities in musical arts and life circumstances. Performance composition, as sonic, choreographic, or dramatic narrative, must make delectable artistic sense while interpreting event-meaning and emotions. It commands spontaneity in creative con-figurations and sequencing intended to sonically direct or translate as well as broadcast event narratives, and also evoke adequate situational mood and functional aesthetic. A mother musician (woman or man) is thus in astute command as she communicates through performance transpiring event procedures and contingencies. Improvisation as abstract, aesthetic, elaborations (usually internal variations) on a theme could feature in ensemble roles that spiritually enrich overall sonic aesthetic. Sheer improvisation also marks a delightful musicianship reckoning in music-events such as solo/relaxation music making. The only exception is the *phrasing reference* instrument role, which acts as the invariable phrasing signpost for the rest of ensemble instrument players. The capability to demonstrate original creative acumen, no matter how minimal, is commended as the demonstration of one's original personality attribute that is essential for life. Performance composition as exceptional expertise that creatively effectuates a transpiring event is assessed and acclaimed in the public space as the hallmark of mother musicianship.

Modern Assessment Policy Pointers

Creative and performance composition expertise that is ingrained in every child through musical arts education activities becomes a useful aptitude in other life situations. Assessment policy should reckon positively with demonstrations of spontaneous interpretive and creative explorations in children's as much adult's musical arts activities at education sites. Creative presence should be progressively actuated through adult-hood and should be purposive. Event-oriented and interpretive capability should be encouraged. At the affective level, a group's overall output as much as individual artistic distinctions are to be noted, credited, and discussed for spurring growth. Assessment policy should not program for failure in creative or practical musical arts knowledge acquisition activity; a deemed error or mistake could be a chance token that, when positively explored, could boost self-confidence and creative presence.

Participation

Participation is coerced as per cultural musical arts type so that all will benefit from the central indigenous musical arts intentions of managing mind, body, and societal wellness. Group comes before the individual; and every capability as well as quality of effort is appreciated in inclusivity ideology. Peculiar ingenuities and competencies in the manipulation of standard frameworks should manifest and blossom. Individuality-in-conformity becomes inculcated for societal living. An indigenous adage posits that *all fingers are not equal; each has peculiar capacity as per size and position, but all do complementally collaborate to ordinarily fulfill life tasks.*

Children have the proclivity to express aptitudes, and are encouraged to enthusiastically participate in their autonomous, life skill and education-intensive, genres, whether the home species such as folk tales or the public arena play-team types. Every baby in indigenous Africa was born musical, being implicitly sensitized from the womb by musicking-dancing pregnant mothers. At birth the intuitive efforts in experimenting with the use of the body parts is musically spurred by the vocal appreciation of adults and peers. Indigenous assessment policy canons respected a child's inhered cultural knowledge sensibility and expressions. Children exercised absolute creative autonomy without utilitarian constraints. They could creatively adapt adult musical arts types and materials. Adults would be circumspect in proffering any suggestions, but not indulge in negative, controlling, judgmental, or instructional supervision in the child's productive domain. Some children's original creations did compare to adult types in structural and performance expertise.

Cultural education canons imperative in classroom assessment policy encourage children to explore and advance genius through practical experimentation and participation in group productions with adult facilitation and participation as applicable. The underpinning moral dictum must be enunciated for every musical arts creation; critical acumens and dispositions should be interactively kindled and manifested progressively. Rehearsals and public presentations are sites for robust but playful mutual peer assessment and critical interlocutions. In these conversations, the group resolves and endorses the best practice. The community adults observe and take note of emerging special aptitudes for possible recruitment or apprenticeship in specialist adult musical arts genres, mostly instrumental. Children also grow in skill by participating with aplomb alongside adults in a community's mass musical arts events that coerce all-inclusive partaking. The very little children freely test their capabilities at the sidelines of even specialist or exclusive musical arts activities staged in public without inhibition or restriction. Child prodigies are known to have emerged. The life benefits of encouraging children's autonomous productions are immense. They include:

1. effortless acquisition of the culture's structural and performative grammar and vocabularies for music, dance, and drama;
2. objective and forthright critical acumen and disposition;
3. psychophysiological health;
4. competent and specialist performance skills;
5. creative aptitude;
6. self-esteem and self-discovery;
7. actuation and honing of multiple artistic capabilities;
8. consciousness of personal preferences;
9. self-discipline;
10. spirit of mutual respect and other support; and
11. life skills and general socialization.

A child who dodges participation in children's play sessions is teased by peers and scolded by parents/adults for exhibiting signs of antisocial disposition, normally curbed and corrected in children's group musicking, by coercion if necessary. For adults, participation in musical arts groups and types could be in mass categories or in delimited, compulsory (age/gender/associational) interest group types, or participant audience in event-music types that select specialist performers, especially for discharging specialized institutional functions.

Modern Assessment Policy Pointers

Effort matters most; no capability in participating in group or solo activity should be adjudged a failure. Ab initio, it must be cautioned that self-deceit or self-exclusion (non-participation) incurs a sick mind that harms the self for life. Merit is assessed in overall group terms or score, before extra individual inputs or flairs earn additional points. Competing to win money, material, or ego advantage induces immoral dispositions and subterfuges. Rather, exhibited special capabilities should be compared and mutually appreciated to attain best results within or between groups and their objectives. Above all, in children and indeed at all education sites, learners should be accorded freedom to interact with many creative opinions, options, and originations in manageable group productions, both cultural and multicultural. These experiences humanize and affirm, as well as liberate dormant capabilities and purge introverted dispositions.

Solidarity Agenda of Age/Group Criteria

No citizen must feel or be excluded. In old African cultures, it was rare to encounter anybody who did not belong to an interest or solidarity group, often organized along age, gender, occupational, titular, or other common-interest lines. All interest groups have representative musical arts. Rulers would have special music that signifies the elevated office, and to which s/he must dance with the support of designated persons as a public demonstration of egalitarian spirit and community belonging. An individual, a group, or a community event could invite a specified musical arts type to facilitate sonically certain event activities. Since music underscores most societal institutions and events, everybody has the opportunity to experience musical arts actively as a performer or audience member and evaluate the normative outcome. Basic standard indices of assessment focused on appraising situational creativity and performance, the generation of solidarity or shared emotions, or the activation and fulfillment of designated societal purpose. Specialist mother musicians command the event scenario (interpretive or marshaling compositional expertise), and are in demand for their event music styles/ types that facilitate funerary, religious, sporting, healing, social sanction, and festival events. Because mother musicianship was a divine attainment, specialist expertise was not reckoned as an economic or full-time occupation. Specialists received compensation only in kind for time taken off a known, daily subsistence occupation to fulfill specialist performance obligations.

Modern Assessment Policy Pointers

In practice, the group and other observers of the process and final performance reflectively discuss and evaluate the degree to which the performers accomplished the intention of their performance. They note special merit and offer commendations. In this process, the assessors do not accommodate a competition mentality. Competition warps communality spirit and generates stresses. Judgmental dispositions (Ruddock, 2012) that apportion elusive excellence are invariably subjective and self-serving, as no human is perfect or omniscient. Comparing capabilities for mutual enrichment is godly, and all participants share equitably any rewards, inducements, or prizes. Sharing accords essential mental health and spiritual bonding of all, young and old.

AFRICA IN GLOBAL ASSESSMENT POLICY INTERVENTIONS

Northern Hegemonic Curricula and Assessment Policy Constructs

Coping with overriding Northern hegemonic curricula and assessment policy constructs that do not necessarily resonate with African indigenous canons, and concerns to interrelate music education transmission and assessment formulations as well as practices globally, resulted in the formation of the International Society for Music Education (ISME), with Africa as a regional group. Special interest groups concerned with aspects of global music education include the International Symposium on Assessment in

Music Education, founded and chaired by Timothy Brophy. Since the genesis of elitist classroom music education, Northern classical music scholars have consistently continued to cogitate, research, invent, regulate, test, discard, and refine theories on curricula content development, teaching methodology, and assessment models internationally. Classroom implementation relies often on control-ridden policies for classroom transmission praxes. Regarding assessment theorization and innovation, scholars have championed perspectives that include social, emotional, physical, and cognitive domains of classroom music education (Airasian, 1977; Brophy, Lai, & Chen, 2014; Murphy, 2007; O'Leary, 2004; Staggins, 1977); peer as sessment (Blom & Poole, 2004; Daniel, 2004; Falkchikov, 1995; Marlatt, 2014; Nierman, 2014); cultural integrity of content (Brophy & Lehmann-Wermser, 2013; Eisner, 2007; Elliot, 1995); teachers' disposition (Farrel, 2014; Holcomb, 2014; Nordlund, 2014; Parkes, Doerksen, & Ritcher, 2014); and learners' understanding about music (Brophy, 2000; Edmund & Edmund, 2014; Hudson, 2014; Murphy, 2007; Pitts, 2005; Wang, 2014; Woodward, 2002). Research and theoretical positions are informed primarily by knowledge orientations based on Western classical music history and logics. Historic African music prototypes, which are purposively conceived and designed to serve as a functional agency for societal and human management, remain snubbed even by both Africa governance and scholarship elite who dictate policy. They adopt, without adequate cultural rationalization, the dominant Northern hegemonic knowledge models and dissemination policies. Where bureaucratic recognition has been accorded cultural musical arts heritage, possible economic viability is prioritized as a mere entertainment commodity instead of as a powerful utilitarian institution. The modern educational music therapy subdiscipline equally copies Northern sophistications of theory and technology, snubbing the historic potency of indigenous music as a soft science, a healing phenomenon that remains an effectual agency for managing mind, body, and societal wellness if appropriately advanced and applied.

Colonial school education and church doctrines implanted in Africa ignorantly negated and silenced the prodigious genius and functional capacities of indigenous musical arts practices and education ideology. Thus, music was excluded as a learning or examinable subject in school syllabi for a long time in most African countries, even after political, though not much mentality, independence. The postcolonial governance mindset was indoctrinated to discriminate cultural knowledge systems as irrelevant in classroom education. This persistent, exogenous mentality disposes African intellectuals and bureaucrats to continue disavowing the relevance of most indigenous knowledge heritage, including music, in contemporary social systems. Music education in the colonial period, where offered, focused exclusively on abstract Western classical music. This process produced literate, certified practitioners who did not obtain basic knowledge of the conceptualizations, theories, and purposes of African cultural music heritage. Western classical music education disavows and discriminates common human musicality, instating the jargon of talent. Yet modern music experiences, be they classical, popular, traditional, or global, address the patronage of supposedly unmusical mass audiences. The intimidated mass consumers, ironically, are expected to appreciate the sonic specialties of classical music for instance, or to dance with rhythmic acuity to popular music. Music education policy, at least in Africa, must cultivate the innate musicality of every normal human as a genetic truth and for psychophysical health: If you can walk, you can dance; if you can talk, you can vocalize; if you express yourself with gestures, you can dramatize. Some who are rejected as nonmusical in institutional music education admission tests, but who are passionate about their musicality, do become stars in the popular musical arts genres that now dominate global musicking. Officially recognized academic music specialization has minimal public patronage. The propagation of the utilitarian tenets of original music in institutional education has become further alienated with the invention of captivating technology for music education, creativity, dissemination, and farcical evaluation. Technology creates an age of techno-human minds, and promotes a mechanistic music experience. Narrative procedures (including those applied to musical arts production and assessment) do subtly expose guarded truths. As I have stated before: *The salutary potency of the indigenous musical arts episteme can rescue mankind from the prevailing plague of high-minded political, technological, religious, social, and business inhumanities and insincerities.* Still, Africa must not be a modern ghetto; dialogic exchanges with compatible global human knowledge typologies and assessment policy inventions can harmonize with the virtues and values of its salubrious heritage.

Cultural and Human Integrity of Current African School Music Education

Systematic and informed cultural heritage education to reinstate genuine African mentality was not a post-independence agenda in arbitrarily forged African countries. Sparks of culture consciousness started after independence in a few countries where government elites attempted to include tentatively indigenous music and other cultural arts studies in school education. However, indigenous musical arts performances were being featured in modern public events, albeit as entertainment side attractions. Bresler (2000) samples initial policy sorties at culture-promotion in the *Symposium on Arts Education in Africa*, in which Mans (2000) reviewed the Namibian experience, Opondo (2000) the Kenya experience, and Flolu (2000) the Ghanaian experience. The few ventures to introduce culture-derived school music education in African countries were not authoritative because governments relied on ignorant experts (Nzewi 2006), foreign and local, whose research and scholarship credentials lacked uniquely Africa-sensed discernment integrity for advancing indigenous cultural intellectual lore (Africa-common or culture-peculiar) in classroom and public education sites. Curricular orientation and design in the few African countries focused on Western classical music, whether or not as an examinable subject area. Examination makes a subject important in the estimation of learners, parents, and teachers, irrespective of interest or value. The officially promoted choral (secular and church) and indigenous musical arts festival interactions adopted the perverse ideology of competitions for monetary or other exclusive prizes.

In Africa, so far, cultural epistemologies and the humanity-based principles of heritage knowledge systems have not been taken into much reckoning even at tertiary education levels due to the availability of few cognitive literature texts on authoritatively indigenous African creative theory, transmission ideology, and methodology. Agawu (2004) stresses that African functional music requires factoring the morphology of its social function in analysis. Curricular and policy designs remain largely exogenous-minded for the obvious reason that education policy bureaucrats are mostly not musical arts specialists, and are not enthusiastic about prescribing an authoritative Africa cultural civilization imperative in classroom studies. The consulted subject advisers, supervisors, and educators in music, local and foreign, prescribe Western classical music for African schools. The educational renaissance in African musical arts should start making Africa-sense when it emphasizes cultural canons, starting with reintegrating the indigenous holistic knowledge integrity.

The Roles of Literature and Modern Technology in Transmission and Assessment

Human as well as societal management intentions mark cultural musical arts ideations and expressions. Hence, Kermode (1979) writes about the hidden meanings of African musical lyrical narratives patterned by cultures. Factual published literature for education is of the essence. So far, contemporary classroom education mostly parrots extrinsic conjectures about African cultural intellect and knowledge constructs. Cosmopolitan valuation and theories about music are entertainment- and commodity-fixated, with increasing overreliance on technology for production, transmission, access, and education. Contemporary education in Africa illogically copies hegemonic conventions, while negating what is relevant for inculcating Africanness. Further, global humanity must reckon with the fact that technology has no emotion and therefore deadens human sensitivity, emotion, conscience, and morality over time. Super-refinement or purification of materials and procedures insidiously destroys the mind and body. An attempt at the Centre for Indigenous Instrumental Music and Dance practices of Africa (CIIMDA) in South Africa showed that modern transcription technology, for instance, could not cope with the unique logic of linear harmonization of structural components that mark indigenous African ensemble music theory. Similarly, quantitative or statistical data elicitation and assessment designs are of limited reliability in accessing mind-truth in African human research situations. Music that is produced with natural materials generates and infuses healing vibrations into minds and tissues; activity-framed musical arts interactions generate somatic energy, humanizing and promoting spiritual and physiological wellness. Hence, music education assessment policy in Africa should primarily stress ecologically sourced materials as well as interactivity in classroom musicking intended to humanize knowledge acquisition and bond instead of isolate humans. Compatible global perspectives should, of course, be accommodated.

Samples of Current Assessment Policy Integrity in African Countries

Human-Focused Imperatives of Interactive Music Education Assessment Policy in Schools

Somatic sensations generated in practical musicking mend any lurking antisocial tendencies and dispositions. Music assessment policy at all levels, particularly in early schooling, must prioritize the indigenous African exemplar of engineering autonomous children's practical experiences of creativity and performance learning interactions that positively credit every degree of participation skill. Postproduction reflections, personal as well as group, provide an ideal mind-priming forum for the analysis of musical arts knowledge. Basic notation skill is acquired easily through activity-based learning (Nzewi, 2006). Stress in learning situations is obviated in all-inclusive learning and assessment edu-play interactions, which relax the mind and emotions while embedding knowledge through experience. At the tertiary education level, the use of autonomous group productions anchored by individual written analytical reflections on the humanning and intellectual experiences gained was also preferred as the primary Africa-sensed annual assessment criterion at the University of Pretoria, South Africa (Nzewi & Omolo-Ongati, 2014).

Cultural Background of Official Attitude Toward Musical Arts Education in Schools

As stated earlier, in indigenous African societies, participatory knowledge acquisition in the musical arts was everybody's privilege and started from childhood. Music making was not regarded as a livelihood occupation, as specialists do not receive compensation when engaged for some event-music services. As such, the idea of engaging in music as a subsistence occupation in postcolonial African was not favored as an economically viable full-time occupation. This cultural attitude partly accounted for parents and students not initially favoring music as subject of specialization in modern job-training education, even though singing and instrumental performances in school and church groups were commendable extracurricular socialization activities. Such lingering cultural attitudes could account for the African bureaucratic elite's initial neglect to rationalize music as a serious and examinable school subject at any level, as only a few elites who studied abroad observed school-trained livelihood practitioners. The general official reluctance to institute heritage-derived holistic musical arts education and assessment as a compulsory subject in classrooms could also derive from latent cultural fear of functional music: the performative phenomenon retains the historic capacity to intrepidly censure and sanction official malfeasance and immoral acts in the public space.

Extrinsic Factors That Continue to Suppress Culture-Based Music Education and Assessment Policies in Africa

At the national level, leaders globally are now prioritizing governance policies and legislation that would consolidate their stranglehold on political power as well as maximize economic advantages for the privileged. Thus, despite decades of political independence, African ego-inebriated leaders, who suppressed the masses, generally remain mentally colonized, avidly aspiring to copy Northern hegemonic lifestyles and polity practices. Religious leaders are equally consumed with consolidating their earthly power through chasing new converts, controlling members' allegiance, and exerting doctrinal obeisance to boost their worldly ego and wealth. Music is central to any religion. African worldview and life orientation was permeated by intense, musically processed religiosity and reverence for the Supreme Deity, the overseeing minor deities, and intangibly interactive ancestors. The sonic phenomenon was collectively guarded as the intrepid conscience of spirituality-suffused societies, and fearlessly oversaw public secular and religious policies and polity actions. Public ridicule was an incontrovertible intangible weapon of the musical arts, a primary correctional force that none, regardless of eminence, could withstand or countermand in the indigenous and even modern milieu. There was scarcely need for employing tangible weaponry or imprisonment to police society; rather public shaming resulted in self-banishment in very extreme violations. The effectuality of the musical arts as societal overseer was possible because, according to Anyahuru, indigenous corrective music specialists enjoyed "sacrosanct immunity" (Nzewi, Anyahuru, & Ohiaraumunna, 2008) to impartially, sonically pronounce the truth without fear or favor. However, such intangible, proactive, societal management roles are now silenced by modern governance policy and protected by modern technology and legal systems that intimidate the underprivileged. The functional essence of cultural musical arts and science has become severely silenced by technology-focused humans; trivialization is in ascendance. The privileged prefer to encourage and glamorize the Western classical and popular music genres that pose no danger of confronting and sanctioning escalating malpractices in governance, business, and other polity sites.

Diagnosis of the *Sense* of Current Assessment Policies

This exposition argues the viable nature of indigenous African knowledge base that should command fast-tracking culture-sensitive and human-conscious classroom musical arts education as well as situated assessment policies in African countries. What I stridently advocate is the restoration of the essence of musical arts that resolutely coheres and organizes a stable society as proactive symbiotic siblings of music, dance, and drama. The invasion of rarefied theories and elusive excellence propounded by ensconced academics and policymakers has subverted the musical arts' utilitarian societal mission. Senoga-Zake (1986) has tendered the truth that in indigenous Africa nothing important happens without music. This means that the idea of musicking was originally utility grounded. African, and indeed global, governance leaders appear blinded by the mania of boosting economic benefits for the nation (which implies themselves and the privileged). There is scant visible concern for the basic well-being of the deprived and depressed majority, which thereby escalates social tensions, insecurity, mental distress, and traumatic conflicts globally. The viable cultural mandate of the musical arts is to engrave consciousness of what is beneficial to all from infancy, and should be the primary objective of school music curricula and assessment. Instituting proactive, culture-based music education is predicated on sound knowledge of the functional integrity of indigenous epistemology and its purposive-creativity methodology. A competent and passionate education work force as well as support materials must be available.

The curricular tonality of music education practice and assessment policy in African countries should take account of the Africa-common epistemological framework (much positioned already, and tested in CIIMDA), which could be adapted to suit cultural peculiarities (Nzewi, 2009). The African countries sampled hereafter provide evidence of the varied consciousness of the pressing human need and national prestige of culture-sensed musical arts education curricula and assessment policy. Northern hegemonic knowledge models theorize that the contemplative aesthetics of Western classical music history reign supreme in African education philosophy mindset. Economic objectives take undue precedence over pressing human-making ideology prioritized in the functional aesthetics of African heritage, which engages proactively with societal and moral issues. An overwhelming majority of knowledge givers at all education levels in Africa have scant knowledge of cultural music epistemology, philosophy, and praxis. Although measures for training Africa-cognizant indigenous knowledge givers have been developed and tested in the CIIMDA project on policy and implementation (Nzewi, M., & Nzewi, O., 2007), education bureaucracy in African countries still prefers to rely on exogenous research and knowledge regimens parodied by entrenched ignorant expert advisers (Nzewi, 2006).

Samples of African Policy

East Africa—Uganda, Tanzania, and Kenya

Emily Akuno (2013) provides an overview on attempts at culture-conscious school music education, from which assessment policy derives in the three East African countries. She observes that although Uganda became independent in 1962, the education system maintained a "total eclipse of music and the arts" (p. 21). The report of the country's Ministry of Education and Sports (MOEST) to UNESCO in 2004 on school education, declares the characteristic modern African rhetoric of promoting economic productivity, African renaissance, Millennium Development Goals, and emphasizing science education and technical skills. There is typically no report on governance polity measures that would instate a culture-conscious education. Leaders continue to stress money and the economy, instead of policies that facilitate other-human consciousness and sublime life orientation in national and personal priorities. Yet, there is no clear Ugandan policy statement on deploying culture-sensed music education and policy practice to cultivate mind wellness in modern societal practices.

Akuno's survey informs that Tanzania, which gained independence in 1961, proclaimed the Arusha Declaration in 1967, which enabled the inclusion of dance, thereby music, as a tool for promoting culture in the schools as much as to propagate the country's socialist ideology. A 2003 Ministry of Education and Culture document requires that music teacher education along with dance and theater should "promote the acquisition and appropriate use of culture, customs and traditions of the people of Tanzania" (Akuno, 2013, p. 29). Theater and dance are required to be strong cocurricular activities in schools, although there is no sustained culture-focused music education, and thereby no assessment policy. The country's Vision 2025 emphasizes science and technology education. The Bagamoyo College of Arts trains theater personnel, while the University of Dar es Salam offers the music degree.

Kenya gained independence in 1963. Music education was a compulsory examinable primary school subject in the country's 1985 "8-4-4" system of education until it was removed from primary and secondary education as a result of the 2001 national curriculum review. It was reinstated in 2002 as a non-examinable subject in primary school, and an elective at secondary level. Five universities offer music degrees. Akuno's study establishes that by 2005 no music education or assessment policy existed in Kenya. What is unique about Kenya among African countries is the president's action of setting up the Permanent Presidential Music Commission (PPMC), which was concerned with all musical matters in Kenya in 2007. The mandate of the Commission officially identifies "the role music plays in the emotional, cognitive, intellectual, psychological, physical and cultural development of the individual" (p. 33). The activities of the Commission have resulted in a vibrant Kenya Music Festival competition. Competition for the sole purpose of winning money prizes is not African. It generates acrimony, despondence, and often-dishonest practices and subjective/prejudicial judgments, unlike the inspiring African ideology of comparing and sharing capabilities at intra- or intercultural festivals. In 2015, the Republic of Kenya released an elaborate National Music Policy. In the main, the policy discussed music as a commodity, with a vision to generate youth employment, facilitate national cohesion, and enhance the gross domestic product. The document delineates policy statements along with implementation provisions. It takes into account UNESCO's Convention in 2003 for the Safeguarding of the Intangible Cultural Heritage (CSICH) policy of "promoting the function of the intangible cultural heritage in society" (Akuno, 2013, p. 35). What is missing is that a truly African national education assessment policy in music should provide for practically implanting fellow-humanity consciousness in the life aspiration of all learners. Policy should facilitate national cohesion of all citizenry and enhance stable society as in indigenous cultures predating evangelization and colonization of Africa. Where music is taught in Kenyan schools the bias remains "towards Western music content in material and delivery" (p. 34). There is no systematic music education assessment policy. The Kenyan National Music Policy boldly captures the country's elite perceptions of contemporary music landscape in Africa as an economic commodity aspiration. The policy statement on the Music Education and Training section provides for practice-oriented music curriculum and evaluation of performances, although it fails to specify the historic human-making intentions and functions (value benchmarks), which African music education assessment policy should define authoritatively.

Nigeria

Nigeria gained political independence in 1960. In 1976, Compulsory Universal Primary Education (UPE) was instituted. A national policy on education was promulgated in 1977. The first national curriculum for music education within the cultural and creative arts (CCA) in junior secondary schools was published 1985 by the National Education Research and Development Commission (NERDC). In 1999, universal basic education (UBE) for the first 9 years of free schooling replaced UPE with a revised CCA curriculum to align it with National Economic Employment Strategies (NEEDS) and Millennium Development Goals (MDGs). It reflected biculturalism, delving more into foreign music culture by the middle primary education level (Olorunsogo, 2015). Olorunsogo designed a culture-oriented elementary school curriculum model, in which she argues, "children, the world over are more alike than different . . . believed to be natural musicians . . . eager to participate in the events and activities within their experience" (Olorunsogo, 2015, p. 13). Government assessment guidelines started with the conventional summative framework. Then, the Federal Ministry of Education in 1980 adopted the Continuous Assessment convention, which is formative, although subject to abuse by biased assessors. Elui (2015), in her diagnosis of continuous assessment in Nigerian schools, deposes that there is little concern for "higher mental tasks, thinking and application of skills such as ability to apply the knowledge to real life problems" (p. 9), which should be central to music education assessment policy. At the tertiary education level, the National Universities Commission of Nigeria released a document, *Benchmark Minimum Academic Standards for Undergraduate Programs in Nigerian Universities* (2007). The section on music emphasizes Western music theory, performance, and technology. However, African music is included as an area of specialization and all final year students should take three courses in African music. The document provides no culture-informed assessment policy guidelines.

South Africa

In 2011, South Africa designed a detailed Curriculum and Assessment Policy Statement (CAPS) for the grades R-12 (ages 5–17) schooling sector, which has three phases. In the foundation phase (grades R-3, ages 6–8) learners should experience music as part of the life skill subject; observational assessment pointers are suggested for each term under arts and crafts. In the intermediate phase (grades 4–6, ages 9–11) music features as part of the creative arts subject, and in the senior phase (grades 7–9, ages 12–14) under the arts and culture subject. The artistic components are not, however, required to be learned as holistically integrated from conception to performative experiences as per the indigenous African paradigm. The policy prescribes weighted informal and formal assessments, emphasizes practical tasks, and culminates in end-of-year examinations. In the further education and training (FET) phase (grades 10–12, ages 15–17), students can study music as an elective subject. For final matriculation, candidates who wish to study music in their tertiary education take a required examination. The 2011 FET curriculum includes an Indigenous African Music stream adapted from the CIIMDA generic Africa-sensed curriculum with assessment stipulations for studying African music in primary education.

Judging from this sampling, African countries have, to some extent, been aware of the need to produce and institute cultural policies such as the elaborate Cultural Policy of Ghana (2004). From these, music education curricula, practice, and assessment statements take some account, albeit superficial, of indigenous cultural knowledge heritage. However, and in spite of promulgated national cultural policies, factual Africa-sensed school music education and assessment policies remain quite elusive. Curricular imagination and content of school music education, along with transmission designs and assessment procedures as well as purposes, mostly parrot elitist Northern theoretical, methodological, and philosophical models. Governance and academic leaders are preoccupied with technologizing and commodifying music in education to the exclusion of regenerating and advancing the overriding beneficial societal functions stressed in indigenous African cultures. Indigenous assessment canons emphasize an interactive theory-in-practice approach that engraves knowledge in mind and body, from children's autonomous musical arts to adult domains. A major setback is that cognitively researched, discerned, and explicated literature and methodology to guide graded levels of modern classroom and public knowledge transmission are scarce and not of concern to policy makers. Additionally, there are published and ignorantly applied terminologies that block contemporary mental perceptions of prodigious values and virtues of indigenous knowledge constructs and methods. Uninformed and prejudiced scholars/writers have invented pejorative terms such as "orality," "informality," "repetition," and so forth, to derogate African heritage knowledge designs and proactive practices in contemporary literature, classroom, and scholarly as well as public discourses. What is mal-perceived as informality is actually a subtly systematic, play-mode formality rationalized to obviate control and stress in knowledge creation, acquisition, and transmission procedures. Orality remains the dominant mode of instruction and disputation at all modern levels of classroom delivery, as much as technology-contrived or remote learning is becoming a popular vogue for developing techno-minded humans. The primary virtue of oral learning is its spontaneous interactivity, which has immense human and humane benefits. Self-isolated, technology-transacted, or distance learning as well as social media exchanges induce antisocial dispositions, inhibiting other-human consciousness/conscience and communication life-skills acquired through somatic interactions. I have already remarked that repetition is a psychical force (in traditional or modern communication milieux), which, depending on perception, unsettles closed minds but regenerates perception of key idea or routine in memory or reflex among other functions.

POSITING HUMANITY-SENSITIVE ASSESSMENT POLICY FOR PURPOSIVE CLASSROOM EDUCATION IN THE MUSICAL ARTS AND SCIENCE

Trans-African, Intercultural/Multicultural Collaboration in Policy Rationalizations

Grounded humanity-framed assessment policy will remain a mirage in African countries for as long as governance bureaucracies and education policymakers indiscriminately copy flashy exogenous intellectual and existential models, and indulge the global consumption of music as the monetary equation of human existential issues. Stone-heart brilliance propels technology demonism, and therefore subverts individual human conscience. Sublime humanity-sensitive education policies are of the essence. Purposive musical arts that derive from the indigenous African model of impartial, non-brutal agency for imbuing humane conscience and overseeing moral integrity in societal polity processes remains a divinely inspired savior. It has become severely subverted and subdued, but needs revitalization as already stressed. The persuasive research-derived testimony is that natural musical arts science, by its divine power to instigate minds, prompts and manifests hidden truths in performance, while instilling morality attributes. Wholesome education of the impressionable young is a critical human developmental commission and a stable-society-building task. It must eschew subversion by self-aggrandizement or money- and notice-chasing dispositions in policy, theory, and methods. Human-based ideology in music education or assessment policy is compromised when grandiose theories and glamorous devices override human-focused measures in testing and measurement, thereby undermining or controlling each human's unique, legitimate mental disposition, or capability. Hence modern policy constructs must be circumspect about apportioning failures in narrative and practical knowledge interactions, processes that are prioritized and cherished in African cultural milieux.

Cultural Integrity and Regeneration

Cultural integrity and regeneration imperatives of virtues and values are grounded in applied transmission methodologies. The common standard policy pointers provided so far underpinned all extant sub-Saharan African knowledge acquisition and assessment lore. They are being posited as steppingstones for rationalizing curricula content and assessment policy that demonstrate cultural integrity with a requisite expanded world-view. The cultural location and mix of every school and class presents illustrative local peculiarities applicable to learners' human background and relevant social milieu. Regenerating indigenous authenticity will take into account literacy imperatives and relevant universal variables of sonic constructs that will facilitate cross-pollination for progressive growth.

Attaining Human-Focused Assessment Policy

To attain human-focused assessment policy, we must consider reinstating humanity-based imperatives and polity conscious transmission designs with a global outlook. Theory could be demonstratively practical or written. Modern literacy intelligentsia did not originate the ideas of theoretical procedure and research in transacting knowledge. African indigenous knowledge designs and creations in the musical arts derive from systematically replicable frames of reference, hence the indigenous expression, theory-in-practice: "Illustrate or see it as real." Such a performatively interacted theoretical canon now needs a literacy focus from cognizant, respectful scholars and learners for posterity. Fashionable abstract theorizing (floating theory) of music has gained ascendancy in glamorous scholarship as scholars invent and reinvent self-brilliance in established knowledge practices. Extraneous policy designs, which do not embody the ideal of humanizing integrity that marked African cultural musical arts intellect and knowledge constructs, have been contested as eroding the original African mentality and world-view. I hereby stress that the primary purpose of music in and out of the classroom must not be as an economic enterprise. Avid modern promotion of technological/electronic production and dissemination renders humans redundant, including in music production, diminishing job opportunities in both the classical and popular genres. In music knowing and appreciation, assessment policy and designs should reckon principally with interhuman narratives, verbal or gestural (performative), which reveal real feelings and impressions of experience. African music scholars and policy designers should resist the modern vogue of nonperforming "experts" in a genre pontificating merits in musical arts created and produced by others. The academic exercise merely flatters the high-mindedness of the dubbed experts.

Reorienting the Knowledge Competence of Trainers and Assessors for Viable Advancement

I have remarked that technology has increasingly short-circuited the instilling of human-focused sentiments, emotions, and fellow-human conscience and conscious-ness that underpinned indigenous African ideology. Most fanciful modern teaching and research theories distract from knowing and learning by experiential doing and experimenting. For emphasis, in Africa, musical arts pedagogy and assessment policy, particularly for younger age learners, should prioritize edu-play experiential interactions in original creativity and production with available natural facilities preferably. Every passionate music-teacher-aspirant should be given the opportunity to demonstrate practically the capability to stimulate the innate abilities of learners. Mechanistic or virtual quantitative (questionnaire) assessment of disposition, liable to subjective opinions, could be deceptive. The CIIMDA project reoriented and sensitized African musical arts educators and learners in 10 Southern African Development Countries (SADC) on the theoretical, creative, and performative paradigms of indigenous musical arts and science, which should be foundational knowledge for contemporary classroom education and practice in Africa. Assessment policy stipulated interactive experiences in lecture and practical modules for intercultural participants, irrespective of age and qualification. The practical assessment demonstrated impressive latent heritage knowledge in the groups' creative, production, and literacy play-shopping activities packaged during 2 weeks' courses. There were minimal exotic theories and assessment yardsticks beyond stimulating latent cultural norms.[3]

CONCLUSION

I conclude with the close of the opening allegory in Box 4.2.

Box 4.2 The Allegory of the Child, Adult, and the Womanly Sage

The Feminine Sage in her ancient to modern wisdoms of Africa conclusively instructs: High-minded scholars and education officialdom should be mindful of extrinsic, control-ridden knowledge constructs and technological or statistical assessment procedures. Patiently stimulate the intuitive voices of culturally connected children. When not intimidated, such children as much as indigenous knowledge experts provide original essentials. To instate authoritative African assessment ideology and logic in global imagination of knowledge assessment commands circumspection in imposing modern theoretical or policy sophistries. Aspire to restore the essential capacities of the musical arts and science as a Divine intangible gift for humanizing mankind. Prioritize the functional aesthetic of ordering and overseeing salubrious societal systems on Earth. The modern hi-mind is not necessarily wiser than her/his knowledge progenitor, who cherished virtuous intellect in exercising inventive acumen. Modern humans, globally, should cherish mind sobriety in advancing the known so as to endear ethical, other-human conscious creativity and interactions on Earth. Music education assessment policy in Africa must engineer transmitting humanning musical arts emotions. Artistic-creative aspirations that sublimate minds and hearts should freely flow in all learners performatively. The sonic-dramatic-choreographic phenomenon remains a primary agency for engendering stable human existence and relationships among culture groups, countries, and regions without discriminating elites and commoners. Note that a knowledge provider who contrives failures in a general human knowledge capability such as the musical arts is already a failed or jaundiced mind.

Acknowledgments

I acknowledge the cooperation of the following colleagues who supplied me documents on cultural and assessment policy in various Africa countries: Jenny Kinnear (South Africa), Mellitus Wanyama (Kenya), James Thole (Malawi), Jorge Mabunda (Mozambique), Nasilele Imbwela (Zambia), Grace Ekong (Nigeria), I. Idamoyibo (Ghana), B. Chinouriri (Zimbabwe).

Notes

1. This contribution on music assessment policy in Africa privileges the indigenous African narrative style and morality anecdotes for engraining knowledge in the introduction and conclusion to urge policies that would entrench virtuous societal practices and living with purposive and proactive music. The style also strategizes calculated repetition of key themes with varied insights for emphasis.
2. Musical arts in Africa is conceived and applied as a soft science. "Musical arts science," "musical arts," and "music" are, therefore, used interchangeably as translating Africa's indigenous terminological sense of the holistic conceptualization of music, dance, drama, and performance materials as integrated creative and performative phenomenon discussed in singular terms. In tradition, adjectival terms are used as need arises to distinguish the peculiar features, actions, and functions of the components. The holism is crafted and applied as a proactive soft science of humanity and societal management.
3. The CIIMDA project, based in South Africa, was funded by the Norwegian Concert Institute from 2004 to 2012, and resulted in the publication of 15 books for various levels of theoretical and philosophical studies and concert performance compositions informed by indigenous knowledge heritage in African musical arts science, also the research and writing of Africa-generic music curricula for pre tertiary music education and assessment.

References

Agawu, K. (2004). Aesthetic inquiry and the music of Africa. In K. Weredu (Ed.), *A companion to African philosophy* (pp 404–414). London, UK: Blackwell.

Airasian, P. W. (1977). *Classroom assessment* (3rd ed.). New York, NY: McGraw-Hill.

Akuno, E. A. (2013). *Kenyan music: An education perspective*. Nairobi, Kenya: Emak Music Services.

Blacking J. (1970). Tonal organization in the music of two Venda initiation schools, *Ethnomusicology, 14*(1), 1–54. doi: 10.1177/0255761411408503

Blacking, J. (1976). *How musical is man?* London, UK: Faber & Faber.

Blom, D., & Poole, K. (2004). Peer assessment of tertiary music performance: Opportunities for understanding performance assessment and performing through experience and self-reflection. *British Journal of Music Education, 21*(1), 111–125. doi: 10.1017/S0265051703005539

Bresler, L. (Ed.). (2000). *Arts Education Policy Review—Symposium on Arts Education in Africa, 101*(5).

Brophy, T. S. (2000). *Assessing the developing child musician*. Chicago, IL: GIA Publications.

Brophy, T. S., & Lehmann-Wermser, A. (Eds.). (2013). *Music assessment across cultures and continents—The culture of shared practice*. Chicago, IL: GIA Publications.

Brophy, T.S., Lai, M.-L., & Chen, H.-F. (Ed.). (2014). *Music assessment and global diversity: Practice, measurement, and policy.* Chicago, IL: GIA Publications.

Campbell, P. S. (2007). Musical meaning in Children's cultures. In L. Bresler (Ed.), *International handbook of research in arts education* (pp. 881–894). Dordrecht, Netherlands: Springer.

Daniel, R. (2004). Peer assessment in music performance: The development, trial and evaluation of a methodology for the Australian tertiary environment. *British Journal of Music Education, 21*(1), 89–110.

Edmund, D., & Edmund, J. C. (2014). Performance assessment in music teacher education: Models for implementation. In T. Brophy, M. Lai, & H. Chen (Eds.), *Music assessment and global diversity: Practice, measurement and policy* (pp. 321–340). Chicago, IL: GIA Publications.

Eisner, E. (2007). Assessment and evaluation in education and the arts. In L. Bresler (Ed.), *International handbook of research in arts education* (pp. 423–426). Dordrecht, Netherlands: Springer.

Elliot, D. (1995). *Music matters: A new philosophy of music education.* Oxford, UK: Oxford University Press.

Elui, E. P. (2015). *School based assessment in Nigeria primary school.* (Unpublished paper).

Falkchikov, N. (1995). Peer feedback marking: Developing peer assessment. *Innovation in Education and Training International, 32*(2), 175–187.

Farrel, F. (2014). The blind assessor: Are we constraining or enriching diversity of music development and learning? In T. Brophy, M. Lai, and H. Chen (Eds.), *Music assessment and global diversity: Practice, measurement and policy* (pp. 211–232). Chicago, IL: GIA Publications.

Flolu, J. E. (2000). Re-thinking arts education in Ghana. *Arts Education Policy Review, 101*(5), 25–29. doi: 10.1080/10632910009600270

Holcomb, A. (2014). An investigation into the development of assessment disposition of pre-service music teachers. In T. Brophy, M. Lai, & H. Chen (Eds.), *Music assessment and global diversity: Practice, measurement and policy* (pp. 387–397). Chicago, IL: GIA Publications.

Hudson, M. (2014). Assessment in music education: A Colorado perspective. In T. Brophy, M. Lai, & H. Chen (Eds.), *Music Assessment and global diversity: Practice, measurement and policy* (pp. 233–246). Chicago, IL: GIA Publications.

Kermode, F. (1979). *The genesis of secrecy: On the interpretation of narrative.* New York, NY: Harvard University Press.

Mans, M. E. (2000). Creating a cultural policy for Namibia. *Arts Education Policy Review, 101*(5), 11–17.

Marlatt, J. (2014). Benchmarks and milestones: Assessing the undergraduate music teacher. In T. Brophy, M. Lai, & H. Chen (Eds.), *Music assessment and global diversity: Practice, measurement and policy* (pp. 341–350). Chicago, IL: GIA Publications.

Murphy, R. (2007). Harmonizing assessment and music in the classroom. In L. Breslar (Ed.), *International handbook of research in arts education* (pp. 361–380). Dordrecht, Netherlands: Springer.

Nierman, G. (2014). Music teacher evaluation: Don't forget the affective side of the house. In T. Brophy, M. Lee, & H. Chen (Eds.), *Music assessment and global diversity: Practice, measurement and policy* (pp. 397–406). Chicago, IL: GIA Publications.

Nketia, J. H. K. (1974). *The music of Africa.* New York, NY: Norton.

Nordlund, M. (2014). Assessing quality standards of teacher disposition. In T. Brophy, M. Lai, & H. Chen (Eds.), *Music assessment and global diversity: Practice, measurement and policy* (pp. 407–413). Chicago, IL: GIA Publications.

Nzewi, M. (1991). *Musical practice and creative—An African traditional perspective.* Bayreuth, Germany: Iwalewa-Haus, University of Bayreuth.

Nzewi, M. (1997). *African music: Theoretical content and creative continuum—The culture-exponents definitions*. Oldershausen, Germany: Institut fur Didaktik popularer Musik.

Nzewi, M. (1999). The music of staged emotions—The coordinates of movement and emotions in African music performance. *Musikunterricht Heute*, 2, 192–203.

Nzewi, M. (2003). Acquiring knowledge of the musical arts in traditional society. In A. Herbst, M. Nzewi, & K. Agawu (Eds.), *Musical arts in Africa—Theory, practice and education* (pp. 13–37). Pretoria, South Africa: Unisa Press.

Nzewi, M. (2006). Growing in musical arts knowledge versus the role of the ignorant expert. In M. Mans (Ed.), *Centering on African practice in musical arts education* (pp. 49–60). Sommerset West, South Africa: African Minds.

Nzewi, M., Anyahuru, I., & Ohiaraumunna, T. (2008). *Musical sense and musical meaning: An indigenous African Perception*. Amsterdam, Netherlands: Rozenberg Publishers.

Nzewi, M. (2009). The CIIMDA initiative for culture-sensitive musical arts education in Africa. In M. Masoga, M. Nzewi, & O. E. Nzewi, *African knowledge-sensed musical arts education: Policy considerations* (pp. 159–174). Sommerset West, South Africa: African Minds.

Nzewi, M., & Nzewi, O. E. (2007). *A contemporary study of musical arts informed by African indigenous knowledge systems*. Vols. 1–5. Pretoria, South Africa: CIIMDA series.

Nzewi, M., & Omolo-Onganti, R. (2014). Injecting the African spirit of humanity into teaching, learning and assessment of musical arts in the modern classroom. *Journal of the Musical Arts in Africa*, 11, 55–72. doi: 10.2989/18121004.2014.998403

O'Leary, M. (2004). *Towards a balanced assessment for Irish schools*. Keynote address to the Department of Education and Science Inspectorate, 2004.

Olorunsogo, I. (2015). *Developing a culture-oriented or indigenous knowledge curriculum for elementary school music education in Nigeria*. (Unpublished paper).

Opondo, P. A. (2000). Cultural policy in Kenya. *Arts Education Policy Review*, 101(5), 18–24.

Parkes, K., Doerksen, P., & Ritcher, G. (2014). Measuring professional dispositions in pre-service music teachers in the United States. In T. Brophy, M. Lai, & H. Chen (Eds.), *Music assessment and global diversity: Practice, measurement and policy* (pp. 351–387). Chicago, IL: GIA Publications.

Pitts, S. E. (2005). "Testing, testing..." How do students use written feedback? *Active Learning in Higher Education*, 6, 218–229. doi: 10.1177/1469787405057663

Ruddock, E. (2012). "Sort of in your blood": Inherent musicality survives cultural judgment. *Research Studies in Music Education*, 34, 207–221. doi: 10.1177/1321103X12461747

Senoga-Zake, G. (1986). *Folk music of Kenya*. Nairobi, Kenya: Uzima Press.

Staggins, R. (1997). *Student-centered classroom assessment* (2nd ed.). Upper Saddle River, NJ: Prentice Hall.

Wang, D. P. (2014). Rhetoric of reality? Assessing the reliability of the assessments to the elementary school general music classes and the graduates' music achievements. In T. Brophy, M. Lai, & H. Chen (Eds.). *Music assessment and global diversity: Practice, measurement and policy* (pp. 169–182). Chicago, IL: GIA Publications.

Woodward, S. (2002). Assessing young children's musical understanding. *Music Education International*, 1, 112–121.

....

CHAPTER 5

CURRICULUM-BASED POLICY IN MUSIC ASSESSMENT
Asian Perspectives

....

HSIAO-FEN CHEN

BECAUSE of traditional cultural influences, countries in the Asia-Pacific region place a heavy emphasis on the importance of education. As globalization continues to draw the world closer, the revision of curriculum guidelines has become a major part of educational reform. At the same time, the importance of music assessment in international circles is increasingly reflected in the music curriculum guidelines/standards in countries of the Asia-Pacific region.

The officially designated curriculum syllabus of each country can be viewed as a reflection of their respective educational policies. These syllabi also serve as important markers that guide the implementation of education policy in schools. Despite many revisions over the years, the representative and authoritative weight of such syllabi make them valuable sources of information for any research into educational policies. This chapter is an overview of the music curriculum assessment policies in the following countries of the Asia-Pacific region: China, Hong Kong, Japan, Singapore, South Korea, and Taiwan. Most of the literature from which the ensuing policy discussions draw is published by the educational authorities of each country, or is on their official websites. Each policy review begins with a brief introduction of the country's educational context and music curriculum, followed by a review of the country's music assessment policy. The chapter closes with a discussion of Asian perspectives on shared policy features, challenges, and trends and issues regarding music assessment.

CURRICULUM-BASED MUSIC
ASSESSMENT POLICIES

China

After its founding in 1949, the People's Republic of China (PRC), with the Soviet educational experience as a model, established a system of curriculum management, government-designated guidelines, and centralized publication of textbooks. In the 1980s, the PRC began to slowly experiment with educational reform, with the National People's Congress passing the implementation of a 9-year compulsory education system in 1986 and the State Council's administrative educational unit, the State Education Commission (renamed the Ministry of Education [MOE] in 1998) was given responsibility for the examination and approval of teaching plans, textbooks, and other related materials (Gao, 1992). In accordance to the *Guidelines for Basic Education Curriculum Reform (Trial)* disseminated in 2001, China implemented a curriculum management system at the national, local, and institutional levels. First, at the national level, curricula were formulated in the development of an overall educational plan with subject and instructional hours, and national curriculum standards were developed. Next, at the local level, the formulation of curriculum implementation plans in consideration of the requirements of different regions took place—a step that included the development and selection of local curricula. Finally, at the institutional level, schools could develop or choose curricula that best fit their particular needs (Zhou, 2008). Currently, curricula at the compulsory educational stages (elementary through junior high school) are planned in accordance with the 2001 *Compulsory Curriculum Pilot Program* and the 2011 *Full-Time Compulsory Education Curriculum Standards*. As for curricula at the senior high school level, they are carried out in accordance with the *High School Curriculum Program (Experimental)* and the *High School Curriculum Standards (Experimental)*, both promulgated in 2003.

China's arts curriculum for the three educational levels—elementary, junior high, and senior high—includes the subjects of music, the fine arts, and general arts. Schools may offer courses in general arts, or alternatively choose either the fine arts or music. Music at the senior high school level, as a three-credit course, includes music appreciation, singing, composition, the study of musical instruments, dance, and theater, for a total of six categories. Music appreciation, worth two academic credits, is usually given priority to ensure that students possess, at the very minimum, basic music literary (PRC MOE, 2003a).

The music curricula at the elementary and junior high school levels include music perception and appreciation, performance, composition, and music and culture. Each area, in turn, is divided into three to four key areas, with content taught over three learning stages—grades 1 to 2, grades 3 to 6, and grades 7 to 9. Musical perception and appreciation, for example, includes the areas of *elements of musical performance*, *music and emotion*, *musical forms and genres*, and *musical styles* (PRC MOE, 2011). Music curricula at the senior high school level, however, place a heavier emphasis on experience, comparison, exploration, and cooperation in order to cultivate a greater sense of musical aesthetics, as well as performance and composition skills in students (PRC MOE, 2003a).

Assessment criteria of elementary and junior high school music curricula are drawn from curriculum content goals and are currently divided into three areas (PRC MOE, 2011):

1. *Combination of formative and summative assessments.* The goal here is to understand changes to a student's emotional life, attitude, methods used, knowledge acquired, and skills developed over the course of his or her studies. Assessments are based on observation, conversation, asking questions, discussion, singing, musical instrument performances, and so forth. Summative assessments evaluate a student's overall progress at each educational stage and are carried out at semester's or academic year's end. Evaluations are based on listening skills, singing, instrument playing, integrated artistic performances, and so on.
2. *Combination of qualitative review and quantitative evaluation.* The goal of qualitative review is to evaluate a student's attitude and values, processes and methods, knowledge and skills over the course of his or her musical study; quantitative evaluation is based on a quantitative assessment of various course content, for example, the number of songs sung or musical pieces played.
3. *Combination of self-assessment, peer assessment, and other assessment.* Self-assessment is mainly descriptive and focused on a student's personal development over the course of different educational stages; peer assessment involves a mutual evaluation of students participating in singing together, musical ensembles, or musical talent showcases; other assessment refers to a teacher's evaluation of students over the course of different educational stages and is based on musical listening skills and recognition as well as musical (vocal or instrumental) concerts.

Senior high school music curriculum assessment further includes another set of four principles (PRC MOE, 2003a):

1. *Guiding principle.* Help students to understand their own progress, to discover and develop their music potential, to further improve their cultural literacy and value judgments, and to establish a sense of social responsibility.
2. *Scientific principle.* Assessment indicators and methods are to be based on features characteristic to the discipline of music and the content standards of different teaching modules.
3. *Holistic principle.* Assessment should cover course objectives at different levels and various content.
4. *Operability principle.* Assessment indicators and methods should be clear and simple to understand, as well as easy to implement and use.

The *2003 High School Curriculum Program (Experimental)* stipulates the establishment of high school assessment schemes that offer an integrated assessment of a student's academic performance and growth record. Furthermore, while acknowledging the diverse goals before them and various methods available to achieve these goals, and adhering to the stated principles of the assessment process, school faculty may use observation, interaction, tests, performance, displays of finished work, self-assessment, and mutual assessment among other methods to keep track of a student's growth. At the same time, these assessment efforts at the high school level are monitored by officials from education administrative departments (PRC MOE, 2003b).

The use of diagnostic, incentive, and improvement tools is encouraged in music curriculum assessment, to help students better understand their own progress and increase their confidence and motivation to learn, thereby contributing to the overall enhancement of teaching quality (PRC MOE, 2011). In order to further examine the results of arts education in schools, the Ministry of Education promulgated the *Elementary and Junior High School Student Arts Quality Evaluation Regulations*, later implemented in 2015, so as to better understand artistic development in students and improve aesthetics education and students' overall sense of aesthetics and literacy in the humanities (PRC MOE, 2015).

Summary

In China, multiple forms of assessment are employed—for example, formative, summative, qualitative, quantitative, self, other, and peer assessments—to ensure that assessments accurately reflect students' learning outcomes. They give students a chance to observe their own progress, improve confidence and the desire for learning, and contribute to an overall improvement in teaching quality. Moreover, in order to further strengthen arts education in schools, in 2015 an evaluation system targeting arts education in elementary and junior high schools was implemented to enhance artistic competency in students and advance arts education goals through assessment policies.

Hong Kong

Following the return of Hong Kong to Chinese control in 1997, the territory began to actively implement a series of far-ranging educational reforms. In 2002, Hong Kong's top educational authority, the Education Bureau, published the *Basic Education Curriculum Guide*, introducing curriculum reform at the primary school level and establishing a new curriculum framework for grades Primary Three through Secondary Three (ages 9 to 15). In 2007, the Education Bureau released a curriculum guide for senior secondary (ages 16 to 18), a step later followed by the reform of the school system in 2009 that greatly expanded the number of electives for students at the senior secondary level (Education Commission, 2015). Each of the two educational levels—elementary and secondary—offers music and visual arts for a total of 12 years of study (Education Bureau, 2003).

Music curricula from Primary One through Secondary Six (ages 6 to 18), share four common learning targets: *developing creativity and imagination, developing music skills and processes, cultivating critical responses in music,* and *understanding music in context*—with related content being tailored to the grade in question. From Primary One to Secondary Three, focus is on the building of musical elements and emotions and finding methods of expression through the use of creativity, performance techniques, and listening skills. From Secondary Four through Secondary Six (ages 16 to 18), the curriculum consists of both required and elective courses. Required courses focus on the use of listening, performance, and composition skills in the cultivation of musical creativity, sensitivity, and ability. Electives, on the other hand, encourage students to choose a field of specialization and emphasize the cultivation of professional music skills.

The principles of assessment used in Hong Kong are (Education Bureau, 2003):

1. Set assessment areas, methods, and criteria that focus on the four learning targets and the learning objectives;
2. Assess both the learning process and outcome;
3. Select and adopt a combination of diversified modes of assessment according to learning and teaching needs;
4. Emphasize simple but effective methods of recording students' performance;
5. Clearly explain the assessment areas, methods, and criteria to students prior to the assessment, which may also be developed with students if necessary;
6. Provide students with appropriate feedback as soon as the assessment is completed;
7. Stress the quality of assessment rather than the quantity of assignments or the frequency of assessment.

The modes of assessment recommended by the Hong Kong Education Bureau are:

1. *Elementary Three to Secondary Three*: includes classroom performances, worksheets, practical tests, listening tests, concert reports, project learning, self- and peer assessment, music activities recording, portfolios, and reporting (Education Bureau, 2003).
2. *Secondary Four to Secondary Six*: Assessment should include "assessment for learning" and "assessment of learning." "Assessment for learning" is especially important in the process of music learning and teaching, whereby teachers immediately give appropriate feedback on student performances, while letting them know their level of achievement. "Assessment of learning" is usually conducted regularly at a certain period of the school term, and is mostly used for selection and reporting purposes.
   (1) "Internal assessment" refers to the assessment practices that teachers and schools employ as part of the ongoing learning and teaching process during the 3 years of senior secondary study, includes the use of classroom performances, worksheets, practical tests, listening tests, concert reports, project learning, and portfolios.

(2) "Public assessment" (public examinations and the moderated school-based assessment, SBA) refers to the assessment conducted as part of the assessment processes in place for all schools and aims to provide summative assessments of the learning of each student (Education Bureau, 2015).

The areas of assessment identified by the Hong Kong Education Bureau are:

1. *Elementary to Secondary Three*
   (1) *Creating.* There is a wide variety in the scope of creating, such as creating rhythms, creating melodies, sound projects, music arrangements, creative works, improvisation, and creating movements. The focus of assessing creative works may include the use of musical elements, grasp of compositional devices, structure, and level of creativity.
   (2) *Performing.* Singing, instrumental playing, and music reading are the main areas of assessing students' performing abilities. Solo singing or choral singing, solo playing or ensemble playing, and singing at sight or playing at sight are suggested. The focal points in assessment may include pitch, rhythm, timbre, dynamics, tempo, mood, phrasing, diction (in singing), tonguing (in recorder playing), and so forth.
   (3) *Listening.* Oral and/or written forms can be adapted for assessing students' listening abilities. For example, the following focal points in the assessment of pitch are suggested: Identifying a specific melody heard from a number of melodies, identifying the sol-fa names of a melody, identifying the wrong notes played intentionally of a familiar melody, or correcting the wrong notes played or written intentionally on a score (Education Bureau, 2003).
2. *Secondary Four to Secondary Six*

The Hong Kong Examinations and Assessment Authority (HKEAA) explains that tests targeting musical subjects are, content-wise, similar to that of the average professional music exam. For example, the 2015 External School Review (ESR) exams include both compulsory and optional testing in the areas of musical composition, musical performance (instrumental or vocal), and musical listening. These areas also serve as the basis for SBA. Through 2018, schools have the option to not provide assessment scores; however, starting in 2019, following the program's full implementation, score submission will be compulsory and will account for a full 20% of grades given for music-related courses (HKEAA, 2015).

Summary

Hong Kong has particularly strict standards when it comes to music curriculum assessment. Assessment goals from Primary One to Primary Three focus on the interaction between student, teacher, school, and parent to better understand a student's performance and enhance his or her musical skills in the areas of musical composition, musical listening, and musical performance. From Secondary Four to Secondary Six, the focus is on the relationship between—and the application of—music appreciation, performance, and composition, with listening skills given particular weight in the instruction of musical appreciation. Regarding assessment methods, a plurality of methods are used from Primary One to Primary Three, while, from Secondary Four to Secondary Six, professional competency tests are used to evaluate a student's learning outcomes. Before graduating from Secondary Six, students must take part in both the SBA and ESR public examinations—a process that clearly highlights the strict nature of assessment protocols in Hong Kong.

Japan

At the end of World War II, Japan's Ministry of Education set down the direction of the country's postwar educational policy in a paper titled *Educational Policy for the Construction of a New Japan*, published in September 1945 (Ministry of Education, Culture, Sports, Science and Technology [MEXT], 2015a). Two years later, in 1947, a trial version of curriculum guidelines was released. The guidelines were later finalized in 1958, becoming the country's first educational standards (National Institute for Educational Policy Research, 2015a). Since 1958, Japan's educational authority, the MEXT, has amended the country's curriculum guidelines on several occasions—on average once every decade. In the most recent round of amendments of 2015, however, outside of changes to moral education, course guidelines remained unchanged from the 2008 curriculum guidelines (MEXT, 2015b).

School education in Japan is divided into three educational levels—elementary, junior, and senior high levels. Arts curricula are planned for grades 1 to 12 and include music and drawing at the elementary level, music and fine arts at the junior high level, and a selection of music, fine arts, arts and crafts, or calligraphy (one of four) at the senior high level. In other words, music is required at the elementary and junior high school level, but is an elective for high school students (MEXT, 2008, 2010). The overall objective of music curricula at the elementary school level is to nurture basic musical competency in addition to the cultivation of a sensibility for, and an interest in, music. At the junior high school level, the emphasis is on developing basic musical skills, understanding elements of music culture, and cultivating a sense of enjoyment and feeling for music. Building on this foundation, students at the senior high school level are then guided to a further understanding of music culture and creativity (MEXT, 2105c).

Music curricula are built on the two pillars of "expression" and "appreciation." Expression includes performance-related activities such as singing, musical instrument playing, and musical composition, while appreciation emphasizes an understanding of culture through the experience of music. From a learning content standpoint, this means that elementary school students are encouraged to develop a sense of, and an interest in, the musical elements to which they are exposed and junior high school students learn how to better express music's emotive aspects, while high school students are expected to begin to display musical performance skills or a grasp of music theory.

From elementary to senior high school, the process of musical acquisition is overall one of gradual deepening (MEXT, 2105d).

Assessment of music curricula is based on learning goals, assessment perspectives and spirit, and music learning content. The selection of content for musical study is done in accordance with the most current curriculum guidelines, while assessment methods are drawn from a National Institute for Educational Policy Research publication detailing assessment criteria and methods (National Institute for Educational Policy Research, 2015b). Traditionally, assessment perspectives have focused on the domains of *interest, motivation, and attitude; thinking and decision-making; expression and skills*; and *knowledge and comprehension*. In alignment with these four assessment domains, the musical assessment components of *interest, motivation, and attitude; creative expression; performance competency*; and *musical appreciation* are advanced in consideration of the goals and content of each of the three educational stages. These components are elaborated here.

1. *Musical interest, motivation, and attitude.*

At the elementary school level, children start to find a familiarity and interest in music. They also begin to develop musical appreciation and perform music to express themselves. The process at the junior high school level remains essentially the same, however, students are asked to take more initiative in their musical expression. At the senior high school level, attention is paid to the intersection of music and culture and to the study of singing, musical instrument playing, musical composition, and musical appreciation.

2. *Musical creative expression.*

For all three educational stages, students are required to familiarize themselves with a range of musical elements so as to be able to enjoy musical performances and the intent behind them, in addition to being able to perceive the beauty and joy of music.

3. *Musical performance.*

Students at the elementary and junior high school level learn to perform musically, thereby giving them a basic music skill set that includes singing, musical instrument playing, and musical composition. At the high school level, students continue to study musical performance with the further goal of conveying original interpretations.

4. *Music appreciation.*

At the elementary school level, students learn to shape and create musical elements at the same time that they perceive the beauty and joy of music—specifically, when they convey different musical styles and aesthetics. At the junior and senior high school level, content on how to reflect on and interpret music is added, deepening the students' understanding of music and their ability to listen and find emotional resonance within musical aesthetics.

Suggested assessment methods include observation, student and teacher interaction, note taking, worksheets, study sheets, self-work reports, written exams, questionnaire surveys, interviews, self-assessments, and mutual assessments. Each class year uses a same ranking system ranging from 1 to 5: 5 = Very satisfactory and high level exhibited,

4 = Very satisfactory, 3 = Satisfactory, 2 = More effort required, 1 = Significantly more effort required (National Institute for Educational Policy Research, 2015b).

Summary

The music curriculum assessment areas put forth by the National Institute for Educational Policy Research (2015b) are: *interest, motivation, and attitude*; *creative expression*; *performance competency*; and *music appreciation*. Teachers are given flexibility in the choice and use of assessment methods, with no obvious restrictions in place and no particular case or model to which they are required to adhere. The ranking system for assessment criteria is on a simple scale of 1 to 5; however, in the reference manual for assessment criteria, there are many models that teachers may refer to and use.

Singapore

Starting in 1966, Singapore began to gradually implement an English-based bilingual education system in which mother tongues and English were given equal educational weight by Singapore's top educational authority—the Ministry of Education (MOE [Singapore MOE]). In 2003, Singapore implemented a nationwide 10-year compulsory education system in two major stages, covering 6 years of primary and 4 years of secondary schooling (ages 6 to 16) (Singapore MOE, 2015a). In the fifth grade of primary school, classes in English, the student's mother tongue, mathematics, and science are offered in accordance with the academic aptitude of each student. Before graduating from primary school, all students take the Primary Student Leaving Examination (PSLE; Singapore MOE, 2015b). Depending on their individual performance, students then enter one of three academic tracks in secondary school: *Express, Normal (Academic)*, or *Normal (Technical)* (Singapore MOE, 2105c). The placement of students in one of these tracks is based on their individual ability and interest, and is one of the main distinguishing factors of the educational system in Singapore.

Music courses in Singapore are taught under the discipline of the Humanities and the Arts. From Primary One through Secondary Two (ages 6–14), music is compulsory for all students. When part of the lower secondary subjects (secondary grades 1–2), music is compulsory for all students; whereas, among upper secondary subjects (secondary grades 3–4), music courses are offered as electives (Singapore MOE, 2015b, 2015d). Currently, the *2015 General Music Syllabus Program* provides the guidelines for the country's music curricula (Singapore MOE, 2014).

The music syllabus spans four key stages, from Primary One to Secondary Two. Each stage includes two levels and builds on the competencies introduced in previous stages (MOE, 2014). The five main learning objectives of the music syllabus are as follows (Singapore MOE, 2014, pp.4–7):

LO1: Perform music in both instrumental and vocal settings, individually and in groups.

LO2: Create music in both instrumental and vocal settings, individually and in groups.

LO3: Listen and respond to music.

LO4: Appreciate music from local and global cultures.

LO5: Understand musical elements and concepts.

In accordance with the five main learning objectives just described, at the completion of their primary school education, students are expected to be able to: (1) play a classroom percussion instrument and a major melodic instrument (e.g., recorder or guitar); (2) perform simple musical composition and improvisation; (3) evaluate music using the appropriate vocabulary to describe musical characteristics; (4) appreciate the music of Singapore and other local cultures as well as that of the Western classical music tradition; (5) describe and express musical elements and concepts while listening, playing, or composing different styles of music and music from different cultures. At the end of their second year of secondary schooling (Secondary Two, age 14), students are expected to be able to perform on a musical instrument; communicate ideas through music; respond to music actively; discuss in-depth various musical styles and cultures; and express their understanding of musical elements and concepts through the listening, playing, and composing of music.

Therefore, it is clear that the role of primary school is to create a foundation on which students at the secondary school level work to strengthen their abilities in musical performance, composition, expression, appreciation, and understanding. Referring to the development of these skills and learning content at each educational stage, teachers are then able to examine instructional design and student performance as the basis for further teaching and learning assessments.

Assessment is implemented in alignment with the five learning objectives listed previously, and teachers ensure that all learning objectives are addressed over the course of the academic year. For teachers, assessment helps them review teaching approaches and strategies and facilitate student learning. It is carried out in a variety of ways, including through listening activities, responding through movement, musical performances, improvisation or composition tasks, and written assignments or reflection journals. For students, assessment is integral to helping them better understand themselves over the course of the learning process, with assessment implemented on a regular basis to assist them in understanding their strengths and weaknesses and quickly fill in any learning gaps (Singapore MOE, 2014).

Summary

The importance of assessment is addressed from both the teaching and learning aspects. Music curricula in Singapore emphasize learning content and assessments that lie closely linked with the five learning objectives. The five learning objectives are the basis on which teachers decide contents for teaching and assessment. Music assessment using multiple methods is recommended to assist in student learning and in offering immediate feedback.

South Korea

National curricula in South Korea have been revised approximately every 7 to 10 years since the nation's first curriculum was released in 1954. With the advent of globalization and an information society from the mid-1990s on, the demand for national curriculum revisions has continued to grow. The 2009 revised curriculum is currently the newest iteration of these revisions, with the Korea Institute for Curriculum and Evaluation (KICE) responsible for conducting basic research regarding curriculum development (KICE, 2012). However, the country' music curriculum continues to follow the 2007 curriculum.

With the introduction of the 2009 curriculum, learning at the elementary school level has been divided into 2-year learning stages, while the division of academic subjects has shifted to subject clusters. In recent years, focus has been on school-based curricula and the decentralization of curriculum planning, thus giving schools further autonomy in curriculum creation. At the elementary and junior high school level (ages 6–15), 20% of total teaching hours are given over to school planning, while, at the senior high school level (ages 16 to 18), 64 academic credits are open to planning by schools. As for arts curriculum, the instruction of music and the fine arts is offered from grade 3 of elementary school up through high school, with such classes being part of the life curriculum at grades 1 and 2 (ages 6–8) of elementary school (KICE, 2012). Music course content follows regulations laid out in the 2007 curriculum guidelines and, from grade 3 of elementary school until the first year of senior high, the planning of learning content and corresponding assessments revolves around the areas of *musical activities, musical understanding,* and *practical applications* (Ministry of Education, Science and Technology [MEST], 2007).

Assessment is considered an important aspect of the 2009 curriculum guidelines (KICE, 2012). Guidelines place an emphasis on school accountability based on the results of the national-level achievement test given to students in the sixth grade of elementary school, third year of junior high school, and second year of senior high school. In addition, the promotion of creativity in curriculum design has encouraged many high schools at the junior and senior high level to reform their curricula through school-based curriculum development (SBCD) policies and develop creative activities for their students (KICE, 2012).

As stated in *The School Curriculum of the Republic of Korea* (MEST, 2009), schools are charged with the evaluation of the suitability, validity, and effectiveness of their curriculum organization and implementation and with the responsibility to identify any problems and make improvements in the following year. Generally, the assessment of curricular activities for primary school students is recorded in descriptive form so that a student's status and progress can be easily identified. Assessment results, provided in descriptive form, accompany a student's report card received at the end of each semester. Assessment of secondary school students includes a review of school records, which is used later on for admission to higher levels of education (KICE, 2012).

In the assessment of musical learning, various methods of assessment—which should all reflect a high level of reliability and validity—are used in accordance with the nature of the music being taught and the overall learning content of the curriculum. Evaluations are based on the regulations and standards laid out in the national music curriculum, with range of content and level of difficulty selected in accordance to the characteristics of the school and/or student in question. Students are to be notified in advance of the content, difficulty level, and assessment methods used (MEST, 2007). Following is the role of assessment within music curriculums:

1. A high level of validity and reliability of the assessment is ensured by its comprehensive inclusion of each curriculum area.
2. The students' mastery of learned materials should be emphasized during assessment. In addition, changes in behavior and attitude among students during the teaching and learning process are to be considered in the assessment.
3. Various evaluation methods, including performance assessment, paper and pencil tests with sounds, observations, self-assessments, peer assessments, portfolios, and online evaluations should be used.
4. A balanced administration of scheduled and nonscheduled evaluation is advised.
5. The content, projects, and media for performance assessment should be presented to students in a way that acknowledges the unique characteristics of each school and its students. Students should be able to choose assessment materials whenever possible (MEST, 2007).

For musical activities, a balanced focus on basic skills, methods of expression, and attitude is recommended in the evaluation of singing, playing, and creating of music, while the comprehensive understanding of music should be the focus during the assessment of any listening activities. In the case of musical understanding, a student's understanding of musical terms and concepts should be assessed through the use of various sounds and pieces of music. For practical applications, the frequency of participation in music-related occasions inside and outside of school, a positive attitude toward music, and a willingness to use music are all areas to be noted. Assessment results may be used for the improvement of teaching and learning strategies. Results may also be used for the development of special instructional strategies for students having difficulties in meeting curriculum standards (MEST, 2007).

Summary

Music curriculum assessment in South Korea is carried out with the understanding that assessment addresses national music curriculum content, while also taking into consideration local learning environments and factors. Design and selection of assessment methods echo recent curriculum reforms at the national level emphasizing school-based curricula. Prior to the commencement of any assessment, students are first informed of the content, difficulty level, and assessment method. Assessments use a variety of methods including performance assessment, paper and pencil tests with sounds, observation, self-assessment, peer assessment, portfolio assessment, and online evaluations, among others. As for the three main curriculum facets—musical activities, musical understanding, and practical application—assessment reflects corresponding content. Finally, the assessment results are to be used by teachers to improve their instruction and also to develop special strategies targeting students who are struggling to meet curriculum standards.

Taiwan

In 1946, Taiwan implemented a national education policy, making education compulsory for elementary school children from ages 6 to 12. Later, in 1968, compulsory education was extended through grade 9 (ages 6 to 15). Class curricula at these elementary and junior high school levels were planned in accordance to the curriculum standards promulgated by the Ministry of Education (MOE), with these standards revised many times over the years. The 2001 *Grade 1–9 Curriculum Guidelines* was one of the most important of these revisions, organizing subjects into seven major learning areas. Instruction in the arts and humanities, being part of the life curriculum at grades 1 and 2, includes music instruction and instruction in the visual and performing arts, and is required for grades 3 through 9. The subjects of music, fine arts, and arts and life were offered at the senior high level, with every subject a minimum of 2 credits for a total of 10 credits required in the arts area. In 2014, Taiwan passed the *12-Year Basic Education Plan* based on the framework of three educational levels and five learning stages, covering three 2-year learning stages in the elementary school level, one 3-year learning stage in the junior high school level, and one 3-year learning stage in the senior high school level. The plan emphasized the continuity and integration of elementary and junior high school curricula as well as core competency-oriented curricula and instruction. The various curriculum guidelines of the *12-Year Basic Education Plan* are slated to be implemented starting in 2019 (MOE, 2014). Guidelines for arts education use the three learning domains of *expression*, *appreciation*, and *practice* in the development of curriculum frameworks and in the establishment of key content (including learning performance and content), which are then used in the curriculum design, teaching material development, textbook compilation, and teaching and learning assessment (National Academy for Educational Research [NAER], 2015).

According to the *Grade 1–9 Curriculum Guidelines for Elementary and Junior High School*, a student's academic assessment shall be carried out in accordance with the relevant regulations of the Elementary and Junior High School Student Achievement Assessment Criteria Act (MOE, 2008). Assessment for elementary and junior high school students is based on ability indicators, level of student effort, level of progress, and also take into account the cognitive, affective, psychomotor, and performance domains with an emphasis on the analysis of learning progress and results that are recorded through the use of rankings, grading, or descriptive methods (MOE, 2015).

Assessment in the arts and humanities must align with the relevant competence indicators—the basic knowledge and skills to achieve by a certain stage—and teaching materials, and include the adoption of multiple assessment methods in both formative and summative measures. Teachers can choose between performance assessment, dynamic assessment, authentic assessment, or portfolio assessment, among other assessments to demonstrate the various facets of a student's performance. The scope of the assessment covers the areas of exploration and expression, aesthetics and under-standing, and practice and application. Furthermore, to better understand a student's cognitive abilities, psychomotor skills, affective growth, and social responsibility (in addition to any other art related behaviors), performance in various art learning activities is recorded. Qualitative and quantitative assessment data are collected to help students achieve the basic skills. In addition, the proper use of other assessment methods, such as class discussion, questionnaires, anecdotal records, testing, self-reports, rating scales, checklists, baseline assessments, and discussion are also included to help ensure curricular goals are achieved (MOE, 2008).

Regulations within the nation's *High School Curriculum Guidelines* declare that teachers at the high school level must consider using formative, summative, and diag-nostic assessments. Furthermore, assessments must address the cognitive, affective, and psychomotor domains as well as the core competencies and connotations of each field and academic discipline. Teachers are also suggested to reference the learning objectives, teaching materials, and student diversity to select and administer appropriate assessments to strengthen high levels of cognitive thinking and cultivate demonstrative, investigative, critical, and creative thinking skills. In music curricula, teachers are recommended to employ appropriate and multiple assessment methods that align with learning goals and music content, while also taking into account the individual differences between stu-dents and focusing on the inspiration of thinking and creative skills in students. Schools may furthermore undertake teaching effectiveness assessments to serve as a reference for teachers in their improvement of teaching materials and methods that are to be based on and implemented with regard to individualized student instruction and guidance (MOE, 2009).

In order to provide the nation's teachers with a unified index as a reference, the MOE commissioned National Taiwan Normal University's Research Center for Psychological and Educational Testing to develop *Standard-Based Assessment of Student Achievement for Elementary and Junior High School Students* (SBASA). These standards are used to describe a student's achievements to represent the level of mastery he or she displays toward learning content. Currently, ahead of the implementation of the *12-Year Basic Education Plan*, the transition from the competence indicators used in the *Grade 1–9 Curriculum Guidelines* to these new standards is taking place (Research Center for Psychological and Educational Testing, NTNU, n.d. a, n.d. b).

Music assessments are based on the goals of the *Grade 1–9 Curriculum* as well as the competence indicators established for Stage 4 in the Arts and Humanities learning area. There are six subthemes within the content standards: performance capability, creative capability, appreciation capability, basic knowledge, life application, and cooperative participation, for the purpose of assessing students' ability in expressing themselves through singing, playing musical instruments, and conducting, in identifying and describing musical works, and in understanding the connection between music and life. In accordance with the content of the *Grade 1–9 Curriculum Guidelines*, performance within these six subthemes is graded from A to E (from Excellent to Poor). Also available are assessment formulas in the areas of singing, recorder playing, conducting, and creating to be used as reference for teachers (Research Center for Psychological and Educational Testing, NTNU, n.d. a, n.d. b).

Summary

Taiwan's assessment methods have undergone a transformation from norm-referenced to standards-referenced systems, while rankings have replaced grade point systems in the effort to enable students to better view and understand their learning achievements through assessments and also lower the pressure students are under to compete for a high score. Currently, for all subjects at the junior high school level, scoring criteria and models are available for teachers as reference, with teachers additionally encouraged to develop their own scoring criteria.

Discussion

Policy: Shared Features

With the structure and content of educational systems varying from country to country, it is often difficult to carry out direct comparisons between them. However, trends in globalization mean that countries are now looking to each other for ideas in the realm of educational policy and thus sharing commonalities across borders. In other words, although the countries discussed in this chapter have instituted different curriculum assessment policies, these policies share several common features.

Policies Emphasize the Value of Assessment; in Particular,
the Use of Multiple Assessments

For the countries discussed in this chapter, all have directives in place detailing the use of music assessment within corresponding curricula. The significance of assessment in the areas of teaching and learning, as well as the relationship between the two, has been gaining much attention. Assessment has both guiding (formative) and summative functions and is a systematized process—one part of effective teaching (Miller, Linn, & Gronlund, 2009). In the past, if music teachers had an insufficient understanding of assessment, they generally focused on summative assessment. However, as policy guidelines regarding the explanation and implementation of assessment content continue to mature, the result has been increased expertise in the use of assessment tools by teachers and gradual changes to the implementation of music education itself.

In recent decades, societies in Asia have undergone a gradual transition from homogeneity to pluralism in many areas. These changes in social mainstream values have also been reflected in gradual revisions to previously enshrined educational concepts—for instance, the region's competitive exam culture. Long used to determine a student's future, such exams placed a heavy emphasis on the display of scholastic aptitude. Although such paper and pencil exams can effectively assess a student's cognitive performance, are easily administered, and are generally fair, they are, however, unable to assess higher order thinking skills. The region, therefore, is seeing education heading toward a more holistic direction. Furthermore, as educational goals become more pluralistic, a system of multiple assessments has risen to acknowledge these goals.

Music, much like other subjects, holds educational goals in the cognitive, psychomotor, and affective domains. Additionally, however, its learning elements and activities are infused with artistic influences, progressive learning, and topics of diversity. For example, in addition to cognitive concepts, psychomotor learning in the field of music includes instrument playing, composition, and listening skills, while the affective domain includes, among other things, music appreciation, music criticism, and feelingful response (Brophy, 2000). It is no surprise, therefore, that the assessment of music learning tends to be more complex than the assessment of learning in other subjects and that multiple assessment formats are emphasized. The strength of multiple assessments is that they offer music teachers a way to observe a student's performance in a manner that aligns with the nature of music, thus helping achieve pluralistic educational goals.

Use of Ranking Systems to Present Assessment Results; Positive Interpretations of Assessment Data

In light of the stiff competition for acceptance into top schools throughout Asia, test scores are seen as essential and grading policies extremely strict. Although exams are still often the gatekeepers of scholastic advancement—for example, Singapore's *Primary School Leaving Examination* (Singapore MOE, 2015b) or Hong Kong's *HKDSE* for high school students (Hong Kong Examinations and Assessment Authority, 2015)—attitudes toward assessment are changing and test results are being looked at in a more forgiving light. Curricula in Hong Kong, Japan, South Korea, and Taiwan are now beginning to adopt a ranking system for grading purposes. Although such changes are difficult for some schools or parents to accept, traditional concepts of education are slowly changing as it becomes clear that these pluralistic assessment formats do a better job at meeting the expectations and needs of today's society.

In addition to ranking systems, standards-based assessments have become the new trend in educational assessment in the Asia-Pacific region. Hong Kong, for example, has moved gradually from norm-referenced to standards-based assessment by increasing school-based assessments in its secondary schools (Yip, 2008). Taiwan is currently testing the implementation of its *Junior High School Student Learning Achievement Assessment Standards*, a standards-based assessment aligned with curriculum guidelines, in an effort to address the inability of quantitative scoring to adequately present a student's learning achievements in totality. Instead, qualitative descriptions, corresponding to performance levels, are used to present the knowledge and skills a student currently possesses. Such steps not only allow assessment systems to play a more positive and diagnostic role, but, when compared with quantitative scoring or norm-referenced testing, they offer more educationally pertinent information and help expand the role of assessment in the educational arena.

Curricula Are Performance-Standard Orientated, Facilitating the Implementation of Assessment Protocols

At the time of this publication, music curricula in Asia-Pacific region are becoming oriented toward performance standards. One example is Mainland China, whose music curriculum holds student performance competency at its core and clearly addresses specific goals for students at different learning stages. Furthermore, in a trend common to the region, China's curriculum descriptions are usually framed using active tense and verb-based sentences. In Hong Kong something similar can be seen with the region's music syllabus using the phrase "Students should be able to..." when discussing learning targets and the four learning goals—*developing creativity and imagination, developing music skills and processes, cultivating critical responses in music, understanding music in context*—among different learning stages. Similar to both China and Hong Kong, music syllabi in Japan make use of active-tense, verb-based sentences when describing the learning of grade-appropriate content in the areas of singing, musical instrument playing, musical composition, and musical appreciation. Singapore's music syllabus, which in this case revolves around five main learning objectives, also makes use of sentences such as "Students should be able to..." when explaining learning objectives at different stages of learning content. South Korea's music syllabus includes a description of classes in the areas of musical activities, musical understandings, and practical applications for each grade level as part of its description of the characteristics of its music curriculum.

Finally, in Taiwan, the existing grades 1–9 curriculum uses a learning stage-based competence indicators to show which skills a student should have achieved. Whereas, at the high school level, desired core competencies, themselves a reflection of curriculum goals, are clearly listed. In both cases, descriptions make use of active tense and verb-based sentences. Finally, Taiwan's *12-Year Basic Education Plan* is written in terms of desired learning content and performance. Because the plan clearly states the learning content and essential skills to which a student should have access, this has helped to form assessment standards and strengthen the connection between instruction and assessment policies.

Challenges

The educational reforms currently taking place in Asia principally stem from concerns about the overcentralization of education, the region's overly monolithic educational values, and the excessive pressure educational content places on students, as well as from reflections on the necessary competencies and skills that a new generation of students should possess. Therefore, in the 21st century, countries in Asian-Pacific region have been busy instituting educational reform, revising curriculum guidelines/standards, and giving local governments, schools, or teachers further decision-making autonomy.

In China, Japan, and Hong Kong, music is now a required subject for grades 1 through 9 (ages 6–15). In Singapore, music is compulsory from Primary One to Secondary Two (for a total of 8 years). South Korea and Taiwan has music as a required course from the third year of elementary through senior high school (ages 8–18), while South Korea requires music from third year of elementary through first year of senior high (ages 8–15). When compared to the proportional time and weight music-based classes have in curricula in other parts of the world, the importance of music education in these countries in the Asia-Pacific region is clear, and these music curricula reflect the status of assessment policies and programs. However, following any research or exploration into policy inputs, the question of policy implementation is important to consider (Jones, 2008). Therefore, in the following section, some of the challenges that music assessment currently faces are discussed.

From Policy to Practice

Although music teachers generally support the idea of music assessment, with too many classes, large class sizes, and not enough time per class, there is often insufficient time for assessment, resulting in poor implementation. For example, Taiwan's junior high school music teachers generally have around 20 classes of 30 students each, with each class only meeting once per week. This means music teachers often have to carry out assessments for several hundred students at a time—an undue burden for most. As for the use of multiple assessments, even if the majority of music teachers make use of diverse teaching methods, this has not necessarily translated into the use of multiple assessment strategies. Correcting large amounts of homework, collecting qualitative data, or assessing each student's musical instrument performance in the limited time allotted often make the use multiple assessment protocols extremely difficult (Lin, 2001). In addition, as the fairness and objectivity of multiple assessment continues to be questioned, it is no surprise that it has been ineffective as an assessment strategy.

The average music teacher also lacks the knowledge and skills to carry out multiple assessments. Research in Taiwan shows that only one-quarter of Taiwan's junior high school music teachers offer students time to carry out self-assessment or peer assessment. Moreover, when using multiple assessment strategies, teachers generally focus on performance assessment over other forms (Chi, 2007). Music assessment in junior high school focuses on written exams and on tests for singing and playing the recorder. Paper and pencil tests are gradually being replaced by worksheets, however, worksheets are not necessarily included in a student's final grade. And although performance assessments for the areas of singing, musical instrument performance, and creative composition are used, they run the risk of being only a teacher's subjective judgment; thus, quantitative scoring is often used instead to give performance results. In fact, regardless of which type of assessment is being discussed, what is clear is that assessment goals often fail to harmonize with teaching and learning goals. Furthermore, with formative assessments often ignored, the interpretation of assessment results also lacks a corresponding incentivizing effect (Lai, 2002). Some teachers have argued that music assessment methods proposed in the curriculum guidelines are too extensive, complicated, and limited in use, while there exists a gap between knowing about the assessment methods and putting them into practice (Wu & Chuang, 2013). Research in the field has suggested using authentic assessment in the instruction of aural skills, performance assessment in the instruction of musical instruments, and portfolio assessment in the area of music appreciation (Lin, 2001). However, at the time this chapter was written, issues regarding the implementation of multiple assessments were still being discussed.

On Assessing Artistic Ideals of Music

When discussing the effect of policy on music education, an important question emerges: "Can there be conflict between what our legislatures are demanding of us and what we feel our true art is?" (Goldie & Chen, 2014, p. 435). In other words, should policy development invite the participation of more music teachers? Are such government policies in fact suitable for a field of learning such as art? Regardless of the field— whether scientific, functional, or aesthetic—traditionally assessment formulas have favored the knowledge domain over the affective or psychomotor domain, written tests over actual performance, summative over formative strategies, and results over process. The end result has been that assessment has failed to accurately capture the essence that the field of arts encompasses (Lin, 2001).

Regarding assessment protocols that successfully tally with the nature of art, Thompson (2003) had this to say:

> Feelingful responses to music are generally considered the ultimate goal for any musical experience. If such responses are a goal for teaching music, then they should be assessed.   (p. 22)

> I believe that most musicians would agree the human response to music is what music is really about. Some call this musicianship. I prefer to call it musical sensitivity. I must admit that these very deep and personal responses are very difficult to talk about.... If we cannot find ways to assess this, our most important goal, we are in deep trouble in today's education environment.   (p. 40)

Suggested multiple assessment strategies include stressing the importance of worksheet implementation through the design of questions that make use of the collected data in the areas of musical appreciation, singing, or musical instrument playing, or stressing affective learning through the design of questions relating to the study of emotion, attitude, interest, and values (Lai, 2002). The nature of multiple assessment is that, as a system, it is flexible enough to adapt to needs of the subject in question. With regard to music, the goal has been to let students carry out educational assessment as they engage in their artistic activities. Despite the inherent difficulties, giving students of varying potential and skills the chance to express their individual musical achievements, has always been a goal worth working toward.

Trends and Issues

Assessment Redefined

Traditionally, the role of assessment was defined as an "assessment of learning." That is to say, assessment was a tool to judge a student's learning progress or results, or a summative function with an emphasis on learning outcomes. Its priorities, however, often hid the fact that there existed a disconnect between assessment protocols and actual learning. Yet over the past few years the definition and concept of assessment has gone through many changes. One transformation has been toward "assessment for learning," in which assessment has become a source of helpful feedback for students, assisting them on the path of learning. Also emphasized here is a well-defined relationship between assessment strategies and learning outcomes. The second transformation has been toward "assessment as learning"—a process through which students learn from the assessment itself. Here students are no longer passive, but active partners in the assessment process. Some examples of "assessment as learning" would be self-assessment, peer assessment, and portfolio assessment (Sung, Chang, Chiou, & Hou, 2005).

The relationship between education and assessment can also be examined from the viewpoint of establishing performance standards. After the *National Standards for Music Education* was published in 1994 by the US Music Educators National Conference (MENC, now the National Association for Music Education, or NAfME), state governments across the United States begin to look anew at the framework and strategies surrounding performance standards. What followed was a decade often described as the decade of "academic standards." The first decade of the 21st century, on the other hand, has been described as a decade of "student assessment" (Lindeman, 2003). This phenomenon has not gone unnoticed in Asia. During the spate of curriculum revisions at the turn of the 21st century, the move was toward performance standards, which countries then used to revise and update music curriculum guidelines/standards. However, in any operational curriculum, unless a teacher thinks about how students will demonstrate knowledge and skills from the moment s/he begins to write her/his objectives, assessment content and performance standards will often fail to find unity (Niermann, 2013). This is the reason behind the previously stated problem of assessment and teaching goals failing to work in harmony. As this review shows, current trends in assessment continue to place high value on the interplay between learning content, performance standards, and assessment goals, while emphasizing the mutual cohesion and transformation of the educational trinity of curriculum, instruction, and assessment.

Teacher Empowerment

An important aspect to consider when discussing policy issues is "the flexibility/ ambiguity inherent in national, regional, and local curriculum mandates and supporting legislation" (Freed-Garrod, Kojima, & Garrod, 2008, p. 27). Teachers are key to the implementation of policy, possessing pedagogical decision-making power, and some choice about which aspects of the curriculum they will concentrate on (Freed-Garrod et al., 2008). Music teachers typically have more autonomy in the selection of methods and materials than do teachers of other subjects. However, they are still subject to policies that are either made overtly in the curricular documents, or covertly embedded in the culture of schools and music education (Jones, 2008). These policies often have a great impact on teachers; conversely, the role of teachers in accepting, neutralizing, or even reversing the impact of such policies can play a large part in their implementation (Jones, 2008). Due to teachers' different personal backgrounds and professional training, there will be variances in the scope and extent of implementation; therefore, policies should empower music teachers' professionalism and autonomy and should allow teachers who work within a mandated curriculum more input when it comes to policy development and implementation.

Music teachers should have more confidence in the use of assessment. In Asia, as music is not a subject tested on entrance exams, the results from the implementation of music assessment are often far from ideal. Music teachers, therefore, need to find ways to make music assessment more meaningful for students. Informing students of assessment content will help not only clarify the focus of musical learning but also improve motivation in students (Brophy, 2000). Offering feedback during assessment, teachers can help students better understand their current skill level or compare learning achievements at different stages, thus encouraging further self-learning (Lai, 2002; Wu & Chuang, 2013).

Global Thinking Versus Local Features

Music curricula in Asian countries grow more international by the year. Emphasizing instrument playing, singing, creative composition, and listening responses, they exhibit both aesthetics and their practice and have successfully integrated technological and interdisciplinary elements. Overall, music curriculum content is very broad and encompassing; curriculum guidelines are loosely worded and depend, to a large extent, on an individual teacher's decisions and choices. "Education, thus assessment" is how one could describe the present era. Teachers need to decide what to prioritize in class and, while remaining true to their art, assess those things that are most important for students to learn about music (Thompson, 2003). What they will find is that the areas most worth teaching are precisely where the focus of teaching and learning assessment should lie.

It is also necessary to mention the large role schools play in the development of educational policies. Currently Hong Kong, South Korea, and Taiwan attach great importance to school-based curricula, encouraging the use of music or arts in the development of interdisciplinary learning or locally based curricula. Schools serve as the bridge linking administration, parents, and teachers together. They also form a powerful framework or system of assessment policies, with music teachers able to ensure assessment finds its place in school-based curricula. Despite the globalization of educational policy and the continual innovation of assessment methods, at its core, music comes from life and returns to it; therefore, assessment policies do not need to intentionally pursue any grand schemes but simply consider the circumstances and characteristics of the area, school, or class in which they find themselves and adapt to the needs therein.

CONCLUSION

In the face of globalization, educational policy in Asia is becoming well rounded and capable of adapting to the requirements of the era or locale. However, even if music is mandated in public schools as a subject, translating policy into practice is rarely a straightforward process (Burnard, 2008). Syllabi may offer guiding principles for music assessment, yet it is only through their implementation that the effectiveness of such principles can be understood.

Assessment is currently a popular topic in education, and the relevant literature is abundant, but research papers discussing the music assessment policies of multiple countries are few in number. Although this chapter's review of assessment policies in the Asia-Pacific region only does so from a short-term perspective, the author hopes that highlighting the vital role that assessment plays in music education can stimulate further discussion and reflection among policymakers and music educators alike.

REFERENCES

Brophy, T. S. (2000). *Assessing the developing child musician*. Chicago, IL: GIA.

Burnard, P. (2008). Preface. In C. C. Leung, L. C. R. Yip, & T. Imada (Eds.), *Music education policy and implementation: International perspectives* (p. xi). Aomori, Japan: Hirosaki University Press.

Chi, Y. C. (2007). *An investigation of the practice status of junior high school music assessment* (Unpublished master's thesis). National Taiwan Normal University. Taipei.

Education Bureau. (2003). *Music curriculum guide (P1—S3)*. Retrieved from http://www.edb.gov.hk/attachment/en/curriculum-development/kla/arts-edu/references/music%20complete%20guide_eng.pdf

Education Bureau. (2015). *Music curriculum and assessment guide (Secondary 4–6)*. Retrieved from http://www.edb.gov.hk/attachment/en/curriculum-development/kla/arts-edu/pdp-nss-mus/Music%20CnA%20Guide_e_25-11-2015.pdf

Education Commission. (2015). *Education reform*. Retrieved from https://english.moe.gov.tw/public/Attachment/69810435871.pdf

Freed-Garrod, J., Kojima, R., & Garrod, S. (2008). Policy and practice in music education: Elementary education through an integrated arts approach in two cultural contexts, Canada and Japan. In C. C. Leung, L. C. R. Yip, & T. Imada (Eds.), *Music education policy and implementation: International perspectives* (pp. 25–40). Aomori, Japan: Hirosaki University Press.

Gao, J. (1992). A comparative study of cross-straight compulsory education curriculum management systems. In Chinese Taipei Comparative Education Society (Ed.), *A comparison of cross-straight educational development* (pp. 189–210). Taipei: Lucky Bookstore.

Goldie, S., & Chen, H.-F. (2014). (Transcription). Key issues for assessment in music education: Practice, measurement, and policy. English focus group summary. *Selected papers from the Fourth International Symposium on Assessment in Music Education* (pp. 427–435). Chicago, IL: GIA.

Hong Kong Examinations and Assessment Authority (HKEAA). (2015). *Exam registration.* Retrieved from http://www.hkeaa.edu.hk/tc/candidates/exam_registration/

Jones, P. M. (2008). Policy studies as a component of music teacher education: Building the profession's capacity for strategic action. In C. C. Leung, L. C. R. Yip, & T. Imada (Eds.), *Music education policy and implementation: International perspectives* (pp. 72–82). Aomori, Japan: Hirosaki University Press.

Korea Institute of Curriculum and Evaluation (KICE). (2012). *Education in Korea research report.* Retrieved from http://www.kice.re.kr/sub/info.do?m=0106&s=english

Lai, M. L. (2002). *A study of implementing multiple assessments in music teaching: Assessment strategies for Arts and Humanities curriculum* (NSC 91-2411-H-003-036). Unpublished manuscript.

Lin, S.-Y. (2001). The essence and implementation of the multiple assessment approaches in music teaching: On the art of music. *Journal of Musical Arts, 1*, 61–88.

Lindeman, C. A. (2003). Preface. In. C. A. Lindeman (Ed.), *Benchmark in action: A guide to standards-based assessment in music* (p. vii). Lanham, MD: Rowman & Littlefield Education.

Miller, M. D., Linn, R. L., & Gronlund, N. E. (2009). *Measurement and assessment in teaching* (10th ed.). Upper Saddle River, NJ: Pearson.

Ministry of Education (MOE). (2008). *Grade 1–9 curriculum guidelines.* Taipei, Taiwan: Author.

Ministry of Education (MOE). (2009). *General high school curriculum guidelines.* Taipei, Taiwan: Author.

Ministry of Education (MOE). (2014). *General curriculum guidelines for 12-year basic education.* Retrieved from http://www.naer.edu.tw/ezfiles/0/1000/attach/87/pta_5320_2729842_56626.pdf

Ministry of Education (MOE). (2015). *Elementary and junior high school student achievement assessment criteria act.* Retrieved from http://edu.law.moe.gov.tw/LawContent.aspx?id=FL008949

Ministry of Education, Culture, Sports, Science and Technology (MEXT). (2008). *Elementary school teaching hours per subject area.* Retrieved from http://www.mext.go.jp/a_menu/shotou/new-cs/youryou/syo/index.htm

Ministry of Education, Culture, Sports, Science and Technology (MEXT). (2010). *Junior high school teaching hours per subject area.* Retrieved from http://www.mext.go.jp/a_menu/shotou/new-cs/youryou/chu/index.htm

Ministry of Education, Culture, Sports, Science and Technology (MEXT). (2015a). *One hundred years of a general education system.* Retrieved from http://www.mext.go.jp/b_menu/hakusho/html/others/detail/1317552.htm

Ministry of Education, Culture, Sports, Science and Technology (MEXT). (2015b). *Current curriculum guidelines, life skills.* Retrieved from http://www.mext.go.jp/a_menu/shotou/new-cs/idea/1304372.htm

Ministry of Education, Culture, Sports, Science and Technology (MEXT). (2015c). *Standardized credit hours for common core courses at colleges and universities.* Retrieved from http://www.mext.go.jp/component/a_menu/education/micro_detail/__icsFiles/afieldfile/2011/03/30/1304427_004.pdf

Ministry of Education, Culture, Sports, Science and Technology (MEXT). (2015d). *Current curriculum guidelines.* Retrieved from http://www.mext.go.jp/a_menu/shotou/new-cs/youryou/1356248.htm

Ministry of Education of the People's Republic of China (PRC MOE). (2003a). *General high school music curriculum standards (experimental)*. Retrieved from http://www.ibe.unesco.org/curricula/china/cc_us_mu_2008_chi.pdf

Ministry of Education of the People's Republic of China (PRC MOE). (2003b).*General high school curriculum program (experimental)*. Retrieved from http://www.moe.gov.cn/srcsite/A26/s8001/200303/t20030331_167349.html

Ministry of Education of the People's Republic of China (PRC MOE). (2011). *Compulsory education music curriculum standards*. China: Beijing Normal University.

Ministry of Education of the People's Republic of China (PRC MOE). (2015). *Ministry of Education notification on the printing and distribution of the regulations for the testing and evaluation of art quality in elementary/middle school and sister regulations*. Retrieved from http://www.moe.edu.cn/srcsite/A17/moe_794/moe_795/201506/t20150618_190674.html

Ministry of Education, Science and Technology (MEST). (2007). *The school curriculum of the Republic of Korea: Music curriculum*. Retrieved from http://ncic.kice.re.kr/english.kri.org.inventoryList.do;jsessionid=B0D%2014812E4BC8242863AF54627BF2401#

Ministry of Education, Science and Technology (MEST). (2009).*The school curriculum of the Republic of Korea*. Retrieved from http://ncic.kice.re.kr/english.kri.org.inventoryList.do;jsessionid=B0D%2014812E4BC8242863AF54627BF2401#

Ministry of Education, Singapore (Singapore MOE). (2014). *2015 General music programme syllabus (primary/secondary)*. Retrieved from https://www.moe.gov.sg/docs/default-source/document/education/syllabuses/arts-education/files/2015_Music_Teaching_and_Learning_Syllabus_(Primary_and_Lower_Secondary).pdf

Ministry of Education, Singapore (Singapore MOE). (2015a). *Compulsory education*. Retrieved from https://www.moe.gov.sg/education/education-system/compulsory-education

Ministry of Education, Singapore (Singapore MOE). (2015b). *MOE corporate brochure*. Retrieved from https://www.moe.gov.sg/docs/default-source/document/about/files/moe-corporate-brochure.pdf

Ministry of Education, Singapore (Singapore MOE). (2015c). *Secondary school*. Retrieved from http://www.moe.gov.sg/education/secondary/

Ministry of Education, Singapore (Singapore MOE). (2015d). *Booklet on primary school education*. Retrieved from https://www.moe.gov.sg/education/primary/primary-school-education-booklet

National Academy for Educational Research (NAER). (2015). *Curriculum guidelines for arts area in 12-year basic education*. Retrieved from http://12basic-forum.naer.edu.tw

National Institute for Educational Policy Research. (2015a). *Current curriculum guidelines database*. Retrieved from http://www.nier.go.jp/guideline/index.htm

National Institute for Educational Policy Research. (2015b). *Reference materials for the improvement of music curriculum evaluation criteria and evaluation methods*. Retrieved from http://www.nier.go.jp/kaihatsu/shidousiryou.html

Niermann, G. E. (2013). Making the case for high-stakes assessment in music. In T. S. Brophy & A. Lehmann-Wermser (Eds.), *Music assessment across cultures and continents: Proceedings of the 3rd international symposium on assessment in music education* (pp. 97–107). Chicago, IL: GIA.

Research Center for Psychological and Educational Testing, NTNU. (n.d. a). *Junior high school student achievement assessment standards (trial)-Arts and Humanities learning area (music)*. Retrieved from http://www.sbasa.ntnu.edu.tw/SBASA/documents/ArtMusic.pdf

Research Center for Psychological and Educational Testing, NTNU. (n.d. b).*Junior high school student achievement assessment standards (trial)*. Retrieved from http://www.sbasa.ntnu.edu.tw/SBASA/Assessment/sbasa.pdf

Sung, Y.-T., Chang, K.-E., Chiou, S.-K., & Hou, H.-T. (2005). The design and application of a web-based self- and peer-assessment system. *Computers and Education, 45*, 187–202. doi: 10.1016/j.compedu.2004.07.002

Thompson, K. (2003). Assessing music learning. In H. F. Chen (Ed.), *2003 International Conference in Music Education* (pp. 23–45). Taipei: National Taiwan Normal University.

Wu, Y. L., & Chuang, M. J. (2013). A survey of elementary music teachers' perspectives on instructional assessment proposed by the Ministry of Education in Taiwan. In T. S. Brophy & A. Lehmann-Wermser (Eds.), *Music assessment across cultures and continents: Proceedings of the 3rd international symposium on assessment in music education* (pp. 187–199). Chicago, IL: GIA.

Yip, L. C. R. (2008). Establishing standards-based assessment in music performance. In C. C. Leung, L. C. R. Yip & T. Imada. (Eds.), *Music education policy and implementation: International perspectives* (pp. 141–156). Aomori, Japan: Hirosaki University Press.

Zhou, Q. (2008). Examining curriculum reform in basic education in China through global perspective. *Hong Kong Teachers' Centre Journal, 7*, 127–131.

....

CHAPTER 6

ASSESSING MUSIC TEACHING AND LEARNING IN SPANISH-SPEAKING COUNTRIES IN SOUTH AMERICA

....

ANA LUCÍA FREGA WITH RAMIRO LIMONGI

HISTORICAL FOUNDATIONS

....

Spanish Colonial Educational Influences

SPANISH-SPEAKING Latin American countries share some cultural identity traits, other than language, due to their educational history and approaches and their shared past as Spanish colonies. In this vast region, Portuguese-speaking Brazil also has a colonial origin, but, in addition to language, differentiation goes back at least to the early 15th century, when Spain and Portugal established mutual competition and rivalry as a result of disputes over newly discovered territories while exploring the Atlantic Ocean.

When the Spanish and Portuguese explorers finally reached America, the papacy followed medieval Christian practices and commanded faithful Christian rulers to evangelize the "infidel" people, even if it meant they would become enemies. During this time both crowns had a tumultuous relationship as their possessions expanded and they struggled to obtain commercial benefits, and other nations' interests got also involved in their confrontation. Whether through wars or diplomacy, agreements and disagreements over the centuries eventually culminated in the Independence period. As a consequence, not only did two distinct cultures evolve in South America, but also occasionally, traces of the old enmity between conquerors remain and may still estrange Brazil from the Spanish-speaking countries (Escudé & Cisneros, 2000).

When Europeans first arrived, religious and political ideas were decisive factors in defining perspectives to address both education and artistic activities. During the conquest and evangelization periods, the Catholic Church was a key agent for spreading the arts and early developing music education (Frega, de Couve, & Dal Pino, 2010a). As part of a transculturation process, religious orders appointed by the Spanish crown were in charge of setting an educational system that would erase radical differences between cultures by changing the indigenous worldview (de Couve, Dal Pino, Fernández Calvo, Frega, & Souza, 1998). Within this context, European residents in Latin American territories received arts education similar to that imparted in Europe. When offered to aboriginal communities, this kind of training was understood as a powerful tool for instilling the conqueror's cultural patterns (Frega, de Couve, & Dal Pino, 2010b).

During the colonial years, as settlements grew into towns and cities, arts were also an essential part of civic education (Frega et al., 2010b), a sign of social status and power (de Couve & Dal Pino, 1999; de Couve, Dal Pino, & Frega, 2004), and an effective tool for cultural control (de Couve & Dal Pino, 1999). The first music educators were European priests who soon had layperson, and even native, assistants (de Couve et al., 2004). Indigenous musical practices, related to pre-Columbian idolatry, were to be eradicated and replaced by European music styles all through Latin America. However, showing typical Christian syncretic pragmatism, priests would, in many cases, adapt native melodies to religious texts (Moreno Andrade, 1930, cited in de Couve et al., 2004, p. 86), compose religious songs in the minor pentatonic scales traditionally used by native people, or even allow indigenous children to perform their dances, once dedicated to their gods, to honor Christ and the saints (Saldivar, 1934, cited in de Couve et al., 2004, p. 87). Similarly, after Europeans brought their slaves to America, African elements also influenced Christian music in the New Continent, despite ecclesiastical controversy. Thus, the American experience led to fusion styles, such as the Colonial, or the *Tropical Baroque* (de Couve et al., 1998).

During the 16th century, as the protector and custodian of the Christian faith in these territories, the Spanish crown supported musical development in American churches. The Spanish crown also supported the private sphere, disregarding the ecclesiastical authority's need for control. As stated by de Couve et al. (2004), "From the beginning of the conquest, colonizers taught vocal and instrumental performance both to Indians and to the first settlers without any connection with the incipient educational institutions" (p. 90).

As schools developed—first as religious schools and later run by civil administration— singing was considered a valuable tool for catechizing, beginning at the elementary level. Instrumental instruction for children, if it existed, is not documented. Only servants were explicitly declared as trainees, and quality music players came mostly from the Missions. The ability to perform European music was considered a sign of civilization (Frega et al., 2010b). Locally educated priests and nuns were required to acquire a considerably high level of musical knowledge and, following the Italian model, girl asylums taught music, training as teachers those considered most talented (de Couve et al., 2004).

Gradually, local *Cabildos* (town councils) had a more prominent role in supervising music teaching within general school education. Additionally, an increasing presence of private teachers, many of whom established music schools or academies at their own home with state approval, signaled the relevance attained by music education. Later on, these private enterprises frequently served as the basis for the creation of conservatories (de Couve et al., 2004). By the end of the 18th century, urban societies, especially wealthy upper classes, recognized music education as an important aspect of their children's upbringing, and mostly private teachers, frequently European artists, provided instrumental instruction with special emphasis on dance repertoire. Talented individuals from lower strata were also considered for this kind of training, thus gaining access to convenient job opportunities and improving their social status (de Couve & Dal Pino, 1999, de Couve et al., 2004).

Common Principles, Rules, Facts, Examples, and Conflicts in South America During the Independence Days of the Early 19th Century

Likewise, music was important for the patriots who led the revolutionary process toward Independence. The arts, as a whole, served for the promotion of values that supported the emerging national spirit, and education was conceived as instrumental for giving deprived people the opportunity for social inclusion (Frega et al., 2010b). Although it was not yet considered a school subject, music was taught in several institutions, and students usually sang a repertoire of recently composed patriotic songs at public celebrations (Frega et al., 2010a).

In Buenos Aires, private enterprises flourished, offering instrumental and vocal teaching and organizing various artistic events, often supported by public funding from local authorities (Frega, 1995; Frega et al., 2010a). Looking to European and North American models to consolidate and modernize the country, "intellectual figures encouraged music education and pointed out its values" (Frega et al., 2010a, p. 140), and most of them explicitly stated that offering education, in general, was a government duty (de Couve et al., 1998).

During the second half of the 19th century, states redirected public funds, and created and supported public conservatories, thus promoting training for national artists. Italian and French conservatories, particularly those in Paris, were observed as prototypes for organizing these kind of proposals, which still prevailed at the end of the millennium, for example, in Argentina, Bolivia, and Ecuador. As long as the hazardous political, institutional, and economic life of Latin American countries allowed it, conservatories developed and state-funded scholarship programs granted local musicians the possibility of further pursuing their education in Europe (de Couve & Dal Pino, 1999).

As elementary education became compulsory, music was frequently included, and at the start of the 20th century, music theory was added to the curriculum. There were some innovative proposals, such as the Argentinian Josefina Farnesi's, that anticipated later advances, but, in general, because of uneven results, authorities became concerned with the training of specialized music teachers (Frega et al., 2010a).

During the early 1930s, innovative music education methods that were developed in Europe influenced the explorations of leading music education professionals, and texts were translated into Spanish. Music curricula were revised with the aim to introduce local musical aesthetics (Frega, 1998). During the previous decade, professional associations, such as the Chilean Bach Society, encouraged curricular renewal, firmly opposing old-fashioned approaches that had come to define conservatory practices (de Couve et al., 1998). Concurrently, renowned musicologists and folklorists promoted the inclusion of local traditional expressions as the basis of school artistic education (Aretz, 1995).

During the last three decades of the 20th century, several educational modifications took place. Curricular guidelines were updated, administrative and pedagogical decentralization promoted (or even demanded) jurisdictional accords, and revised subjects were included as compulsory. As an outcome of these actions, other arts entered the school curriculum and, sometimes, music was either excluded, offered as an optional subject or with a reduced course load. Nonetheless, education laws generally prescribe some kind of arts education. As is the case with many other teaching programs, arts teacher training tends to be exclusively part of higher education (Frega et al., 2010a).

Paraphrasing Hobsbawm (1962/1996), after the establishment of the independent nations along the 19th century, Latin American education systems have had a long 20th century of organization. Beginning around the 1880s, with the regulation of compulsory schooling, a first stage comprised the diffusion of methods whose main aim was *plainly* teaching music, with no reflection on social or holistic effects of music education. After World War II, planning and assessment theories became widespread, at least within decision-making spheres, and led to recent reforms that, after what Gainza (2003) calls "the child's century," according to its main focus, may initiate "the teacher's century," mostly involved with setting high standards for music educators' qualifications.

MUSIC EDUCATION IN SOUTH AMERICA

As a result of its history described briefly here, the concept of music education has been multifarious and changeable through the years. As part of Church practices, music has been a powerful tool for spreading religion (de Couve & Dal Pino, 1999), much in the sense it had had in Europe during the early Middle Ages. Concurrently, it was an adequate vehicle for inculcating cultural values, introducing moral precepts, easing social control (de Couve & Dal Pino, 1999; de Couve et al., 2004), achieving group cohesion (Frega et al., 2010b), and finding a meeting point for two completely different worldviews (de Couve et al., 1998; de Couve et al., 2004; Frega, 2010b). In the same spirit, music education fostered emerging nationalistic principles, building a new identity and strengthening communal feelings. Even in consonance with the French Revolution motto and the ideas of the Enlightenment that supported it, education was favored as the proper means for liberating and empowering the people of recently independent countries.

Later reflecting Romantic European trends, leaders gradually promoted the inclusion of music in state-funded school education. On the one hand, it was considered an essential part of an integral education. On the other, it was instrumental for integrating massive amounts of immigrants that arrived between the end of the 19th and until the mid-20th century. The national language was taught through vocal music, and, as a component of a nascent culture, it was a key factor for defining the national idiosyncrasy (Frega et al., 2010b).

The Concept and Meaning of Music Education in General Compulsory Education

When legally regulated, music was, at first, mostly assigned as an activity for the spare time (e.g., Argentinian *Ley 1.420 de Educación Común*, 1884, article 14). Reasons that founded its inclusion went from its motivational value (Granado, 1912, cited in García, 2009) to its uniqueness as a means of human communication in the context of a comprehensive education (Frega, 1998), going through discipline issues (Sarmiento, 1848, cited in Frega et al., 2010a), emotional development (Frega & Cash, 1980), socializing and communal bonding (Frega et al., 2010b), cultural experience, multiculturalism awareness, and national identity (Aretz, 1995; Consejo Nacional de Educación, 1913, cited in Frega et al., 2010a; Gainza, 2003), critical thinking (Frega, 1997a), creativity stimulation, personal identity, intellectual (Ministerio de Cultura y Educación de la Nación, & Consejo Federal de Cultura y Educación, 1995), or even physical development (Granado, 1912, cited in García, 2009; Torres, 1887, cited in Frega et al., 2010a).

Given the esteem granted to the subject, it soon became mandatory in Argentina and Chile. In other countries, although music is an important part of their culture, its acceptance within school teaching has not been so unproblematic. For instance, in Venezuela, there was a longer period of national organization during which education was neglected. Singing lessons were offered at elementary schools just in 1912, and it was not until 1936 that some theoretical content and music appreciation exercises were added. Music making was encouraged as an extra class activity. While some improvements were made in the 1960s and 1970s, by then, music education had begun flourishing in a different context, described later in this chapter. During the 1980s and early 1990s, a more thorough transformation planned by experienced specialists proposed a considerable update of practices. However, it was not successfully implemented and classroom realities remained mostly unchanged (García, 2009). Although currently music is a mandatory subject within general education, it still lacks the proper recognition from society that tends to regard it "as simply providing a superficial kind of entertainment" (Sánchez, 2015, p. 185).

Social circumstances have also determined the status of music education. In Colombia, it had been a substantial part of curricular proposals made in the 1960s aiming at the equalization of schooling conditions all across the country. These actions were especially reinforced by the German Pedagogical Mission (1965–1978), which was the result of an intergovernmental agreement in order to improve teacher education (Rojas de Ferro, 1982). However, after 15 years (1993), authorities had to question the role of school in a society that had become alarmingly violent, and considered that attention had to be paid to concrete realities and necessities of each community. As a consequence, even when some general requirements should still be fulfilled, since 2000 it has been up to each individual institution whether or not to include music within the area of arts education (M. E. Rodríguez Melo, personal communication, March 15, 2016).

In Peru, music has never been an independent mandatory subject at the general education level. Nonetheless, current curricular guidelines (Ministerio de Educación, República del Perú, 2005) incorporate it in a broadly defined "communication/education through art" area, with remarkable detail in content lists and articulation.

Professional Training: Institutions and Degrees

Beside the offer of early private teachers, already in 1784, Father Sojo created a Music Academy in Venezuela that provided training for about 30 composers and 200 performers and teachers (Calcaño, 1962, cited in de Couve & Dal Pino, 1999). Although some other private enterprises appeared during the early decades of the 19th century, music educators usually studied abroad or took private lessons. In Argentina, only after the national organization period had advanced, new private conservatories, opened by Esnaola (in 1874), Gutiérrez (in 1880), or Williams (in 1893), "obtained state subsidies and [their] qualifications received official recognition" (Frega et al., 2010a, p. 147).

Music entered university curricula already by the 17th century. Institutions in Venezuela and the Dominican Republic offered a doctor in arts degree (de Couve & Dal Pino, 1999). However, music schools that depended on national state universities adopted the dominant conservatory paradigm (Frega, 1995a). The transformation toward more typical university standards has been recent.

In Buenos Aires, Argentina, municipal music schools were unified as the Conservatorio Municipal de Música Manuel de Falla in 1927, and the Conservatorio Nacional de Música was created in 1924 by the National Ministry of Public Instruction. "Both institutions offered degrees in several instruments and singing and were the main training ground for school music educators in [the] city" (Frega et al., 2010a, p. 147). Adopting the same curriculum or adapting it, many conservatories and music schools were founded during the 20th century.

Today, specialists point out the need for a serious revision of higher education offerings. The old conservatory model should be revitalized, long-established fields of study renovated, and new programs should attend to contemporary realities and interests (Gainza, 2003).

Artistic Training

In Argentina, early antecedents in institutional music training with a specifically artistic approach go back as far as 1810, when documents indicate the existence of de la Prada's Academy of Instrumental Music (Frega, 1995). The advocacy of national arts motivated the creation of state-supported conservatories all over the continent (de Couve & Dal Pino, 1999): Venezuelan Instituto de Bellas Artes in 1877 (Conservatorio de Música y Declamación since 1913), Academia Nacional de Música in 1879 in Colombia, in 1908 in Peru (in 1946 this became the Conservatorio Nacional de Música); the Conservatorio Nacional de Música in Colombia in 1910, and in Argentina in 1924; the music program of Universidad de Chile in 1945; and the Venezuelan Conservatorio de Música José Ángel Lamas in 1957.

Currently, institutions in these countries offer the following degrees: *Licenciatura en Artes Musicales, con orientación* (Bachelor of Music—specialty), and *Tecnicatura Superior en Música* (with no exact English equivalent) in Argentina; *Licenciatura en Interpretación, Composición o Musicología* in Chile (Bachelor in Performance, Composition, or Musicology); *Bachiller en Música* (Bachelor in Music) and *Licenciatura en Interpretación Musical* con especialidad (Bachelor in Music Performance—specialty) in Peru; *Licenciatura en Música* con mención (Bachelor of Music—specialty) or *Técnico Superior Universitario en Música* (with no exact English equivalent) in Venezuela; and *Músico con énfasis en...* (Musician—specialty) in Colombia.

Specialists in School Music Education

Initially, classroom teachers, trained within the Spanish and French normal school tradition, were expected to teach music at elementary schools. However, "school inspectors, having detected unequal musical achievements in classrooms, gradually promoted the appointment of specialist music educators" (Frega et al., 2010a, p. 147). Through this measure, the authorities were looking for a higher degree of standardization.

Although institutions had been training musicians since the beginning of the 20th century, graduates were composers or performers with no pedagogical training or specialization in music education who would eventually teach in schools (Frega, 1995). By 1910, schools began to employ specialists, or technical assistants to the general educator (Frega, 1998), and by 1912, according to Moreno Andrade (1930/1966, cited in de Couve & Dal Pino, 1999), there was a specialist in every major school in Ecuador. Formal music education programs, though, were developed considerably later, as found in the Colombian Conservatorio Nacional (around the 1960s), Venezuela's Instituto Pedagógico de Caracas (1977) or the Chilean Universidad Metropolitana de Ciencias de la Educación (1981). Since then, many public and private institutions were created in different places over Colombia and Peru, some in Chile, and a few public ones in Venezuela offering both artistic and pedagogical programs. In 2008, the Culture Ministry in Colombia launched a program, Colombia Creativa, to professionalize de facto teaching artists, recognizing their background and experience.[1] At present, music teaching degrees offered are: *Profesor de Música*, *Educación Musical* or *Artes Musicales* (Music, music education, or musical arts teacher) in Chile; *Licenciatura en Pedagogía o Educación Musical* (Bachelor in Music Pedagogy or Music Education) in Colombia; *Bachillerato* or *Licenciatura en Educación Musical* (Bachelor in Music Education) in Peru; and *Licenciatura en Educación para las Artes, mención Música* (Bachelor in Arts Education, Music) in Venezuela.

As programs began to appear, new teaching methods were changing the scene of music education worldwide, and South American countries received them enthusiastically. Early on, books on Jaques-Dalcroze, and later on Orff and Kodály methods, were translated, adapted, and published in Argentina (Frega, 1998; Gainza, 2003). Those by Willems and Martenot came soon after (Frega, 1998). Beginning in the 1950s, new approaches to the philosophy of music and interaction with music educators from other parts of the world had raised awareness of global trends (Frega, 1995). Through the practice of pioneering teachers, and also professional associations in Peru and Venezuela, these methods have had different degrees of diffusion and acceptance in different countries of the region. Orff Schulwerk seems to be the most popular, being applied in Colombia, Chile, and Peru. Kodály's and Suzuki's methods were also promoted in these three countries. The adoption of Jaques-Dalcroze methods in Colombia and Peru were limited, while Willems's was early and widely known in Colombia and moderately implemented in Chile. Martenot's method was employed in Colombia, and Murray Schafer's was implemented in Chile. Most of these methods were known and even included in the official curricula of Venezuelan specialized schools, but they did not reach the general education classroom.

Simultaneously, professional societies promoted further teaching training by organizing meetings, symposia, and conferences, and offering courses to members in Chile, since the 1950s, although intermittently (C. Sánchez Cunill, personal communication, March 5, 2016); or to members and the community, as done, for example by the Asociación Suzuki and FLADEM in Peru (I. Petrozzi Helasvuo, personal communication, March 4, 2016); and the Sociedad Venezolana de Educación Musical Juan Bautista Plaza until 2000, when it ceased activities (F. Sánchez, personal communication, March 4, 2016). Supported also by international organizations such as the Organization of American States (OAS), these exchanges among music educators inspired a search for a regional identity (Valencia, 1995). At that time, Argentina assumed a pedagogical leadership role in the region. Chile set trends, too, especially through the action of the INTEM (Inter-American Institute for Music Education), which, implementing a scholarship program, gathered professionals from all over the continent for further education (Gainza, 2003). Today, and since 1997, regional conferences organized by the International Society for Music Education (ISME) are an essential contribution for encouraging improvement in music education practices.

Over time, professional interests have been changing. Twenty years ago, Frega pointed out "that seminars or workshops related to 'tools' (strategies) are more popular among [Argentinian] music educators than those related to psychological rationales or philosophical thinking" (1995, p. 49). Since then, a more reflective attitude favored the undertaking of systematic research studies, as shown, for example, by university-funded programs and a constantly increasing graduate school offering (Gainza, 2003).

The status reached by music education within general education determined that teaching should be provided by specialists in Argentina, Chile (C. Sánchez Cunill, personal communication, March 5, 2016), and Venezuela (F. Sánchez, personal communication, March 4, 2016). In Colombia, Institutional Educational Projects define the need for graduated specialists (M. E. Rodríguez Melo, personal communication, March 15, 2016).

Details About Laws and Regulations with Policy as Focus

After Independence, governments advanced in the organization of educational systems. The Argentinian *Ley de Educación Común N° 1.420* instituted compulsory schooling for primary level in 1884, including singing as a mandatory form of music instruction. Consequently, music courses were also included in teacher training curriculum (Frega, 1995). In Venezuela, a decree prescribing public, free, and compulsory education had already been issued in 1870. In 1884, a report of the Ministry for Public Education incorporated music in pedagogical training, but it did not appear in primary school until 1933, when official programs were implemented, later becoming mandatory in 1944 (García, 2009). In Chile, teacher education was first regulated in 1847, and, after profound changes in the system's organization, music was included for all levels in 1893 (Poblete Lagos, 2010).

As early as 1910, a music program for primary school appeared in Argentina mainly comprising singing and dancing. In 1937, Athos Palma, a leading figure in Argentinian musical life, elaborated an updated proposal in which new European methodological approaches were already tested (Frega, 1995). The Venezuelan education system developed along considerably prescriptive guidelines, heavily determined by official programs. However, according to García's (2009) review of legal documents, the emphasis was on professional training, institutional organization (decrees from 1913, 1915, 1936; Report of the Ministry for Public Education from 1937; regulations from 1941; *Ley Orgánica de Educación* from 1948; and subsequent regulations), and curriculum (resolutions from 1914, 1921). Primary education was consistently regulated around the 1950s, including music instruction (still limited to singing) from the beginning of the process.

Government organizations formulated curricular guidelines, usually in collaboration with experts. Since the 1960s, the Argentinian National Ministry of Education, together with the Federal Board of Education, issued general aims for music instruction, emphasizing sensitivity, national and local identity, contributions for general knowledge, promotion of artistic occupations, and social interactions. These aims have stimulated changes in music teaching strategies and, subsequently, the development of new teacher training courses or programs (Frega, 1995).

Frega, de Couve, and dal Pino (2015) provide an interesting example. These researchers compared three curricular documents for music education at the kindergarten level successively in force in the city of Buenos Aires (1980, 1989, and 1996) and identified and aligned different perspectives. In these curricula, proposed aims moved from specific technical, production-oriented goals to consideration of music's expressive value and its importance for both individual and social development. As teacher specialization was increasingly required, his/her role description changed from being the leader of pleasant experiences to the conductor of possibilities that flexibly take into account children's interests, abilities, and necessities based on a wide knowledge of teaching methods and music varieties. The most recent documents emphasize creativity but leave specifics to professional music educators. While earlier documents state some general methodological proposals, the newest one offers a detailed list of aspects that define teaching strategies. Activities and repertoire are precisely prescribed for the 1980s but only characterized toward the turn of the 21st century. While music is conceived as an important factor for personal growth in older documents, the latest guidelines emphasize social skills development and art's essential role in identity, culture, and society building.

Today official curricular guidelines for music instruction at preschool, elementary, and high school education are also in force in Colombia, Peru, and, for the two higher levels, in Venezuela. In all three countries, these standards are applied nationwide, and some jurisdictional specifications may be found in Colombia. As a consequence of the urgent need to address social issues, *Lineamientos Curriculares de Educación Artística* (Ministerio de Educación Nacional. República de Colombia, 1997), developed between 1993 and 1997; *Ley General de Educación 115* (LGE 115), developed in 1994; and *Orientaciones Pedagógicas para la Educación Artística en Básica y Media* (Ministerio de Educación Nacional. República de Colombia, 2010), all propose, "the Institutional Educational Project must attend to students' needs and circumstances, as well as those of the community, the region, and the nation; it must be specific, feasible, and evaluable" (LGE 115, 1994, article 73). According to regulations, arts instruction within basic education is not meant to train artists, but contribute to human integral development, and teachers should address students' interests in order to provide meaningful experiences (M. E. Rodríguez Melo, personal communication, March 15, 2016).

In Peru, where government curricular guidelines for music date from 2005, there is also an alternative possibility. Primary and secondary schools may adopt the title of "experimental school," and are therefore free to develop a different curriculum, either its own design, taken from another country, or from the International Baccalaureate organization, with no obligation to consider any Ministry regulation (I. Petrozzi Helasvuo, personal communication, March 4, 2016). In Venezuela, although *Ley Orgánica de Educación* (1980) still included music in the mandatory curriculum, it conforms the area of aesthetic education or training for the arts, requiring no specialist teacher for the first cycle (grades 1 to 3) of basic education. Considering arts as a means for creativity development, a decree issued in 1986 reserves specialized music education for specialized schools. However, in 1989, the Education Ministry and the National Culture Council unified criteria, and in 1991 the *Basic Music Studies* curriculum was adopted nationwide by basic education schools. As mentioned earlier, until now, the implementation was unsuccessful (García, 2009) and proposals have already become outdated (F. Sánchez, personal communication, March 4, 2016).

Beyond differences, all curricular documents set aims for music education. In Chile and Venezuela, schools may consider them flexibly, according to institutional projects, but teachers should strictly conform their plans to official requirements. In Colombia and Peru, both teachers and institutions may select aims, adjusting them to specific proposals (personal communications). In Argentina, strict programs used to organize instruction, but, since updated planning theories and philosophical and psychological foundations for education were taken into account around the early 1960s, "there is a considerable amount of freedom in the planning of the curriculum for each school, provided 'basic content' is included and nothing against national and/or provincial Constitutions is being taught" (Frega, 1995, p. 47).

Legal documents also presented professional qualification requirements. Early on, regulations established that professionally trained teachers, soon afterward music specialists, should be appointed for all levels (Frega, 1995). Still, a precise description of expected competences had to wait for further developments in music teacher training programs. Additionally, as the population grew, especially in metropolitan areas and countries with centralized administration, teachers' status and working conditions became complex. In Argentina, through union actions and after meticulous deliberations, *Ley 14.473*, known as the Teacher Statute, was enacted in 1958. It regulated the teaching profession and brought certifications under scrutiny. From 1940 on, legal provisions also demanded the hiring of graduate teachers in Venezuelan schools. Nevertheless, administrators' goals are still difficult to fulfill and graduate teachers are not enough to satisfy the system's demands. Students and even popular artists are often hired to cover vacancies (Aretz, 1995; Frega, 1995; Sánchez, 2015).

Successive reforms have updated the Argentinian education system. In 1993, *Ley Federal de Educación Nº 24.195* and its subsequent *Contenidos Básicos Comunes para la Educación General Básica* (Ministerio de Cultura y Educación de la Nación, & Consejo Federal de Cultura y Educación, 1995) proposed common curricular elements to be covered in every jurisdiction. Revisions in the law introduced a mandatory arts education area, within which proposals should be articulated, optionally including music, and resulting in enriched experiences and reduced credit hours (Frega et al., 2010a). Thoroughly founded by state-of-the-art theories and strategies, the implementation was limited, since teachers were not adequately trained and the required changes posed occupational and budgetary issues that could not be satisfactorily solved. In 2006, *Ley de Educación Nacional Nº 26.206* prescribed arts education as sensitivity and creativity stimulation, and sanctioned that only higher education institutions could grant teacher degrees.

PRINCIPLES OF ASSESSMENT IN MUSIC EDUCATION

The culture of assessment is still incipient in Spanish-speaking Latin America, as it is in Spain. Resistance to its adoption in university environments, more likely to show than to be observed (Callejo, Aguado, Ballesteros, Gil Jaurena, & López, 2001), lack of consensus within the communities that would implement it, mistrust of the treatment given to its results (Dirección Nacional de Información y Evaluación de la Calidad Educativa, Ministerio de Educación, 2009) or difficulties in making a profitable use of them (Moreno Olivos, 2011) are commonplace. In particular, assessing "failure" is not usually considered a useful tool for planning improvement, but a shameful instance that may cause stigmatization (*Ley de Educación Nacional N° 26.206*, 2006).

Furthermore, establishing assessment criteria may be troublesome because of the diverse approaches when determining the role of music education and its consequent aims. Yet, in Latin America, state-of-the-art theorizing often collides with actual practices, remarkably so when proposals are made by those at higher decision-making levels, advised by expert consultants, but who never contemplate the characteristics, needs, and possibilities of those who would accomplish what is planned. An active participation implies making sense and acknowledging expectations (López León, 2014). However, convulsive political changes and unstable economies, in addition to more general cultural traits, are causes for frequent unsustained efforts that start with outstandingly elaborated policies, but continue with deficient monitoring and assessment of the implementation process and finally end in failure, followed by careless rejection. A real awareness of what assessment involves, its deep implications and vast benefits—in fact, its inevitability—is yet to be achieved (Dirección Nacional de Información y Evaluación de la Calidad Educativa, Ministerio de Educación, 2009). As Frega states, "The assessment of learning processes is vital for **education**. [...] Either focused on student achievements [...] or on consideration of the teacher's own practices, we may state that *there is no education without permanent assessment*" (1997b, p. 5; emphasis in original).

Relevant Examples in General Education

In the light of contemporary theories considered in the region, in order to set effective assessment policies and develop successful assessment practices, projects should be realistic and internally coherent. This requires a calculated articulation of all aspects involved in the process: purpose, aims, contents, activities, resources, time, and assessment (Frega & Cash, 1980). Whatever the approach, the initial goals for music education should be set taking into account the teacher's profile, the students' characteristics, and their community contexts. When music is supposed to stimulate creative and collaborative thinking, implying expressive and experiential features, students assume an active role rather than passively adapting to a standard model. Consequently, assessment must comprise not only productions and skills but also processes, attitudes, habits, and participation (López-León, 2014). Yet, narrow-minded conceptions still persist and, despite grandiloquent aim statements, assessment is often reduced to performance results.

Regarding assessment tools, until recently, formal reports were rarely written for the preschool level in Argentina. At present, music educators commonly complete checklists either by themselves or in team evaluation, collaborating with classroom teachers.

The practice could be part of a continuous process, but, more often than not, it just takes place summarily at the end of certain stages during the school year. At the elementary school level, in addition to public performances, more varied, frequent, and reflective ways of assessment were developed throughout the years. End-of-term school reports present marks either on a numeric or Likert-type scale, but low marks in music education have never prevented promotion, assessment serving primarily as a kind of feedback to students and families. In secondary schools, when orientation includes mandatory music courses, these must be approved in similar conditions to other subjects. Nonetheless, whenever a student fails, he/she usually passes through additional examinations, and promotion would rarely depend on music education (Frega, 1995).

Previously described official documents also establish student assessment criteria for the compulsory education system. According to the role music education plays in it, general criteria may apply or more specific ones may be offered. In Colombia, for example, where music courses are not mandatory, criteria are selected by institutions (M. E. Rodríguez Melo, personal communication, March 15, 2016). As established by curricular guidelines in force in Peru, assessment within general education must be an integral, continuous, systematic, participative, and flexible process, tending to improve learning experiences and considering both processes and results. Grading scales and approval criteria are succinctly but precisely presented, and are valid for any of the areas included in the curriculum (Ministerio de Educación, República del Perú, 2005). Chilean and Argentinian curricula also present sections considering assessment issues.

However, practices reflect a more uncertain reality. Sánchez Cunill (personal communication, March 5, 2016) declares that, in Chile, elementary and high schools tend to standardize student assessment, and practices are usually updated regularly. Authorities also regulate project and teacher practice assessment. Other countries, though, present a less ideal situation. Although student assessment criteria are quite accurately defined, they may be outdated, as in Venezuela (F. Sánchez, personal communication, March 4, 2016), or inconsistently applied or even ignored. Approaches and tools are scarcely standardized only in Peru and Venezuela (A. Chang Arana, personal communication, March 5, 2016; F. Sánchez, personal communication, March 4, 2016). Concerning assessment of institutional projects and teacher practices, the situation is still more erratic. Even in cases where this type of evaluation is required by law, and tools are consistently standardized (e.g., teacher assessment in Argentina), actions are carried out as mere empty formalities and results reported for the most part without further implications.

Professional Training Programs

Whenever professional meetings presented an opportunity for reflection on teaching practices, the issue of evaluation has been considered from a variety of perspectives. In Argentina, González and Lobato (2014) have offered a critical view, proposing the analysis of challenges facing professional music training programs, with either artistic or teaching orientation. They recognize the persistence of old traditions based on rigid and repetitive concepts, particularly in reference to assessment practices, standing in clear contradiction with existing curriculum proposals, founded on contemporary theories. The authors also criticize the centrality of production as an end in itself. According to this approach, "teachers [...] expect to see in students a reproduction of their own representations, speeches, and account of musical discourse" (Gonzalez & Lobato, 2014, p. 5). Even course approval often depends on identification, and hegemonic teachers become even models from which their peers are evaluated.

From a more practical stance, Malbrán and Ramallo (2014) presented in a Latin American international conference an experience that took place in Buenos Aires, implementing the use of portfolios, an assessment instrument quite new in the region. Portfolios are offered as a possibility to evaluate students very flexibly and thoroughly through different stages of their learning processes as they become independent pro-fessionals, appraising their background, style, interests, and personality by means of completing a variety of productions. Evaluation is presented as ubiquitous, always sup-porting decision-making. In order for it to be possible, planning and design, as well as the implementation of relevant instruments, are essential. The undertaking is remarkably personalized. Evaluation opportunities are frequent, and activities range from more prescriptively patterned exercises to research activities, including musical analysis, multimedia artistic production, and theoretical reflection. The authors acknowledge the task is notably time-demanding for students to complete, also needing the sustained collaboration and interaction of every member of a large teaching team. In general, Latin American institutions for professional training offer neither one nor the other.

Considering regular practices, official documents establish assessment criteria for students in professional music training in Chile (for pedagogical programs), Peru (for artistic programs), and Venezuela. In Argentina and Colombia, these criteria are just part of the institutional course description. Assessment practices tend to be standard-ized by each institution in Peru (by the use of rubrics), Chile, and Colombia, but not in Argentina and Venezuela. According to informants (I. Petrozzi Helasvuo, personal communication, March 4, 2016; F. Sánchez, personal communication, March 4, 2016; C. Sánchez Cunill, personal communication, March 5, 2016; A. Chang Arana, personal communication, March 5, 2016; M. E. Rodríguez Melo, personal communication, March 15, 2016), only Chile regularly updates them. In Chile and Venezuela, program offers are regularly assessed by institutions and national authorities, while teaching practice evaluation is performed in Chile, Colombia, and Venezuela, without standard-ized tools and only required by law in the latter. In Argentina, academic offerings are occasionally reviewed, but it has not become a systematic, regular practice.

Artistic Training

Assessment in arts education evidences critical issues that tend to remain unnoticed in other fields. Controversies become explicit, and the very essence of teaching and assessing comes under scrutiny, covering criteria, references, moments, interpersonal relationships, subjectivity, judgment faculties, assessment tools, and formal institutional requirements.

During recent years, assessment practices, nurtured by most heterogeneous theoretical approaches, have frequently collided with perspectives explicitly adopted as educational bases. Despite specialists' valuable warnings raising awareness of constructs that inevitably condition observation, teachers apply criteria showing great intra- and interpersonal variability. There is hardly a common ground that allows any standardization and coming to terms with attributing responsibilities for criteria definition. Extensive research in different contexts indicates arts education is a particularly problematic field, where decisions seem to be always debatable and controversial. Different aesthetic and/or pedagogical conceptions, multiple considerations on art itself, contrasting definitions of the work of art, and extensive debates on creativity, its measurement, cognition, and consciousness demarcate an intricate area for reflection.

Amid uncertainties, assessment in professional arts education frequently becomes authoritarian, either manifested through impressionistic, intuitive value judgments, or by strictly adhering to rules, technical matters, and even models to be reproduced.

Yet another difficult issue is that of the object of assessment. Professional arts education tends to be extremely product-centered, even when the very notion of a work of art proves to be vast and kaleidoscopic. The prominence of results is hard to combine with consideration of processes. On the other hand, teachers sometimes evaluate student school history, talent, and personality, even appraising empathy, and ignore his/her specific production or reflection. Efforts to improve assessment reliability are limited to only a few Spanish-speaking South American countries that have systematically adopted the use of auxiliary tools (Camilloni, 2015).

The use of rubrics in the assessment of instrumental performance was recently discussed at an international meeting held in the region (Correa Ortega, 2014). Their implementation may allow feedback to reach students in a more constructive, less biased manner and to support teacher planning, overcoming extreme degrees of subjectivity and offering more than a final grade for a course. For attaining assessment reliability, observable and measurable categories in musical performance should be established and clearly defined, as well as achievement levels for each one.

The report also refers to negative aspects such as the lack of technical training for the teachers who design the tools, a concern many of them expressed about the possible loss of a holistic view in understanding the complex phenomenon of musical performance, and the tendency to consider results of review processes as final products. Once established, most rubrics were neither reviewed nor updated and, after a first stage of implementation, professionals did not consider them useful anymore. Student appraisal was even less favorable, as teachers did not integrate them into debates relating to the development of assessment tools, and influential factors were kept out of the analysis.

Teacher Training

Coherence between assessment practices and contemporary pedagogical thought is also evaluated within the context of music teaching training programs (Barco, 2008), as traits of resistance to renewal become evident within mostly conservative education systems frequently found in Latin America. On the one hand, a gap between discourse and action often appears in the practice of teachers that have a solid artistic training but little or no pedagogical background. On the other hand, students may considerably benefit from being assessed with a similar approach to the one they are supposed to adopt for their future professional practice. Researchers also encouraged the appraisal of assessment as something other than the final grading of a course that measures the level of adaptation to established rules shown by results. Once again, the need for clear criteria, adequate systematization, and solid grounds is strongly emphasized, and unfavorable working conditions are noted as possibly hindering the adoption of updated perspectives. Students, who are inevitably involved in assessment practices, need to explicitly know about guidelines, criteria, and forms of participation in such processes.

In order to develop a solid assessment culture, one that sustains a consistent practice and makes profitable uses of its results, music teacher training programs first confront the challenge of supplying teachers with an education that allows them to attain the proposed learning objectives, update practices to flexibly address contemporary school realities and social demands (Frega, 1998), and make use of planning strategies for formulating organic proposals leading to effective assessment. At the end of the 20th century, Hansen (cited in Frega & Cash, 1980) considered planning to be the essence of reflection in Latin American education debate. Today, in a century that needs to focused in teacher training (Gainza, 2003), it still is.

For teachers, assessment implies the observation of comprehension, information, application, attention, habits, attitudes and skills, and the selection of proper tools for its implementation. From goals, through processes, to results, adjustment and improvement are only possible if assessment is carried out all along the way instead of being understood just as an additional final stage. The validity and appropriateness of aims, methodology, resources, and interests should also be evaluated (Frega & Cash, 1980). This delicate and rewarding task calls for an expertise whose development should be at the top of institutions' priorities.

ASSESSMENT IN SPECIFIC COUNTRIES

This section presents some cases with particular emphasis on outstanding traits related to assessment tools and practices that may stimulate enriching reflection. Although they are organized by nation, a thorough consideration of assessment in every aspect of each educational system is not intended. For similar reasons, there is no common structure describing equivalent categories.

Argentina

Although it is not really an integral part of Argentinian culture, assessment, being inevitable, has been addressed by pedagogical debates and official documents. However, preferred focuses tend to be the concept of music education, its aims and contents, and, when it comes to more technical consideration, methods, activities, and resources are the object of study. Planning, as previously mentioned, has lately been significantly examined and, in current practice, is normally included as a specific subject within teacher training curricula. Assessment may well be part of these courses' syllabi, but until a new generation of teachers is fully active, theorizing and development of effectively articulated tools remain as part of decision-makers and experts' discussions and hardly reach the level of classroom practitioners.

Student assessment in institutional contexts has been conducted using different instruments:

- Traditionally, essay exams were used almost exclusively. "Standardized" tests were occasionally adopted but usually created by each teacher him/herself for a particular class, there has been no standardization.
- Anecdotal records are frequently used for assessing preschool students or performance activities in other levels of general education. Contemplating participation, attitudes, and reactions, even when they are not actually written, they tend to be a popular though informal assessment practice through college.
- Checklists, often combined with grading scales, eventually becoming rubrics, are now commonly employed. But once again, they are formulated ad hoc by the teacher and lack the standardization that would better guarantee some objectivity. At the college level, theoretical contents are usually tested orally.

As the secondary school system is about to be reformed nationwide, documents elaborated and published by the Education Ministry of Buenos Aires City are currently considered to be a valuable model. The arts curricular design for the New Secondary School (Ministerio de Educación, Buenos Aires Ciudad, 2015) presents general guidelines for assessment that point out the need for articulating all the elements that intervene in educational processes in order to achieve a real improvement. Assessment richness and complexity comprises its implementation at different stages, including diversified aspects of what needs to be assessed, regarding individuality, multiple formats and tools, the importance of feedback in order to make a profitable use of evaluation results, and the role of expectations. Additionally, assessment performance is attributed not only to teachers and authorities but also to students in terms of peer and self-evaluation.

Also here, coherence between assessment and proposed aims is advised as essential for a process that comprehends development, creativity, collaborative abilities, critical thinking, expressive and communication skills, and awareness of historical, social, and cultural contexts. The teacher is expected to approach assessment creatively through manifold activities, involving students, and making a formative instance out of it. Standardized assessment tools are neither observed, nor searched for, although possibilities are enlisted. The main focus of music education remains on production, and students' reflective participation is much appreciated. Final suggestions present practices that consistently integrate educational processes as a whole.

Searching for new perspectives, and given the flexibility needed when assessing creative processes involved in arts education, recent studies have considered the development of tools for evaluating strategies that underlie such processes. To this end, researchers have pointed out the importance of clearly establishing descriptors for creative behavior, allowing the recognition of results of systematic stimulation, and evaluated the appropriateness of applying in educational contexts a measurement tool that has been developed in the field of music therapy (Frega, 2009).

In later instances, after the validation of the aforementioned tool, its combination with the latest technology (fMRI), applied in neurological studies, raised new possibilities from a multidisciplinary approach that brings music education together with the neurosciences. However, extensive development is still required for a more consistent interpretation of results and an adequate application to the study of classroom situations (Frega, 2013).

Chile

Since the late 1950s, Chile has been at the avant-garde of Latin American musical education. Considering it as one of the basic aspects in cultural instruction for its ethical values, its unique way of connecting with the world, and its contribution to personality and social development, in 1956 the OAS created the Inter-American Music Council that, four years later, recommended the creation of the INTEM under the sponsorship of the University of Chile Music Department. Selection of this location acknowledged long-established institutions such as the National Conservatory (1849), and the University of Chile (1842), which included arts in higher education programs in 1929 and founded its Music Department in 1948. Since 1966, INTEM offered scholarships for the academic training of specialized music educators, and provided technical assistance to whoever requested it, be it government, individual, or institution. Updated, flexible curricula and state-of-the-art planning theories supported at least a decade of activities that reached professionals from 19 countries in the region, creating productive bonds and originating several research studies. Positive assessment reports highlighted the scope of the endeavor and its functional approach, specifically taking into account concrete realities of Latin American music education. Further projects integrated the Institute as a Multinational Center of OAS's Regional Program for Cultural Development, promoted the creation of institutional development missions that would enhance conditions for music education professional training all over the continent, and looked for the setting of a subsidiary center in charge of producing didactic materials focused on folklore in collaboration with Venezuela's American Institute of Ethnomusicology and Folklore (INIDEF) (Comité Editorial, 1976). Efforts were well planned, processes properly assessed, and synergies took advantage of previous and coexisting projects. However, political changes limited possibilities and resulted in decay and extinction. Political instability also affected education policies as shown in successive curricular adjustments (Poblete Lagos, 2010).

After early organization of a national education system, 1965 reforms transmitted the spirit of the "Revolution in Liberty" (1964–1970), seeking to expand access to education, the professionalization of specialized teachers, the adoption of updated approaches to education and the reorganization of elementary and high schools. Curricular documents presented a new purpose, aims and content arrangement for music education, avoiding encyclopedic teaching, didacticism, and rote learning. In tune with INTEM perspectives, the proposal focused on production and aesthetic appreciation, working on a varied repertory. Beyond technical objectives, music education was conceived in wide terms, valued for its formative influence.

After the 1973 military coup, liberal economic principles were adopted, individual liberties restricted, and unions and professional associations either dissolved or suspended, and the education system was reformed once more. The university system was dismantled and restructured, and programs reorganized in universities, professional institutes, and technical training centers, which resulted in undesirable stratification. For compulsory education, the 1965 guidelines were maintained but stripped of any potentially controversial or politicized content, moving back to a traditional view of education. Policies established objectives or expected behaviors rather than content or coordinating concepts for actions. Educators had a broad choice of methodological options, and institutions could flexibly adapt the curriculum. However, by relying so much on professional skills, schools that could not count on expert teachers were left without music lessons.

In 1990, when democracy returned, a new Education Law (*Ley Orgánica Constitucional de Enseñanza N° 18.962*) kept the system under government control, but granted still a greater freedom for institutions to develop their proposals attending to their own orientation and community profile, once Fundamental Objectives and Minimum Compulsory Contents had been covered. Although the area of arts education was mandatory for all levels within general education, individual arts were optional and curricular structure favored visual arts rather than music. These instances present three different perspectives for music education that reflect social needs and conceptions. The first one contemplates music as a unique contribution for human development, but it is restricted to a Eurocentric model. Social issues are disregarded by the second one, and declared purposes seem to dilute because of curricular structural looseness. The third proposal is subject-centered, emphasizing social aspects and aiming for educating critical thinkers who are aesthetically sensitive, although its ambitious goals lack a more solid theoretical framework. Presenting still further changes, a new *Ley General de Educación N° 20.370* was passed in 2009, but is still the source of intense debate.

Venezuela

Venezuelan political instability prevented the development of traditions and institutions that may have occurred in other former Spanish colonies during the 19th century (Carlson, 2016). Many of the achievements in the field of music education observable during the early 20th century only reached the upper classes. Inside schools, music experiences "were overall ineffective due to scarce resources and faulty implementation" (p. 66), and alternatives did not contemplate offerings for children's education. Subsequent political and economic problems still inhibited real improvement (Carlson, 2016).

In the 1970s, the national economy recovered, which was also reflected in cultural life. Scholarship programs, new educational institutions, and professional orchestras throughout the country (Carlson, 2016) set the conditions for transformation in music education. The Venezuelan Society for Music Education was active and influential (F. Sánchez, personal communication, March 4, 2016), and government organizations seriously promoted, for the last quarter of the 20th century, the inclusion of native folk music in general education through the INIDEF led by Isabel Aretz, and supported by the OAS (Aretz, 1995).

The rise of a program that originated the national network of youth orchestras, known as *El Sistema*, was enthusiastically received (Baker, 2014; Carlson, 2016; Sánchez, 2007). The proposal had important antecedents both in Chile in Jorge Peña Hen's 1964 project, some of whose teachers were responsible for the first Venezuelan children orchestra (Carlson, 2016), and in the Youth Program of the National Symphony Orchestra in Costa Rica, initiated in 1972 (López, 2011). In Venezuela, the program emerged in 1975 as an alternative to traditional conservatory training; "new methodologies and new institutions [...] that converge in an essential aim: the training of musicians through ensemble practice [...] with a high quality repertoire." (Garmendia, 1995, p. 12). Despite this spirited reception, the program left little space for music theory, and historical or musicological perspectives, narrowing down the curriculum prescribed by the Ministry of Education in 1964 (Baker, 2014). Consequently, "[m]any students emerge as skilled orchestral players, but their practical skills often have little foundation in knowledge" (Baker, 2014, p. 145).

By promoting a positive social change through classical music, collective learning in orchestral practice, and an intensive work schedule, *El Sistema* has become a huge, powerful institution. It currently receives almost all state funds for culture, and is even seen as a global franchise for music education, expanding in more than 60 countries.

Undoubtedly, the program has brought cultural activities and opportunities to many children. Nevertheless, both its deep social effects and the quality of the education offered are at present heavily questioned. Endorsement by international figures seems to examine only artistic results, and most analysis attempts actually reproduce the official, propagandistic discourse. "Combining children, a repertoire of classical favorites, and a heartwarming backstory, El Sistema has an extraordinary capacity to appeal to the emotions. [...] Yet [...] this emotional effect is carefully calculated" (Baker, 2014, p. 3) and designed to impress visitors and donors.

While Garmendia (1995) praises the inclusion of Latin American repertoire, *El Sistema* "[m]usicians play the same pieces [among which, some Latin American flavored, technically European, hits] repeatedly rather than constantly exploring new repertoire" (Baker, 2014, p. 140). Refuting Garmendia's esteem for innovations, *El Sistema* teaching methods are largely based on repetition, and according to an experienced Sistema teacher, "peer teaching covered up a lack of systematic teacher training" (cited in Baker, 2014, p. 141), replicating hierarchical dynamics and resulting in mere reproduction rather than in creativity stimulation. Rehearsals can be inconceivably long, even for adult professional musicians, and conductors, driven by artistic goals, leave no place for critical thinking. "El Sistema [...] proposes a model of citizenship that [...] is unitary rather than pluralistic, obedient rather than critical, and politically passive rather than active" (Baker, 2014, p. 250), thus perpetuating the very social stratification and the inequalities it is supposed to fight.

Contemporary progressive trends in music education emphasize the importance of processes, multilayered experiences, and inventiveness. This may be considerably favored by many genres other than European art music, and multicultural diversity acknowledgment, respect, and valuation, building identity from one's very own roots. *El Sistema*, in contrast, proposes socioeconomic and moral salvation by isolating children from their own culture, and leaving no place for their active participation in the construction of knowledge, relationships, and society. As Latin America began to develop an emancipatory approach to any educational activity, *El Sistema* chose to go back to old-fashioned practices. A proper assessment of the program is still due, asking accurate questions instead of repeating official formulas, and critically considering declared aims, teaching methods, processes, and results, within an adequate research framework.

At the university level, for the last 20 years, different experimental curricula have been in the trial stage at several institutions both for artistic and pedagogical training, without satisfactory results. Implementation has been generally met with rejection, since planning omitted the community's participation, official guidance has been ineffective, no links between teaching and research activities have been established, and social, possibly ideological, struggles have originated considerable controversy leading to resistance (Sánchez, 2015). Disjointed efforts result in failure, and lack of assessment prevents its proper detection and consequent improvement.

CONTEMPORARY RELEVANT ISSUES AND CONCLUSIONS

Conflicts in Artistic Education Assessment

Gratuity Versus Payment in Higher Education

Since the inception of compulsory schooling, Argentinian public education has been free for all mandatory levels, and already in 1918, the University Reform movement demanded gratuity also for higher education. It was not until the mid-20th century, though, that the complete education system became free of fees at public institutions. Nowadays, impassioned debates deeply rooted in contrasting ideologies addressed the issue, while the quality of education decays for lack of sufficient funds (Frega, 1995).

State-funded higher education is also free in Peru and Venezuela, but not in Colombia (I. Petrozzi Helasvuo, personal communication, March 4, 2016; F. Sánchez, personal communication, March 4, 2016; M. E. Rodríguez Melo, personal communication, March 15, 2016). It used to be free in Chile, until reforms passed in 1981 ended the benefit. Since then, music education, both artistic and pedagogical, has considerably grown, either at universities or professional institutes and conservatories. However, since it is not free but expensive, many interested people cannot enter the system or successfully finish their studies. Currently, the national administration is expected to gradually establish gratuity for all state-funded education (C. Sánchez Cunill, personal communication, March 5, 2016).

Free Admission Versus Talent Selection

At the higher education level, another controversial matter is requirements for admission. Traditionally, "it was believed that art education should be reserved only for the most talented" (Frega, 1998, p. 1). For professional training, the conception clashed with another of the principles set by the 1918 reformist movement that rejected admission proofs as unfair and discriminatory. The conflict remains unresolved today, and in Argentina, even though access to music higher education requires generally either the approval of an entrance test or the completion of specialized secondary school, there is currently considerable debate with those who demand free access for all undergraduate art programs (as is the case for fine arts).

In Colombia, Peru, and Venezuela access to music higher education is gained through an admission examination, while in Chile, such a test must be passed for artistic training. Pedagogical higher education only requires approval of secondary level studies.

"Ideological Rationales" Behind Political Issues

Policy adjustments are strongly attached to political changes and historical ups and downs in South American Spanish-speaking countries. When performed, assessment is rarely autonomous.

As previously discussed, assessment is central to contemporary debates in every professional meeting. However, teachers are frequently influenced by populist, demagogic ideologies. Even in higher education contexts, including fee-free, tax-funded institutions, many proposals remain at an entertainment level, whereas certain sectors of society are demanding a quality education that allows them to grow. On the contrary, other social groups adhere to this short-lived conception. Government official answers are often tentative. Highly prescriptive state policies, such as those in Venezuela, leave no room for the participation of those involved (Baker, 2014). Legal changes in Argentina (Ley de Educación Nacional N° 26.206, Art. 97) tend to hide problems by forbidding diffusion of information even for statistical or study purposes. Further developments are required, as issues remain for the most part unsolved.

Challenges in Policies, Planning, and Assessment of Music in the General Compulsory System of Education

Despite recent attempts at educational improvement in most Latin American countries, there are still particular challenges that need to be tackled.

Proposals, such as legal frameworks, curricular guidelines, or pedagogical materials, frequently adopt international trends and are carefully designed (e.g., Ministerio de Educación, República del Perú, 2005). Nonetheless, implementation processes tend to be insufficiently examined. Not all intervenient parts are adequately trained or allowed time, space, or participation in planning, assessing, and proposing (Correa Ortega, 2014). Program developers often ignore specific contexts and neglect assessment, so that classroom realities remain unchanged (Fajardo & Wagner, 2003). Everyday *practice fields* need to come under scrutiny, in order to learn from experience and overcome rejection to renewal whenever it appears (Barco, 2008).

State-of-the-art research results and theoretical thought must be taken into account (Barco, 2008) but not only at initial stages and hierarchical levels. Since processes are not automatic, they should be assessed all along the way (Malbrán & Ramallo, 2014).

Conclusions and Questions for Future Research, Analysis, or Study

Teacher training conditions should be carefully revised in order to consider not only updated theories developed internationally but also the actual demands of each context, involving representatives from all contributing groups. Cultural diversity should be acknowledged and respected, and creativity stimulated. Polarization between academic and popular music must be avoided, and music education must consider all kinds of productions implicating students in their social and cultural environment. Old-fashioned music education models contradict contemporary progressive pedagogical trends, many of them developed by leading Latin American intellectuals (e.g., Paulo Freire). Research needs to address local traditions and regional cultural heritage, aiming for a deep understanding of meaning and value and promoting the production of appropriate teaching materials and teacher training.

Better working conditions should be offered, granting not only decent wages but also sufficient materials, adequate physical spaces, small groups of students, and time for sharing, reflecting, and professional development as well as opportunities for participating in processes intending improvement.

If assessment is to be adequately performed and results conveniently used, professionals need to update their knowledge. Basic teacher training has recently undergone a thorough revision in some Argentinian jurisdictions, resulting in refined curricular proposals. Their implementation is now to be carefully assessed in all stages and with the active participation of every participant.

As a final thought, we suggest that once processes of change are evolving, accompaniment, assessment, and optimization of results should be the rule, instead of constant, nonarticulated attempts that start over from scratch.

NOTE

1. Most national information was provided by Carlos Sánchez Cunill (Chile), Martha Enna Rodríguez Melo (Colombia), Inkeri Petrozzi Helasvuo and Álvaro Chang Arana (Perú), and Freddy Sánchez (Venezuela), through personal communications, for which we are very grateful. At the time of writing, the authors could not find trustworthy information about Bolivia, Ecuador, Paraguay, or Uruguay.

REFERENCES

Aretz, I. (1995). Latin American folklore in music education. In A. L. Frega (Ed.), *Music education in Latin America: A festschrift for Rodolfo Zubrisky* (pp. 43–45). Reading, UK: International Society for Music Education.

Baker, G. (2014). *El Sistema: Orchestrating Venezuela's youth*. New York, NY: Oxford University Press.

Barco, J. M. (2008). Indagaciones en torno a la evaluación en la educación artística. *Praxis Pedagógica, 8*(9), 80–93.

Callejo, J., Aguado, T., Ballesteros, B., Gil Jaurena, I., & López, B. (2001). Indicadores de evaluación de la educación a distancia en un sistema universitario. *RIED. Revista Iberoamericana de Educación a Distancia, 4*(1), 35–50. doi: 10.5944/ried.4.1.1190

Camilloni, A. W., de. (2015, September). *La evaluación de los aprendizajes en la enseñanza artística*. Paper presented at the 2ª Jornada de Arte y Educación 2015: "La evaluación en las enseñanzas artísticas," Academia Nacional de Educación, Buenos Aires.

Carlson, A. (2016, February). The story of Carora: The origins of El Sistema. *International Journal of Music Education, 34*(1), 64–73.

Comité Editorial. (1976). Informes: El Instituto Interamericano de Educación Musical. *Revista Musical Chilena, 30*, 111–115.

Correa Ortega, J. P. (2014). Uso de rúbricas en la evaluación de instrumento principal: Estudio de caso en un programa profesional de estudios musicales. In C. Poblete Lagos (Ed.), *Actas de la 9ª Conferencia Latinoamericana y 2ª Panamericana de la Sociedad Internacional de Educación Musical, ISME* (pp. 1015–1024). Santiago, Chile: Facultad de Artes, Universidad de Chile.

de Couve, A. C., & Dal Pino, C. (1999). Historical panorama of music education in Latin America: Music training institutions. *International Journal of Music Education, 34*, 30–46.

de Couve, A., Dal Pino, C., Fernández Calvo, D., Frega, A. L., & Souza, J. (1998). Arts education policy in Latin America. *Arts Education Policy Review, 99*(4), 18–28.

de Couve, A., Dal Pino, C., & Frega, A. L. (2004, April). An approach to the history of music education in Latin America, Part II: Music education 16th–18th centuries. *Journal of Historical Research in Music Education, 25*(2), 79–95.

Escudé, C., & Cisneros, A. (2000). *Historia de las relaciones exteriores argentinas*. Buenos Aires: Consejo Argentino para las Relaciones Internacionales (CARI). Retrieved from http://www.argentina-rree.com/historia.htm

Fajardo, V., & Wagner, T. (Eds.). (2003). *Métodos, contenidos y enseñanza de las artes en América Latina y el Caribe*. París: Organización de las Naciones Unidas para la Educación, la Ciencia y la Cultura.

Frega, A. L. (1995). Argentina. In Laurence Lepherd (Ed.), *Music education in international perspectives: National systems; England, Namibia, Argentina, Russia, Hungary, Portugal, Singapore, Sweden, the United States of America* (pp. 37–50). Toowoomba, Australia: University of Southern Queensland Press.

Frega, A. L. (1997a). Educación Artística. In *Fuentes para la transformación curricular: Educación Artística y Educación Física* (pp. 13–64). Buenos Aires, Argentina: Ministerio de Cultura y Educación de la Nación.

Frega, A. L. (1997b). Prólogo. In M. A. Pujol I Subirà (Ed.), *La evaluación del área de música* (pp. 5–6). Barcelona, Spain: Eumo-Octaedro.

Frega, A. L. (1998). *All for music, music for all*. Pretoria: Centre for Music Education, Department of Music, University of Pretoria.

Frega, A. L. (2009). *Educar en creatividad*. Buenos Aires, Argentina: Academia Nacional de Educación.

Frega, A. L. (2013). Final report on creativity as assessed by functional magnetic resonance imaging and SCAMPER tool. *Journal for Educators, Teachers and Trainers JETT, 5*(1), 68–79.

Frega, A. L., & Cash, I. (1980) *Planeamiento de la educación musical escolar y su evaluación*. Buenos Aires, Argentina: Casa América.

Frega, A. L., de Couve, A. C., & Dal Pino, C. (2010a). Argentina: From "música vocal" to "educación artística: Música." In G. Cox, & R. Stevens (Eds.). *The origins and foundations of music education: Cross-cultural historical studies of music in compulsory schooling*. London, UK: Continuum.

Frega, A. L., de Couve, A. C., & Dal Pino, C. (2010b). Las enseñanzas del arte en la Argentina: Una visión desde la Colonia hasta la Independencia. (Informe de un trabajo de investigación en curso). In Academias Nacionales (Eds.), *En torno a 1810* (pp. 209–228). Buenos Aires, Argentina: Abeledo Perrot.

Frega, A. L., de Couve, A. C., & Dal Pino, C. (2015). *Comparative analyses of Argentine documents for kindergarten level (1980–1996) according to FAD: Example of categorization of quotations referred to the vocal aspect*. Unpublished manuscript.

Gainza, V. (2003). *La educación musical entre dos siglos: Del modelo metodológico a los nuevos paradigmas*. Victoria, Buenos Aires: Universidad de San Andrés.

García, Z. (2009). Inclusión de la música en los planes y programas de estudio en las escuelas venezolanas. *Revista de Pedagogía, 30*, 333–353.

Garmendia, E. (1995). Youth orchestras: The first Latin American experience. In A. L. Frega (Ed.), *Music education in Latin America: A festschrift for Rodolfo Zubrisky* (pp. 46–48). Reading, UK: International Society for Music Education.

González, G., & Lobato, S. (2014). *Articular prácticas, discursos y estado del conocimiento en las instituciones superiores de formación musical: Un desafío posible*. Paper presented at VIII Congreso Iberoamericano de Docencia Universitaria y de Nivel Superior, Rosario, Argentina. Retrieved from http://cedoc.infd.edu.ar/upload/Articular_practicas_discursos_y_estado_del_conocimiento_en_las_instituciones_superiores_de_formacion_musical.pdf

Hobsbawm, E. (1962/1996). *The age of the revolution 1789–1848*. New York, NY: Vintage Books.

López, M. O. (2011). Costa Rica: Culture creates opportunities for young people. *Americas, 63*(6), 32–35.

López León, R. N. (2014). Desarrollo del criterio para la evaluación en educación musical. *Pensamiento y Acción, Cuarta época, 19*, 198–206.

Malbrán, S., & Ramallo, H. D. (2014). La producción musical de competencias versátiles en la carrera de grado: Evaluación en la acción. En C. Poblete Lagos (Ed.), *Actas de la 9ª Conferencia Latinoamericana y 2ª Panamericana de la Sociedad Internacional de Educación Musical, ISME* (pp. 582–590). Santiago, Chile: Facultad de Artes, Universidad de Chile.

Moreno Olivos, T. (2011). La cultura de la evaluación y la mejora de la escuela. *Perfiles educativos, 33*(131), 116–130.

Poblete Lagos, C. (2010). Enseñanza musical en Chile: Continuidades y cambios en tres reformas curriculares (1965, 1981, 1996–1998). *Revista Musical Chilena, 64*(214), 12–35.

Rojas de Ferro, M. C. (1982). Análisis de una experiencia: La misión pedagógica alemana. *Revista Colombiana de Educación, 10*, 25–75.

Sánchez, F. (2007). El Sistema Nacional para las Orquestas Juveniles e Infantiles. La nueva educación musical de Venezuela. *Revista da ABEM, Porto Alegre, 18*, 63–68.

Sánchez, F. (2015). Music teacher education in Venezuela. In S. Figueiredo, J. Soares, & R. F. Schambeck (Eds.), *The preparation of music teachers: A global perspective* (pp. 161–191). Porto Alegre, Brazil: ANPPOM.

Valencia, G. (1995). A Colombian look at music education in Latin America. In A. L. Frega (Ed.), *Music education in Latin America: A festschrift for Rodolfo Zubrisky* (pp. 49–51). Reading, UK: International Society for Music Education.

Official Documents

Argentina

Dirección Nacional de Información y Evaluación de la Calidad Educativa, Ministerio de Educación. (2009). *Hacia una cultura de la evaluación. ONE 2009/Censo.*

Ley 14.473. Estatuto del Docente. (1958). Retrieved from www.bnm.me.gov.ar/giga1/normas/8178.pdf

Ley Nº 1.420 de Educación Común. (1884). Retrieved from http://www.bnm.me.gov.ar/giga1/normas/5421.pdf

Ley de Educación Nacional Nº 26.206. (2006). Retrieved from http://www.me.gov.ar/doc_pdf/ley_de_educ_nac.pdf

Ley Federal de Educación Nº 24.195. (1993). Retrieved from http://servicios.infoleg.gob.ar/infolegInternet/anexos/15000-19999/17009/texact.htm

Ministerio de Cultura y Educación de la Nación, & Consejo Federal de Cultura y Educación. (1995). *Contenidos Básicos Comunes para la Educación General Básica.* Retrieved from http://www.bnm.me.gov.ar/giga1/documentos/EL001215.pdf

Ministerio de Educación. Buenos Aires Ciudad. (2015). *Diseño Curricular. Ciclo orientado del Bachillerato: Arte. Artes Visuales. Música. Teatro.*

Chile

Ley General de Educación Nº 20.370. (2009). Retrieved from https://www.leychile.cl/Navegar?idNorma=1006043

Ley Orgánica Constitucional de Enseñanza (N° 18.962). (1990). Retrieved from http://www. uchile.cl/portal/presentacion/normativa-y-reglamentos/8386/ley-organica-constitucional- de-ensenanza

Colombia

Ley General de Educación 115, de Febrero 8 de 1994. Retrieved from http://www.mineducacion. gov.co/1621/articles-85906_archivo_pdf.pdf

Ministerio de Educación Nacional. República de Colombia. (1997). *Lineamientos Curriculares de Educación Artística.* Retrieved from http://www.mineducacion.gov.co/1759/articles-339975_ recurso_4.pdf

Ministerio de Educación Nacional. República de Colombia. (2010). *Orientaciones Pedagógicas para la Educación Artística en Básica y Media.* Retrieved from http://www.mineducacion. gov.co/1759/articles-340033_archivo_pdf_Orientaciones_Edu_Artistica_Basica_Media.pdf

Peru

Ministerio de Educación. República del Perú. (2005). *Diseño Curricular Nacional de Educación Básica Regular. Proceso de Articulación.* Retrieved from http://www.minedu.gob.pe/ normatividad/reglamentos/DisenoCurricularNacional.pdf

Venezuela

Ley Orgánica de Educación. (1980). Retrieved from http://www.oei.es/quipu/venezuela/Ley_ Org_Educ.pdf

CHAPTER 7

....

ASSESSMENT POLICY AND MUSIC EDUCATION

Perspectives from North America

....

GLENN E. NIERMAN AND
RICHARD COLWELL

POLICIES exist to guide and to determine present and future actions.[1] They are not developed in a vacuum. Policies are (or at least should be) formulated and selected from among alternatives in light of given conditions existing in a particular time and place. Consider, for example, the history of income tax policies in the United States (Doris, 1994). This tax was occasionally considered to be unconstitutional and was often viewed as a response to the need for money to finance various wars. The first federal US income tax, levied to finance the Civil War, was repealed soon after that war ended. In 1894, Congress enacted a flat rate federal income tax, which was then ruled unconstitutional the following year by the US Supreme Court because it was a direct tax not apportioned according to the population of each state. Then, perhaps in response to projecting the need for resources for the impending World War I, the 16th Amendment (1913) removed this objection, and the United States has had a federal income tax ever since. The point is, policies can and should be responsive to what is going on in a particular time and place.

Policies affecting music education in general are no less impacted by time and place. Why was Lowell Mason successful in convincing the Boston School Board to institute a policy to bring music into the public schools of Boston, Massachusetts? One explanation is that he was mindful of time and place. In the United States education is primarily in the hands of state and local officials. There were a number of grammar schools in the Boston Public Schools of the mid-19th century modeled on the British concept of such schools (Dorn, 2003). The curriculum for these grammar schools included an emphasis on Latin, the original purpose of medieval grammar schools, and the development of good reading and speaking skills, to include precise enunciation and diction. Can you think of more fertile ground for the growth of vocal music education? It is important to note that the local Boston community also supported music education, particularly influential members of the community such as members of the Handel and Haydn Society. Further, the Boston School Board members were most certainly attuned to an opportunity to improve the state of singing in the church service on Sunday morning through music instruction in the schools. Thus, thanks to Lowell Mason's political and policy astuteness, music education found its way in policy to the schools of the United States.

Looking back over the history of public school music in the United States since its beginnings in Boston in 1838, there has been a clear upward trajectory for music in schools. Even though in today's world music educators (indeed, most educators in the arts) look longingly at those who teach in the disciplines of science, technology, engineering, and math (STEM) and wonder why the battle for equal relevance of education in the humanities has been so contested by many decision makers, policies promoting education in the arts in general and in music specifically have been profoundly successful. According to Parsad and Spiegelman (2012), the following demographics describe music in the kindergarten through 12th grade levels in schools in the United States:

- 94% of elementary schools offer music
- 91% of elementary schools employed music specialists
- 93% of elementary schools that offered music offered it at least once per week
- 91% of secondary schools offer music
- 81% of schools with the highest poverty level offered music
- 96% of schools with the lowest poverty concentration offered music
- 57% of schools required some arts coursework for graduation (excerpted from pp. 5–20)

Likewise, in Canada, music education and arts education appears to be healthy, and the "highly populated areas in the south of the country have greater access and a greater variety of offerings in arts education" (Canadian Commission for UNESCO, 2005, p. 1). As in the United States, education is not a function of the federal government. It falls under the purview of the provincial and territorial governments. In Canada there is no federal ministry of education or integrated national education system.

By contrast, education in Mexico can be described "as a highly centralized system, regulated by the Secretariat of Public Education (Secretaría de Educación Pública, SEP), which establishes national educational policies at all school levels" (Gonzales-Moreno, 2015, p. 99). It is not as easy to proclaim that music education is on an upward path in Mexico, however, as there appears to be a wider variation in the quality of Mexican music programs in schools, depending on the type of school (state, federal, private) examined and the state in which the schools are located. For example, Gonzales-Moreno reports that it is a positive sign that there "are more music teacher educations programs in the country, and therefore more qualified teachers. However, in some federal schools, parents pay the cost of a music teacher. The majority [of schools] lack a music specialist, and classroom teachers are supposed to teach arts and music education" (personal communication, April 23, 2016).

Regardless of the current state of music education in Mexico, Canada, or the United States, there is more policy work to be done to make music education an accepted part of a well-rounded education. Benyon et al. (2005, p. 1) report that this is certainly true in Canada. There are individuals and institutions at work within Canada (and indeed throughout North America) with priorities, ideas, and values different from those of supporters of music and the arts. These individuals (some of whom are experts in a particular field and others who are laypersons) and institutions (some public, some private) have different aspirations, different organizational structures, and different funding/gifting patterns. Such diversity is also present among individuals and institutions that support music and the arts.

The priorities, ideas, and values of various institutions and individuals are aligned and realigned, influenced by time and place, into policy frameworks that seek to influence policy decision-making. Hope (2002) defines a *policy framework* as "a constellation of such forces and resources moving together or in parallel to fulfill a common purpose" (p. 5). Hope further observes:

> The influences of various policy frameworks are as complex as life itself, and as difficult to understand. It is easy to be blinded by simplicity, to get lost in complexity and to be so involved in one policy framework that the others are obscure, unreal or beyond reasonable engagement. All of these positions are dangerous.   (p. 5)

A *policy framework* might be conceptualized as the "lay of the land," the political environment, in which a policy was conceived. The *policy framework* surrounding the Every Student Succeeds Act (ESSA) (Public Law 114-95 [S.1177], 2015), recently passed legislation in the United States to be described in detail later in the chapter, like a rectangular frame surrounding a picture, could be conceptualized as having four sides: (1) special interest groups (the Music Education Policy Roundtable, the National Association for the Advancement of Colored People [NAACP], Partnership for 21st Century Skills [business interests], etc.); (2) politicians who are interested in accountability; (3) parents who are so concerned about overemphasis on testing in No Child Left Behind (NCLB) that they help their children "opt out" of high-stakes testing; and (4) state education decision makers, concerned about loss of control when it comes to educational decision-making. This "policy framework" united behind a common cause: Rewrite No Child Left Behind (NCLB)! Policy frameworks can be powerful and persuasive in terms of decision-making.

The purpose of this chapter is to examine several issues that emerge at the intersection of assessment policy and music education, as well as trends that impact these issues from a North American (delimited to Canadian, Mexican, and US) perspective. There are several key questions that arise at the point of this intersection: What issues in music education arise from assessment policy? How will trends in policymaking affect assessment in music education? After exploring several policy frameworks and types of policies that seem to be impacting music education, this chapter begins by positing a definition of assessment policy. Issues in music education that have arisen because of various explicit or implicit assessment policies form the body of the chapter content. The chapter then concludes with a discussion about trends in policymaking affecting assessment in music education.

Toward a Definition of
Assessment Policy

There are many viewpoints about what constitutes education policy in general and what constitutes assessment policy in education specifically. Evidently, the boundaries regarding just what is assessment policy are not clearly and distinctly drawn. It seems logical to begin the discussion of defining assessment policy by exploring the nature of policies in general and the concomitant, parental policy frameworks that wield powerful influences on policy decision-making.

The Nature of Policy and Its Frameworks

In its most basic form, a policy is an endorsed plan of what to do in particular situations. Governments, rulers, political parties, businesses, or individuals may formulate policies. Policies may be based theoretically on knowledge provided by research; but in practice, values, attitudes and opinions often are also part of the decision-making process. Some policies are based simply on tradition. Policies are often enacted to enable the realization of long-term goals or objectives.

Because, as presented previously, effective policies are based in place and time, policies must change to be effective. Who is responsible for change in education policy, including assessment policy? In the United States, education is primarily a function of each of its states. It was a sentence in the 10th Amendment to the US Constitution that solidified concept of education as a state function: "The powers not delegated to the United *States* by the Constitution, nor prohibited by it to the *States*, are *reserved* to the *States* respectively, or to the *people*." In fact, the federal government is prohibited from direct control over the curriculum and management of schools, not only by the 10th Amendment, but by the Elementary/Secondary Education Act and the Arts and Humanities Act establishing the two endowments, the National Endowment for the Arts (NEA) and the National Endowment for the Humanities (NEH), as well (Hope, 2002, p. 6). So, the states ultimately have statutory authority for education; but in practice, it is the local school boards who determine how allocated monies are to be spent and what is to be taught in US public schools. The primary impact of federal education policy is its influence on state and local policy through funding, as observed in the Department of Education's Race to the Top competitive grant competition (US Department of Education, 2010), which was in large part responsible for a renewed emphasis on teacher evaluation and the concomitant measurement of student achievement.

In Canada, the federal government has relatively little responsibility for education. Elementary and secondary education in Canada, as in the United States, is the responsibility of a smaller subdivision, the province, which in many respects is similar to a

US state. There are 10 provinces in Canada, and each has different educational policies. The Canadian provinces perhaps fund their schools more generously than in either Mexico or in the United States (Herman, 2013).

In contrast to the United States and Canada, there is a national curriculum mandated by the Secretariat of Public Education in Mexico. Helper, Levine, and Woodruff (2006), however, report the education in Mexico was decentralized by changing policies in 1992, giving the states more responsibility in the education system. This decentralization, however, was more financial than it was operational (Fierro-Evans, Tapia-García, & Rojo-Pons, 2009, p. 4). What is offered in Mexican schools, however, seems to vary greatly between public and private schools, between state and federal schools, and often between states across the country.

While government's impact on policy decisions affecting education and music education is robust, it is not ubiquitous. There are a number of nongovernmental policy frameworks that rival government in their influence in educational policy matters. Consider publishing companies, for example, who have much to gain from policies requiring assessment of basic skills at certain levels of education; large corporations seeking a workforce who have mastered reading, writing, and mathematics; or civil rights groups concerned about biases in mandated assessment measurement tools.

As referenced in the previous examples and in the introductory materials to this chapter, there are indeed a large number of policy frameworks with fundamentally different priorities, ideas, and values. Competition and ideological differences often emerge among these policy frameworks, particularly in policy discussions. Policy discussions involving music education interests are not immune to such disagreements. Superintendents and principals who see music performances as public relations tools rather than celebrations of excellence of the learning that has occurred in the music classroom might be at odds with dedicated music educators over policies regarding the number of athletic contests that need to be supported by the pep band. Business leaders in the community might come to a school board meeting demanding that cocurricular outings such as district music festivals or contests be suspended and that those funds saved be diverted to offset costs for purchasing computers for all secondary students. District curriculum specialists concerned about math and reading assessment scores that will be reported to the public via the Internet may be reluctant to support policies limiting the number of days that students in music and other "nontested" subjects can be excused from class to prepare for high-stakes reading or math assessments.

Music educators cannot necessarily change these policy frameworks, but they can act with more knowledge and political astuteness as to how various policy frameworks ideas might impact their ability to achieve their goal of a comprehensive, sequential music education for all students taught by qualified music specialists. With the emerging prominence of the STEM culture and high-powered technology industry thinking about education, failure to build new bridges with those outside of music, for example, may result in fewer opportunities for students to encounter music in their schools.

Assessment Policy Types

The concept of policies might further be refined and developed through understanding various types of policies. Barresi and Olson (1992) simply divided policy into two basic types—"explicit policy, which is formally stated and clearly defined, and implicit policy, which occurs 'where the absence of specific policy, in effect, constitutes a policy or where the behavior of decision makers or administrators alters the stated goals or implementation strategies of policy' (Pankratz, 1989)" (p. 761). They further subdivided *explicit policy* into three subsets—*imposed policy, endorsed policy*, and *advocated policy* and implicit policy types into two subsets—*adjusted policy* and *resultant effects*.

Explicit Policy Types

According to Mayer and Greenwood (p. 14), cited in Barresi and Olson,

> the effectiveness and feasibility of an explicit policy is related to the effects of the policy on its constituency. Compliance, therefore, is a major determinant of policy success or failure, and the relative power of the policymaker is related directly to the ability to require compliance.   (1992, p. 761)

Therefore, te three explicit policy types—*imposed policy, endorsed policy*, and *advocated policy*—are based on the policy maker's ability to demand compliance.

Imposed policies include the authority to require conformity with a policy under the penalty of some kind of sanction, usually economic or professional. Institutions that often make imposed policies affecting education are the federal government, state departments of education, and the courts. An example of imposed policy from the United States involves the Artist-in-Education program, a program designed to accomplish the policy initiatives of the NEA by placing artists in schools to teach by demonstrating their art. Federal funding, administered by state arts agencies, supports this program. Program policies are enforced through the possibility of removal of these funds, thereby making these Artist-in-Education policies an example of an imposed policy. Likewise, the granting of licensure for teaching by state departments of education in the United States, provincial governments or a provincial College of Teachers in Canada, or one of the state ministries of education in Mexico is an example of imposed policy administration. Teachers must complete certain courses and engage in a certain number of hours of field experiences in schools as part of a state-approved teacher education program. Failure of music teacher education programs in institutions of higher education to comply with state teacher education imposed policies could result nonlicensed, unemployable graduates.

Endorsed policies also require conformity with policy rules and regulations, but the penalties imposed for noncompliance often involve failure to receive some benefit from the policy-making institution, rather than the economic or professional sanctions characteristic of imposed policies. An example of the endorsed policy type in the United States involves the accreditation policies of the National Association of Schools of Music (NASM). The NASM has explicit policy related to the courses of study in music education programs. Currently, the following proportional standards are listed for music education programs seeking NASM approval: music studies (at least 50%), general studies (30%–35%) and professional education (15%–20%); and the NASM *Handbook* further describes desirable attributes, professional competencies, and professional procedures to be used in the preparation of music educators seeking to be licensed to teach (NASM, 2015, pp. 116–118). Teams of evaluators are sent to departments and schools of music to monitor compliance with these policies. Failure to comply with NASM policies for accreditation will not directly result in lost revenue or the inability to recommend music education graduates for licensure (characteristics of imposed policy sanctions); but noncompliance could result in the withholding of the designation of an NASM-approved program, thus making recruiting more challenging. Because NASM policies may result in failure to receive the benefit of NASM program approval, the NASM accreditation policy would be classified as an endorsed policy type.

Advocated policy, by contrast to both imposed policy and endorsed policy, has no sanctioning power to enforce its guidelines; compliance with advocated policy is completely voluntary. Barresi and Olson (1992) suggest that those who make advocated policy may not see "themselves as policymakers but rather as leaders in educational thought and action who look to and rely on their constituency for the implementation of ideas" (p. 761). Nevertheless, it seems that if the guidelines of a body are developed systematically and call for consistency in a course for action, they constitute policy. Recently the National Executive Board (NEB) of the National Association for Music Education (NAfME) in the United States endorsed the National Core Arts Standards (National Coalition for Core Arts Standards, 2014), which include the voluntary recommended use of Model Cornerstone Assessments (MCAs) as templates to determine whether the Performance Standards of the Core Arts Standards are being met. The NAfME NEB has no sanctioning power to encourage adoption and use of the National Core Arts Standards or its MCAs that recommend a process-oriented approach to curriculum and assessment. Yet because there is substantial philosophical agreement among NAfME members regarding the purpose and function of music education in the schools, and because the number and influence of NAfME members in most states is robust, the tenets of the Core Arts Standards, endorsed by the NEB, are finding their way into many state's arts standards. This is an example of advocated policy at work.

Implicit Policy Types

Implicit policies, much more subtle and far less specific than explicit policies, are of two types—*adjusted policy* and *resultant effects*. *Adjusted policy*, according to Barresi and Olson (1992), "refers to a new policy resulting from alteration of an explicit policy by its formulators. Such alteration, often covert, may occur in stated goals or in implementation strategies that result in an adjusted policy that is active but unstated" (p. 761). Drawing on examples from US policy, the alterations to the Adequate Yearly Progress stipulations of No Child Left Behind through subsequent waiver policies would constitute an example of adjusted policy.

Resultant effects, on the other hand, do not have a stated policy, neither an initial policy nor an adjusted policy that actually exists. *Resultant effects* are "policy-like initiatives that occur as a covert consequence of the imposition of an explicit policy causing constituents to take action in response" (Barresi & Olson, 1992, p. 762). Again, from US policy, the elimination of the definition of "highly qualified teacher" in the ESSA is an example of policy with *resultant effects*. Some states, Michigan, for example, are concerned that without a definition of "highly qualified teacher," from the federal level, doors might be opened for noncertified teachers to lead music instruction in schools.

Defining *Assessment Policy*

Having established a general understanding of the meaning of policies in consideration of the diverse, powerful policy frameworks that seek to influence policy decision-making and with reference to various explicit and implicit policy types, it is now appropriate to consider the nature and meaning of assessment policy specifically. A good working knowledge of what assessment policy is and what it is not should deepen understanding of the issues for music education arising from such assessment policies.

First, it should be recognized that there is considerable confusion surrounding the many assessment terms that Herman and Baker (2009) call "the assessment argot." They suggest, without considering any psychometric terms (e.g., item analysis, alphas, congruent validity, etc.), that the overlapping meanings of common assessment terms may cause miscommunication among stakeholders in various policy frameworks, and a presumed policy consensus in the assessment policy arena may not be consensus at all. As an example, Herman and Baker point to the confusion and overlapping meanings surrounding the term "assessment" itself:

> Assessment, test, measure, instrument, examination, metric? Tests or assessments are instruments used to collect and provide information; they are composed of measures that can be numerically summarized. Summarized quantitatively, singly, or in simple or weighted combination, assessment results can be used to produce an indicator. A metric is an indicator divided by some other variable, such as time or cost. Although the term "test" often connotes more traditional kinds of measures (multiple-choice or short-answer items, easily hand-scored or machine-scored), and assessment a wider array of task and item types, we use the two terms interchangeably.   (p. 176)

There are other examples of overlapping meanings in the "assessment argot." Even distinctions between terms such as "norm-referenced" and "criterion-referenced" seem muddled in today's world.

For purposes of this chapter, the term "assessment," however, has very broad parameters. Often writers make distinctions among the terms "measurement," "assessment," and "evaluation." *Measurement* can be understood to refer to the use of some kind of testing device to gather quantitative or qualitative data. For example, a quantitative measurement tool to determine the student's ability to read compound rhythmic notation correctly might involve the composition of a 16-measure rhythm pattern to be read at sight—one point per measure; a qualitative measurement tool might involve the use of a rubric to select the most accurate verbal description of students' phrasing choices and tone quality execution for a song or piece of music. *Assessment,* on the other hand, simply involves the determination of growth. It typically involves measurement from two points in time—a teacher may use the quantitative rhythmic measurement tool described above to *assess* a student's rhythmic reading ability before the use of a pre-scribed rhythmic reading system and after study/practice with such a system. The assessment might reveal that the student increased his/her score by 15 points between the times the two measurements were taken. Assessment simply involves determining whether growth has occurred—nothing more or less. When a standard is applied to an assessment, the teacher has engaged in *evaluation*. So, the teacher might determine that if a student's score on the second assessment is 5 points above or below the mean score, that student would be evaluated as performing "at level" and would be given the grade (evaluation mark) of C. In this evaluation of the student's work, the teacher applied an arbitrary, fixed standard to the growth of plus or minus 5 points from the mean to arrive at a grade, an appraisal (evaluation) of the student's rhythmic reading ability. For purposes of this chapter, the word "assessment" in the term "assessment policy" is understood to encompass all of the parameters of the terms "measurement," "assess-ment," and "evaluation." In other words, an assessment policy examined in this chapter could involve measurement, assessment, and/or evaluation.

Secondly, the multiplicities of the purpose of assessment add to the complexity of defining the term "assessment policy." Historically, the purposes of assessment have centered on diagnosis, accountability, and communication. The music education pro-fession has been about the business of assessment almost since its inception (Seashore, Lewis, & Saetveit, 1919). More attention, however, has been given to the diagnostic function of identifying students' music aptitude (measuring students' capability to learn music, as opposed to measuring what has been learned [achievement]), or what Brophy (2000) terms "enabling competencies and fundamental aural discriminations" (pp. 88–92). Whether aptitude or achievement are being measured/assessed, relatively little instructional time is been devoted to these activities in either general music classes or performance-based classes, perhaps because educators believe that music is all process or because they believe that their classes/ensembles—recorders, choruses, bands, orchestras—are continually being assessed in public performances or by outside adjudicators in contests or festivals. (In some US states, contest ratings count for value added growth!) Hours upon hours are devoted to the assessment and selection of students for honors ensembles in a fair and equitable manner, however. At the collegiate level, the NASM holds music programs accountable to certain accreditation standards. Assessment is also used by the music education profession to communicate and reassure the public (music students' parents in particular) that quality music education is occur-ring in the district. Although some music educators would disagree with presenting superior contest ratings as evidence of quality music instruction, others would approve of this use of this outside expert evidence to ascertain quality, for example.

Perhaps, however, in reality the scenario surrounding assessment's purposes is much more complex than simply the diagnosis, accountability, and communication purposes of assessment resulting from the acquisition of technical data. Testing/assessments do provide technical data in the form of scores that can inform decision makers pondering policy decisions, but this data also carries additional consequences and meanings. A case in point: In Nebraska, as well as in many other states in the United States, schools are now required to test students' reading and writing achievement. The results of these tests are reported to individual students and their parents, and these data are then aggregated at the school, district, and state levels and reported publicly in newspapers, the news media, and on the Nebraska Department of Education website. The publicized purpose of this test is to certify that students can read and write at levels the state has determined are expected of students at specific grades in school, in theory, to assure that the students are developing proficiencies to be successful in life after their K-12 diploma is received. Because this test is mandated, those who make policy communicate that they are concerned that students be prepared to be successful in their adult lives, that they care about education, and that they are serious about holding teachers and schools accountable. Because reading and writing are perceived to be important to students in the future, the specter of "the test" is expected to motivate students to learn and to prepare for the test. Not only are the students themselves expected to be motivated but also the test ostensibly could motivate the students' parents to support their children's reading and writing development. Teachers too could be motivated to help students succeed on the test, by modifying curricular content to the test content and format, purchase new instructional materials to aid reading/writing development, or to design practice tests to monitor student growth, and so forth. The scenario could hypothetically continue. The results of the tests might be used in a number of ways. Teachers might place students who do not pass the test in special classes or provide them with extra tutoring options. Those same test results might be aggregated at the school level and used to reinforce curriculum strengths or to make adjustments for weaknesses or to identify particular teachers who might benefit from selected professional development opportunities. Leaders at the district and state levels might be pondering similar curriculum, staffing, and equipment adjustments based on the aggregated reading/writing scores. This example illustrates the confounding of a test designed for a singular purpose and shows how a single test with a very specific purpose could spawn a series of related actions that go well beyond a test's initial, singular purpose.

Despite the confusion surrounding the "assessment argot" and the multiplicities of assessment purposes, it is both necessary and possible to bring together these complexities of assessment with a general understanding of policy to operationally define assessment policy for educational contexts. *Assessment policy*, for purposes of this chapter, will be defined as any set of principles or guidelines constructed for the purpose of bringing consistency and fairness to a course of action involving measurement, evaluation, or growth related to any dimension of an individual's learning.

Issues for Music Education Arising from Assessment Policy

Assessment policies often create issues for a discipline in their attempt to bring consistency and fairness to a course of action. Issues for assessment in music education that have arisen because of various explicit or implicit policies are examined in this section. In addition to naming and explaining the specific issues, possible policy modifications or new policies that would alleviate problems from music educators' points of view are suggested. The issues examined in this section concern the assessment aspects of policies surrounding the status of music as a basic/core subject essential for a well-rounded education and the jurisdiction for the teacher certification process.

Policies Surrounding Music as a Basic/Core/ Well-Rounded Subject

The battle for music to become one of the subjects recognized as important enough to be emphasized in the curriculum like reading and math is a clash that has echoed throughout North America for several decades. Governali (1983) reported that the emphasis on student needs and interests; humanness; and the "whole child," so prevalent in the 1960s and 1970s, were replaced in the 1980s (and three decades that followed) by "a return to a time when schools were primarily interested in the so-called academic areas and their goals revolved around the 3 R's."[2] (p. 564). The academic subjects, areas deemed most important to a child's education, were termed variously: *basic* subjects, *core* subjects, *STEM* subjects, and most recently *well-rounded* subjects. Although space limitations do not permit a detailed discussion of the rise of the arts and music education to the status of a well-rounded subject, equal, at least in statute to the 3 R's, suffice it to say that music is now designated as a well-rounded subject in Mexico, Canada, and the United States.

In Ontario, Canada, the Ministry of Education (2014) describes the province's vision for their students (tomorrow's leaders): "They will be *well-rounded* [emphasis added] individuals who have not only strong basic skills but also the critical thinking skills, imagination and resilience to excel in—and create—the new jobs of tomorrow" (p. 19). Gonzales-Moreno (2015) describes the current policies in Mexico designating music as a well-rounded subject:

> The value and importance of music and arts education in a well-rounded formation of all children has been acknowledged within national educational policies, which at the same time provide opportunities and impose challenges to novice and experienced music teachers. In the previous Presidential term of office (sexenium), the Federal Government, through its National Development Plan (PDN, Plan Nacional de Desarrollo 2007–2012), proposed "to promote a well-rounded education in which

opportunities for students to participate in arts education would be increased in schools, as a means of enhancing students' development as human beings" (Presidencia de la República, 2007, p. 225). While this statement promoted the provision of a quality arts education, it was not fully operationalized. Yet, it permeated the possibility of advocating for the public acknowledgment about the role of arts and music educators within the education system.   (p. 112)

In the United States, ESSA specifically names music as a well-rounded subject. This US legislation is used here to highlight some of the issues for music education that arise as a result of some of the assessment policies that accompany legislation that designates well-rounded subjects.

Background for ESSA

To understand the potential issues for assessment in music education that could arise because of assessment policies embedded in legislation that designates well-rounded subjects, a brief historical journey is warranted. Remembering that in the United States, education is fundamentally a state function, perhaps the most far-reaching federal legislation affecting education ever passed by the United States Congress was Public Law 89-10, the Elementary and Secondary Education Act (ESEA) of 1965. The ESEA is an extensive statute that emphasizes equal access to education, establishes high standards, requires accountability, and provides federal funding to implement its goals. Since its enactment in 1965, the government has typically reauthorized the Act every 5 years. The reauthorization of ESEA by President George W. Bush, Public Law 107–110, was known as the No Child Left Behind Act (NCLB) of 2001. Many provisions of this imposed policy were unpopular, including adequate yearly progress (AYP), the barometer by which the law required states to measure how public schools and school districts performed academically as determined by each state's mandated tests.

In 2007, NCLB (ESEA) was supposed to be reauthorized, but political problems surrounding the law abounded. In the absence of a reauthorized ESEA, the Department of Education, under the leadership of Arne Duncan, exercised its authority to try to improve education through a 4.35-billion-dollar competitive grant program—Race to the Top (RTTP). This competitive grant program could be characterized as imposed policy because there were financial penalties for those states not meeting RTTP policy guidelines (US Department of Education, 2010). The RTTP selection criteria (policy guidelines) that involved assessment included developing and implementing common, high-quality standards and assessments. Further, with respect to teacher evaluation, student achievement was required to be a "significant" part of any teacher evaluation system. A number of models were conceptualized based on the policy criterion (Nierman, 2012). Meanwhile, in the fall of 2011, the Obama administration announced that it would offer waivers to states from certain requirements of NCLB in return for their assent to implement certain reform measures, several of which were related to assessment: the adoption of the Common Core Standards for college and career readiness and the creation of guidelines for teacher evaluation that included student performance.

ESSA and Assessment Policy

This is the environment in which ESSA was birthed and signed into law by President Obama in the fall of 2015. In addition to a provision that names *music* specifically as a subject needed for a well-rounded education (Public Law 114-95 [S.1177], 2015, December, Sec 8002, p. 2980). There are several policies in ESSA that pertain to assessment, more specifically, that pertain to teacher evaluation and assessing student achievement.

The federal mandate on teacher evaluation linked to student growth and test scores, a stipulation of the waiver agreement policies in 2011, has been eliminated under ESSA. States may use federal funds to continue such programs, but they are not required to do so. In fact, ESSA permits states to change their teacher evaluation strategies entirely. States will, however, no longer be required to include these policies as a condition of federal funding. The NAfME's Christopher Woodside, Deputy Executive Director, Center for Advocacy, Policy and Constituency Engagement, observes:

> This [the elimination of teacher evaluation linked to student growth and test scores] is such a significant element of ESSA that the law now contains explicit language prohibiting the U.S. Secretary of Education from mandating any aspect of a teacher evaluation system, or even from mandating that a state conduct the evaluation altogether (S. 1177, Sec 1111(e)(1)(B)(iii)(IX); and (X), section 2101(e); & section 8401(d)(3)). Without drawing much attention to itself, however, ESSA continues a separate, competitive funding program, entitled the "Teacher and School Leader Incentive Fund," which allows states, school districts, non-profits, and/or for profits, in partnership with a state or school district, to apply for competitive grants aimed at implementing teacher evaluation systems as a means of trying to learn more about effective and equitable ways of linking student performance to teacher performance (S. 1177, Secs. 2211 & 2212).   (personal communication, April 10, 2016)

This would seem to be an example of an endorsed, explicit policy, because the entities that do not apply fail to receive a benefit from the policymaking institution. Further, an adjusted policy in ESSA eliminates the definition of a "highly qualified" teacher that was included in NCLB. States are now free to define "highly qualified" themselves.

In the area assessing PreK-12 student achievement, the ESSA legislation is largely silent, with one exception—in Title II of the legislation, policy states that school districts may use Title II funding to aid teachers and principals in better understanding how to work with, *assess*, and generally meet the needs of students through age 8 (S. 1177, Sec 2103(G)(ii)). This is consistent with the Obama administration's emphasis on early childhood education.

Issues as ESSA and Music Education Intersect

There are several issues that may arise for music education as a result of ESSA policy stipulations. One such issue involves the use of student growth measures as a part of teacher evaluation, and the other involves funding for assessment through Title II of ESSA.

There are a number of music educators in the United States who are celebrating the fact that the newly reauthorized ESEA (ESSA) no longer mandates that teacher evaluation be linked to individual student growth and test scores, although required testing still exists annually in the STEM subjects. In fact, states can change their teacher evaluation strategies entirely. Many in the profession feel that the group evaluation that occurs at contests and festivals is sufficient to provide evidence of the teacher's effectiveness.

Music educators at the K-12 level should not be so quick to "make merry," however. Many states already have built into state statutes and policies the measurement of the individual student's growth and the use of that evidence as a significant factor in teacher evaluation. The ESSA policies on teacher evaluation do not negate such policies at the state level. Further, philosophically, it is in the best interests of the music education to assess the individual's growth, just as is often mandated in the STEM subjects. Yes, music may be named in fact as one of the subjects necessary for a well-rounded education; but the profession has a long road ahead to have music accepted by some decision makers and the public at large as a subject that truly is central to a well-balanced education. One definition of the law is that it is the minimum legal ethic that society will accept. Placing the discipline of music outside of the parameters of the other subjects with respect to individual assessment does not move the case that music belongs in the list of well-rounded subjects forward in the United States, Mexico, or Canada.

If individual assessment is to be an important component of music education, then from where is the funding to come to develop such measures and to provide professional development to use the measurement tools appropriately? Music educators in the United States can take heart from the fact that by virtue of music being a part of a well-rounded education, music programs in school districts may use Title II funding to aid teachers in better understanding how to work with, *assess*, and generally meet the needs of students through age 8. So, there could be monies available for the development of diagnostic music assessment tools and professional development in this area, according to S.1177 in the United States. Yes, the funding only applies to the education of primary children now, but that funding does represent a beachhead that could lead to future funding for upper elementary and secondary students' individual music assessment.

Summary

In brief, the *resultant effect*, a type of implicit policy, of ESSA is that it largely places authority for many important education decisions, including teacher evaluation, back at the state level. Some in the United States would say that this was the intent of the writers of the US Constitution; education should be a state function.

Teacher Certification

Another area in which assessment policies and music education intersect in North America involves teacher certification, both for teacher educators and preservice teacher education students who are part of traditional teacher education preparation programs and for those who are part of alternative certification programs. The route to certification through traditional programs is widely known and similar across North America. As described by Waziak (2015), most programs include some combination of academic courses in music (e.g., music theory, history, musicianship, studio and ensemble performance, conducting) along with professional studies in education (e.g., curriculum and instruction, assessment, educational psychology, practicum). Alternative certification routes seem to be more prevalent in the United States than in Canada or Mexico and are much less similar, even among states in the United States. Feistritzer's (2005) description of the alternative certification landscape in the United States is still accurate: Demand for teachers, particularly in large cities and in rural areas, drives many teachers to enter the profession through alternative certification routes. Not only are alternative programs designed specifically to meet the needs of schools in these areas but also they are designed to meet the specific needs of prospective teachers who come from other careers and with considerable life experiences. The assessment policies that govern the granting of a license to teach via alternative teacher certification programs are often complex and vary greatly from state to state, province to province. Nevertheless, teachers who are prepared to teach music through nontraditional programs are becoming more commonplace. According to Feistritzer's (2011) demographic analysis of teachers in the United States, "One-third of first-time public school teachers hired since 2005 entered the profession through an alternative program other than a college campus-based teacher education program" (p. ix).

Background

Traditional teacher education programs in North America typically are based in colleges or universities and are organized in one of two ways. In one model, preservice teachers typically earn a bachelor's degree in a subject (music), followed by additional coursework that may take the form of a postbaccalaureate credential or master's degree. In a more prevalent model, preservice teachers study a subject (music) and the ways of teaching that subject concurrently, leading to a bachelor's degree. (It should be noted that in Canada and particularly in Mexico [less so in the United States], those teaching music in PreK-12 schools may or may not be music specialists.)

Simply put, alternative teacher certification is a process by which an individual can receive a license to teach without having completed a traditional teacher education program. Alternative certification seems to be a concept unique to the United States on the North American continent. It began around 1980 in response to a proliferation of emergency certification practices designed to supply the market with needed teachers. Graduates with bachelor's degrees in a particular subject (without teaching coursework) were seen as already having completed a large part of the traditional teacher preparation program. Therefore, alternative certification programs began as a way to educate people who had already earned a 4-year degree and wanted to become teachers. These programs get prospective teachers into the classroom early, usually as a full-time teacher, earning a salary, while working with experienced teachers. While alternative certification requirements differ from state to state, there are certain characteristics of these programs that are similar:

- Routes specifically designed to recruit, prepare, and license talented individuals who already had at least a bachelor's degree—and often other careers—in fields other than education.
- Rigorous screening processes, such as passing tests, interviews, and demonstrated mastery of content.
- Field-based programs.
- Coursework or equivalent experiences in professional education studies before and while teaching.
- Work with mentor teachers and/or other support personnel.
- High performance standards for completion of the programs. (National Center for Alternative Certification, 2006, para. 18)

Jurisdiction for Teacher Certification and Assessment Policies

Just as alternative certification is unique to the United States, so one of the major issues arising at the intersection of teacher certification and assessment policy—required exit or bar exams—is uniquely American. Whether preservice teaching candidates are educated in a traditional or an alternative certification program in the United States, most state certification policies are imposed policies, requiring a minimum score to be achieved on a standardized exit or bar exam that measures teaching knowledge and/or skills. This score, established by policy, sets a standard—a bar—for entering the profession. Just as in the legal profession, states can to set their own minimum passing scores for their teacher licensure exams. Therefore, testing requirements can and do vary from state to state. In California, for example, teacher candidates must pass the California Basic Education Skills Test (CBEST). Texas, however, uses two test batteries that are unique to the state: the Texas Examinations of Educator Standards (TExES) and the Texas Examinations for Master Teachers (TExMaT).

In the United States, there are a several national standardized teacher examinations that are specified in policy to be used as "teacher bar exams" in various states across the country. Among the most widely used exams typically encountered by preservice music educators are the Praxis Subject Assessments (formerly Praxis II) and the edTPA (Teacher Performance Assessment). (The National Evaluation System [Pearson Education Incorporated, 2016b], a new computer-based program administered by Pearson Education, that measures the knowledge and qualification of potential teachers, including music teachers, is available; but it is used less frequently.)

The Praxis Subject Assessments are administered by the Educational Testing Service (ETS) and used by over 40 states as a criterion for professional licensing decisions. These assessments (ETS, 2016) measure knowledge of specific subjects that K-12 educators will teach, as well as general and subject-specific teaching skills and knowledge. They are delivered via computer and are administered through an international network of test centers. In music, there are two different examinations available: *Music: Content: The*

Praxis Study Companion 5113 (ETS, n.d. a) with content in four categories (music history and literature; theory and composition; performance; and pedagogy, professional issues, and technology) and *Music: Content and Instruction: The Praxis Study Companion 5114* (ETS, n.d. b) with content also in four categories (music history and theory; performance; instruction, professional issues, and technology; and instructional activities).

Stanford University faculty and staff at the Stanford Center for Assessment, Learning, and Equity (SCALE) and the American Association of Colleges for Teacher Education (AACTE) formed a partnership to develop and share edTPA, formerly the Teacher Performance Assessment. Later Stanford University engaged the Evaluation Systems, Group of Pearson Education, as an operational partner to help with the distribution and scoring of the edTPA. The edTPA (2017) evaluation tool was designed to

> give teacher preparation programs access to a multiple-measure assessment system aligned to state and national standards—including Common Core State Standards and the Interstate Teacher Assessment and Support Consortium (InTASC)—that can guide the development of curriculum and practice around the common goal of making sure new teachers are able to teach each student effectively and improve student achievement.   (AACTE, n.d., para. 2)

Further, "It [edTPA] is designed to evaluate how teacher candidates plan and teach lessons in ways that make the content clear and help diverse students learn, assess the effectiveness of their teaching, and adjust teaching as necessary" (para. 3), and "includes a review of a teacher candidate's authentic teaching materials as the culmination of a teaching and learning process that documents and demonstrates each candidate's ability to effectively teach subject matter to all students" (para. 4).

Further, the edPTA is described by its authors as being a subject-specific assessment, and there is a handbook available for K-12 performing arts (Pearson Education Incorporated, 2016a) to assist preservice teachers in their preparation of edTPA materials. Institutions in 35 states and the District of Columbia at different levels are currently using the edTPA.

Policies establishing guidelines for bar exams such as the Praxis Subject Assessments and the edTPA in teacher licensure are perhaps more critical for alternative certification programs than for traditional programs because these programs often accelerate the time needed to complete certification and require less formal educational experiences, with fewer formative and summative assessments in formal courses. There are some state policies, for example, that grant certification in a new subject area on the basis of Subject Assessment (Praxis II) scores alone, provided the candidate has previously been endorsed in another subject. Thus a teacher endorsed to teach English could also be granted a license to teach music on the basis of an acceptable Praxis II score alone.

Issues as Certification Policies and Music Education Intersect

The central question raised by imposed certification policies that require a standardized bar exam before the granting of licensure is: Who should be ultimately responsible for evaluating the teaching candidates? Music teacher educators, in partnership with cooperating teachers (and now sometimes mentor teachers and/or other support personnel alone in alternative licensure programs) have long been the final arbitrators of who is ready to enter the teaching profession. Student-teaching/field-based work is conceptualized by most teacher educators in traditional or alternative settings as the culminating experience in a music teacher education program because it is the arena in which their students can demonstrate authentically their ability to apply theory and life experiences to practice, that is, demonstrate their ability to teach successfully.

When certification policies, mandated exit exams, demonstration of successful student-teaching/field-based experiences no longer became the final bar for licensure. It is possible that a student could have an acceptable grade point average and/or successful field-based experiences, and still not be recommended to teach because of failure to meet state-mandated Praxis Subject Assessments or edTPA cut scores mandated by state teacher certification policies.

Music teachers educators are concerned that when policy shifts the burden of proof for readiness to enter the teaching profession from local professionals who are familiar with the preservice teacher's knowledge and skills from multiple modes of demonstration in multiple, diverse settings over an extended period of time to a single outsourced, corporate, computer-based assessment (Praxis) or portfolio-based evidence from a single setting to be assessed by outside evaluators (edTPA), the validity and reliability of the assessment process are compromised. There is no compelling evidence to suggest that the edTPA as used in arts classrooms is either valid or reliable (Parkes & Powell, 2014). Further, test results must now be reported by subgroups. The research of Elpus (2015, 2016) suggests that there may be biases in the Praxis Music Subject Assessments. In his research, Elpus examined the scores of 20,521 individuals who took either the Praxis Music: Content Knowledge or Music: Content and Instruction tests from 2007 to 2012 and found that

> Praxis II score[s] were significantly associated with race, sex, and other demographic characteristics. Analyses indicated that White candidates earned significantly higher Praxis II scores than did Black candidates and that male candidates earned significantly higher scores that did female candidates.   (Elpus, 2015, p. 314)

Thus some of the very minorities that the profession is desperately trying to recruit are completing requirements through either traditional or alternative music teacher certification programs, only to be denied licensure because of substandard Praxis scores.

A second issue concerning teacher certification policies requiring bar exams for licensure also involves questions of validity: Is performance on a standardized test alone sufficient (valid) evidence on which to predict the success of the teacher education candidate in schools? Should authorities grant certification in a new subject area on the basis of bar exam scores alone, provided the candidate has previously been endorsed in another subject area, for example? Space limitations do not permit a thorough examination of this issue, but suffice it to say that a single measurement tool without documented predictive or congruent validity is questionable as a source for high stakes decisions.

TRENDS IN POLICYMAKING
AFFECTING ASSESSMENT
IN MUSIC EDUCATION

Having examined some current issues at the intersection of policy with music education, we conclude with an exploration of several trends in policymaking affecting assessment in music education. Among the trends to be examined are the decreasing federal government involvement in education, the extending of educational agendas across boundary lines, and the growing power of arts advocacy groups.

Decreasing Federal Government Involvement

After years of expansion, US federal government involvement in education since the turn of the century as evidenced by NCLB, the President's Committee on the Arts and Humanities activities (Dwyer, 2011), and RTTP, this trend seems to be in reverse. ESSA, for example, could be seen as a firm reaction (some might even say an overreaction) to a national perception that NCLB and RTTP policies went too far in their educational dictates to states. The elimination of the federal mandate on teacher evaluation linked to student growth and test scores, a stipulation of the waiver agreement policies in 2011, is one example. Another example is the elimination of the concept of AYP from the NCLB legislation.

ESSA not only eliminated AYP but also shuns federal involvement in other areas, including NCLB waivers and rewards attached to implementing the Common Core. In fact, ESSA goes so far as to include a lengthy list of stipulations specifying areas in which the secretary of education may *not* be involved. The demise of teacher evaluation linked to student growth and tests scores mentioned earlier is one of those now forbidden areas.

Further, ESSA policies reducing the federal government's involvement in testing in general has, no doubt, been influenced by the public's concern about the extensive amount of time devoted to previously required high-stakes testing of K-12 students in the STEM subjects and their concern about basing decisions affecting their children's future on measurement tools with questionable validity. Prior to 2015, it was the Obama administration's vision to test students across the country on a common set of exams in math and English. As a result of what was termed the Common Core Standards Initiative (National Governors Association Center for Best Practices & Council of Chief State School Officers, 2010) and federal government policies, students in as many as 40 states took or were scheduled to take one of two standardized tests of Common Core objectives. Then came an outcry from state legislators, angry at spending money for a federally funded test, and from parents who saw the tests as a move toward a national curriculum. Many parents, at first from suburban schools, but later from a more diverse community base, participated in an antitesting movement labeled the "Opt-Out Movement" in which they held their children out of school on test days in protest of an experience they deemed harmful to their children. All of this unrest, along with other political frameworks, has led to the inclusion of policies in ESSA designed to return control of education to the states and the people. To date, however, little has been legislated about assessing all of these "forthcoming" well-rounded programs. The consequences—resultant effects—of this lack of existing policy means that if something is done, it will be done at the state level, where music educators are least prepared to wage a successful lobbying effort against well-organized, well-funded publishing and STEM interests. Decreasing federal government involvement in education is likely to continue in the United States.

Likewise, federal involvement in education seems to be reduced in Mexico. Rolwing (2006) reports that until the early 1990s, teacher education in Mexico was "under the direct control of the federal government, specifically through the offices of the *Secretaría de Educación Pública/SEP* (Secretariat of Public Education)....Since 1993, the SEP has gradually been devolving educational authority to the 31 state ministries of education, and now plays a role that is more supervisory than regulatory in nature" (para. 3). Again, it should be noted that these reductions are mostly financial in nature. The SEP still mandates a considerable number of educational policies.

Extension of Educational Agendas Across Boundaries

The Common Core Standards Initiative is an example of another trend in policymaking—the extension of educational agendas across state/province boundaries. This initiative was designed to establish consistent educational standards across the states as well as ensure that high school graduates were prepared to enter college or the workforce.

Another example of educational agenda extensions comes directly from assessment policy. Recently, Colorado has experimented with new competency-based assessment systems, based on similar efforts in New Hampshire, Georgia, California, and several other states. Colorado policy, for example, "allows districts to advance aggressively toward a competency-based system, but also allows others to continue to be time-based and credit-based in their structures" (Sturgis, 2013, para. 2). Thus it might be possible for a student to get a certain AP Math score and use this score as evidence of meeting minimum high school math graduation requirements in Colorado.

Likewise, experimenting with the use of social and emotional growth as a performance measure is another idea embodied in policy that is crossing state boundaries that has very exciting implications for the field of music education, because such growth is often cited as an outcome of music participation in the schools. "The reason for the interest (other than national backlash against high stakes testing) is that our system tends to provide instructional dollars for things that can be tested ('what's measured gets tested')," said Christopher Woodside, NAfME Deputy Executive Director. He continued:

> This focus on assessing non-cognitive skills has led to a fascinating and controversial experiment in the California CORE districts, where data related to such factors is being collected using the School Climate Assessments Instrument (SCAI) model and has interesting implications, given ESSA's new requirement that states permit at least one non-academic performance indicator in their accountability systems.
> (personal communication, April 10, 2016)

It may be in the end that such assessments will, by policy, be voluntary.

The Increasing Power of Music Education Advocacy Groups

A final trend in policymaking that affects assessment in music education to be considered here is one that forms a fitting conclusion to this chapter—the increasing power of *music education* advocacy groups. For some time, there have been three primary advocacy groups lobbying on behalf of *music* (and the other arts) that have had a presence on Capitol Hill in Washington, DC—Americans for the Arts, the League of Symphony Orchestras, and the National Association for Music Merchants (NAMM). These groups have advocated admirably for the needs of music education over the years, but they also have other interests that command the attention of their lobbyists. Other groups that have sought to influence policy affecting music education, particularly in the NCLB days, are the Arts Education Partnership (AEP) and the Arts Education Policy Working Group (which includes the Kennedy Center). These groups now have an influential new partner in their advocacy efforts. In June of 2012, a new group, the Music Education Policy Roundtable, was founded by NAfME, with the American String Teachers Association (ASTA) as the first Roundtable member. The Roundtable shield now represents 36 different organizations with musical interests unified under a single policy banner, working together in efforts to achieve a consensus set of federal legislative recommendations, on behalf of the music education profession and all of those who stand to benefit from its contributions to education.

While the number of such organizations has not grown significantly in North America, their power and prestige certainly has. Over 90% of the Roundtable organizations, for example, were not involved in music education advocacy 5 years ago. Today the united voices of this group are a powerful force on Capitol Hill in Washington. The Policy Roundtable joined with others to ensure that music would "stand by itself" not just as one of the arts, as a subject necessary for a well-rounded education in the ESSA legislation referenced earlier in the chapter. As ESSA regulatory policies are now being developed, the possibility of funding for professional development that could include the development of new measurement tools and assessment processes now exist because music is designated in the ESSA policies as necessary for a well-rounded education.

Expect music education advocacy groups to continue to grow in their ability to press for policies that will make it possible for new assessments to promote the musical growth of children and orchestrate success in their lives.

NOTES

1. The authors acknowledge the following persons, who assisted in providing information and resources for this chapter: Dr. Dale Bazan, University of Nebraska-Lincoln; Dr. Patricia A. Gonzales Moreno, University of Chihuahua; and Mr. Christopher Woodside, National Association for Music Education, United States.
2. Reading, writing, and mathematics.

REFERENCES

American Association of Colleges for Teacher Education. (n.d.). *About EdTPA*. Retrieved from http://edtpa.aacte.org/about-edtpa

Barresi, A., & Olson, G. (1992). The nature of policy and music education. In R. Colwell (Ed.), *The handbook of research on music teaching and learning* (pp. 760–772). New York, NY: Oxford University Press.

Benyon, C., Bowman, W., Lowe, A., Mathieu, L., Rose, A., & Veblen, K. (2005). *Music education in Canada: What is the state of the art?* London, Ontario, Canada: Canadian Music Education Research Cooperative.

Brophy, T. S. (2000). *Assessing the developing child musician: A guide for general music teachers*. Chicago, IL: GIA Publications.

Canadian Commission for UNESCO. (2005). *Learning to live, living to learn: Perspectives on arts education in Canada*. Ottawa, Canada: Author.

Doris, L. (Ed.). (1994). *The American way in taxation: Internal revenue, 1862–1963*. Buffalo, NY: Hein.

Dorn, C. (2003). Grammar school. In P. S. Fass (Ed.), *Encyclopedia of children and childhood in history and society*. Retrieved from http://www.encyclopedia.com/topic/Grammar_School.aspx

Dwyer, M. C. (2011). *Reinvesting in arts education: Winning America's future through creative schools*. Retrieved from https://eric.ed.gov/?id=ED522818

Educative Teacher Performance Assessment. (2017). Amherst, MA: Pearson Education.

Educational Testing Service. (2016). *Praxis subject assessments overview*. Retrieved from http://www.ets.org/praxis/about/subject/

Educational Testing Service. (n.d. a). *Music: Content: The praxis study companion 5113*. Retrieved from https://www.ets.org/s/praxis/pdf/5113.pdf

Educational Testing Service. (n.d. b). *Music: Content and instruction: The praxis study companion 5114*. Retrieved from https://www.ets.org/s/praxis/pdf/5114.pdf

Elpus, K. (2015). Music teacher licensure: Candidates in the United States; A demographic profile and analysis of licensure examination scores. *Journal of Research in Music Education, 63*, 314–335. doi: 10.1177/0022429415602470

Elpus, K. (2016, March). *Exploring racial gaps in Praxis II music test scores: Do institutional effects matter?* Paper presented at the National Association for Music Education Research and Teacher Education Conference. Atlanta, GA.

Feistritzer, C. E. (2005, September). *State policy trends for alternative routes to teacher certification: A moving target.* Paper presented at Conference on Alternative Certification: A Forum for Highlighting Rigorous Research, Washington, DC. Retrieved from http://citeseerx.ist.psu.edu/viewdoc/download?doi=10.1.1.420.25&rep=rep1&type=pdf

Feistritzer, C. E. (2011). *Profile of teachers in the U.S. 2011.* Washington, DC: National Center for Education Information. Retrieved from https://www.edweek.org/media/pot2011final-blog.pdf

Fierro-Evans, C., Tapia-García, G., & Rojo-Pons, F. (2009). *Descentralización educativa en México: Un recuento Analítico.* Retrieved from https://www.oecd.org/mexico/44906363.pdf

Gonzales-Moreno, P. (2015). Music teacher education in Mexico: Current trends and challenges. In S. Figueiredo, J. Soares, & R. Schambeck (Eds.), *The preparation of music teachers: A global perspective* (pp. 99–122). Porto Alegro, Brazil: Associação Nacional de Pesquisa Epós-Graduação em Música.

Governali, J. F. (1983). Health education and "Back to the Basics" movement. *Journal of School Health, 53,* 564–567. doi: 10.1111/j.1746-1561.1983.tb01157.x

Helper, S., Levine, D., & Woodruff, C. (2006). *How does economic liberalization affect investment in education? Evidence from Mexico.* Retrieved from ilar.ucsd.edu/assets/015/8804.pdf

Herman, J. L., & Baker, E. L. (2009). Assessment policy: Making sense of the babel. In G. Sykes, B. Schneider, & D. N. Plank (Eds.), *Handbook of education policy research* (pp. 176–190). New York, NY: Routledge.

Herman, S. (2013). *Canada's approach to school funding.* Washington, DC: Center for American Progress.

Hope, S. (2002). Policy frameworks, research, and K-12 schooling. In R. Colwell, & C. Richardson (Eds.), *The new handbook of research on music teaching and learning* (pp. 5–16). New York, NY: Oxford University Press.

National Association of Schools of Music. (2015). *Handbook 2015–16.* Reston, VA: Author.

National Center for Alternative Certification. (2006). *Alternative teacher certification: A state by state analysis.* Retrieved from http://web.archive.org/web/20061003233050/http://www.teach-now.org/overview.cfm

National Coalition for Core Arts Standards. (2014). *National core arts standards.* Retrieved from http://www.nationalartsstandards.org

National Governors Association Center for Best Practices, & Council of Chief State School Officers. (2010). *What is Common Core?* Retrieved from et2core.org/national/what-is-common-core/standards

Nierman, G. E. (2012). Toward a model for assessing teacher effectiveness. In W. L. Sims (Ed.), *Proceedings of the XXX World Congress of the International Society of Music Education, Thessaloniki, Greece* (pp. 281–288). Nedlands, Western Australia: International Society for Music Education.

Ontario Ministry of Education. (2014). *Achieving excellence: A renewed vision for education in Ontario.* Ontario, Canada: Queen's Printer for Ontario. Retrieved from http://www.adsb.on.ca/.../Schools/.../Achieving Excellence A Renewed Vision

Parkes, K. A., & Powell, S. R. (2014). Is the EdTPA the right choice for evaluating teacher readiness? *Arts Education Policy Review, 116,* 103–113. doi: 10.1080/10632913.2014.944964

Parsad, B., & Spiegelman, M. (2012). *Arts education in public elementary and secondary schools: 1999–2000 and 2009–10* (NCES 2012014REV). Retrieved from National Center for Education Statistics website: http://nces.ed.gov/pubsearch/pubsinfo.asp?pubid=2012014rev

Pearson Education Incorporated. (2016a). *K-12 performing arts handbook.* Retrieved from https://secure.aacte.org/apps/rl/resource.php?ref=edtpa

Pearson Education Incorporated. (2016b). *National evaluation series*. Retrieved from http://www.nestest.com/

Public Law 89-10—H.R.2362—Elementary and secondary education act. (1965). Retrieved from https://sites.google.com/site/publicedforparents/original-text-of-1965-esea-act

Public Law 107-110—An act to close the achievement gap with accountability, flexibility, and choice, so that no child is left behind. (2001). Retrieved from US Government Printing Office website: http://www.gpo.gov/fdsys/pkg/PLAW-107publ110/content-detail.html

Public Law 114-95 (S.1177). (2015, December). *Every student succeeds act*. Retrieved from https://www.congress.gov/bill/114th-congress/senate-bill/1177

Rolwing, K. (2006). Education in Mexico. *World Education News and Reviews, 19*(3), 1.

Seashore, C. E., Lewis, D., & Saetveit, J. G. (1919). *The Seashore measures of musical talents*. New York, NY: The Psychological Corporation.

Sturgis, C. (2013, June 28). *Competency education in Colorado takes a giant step forward* [Online resource]. Retrieved from https://www.competencyworks.org/reflections/competency-education-in-colorado-takes-a-giant-step-forward/

US Department of Education. (2010). *Race to the Top executive summary*. Retrieved from https://www.scribd.com/document/61483450/Race-to-the-Top-Executive-Summary

Waziak, E. (2015). The preparation of music teachers in Canada. In S. Figueiredo, J. Soares, & R. Schambeck (Eds.), *The preparation of music teachers: A global perspective* (pp. 67–98). Porto Alegro, Brazil: Associação Nacional de Pesquisa Epós-Graduação em Música.

CHAPTER 8

··

MUSIC ASSESSMENT IN AUSTRALIAN HIGHER EDUCATION

··

DON LEBLER

It is difficult to overstate the importance of assessment in any formal learning process, and this is true for music education. Informal learning of music can also be influenced by the feedback received by the learner and this feedback can be thought of as a form of assessment, though this has not been investigated as thoroughly as assessment in formal learning contexts. The substantial literature on assessment supports the view that assessment has a powerful influence on what and how students learn. As David Boud and Associates write:

> Assessment is a central feature of teaching and the curriculum. It powerfully frames how students learn and what students achieve. It is one of the most significant influences on students' experience of higher education and all that they gain from it. The reason for an explicit focus on improving assessment practice is the huge impact it has on the quality of learning.   (Boud & Associates, 2010, p. 1)

The assessment of musical performances is a characteristic of those music programs that intend to develop advanced musical performance skills in their graduates, so that particular kind of assessment is the focus of this chapter.

Higher music education is conducted in every state and territory in Australia in a range of institutions including 10 private for-profit and vocational education institutions (National Register of Higher Education Providers, 2016), though about 30 public universities provide a large majority of higher music education. When there is a focus on the development of high levels of performance ability, the European Conservatoire model is commonly adopted in Australia, with the associated emphasis on one-to-one performance tuition. There is considerable diversity in specializations, and while not all specializations are available in all institutions, the author's institution for example offers classical instrumental studies, vocal performance and opera, composition, pedagogy, jazz, new music, popular music, musical theater, music technology and electronic music along with a comprehensive range of postgraduate and research programs. As would be expected, assessment practices also vary between institutions, but recently, strengthened regulations have produced increased coherence in practices across the sector.

The regulatory context is important in any discussion about assessment, so this chapter describes the Australian regulatory environment before providing an account of assessment in music in the earlier stages of education. Assessment practices will be described and discussed in broad categories including both formative and summative practices, along with formal and informal feedback processes. The development of effective self-assessment abilities is included because it is essential for the continuation of independent learning. I also discuss the development of an appreciation of standards of achievement because this is necessary for self-assessment to be reliable, as is also the case for all other forms of assessment. These aspects of assessment are contextualized in the formal assessment of musical performances, group assessment, participatory assessment, and e-assessment as well as the informal contexts that are important for the 21st-century music student.

AUSTRALIAN HIGHER EDUCATION REGULATORY CONTEXT

The overarching regulatory environment has become increasingly important in the Australian higher education context following a comprehensive review of Australian higher education (Bradley, Noonan, Nugent, & Scales, 2008), which enabled a much broader range of providers of higher education to operate in Australia. A new regulatory body was needed to replace the Australian Universities Quality Agency so that nonuniversity providers of higher education could be included. As a consequence, the Tertiary Education Quality and Standards Agency (TEQSA) assumed oversight of higher education in 2012. The Higher Education Standards Panel (HESP) was established to provide advice to TEQSA and to the responsible minister, and it has developed a range of standards including course design standards and learning outcomes standards (Lebler, Holmes, Harrison, Carey, & Cain, 2015). In addition, a strengthened Australian Qualifications Framework (AQF, 2013) specifies a range of learning outcomes that should be demonstrated by all graduates in their responses to assessment tasks. These regulations are embodied in the Australian Higher Education Standards Framework, which is under review at the time of writing (Australian Government Department of Education and Training, 2014). As a consequence of these developments, a more transparent process replaced the era of Australian conservatoires and university music departments acting more or less autonomously, just as was the case for the rest of Australian higher education.

The AQF has published detailed specifications for each of 10 levels of postsecondary education, from Certificate 1 at Level 1 through to Doctorates at Level 10. A bachelor degree is at AQF Level 7, which describes graduates as having:

1. Broad and coherent knowledge and skills for professional work and/or further learning,
2. well-developed cognitive, technical and communication skills, and
3. the ability to apply knowledge and skills to demonstrate autonomy, well-developed judgement and responsibility. (AQF, 2013)

Successive Australian governments have supported the development of learning and teaching through such bodies as the Carrick Institute for Learning and Teaching in Higher Education, established in 2004 then replaced in 2008 by the Australian Learning and Teaching Council. The Office for Learning and Teaching took over this role in 2012, to be replaced by the National Institute for Learning and Teaching in 2016. All of these organizations have supported research and acknowledged excellence in learning and teaching, including an increased focus on developing innovative and robust assessment practices and related scholarship. These capabilities have proved useful because changes in the regulatory environment have provided an opportunity for disciplines to have a voice in drafting the regulations that apply to their sectors of higher education.

The development of Threshold Learning Outcomes statements (TLOs) for each of a number of discipline clusters was an important aspect of the revised regulations and they are a reference point for institutions when they report to TEQSA. The Australian Learning and Teaching Council was responsible for the development of the TLOs through its Learning and Teaching Academic Standards project. Music was included as part of the Creative and Performing Arts (CAPA) discipline cluster, and Professor Jonathan Holmes led a highly consultative process for this cluster that included numerous meetings with stakeholders and a sequence of workshops and symposia presentations (Holmes & Fountain, 2010).

The CAPA TLOs are as follows:

Upon completion of a bachelor degree in Creative and Performing Arts, graduates will be able to:

a) Demonstrate skills and knowledge of the practices, languages, forms, materials, technologies and techniques in the Creative and Performing Arts discipline.
b) Develop, research and evaluate ideas, concepts and processes through creative, critical and reflective thinking and practice.
c) Apply relevant skills and knowledge to produce and realize works, artefacts and forms of creative expression.
d) Interpret, communicate and present ideas, problems and arguments in modes suited to arrange of audiences.
e) Work independently and collaboratively in the Creative and Performing Arts Discipline in response to project demands.
f) Recognize and reflect on social, cultural and ethical issues, and apply local and international perspectives to practice in the Creative and Performing Arts Discipline. (Lebler, Holmes, et al., 2015, pp. 43–44)

In her focus group study conducted in an Australian Conservatorium, Cain reports that all teacher participants "agreed that current methods of assessment successfully addressed the CAPA TLOs in an ongoing, developmental manner," though they "questioned the extent to which the CAPA TLOS represented a professional industry standard—a theme also explored by the student focus groups" (2015, p. 100). Teachers cross-referenced their professional standards with institutional standards when assessing their students' performances, which is "not necessarily problematic and may even serve to ensure the appropriateness of institutional standards in a broader professional context" (Cain, 2015, p. 102).

Graduates of music bachelor programs in Australian must have the opportunity to demonstrate their achievement of high standards in music as well as the generic learning outcomes specified by the AQF and the CAPA TLOs. All of these attributes and skills must be evident in student responses to assessment tasks that can be demonstrated to be robust and where the grades awarded are comparable with those awarded in other similar courses and programs of study in other institutions (Lebler, Holmes, et al., 2015). This raises the question of how understandings of standards of achievement can be effectively shared between markers, and that is the topic of the following section.

Setting Standards

For the purposes of this chapter, standards are measures of the degree to which students are able to demonstrate their mastery of the criteria for an assessment task (Sadler, 1985). One of the methods in widespread use for communicating standards in the higher music education context is the use of detailed verbal descriptions of the characteristics of various standards of achievement, usually several sentences describing each category of achievement for each criterion. This is often presented as a rubric or table with standards of achievement associated with a marks range or grade. Sadler (2007) points out that when this approach is taken to the degree that complex learning objectives are broken down into their constituent parts, the result is a list of microcompetencies that are sometimes assessed as being either present or absent, such as is common practice in the vocational education sector, for example. Holistic judgements of assessments where "the appraiser... makes a qualitative judgment as to its overall quality" are more effective than those where "the teacher makes separate qualitative judgements on each of the preset criteria" according to Sadler (2009a, p. 161). This is developed further in Sadler's *backward assessment* approach (Sadler, 2015) in which complex assessment tasks are assessed holistically for their overall quality without reference to predetermined criteria, and feedback is given on the noteworthy aspects of the submission to elaborate on the mark awarded.

Australian higher education institutions are responsible for their own assessment processes that must comply with the regulations set out by TEQSA and a variety of processes are employed to ensure valid and reliable assessment of musical performances. While there is no requirement for external examiners, the use of external examiners for such assessments as recital performances is not uncommon. The European Union's Polifonia Working Group on Assessment and Standards found that "external examiners help institutions reflect on their assessment procedures and standards in addition to making assessment more reliable and providing external measures against which to measure standards of student achievement" (Polifonia Working Group on Assessment and Standards, 2013, pp. 30–31). Although this view has general support in the European higher music education community, some question the effectiveness of external examiners as custodians of interinstitutional standards. In their UK study, Bloxham and her colleagues have found "the potential of experienced peers in a subject discipline to provide the assurance of standards is limited" (Bloxham, Hudson, Outer, & Price, 2015, p. 1). In their final report, the Polifonia Working Group on Assessment and Standards recognized "the potential of the consensus moderation approach in working towards the goal of inter-institutional consensus on standards in European HME" (Polifonia Working Group on Assessment and Standards, 2013, p. 19). This approach is discussed in more detail later.

Various interinstitutional projects in the Australian university sector (Barrie, Crisp, Hughes, & Bennison, 2011; Boud & Associates, 2010; Krause et al., 2014) have provided extrainstitutional perspectives on assessment processes and standards, including some with a focus on higher music education (Lebler, Carey, & Harrison, 2015; Lebler, Harrison, Carey, & Cain, 2013a; Monkhouse, 2010). Among nonuniversity providers, such processes as the use of an external examiners panel to report to institutional academic boards are effective mechanisms to demonstrate that the standards being applied and the grades being awarded are comparable with those awarded by other similar Australian and international institutions. A national Peer Review of Assessment Network (Peer Review of Assessment Network, 2016) has been established to facilitate interinstitutional collaboration in assuring comparability of assessment standards and practices. In the Australian higher education context, assessments are now required to be made against predetermined standards, ruling out norm-referenced assessments where the proportions of submissions assigned particular grades is predetermined, so the setting of standards and ensuring that they are comparable with standards applied in other similar courses of study is very important in the Australian context.

Sadler (2010a) recommended the process of *consensus moderation* as an appropriate strategy for sharing understandings of the standards to be applied when multiple assessors are involved in marking student responses to a single assessment task. In this process, all assessors grade a representative sample of work, compare marks, and engage in focused discussion on what constitutes quality and on the standards that should be applied to the work of the remaining students in the course. The meaning of various levels of student achievement can be communicated among examiners through sharing collections of responses to assessment tasks that have been judged to be of particular standards. This is more likely to produce a consensus than written descriptors alone (Sadler, 2010b, 2010c).

This process can also be used to ensure consistency of standards between units of study within and between degree programs as well as between institutions as described later.

Consensus moderation has been found to be effective at the author's institution. In this location, performances are assessed by at least two or three teachers, not always including the teacher of the student being assessed, and sometimes including a teacher who is not a specialist in the instrument being assessed. Each marker works independently, then the panel discusses their views before finalizing the assessment, ensuring the maintenance of consensus as to the standards represented by the grades awarded. Markers are familiar with the standards that are applied through the consensus moderation process described above. A bank of video-recorded exemplars has been developed as reference points for assessment, and these are available to teachers from all departments so that consensus can be assured across departmental boundaries (Lebler, 2013a).

The Australian Assessment in Music (AiM) project conducted a trial of a method by which interinstitutional consensus on standards could be developed (Lebler et al., 2014). The trial included all three AiM project partners—the Queensland Conservatorium of Griffith University, the University of Newcastle, and the University of Tasmania. Example files were shared in advance using Dropbox, e-mail was used to inform all the participants about the process, and the meeting itself was conducted using Skype Premium, which enables video conference calls. All of these aspects of the exercise were completely satisfactory, demonstrating that such activities can be conducted at almost no cost. The process is reported on the project website as follows:

> The first 10 minutes of two audio recordings of 4th year, second semester, Bachelor of Music exams from the lead institution were considered first for their overall quality rather than highly specified criteria. Feedback was provided based on the most noteworthy aspects of the performances, both strengths and weaknesses, and criteria may be used to categorize aspects of this feedback. This process conforms to Royce Sadler's (2013) notion of *backwards assessment*. The design of this exercise was also influenced by the project leader's experience of assessment exercises in Greece (at the International Society for Music Education World Conference), Finland (at the Pentacon+ Assessment Seminar) and Austria (at the Polifonia Working Group on Assessment and Standards seminar "Enhancing Standards for Assessment through Effective Practice") that were designed to explore various degrees of criteria specification and enhance assessment practices through sharing understandings of standards.   (Lebler et al., 2014, para. 2)

The consensus moderation process has been adopted by the author's institution as part of university-wide assessment practice under the Griffith University Assessment Policy (Griffith University Assessment Policy, 2014). This did not present any major challenge for Conservatorium staff, because most assessment practices already included this kind of collaboration, and many had prior experience of this kind of process. While the consensus moderation process itself is not in widespread use in Australian higher education, remarkably similar processes can be found in other contexts. Music examination boards in Australia and elsewhere conduct similar training processes for their examiners and there are also examples in secondary education. These instances from other educational contexts are described in the following section.

Pretertiary Assessment in Music

Kindergarten through 12th grade (ages 5–18) education in Australia is managed and largely delivered by state and territory governments, though recently a national curriculum has been implemented for most fields of education including music (The Australian Curriculum, 2013). Robust processes have been adopted by pretertiary educators, and one example is Queensland's system of externally moderated school-based assessment (Queensland Curriculum and Assessment Authority, 2016) that is used in the latter stages of secondary education. In this process, schools are required to make provisional assessments of student work and then submit samples for the external moderation process. Pairs of trained assessors independently assess the submitted samples of student work then meet to discuss their initial views in order to reach consensus on the quality of each piece of work. They then provide feedback to the schools, which enables appropriate standards to be applied at all stages of the assessment process and in all Queensland schools.

There are authentic assessments available to secondary music students that are complex and realistic representations of musical activities students might experience outside their educational contexts. Drawing on a Queensland example again, the senior secondary subject Music in Practice includes a performance and "a written, visual or audio journal that documents and evaluates the effectiveness of the processes used to produce a concert performance" (Queensland Curriculum and Assessment Authority, 2015, p. 5). Students participate in all aspects of the preparation and staging of the performance, so there are many learning outcomes in addition to the core musical outcomes that are developed through these activities and assessment tasks.

In addition to the school system, there is another major field of assessment in music—the independent commercial provision of musical syllabuses and examinations. Although there are a number of reputable organizations operating in Australia, the Australian Music Examinations Board (AMEB) are leaders in the Australian context (AMEB, 2016). The AMEB and its British equivalent, the Associated Board of the Royal Schools of Music (ABRSM)[1] are both large and very sophisticated organizations, with boards of directors that include very senior people from government education departments as well as from the university higher music education community. Their examiners undertake regular high-quality training that ensures their results are reliable and consistent between specializations and in all locations, and their training processes are remarkably similar to the consensus moderation approach. The AMEB website rightly claims that its qualifications are recognized as a national benchmark across Australia, and the attention paid to the maintenance of shared understandings of quality in assessment performances is an important aspect of this reputation.

BROAD CATEGORIES OF ASSESSMENT

As discussed at the start of this chapter, regulations now provide clarity about what is acceptable practice in the Australian higher music education context, ensuring that the certification of students' achievements is carried out using consistent standards and robust processes. However, assessment can also contribute to students' learning through the provision of constructive feedback that will inform and direct the future learning of students. Furthermore, if assessment tasks are realistic and authentic representations of what musicians are likely to do in their professional lives after graduation, students' learning will benefit directly from the completion of the assessment tasks. Musical performances are almost always present in the professional lives of musicians, so musical performances are an authentic assessment activity because they replicate one of the activities that students would expect as an outcome of their higher music education. This kind of assessment is particularly beneficial for music students because the preparation required is the same as would be needed for any other musical performance, so students experience an aspect of their future professional lives as part of their studies.

Assessment tasks should be capable of measuring the achievement of the learning objectives of the course of study, and should be sufficiently authentic to encourage the attributes and abilities that we intend our students to develop and use after graduation. Biggs (1999, 2008) tells us that assessment not only directs students' learning to what it is that will be assessed, but also shapes the way in which students undertake and customize their learning to be effective in the context of the assessments they will experience. David Boud has developed the notion of *sustainable assessment* (Boud, 2000; Boud & Soler, 2016), which includes a focus on the future benefits of assessment after graduation. In higher music education, the preparation of students for their continuing development after their formal studies should be a primary consideration. Many would argue that the ability to be self-monitoring after graduation should be one of these abilities (see for example Sadler, 2009b, 2010b, 2013), so some focus on the development of self-assessment abilities should be included in higher music education.

SUMMATIVE AND FORMATIVE ASSESSMENT

Summative assessment is usually conducted at the end of a unit of work to document students' achievement of the unit's learning outcomes. While the dominant role of summative assessment is to provide a measure of students' achievement of the learning outcomes of a course, the provision of feedback along with marks is not uncommon in summative processes, so an element of formative assessment is frequently present. Summative assessment tasks often act as important motivators because they provide goals for learners to aim for and milestones to record their achievements. Indeed, this is one of the arguments used to support engagement with such organizations as the AMEB (2016). The preparation for a successful performance assessment usually includes very systematic learning processes at all levels of study; students need to identify those aspects of the performance that need particular attention and find a means to develop the required skills and abilities, usually under the guidance of a teacher.

Formative assessment occurs in many contexts in higher music education, sometimes in formal, low-stakes assessment activities, and frequently as part of the informal interactions between musicians, including the interactions between music students and their teachers. Letting students know how they are progressing toward their learning goals is the main function of formative assessment, even though some formative assessment tasks may contribute to a student's grade, thereby also functioning as summative assessment. The provision of feedback by any means has very widespread support in the literature, but even so, some caution is warranted. The eminent assessment scholars cited in this chapter all stress that the development of effective self-assessment abilities should be a core goal, because of its many benefits including the ability to independently monitor the quality of work in progress. Frequent feedback that consists mainly of teachers expressing their views and giving direction can potentially encourage students to become unduly dependent on external judgments, which may not be helpful in the development of lifelong independent learning abilities. Boud (1995b), Lerman and Borstel (2003), and Partti, Westerlund, and Lebler (2015) all describe feedback processes that avoid the risk of creating dependency in the learner and actively encourage the development of self-assessment abilities that will be beneficial in students' future lives.

INFORMAL ASSESSMENT

Interactions between teachers and students in the one-to-one learning context are an example of less formal assessment and feedback processes, where the provision of highly customized feedback is a central feature of this form of learning. As indicated previously, the nature of this feedback will have important consequences for students. Carey and her colleagues have conducted an extensive study of interactions in the one-to-one learning context and they have identified two key pedagogical approaches in their teacher-participants—*transformative pedagogy*, which emphasizes the depth of student understanding and ownership, and *transfer pedagogy*, which is largely didactic (Carey, Bridgstock, Taylor, McWilliam, & Grant, 2013). All teacher-participants in their pilot study used both approaches but in varying proportions. The feedback provided in the transformative mode was frequently dialogic, with the teachers asking questions to draw attention to noteworthy aspects of their students' performances, rather than the direct communication of the teachers' opinions and instructions that is characteristic of the transfer approach.

Informal assessments are common in the interactions between members of musical ensembles, particularly small ensembles that are not conducted. For example, popular musicians are known to learn with and from each other (Green, 2001, 2006, 2008), and informal peer assessment is an important aspect of this learning process. It is not uncommon for musicians to use Facebook, YouTube, and Twitter to solicit feedback on the videos of their performances they post to these sites, and this is also true in the Australian context. This is a form of informal peer assessment that has intrinsic value to its users, and the emerging area of e-assessment is addressed later in this chapter. Some instances of peer and self-assessment in formal learning contexts are included in the following section.

Formal Assessment Practices

Assessment in Nonperformance Music Courses

A conservatory education is characterized by the intensive study of performance, so it is not surprising that the assessment of musical performances is a major topic in the research literature about higher music education. However, in the Australian context and elsewhere, it is not enough for students to devote all of their attention to their performances, because they also must demonstrate the other learning outcomes discussed earlier in this chapter. Bachelor of music programs will typically include courses in music theory, music history and analysis, and a variety of other topics in addition to the core study of performance (Carey & Lebler, 2012; Monkhouse, 2015), and in these courses, the normal range of assessment types will be found. These could include the writing of essays, assignments, research projects, and tests and examinations, and they will be assessed in accordance with the institutional policies at each location.

The assessment of the various forms of musical performances presents particular challenges, and there is some variation in the specific processes employed, depending on the musical and institutional contexts, and these are discussed in the following section. However, given the apparent importance of this aspect of students' experiences, there is a surprisingly low incidence of innovation or even variation in the ways musical performances are assessed in the Australian context (Zhukov, 2015).

Recital Performance

Performance examinations are usually conducted at the end of each learning period, normally one semester long with two semesters being undertaken each year (Lebler, Harrison, Carey, & Cain, 2013b). However, higher education in Australia is experiencing increased adoption of the trimester model with three learning periods each year, which may well result in three performance exams each calendar year. To prepare for three recital assessments each year would be a substantial workload for an undergraduate student, and there is a view that a slower learning pace might be beneficial for the development of students' abilities to perform music. Clearly Australian institutions will need to pay attention to the frequency of complex assessments such as recitals when they consider alternative academic calendars.

In response to the concerns about the frequency of recital assessments that have been expressed by performance teachers at the author's institution, performance courses at the time of writing are two semesters in duration, with a 25% technical assessment at the end of the first semester and a 60% recital assessment at the end of the second semester. Students receive a written report on their recital performance that provides a permanent record of the stages of their development. Reports can enhance students' reflections on their performances, particularly if recordings of the examination performances are available, as is the case at this institution, enabling a triangulation with the performers' recollections. The remaining 15% is allocated to a Performance Studies Portfolio—7.5% each semester—containing students' critical reflections on their learning.

Zhukov (2015) reports a fairly consistent approach to recital performance assessment in Australian higher music education but draws attention to a number of innovations and variations that may provide additional benefits. These include initiating a broader range of evaluation tasks including peer assessment and self-assessment of recorded performances, reflective journals, group work, engaging students in the development of assessment criteria, and paying attention to the development of entrepreneurship and other skills that will be useful in a portfolio career. Such additional assessment tasks are likely to demonstrate some of the learning outcomes specified in the AQF that may be difficult to demonstrate in a recital performance alone.

Earlier research at the author's institution investigated ways to improve the quality of music performance evaluation in an effort to address the accountability imperative in tertiary music education, developing "an instrument-specific, criterion-referenced rating scale for empirically measuring music performance outcomes that demonstrated levels of standards in music performance" (Wrigley, 2005, p. i). This model was not adopted because most members of the teaching faculty had a strong preference for more holistic assessment even after participating in the study and the trials of the proposed method. This is still the case at this institution, where detailed criteria are not used in the assessment of performances, favoring instead the backward assessment approach as described by Sadler (2015). This approach is not uncommon in the assessment of musical performances and is not problematic under Australian regulations, provided assessments are referenced to appropriate predetermined standards.

Group Assessment

The assessment of group work poses particular complexities, particularly in relation to the degree to which process should be assessed along with product, and Harrison and his colleagues have conducted studies of ensemble assessment in the Australian context (Harrison, Lebler, Carey, Hitchcock, & O'Bryan, 2013; Harrison, O'Bryan, & Lebler, 2013). Teachers and students participating in these studies shared their views about peer and self-assessment of ensemble work, and there was a general view that there are tensions between assessment that is seen as necessary for compliance with institutional regulations and preparation for performing in the music industry. Many students are performing outside their course requirements while studying, and ensemble work is likely to be part of the professional portfolio careers of graduates, so the experience of ensemble music-making is acknowledged as an important aspect of the undergraduate experience for most students. As Orr (2010) rightly asserts, "Group work is central to pedagogy in the performing arts. It is the norm, not the exception" (p. 302).

In some locations, participation in ensembles is required but is not marked and does not contribute to students' grades, and there is a wide variation in the assessment of ensemble performances in Australia as is the case elsewhere (see, for example, Ginsborg & Wistreich, 2010). Australian academics have explored alternatives to the assessment of performances by teachers, including Blom and Poole (2004), Daniel (2004), Harrison et al. (2013), Lebler (2006, 2007, 2008, 2010, 2012, 2013b, 2014, 2015), and McWilliam, Lebler, and Taylor (2007), but the established practice of the individual assessment of individual performers in ensembles by teachers continues to be the dominant method used for ensemble performance assessment. At the author's workplace, jazz instrumental students were assessed while playing with an ensemble of teachers rather than with their fellow students, and this enabled immediate feedback to be provided to students by teachers, emulating normal practice in jazz ensembles. This method was extremely costly and has been discontinued. Chapman (2015) describes another interesting variation to ensemble assessment in which multiple assessors each mark various individuals in an ensemble simultaneously, thereby reducing the time needed to complete the assessment. At the time of writing, participants in large ensembles at the author's institution are assessed on a pass/fail basis and participants in small ensembles are marked by their ensemble coach on the basis of a written summary of learning activities weighted at 30%; their ensemble participation, dedication, development, application of coaching suggestions and other ensemble skills defined in the Course Profile weighted at 30%; with the remaining 40% being awarded for the quality of their end of semester performance.

Participatory Assessment

Boud and Associates tell us, "students themselves need to develop the capacity to make judgements about both their own work and that of others in order to become effective continuing learners and practitioners" (2010, p. 1). Partti et al. (2015) describe these assessment practices as *participatory assessment*, involving the active participation of students in the assessing process. Peer assessment sometimes contributes to the grades or marks awarded to the student being assessed and might also produce a mark or grade for those conducting the assessment. Self-assessment is also a participatory activity and is arguably the most important of all assessment types, whether or not it is included as part of an official process, because it is the form of assessment that will serve the student for life (Boud, 1995b, 2000; Boud & Associates, 2010; Boud & Soler, 2016). Higher education institutions in Australia frequently cite an ability to engage with lifelong learning as one of their graduate attributes, and the ability to make well-founded judgments about work while it is in progress is a core skill for lifelong learning (Sadler, 2013). This is particularly important for musicians because they typically practice alone, so they must be able to evaluate their performances and respond to any weaknesses that they identify in constructive ways. When students assess their own work or the work of their peers they will develop their abilities to make valid judgments about the quality of their own work while it is in progress, which is a core skill for autonomous professionals in all fields (Lebler, 2014). Given the demonstrated benefits of participatory assessment for students and its widespread support in the literature, it is difficult to understand why the implementation of such practices is so limited in higher music education, not just in Australia but also elsewhere.

One example of participatory assessment can be found in the Bachelor of Popular Music (BPM) program at the Queensland Conservatorium Griffith University. Students in this program conduct a criteria-referenced self-assessment of their recorded creative works, which they submit online at the same time as the recordings. This self-assessment informs discussions that take place in assessment panel meetings, where seven or eight students and a teacher meet to discuss their responses to the submissions they have each been assigned and have provisionally assessed through an online system in advance of the panel meetings. In this example, the process makes extensive use of online technologies at all stages of the assessment process, employing a sophisticated bespoke online application called the Bachelor of Popular Music Assessment Tool (BoPMAT);[2] this is particularly appropriate in the popular music context, where technology is prevalent.

The critical response process (Lerman & Borstel, 2003) is a feedback method that is informing practice in the Australian context, including at the author's institution and as part of the Transforming One-to-One project[3] workshop activities that have been conducted at a number of other Australian universities. This process is based on a dialogue between the creator of the work being assessed and the assessors that relies on the asking of nonjudgmental questions rather than the direct communication of the views of the assessors about the work.

E-assessment

The use of information technologies and e-learning strategies has been under consideration in higher education for more than a decade (Buzzetto-More & Alade, 2006) and has been recognized as an efficient and effective means of assessing teaching and learning effectiveness as part of a broader suite of assessment methods. For example, Demirbilek has identified "an increasing interest in using social networking tools (e.g., Facebook, Twitter, YouTube) and Wikis in the teaching and learning process, and these can be utilized as peer feedback and collaboration tools" (2015, p. 212). The use of social media in higher education has emerged as a theme in the literature, particularly since 2011.

There are reports of studies that include social media to provide content to students, as well as its use in assessment processes, particularly peer assessment processes, across a range of disciplines (Denton & Wicks, 2013; Donlan, 2014; Hilscher, 2013; Jacquemin, Smelser, & Bernot, 2014; Jaffar, 2014; Meishar-Tal, Kurtz, & Pieterse, 2012; Mok, 2012; Shih, 2011; Smith, 2011).

E-assessment is now attracting considerable attention in Australian higher education, as institutions adapt to students' increasing engagement with the online world. The author's institution has been investigating e-assessment as it looks to improve the efficacy and efficiency of its assessment processes (New Worlds of Assessment, 2015). Trials of the provision of off-campus online examination processes have been conducted, using such technologies as keystroke recognition and webcams to ensure that online assessments are reliable indicators of students' achievement.

The assessment of recorded performances is also in use in the Australian context. The Bachelor of Popular Music Assessment Tool referred to previously is one example of a complex and comprehensive assessment process being conducted largely online, and this kind of process is likely to become more common as institutions adopt fully online delivery of their programs. Other courses at the author's institution conduct online examinations using the institution's learning management system Blackboard, though most are conducted in computer labs on campus rather than remotely to enable appropriate invigilation.

People applying for Australian music programs from overseas or from remote Australian locations are often able to submit recordings of their audition performances as part of the application and selections processes for entry to music programs, and this would be likely to be the most common form of e-assessment in use in Australia at the time of writing. YouTube provides one extremely accessible method for applicants to provide video recordings as a substitute for attending auditions in person.

Another example of a music program that has embraced e-assessment can be found at the University of Southern Queensland, where the music major in the bachelor of creative arts is available as an external study, with remote location students completing assessments in nonperformance courses by submitting electronic documents via the university's learning management system, just as is the case for students undertaking these courses on campus. The external students' performances are videoed and uploaded to a private YouTube channel, and this has been found to be an entirely satisfactory process in this context (M. Forbes, personal communication, February 18, 2016; assessment of off-campus music students).

INFORMAL ASSESSMENT PRACTICES

In addition to the formal assessment applications discussed in the previous section, YouTube has become a substantial resource for learning since its inception in 2005 (Cayari, 2011). A search for "learn piano" on YouTube on February 18, 2016, yielded over

3,000,000 results, and a similar search for "learn music" produced over 28,000,000 results. Even a search for "assessment in music" yielded almost 650,000 results, a few of which were training videos for formal music assessment practices. The quality of these offerings may be inconsistent, but the level of engagement with this site as a location for learning music is evident. Interestingly, when a teacher posts an instructional clip on YouTube, it is not the quality of the learners' achievements that is being assessed, but rather the users are able to like or dislike a particular clip, providing a measure of user-satisfaction as a proxy for a measure of quality. Similarly, Facebook posts can be liked with a click, and negative responses can be made in a text comment. The value placed on peer review in informal contexts like Facebook "likes," YouTube views and shares, and positive Twitter comments may be an indicator that the inclusion of similar processes in formal contexts might enhance students' engagement with the assessment processes they are engaged with in higher education.

Conclusion

This chapter has provided a description of assessment practices in Australian higher education including placing it in its regulatory context. While the work of Australian scholars in this field is included, the chapter also draws on the broader assessment literature, using Australian examples of practice. Largely as a consequence of the Australian regulatory context, the attention of Australian music academics and scholars has been drawn to assessment and the development of a shared understanding of the standards to be applied to student work, not just in higher music education, but also in pretertiary and extracurricular music.

Australian examples of summative and formative assessment practices have been described in formal and informal contexts, leading to the assessment musical performance, the characteristic assessment for higher music education institutions that are focused on developing high levels of musical performance in their students. The higher music education sector provides fertile ground for a range of assessment practices including the assessment of complex authentic tasks like musical performances, the assessment of group work that is central to most music programs, the opportunity to implement participatory assessment practices effectively, and the opportunity to capitalize on the networked dispositions that are common to the post-Internet generations.

Those interested in the learning benefits of effective assessment practices can look to a future that will include access to rich media and information on a scale far greater than what is currently available, allowing possibilities for greater efficiencies and flexibility in assessment tasks. For example, the complexities of managing meaningful peer assessment processes on a large scale will no longer be a disincentive to innovation. Importantly, as higher education programs in Australia continue to refine their responses to regulations that demand the achievement of a range of learning outcomes, musical performances will remain a sustainable form of assessment because they are complex and authentic tasks that emulate important aspects of the professional lives of most performing musicians. This is precisely the kind of assessment that can meet the demands of the regulations and respond to the recommendations of leading scholars in the field, enabling the demonstration of a broad range learning outcomes through authentic tasks that have relevance to the broader profession.

It is important that teachers in Australian higher music education and those working in other locations continue to be rigorous in their assessment practices and eloquent in their advocacy for the validity of musical performances as an assessment task. This is needed because of the substantial impact assessment has on learning. As the Australian assessment scholar David Boud writes, "[s]tudents can, with difficulty, escape from the effects of poor teaching, [but] they cannot … escape the effects of poor assessment" (1995a, p. 35).

NOTES

1. The AMEB, the ABRSM, and Trinity (http://www.trinitycollege.com.au) are all active in Australia, along with a number of smaller less established organizations.
2. More details on this process can be found on the Assessment in Music website at http://assessmentinmusic.com.au and in Lebler (2007, 2008, 2012, 2013a).
3. The Transforming One-to-One project (www.transformative121.com) is funded by the Australian Government Office for Learning and Teaching www.olt.gov.au.

REFERENCES

The Australian Curriculum. (2013). Retrieved from http://www.australiancurriculum.edu.au/
Australian Music Examinations Board (AMEB). (2016). *About*. Retrieved from http://www.ameb.edu.au/about-ameb
Australian Government Department of Education and Training (2014, December). *Final proposed higher education standards framework—Advice to the Minister—December 2014*. Canberra: Author. Retrieved from https://docs.education.gov.au/node/37863
Australian Qualifications Framework (AQF). (2013, January 2013). *Second edition*. Retrieved from https://www.aqf.edu.au
Barrie, S., Crisp, G., Hughes, C., & Bennison, A. (2011). *Assessing and assuring graduate learning outcomes: Principles and practices within and across disciplines (2011–2012)*. Retrieved from http://www.itl.usyd.edu.au/projects/aaglo
Biggs, J. B. (1999). *Teaching for quality learning at university: What the student does*. Philadelphia, PA & Buckingham, UK: Society for Research into Higher Education; Open University Press.
Biggs, J. B. (2008). *Constructive alignment*. Retrieved from http://www.johnbiggs.com.au/academic/constructive-alignment
Blom, D., & Poole, K. (2004). Peer assessment of tertiary music performance: Opportunities for understanding performance assessment and performing through experience and self-reflection. *British Journal of Music Education, 21*, 111–125. doi: 10.1017/S0265051703005539

Bloxham, S., Hudson, J., Outer, B. D., & Price, M. (2015). External peer review of assessment: An effective approach to verifying standards? *Higher Education Research and Development, 34*(6), 1069–1082. doi: 10.1080/07294360.2015.1024629

Boud, D. (1995a). Assessment and learning: Contradictory or complementary? In P. Knight (Ed.), *Assessment for learning in higher education* (pp. 35–48). London, UK: Kogan Page.

Boud, D. (1995b). *Enhancing learning through self assessment.* London, UK: Kogan Page.

Boud, D. (2000). Sustainable assessment: Rethinking assessment for the learning society. *Studies in Continuing Education, 22,* 151–167. doi: 10.1080/713695728.

Boud, D., & Associates. (2010). *Assessment 2020: Seven propositions for assessment reform in higher education.* Retrieved from http://www.assessmentfutures.com

Boud, D., & Soler, R. (2016). Sustainable assessment revisited. *Assessment and Evaluation in Higher Education, 41,* 400–413. doi: 10.1080/02602938.2015.1018133.

Bradley, D., Noonan, P., Nugent, H., & Scales, B. (2008). *Review of Australian higher education.* Retrieved from http://hdl.voced.edu.au/10707/44384

Buzzetto-More, N. A., & Alade, A. J. (2006). Best practices in e-assessment. *Journal of Information Technology Education, 5,* 251–269.

Cain, M. (2015). Participants' perceptions of fair and valid assessment in tertiary music education. In D. Lebler, G. Carey, & S. Harrison (Eds.), *Assessment in music education: From policy to practice* (pp. 87–106). London, UK: Springer.

Carey, G., Bridgstock, R., Taylor, P., McWilliam, E., & Grant, C. (2013). Characterising one-to-one conservatoire teaching: Some implications of a quantitative analysis. *Music Education Research, 15,* 357–368. doi: 10.1080/14613808.2013.824954

Carey, G., & Lebler, D. (2012). Reforming a bachelor of music program: A case study. *International Journal of Music Education, 30,* 309–326. doi: 10.1177/0255761412459160

Cayari, C. (2011). The YouTube effect: How YouTube has provided new ways to consume, create, and share music. *International Journal of Education and the Arts, 12*(6), 1–30.

Chapman, J. (2015). The amazing marking machine, a process for efficient, authentic assessment. In D. Lebler, G. Carey, & S. Harrison (Eds.), *Assessment in music education: From policy to practice* (pp. 237–250). London, UK: Springer.

Daniel, R. (2004). Peer assessment in musical performance: The development, trial and evaluation of a methodology for the Australian tertiary environment. *British Journal of Music Education, 21*(1), 89–110. doi: 10.1017/S0265051703005515

Demirbilek, M. (2015). Social media and peer feedback: What do students really think about using Wiki and Facebook as platforms for peer feedback? *Active Learning in Higher Education, 16,* 211–224. doi: 10.1177/1469787415589530

Denton, D. W., & Wicks, D. (2013). Implementing electronic portfolios through social media platforms: Steps and student perceptions. *Journal of Asynchronous Learning Networks, 17,* 125–135.

Donlan, L. (2014). Exploring the views of students on the use of Facebook in university teaching and learning. *Journal of Further and Higher Education, 38,* 572–588. doi: 10.1080/0309877X.2012.726973

Ginsborg, J., & Wistreich, R. (2010). *Promoting excellence in small group music performance: Teaching, learning and assessment.* Retrieved from https://www.heacademy.ac.uk/knowledge-hub/promoting-excellence-small-group-music-performance-teaching-learning-and-assessment

Green, L. (2001). *How popular musicians learn: A way ahead for music education.* Burlington, VT: Ashgate.

Green, L. (2006). Popular music education in and for itself, and for "other" music: Current research in the classroom. *International Journal of Music Education, 24,* 101–118. doi: 10.1177/0255761406065471

Green, L. (2008). *Music, informal learning and the school: A new classroom pedagogy.* Aldershot, UK; Burlington, VT: Ashgate.

Griffith University Assessment Policy. (2014). Brisbane: Griffith University. Retrieved from http://policies.griffith.edu.au/pdf/Assessment Policy.pdf

Harrison, S., Lebler, D., Carey, G., Hitchcock, M., & O'Bryan, J. (2013). Making music or gaining grades? Assessment practices in tertiary music ensembles. *British Journal of Music Education, 30*(1), 27–42. doi: 10.1017/S0265051712000253

Harrison, S., O'Bryan, J., & Lebler, D. (2013). "Playing it like a professional": Approaches to ensemble direction in tertiary institutions. *International Journal of Music Education, 31,* 173–189. doi: 10.1177/0255761413489791

Hilscher, J. (2013). *A case study examining how students make meaning out of using facebook as a virtual learning community at a midwestern university.* ProQuest Dissertations & Theses Global. Retrieved from http://search.proquest.com.libraryproxy.griffith.edu.au/docview/14 16379218?accountid=14543

Holmes, J., & Fountain, W. (2010). *Creative and performing arts learning and teaching academic standards statement.* Retrieved from http://www.olt.gov.au/resource-creative-performing-arts-ltas-statement-altc-2010

Jacquemin, S. J., Smelser, L. K., & Bernot, M. J. (2014). Twitter in the higher education classroom: A student and faculty assessment of use and perception. *Journal of College Science Teaching, 43*(6), 22–27.

Jaffar, A. A. (2014). Exploring the use of a Facebook page in anatomy education. *Anatomical Sciences Education, 7,* 199–208. doi: 10.1002/ase.1404

Krause, K.-L., Scott, G., Aubin, K., Alexander, H., Angelo, T., Campbell, S.,...Vaughan, S. (2014). *Assuring final year subject and program achievement standards through inter-university peer review and moderation: Final report of the project.* Retrieved from http://www.uws.edu.au/__data/assets/pdf_file/0007/576916/External_Report_2014_Web_3.pdf

Lebler, D. (2006). The masterless studio: An autonomous education community. *Journal of Learning Design, 1*(3), 41–50.

Lebler, D. (2007). Student-as-master? Reflections on a learning innovation in popular music pedagogy. *International Journal of Music Education, 25,* 205–221. doi: 10.1177/0255761407083575

Lebler, D. (2008). Popular music pedagogy: Peer-learning in practice. *Music Education Research, 10,* 193–213. doi: 10.1080/14613800802079056

Lebler, D. (2010, July 27–30). *Informal learning in formal learning: Web 2 to the rescue.* Paper presented at the Musician in Creative and Educational Spaces of the 21st Century [electronic resource]: Proceedings from the International Society for Music Education (ISME) 18th International seminar of the Commission for the Education of the Professional Musician, Shanghai Conservatory of Music.

Lebler, D. (2012). Technology and students' musicking: Enhancing the learning experience. *Theory into Practice, 51,* 204–211. doi: 10.1080/00405841.2012.690302

Lebler, D. (2013a, 30 July). *Performance standards exemplars.* Retrieved from http://assessmentinmusic.com.au/reference-bank/performance-standards

Lebler, D. (2013b). Using formal self- and peer-assessment as proactive tools in building collaborative learning environments: Theory into practice. In H. Gaunt & H. Westerlund

(Eds.), *Collaborative learning in higher music education: Why, what and how?* (pp. 111–122). Farnham, UK: Ashgate.

Lebler, D. (2014, July 15–18). *Promoting professionalism: Developing self-assessment in a popular music program.* Paper presented at the Relevance and Reform in the Education of Professional Musicians, 20th International Seminar of the ISME Commission for the Education of the Professional Musician (CEPROM), Belo Horizonte, Brazil.

Lebler, D. (2015). *The BoPMAT: Bachelor of Music Popular Music program.* In D. Lebler, G. Carey, & S. Harrison (Eds.), *Assessment in music education: From policy to practice* (pp. 221–236). London, UK: Springer.

Lebler, D., Carey, G., & Harrison, S. D. (Eds.). (2015). *Assessment in music education: From policy to practice.* London, UK: Springer.

Lebler, D., Carey, G., Harrison, S. D., & Cain, M. (2014). *Consensus moderation.* Retrieved from http://assessmentinmusic.com.au/reference-bank/consensus-moderation-excercise

Lebler, D., Harrison, S., Carey, G., & Cain, M. (2013a). *Assessment in music.* Retrieved from http://www.assessmentinmusic.com.au

Lebler, D., Harrison, S., Carey, G., & Cain, M. (2013b). *Assessment university assessment summary.* Assessment in Music: An Approach to Aligning Assessment with Threshold Learning Outcomes in the Creative and Performing Arts website. Retrieved from http://assessmentinmusic.com.au/wp-content/uploads/2012/06/Australian-University-Assessment-Summary3.docx

Lebler, D., Holmes, J., Harrison, S., Carey, G., & Cain, M. (2015). Assessment in music in the Australian context: The AiM project. In D. Lebler, G. Carey, & S. Harrison (Eds.), *Assessment in music education: From policy to practice* (pp. 39–54). London, UK: Springer.

Lerman, L., & Borstel, J. (2003). *Critical response process: A method for getting useful feedback on anything you make, from dance to dessert.* New York, NY: Liz Lerman Dance Exchange.

McWilliam, E., Lebler, D., & Taylor, P. G. (2007, June 17–21). *From passive consumers to active prod-users: Students as co-teachers in a popular music program.* Paper presented at the 13th International Conference on Thinking—Curious Minds Think and Learn by Exploring the Unknown, Norrköping, Sweden.

Meishar-Tal, H., Kurtz, G., & Pieterse, E. (2012). Facebook groups as LMS: A case study. *International Review of Research in Open and Distance Learning, 13*(4), 33–48.

Mok, J. C. H. (2012). Facebook and learning: Students' perspective on a course. *Journal of the NUS Teaching Academy (Singapore), 2*, 131–143.

Monkhouse, H. (2010). *Developing effective learning environment for tertiary music students and staff.* Retrieved from http://www.olt.gov.au/system/files/resources/Monkhouse%20H%20UTAS%20Fellowship%20report%202010.pdf

Monkhouse, H. (2015). The bachelor of music: Purpose, desires and requirements. In D. Lebler, G. Carey, S. Harrison, & M. Cain (Eds.), *Assessment in music education: From policy to practice* (pp. 71–86). London, UK: Springer.

National Register of Higher Education Providers. (2016). Retrieved from https://www.teqsa.gov.au/national-register

New Worlds of Assessment. (2015). Retrieved from https://www.griffith.edu.au/learning-teaching/news-events/celebrating-teaching-week/new-worlds-of-assessment

Orr, S. (2010). Collaborating or fighting for the marks? Students' experiences of group work assessment in the performing arts. *Assessment and Evaluation in Higher Education, 35*, 301–313.

Partti, H., Westerlund, H., & Lebler, D. (2015). Participatory assessment and the construction of professional identity in folk and popular music programmes in Finnish and Australian music universities. *International Journal of Music Education, 33,* 476–490. doi: 10.1177/0255761415584299

Peer Review of Assessment Network. (2016). Retrieved from http://www.utas.edu.au/student-evaluation-review-and-reporting-unit/peer-review-of-assessment-network

Polifonia Working Group on Assessment and Standards. (2013). Retrieved from http://www.aec-music.eu/polifonia/working-groups/assessment--standards

Queensland Curriculum and Assessment Authority (2015). *Music in practice SAS 2015.* Brisbane: Author. Retrieved from https://www.qcaa.qld.edu.au/downloads/senior/snr_music_prac_15_unit_work_contemp_music.pdf

Queensland Curriculum and Assessment Authority. (2016). Retrieved from https://www.qcaa.qld.edu.au

Sadler, D. R. (1985). The origins and functions of evaluative criteria. *Educational Theory, 35,* 285–297. doi: 10.1111/j.1741-5446.1985.00285.x

Sadler, D. R. (2007). Perils in the meticulous specification of goals and assessment criteria. *Assessment in Education: Principles, Policy & Practice, 14*(3), 387–392. doi: 10.1080/09695940701592097

Sadler, D. R. (2009a). Indeterminacy in the use of preset criteria for assessment and grading. *Assessment and Evaluation in Higher Education, 34,* 159–179. doi: 10.1080/02602930801956059

Sadler, D. R. (2009b). Transforming holistic assessment and grading into a vehicle for complex learning. In G. Joughin (Ed.), *Assessment, learning and judgement in higher education* (pp. 45–64). London, UK: Springer.

Sadler, D. R. (2010a). *Assuring academic achievement standards at Griffith University.* Retrieved from http://app.griffith.edu.au/assessment-matters/pdfs/assuring-academic-achievement-standards-second-edition.pdf

Sadler, D. R. (2010b). Beyond feedback: Developing student capability in complex appraisal. *Assessment and Evaluation in Higher Education, 35,* 535–550. doi: 10.1080/02602930903541015

Sadler, D. R. (2010c). Fidelity as a precondition for integrity in grading academic achievement. *Assessment and Evaluation in Higher Education, 35,* 727–743. doi: 10.1080/02602930902977756

Sadler, D. R. (2013). Opening up feedback: Teaching learners to see. In S. Merry, M. Price, D. Carless, & M. Taras (Eds.), *Reconceptualising feedback in higher education: Developing dialogue with students* (pp. 54–63). London, UK: Routledge.

Sadler, D. R. (2015). Backwards assessment explanations: Implications for teaching and assessment practice. In D. Lebler, G. Carey, & S. Harrison (Eds.), *Assessment in music education: From policy to practice* (pp. 9–20). London, UK: Springer.

Shih, R.-C. (2011). Can Web 2.0 technology assist college students in learning English writing? Integrating "Facebook" and peer assessment with blended learning. *Australasian Journal of Educational Technology, 27,* 829–845.

Smith, A. K. (2011). Web and software engineering the Facebook way—An undergraduate mini project. *Innovation in Teaching and Learning in Information and Computer Sciences, 10*(103), 58–67.

Wrigley, B. (2005). *Improving music performance assessment* (PhD dissertation). Griffith University, Brisbane.

Zhukov, K. (2015). Challenging approaches to assessment of instrumental learning. In D. Lebler, G. Carey, & S. Harrison (Eds.), *Assessment in music education: From policy to practice* (pp. 55–70). London, UK: Springer.

NATIONAL PERSPECTIVES

CHAPTER 9

ASSESSMENT POLICY AND PRACTICE IN SECONDARY SCHOOLS IN THE ENGLISH NATIONAL CURRICULUM

MARTIN FAUTLEY

IN this chapter the policy and practice of assessment in English schools is discussed and examined. There are many aspects of the English experience that not only are singular but also act as warnings to the wider international music education community, which this chapter points out. The policy situation in England should, at first glance, be openly transparent as a National Curriculum has been operating for many years. However, as we shall see, that has not necessarily helped with ensuring that curriculum and assessment, both as viewed by policymakers and as interpreted by schools and teachers on the ground, have been as straightforward and unambiguous as might be thought to be the case.

THE POLICY BACKGROUND TO ASSESSMENT IN MUSIC EDUCATION IN ENGLAND

The curriculum in English secondary schools has been in a process of flux for a number of years as a result of policy directives and the subsequent policy changes and alterations in emphasis that flow from them. Indeed, changes in education policy, which happen as the political hue of parliament changes, show that control of the curriculum in schools is often one of the first tasks that an incoming government concerns itself with. When there is a change of party controlling government, this tends to assume an even greater importance. In order to understand how this happens, and how it has affected music education, we need to begin with an understanding of what the very notion of "National Curriculum" means in the English political context, and what this means for teaching and learning in schools themselves.

In 1988 the first National Curriculum for all subjects in both primary schools (up to age 11) and secondary schools (from age 11) was introduced (http://www.legislation.gov. uk/ukpga/1988/40/contents). This laid down in statute for the first time what subjects should be taught in schools, with a division established between core subjects: maths, English, and science; and foundation subjects, which numbered music among them. Not only did the National Curriculum introduce these core and foundation subjects but also it established what should be taught and learned in each of them and, importantly, how it should be assessed. In this first iteration, assessment was laid out in scalar fashion, in the form of a series of what were known as "National Curriculum levels," which were designed to be used only at the end of substantial periods of teaching and learning, *key stages*, in the English nomenclature. Despite being labeled a *National* curriculum, it has never applied to independent schools, and over time has increasingly become disapplied in other types of school too.

The 1988 National Curriculum was introduced by the Conservative government of Margaret Thatcher, and was meant to be a significant apparatus involved with raising standards in schools in England. As well as this it would be a key tool in what the right-wing government of the day saw as a mainstay of their political viewpoint, that of promoting "parental choice" of schools, which function would be aided by publishing examination results of National Curriculum and other assessments in local and national newspapers. This does not mean Thatcher fully approved of the final published version of the new National Curriculum, especially when she found out who was in favor of it. Assessment in the National Curriculum was based, by-and-large, on proposals suggested in a report by the Task Group on Assessment and Testing (TGAT, 1988), a body set up with the purpose of advising on how assessment might be achieved. Thatcher herself viewed this report with considerable suspicion: "The fact that it was welcomed by the Labour party, the National Union of Teachers and the Times Educational Supplement was enough to confirm for me that its approach was suspect" (Thatcher, 1993, p. 595). However, she was too late to prevent its transfer into statute. But this discomfort at the birth of an entirely new thing—a National Curriculum—sets the tone for what has happened since, with successive governments wanting to establish political control over *what* is taught in schools. Increasingly this has also included *how* it is taught as well, which has important ramifications for music, as we shall see.

The National Curriculum has not remained fixed since 1998, however. The first of a series of changes took place in 1995, still under a Conservative government. These alterations addressed the issue that the National Curriculum had been conceived of as a series of separate unrelated subject-specific entities, with what was felt to be too much by way of content for each of the subjects in it.

With a subsequent change of government in 1997, and with political control swinging to the left to New Labour under Tony Blair, more changes were made to the National Curriculum, and these became statutory from 2000. Further alterations again were enacted in 2007, with a substantially slimmer curriculum document being produced. With another change of government in 2010, this time to a center-right coalition government led by David Cameron, an "expert panel" was convened to look into the National Curriculum, and make recommendations. The notion of political intervention can be seen clearly in the actions of the coalition government and the expert panel on assessment it convened. After a period of time, two members of the expert panel, Professors Andrew Pollard and Mary James, very publicly resigned from it, stating the following among their reasons:

> We do so because we are concerned with the directions which the Department [of education] now appears to be taking. Some of these directions fly in the face of evidence from the UK and internationally and, in our judgement, cannot be justified educationally. We do not therefore believe that the review, if it continues on the course which now appears to be set, will provide the quality of education which pupils, parents, employers and other national stakeholders have a right to expect.
> (James & Pollard, 2011, para. 2)

Meanwhile, alongside the outward-facing expert panel, the then education minister, Michael Gove, had apparently appointed a secretive team of political (not educational) advisers, from whom he was taking far more advice than from the expert panel: "A shadow team of advisers, whose identity has not been made 'transparent', was advising Gove and bypassing the official panel in a move that raised concerns among the experts" (Guardian, 2012, para. 6).

The reforms went on, but a number of the expert views, like the experts themselves, were disregarded. A new National Curriculum was produced in 2013 for first teaching in 2014. In terms of assessment in music education, this contained a significant development. It was announced that:

> As part of our reforms to the national curriculum, the current system of "levels" used to report children's attainment and progress will be removed. It will not be replaced.
>
> We believe this system is complicated and difficult to understand, especially for parents. It also encourages teachers to focus on a pupil's current level, rather than consider more broadly what the pupil can actually do.
> (National Archives, 2013, para. 2 and 3)

This is the situation currently pertaining in England, with new policy announcements being made on a very regular basis—for example, since 2010 there have been over 70 centrally published policy and policy-related documents (Education England, n.d.), this number will doubtless have changed by the time this chapter is being read.

In order to understand why these issues are significant for music education in England, and why they provide a useful informant for other jurisdictions, we need to consider both the nature of music education in English secondary schools and how the assessment regime pertaining during the years of compulsory National Curriculum assessment outlined in previous paragraphs has been operationalized in schools.

THE ORGANIZATION OF MUSIC IN ENGLISH SECONDARY SCHOOLS

The nature of music education in secondary schools in England is that it is taught and learned as a generalist subject. This means that specific and detailed musical learning does not take place using a single instrument, as is the case in some jurisdictions; instead musical learning is divided by the National Curriculum into three principle but interrelated components, namely *composing, listening,* and *performing,* and music is taught through and using these. There are some important distinctions to make regarding how these terminologies are used and understood, both from policy and practice perspectives. Composing normally causes the most concern from an international perspective. What composing is *not* is systemic staff notation-based written exercises, instead it is viewed as creating ideas directly into sounds, using classroom instruments, and realized directly into performance. This suggests the intent of National Curriculum music is that it be a musical education for all. The aims are expressed thus:

> The national curriculum for music aims to ensure that all pupils:
>
> perform, listen to, review and evaluate music across a range of historical periods, genres, styles and traditions, including the works of the great composers and musicians;
>
> learn to sing and to use their voices, to create and compose music on their own and with others, have the opportunity to learn a musical instrument, use technology appropriately and have the opportunity to progress to the next level of musical excellence;
>
> understand and explore how music is created, produced and communicated, including through the inter-related dimensions: pitch, duration, dynamics, tempo, timbre, texture, structure, and appropriate musical notations.
>
> (Department for Education, 2013, p. 217)

This generalized version of music education has important implications not only for teaching and learning but also for assessment. We have already had a brief introduction to the National Curriculum levels earlier in this chapter, it is now time to consider them in more detail.

Given the generalist nature of the National Curriculum, which has persisted almost unchanged through its various iterations, it is unsurprising that assessment of it is also of a general nature. In early versions of the National Curriculum this was done via the use of *level statements.* These entailed holistic phrases of musical accomplishment, and the original intent was that they be used once only at the end of each stage of education, so at 7, 11, and 14 years of age, known as the *end of a key stage* in the local parlance. As an example, here is the wording of the statement for level 5, deemed to be the average level of attainment that would be reached by pupils at the age of 14 years. This wording is taken from the 2007 version of the National Curriculum:

> Level 5
>
> Pupils identify and explore musical devices and how music reflectstime, place and culture. They perform significant parts from memory and from notations, with awareness of their own contribution such as leading others, taking a solo part or providing rhythmic support. They improvise melodic and rhythmic material within given structures, usea variety of notations, and compose music for different occasions using appropriate musical devices. They analyse and compare musical features. They evaluate how venue, occasion and purpose affect the way music is created, performed and heard. They refine and improve their work.
> (Qualifications and Curriculum Authority, 2007, p. 186)

As can be seen, there is little by way of specificity of musical accomplishment in this statement. It is a holistic overall viewpoint that encompasses all of the elements of National Curriculum music, composing, listening, and performing, wrapped up together in a single statement. Eight of these statements were produced, with an extra available for what was termed "exceptional performance." Teachers were to use these descriptions in arriving at a "best fit" judgment of learner achievement:

> The level descriptions may be seen as describing the complex of attainments of the typical pupil at that level. Their main purpose is to assist teachers in making their judgements of pupils' performance at the end of the key stage. The mode of use of the level description is to form a "best fit" judgement, considering the range of the pupil's attainments against the complex descriptions. This judgement should be made bearing in mind the scale of levels, and balancing strengths and weaknesses in the pupil's overall performance.   (Sainsbury & Sizmur, 1998, p. 187)

In practice, teachers used their own professional judgment rather than relying on any external testing regime to produce a result:

> A consensus of professional judgement is built up about the interpretation of the standard set out in each level description. The consensus is based on the wording of the level description.   (Sainsbury & Sizmur, 1998, p. 191)

This in itself presented problems, though, especially as teachers had to impose their own personal understandings of coherence on the assessment levels in order for them to make any sense at all. Sainsbury and Sizmur (1998) again:

> The level descriptions contain, in themselves, collections of varied attainments that have no necessary unity or coherence. It might be argued that this is a collection of descriptions, not of linked performances, but rather of a typical pupil working at that level. But why should this collection of performances be typical of such a pupil? The answer is that this is a pupil who has been following the programmes of study of the National Curriculum. By teaching the programmes of study, teachers are to impose order upon the attainment targets.   (p. 190)

An implication of this is that the way to "impose order" is to teach the National Curriculum, such that assessment will make sense. In practice, however, teachers tended to invert the assessment and curriculum planning processes, so that what resulted could be termed *assessment-led curriculum*; in other words in order to teach and assess musical attainment according to the National Curriculum, the classroom teacher had to begin with the assessment criteria, and then look to what curricula materials would be appropriate that could follow the assessment regime. This is the opposite way to which the curriculum was intended to be used, wherein assessment practices would follow teaching materials.

THE ROLE OF THE OFFICE FOR STANDARDS IN EDUCATION—POLICING EDUCATION IN ENGLAND

I have shown how issues arose early on with the notion of policy being made and then interpreted in different ways at the local level. In order to investigate this further, and explain the context for an international audience, we need to look into the role and importance of Ofsted, the Office for Standards in Education, a quasi-independent nongovernmental body charged with inspecting schools and reporting on what they find. This anodyne statement does not adequately convey the strength of feeling and very real fear that Ofsted's name strikes into teachers, head teachers, and governors in English schools.

To understand how this came to be, a very peculiarly English division of legislature and judiciary in education needs to be understood. The procedure for enacting policy at a national level rests with the government. There are different policymaking mechanisms for each of the constituent countries of the United Kingdom—England, Wales, Scotland, and Northern Ireland. Proceeding from central policymakers it then devolves to local authorities (although increasingly less so nowadays) and individual schools and chains of schools to interpret how policy will be enacted in each of their specific circumstances. Then, acting as a sort of uneasy mixture of judiciary and the police, is Ofsted, whose role is defined as being both "independent and impartial" (Ofsted website). Ofsted reports directly to parliament. Fear of the results of a bad outcome from an Ofsted inspection cannot be overemphasized for an international audience. There have been teachers who have committed suicide as a result of a poor Ofsted inspection result,[1] so intense is the pressure that these inspections place on head teachers, teachers, and schools.

Ofsted inspections of schools are reported in local press, and this, combined with examination results being published in newspaper "league tables," means that schools feel considerable public pressure to present themselves in the best possible light. One of the effects of this is that Ofsted utterances are seen as being of significant importance by schools themselves, and any discussion of assessment or pedagogic innovation is suffixed by the question "Would Ofsted like it?" rather than by the more personal "Will this be good for the learners in our school?" Another of the effects of this has been that fear of Ofsted has spawned a whole series of what have become known as "Ofsted myths." These can spread rapidly thorough the education system. An example of this is when in one school, allegedly, Ofsted inspectors stopped pupils in school corridors and quizzed them as to what National Curriculum levels they were currently working at in all of their various schools subjects. The upshot of this was that suddenly schools started ensuring that all of their pupils were drilled in this knowledge!

Consequentially there came a marked departure from the practice of awarding levels only at the end of a key stage, and they came to be awarded to pupils far more frequently, notably at the end of each project or piece of work. Indeed, so widespread did the usage frequency increase that holistic level statements, as outlined in the example above, become inadequate to show fine-grained progression of the sort that it was believed "Ofsted wanted," and so an entirely spurious set of sublevels was introduced. This subdivided the extant level statements into what, it must be said, was an entirely ad hoc system more or less invented and reinvented in each school, of what came to known as "sublevels." These were (and in some cases still are) ubiquitous, their use coming to be a regular and common part of teaching and learning encounters (Fautley, 2012). The reason that these sublevels were and are a problem is to do with enactment of policy at a local level, the resultant classroom practice that ensued, and misunderstandings of what teaching and learning in generalist music education look and, importantly, *sound* like.

As I have shown, the level statements themselves were designed and written as holistic and overarching comments on overall musical attainment. Subdividing them was done to show either progression through the levels or to produce rewritten atomized statements of musical progression, both of which are a long way from the original intention of the authors of the levels. As sublevels had no origin in statute, interpretation of what they meant, and how they should be written, was very much left to the individual whimsy of schools. Indeed, such was the variation in practice that even the number of sublevels was not standardized! Although over time most schools opted for three, usually labeled a, b, and c, giving level markings such as 4b, 5c, and so forth. In some schools, though, tenths of a level were used, giving a decimal grade, 4.4, 5.1, and so on, while a few schools used a percentage, somehow dividing the levels into hundredths, giving marks of 4.45%, 5.17%, and so forth. Confusion was rife, and this was amplified by the fact that very few schools undertook any form of standardization of their sublevels with other institutions.

PROGRESS, PROGRESSION, ATTAINMENT

Those from other countries who look in on the English system of assessment in classroom music education are often confused by the way in which English schools have a somewhat idiosyncratic notion with regard to what progress and progression entail. Indeed, these two words have come to have related, but strangely discontiguous meanings. "Progress" is operationalized as the speed at which attainment points are met, whereas "progression" is often viewed as the ways in which learners move through programs of study, or schemes of learning. Again, this is largely due to the way in which schools have interpreted Ofsted utterances. In 2014, Ofsted wrote to all schools saying that they would henceforth be looking at pupil work to ascertain what *progress* had been made. This caused a flurry of worry among schools, as suddenly a focus on progression became the order of the day. This has had the interesting and unintended consequence of schools moving their attention away from attainment and onto progression. As one teacher remarked in an interview:

> TEACHER: My school aren't so bothered about attainment any more, it's only progress they are interested in
> RESEARCHER: How can they concentrate on progress without also looking at attainment?
> TEACHER: I don't know, they just do! (Fautley, 2016)

This is all rather odd, as progress is clearly by-and-large about the rapidity—or lack thereof—of speed at which pupils move through various attainment milestones. To say that attainment is something that schools "aren't so bothered about" seems to be counterintuitive, if not plain wrong! But this focus on progress has also highlighted another policy-practice disjunct in the way the notion of *visible progress* has taken hold. As a result of the aforementioned Ofsted pronouncement, two other Ofsted statements, made in the 2012 *Handbook for Inspection* (Ofsted, 2012), also had a significant impact on thinking at a local level:

> [J]udgement on the quality of teaching must take account of evidence of pupils' learning and progress over time.   (p. 34)
>
> Observing learning over time … scrutiny of pupils' work, with particular attention given to … pupils' effort and success in completing their work and the progress they make over a period of time.   (p. 35)

The question that schools asked themselves was that if Ofsted visits, and inspections of individual teachers and their lessons last on average for 20 minutes, what sort of progress might it be expected that pupils could make in this time? This requirement arose from the same Ofsted fear that was discussed earlier, with serious consequences, it was felt, if this production of visible learning was not done. As one commentator observed:

> The twenty-minute "outstanding lesson" now endemic, with its enforcement by terrified leadership teams, and even training courses offered by the usual suspects who are making a fast buck out of teaching schools how to game the system. This concept requires teachers to split lessons into 20-minute segments (the length of time an inspector will attend a lesson), and in that twenty minutes, tick every box on the inspection framework, which itself would take most adults at least five minutes just to read and decode. Chief amongst the hoops teachers are required to jump through is that of demonstrating that every student in the class has made measurable progress inside twenty minutes.   (Royal Society of Arts, 2013, para. 11)

What is interesting about this comment, and the fear that led to the described actions being commonplace, is that it is a terror of the *consequences* of not being compliant that has led to this situation, rather than the activity itself. In other words this is an example of the policing of policy coming to replace the policy itself; this in turn being due to culture of performativity, resulting in and from a climate of fear.

THE ROLE OF ASSESSMENT IN ACCOUNTABILITY

This point takes us to a key issue in the English education system, and of music education in particular. This is the role of assessment in accountability processes. Performativity, and what has come to be known as "the standards agenda," are driving many aspects of learning in music lessons, as elsewhere across the school curriculum. Performativity was defined by Ball (2003):

> Performativity is a technology, a culture and a mode of regulation that employs judgements, comparisons and displays as means of incentive, control, attrition and change—based on rewards and sanctions (both material and symbolic). The performances (of individual subjects or organisations) serve as measures of productivity or output, or displays of "quality," or "moments" of promotion or inspection. As such they stand for, encapsulate or represent the worth, quality or value of an individual or organisation within a field of judgement.   (p. 216)

Elsewhere, Ball (2006) observes, "as part of the transformation of education and schooling and the expansion of the power of capital, performativity provides sign systems which 'represent' education in a self-referential and reified form for consumption" (p. 70). Ball (2003) describes performativity as being a "terror," with teachers feeling it "in their soul" as being something they are struggling against: "[T]hese struggles are currently highly individualized as teachers, as ethical subjects, find their values challenged or displaced by the terrors of performativity" (p. 216).

It is performativity that causes a very tight focus on assessment and testing, but England is not alone in this. The Finnish commentator Pasi Sahlberg (Sahlberg, 2014) has observed this, characterizing it as being part of what he calls the GERM, a global educational reform movement:

> GERM has gained global popularity among policymakers and change consultants because it emphasizes some fundamental new orientations to learning and educational administration. It suggests strong guidelines to improve quality, equity, and the effectiveness of education, such as making learning a priority, seeking high achievement for all students, and making assessment an integral part of the teaching and learning process....GERM assumes that external performance standards, describing what teachers should teach and what students should do and learn, lead to better learning for all. By concentrating on the basics and defining explicit

learning targets for students and teachers, such standards place a strong emphasis on mastering the core skills of reading and writing and mathematical and scientific literacy. The systematic training of teachers and external inspection are essential elements of this approach.   (p. 150)

Sahlberg's notion of "defining explicit learning targets for students and teachers" is an important one in the English educational system. This is because targets set by teachers for the work of their pupils turns out, in many cases, to be the means by which the teachers themselves are judged. This links back to the earlier description of sublevels, in that the way that many schools use these is to set a minimum requirement of prog-ress which the pupils *have* to make, delineated in terms of how many sublevels the pupils have covered per year. The way in which this target setting was arrived at was by the simple arithmetic division of the expected National Curriculum level at age 11, and then how to get to the expected National Curriculum level 5 by age 14. What this resulted in was a requirement of pupils making a specified number—usually two or three—sublevels progress per year. This in itself sounds like a reasonable requirement, but what happened in many cases was that the requirement became not a means of monitoring progress (and progression), but an end in its own right, with teachers having to produce data showing that their pupils *had* made the necessary number of sublevels required in all cases. These were statistical data, in many cases school leadership teams cared little for the individual stories of pupils, of the names behind the numbers, they were simply concerned with numbers on a spreadsheet. This is a clear example of what the educa-tional commentator Warwick Mansell calls "the obsessive, sceptical, and politicised emphasis on statistics which characterises our education system" (Mansell, 2007, p. 210).

What we find, when looking into this further, is that these statistical levels of progress targets which the learners make, have become instead a proxy measure of school, and, importantly, teacher efficacy. This is because the target has become itself a measure, a clear example of what has become known as "Campbell's law." This states, "the more any quantitative social indicator is used for social decision-making, the more subject it will be to corruption pressures, and the more apt it will be to distort and corrupt the social processes it is intended to monitor" (Campbell, 1976, p. 49).

More specifically, Campbell describes what this means in relation to education in the form of test scores:

achievement tests may well be valuable indicators of general school achievement under conditions of normal teaching aimed at general competence. But when test scores become the goal of the teaching process, they both lose their value as indica-tors of educational status and distort the educational process in undesirable ways
(Campbell, 1976, pp. 51–52).

This is exactly what happened in the English situation. Test scores, in this case taking the form of National Curriculum assessment levels, had "become the goal of the teaching process," with the result that processes of monitoring pupil attainment had switched instead to processes of monitoring teaching via grades (National Curriculum levels) that teachers were giving their pupils.

Of course, all of these notions of progress and progression in secondary schools assume that the starting points from which progression can be measured are more-or-less accurate. But the National Association of Head Teachers in the United Kingdom has pointed out that this cannot be automatically taken to be the case. The grades that teachers in primary schools are giving are subject to exactly the same sort of performativity issues that the grades in secondary schools as described previously have been:

> with the lack of trust exhibited by the profession itself—junior schools often report that infant schools' assessments of their pupils are over-inflated, secondary schools argue that they need to test pupils on arrival because primary assessments, including national tests, cannot be relied upon. In part, this lack of trust is due to a lack of consistency and in part to the perverse incentives resulting from a high stakes accountability model...secondary schools were likely to test pupils as they came into year 7 rather than trust the KS2 assessments. This was generally seen as a problem caused by the nature of the accountability system rather than any underlying lack of ability within the profession.
>
> (National Association of Head Teachers, 2014, pp. 15–16)

What all this means is that:

> pupil outcomes are of enormous individual significance and schools have a social and perhaps moral obligation to maximise individual student attainments, raise aspirations, and enhance employment and educational opportunities. However, translated from measure of individual attainment to institutional indices of success on which careers and institutional fates depend, pupil outcomes begin to serve a quite different purpose.   (Husbands, 2001, p. 7)

And this is the situation that currently pertains in England, where teachers are judged by how many of their pupils have made a statistically stipulated amount of progress, using measures that the teachers have devised themselves. The tail is certainly wagging the dog here!

Implications for Policy and Practice in Secondary School Music Classes

There are serious implications for music teachers from the policy and practice situations described in this chapter, not just locally but also nationally and internationally. Notions of performativity and measurement, teacher efficacy, and the primacy of pupil scores are international issues. In America, Diane Ravitch (Ravitch, 2013) has observed:

> The thirst for data became unquenchable. Policy makers in Washington and the state capitals apparently assumed that more testing would produce more learning. They were certain that they needed accountability and could not imagine any way to

hold schools "accountable" without test scores. This unnatural focus on testing produced perverse but predictable results: it narrowed the curriculum; many districts scaled back time for the arts, history, civics, physical education, science, foreign language, and whatever was not tested. Cheating scandals occurred in Atlanta, Washington, D.C., and other districts. States like New York manipulated the passing score on state tests to inflate the results and bring them closer to Washington's unrealistic goal. Teaching to the test, once considered unprofessional and unethical, became common practice.   (pp. 13–14)

But what does this mean for the classroom music educator? There is no doubt that assessment in music education, in and of itself, is not a bad thing. After all, as Swanwick (1988) long ago observed, "to teach is to assess" (p. 149), and in music education in England and elsewhere there is a long and proud history of doing music assessment, and getting it right, and as reliable and valid as it can be. The history of ABRSM and Trinity College graded examinations presents strong examples of this. We also know that music educators are really good at formative assessment, and that this is a vital aspect of developing high-quality learning outcomes in our pupils. What we are witnessing now is the all-pervading eye of neoliberalism being cast firmly over every aspect of schooling and education. Music education and music educators are not immune from this, and the English examples outlined in this chapter show that very real dangers can accrue from too much political interference in the curriculum. But there is also a danger for music as a school subject if music educators try to argue that music should stand outside such measures, as the danger becomes then that the same neoliberal reformers will simply cut music and the arts from schools, as they do not understand that which they cannot measure. In the United Kingdom we already have the example of the secretary of state for education warning against studying the arts: "Education secretary Nicky Morgan has warned young people that choosing to study arts subjects at school could 'hold them back for the rest of their lives'" (Hutchison, 2014, para. 1).

So, removing the necessity for assessment from music could well be counterproductive. But what would help music educators is for assessment to be placed as servant, rather than master. Nowhere is this truer than in curriculum time for school music lessons.

With finite budgets, and the perils of performativity biting hard, a clear focus on curriculum would be of serious benefit to the classroom music practitioner. None of the egregious cases of assessment problems outlined in this chapter are the result of teachers making free choices. They have all been made under the constraints of externally imposed systems. In order for music teachers to reclaim assessment as their own, we need to look very carefully at what we think the purposes of schooling are, and what they should be. While it can be argued that assessment *is* learning, the very future of the subject itself is in question if music education becomes reduced to the teaching and learning of only that which can be easily assessed. One of the things we know about music as a truly *musical* experience is that overly simplistic assessment schedules cannot possibly capture the subtleties and nuances of skillful music making, whatever the style, type, or genre. After all, as Janet Mills (Mills, 2005) noted,

As I leave a concert, I have a clear notion of the quality of the performance which I have just heard. If someone asks me to justify my view, I may start to talk about rhythmic drive, or interpretation, or sense of ensemble, for instance. But I move from the whole performance to its components. I do not move from the components to the whole. In particular, I do not think: the notes were right, the rhythm was right, the phrasing was coherent, and so on—therefore I must have enjoyed this performance. And I certainly do not think something such as SKILLS + INTERPRETATION = PERFORMANCE.   (p. 176)

Reclaiming assessment, then, is one of the most important tasks facing music educators in England and elsewhere in the coming years. But it is to be hoped that there are also lessons to be learned for the international community from what has been happening in England. The effects of Campbell's law, the chasing of statistical targets at the expense of real learning and music making by children and young people, the judging of teaching efficacy by pupil grades, and the other issues outlined in this chapter, all of these divert time away from the teaching and learning of music. Indeed, the very reason many music educators enter the profession in the first place, to help young people make music both individually and together, has been sadly replaced for many by a narrow focus solely on measuring the measurable. We need to look forward to a time when we value music as whole, not just the isolated atomistic components of it that we often struggle to measure. This is the real lesson for international music education, that music lessons are better when they are musical.

Note

1. For example: "An award-winning headteacher hanged herself shortly after Ofsted downgraded her school, an inquest has been told" (Guardian, 2015).

References

Ball, S. (2006). *Education policy and social class: The selected works of Stephen J. Ball.* Abingdon, UK: Routledge.

Ball, S. J. (2003). The teacher's soul and the terrors of performativity. *Journal of Education Policy, 18*, 215–228. doi: 10.1080/0268093022000043065

Campbell, D. (1976). *Assessing the impact of planned social change.* Occasional Paper #8. Hanover, NH: Public Affairs Center, Dartmouth College.

Department for Education. (2013). *Music programmes of study: Key stage 3.* Retrieved from https://www.gov.uk/government/uploads/system/uploads/attachment_data/file/239088/SECONDARY_national_curriculum_-_Music.pdf

Education England. (n.d.). Retrieved from http://www.educationengland.org.uk/history/timeline.html

Fautley, M. (2012). Assessment issues within National Curriculum music in the lower secondary school in England. In T. S. Brophy & A. Lehmann-Wermser (Eds.), *Proceedings of the Third International Symposium on Assessment in Music Education* (pp. 153–164). Chicago, IL: GIA Publications.

Fautley, M. (2016, October). *Assessment in music education—Some current issues*. Paper presented at the Royal Society Assessment Conference, London.

Guardian. (2012, June 17). Michael Gove's own experts revolt over "punitive" model for curriculum. *The Guardian*. Retrieved from https://www.theguardian.com/politics/2012/jun/17/michael-gove-national-curriculum

Guardian. (2015, November 20). Headteacher killed herself after Ofsted downgrade inquest hears. *The Guardian*. Retrieved from http://www.theguardian.com/uk-news/2015/nov/20/headteacher-killed-herself-after-ofsted-downgrade-inquest

Husbands, C. (2001). Managing "performance" in the performing school. In C. Husbands & D. Gleeson (Eds.), *The performing school* (pp. 7–19). London, UK: RoutledgeFalmer London.

Hutchison, N. (2014, November 11). Education Secretary Nicky Morgan: "Arts subjects limit career choices." *The Stage*. Retrieved from https://www.thestage.co.uk/news/2014/education-secretary-nicky-morgan-arts-subjects-limit-career-choices/

James, M., & Pollard, A. (2011, October 10). *Letter to Mr. Gove*. Retrieved from https://www.bera.ac.uk/wp-content/uploads/2014/03/4.-AP-MJ-letter-to-MG-final-101011.pdf?noredirect=1

Mansell, W. (2007). *Education by numbers: The tyranny of testing*. London, UK: Politico's Publishing.

Mills, J. (2005). *Music in the school*. Oxford, UK: Oxford University Press.

National Archives. (2013, June 14). *Assessing without levels*. Retrieved from http://webarchive.nationalarchives.gov.uk/20130904084116/https:/www.education.gov.uk/schools/teachingandlearning/curriculum/nationalcurriculum2014/a00225864/assessing-without-levels

National Association of Head Teachers. (2014). *Report of the NAHT commission on assessment*. Haywards Heath, Sussex, UK. Retrieved from www.naht.org.uk/assets/assessment-commission-report.pdf

Ofsted. (2012). *The framework for school inspection from January 2012*. Report Number 090098. London, UK: Ofsted.

Ofsted (2014). *Letter to schools*. Retrieved from https://www.gov.uk/government/uploads/system/uploads/attachment_data/file/379634/Letter_20to_20schools_20from_20HMCI_20-_20July_202014.doc

Ofsted. *About*. (n.d.). Retrieved from https://www.gov.uk/government/organisations/ofsted/about

Qualifications and Curriculum Authority. (2007). *Music: Programme of study for key stage 3*. Retrieved from http://archive.teachfind.com/qcda/curriculum.qcda.gov.uk/uploads/QCA-07-3341-p_Music_KS3_tcm8-406.pdf2007%20programme%20of%20study%20for%20key%20stage%203.pdf

Ravitch, D. (2013). *Reign of error: The hoax of the privatization movement and the danger to America's public schools*. New York, NY: Random House Digital.

Royal Society of Arts. (2013). *Inspector inspect thyself*. Retrieved from https://www.thersa.org/discover/publications-and-articles/matthew-taylor-blog/2013/12/inspector-inspect-thyself-

Sahlberg, P. (2014). *Finnish lessons 2.0: What can the world learn from educational change in Finland?* New York, NY: Teachers College Press.

Sainsbury, M., & Sizmur, S. (1998). Level descriptions in the National Curriculum: What kind of criterion referencing is this? *Oxford Review of Education, 24*, 181–193.

Swanwick, K. (1988). *Music, mind, and education*: London, UK: Routledge.

Task Group on Assessment and Testing (TGAT). (1988). *Task group on assessment and testing: A report*: London, UK: DES.

Thatcher, M. (1993). *The Downing Street years*. London, UK: HarperCollins.

CHAPTER 10

ASSESSMENT IN GERMAN MUSIC EDUCATION

ANDREAS LEHMANN-WERMSER

Assessment does not play a major role in German music education. Scanning the existing handbooks with introductions to music education, one finds a surprisingly small body of literature on assessment. Indeed, quite a few publications omit the topic completely. This can in part be explained by the history of music education both as an academic subject and in schools. Therefore, the first section of this chapter outlines the historical background of assessment in music education. Another section sketches the praxis of assessment in today's schools. Finally, the chapter closes with a description of current research in German universities.

ASSESSMENT IN MUSIC IN GERMAN MUSIC EDUCATION FROM A HISTORICAL PERSPECTIVE

From the turn of the 20th century until the late 1960s, music in schools was deeply influenced by scholars following a philosophy labeled "musische Bildung," or "artistic formation." Although they varied in their understanding of what should constitute music lessons in schools, expounders of this philosophy agreed that music should not line up with other subjects in school, which demanded that children and youths learn something. Their concepts were "nourished by the Romantic idea of the 'holy child' and of the irrational powers of life and music" (Vogt, 2007, p. 8). In this way of thinking, it is only logical *not* to assess achievement in music. Influential practitioners like Jöde in the 1920s despised the then common practice in which students had to go up to the teacher and sing alone to be graded or to learn "technical facts" about works of music history (Jöde, 1924, pp. 10–14). Although teaching practices and styles changed over the years, and due to political influence during fascism, the underlying notion of music being a subject where achievement was *not* assessed remained strong for a long time.

"Musische Bildung" still formed the basis of teaching music after World War II. Therefore, it is not astonishing that up until the 1960s, when a broad discourse emerged on the foundations of society and its recent history (including the lack of critical discussion about the origins and outcomes of fascism in schools), assessment was not even mentioned. The *Handbook of School Music*[1] (Valentin, 1964), which claimed to represent music teaching "as a whole" (p. 7), not only lacks a chapter (or even an entry) on assessment but makes no mention of it at all. The same holds true for Fischer (1954, 1964).[2] This is even more surprising because achievement as such was valued at least in the Gymnasium, the high-ranking type of school leading to university entrance. German teachers almost always teach to subjects. Music teachers often found themselves in a position of very different assessment practices and value systems in a school that only the top 15% of all pupils attended (cf. Gruhn, 2003).

To my knowledge, the first to deal with the results of learning processes in music is the influential scholar Sigrid Abel-Struth. She dedicated a large section of her book *Compendium of Music Education* (Abel-Struth, 1985) to the results of music learning, which she understood as a unity of cognitions, perceptions, attitudes, and motoric skills. Abel-Struth's perspective was not primarily directed toward the schools, although she was aware of the implications when she stated:

> The methods to assess successful learning in music classes present multiple tasks. These methods are linked to the difficult problem of defining learning objectives. "Informal tests" that are used in schools to assess the achievement of given objectives are vague; practical uses have overrun the necessary methodical development.
>
> (p. 134)[3]

The notion of necessary research was mostly triggered by the American discourse. It was no coincidence that a publication by Edwin Gordon was translated into German during those years (Gordon, 1986). However, only a few years later when sketching future fields of research, Abel-Struth mentioned interaction analysis (in the tradition of Flanders), teacher behavior, and students' attitudes—but not assessment (Abel-Struth, 1984).

However, some handbooks from these years did pick up the topic. Füller (1977) dedicated a chapter in his own introduction but referred mostly to general questions of assessment, such as summative or formative evaluations and their inherent assessment procedures. To Füller, this was justifiable, as "according to experience there is less frequent and less rigorous testing than in many other subjects" (Füller, 1977, p. 106). It is remarkable that even a scholar like him, who was then a leading expert on the topic, could not rely on evidence to comment on assessment practices. Instead, facing a lack of data in the field, he based his argument on "experience." The notion of discussing assessment detached from everyday schoolwork can be traced through the literature of the past 40 years; we return to that later in the chapter. In the *Handbook for Music Lessons in Primary School* (Gieseler, 1986), Schmitt took a unique position for that time period. His starting point was also general considerations on the nature of assessment within school and society. He stressed that assessment should document "the progress of learning processes [...], the learners' understanding of content [...], the efficiency of methods, modes of working and media [...], compliance with general and subject specific objections" (Schmitt, 1984, p. 341). Given all that, he viewed the assessment procedures of his time critically: "It is obvious that for such precise and compulsory assessment of learning processes, traditional tests are not sufficient as assessment and testing are not only embedded in ongoing lessons, but also in a net of either stable or variable factors such as aptitude, item difficulty [sic], effort and luck" (p. 341). It is striking how little understanding of assessment practices is displayed in quotes like this one, a fact that can only be explained by the little attention that was paid to American and British music education publications in general and especially to the discourse on assessment. Like Schmitt, other authors, too, focused on the problems of assessment not on the opportunities (Eicke, 1970, 1973). What they commented on and criticized was not the existing school practice where music teachers graded and marked all students without a sound basis but some inconsistencies and pen questions.

The ambiguity toward assessment remained until the millennium. Some authors did not even include assessment in their introductions (e.g., Gieseler, 1978; Meyer, 1978). Other authors provided a rough outline but often neglected recent publications: for instance, Lohmann cited only publications up to 1989 in the three-volume *Handbook of Teaching Music* (Lohmann, 1997a, 1997b, 1997c).

The year 1997 is usually marked as a major break in the development of the German school system and the national perspective on teaching. In 1997 the results of the Third International Math and Science Study (TIMSS) were published (Baumert & Lehmann, 1997; Martin, 2000). They revealed that German students lagged in their achievement on the international scale. Even more important, they documented that "schools and teachers cause relevant differences in the average achievement and progress of the students" (Weinert, 2002, p. 18). Though this may seem to be common sense, it shook sound beliefs. One of these beliefs was that educational reform should start with structural changes in the school system—for instance by postponing the time of distributing children to different schools much as it is done in American high schools. From this point forward, the paradigm of reform changed.

The TIMSS findings showed that students' achievement varied considerably across schools of the same type or even of comparable status. But the results were not used to compare schools, to influence parental appreciation, or to direct student enrollment; the names of outstanding schools were not even disclosed (Baumert & Köller, 1998, Köller, Baumert, & Bos, 2001, p. 283). Rather it was used to insist on the necessity of *all* schools to improve. The German term used in this context is "Schul- und Unterrichtsentwicklung" (which translates to "development of schools and classes"). It stresses the potential of schools as a bounded but complex system and underlines the potential of individual teachers to improve.

The TIMMS was followed by the Program for International Student Assessment (PISA), which initiated in Germany in 2000 and biennially thereafter (OECD, 2000; PISA-Konsortium Deutschland, 2003a, 2003b). The impact of the published results was even greater, as more subjects were involved, but the results remained the same: On an international scale students' achievement was just average; equal opportunities were not provided.[4]

CURRENT SITUATION OF ASSESSMENT IN MUSIC

Beginning with the TIMSS in 1997, German officials changed to an output-oriented look on education and deepened their international cooperation in large-scale assessment. In 1997 the Standing Committee of the Secretaries of Education (KMK) decided to participate regularly in international and comparative large-scale assessments. In particular, the PISA gave detailed information about subject-specific achievement, but also on the opportunities German schools offered with special regard to gender, cultural, and socioeconomic background. The reports were read equally by the public and the academic community. Vivid and controversial discussions were triggered about the state of education and schooling, the financial resources needed to secure a broad social consensus, and a qualified labor force (Brügelmann, 2002). One of the questions focused on was whether the money for testing was well invested. Teachers and teachers' unions had doubts, while political and administrative officials underlined the value of testing for long-term development. The many voices spoke out on three different levels: the *political* discourse stressed the need for qualified workers in a nation with very few natural resources. The *research-centered* discourse focused on the quality of the instruments used in large-scale assessments and the chances and risks of these as reports on their development in the United Kingdom were read in Germany. Finally, the use of assessment as a means for reforming schools was vividly discussed. In any case, the focus was *not* on single schools (or even teachers in the sense of value-added measurements), but on the education system as a whole with regard to structures and constraints.

One would expect to find some reaction to the new output orientation as a leading paradigm in the music education discourse. However, even after the turn of the century, authors constrained themselves to general categories when discussing output orientation and assessment. Meißner (2005) may serve as a good example. In the *Dictionary of Music Education*, he stated: "The term 'achievement' points towards a crucial contradiction of the institution *school* (between advancement of the individual and selection processes demanded by society); therefore it is discussed controversially. [...] In music, problems of assessment are deepened by the subject's content (as an esthetic subject), the major share of affective objectives, and its procedural nature" (Meißner, 2005, p. 142—italics in the original). Not only did Meißner mix the terms "achievement," "assessments," and "grades," but also he made no mention of the rubrics, or of assessing singing, playing, composing, and the like. Like other scholars before him he does not focus on everyday teaching. At least in the Gymnasium, music teaching up to then focused on music theory and music history. Since 2000, performance has gained ground at least as a medium for demonstrating content or experiencing the musical phenomenon. Additionally, special performance-based classes such as string or woodwind classes began to appear. For practitioners, a wide array of questions arose: How do you assess in a just and fair yet time-economic way? How can you assess individual students within an ensemble? How do we factor into our assessments the fact that some pupils take private instrumental lessons? Therefore, while the scholarly discussion focused on serious and important questions, school music teachers were largely left alone.

Meißner was not alone in his appraisal of assessment. Niessen (2005), in Jank's very popular *Handbook of Practical Teaching in Secondary Schools*, outlined the broad variety of approaches to evaluation and assessment. She pointed to the fact that both fulfill various functions as they are intended to give individual feedback, delineate the quality of single lessons or a series of lessons, indicate the quality of schools or even the school system, or allocate formal certificates of education that give students access to different levels of education. She concluded, "Due to the obligation of grading, various forms of assessment take place in music lessons which ordinarily are not up to the scientific benchmarks" (Niessen, 2005, p. 137). In other words, neither did she offer practical help to beginning teachers as could be expected in a guide to practical teaching, nor did she show a positive attitude toward assessment at all.

Other contemporary handbooks displayed the same weakness. Schatt (2007) left out all aspects of assessment, as did Kraemer (2004), although his book is meant as a compulsory introduction into all aspects of studying music education. Of these publications, only Schilling-Sandvoß (2015) took a different position. She, too, referred to the ongoing discourse on the contradiction between "Bildung" in aesthetic subjects and the needs of learners to get some feedback on their progress in the learning process. But she also mentioned a number of studies on how assessment and grading are done in schools, and she looked for alternatives. Regarding general music education in primary schools, the most obvious form of assessment is feedback as verbal report. In Germany, usually schools up to 10th grade, when students are about 16 years of age, issue report cards with a single number for each subject ranging from "1" ("very good") to "6" ("insufficient"). However, in primary schools, most states have abandoned these marks, and schools now give written comment on the pupil's learning behavior and progress. Although this may be considered progress, as the comments take into consideration the multitude of achievements and accomplishments by children, they can rarely act as assessment *for* learning in a formative way. The last reference to be mentioned in this section is Biegholt (2013). He paid attention to music performance and mentioned criteria such as *effectiveness, creativity, absence of errors*, and *identity of performance* (p. 221). Clearly, these criteria cannot be easily operationalized and remain unclear in everyday schoolwork. In summary, it is obvious that assessment and all related topics do not have a prominent place in the scientific discourse and are not deeply rooted in the professionalization of future music teachers.

So, what may cause that narrow perspective that seems to be typical of German music education? One answer can be found in the specific tradition of "Bildung" (translates to "formation") that is still valid in the German education system; another is in the overall role of assessment within the German school system.

Bildung as a Fundamental Category in German Education

The idea of *Bildung* came up at the beginning of the 19th century; the term and the notion is inseparably linked to Wilhelm v. Humboldt (1767–1835), a great reformer of the Prussian school system. Although he himself was more interested in languages and philosophy, the arts became more important in formal education. As the ideas of the Enlightenment came into reality and gained ground in the school system, individual rights and careers were stated as the objectives of schooling (at least for the minority of bourgeois sons). From then on, schools did not assign places in society according to the interests of the nobility, but provided opportunities for learning and developing freely. With respect to music education, Vogt stresses the importance of the term. *Bildung* thus "includes all aspects of education designed to help human beings become individuals. [...] However, *Bildung* always also includes *adaptation* to the given circumstances and, at the same time, *resistance* to them in the name of the individual's uniqueness" (Vogt, 2007, p. 5—text in English). Critical pedagogy picked up the concepts of emancipation as objective in education in general and in schools in particular (see Abrahams, in this volume). Although Vogt went on to state that the term is "too fuzzy [...] and too complicated," it nevertheless forms the basis of teachers' beliefs and often structures teaching (cf. Lehmann-Wermser, 2017).

If school is about individual progress, there is little sense in assessing, which always implies the existence of collective standards. Although this notion may often be merely implicit, and other mechanisms that are more conservative are effective, a generally critical attitude toward assessment, voiced in the context of large-scale assessments and in-state school testing introduced after 1997, remains. Music education scholars supported that notion partly because they shared the idea of *Bildung*, partly because the unique nature of music is basically unstandardized and ambiguous. Assessment and testing would counteract all attempts to establish the top-level goal of *Bildung*, a fundamental discrepancy that teachers and schools could not possibly solve (Vogt, 2008). Rolle therefore decided to "drop all practices and tasks in school lessons either completely or to a large degree which would imply such difficulties" (Rolle, 2008, p. 72).

While *Bildung* merely refers to a philosophy of educating that is a vague general attitude, the structures of school policies and administration detached from the philosophy weaken the idea of assessment. Although these mechanisms cannot be laid out in detail, some features are directly related to assessment practices.

First, formal allocations for careers are to a large degree not based on individual achievement but on formal certificates acquired in school. With exceptions of highly specific study programs with auditions (e.g., music education) or degrees much sought after (e.g., medicine), access to public universities is based on a completed high school program ("Abitur"), not the average grades achieved. Although centralized tests for grade 12 (age 18) that were introduced in the first decade of the 21st century have altered attitudes somewhat (Lenord, 2010), assessment and testing carry less weight. Furthermore, for students headed to job careers that require less qualifications, the results of assessment in schools are not crucial compared to the formal status of having completed 10th grade. For this group of pupils access to music education declines rapidly. Job training is usually done in what is called the "dual system." Trainees spend 75% of the time in companies to learn, and 25% in vocational schools, where time is spent on core and job-related subjects. There are hardly any music classes. With the diminished weight of music, the importance of assessment vanishes.

Second, assessment and testing do not modify the status or the salary of teachers. Teachers are paid on a statewide homogeneous basis, so success in teaching and efficiency does not function as a reward. Although a paradigm shift has taken place from input- to output-orientation on a national level, aggregated data on class- or even school-level results are never made public. Therefore, the publication of PISA results may be much discussed and may lead to more money in the school system or changes in teacher preparation programs—but it does not really impact individual teachers, classes, or schools. This holds true for the core subjects but even more so for music, which has never been included in national tests. Both features may explain to a certain degree the limited role of assessment. However, grading does take place, and therefore one needs to examine the current practices in schools.

CURRENT ASSESSMENT PRACTICE IN SCHOOLS

German schools issue report cards only twice a year. While up to grade 7 (age 13) in lower secondary school there are only compulsory subjects, and music may be taught alternatively to arts or drama. Students are marked most commonly on a scale from "1" to "6" with "1" indicating the best results. As discussed earlier, these marks are used to allocate opportunities for formal education careers. Secondary schools remain largely divided into three different types. The "Gymnasium" is the supposedly most ambitious one, and offers 12 or 13 years of schooling and completion entitles students to attend universities without further entrance examination (with a few exceptions like music, medicine, or psychology). Two models of schools rank below Gymnasium and offer only 10 years of education that lead to a diploma for managerial professions (middle school) or craft or industrial art jobs (main school). The report cards not only document the student's formal education status aligned with the school type but also verify the student's success in the previous year. Students with a grade "5" in two subjects may be forced to leave the higher school or to repeat the previous year—a fate which less than 1% of all primary school children, but 23.2% of all secondary school pupils in their last 2 years before graduation share.

There have been no German publications on marking practices in music in the 15 years prior to the time this chapter was written. Subsequently, we do not know the distribution of grades or the different areas, such as music appreciation, singing, or composing, that teachers cover in music lessons. There are no studies on teachers' knowledge about assessment techniques or related assumptions and beliefs. However, from an ongoing exploratory study on feedback in music lessons (Lehmann-Wermser & Weyel, 2018) there is evidence that teachers base secondary school grades on two sources. One is cognitive content, like music theory or music history facts, that can effectively and easily be tested and marked four or five times during the school year. The other one is students' general interest or active participation in the classes, which may be observed in general music education as well as in performance-based lessons. Therefore, Füller's (1974b) assumption that teachers do not make use of all six grades on the exist- ing scale probably still holds true. Typical music lessons bear different features today compared to 40 years ago, but it is questionable whether this alters assessment practices in school if it is not part of an intense discourse as it has been in other areas. Given the fact that assessment in this field is underrepresented both in scholarly writing and in teacher training, it becomes clear why Niessen (2005) remained so skeptical.

The marking system described previously has been abandoned in two cases. First, in the upper grades in secondary schools, students are graded on a scale from "0" being the worst grade to "15" being the best. Using these grades, teachers are encouraged to map content and expectations more precisely, much in the way a syllabus at the tertiary level in the United States is presented. This has led to a higher acceptance of grades (Lenord, 2010), but covers only a minority of the students, as only about 40% of all students continue school until grade 12 or 13 (ages 18–19).

The other case in which grades from 1 to 6 are not used is in the compulsory high schools (*Gesamtschule*) that have been in existence since the mid-1970s. These schools typically develop special concepts for teaching and for school life. As they stand in the tradition of the *Reformpädagogik* (pedagogical reform), a movement quite strong before Hitler came into power in 1933, the individual development of children is held high, and the arts and crafts are valued following Pestalozzi's ideas of learning with "head, heart, and hand." Consistent with this approach, achievement is not assessed based on standards valid for all, but rather on individual development. Here, this notion touches the philosophy of *Bildung* mentioned earlier.

Figure 10.1 shows a typical report card from one of these schools in Lower Saxony. It is located in a midsize town and is widely acclaimed for its emphasis on arts (Lehmann- Wermser, 2013a). The report card displays the topics covered in class. It is divided in four dimensions that roughly resemble standards published in other countries: singing and playing, listening and appreciating, knowing about music and music theory. For each of the dimensions four statements have been formulated that that are meant to describe levels of achievement and form an implicit four-step-scale.

	Learning progress report		2016/17	Term 2, Year 6
IGS Querum		Music		
	Name Class			

	Topics covered
a	Making music in class
b	A composer's portrait: W.A. Mozart
c	Listening and analyzing music of various genres (i.e. concert, classical music, contemporary music)
d	Music theory (i.e. using a keyboard or boomwhackers)
e	Musical aspects of this year's joint project: *love & friendship*

Areas of competence	Levels of competence			
Making music	When singing or playing you should use your voice more deliberately and get more engaged.	You can use your voice or instrument on a basic level with some assistance.	You can use your voice or instrument rather confidently and most of the time goal oriented.	When singing or playing you achieve goals in an impressive manner.
Listening to and describing music	You should show more interest in musical details.	With some assistance you can hear and present musical details.	Rather often you are able to pick up musical information and to present it in a way that is easy to understand.	By listening attentively and thinking carefully you contribute a lot to the class.
Basics in music	You should actively try to learn the basics in music.	With some assistance you understand the basics in music.	You can learn the basics in music and reproduce them	Acting very independently you can learn even more complex basis in music and present them in class.

This report card refers to the standards of your current year. It documents your development during the entire year.

Additional Comments:

Braunschweig,	den 21. Juni 2017	Seite 7

FIGURE 10.1 Report card for music classes for 6th grade students in a reform-oriented school. For each dimension the teacher has to tick a box describing best students' achievement during the last period. Topics of the class are indicated above. Below is space for individual comments on special achievement and outstanding activities. Additional recommendations for future learning in class or music making in extracurricular activities may also be added.

©IGS Querum/Braunschweig/Lower Saxony.

It should be noted that these rubrics are a step forward, as they give much more differentiated feedback to students than the single-digit system used in the majority of schools. They are related to competencies and indicate levels just as the more advanced and psychometrically rooted models of Knigge (2011), Jordan, Knigge, Lehmann, Niessen, and Lehmann-Wermser (2012), and Hasselhorn and Lehmann (2014) do (see in what follows). Also their attempt to focus on strengths rather than weaknesses may be motivating to pupils. Especially the "comments" that conclude these report cards are used by teachers to give individual feedback and make recommendations for future musical engagement. As many of these compulsory high schools ("Gesamtschule") are located in school districts with a high percentage of pupils from migrant worker families or weak economic status, they may serve as an encouragement to those whose families are not able to or willing to give support to musical participation (cf. Hille & Schupp, 2013).

However, the rubrics are developed with little support by research. In the previous example it is obvious that the statements in each of the areas of competence for the four levels are not specifications of a one-dimensional scale as it is suggested. The first level of music making, for instance, addresses a motivational question ("you should be more engaged"). The second refers to a competency ("use your voice [...] with some assistance"), while the third speaks of a personality trait ("confidently"). While this seems reasonable and maybe practical, it is certainly problematic in terms of psychometric testing. Also, the more advanced rubric systems are much clearer in the relationship between task descriptions, dimensions, and scale levels (i.e., Stevens & Levi, 2013).

The form is meant to provide detailed feedback for learners. There is, however, anecdotal evidence that students do not make use of the opportunity. In our visits to schools, teachers report that pupils simply count the "rights" and "lefts" and "in-betweens" for all subjects and all dimensions rather than studying the reports carefully and taking them as a starting point for an intense self-reflection of achievement. Therefore, the effect of feedback is in part destroyed.

RESEARCH ON ASSESSMENT IN GERMANY

As mentioned earlier, there is only a limited number of papers dealing with assessment from a scientific perspective. In the 1970s and 1980s, when the first wave of empirical research hit music education, there were attempts to put assessment and grading on solid ground. Especially Füller (1974a, 1974b) introduced psychometric standards and paradigms into the discourse. His publications were meant as steps toward a taxonomy in music and "objective" assessment. However, looking back from today's point of view, it is obvious that Füller's attempt simplified the problems of adjusting existing taxonomies to music: The models lag behind the current more sophisticated Item Response Thoery (IRT) models, and they still do not reinforce the use of objective standards in everyday classroom teaching. Not surprisingly, his approach was not picked up by scholars and was virtually unnoticed by practitioners (see Füller, 1981).

Since 2005, a wave of publicly financed research projects has dealt with assessment in general and in almost all subjects. If Germany was to catch up in international comparisons, the quality of teaching would have to get better. New models of professionalization were developed. New ways to enhance students' performance were studied. Research in these fields was promoted to support teachers. The key term in the discourse is "competencies." In Germany, the definition follows the influential educational psychologist Franz E. Weinert, who understood "'competence' as referring to combinations of those cognitive, motivational, moral, and social skills available to (or potentially learnable by) a person [...] that underlie the successful mastery through appropriate understanding and actions of a range of demands, tasks, problems, and goals" (cited in Klieme et al., 2003, p. 16). This definition constituted the core of a national expertise. It has been the basis of all assessment efforts, state curricula, teachers' on the-job-training, and textbooks since 2004.

In the research programs, psychological paradigms prevailed. Therefore, the questions in general and for all subjects were seldom, Does it work in schools? Is it manageable for teachers? Rather, the questions were: Is it up to the standards derived from large-scale assessments? Have the testing criteria been met? Can the teaching and learning be modeled? What can we learn in the international assessments from other countries? To answer these questions, federal ministries and research associations financed various projects, among which were two extended ones in music.

The KoMus-project[5] (Niessen, Lehmann-Wermser, Knigge, & Lehmann, 2008) ran from 2005 until 2008. KoMus followed the paradigm just mentioned and applied it to a key field in German music education. Up to today, music as a school subject follows the idea of general music education even in higher grades. Although the notion of connecting learning in music to music making has gained ground, the curriculum's objectives are still looking for understanding music and less performing as an end. Therefore, the research group from the universities of Bremen and Cologne picked the field of "perceiving and contextualizing."[6] Perceiving was assumed to be an independent dimension in the field with questions of capacity of working memory playing an important role in the process. The aim was to develop a test that would measure up to the test standards regarding item discrimination, level of difficulty, and so forth. For more than a year, a group of scholars and music teachers developed 183 items that were immediately tested in classes to check for practical difficulties and test criteria. Afterward, 104 items were selected. While at first paper and pencil tests were used, the research group then changed to computer testing. However, the students' distraction by noise or questions of other classmates proved to be too irritating not to influence the results. Subsequently, a computer-based test was developed. Since school Internet did not always reach the capacity necessary, local networks were developed. A laptop functioned as a server with up to 30 other laptops providing the test items, listing examples, or score sheets (for details, see Knigge [2011]). The final set of items was distributed in nine series to 941 6th graders.

For the first time, IRT scaling was used systematically to develop a model that would show the dimensional structure of the learning field and display the thresholds of different levels of competence by revealing item difficulty and the person's competence on the same scale (Jordan, 2014). The analysis revealed a three-dimensional structure of the KoMus model of competencies in the domain of listening, contextualizing, and perceiving as a dimension of its own (see Figure 10.2).

Although the sample did not meet the criterion to be representative, various calculations were done for all four dimensions in order to gain insight into the importance of background variables. Gender; musical self-concept; prior experience in orchestra, band, or choir; and familiarity with cultural activities in general could explain between

	Dimension 1 perception and musical memory	Dimension 2 verbalizing, specific terminology related to perception	Dimension 1 notation in relation to perception	Dimension 1 historical and cultural (re-) contextualizing in relation to perception
Dimension 1	–			
Dimension 2	.83	–		
Dimension 3	.80	.84	–	
Dimension 4	.71	.67	.56	–

FIGURE 10.2 Correlations among competency dimensions (Jordan, 2014).

15% and 27% of the variance (Jordan, 2014, p. 143). The project seemed to lay a solid basis for future studies aimed at examining more closely the importance of family background, the quality of lessons, and so on.

The reaction of the scientific community was harsh. Some stated that education in the arts could not be measured (i.e., Rolle, 2008, p. 42); others feared that modeling music competencies and defined levels would be a first step to national standards and warned of negative consequences as observed in Britain and elsewhere (Feucht, 2011; see also Fautley, 2010). Even after some years now the idea of modeling and assessing competencies has not been broadly accepted.

In the project KOPRA-M, a research team led by Andreas C. Lehmann carried on with the idea and modeled practical competencies (Hasselhorn, 2015; Hasselhorn & Lehmann, 2014). They tested a sample of 9th-graders ($N = 420$) in singing, instrumental playing, and rhythm-tasks. Play-backs and play-alongs were used to synchronize and standardize the recordings. Expert raters judged the recordings and reached good inter-rater reliability ($r > .77$). Hasselhorn and Lehmann succeeded in constructing items that fit the criteria for IRT models. Thus, they could explain a good deal of the occurring variance by background variables. Among those, private instrumental lessons, which are still common for roughly 10% of all German youths, was an important factor: It could explain about 15% of occurring variance (Hasselhorn & Lehmann, 2014). Of high importance also was the finding that showed girls doing significantly better than boys even if background variables such as income were being controlled.

Using Assessment to Research External Factors in Education

The two studies mentioned answered the questions of whether it is possible to model musical competencies at all. They also shed light on the dimensional structure with respect to validity and criterion quality. They did not research the questions that had dominated the German discourse since the millennium regarding the identification of factors that support or hinder musical achievement in terms of the German curriculum. Are there discernable impacts of the school system, of classroom quality, of family background, or of socioeconomic status? What personality traits could have an impact? While for other school subjects there is plenty of evidence, for music there is just a beginning. Krupp-Schleußner and Lehmann-Wermser (2017) reanalyzed data from the national panel survey (SOEP) that asked 17-year-olds about their professional and private activities, their background, civic engagement, and so on. Out of $N = 5,799$ youths, 38.4% of the pupils from Gymnasium indicated that they were actively making music, while this was true for only 18.5% of pupils from all other schools. Even more distressing was the percentage of those who took music lessons privately. Here a social status factor becomes more prominent, as this would imply some sort of financial investment—even if German community music schools are subsidized by the state (Lehmann-Wermser, 2013b). In the Gymnasium group, 31.8% take private lessons; only 10.2% of students in the other schools take private lessons. However, there is no evidence of what exactly brings pupils to music—or keeps them away. To learn more about that large-scale assessment would be needed. Large-scale assessment data would make it possible to estimate the outreach of school music and understand the good work that is happening as well as shortcomings.

Hasselhorn and Lehmann (2015) used the test they developed to study the heterogeneity in achievement that has long been stated by practitioners but had never been documented. They administered their computer-based test on singing, playing melodies and rhythms to 9th graders from regional secondary schools ($N = 420$). They also gathered information on private instrumental lessons and gender. Test results (scores) were analyzed as independent variables in all subsequent calculations. Results showed that indeed heterogeneity exceeded by far the expected value of ± 2 SD, that is, a range of 4.00. To reduce the weight of extremes, only the middle 95% were used. For singing, the range was 7.68, 5.54 for playing melodies, and 4.37 for playing rhythms. To investigate the effect of the factors mentioned earlier, the mean and standard deviance was calculated. Not surprisingly, Hasselhorn and Lehmann found a gender effect in favor of girls and of private lessons. With singing they found a large effect of $d = 1.01$, with playing melodies a medium effect of $d = .68$ and with playing rhythms of $d = .41$. Likewise, there was more than a standard deviation difference for pupils from schools facilitating special music programs.

To understand these findings, Knigge and Harnischmacher (2017) examined the heterogeneous nature of German secondary school pupils for explanatory factors. They checked for intrapersonal factors such as motivation of musical practice and self-perception of musical competence (Carmichael & Harnischmacher, 2015), but also contextual factors such as interest in music within the family and out-of-school activities in music to explain variance in an achievement assessment. Like Hasselhorn and Lehmann, Knigge and Harnischmacher wanted to explain the observed differences in achievement. They administered a shortened test that consisted of 27 test items from KoMus (Jordan, 2014) to 803 pupils. Of these, $N = 600$ who completed the test routine were chosen at random for analysis; 50% were boys, 94 were born in Germany, and 48% had played an instrument for a long period of time.

Knigge and Harnischmacher (2017) found a significant correlation between the perceived musical competence and the competence as predicted ($r = .11; p = .045$), but the effect was rather small. Out of the context variables, the interest in music in the family was a significant influence ($\beta = .28, p \le .001$). Both studies show that present research in assessment in music education in Germany is hardly designed to support teachers or to improve assessment practices, although they may be methodologically sophisticated.

Because of that, an ongoing study intends to bridge the gap between high-level psychometric paradigms and everyday music lessons. An interdisciplinary group of music educators and computer scientists is researching the potential usefulness of testing and feedback (see http://www.posymus.de). In a first step, test items from KoMus and KOPRA-M are being adapted for administration in the classroom via electronic tablets. The objective is to design an interface that gives teachers necessary information to give feedback to the students. This has to be done with respect to the statistical literacy of teachers (Gal, 2002), the usability for pedagogical objectives, accessibility, and flexibility. Semistructured interviews are being conducted in order to explore teachers' beliefs about the usefulness of assessment and the use of tablets in the music classroom and related questions. First findings document that teachers are interested and open to electronic feedback systems if they are used to and open for IT in the music classroom (Lehmann-Wermser & Weyel, 2018).

Time will tell whether research like this can bridge the gap between high-stakes psychometric research and the rudimental and unsystematic practices of music teachers in schools. On the teachers' side one may expect that young teachers are more used to technology in general and will easily incorporate new devices even if they imply a change of habits on a broad basis. On the other hand, assessment as such must be included in the scientific discourse as well as in the discourse on practice. It must become a part of study programs, on-the-job-training, in supervision, or of the school development process.

NOTES

1. Book titles are usually translated by the author. The original title can be found in the references.
2. It is interesting that although achievement (and a tough system of selecting students) was important in East Germany, the specific handbooks show the same features (e.g., Bimberg, 1973).
3. If not otherwise indicated, all quotations from German books are translated by the author.
4. In Germany, the socioeconomic status of families has less impact on success in education compared to the degree of education parents acquired. The portion of students attaining higher degrees than their parents is well below the OECD-average (OECD, 2014, p. 84), see also OECD (2011).
5. *Kompetenzmodellierung im Fach Musik* (modeling competencies in the subject of music).
6. The terms "listening and understanding" ("Hören und Verstehen") come close to what was meant, but they were not chosen for fear of getting mixed up with the German concept of music education by Ehrenforth (1971) and Richter (1975, 1976), who use the terms in the context of phenomenology.

References

Abel-Struth, S. (1984). Allgemeine und musikpädagogische Unterrichtsforschung: Gegenstand—Methoden—Probleme [General and subject specific classroom research]. In G. Kleinen & H. Antholz (Eds.), *Musikpädagogische Forschung: Vol. 5. Kind und Musik* [Music education research: Vol. 5, Children and music] (pp. 360–374). Laaber, Germany: Laaber-Verl. Retrieved from http://www.ampf.info/index/publikationen/band05/Bd%205%2023%20Abel-Struth%20S.%20360%20-%20374.pdf

Abel-Struth, S. (1985). *Grundriß der Musikpädagogik* [Compendium of music education]. neue aktualisierte Ausgabe 2005. Darmstadt, Germany: Wissenschaftliche Buchgesellschaft.

Baumert, J., & Köller, O. (1998). Nationale und internationale Schulleistungsstudien: Was können sie leisten, wo sind ihre Grenzen? [National and international school performance studies: What can they do, where are their limits?]. *Pädagogik, 50,* 12–18.

Baumert, J., & Lehmann, R. (1997). *TIMSS—Mathematisch-naturwissenschaftlicher Unterricht im internationalen Vergleich: Deskriptive Befunde* [Math and science teaching in international comparison]. Wiesbaden, Germany: VS Verlag für Sozialwissenschaften; Imprint.

Biegholdt, G. (2013). *Musik unterrichten: Grundlagen—Gestaltung—Auswertung* [Teaching music]. Seelze, Germany: Kallmeyer.

Bimberg, S. (1973). *Methodisch-didaktische Grundlagen der Musikerziehung* [Basic methods and didactic in music education]. *Handbuch der Musikerziehung Teil III.* Leipzig, Germany: VEB Breitkopf & Härtel.

Brügelmann, H. (2002). Kontroversen um die Schulleistungsmessung in Deutschland. Eine fiktive Diskussion über Positionen und Perspektiven in verteilten Rollen [Controversy over assessment of school achievement in Germany]. In F. E. Weinert (Ed.), *Beltz Pädagogik. Leistungsmessungen in Schulen* (2nd ed., pp. 33–44). Weinheim, Germany: Beltz.

Carmichael, M., & Harnischmacher, C. (2015). Ich weiß, was ich kann! Eine empirische Studie zum Einfluss des musikbezogenen Kompetenzerlebens und der Motivation von Schülerinnen und Schülern auf deren Einstellung zum Musikunterricht. [I know what I can do! An empirical study on the influence of music related competence perception and the motivation of pupils]. In A. Niessen & J. Knigge (Hrsg.), *Theoretische Rahmung und Theoriebildung in der musikpädagogischen Forschung* (pp. 177–198). Münster: Waxmann.

Ehrenforth, K. H. (1971). *Verstehen und Auslegen: Die hermeneutischen Grundlagen zu einer Lehre der didaktischen Interpretation von Musik* [Basics of hermeneutics for learning of didactical interpretation of music]. Frankfurt, Berlin, München, Germany: Diesterweg.

Eicke, K.-E. (1970). Erfolgsmessung im Musikunterricht [Measuring success in music classes]. In E. Kraus (Ed.), *Bildungsziele und Bildungsinhalte des Faches Musik. Vorträge der achten Bundesschulmusikwoche Saarbrücken 1970* [Educational goals and educational content of the subject music: Lectures from the eighth Federal School Music Week, Saarbrücken, 1970] (pp. 198–208). Mainz, Germany: B. Schott's Söhne.

Eicke, K.-E. (1973). Lernzielbestimmung und Leistungsermittlung im Musikunterricht—ein Problem der Curriculumforschung [Estimating learning objectives and achievement in music classes]. In A. Bentley, K. E. Eicke, & R. G. Petzold (Eds.), *Research series/International Society for Music Education (ISME): Vol. 1. International Seminar on Research in Music Education* (pp. 117–127). Kassel, Germany: Bärenreiter.

Fautley, M. (2010). *Assessment in music education.* Oxford, UK: Oxford University Press.

Feucht, W. (2011). *Didaktische Dimensionen musikalischer Kompetenz: Was sind die Lehr-Lern-Ziele des Musikunterrichts?* [Didactical dimensions of musical competence: What are objectives for teaching and learning in music lessons?]. Aachen, Germany: Shaker.

Fischer, H. (Ed.). (1954). *Handbuch der Musikerziehung* [Handbook of music education—neu durchgesehene Auflage]. Berlin, Germany: Rembrandt.

Fischer, H. (Ed.) (1964). *Handbuch der Musikerziehung* [Handbook of music education—revised edition]. Berlin, Germany: Rembrandt.

Füller, K. (1974a). *Lernzielklassifikation und Leistungsmessung im Musikunterricht* [Classification and assessment of learning objectives in music lessons]. Weinheim, Germany: Beltz.

Füller, K. (1974b). *Standardisierte Musiktests* [Standardized tests in music]. Frankfurt, Germany: Diesterweg.

Füller, K. (1977). *Kompendium Didaktik Musik* [Compendium didactics in music]. München, Germany: Ehrenwirth.

Füller, K. (1981). Bewertungskriterien im Musikunterricht der Sekundarstufe I [Criteria for assessment in music lessons in lower secondary school]. In K. H. Ehrenforth (Ed.), *Musikerziehung als Herausforderung der Gegenwart. Didaktische Interpretation von Musik.* [Music education as a challenge of the present: Didactic interpretation of music.] (pp. 162–170). Mainz, Germany: Schott.

Gal, I. (2002). Adults' statistical literacy: Meaning, components, responsibilities. *International Statistical Review, 70*(1), 1–51.

Gieseler, W. (1978). Curriculum. In W. Gieseler (Ed.), *Kritische Stichwörter: Vol. 2. Kritische Stichwörter zum Musikunterricht* [Critical keywords: Vol. 2, Critical keywords to music lessons] (pp. 59–65). München, Germany: Fink.

Gieseler, W. (1986). Curriculum-Revision und Musikunterricht [The revision of curriculum and music lessons]. In H. C. Schmidt (Ed.), *Handbuch der Musikpädagogik: Bd. 2. Geschichte der Musikpädagogik* [Handbook of music teaching: Vol. 2, History of music education] (pp. 215–266). Kassel, Germany: Bärenreiter.

Gordon, E. (1986). *Musikalische Begabung* [Musical aptitude]. Mainz, Germany: Schott.

Gruhn, W. (2003). Geschichte der Musikerziehung. Eine Kultur- und Sozialgeschichte vom Gesangunterricht der Aufklärungspädagogik zu ästhetisch-kultureller Bildung. 2., überarb. und erw. Aufl. [History of music education: A cultural and social history from singing instruction of educational education to aesthetic-cultural education, 2nd, revised ed.]. Hofheim, Germany: Wolke.

Hasselhorn, J. (2015). *Messbarkeit musikpraktischer Kompetenzen von Schülerinnen und Schülern: Entwicklung und empirische Validierung eines Kompetenzmodells* [Measuring practical competencies of students: Development and empirical validation of model of competencies]. *Perspektiven musikpädagogischer Forschung, Vol. 2.* [Perspectives of music pedagogical research, Vol. 2]. Münster, Germany: Waxmann.

Hasselhorn, J., & Lehmann, A. (2015). Leistungsheterogenität im Musikunterricht. Eine empirische Untersuchung zu Leistungsunterschieden im Bereich der Musikpraxis [Heterogeny of achievements in the music classroom—An empirical investigation regarding differences in practical musical competencies in 9th grade]. In A. Niessen & J. Knigge (Eds.), *Theory framework and development in music education research.* (pp. 163–176). Münster, Germany: Waxmann.

Hasselhorn, J., & Lehmann, A. C. (2014). Entwicklung eines empirisch überprüfbaren Modells musikpraktischer Kompetenz [Development of an empirically tested model of practical competencies]. In B. Clausen (Ed.), *Teilhabe und Gerechtigkeit* [Participation and justice] (pp. 79–95). Münster, Germany: Waxmann.

Hille, A., & Schupp, J. (2013). How learning a musical instrument affects the development of skills. *SOEP Papers, 591*, 1–33. Retrieved from https://www.sciencedirect.com/science/article/abs/pii/S0272775714000995

Jank, W. (Ed.). (2005). *Musikdidaktik: Praxishandbuch für die Sekundarstufe I und II* [Didactics in music: Practical handbook for lower and upper secondary school]. Berlin, Germany: Cornelsen Scriptor.

Jöde, F. (1924). *Musik und Erziehung: Ein pädagogischer Versuch und eine Reihe Lebensbilder aus der Schule* [Music and education. A pedagogical attempt and a series of pictures of life in a school]. Wolfenbüttel, Germany: Kallmeyer.

Jordan, A.-K. (2014). *Empirische Validierung eines Kompetenzmodells für das Fach Musik: Teilkompetenz "Musik wahrnehmen und kontextualisieren"* [Empirical validation of a model of competencies: Subdomain "Perception of music and contextualizing"]. Münster, Germany: Waxmann.

Jordan, A. K., Knigge, J., Lehmann, A. C., Niessen, A., & Lehmann-Wermser, A. (2012). Entwicklung und Validierung eines Kompetenzmodells im Fach Musik—Wahrnehmen und Kontextualisieren von Musik [Development and validating a model of competencies in music]. *Zeitschrift für Pädagogik* [Journal of Education], *58*, 500–521.

Klieme, E., Avenarius, H., Blum, W., Döbrich, P., Gruber, H., Prenzel, M., Reiss, K., et al. (2003). *Zur Entwicklung nationaler Bildungsstandards. Eine Expertise* [Toward the development of national standards of education]. Berlin, Germany: Bundesministerium für Bildung und Forschung. Retrieved from https://www.bmbf.de/pub/Bildungsforschung_Band_1.pdf.

Köller, O., Baumert, J., & Bos, W. (2001). Die Dritte Internationale Mathematik und Naturwissenschaftsstudie—Third International Mathematics and Science Study (TIMSS). In F. E. Weinert (Ed.), *Leistungsmessungen in der Schule* [Performance measurements in schools] (pp. 269–284). Weinheim, Germany: Beltz.

Knigge, J. (2011). *Modellbasierte Entwicklung und Analyse von Testaufgaben zur Erfassung der Kompetenz "Musik wahrnehmen und Kontextualisieren"* [Model-based development and analysis of test items for the competencies in "music perception and contextualization"]. Münster, Germany: Lit.

Knigge, J., & Harnischmacher, C. (2017). Motivation, Musizierpraxis und Musikinteresse in der Familie als Prädiktoren der Kompetenz Musik wahrnehmen und kontextualisieren" und des Kompetenzerlebens im Musikunterricht [Motivation, musical practice, and the family's interest in music as predictors of musical competence (perceiving and contextualizing music) and beliefs in music competence]. *Bulletin of Empirical Music Education Research, 8*, 1–21. Retrieved from http://www.b-em.info/index.php?journal=ojs&page=article&op=view&path%5B5D=136&path%5B5D=292

Kraemer, R.-D. (2004). *Musikpädagogik—eine Einführung in das Studium* [Music pedagogy—An introduction]. Augsburg, Germany: Wißner.

Krupp-Schleußner, V., & Lehmann-Wermser, A. (2017). *Zur musikalischen Teilhabe 17-Jähriger in Deutschland.* [On musical participation of 17-year-olds in Germany]. Gütersloh, Germany: Bertelsmann Stiftung.

Lehmann-Wermser, A. (Ed.). (2013a). *Hammer, Geige, Bühne. Kulturelle Bildung an Ganztagsschulen.* [Hammer, violin, and stage: Cultural education at all-day schools.] Baltmannsweiler: Schneider-Verl. Hohengehren.

Lehmann-Wermser, A. (2013b). Music education in Germany: On politics and rhetoric. *Arts Education Policy Review, 114*, 126–134.

Lehmann-Wermser, A. (2017). Lower Saxony (Germany) plus Scotland: How lessons are structured. In C. Wallbaum (Ed.), *International comparison of music lessons on video* (pp. 97–126). Hildesheim, Germany: Olms.

Lehmann-Wermser, A., & Weyel, B. (2018). Using mobile devices to assess students' achievement as a basis for teachers' feedback. In T. S. Brophy & M. Fautley (Eds.), *Context matters:*

Selected papers from the 6th International Symposium on Assessment in Music Education (pp. 279–292). Chicago: GIA.

Lenord, C. (2010). *Abitur nach Partitur? Auswirkungen der Zentralabitureinführung auf die Individualkonzepte von Musiklehrern* [High school by score? Effects of the zentralabitur introduction to the individual concepts of music teachers] (Unpublished dissertation). Universität Bremen, Bremen, Germany. Retrieved from http://elib.suub.uni-bremen.de/diss/docs/00011752.pdf

Lohmann, W. (1997a). Leistungserfassung—Leistungsbeurteilung—Leistungsbewertung [Recording—assessing—grading achievement]. In S. Helms (Ed.), *Handbuch des Musikunterrichts. Sekundarstufe II* [Handbook of music education: Secondary education] (pp. 43–45). Kassel, Germany: Bosse.

Lohmann, W. (1997b). Leistungserfassung—Leistungsbeurteilung—Leistungsmessung [Recording—assessing—grading achievement]. In S. Helms, R. Schneider, & R. Weber (Eds.), *Handbuch des Musikunterrichts, Bd. 1* [Music instruction manual, Vol. 1] (pp. 63–70). Kassel, Germany: Bosse.

Lohmann, W. (1997c). Leistungserfassung—Leistungsbeurteilung—Leistungsbewertung [Recording—assessing—grading achievement]. In S. Helms, R. Schneider, & R. Weber (Eds.), *Handbuch des Musikunterrichts—Sekundarstufe I* [Handbook of music education: Secondary education] (pp. 49–56). Kassel, Germany: Bosse.

Martin, M. O. (2000). *TIMSS 1999: International science report: Findings from IEA's repeat of the Third International Mathematics and Science Study at the eighth grade.* Chestnut Hill, MA: Boston College, Lynch School of Education.

Meißner, R. (2005). Leistungsmessung/Zensuren [Assessing achievement/Grading]. In S. Helms, R. Schneider, & R. Weber (Eds.), *Lexikon der Musikpädagogik* [Lexicon of music pedagogy] (pp. 142–143). Kassel, Germany: Bosse.

Meyer, H. (1978). *Musik als Lehrfach. Materialien zur Didaktik und Methodik des Musikunterrichts* [Music as a subject: Materials on didactics and methods of music teaching]. Wiesbaden: Breitkopf & Härtel.

Niessen, A. (2005). Evaluation und Leistungsmessung [Evaluation and measuring achievement]. In W. Jank (Ed.), *Musikdidaktik. Praxishandbuch für die Sekundarstufe I und II* [Music didactics: Practical handbook for upper secondary education] (p. 139). Berlin, Germany: Cornelsen Scriptor.

Niessen, A., Lehmann-Wermser, A., Knigge, J., & Lehmann, A. C. (2008). Entwurf eines Kompetenzmodells "Musik wahrnehmen und kontextualisieren" [Sketches of a model of competencies "Music perception and contextualization"]. *Zeitschrift für Kritische Musikpädagogik* [Journal of Critical Music Pedagogy], 7 (special issue), 3–33.

OECD. (Ed.). (2000). *Measuring student knowledge and skills: The PISA 2000 assessment of reading, mathematical and scientific literacy.* Paris, France: OECD.

OECD. (Ed.). (2011). *Overcoming social background: Equity in learning opportunities and outcomes* Paris, France: OECD. Retrieved from http://browse.oecdbookshop.org/oecd/pdfs/free/9810081e.pdf/

OECD. (Ed.). (2014). *Education at a glance 2014: OECD indicators.* Paris, France: OECD. Retrieved from http://www.oecd.org/edu/Education-at-a-Glance-2014.pdf

PISA-Konsortium Deutschland. (Ed.). (2003a). *PISA 2003: Der Bildungsstand der Jugendlichen in Deutschland—Ergebnisse des internationalen Vergleichs* [Level of education of adolescents in Germany: Results of the international comparison]. Münster, Germany: Waxmann.

PISA-Konsortium Deutschland. (Ed.). (2003b). *PISA 2000—ein differenzierter Blick auf die Länder der Bundesrepublik Deutschland* [PISA 2000—A differentiated view on the states of the Federal Republic of Germany]. Opladen, Germany: Leske & Budrich.

Richter, C. (1975). *Musik als Spiel: Orientierung des Musikunterrichts an einem fachübergreifenden Begriff. Ein didaktisches Modell* [Music as a game: Looking at music lessons from a subject's connecting term]. Wolfenbüttel, Germany: Möseler.

Richter, C. (1976). *Theorie und Praxis der didaktischen Interpretation von Musik* [Theory and practice of a didactical interpretation of music]. Frankfurt, Germany: Diesterweg.

Rolle, C. (2008). Argumentationsfähigkeit: Eine zentrale Dimension musikalischer Kompetenz? [The ability to argue: A core dimension of musical competence?]. In U. Schäfer-Lembeck (Ed.), *Leistung im Musikunterricht. Beiträge der Münchener Tagung 2008* [Performance in music lessons: Contributions of the Munich Conference 2008]. München, Germany: Allitera Verlag.

Schatt, P. W. (2007). *Einführung in die Musikpädagogik* [Introduction to music pedagogy]. Darmstadt, Germany: WBG.

Schilling-Sandvoß, K. (2015). Leistung feststellen und bewerten [Assessing and grading of achievement]. In M. Fuchs (Ed.), *Musikdidaktik Grundschule. Theoretische Grundlagen und Praxisvorschläge* [Music didactics in the elementary school: Theoretical basics and practical suggestions] (pp. 342–353). Innsbruck, Austria: Helbling.

Schmitt, R. (1984). Erfolgs- und Leistungskontrolle [Assessing success and achievement]. In W. Gundlach (Ed.), *Handbuch Musikunterricht Grundschule* [Manual for music education in the elementary school] (pp. 340–356). Düsseldorf, Germany: Schwann.

Stevens, D. D., & Levi, A. (2013). *Introduction to rubrics: An assessment tool to save grading time, convey effective feedback, and promote student learning* (2nd ed.). Sterling, VA: Stylus.

Valentin, E. (Ed.). (1964). *Handbuch der Schulmusik* [Handbook of school music]. Regensburg, Germany: Bosse.

Vogt, J. (2007). Nationalism and Internationalism in the philosophy of music education: The German example. *Action, Criticism and Theory for Music Education, 6*(1), 1–17.

Vogt, J. (2008). Musikbezogene Bildungskompetenz—ein hölzernes Eisen? Anmerkungen zu den Theoretischen Überlegungen zu einem Kompetenzmodell für das Fach Musik [Music-related competencies and formation]. *Zeitschrift für Kritische Musikpädagogik* [Journal of Critical Music Pedagogy]special edition), 2, 34–41. Retrieved from http://www.zfkm.org/sonder08-vogt.pdf.

Weinert, F. E. (Ed.). (2002²). *Leistungsmessungen in Schulen* [Measuring achievement in schools]. Weinheim, Germany: Beltz.

Online Resources

Educational statistics for Germany are available at www.destatis.de: https://www.destatis.de/EN/FactsFigures/SocietyState/EducationResearchCulture/EducationResearchCulture.html

CHAPTER 11

ASSESSMENT OF MUSIC LEARNING IN THE ITALIAN EDUCATION SYSTEM

DARIO DE CICCO

MUSIC CURRICULA IN THE ITALIAN EDUCATION SYSTEM

Music Teaching and Its Evolution

THE role and development of music teaching in the Italian school system since 1861 has been linked to (1) the historical and institutional development of the nation, (2) the changes that the sound arts (and their role) have seen over time, and (3) the spread of different educational models for music throughout the country. Beginning with the second half of the 19th century, a debate about music education developed involving leading figures in culture, pedagogues, and music teachers, that wavered between traditional attitudes (with particular reference to the predominance of opera), artistic production, and national identity issues.

Music first entered the Italian school system officially at the primary level (ages 5–10), as an optional course based on choral singing. In 1896, it was introduced permanently into the curricula of the so-called normal schools, where teachers were trained (Law no. 293/1896, 1896; Scalfaro, 2014). From these beginnings, music was gradually introduced at many school levels (kindergarten, junior high, normal, specialist, all-girl, etc.), though still essentially centered around choral singing, and performed many functions: aesthetic, educational, patriotic, recreational, social, and so forth (Agazzi, 1936).

Italian school laws on these matters—marked by repeated series of reforms—show a steady evolution that assigned music an increasingly key role in education and

Table 11.1 Italian Schools Where Music Is Taught

Education level	Type and duration
Basic education	Kindergarten (3 years)
	Primary School (5 years)
	Junior High: general course (3 years)
	or music course (3 years)
Senior High school	Music and Arts High School,
	some Vocational Institutes (5 years)

highlighted this domain as a strategic skill to build "bridges" between education and reality (Wiggins, 1989). An important contribution was Italy's entry into the European Union and the ensuing reception of norms and principles on teaching and learning. Music achieved new esteem and awareness of its educational value. Table 11.1 shows the current distribution of music courses taught in the Italian schools (Scala, 2008).

Furthermore, under their regulations on autonomy (Presidential Decree no. 275/1999, 1999) even schools that are not listed in Table 11.1 may introduce music as part of their curriculum, either compulsory or optional, to complete or develop their educational syllabuses.

Basic Education (Kindergarten, Primary, and Junior High)

In basic education (kindergarten, primary, and junior high schools, ages 3–13), music teachers integrate content with other art forms and various fields of knowledge, supporting educational purposes beyond music learning (Bianconi, 2009; Ficarella, 2009). At this level, music mainly has a practical-performance connotation, where exploration, comprehension, and learning mutually interact.

Kindergarten is a noncompulsory segment of the Italian educational system and serves a formative and caring function for children aged between 3 and 6. Music is part of its curriculum:

> Music is a universal experience that expresses itself in different modes and genres, rich in emotions and cultural heritage. By interacting with the sound landscape, young children develop their cognitive and relational abilities, learn to hear, listen to, look for and distinguish sounds within key learning environments. They explore their own sound-expressive and symbolic-representative possibilities, increasing self-confidence. Listening to personal sound productions opens the child to the pleasure of playing music and sharing repertoires of different musical genres.
>
> (Ministerial Decree no. 254/2012, 2012)

The number of teaching hours is not specified, and teachers—generalist teachers without specific musical knowledge—can freely manage content, objectives, methods, and schedules of teaching/learning (Ministerial Decree no. 254/2012, 2012).

In primary schools, music teaching/learning is a symbolic and relational space suitable for cooperation and socialization processes (Ministerial Decree no. 254/2012, 2012). As such, it is useful for the acquisition of knowledge tools, the enhancement of creativity and participation, and the development of a sense of belonging to a community as well as interaction between different cultures (Ministerial Decree no. 254/2012, 2012). It is unquestionably a subject with disciplinary objectives, primarily relational and social ones.

Music learning is organized into two dimensions: (1) production, through direct action (exploratory, compositional, executive) on and with sound materials, in particular through choir activities and ensemble music; (2) conscious use, which implies the construction and elaboration of personal, social, and cultural meanings relating to facts, events, and present and past works (Ministerial Decree no. 254/2012, 2012). The *National Guidelines* for primary schools prescribe the learning objectives to be reached by the end of the 5th grade:

- Using voice, instruments, and new sound technologies in a creative and conscious way, gradually broadening personal improvisational and creation abilities.
- Playing vocal/instrumental or even polyphonic pieces individually or in a group, paying attention to tone, expressiveness and performance.
- Assessing functional and aesthetic aspects of pieces differing in genre and style, with recognition of different places, time and cultures.
- Recognizing and classifying basic elements of musical language in pieces of different genres and origin.
- Representing basic elements of pieces and sound events through conventional and unconventional symbolic systems.
- Recognizing the uses, functions and contexts of music and sound in multimedia situations (cinema, TV, computer).   (Ministerial Decree no. 254/2012, 2012)

In primary schools, teachers are not required to have specific musical skills, and principals assign generalist teachers to teach the subject.

Italian school regulations provide for two junior high school curricula. One curriculum is an "ordinary" course where music education teaching is provided. Another curriculum is the "music-oriented junior high schools," where an instrument (harp, guitar, clarinet, horn, bassoon, accordion, flute, oboe, drums, piano, saxophone, trumpet, violin, cello) is taught along with basic music knowledge, with the aims of "intercultural integration and enrichment of compulsory music teaching" (Ministerial Decree no. 201/1999, 1999, no. 124, art. 11, para 9).

As for 3-year music courses, previously called "music education," the subject has the same role and functions it has in primary school. The current *National Guidelines* set specific—but still adaptable—learning objectives, allowing some flexibility in managing learners and variability in objectives, methods, and assessment (Ministerial Decree no. 201/1999, 1999, no. 124, art. 11, para. 9):

- To play individually, or in an ensemble, vocal and instrumental pieces of different genres and styles in an expressive way, also using electronic technology.

- To improvise, revise, and compose vocal and instrumental pieces using both open structures and simple rhythmic and melodic schemes.
- To recognize and stylistically classify the most important constituent elements of musical language.
- To know, describe, and interpret musical artworks in a critical way and plan/realize events that mix other forms of art, such as dance, theater, visual and multimedia arts.
- To build personal musical identity, broadening its scope and enhancing experiences, curriculum and the opportunities offered by the field.
- To access online resources and analyze specific software for sound and music editing.   (Ministerial Decree no. 254/2012, 2012)

Teachers have specific degrees in music and humanities, and current junior high music teaching staff have a conservatory degree. Music lessons generally take up 2 hours a week.

Music-oriented junior high schools entered the Italian school system at an experimental stage in 1975 (Ministerial Decree no. 8/1975, 1975; Scalfaro, 2014, p. 114), and have been a fixture since 1999. Access to "music-oriented" junior high schools is left up to students and their families, and admission is selective based on the results of a musical skills aptitude test.

The study of a musical instrument aims to broaden students' cross-curricular skills, thus promoting the overall education of an individual (Ministerial Decree no. 201/1999, 1999, no. 124, art. 11, para. 9). Teaching focuses on the following areas, based on cooperative activities: development of instrumental techniques and performance skills, competence in sight-reading, study of repertoires from different genres and musical styles, development of re-elaboration skills (free and/or conducted improvisation), and development of proprioceptive, respiratory, postural, muscular, and emotional feedback. The teaching of an instrument in this kind of school is reserved for those who, apart from junior and senior high school education, have a degree from a music conservatory or a certified music institute.

Senior High School

A specific type of 5-year senior high school—the Higher Institutes of Music and Art of Dancing—was established in 2008 (Law no. 169/2008, 2008, no. 137; Scalfaro, 2014, p. 148). Here students are given "the cultural and methodological tools to gain a deeper understanding of facts." Classes are aimed at "learning the technical and practical aspects of music and dance while studying their role in history and tradition" (Presidential Decree no. 89/2010, 2010, art. 2; Scalfaro, 2014, p. 149). The syllabus focuses on the following areas: composition, performance, and interpretation. The following subjects are taught: (1) Music History; (2) Theory, Analysis, Composition; (3) Music Technology; (4) Ensemble Music; and (5) Performance and Interpretation (Presidential Decree no. 89/2010, 2010). Table 11.2 shows the numbers of hours dedicated to each of these subjects.

Table 11.2 Music Lesson Timetable in Musical Schools

Disciplines	Hours per class per Week				
	I class	II class	III class	IV class	V class
Music History	2	2	2	2	2
Theory, Analysis, Composition	3	3	3	3	3
Music Technology	2	2	2	2	2
Ensemble Music	2	2	3	3	3
Performance and Interpretation	4	4	2	2	2

To access this high school, an entry test is scheduled to assess "specific musical or dance skills" (Presidential Decree no. 89/2010, 2010, art. 7, no. 2). School personnel are free to set their own test structure according to rules shared with other teachers.

Conservatories and Universities

Conservatories are state educational structures with a historical origin that is deeply rooted in Italian culture, and are responsible for the training of music professionals: singers, composers, choir and orchestra conductors, instrumentalists, teachers, and so forth (Spirito, 2012).

The current regulation is rather varied and has been structured since Law no. 508 of 1999, which reformed conservatories—also called Institutes of High Culture—and gave them full planning and institutional autonomy while designating them as "university-level" institutes (Law no. 508/1999, 1999, art. 4). In the Italian music education system, there are also "Recognized Music Institutes" (the so-called *Istituti Musicali Pareggiati*), that is, institutions that are structurally akin to conservatories though not managed by the State (Royal Decree no. 1170/1930, 1930; Spirito, 2012). Conservatories, Certified Music Institutes, Fine Arts Academies, and Drama Academies make up the AFAM system (*Alta Formazione Artistica e Musicale*—Higher Education in Art and Music).

Following the enactment of Law 508 (Law no. 508/1999, 1999), courses have been revised in order to conform to European standards and each conservatory is free (within certain national limits) to plan its own syllabi, contents, and practical aspects. Academic courses can be accessed with a senior high school qualification, except for students endowed with special and exceptional musical qualities. In most Italian conservatories, there are classes in music and instrument teaching intended for the training of junior and senior high school teachers. Musicology faculties teach music theory and other courses where music is part of the curriculum as required by each institute (Law no. 240/2010, 2010; Ministerial Decree no. 509, 1999; Ministerial Decree no. 270/2004, 2004).

ASSESSMENT IN THE ITALIAN
EDUCATION SYSTEM

Historical and Evaluative Overview

The assessment of learners—in its pedagogical, legal, and administrative meaning—has recently registered a *crescendo* in interest by pedagogues, schools, and society, due to the changing focus from "knowledge schools" to "skills schools" brought about by the recent Italian school system reforms (Domenici, 2006; Vertecchi, 2003). Reforms—derived from a new concept of *teaching* and *learning* (Delfrati, 2008) and the reception of European principles—have focused on the assessment process as a means to renew education (Castoldi, 2012) and rethink it.

> Assessment represents an important dimension in teaching, since it affects the education of a person, helps form a young person's identity, and can increase self-confidence to become successful both at school and in life in general.
> (Ministerial Circular no. 3/2015, 2015, p. 6)

Assessment is defined as an elaborate and systematic procedure aimed at establishing social, relational, and subject learning within a personal context, rather than the use of routine assessment procedures (Castoldi, 2012).

The Current Legislative Framework

The current regulations on assessment are varied, since they are the result of the stratification of rules at different "hierarchical" levels: *European regulations* from cross-national projects such as the DeSeCo project PISA survey (Council of Europe, 2003); key competencies (Castoldi, 2015, pp. 31–46; European Qualifications Framework, 2006) and *national regulations* (constitutional rules, laws, decrees, etc.). National legislation safeguards learning assessment (Italian Constitution, 1947). The constitution ratifies freedom in teaching with this statement: "Art and science are free and the teaching of them is free." Article 33, paragraph 1 of the constitution includes assessment as a substantial part of the teaching/learning process (Fautley, 2010). In the application of this principle of freedom and the implementation of the *Regulation for School Autonomy* (Presidential Decree no. 275/1999, 1999, art. 21; Law no. 59, 1997, art. 10), schools and teachers have full autonomy regarding learning assessment and skills certification. They choose the subject to be assessed, the assessment tools, the assessment time frame (initial, intermediate or ongoing, final), data interpretation, and so forth (Castoldi, 2012).

Individual tests are the most prevalent assessment method. These include written tests (structured, semistructured essays, translations, math problems, drawings, etc.), and oral and practical examinations. Certification and assessment are handled confidentially among students and those who are jointly responsible for their growth, specifically, teachers and families (Tafuri, 1995). In the space of a school year, different assessment models can coexist (Fautley, 2010): diagnostic, formative, measurative, summative, and so on. Final assessments (every 2, 3, 4, or 5 months, at the end of the school year, or after the exams) have a certification value, recognized by law, for the awarding of a degree (Ministerial Circular no. 84/2005, 2005).

Assessment is a compulsory skill for teachers—a "right/obligation"—and it involves personal opinion (objective, unappealable, indisputable) in addition to legal prescriptions.

At basic school (kindergarten, primary school, and junior high school), teachers are requested to assess students collectively, distinguishing subject assessment (expressed in numbers on a decimal scale) from behavioral assessment (expressed by a collective statement at primary school and with a numerical coefficient at other school levels):

> Teachers are responsible for assessment and documentation, as well as for the choice of the related tools, within the criteria stated by the governing body. Intermediate tests and recurring and final assessments should be consistent with the objectives and aims laid down in the Guidelines and applied in the curriculum.
>
> Assessment precedes, accompanies and follows the curriculum. It implements actions, regulates them, and promotes a critical outcome. It has an educational function, guides the learning process and fosters continuous improvement.
>
> (Ministerial Decree no. 254/2012, 2012)

At the kindergarten level, assessment—not compulsory but often applied "autonomously" by individual schools—"has a formative function that recognizes, accompanies, describes and documents the growth process of the children, avoiding classifying and judging their performance, since it is oriented to exploring and encouraging the development of their potential" (Ministerial Decree no. 254/2012, 2012). A favored means is observation, which is considered a "fundamental tool to get to know and follow children in all the dimensions of their development, respecting their originality, uniqueness and potential, through listening, empathy and reassurance" (Ministerial Decree no. 254/2012, 2012).

At the senior high school level (high schools and vocational education), subject assessment remains in the context of the regulations applied at junior high school. At this level, two kinds of educational assessment are expected. These are (1) subject assessment done by single teachers (Legislative Decree no. 226/2005, 2005; Law no. 53, 2003, art. 13, no. 1); and (2) behavioral assessment done by the teaching body as a whole (Law no. 169/2008, 2008, no. 137, art. 2, no. 1). Because students gain a qualification at the end of this 5-year school cycle, assessment—with particular emphasis on final assessment—aims to verify the acquisition of key competencies in terms of education, culture, and professional skill. These are the objectives of teaching/learning as required by decree (Legislative Decree no. 226/2005, 2005, art. 1/Law no. 53, 2003, art. 1, para. 5).

The outcomes of assessment processes should be communicated to students and their families in a proper and efficient way. Furthermore, procedures and results should be transparent, comply with the regulations, and promote metacognitive thinking and self-analysis (Castoldi, 2012).

> Students and their families should be informed promptly and transparently of the criteria and results of assessment throughout the different stages of their education by promoting participation and co-responsibility, while separating roles and functions.   (Ministerial Decree no. 254/2012, 2012)

Special regulations for assessment are applied to "foreign students" at every school level. These regulations consider cases such as incoming students and include a diagnostic/predictive assessment to define their starting level, to help develop a personalized education plan. Instead, foreign students who have been in Italy for a longer time are subject to the same assessment criteria as Italian citizens.

Individualized norms are created to assess students with certified learning disabilities (D.S.A.) or special educational needs (B.E.S.), that is, a collective evaluation based on a personalized education plan (Law no. 104/1992, art. 16; Law no. 170/2010, 2010), namely, identifying the learning/assessment procedures based on the student's characteristics. In extreme cases, connected to particular pathologies, it is possible to choose specific kinds of assessment (Ministerial Order no. 126/2000, 2000; 1999–2000 school year) and/or tests that are different from those for other students. For students with learning disabilities or special needs connected to other disorders or socioeconomic/cultural hardships, an appropriate personalized education plan is developed, and teachers must bear in mind the personal situations and the educational action undertaken to deal with them when assessing the student (Ministerial Decree no. 5669/2011, 2011; Presidential Decree no. 122/2009, 2009).

Together with teachers' periodic subject and behavioral assessment, from primary to senior high school, skills certification is also expected (knowledge, ability, attitude, emotions, personal potential and aptitude). This has a "purely educational value" (Ministerial Circular no. 3/2015, 2015) and is issued by the school attended by the student.

> On the basis of the targets set nationally, it is up to the educational autonomy of the teaching staff to plan courses to foster, identify and assess skills. Particular attention is devoted to the ways students use their own resources—knowledge, ability, attitude, and emotions—to cope with real situations successfully and according to their own potential and aptitude.   (Ministerial Decree no. 254/2012, 2012)

Such certification is a document which has an educational function aimed at stimulating motivation in learning and intellectual growth, and is issued following regular observation (using charts, structured protocols, questionnaires, interviews, etc.).

This document states and describes what the student has learned in formal, nonformal, and informal contexts, devoting particular attention to problem-solving skills, autonomy, participation, responsibility, flexibility, and awareness (see Table 11.3).

The reference framework for assessment and certification are the "key competencies" highlighted by the European Union (Communication in L1 [mother tongue], in L2 [a second language], digital competence, etc.), the *National Curriculum Guidelines* (for primary school and junior high school), or senior high school syllabi.

The *National Guidelines* for primary schools point out 12 cross-curricular markers of competence in various subjects, and 4 levels of positive development (advanced,

Table 11.3 Skills Certification in the Italian School System (INVALSI test)

Type of school	Class	Aim of the certification	Subjects
Primary school	II	Describes and declares "mastery of the	All curricular
	V	skills acquired, supports students and	subjects, teachers
Junior high school	III	guides them toward senior high school"	can specify the
		(IN2012, p. 15) using the CEFR definitions	most important
		(ISCED1 and ISCED2). Final qualification	ones.
		corresponding to the first EQF level.	
Senior high school	II	Verifies achievement of all the curricular	Other disciplines
		objectives (D.L. 226/2005 Arts. 20 and 22;	
		D.L. 226/2005 Art. 13 no. 3)	

intermediate, basic, beginners). A similar standardized documentation for acquired competencies is also available for senior high school, this specifies the student's level (basic, intermediate, advanced, "not achieved") on each cultural "axis" (linguistic, mathematical, scientific and technological, historical and social). It is written by each teaching body and communicated to students and families.

The Italian school system also has a National Assessment Service (Law no. 53, 2003; Legislative Decree no. 286/2004, 2004, arts. 1 and 3) to evaluate the national education system compared to European and international standards by "providing schools, families and social communities, Parliament and Government with the essential information on the health and criticalities of our education system" (Ministerial Decree no. 254/2012, 2012). The current regulation (Presidential Decree no. 80/2013, 2013) considers three interacting organizations:

1. INVALSI—the National Institute for the Evaluation of the Education System (Presidential Decree no. 80/2013, 2013, art. 3). Once a year a standardized anonymous test is given to all primary (2nd and 5th grades) and secondary schools, junior high school (3rd grade), and senior high school (2nd grade, 5th grade in future) (Ministerial Directive no. 85/2012, 2012, art. 3). The INVALSI test assesses achievements in certain curricular subjects (mainly Italian and Math) based on the *National Guidelines*;

2. INDIRE—the National Documentation Institute for Educational Innovation and Research (Presidential Decree no. 80/2013, 2013, art. 4), which monitors and documents innovations in educational systems. This organization has sometimes dealt with music;

3. School inspectors and evaluation teams also contribute to the assessment of the school system.

Each school is actively involved in self-evaluation procedures in order to "introduce reflection upon its education offer and organization, to develop effectiveness through social observation or external evaluation" (Ministerial Decree no. 254/2012, 2012). The principal submits annual self-evaluation data to the ministry, together with a Self-Assessment Report and an Improvement Project (Presidential Decree no. 80/2013, 2013, art. 6).

The assessment system applied in State conservatories and recognized music institutes is the same as that of the university. Article 33 (first paragraph) of the Republican Constitution safeguards these contexts, since these institutions are considered places of "free research and education...and critical thinking" (Law no. 240/2010, 2010) that operate "to bring about cultural, civil and economic progress in the Republic...and are inspired by the principles of autonomy and responsibility" (Law no. 240/2010, 2010, art. 1, nos. 1–2).

Assessment tests are set at the end of each course and are of two kinds: exams and certificates of eligibility. For the exams, a Commission—with the subject teacher as a member—gives a mark (out of 30), whereas for "eligibility" the teacher has "exclusive" power to decide whether to assign the certificate or not.

The assessment of Higher Education in Arts and Music (Law no. 508/1999, 1999, art. 27, para. 7) is based on the performance of the teaching staff, with particular reference to organizational aspects and exploitation of resources. Special evaluation teams named *Nuclei di valutazione* are currently active in conservatories and recognized music institutes. They consist of three members (one internal and two external experts) who are in office for 3 years and assess the management—not the learning—based on guidelines provided by ANVUR (National Agency for the Evaluation of the University and Research Systems).

The evaluation of the Italian university system is based on comprehensive regulations (Law no. 240/2010, 2010: *Norms on the organization of Universities, academic staff, and recruitment, and proxy to the Government to support the quality and efficiency of the university system*) that identify the following bodies: ANVUR and the internal evaluation team. The former is responsible for steering the activities of the latter, which has to assess the quality of the educational offer of universities and their research activities.

ASSESSMENT OF MUSIC LEARNING: OVERVIEW

Assessment of musical competencies is a dynamic process involving information about music education in its cognitive, emotional, and psychomotor dimensions (Della Casa, 1985; Freschi, 1998). It takes place "in a situation," that is, in a real education environment focused on learning/teaching processes (Freschi, 1993, p. 108; 1998, p. 15), and serving different functions at any one time: diagnostic, educational, summative, and so forth. (Della Casa, 1985; Fautley, 2010). Here, assessment is more complex than in other subjects (De Cicco, 2012; Fautley, 2010; Freschi, 1993; Tafuri, 1995), especially in performances, where the identities, personal taste, and habits of teachers and students are particularly relevant, and introduce arbitrary and random elements (Freschi, 1993).

Due to possible tension between objectivity and subjectivity, the assessment of music "has been neglected or even ignored on purpose, as there is a sort of incompatibility—acknowledged or theoretical—between an extremely symbolic and emotional discipline, and an assessment procedure which is traditionally logical and quantitative" (Freschi, 1998, p. 15). Within the Italian debate, this has been addressed primarily at the junior high school level (Bordin, Cantamessa, & De Cicco, 2013; Lucisano, Scoppola, & Benvenuto, 2012). Research continues on performance (instrumental teaching, choral singing, etc.).

Other components that make music learning even more complex to assess include determining "what" is assessed—the final result, or the learning process. Should qualitative and quantitative aspects prevail? Should relationships and social objectives be highlighted rather than the subject itself? Answering these questions is preliminary to the assessment process—since "what" to assess is strictly related to "how" to do it—which is almost always left to the teachers' discretionary power (Brophy, 2000; Castoldi, 2012; Tafuri, 1995). This results in nonstandard procedures, depending on personal opinion and/or models, influenced by personal experience in teaching/learning, and on tradition (Biasutti, 2011).

The processes of observation and assessment in music education focus on tasks based on complex abilities (perceptive, logical and analytical, symbolic-imaginary, representative, etc.) and on the activation of processes of analysis, summary, problem-solving, and so on (Freschi, 1993; Tafuri, 1995). It can be difficult to disaggregate the contribution, relevance, and significance of each ability, as teachers must set personal "hierarchies" of learning objectives and use different kinds of tests at the same time (Della Casa, 1985; Freschi, 1993).

The activities carried out, whether ongoing or final, are often recorded on video or tape, thus making observation "more objective," and allowing interaction (teachers, students, etc.) and stimulating a virtuous "interplay between self-assessment and assessment" (Freschi, 1993, p. 110).

Further issues are related to "how" to collect and interpret information. These are functionally connected to those parts of the curriculum that are the focus of assessment: performing (singing, playing, dancing), listening, musical invention (composition, improvisation, and arrangement), history, theory, and so forth (Brophy, 2000; Fautley, 2010; Freschi, 1998). Each area is linked to the learning objectives that are set by the *Guidelines* of the national syllabus (for basic school and junior high school), whereas at university or in conservatories they are left up to the teachers' discretion.

At the primary school level, "performance-based" assessment prevails (Brophy, 2000, p. 17), and is integrated with "global listening and production events" (Freschi, 1998, p. 18; Piatti, 1993). Such a data collection mode ensures constant monitoring of education, but on the other hand is exposed to subjectivity, since observing always means "assuming a point of view" (Freschi, 1993, p. 108; see Brophy, 2000).

Observation makes interaction between teaching and learning easier, since "teachers are no longer external observers judging an object different from themselves, but are the stakeholders and an integral part of a self-assessing system" (Freschi, 1998, p. 16). Freschi (1998) declared that in this way, they develop a consistent global assessment, bearing in mind all the components that interact in both the learning process and assessment, thereby creating a "new paradigm of assessment reliability" (p. 16).

For periodic learning assessments, the regulations put the teachers in charge of the process, although they should share this responsibility with students and their families (at the information stage, at least). To record results, teachers at both primary and senior high school use a register (paper or digital) with a certifying value. In universities and conservatories, credits are assigned on the basis of a mark or qualification entered in the students' personal register. In the primary school, there is a notable difference in teachers' behavior. This is a result of their training, and impacts assessment as well; generalist teachers (kindergarten and primary school) favor objectives that link to students' educational needs, socialization, and relationships. Junior and senior high school subject teachers—often with conservatory degrees—support and develop subject-related objectives (Biasutti, 2012; Biasutti & Bergonzi, 2006). The validity and effectiveness of assessment, also in the music field, are conditioned by various factors: (1) sharing and transparency in identifying, clarifying, testing, and assessment of objectives (Freschi, 1993); (2) the time required for assessment (conditioned by any special needs and disabilities); and (3) the creation of a positive and motivating environment (Brophy, 2000).

Primary Education (Kindergarten, Primary, and Junior High Schools)

In kindergarten, no curricular certification is required, and "generalist" teachers are given full freedom in assessment, provided that it is educational and diagnostic. *National Guidelines* identify the following tools as key for this level:

- *Observation*: functional to positive dynamics, that is, "listening, empathy and reassurance" (Ministerial Decree no. 254/2012, 2012), respecting children's overall identity and emotional experience;
- Progressive *documentation* of experiences and learning processes involving music. This makes it possible to share and monitor learning progress and assessment among all those involved in the educational process.

                    (Ministerial Decree no. 254/2012, 2012)

These are techniques which are consistent with a stage in children's development where they come to know their "musical self" through play, manipulation, discovery, experimentation, and so on, in which "know-how" and sensory faculties interact.

Considering that kindergarten is targeted to the global education of children—especially as far as identity, autonomy, skills development, and citizenship are concerned (Ministerial Decree no. 254/2012, 2012)—relational and social objectives are of the utmost importance. Primary music experiences are mostly performance-based: use of the voice (speaking and/or singing), playing (Orff and/or ethnic instruments), and dancing (free movement or structured activity based on sound stimuli). There is no doubt that the observation of this kind of activity poses difficulties related to the observer's disciplinary skills and their "point of view." Observing and assessing children aged 3–6 is a delicate operation in which naturalness and cognitive development must be suitably balanced.

Assessment of music education at primary and junior high schools mainly has an educational and diagnostic function. It focuses on processes and behavior linked to the curriculum: (1) individual and group production (singing, composing, dancing, playing); and (2) conscious use (comprehension, theoretical and historical knowledge, etc.). Learning objectives are laid down by the *National Guidelines* (Ministerial Decree no. 254/2012, 2012), and they should be achieved by the end of the 5th grade. Teachers are thus expected to distribute the content and objectives over a 5-year period, while a sequential numerical scale—from 0 (insufficient) to 10 (excellent)—is used for assessment.

Certification of competencies—at the end of the 5th grade in primary school—refers to the following goals, which are set as standard throughout Italy:

- Students explore, discriminate, and develop sound events from a qualitative and spatial point of view, with reference to their source.
- They explore the different expressive possibilities of the voice, objects and musical instruments, learning to listen to themselves and others; they use coded or analogue notation systems.
- They develop timbre, rhythm, and melodic combinations using simple schemes, they perform them using the voice, body and instruments, including ICT.
- They improvise freely and creatively, gradually learning how to manage techniques and materials, sounds and silences.
- They perform simple vocal or instrumental pieces of different genres and from diverse cultures *solo* or in a group, using educational instruments or self-made ones.
- They recognize the basic constituent elements of simple musical pieces, using them in their practice.
- They listen to, interpret, and describe musical pieces of different genres.

(Ministerial Decree no. 254/2012, 2012)

Assessment of the subject of "Music" (previously called "Music Education") at the junior high school level refers to the *National Guidelines* that state the educational objectives to be met by the end of the 3-year course:

- Students actively participate in the realization of musical experiences by performing and interpreting instrumental and vocal pieces from different genres and cultures.
- They use several notation systems to read, analyze, and produce musical pieces.
- They can design and produce music and multimedia messages by improvising or participating in group work; they can critically manage models from their own musical heritage and also use ICT tools to this end.
- They can understand and evaluate events, material, musical pieces, and define their meaning, referring to their own personal experience and to various cultural and historical contexts.

- They complete their musical experience with other know-how and arts, and can use appropriate codes and coding systems.

(Ministerial Decree no. 254/2012, 2012)

Assessment of music learning in music-oriented junior schools whose music curriculum has both an educational and diagnostic function is carried out by supplementing the *National Guidelines* with components specified by special decree (Ministerial Decree no. 201/1999, 1999, art. 11, para. 9). Assessment of results related to the teaching of musical instruments is based on competence, seen as mastery of the operational features of the instrument, at preset levels. The aim is the correct production of a musical event, as regards its parameters: meter, rhythm, harmony, melody, and phrase structure, together with their agogic dynamics (Law of May 3, 1999, no. 124, art. 11, para. 9).

Instrumental teaching and its assessment is an ideal continuation of curricular "music" teaching and integrates with other subjects in cross-curricular ways. Assessment can be complex, since teachers need to take into account multiple aspects and interconnections between different branches of knowledge, balancing them within a numerical—often summative—framework. According to Ministerial Decree no. 201/1999 (1999), instrumental performance is a convergence of many abilities (cognitive, critical and aesthetic, expressive, interpretative, logical, operational and practical, sensorimotor, technical, etc.). Therefore, performance is the operational translation of the competencies acquired during a standardized educational process (Fautley, 2010; Ministerial Decree no. 201/1999, 1999/Law of May 3, 1999, no. 124, art. 11, para. 9).

Given these assumptions, it is understandable why observation is considered the best technique to assess students' individual or group instrumental performances, provided that the teachers make their objectives and assessment methods clear. At junior high schools with a specific music curriculum, an "entry test" is obligatory. This has predictive and diagnostic purposes, to define the "students' starting level, the quantity and the quality of the information and skills they possess" (Della Casa, 1985, p. 147). In such a context, assessors are free to set the assessment parameters and methods.

As for the certification of musical competencies issued by primary schools at the end of the 5th grade and after the 3rd grade of the junior high, the ministerial guidelines for the enforcement of Ministerial Decree no. 8/2011 (2011), *Introduction of Practical Music Courses in Primary Schools*, is a further series of "quality markers" dealing with two macro areas in the curriculum: instrumental and choral practice. Starting from an enrichment of the final goals of music education at school, these should be:

- Encounter and interaction between people and identities;
- Significance of experience;
- Performance and identity development;
- Experimentation with different styles, musical techniques and learning tools;
- Cross-reference between music experience and practice and other curricular subjects;
- Knowledge of one or more music-writing systems;

- Fostering of discussion at national events;
- Development of techniques and improvisation practices.

In curricular and extracurricular choral experiences, the following points are specified:

- Experimentation with use of multiple repertoires;
- Awareness in using the voice and activation of self-perceptive feedback;
- Ability to be an active part of a choral group, respecting the roles, functions and relational dynamics;
- Stimulation and development of music reading skills;
- Activation of self-assessment processes for musical performances, also using audio-visual equipment;
- Implementation of methods and effectiveness of individual and collective study;
- Development of improvisation techniques.

Senior High Schools for Music and Dance, and Others

Teachers are required to use a decimal coefficient, which expresses an "evaluative summary" deriving from the sum of a "series of tests of different kinds, consistent with the teaching methods and strategies used by the teachers" (Ministerial Circular no. 89/2012, 2012).

For teachers who teach performance and interpretation, theory, analysis and composition, music history, ensemble music workshop, and music technologies, it is necessary to describe fully the objectives and content of the syllabus. The final goals, achieved after 5 years are:

- To execute and interpret pieces of different periods, genres, and styles, proving autonomy and self-assessment skills;
- To participate in vocal and instrumental ensembles, being able to interact in a group context;
- To use, together with the major monodic or polyphonic instrument, a second instrument, either monodic or polyphonic;
- To know the fundamentals of proper vocal emission;
- To use the most popular electroacoustic and music-related ICT;
- To know and use the most important codes in music writing;
- To know music history in its essential lines, as well as the main categories used to describe musical tradition, both written and oral;
- To recognize the traditions and contexts of works, genres, authors, artists, movements, referring to both music and dance and linked to historical, cultural and social developments;
- To grasp the aesthetic values in musical works of various genres and periods;

- To know and analyze important pieces from the musical repertoire;
- To know the morphological and technological evolution of musical instruments.

(Presidential Decree no. 89/2010, 2010)

The testing and assessment phase should be well timed, functional, and consistent with these objectives, in order to fulfill "coherent, motivating, transparent criteria, as well as documentability" (Ministerial Circular no. 89/2012, 2012). In particular, schools are asked to clearly state the "types of ongoing testing, the methods and criteria of assessment used at the end of each period" (Ministerial Circular no. 89/2012, 2012). These criteria must be presented in the Triennial Plan for the Educational Offering (PTOF), which is prepared by each school.

The entry test to this school type and the collective assessment by a special exam board has a diagnostic function, since it is aimed at verifying students' starting level.

In other senior high schools, where music education is present (in accordance to the autonomy in partially defining their curriculum) assessment is the same as that used in the other senior high schools.

High-Level Arts and Music Education Institutions (AFAM)

Assessment procedures at AFAM schools are consistent throughout each student's education, serve subject-specific functions, and complement the teaching and learning process (Cox, 2010). At both the BA and MA academic levels, assessment takes place at the beginning, and at the end of each course as the final exam.

To access AFAM academic courses (*numerus clausus*) students take an entry exam to prove their competence and skills in different tests prepared by each institution. These mostly consist of vocal or instrumental performance tests, presentations of original pieces (as composers), conducting (orchestra or choir), together with an interview to assess motivation, knowledge, and so forth (Cox, 2010; Rossi, Bordin, & De Cicco, 2014). The examining board gives a mark out of 30 and compiles a shortlist.

At the end of each course of the curriculum, students take a final exam. They receive a mark (in thirtieths) and a qualification along with European Credit Transfer System (ECTS) credits. The organization of academic musical curricula according to the university model (i.e., courses awarding ECTS credits) has increased the importance of the final course assessment, since continuous assessment no longer has a legally certifying value.

At the end of BA or MA courses, students must have earned the prescribed ECTS credits (180 at BA level and 120 at MA level) and taken the final exam to obtain the corresponding "academic degree." This last exam can differ according to the course attended and the institution. Final assessment is expressed as hundred-and-tenths and is the sum of the weighted average of the results from the courses, plus extra points (highest 10) for the final test. This assessment often plays a pivotal role between the educational cycles exercising a guiding role for the remainder of the student's educational and artistic life.

At institutes for higher education in music and arts, the teachers determine the assessment. A great part of the evaluation process is managed individually between teachers (and/or the board) and students, in accordance with the regulations set by each "autonomous" institution.

Similar considerations apply to university courses in musical subjects, where teachers are free to plan content, educational syllabuses, and methods for knowledge assessment. The regulations for universities are included in the individual statutes of each institution and in the implementation regulations.

Exams are evaluated using a grade or a simple "pass" statement. As for final exams (BA or MA), the result is the sum of the weighted average of the results from the courses, plus the mark for the final written paper.

CONCLUSION

Assessment evolves continuously and is an important issue in political, educational, and teaching debates in Italy. Assessment drives forces that affect education, most importantly the relationship between education and the world of work. It also drives the implementation of internationalization processes (in both European and extra-European dimensions), the progressive updating of school curriculums, the evolution in professional status and teaching competencies, and so on. As a result, the regulatory framework and subsequent assessment practices used are subject to constant change.

The assessment of music learning in the Italian school system is also being affected by this dynamism. Assessment aims and processes change according to the type of school, and correlate with the unique characteristics of each educational segment, while safeguarding respect for democratic rights and transparency in both procedures and results. Further developments in the context of assessment will occur in the future, with the implementation of more incisive planning that allows communication between the various school types in which art and music are taught.

REFERENCES

Agazzi, R. (1936). *L'abbici del canto educativo ad uso delle scuole materne e del corso elementare inferiore* [The ABC of educational singing for use in nursery and primary schools]. Brescia, Italy: La Scuola.

Bianconi, L. (2009). La musica al plurale [Music in the plural]. *Annali della Pubblica Istruzione, 3–4*, 13–18.

Biasutti, M. (2011). Investigating trainee music teachers' beliefs on musical abilities and learning: A quantitative study. *Music Education Research, 12*(1), 47–69.

Biasutti, M. (2012). Music teaching beliefs: A quantitative study. In G. K. Konkol & R. Nieczyporowski (Eds.), *Teaching and learning processes* (pp. 21–31). Gdansk, Poland: Stanislaw Moniuszko Academy of Music.

Biasutti, M., & Bergonzi S. (2006). Una ricerca sulle pratiche di valutazione degli insegnanti di scuola elementare, secondaria di primo e secondo grado [Research into assessment practices for teachers in primary, junior and senior secondary schools]. In G. Domenici (Eds.), *La ricerca didattica per la formazione degli insegnanti. Atti del V Congresso Scientifico* (pp. 339–349). Rome, Italy: Monolite.

Bordin, A. M., Cantamessa, M., & De Cicco, D. (2013). Musical learning and assessment: Norms, practices and methods in the context of the Italian education system. In T. S. Brophy & A. Lehmann-Wermser (Eds.), *Music assessment across cultures and continents: The cultures of shared practices of the 3rd International Symposium on Assessment in Music Education* (pp. 175–185). Chicago, IL: GIA Publications.

Brophy, T. (2000). *Assessing the Developing Musician. A Guide for General Music Teachers.* Chicago, IL: GIA Publications.

Castoldi, M. (2012). *Valutare a scuola: Dagli apprendimenti alla valutazione di sistema* [Assessing at school: From learning to evaluation of the system]. Rome, Italy: Carocci.

Castoldi, M. (2015). *Valutare le competenze: Percorsi e strumenti.* [Assessing skills: Itineraries and instruments]. Rome, Italy: Carocci.

Council of Europe. (2003). *DeSeCo project. PISA Survey.* Retrieved from https://www.coe.int/t/dg4/highereducation/recognition/lrc_en.asp

Cox, J. (2010). *Admission and assessment in higher music education.* Brussels, Belgium: Association Européenne des Conservatoires, Académies de Musique et Musikhochschulen.

De Cicco, D. (2012). Assessment of musical learning in the Italian basic school: The reasons for a specificity. *ICERI 2012 Proceedings, I,* 4420–4428.

Delfrati, C. (2008). *Fondamenti di pedagogia musicale: Un paradigma educativo dinamico* [The foundations of musical pedagogy: A dynamic educational paradigm]. Turin, Italy: EDT.

Della Casa, M. (1985). *Educazione musicale e curricolo* [Music education and curriculum]. Bologna, Italy: Zanichelli.

Domenici, G. (2006). *Manuale della valutazione scolastica* [School assessment manual]. Bari, Italy: Laterza.

European Qualifications Framework. (2006). *Recommendation of the European Parliament and Council of 18 December 2006 on key competencies for lifelong learning,* 2006/962/EC.

Fautley, M. (2010). *Assessment in music education.* Oxford, UK: Oxford University Press.

Ficarella, A. (2009). Per un curricolo verticale delle discipline musicali: Storia di utopie e dicotomie [For a vertical curriculum of musical disciplines: A history of utopias and dichotomies]. *Annali della Pubblica Istruzione, 3*(4), 19–26.

Freschi, A. M. (1993). Valutare la valutazione [Assessing assessment]. In Valeria Ventura (Eds.), Educazione al suono e alla musica nella scuola primaria, Linee-guida per la formazione del docente (pp. 105–112). Bologna, Italy: Milano.

Freschi, A. M. (1998). La valutazione fra opportunità e tabù [Assessment between opportunities and taboo.] *Musica Domani, 108,* 15–20.

Italian Constitution. (1947, December 22). Official Gazette no. 298/1948. Retrieved from https://www.senato.it/documenti/repository/istituzione/costituzione.pdf

Law no. 293/1896. (1896, July 12). *On teaching in male and female normal schools.* Official Gazette no. 167/1896. Retrieved from http://augusto.agid.gov.it/gazzette/index/download/id/1896167_PM

Law no. 104/1992. (1992, February 5). *Framework act for social assistance, integration, and rights of disabled people.* Official Gazette no. 39/1992, Ordinary supplement n. 30. Retrieved from http://www.gazzettaufficiale.it/eli/id/1992/02/17/092G0108/sg

Law no. 508/1999. (1999, December 21). *Reform of Academies of Art, National Dance Academies, National Drama Academies, Institute of Higher Education for Industrial Art and Design,*

Conservatories and Recognized Music Institutes. Official Gazette no. 2/2000. Retrieved from https://archivio.pubblica.istruzione.it/normativa/1999/legge508_99.pdf

Law no. 169/2008. (2008, October 20). *Turning into law, with amendments, of the law decree dated 1 September 2008, no. 137, on urgent issues in the fields of education and university.* Official Gazette no. 256/2008. Retrieved from http://www.gazzettaufficiale.it/atto/serie_generale/caricaDettaglioAtto/originario?atto.dataPubblicazioneGazzetta=2008-10-31&atto.codiceRedazionale=08A08012&elenco30giorni=false

Law no. 170/2010. (2010, October 8). *New rules on specific learning disorders in schools.* Official Gazette n. 244/2010. Retrieved from http://www.istruzione.it/esame_di_stato/Primo_Ciclo/normativa/allegati/legge170_10.pdf

Law no. 240/2010. (2010, December 30). *Norms on the organization of universities, academic staff, and recruitment, and proxy to the government to support the quality and efficiency of the university system.* Official Gazette no. 10/2011, Ordinary Supplement no. 11. Retrieved from http://www.camera.it/parlam/leggi/10240l.htm

Legislative Decree no. 286/2004. (2004, November 19). *Founding of the National Assessment Service for the Education System, and the management of the institution, according to arts. 1 and 3, Law no. 53, March 28, 2003.* Official Gazette no. 282/2004. Retrieved from http://www.camera.it/parlam/leggi/deleghe/04286dl.htm

Legislative Decree no. 226/2005 (2005, October 17). *General norms and threshold levels for the second grade of education, according to Law no. 53, March 28, 2003.* Official Gazette n. 257/2005, Ordinary Supplement no. 174. Retrieved from https://archivio.pubblica.istruzione.it/comitato_musica_new/normativa/allegati/dl226_05.pdf

Lucisano, P., Scoppola, L., & Benvenuto, G. (2012). Measuring the learning outcomes in music education. *Giornale Italiano della Ricerca Educativa* [*Italian Journal of Educational Research*], V, special number, 44–60.

Ministerial Circular no. 84/2005. (2005, November 10). *Guidelines for the definition and use of the portfolio of competencies at kindergarten and primary schools.* Retrieved from https://archivio.pubblica.istruzione.it/normativa/2005/cm84_05.shtml

Ministerial Circular no. 89/2012. (2012, October 18). *Periodic assessment in senior high schools: Guidelines for the assignation of term marks in the 2012–13 school year.* Retrieved from http://hubmiur.pubblica.istruzione.it/web/istruzione/cm89_12

Ministerial Circular no. 3/2015. (2015, February 13). *Pilot adoption of new national models for skills certification in primary schools.* Retrieved from http://www.indicazioninazionali.it/documenti_Indicazioni_nazionali/CM_certificazione_comp_primo_ciclo.pdf

Ministerial Decree [without number]. (1975, September 8). *Pilot three-year courses with musical guidance.* Retrieved from http://wwcat.saggiatoremusicale.it/saggem/ricerca/bibliografia/emer_insegnamento_dello_strumento_musicale.pdf

Ministerial Decree no. 201/1999. (1999, August 6). *Regulations on music courses at junior high school according to Law of May 3, 1999, no. 124, Art. 11, par. 9.* Official Gazette n. 235/1999. Retrieved from https://archivio.pubblica.istruzione.it/comitato_musica_new/normativa/allegati/dm0608_99.pdf

Ministerial Decree no. 270/2004. (2004, October 22). *Amendments to the regulations for university autonomy, approved with Ministerial Decree no. 509 on November 3, 1999.* Official Gazette no. 266/2004. Retrieved from http://www.gazzettaufficiale.it/eli/id/2004/11/12/004G0303/sg

Ministerial Decree no. 5669/2011. (2011, July 12). Retrieved from http://www.istruzione.it/esame_di_stato/Primo_Ciclo/normativa/allegati/prot5669_11.pdf

Ministerial Decree no. 8/2011. (2011, January 31). *Introduction of practical music courses in primary schools*. Retrieved from http://www.istruzione.it/allegati/2014/prot151_14.pdf

Ministerial Decree no. 254/2012. (2012, November 16). *National guidelines for the curriculum at kindergarten and primary schools*. Official Gazette no. 30/2013. Retrieved from http://www.gazzettaufficiale.it/eli/id/2013/02/05/13G00034/sg

Ministerial Directive no. 85/2012. (2012, October 12). *Strategic priorities of INVALSI for the school years 2012–13, 2013–14 and 2014–15*. Retrieved from http://www.invalsi.it/download/direttiva_MIUR_85_2012.pdf

Ministerial Order no. 126/2000. (2000, April 20). *Norms for the assignation of term marks and exams in state and private primary, junior, and senior schools. 1999–2000 school year*. Retrieved from https://archivio.pubblica.istruzione.it/news/2000/om126_00.shtml

Piatti, M. (1993). *Con la musica si può* [With music you can cope]. Rome, Italy: Valore Scuola.

Presidential Decree no. 275/1999. (1999, March 8). *Regulations for the autonomy of school institutions, according to Art. 21 of Law no. 59, March 15, 1997*. Official Gazette no. 186/1999, Ordinary Supplement no. 152/L. Retrieved from http://www.gazzettaufficiale.it/eli/id/1999/08/10/099G0339/sg

Presidential Decree no. 122/2009. (2009, June 22). *Regulations for the coordination of current norms for student assessment*. Official Gazette no. 191/2009. Retrieved from http://www.gazzettaufficiale.it/gunewsletter/dettaglio.jsp?service=1&datagu=2009-08-19&task=dettaglio&numgu=191&redaz=009G0130&tmstp=1251275907525

Presidential Decree no. 89/2010. (2010, March 15). *Regulations for the revision of the curricular, organizational, and educational structures at high schools*. Official Gazette no. 137/2010. Retrieved from http://nuovilicei.indire.it/content/index.php?action=lettura_paginata&id_m=7782&id_cnt=9667

Presidential Decree no. 80/2013. (2013, March 28). *Regulations for the national assessment system for education*. Official Gazette no. 155/2013. Retrieved from http://www.gazzettaufficiale.it/atto/serie_generale/caricaDettaglioAtto/originario?atto.dataPubblicazioneGazzetta=2013-07-04&atto.codiceRedazionale=13G00121&elenco30giorni=false

Rossi, T., Bordin, A. M., & De Cicco, D. (2014). Assessment and professors' competence in Italian higher music education between tradition and new goals. *Creative Education, 5*, 341–1352.

Royal Decree no. 1170/1930. (1930, May 15). *Norms for certification of musical institutes*. Retrieved from http://www.cgilconoscenza.it/area_riservata_rsu_delegati/ipertesto_ccnl/materiali/rd19301170.htm

Scala, S. (2008). La presenza della musica nella scuola italiana [The presence of music in Italian schools]. *Annali della Pubblica Istruzione, 123*, 1–6.

Scalfaro, A. (2014). *Storia dell'Educazione Musicale nella Scuola Italiana: Dall'Unità ai giorni nostri*. [History of music education in Italian schools: From unification to our own times]. Milan, Italy: Franco Angeli.

Spirito, N. (2012). *Disciplina giuridica dei Conservatori di musica (Istituti di Alta Formazione Artistica e Musicale)* [The legal framework of music conservatories (Institutes of higher education in the arts and music)]. Turin, Italy: Giappicchelli.

Tafuri, J. (1995). *L'educazione musicale: Teorie, metodi, pratiche* [Music education: Theories, methods, practices]. Turin, Italy: EDT.

Vertecchi, B. (2003). *Manuale della valutazione: Analisi degli apprendimenti e dei contesti* [Assessment manual: Analysis of learning and contexts]. Milan, Italy: Franco Angeli.

Wiggins, G. (1989). A true test: Toward more authentic and equitable assessment. *Phi Delta Kappan, 70*, 703–713.

CHAPTER 12

....

MUSIC EDUCATION ASSESSMENT POLICY AND PRACTICE IN TURKEY

....

DILEK GÖKTÜRK-CARY

INTRODUCTION

....

MUSTAFA Kemal Atatürk (1881–1938) established the Republic of Turkey on October 29, 1923. Following the foundation of a new government based on secular democratic principles, Atatürk initiated aggressive programs of social and cultural changes. Educational reform was one of the first areas he addressed. Although his educational proposals were based on European models, Atatürk's policies stressed the importance of a strong national identity as the primary foundation for his new educational system (Williamson, 1987). According to Çakar, "The founding philosophy of the Republic of Turkey was creating a new state, capital city, society and citizen" (2015, p. 12). In an attempt to obliterate the cultural capital of the Ottoman past, from 1924 through 1928 Atatürk instituted a set of religious (1924/5), sartorial (1925), economic (1927), and linguistic (1928) reforms that served to underscore the modernist and westernizing aspirations of his new state. These reforms were subsequently legitimated in article no. 2 of the 1937 Constitution according to the ideological tenets of revolutionism (*inkılâpçılık*), and nurtured a discourse about change that permeated many aspects of Turkish life (O'Connell, 2000). As one of these changes, *Resmi Gazete* (The Official Gazette) published the "Tevhid-i Tedrisat Kanunu" (Law on Unification of Educational Institutions) on March 3, 1923. "Tevhid-i Tedrisat Kanunu" called for the unification of all educational institutions under the control of the Ministry of National Education. The primary reason for this law was the abolition of religious instruction in all schools. This action was central to the development of secularism in modern Turkey (Göktürk-Cary, 2014).

While this discourse had a substantial historical pedigree and had appeared in many contemporary publications, Atatürk was in a position to implement his vision of a new

Turkish society with legislative effect and to validate (albeit in retrospect) his revision of this society by co-opting the evolutionary language of a long-established discursive tradition. As a result, Atatürk has been credited with the rapid transformation of Turkish culture during the period (O'Connell, 2000).

It is difficult to assess or even describe the exact nature of Kemal Atatürk's influence on the development of Turkish education, primarily because that development became intertwined with other factors in the growth of the modern Turkish Republic. However, it is safe to say that, for Atatürk, education was vital to the new nation and that educators were highly prestigious professionals (Özeke, 2003). İlhan Başgöz and Howard E. Wilson (1968) describe the new educational system as follows:

> After the establishment of the Turkish Republic, the new government began to search for a general system of education. Previously, the Ottoman Empire had included diverse religions and nationalities. After the collapse of the Empire, the new Turkish government began to develop a national system of education. Some of the biggest difficulties faced by the new government were an insufficient number of schools and teachers, a high illiteracy rate, and a lack of sufficient funds.
>
> (cited in Göktürk-Cary, 2014, p. 15)

Despite these challenges, Atatürk was persistent in the implementation of his reforms of music and the arts. During a speech at İzmir Teacher Training School for Girls in 1925, he described his sensitivity to and support of music: "Creatures who do not have any connection with music cannot be humans. Music is the joy, spirit, pleasure, briefly everything in life" (Kavcar, 1982, p. 16). Atatürk's preoccupation with his revolutionary changes also resulted in the emergence of a national style that sought to alter Ottoman music practice using Western musical principles (O'Connell, 2000).

FOUNDATIONS OF MUSIC EDUCATION IN TURKEY

The Ottoman Empire's "period of glory" began in the 16th century and lasted until the 20h century. After two centuries of slow decline and a century of efforts to reverse the decline through increasing westernization, the empire collapsed at the close of World War I. This ultimately resulted in the birth of Turkish Republic in 1923 (Öztürk, 1996).

Pedagogical experts noted the need for teacher education in Turkey before the Republic was established, but official policies toward teacher education began during the Republican period. The founding of the Republic also led to major changes and developments in the nation's socioeconomic structure. At the same time, improvements in science and technology resulted in broader educational needs and expectations on the part of the Turkish people. Changes in the roles of teachers created significant burdens for Turkish teacher education institutions (Özeke, 2003), because the need to balance Turkish identity with Western modernism was (and still is) arguably the most challenging aspect of Turkish educational policies in modern days (Başgöz & Wilson, 1968; Özeke, 2003).

Nowhere is this challenge more evident than in the evolving curricula of Turkish public schools, colleges, and universities (Göktürk, 2008), and music teacher education was no exception (Özeke, 2003).

Music education practice today has been influenced by modernist movements that emerged in the first quarter of 1800s. Through such movements, Ottoman music, which had originated in Middle Asia (the ancient motherland of the Turks) and had been influenced by Anatolian culture and the surrounding cultures for centuries, gained a rather different dimension. Following these attempts, Ottoman music and music education was under the influence of the sultans. For instance, Sultan Abdülmecit was very keen on Western music and opera. During his reign, bowed string instruments, singing, dancing, and the new military band were established with the contributions of the Italian musician Giuseppe Donizetti (1788–1856). Music took its place as a subject in secondary education in the 1910s, starting with secondary schools and teacher training school programs for girls, and later in teacher training schools for boys (Uçan, 1994). During these years, another important development was the foundation of Darül'elhan in İstanbul, which would function as a conservatory after the Republic (Tufan, 2006).

Following the foundation of the Republic, a number of foreign music specialists were invited to Turkey after 1930. These specialists were employed to develop Western art music at the new music institutions in İstanbul and Ankara. An impressive number of foreign artists were attracted to Turkey, including Joseph Marks (1882–1964), Paul Hindemith (1895–1963), Ernst Praetorius (1880–1946), Carl Ebert (1887–1980), and Eduard Zuckmayer (1890–1972). These musicians were drawn to Turkey (following Hindemith's lead) by the availability of new job opportunities, and they also wished to flee the increasingly difficult political situation at home (O'Connell, 2000).

There is no doubt that Turkish education, including music education and music teacher education, began the path to its present position through the special efforts of Mustafa Kemal Atatürk. This was true for all Turkish education, but perhaps it was especially so in music teacher education due to the influential consultants he brought into the country (Göktürk-Cary, 2014). Today, the Turkish government continues to build and develop music education based on the foundations established during the early years of the Republic.

Music Assessment at Primary Schools in Turkey

Brief History of Music Education at the Primary-School Level in Turkey

Music became an academic subject in urban elementary schools in 1924 and in rural elementary schools in 1948 (Küçüköncü, 2006). It became a compulsory subject in the Turkish elementary school curriculum in 1968. Goals, objectives, and evaluation tools were clearly described for each stage of instruction in this curriculum. The evaluation tools in the 1973 pilot curriculum for elementary and secondary school levels required that a list of topics and activities be specified without determining goals for the music class. The music curriculum for students with learning disabilities was developed in 1976. After an analysis of these three music curricula, the draft of the 1982 curriculum was prepared. This revised draft curriculum presented specific goals and evaluation tools for each unit and subject at each stage of the elementary level (Özgül, 2009).

Music education has also been compulsory in nursery schools since the 1920s. At this level it is offered as a games, art, and music program taught by the nursery school teachers. In elementary schools it is offered as a general music course and taught to grades 1, 2, and 3 by the classroom teachers, and to other grades by music teachers. Students receive 2 hours of music per week in the first 3 years of elementary schooling, and 1 hour per week in the last 5 years. The basic aim of music education in Turkey is to help students develop their individual and common music capabilities in a systematic way in order to function effectively in the community (Özgül, 2009).

The Primary School Music Teaching Curriculum was accepted and published by the Ministry of National Education in April 1994, and the 2006 revision of this curriculum was prepared by a special commission appointed by the Ministry of National Education Elementary School Public Directorship. This revised version was undertaken with the understanding that public music education is oriented toward a balanced program in terms of aesthetics, using suitable methods and approaches. The content and approaches of the 1968, 1973, and 1994 curricula were also taken into consideration. The 2006 curriculum was developed with constructivism as a theoretical foundation. Developed first for the primary school music curriculum, constructivist-based curricula are recent in the Turkish educational system (Göktürk, 2010). The 2006 music curriculum consists of an introduction, general objectives of Turkish national education, the vision for the curriculum, basic approach and structure, teaching and learning processes, acquisitions, methods and techniques, measurement and evaluation, and texts and resources (Türkiye Cumhuriyeti MEB, 2006). Although there have been several positive effects on student learning and creativity as a result of this new approach, challenges and misunderstandings also exist in practice (Göktürk, 2010, p. 3076). Behaviorist approaches were used in the 1994 music curriculum, which was used for 15 years. However, they were replaced by constructivist approaches grounded in emerging educational philosophies (Albuz & Akpınar, 2009).

Assessment in the Primary-School Music Curriculum

Scholars have examined the measurement and evaluation tools in the 2006 music curriculum in a variety of studies. The main goal of this research is to investigate the effectiveness of assessment tools in the curriculum.

Türkmen (2009b) found that measurement and evaluation practices that result in receiving good grades are the most effective strategies to motivate and to increase the involvement of 5th-grade students in the music classroom. In another study, Türkmen

(2009a) found that music teachers were familiar with the measurement and evaluation processes of the 2006 music curriculum. However, teachers complained about the limited weekly class time (only 40 minutes per week) and crowded classroom settings that inhibit efficient student evaluation. Teachers also stated that they developed their own unique strategies to evaluate student learning effectively. Türkmen further indicated that students were taking music more seriously as a subject as long as the teacher used evaluation tools in the curriculum correctly.

Demirci and Albuz (2010) found that among primary-school music teachers ($n = 20$), 55% responded positively regarding the evaluation part of the curriculum. The purpose of their study was to evaluate the effectiveness of the teacher's book for 6th-grade music class. They found that most of the teachers believed the evaluation section to be adequate. However, the participants made a common critique that after the subject of the course was taught, evaluating students' comprehension remained problematic.

Demirci and Albuz (2010) also examined the music teachers' use of student self-evaluation tools included in the evaluation section of the curriculum. The majority of these teachers (65%) responded negatively, indicating that the "inadequacy of the evaluation part on account of self evaluation and intensifying the subjects of the students" (p. 279). In a similar way, Kırmızıbayrak (2012) also suggested that multiple assessment activities should be included and students should also be evaluated based on their class participation, general behavior, and relationship with others in addition to their musical knowledge.

Köroğlu (2014) found that music teachers complain about the measurement and evaluation segment of the curriculum because it is difficult to apply. Her participants responded that students struggled to comprehend the topics, which made it quite difficult for teachers to achieve the goals in the curriculum. Similarly, Aksu's (2007) results also indicated that music classroom subjects (particularly solfège reading) were above the level of eighth-year primary-school students. Based on these findings, students could not be evaluated properly with the measurement tools in the curriculum.

Another problem with the evaluation process that music teachers indicate is the uniform structure of exam types and the ineffective use of measurement tools that cannot be used to evaluate students fairly. The structure of these tools emphasizes rote learning instead of meaningful learning for students (Baş, 2011).

Regarding the assessment segment of the primary-school curriculum, two studies (Göktürk-Cary, 2012; Holmes, Aguilar, Chen, & Göktürk, 2009) focused on existing problems. In Göktürk's collaborative study (Holmes et al., 2009), music teachers responded that providing different assessment tools would help them assess student learning in diverse classroom settings. Also, the participants complained about the amount of paperwork for evaluation and recommended less paperwork for assessment. Göktürk-Cary (2012) and Toraman (2013) found similar results regarding evaluation tools, such as checklists and observation reports. Other issues were:

- negative effects of the standardized measurement and evaluation tools on students about learning music (one of the respondents indicated that preparedness, motivation, participation, and interest of the student could be used as measurement tools in the classroom),

- because of the 1-hour time period for music class, lack of time to pay attention to students individually,
- lack of student interest in oral exams and higher interest level in written exams (music teachers prefer oral exams rather than preparing written tests),
- lack of balance among written homework/assignment or project, written exam, and oral exam/performance (more weight on written exams),
- difficulty of grading written exams because of the high number of students,
- assessment tools that are not functional in the classroom, and
- difficulty level of using the assessment tools (Göktürk-Cary, 2012; Toraman, 2013).

Respondents in Göktürk-Cary's (2012) study also offered the following recommendations for the improvement and effectiveness of music teaching and learning through assessment tools in Turkey:

- a standardized grading scale that would help to clarify the criteria and allow teachers to be more objective when evaluating students,
- adding projects and performances would help students to improve their attention and self-confidence,
- developing measurement tools that are easier to use, and
- reducing the amount of paperwork for evaluation. (Göktürk-Cary, 2012, p. 170)

The music teachers also indicated that measurement tools which can assess the individual abilities of students would be the best option for the music classroom. With individualized tools, students could be evaluated fairly based on their musical background, interest, and inborn ability (Göktürk-Cary, 2012).

MUSIC ASSESSMENT AT SECONDARY SCHOOLS IN TURKEY

Assessment in the Secondary-School Music Curriculum

Music has been a subject in high school curriculum since 1952 (Uçan, 1990). Today, music is an elective course at general high schools, but there is no music course in vocational schools' curricula (Tufan, 2006). As a subject for secondary schools, the Ministry of National Education stated that the goal of "music" was to educate students to embrace national and international musical culture, train them to be able to complete the following tasks: sing and play a musical instrument, describe music through listening, improvise and compose, express their creativity, think musically, build up self-confidence, and develop musical reading skill (MEB, 2009). The 2009 high school music curriculum was also developed using a constructivist approach similar to the 2006 primary school music curriculum (Secondary School Music Curriculum, 2016).

Because music is an optional subject, only a portion of high school students study music. As another issue, a music teacher shortage led to music teaching positions being filled by unspecialized teachers. Under these circumstances, music courses were lacking the necessary artistic foundations and understandings (Tufan, 2006).

The *Measurement and Evaluation* part of the secondary-school music curriculum is a combination of 10 segments as follows:

- Classroom Performance (based on general participation and attitude of students in the music classroom)
- Projects (original topics in music that students choose to investigate, develop, and write/can be personal or group projects)
- Musical Performance (playing musical instruments, singing solfège, sight-reading, etc., by students)
- Observation Report (teacher keeps records of students through observing them in the class)
- Classroom Presentation (by students)
- Self-evaluation (students evaluate themselves)
- Peer evaluation (students evaluate each other)
- Classroom Interviews (teachers evaluate students by asking them questions)
- Portfolio (students prepare files that include all of their activities in music classroom. Portfolios show musical development of students, and can be exhibited at school or given to parents.)
- Written Exams (multiple choice, open-ended questions with short answers, pairing items, etc.). (Secondary School Music Curriculum, 2016)

Separate forms and criteria that include measurement tools and sample exams with detailed information are also provided for each segment.

Varış and Cesur (2012) decided to develop a music achievement test for secondary school students, but their study of music tests revealed that most tests in music education are based on performance. They concluded that instead of having a solely performance-based evaluation, these tests should combine all three learning domains (cognitive, affective, and psychomotor) to assess students.

Assessment in the High Schools of Fine Arts Music Departments

The first high school of fine arts was opened in İstanbul on November 16, 1989, as the İstanbul Anatolian High School of Fine Arts. This was followed by the Ankara Anatolian High School of Fine Arts and İzmir Anatolian High School of Fine Arts in 1990.

These schools brought a new perspective to arts education in Turkey. The main purpose of these institutions was to develop students for undergraduate-level music schools, such as music teacher training schools, conservatories, and music departments at colleges of fine arts (Özden, 2010). Today there are 83 high schools of fine arts in Turkey,[1] and studies show that between 67.41% (Köse, 2006) and 69.41% (Bozkaya, 2006) of the students at music teacher training schools come from high schools of fine arts.

The music curricula of schools of fine arts were developed in 2006 in the following areas:

- Instrumental (Violin, Viola, Cello, Double Bass, Flute, Piano, Guitar, Kanun, Oud, Bağlama)
- Music theory (Introduction to Music, PC Use in Music, Musical Forms, Solfège)
- Music history (History of Western Music, History of Traditional Turkish Music)
- Ensembles (Western Music Ensemble, Turkish Music Ensemble, Western Music Choral Ensemble, Turkish Music Choral Ensemble)
- Other (Drama, Studio Voice, Instrumental Care)

As in the secondary school music curriculum, all 23 curricula for high schools of fine arts were constructivist based. The *Measurement and Evaluation* segment of each curriculum also includes exam samples and forms similar to the secondary school music curriculum. These forms have detailed information on the assessment process.

MUSIC ASSESSMENT AT THE COLLEGE LEVEL IN TURKEY

Assessment in Music Teacher Training Schools in Turkey

Music teacher education at the collegiate level in Turkey was first offered in 1924 at the Musikî Muallim Mektebi [Music Teacher Training School] in Ankara, the newly established capital of Turkey. The purpose of this educational institution was to prepare students to become general music instructors in secondary schools (Yayla, 2004). Instruction began on November 1, 1924. Atatürk opened this institution because he valued the role of music education in the development of better life standards for the citizens of the newly established state (Uçan, 1994).

For 13 years from 1924 to 1937, the Music Teacher Training School emphasized musical performance training despite its name. In 1936, the Ankara State Conservatory was established in the nation's capital city as a branch of the Music Teacher Training School. In 1937, the Gazi Orta Öğretmen Okulu ve Terbiye Enstitüsü Müzik Şubesi (Music Branch of the Gazi Secondary Teacher School and Training Institute) opened in

Ankara and took on responsibilities for music teacher training. The name of this institution was later changed to Gazi Eğitim Enstitüsü Müzik Bölümü (Gazi Education Institute Music Department). It became the Gazi Yüksek Öğretmen Okulu Müzik Bölümü (Gazi Higher Teacher School Music Department) in 1980. By 1978, education institutions in İstanbul, İzmir, and Nazilli had added music branches. The Nazilli Education Institute closed in 1980, but the university in Bursa added a music department in 1981. By the 1981–1982 academic year there were four institutions with music teacher education programs, all of which had passed through similar stages in their development (Özeke, 2003). At the time this chapter was written, all four continued to support music teacher education programs.

In 1982, the Turkish constitution was changed to include new provisions for higher education. As a result of this restructuring, higher education was placed under the Yüksek Öğretim Kurulu (Higher Education Council). Previously, teacher education programs had been associated with education institutions affiliated with the Milli Eğitim Bakanlığı (Ministry of National Education), after which they were transferred to the Higher Education Council. Therefore, in 1982, The Gazi Higher Teacher School of Music Department changed its name to Gazi Üniversitesi Gazi Eğitim Fakültesi Müzik Eğitim Bölümü (Gazi University Gazi Education Faculty Music Education Department) (Özeke, 2003). By April 2016, the number of independent higher-education music institutions had gradually increased to the present number of 34, but only 25 of them were actively accepting students.[2]

Regarding the assessment segments of the curricula that have been used in music teacher training institutions, there was no detailed information in 1924 and 1931. However, students could not advance to a higher level of class unless they were successful. By 1970, the goals of the curriculum were more detailed and students were expected to be equipped to achieve them. The first actual measurement and evaluation segment was included in the 1978 curriculum, and by 1980, the measurement tools, particularly for instrumental performance, were included in detail (Tebiş, 2004). After 1997, however, the curricula did not contain an adequate assessment segment but only brief course descriptions (Tebiş, 2004), and the evaluation section of the curriculum was deficient regarding the number of exams and the measurement of course objectives. The assessment processes needed both theoretical foundations and practical applicability (Şaktanlı, 2004).

Regarding assessment at music teacher training schools (particularly with the instrumental juries), Çoban (2011) states the lack of standardization and cursory evaluation for students as the most pressing problems. She found that student participants complained about inadequate assessment criteria, and, as a result, mistrust for their professors. As a similar concern, Saraç and Şeker (2008) revealed that due to the lack of studies on the evaluation of psychomotor development in music education, objective measurement of instrumental performances is problematic. To address this and attempt to standardized the process, the authors developed a performance evaluation form that can be used to assess string teacher education students. The form has 26 different criteria to assess string students. These include, among others, criteria that address the positions of the fingers that hold the bow, the position of the right hand, technical issues, sight-reading ability, general posture of the student, and the use of dynamics and musicality.

According to Alpagut (2004), the main issues regarding the evaluation processes in the violin curriculum were:

1. lack of measurement scale development to evaluate violin students,
2. insufficient amount of sources that teachers can systemize to achieve the goals in the curriculum,
3. usually only one "subjective" midterm exam because it is conducted by only the instructor (not by a jury and also 30% of the overall score), and
4. a final exam that students have to play in front of a jury (final exam percentage may differ according to the institution, varying from 60% to 70%, and these exams are usually not standardized) (Alpagut, 2004).

Along with Alpagut's concerns over the evaluation processes of instrumental training at music teacher training schools, Yayla (2003) suggests that faculty should develop different criteria to evaluate students regarding their instrumental education. According to him, professors who teach instruments should gather evaluation data at certain times every academic year and make necessary changes for the evaluation processes. Yayla also suggested that measurement tools be developed based on the new methods of evaluation, and that students' general level of success should be reviewed by an academic committee.

In a similar study of 55 professors from 3 music teacher training institutions, Atak Yayla (2004) found that performance assessment at music teacher training schools was somewhat, but not completely, objective. While participants reported the use of some type of form to evaluate students, she recommended and developed a more detailed evaluation form. Dalkıran (2006) studied 30 violin professors from 7 different music teacher training schools, and noted the pervasive concern regarding the lack of standardization in violin performance assessment. In 2009, she developed an assessment tool for violin performance. Dalkıran's participants included 23 violin professors and 330 violin students from 6 different music teacher training schools. Her study focused only on the measurement of violin performance, but her results led her to suggest that her scale could be used as a measurement tool for musical auditions and for other instruments (see Table 12.1). Dalkıran further explained her findings as follows: "The component load that was serving for the general purpose of the measurement tool varied between .98 and .34, which is between −1.00 and +1.00. This explained to us that each criteria that was chosen would help to measure violin performance effectively" (Dalkıran, 2009, p. 4).

Piji Küçük (2010) studied the exam anxiety and self-esteem of music teacher candidates ($n = 66$), and concluded that it was important to develop a guide for students to better control anxiety and strengthen self-esteem. Her results revealed a significant negative relationship ($p < .01$) between music students' exam anxiety and scores in instrument classes and between exam anxiety levels and those of self-esteem. No significant

Table 12.1 Dalkıran Violin Scale for Jury Exams and/or Music Auditions

Criteria		Component
		1
1	Playing etudes, exercises, and pieces artistically and competently	.986
2	Playing the sounds in etudes, exercises, and pieces with correct intonation and producing good sound	.980
3	Producing correct sound and intonation while fluidly shifting	.978
4	Staying in tune while shifting	.978
5	Correct posture and body position while playing	.978
6	Symmetrical use of the bow	.970
7	Using different bowing techniques correctly and effectively while playing etudes, exercises, and pieces (e.g., detache, legato, martele, staccato, spiccato)	.968
8	Playing etudes, exercises, and pieces with correct meter and rhythmic structure	.957
9	Using correct articulation while playing etudes, exercises, and pieces	.953
10	Playing etudes, exercises, and pieces continuously	.951
11	Playing etudes, exercises, and pieces with an effective and beautiful tone	.753
12	Playing etudes, exercises, and pieces with good phrasing and appropriate stylistic considerations	.643
13	Playing etudes, exercises, and pieces with appropriate speed	.629
14	Using dynamics while playing etudes, exercises, and pieces	.493
15	Using effective vibrato technique	.369
16	The interest, work, and effort of the student in general	.348
Variance %		70.54
Cronbach's α		.87

relationship was found between the student's self-esteem scores and exam anxiety, and also the variables of gender, grade, and type of school where they graduated. In line with the results of her study, as the level of exam anxiety of music teacher candidates decreases, their success in instrument education increases, and as the students' self-esteem rises, their exam anxiety level decreases (Piji Küçük, 2010).

Ece and Bilgin (2007) studied the differences between the student success levels ($n = 41$) at music teacher training schools based on the type of high school from which they graduated. The results showed no significant deviation between the music students who graduated from high schools of fine arts and those from other types of high schools, although the authors' hypothesis was that the students from high schools of fine arts would have higher success levels. However, Ece and Bilgin recommended that when there are performance differences between these two groups of students, the professors at music teacher training schools should reconsider their measurement tools to evaluate them to accommodate these differences.

In the music teacher training school curriculum, Measurement and Evaluation is a fourth-semester course and Teaching Practice is a seventh and eighth-semester course. In their study, Berki and Karakelle (2009) recommended that because the content of these two courses was related, they should offered in the sixth-semester so that these two courses could be delivered simultaneously.

Assessment in Music Departments at Colleges of Fine Arts in Turkey

The first music department within a college of fine arts was opened at Ege University in İzmir in 1975. The main purpose of this department was to support research and education in musicology (Kavcar, 1982). At the time this chapter was written, there were 18 music departments at colleges of fine arts.[3]

Music departments at colleges of fine arts in Turkey have different areas of concentration, such as musicology, performance, and music technologies, and each area has its unique curriculum. Unlike the music teacher training schools that have a centralized curriculum, the professors have the freedom to develop their own courses in their area; therefore, there is little uniformity regarding the number, nature, or content of the subjects among these institutions. However, similar to music teacher training schools, assessment criteria are lacking, particularly for the performance area, where professors evaluate students in a similar way but with almost no standardization. In theory and history courses, likewise, professors develop their own assessments for midterm and final exams.

MUSIC ASSESSMENT AT CONSERVATORIES IN TURKEY

Formal music instruction dates back to Ottoman Empire times, when classical Turkish music was the main subject at Enderun-ı Hümayun (The Palace School) and Acemi Oğlanlar Ocağı (Novice Boys Quarry). The first Western musical training began during the reign of Sultan Mahmud II. After he abolished the Janissaries (Yeniçeriler) he established the Muzika-yı Hümayun (Imperial Music School) and brought musicians from European countries as instructors (Kavcar, 1982).

İstanbul Municipality Conservatory was founded in 1917 as Turkey's first music training institution. This institution emphasized musical literacy over oral transmission and encouraged (for the first time) both men and women to participate in musical instruction and musical performance. The creation of the Darül'elhan was a momentous event in the history of Turkish music. Founded in 1912 as the Darülbeday-î Osmanî, renamed in 1916 as the Darül'elhan, closed in 1918, and reopened in 1923, the Darül'elhan was the first public institution to offer a comprehensive system of instruction in Turkish music: a system that loosely imitated a European precedent and emphasized musical literacy over oral transmission (O'Connell, 2000).

Ankara State Conservatory was founded in 1936 with the help of the famous German composer and musicologist Paul Hindemith, who was invited as a consultant. He did not accept a permanent position in Turkey, and visited four times (April–May 1935; March–May 1936; February 1937; and October–November 1937) to help to establish the conservatory (Çakar, 2015, p. 18). Hindemith wrote various reports about music in Turkey after observing the music institutions and their facilities, and he mentioned the Turkish priorities regarding music education. He continued to visit from time to time and audited the efforts in the area until Atatürk died (Anıl, 1977). The purpose of the Ankara State Conservatory was to provide education in music and performing arts with a Western approach. As another important development in 1936, the Hungarian composer, music educator, and musicologist Béla Bartók (1881–1945) also came to Turkey and established the Turkish Folk Music Archive in 1937 (Kavcar, 1982). İzmir State Conservatory (founded in 1958), İstanbul State Conservatory (founded in 1971) and İstanbul Technical University Turkish Music State Conservatory (founded in 1976) followed Ankara State Conservatory (Kavcar, 1982, p. 20). At of the time this chapter was written, there were 48 Western and Turkish music conservatories.[4]

Music departments at conservatories in Turkey may have different discipline areas, including performance, musicology/ethnomusicology, Turkish folk music, traditional Turkish music, and jazz. As in the case of music departments at colleges of fine arts, each discipline area has its own curriculum. Because of this diversity, again, as in the music departments of colleges of fine arts, there are dissimilarities regarding the number, nature, or content of the courses among conservatories in Turkey. Regarding assessment criteria, professors in the performance areas evaluate students in a similar way as in other music schools. For example, in voice instruction at all music schools (including conservatories) at the collegiate level, due to lack of measurement tools and standards to evaluate students, the assessment is not objective and the validity of the evaluation is questionable (Töreyin, 1999). In other areas, instructors have the freedom to develop their tests and examinations based on the goals of their curriculum.

AUDITION PROCESS FOR MUSIC SCHOOLS IN TURKEY

How Music Schools Accept/Recruit Students in Turkey

All music students are recruited through an audition process at high schools of fine arts, music teacher training schools, colleges of fine arts, and conservatories in Turkey. Every year, music schools in Turkey post their requirements regarding that particular year's audition on their websites, including the types of questions they will ask, so that the students are knowledgeable about the process. Candidates from high schools of fine arts have an advantage over students who are from other high schools. The audition process often has two or three phases that may vary depending on the school. The purpose of the first phase is to measure the student's level of musical aptitude. This stage is considered to be the most important part of the audition process. Candidates who can pass the first phase are accepted to take the second (and—if needed—the third) phase of the audition. Certain percentages of the score from the second and third phases of the audition, standardized test score (YGS), and student's secondary school grade point average (GPA) are added together. The ratio of these scores are determined by ÖSYM (Öğrenci Seçme Yerleştirme Merkezi/Student Selection and Placement Center). A student's total score determines his/her acceptance to the music school (Dicle, 2004). During the audition process, students who apply for music teacher training schools or for musicology programs have to take musical auditions, but they also are interviewed and evaluated in terms of their qualifications and desire to become a music teacher or a musicologist (Küçüköncü, 2006).

The auditions at high schools of fine arts are designed to determine the student's musical aptitude. In general, a student's musical aptitude is measured by his her/recognition of a single pitch up to four-voice chords and repetition of rhythmic patterns and simple melodic lines. Yağcı (2009) considered the melodic component of the auditions at high schools of fine arts somewhat problematic because of their length and the difficulty level. He recommended that jury members reevaluate the melodic section of musical auditions depending on the age and the biological development of early adolescents.

The auditions at music teacher training schools have included varying components. In the 1950s, they included an essay question, a musical aptitude test, singing, and playing a musical instrument. Auditions included a certain percentage of the standardized test score, essay question, musical aptitude test, singing, and playing a musical instrument in the 1960s. This approach changed in the 1970s to a certain percentage of the standardized test score, essay question, and a two-phase audition (the first phase measured the musical aptitude of students, and the second phase included the components of musical dictation, singing, and playing a musical instrument) (Ece & Sazak, 2006b). During the 1990s, fine arts high school graduates began applying to undergraduate music schools; therefore, some changes were made in the audition process. The first centralized audition system was implemented at music teacher training schools in 1994. This audition consisted of two phases and eased the process for students. However, it was not used very long, and it was changed back to the older system shortly thereafter (Coşkun Yüksel & Tufan, 2012). There is not much information about this system due to the preference of the Student Selection and Placement Center not to release any reports about this short-lived experience (Tarman, 2002). The criteria most often used in auditions at music teacher training schools are presented in Figure 12.1 (Tarman, 2002, pp. 60–63). Beside the musical audition, an essay about students' musical past may also be required, and students are interviewed by the jury members to be evaluated based on their interest and knowledge on music and music teaching (Tankız, 2011).

First Phase (musical aptitude)							
Single Pitch	Intervals	Three-voice chords	Four-voice chords	Melody	Rhythm		Total
$10 \times 2 = 20$	$7 \times 2 = 14$	$4 \times 3 = 12$	$1 \times 4 = 4$	$8 \times 5 = 40$	$8 \times 1.25 = 10$		100

Second phase (musical theory)				
Dictation			Sight reading	Total
Melody #1	Melody #2		$4 \times 12.5 = 50$	100
$4 \times 6.25 = 25$	$4 \times 6.25 = 25$			

Second phase (singing)								
Dimensions	Vocal volume	Vocal range	Vocal timbre	Pitch accuracy	Speech clarity	Musical interpretation	Entirety	Total
Scores	15	15	10	30	10	15	5	100

Second phase (playing a musical instrument)					
Comfort (in playing)	Playing correctly and accurate	Entirety/ Technical Level	Musical interpretation	The level of the piece	Total
10	35	20	20	15	100

FIGURE 12.1 Musical audition form used for admission to Gazi University Music Teacher Training School.

The auditions at music departments of colleges of fine arts are similar to those at music teacher training schools except for the musicology and music technology programs. For these areas, students have to write essays or take a multiple-choice test (based on the program) if they pass the musical aptitude test.

Conservatory musical auditions are conducted based on the area that students apply for, and all students must take a musical aptitude test. A set of sample musical aptitude test criteria for all areas (except musicology at Hacettepe University Ankara State Conservatory) is presented in Figure 12.2.[5] There is one exception, as students have to take a different type of musical aptitude test for the musicology program. The second phase of the performance area auditions is based on the level of musical playing. A list of the required repertoire for each instrument is determined by the jury members and released on the school's website. As an example, the list of pieces and études that are required for the piano performance area at Hacettepe University Ankara State Conservatory is presented in Figure 12.3,[6] and sample criteria used for their musicology undergraduate program are presented in Figure 12.4.[7]

The assessment process for musical auditions has become a keen interest among scholars in Turkey. Erol Demirbatır (2004) evaluated the reliability of the auditions at Uludağ University Music Teacher Training School. The findings revealed that the first phase of the test to evaluate students' musical aptitude is valid and highly reliable (see Table 12.2). Ece and Kaplan (2008) analyzed the interrater reliability of the musical auditions for the 299 applicants for the Music Teacher Training School in Bolu, Turkey in 2006. Using

First phase (music theory)		
Area	*Definition*	*Total*
Dictation	Advanced-level dictation	50
Harmonic analysis	Analysis of figured bass (4–8 measures)	20
Harmonic analysis	Harmonic analysis of a piece from the literature (at least 10 measures)	30
Total		100

FIGURE 12.2 Musical aptitude test scoring criteria for all areas except musicology undergraduate program at Hacettepe University Ankara State Conservatory.

Second phase (instrumental performance/piano)		
Area	*Explanation*	*Total*
Performance	1 (one) Etude	20
Performance	1 (one) piece from the Baroque Period	20
Performance	1 (one) piece from the Classical Period	20
Performance	1 (one) piece from the Romantic Period	20
Performance	1 (one) piece from the 20th Century	20
Total		100

FIGURE 12.3 Musical audition from for piano performance undergraduate program at Hacettepe University Ankara State Conservatory.

"Kendall's W" coefficient of concordance, the interrater reliability for the music auditions was found to be quite high (.872–1.00). However, in their study, Sevgi and Şengül (2003) recommended the following list of components for musical aptitude tests:

- Single-pitch recognition should be excluded.
- Intervals should only be asked in the first phase of the audition.
- Because of their difficulty to be heard, major 7 and minor 2 intervals, dissonant three-voice chords, and four-voice chords should be asked in the second phase of the audition.
- Rhythmic and melodic patterns should be assessed in their entirety instead of measure-by-measure evaluation.
- Modal melodies should be asked in the second phase of the audition.

Ece (2007) found that the majority of the students who applied for the Music Teacher Training School in Bolu, Turkey (30.5%) graduated from high schools of fine arts, and the standardized test scores and the GPAs of these students were calculated in a different way (to their advantage). However, in general, the students who come from high schools of fine arts have lower standardized-test scores than those coming from other high schools.

First phase (musical aptitude test)		
Category	*Number of Questions*	*Total*
Sense of sound clusters	40	$1 \times 40 = 40$
Sense of musical dynamics	10	$1 \times 10 = 10$
Sense of rhythmic patterns	10	$1 \times 10 = 10$
Sense of tempo	10	$1 \times 10 = 10$
Sense of alteration/modulation in melodies	30	$1 \times 30 = 30$
Total	100	100

Second phase (essay)			
Assessment Criteria		*Score*	*Total*
Grammar		50	50
Expression	Consistency of paragraphs	15	50
	Consistency of sentences	10	
	Vocabulary	10	
	Justification	10	
	Consistency between the title and the text	05	
Total			100

Third phase (interview)
to measure the level of interest and knowledge of students in musicology

FIGURE 12.4 Assessment criteria and scoring scheme for musical auditions used for the musicology undergraduate program at Hacettepe University Ankara State Conservatory.

Regarding the auditions at music teacher training schools, the ratios (the percentage of weight in the total score out of 100) of the YGS, the score of the music audition, and GPA of students may vary as below:

- YGS score: between 41%and 45%
- music audition score: between 34% and 35%
- student's GPA: between 20% and 25%

These ratios may change year to year within the range, and, as stated earlier, the Student Selection and Placement Center is the decision maker for such matters (Arapgirlioğlu & Tankız, 2013; Ece & Sazak, 2006b). Regarding these ratios, Sungurtekin (2006) found a meaningful positive correlation between the YGS score and the music audition score in his study, while Atak Yayla (2006), Ece and Sazak (2006a), Aşkın Kumova and Demirbatır (2012), Eroğlu and Gençel Ataman (2013), and Arapgirlioğlu and Tankız (2013) advocate for a higher percentage of music audition score and lower ratio of YGS score.

Table 12.2 Demirbatır's (2004) Item Analysis of the First Phase Scores for Music Auditions at Uludğ University

Parts of the Audition (1st Phase)	Number of Items	Correct answers in the upper group f %		Correct answers in the lower group f %		Discrimination Index of the Item (D)	Difficulty Level of the Item (P)	Difficulty Level of the Parts of the Audition (1st Phase)
Part I Single Sound	1	48	96	14	28	.68	.62	.62
	2	46	92	26	52	.40	.72	
	3	44	88	13	26	.62	.57	
	4	27	54	6	12	.42	.33	
	5	43	86	9	18	.68	.52	
	6	49	98	31	62	.36	.80	
	7	49	98	30	60	.38	.79	
Part II Rhythm and Melody	1	44	88	23	46	.42	.67	.72
	2	47	94	24	48	.46	.71	
	3	48	96	32	64	.32	.80	
	4	49	98	36	72	.26	.85	
	5	43	86	21	42	.44	.64	
	6	46	92	16	32	.60	.62	
	7	49	98	28	76	.42	.77	
Part III Intervals and Chords	1	48	96	18	36	.60	.66	.56
	2	46	92	6	12	.80	.52	
	3	46	92	20	40	.52	.66	
	4	46	92	9	18	.74	.55	
	5	48	96	28	56	.40	.76	
	6	39	78	12	24	.54	.51	
	7	35	70	16	32	.38	.51	
	8	48	96	32	64	.32	.80	
	9	19	38	14	28	.10	.33	
	10	36	72	8	16	.56	.44	
	11	42	84	9	18	.66	.51	

A Critique of the Audition Process for Music Schools in Turkey

Based on the data that presented thus far, the following criticism for musical auditions at music schools in Turkey can be stated:

- Compared to the auditions at music teacher training schools where criteria are provided clearly for each stage of the evaluation, there is a lack of written criteria for the auditions at the conservatories, particularly regarding the performance and interview phases. This factor may cause inconsistent subjective assessment by jury members.
- Questions for music auditions at high schools of fine arts and sports were prepared by committee members; therefore, questions at each institution differ. As a result, the lack of standardization regarding number and difficulty level of questions disrupts the objectivity of the evaluation process (Yayla & Yayla, 2009).
- The fear of negative evaluation may cause individuals to refrain from their performances, and may eventually end with a poor performance. Considering that social phobia can develop at the beginning of adolescence (around ages 10 to 16), it can lead to depression. Creating a judgmental environment during musical auditions may cause lack of confidence in students, which may effect their performances (Yokuş, 2013).
- Music teacher training schools accept students based only on their musical aptitude and do not assess them regarding their interest in becoming music educators (Apaydın, 2006) or evaluate them physiologically in case of problems that students may have (issues with voice, fingers, etc.) (Töreyin, 2002).

Perhaps the most important criticism of the musical auditions in Turkey has to do with the highly challenging nature of the auditioning process in many music schools. Most institutions prepare auditions with the expectation of receiving students from high schools of fine arts. This expectation often causes audition jury members to prefer evaluating students based on their musical knowledge instead of measuring their musical aptitude. This situation may cause intimidation among many students coming from other high schools, who may also recoil from auditions. (Yayla, 2003).

CONCLUSION AND RECOMMENDATIONS

The main points of this chapter are summarized here:

- Assessment in music education has become an increasing interest among Turkish scholars since the 1990s, and continues to build in the 21st century.

- Although there is a vast amount of research on music education assessment for primary schools and music teacher training institutions, studies on this topic for secondary schools, music departments at colleges of fine arts, and conservatories are insufficient.
- Music education curricula for primary schools lacked assessment tools until 1994. The curricula from 1994 and 2006 included proper and detailed assessment criteria.
- Although primary-school music curriculum provides effective assessment tools, lack of time (1 hour per week), and crowded classrooms are obstacles to the process of efficient student evaluation.
- The self-evaluation segment of the curricula for primary and secondary schools is inadequate.
- Regarding the assessment of instrumental performance at the collegiate level, lack of standardization, cursory evaluation, and inadequate assessment tools prevent objectivity and cause students to mistrust their professors.
- Performance anxiety is an issue for many music students.
- There are several issues and concerns regarding the musical auditioning process. (These issues were stated in the previous chapter).

Based on these points, the following recommendations may serve to improve the practices of musical assessment in Turkey:

- Although there is a growing interest in music education assessment in Turkey, there is more need for studies, particularly on the secondary school and collegiate levels.
- Since the assessment tools for primary school music classes cannot be used effectively (mainly because of the lack of weekly hours), either specialists should reexamine and rebuild the amount of these tools or the Ministry of National Education should be informed about this issue and consider increasing the insufficient amount of music class hours.
- The self-evaluation segment of the curricula for primary and secondary schools should be reexamined because of their inadequacies.
- Regarding the lack of standardization of instrumental performance evaluations, Alpagut (2004) recommended that the assessment tools should be standardized for violin (and other instrumental) training and should be similar to what is presented in Table 12.3 (Alpagut, 2004).
- Professors should help their students learn how to effectively deal with performance anxiety through the development of self-esteem.
- Although having the freedom to develop their own curricula can be considered as a positive quality for music departments at colleges of fine arts and conservatories, standards for courses and assessment tools should be determined nationally.
- The audition processes for music teacher training schools should be reexamined and restructured based on the source of recruitment of the students as they may

Table 12.3 Instrumental Evaluation Chart
for Music Schools (Alpagut, 2004)

Type of exam	Number of exams	Percentage (%)
Quiz	3	9–10
Midterm	2	19–21
Final	1	44–46
Attendance	–	4
Total	6	100

come not only from the high schools of fine arts but also from regular high schools (Yayla, 2003).

- For music teacher training schools, students should be evaluated based on their interest in becoming music teachers along with their musical aptitude and abilities (Apaydın, 2006; Yayla, 2003).
- The high ratios of the standardized test score and GPA for the acceptance of music teacher training schools should be reconsidered and reevaluated by the policymakers.
- It is important to detect students with permanent voice problems when they audition at music teacher training schools because music teachers with physiological voice problems cannot perform effectively. Therefore, if there were greater awareness of this issue during the audition process, it would be easier to identify potential deficiencies before the students enter the school (Otacıoğlu, 2006; Töreyin, 2002).
- A committee of professors from music schools should be assigned by the Higher Education Council to develop standardized assessment tools (Arapgirlioğlu & Tankız, 2013).

Assessment in music education can be considered a relatively new topic among Turkish academicians. If we examine past history, this matter was often neglected and left to music teachers and professors. However, due to globalization after the 1990s, Turkey opened itself to other cultures along with many countries. These encounters resulted in many positive effects on music education assessment. A good example of this transition is the recent interest in constructivism, the latest educational trend in Turkey. Constructivism was adopted from the West and adapted into our music education system. Although there are problematic areas of this adaptation due to the traditionally rigid educational system and culture of Turkey, it is nevertheless a positive development. Finally, there is no reason that Turkish music educators cannot develop appropriate approaches to music education, and perhaps develop a Turkish school of assessment if the Higher Education Council and Ministry of National Education provide more support for further research and attend to scholars who tirelessly work on these issues.

Notes

1. See http://www.muzikegitimcileri.net/
2. See http://www.yok.gov.tr/
3. See http://www.muzikegitimcileri.net/
4. See http://www.yok.gov.tr/
5. See http://www.konser.hacettepe.edu.tr/sayfa/belgeler/belgeler
6. See http://www.konser.hacettepe.edu.tr/sayfa/belgeler/belgeler
7. See http://www.konser.hacettepe.edu.tr/sayfa/belgeler/belgeler

References

Aksu, C. (2007). *İlköğretim 8. Sınıf Müzik Programının Hedeflerine Ulaşma Düzeyinin Değerlendirilmesi* [Evaluation of the eighth-year primary school music curriculum regarding the achievement level of goals]. (Unpublished doctoral dissertation). Erzurum: Atatürk University.

Albuz, A., & Akpınar, M. (2009). *2006 İlköğretim Müzik Dersi Öğretim Programı ve Yeni Yaklaşımlar* [2006 primary-school music curriculum and new approaches]. Paper presented at the 8. Ulusal Müzik Eğitimi Sempozyumu, Ondokuz Mayıs University, Samsun, Turkey.

Alpagut, U. (2004). *Keman Eğitiminde Kurul Önünde Gerçekleşen Sınavlarda Değerlendirmede Standardizasyon* [Standardization of the evaluation of violin performance with jury]. Paper presented at the 1924–2004 Musiki Muallim Mektebinden Günümüze Müzik Öğretmeni Yetiştirme Sempozyumu, Süleyman Demirel University, Isparta, Turkey.

Anıl, M. (1977). Türkiye'de Konservatuvar Eğitimi [Conservatory education in Turkey]. *Eğitim ve Bilim* [Education and Science], 2(8), 46–51.

Apaydın, M. (2006). *Eğitim Fakülteleri Güzel Sanatlar Eğitimi Bölümü Müzik Öğretmenliği Anabilim Dallarına Özel Yetenek Sınavları ile Öğrenci Alımına Yönelik Eleştirel Yaklaşımlı Bir Değerlendirme* [A critical evaluation for the musical auditions at music teacher training schools]. Paper presented at the Ulusal Müzik Eğitimi Sempozyumu, Pamukkale University, Denizli, Turkey.

Arapgirlioğlu, H., & Tankız, K. D. (2013). Özel Yetenek Sınavlarında AOBP ve YGS Puanlarının Yerleştirme Puanları İçerisindeki Dağılımının İncelenmesi [Examining the ratio of GPA and standardized test scores in overall musical-audition score at music teacher training schools]. *Hacettepe Üniversitesi Eğitim Fakültesi Dergisi* [Hacettepe University College of Education Journal], 28(2), 14–26.

Aşkın Kumova, P., & Demirbatır, E. (2012). Müzik Öğretmenliği Programları Kapsamında Özel Yetenek Sınavlarının Karşılaştırılarak İncelenmesi [A comparative study of musical auditions at music teacher training schools]. *Gazi Üniversitesi Gazi Eğitim Fakültesi Dergisi* [Gazi University Gazi College of Education Journal], 32(1), 103–127.

Atak Yayla, A. (2004). *Müziksel Performansın Ölçülmesi* [Evaluation of the musical performance]. Paper presented at the 1924–2004 Musiki Muallim Mektebinden Günümüze Müzik Öğretmeni Yetiştirme Sempozyumu, Süleyman Demirel University, Isparta, Turkey.

Atak Yayla, A. (2006). *Müzik Eğitimi Anabilim Dalları Özel Yetenek Sınavlarında ÖSS ve Ağırlıklı Orta Öğretim Başarı Puanlarının Yerleştirme Puanına Etkisi* [The effect of the standardized test score and high school GPA on the overall score of musical auditions at music teacher training schools]. Paper presented at the Ulusal Müzik Eğitimi Sempozyumu, Pamukkale University, Denizli, Turkey.

Atak Yayla, A., & Yayla, F. (2009). *Müziksel Algılama Ölçeği* [Scale of musical perception]. Paper presented at the 8. Ulusal Müzik Eğitimi Sempozyumu, Ondokuz Mayıs University, Samsun, Turkey.

Baş, G. (2011). *Türkiye'de Eğitim Programlarında Yapılandırmacılık: Dün, Bugün, Yarın* [Constructivism in Curricula in Turkey: Past, Present and Future], Eğitişim Dergisi [Eğitişim Journal], 32.

Başgöz, I., & Wilson, H. E. (1968). *Educational Problems in Turkey: 1920–1940*. Bloomington: Indiana University Publications.

Berki, T., & Karakelle, S. (2009). *2006–2007 Akademik Yılında Uygulamaya Konulan Merkezi Müzik Öğretmenliği Lisans Programının İncelenmesi* [Evaluation of the centralized 2006-curriculum for music teacher schools]. Paper presented at the 8. Ulusal Müzik Eğitimi Sempozyumu, Ondokuz Mayıs University, Samsun, Turkey.

Bozkaya, İ. (2006). Anadolu Güzel Sanatlar Liseleri Mezunlarının Müzik Öğretmenliği Programı Kontenjanları İçindeki Yeri (Place for Anatolian High School of Fine Arts Graduates in Music Teacher Training Schools). Paper presented at the Ulusal Müzik Eğitimi Sempozyumu, Pamukkale University, Denizli, Turkey.

Çakar, D. (2015). Hacettepe Üniversitesi Ankara Devlet Konservatuvarı (Cebeci'den Beşevler'e) [Hacettepe University Ankara State Conservatory (from Cebeci To Beşevler)]. *Hacettepe Üniversitesi Ankara Devlet Konservatuvarı Sahne ve Müzik Eğitim Araştırma e-Dergisi* [Hacettepe University Ankara State Conservatory Performing Arts and Music Education E-Journal], 1, 9–34.

Çoban, S. (2011). Müzik Öğretmeni Adaylarının Bireysel Çalgı Eğitimi Dersi Dönem Sonu Sınavları ile İlgili Düşünceleri: Marmara Üniversitesi Örneği [The views of the music teacher candidates on the final-exam evaluation of their primary instrument: Marmara University case study]. *Buca Eğitim Fakültesi Dergisi* [Buca College of Education Journal], 31, 115–127.

Coşkun Yüksel, G., & Tufan, S. (2012). Müzik Eğitimi Anabilim Dalı Özel Yetenek Sınavını Kazanan Öğrencilerin Ezgi İşitme ve Ritim İşitme Boyutu Başarı Düzeylerinin İncelenmesi [Examining rhythmic and melodic scores in musical auditions of first-year students at music teacher training schools to determine levels of success]. *İDİL, 1*, 379–393.

Dalkıran, E. (2006). *Müzik Eğitimi Anabilim Dalları Keman Eğitimi Yarıyıl Sonu Sınavlarında Performansın Ölçülmesine İlişkin Öğretim Elemanı Görüşleri* [The views of the professors on evaluating violin students at music teacher training school in final exams]. Paper presented at the Ulusal Müzik Eğitimi Sempozyumu, Pamukkale University, Denizli, Turkey.

Dalkıran, E. (2009). *Keman Eğitiminde Performansa Yönelik Ölçme Aracı Örneği* [A performance scale model for violin teaching]. Paper presented at the 8. Ulusal Müzik Eğitimi Sempozyumu, Ondokuz Mayıs University, Samsun, Turkey.

Demirbatır, R. E. (2004). *U. Ü. E. F. Güzel Sanatlar Eğitimi Bölümü Müzik Eğitimi Anabilim Dalı 2001–2002 Öğretim Yılı Giriş Yetenek Sınavında Uygulanan Müziksel İşitme Test Sınavının Değerlendirilmesi* [The evaluation of the musical aptitude test scores of the auditions at Uludağ University music teacher training school during 2001–2002 academic year]. *Uludağ Üniversitesi Eğitim Fakültesi Dergisi* [Uludağ University Journal of College of Education], 17(1), 29–38.

Demirci, B., & Albuz, A. (2010). An evaluation on practicing of teacher's book and student's workbook based on music classes [of the] 2006 primary education teaching program, *International Journal of Human Sciences, 7*, 267–283.

Dicle, H. (2004). *Üniversitelerin Güzel Sanatlar Eğitimi Bölümlerinde Verilen Eğitim Nitelikli Müzik Öğretmeni Yetiştirmek İçin Uygun ve Yeterli midir?* [Is the education at music teacher training schools adequate and sufficient to train qualified music teachers?]. Paper presented at the 1924–2004 Musiki Muallim Mektebinden Günümüze Müzik Öğretmeni Yetiştirme Sempozyumu, Süleyman Demirel University, Isparta, Turkey.

Ece, A. S. (2007). Özel Yetenek Sınavlarında Yerleştirmeye Esas Olan Puan ve Katsayıların Alan ve Alan Dışından Gelen Adaylara Yansıması (Karşılaştırmalı Durum Saptaması) [The reflection of the scores and the coefficients as the criteria for the musical auditions (A comparative study)]. *Mehmet Akif Ersoy Üniversitesi Eğitim Fakültesi Dergisi* [Mehmet Akif Ersoy University College of Education Journal], *8*, 121–132.

Ece, A. S., & Bilgin, A. S. (2007). Mezun Oldukları Lise Türlerine Göre Müzik Eğitimi Anabilim Dalı Öğrencilerinin Başarı Durumlarının İncelenmesi [An examination of the students' level of success at music teacher training schools based on the high schools that they graduated from]. *İnönü Üniversitesi Eğitim Fakültesi Dergisi* [İnönü University College of Education Journal], *8*, 113–130.

Ece, A. S., & Kaplan, S. (2008). Müzik Özel Yetenek Seçme Sınavı'nın Puanlayıcılar Arası Güvenilirlik Çalışması [A study on the reliability of music auditions regarding inter-scorer]. *Milli Eğitim Dergisi* [Journal of National Education], *177*, 36–49.

Ece, A. S., & Sazak, N. (2006a). *Özel Yetenek Sınavlarında ÖSS & AOÖB Puanlarının Yerleştirme Puanları İçerisindeki Yeri ve Adayların ÖSS Puanları ile Akademik Ortalamaları Arasındaki İlişkilerin İncelenmesi (AİBÜ ÖRNEĞİ)* [The effect of the standardized test Score and high school GPA on musical auditions at music teacher training schools and an investigation of the relationship between candidates' standardized test score and high school GPA]. Paper presented at the Ulusal Müzik Eğitimi Sempozyumu, Pamukkale University, Denizli, Turkey.

Ece, A. S., & Sazak, N. (2006b). Özel Yetenek Sınavlarında ÖSS Puanı ile Yetenek Puanları (İşitme Alanı, Ses Alanı, Çalgı Alanı) Arasındaki İlişkilerin İncelenmesi [An investigation on the relationship between the standardized test scores and scores of the musical auditions]. *Trakya Üniversitesi Sosyal Bilimler Enstitüsü Dergisi* [Trakya University Journal of Social Sciences Institute], *8*, 133–144.

Eroğlu, Ö., & Gençel Ataman, Ö. (2013). Müzik Eğitimi Anabilim Dalı Mezunlarının Yetenek Sınavı Puanları ile Mezuniyet Notlarının Karşılaştırılması [The comparison of aptitude test scores and undergraduate GPA of music teacher training school graduates]. *Eğitim ve Öğretim Araştırmaları Dergisi* [Journal of Research in Education and Teaching], *2*, 332–337.

Göktürk, D. (2008). *Current status of string teacher education at university music teacher training schools in Turkey.* (Doctoral dissertation; published as a book by LAP Publishing in 2010). University of Florida, Gainesville, Florida.

Göktürk, D. (2010). The role of the constructivist approach on creativity in primary school music curriculum in the Republic of Turkey. *Procedia Social and Behavioral Sciences, 2*, 3075–3079.

Göktürk-Cary, D. (2012). Assessment in primary-school level music curriculum in Turkey: How can we improve music teaching and learning? In T. S. Brophy, & A. Lehmann-Wermser (Eds.), *Music assessment across cultures and continents: Proceedings on the Third International Symposium on Assessment in Music Education* (pp. 165–174). Chicago, IL: GIA Publications.

Göktürk-Cary, D. (2014). The evolution of music education in Turkey. *DEBATES, 13*, 13–22.

Hacettepe University Ankara State Conservatory Music Audition Requirements. (2016). Retrieved from http://www.konser.hacettepe.edu.tr/sayfa/belgeler/belgeler.

Holmes, A., Aguilar, B., Chen, J. J., & Göktürk, D. (2009). Assessment "Over the Ocean"—Outside of the US. In T. S. Brophy (Ed.), *The practice of assessment in music education—Frameworks, models and designs: Proceedings of the 2009 Florida Symposium on Assessment in Music Education* (95–96). Chicago, IL: GIA Publications.

Kavcar, C. (1982). Cumhuriyet Döneminde Müzik Eğitimi [Music education during the Republic Period]. *Eğitim ve Bilim* [Education and Science], *6*(35), 16–26.

Kırmızıbayrak, N. (2012). İlköğretim Okullarında Müzik Ders Programının Öğretmen Görüşlerine Dayalı Olarak Değerlendirilmesi (Kars İli Örneği) [The evaluation of music curriculum according to teachers' opinions (A Sample of Kars Province)]. *Kafkas Üniversitesi Sosyal Bilimler Enstitüsü Dergisi* [Journal of the Institute of Social Sciences], *10*, 91–105.

Köroğlu, G. N. (2014). İlköğretim İkinci Kademe Müzik Öğretmenlerinin 2006 Müzik Dersi Öğretim Programına Yönelik Görüşleri [The views of middle-school music teachers on the 2006-music curriculum]. *Sanat Eğitimi Dergisi* [Journal of Art Education], *2*, 127–141.

Köse, S. (2006). *Müzik Öğretmenliği Eğitiminde Öğrenci Kaynağı Olarak Anadolu Güzel Sanatlar Liseleri Müzik Bölümleri* [High schools of fine arts as the source for music teacher training schools]. Paper presented at the Ulusal Müzik Eğitimi Sempozyumu, Pamukkale University, Denizli, Turkey.

Küçüköncü, H. Y. (2006). *Türk Eğitim Sistemindeki Yeniden Yapılanma Sürecinde Müzik Öğretmeni Modelleri* [Music teacher models during the time of reconstructional period in Turkish educational system]. Paper presented at the Ulusal Müzik Eğitimi Sempozyumu, Pamukkale University, Denizli, Turkey.

O'Connell, J. M. (2000). Fine art, fine music: Controlling Turkish taste at the Fine Arts Academy in 1926. *International Council for Traditional Music, 32*, 117–142.

Ortaöğretim Müzik Dersi Öğretim Programı [Secondary-school music curriculum]. (2016). Retrieved from http://ttkb.meb.gov.tr/program2.aspx

Otacıoğlu, S. (2006). *Türkiye'de Müzik Öğretmeni Yetiştiren Kurumlarda Yapılan Giriş Yetenek Sınavlarında Adayların Ses Kapasitelerini Değerlendirme Kıstasları Üzerine Bir Çalışma* [A study on the evaluation of candidates' vocal capacity in musical auditions at music teacher training schools]. Paper presented at the Ulusal Müzik Eğitimi Sempozyumu, Pamukkale University, Denizli, Turkey.

Özden, Ö. (2010). Üniversitelerin Özel Yetenek Sınavlarında Anadolu Güzel Sanatlar Lisesi Müzik Bölümü Öğrencilerinin Başarı Düzeyleri [The success level of the graduates from Anatolian high schools of fine arts in musical auditions]. *E-Journal of New World Sciences Academy, 5*, 312–323.

Özeke, S. (2003). *A history of music teacher education in the Republic of Turkey: 1982–1998.* (Unpublished doctoral dissertation). Arizona State University, Tempe, AZ.

Özgül, İ. (2009). An analysis of the elementary school music teaching course in Turkey. *International Journal of Music Education, 27*, 116–127.

Öztürk, C. (1996). *Cumhuriyet Dönemi Öğretmen Yetiştirme Politikası* [Policy of Training Teachers during the Republic Period], Türk Tarih Kurumu Basımevi.

Piji Küçük, D. (2010). Müzik Öğretmeni Adaylarının Sınav Kaygısı, Benlik Saygısı ve Çalgı Başarıları Arasındaki İlişkinin İncelenmesi [Assessment of relation between test anxiety, self-esteem and success in instrument for candidates of music teacher]. *Ahi Evran Üniversitesi Eğitim Fakültesi Dergisi* [Ahi Evran University College of Education Journal], *11*(3), 37–50.

Şaktanlı, S. C. (2004). *Son Sınıf Öğrencilerinin Lisans Programlarında Verilen Müzik Eğitimi Derslerine İlişkin Görüşleri* [The views of the senior-year students on the undergraduate music education courses]. Paper presented at the 1924–2004 Musiki Muallim Mektebinden

Günümüze Müzik Öğretmeni Yetiştirme Sempozyumu, Süleyman Demirel University, Isparta, Turkey.

Saraç, G., & Şeker, H. (2008). Güzel Sanatlar Eğitimi Bölümlerinde Çalgı Öğretimindeki Performansın Değerlendirilmesi [Assessment of instrumental training at Departments of Fine Arts Education]. *Atatürk Üniversitesi Güzel Sanatlar Enstitüsü Dergisi* [Atatürk University Institute of Fine Arts Journal], *20*, 99–110.

Sevgi, A., & Şengül, A. (2003). *Müzik Eğitimi Bölümlerinin Giriş-Yetenek Sınavlarına Başvuran Adayların Müziksel İşitme-Yineleme Sınavındaki Soru Tiplerine Göre Başarı Durumlarının Belirlenmesi* [Determining the achievement level of applicants of music teacher training schools based on the types of questions in musical aptitude test]. Paper presented at the Cumhuriyetimizin 80. Yılında Müzik Sempozyumu, Ankara, Turkey.

Sungurtekin, M. (2006). U. Ü. Eğitim Fakültesi Güzel Sanatlar Eğitimi Bölümü Müzik Eğitimi Anabilim Dalı 2004–2005 Yetenek Sınavının Genel Değerlendirmesi [An evaluation of the musical auditions at Uludağ University music teacher training school in 2004]. *Uludağ Üniversitesi Eğitim Fakültesi Dergisi* [Uludağ University College of Education Journal], *19*, 399–414.

Tankız, K. D. (2011). *Müzik Öğretmenliği Programı Özel Yetenek Sınavına Başvuran Adayların Başarı Durumlarının Çeşitli Değişkenlere Göre İncelenmesi* [Examining the applicants' achievement level on musical auditions at music teacher training schools based on different variables] (Unpublished master's thesis). İnönü University, Malatya, Turkey.

Tarman, S. (2002). *Gazi Üniversitesi Müzik Eğitimi Anabilim Dalı Giriş Müzik Yetenek Sınavlarının Geçerlik ve Güvenirlik Yönünden İncelenmesi ve Değerlendirilmesi* [An investigation and evaluation of musical auditions at Gazi University music teacher training school regarding validity and reliability]. (Unpublished doctoral dissertation). Gazi University, Ankara, Turkey.

Tebiş, C. (2004). *Musiki Muallim Mektebinden Günümüze Müzik Öğretmeni Yetiştirme Kurumlarındaki Yaylı Çalgı Öğretimine İlişkin Sınama-Ölçme-Değerlendirme Durumlarının İncelenmesi* [An examination of measurement and evaluation part of the string education curricula in university music teacher training schools from past to present]. Paper presented at the 1924–2004 Musiki Muallim Mektebinden Günümüze Müzik Öğretmeni Yetiştirme Sempozyumu, Süleyman Demirel University, Isparta, Turkey.

Toraman, M. (2013). *Müzik Öğretmenlerinin İlköğretim Programında Yer Alan Müzik Dersine Yönelik Görüşleri Üzerine Nitel Bir Araştırma* [A qualitative study on the primary-school music curriculum with the music teachers as respondents]. (Unpublished master's thesis). Pamukkale University, Denizli, Turkey.

Töreyin, A. M. (1999). *Eğitim Fakültelerinin Müzik Öğretmenliği Lisans Programlarındaki Şarkı Söyleme Eğitimi 'Bireysel Ses Eğitimi' Dersinin Ölçme ve Değerlendirme Sorunları* [The problems of evaluating voice studio lessons at music teacher training schools]. Paper presented at the 8. Ulusal Eğitim Bilimleri Kongresi, Ondokuz Mayıs University, Samsun, Turkey.

Töreyin, A. M. (2002). *Müzik Eğitimi Anabilim Dallarına Giriş Özel Yetenek Sınavlarının Müziksel Söyleme (Ses ve Şarkı Söyleme Yeteneği) Boyutu* [Singing part of the musical auditions at music teacher training schools]. Paper presented at the 11. Eğitim Bilimleri Kongresi, Ankara, Turkey.

Tufan, E. (2006). *The history of music education in Turkey: The role and importance of Gazi faculty of education.* Paper presented at *APERA Conference*, Hong Kong Institute for Education.

Türkiye Cumhuriyeti MEB [Republic of Turkey Ministiry of National Education]. (2006). *İlköğretim müzik dersi öğretim programı* [Primary School Music Curriculum].

Türkiye Cumhuriyeti MEB. (2009). *Lise Müzik Dersi Öğretim Programı* [Republic of Turkey, Ministry of National Education, High School Music Curriculum].

Türkmen, E. F. (2009a). *Yeni Öğretim Programlarına Uyum Sürecinde Müzik Öğretmenlerinin Yaşadığı Sorunlar* [Problems that music teachers encounter with the new music curriculum]. Paper presented at the 8th Ulusal Müzik Eğitimi Sempozyumu, Ondokuz Mayıs University, Samsun, Turkey.

Türkmen, E. F. (2009b). İlköğretim 5. Sınıf Müzik Derslerindeki Ölçme Değerlendirme Uygulamalarının Öğrencilerin Müziksel Davranış ve Başarılarına Etkisi [The effects of the measurement and evaluation practices on musical behavior and success of 5th-year music students at primary schools]. *Afyon Kocatepe Üniversitesi Sosyal Bilimler Dergisi* [Afyon Kocatepe University Journal of Social Sciences], *11*, 179–193.

Uçan, A. (1990). *Ülkemizde Müzik Öğretimine Genel Bir Bakış* [A general view on music education in Turkey]. Paper presented at the Ortaöğretim Kurumlarında Müzik Öğretimi ve Sorunları: Türk Eğitim Derneği VII. Öğretim Toplantısı, Ankara, Turkey.

Uçan, A. (1994). *Müzik Eğitimi Temel Kavramlar-İlkeler-Yaklaşımlar* [Music Education: Foundational Concepts, Principles, Approaches]. Ankara: Müzik Ansiklopedisi Yayınları.

Varış, Y. A., & Cesur, D. (2012). Ortaöğretim Müzik Dersine Yönelik Başarı Testinin Geliştirilmesi [Developing an achievement test for the music course at secondary-schools]. *Turkish Studies—International Periodical For The Languages, Literature and History of Turkish or Turkic, 7*, 3189–3198.

Williamson, B. (1987). *Educational change in Egypt and Turkey: A study in historical sociology.* London, UK: Macmillan Press.

Yağcı, U. (2009). *Türkiye'deki Anadolu Güzel Sanatlar Liseleri Müzik Bölümleri Öğrenci Özel Yetenek Giriş Sınavlarının Müziksel İşitme-Algılama Boyutunun Değerlendirilmsi* [An evaluation of the musical auditions at high schools of fine arts music departments in Turkey]. Paper presented at the 8. Ulusal Eğitim Bilimleri Kongresi, Ondokuz Mayıs University, Samsun, Turkey.

Yayla, F. (2003). *MEABD Öğretim Elemanlarının Müzik Öğretmeni Yetiştirme Sistemine İlişkin Görüşleri* [The views of the professors at music teacher training schools on the music teacher education system]. Paper presented at the Cumhuriyetimizin 80th Yılında Müzik Sempozyumu, Ankara, Turkey.

Yayla, F. (2004). *Musiki Muallim Mektebinden Günümüze Müzik Öğretmeni Yetiştiren Kurumlar ve Müzik Öğretmeni Yetiştirme Yaklaşımları Işığında Genel Durum* [Music teacher training institutions from their foundations to the present]. Paper presented at the 1924–2004 Musiki Muallim Mektebinden Günümüze Müzik Öğretmeni Yetiştirme Sempozyumu, Süleyman Demirel Üniversitesi, Isparta, Turkey.

Yokuş, H. (2013). The relationship between the fear of negative evaluation and the achievement in special aptitude test in music of prospective music teacher candidates. *International Journal of Academic Research, 5*, 184–189.

CHAPTER 13

CURRICULUM AND ASSESSMENT IN MUSIC EDUCATION IN RUSSIA

Perspectives from the Past and the Present

ALENA V. HOLMES

HISTORICAL AND POLITICAL CONTEXTUAL INFLUENCES

THE Russian Federation, with a population of about 146 million and covering one-eighth of the surface of the world, has contributed many outstanding composers and performers to the world of music during the past 300 years. There is very limited research and literature in English-speaking countries related to Russian music education. It is not within the scope of this chapter to evaluate or cast judgment on the Russian system of music education in comparison to music education programs in the United States. The intent is to present a factual, objective view of the system, curriculum, and assessment in music education; describe historical influences; and share perspectives from Russian educators and researchers.

Education During the Imperial Period

For centuries, education in Russia has been a vital part of life. The Orthodox Church has been called the mother of Russian general and music education. During the 10th- and 11th-century church, singing instruction was established in older Russian cities such as Kiev and Novgorod. Later, the centers for singing education were established in the city of Vladimir (12th century) and Moscow (13th century) (Doroshenko, 2016). In 1633 the Metropolitan of Kiev, Peter Mojilla, established an academy in Kiev at which the curriculum included the classics, theology, philosophy, and rhetoric. The history of school education started during Tsar Peter the Great's leadership in the beginning of the 18th century. As his first act as tsar, Peter departed Russia to study abroad in Germany and Holland. When he returned, he placed great emphasis on establishing modern education systems in Russia, as he had seen in Western countries. Under Peter's system, school education took place in educational institutions call "gymnasiums"—which were later divided into boys' and girls' schools. Students attended the gymnasiums for 10 to 12 years. Initially, not everyone could afford to send their children to these schools. But later, in the late 18th and early 19th centuries, schools began to open to the general public. The institutionalization of secular music education began in the first half of the 18th century in Saint Petersburg. The empress of Russia, Anna Ioannovna, continued the westernization of the country and opened establishments such as the Academy of Science, cadet corps education, theater and opera, and training institutions for professional musicians (Fedorovich, 2014). Starting from the middle of the 18th century, higher education as a system started with the foundation of universities in Moscow and St. Petersburg. The system was modeled after the German system of higher education: it was open to secondary school graduates and took 5 years to complete. Upon completion, a "Diploma of Higher Education" in a specialized area was granted. Since then, the system has not undergone many changes.

Catherine the Great also tried to introduce Western enlightenment into Russia, and she made many reforms. At her command, Diderot, the French philosopher, prepared a plan for the organization of a state system of public instruction in Russia. The educational system included an introduction of instruction in mathematics, modern sciences, literature, history, drawing, and music. The entire structure of education was designed to give advantages most exclusively to the middle and upper classes. The first private music schools opened in 1830. The curriculum of the music school included individual instruction in vocal and instrumental techniques and music theory (Fedorovich, 2014). The owners of the music schools decided on structure, curriculum, and assessment. Private music schools became very popular by the second half of 19th century; just in the city of Saint Petersburg there were 130 music schools (Bosova, 2003). In 1804, Alexander I launched an ambitious project; he encouraged the establishment of public primary schooling among the peasants finally opening in 1861. In 1864 the first education law was passed, setting up the system of education that was available to all children without distinction, but also without compulsion. In the 1860s free public music and art schools opened. The famous composer Balakirev was a founder of the first free music school in Saint Petersburg. In 1866 the Russian Music Society was formed and played a highly important role in the development of Russian public and private music education (Novikova, 2013). The Russian Music Society helped to open conservatories, choral clubs, and public music schools. The imperial government generously subsidized the Russian Music Society, and by the beginning of the 20th century, 50 branches were opened in different cities throughout Russia.

In the 1860s, the roots of Russia's excellence in performance began when the Rubinstein brothers, Anton and Nikolai, founded the St. Petersburg and Moscow conservatories. By the beginning of the 20th century, Russia had produced numerous artists of the highest levels of achievement, such as the pianists Sergei Rachmaninoff, Josef Lhevinne, and Vladimir Horowitz; the violinists Mischa Elman and Jascha Heifetz; the cellist Gregor Piatigorsky; and the composers Alexandr Glazunov, Alexandr Skryabin, and others. (Fedorovich, 2014).

In 1889 the Russian Ministry of Education announced the first declaration regarding compulsory music lessons in schools (Novikova, 2013). Great educational changes were instituted by the Duma, the elective state council after the 1905 Russian Revolution. A series of reforms allowed for the expansion and support of secular elementary schools, in an attempt to promote universal education among the peasant population. In 1908, the government approved a law that made education compulsory and free to all children in the empire ages 8–11 (Bereday, Brickman, & Read, 1960). In 1914, 91% of Russian children were receiving scholastic instruction.

Education During the Soviet Era

In 1917, two revolutions swept through Russia, ending centuries of imperial rule and setting in motion political and social changes that would lead to the formation of the Soviet Union. In 1917, the People's Commissariat of Education was founded and given the task to focus on schooling. Under the plan of the Commissariat, the policy of *likbez* ("liquidation of illiteracy") was introduced. It was the first mandate of compulsory education for children in Russian history. By September of 1918, they made a start in replacing the prerevolutionary school system with a 9-year unified labor school. According to the October 1918 government document, "Statute of the Unified Labor School of the Russian Socialist Federative Soviet Republic," the school system was divided up in two levels. The first level consisted of grades 1 through 5 for children 8 to 13 years of age; the second level included the grades 6 through 9 for students between the ages of 13 and 17. With every following year, literacy among the citizenry increased substantially. The pre-Stalin period of Soviet education was marked by the encouragement of diverse educational practices and new reforms. In 1920, after the demand came for a common curriculum, leaders began to look abroad for examples of new education techniques. Soviet schools soon showed signs of influence from a number of foreign sources, including John Dewey and elements of the Montessori system (Bereday, Brickman, & Read, 1960). Schools were centralized and brought under the full control of the state. The Soviets fully subsidized education at all levels. Education was to be free, coeducational, and compulsory for all children. According to Kabalevsky (1973), the very first Soviet decree on education made music and drawing lessons obligatory for all children beginning with the first grade, regardless of the social standing and status of their parents.

Soviet musical life and education underwent radical transformation in the 1930s as the Communist Party of the Soviet Union began to play an active role in shaping artistic affairs. The focus of education during Stalin's years in power abandoned the experimental educational practices and learning by inquiry, instead adopting a traditional approach with strong political and ideological components. The ideological hegemony of Stalinism infiltrated the character of the schools; therefore, inquiry and exploratory education ceased to exist during that period. Memorization and unquestioned accept-ance of the factual authority of the teacher became the norm for schools. Over the next few years, the government created a centralized group of textbooks, fixed lesson plans, homework, grading systems, and every other detail of educational policy down to the timetables for each grade. Creating a fully literate population remained a central goal of the Soviet education system. Primary education was made compulsory in 1930, and in 1934 the 9-year school system was replaced by a 10- year system. This consisted of a 4-year primary school (ages 7–10), a 3-year middle school (ages 10–13), and a 3-year secondary school (ages 14–17).

A general curriculum was also established, and with the exception of occasional minor modifications, this curriculum remained as the basic foundation for the general education program to the mid-1980s. In the general education school curriculum, 1 hour per week of music was required in grades 1 through 7 (ages 7–14). Music was available as an elective subject in grades 8 through 10 (ages 15–17). Many secondary students participated in school instrumental and choral organizations, while others were members of the various music clubs/listening groups. Prior to the adaptation of Kabalevsky's program in the early 1980s, the primary curricular emphasis was on singing and music listening.

New reforms of professional music education were established in 1933. The system of 7-year music schools, which run parallel to general schools, was established. Music schools have been founded in many cities and towns throughout Russia, providing a more concentrated training in various aspects of music (performance training, choir, ensemble practice, solfeggio, music theory, music literature). The Soviet curriculum theorists Kraevskij and Lerner (1984) provide an overview of Soviet curriculum history. They state:

> since its inception, Soviet curriculum has had more classroom time for humanities (languages, literature, history, social sciences, geography, study of the constitution, elements of state and law, drawing and music) than natural sciences (mathematics, physics, chemistry, biology, astronomy, technical drawing, and natural history).
>
> (p.12)

In the organization of Soviet curriculum, music education occupied an important place not only in general education schools but also in the preschool institutions. Soviet educators believed that the foundation of the person's future musical culture is estab-lished during preschool years (Remeta, 1974). Soviet music pedagogy was based on the optimistic view that all children have the potential for development in music and "musi-cal ability" is formed by training and teaching. According to the program adopted in 1919 at the Eighth Party Congress, the preschool institutions were to foster social and intellectual education and women's emancipation. It was decided that preschools pro-viding 9 to 10 hours of daily care on a year-round basis should be developed to meet the needs of working mothers. Music education, therefore, became an important part of the preschool curriculum.

Education in the Soviet Union had undergone little meaningful change since the 1930s, largely due to the lack of debate permitted concerning teaching methodology and school structure. Centralized control of education became the norm until the reform efforts of Perestroika. In 1989, Mikhail Gorbachev, then the general secretary of the Communist Party and the leader of the USSR, tried to reform the country's education system. He allowed schools more local control. However, the efforts, which aimed at educational reform, were hampered because the nation was suffering from political upheaval and a weak economy.

Education in the Post-Soviet Era

With the fall of the Soviet Union in 1991, the former Soviet republics, such as Russia, Ukraine, and Belarus, became independent nations. They controlled their own political and educational systems. The end of the Communist Party dominance opened methodology to differing theories that had been blocked by party ideology since the Cultural Revolution in the late 1920s. New policies for Russian education stemmed from the reform movements of the late 1980s and early 1990s. This necessitated not only the removal of Soviet ideology from the school curriculum but also the modification of education to a child's specific needs and to the development of nonstate schools and art institutions. The teacher-reform groups that pioneered Perestroika education reforms heavily relied on theories based on individualization and humanization in education. In 1992 the "Law of Education in the Russian Federation" was drawn up. This law stressed humanization, democratization, and "personal self-determination" as educational aims (Elliott & Tudge, 2007). Since the reform era of the early 1990s, the Russian system of education has faced several reform setbacks, including financial difficulties, a conflict between regional and national interests, and conflicting views on the educational requirements of the modern Russian Federation. A period of reform stagnation followed the economic collapse of 1998, and many educational reforms had done little to impact the reality of the schools. The removal of Soviet ideology from textbooks and the incorporation of different social theories and ideas opened up the schools to influences from the outside world. Prior to 1991, the state controlled the curricula of all schools, including institutions of higher education, and regulated traditional music study and pedagogy, requiring the study of philosophy, aesthetics, Soviet folk music, and Russian music history. Studies in psychology and learning theory were forbidden (although now students can choose elective coursework outside their area of specialization, and the study of ideology and political theory has been abolished [Larimer, 1993]). However, fundamental change to the structure and operation of schools had never been successfully implemented. Despite multiple reform efforts, what was happening from day to day in many Russian schools looked quite similar to what happened in Soviet schools a generation before (Kerr, 2005). The changes that have taken place in Russia and the Soviet Union since 1991 have affected the values and beliefs of the people; a new post-communist mentality has been formed. During the 1990s old ideology-laden textbooks were replaced with new ones. Syllabi have changed accordingly and now include new subjects such as civil rights, religion, environmental studies, and basic market economics. In addition, students are now encouraged to be generally more inquisitive and questioning in their approach to learning. In general, the system of public education in the country was supposed to be rebuilt on the basis of the following principles: decentralization, de-ideologization, democratization, diversification, humanization, and "humanitization" (increasing the number of humanitarian subjects in the school curriculum). After two visits to St. Petersburg, the distinguished American music educator Frances Larimer wrote in his article "Music Education in Russia: A Recent Perspective" (1993):

> I have observed monumental changes occurring in the cultural activities as well as the day-to-day lives of the Russian people. Yet education in the arts remains a strong force in the lives of most Russians, regardless of social or educational status. Highly motivating forces remain in evidence, especially the traditional Russian pride in the nation's history and cultural heritage. Clearly, the Russian people have a strong dedication to preserving the best of their nation's cultural traditions. To this is being added a new and powerful eagerness to discover new ways of improving cultural education.   (p. 66)

New Reforms and New Standards

In October 2003, Russia joined the all European Bologna process, which sought to unify the requirements and approaches to higher education across all European universities. The reforms led to the establishment of two levels of higher education, the bachelor's and master's programs, which replaced the previous 5-year "specialist" degrees. At the same time, the Russian system retained its two-level postgraduate education in the form of the Candidate of Sciences (roughly, a PhD equivalent) and advanced Doctoral degree. In general terms, the new system resembled the American model, with 4 + 2 years of education (Kurilla, 2013). In November 2010, the Russian Government adopted a new "Federal Program of Education Development for 2011–2015," which was the basis of the presidential program Our New School with the goal to develop new standards of general education, school and afterschool programs, information service centers, systems and methods, and finally, electronic forms of information delivery. This program was meant to modify the role and standards of public education, and refocus it toward developing Russian identity and strengthening such civic values as justice, freedom, interethnic peace, family traditions, individual and public safety, and security. Minister of Education and Science Andrei Fursenko stated:

> "Our New School" aims at the gradual transition to new education standards, some changes in the infrastructure of the school network, at keeping up and building up the health of schoolchildren, and at developing the teaching potential and the support system for talented children.   (cited in Cox, 2011, p. 67)

New state education standards were developed by a large group of academics under the supervision of Kondakov, CEO of the most prestigious Russian educational publishing house "Prosvetschenie," in 2011. The standards specify requirements for a compulsory core curriculum. According to the new standards, music is part of core curriculum in grades 1–9 (ages 6–14) and part of elective curriculum in grades 10–11 (ages 15–17). The new standards outline six main objective of music lessons: (1) development of foundation of musical culture of pupils, fostering the love of music; (2) development of music aptitude and critical and creative thinking; (3) development of enthusiasm toward music-making activities; (4) development of creative abilities in different genres of music and integration of music with different subjects including theater, cinema, literature, and art; (5) development of "musical taste" and understanding; and (6) acquisition of music literacy (Kezina & Kondakov, 2011).

The new reform program, originally scheduled for implementation beginning in 2013, is still a "work in progress" due to protests and debates around the plan. Dmitry Medvedev told an audience in April 2011, "We will not hurry with the education reforms. No one is going to mess up our education system. We will act very cautiously" (cited in Cox, 2011 p. 68). The dismissal of Russia's education minister Dmitry Livanov in August 2016 and his replacement with Olga Vasilyeva, an official who worked in Russia's presidential administration, indicates that Russia's educational system still is in need of reform. Education reform in Russia is historically highly politicized and integrated with sociopolitical trends. The discrepancy between educational policy and classroom practice was problematic throughout the Soviet Union, and remains difficult in the Russian Federation today.

CURRENT STRUCTURE OF THE RUSSIAN EDUCATIONAL SYSTEM

Russia is the largest country in the world, occupying about one-third of Eurasia. It is a large multiethnic nation, and three-quarters of the population reside in urban areas. The federal government comprises 83 "regions." These regions are relatively autonomous and responsible for the provision of educational services in their jurisdictions, but they are accountable to the federal government for the quality of education (Bolotov Kovaleva, Pinskaya, & Valdman, 2013). The country inherited a strong tradition of universal education from the Soviet era. The education system is divided into preschool, primary (ages 6–10), basic (ages 10–15), secondary (ages 15–17), and tertiary education. According to the Organization for Economic Co-operation and Development (2012), in 2010 a large proportion of adults in the Russian Federation had attained at least upper secondary high school education (88%, compared to 56% on average among G20 countries), and a high proportion of adults had attained tertiary education (54%, compared to 26% on average among G20 countries). The right to education is stated in the constitution of the Russia Federation (Russian Federation, n.d.). Education in Russia is organized and coordinated by the state, which ensures that general education is free and available for everyone. General education comprises (1) preschool education; (2) primary general education; (3) basic general education; and (4) secondary (high school) general education.

Preschool Education

According to the OECD (Organization for Economic Co-operation and Development (2012), 68% of 3-year-olds and 75% of 4-year olds attend government-subsidized preschools. The Russian Federation has approximately 57,000 preschool establishments of various types with enrollment of more than 5.3 million children (UNESCO, 2010). According to federal requirements, the content of preschool education must cover all areas of the preschool child's development: social/personal, intellectual, artistic, and aesthetic (Ministry of Education and Science of Russian Federation, 2016). Parents (or legal guardians) pay a fee for enrolling their children in preschool. By law, the amount paid by parents cannot exceed 20% of the total cost of the preschool expenses on the care and education of the child. Parents of children with disabilities are not required to pay (UNESCO, 2010). In "the Federal state educational standards of preschool education" approved in 2013, the five education areas are (1) sociocommunicative development; (2) cognitive development; (3) speech development; (4) artistic and aesthetic development; and (5) physical development. Music is an integral and compulsory part of the preschool curriculum. Music teachers in preschool are required to have at least an associate's degree in music education (Holmes, 2014).

General Education

Russia has an 11-grade system of general education, which is separated into elementary (grades 1–4, ages 6–10), middle (grades 5–9, ages 11–15) and senior (grades 10–11, ages 16–17) classes. Education usually begins with preschool before the age of 6, although it is not compulsory. The next step is primary school, which is part of the general education. Since 2007, 11-year education is compulsory. Every school has a "core curriculum" of academic subjects. After finishing the 11th grade, students must pass the EGE (Unified State Examination) and are then awarded a Certificate of Complete Secondary Education in June. Within the general school program, music is a required subject at elementary and middle levels and is taught by music specialists. At most schools, general music is taught 1 hour a week. At the upper secondary level (grades 10–11) music is not part of the curriculum of the general school, however, there are special courses available as elective subjects in areas of music, fine arts, world culture, and national culture.

Higher Education

Professional education is designed for individuals who wish to acquire a professional qualification. Professional education includes the following: (1) vocational education (technical or vocational schools); (2) non-university-level higher education (colleges); (3) university-level higher education; and (4) postgraduate education. The Ministry of

Education of the Russian Federation has developed and approved the State educational standards for higher professional education. State educational standards stipulate federal minimum requirements relating to the content of education and to teacher training, and imply regional and institutional components. Based on the state educational standards and its suggested curricula, each educational institution develops its own curriculum and program of studies. According to the state standards, the typical time for completing a program in music education is 5 years for full-time undergraduate students. In 2003, Russia became a member of the European Higher Education Area, the cooperative system for higher education in Europe whose foundations were laid by the 1999 Bologna declaration. As a result of that membership, the "Guidelines for Calculating Workload in Credits in the Educational Programs" have been developed and distributed among the institutions and a new system of bachelor's and master's diplomas was introduced. The education at the state institutions of higher education is free. At present, Russia has around 700 state-run institutions for higher education. There are also several hundred private institutions, at which programs in law, economics, business, management, and finance are strongly represented (EP NUFFIC, 2015).

The preparation of music teachers in Russia has traditionally been carried out by music departments in pedagogical universities and colleges. However, there are few cultural institutes and conservatories that offer a music education degree. There are three possible levels in the preparation of music teachers:

1. Training of preprimary and primary/basic teachers, including music specialists in preschools or lower elementary schools. This normally takes place in non-university-level educational institutions (colleges). The duration of the program ranges from 2 (for those students who have completed high school) to 5 years (students who only completed middle school). This degree is the equivalent of an American associate's degree.

2. Training of elementary/secondary teachers. Teacher training is carried out in teacher training university-level institutions, mostly at pedagogical universities. The program lasts for at least 4 years. In many universities, once students receive their bachelor's degree, prospective teachers can continue their studies to improve their professional music pedagogical education by studying toward a master's degree.

3. Training of higher education teachers. University teachers must follow postgraduate training. A candidate of pedagogical science degree (roughly equivalent to the PhD in the United States) is compulsory. There is also a doctor of science degree (has no equivalence in the United States), which is the highest degree in Russia. The candidate of sciences degree normally requires at least 3 years of study beyond graduation from a university-level higher education institution. The doctor of sciences degree can be earned after a period of further study following the award of the candidate of sciences degree (Holmes, Gokturk, Aguailar, & Chen 2010).

Music Schools

A children's music school is an educational establishment in which children receive musical education and skills in addition to the academic education of their normal school. The Ministry of Culture is responsible for coordinating the development of musical excellence through the system of specialized music schools for gifted children and 7-year music schools that run parallel to general schools. Music schools operate in most cities and towns throughout Russia and provide concentrated training in various aspects of music: performance training, choir, ensemble practice, solfeggio, music theory, and music history. Children are enrolled in a music school based on the results of entrance exams that assess their musical ability. The number of applicants depends greatly on the size of the population of the region where the school is located. The standard program includes lessons on how to play a musical instrument, as well as instruction in music theory (solfeggio) and the history of music. Lessons are held in the second half of the day so as not to interfere with studies in regular school. Usually children attend lessons at music school four to five times a week. The education in music schools is not free. Parents pay for tuition; however, it is relatively inexpensive, since the government subsidizes most of the music schools. Currently, there are approximately 3,000 children's music schools in Russia.

Special Music Schools

Musically gifted children may obtain admission (between 5 and 8 years of age) to one of a small number of fully residential "special" music schools attached to conservatories, where music education from expert teachers (as well as general education subjects) may continue up to the age of 18. The curriculum includes performance (piano and orchestral instruments), ensembles, theory (solfeggio), and music history (see Figure 13.1).

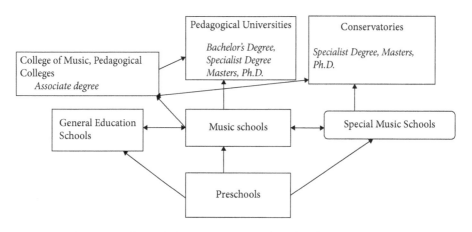

FIGURE 13.1 Structure of Music Education in Russia (Word and EPS)

Music Education Curriculum

After the collapse of the Soviet Union in 1991, the unified curriculum was no longer enforced, and each former Soviet country developed its own standards and curricular guidelines. Alternative programs with new approaches to content and methods of education have been developed, and some programs were officially accepted and recommended for implementation by the Ministry of Education and Science. Currently, music education is an integral part of the preschool, elementary, and secondary curriculum even though the quality of music program varies depending on the region, setting, administration, and teacher. Kodaly and Orff specialists from Hungary, Germany, and the United States have been presenting workshops and short teacher-training courses throughout the country. Currently, there are several music curricula recommended by the Russian Ministry of Education and Science. Teachers have the right to choose any of the approved curricula or develop their own programs with approval/examination of the State Department of Education. New curriculum development is now taking place in the general school settings; however, most of it is still based on the guiding philosophy and methodology of Dmitry Kabalevsky (Kabalevskaya, 2012).

Kabalevsky's Method

As a composer, Dmitri Kabalevsky is well recognized all over the world. His symphonies, operas, requiem, concertos, songs, and many other musical works have been performed around the globe. However, the pedagogical and methodological side of Kabalevsky's legacy is far less known outside of former Soviet Union countries. Music for children played a special role in Kabalevsky's creative endeavors from his earliest days. For younger audiences he dedicated concertos, as well as preludes, choral cantatas, and instrumental and vocal pieces. *ISME-Fanfares* (1974) is commonly heard at the opening ceremony at ISME (International Society for Music Education) conferences. Kabalevsky was an honorary president of the ISME. Aside from the plethora of musical compositions, he wrote many manuscripts and articles in the field of music education. One of the most important contributions was the development and implementation of music education curriculum in public schools.

Kabalevsky's program of general music education is based on his more than 30 years of experience talking to children and adults about music. He lectured on the radio, TV, and in concert halls; his face and his voice were known all over the country. At the end of 1960s Kabalevky began to work at a regular public school in Moscow as a music teacher with a goal to test his methodology in practice. He taught music at school once a week for 7 consecutive years. Government officials, politicians, researchers, teachers, and parents observed Kabalevsky's lessons. Some of the lessons were recorded and broadcast. The National Television Company showed these recordings in the program "Music

Lessons for Teachers." The program featured music teachers from different towns across Russia, Belarus, and Kazakhstan. In 1974, Kabalevsky approached the Government of the Soviet Union to support his idea of the development of a special research laboratory. He also proposed a new journal—*Music in School*. In the laboratory, specialists from different areas of music and education worked together to develop the rationale and curriculum of a new program. The laboratory included a composer, a musicologist, a psychologist, a specialist from higher education institution, and music teachers. The journal was intended for the program to be better known and to provide the opportunity for discussion and communication with music teachers all over the country. The number of schools that adapted Kabalevsky's method increased with each year. Teachers attended special professional development courses, and by the end of the 7-year experiment, over 2,000 teachers taught music at their school according to Kabalevky's method. Since the beginning, in the 1980s all schools in Russia adopted the Kabalevsky program, and it became compulsory in the general schools until 1991.

Kabalevsky's methodology stemmed from a growing dissatisfaction in Soviet society with public school music education. His intent was to enrich the life of every child by making music an integral part of the school curriculum. He was trying to bring music closer to society and society closer to the arts. Kabalevsky's philosophy constitutes four concurrent parts, including a focus on the harmonious development of the individual; a focus on his belief in the power the arts exerts on children and all aspects of culture; a focus on the close relationship between music (as art and a school subject) and the child's life; and a focus on music content (musical material). The cornerstone of Kabalevsky's educational philosophy was his concern with the general education of the individual. To support this point, Kabalevsky used as the epigraph for his general school music program a phrase by the Soviet educator Vasili Sukhomlinsky: "Music education does not mean educating a musician—it means first of all educating a human being" (quoted in Kabalevsky, 2001, p. 12).

Kabalevky's program has a clear objective: to foster the love of music. Kabalevsky believed that with the correct models, principles, materials, and tools he would be able to persuade children to study music, thus spiritually enriching each human being. To achieve these results three main problems in music must be solved: (1) To awaken and develop children's interest in music as an art and consequently in music studies; (2) To develop systematically a conscious perception of music and artistic thinking; and (3) To develop a musical ear.

Kabalevsky sought to focus the study of music into basic genres—a song, a dance, and a march. He called them "The three whales of music" referring to an old Russian fairy tale that describes earth as a flat surface that rests on the backs of three giant whales. He extends that fairy tale and suggests that three whales carry the entire world of music on their back. Kabalevsky explains that all music that exists in the world also rests on three whales—a song, a dance, and a march. Children know them from the first hours of their lives, so they easily understand them as a real part of everyday life. He strongly believed that these "whales" are the simplest, and therefore, the most accessible musical genres. Every child sang the song or at least heard the song sung by someone. Furthermore, there is no child who has not seen or been involved in a dance or marched to the music. He believed that children should know about song, dance, and march before they step into the classroom, and a foundation for learning exists before any formal schooling takes place.

Choosing material for music class must be done with great care. The primary considerations are: (1) musical materials must be educationally sound (it should teach something that is necessary and valuable), (2) the music should fulfill an ideological role: be able to shape morality and the aesthetic taste of the student, and (3) the music has to be appealing to the students, stimulating their desire to participate in learning. Overall, the content of Kabalevsky's program is organized according to specific themes and divided into six parts according to the years of study: the first year of study, the second year, and so on. The major theme of first year is "How may we hear music." What does it mean, "to hear music"? Kabalevsky writes that it means "to listen to, discover, sink into, plunge into, touch (lightly), experience, go through; endure, watch, keep an eye on it, distinguish; tell apart; modify, evaluate, perceive and so on" (Kabalevsky, 2001, p. 34). The list of music includes the following: "Kikimora," by Lyadov; a variety of the Russian lullabies; folk and composed songs ("The Wind," by Frid; "The Squirrels," by Levina; "The Trees," by Tilicheeva); the Russian folk songs ("Under Our Gates"); the Ukrainian folk songs ("The Sweep") and so on; the children's singing game "The Old Man and the Turnip." It also includes classical masterpieces such as "The Mother," "Baba Yaga," "Waltz" from Album for Children, and fragments from Symphony No. 2 by Tchaikovsky. There are a number of pieces from *The Anna Magdalena Notebook* by J.S. Bach. Music by Kabalevsky is represented by *Novella* and *Preludes* (for piano), fragments from his *Concerto for Violin and Orchestra* (II part), and other pieces for piano and songs. The content for the second year is devoted to the theme "Three whales in music—song, dance, march." Students engage in listening, performing, and composing activities and are expected to recognize and define all three genres of music. The theme of the third year is "Where the three whales lead us". Students learn about opera, ballet, symphony, and concerto. The theme in the fourth year is, "What is musical language?" Students learn about musical terminology and concepts: melody, tempo, form, dynamics, texture, tonality, rhythm, register, and timbre. During year 4 they also learn about characteristics of the traditional and classical music instruments and the role of instruments in creating musical images.

Other curricula

Kritskaya's program *Muzika* is another popular curriculum (and textbook) for the first 4 years of elementary general music. In her method, music and its elements are introduced and taught in integration with visual arts and literature. The method is based on the main principles of Kabalevsky's ideas, but the principle position of the author is that "the child's entrance into the world of musical art should take place in connection to Russian music—its inflexions, themes and imagery" (Kritskaya, Sergeeva, & Shmagina, 2001, pp. 211–212). All masterpieces of Western music are taught by comparing them to Russian music thereby strengthening the relevance of music to the Russian culture, and consequently, to each child's life. Each page of the textbook and the exercise book includes the musical material (the title of the piece, scores of the major themes), illustrations (photos, reproductions of paintings), text (fragments of poems and narratives, correlating to the topic of the double page), lists of musical terminology necessary for the children on this level of education, and questions and activities.

The Zankov (2000) music curriculum emerged in 1991. The Zankov program was developed in the 1970s, but it was not recommended for adaptations in schools because it did not meet the requirements of the ruling Communist Party. Asmolov (1999) described the Zankov theory as "an innovative form of pedagogy" based on Vygotsky's theories. Zankov recognized Vygotsky's notion of the zone of proximal development, and based his educational system on the principle of presenting tasks according the degree of difficulty. He emphasized that in the educational process every child must meet the cognitive challenge.

There is variety of curricula for lower elementary schools in Russia. For teaching children in upper elementary and secondary schools, many teachers use the unified program for general music that was developed by Abdulin, Beider, Vendrova, Kadobnova, and others, under the guidance of Kabalevsky (Hrennikov, 1994).

ASSESSMENT AND EVALUATION
IN RUSSIA

Assessment and evaluation had a very interesting history in the system of Russian education. During first days after the October 1917 Russian revolution, a new government commission for education was established. The new declaration titled "Main Principles of Unified School Education" was adopted. In May 1918 the People's Commissariat of Education declared a statute canceling all kinds of assessments and grades at all levels of public school education. Along the way, homework was abandoned too. The new system intended the school to be a place of exploration rather than dictation and memorization, meanwhile eliminating many long-held educational traditions, such as grades, homework, and entrance examinations. The main idea about the termination of grades was to abolish old, prerevolutionary authoritative views and to develop new citizens: free of boundaries, creative, in control of their own education and life. Decisions about completion of each grade level and about completion of degree were based on teacher recommendations. The predominant philosophy of education was based on theory of free education without any boundaries and grading. According to Amonashvili (2012), that decision had a very negative impact on the educational process. In September 1935 the government of the USSR re-established the prerevolutionary system of assessment and established the differentiated 5-scale system of grading that used verbal terminology:

Numerical Mark	Russian Description	Russian Words	Meaning
5	*Otlichno*	*Pyat*	Excellent
4	*Khorosho*	*Tchetyri*	Good
3	*Udovletvoritel'no*	*Trie*	Satisfactory
2	*Neudovletvoritel'no* (also: plokho)	*Dwa*	Poor (fail)

FIGURE 13.2 Russian Educational System Grading Scale (Word and EPS)

"excellent," "good," "satisfactory,"" unsatisfactory," "very unsatisfactory." In 1944, verbal terminology was replaced with a "digital" format, with a score of "5" equal to excellent, "4"—good, "3"—satisfactory; "2"—unsatisfactory, "1"—very unsatisfactory. As shown in Figure 13.2, the current Russian education system uses a 5-2-assessment scale (EP NUFFIC, 2010/2015, January).

In the first decade of the 21st century, Russia launched a comprehensive reform of the assessment system. This mission was part of a broader reform of the education system, which aimed to ensure that students developed the skills required for the country's social and economic development. The reform was also part of a greater decentralization of educational administration in Russia. During the 1990s the country completed the journey from the school/institution level examination to a standardized examination for school graduation and admission to higher education institutions. The Russian program has a well-established system of assessment that provides measurement and evaluation for different educational purposes. The system incorporates three main types of assessment: (1) primary and secondary school examinations for certification and admission to higher education institutions; (2) national and international large-scale assessments for monitoring and evaluation of educational quality; and (3) classroom assessments for the purposes of grading students and improving teaching and learning. The Law on Education (passed in 1992 and amended in 2010) provided the legal basis for the national examination in grade 9 (age 15) (Final State Certification [FSC]) and the unified examination (Unified State Examination [USE]) in grade 11 (age 17). Starting in 2009, the USE became an official tool for finishing secondary education and starting higher education. Russian language and mathematics are mandatory subjects on the USE, and are required for graduating high school. Three or more subjects are necessary to apply for university admissions; music is not included as a possible elective subject of the USE. The USE became an authentic mechanism of modernization in educational assessment in Russia. Every secondary school graduate, regardless of social background or place of residence, has the opportunity to send his/her USE certificate and scores to any university (or several simultaneously) and take part in an admissions competition. In 2010 the FSC-9 exam became a requirement for all students. This exam is a central-level standardized examination at the end of basic education (grade 9, ages 14–15) and includes the Russian language and mathematics, plus two examinations chosen by the student from among subjects taught in grade 9. Even though music is a mandatory part of the curriculum in grades 1 through 9 (ages 6–14), music as a subject is not offered at examination. The purpose of the FSC-9 is to certify that students have met the requirements of basic education, which align with federal learning standards. Beyond certification, examination results can be used to "track" students in secondary education (i.e., the vocational or academic track), as well as in school accreditation and teacher evaluation processes (Bolotov et al., 2013).

The national assessment system operates through a complex network of federal and regional institutions. Each institution is in charge of a different aspect of the system, including policy decisions, design, implementation, and research.

- The Federal Institute of Pedagogical Measurements develops standardized assessments, trains examination administrators, and analyzes examination results.
- The Federal Testing Center provides technology and information support in administering assessments, including data processing and maintenance of the examinations database. It is also responsible for producing and distributing examination materials to the regions.
- The Russian Academy of Education pursues research in assessment and evaluation through the activities of two institutes: The Institute of Content and Methods of Education and the Institute of Management in Education. The Center for Evaluating the Quality of Education, part of the Institute of Content and Methods of Education, is responsible for administering international assessments. (Bolotov et al., 2013)

In addition to federal institutions, regional entities are in charge of core assessment activities. Every Russian region sets up a state examination board during the secondary school examination period. This board is responsible for preparing and implementing examinations and for approving the results.

Classroom Assessments

Russian teachers use classroom assessments for different purposes. According to the Progress in International Reading Literacy Study (PIRLS, 2006), Russian teachers mainly use classroom assessments to assign student grades, identify students in need of remedial instruction, and as a way of informing parents about student progress. Teachers also use classroom assessments to modify their instruction, assign students for specific instruction, and provide data to national or local educational administrators. Teachers enter students' grades in the class book, following a standard procedure. The class book is the official instrument for reporting grades at the regional level. Based on grades recorded in the class book, teachers report final grades for a 3-, 6-, or 12-month period. Grades are recorded in student report cards, which are the main tool for informing parents about their student's performance. In some schools, new electronic forms (e-book) of grading and report cards have been introduced, and there is the prospect of implementing electronic grading throughout the country. Teachers currently grade students using a scale that was established by the Commissariat of Public Education in 1937, and that scale applies to both formative and summative assessment. Scoring is based on a five-point scale that goes from "1"—fail to "5"—excellent. This grading system is highly criticized by teachers, students, and the educational community for: (1) lack of transparency, together with the subjectivity of assessment criteria and procedures; (2) the fact that in practice, only positive marks are given, reducing the effective range of the scale to 3–5 points; and (3) the scant information provided by the grades (Bolotov et al., 2013).

Assessment in the Music Classroom

Currently there is debate on national music assessment practices and implementation policies. While most Russian music educators largely promote informal assessment in music, many remain strongly opposed to a standardized music assessment. I had several opportunities to discuss the topic of assessment with a few Russian music education professors and music teachers, and according to their feedback, most of the teachers resist the notion of standardized exams in music and the USE in music. One of the main arguments posited by music educators is that music is an artistic expression and cannot and should not be academically tested. Dmitry Kabalevsky was a strong promoter of group/class assessments and believed that measuring students' growth is more imperative than measuring students' achievement. According to Koroleva (2003), Russian music teachers measure the "individual progress" of students and "active participation" in music class. An individual approach to each student is a priority of assessment policy in music. Because musical aptitude, background, and experiences in music differ significantly among students, teachers evaluate progress of each student, not a particular achievement. Group assessment is widely used, and teachers assess student's participation in music activities. Grading in music class plays a stimulating role and most of the students traditionally receive good grades in music. The famous Russian music educator Eduard Abdulin developed recommendations for assessment in the general music classroom. According to Abduin and Nikolaeva, the following criteria should be used:

Criterion # 1:   Interest in music, emotional response to the music, participation in discussion, feedback/critical evaluation of listening and performing experience.

Criterion # 2:   Effort of the student, ability to use musical knowledge and skills in the process of reflecting on music listening experiences and performances.

Criterion # 3:   Growth of performing skills based on initial level of music preparation.

Abdulin recommends the following rules for grading:

"5"—demonstration of at least two criteria
"4"—demonstration of at least one criterion
"3"—no demonstration of any criterion
"2" and "1"—should not exist in music classes.

Many Russian music educators (Abdulin & Nikolaeva, 2006; Ksenzova, 2001) do not recommend assigning grades "2" and "1" even if a child misbehaves or does not participate at any activities. There is a recommendation to give more then one grade for different types of activities (Abdulin & Nikolaeva, 2006; Koroleva, 2005) Many teachers recommend including comments about students' progress in students journals.

Assessment of Preservice Music Teachers

At the higher education institutions the assessment of knowledge of future music teachers can be divided into two components: course assessment and state examinations.

Course Assessment

After completing each course, during exam weeks students have to participate in oral examinations. Prior to examination dates, students usually receive a study guide or preparation questions from the professor. During the examination, students have to "draw questions from a hat" with one or two questions (depending on the course of study, exam can contain two to five questions). Students have approximately 10–15 minutes to review the exam questions and prepare their answers after which he/she has to present it orally in front of the professor(s) (if the course has been taught by two or more professors during two or more semesters of study, exams will be administered by two or more professors). The marking scale is the same as in primary and secondary schools, with "5" = excellent "4" = good "3" = satisfactory "2" = unsatisfactory.

State Examinations

In order to be certified for the teaching profession every student has to pass two state examinations after completing all coursework. Typically, the content of each examination includes two parts: practical (performance) and theoretical. The performing part of music performance examinations include a solo recital, which comprises at least three compositions of various styles and forms (polyphony, sonata or variation form composition, and romantic or contemporary piece). The theoretical part of the examination includes assessment of the knowledge of the major methodologies, history and theory of music, psychology, pedagogy, theories, and history of music education. The marking and assessment strategy are same as used in course assessment.

Challenges and Future of Assessment

In 2014, the new program for the development of the system of Russian music education for 2014–2020 was published. According to that program, the new assessment reforms in music education will be implemented during the next few years. This includes: (1) the development of preservice and in-service teacher training programs that provide training on assessment, (2) the development of uniform entrance examinations to music schools, (3) the development of standardized examinations in music and art for FSC, and (4) improvement of quality (including quality of evaluation) of current music competitions and festivals.

Currently reforms in classroom assessments have been hard to introduce, although some changes are taking place. Music education programs do not provide training in the topic of assessment and evaluation. Traditional assessment practices used for bureaucratic and control purposes are deeply engrained in the culture of Russian teachers. Changing that culture takes time, training, and resources. Progressive Russian educators (Bolotov et al., 2013) recommend the following efforts: (1) aligning classroom assessment with federal standards, (2) using explicit criteria to judge student learning, (3) employing self-assessment and peer assessment, (4) using ongoing assessment of students learning, (5) using a wider range of assessment instruments and formats, (5) using student portfolios, (6) using a new 10-point scale to describe learning levels, and (6) using effective communication tools to provide assessment information to students and parents.

CONCLUSION

Music education in Russia plays an important part of the educational and cultural experience. Since beginning of the 20th century the Russian government has succeeded in developing an impressive system of music education that is available to all citizens. This is evidenced in the compulsory music lessons in grades 1–9 (ages 6–15) the availability of elective music courses in grades 10–11 (ages 15–17), the existence of music schools and special music school for gifted children, and the presence of music clubs and music societies. Russian general music education has a well-established successful music education curriculum based on Kabalevsky's methodology. Many progressive musicians regard Kabalevsky's system as a revolution in music education (Pozhidayev, 1993). Dmitri Kabalevsky's contributions to music education in the general schools have been truly transformational. Once Kabalevsky said, "There are people who composed music better than mine. But the music syllabus is my lifework!" (1988). Currently, teachers have wide choices when they select syllabi and textbooks; they no longer are locked into a single, centralized curriculum. However, most of the general music teachers still used curriculum developed by Dmitri Kabalevsky. According to the new 2011 state educational standards music is part of core curriculum in grades 1–9 (ages 6–14) and part of elective curriculum in grades 10–11 (ages 15–17). According to the state educational standards the goal of music lessons is to develop well-rounded aesthetic and cultural knowledge by learning Russian and world music heritage through the involvement in creative and aesthetic activities.

Currently education in Russia is going through radical and at times controversial changes. New State Educational Standards and the New Educational Program have been highly criticized by educational professionals and are still in the process of adaptation and implementation. Russia has taken important steps to develop a national student assessment system. The implementation of the USE has led to changes to the school graduation examination system and entrance exams to higher education institutions. Currently it is viewed as one of the most significant elements of the assessment system reform and the national education system reform. Since 2009, the USE is the only form of graduation examination in schools and the main form of preliminary examination in universities. A student can take a USE in Russian language, mathematics, foreign languages, physics, chemistry, biology, literature, history, geography, social sciences, and computer sciences. Music as a subject is not offered as a USE. The USE became a real mechanism to support democratization of education. This has brought more equity of opportunities, particularly for students of remote Russian regions, who can now enter the best universities without spending a lot of money on travel. External exams have provided excellent feedback into the system, allowing decision makers to compare schools and university entry requirements. Nevertheless, many important steps remain ahead in order to consolidate these assessment reforms. Assessment policies in music education have been in the stage of development since 2014. According to the new 2014 program for the development of Russian music education, the new assessment reforms in music education will be published and implemented during 2016–2020.

With the absence of the communist ideology and centralized curriculum the Russian nation is circumstantially forced to rethink and transform its concepts and policy toward structure, content, and pedagogy of modern education in order to keep up with current global trends and the needs of the Russian community. As it faces a number of political and economical problems, the solutions for transformation and reformation will determine the future of both students and music teachers. The former president of the USSR, Mikhail Gorbachev, wrote in his most current book, *The New Russia* (2016): "We need now to realize that we are facing a wave of social problems that will determine Russia's future, the situation in education, healthcare and other areas. If we cannot find solutions to these problems, Russia will not modernize" (p. 257). Gorbachev insists that Russia will have to be reformed, and there is no other way: Every aspect of society needs transformation. He writes,

> The Russian people in the course of their long history have incorporated and defended vast territories, given the world outstanding politicians, thinkers, writers, composers and artists. We are a talented people, capable of great feats of endurance and dogged, routine hard work. Russians, both at home and abroad, achieve enormous success when they are able to work in normal conditions.   (p. 424)

References

Abdulin, E., & Nikolaeva, E. (2005). *Muzikalno-pedagogicheskoe obrzobvanie v Rossii v 20 I 21 stoletii* [Music pedagogical education in Russia in the 20th & 21st centuries]. Moscow, Russia: Prometheus.

Abdulin, E., & Nikolaeva, E. (2006). *Bringing up a teaching musician with broad background.* Paper presented at the 2006 Conference of International Society for Music Education, Kuala Lumpur, Malaysia.

Amonashvili, S. (2012). *Osnovi Gummannoi Pedagogiki; Ob Ocenkah.* [Foundation of human pedagogy: About grades]. Moscow, Russia: Amrita.

Asmolov, A. (1999). Obrazovanie v Pronstranstve SNG [Education in the Post-Soviet Independent States]. *World of Psychology, 1,* 205.

Bereday, G. Z. F., Brickman, W. W., & Read, G. H. (1960). *The changing Soviet school.* Cambridge, UK: The Riverside Press.

Bolotov, V., Kovaleva, G., Pinskaya, M., & Valdman, I. (2013). *Developing the enabling context for student assessment in Russia.* Washington DC: The International Bank for Reconstruction and Development.

Bosova, G. (2003). *Myzikalnoe Obrazovanie v Peterburge XIX veka* [Music education in Petersburg in the 19th century]. Paper presented at National Conference of History of Saint Petersburg, Russia.

Cox, A. (2011). *Policy and Practice: Russian and Soviet Education during Times of Social and Political Change* (Unpublished senior honors thesis). Boston College, Boston, MA.

Doroshenko, S. (2016). History of Russian music education from the perspective of the dialogue of cultures between the capital cities and the provinces: Specifics of periodization. In *Selected Articles about the World of Music Arts and Education 1*, 10c.–beginning of 20c. Moscow: UNESCO Chair in Musical Arts and Education in Life-Long Learning.

Hrennikov, B. (1994). 5–8 Klassi. *Programmi dlya obsheobrazovatelnih uchebnih ucherezhdenii. 1 class chetirehletnei nachalnoi shkoli.1–3 klassi trehletnei nachalnoi shkoli* [Grades 5–8. Syllabus for general educational institutions. Grade 1 of four-year primary school. Grades 1–3 of three-year primary school (with brief recommendations)] (pp. 93–223). Moscow, Russia.

Elliott, J., & Tudge, J. (2007). The impact of the west on post-Soviet Russian education: Change and resistance to change. *Comparative Education, 43*(1), 93–112.

EP-Nuffic. (2010/2015, January). The Russian education system described and compared with the Dutch System. *Education system Russian Federation* (2nd ed., version 2). Retrieved from https://www.nuffic.nl/en/publications/find-a-publication/education-system-russian-federation.pdf

Fedorovich, E. (2014). *Istoria professionalnogo musicalnogo obrazovania v Rossii (XIX–XX veka)* [The History of professional music education in Russia (19th–20th century)] (2nd ed.). Moscow, Russia: Direct-Media.

Gorbachev, M. (2016). *The new Russia.* Cambridge, UK: Polity Press.

Holmes, A. (2014). Music in the Russian preschool curriculum. *Perspectives: Journal of the Early Childhood Music and Movement Association, 9*(3), 19–23.

Holmes, A. V., Gokturk, D., Aguailar, B. E., & Chen, J. (2010). Assessment "Over the ocean"—Outside of the US. In T.S. Brophy (Ed.), *Proceedings of Second International Symposium on Assessment in Music Education: The practice of assessment in music education: Frameworks, models, and designs.* Chicago, IL: GIA Publications.

Kabalevskaya, M. D. (2012). *The world's best kept secret for the excellence in music education—The legacy of Kabalevsky method.* Paper presented at 2012 ISME World Conference on Music Education, Thessaloniki, Greece.

Kabalevsky, D. (1973). Soviet music education: As seen by a Soviet composer. *Music Educators Journal, 60*(9), 91–94.

Kabalevsky, D. (1988). *Music and education.* London, UK: Jessica Kingston Publishers.

Kabalevsky, D. (2001). Osnovnie Principi i metodi pogrammi po myzike dlya obrazovatelnoi shkoli [The main principals and methods of music program for general school]. In Yaryomenko (Ed.), *Curricular and methodical materials: Music; Primary School* (pp. 10–130). Moscow, Russia: Drofa.

Kerr, S. T. (2005). Demographic change and the fate of Russia's schools: The impact of population shifts on educational practice and policy. In B. Eklof, L. E. Holmes, & V. Kaplan (Eds.), *Educational reform in post-Soviet Russia* (pp. 153–175). London, UK: Fran Cass.

Kezina, L., & Kondakov, A. (2011). *Federal state educational standard of general education.* Moscow: Russian Academy of Education.

Koroleva, T. (2003). *Metodicheskaya podgotovka uchitelya* muziki [Methodological preparation of music teachers]. Minsk, Belarus: Technoprint.

Koroleva, T. (2005). *10 Leksii po Methodike Muzikalnogo Vospitanuya: Uchebnoe posobiye dlya vyzov* [10 lectures about music education: Textbook for higher education institutions]. Minsk, Belarus: Technoprint.

Kraevskij, V. V., & Lerner, I. Y. (1984). *The theory of curriculum content in the USSR.* Paris, France: UNESCO.

Kritskaya, E., Sergeeva, G., & Shmagina, T. (2001) *Myzika* [Music]. Moscow, Russia: Prosveschenie.

Ksenzova, G. (2001). *Ocenochnaya deyatelnost uchitelya* [Evaluation strategies of the teacher]. Moscow, Russia: Pedagogicheskoe obschestvo.

Kurilla, I. (2013). Education reform in Russia. *Russian Analytical Digest, 137*(9), 2–8.

Larimer, F. (1993). Music education in Russia: A recent perspective. *The Quarterly, 4*(3), 64–68.

Ministry of Education and Science of Russian Federation. (2016). *State standards of education.* Retrieved from http://минобрнауки.рф/документы?keywords=253

Novikova, I. (2013). Razvitie Teorii Muzikalnogo Obrazovaniya [Development of theory of music education in Russia]. *Srednee Porfessionalnoe Obrazovanie, 2,* 57–59.

OECD. (2012), *Education at a glance 2012: Highlights.* OECD Publishing. Retrieved from http://dx.doi.org/10.1787/eag_highlights-2012-en

Pozhidayev, G. (1993). Music education in Russia. *The Quarterly, 4*(3), 5–7.

PIRLS. (2006). *International report.* Retrieved from http://timssandpirls.bc.edu/pirls2006/intl_rpt.html

Remeta, D. R. (1974). *Music education in the USSR* (Unpublished doctoral dissertation). University of Southern California, Los Angeles, CA.

United Nations Educational, Scientific and Cultural Organization. (2010). *Early childhood. care and education country report. Russian Federation.* World Conference on Early Childhood Care and Education. Retrieved from http://unesdoc.unesco.org/images/0018/001893/189374E.pdf

Zankov, L. (2000). *Muzika. V Sbornike Program Dlya Chetirehletnei Nachalnoi Shkoli. Sistema Zankova* [Music. In Collection of syllabi for four-year primary school: The Zankov system] (pp. 164–183). Moscow, Russia: Zentr obshego rasvitiya.

CHAPTER 14

BRAZILIAN POLICIES ON EDUCATION ASSESSMENT

Higher Education Perspectives

SERGIO FIGUEIREDO AND
LUCIANA DEL-BEN

INTRODUCTION

THE Lei de Diretrizes e Bases da Educação Nacional (Law of Guidelines and Bases of National Education) states that the Brazilian education is composed of basic education (0–17 years, approximately) and higher education (from 18 years on, approximately). The same law, approved in 1996 and updated subsequently, determines the "free and compulsory basic education of four (4) to seventeen (17) years of age " (Brasil, 2015, art. 4). Therefore, it is compulsory that the Brazilian States offer free access to basic education and also that all students in this age group—between 4 and 17 years—have the right of attending basic education in public institutions, maintained by federal, state and city governments.

Basic education in Brazil is divided into 3 levels: early childhood education (0–5 years), fundamental teaching (6–14 years) and middle teaching (15–17 years). Higher education includes several university undergraduate courses, and also graduate programs (*lato* and *stricto sensu* programs).

For each level of basic education and higher education, rules are defined regarding assessment, with different aims and objectives. Two national assessment systems were officially established for the development of proposals and processes, with very comprehensive approaches, covering all levels of basic education and all types of higher education courses: SAEB—Sistema de Avaliação da Educação Básica (Assessment System of Basic Education) is directed to the national assessment, mainly fundamental teaching (6 to 14 years) and middle teaching (15 to 17 years) (Brasil, 2005); SINAES—Sistema Nacional de Avaliação da Educação Superior (The National System of Higher Education Assessment) refers to the assessment of institutions, undergraduate courses, and students' performance (Brasil, 2007). Both assessment systems include different programs and types of evaluation, applied to specific levels of education in Brazil.

Several types of assessment have been designed and implemented from the official rules established by SAEB and SINAES. Additional documents guide the evaluation systems also considering the results presented from the performance of each type of test or evaluation. In a very broad and diversified format, Brazilian educational policies have been configured from various modes of evaluation, which generate key indicators for the diagnosis of the quality of Brazilian education at different levels. From this diagnosis, specific actions are carried out continuously in order to reinforce positive results and seek specific solutions to the problems detected.

> If there is a policy that advanced in Brazil, over the past 15 years, it was the implementation of educational assessment systems. During this period, several initiatives have formed a robust and efficient evaluation system at all levels and types of education, consolidating an effective educational assessment policy. Considered today one of the world's most comprehensive and efficient, the assessment policy includes various programs such as the Assessment System of Basic Education—*SAEB*, the National Exam of Middle Teaching—*ENEM*, the National Course Exam—*ENC* known as *Provão* and subsequently replaced by the National Exam of Students' Performance in Higher Education—*ENADE*, the National Exam for Youth and Adult Certification—*ENCCEJA*, the National System of Higher Education Assessment—*SINAES*, the Brazil Exam and the Basic Education Development Index—*IDEB*. Together, these systems, along with the CAPES [Brazilian educational agency connected to the Ministry of Education], the oldest evaluation system in the education sector in Brazil—constitute the macro-system of the assessment of the quality of Brazilian education.   (Castro, 2009, p. 5)

In this chapter, we describe and analyze public policies for evaluation in Brazil, focusing on undergraduate and graduate levels, with the objective of discussing how music education has been treated in these assessment policies. We also analyze aspects related to different evaluation models, discussing the implications of such models to improve the quality of Brazilian education. The analysis and discussion of the assessment perspectives of undergraduate and graduate levels also reflects on the current policies and practices, and how such policies are connected and articulated in practice.

HIGHER EDUCATION ASSESSMENT

The evaluation of higher education courses and institutions in Brazil has shown a steady and consistent evolution, from different procedures (Dias, Horiguela, & Marchelli, 2006). Such evolution can be verified from "a critical analysis of the assessment policies of quality in higher education" (Bittencourt, Viali, Cassartelli, & Rodrigues, 2008, p. 249).

The SINAES was established by Law 10.861/2004 as part of the Brazilian educational policies, in order "to ensure national evaluation process of higher education institutions, undergraduate courses and performance of their students" (Brasil, 2004, art. 1). The processes established by SINAES strengthen the assessment instruments as a means of guaranteeing the quality of education offered in higher education. This assessment system, established in 2004, has been promoting a number of changes that are necessary when considering the growing number of new institutions and undergraduate programs in Brazil: "Changes in assessment processes have been intended, by the State, to ensure the quality of education offered in the country, especially in expansion and access times" (Griboski, 2012, pp. 181–182). The process forms "an evaluative tripod, which allows to know the quality of courses and Higher Education Institutions (HEIs) throughout Brazil" (http://portal.inep.gov.br/enade) involving a number of factors to improve the quality of higher education in Brazil.

In the evaluation of institutions, "the policy for teaching, research, graduate and their ways of operation" (Brasil, 2004, art. 3), as well as the social responsibility of institutions, physical infrastructure, organization, management, and financial sustainability are considered. For institutional evaluation, various procedures and instruments are used, including self-evaluation and external review by the appropriate individuals and groups.

The assessment of undergraduate courses is applied to programs in all areas of knowledge, in order to identify issues related to faculty, facilities, and didactic-pedagogical organization. Evaluation of the courses is done using various methods, including visits by committees of experts in each field of knowledge.

The students' performance assessment is conducted by the ENADE—Exame Nacional de Desempenho dos Estudantes—National Exam of Students' Performance. Two indicators are associated with ENADE in terms of evaluation. One of these indicators is the ENADE written exam, performed for each specific knowledge area; another is the performance difference indicator, "where students are assessed in relation to the average performance expected for students in supposedly similar circumstances" (Bittencourt et al., 2008, p. 250).

The ENADE exam syllabus is based on the curriculum guidelines for each undergraduate course, and assesses students' skills and competencies in relation to their area of study, as well as with respect to Brazilian and global reality. The ENADE is applied periodically. Every year, tests for undergraduate programs are carried out in some predetermined locations. Every 3 years, at most, all students in Brazilian higher education are evaluated by the ENADE. Initially, this exam was applied to "a sample of students from each course in the areas selected each year, with a guaranteed new application in such areas in a maximum of three years" (INEP, 2004, art. 1). Currently, ENADE is mandatory for all students in higher education in all areas of knowledge. According to the legislation, students who are in the first and in the last year of courses must take the ENADE. According to Limana and Brito (2006), assessing the performance of the students,

> could show if he/she had or not competencies development, if he/she is capable of working the learned contents and, mainly, the capacity of the student to use the knowledge for his/her own development. ENADE intends to verify what the student is capable of doing with the acquired knowledge and not "what" and "how much" he/she learned.   (p. 22)

This set of assessments—institutional, undergraduate courses, and students' performance—is coordinated by the CONAES—Comissão Nacional de Avaliação da Educação Superior (National Commission for Higher Education Assessment), which is directly connected to the Ministry of Education. The implementation of these assessments at the national level, is under the responsibility of INEP—Instituto Nacional de Estudos e Pesquisas Educacionais Anísio Teixeira (Anísio Teixeira National Institute of Educational Studies), the official agency bound to the Ministry of Education, which acts directly in the formulation and implementation of public policies related to the assessment of Brazilian education.

From the evaluations obtained in the institutions in undergraduate courses and from students, the results are disseminated through reports that contain different information, used

> by the HEIs for guidance of their institutional effectiveness and academic and social effectiveness; by the government agencies, to guide public policies and by students, students' parents, academic institutions and the general public, to guide their decisions about the courses and institutions. (http://portal.inep.gov.br/enade)

Despite the existence of the reports and their acknowledgment of the complex task of gathering and analyzing data from various sources, many higher education institutions make little or no use of this information in their curriculum reorganization process: "In general, it is observed that both reporting information and evaluation data and characteristics are not known by the undergraduate courses, contributing little or nothing if they do not motivate reflection and analysis for possible improvements" (Griboski, 2012, p. 194).

Even after several years of ENADE implementation, its utility is still questioned. For many the test is performed because it is mandatory and not necessarily because it would be a tool to contribute to the improvement of the courses. The existence of this exam promotes, in some cases, institutional competition, internally and externally, which could be questioned in terms of evaluation. The final notes of the analyzed courses should serve as benchmarks for changes or continuities regarding the formative aspects that are part of the curriculum, including teaching, research, and university extension.

The purpose of SINAES is to improve the quality of Brazilian education, but the outcome of the assessment is not always assumed as a factor that motivates this desired improvement. Agreeing with Griboski (2012),

> it is necessary a broad movement that mobilizes government, teachers and students not only for the participation of students in ENADE, but also to the responsibility with the consolidation of the evaluation culture within the higher education institutions.
>
> (Griboski, 2012, p. 190)

It should be noted that the ENADE is one of the components of the assessment provided by SINAES policy. However, "the majority of higher education institutions and the press give more prominence to ENADE and the Performance Difference Indicator (IDD), both based on student performance" (Bittencourt et al., 2008, p. 249). Reinforcing this perspective, Ristoff and Giolo (2006) affirm that many students, the press, and much of society are unaware of the broad SINAES policy, understanding that this policy comes down only to ENADE.

The consolidation of an "evaluation culture," as posed by Griboski, is necessary to reach the outcomes of the SINAES. The ENADE is one of the inductive elements to improve Brazilian education in undergraduate programs. More interest, participation, and consequently, more analysis of the evaluation processes as a whole are mandatory to assure that assessment policies make sense, for both those who assess and those who are assessed.

ENADE Music

Since the implementation of SINAES, the ENADE examinations for the music area were conducted in the years 2006, 2009, 2011, 2014, and 2017 (the most recent ENADE *Música* was administered in November of 2017, keeping the same structure of the ENADE, 2014). The following descriptions reference the 2014 administration for students of the Licenciatura em Música (Bachelor of Music Education equivalent). The undergraduate courses named "Licenciatura" in Brazil prepare teachers for all areas of school knowledge, so the Licenciatura em Música prepares music teachers.

The ENADE is administered on a specific date for all students of various undergraduate courses in Brazil. The exams are organized in two parts that total 40 questions in different formats. The first part has 10 questions about general issues, and the second part contains 30 questions about a specific area of studies.

In 2014, the first section comprises the common questions given to all students in all undergraduate courses. This consisted of eight multiple-choice questions and two essay questions. These questions addressed the following elements:

> ethical attitude; social commitment; understanding of issues that transcend the environment of the students' formation, relevant to the social reality; scientific spirit, humanistic and reflexive; capacity for critical integrative analysis of reality; and ability to socialize knowledge in various contexts and for different audiences.
> (ENADE, 2014, p. 9)

The intention of the first part of the ENADE is also the verification of competencies in reading, interpreting, and writing, "establishing relationships, comparisons and contrasts in different situations" (ENADE, 2014, p. 9). The ENADE also provided evidence of the students' ability to develop arguments and their capacity to propose solutions for some problems presented in the questions. The themes of the first part of the exam were:

> culture and art; technological advancements; science, technology and society; democracy, ethics and citizenship; ecology; globalization and international politics; public policies (education, housing, sanitation, health, transportation, security, defense and sustainable development); work relationships; social responsibility (public, private and third sector); social diversity and multiculturalism (violence, tolerance/intolerance, inclusion/exclusion and gender relations); information and communication technologies; and urban and rural life.   (ENADE, 2014, p. 9)

The second section of ENADE addressed the specific components of the music area, and the questions presented diverse levels of complexity, allowing responses from the first- and last-year students. It is important to emphasize that the objective of this exam was to analyze the students' performance and not necessarily their accumulated knowledge or information obtained in the course. So, the first-year students' answers could be different from the final-year students, based on the different topics approached in the curriculum.

The second part of the exam presented 30 questions (27 multiple choice and 3 essays), designed to evaluate the students' skills and competencies acquired in their training processes. These skills and competencies included the following areas: ethical, critical, and human understanding of music as immaterial cultural patrimony; integration of musical and educational knowledge; interaction with music in different contexts; planning and realization of didactic and pedagogical actions in several social contexts; the comprehension of the basis of scientific research as a form of music knowledge systematization; the use of technology; and the use of teaching and learning creative processes (ENADE, 2014).

Curricular components were also evaluated in the ENADE (2014). These were musical perception, music theory, musical practice, creation, composition and improvisation, teaching methodologies for different educational contexts, music form in diverse cultures, technology, research possibilities, and implications for the music area (ENADE, 2014).

Each edition of ENADE sought to improve the process of evaluating students' performance, reviewing the procedures of the preparation of issues and specific contents, and analyzing alternatives that could bring more significance to the exam. However, there are still challenges to be faced, particularly those related to the assessment of practical aspects of the curriculum. The exam is completely written and there are no sound stimuli of any nature to assess and evaluate specific music issues. Similarly, musical practice, which occupies a significant portion in the Licenciatura undergraduate course in music, is also not evaluated by ENADE. So, a big gap in the assessment of undergraduate music courses exists because key parts of the curriculum are not addressed in the ENADE. The exam is an essentially theoretical evaluation, despite the inclusion of questions that consist of a reflexive exercise with regard to aspects related to musical hearing, performance, and creation. Being completely silent, the exam does not gauge the different musical practices that are intensely integrated into the curricula of undergraduate music programs, even though these practices are indicated in ENADE objectives.

The condition of the ENADE music exam lacking real sound elements, for instance, could be viewed from the discussion proposed by Biesta (2009) in terms of methodological issues related to measurement.

> More than just the question of *technical validity* of our measurements—i.e., whether we are measuring what we intend to measure—the problem here lies with what I suggest to call the *normative validity* of our measurements. This is the question whether we are indeed measuring what we value, or whether we are just measuring what we can easily measure and thus end up valuing what we (can) measure.
>
> (Biesta, 2009, p. 35)

In this sense, the ENADE music exam addresses some aspects of the students' performance, and not the complete elements of the curricula that prepare them. So, ENADE is measuring what can be measured according to convenient methodological procedures, not necessarily measuring the quality of education that is offered in higher education institutions. When the exam is directed to some components of the students' performance, the results also show the quality of education only in those components: "means become ends in themselves so that targets and indicators of quality become mistaken for quality itself" (Biesta, 2009, p. 35). This is a point to be considered for the future editions of the ENADE music exam.

POSTGRADUATE ASSESSMENT

The Brazilian National System of Postgraduate Studies (NSPS) aims at the postgraduate training of teachers and professors for all levels of education, the training of qualified human resources for the nonacademic market, and the strengthening of scientific, technological, and innovation bases (http://www.capes.gov.br/avaliacao/sobre-a-avaliacao). Music education is not an independent area in the NSPS. In most cases, music education is configured as a subarea, an area of concentration or a discipline in the field of music; or as an area of expertise in the field of education or even of arts education. As the first configuration is the most frequent in the NSPS, in this chapter we approach only the evaluation of postgraduate studies in music. Furthermore, although the evaluation of postgraduate studies is based on standardized criteria and procedures for all areas of knowledge, each area has its own particularities.

Postgraduate programs in music are allocated currently in the area of arts, one of the 49 areas of assessment of the NSPS. Postgraduate studies in arts—which covers music, dance, drama, and visual arts—began, in Brazil, in 1974, with the opening of the master's course at the School of Communication and Arts of the University of São Paulo. The growth of the area has been significant over the past 40 years. In 1996, there were 15 programs, only 2 of them offering doctorate courses. In 2000, this number rose to 19 programs; in 2003, to 22 programs; and in 2009, to 37 programs, 21 of which offering master's courses and 16 master's and doctorate courses. In 2012, there were 39 programs, 19 of them offering master's courses and 20 offering master's and doctorate courses (CAPES, 2016). Currently, there are 59 programs in operation in the area that offer 52 academic master's degrees, 28 doctoral degrees, and 7 professional master's degrees (Plataforma Sucupira, 2018).

The first postgraduate program in music was created in 1980 at the Music School at the Federal University of Rio de Janeiro. Currently, there are 16 postgraduate programs in music in Brazil, distributed in four out of the five regions of the country. There are also two programs in arts that include music as one of the areas. There are also three programs offering professional master's courses in music and a network professional master's program for the training of teachers in the arts, including music.

The evaluation of the NSPS is guided and conducted by the Coordenação de Aperfeiçoamento de Pessoal de Ensino Superior—CAPES (Coordination for the

Improvement of Higher Education Personnel), an agency of the Ministry of Education (MEC), created in 1951, aiming to "ensure the availability of specialized personnel in sufficient quantity and quality to meet the needs of public and private enterprises that [aimed at] the development of the country" (http://www.capes.gov.br/historia-e-missao). Since its creation, CAPES has been fulfilling a key role in the expansion and consolidation of postgraduate studies in the country, in all areas of knowledge. Besides the evaluation of *stricto sensu* postgraduate programs, currently CAPES activities involve the following:

> access and dissemination of scientific production; investments in the higher level training of human resources in the country and abroad; promotion of international scientific cooperation; induction and development of initial and continuing training of teachers for basic education at presence and distance education formats. (http://www.capes.gov.br/historia-e-missao)

The evaluation system of postgraduate courses is the oldest one in the Brazilian educational system. Its origin dates back to 1976, when CAPES organized its first evaluation process, designed, as reported by Balbachevsky (2005, p. 282), to generate parameters that could guide the distribution of scholarships. The author continues:

> To give credibility to this endeavor, Capes focused its assessment on the scientific production of researchers linked to each program. In every field of knowledge, the agency [CAPES] formed committees with the participation of the most prestigious researchers. These committees were responsible for evaluating and classifying each program. Over the years, and with the repetition of these evaluation processes, these committees have become important forums for fixing the quality standards of research and academic career, legitimizing objects of studies, theories and methodologies and valuing certain standards of publication and interaction with the international community (Coutinho, 1996). Thus, the activity of these committees had important consequences for the process of institutionalization of the fields of knowledge and the construction of the Brazilian scientific community.
> (Balbachevsky, 2005, p. 282)

In 1998, a new evaluation model was established that combined the authority of the evaluation by peer review committees to a set of well-defined criteria, which were to be adopted by the evaluation committees in all areas of knowledge (Balbachevsky, 2005, p. 283). These foundations remain today. The criteria are updated at the end of each evaluation cycle, which, currently, comprises a period of 4 years. Transparency was also established as a principle in the evaluation process, guaranteed by the online dissemination of decisions, actions, and evaluation results. At the end of each evaluation cycle, the programs in each area are ranked on a scale from 1 to 7, with 3 being the minimum rank for a program to remain in the NSPS. Ranks 6 and 7 indicate levels of excellence and international standards. The evaluation system, therefore, is classificatory and comparative. The results of the evaluation process are used as a basis to distribute scholarships and resources for the promotion of research. The same principles also guide the evaluation of proposals for new courses. Therefore, the evaluation system results are used to control both the entry and the permanence of the programs in the NSPS.

All areas adopt the same system and the same set of evaluation items. There is room, however, for some differentiation in the areas to be covered, such as the priority given to some items and the types of intellectual production to be considered. These particularities are explained in the *Documento de Área* (Area Document), which serves as a reference for the evaluation. Area Documents are flexible enough to allow programs to be organized according to specific pedagogical proposals, consistent with the profile of the faculty, its trajectory, and the demands of the educational, social, and cultural context of each program. Specifically in the music programs, this has generated a broad production in terms of research themes and paradigms as well as theoretical and methodological frameworks.

In 2017, when the last evaluation cycle ended, the set of evaluation items adopted by the area of arts and their weights were the following ones, displayed in Table 14.1.

For each evaluation item, some indicators are defined in order to demarcate the types of evidence to be provided by the programs about their organization, operation, and production. These indicators define what is expected from the programs.

As stated in the Area Document, "the program proposal, despite not receiving weight, guides all the process of analysis, since the items are evaluated taking into account the consistency and specificity of the proposal" (CAPES, 2016, p. 12). The analysis focuses on the "coherence, consistency, scope and updating of the focus areas, lines of research, ongoing projects and the curriculum" (CAPES, 2016, p. 15), the program planning for its future development, and the infrastructure for teaching, research, and extension.

The evaluation of the faculty members that are involved with postgraduate programs includes information in terms of training and experience and their suitability to the program proposal, the dedication to research activities and teaching, how these activities are distributed in the program, and the participation in teaching and research activities in undergraduate programs, and what signals the need for integration between undergraduate and postgraduate levels. In relation to students, the time spent to conclude theses, dissertations, and intellectual production constitute part of the evaluation. In the process, the number of completed theses and dissertations and the adequacy of the products with regard to the research lines of the program are also considered, compounding the evaluation of the item.

Table 14.1 Evaluation Items and Weights

Items	Academic Proposals	Professional Proposals
	Weight	Weight
Program proposal	0%	0%
Faculty	20%	20%
Students, theses and dissertations	35%	30%
Intellectual production	35%	30%
Social relevance	10%	20%

Source: Adapted from CAPES (2016).

Intellectual production refers to bibliographic products (papers, book chapters, books, and proceedings), artistic products (such as recitals, recordings, and compositions), and technical production (such as participation in conferences, consulting, and representation activities) of the faculty members. This production is expected to be linked to the research projects and be evenly distributed among the professors in the program. Both the quantity and the quality of production are considered. Quality is measured by means of a classification system that includes journals, books, events, and artistic production. "Stratification of the quality of this production is done indirectly," as exemplified by the classification system called *qualis periódicos* (journal qualification), in which the quality of a paper is measured not from the quality of the text itself, but "from the analysis of the quality of the vehicles where the text is disseminated, i.e., the journals" (http://www.capes.gov.br/avaliacao/instrumentos-de-apoio/classificacao-da-producao-intelectual).

Social inclusion and relevance of a postgraduate program are evaluated through indicators of cultural, educational, social, and technological impact, such as the training of human resources for different levels of education and for the nonacademic market, scientific and artistic dissemination actions, contributions to improve undergraduate programs and basic education, and the development of innovative proposals and educational materials, signaling, once again, the importance of integrating postgraduate education with other educational levels.

The Plano Nacional de Pós-Graduação (National Plan for Postgraduate Studies) for the period 2011–2020 indicates that new parameters and procedures should be introduced in the evaluation, aiming both to improve the current model and to correct some distortions, such as the induction of certain conservatism and subsequent accommodation of the programs and the primacy of quantity (Brasil, 2010, p. 22). However, the creation of a new evaluation model is not intended, since it is argued that the current model has been effective as a strategy to ensure and control the quality of programs. As explained by Sguissardi (2006, p. 50), it is not an "educational and diagnostic-formative assessment," but "a specific type of assessment, with the precise scope to serve the regulation and control for the public guarantee of the programs' quality and conferred titles" (Sguissardi, 2006, p. 78), a result of a postgraduate funding agency.

On the one hand, the clear delineation of a postgraduate evaluation system has positively affected the area of music that was developed to adopt recognized procedures and parameters shared by other areas. This contributed to its consolidation as an area of research and training, also strengthening the recognition of music as a field of knowledge at the universities. On the other hand, the evaluation model has also been criticized, as it does not cover some important aspects of postgraduate programs. As stated by Trevisan, Devechi, and Dias (2013),

> it is necessary to discuss evaluation not only to achieve the improvement of each postgraduate program or emerging groups. Our understanding is that if the discussions did not return to practical objectivity, we will have difficulty to continue justifying the ideal of excellence.   (p. 378)

The evaluation system makes clear that this excellence is built mainly from research, which is central in the Brazilian postgraduate system, both as a strategy of knowledge production and as an axis of preparing master's and doctoral students (see Kuenzer & Moraes, 2005; Macedo & Sousa, 2010). The weights assigned to the evaluation items related to students, theses and dissertations, and intellectual production confirm this perspective. However, one cannot lose sight of the fact that excellence, or, even better, different standards of excellence, are built into the daily work of the programs by their professors and students, in their actions, and procedures of training and production of knowledge.

To reflect on the preparation of master's and doctoral students and the production of knowledge in music is, therefore, an essential task for the continuous strengthening of postgraduate training in music. This is particularly relevant at the time this chapter was written because science, technology, and innovation are treated as axes that structure the development of countries around the world. The current policy of science, technology, and innovation in Brazil (Brasil, 2012) requires that researchers explain better the origin of their interests of knowledge (or their research problems) and also make clearer both the expected and the achieved results of their research (Del-Ben, 2014, p. 137).

Scientific thinking or reasoning is not "natural," but the result of "a deliberate and disciplined mental effort," having an "artificial" character (Dieterich, 1999, p. 24). Research is therefore something that one must learn to do. According to Meglhioratti, Andrade, Brando, and Caldeira (2008),

> The preparation of a scientist [a researcher] happens through his/her immersion in a different context from that found in daily life. The scientist is formed when in contact with certain problems, theories and discussions of his/her field of research. The preparation as a researcher is related to experiencing the difficulties of the area, participation in a research group, raising hypotheses and trying to get solutions.   (p. 32)

Louzada and Filho (2005) add that one of the characteristics of the preparation of researchers

> is the close relationship with an established researcher and the mastering of an activity that is not fully coded. Not everything that is done in research can be found in books and papers. Learning to research refers to an acquisition of everyday, tacit knowledge, what happens gradually, through the direct contact "with who knows how to do."   (Louzada & Filho, 2005, pp. 272–273)

The preparation of researchers in those perspectives signals the need to consolidate a research tradition and a structure for research in the institutions. Eventual or occasional research, even if they are good research efforts, are not enough (Nosella, 2010, p. 182). It is necessary to institutionalize the practice of research, that is, "to create a research culture" (Nosella, 2010, p. 182) that, as such, spreads itself to different spaces, reaching teaching practices at the undergraduate level, especially the preparation of music teachers, both nurturing them and being nurtured by them. One of the current challenges in the area of music in Brazil, and more specifically music education, is to adopt this research culture, which also depends on the quality of scientific production.

Unfortunately, few studies discuss the quality of scientific production in music and music education in Brazil. Some of them highlight problems such as the difficulty of developing group work (Souza, 1997; Ulhôa, 1997), the lack of continuity of research (Souza, 1997), and, as a consequence, the dispersion of the production about the same problem (Del-Ben, 2014; Del-Ben & Souza, 2007; Oliveira, Santos, Macedo, & Del-Ben, 2012), and the lack of referential texts on certain themes produced in the country (Oliveira et al., 2012). Furthermore, in the national music education literature one can find studies about the same theme, which, although carried out in different periods, bring very similar results, because they are originated from similar research questions. This is worrisome because it suggests "a low capacity of accumulation of knowledge, derived from the horizontal proliferation of case studies" (Arretche, 2003, p. 8) and little dialogue among the studies (Del-Ben & Souza, 2007; Oliveira et al., 2012). It should be emphasized that, despite not having a consolidated research culture, we have a production environment, which can lead us to the so-called publish or perish situation.

In-depth analysis of scientific production does not fit in the current evaluation system of postgraduate programs in Brazil. Evaluating how to do and how to learn to do research in postgraduate programs in music, therefore, is a critical task for the area, because the way the programs do research and produce knowledge (or try to produce it) says something about what we mean by scientific research, and, unintentionally, shapes the way master's and doctoral students are prepared through research and to be researchers.

The current evaluation model of postgraduate programs in Brazil, despite the many advances it brought to music area, seems unlikely to receive a more detailed analysis of the dimensions here mentioned. An alternative is to include this sort of analysis in the music research agenda, assuming that the evaluation is not only a government task, which regulates, controls, and finances postgraduate programs, but also a responsibility of all involved with them.

CONCLUSION

Brazilian educational administrators have been working in recent years to build not only instruments but also assessment systems in order to develop more accurate diagnoses of school education, at different levels and stages. The diagnostics are essential to the identification of problems and needs and also to verify the advances already established. In sum, diagnostics are fundamental to support educational policies. Whereas education is conceived as a social right, assessment reinforces the recognition of this right and legitimizes the right to education, especially compulsory education (from 4 to 17 years). Evaluation validates the formal school education and shows that it is important for the country project so far established. Systems and assessment tools also indicate concern for transparency, because it is a way for the government to be accountable to society for its investment in education and the results of educational policies and specific educational programs.

The assessment systems are comprehensive and address all areas of knowledge, including music and music education. Because of the complexity of this task, not all of the important components of the area of music and music education are covered. Music is absent from the evaluation of basic education, at least at the time this chapter was written, but has some of its unique characteristics included in the ENADE. In the postgraduate evaluation system, this problem does not occur. The gains for music as an area seem to become more evident when it entered the system and gained consistency as a research field and recognition at the university.

In general, although the documents for the diverse levels of Brazilian education have internal coherence, more interactions that promote dialogue among the educational levels and more consistency for the assessment process as a whole are needed. Verhine and Dantas (2009), discuss the need for more articulation between SINAES, the assessment policy, and CAPES, the Brazilian agency responsible for postgraduate programs.

> The SINAES, implemented in 2004 by Law 10.861/04 was conceptualized as an integrated system that included the CAPES as one of its key components. However, there is little correlation between the instruments developed by INEP for evaluation of higher education institutions and undergraduate courses and those used by CAPES to evaluate postgraduate programs. There is also little correlation between their indicators and the frequency of collection. More importantly, there has been an effort to incorporate CAPES huge database by INEP database for the National Census of Higher Education. Over time, the demands for a national and unified database, powered by collections made by complementary instruments should be increased, and when this occurs, CAPES will need to rethink its model in order to adapt it to the role of a subsystem integrated into the SINAES structure.
>
> (Verhine & Dantas, 2009, p. 308)

One of the challenges is to develop a culture of evaluation in the institutions that assumes the task of assessment is their responsibility and establishes self-assessment as a continuous practice independent of the external evaluation that the government does. In this sense, external evaluation is important, but not sufficient. It would be desirable to combine internal and external evaluation, but this seems not to be a priority in the policies. It is necessary to consolidate a more participatory evaluation, to promote emancipatory assessment, not only regulatory. This is a challenge for the future.

References

Arretche, M. (2003). Dossiê agenda de pesquisa em políticas públicas. Apresentação [Dossier research agenda in public policies. Presentation]. *RBCS—Revista Brasileira de Ciências Sociais* [Brazilian Journal of Social Sciences], *18*(51), 7–9.

Balbachevsky, E. (2005). A pós-graduação no Brasil: Novos desafios para uma política bem-sucedida [The postgraduate in Brazil: New challenges for a successful policy]. In C. Brock, & S. Schwartzman (Eds.), *Os desafios da educação no Brasil* [Challenges of education in Brazil] (pp. 285–314). Rio de Janeiro, Brazil: Nova Fronteira.

Biesta, G. (2009). Good education in an age of measurement: On the need to reconnect with the question of purpose in education. *Educational Assessment, Evaluation and Accountability*, *21*(1), 33–46.

Bittencourt, H. R., Viali, L., Cassartelli, A. O., & Rodrigues, A. C. (2008). Uma análise da relação entre os conceitos Enade e IDD [An analysis of the relationship between the Enade and IDD concepts]. *Estudos em Avaliação Educacional* [Studies in Educational Assessment], *19*, 247–262.

Brasil. (2004). *Lei 10.861/2004*—Institui o Sistema Nacional de Avaliação da Educação Superior—SINAES—e dá outras providências [*Law 10.861/2004*—Establishes the national system of higher education assessment—SINAES—and gives other measures]. Brasília, Brazil: Presidência da República.

Brasil. (2005). *Sistema de Avaliação da Educação Básica—SAEB* [Basic education assessment system—SAEB]. Brasília, Brazil: INEP/MEC.

Brasil. (2007). *Sistema Nacional de Avaliação da Educação Superior—SINAES* [National System of Higher Education Assessment—SINAES]. Brasília, Brazil: INEP/MEC.

Brasil. (2010). Ministério da Educação. Coordenação de Aperfeiçoamento de Pessoal de Nível Superior. *Plano Nacional de Pós-Graduação—PNPG 2011-2020*. V. 1. Coordenação de Pessoal de Nível Superior [Ministry of Education. Coordination of improvement of higher level personnel. *National Postgraduate Plan—PNPG 2011-2020*. V. 1. Coordination of Higher Level Personnel]. Brasília, Brazil: CAPES.

Brasil. (2012). Ministério da Ciência, Tecnologia e Inovação. *Estratégia Nacional de Ciência, Tecnologia e Inovação 2012-2015. Balanço das Atividades Estruturantes 2011*. [Ministry of Science, Technology, and Innovation. *National Strategy for Science, Technology and Innovation 2012-2015. Balance of 2011 Structuring Activities*]. Brasília, Brazil: MCTI.

Brasil. (2015). *Lei 9.394/96*—Estabelece as diretrizes e bases da educação nacional.—LDBEN [*Law 9.394/96*—Establishes the guidelines and bases of national education.—LDBEN]. (11ª ed.). Brasília, Brazil: Edições Câmara, Retrieved from http://www2.camara.leg.br

CAPES. (2016). Coordenação de Aperfeiçoamento de Pessoal de Nível Superior. *Documento de Área 2016*. Área 11—Artes/Música. [Coordination of improvement of higher level personnel. *Area Document 2016*. Area 11—Arts/Music]. Brasília, Brazil. Retrieved from http://capes.gov.br/images/documentos/Documentos_de_area_2017/11_arte_docarea_2016.pdf

Castro, M. H. G. (2009). Sistemas de avaliação da educação no Brasil: Avanços e novos desafios [Systems of evaluation of education in Brazil: Advances and new challenges]. *São Paulo em Perspectiva* [São Paulo in Perspective], *23*(1), 5–18.

Del-Ben, L. (2014). Políticas de ciência, tecnologia e inovação no Brasil: Perspectivas para a produção de conhecimento em educação musical [Science, technology and innovation policies in Brazil: Perspectives for the production of knowledge in music education]. *Revista da ABEM* [Journal of the Brazilian Association of Music Education], *22*, 130–142.

Del-Ben, L., & Souza, J. (2007). Pesquisa em educação musical e suas interações com a sociedade: um balanço da produção da ABEM [Research in music education and its interaction with society: A balance of ABEM's production]. In *Congresso da Associação Nacional de Pesquisa e Pós-Graduação em Música—Anppom* [Conference of the National Association of Research and Post-Graduation in Music—Anppom]. São Paulo, Brazil: Anppom.

Dias, C. L., Horiguela, M. L. M., & Marchelli, P. S. (2006). Políticas para a avaliação da qualidade do ensino superior no Brasil: Um balanço crítico [Policies for the evaluation of the quality of higher education in Brazil: A critical balance]. *Educação e Pesquisa* [Education and Research], *32*(3), 435–464.

Dieterich, H. (1999). *Novo guia para a pesquisa científica [New guide to scientific research]*. Blumenau, Brazil: Editora da FURB.

ENADE. (2014). *ENADE 2014—Exame Nacional de Desempenho dos Estudantes—Relatório de Área—Música (licenciatura) [National Exam of the Student Performance—Area Report—Music (licenciatura)]*. Brasília, Brazil: INEP, Diretoria de Avaliação da Educação Superior.

Griboski, C. M. (2012). O ENADE como indutor da qualidade da educação superior [The ENADE as an inducer of the quality of higher education]. *Estudos em Avaliação Educacional* [Studies in Educational Assessment], *53*, 178–195.

INEP. (2004). *Portaria n. 107/2004 [Normative document n. 107/2004]*. Brasília, Brazil: INEP.

Kuenzer, A. Z., & Moraes, M. C. M. (2005). Temas e tramas na pós-graduação em educação [Themes and plots in postgraduate education]. *Educação e Sociedade* [Education and Society], *26*, 1341–1362.

Limana, A., & Brito, M. R. F. (2006). O modelo de avaliação dinâmica e o desenvolvimento de competências: Algumas considerações a respeito do ENADE [The dynamic evaluation model and the development of competences: Some considerations about ENADE]. In D. Ristoff, A. Limana, & M. R. F. Brito (Eds.), *Enade: Perspectiva de avaliação dinâmica e análise de mudanças* (pp. 17–44). Brasília, Brazil: Instituto Nacional de Estudos e Pesquisas Educacionais Anísio Teixeira.

Louzada, R. de C. R., & Filho, J. F. da S. (2005). Pós-graduação e trabalho: Um estudo sobre projetos e expectativas de doutorandos Brasileiros [Postgraduate and work: A study on projects and expectations of Brazilian doctoral students]. *História, Ciências, Saúde—Manguinhos* [History, Sciences, Helath—Manguinhos], *12*, 265–282.

Macedo, E., & Sousa, C. P. de. (2010). A pesquisa em educação no Brasil [Brazilian research in Education]. *Revista Brasileira de Educação* [Brazilian Journal of Education], *15*, 166–176.

Meglhioratti, F. A., Andrade, M. A. B. S., Brando, F. R., & Caldeira, A. M. A. (2008). Formação de pesquisadores: O papel de um grupo de pesquisa em Epistemologia da Biologia [Formation of researchers: The role of a research group in Epistemology of Biology]. *Revista Brasileira de Biociências* [Brazilian Journal of Biosciences], *6*(1), 32–34.

Nosella, P. (2010). A pesquisa em educação: Um balanço da produção dos programas de pós-graduação [The research in education: A balance of the production of the graduate programs]. *Revista Brasileira de Educação* [Brazilian Journal of Education], *15*, 177–203.

Oliveira, M. A. W., Santos, C. P., Macedo, V. L. F., & Del-Ben, L. (2012). *Produção científica sobre educação musical escolar: Uma análise das referências de artigos da Revista da ABEM* [Scientific production on school music education: An analysis of the references of ABEM Journal articles]. In *Congresso da Associação Nacional de Pesquisa e Pós-Graduação em Música—Anppom* [Conference of the National Association of Research and Post-Graduation in Music—Anppom], João Pessoa, Brazil: Anppom.

Plataforma Sucupira. (2018). *Cursos avaliados e reconhecidos. [Assessed and recognized courses].* Retrieved from https://sucupira.capes.gov.br/sucupira/public/consultas/coleta/programa/quantitativos/quantitativoIes.jsf?areaAvaliacao=11&areaConhecimento=80300006

Ristoff, D., & Giolo, J. (2006). O Sinaes como sistema [The Sinaes as a system]. *RBPG-Revista Brasileira de Pós-Graduação* [Brazilian Journal of Postgraduate], *3*(6), 193–213.

Sguissardi, V. (2006). A avaliação defensiva no "modelo CAPES de avaliação"—É possível conciliar avaliação educativa com processos de regulação e controle do Estado? [The defensive evaluation in the "CAPES evaluation model"—Is it possible to reconcile educational evaluation with processes of regulation and control of the State?]. *Perspectiva* [Perspective], *24*(1), 49–88.

Souza, J. (1997). A pesquisa em educação musical na universidade: Algumas questões [Research in music education at the university: Some questions]. In *Encontro Anual da Associação Nacional de Pesquisa e Pós-Graduação em Música* [Annual Meeting of the National Association of Research and Post-Graduation in Music—Anppom], Goiânia, Brazil: Anppom.

Trevisan, A. L., Devechi, C. P. V., & Dias, E. D. (2013). Avaliação da avaliação da pós-graduação em educação do Brasil: Quanta verdade é suportável? [Evaluation of postgraduate education in Brazil: How much truth is bearable?]. *Avaliação* [Assessment], *18*, 373–392.

Ulhôa, M. (1997). Relatório da mesa redonda A Pesquisa em Música na Universidade Brasileira [Round Table Report The Music Research at the Brazilian University]. In *Encontro Anual da Associação Nacional de Pesquisa e Pós-Graduação em Música* [Annual Meeting of the National Association of Research and Post-Graduation in Music—Anppom], Goiânia, Brazil: Anppom.

Verhine, R. E., & Dantas, L. M. V. (2009). Reflexões sobre o sistema de avaliação da Capes a partir do Plano Nacional de Pós-graduação [Reflections on Capes' evaluation system based on the National Graduate Plan]. *Revista Educação Pública* [Public Education Journal], *18*, 295–310.

CHAPTER 15

ASSESSMENT IN MUSIC CLASSES IN CHINA

DENNIS PING-CHENG WANG

INTRODUCTION AND OVERVIEW OF THE EDUCATION SYSTEM IN CHINA

Historical Background

CHINA has a more than 5,000-year history, and both its culture and economy have been particularly impressive and prosperous in the past 20 years. Until recently, however, because of the closed trading policies of 18th-century China and lack of access to the outside world, China's science and technology development has lagged. China's colonial history and invasions by foreign countries also contributed to the chaotic situation in the country for hundreds of years. However, the rapid economic growth of the past 20 years has again made the nation influential in the world.

Traditionally in China, music education has centered on aestheticism and Confucius's idea of ceremony versus music. As various Western education ideas were introduced to China in the middle of the last century, Chinese education began to absorb foreign practices and educators tried to combine these new ideas with the ancient Chinese traditions. As one of the world's four ancient civilizations, China has extensive and diversified artistic and musical resources. Not only does mainland China have nearly 60 ethnic groups, each with its own unique music tradition, but also the nation has over 600 traditional folk musical instruments and nearly 10,000 composed and recorded folk songs.

Current School Setting and Music Education

With accelerated economic development and cultural modernization, China has increasingly become open to global business and participation in international affairs. Education is considered essential to strengthening a nation, and the Chinese government stresses it to cultivate the next generation.

Education clearly has become a high-priority area for the government, and China now has the world's largest school-based music education system. According to the official statistics, there are more than 200,000 music teachers, nearly 600,000 schools with 300 million elementary and secondary students, and 388 colleges and universities that provided teacher training as of 2008 (Ministry of Education, PRC, 2008). Moreover, 80% of the schools are located in the countryside. However, due to the varieties of music cultures, the nation's size, and knowledge-delivery logistics, music education in mainland China still faces lots of challenges, such as gradual loss of interest in traditional Chinese music, unsystematic music education policies in some provinces, and the uneven quality of music teachers' competency and teaching approaches throughout the nation.

To address these problems, the government promulgated the *National Music Curriculum Standard for Compulsory Education* (Ministry of Education, PRC, 2011) and the *National Music Curriculum Standard for Senior High School (Trial)* (Ministry of Education, PRC, 2003) to provide systematic school music education systems for China and create compulsory music courses at the elementary and secondary levels. The national standards clearly state that music is one of the country's most important cultural assets. Through music, aesthetics and creativity are delivered and promoted, and students are expected to gain these values through listening, singing, and performing. Moreover, not only do the national standards clearly state that music is one of the compulsory subjects for the 9 years of compulsory education but also the standards detail the curriculum for each grade, such as singing, appreciation, notation reading, sight-reading, instrumental learning, and so forth. Furthermore, the national standards list music instrument expectations for students in lower levels of elementary school, and specify the number of instruments students are expected to learn (Tian, 2012).

However, compared with core subjects such as language, sciences, and literature, music is still considered less important at all school levels. Also, competency variances among individual music teachers and differences in regional economies across the nation result in uneven promotion of music education in China.

The Current Education System in China

In 2014, 94,510,651 students were enrolled at 201,377 elementary schools, 438,463 students were enrolled at 37,958 junior high schools, and 24,004,723 students were enrolled at 13,799 senior high schools in mainland China (National Bureau of Statistics of the People's Republic of China, 2015). Like most countries, the school setting in China is kindergarten (ages 4–6), elementary school (ages 6–12), junior high school (ages 12–15), and senior high school (ages 16–18). Under the statement of the *National Music Curriculum Standard for Compulsory Education*, music is one of the compulsory courses for elementary school and junior high school students (Ministry of Education, PRC, 2011). The 9 years of compulsory education in China consists of elementary school and junior high school. Music class is offered three times a week for grades

1 and 2 and twice a week for students grade 3 and above. In junior high school, students have music class once a week. Elementary school music education stresses arousing students' interest, while for junior high school students the focus is cultivating a sense of aesthetics.

According to official data, there are 1,040 elementary schools, 337 junior high schools, and 306 senior high schools in Beijing, the capital of mainland China; there are 757 elementary schools, 522 junior high schools, and 246 senior high schools in Shanghai; and there are 8,979 elementary schools, 1,538 junior high schools, and 402 senior high schools in the province of Gansu, which is one of the major provinces in the west side of China (National Bureau of Statistics of the People's Republic of China, 2015).

Traditional one-way teaching and a singing-centered approach along with basic body movement are still the most frequently used techniques in music classrooms at all school levels in China. Instead of preparing and designing new course contents, materials, and activities for music students, most local music teachers still prefer the traditional teaching method, which hinders the promotion of international music approaches, such as those based on the theories of Orff, Kodály, and Dalcroze. Moreover, Chinese folk songs/children's songs are more often used than Western classical music in the music classroom. Furthermore, numbered musical notation (simplified music notation and *jiǎnpǔ* in Chinese) is still more often used than the music staves that are common in the Western world.

Teachers are required to have at least a bachelor's degree in the relevant subject areas. So, for example, music majors can teach only music in the public schools in China. Regarding the recruitment of new teachers, there are basically two types of exams: the Teachers Qualified Exam and the Recruitment Exam for the Professional Personnel in Education (Hai-Ding Education Committee, 2015). The Teachers Qualified Exam is designed for new graduates, while the Recruitment Exam is offered for the public in general. New graduates also need to take personal interviews with school officers, most often the local school principal. Whoever meets the requirements can go on to the next-level written exam. The written exam usually consists of two subjects: an introduction to education, and psychology. All of the exams are held in each province, where certain cities are designated as recruitment centers for new teachers. The number of new recruitments usually is very limited; therefore, it is a quite challenging and competitive exam. Furthermore, to enhance and ensure the quality of current teachers' teaching, the local government of every city in China also provides frequent teacher training and seminars. Besides music classes, in order to let students have various opportunities to learn music and to collaborate musically with other students, most public schools in China provide ensemble experiences, such as marching band, choir, and orchestra.

The music graded exam is another highlight of music education in China. Whoever achieves highly on the music exam offered by the Central Conservatory of Music and/or the Royal Conservatory of Music (and others) is considered a talented and specially skilled student; this can earn them a bonus and priority consideration on the entrance exam for the next school level and/or other admission opportunities; therefore, learning musical instruments after school has become a privilege and/or useful tool for entering the next school level in China.

THE CONTEXT OF NATIONAL MUSIC CURRICULUM STANDARDS FOR COMPULSORY EDUCATION

Given China's rapid societal development and education reform, the Beijing government expects music education to not only emphasize the aesthetic but also inspire students' musical creativity. The *National Music Curriculum Standard for Compulsory Education* (Ministry of Education, PRC, 2011) provides a new concept for school music education and integrates the categories of singing, music appreciation, instrument performance, and sight-reading from the previous guidelines into aesthetic and expression, music competency, creativity, and cultural influence.

There are two types of developments in the curriculum: center-periphery curriculum development and school-based curriculum development. The first is controlled by the government, and the second provides schools more freedom and flexibility in terms of teaching contents and teaching approaches (Keiny, 2006). Most schools in China use the center-periphery curriculum development approach, meaning the government designs a series of standards for schools at all levels and expects teachers and students to follow their plan for accomplishing these.

In China, textbooks are common core teaching materials for music classes at public schools. The music textbooks published by People's Education Publisher are officially authorized for use at the public schools in Beijing, while those published by the Guangdong Flower City Publishing House are the officially authorized textbooks for the public schools in Shenzhen (Hai-Ding Education Committee, 2015; Lau, 2007). The textbooks include all the learning concepts that are based on the *National Music Curriculum Standard for Compulsory Education* (Ministry of Education, PRC, 2011). Music teachers need to follow the curriculum standards and include them in their teaching materials and classroom lectures. Furthermore, to ensure students' learning, an official certified exam is given to randomly selected public schools in every city every year by the local government. Normally, the local government informs the selected schools one week before the end of the semester. The teachers' self-designed written test and singing test are the majority of the assessment for students at all levels in Beijing. The contents of the written test are all based on the materials that were taught in the class (Hai-Ding Education Committee, 2015).

The revised curriculum standards include music appreciation, music performance, and creativity. Not only do the revised standards inspire students' music learning but also they include more music activities and expectations that students will actively participate in the activities in class. Under this revision, music teachers are expected to design complete and inspiring course contents so that the subject can attract students' interest and further enhance their music competency. Moreover, music competency needs to be precisely and professionally introduced to students. It also needs to be collaborated with different cultures and other subjects. Not only do the standards state systematic music competencies that students need to learn during different school levels but also the government expects students to have concrete aesthetic experiences through the music subject. Also, in order to provide efficient learning, the design of music competency in the standards is based on both students' mental and physical maturity and development at each school level. Finally, in order to make the subject more interesting and acceptable to both students and teachers, the revision of curriculum standards provides music teachers flexibility and freedom in terms of designing course content and materials.

Aesthetics are the core foundation and essence of the revised music curriculum standards. The government expects music teachers to integrate basic music knowledge with artistic aesthetics and different cultures. In the meantime, inspiring students' interest in music is the essential element for the music subject. Moreover, the national standards also focus on students' practical outcomes, such as singing, performance, listening, and improvisation. Not only can those activities ensure students' learning achievement but also they can build students' confidence through teamwork and/or various types of performance. In order to provide students with a concrete understanding of the subject, the standards also incorporate other subjects, such as drama, dance, arts, and film production. It can both broaden students' artistic understanding and help students further relate music to other disciplines. Another highlight of the revised standards is the promotion of patriotism. In the national standards, not only does the government expect students to be able to sing Chinese folk songs but also it expects them to sing and memorize certain numbers of Chinese folk songs for each grade. Moreover, the higher grades of elementary school and high school students are expected to learn Chinese opera and regional operatic arias. It is expected that through these standards students will not only learn to respect different races and tribes in China but also will be aware of the importance of patriotism and nationalism. Priorities for students and student success are another unique feature of the revision. The standards respect each individual and encourage students to fully express themselves artistically.

The Content of the National Curriculum Standards for Elementary and Middle School

The content curriculum standard for music consists of four parts: aestheticism and expression, music competency, creativity, and culture influence for students from grade 1 to grade 9. The students are expected to develop overall musicianship from the four aspects. Not only do the national standards clearly describe systematic music learning and course content but also they point out the importance of musical ensemble experiences and expectations that students can enhance their music understanding from various approaches.

In the aestheticism and expression standard, music appreciation is not only the foundation of music but also the best way to cultivate aestheticism in students. Under this part of the standards, there are four training expectations for each grade of students: general ability, expressions, form and analysis, and music styles and genres (see Table 15.1). It is necessary to inspire students' interest in music and train students to have critical thinking of music appreciation. Students need to have general music ability and expression

Table 15.1 The Training Expectations for Students of Aestheticism and Expression under the National Curriculum Standards for Elementary School and Middle School

Curriculum area	Grades 1–2	Grades 3–6	Grades 7–9
General Ability	*Be able to feel various sounds of nature and use their own voice/sounds to imitate nature sounds. *Be able to distinguish the voices of different genders. *Be able to distinguish different percussion instruments and perform sounds different in length and strength. *Be able to distinguish different tempo, speed, and strength of music. *Be able to differentiate 2/4, 3/4, and 4/4 music.	*Be able to feel various sounds of nature and use their own voice/sounds to imitate nature sounds. *Be able to sing familiar melodies and songs. *Be able to distinguish and explain different genders' voices. *Be able to know the common Chinese and Western musical instruments and recognize their tone color. *Be able to differentiate 2/4, 3/4, and 4/4 music and further follow the rhythms. *Be able to differentiate high-low, fast-slow, strong-soft, and have basic understanding of music structures.	*Be able to use different way to imitate sounds. *Be able to distinguish and explain the different tone colors of human voices and instruments. *Be able to feel and understand the strength, tempo, tone color, rhythm, keys, and harmony of music. *Be able to express the contrast and changes of different sections of music.
Expression	*Be able to feel the different mood of music and express corre-spondent response. *Be able to express and say the same and different mood of music	*Be able to distinguish and describe different mood of music. *Be able to describe the mood changes of music	*Be able to use music terms to describe different mood of music. *Be able to describe the mood change and development of music.

Curriculum area	Grades 1–2	Grades 3–6	Grades 7–9
Form and Analysis	*Be able to feel different types of music, such as dancing, marching, etc. *Be able to respond and follow the tempos of various types of music, such as dancing, marching, etc.	*Introducing some popular music with "healthy lyrics." *Introducing some easy binary form of music. *Be able to recognize the title of music composition by listening to the theme of music	*Introducing big ensembles, such as choir, opera, chamber music, orchestra, concerto, and symphony works, and sing along with played music. *Be able to describe and recognize the title of music by listening to the melody. *Be able to comprehend and understand the forms and structures of music in general.
Music Styles and Genres	*Introducing various folk songs, children's songs, and music from different regions and nations.	*Be able to understand and distinguish the styles of folk songs from various provinces of China. *Be able to understand and distinguish the styles of folk songs from various nations.	*Be able to describe the regional characteristics and style of folk songs from various provinces of China. *Be able to describe the regional characteristics and style of folk songs from various nations. *Be able to recognize and describe the representatives of composers from the Western classical music history.

Source: Adapted from Ministry of Education, People's Republic of China. (2011).

and the ability to understand the form of music and to analyze music. Not only does this part of curriculum standard list detailed guidelines for the students but also it provides directions for teachers to follow in the music classes.

In the music competency standard, the government believes that music competency is not only the foundation of music learning but also the demonstration of a student's capability of music learning. It is also the way teachers can deliver and teach aestheticism. Under this part of the standards, there are four training expectations for each grade of students: singing, performance, ensemble, and sight-reading (see Table 15.2).

Table 15.2 The Training Expectations for Students of Music Competency under the National Curriculum Standards for Elementary School and Middle School

Curricular Area	Grades 1–2	Grades 3–6	Grades 7–9
Singing	*Be able to sing basic children's songs and folk songs and participate in any music activities. *Be able to sing with correct pause and make correct resonance. *Be able to have basic response to conductor's pause. *Be able to use different strength and tempo to sing songs. *Be able to memorize and sing four to six songs, among which one or two songs have to be Chinese folk songs.	*Willing to participate in any music activities. *Be able to sing with correct approaches and breathing. *Be able to sing alone with expression and participate in choirs. *Understand the voice changes that frequently occur in a teen's breaking voice. *Be able to have basic comments about self and classmates' singing. *Be able to memorize and sing four to six songs, among which one or two songs have to be Chinese folk songs. *Be able to have basic singing techniques of Chinese opera.	*Be able to participate in various singing activities actively. *Be able to sing with confidence. *Be able to understand basic conductor pauses and have correspondent responses to the conductors. *Be able to have basic skills of analyzing art songs. *Understand the voice changes that frequently occur in a teen's breaking voice. *Be able to memorize and sing two to four songs, among which one song has to be a Chinese folk song. *Be able to have basic singing techniques of Chinese opera.
Performance	*Be able to distinguish small percussion and participate in any music activities. *Be able to accompany other instruments along with small percussion	*Willing to participate in any performance opportunities. *Be able to play recorder and harmonica, and accompany with songs. *Be able to demonstrate basic comments about other's performances. *Be able to perform one or two songs with music instruments.	*Be able to actively perform in any music activities. *Be able to choose at least one musical instrument and perform. *Be able to demonstrate basic comments about other's performances. *Be able to perform two or three songs with musical instruments.
Ensemble	*Be able to participate in any music activities. *Be able to move around along with music.	*Be able to actively participate in any music activities. *Be able to perform a scenario of music activities.	*Be able to perform and participate in music activities with confidence. *Be able to combine with learned music and compose simple-scenario music activities.

Curricular Area	Grades 1–2	Grades 3–6	Grades 7–9
	*Be able to move around, demonstrate basic movement, and participate in music activities along with others.		*Be able to sing simple operatic and musical techniques and works. *Be able to demonstrate basic comments about other's performances.
Sight-reading	*Be able to understand the basic music signs and sing along with music and body movement. *Be able to sing and recognize note names on the staffs.	*Be able to comprehensively understand the note names, rests, and basic music notation. *Be able to sight-read simple music along with piano accompaniment.	*Be able to sight-read music along with piano accompaniment. *Be able to sight-read music fluently.

Source: Adapted from Ministry of Education, People's Republic of China. (2011).

It focuses on students' capability and confidence in performing. Sight-reading is also a requirement of music learning. Students are expected to sing and perform music with their own expression. Comparing with the previous aestheticism and expression, this focuses on students' music competency in both individual skills and group collaborating works.

Besides performance and music skills, the government also stresses on students' creativity in music. Creativity is combination of students' imagination and understanding in a subject. Teaching music creativity in music class should include both inspiring students' potential and applying music knowledge on creative activities. Under this part of the standards, there are three training expectations for each grade of students: exploration, improvisation, and composition (see Table 15.3). By graduation, students are expected to improvise music with musical instruments and compose music.

Music and culture are indivisible, and they influence each other. In the cultural influence standard, music and cultures are closely related. Not only do they impact students' recognition of their own culture but also they help students understand their own cultural heritage. This can be seen in music appreciation, listening practice, and music creativity. Under this part of the standards, there are three training expectations for each grade of students: music and society, music and application, and collaboration with other subjects (see Table 15.4). The government expects students not only to understand their own cultures and the nation but also to appreciate their own culture and understand how cultures have been formed and how they affect our daily life.

Table 15.3 The Training Expectations for Students of Creativity under the National Curriculum Standards for Elementary School and Middle School

Curricular Areas	Grades 1–2	Grades 3–6	Grades 7–9
Exploration	*Be able to apply human voice and musical instruments to imitate the natural sound. *Be able to demonstrate loud and soft with percussion instruments.	*Be able to express natural sounds with human voice and musical instruments. *Be able to hand make own musical instruments.	*Be able to express mood changes with human voice and musical instruments. *Be able to comment on student's own and other's music
Improvisation	*Be able to use different tempo, rhythm, and strength in children's songs. *Be able to make some movement when students are singing and listening music. *Be able to express mood changes based on storytelling and music activities with musical instruments.	*Be able to improvise musical movement and dances based on the played music and/or songs. *Be able to improvise music and use different music instruments along with the played music and/or songs.	*Be able to improvise music or rhythms. *Be able to make music activities and/or performances based on the content of music.7
Composition	*Be able to use lines, colors, and shapes to represent music heard in class. *Be able to compose short one or two measures of music with human voices and musical instruments.	*Be able to write music on the music staffs under teacher's guidance. *Be able to compose two to four measures of rhythm or melody.	*Be able to compose four to eight measures of rhythm or melody and write them down on music staffs. *Be able to compose music with computer/MIDI.

Source: Adapted from Ministry of Education, People's Republic of China. (2011).

The Content of the National Music Curriculum Standard for Senior High School

The Objective

The *National Music Curriculum Standard for Senior High School (Trial)* (Ministry of Education, PRC, 2003) is based on cultivating in students a lifetime music habit, the

Table 15.4 The Training Expectations for Students of Cultural Influence under the National Curriculum Standards for Elementary School and Middle School

Curricular Areas	Grades 1–2	Grades 3–6	Grades 7–9
Music and Society	*Be able to feel music in their daily life and be willing to share their music with others. *Be able to listen to music through radio, films, TV, and other media.	*Be able to pay attention and be aware of music in their daily life. *Be able to appreciate music from radio, films, TV, and other media. *Be able to actively participate in various music activities in the community.	*Be able to have the habit of listening to music and understand the importance of music in their daily life. *Be able to appreciate music from performing media and live performances. *Be able to participate in music activities and conversations about music in the community.
Music and Application	*Be able to make simple movement along with music. *Be able to express feeling and mood along with music. *Be able to use colors, lines, and shape to express heard music.	*Be able to watch and appreciate drama and dances and understand the function used in the performances. *Be able to understand the function of music played in films and drama.	*Be able to distinguish the application and differences between visual and aural arts. *Be able to describe background music in drama and films. *Be able to collaborate with others and make an activity and music production by applying various arts.
Collaboration with other subjects	*Be able to illustrate the sounds in daily life and natural environment. *Be able to make simple body movements with different rhythms and tempo.	*Be able to use appropriate background music in any children's story. *Be able to identify music from different nations, regions, and historical periods.	*Be able to express the influence of music to mood changes and use appropriate music to adjust students' emotion. *Be able to use music to accompany ancient rhythms and stories. *Be able to identify and state significant composers and music works from China and other countries around the world.

Source: Adapted from Ministry of Education, People's Republic of China. (2011).

ability of music appreciation, and creativity. Promulgated in 2003, it proposed a systematic music curriculum standard for senior high school students. In this standard, music class becomes an elective course that includes 54 class periods and 3 credits per semester. Not only does this new standard provide students a flexible approach to learning music but also it allows schools to rethink what students really need in the high school period. The objectives are to (1) cultivate students with love and sympathy for others, (2) ensure students enjoy the learning process as an inspiring experience, and (3) by introducing different genres of music, ensure students understand the development of music history and its function in society.

The philosophy of the *National Music Curriculum Standard for Senior High School (Trial)* requires aesthetics to be at the center of the curriculum standards. It stresses providing students with informative, fundamental, and essential music knowledge and ensuring music becomes a lifetime learning goal. The philosophy and ultimate goals are (1) to provide students a musical habit with music aesthetics as the core of learning, (2) that students come first with an emphasis on individual personality development, (3) to stress practical learning outcome and ensure students' creativity and improvisational capability, and (4) to respect and understand the multicultural society with a strong sense of nationalism (Ministry of Education, PRC, 2003).

The Content

The contents of the learning area include the following six categories: music appreciation, singing, performance, creativity, music and dance, and music and drama. The government expects the standards to not only cultivate students' music competency but also help them with aesthetic capability and cultivate them through creativity. By the time students graduate from high school, students are expected to understanding basic music theories and apply them in creative works. Furthermore, students are expected to demonstrate basic movement and choreography with corresponding music and drama (see Table 15.5).

CURRENT MUSIC EDUCATION AND ASSESSMENT PRACTICE IN CHINA

A. Wang (2012) believes that educational assessment should include multiple measures and opportunities for both teachers and students to understand what they can do in the subject. The purpose of assessment is to find out the current reality and challenges for both teachers' teaching and students' learning based on responses to questions they provide and then to offer recommendations for improvement. What makes assessment more effective is how well the information is provided.

Table 15.5 The Content of the National Music Curriculum Standard for Senior High School

Curricular Areas	Grades 10–12
Music Appreciation	* Providing students with aesthetics capability * Understanding the history of music development, importance of multicultural value, and its connection to the society * Understanding musical composers' music styles and their historical background * Understanding the traditional Chinese musical instruments and music history
Singing	* Being able to appreciate musical works by the composers * Actively involving choir and being able to listen to all other voices in the choir * Being able to sing both part/voices in duet and harmoniously work with others * Demonstrating interest in folk songs and researching local folk songs and rhythms
Performance	* Actively participating and performing in any music ensemble * Being able to perform two to four pieces in any music ensemble * Being able to play a part in any music ensemble * Being able to perform folk songs and research local folk songs and rhythms
Creativity	* Understanding basic music theories and applying them in any creative works * Being able to use modern technology and musical software in composing music * Being able to compose music and write simple accompaniment for music
Music and Dance	* Actively participating in dancing rehearsal and performance * Understanding basic dancing movement * Demonstrating the ability of choreography with corresponding music
Music and Drama	* Actively participating in drama rehearsal and performance * Being able to write a drama and/or musical with corresponding music * Being able to express and understand the content of drama from the story, characteristics, and music

Source: Adapted from Ministry of Education (2003).

Teachers are the soul of education; therefore, the teachers' music competence and teaching materials need to be systematically described, examined, and analyzed. Music teachers need to know how well their students have learned so that they can make appropriate adjustments to what is taught and included in the class (Hoffer, 2008). Orzolek (2008) also believes that assessment helps to explain, determine, monitor, and promote students' learning, which can benefit communication between teachers and students. I acknowledge that a teachers' effectiveness contributes significantly to students' learning achievement.

To provide comprehensive learning and student success, teachers should strive to create effective strategies of teaching. In order to understand the current status of assessment in music education in China, I investigated teachers' teaching materials, teaching approaches, and assessment criteria for students in music class. I then analyzed the results, and I offer recommendations.

Because China covers a huge territory and also many schools and teachers were conservative about interviewing and releasing related information, it was a challenge to collect all the necessary data. I randomly and anonymously selected 235 music teachers from a total of 128 elementary schools, 56 middle schools and 51 high schools from Beijing, Shanghai, Shenzhen, and Lanzhou, which are the major cities from the north, center, south, and west of mainland China. The study lasted 1 year, from November 2015 to November 2016, and the research consisted of a review of the teachers' portfolio assessments. The portfolio assessments included teachers' self-evaluations, a collection of teaching plans, teaching materials, and teachers' reflection journals. Information regarding student assessments, such as assessment criteria, evaluated items, and grading percentages for each item, were also included in the teachers' self-evaluation (see Appendix 15.1). All of the documents were completely anonymous and confidential, and were kept locked in an office cabinet and destroyed 3 months after the study was completed.

The Portfolio Assessments

Teachers' Self-Evaluation

After detailed student assessment analysis, I found that the national curriculum guideline is the foundation of music teaching and the music textbook is the major teaching material for most music teachers (94.6%) at all school levels in China. Most (95.2%) of the participants' teaching plans and materials were based on the textbooks. The two officially authorized textbooks published by People's Education Publisher and the Guangdong Flower City Publishing House were the most-used music textbooks in the local public schools in China (Hai-Ding Education Committee, 2015; Lau, 2007).

Regarding the teaching content, 98.4% of music teachers used singing as the main contents for music classes, while 71.2% of teachers introduced music theory in class. Body movement and memorization of lyrics along with singing were the major activities and the basis for student assessments in the local music classes. However, even with singing as the major component of music class, only one-third of teachers (33.7%) focus on students' pitch and rhythm. Teachers need to focus on students' pitch, rhythm, and other music elements rather than merely sing music.

Due to the use of different music notation systems in China compared to countries of the Western world, the majority of Chinese teachers in public schools use numbered musical notation rather than music staves. Because singing is the major teaching content in public schools in China, a singing test is the most common assessment of elementary school students for the majority of music teachers; only 18.3% of the nation's teachers use a written test as their assessment. The results show that a majority of music teachers still choose the traditional approach to assess their students' music competency. Besides singing, students' assessment in music should include a broader range of assessment, such as music theory and rhythm, and so forth. The results also show that 71.7% of music teachers have never used international music methods, such as Orff, Kodály, and Dalcroze methods, in their music class, and surprisingly also found that nearly 40% of the participants have never heard about the methods. This reveals the potential for promoting international music methods in the nation. Regarding the content of music class, 70.6% of participants admitted that teaching focuses on Chinese music more than Western classical music.

Even for music notation reading, the numbered *musical* notation is still the dominant method over music staves for most music teachers in China. All of the above show that music classes can be more creative and motivated if new assessment strategies and teaching approaches are included and implemented.

Including elements of patriotism and nationalism is another highlight of the nation's music classes. The spirit of patriotism and nationalism is easily found in textbooks and teaching in every subject—music definitely not excluded—so that students can not only understand the nation better but also recognize the national identity.

Regarding additional assistance, although 78.1% of participants said that they are satisfied with what they have, more than 60% of teachers hope their schools can provide more support for the subject and nearly 50% of participants said that they felt music does not carry the same respect as other core subjects, such as mathematics, Chinese, and so forth, among both the school and parents. Faced with the pressure of studying other subjects, students often neglect music, especially at the high school level. This seems to be a universal problem, making it worth rethinking the value and purpose of the music subject at each level.

Teachers' Reflection Journals

Participants were required to write down their teaching progress in a reflection journal. The participants were encouraged to comment regarding their teaching so that I could understand their class challenges. I believe that the reflection journal provides a private space where teachers can have time to not only reflect on teaching but also calmly figure out various challenges they might have and devise possible constructive solutions.

The majority of the participants believe that the national curriculum guideline provides clear and systematic standards in the subject. Of the participants, over 90% think the inclusion of nationalism can cultivate students' patriotism and self-identity, which is necessary and important for education. "We were educated this way and believe that teaching students patriotic songs can stimulate students' unity and self-identity," said Teacher G.

Nearly 30% of teachers have never heard about any international music method. After cross-analyzing responses, it became clear that the participants from Lanzhou, the capital of Gansu province, were relatively conservative and traditional in terms of their teaching philosophy and teaching approach. "I have heard about the Orff music method but I don't know how to get such information," said Teacher C. "I don't need to learn those methods. I am fine with what I have so far in my class," said Teacher Z. "Most of my students have difficulty to understand and clap rhythms. I really don't know how to make them become easier," was admitted by teachers A and G. It appears that the success of international music methods such as Orff, Kodály, and Dalcroze lies in that not only do they provide a chance for teachers to interact with their students rather than take a traditional one-way lecturing approach but also the methods inspire and motivate students with creative music activities, which helps students understand concepts. According to the survey, some music teachers also reflected that music did not seem to get the same attention and respect as other core subjects, which makes some teachers unmotivated and unenthusiastic. "Comparing with other core subjects, music is often being neglected and disrespected in terms of assessment, school support, and activities," said Teacher C.

It is worth mentioning that although some participants are not currently living and teaching in rural areas, they still mentioned that the teaching contents are not systematic or professional in some rural cities in China. "In my hometown, there are still many public schools that need complete music facilities and qualified music teachers," said Teacher A. "Compared to the rural areas, the teaching quality and standards are much better in Shanghai," Teacher A further said. B. Wang (2004) also points out that a lack of music facilities as well as school/parents' supports, unsystematic teaching contents, and poor quality of students are the main challenges in rural areas, which matches the results of this study. Tian (2012) also states that due to neglect by schools, many music classes were canceled and replaced by other so-called core courses without further rescheduling in many public schools in rural areas. Ma (2012) also states that the government was aware of the challenges in rural China and strongly advocated for education improvements, such as changes in leadership and teaching management and concepts. Moreover, there were calls for increasing manpower and budgets in elementary and secondary schools (Ma, 2012). Indeed, the lack of teaching materials, manpower, and facilities were the main concern for survey participants in some rural areas in China. The results revealed the unbalanced situation in music teaching between city and rurality in China.

Discussion and Recommendations

The current practice and implementation of the national curriculum guidelines in all public schools in China are accurate and practical. Not only does every school have a systematic guideline to follow but also the guideline provides both teachers and students a clear direction and systematic plan for the subject; therefore, implementing the national curriculum guideline needs to be encouraged throughout the whole of China. Teachers are the soul of education. In order to raise students' music standards, it's important to cultivate music teachers with complete professional competence. Revising music content and being more practical so that students can connect the learned music knowledge with their daily life is suggested. Moreover, music teaching should have broader and deeper purposes and implications. Not only are teachers at all school levels responsible for delivering music knowledge, but also they need to cultivate students' aestheticism in the subject rather than just competition and extra credit.

I was aware that the current practice of music assessment for assessing students' learning achievement from all school levels was too simple and lacked diversification, and my research confirmed this. Singing children's songs from the textbooks seems to be the only assessment for the students' learning achievement for the majority of the music teachers. Teachers are responsible to provide a diverse musical creativities and learning experiences; therefore, at the same time, students should have opportunity to demonstrate mastery of what they have learned (Burnard, 2016).

Moreover, appropriate and consistent administrative procedures of assessment should be implemented so that the result can be fair and reliable (Brophy, 2000). Not only should assessment provide evidence that students can master the music ability through performance, but also it should demonstrate reliable results through various forms of assessment. Designing a valid assessment that can allow students at all levels to demonstrate their learning outcomes seems to be necessary for music education in China.

Due to China's vast territory, it is urgent and important to unify and standardize music teachers' competency throughout the country so that all students from all school levels and all areas can benefit from professional music teachers. Also, in order to promote common learning content and unified learning standards, standardized course content provided by the government is needed in every province throughout the nation. China has been through many wars and chaotic experiences in the past, which hindered its progress and development. The promotion of nationalism and patriotism through music and other subjects is understandable and explicable. However, in order to be international and have better communication with the world, besides the traditional numeric notation, music staff and notation should be promoted to students at all school levels.

There are two major systems of music reading and both of them provide different training to students. Fixed-Do stresses reading notes on the staff, while the Movable-Do focuses on the perceived relationships between pitches as they occur within scales. The value of Movable-Do system is that the intervals are consistent, which benefits students' aural training (D. Wang, 2016). However, often teachers and students neglect that the importance of notation reading on the music staves, which the Fixed-Do system can provide, and which is the basis and foundation of music learning; therefore, it is teachers' responsibility to help students with such training. Not only can studying the two systems enhance students' music competency and understanding in terms of rhythm and notation reading but also it can broaden students' points of view on the international level and improve their ability to communicate with others outside the nation.

World music methods, such as Orff, Kodály, and Dalcroze, also need to be encouraged and promoted at all school levels, especially the rural areas of the nation. Implementing various international music approaches will make the subject more inspirational and motivational. Not only can students explore the contents delivered by the new teaching methods from the Western world but also they can be inspired by and benefit from the motivating music approaches. Most important, the students are connected to the world and are able to exchange new ideas globally. The current international music methods not only provide motivating approaches in music learning but also focus on improvisation and creativity, which will tremendously help students in every aspect of learning.

Finally, personnel shortages in rural China are constant challenges in every respect, education included. Bridging the gap between city and rural communities will require the provision of qualified music graduates with more attractive benefits and assistance to teach in the remote areas of the nation. Doing so will ensure that all students have equal opportunity in education and also reduce potential social problems.

APPENDIX 15.1

THE PORTFOLIO ASSESSMENTS: TEACHERS' SELF-EVALUATION

Categories	Items		Performance Rating (1 as lowest and 10 as highest)
Teaching Context	Music Theory		
	Singing		
	Rhythm		
	Musical Instruments		
	Music Appreciation	Chinese Music	
		Western Classical Music	
Class Activities	Body Movement		
	Singing		
	World Music Approaches: Orff, Kodaly, and Dalcroze Methods		
	Music Theory		
	Rhythm		
	Composing/Improvisation		
Assessment Criteria	Music Theory		
	Rhythmic Dictation		
	Singing	Pitch	
		Rhythm	
		Memorization	
Guidelines Used in Music Class	National Curriculum Standards		
	Self-Designed Teaching Materials		
	Textbook		
Comments	School Support		
	Parental Support		
	Others		

REFERENCES

Brophy, T. (2000). *Assessing the developing child musician: A guide for general music teachers.* Chicago, IL: GIA.

Burnard, P. (2016). Assessing for real world learning of diverse musical creativities. In T. S. Brophy, J. Marlatt, & G. K. Ritcher (Eds.), *Connecting practice, measurement, and evaluation: Selected papers from the 5th International Symposium on Assessment in Music Education* (pp. 29–40), Chicago, IL: GIA.

Education Mission. (2000). *The discussion of the educational system.* Hong Kong: Hong Kong Government.

Hai-Ding Education Committee. (2015). *The Hai-Ding education document #24.* Beijing: Beijing Normal University. Unpublished manuscript.

Hoffer, C. (2008). *Introduction to music education.* Long Grove, IL: Waveland Press.

Keiny, S. (2006). School-based curriculum development as a process of teachers' professional development. *Educational Action Research, 1*(199), 65–93.

Lau, F. (2007). *Music in China: Experiencing music, expressing culture.* London, UK: Oxford University Press.

Ma, L. (2012). On music education in China's rural primary and middle schools. *World Rural Observations, 4*(1), 45–48.

Ministry of Education, People's Republic of China (PRC). (2003). *National music curriculum standard for senior high school (trial).* Beijing: Beijing Normal University.

Ministry of Education, People's Republic of China (PRC). (2008). *National curriculum standard in music of compulsory education.* Beijing: Beijing Normal University.

Ministry of Education, People's Republic of China (PRC). (2011). *National music curriculum standard for compulsory education.* Beijing: Beijing Normal University.

National Bureau of Statistics of the People's Republic of China. (2015, February 26). *Statistical communique of the People's Republic of China on the 2014 national economic and social development.* Retrieved from http://www.stats.gov.cn/english/pressrelease/201502/t20150228_687439.html

Orzolek, D. (2008). Navigating the paradox of the assessment in music education. In T. S. Brophy (Ed.), *Integrating curriculum, theory, and practice: Proceedings of the 2007 Symposium on Assessment in Music Education* (pp. 37–44). Chicago, IL: GIA.

Tian, L. (2012). *The current music education in China.* Hunan, China: Hunan Normal University. Unpublished manuscript.

Wang, B. (2004). *The research on music education in county of Hunan Province.* Hunan, China: Hunan Normal University. Unpublished manuscript.

Wang, A. K. (2012). The new beginning of the music education for the curriculum reform and development. *People's Music, 6,* 64–68.

Wang, D. (2016). Assessing the influence of music courses on pre-service teachers' teaching competency. In T. S. Brophy, J. Marlatt, & G. K. Ritcher (Eds.), *Connecting practice, measurement, and evaluation: Selected papers from the 5th International Symposium on Assessment in Music Education* (pp. 217–230). Chicago, IL: GIA.

CHAPTER 16

POLICY AND PRACTICE OF ASSESSMENT IN MUSIC EDUCATION: THE CASE OF SINGAPORE

WEI SHIN LEONG AND JULIE TAN

GAINING its independence from Britain and Malaysia only in 1965, Singapore's current education system and consistently stellar student performance in international comparative measures of educational achievement have been widely reported (OECD, 2013; World Economic Forum, 2009) and celebrated as a milestone achievement in its 50 years of nationhood. What is perhaps less exalted is that this city state of 5.61 million people (as of 2017) has inherited a colonial legacy of the English examination system that has been in place since its founding. Through and in it, the current achievement can be deemed an expression of a powerful ideological and cultural consensus on the significance of examination and education (Sharpe & Gopinathan, 2003). The current initiatives articulate a different order of worth and value of a more "holistic education" that should help students to be more confident and curious and (consequentially) to place less emphasis on exclusive academic pursuits and examination results (Heng, 2011; Ministry of Education [MOE], 2005; C. M. Ng, 2016; E. H. Ng, 2008). E. H. Ng's keynote address (2008), as minister for education at the time, outlined the challenges of educators today in preparing students not only for and through a more diversified curriculum but also for the challenges that arise beyond schooling. A logical implication of "holistic education" is subsequently given further attention by listening to various aspirations and desires of school leaders and teachers for "student-centricity" in education (Heng, 2011; C. M. Ng, 2016): in other words, how students should have more time and space to pursue their interests. The progressive introduction of new "holistic education" policies articulate in different ways, and to varying degrees, the espoused school and classroom assessment practices that teachers must introduce to help students access opportunities for "holistic learning." Put another way, students can strive beyond narrowly defined academic excellence to develop a wider set of appropriate attributes, skills and knowledge, mindsets, and values.

Arts education, including music, has been highlighted as a key area of focus in pursuing the goals of such a holistic education (Lum & Dairianathan, 2014), both within and outside classrooms, particularly in terms of developing students' dispositions and abilities to perceive, conceptualize, and express ideas (E. H. Ng, 2010). In the past 50 years, subjects such as music and art have tended to be deemed less important subjects in public school curricula, even being termed "non-core" subjects. This is in sharp contrast with the heavy investment by some Singaporean families in supporting their children in private art and music tuition programs outside of school. Recognition and signaling of the ascendancy of the arts within public education (Lum & Dairianatham, 2014) is unprecedented but unsurprising, as policymakers and teachers grapple with the full meaning of a "holistic education," while addressing issues of social equity and reviewing meritocratic education provisions. The question "What next for Singapore's education system in the next 50 years?" affects all sectors of education, including music. Such a deep predictive question cannot find its lineage within Singapore or in any other educational systems that are, for instance, grappling with falling standards of student academic achievement, while managing budgetary cuts in funding in arts education.

In this chapter, we situate the policy and practice of assessment in music education within Singapore based on these unique confluences of local and global educational contexts. As in other subjects, the British examination system is also present in music education, if not even more deeply entrenched. The British music examining boards first introduced their graded music examinations within "private music education" in Singapore as early as 1948 (Stead & Lum, 2014). The early semblance of music education in "public music education" within mainstream schools in the 1950s was heavily influenced by the requirements of British music examination boards. Their influence undoubtedly was, and still is, extremely significant today in what constitutes being "musically educated" in Singapore, in both the private and public sectors of music education. Withstanding the challenges of uncertainty in the 21st century, and the need for time and space for a different vision and values in education, the question "What is next?" in music education, and particularly how the policy and practice of assessment will remain or change, is central in this chapter.

We define the discourse of policies within both public and private education as the orchestration of an ensemble of ideas and concepts that are "produced, reproduced and transformed in a particular set of practices" (Hajer, 1995, p. 44). Such orchestration and performance can be explicit, tacit, hidden, or even nonexistent, leading to consequences that require negotiation of contingencies and creative negotiations. The contested and creative social interactions of policy activities cannot be hidden behind "clean" policy text (Ball et al., 2012). A practice, therefore, is not just the executive arm of policy; neither is it just an action. Rather, it is part of sets of dialectical and concerted human activities, both individual and collective ways of negotiating the world, with its own affective, cognitive, and moral demands that are contextually bounded by different considerations (Torgerson, 2003, 2010). Assessment researchers and scholars (Gipps & Murphy, 1994; Klenowski & Wyatt-Smith, 2013) have besieged educators to consider assessment policy and practices as important aspects of gatekeeping by asking four overarching questions: What knowledge is assessed and deemed as achievement and learning? Is the range of knowledge well reflected in definitions of appropriate achievement and learning? Are the form, content, and mode of assessment appropriate for different groups and individuals? How does specific cultural knowledge mediate individuals' responses to assessment in ways that need to customize how certain knowledge and skills are assessed within a local context? A particular set of assessment policies and practices would provide a response to these questions. There are, therefore, diverse permutations and possibilities of ensembles of assessment policies and practices, with their own unique set of logic, standards, orientations to society, and their own public image. This engenders careful micro- and macro-level analyses to obtain a fuller understanding of the interrelations of policies and practices of assessment, as enacted and experienced by the same teacher and student, for instance. Such policies, once enacted, can become the focus of struggles over allocation resources such as the hiring and deployment of teachers and allocation of curriculum time. We concur with Ball et al. (2012) in highlighting that assessment policies and practices can empower some and displace others.

This chapter describes and provides critical perspectives on questions such as: What are the music assessment policies and practices in Singaporean music classrooms in both public and private education settings? How are assessment practices enacted that go beyond the mere "enactment" of certain explicit policies (if any)? How do hidden or implicit policies in both national and private music education settings dictate music assessment practices that have their own unique moral and cultural demands? Ultimately we want to arrive at some conclusions about the tenacity of certain policies and practices of music assessment, and how a more collaborative orchestration of ensembles between the public and private sectors of music education can point meaningfully to the composition of a "What's next?" piece.

National Music Curriculum, Program, and Assessment System

The general music program (GMP) is offered to all students in primary and secondary schools. Although it is limited to between 35 minutes and 1 hour of lessons each week, it is positioned in the school curriculum as a key platform on which every child in Singapore is provided a foundational music education. Hence, it is worthwhile reproducing here the aims of such a significant program, in accordance with the syllabus document from the Ministry of Education (MOE), Singapore (MOE, 2014):

   i. Developing an awareness and appreciation of music in local and global cultures;
  ii. Developing an ability for creative expression and communication through music; and
 iii. Providing the basis for developing an informed and lifelong involvement in music.

Such aims are further enacted through a British model of teaching and learning music through the prescription of balanced curricular emphasis on performing, listening, and creative music-making activities (Swanwick, 2002; Swanwick & Taylor, 1982) typically located within, but not limited to, classrooms. The GMP syllabus spans four key stages from grades 1 to 8 (6–14 years old), with each stage comprising two grades. More details of the syllabus can be found in Appendix 16.1. The diligent curricular debates and revisions through the decades include an increasing emphasis on world and popular music, particularly understanding the indigenous musical cultures of Singapore and the neighboring regions, the use of information and communications technology (ICT), and giving prominence to the music classroom as a conduit to teaching 21st-century competencies (MOE, 2014) in more recent times.

Yet, the rhetoric of policy and official documents does not shed light on the deeper discontinuities, such as the persistent "out-of-balance" nature of the enacted GMP curriculum, with its overemphasis on performative and recreative music tasks (Stead & Lum, 2014; Tan, 1997), coupled with a chronic shortage of qualified music teachers (Lum & Dairianathan, 2014) within the entire fraternity of MOE-hired civil servant teachers. Many GMP teachers currently hold a music teaching diploma at the very least (or its equivalent), although these are still in short supply and most do not hold a degree in music or performing arts. One can then expect that the professional development of music teachers at in-service level is paramount. Over the past 50 years, we have witnessed substantial investment in developing a wide repertoire of professional development courses, particularly in introducing a variety of classroom-based music pedagogies. Classroom assessment, on the other hand, seems to receive less attention in GMP (Leong, 2014).

On the assessment policy front, the new "holistic" or "balanced assessment" policy, which is currently applicable to other academic subjects, ironically does not affect GMP teachers as much, since the GMP has been declared a nonexamination subject since 1968. The achievement score of student performances in the GMP is not critical for the summative consideration of promotion or certification; hence, for the past five decades, music teachers have enjoyed autonomy in awarding assessment grades.

The O level music program and music elective program (MEP) is designed to enable select secondary school and junior college students (grades 7–12, 12–18 years old) with both academic and musical abilities to undertake a challenging music program, with a final accreditation in GCE University of Cambridge-Singapore O and/or A level music or its equivalent at the end of grades 10 and 12 (15–16 and 17–18 years old), respectively. From their inception in 1980, the assessment policies of these examination-based music curricula, contrary to the GMP, have been highly prescriptive in accordance, standards, and practices set on collaboratively by the University of Cambridge Local Examinations Syndicate (UCLES) and the Singapore Examination and Assessment Board (SEAB). The syllabus structure (see Appendix 16.2) clearly delineates a comprehensive assessment regime in broad learning areas of music studies (including listening and analysis), performing, and music writing (including counterpoint, imitative writing). While the substantial basis of the assessment requires teachers and students to be widely familiar with Western classical music repertoires and rudiments, increasingly it offers study assessment areas in Asian music, even allowing students to perform on non-Western musical instruments.

Since its inception in the 1980s, the MOE has recommended that a student must satisfy the prerequisites of passing external private music examinations, such as the Associated Board of the Royal Schools of Music (ABRSM), or its equivalent, before being admitted to these examination-based music elective programs. Such prerequisites are necessary, as the curriculum and assessment requirements assume advanced knowledge and skills in music that are not likely to be addressed in the GMP lessons. In contrast to the GMP, qualified music teachers, typically with a degree in music or its equivalent, are deployed by the Ministry to teach in schools as part of such a program. Such a process also ensures that students are competitively prepared for even higher levels of music studies at post-secondary and tertiary institutes.

A more recent examination-based normal-technical (NT) music syllabus with an emphasis on music technology and its applications has been developed for students bound for vocational studies in post-secondary schools. Even more recently, some secondary schools have been selected to offer the enhanced music program (EMP). These schools will provide an enriched learning environment for select grade 9 and 10 students (14–15 and 15–16 years old) with an inclination toward more practice-oriented music learning that is less "examination-focused." Beyond being required to sit for the O level examination syllabus, students have opportunities to interact with and learn from practitioners from arts and creative industries.

Cocurricular Activities and Singapore Youth Festival

Cocurricular activities (CCAs), previously known as extracurricular activities (ECAs), are nonacademic activities in which all students must participate outside the classroom. This policy was introduced by the MOE as a means to enhance social interaction, character development and leadership, and healthy recreation. The aesthetics CCA includes band, choir, string ensemble, and ethnic music ensembles such as Chinese Orchestra, Guzheng, and Gamelan. The MOE also organizes the biennial Singapore Youth Festival (SYF) for the aesthetics CCAs. Typically, these music CCA ensembles are led and directed by private music instructors hired by the schools, albeit supported by the music teachers in schools. The humble beginnings of the SYF can be traced back to its roots on July 18, 1967, by (then) President Yusof Ishak. It was a festival that involved 24,000 students from primary and secondary schools in a 2-week celebration, as a means to showcase both the achievements of the initial nation-building and the vibrancy of Singaporean youths. It has metamorphosed into an annual kaleidoscopic showcase of talent involving more than 40,000 students between April and July every year. The "examination syndrome" eventually crept into the psyche of many as early as the 1970s, as the SYF has become an annual adjudication event of the quality of performance of the various school-based aesthetics CCA performing groups. The hours of preparation that go into the biennial adjudication can take its toll on students, teachers, and instructors, as the results can have high-stakes consequences for students, teachers, and schools. External adjudicators' assessment of a single performance will determine the quality of certification (MOE, 2017) that the ensemble will carry for the school (and themselves) for at least 2 years and into their CCA record. The students are finally assessed and rewarded with CCA points, based on the extent of their participation and achievements in SYF, for competitive admissions to postsecondary institutions and universities.

Overall, the MOE makes a huge investment to ensure a wider offering of music curricula and programs for students across age groups, schools, and differing levels of interest in music. There is regular review of the music curriculum and examination syllabi to ensure that the curricular content and pedagogy are up-to-date. The differences in the music syllabi in terms of their design issues for different target audiences and aims result in assessment policies and practices in the music classrooms within a school or even classroom that can be quite different. While assessment in the GMP is recognized as being integral to teaching and learning, and a variety of modes of assessment (e.g., the use of rubrics, portfolios, and reflection journals) have been suggested in the syllabus (MOE, 2014), the absence of a systemwide policy and comprehensive evaluation of achievement standards of learning in the GMP could mean that its aims have not been met adequately in some areas (and more in others) in all its years of implementation. Without clear policy guidance, it is common to hear of GMP teachers being uncertain of whether their assessment is sound. The assessment practices in O and A level–driven syllabi will be much more standardized and prescriptive, as compared to the GMP. The same teacher who teaches both GMP and MEP will experience stark differences in enacting assessment policies and practices. The assessment of participation and achievement in CCA and SYF provides another context of differences in policy and practice in mainstream schools, whereby partnership with external music instructors is the norm. This is a case of an interesting juxtaposition of tightly regulated assessment policies and practices within the examinable and publicly adjudicated music performance events and a much looser control within the GMP, all within the public music education sector.

PRIVATE MUSIC INSTRUCTION AND EXTERNAL EXAMINATION BOARDS

Beyond the school sector, the private sector of instrumental/vocal teaching is the main sphere in which music learning takes place. It is the primary source that provides the general public with access to music lessons, from beginner to advanced levels. Lessons are taught by either self-employed, private studio teachers or those who teach within commercial music schools. In the standard weekly one-to-one lesson, ranging from

45 minutes to an hour, the primary aim is to develop instrumental proficiency and performance skills.

Independent Studio Teachers

Unlike mainstream schools, which fall under the jurisdiction of the MOE, the fraternity of independent studio music teachers is autonomous and does not report to any authority. It is an open, unregulated industry in which any interested person (i.e., with or without qualifications) can become a teacher without a license. Lesson policies are decided by mutual agreement between teacher and student/parent. Teachers are therefore at liberty to decide on all matters (including curriculum, syllabus, pedagogy, assessment, and fees), and undergo no external audit. Indeed, such unrestricted entry to the profession makes music teaching both viable and lucrative. This "openness" adds vibrancy to the music teaching industry, invariably attracting diverse teaching methods, standards, and quality. Students' music standards are therefore wide-ranging, from mediocre to extremely high, world-class standards.

Commercial Music Schools

In contrast, commercial music schools (CMSs), which generally operate as business entities, come under the auspices of the Private Schools Section (PSS) in the Higher Education Division of the MOE. Such schools, their teachers, and courses are subject to registration, and permission must be granted prior to operation. To further grasp the extent of polarity between the "autonomy" and "authority" experienced by self-employed studio teachers and commercial schools respectively, it is useful to understand the requirements and policy on CMS registration:

> MOE registers private schools, the courses they offer and the teachers conducting the registered courses. To be registered, private schools need to meet basic statutory requirements, such as building and fire safety requirements, and have an acceptable curriculum and qualified teachers. As all private schools are owned by private entities, the operators themselves are responsible for the management and administration of their private school and courses.   (MOE, 2016, para. 1)

While registration is mandatory, the MOE stipulates that "registration … does not in any way represent an endorsement or accreditation of the quality of the courses offered" (MOE, 2016, para. 1). With much attention placed on registration matters, there is, however, no policy on music assessment. Neither is there a national or standardized instrumental syllabus or examination. Instead, assessment via grade exams (comprising grade levels 1–8) provided by external music examination boards fills the void of a national music examination and thus serves as the benchmark for the vast majority of teachers and their students in both independent and CMS settings.

External Music Examination Boards

The ABRSM from the United Kingdom is arguably the world's leading (ABRSM, 2017, para. 1) and highest subscribed music examination body in the Republic. Since its afore-mentioned introduction to Singapore in 1948, its "open-door" policy has enabled anyone to register and undergo music examinations without any prior conditions, including the need to study with a "qualified" music teacher or be registered with a school. This is similarly practiced by other external music examination boards such as Trinity College London (TCL), the London College of Music (LCM), and Australian & New Zealand Cultural Arts Limited (ANZCA), whose examinations are also undertaken locally, albeit in smaller numbers than the ABRSM. Such open policy for music stands in stark contrast to that for dance students, who can only be entered for a Royal Academy of Dance (RAD, UK) examination by a qualified teacher who holds the Academy Registered Teacher Status (Royal Academy of Dance, 2015, para. 5). We view such unrestricted policy as being consistent with the ABRSM founders' vision of a music examining board that offers an alternative to privately owned examining institutions widely perceived to be "motivated more powerfully by mercenary concerns, than promoting high standards of musical education and assessment" (ABRSM, 2016, para. 1). Yet, we need to question whether the proliferation of such music examinations across the world continues to hold fast to the founders' vision. Each year, Singapore sees an excess of 65,000 candidates (with an approximate examination revenue of SGD20.39 million/USD14.83 million) undertaking the ABRSM music examinations (A. Brice, personal communication, September 16, 2013).

The local teaching fee structure, which shadows the external examination boards' numeric step system of grades 1 to 8 and diploma-level exams (i.e., the fee increases as the grade level ascends, rather than being time-based or age-based), speaks more to the reliance on, and predominance of, such assessment than to teachers' active participation in the examination process. (The terminology of "grade" used here should not be confused with the "grade" used in a school context, which is age-related.) It is common for a student to be pegged arbitrarily against a particular "grade" (level), whether or not s/he is ready or has even been entered for graded examinations by the teacher. This peculiarity, which also pervades music assessment in other former British colonies (e.g., Malaysia and Hong Kong) results in a "default" curricular setting in which graded music examinations drive teaching and learning in private music classes. Further details of the contents of the ABRSM and Trinity College London Grades 1 to 8 Piano exam syllabi can be found in Appendix 16.3.

Private graded music examinations constitute one of the largest criterion-referenced testing systems in the world (Peggie, 1994, p. 5). They are summative, criterion-referenced music examinations in which the same performing criteria are applied to all examination candidates, irrespective of instrument/voice and level. Generalist examiners, rather than specialists, assess all instruments, including voice, regardless of their major instruments. In other words, they assess the outcome of the musical performance, and not necessarily the technique used to achieve it (ABRSM, 2015a, para. 2). For the ABRSM, their marking criteria set the standards while ensuring marking consistency across the world. The Board states:

> The ABRSM marking criteria underpin the standards and consistency of all examiners' marking as they form the basis of assessment for practical graded music exams. So wherever you take an exam—in Solihull or Singapore—the examiner will be following exactly the same marking guidelines, with the aim of exactly the same assessment.
>
> (ABRSM, 2013, p. 8)

Some private music examinations (e.g., at Trinity College) have a more flexible system that provides more choices (such as performing one's own music compositions) to support the personalization of music learning. Other alternatives, such as the Music Certificate Examinations by Trinity College and the Performance Assessment by ABRSM, which feature no assessment of scales, sight-reading, or aural tests, instead focus solely on students' prepared performance with partial or no prescribed works, respectively. For ABRSM, constructive comments (with no pass or fail nor marks) are written on the certificates, which are awarded to candidates at the end of the assessment. With ABRSM's introduction of its new performance assessment (in 2015) open to all ages and levels, it remains to be seen whether such a formative-oriented assessment would be well-received and used by local teachers and students.

Although music assessment has traditionally been provided by external British examination boards, recent years have witnessed the development of pan-Asian Pacific music examination boards such as the Australian & New Zealand Cultural Arts Limited (ANZCA), which was formed in 1983 in response to "a growing need amongst private music teachers for an examination system catering for a greater diversity of musical styles" (ANZCA, 2018, p. 1). In Singapore, the now defunct National University of Singapore Centre for the Arts Chinese Instrumental Examination was conducted since December 2004 (discontinued from 2017). Apart from promoting an appreciation of, and education in, Chinese music in Singapore and the region, the main objective of creating such an examination system was to "establish a coherent and consistent set of guidelines for facilitating systematic training of various Chinese musical instruments" (National University of Singapore Centre for the Arts, 2016). Another example is the Graded Examination for Chinese Instruments, which is jointly organized and offered by the Nanyang Academy of Fine Arts (NAFA) and the Beijing Central Conservatory of Music.

The Singapore Performers' Festival

An authentic assessment approach that replicates the real-world situation comes in the guise of the biennial Singapore Performers' Festival, in which participants (piano, piano duet, strings, voice, and chamber groups) receive critiques from *public performances* that they give before a live audience and a small panel of international pedagogues in *specific* instrumental areas (The Singapore Music Teachers' Association, 2017). Introduced in 2006, this newer platform, inaugurated by The Singapore Music Teachers' Association (founded in 1952 as The Singapore Music Teachers' Society and reformed in 1966, it is the only independent, nonprofit professional teaching body in the Republic), advocates music as a performing art and puts the learner at the forefront. Participants of all ages and levels undergo the entire performing experience, from preparation (planning one's own program and writing of program notes) and performing to learning how to promote, publicize, and garner audience support for their performances. With an open choice of performing repertoire, teachers do not have to teach to any prescribed repertoire, unlike the mandated graded examination repertoire. The teaching syllabus can be jointly decided by teachers and students, and the repertoire learned can continue to be presented for external assessment. Post-performance, participants have the opportunity to consult with the adjudicators in open classes. In addition, a video recording of their performances (given to each participant) serves as a reference for self-critique to help further improve their playing skills and stagecraft. Participants can continue to learn from peer-critiquing other participants' performances in the recordings. This results in better alignment of syllabus, pedagogy, and assessment. Such an iterative system is useful and in line with leading scholars' thinking on sustainable assessment and learning (e.g., Boud, 2000). Students need to be able to appreciate the values and limitations of different forms of external assessment and make attempts on their own to appreciate self-assessment as being significantly more critical to a much longer lifelong learning journey. As Boud and Associates note, "Students themselves need to develop the capacity to make judgements about both their own work and that of others in order to become effective continuing learners and practitioners" (2010, p. 1). The Performers' Festival, although relatively young, has the potential to counterbalance the summative-oriented private music examination system, with all its negative backlashes. However, we are cognizant that there is still plenty of room for such a platform to evolve so that the formative orientation of music assessment can be fully optimized.

Therefore, even with new and diverse local initiatives, it appears that the time-tested tradition of externally graded examinations will continue to cast a heavy influence over Singapore's private music education sector. Such examinations prescribe or instantiate a curriculum for private music teachers, such that little else is taught besides what will be examined. In short, "what is tested is what [is] taught" (Colwell, 2006, p. 201). Given that governmental agencies and education institutions have been using these as a reference for advising the public, it will be difficult to question reliance on such examinations even in the public education sector, perhaps until alternative reliable and valid systems of assessment can be given due consideration. We are hopeful that new local initiatives such as the Performers' Festival can provide an impetus for the dissemination and professional learning of new assessment music practices. It will have to begin with a smaller group of like-minded private music teachers, helping others to tap into their self-agency in fostering learning and changes in private studio practice, in which graded examinations play a more subsidiary (rather than dominant) role.

Interweaving National and Private
Music Education Assessment Systems

There is a polarization and yet a curious coexistence of the mainstream school and private music education sectors. While there are currently limited or nonexistent connections, communication, and collaboration between both sectors, the "third-party assessment/certificate" is used openly by and within governmental agencies, mainstream, and commercial music schools as a form of "currency." The current policies of certain governmental and statutory board agencies such as the MOE and the People's Association, which require students to acquire private music examination certifications before being accepted for enrollment on their music courses—even for a job application as a private music teacher or instructor—inevitably exacerbate the prevailing dependencies on external private music examination subscription. It is commonplace for higher education institutions (for music-related courses) to make use of external private music examination board qualifications as minimal prerequisites for students to apply for a place. Indeed, without the private music sector and external private music examinations, it would be extremely challenging to identify and attract students who have sufficient musical competencies and readiness to undertake the rigorous and challenging examinable music studies at the mainstream school level and beyond. For instance, the performing component of the examinations in the MEP relies on students' own private teachers for preparation and coaching. We note that there is also a disparity in assessment standards within mainstream schools, with GMP assessment tending to be much more unrestrictive compared to the requirements of MEP examinations, even within the same school and taught by the same teacher. The same GMP and MEP teacher could expect much less of a GMP student than an MEP student (or a student who has private music examination qualifications), as a result of the wide disparity in standards. Therefore, there are both symbiotic *and* nonsymbiotic relationships between and within national music assessment policies and examinations and private music board examinations. There are consequentially discomforts and even tensions in music assessment practices, which nevertheless somehow continually fuel the interest and aspirations of students pursuing music or music-related careers.

We acknowledge that external private music examinations have been widely appreciated in past decades, giving Singaporeans opportunities to access a rigorous (pan-Western) music education. However, in practice such examinations are less egalitarian than they appear, particularly as private music tutoring fees are not regulated, and, increasingly, only the more affluent families can afford private music lessons. We note the argument from private music education tutors and agencies that the sector is essential, because of its flexibility and freedom in the choice of music curriculum, teaching, and assessment. This stands in contrast with the regulated public music education, which cannot be customized to the needs of individuals. These advocates have a point, but they represent an increasingly untenable position because of the variation in teaching provision quality standards and inequitable access to their programs.

Moreover, we find the narrowing of musical creativities to the simplistic pursuit of (pan-Western) music examination "grades" through external private music examinations to be deeply problematic. It is troubling that local and pan-Asian examination boards seem to adopt a similar approach and model of the examination system, through an exclusive focus on performance on a single music instrument, for instance. We concur with Burnard (2012) that musical creativities reside in a wide spectrum of real-world musical practices, not in the singular "creativity" of an exclusive (classical) kind. Policies and practices from both national and private music education assessment systems need to draw their meanings from a wide pool of musical creativities residing in different communities of practitioners. It is not within the purview of a single agency (e.g., the MOE or ABRSM) to create this dialogue and deliberation. Rather, we need to hear the voices of music teachers, students, and practitioners on creative musical activities that are worth pursuing in schools as well as within the private studio. We also need to hear which of these activities distinguish and support individuals to become lifelong music appreciators and advocates, even "musicians" in all the current senses of the word.

We contend that the private music education sector is underregulated and in need of attention. The enforcement of regulations relating to assessment policies and practices can be resource-intensive, and we note that the MOE may not want to be excessively burdened or invest in such efforts. There are many "softer" approaches to regulation, including facilitating "bottom-up" self-regulation. This can be in the form of dissemination of information and advice about how to select private music teachers and appropriate external examination boards, encouraging self-regulation through unions, community bodies, and the media. There are currently promising developments of "ground-up" initiatives for the self-regulation and promotion of good assessment policies and practices that can help teachers and students to make more informed choices. Such initiatives may however run in dissonance to the more widely entrenched view of some music teachers that assessment is external to their teaching (Fautley, 2010). These music teachers need to be updated of instrument-specific pedagogy and curriculum-building know-how that will better use assessment to support student's learning. Only then can they be better equipped and empowered to recontextualize assessment; assessment as not simply viewed and undertaken externally as a standalone, summative evaluation tool for the purpose of accounting to fee-paying parents or as one's teaching fee barometer.

With regard to the Ministry of Education, we note that there is ongoing assessment research (Leong et al., 2016) to evaluate the extent to which GMP teachers' formative and summative assessment practices are developmentally appropriate and the extent to which students' progression of formative works and summative artifacts in GMP classes are developmentally appropriate for their levels. Such research has the potential to develop a framework of assessment progressions for informing music teachers in *both* the public and private music education sectors, standards of learning, and assessment across stages of musical development in all students.

Moving Forward

When we envision the future of music education, it is possible to expect that a more collaborative interplay between public and private assessment policies and practices may not actually evolve. As noted earlier, there is a compelling argument not to regulate private music education assessment policy, just as the rationale to keep these separate is still relevant. The ensembles are ultimately conducted and performed by different players and to different audiences, and can exist both connected *and* independently at the same time. Over time and through a process of complex iterations between and across policy stipulations, institutional and individual transformation and regeneration of practices can be effected (Ball et al., 2012). Such an existence can be described as "heterotopic" and, according to Foucault (1971), a society needs to have many heterotopias, not only as a space with several places of/for the affirmation of collective similarities and differences but also as a means for citizens to express their individual (musical) identities within different spaces of existence. One is assessed as "musically educated" through neither the public nor the private music education system per se; rather, one can explore these two spheres and even be content to develop, individually and collectively, new identities of being "musically educated." We can and should anticipate and encourage a greater diversity of individual identities while sustaining collective aspirations underpinning the explorations.

According to Castells (1997), there are three possible forms of collective identity-building as a result of policies and practices: (1) a legitimizing identity whereby a dominant institution decides on what constitutes good outcomes; (2) identities of resistance that emerge as a response to processes of perceived biases and stigmatization; and (3) particular social actors that propose and construct new identities, thus challenging the prevailing patterns of allocation of resources. Applying this to the case of music assessment policies and practices in Singapore, the current deference to private music examination qualifications to access the public school, examination-based music curriculum can result in an emergence of identities of resistance to what it takes to be "musically educated." Such resistance can take the form of identifying alternative means of qualifications, such as affirming local musical practices that are not currently assessable within the means of both private and public music examinations. The subsequent introduction of interactive practices, constituting possible fusions that are internationally and locally recognized musical practices (and standards of achievement), can lead to promising transformations of resistance into truly local Singaporean musical identities.

We propose two main directions in which assessment policies and practices should move, both internationally and locally.

Assessment Supporting Equity and Wide Access to Musical Practices

An assessment system must be sufficiently broad to support the personalization (not just standardization) of music learning (Fautley, 2010). Different models of progressions of assessment could be helpful in facilitating teachers to decide what is best for students. Supporting the growth of local music authorities (not necessarily through policymakers alone) can facilitate the identification and promotion of different progressions of assessment that will recognize international and local musical practices that are more congenial to Singaporean musical practices and identities. The shift from governmental policymaking, whereby the policymaker is automatically the "agent and locus of change" (Castells, 1997), should gradually give way to a more democratic governance, whereby a range of nonstate actors are actively mediating new processes of policymaking and practices. The current grassroots attempt to recognize and even create alternative platforms of music assessment systems within the private music education sector represents a promising start.

Looking at the system view of policymaking again, a new national movement called "SkillsFuture" is a powerful governmental enabler for all "Singaporeans to develop to their fullest potential throughout life" (Singapore Work Development Agency, 2016). Such a national endeavor attempts to help individual Singaporean citizens make well-informed choices in education, training, and careers, and ultimately to foster a "culture that supports and celebrates lifelong learning" (Singapore Work Development Agency, 2016). While the collective economic benefits of such an initiative are palpable in its current discourse, we can also look forward to, through such a pragmatic governmental initiative to stimulate productivity, greater aspirations for an individual's pursuit of interests and learning. We can anticipate that international and local music education assessment bodies need to work closely with Singaporean partners in local industry, professional training institutions, and continuing education ecosystems in supporting music teachers with a wide spectrum of relevant musical skills and knowledge. Such innovation and transformation of music teaching can then build a more pervasive music learning culture that is flexible, accessible, and relevant to Singaporean students in the near and far future.

Assessment That Drives Meaningful Curricular and Pedagogical Practices

Music assessment policies and practices that guide differential and atomistic performing–composing–listening–responding activities make sense only if all the elements interact with one another, culminating in what Paynter (1997) refers to as "essential unity of creativities of musical thoughts" (p. 140). Assessing students' listening skills per se in GMP classrooms, without or even in place of firsthand experience of performing and composing, is unlikely to encourage them to respond in the assessment to their potential to reach higher levels of musical understanding. Instead, it seems the assessment is limited to responding to immediate and surface conditions of music listening. Much the same thing can happen in private music instrumental teaching when the emphasis is on drilling the performance of a fixed number of music pieces, without helping students to acquire musical understanding through listening and composing. Similarly, assessing student learning of historical music information, the technique of harmony and counterpoint, and analysis are important and worthwhile so long as they are intended to relate to actual performing, creating, and listening activities. When they become ends in themselves, inevitably imagination and creativity are downgraded and real musical understanding moves beyond reach. Development of musical understanding arises not just through encounters with different interactions of activities but also with different types of music. Thus, it is imperative that policymakers continue to review and include music from a range of traditions, styles, and genres for inclusion within the national music curriculum.

Assessment policies and practices need to help teachers and students to de-emphasize which music activities can, and should, be (easily and) objectively summatively evaluated, and emphasize the valuing of the formative assessment of interactions (that may not easily be evaluated using a numerical grade) of music activities that can better support the lifelong appreciation of, and participation in, music. Do we help teachers and students to prioritize what can most easily be assessed rather than valuing what is important? How do we help them to pay attention to different forms of assessment, even in areas of music activities that are typically not easily assessed and taught? If composing, for instance, is not just an optional event in the curriculum, it can possibly underpin the whole curriculum by helping students to develop judgment that is contingent on different principles and values from different segments of the world. The assessment would focus not just on the assessment of certain compositional/technical music skills but also on moving students to aspire to achieve the ideals of self-actualization to understand the world around them and, ultimately, their own expressive beings. Assessment policies and practices need to encourage teachers and students to exercise their imaginations, defend creative and critical responses, and encourage the expression of independent artistic views. The issue here involves not just protecting music teachers and students from inappropriate assessment practices but also realizing the uniqueness of music assessment policies and practices beyond music performing venues, studios, jamming spaces, and the individual classroom to even other disciplines and fields. Only then can we truly say that a holistic assessment has been effected to not only capture but also support the whole range of learning that is possible through, in this case, the example of assessing music learning.

In this chapter we have attempted to portray the different assessment processes within the case of Singapore music education, how public and private music assessment policies interweave, and to show the interrelatedness and disjuncture of practices. We acknowledge how the way in which we arrive at our "best" interpretation can leave space for others to "see" the case differently. Through the interweaving of these contexts, as well as the particulars of the ensembles of policies and practices, we have attempted to present the textural nuances and dynamics within and between these levels of context to arrive at a more holistic understanding. In doing so, we hope to have discovered and shared something of significance, which is a strange paradox indeed (Simons, 2015) that assessment both in and through music education can offer to the rest of the world.

APPENDIX 16.1

EXTRACT FROM THE GENERAL MUSIC PROGRAMME (GMP) SYLLABUS

The learning outcomes are organized around five overarching learning objectives (LOs). All learning outcomes should be addressed and learned in an integrative manner, where elements and concepts are learned through active musical experiences, such as music creation and performance, as well as movement in music. Where the display of musical skills (listening, creating, and performing) is involved, it should draw on students' learning and understanding of musical elements and concepts. Figure 16.1 summarizes the approach in which the five LOs can be achieved.

ASSESSMENT

Assessment is integral to the teaching and learning process and should be carried out regularly to provide students with information about their strengths and to help them bridge gaps in learning. The information also allows teachers to review their teaching approaches and strategies. Music assessments could be carried out in a variety of ways to facilitate students' learning. These include listening activities (which could include responding through movement), music performances, improvisation or composition tasks, written assignments, or reflective journals.

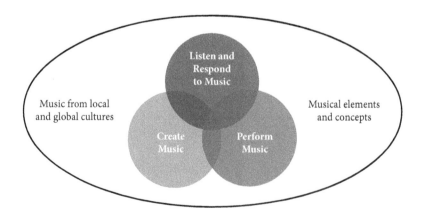

FIGURE 16.1 Summary of the five learning outcomes in GMP.

While it is not necessary to assess all the learning outcomes in one specific assessment task, teachers should ensure that all five learning objectives are addressed in the course of the year.

APPENDIX 16.2

ASSESSMENT OBJECTIVES OF 2016 O LEVEL MUSIC (6085)

The examination will reward candidates for positive achievement in:
Component 1: Music studies

- Aural awareness, perception and discrimination in relation to music for voice, theatre, instruments, and ensemble;
- Identification and explanation of music concepts in the context of the genre/tradition/style;
- Identification and description of chords, modulations, and melodic features in western music;
- Knowledge and understanding of one Prescribed Work and one Prescribed Source Materials.

Component 21: Performing (major)

- Technical competence in one instrument or voice;
- Technical competence either in a second instrument or in an ensemble setting (first/second instrument);
- Interpretative understanding of the music performed.

Component 22: Performing (minor)

- Technical competence in one instrument or voice;
- Interpretative understanding of the music performed.

Component 31: Music writing (major)

- Use of functional harmony and counterpoint in two-part writing.

Component 32: Music writing (major and minor)

- Competence in, and understanding of, the processes of composing, through setting a short passage of poetry for voice with accompaniment.

Source: https://www.seab.gov.sg/pages/nationalExaminations/GOL/School_Candidates

Table 16.1 Contents of ABRSM and Trinity Piano Exam Syllabi Grades 1–8

Contents	ABRSM	Trinity College London
Technical Work	Scales & arpeggios • Staccato is required only at Grades 7 & 8	Scales & arpeggios • Dynamics and staccato are required. • Three short exercises focusing on tone, balance and voicing, coordination, finger & wrist strength, and flexibility.
Pieces	Three pieces, chosen from the published list(s)	Three pieces, chosen from the published list(s). *One piece may be replaced by one's own composition.*
Supporting Tests	Sight-reading and Aural	Up to and including Grade 5, *any two tests* to be chosen from: • Aural • Sight-reading • Improvisation • Musical knowledge For Grades 6, 7, & 8: • Test I: Sight-reading • Test II: Aural *or* Improvisation

Source: ABRSM (2015b); Trinity College London (2015).

APPENDIX 16.3

Examination Board Summaries

Table 16.1 summarizes the music examination content of two examination boards.

For the ABRSM, a minimum of Grade 5 theory is required for students to advance to Grades 6–8 practical exams. Trinity, however, does not have such a requirement.

With regard to assessment criteria, a minimal demonstration of playing the correct notes and timing, for example, would enable a "Pass." In general, quantitative marks coupled with qualitative comments describe the nature of the assessment.

References

Associated Board of the Royal Schools of Music (ABRSM). (2013). Revised assessment criteria from 2014. *Libretto, 2*. London, UK.

Associated Board of the Royal Schools of Music (ABRSM). (2015a). *About our examiners.* Retrieved from http://sg.abrsm.org/en/exam-support/your-guide-to-abrsm-exams/about-our-examiners/

Associated Board of the Royal Schools of Music (ABRSM). (2015b). *Piano syllabus 2015 & 2016*. London, UK: Author.

Associated Board of the Royal Schools of Music (ABRSM). (2016). *History of ABRSM*. Retrieved from http://www.abrsm.org/en/regions/singapore/singapore/about-abrsm/history/

Associated Board of the Royal Schools of Music (ABRSM). (2017). *About ABRSM*. Retrieved from http://sg.abrsm.org/en/about-abrsm/

Australian and New Zealand Cultural Arts. (2018). *Examination syllabus 2018–20: pianoforte/keyboard, theory of music*. Victoria, Australia: Australian and New Zealand Cultural Arts Limited. Retrieved from http://www.anzca.com.au/Syllabus%20PDFs/ANZCA%20Piano%20Syllabus%202018-20.pdf

Ball, S. J., Maguire, M., & Braun, A. (2012). *How schools do policy: Policy enactment in secondary schools*. Abingdon, UK: Routledge.

Boud, D. (2000). Sustainable assessment: Rethinking assessment for the learning society. *Studies in Continuing Education, 22*, 151–167.

Boud, D., & Associates. (2010). *Assessment 2020: Seven propositions for assessment reform in higher education*. Sydney, Australia: Australian Learning and Teaching Council.

Burnard, P. (2012). *Musical creativities in practice*. Oxford, UK: Oxford University Press.

Castells, M. (1997). *The power of identity*. Oxford, UK: Blackwell.

Colwell, R. (2006). Assessment's potential in music education. In *MENC handbook of research methodologies* (pp. 199–269). Oxford, UK: Oxford University Press.

Fautley, M. (2010). *Assessment in music education*. Oxford, UK: Oxford University Press.

Foucault, M. (1971). *The order of things*. New York, NY: Vintage Books.

Gipps, C. V., & Murphy, P. (1994). *A fair test? Assessment, achievement and equity*. Philadelphia, PA: Open University Press.

Hajer, M. A. (1995). *The politics of environmental discourse: Ecological modernization and the policy process*. Oxford, UK: Oxford University Press.

Heng, S. K. (2011). *Opening address by Mr Heng Swee Kiat, minister for education*. Presented at the Ministry of Education (MOE) Work Plan Seminar, Singapore.

Klenowski, V., & Wyatt-Smith, C. (2013). *Assessment for education: Standards, judgement and moderation*. London, UK: SAGE.

Leong, W. S. (2014). Understanding classroom assessment in dilemmatic spaces: Case studies of Singaporean music teachers" conceptions of classroom assessment. *Music Education Research, 16*, 454–470.

Leong, W. S., Onishi, P., Caleon, I., Suradi, S., & Low, T. (2016, July). *A preliminary study of assessment progression: Evaluation of assessment tasks and students' works from General Music Programme (GMP) in Singaporean schools*. Paper presented at 32nd World Conference International Society of Music Education Conference, Glasgow, United Kingdom.

Lum, C. H., & Dairianathan, E. (2014). Mapping musical learning: An evaluation of research in music education in Singapore. *International Journal of Music Education, 32*, 278–295.

Ministry of Education. (2005). *Greater support for teachers and school leaders*. Singapore: Singapore Government Press.

Ministry of Education. (2014). *General Music Program Syllabus (Primary and Secondary)*. Curriculum Planning and Development Division, Singapore.

Ministry of Education. (2016). *List of private schools*. Retrieved from https://www.moe.gov.sg/education/private-education/list-of-private-schools

Ministry of Education. (2017). *About the arts presentation*. Retrieved from https://www.singaporeyouthfestival.sg/arts-presentation/about-the-arts-presentation

Ng, C. M. (2016). *Ministry of Education's Committee of Supply Debate—Speech by acting minister for education (schools), Singapore*. Retrieved from https://www.moe.gov.sg/news/speeches/

moe-fy-2016-committee-of-supply-debate---speech-by-acting-minister-for-education-schools-ng-chee-meng

Ng, E. H. (2008). *Speech by Dr Ng Eng Hen, minister for education and second minister for defence*. Speech presented at the 4th Anniversary of Public Lecture at the Lee Kuan Yew School of Public Policy, Singapore.

Ng, E. H. (2010). *Speech by Dr Ng Eng Hen, minister for education and second minister for defence, at the MOE Work Plan Seminar 2010*. Speech presented at the Ngee Ann Polytechnic Convention Centre, Singapore.

OECD, Newsroom. (2013, November 3). Asian countries top OECD's latest PISA survey on state of global education. Retrieved from http://www.oecd.org/newsroom/asian-countries-top-oecd-s-latest-pisa-survey-on-state-of-global-education.htm

Paynter, J. (1997). The form of finality: A context for musical education. *British Journal of Music Education, 14*(1), 5–21.

Peggie, A. (1994). *The external music examining boards: A comparative survey*. London, UK: Rhinegold.

Royal Academy of Dance. (2015). *Examinations*. Retrieved from http://www.rad.sg/examinations.html

Sharpe, L., & Gopinathan, S. (2003). After effectiveness: New directions in the Singapore education system. *Journal of Educational Policy, 17*, 151–166.

Simons, H. (2015). Interpret in context: Generalizing from the single case in evaluation. *Evaluation, 21*, 173–188.

Singapore Work Development Agency. (2016). *SkillsFuture*. Retrieved from: http://www.skillsfuture.sg

Stead, E. P., & Lum, C. H. (2014). The development of the general music program in primary and secondary schools. In J. Zubillaga-Pow & C. K. Ho (Eds.), *Singapore soundscape: Musical renaissance of a global city* (pp. 235–250). Singapore: National Library Board.

Swanwick, K. (2002). *A basis for music education*. Abingdon, UK: Routledge.

Swanwick, K., & Taylor, D. (1982). *Discovering music: Developing the music curriculum in secondary schools*. Chicago, IL: Trafalgar Square Publishing.

Tan, S. H. (1997). *Teacher perception and pupil achievement in the new primary school music program "the active approach to music-making"* (Unpublished master's thesis). National Institute of Education, Nanyang Technological University.

The Singapore Music Teachers' Association. (2017). *6th Singapore Performers' Festival & Chamber Music Competition 2016*. Retrieved from http://www.smtasingapore.com/section/performers-festival

Torgerson, D. (2003). Democracy through policy discourse. In M. A. Hajer & H. Wagenaar (Eds.), *Deliberative policy analysis: Understanding governance in the network society* (pp. 113–138). Cambridge, UK: Cambridge University Press.

Torgerson, D. (2010). Policy discourse and public spheres: The Habermas paradox. *Critical Policy Studies, 4*(1), 1–17.

Trinity College London. (2015). *Piano syllabus: Piano, piano accompanying 2015–2017 grade exams*: Trinity College London.

World Economic Forum. (2009). *World Economic Forum—Global competitiveness report*. Retrieved from http://www3.weforum.org/docs/WEF_GlobalCompetitivenessReport_2009-10.pdf

CHAPTER 17

....

ASSESSMENT POLICY AND PRACTICE IN MUSIC EDUCATION IN TAIWAN, REPUBLIC OF CHINA (ROC)

....

MING-JEN CHUANG AND SHEAU-YUH LIN

INTRODUCTION

....

EDUCATION is the most critical foundation of human development, because human power is the most valuable source of prosperity for a nation. Hence, all Taiwanese education administrative organizations and institutes have continuously paid extreme attention to forecasting how the country's future is unfolding and using more innovative methods and planning the comprehensive and complete national education system to help children develop their individual potential. With regard to early educational perspectives for helping children and teens find their own path as they become young adults, the Ministry of Education has been focusing Taiwanese educational resources on the development of three areas: educational vitality, athletic vitality, and youthful vitality. According to past governmental achievements of Taiwanese educational departments, the Ministry of Education is working on various innovations in the current educational system to improve administrative efficiency, create robust quality of educational and political strategies, and actively implement and promote national education, sports, and youth educational development.

When it comes to educational policies, the Ministry of Education has worked energetically since 2011 to implement the President's Golden Decade National Vision that focuses on "high-quality education." The components of the President's Golden Decade National Vision comprise the following crucial areas: (1) the Early Childhood

Education and Care Act, and the Quality Preschool Education Development program; (2) establishing quality education environments, and extending basic education up to grade 12; (3) the Technical and Vocational Education Act, and Phase 2 of the Technological and Vocational Education Reform Plan; (4) the Aim for the Top University, and the Promoting University Teaching Excellence projects; (5) amendment of the Family Education Act, and the establishment of locally available ongoing learning and education for all senior citizens; (6) the Study-in-Taiwan Enhancement Program, and the 8-Year Chinese Language Education Export Plan; (7) the White Paper on Teacher Education; (8) Phase I of the 5-year Aesthetic Education Plan to boost arts education; (9) the E-learning Promotion Plan, and the Expansion of Digital Opportunities in Remote Areas project; (10) the Special Education Act, and setting up of an effective support system; (11) amending of the Education Act for Indigenous Peoples, and implementing and promoting the 5-year Indigenous Education Development Program begun in 2011; (12) drafting of the Student Guidance and Counseling Act, which has now been promulgated, working on creating sustainable friendly campuses; (13) the promotion of the Sports Island Project and implementation of the Physical Education and Sports Policy White Paper; and (14) drafting Youth Policy Guidelines and vigorously working to facilitate provision of a diverse range of development pathways for young people (http://www.nownews.com/n/2011/10/12/474621).

The year 2015 was an extremely important year of innovation action for the Ministry of Education because the Ministry not only steadfastly continued our professional collaboration with multifaceted creative approaches but also explored ways to implement new educational thoughts, new educational ways, working with new people, and new perceptions. Particularly in Taiwan, the Ministry of Education has always played a decisively key role in the integration of diversified education resources from all different sectors, for instituting and implementing national education policies and presenting forward-looking and extremely practical government policies that can bring about noticeable positive transformations in the nation's educational system. Table 17.1 presents the education system in Taiwan.

In detail, the current system in Taiwan provides students with up to 20 years of education, which includes 6 years of primary education, 3 years of junior high school, 3 years of senior secondary school, 4 to 7 years of college or university, 1 to 4 years for a master's degree, and 2 to 7 years for a doctoral degree. A 9-year compulsory education system was put into effect in SY1968, which comprised 6 years of elementary education and 3 years of junior high school. To offer more diverse development opportunities for junior high school students, technical arts education is included in addition to the regular curriculum. The practical classes allow students to better realize vocational education and their future career choices including various arts. Twelve-year basic education was carried out in SY2014. Following the 9-year compulsory education requirement, Taiwanese senior secondary education covers 3 years of schooling and includes regular senior secondary schools, skill-based senior secondary schools, comprehensive senior secondary schools, and specialty-based senior secondary schools. After 3 years of secondary school, students may then choose a 2-year or 5-year junior college education and 4-year

Table 17.1 The Education System in Taiwan

Education	School/Level	Grade levels		Age range		No. of years
		From	To	From	To	
Primary	Elementary	1	6	7	12	6
Middle	Junior High School	7	9	13	15	3
Secondary	Senior High School	10	12	16	18	3
Tertiary	Tertiary					

university/college school education. In Taiwan, 2-year and 5-year junior college education can be classified according to admission requirements into 5-year junior colleges and 2-year junior colleges. Five-year junior colleges admit graduates of junior high schools, whereas 2-year junior colleges admit graduates of skill-based senior secondary schools. As to the 4-year university/college and graduate school education, the maximum study period for university education (including universities, colleges, universities of technology, and technical colleges) is 4 years (the postbachelor second specialty program is 1–2 years, while the bachelor's program is usually 2 years), and internships can last one-half to 2 years depending on the needs of the subject. After a 4-year university/college education, students may pursue 1- to 4-year master's degree education. To continue their education, a further 2- to 7-year doctoral education is provided to graduates who are in university/college programs (see http://english.moe.gov.tw/ct.asp?xItem=15742&CtNo de=11434&mp=11).

Furthermore, the Ministry of Education also offers a series of supplementary and continuing education, because supplementary and continuing education institutions provide extensive and comprehensive learning opportunities for the general public. Significantly, this supplementary and continuing education is divided into general supplementary education, continuing education, and short-term supplementary education.

At the start of this chapter, we affirmed our belief that education is the main foundation of a nation; hence, the Ministry of Education has designed teacher education programs for students who desire to be teachers. The Taiwanese teacher education system, consisting of multiple providers, serves to screen potential teacher candidates and establish a pool of prospective teachers. Teachers who teach in preschool, primary school, junior high school, and senior secondary school are trained in universities that house teacher training programs or centers. These institutions are also responsible for supplying in-service training and guidance for local education practitioners. The 2012 Education White Paper published by the Ministry of Education on teacher education elaborated on pre-employment training, counseling-infused teaching, and the teacher's professional development and support system. The paper included 9 developmental strategies and 28 action plans that constituted a comprehensive plan for the education of teachers at all levels and for all subjects. To protect the teacher's professional status and the student's right to education, the Ministry of Education promotes a professional development evaluation system for teachers in primary and secondary education. As a response to the implementation of 12-year basic education, the Ministry of Education plans to improve professional knowledge and skills for effective teaching, multiple evaluations, and differentiated knowledge among teachers.

To consolidate the foundations of arts education in Taiwan, the Arts Education Act was promulgated in 1997 and continuously amended. Regarding its general principles, the purposes of arts education are to cultivate artistic talent, enhance the understanding of the public to the arts, strengthen their sense of aesthetics and creativity, enrich their spiritual life, and raise the overall level of culture. Arts education is implemented in three ways: through professional arts education offered at schools, general arts education offered at schools, and arts education offered to the public. Among them, professional arts education offered at schools is to be provided by the art departments through classes for artistically gifted students at senior high schools, junior high schools, and elementary schools. The general arts education offered at schools aims to implement effective education in art subjects, offering relevant arts courses and art appreciation courses, and enhancing the materials and teaching methods used. The Ministry of Education prescribes unified curriculum standards to ensure consistency in the courses. Arts education for the public refers to the provision of various educational activities relating to art among the general public in addition to the arts education provided in schools (Ministry of Education, 2015).

Music programs in schools include general music programs and artistic talent music programs in Taiwan. K-12 schools offer general music programs; however, artistic talent music programs are offered from the 3rd grade (age 8) to 12th grade (age 18). With this brief introduction to the overall education and arts education system in Taiwan as a foundation, we now discuss several topics related to assessment policies: artistic talent music programs, admissions to the artistic talent music programs in elementary and junior high schools, joint admissions to the artistic talent music program in senior high schools, college joint admissions (first year), music assessment related regulations for compulsory education, and literature related to music assessment in general music instruction. Discussion and implications then follow.

ARTISTIC TALENT MUSIC PROGRAMS

Artistic talent programs in Taiwan, including music, dance, and visual arts, benefit from a significant arts education system created and designed in alignment with the general education system to ensure that the arts education system is inseparable from the general education system. Students with talents in the arts must take general education courses, additional arts training and practical courses simultaneously. The general subjects, including Mandarin and English, have continuously been taught and are part of the entrance examinations in the Program Joint Admission System (PJAS) in the senior high school and university phases.

Regarding artistic talent music programs, the programs begin in 3rd grade (ages 8–9) and continue through the 12th grade (ages 17–18). Artistic talent music programs are offered from grades 3 through 6 (ages 8–12) in elementary schools, grades 7–9 (ages 13–15) in junior high schools, and grades 10–12 (ages 16–18) in senior high schools. Therefore, 2nd grade (ages 7–8) students who have talents in music can audition for studying in the 3rd grade artistic talent music classes. Furthermore, 6th grade students audition for the 7th grade artistic talent music classes and 9th graders do that for the 10th grade classes. Students in grades 3, 4, 5, 7, 8, 10, and 11 may audition as transfer students to study in their next grade level of these programs. However, the number of total students at each grade level is limited to no more than 30 per class.

Admissions to the Artistic Talent Music Programs in Elementary and Junior High Schools

The artistic talent music classes of elementary (grade 3) and junior high school (grade 7) recruit students from April to May each year. The recruitment practical music examination tests basic music capability and music performance ability. The basic music capability test covers three main sessions: sight-singing, dictation, and fundamental music knowledge and conceptions of music theory. Furthermore, some high-performing music students are exempted from the recruitment music test if they have obtained the first, second, and third places in an international music competition or the national music competitions held by the Taiwanese government. The applied admission procedures of the artistic talent music classes of elementary (grade 3) and junior high school (grade 7) are described in Figure 17.1.

The practical examination audition for music usually includes sight-reading and performance on the major instrument, sight-singing, and a rhythm ability test at the elementary school level. There are additional tests, including performance of minor (secondary) instrument, dictation, and a music knowledge test (fundamental music theory, Western, Chinese, Taiwanese music history) at the junior high school level. Students' majors and minors can be Western music instruments or Chinese traditional music instruments. Students are encouraged to choose piano as their major or minor instrument at the elementary and junior high school levels. There are up to six audition groups of Western music instruments: piano, strings, wind/brass, percussion, vocal, and composition. There are three crucial audition groups of Chinese traditional music instruments: blowpipe instruments, bowed strings, and plucked zithers.

Elementary and junior high schools in certain cities or counties in Taiwan conduct joint admission examinations. However, several schools hold student recruitment examinations on their own. Although these schools have their own requirements and criteria for practical examinations, the contents and procedures of their student recruitment examinations are approved by the Board of Education in their own local governments. Therefore, the contents and criteria of the practical examinations vary in different areas of Taiwan.

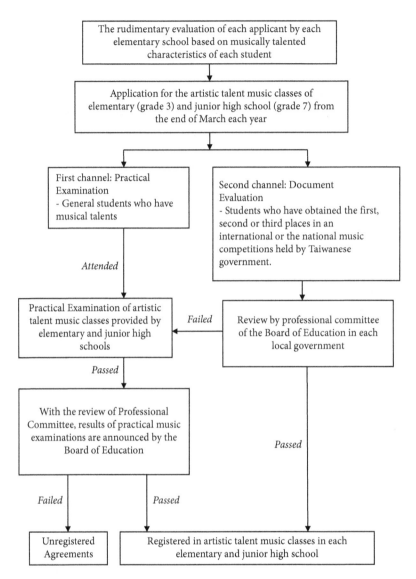

FIGURE 17.1 Framework of application procedures for admission to artistic talent music classes of elementary and junior high schools.

Note: These procedures are also suitable for the recruitment of transfer students.

Joint Admissions to the Artistic Talent Music Programs in Senior High Schools

Based on the Artistic Talent Music Program Joint Admission Prospectus, the Artistic Talent Music Program Joint Admission System (ATMPJAS) for admission to senior high schools (grade 10, age 16) are held and implemented in northern, middle, southern, and eastern Taiwan at the end of April each year. The practical music examination tests basic music knowledge (such as music theory, music history) and music performance (on major and minor instruments).

The practical examination includes the following parts: (1) a sight-singing test; (2) a dictation test (including intervals, rhythms, melody, two-part melody, chords, harmony progression); (3) a music theory test (including basic harmony, Western, Chinese, Taiwanese music history); (4) performance on the major instrument (performance assessment); and (5) performance on the minor instrument (performance assessment).

The content of the dictation test usually consists of the following categories and items: (1) interval recognition (10%), for example, usually 10 items include perfect 4th, perfect 5th, perfect octave, major 2nd, major 3rd, major 6th, major 7th, augmented 4th, and diminished 5th; (2) rhythm (20%), for example, usually three items include duple meter (4/4) and compound meter (6/8), each item consists of 2 measures; (3) single-melody dictation (15%), for example, usually only one item, 3 measures in duple or triple meter; (4) two-part dictation (25%), for example, usually only one item, 3 measures in duple or triple meter; (5) chord recognition (10%), for example, usually 10 items include major triads, minor triads, diminished 3rds, seventh chords (diminished 7th, dominant 7th); and (6) harmonic progression (20%), usually only one item, consists of major or minor keys, includes I, V, vi, IV, V7, ii in a major key.

The music theory test consists of (1) music knowledge (30%), 30 multiple-choice items including listening to music excerpts and then identifying specific music periods or styles, Chinese music history, Taiwanese music history, Western music history; (2) interval identification (10%), 10 items including perfect 4th, perfect 5th, perfect octave, major 2nd, major 3rd, major 6th, major 7th, augmented 4th, or diminished 5th presented on G clef, F clef, C clef, and treble/bass clef; (3) scales (10%), 5 items including major scales, harmonic or melodic minor scales, church modes, pentatonic scales, and whole-tone scales; (4) transposition (20%), usually 4 items, including assigned specific key for melody transposition (for example, A major to D major key), assigned specific interval for melody transposition (for example, each tone is moved upward to major 3rd interval), and transposing instruments; (5) chords (10%), assigned chord inversion, including major triads, minor triads, diminished 7ths, dominant 7ths, augmented triads, or diminished triads; and (6) harmonic progression (20%), only one item, major or minor keys, figured bass offered four-part harmonic progression. The application procedures for admission of the ATMPJAS in senior high schools are shown as Figure 17.2.

College Joint Admissions (First Year)

To be admitted to colleges/universities in Taiwan, there are three paths to choose from: through the stars program, through personal application, and through admission by examination and placement. Please see Figure 17.3.

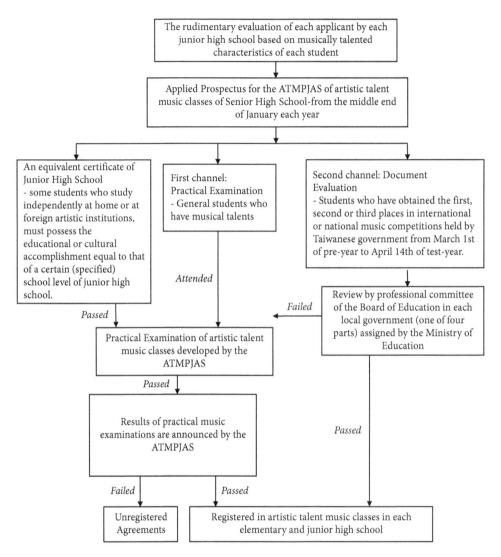

FIGURE 17.2 Framework of application procedures for admission to the ATMPJAS in senior high schools.

Note: These procedures are also suitable for the recruitment of transfer students.

The two institutes that account for college joint admission are the College Entrance Examination Center (CEEC) and the Joint Committee of College Admission Practical Examinations (CAPE). The CEEC is the most important testing institution in Taiwan. One of its primary functions is to develop and administer the General Scholastic Ability Test and the Advanced Subjects Test. These examinations are taken by students in their last year of senior high school, and are an important component of the college admission process. For the past 20 some years, CEEC has helped millions of high school graduates enroll in their desired colleges or universities. On the other hand, the CAPE is the most

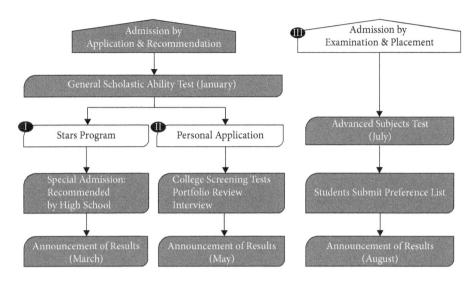

FIGURE 17.3 The three paths to be admitted to colleges/universities in Taiwan.

important practice-oriented subjects-related testing institution in Taiwan. One of its primary functions is to develop and administer the examinations in the disciplines of music, fine arts, and physical education. These examinations are taken by students in their last year of senior high school and are an important component of the college admission process.

According to the College Music Program Joint Admissions Prospectus, the College Music Program Joint Admissions System (CMPJAS) for college joint admissions is initiated by CAPE at the end of October each year. The practical music examination tests basic music knowledge and music performance. Significantly, students who study independently at home or at foreign arts institutions must demonstrate the educational or cultural accomplishment expected at the senior high school level.

The committee of the CMPJAS holds the annual Music Practical Examination for applicants for three to four successive days in January or February. The applicants choose their examination subjects as the basis for their admission to music-related programs in colleges. There are five subject tests to be chosen, namely, dictation, music theory, sight-singing, and performance on their major and minor instruments. All test-taking related regulations are detailed in the annually updated admission handbooks.

Each music department specifies their weighted proportions of academic and music subjects. Table 17.2 presents the Department of Music at University of Taipei as an example.

In terms of the test administration venues, the dictation and music theory tests are taken in the same place, at the same time and on the same date for all test takers. The sight-singing and major/minor instrument performance tests are taken separately and individually, with 7 to 13 judges forming different groups of jury committees and the applicants taking the tests one by one. Special students are offered customized-assistance to meet with their needs.

Table 17.2 Weighted Proportions of Academic and Music Subjects for 2017 Admission to the Department of Music, University of Taipei

Academic subjects calculated and proportions weighted			Music subjects calculated and proportions weighted		
Chinese	1	10%	Major	15	
English	1		Minor	2	
			Music theory	1	90%
			Sight-singing	1	
			Dictation	1	

Dictation Test

The 2016 admission examination dictation test consisted of items in interval recognition (10%), rhythm (20%), single-melody dictation (15%), two-part dictation (25%), chord recognition (10%), and harmonic progression (20%). The test is about 25 minutes long. All dictation answers are written down on answer sheets, and evaluated and scored later by judges through established pre-evaluation and re-evaluation procedures. The test content is posted publicly on the official website afterward.

Music Theory Test

The 2016 admission examination music theory test consisted of items in basic harmony (20%), basic music theory (interval, scale, transposition, modulation, music terminology, and other, weighing 40%), and music basic knowledge (40%). The test is about 50 minutes long. All answers are written down on answer sheets and evaluated and scored later by judges through established pre-evaluation and re-evaluation procedures. Only the multiple-choice items and answers are posted publicly on the official website afterward.

Sight-Singing Test

The sight-singing test is designed for the applicants to sight-sing three different purposefully composed pieces on the spot. The three pieces are normally four measures in length and increase in the difficulty level in terms of tonality, interval, rhythm, and meter. The test-taker can preview the pieces only when the test-taker before him or her is taking the examination. There are a dozen sets of pieces based on the same music schemes to be sung in alternation.

Majors Test

The applicants choose only one major area from seven categories. They are the piano, voice, strings, winds, percussions, composition, and Chinese traditional instrument. These examinations take place in different testing locations on different dates with different repertoire and groups of judges. For example, students who choose the piano as their major instrument have to take the piano tests in two sites: the first site to perform keyboard work by Johann Sebastian Bach (1685–1750) and any fast sonata movement by Joseph Haydn (1732–1809), Wolfgang Amadeus Mozart (1756–1791) or Ludwig van Beethoven (1770–1827); the second site to play assigned scale-arpeggio-cadence and their self-chosen piece of piano music.

Minors Test

The applicants can choose only one minor area from seven categories. Similar to the majors' categories, they are the piano, voice, strings, winds, percussions, composition, and Chinese traditional instruments. These examinations take place in different testing locations on different dates with different repertoire and groups of judges. For example, applicants who choose the piano as their minor instrument have to perform only their self-chosen piece of piano music.

MUSIC ASSESSMENT RELATED REGULATIONS FOR COMPULSORY EDUCATION

The Arts Education Act demanded that the Ministry of Education prescribe unified curriculum standards/guidelines to ensure consistency in the courses (Ministry of Education, 2015). This section deals with music assessment-related regulations of various music curriculum standards and guidelines in general music education offered at schools for compulsory education.

As mentioned before, the general arts education offered at schools aims to implement effective education in art subjects, offering relevant arts courses and art appreciation courses and enhancing the materials and teaching methods used. Since curriculum, instruction, and assessment are closely interrelated, music assessment related regulations can be easily identified in our national curriculum standards/guidelines documents.

Basic education was compulsory for 9 years for elementary and junior high school students in Taiwan for nearly 50 years, and was extended to 12 years in 2014. The Ministry of Education has been mainly playing the role of providing national standards or guidelines for implementation. S.-Y. Lin (2013) studied the six most recently released music-related curriculum standards and guidelines at the compulsory education levels

(Ministry of Education, 1975, 1985, 1993, 1994, 2003, 2008). The former four were music standards, while the latter two were titled "guidelines."

These six documents shared several commonalities: (1) they all addressed music assessment under the session of "implementation approaches/essentials" and presented music assessment issues normally near the ending portion of the standards or guidelines—seeming to reflect the concept that assessment is to comply with the nature of curriculum and instruction, and that curriculum, instruction, and assessment go hand in hand for the success of education; (2) all addressed the importance and need for the balance between both formative and summative assessments; (3) all stated that items related to major instructional content should be feasibly assessed; and (4) all encouraged music educators to strive for objective assessment while taking the needs of special students (for example, those undergoing voice change; those who need remedial instruction) into consideration.

On the other hand, besides the obvious fact that the *Grade 1–9 Curriculum Guidelines* (Ministry of Education, 2003, 2008) were more arts-education-oriented and less specific-discipline-based than other standard documents, there were differences among these policy documents in music assessment at the compulsory education level: (1) the terms changed from "evaluation" to "assessment," indicating the move toward more precision in terminology; (2) the suggested scoring percentages, for instance, among the cognitive, psychomotor, and affective domains, changed from specified to unspecified, indicating the tendency to leave more room for teachers to develop their own scoring approaches; (3) more details such as assessment principles, examples, and approaches were provided for the more updated renditions, particularly the two curriculum guidelines, which seemed to indicate improvement in assessment professionalism; (4) a wider variety of assessment approaches were identified, indicating new trends in the disciplines of music assessment; and (5) they seemed to reveal different interpretations of the affective domain, confirming the complexity of affective assessment (S.-Y. Lin, 2013).

Taking the *Grade 1–9 Curriculum Guidelines* issued by the Ministry of Education (2008) for example, addressed descriptions of the principles and approaches of assessment in general music classes. The principles state that teaching assessment should, based on the curriculum guidelines' competence indicators and the content taught, adopt multiple-assessment approaches to balance formative and summative assessment and to accommodate the various methods of performance assessment, dynamic assessment, authentic assessment, and portfolio assessment when appropriate. This process aims to shed light on students' multifaceted learning outcomes.

With regard to assessment methods, a wide array of approaches are mentioned in the *Grade 1–9 Curriculum Guidelines* (Ministry of Education, 2008), including both traditional methods such as observation and alternatives such as questionnaire surveys, anecdotal records, self-reports, and forms of checklists, rating scales, or rubrics, depending on the instructional objectives. The main point is to take into consideration the cognitive, psychomotor, and affective domains, and to feasibly incorporate quantitative as well as qualitative data to reflect students' learning process and outcomes.

LITERATURE RELATED TO MUSIC ASSESSMENT IN GENERAL MUSIC INSTRUCTION

When considering a broader definition of music assessment, the majority of music education- related literature had something to do with assessment. However, if a narrower definition is adopted, the literature related to music assessment published from 1994 to 2016 in Taiwan can be divided into three main categories: (1) test development driven, (2) instructional assessment oriented, and (3) others.

Test-Development-Driven Literature

Music researchers used formal testing and examination to develop measures for aptitude tests and achievement tests. Chen (2003) designed a computer-based online music aptitude test for primary students. Achievement tests were developed for comprehensive cognitive learning outcomes testing (Chang, 2003; Ho, 2005), and for 5th-grade students in a computerized format (W.-C. Lin, 2013). Specific music element identification or recognition achievement tests dealt with melodic-aural ability (Li, 2004), aural-visual tonal ability (Juan, 2015), rhythm perception (Cheng, 2004), two-part music identification (I.-C. Huang, 2004), and mode melody recognition (Shiu, 2004). Some tests were developed to assess certain musical behaviors, such as music appreciation (Chao, 2013), or creative thinking in music (C.-P. Chang, 2002).

It is interesting to note that among the works just mentioned, four were from a department of educational testing and statistics-related program rather than a music one. Besides, authors developed tests to assess certain musical concepts such as melody, mode, rhythm, texture, and so forth, seeming to reflect the importance of musical elements perception in music instruction. Inaddition, selected tests developed by world-renowned researchers were incorporated for statistical and research reasons. Gordon's *Intermediate Measures of Music Audiation* were used to examine the test's criterion-related validity and the construct validity (H.-W. Chang, 2003). Gordon's *Musical Aptitude Profile* (Cheng, 2004) and Webster's *Measure of Creative Thinking in Music* (C.-P. Chang, 2002) were translated or transformed for test formulation. Lastly, three authors strived to develop computerized on-line tests, emphasizing their beliefs in technology-assisted assessment.

Instructional Assessment-Oriented Literature

This category occupied a major portion of the total literature and was difficult to summarize due to its diverse and complex nature.

Music assessment in formal education has always been the responsibility of music teachers in Taiwan. Music teachers used to assess students for music theory, singing, and recorder playing through paper-and-pencil tests and performance assessments; the implementation of *Grade 1–9 Curriculum of the Arts and Humanities* learning area made students' worksheets replace paper-and-pencil tests while performance assessment remained the same (M.-L. Lai, 2005).

Alternative assessment approaches such as rubrics were used in one study to investigate their development and application in 4th-grade music instruction (Tang, 2006). Portfolio assessment was adopted in several studies to assess students' music learning (Hsu, 2005; P.-H. Huang, 2007), to investigate the learning and teaching effectiveness of a music appreciation course (Chung, 2008) and singing instruction (S.-N. Lai, 2007), and to study certain curricular model such as Arts PROPEL (Fu, 2012; C.-Y. Lin, 2010). Hsieh (2001, 2002) organized a team of music teachers to be engaged in a research project for developing 4th-grade music learning assessment measures. Exemplification materials were designed for a wide variety of music behavior including singing, recorder performing, music appreciation, improvisation and composition, and music reading. The contextual consideration and feedback languages of music assessment were particularly addressed. M.-L. Lai (2005) studied assessment approaches used by junior high school music teachers to investigate how these teachers assessed in response to the implementation of the *Grade 1–9 Curriculum*. Recommendations of this study include the improvement of the structure of worksheets, the improvement of performance assessment, and the establishment of music class portfolios. S.-Y. Lin (2005) developed assessment tools for the implementation of Arts PROPEL curriculum model in music composition instruction. Results of this study indicated positively the use of alternative assessment approaches to music composition.

The authors just mentioned primarily used action research or case study methodologies, probably due to their nontraditional inclination. Besides those studies conducted for degree regulations, the others were funded by the National Science Council (NSC, the predecessor to the Ministry of Science and Technology)—the highest government agency in Taiwan responsible for promoting the development of science and technology.

Other Literature

The third category of music assessment related literature was neither test-development-driven nor instructional assessment-oriented. Several phenomena were observed in theses in this category: (1) the purposes of these theses seemed to be even more varied in nature; (2) the participants included music teachers in many cases; (3) the survey method was used most often; (4) some of them incorporated or modified other research measures as their research instruments; and (5) not only the concepts but also the practices of music assessment were examined. To take some examples, one author conducted content analyses in music assessment-related theses (T.-C. Huang, 2007); one surveyed elementary school students' anxiety for music teaching and assessment activities (S.-T. Chang, 2011); one examined how different testing directions influenced 6th-grade students' mode melody recognition (Liao, 2010); and one researched assessment literacy and implementation for junior high school music teachers (C.-Y. Huang, 2015). Three studies surveyed the concepts and current practices of music assessment at the elementary or junior high school levels (Y.-J. Chen, 2012; Chi, 2007; Wu, 2011).

These assessment-related survey studies investigated a wider scope of music assessment issues, thus they helped to shed light on a wider picture of studies. What were the findings of these surveys related to music assessment? One author concluded that music teachers regarded performance assessment and observation as the most reasonable, practical, and common assessments to use because of their easy implementation and concrete assessing standards (Wu, 2011). Another (Y.-J. Chen, 2012) found that the most frequently used assessments were instrument playing assessment, singing assessment, musical reading and notating assessment, and music listening assessment; less used assessments were music knowledge assessment, ear-training assessment, and composition assessment. Still another concluded that the assessment of music fundamentals, singing, instrument performing, creating, and appreciation each possessed special characteristics and were different from each other in assessment content, method, frequency, people involved, and grading/marking system; the factors of "lack of time to implement assessment" and "overly large class size" were found to be the main obstacles to the practices of music assessment; most music teachers agreed with the ideas of multiple assessments, but their viewpoints diverged when it came to whether multiple assessments caused them teaching burdens (Chi, 2007).

Summary

Content analysis of music assessment related literature in Taiwan reveals positive growth. Most of the studies were from teacher-education-related universities and accomplished by graduate students of music programs, and some were from educational-testing-related institutes. Their participants consisted mostly of higher grade-level general music class students and music teachers. Most of the assessment instruments were generated by teachers in a self-developed way while modifying others' tools whenever feasible. Traditional approaches such as observation and paper-and-pencil tests were not ignored in terms of assessment strategies, while alternative methods including performance assessments gradually obtained attention. Overall, music assessment means and types are found to be increasingly pluralistic in Taiwan.

DISCUSSION AND IMPLICATIONS

Arts education in Taiwan is implemented in three ways: through professional arts education offered at schools, general arts education offered at schools, and arts education offered to the public. This chapter excludes assessment issues concerning music education offered to the public and rather, addresses (1) assessments in joint admissions of the professional music education and (2) assessment in general music education offered at schools.

The assessments in joint admissions in professional music education were similar across school levels. All of the practical examination auditions for music emphasize students' music achievement, including music ability of sight-singing, sight-reading, dictation, music theory and history, major instruments, and minor instruments. Through the examination audition, students who have musical potential could be discovered and have the opportunity to study in artistic talent music programs or be admitted to music departments, enabling students to further develop their professional musical skills. However, appropriate test characteristics (such as content validity, judge reliability) and audition approaches (such as required songs, selective songs, and test administration venues) are challenging for artistic talent music programs to implement. More related research should be conducted.

With regard to the assessment in general music education offered in schools, classroom-based assessments are mostly self-developed instruments and are consistently found in research studies, despite their differences in emphasis on either qualitative or quantitative data, on either conventional paper-and-pencil tests or alternative assessment approaches, on either cognitive, affective, or psychomotor aspects (S.-Y. Lin, 2007). Several issues observed from these studies are noteworthy. The studies were completed mostly by master's students and government-funded project researchers out of music education related departments as well as departments of educational testing or psychology orientations. This phenomenon seems to imply that the assessment concepts and statistics were challenging to music researchers, and that cross-discipline scholarship helped the implementation of music assessment-related investigation. Also, factors such as cultural background, home environment, music learning experience, gender, or age level were recommended in some studies for further investigation. Our deduction is that music assessment researchers tend to believe that music assessment has to be studied under a broader perspective and in a more authentic context. Music assessment should not be studied alone while ignoring its complexity. Additionally, world-renowned measures such as Gordon's *Musical Aptitude Profile* were included for statistical as well as research reasons in some studies. The need for and lack of standardized music assessment measures seems to be an undeniable phenomenon. We hope there will be continued efforts to develop standardized music assessment measures similar to the late Edwin Gordon's work. Finally, in Taiwan there is growing interest research in the development of alternative assessment tools and tests for specific music ability. In order to bridge the gap between assessment practices and assessment research, more effort needs to be taken to build assessment knowledge bases, formulate cross-disciplinary cooperation, and address the contextual integration of curriculum, instruction, and assessment.

REFERENCES

Chang, C.-P. (2002). *The development of the measure of creative thinking in music for elementary school children* (Unpublished master's thesis). National Taichung College of Education, Taichung.

Chang, H.-W. (2003). *A primary music test for fourth graders* (Unpublished master's thesis). National Pingtung College of Education, Pingtung.

Chang, S.-T. (2011). *A survey study of anxiety for music teaching and assessing activities of elementary school students* (Unpublished master's thesis). Taipei Municipal University of Education.

Chao, H.-C. (2013). *Arts and humanities of sixth graders music appreciation computer quiz questions preparation* (Unpublished master's thesis). National Taichung University of Education, Taichung.

Chen, Y.-T. (2003). *Development of music aptitude tests for primary school students* (Unpublished master's thesis). National Taichung College of Education, Taichung.

Chen, Y.-J. (2012). *A survey of current practices of elementary general music teachers using instructional assessment methods in Yunlin County* (Unpublished master's thesis). National Taichung University of Education, Taichung.

Cheng, S.-Y. (2004). *A study of the relationship between the rhythm perception of fourth to sixth grades Taiwanese children and their home environment and music experience* (Unpublished master's thesis). National Taipei College of Education, Taipei.

Chi, Y.-C. (2007). *An investigation of the practice status of junior high school music assessment* (Unpublished master's thesis). National Taiwan Normal University, Taipei.

Chung, C.-C. (2008). *Action research for portfolio assessment application to music teaching: An instance of music appreciation course in the sixth grade of elementary school* (Unpublished master's thesis). National Pingtung University of Education, Pingtung.

Fu, H.-C. (2012). *A study of the arts PROPEL curriculum model applied to eighth-graders music composing* (Unpublished master's thesis). National University of Tainan, Tainan.

Ho, Y.-C. (2005). *The development of a music achievement test for junior high school students* (Unpublished master's thesis). National Taiwan University of Science and Technology, Taipei.

Hsieh, Y.-M. (2001). *Investigation of the development of fourth-grade music learning portfolio assessment measures I.* (NSC 89-2411-H-024-008)

Hsieh, Y.-M. (2002). *Investigation of the development of fourth-grade music learning portfolio assessment measures II.* (NSC 90-2411-H-024-002)

Hsu, H.-W. (2005). *The use of portfolio as assessment in general music class: A case study of the third grade* (Unpublished master's thesis). National Taipei College of Education, Taipei.

Huang, C.-Y. (2015). *A survey on the assessment literacy and implementation in music classes-taken junior high school music teachers in Taipei City* (Unpublished master's thesis). National Taiwan Normal University, Taipei.

Huang, I.-C. (2004). *Two-part music identification abilities of fifth grade students* (Unpublished master's thesis). National Taipei College of Education, Taipei.

Huang, P.-H. (2007). *A case study of elementary music teachers developing teaching portfolios for assessing students' music learning* (Unpublished master's thesis). National Taipei University of Education, Taipei.

Huang, T.-C. (2007). *Content analysis of music assessment related theses between 1994–2007 in Taiwan* (Unpublished master's thesis). Taipei Municipal University of Education, Taipei.

Juan, H.-W. (2015). *A study on design and measurement of an aural-visual tonal test for sixth graders in Taipei City* (Unpublished master's thesis). National Taiwan Normal University, Taipei.

Lai, M.-L. (2005). Assessment approaches used by Taiwanese music teachers in junior high schools. In C. H. Chen & K. C. Liang (Eds.), *Proceedings of 2005 International Symposium* on *Empirical Aesthetics: Culture, Arts and Education* (pp. 151–158). Taipei: National Taiwan Normal University.

Lai, S.-N. (2007). *A study of applying portfolio assessment in singing instruction for sixth graders* (Unpublished master's thesis). National Taiwan Normal University, Taipei.

Li, C.-Y. (2004). *The survey study on melodic-aural ability of fourth-grade children in the elementary school* (Unpublished master's thesis). National Taipei College of Education, Taipei.

Liao, C.-L. (2010). *Effects of testing directions on the results of the mode melody recognition test for sixth-grade elementary students* (Unpublished master's thesis). Taipei Municipal University of Education, Taipei.

Lin, C.-Y. (2010). *A case study of using the arts PROPEL curricular rationales into the fourth grade general music classroom* (Unpublished master's thesis). National Taichung University of Education, Taichung.

Lin, S.-Y. (2005). *An empirical study of music creativity: The implementation of arts PROPEL program in elementary school music composition instruction.* (NSC 93-2411-H-133-002-)

Lin, S.-Y. (2007). Music assessment in Taiwan: Educational practices and empirical studies. In L. Bresler (Ed.), *The handbook of research in arts education* (pp. 383–385). Dordrecht, The Netherlands: Springer.

Lin, S.-Y. (2013, April 10). *The assessment regulations and implications of the music-related national standards and guidelines at the compulsory education levels in Taiwan.* Paper presented at the fourth International Symposium on Assessment in Music Education, National Taiwan Normal University, Taipei.

Lin, W.-C. (2013). *Fifth grade arts and humanities computerized music achievement test* (Unpublished master's thesis). National Taichung University of Education, Taichung.

Ministry of Education. (1975). *The curriculum standards for the subject of music at the elementary school level.* Taipei: Author.

Ministry of Education. (1985). *The curriculum standards for the subject of music at the junior high school level.* Taipei: Author.

Ministry of Education. (1993). *The curriculum standards for the subject of music at the elementary school level.* Taipei: Author.

Ministry of Education. (1994). *The curriculum standards for the subject of music at the junior high school level.* Taipei: Author.

Ministry of Education. (2003). *The grade 1–9 curriculum guidelines for the arts and humanities learning area.* Taipei: Author.

Ministry of Education. (2008). *The grade 1–9 curriculum guidelines for the arts and humanities learning area* (Revised). Taipei: Author.

Ministry of Education. (2015). *Arts education act* (Revised). Retrieved from http://law.moj.gov.tw/Eng/LawClass/LawContent.aspx?PCODE=H0170037

Shiu, J.-L. (2004). *An investigation of mode melody recognition of elementary students in central Taiwan* (Unpublished master's thesis). National Taipei College of Education, Taipei.

Tang, S.-Y. (2006). *A study of developing and applying rubrics to fourth-grade elementary music teaching* (Unpublished master's thesis). Taipei Municipal University of Education, Taipei.

Wu, Y.-L. (2011). *A survey of elementary school music teachers' opinion on the arts and humanities learning area instructional assessment methods from the Nine-Year Curriculum Guidelines in Taichung City* (Unpublished master's thesis). National Taichung University of Education, Taichung.

CHAPTER 18

MUSIC ASSESSMENT POLICY AND PRACTICE IN THE UNITED STATES

BRET P. SMITH

THE public and private education systems of the United States are not subject to direct statutory influence by the national government. Local autonomy and local control of school decisions are deeply rooted values whose influence can be detected on practically every relevant dimension of music education and assessment policy discussed in this chapter. The Tenth Amendment to the United States Constitution explicitly reserves to the states all powers not specifically delegated to the federal government, including education. In the United States, federal influence on education policy is indirect and effected through the leverage that the federal treasury can have on state legislatures and local educational authorities. The purposes of this chapter are to review and summarize aspects of governmental policy at all levels that affect the assessment practices of music teachers, and to similarly examine nongovernmental sources of "external" directives and expectations that may also guide assessment decisions in some musical contexts.

NATIONAL INFLUENCES

The general approach to documenting the history of school-based music education in the United States commences with the 1837 introduction of singing classes in the Boston public schools by Lowell Mason (Mark, 2002). University music degrees and normal school (teacher training) programs emerged in the late 19th century, and secondary schools with instrumental and vocal instruction were in place, in much their current forms, by the 1930s (Cundiff & Dykema, 1923). Each of these manifestations of formal music instruction, by virtue of their aims and objectives, carried with them assessment needs and their attendant practices. For example, to qualify in 1900 as a candidate for admission to the California State Normal School at Los Angeles (then a teacher training institution, now the University of California, Los Angeles), an applicant needed to "be able to sing the major scale, and both sing and write the diatonic intervals" (State Normal School at Los Angeles, 1900, p. 11).

Although a cabinet-level Department of Education existed briefly after the Civil War, it was demoted to a bureau within the Department of the Interior that chiefly served to gather educational data (Urban & Wagoner, 2009), and the Office of Education within the Federal Security Agency, established in 1939, became the Department of Health, Education, and Welfare in 1953 (Johnson, Dupuis, Musial, Hall, & Gollnick, 1996). The increase in federal involvement in education policy during the 1960s and the election of President James E. "Jimmy" Carter in 1976 led to the re-establishment of the current US Department of Education (USDOE). The USDOE is led by a cabinet-level secretary of education.

The Elementary and Secondary Education Act of 1965 (ESEA) represented the most extensive and costly federal education law enacted up to that date (Urban & Wagoner, 2009). The ESEA placed significant focus on disadvantaged students, which stimulated, among other things, interest in early childhood and preschool education with programs like Head Start (Elementary and Secondary Education Act, 1965; US Department of Health and Human Services, 2016). Under Title III of the ESEA, federal grant funds were made available through the Projects to Advance Creativity in Education (PACE) program. By 1969, $427 million had been awarded with 46 funded projects in music (Music Educators National Conference, 1969).

Under the presidential administration of George H. W. Bush in 1991, the America 2000 education strategy was sent to Congress (Tucker, 1992), and elements of its policy recommendations were sustained in the Goals 2000: Educate America Act signed into law by President William J. "Bill" Clinton in 1994 (Goals 2000: Educate America Act, 1994). This education reform act enumerated the areas in which all American students were expected to excel according to rigorous national standards—and in initial drafts, music and the arts were notably absent. The process leading to this act motivated arts organizations to develop the nation's first voluntary National Standards for Arts Education (Consortium of National Arts Education Associations, 1994).

The next major federal policy impact occurred with the enactment of the No Child Left Behind Act of 2001 (NCLB), a reauthorization of the 1965 ESEA (No Child Left Behind Act, 2002). This measure continued the ESEA's emphasis on the achievement of economically disadvantaged students, students from major racial and ethnic groups, and students with disabilities. While initially met with bipartisan support, NCLB sparked numerous controversies and introduced a number of terms to the public lexicon. States were responsible for "challenging academic content standards," accompanied by "challenging student achievement standards," taught by "highly qualified teachers," with student achievement measured by "high-quality, yearly student academic assessments" in order to demonstrate "adequate yearly progress." The act specified that assessments were required in at least mathematics, reading or language arts, and science (No Child

Left Behind Act, 2002). According to the Pew Charitable Trust, annual state spending on testing rose to $1.1 billion by 2008, up from $423 million at the time of the bill's passage (Vu, 2008).

The specific impact of NCLB on music education was increased advocacy to have music and the arts included in state definitions of core learning subjects, the development of assessments of student learning similar to the tests used in other subjects, and a renewed focus on teacher licensure and certification requirements consistent with the notion of a highly qualified teacher (United States Department of Education [USDOE], 2009). While some states may have strengthened the position of the arts as a core subject, there is evidence that access to music classes may have been reduced for those students at risk of failing state proficiency tests in other subjects (Gerrity, 2009; Smith & Hoffman, 2011). Elpus (2014) examined student enrollment patterns in secondary music courses post-NCLB, and concluded that the underrepresentation of Hispanic students, English language learners, and students with individualized education plans that predated NCLB may have been worsened by the implementation of the act.

To reduce the burden of NCLB requirements on local education agencies, in 2011 the USDOE offered states an option for flexibility in some of these requirements surrounding standards and assessments, school accountability and support systems, and teacher/principal evaluation (USDOE, 2012). To receive this flexibility, states were required to demonstrate the development of college- and career-ready standards and assessments in at least reading/language arts and mathematics, as well as a high-quality plan for implementation. In addition, states needed to develop, adopt, and implement teacher and principal evaluation and support systems that met several criteria, including having student growth data as a significant factor. States granted flexibility were able to establish their own annual measurable objectives (AMOs) that were "ambitious and achievable" and to establish their own incremental goals for the AMOs, were relieved of the requirement to identify Title I schools as "in need of improvement, corrective action, or restructuring," were no longer required to publish school status on state and local report cards, and were given increased flexibility to use federal funds for a variety of professional development or school improvement activities (USDOE, 2012). By 2015, 43 states, the District of Columbia, and Puerto Rico applied for and were awarded these NCLB waivers (USDOE, 2016b).

A great deal of anticipation and lobbying effort on the part of music education advocates preceded reauthorization of the ESEA in 2015. The introduction of S.1177, the Every Child Achieves Act (2015), in the US Senate, and HR 5, the Student Success Act (2015), in the House of Representatives, resulted their eventual reconciliation as the Every Student Succeeds Act of 2015 (ESSA), signed into law by President Barack Obama in December 2015. Among music educators, the most prominently publicized feature of the law was the specific inclusion of "activities and programs in music and the arts" as part of the "well-rounded educational experiences" that should be available to all students, and specifically mentioning eligibility for federal funds for magnet school programs to increase student knowledge of music (ESSA, 2015). As in NCLB, states are to maintain statewide accountability systems, which may include "innovative assessment systems" defined as "competency-based assessments, instructionally embedded assessments, interim assessments, cumulative year-end assessments, or performance-based assessments that combine into an annual summative determination for a student, which may be administered through computer adaptive assessments" (ESSA, 2015) As in previous iterations of the ESEA, only reading or language arts and mathematics are specifically required as part of the accountability system. States were required to submit their ESSA accountability plans by September 2017; an early analysis of state plans conducted on behalf of the National Association for Music Education (NAfME) showed that 28% of state plans included data from some element of arts education to be reported within accountability systems at the state level. These measures include arts enrollments, presence of certified teachers, student/teacher ratios, and arts courses offered (Tuttle, 2018).

Given the constitutionally limited federal role in the development of state and local education policies, those seeking reform in public education have relied on the influence of federal agencies and the ability to allocate federal grant funds to pursue their goals. The ESEA, NCLB, and ESSA acts regulate grant funding under Title I, focused on low-income students, and Title II, Part A, focused on teacher quality. Under Title I, schools can be eligible for various grants based on the percentage of low-income students enrolled—if over 40% funds may be used for schoolwide programs (USDOE, 2016c). Title II, Part A, defines highly qualified teachers and makes funds available to state and local education agencies to pursue the provision of them. State and local education agencies receiving these funds are required to provide evidence of gains in student academic achievement (USDOE, 2006). The budget proposal for 2018 presented by the administration of President Donald J. Trump reduces funding for Title II, Part A block grants from $1.65 billion to $400 million, and proposes changes to how the states allocate grant monies, allowing for competitive grants (Office of Management and Budget, 2017). This proposal, and similar proposed reductions in federal funding, have aroused concern among arts advocates, including NAfME (NAfME, 2016a).

Another avenue by which federal or national policy decisions can impact music education assessment is through the role of the National Endowment for the Arts (NEA). The NEA was established as an independent agency in 1965, and its activities have funded a variety of artists, arts presentation organizations, and arts education programs. By 2008, the NEA funded over 11,000 music projects involving over $375 million, and 4,000 opera projects involving over $160 million (Bauerlein & Grantham, 2009).

Reflecting the emerging focus on assessment in education, in 2005 the NEA began requiring a description of assessment practices for applicants seeking arts education funds. The agency commissioned a study published in 2012 that investigated the quality and utility of the arts assessments located through a literature review, and made recommendations for improved practice (Herpin, Washington, & Li, 2012). Among the many findings of this review and survey study were the lack of high-quality assessment tools in the arts (only 20.4% of the items reviewed were found to be relevant to the study and of high quality), the lack of research and technical reports, and a lack of clarity of understanding of the difference between arts *knowledge* and arts *skills*. The majority of publicly available assessment tools were the work of large-scale testing companies and state agencies. The authors called for the development of a clearinghouse for arts assessment information and tools, and increased professional development for the field.

The interest of the NEA in fostering progress in arts assessment is an encouraging development for arts educators, including music educators. In *How Art Works* (NEA, 2012), the agency set out a system model, measurement map, and research agenda to promote the agency's goals. In it, they acknowledge the challenging nature of arts assessment, yet present a detailed roadmap defining variables and suggesting measurable indicators. As access to NEA funds is predicated on the use of valid and reliable assessment tools in funded projects (and if the recommendations of the 2012 study are heeded), an increase in federal resources devoted to arts assessment development might be expected. However, the prospects for such funding rest on the priorities of a given presidential administration and Congress; the 2018 budget proposal of President Donald J. Trump reduces nondefense discretionary spending, eliminating funding for the NEA, the National Endowment for the Humanities (NEH), and other agencies (Office of Management and Budget, 2017).

STATE AND REGIONAL INFLUENCES

Many of the influences on music education assessment practice originate at the state and regional level, with some interactions with national policies (both governmental and nongovernmental). States control K-12 content standards, high school graduation requirements, direct transfer agreements between community and technical colleges and baccalaureate institutions, and licensure policies affecting preservice and in-service music educators.

Several consortia represent state-level policymakers and can serve as a locus of advocacy and consistency in the views of their stakeholders. The Council of Chief State School Officers (CCSSO) brings together the executives of state public school systems, and is sponsor of the Arts Education Partnership (AEP). The ArtScan website provides a searchable database of state policies in 14 areas of concern to arts education (Arts Education Partnership, 2014), illustrating the myriad approaches to state-level requirements, such as arts in the core curriculum at various grade levels, graduation requirements, alternatives for graduation, assessment requirements, and licensure requirements for arts and nonarts teachers; it allows for summaries by state as well as side-by-side comparisons.

Regional accrediting organizations, for example the Higher Learning Commission (HLC) and the Southern Association of Colleges and Schools Commission on Colleges (SACSCOC), establish standards that colleges and universities must meet with regard to many aspects of structure, funding, and governance (Council for Higher Education Accreditation, 2018). The USDOE recognizes accreditation by these organizations as the criterion for receiving funding related to student financial aid and similar programs (USDOE, 2016a). Accreditation standards typically require assessment systems with which an institution's programs monitor and assure student learning, and departments of music are therefore responsible for providing assessment evidence for music majors and the music components of general education curricula (Northwest Commission on Colleges and Universities, 2010).

University departments and schools of music that possess or aspire to accreditation from the National Association of Schools of Music (NASM) need to meet that organization's standards for the structure and content of the music education degree programs (NASM, 2015). The NASM acknowledges considerable autonomy for institutions to "identify, designate, and control... content and methodologies of tests, evaluations, and assessments" (NASM, 2015, p. 29). Within this general framework, the standards for music teacher education require a program of evaluation that "should include an initial assessment of student potential for admission to the program, periodic assessment to determine progress throughout the program, and further assessment after graduation" (p. 120). The NASM *Handbook* additionally describes expectations for music major admissions assessment; assessment of operations; the assessment component of music teacher education, music therapy, and psychology-based research curricula; and the assessment of student performance in music technology internships.

LOCAL INFLUENCES

The ultimate responsibility for establishing specific policies in American public schools rests with local school districts (known as Local Education Agencies, or LEAs in federal statutes), through an elected or appointed school board (Center for Public Education, 2016). While school districts must maintain alignment with federal and state policies, they maintain considerable autonomy to establish music curricula, implement and fund music programs, evaluate music program effectiveness, and hire and evaluate music teachers based on locally developed criteria. The National School Boards Association (NSBA) represents over 90,000 school board members in 49 states (NSBA, 2016). Educational Service Districts or Service Agencies represent districts in larger regions of a state in various endeavors, such as administering grant-funded programs and providing professional development. The Association of Educational Service Agencies (AESA) represents these groups in 45 states, accounting for about 80% of public and private schools, their employees, and students (Association of Educational Service Agencies, 2013).

State and regional music education associations, the constituent organizations of NAfME, exert a large influence on the assessment of musical performance through their sponsorship of local, regional, and state music festivals and competitions. Adjudicator ratings of such large- and small-group events, as well as solo contests, are sometimes a benchmark by which programs and teachers are deemed successful (Barnes & McCashin, 2005). These events operate under a variety of formats and with various assessment approaches, and some research has been undertaken to develop and validate performance rating scales for various ensembles (Norris & Borst, 2007; Smith & Barnes, 2007). The NAfME, in partnership with the National Federation of State High School Associations, Festival Disney, and Disney Honors, formed the National Center for Assessment and Adjudication of Musical Performances (NCAAMP) and in 2008 published *Music Adjudication Essentials*, a brief manual accompanying seminars designed to train adjudicators for national events and foster consistent performance assessment (NCAAMP: The National Center for Assessment and Adjudication of Musical Performances, 2008).

Voluntary National Standards

In addition to the direct influence of governmental bodies, accreditation organizations, and professional organizations, there are more complex interactions between these and other public and private organizations that have influenced the assessment practices of music educators. Perhaps the most influential in recent decades has been the "standards movement," a term that grew out of the dialogues of the 1980s climate of education reform. However, the Music Educators National Conference (MENC, now NAfME) promoted the development of national expectations in the form of the Goals and Objectives (GO) Project of 1969, and one of its stated aims was for evaluation (Andrews, 1970; Hoffman, 1980; Mark, 1980). These goals were primarily organizational and institutional advocacy, rather than learning goals for the nation's students; within the GO Project's work, however, several publications and projects were undertaken pertaining to curriculum and assessment, including *Instructional Objectives in Music* (Boyle, 1974).

Although the terminology of behavioral objectives was altered, the publication of the National Standards for Arts Education (Consortium of National Arts Education Associations, 1994) was a direct response to the federal call for the development of national education standards that accompanied the Goals 2000 Act, previously mentioned in the context of the NCLB legislation (Ravitch, 1995). The nine content standards in this document served as the basis for development of local music standards (and assessments) in several states and generally have served the profession as a reference point (Conway, 2008).

The next manifestation of a national standards movement followed the 2009 development of the Common Core State Standards Initiative, a project of the Council of Chief State School Officers (CCSSO) and the National Governors Association (NGA) (Common Core State Standards Initiative, 2016). In 2014, the National Coalition for Core Arts Standards released the National Core Arts Standards (State Education Agency Directors of Arts Education [SEADAE], 2014) and pilot versions of Model Cornerstone Assessments (National Coalition for Core Arts Standards, 2014; NafME, 2016b). These standards differ from prior iterations in that they are based on a model that focuses on the artistic processes of creating, performing, responding, and connecting. Within these broad process categories, students are able to engage in activities and demonstrate their learning in multiple ways. The Model Cornerstone Assessments are organized by grade band (second, fifth, and eighth grade), ensembles, guitar/keyboard/harmonizing instruments, technology, and composition/theory. Teachers are encouraged to incorporate the assessment projects into their regular curriculum and modify the tasks and rubrics to meet their specific needs (NAfME, 2016b).

The artistic-process model of the National Core Arts Standards, initially presented by Shuler (1996, 2011), was incorporated into the 1997 National Assessment of Educational Progress (NAEP) music assessment (Persky, Sandene, & Askew, 1998). Citing budget restraints, only the responding process at grade 8 was assessed in 2008 and 2016 (Keiper, Sandene, Persky, & Kuang, 2009; National Assessment Governing Board, 2017). The NAEP, or "the nation's report card," was inaugurated in 1969 and included the arts in 1971, 1978, 1997, 2008, and 2016. In the broader sense, the NAEP assessment invites international comparisons, and it is coordinated with the Progress in International Reading Literacy Study (PIRLS), the Program for International Student Assessment (PISA), and the Trends in International Mathematics and Science Study (TIMSS) (Carnoy & Rothstein, 2013; National Center for Educational Statistics, 2013, 2014, 2015; TIMMS and PIRLS International Study Center, 2015).

These large-scale assessment efforts represent a different avenue of policy influence than the "top-down" legislative mandate. By defining the assessment models, formats, and methods of analysis, they illustrate the adage "value what you assess and assess what you value." Designers of curricula, assessments, and instructional materials, as well as teachers themselves, may indeed look to the NAEP and Model Cornerstone Assessments when making their own choices. Lindquist (2010) commented on this state of "entangled influences" in mathematics education. This entanglement is illustrated in music by the fact that the objectives underlying the 1971 NAEP were developed via a contract with the testing company Educational Testing Service (ETS) beginning in 1965 (National Assessment of Educational Progress, 1970). The ETS and other companies remain well invested in the academic assessment market, music included. The framework for the 2008 NAEP in the arts was published by the National Assessment Governing Board, a 28-member group founded in 1998, with funding and assistance from the NEA, the Getty Center for Education in the Arts, the CCSSO, and the College Board—the not-for-profit publisher of the SAT and Advanced Placement (AP) tests, including music (National Assessment Governing Board, 2008; The College Board, 2016).

TESTING COMPANIES

It is fairly straightforward to trace the responses of the teaching field with regard to assessment practices when one begins with a clear policy mandate from an entity, like a government or local education authority, that is vested with the power to reward or sanction adherence to that policy. Just as a distinction can be made for customary behaviors that are de jure, or in accordance with law, and de facto, or existing in fact, we may also consider how precedents and procedures may seep into the professional consciousness of music educators from a variety of nongovernmental entities, and in doing so exert an influence on assessment practices de facto that are every bit as persistent, and effect a similar impact, as policies de jure. One of the most-discussed in recent years has been the role of for-profit testing companies within the overall policy landscape of public education in the United States.

From the contentious 1845 introduction of the first common, timed examinations in Boston (Reese, 2013) to the controversies surrounding state testing today (Hagopian, 2014), the development and provision of large-scale tests for the nation's school systems has developed into a substantial industry. Currently, several entities provide assessments that can be construed as high-stakes, with the potential to steer policies and curricula in music education. While states control the outcomes and assessments associated with K-12 student achievement and graduation requirements, national testing firms have found a resident niche in the form of Advanced Placement and International Baccalaureate programs, multistate teacher licensure consortia, and college examinations in the major fields.

Two programs designed to provide high school music students opportunity for focused study at an advanced level are the Advanced Placement (AP) and International Baccalaureate (IB) programs. The AP examinations in music are developed and administered by the College Board, while the IB exams are administered by the International Baccalaureate Organization (IBO).

The AP courses in high schools prepare students to sit for subject-area examinations resulting in scores that can serve, depending on the college or university, to meet college course credit or placement requirements. According to the College Board (2012), over 90% of American 4-year colleges and universities offer such credit or placement. Exams are scored on a 1–5 scale, with 3, "qualified," aligned with college grades of B–, C+, and C. The AP Music Theory curriculum and examination include music terminology, notational skills, compositional skills, score analysis, and aural skills; the "standard Western tonal repertoire" is assumed, and teachers are encouraged to incorporate examples of "twentieth-century art music, jazz, popular music, and the music of non-Western cultures" (The College Board, 2012, p. 7). The examination makes use of multiple-choice (with and without aural examples), written free-response (including aural dictation), and sight-singing items.

The IB programs were founded in 1968 to address a variety of aims centered on a global vision of education to develop "inquiring, knowledgeable, and caring young people who help to create a better and more peaceful world through intercultural understanding and respect" (IBO, 2015b). According to the IBO's 2015 *Statistical Bulletin*, about 3,200 students worldwide completed IB music assessments at either the Standard Level or High Level in that year (IBO, 2015a). Areas of music in the IB syllabus include music perception, creating, solo performing, and group performing; assessments include a listening paper, the musical links investigation, creating, and solo performing (IBO, 2015c).

In 2013, the ETS released the Major Field Test (MFT) in music. These tests are designed as undergraduate outcomes assessments to be administered at the end of a major course of study, and used by colleges for quality assurance, accreditation, and program improvement (ETS, 2016b). As of 2015, ETS reported *MFT: Music* score distributions for 1,222 students from 70 institutions in the *Comparative Data Guide* (ETS, 2016a). Testing areas include Music Theory (Aural, Fundamentals, and Score Analysis) and Music History (Listening, Before 1750, 1750–1890, and 1890–present), and are in multiple-choice format.

Prospective music teachers in a number of states are required to complete a performance assessment known as edTPA, developed by Stanford University's Center for Assessment, Learning, and Equity (SCALE) and administered by the Pearson corporation's Evaluation Systems group (AACTE, 2016a; Stanford Center for Assessment, Learning, and Equity, 2015). In 2016, 677 teacher preparation programs in 38 states and the District of Columbia participated in some form of edTPA implementation (AACTE, 2016b). The subject-specific assessment (music is included in the performing arts along with theater and dance) requires candidates to complete three tasks: planning for instruction and assessment, instructing and engaging students in learning, and assessing student learning. Candidate written and video evidence is evaluated by trained raters using 15 rubrics (18 in Washington State) with multiple criteria on a 5-point scale. States are able to establish their own cut scores.

Some states participate in a similar testing program for preservice teachers known as PRAXIS, administered by ETS. PRAXIS tests encompass basic academic skills, as well as over 90 subject-specific examinations including Music: Content and Instruction (subsections Music History and Theory; Performance; Instruction, Professional Issues, and Technology, and Instructional Activities) and Music: Content Knowledge (subsections Music History and Literature; Theory and Composition; Performance; and Pedagogy, Professional Issues, and Technology). These tests are computer-delivered, largely multiple-choice exams; both tests include listening examples, and the Content and Instruction exam contains some constructed-response items (Educational Testing Service, 2016c).

We should be curious about the processes used by nongovernmental (yet authoritative) panels, committees, and consortia in defining the scope and content of examinations of advanced secondary achievement and teacher licensure; in other words, how do they define their priorities and make their choices? In a recursive fashion, legislative mandates may in fact follow the test, as may be seen with the edTPA for teacher licensure. It might be presumed that states that changed their licensure requirements (by enacting changes to state law) to require the edTPA did so in part because the test existed. Whether or not it is a direct and valid instrument to assess the nuances of a particular state's philosophy of what it means to be a competent teacher may have taken a back seat to the advantages of the relative ease of implementation (with no development costs to the state) and consistency across state lines as part of a multistate consortium. It is to be expected, in that case, that teacher preparation programs adapt and align their curricula to meet the mandate that was shaped by the test itself. This situation has engendered some pointed commentary and critique on the part of the teacher education community and the public (Singer, 2014).

OTHER INFLUENCES

In this final section, I ask the reader to further consider the origin and malleability of de facto assessment practices within American music education that are not, strictly speaking, the result of policies enumerated through the laws and regulatory apparatus of governments, but may be experienced by teachers and students in a manner that is difficult to distinguish from official mandates. In addition to local school districts, state-level education departments, regional and national educational agencies and associations, and test providers, there have been initiatives promoted by performing arts centers, philanthropic foundations, industry groups, and education unions that have influenced the way that music teachers assess their students.

Opened in 1971, the John F. Kennedy Center for the Performing Arts in Washington, DC, was the culmination of the early vision of the national capital's amenities held by Pierre L'Enfant in the 19th century, First Lady Eleanor Roosevelt's idea of a National Theatre in the 1930s, and the promotion of a National Cultural Center during the Eisenhower and Kennedy administrations, to be jointly funded by federal funds and private donations (Meersman, 1980). In addition to the arts presentation functions of the Center, its advocates foresaw a broader role in the cultural life of the nation. The Center's ArtsEdge website serves as a digital repository of standards-based lesson plans (some including assessments) for elementary, middle, and high school teachers. These lessons typically integrate arts content, for example The Poetics of Hip-Hop, Rhythm and Art: Gesture Drawing, and Amazing Fibonacci lessons at the high school level join music with language arts and mathematics (Kennedy Center, 2014).

A similar effort, the Getty Center for Education in the Arts, was established by the J. Paul Getty Trust and the Getty Museum in Los Angeles in 1982. Focused on the paradigm of Discipline Based Art Education (DBAE), the Getty Center was among the groups that fueled the standards movement of the 1980s and 1990s (Duke, 1988). While primarily oriented toward the visual arts, the Getty Center's website contains lesson and unit plans aligned with music standards (for example, Art and Accessibility of Music). These lessons provide an overview, learning objectives, materials, and a standards alignment— assessment is not specifically addressed (J. Paul Getty Trust, 2016).

While not specifically developing or promoting particular assessment approaches, two organizations traditionally associated with the music industry, the NAMM Foundation and the National Association of Recording Arts and Sciences (NARAS), have entered the arena of music advocacy and bring their unique perspectives to the discussions of what music programs and curricula should encompass. Originally the National Association of Music Merchants, NAMM's advocacy website contains how-to information on creating local music coalitions. One suggestion for such coalitions is to provide annual reports to the local school boards that summarize music student achievement (Benham, 2014). The NAMM Foundation also provides grant funding for research projects on the impact of music education (NAMM Foundation, 2014).

NARAS is most likely known as the sponsor of the annual Grammy Awards. Its Grammy in the Schools program sponsors the Grammy Camp, annual educator awards, and Grammy Career Day as well as highlighting Grammy signature programs and communities. The website also provides exposure to "featured students" in popular genres who have participated in their programs (Grammy Foundation, 2016).

The National Education Association (NEA, not to be confused with the National Endowment for the Arts) and American Federation of Teachers (AFT), as labor unions with significant financial and lobbying resources, appear in the national dialogue from time to time in areas related to music, such as arts advocacy and the perceived conflict between test- and assessment-based accountability efforts and a comprehensive curriculum that includes the arts for all students. A search of the NEA.org website using the keywords "music assessment" resulted in over two million linked results; the same search of the AFT.org site yielded a more modest 1,451 results. Through their broad media access and publications, ideas and projects supported by the teacher's unions would seem to have a great likelihood of increasing their impact.

Since the earliest days of European colonization of North America, the didactic needs of music instructors have stimulated the production of music literature, method books, audio/visual media, and today, online media. This vast body of literature naturally reflects the tastes and teaching trends of the day, and with the advent of heightened interest in common learning standards and valid, reliable assessments, most contemporary music education publishers include assessments of some kind in their offerings. Within the realm of the elementary general music classroom, publishers like Silver Burdett and Macmillan/McGraw-Hill typically offer student quizzes, tests, and informal assessment suggestions in a teacher's manual, supplementary book, or online resources (McGraw-Hill Education, 2016; Pearson Education, 2016). In states like California, Florida, and Texas, which practice statewide textbook adoption, the selection of a particular textbook series or method book can have a large impact both on the teachers and students that use it, as well as the content of the book itself. Diane Ravitch documented the "mad, mad, mad" world of textbook adoptions in her book *The Language Police: How Pressure Groups Restrict What Students Learn* (2003).

A final area of music teaching and learning that should be considered in this survey is the purely private realm of the individual studio. The Music Teachers National Association (MTNA) represents 22,000 members eligible to participate in their certification programs and competitions (Music Teachers National Association [MTNA], 2016a, 2016b). MTNA competitions are sponsored at elementary, junior, senior, and young artist levels for composition, brass, piano, string, voice, woodwind, and chamber music (not all categories available at all levels). In setting the guidelines for ensemble types and repertoire, and by establishing judging criteria, MTNA's values, philosophy, and assessment attitudes will be influential on the practices of its member teachers. To become an MTNA certified teacher, one must demonstrate competence in their standard II.D, Assessing Musical Growth: "Competent music teachers utilize multiple evaluation methods regularly to assess and convey the progress of students' musical growth and performance, and to gather data for planning subsequent courses of study" (MTNA, 2016c).

The American String Teachers Association (ASTA), representing school-based string and orchestra teachers as well as private and collegiate studio string teachers, offers competitions and a Certificate Advancement Program (ASTACAP) for individual students and groups. The ASTACAP offers certificates of achievement for "technical and musical preparedness" at 11 levels (ASTA, 2016). ASTA's National Orchestra Festival, National Solo Competition, and National Youth Orchestras offer adjudicators' feedback and a national showcase for outstanding orchestras and instrumental soloists. ASTA has incorporated "alternative styles" (i.e., not Western classical music) into both solo and ensemble competitions (Williams, 2009), indicating an interest at the organizational level in a broad and inclusive curriculum.

Conclusion

To a considerable degree, American educational assessment policy mirrors the geographic and demographic diversity of the nation itself. Historically, American political discourse presents numerous examples of opposing views of the role of the national government. One contingent argues for a strong federal role in regulating aspects of health, education, and welfare—the other argues for a small federal role with considerable powers retained by the states. Matters of equitable funding, access to services, and attainment of social and educational goods are matters of public concern in either scenario, centralized or decentralized. The ESSA legislation of 2015 represents a retreat from the stronger federal role in assessment policy of the NCLB act of 2001.

The examples described in this chapter help illustrate the complexity of the organizational structures surrounding music assessment policy in the United States. When considered alongside the "extracurricular" influences of private industry and professional associations, the picture becomes more complex still. Advocates for music education in the public schools interact within a network of interrelated agencies and organizations, each with a unique constituency and sphere of influence. When viewed from the perspective of assessment, one must consider how current musical and aesthetic values are reflected in the standards of achievement and criteria for evaluation used by educators in their work. These standards may come from large-scale national efforts, or be quite local. The standards themselves suggest appropriate assessment approaches, and the use of assessment data ranges from feedback for learning to higher-stakes decisions such as teacher licensure. The involvement of for-profit publishers and test developers inspires consideration and critique of the role of the profit motive in the development, administration, and scoring of standardized tests (Fabricant & Fine, 2016; Farley, 2009).

The underlying purposes and uses of assessment—to give feedback and guide student learning, to provide a performance ranking, to provide a quality assurance measure for a teacher or school program—must always be considered by those seeking to understand music assessment in the United States. At the very least, we must hope that the needs and well-being of interested learners do not become obscured by the many voices and disparate promptings that music teachers encounter when making their assessment choices. Is it too optimistic to hope that the motto on our currency, *E pluribus unum* (out of many, one), can be our goal in music assessment? That, from many influences, we can distill one program that best serves the growth of a student? American music educators have been, and are likely to remain, largely responsible for the answer.

REFERENCES

AACTE. (2016a). *About edTPA*. Retrieved from http://edtpa.aacte.org/about-edtpa

AACTE. (2016b). *edTPA: Participation map*. Retrieved from http://edtpa.aacte.org/state-policy

American String Teachers Association (ASTA). (2016). *ASTA Certificate advancement program*. Retrieved from https://www.astastrings.org/Web/Resources/ASTA_Certificate_Advancement_Program__ASTACAP/Web/Resources/ASTACAP/ASTA_CAP.aspx?hkey=477d7064-4568-473b-b26a-9047e0579c60

Andrews, F. M. (1970). Goals and objectives for music education. *Music Educators Journal, 57*(4), 23–26.

Arts Education Partnership. (2014). *ArtScan*. Retrieved from http://www.aep-arts.org/research-policy/artscan/

Association of Educational Service Agencies. (2013). *AESA*. Retrieved from http://www.aesa.us

Barnes, G. V., & McCashin, R. (2005). Practices and procedures in state adjudicated orchestra festivals. *UPDATE: Applications of Research in Music Education, 23*(2), 34–41.

Bauerlein, M., & Grantham, E. (Eds.). (2009). *National Endowment for the Arts: A history: 1965–2008*. Washington, DC: National Endowment for the Arts.

Benham, J. (2014). *Focus on advocacy: Develop an annual report featuring your music education program*. Retrieved from https://www.nammfoundation.org/articles/2014-04-10-focus-advocacy-develop-annual-report-featuring-your-music-education-program

Boyle, J. D. (Ed.). (1974). *Instructional objectives in music: Resources for planning instruction and evaluating achievement*. Vienna, VA: Music Educators National Conference.

Carnoy, M., & Rothstein, R. (2013). *What do international tests really show about U.S. student performance?* Retrieved from http://www.epi.org/publication/us-student-performance-testing/

Center for Public Education. (2016). *The role of school boards*. Retrieved from http://www.centerforpubliceducation.org/You-May-Also-Be-Interested-In-landing-page-level/Audience-The-Public-YMABI/The-Role-of-School-Boards#sthash.EmxfpWxD.dpuf

The College Board. (2012). *Music theory: Course description*. Retrieved from https://secure-media.collegeboard.org/digitalServices/pdf/ap/ap-music-theory-course-description.pdf

The College Board. (2016). *About us*. Retrieved from https://www.collegeboard.org/about

Common Core State Standards Initiative. (2016). *Development process*. Retrieved from http://www.corestandards.org/about-the-standards/development-process/#timeline-2009

Consortium of National Arts Education Associations. (1994). *National standards for arts education: What every young American should be able to know and do in the arts*. Reston, VA: Music Educators National Conference.

Conway, C. (2008). The implementation of the Nationals Standards in Music Education: Capturing the spirit of the standards. *Music Educators Journal, 94*(4), 34–39.

Council for Higher Education Accreditation. (2018). *About accreditation*. Retrieved from https://www.chea.org/about-accreditation

Cundiff, H. M, & Dykema, P. W. (1923). *The school music handbook: A guide for teaching school music*. Boston, MA: C. C. Birchard.

Duke, L. L. (1988). The Getty Center for Education in the Arts and Discipline-Based Art Education. *Art Education, 41*(2), 7–12.

Educational Testing Service. (2016a). *2015 Major field test comparative data guide: Major field test for music*. Retrieved from http://www.ets.org/s/mft/pdf/acdg_music.pdf

Educational Testing Service. (2016b). *ETS major field tests: About ETS major field tests*. Retrieved from http://www.ets.org/mft/about/

Educational Testing Service. (2016c). *ETS praxis: Preparation materials*. Retrieved from https://www.ets.org/praxis/prepare/materials

Elementary and Secondary Education Act of 1965, Pub. L. No. 89–10, 79 Stat. 27 (1965).

Elpus, K. (2014). Evaluating the effect of No Child Left Behind on U.S. music course enrollments. *Journal of Research in Music Education, 62*, 215–233. doi: 10.1177/0022429414530759

Every Child Achieves Act, S. 1177, 114th Cong. (2015–2016).

Every Student Succeeds Act of 2015, Pub. L. No. 114–95, S. 1177. (2015).

Fabricant, M., & Fine, M. (2016). *The changing politics of education: Privatization and dispossessed lives left behind*. Abington, UK: Routledge.

Farley, T. (2009). *Making the grades: My misadventures in the standardized testing industry*. San Francisco, CA: Berrett-Kohler.

Gerrity, K. W. (2009). No Child Left Behind: Determining the impact of policy on music education in Ohio. *Bulletin of the Council for Research in Music Education, 179*, 79–93.

Goals 2000: Educate America Act, Pub. L. No. 103–227, 108 Stat. 125 (1994).

Grammy Foundation. (2016). *Grammy in the schools*. Retrieved from http://www.grammyintheschools.com/programs

Hagopian, J. (Ed.). (2014). *More than a score: The new uprising against high-stakes testing*. Chicago, IL: Haymarket Books.

Herpin, S. A., Washington, A. Q., & Li, J. (2012). *Improving the assessment of student learning in the arts: State of the field and recommendations*. Washington, DC: National Endowment for the Arts. Retrieved from https://www.wested.org/resources/improving-the-assessment-of-student-learning-in-the-arts-state-of-the-field-and-recommendations/

Hoffman, M. E. (1980). Goals and objectives for the eighties. *Music Educators Journal, 67*(4), 48–49, 66.

International Baccalaureate Organization. (2015a). *The IB diploma program statistical bulletin: May 2015 examination session*. Retrieved from http://www.ibo.org/contentassets/bc850970f4e54b87828f83c7976a4db6/dp-2015-may-stats-bulletin.pdf

International Baccalaureate Organization. (2015b). *Mission*. Retrieved from http://www.ibo.org/about-the-ib/mission/

International Baccalaureate Organization. (2015c). *Music*. Retrieved from http://www.ibo.org/en/programmes/diploma-programme/curriculum/the-arts/music/

J. Paul Getty Trust. (2016). *The art and accessibility of music, advanced*. Retrieved from http://www.getty.edu/education/teachers/classroom_resources/curricula/performing_arts/lesson06.html

Johnson, J. A., Dupuis, V. L., Musial, D., Hall, G. E., & Gollnick, D. M. (1996). *Introduction to the foundations of American education* (10th ed.). Boston, MA: Allyn & Bacon.

Keiper, S., Sandene, B. A., Persky, H. R., & Kuang, M. (2009). *The nation's report card: Arts 2008 music and visual arts* (NCES 2009-488). Washington, DC: National Center for Education Statistics, Institute of Education Sciences, US Department of Education. Retrieved from http://nces.ed.gov/nationsreportcard/pdf/main2008/2009488.pdf

Kennedy Center. (2014). *ArtsEdge: Educators: Lessons.* Retrieved from https://artsedge. kennedy-center.org/educators/lessons

Lindquist, M. M. (2010). NAEP, TIMSS, and PSSM: Entangled influences. *School Science and Mathematics, 101,* 286–291. doi: 10.1111/j.19498594.2001.tb17959.x

Mark, M. L. (1980). The GO Project: Retrospective of a decade. *Music Educators Journal, 67*(4), 42–47.

Mark, M. L. (Ed.). (2002). *Music education: Source readings from ancient Greece to today* (2nd ed.). New York, NY: Routledge.

McGraw-Hill Education. (2016). *Spotlight on music: McMillan/McGraw-Hill products.* Retrieved from http://www.mhschool.com/products/music/

Meersman, R. (1980). The Kennedy Center: From dream to reality. *Records of the Columbia Historical Society, 50,* 527–528.

Music Educators National Conference. (1969). Where has all the money gone? *Music Educators Journal, 55*(5), 64–72.

Music Teachers National Association. (2016a). *MTNA: Working for a more musical tomorrow.* Retrieved from http://www.mtna.org/about-mtna/

Music Teachers National Association. (2016b). *MTNA competitions.* Retrieved from https:// www.mtna.org/MTNA/Engage/Competitions/Competitions.aspx

Music Teachers National Association. (2016c). *MTNA professional certification overview.* Retrieved from http://www.mtnacertification.org/certification-overview/

NAMM Foundation. (2014). *Music research.* Retrieved from https://www.nammfoundation. org/educator-resources/music-research

National Assessment Governing Board. (2008). *2008 arts education assessment framework.* Retrieved from https://www.nagb.org/content/nagb/assets/documents/publications/frameworks/arts/2008-arts-framework.pdf

National Assessment Governing Board. (2017). *The nation's report card: Arts assessment 2016: Grade 8.* Retrieved from https://www.nationsreportcard.gov/arts_2016/#/about

National Assessment of Educational Progress. (1970). *National Assessment of Educational Progress: Music objectives.* Ann Arbor, MI: Author.

National Association for Music Education (NAfME). (2016a). *NAfME joins National Education Funding Coalition.* Retrieved from http://www.nafme.org/title-iv_a_coalition/

National Association for Music Education (NAfME). (2016b). *Student assessment using model cornerstone assessments.* Retrieved from http://www.nafme.org/my-classroom/standards/mcas-information-on-taking-part-in-the-field-testing/

National Association of Schools of Music (NASM). (2015). *Handbook 2015–16.* https://nasm. arts-accredit.org/wp-content/uploads/sites/2/2015/11/NASM_HANDBOOK_2015-16.pdf

National Center for Education Statistics. (2013). *About NAEP and international assessment.* Retrieved from https://nces.ed.gov/nationsreportcard/about/international.aspx

National Center for Education Statistics. (2014). *Timeline for National Assessment of Educational Progress (NAEP) assessments from 1969–2017.* Retrieved from https://nces.ed. gov/nationsreportcard/about/assessmentsched.aspx

National Center for Education Statistics. (2015). *Program for International Student Assessment (PISA): Overview.* Retrieved from https://nces.ed.gov/surveys/pisa/

National Coalition for Core Arts Standards. (2014). *Music model cornerstone assessments.* Retrieved from http://www.nationalartsstandards.org

National Endowment of the Arts (NEA). (2012). *How art works.* Retrieved from https://www. arts.gov/sites/default/files/How-Art-Works_0.pdf

National School Boards Association (NSBA). (2016). *State association services*. Retrieved from https://www.nsba.org/services/state-association-services

NCAAMP: The National Center for Assessment and Adjudication of Musical Performances. (2008). *Music adjudication essentials*. Reston, VA: MENC.

No Child Left Behind Act of 2001, Pub. L. No. 107-110, 115 Stat. 1425 (2002).

Norris, C. E, & Borst, J. D. (2007). An examination of the reliabilities of two choral festival adjudication forms. *Journal of Research in Music Education, 55*, 237-251.

Northwest Commission on Colleges and Universities. (2010). *Accreditation handbook*. Retrieved from http://www.nwccu.org/wp-content/uploads/2016/02/Accreditation-Handbook-2017-edition.pdf

Office of Management and Budget. (2017). *Budget of the U.S. government: A new foundation for American greatness: Fiscal year 2018*. Retrieved from https://www.whitehouse.gov/sites/whitehouse.gov/files/omb/budget/fy2018/budget.pdf

Pearson Education. (2016). *Interactive MUSIC (Realize) powered by Silver Burdett with Alfred*. Retrieved from https://www.pearsonschool.com/index.cfm?locator=PS2xXh&PMDbSiteId=2781&PMDbSolutionId=6724&PMDbSubSolutionId=&PMDbCategoryId=818&PMDbSubCategoryId=&PMDbSubjectAreaId=&PMDbProgramId=149981

Persky, H. R., Sandene, B. A., & Askew, J. M. (1998). *The NEAP 1997 arts report card* (NCES 1999-486). US Department of Education, Office of Educational Research and Improvement, National Center for Education Statistics.

Ravitch, D. (1995). *National standards in American education: A citizen's guide*. Washington, DC: Brookings Institution Press.

Ravitch, D. (2003). *The language police: How pressure groups restrict what students learn*. New York: Alfred A. Knopf.

Reese, W. J. (2013). *Testing wars in the public schools: A forgotten history*. Cambridge MA: Harvard University Press.

Shuler, S. C. (1996). Assessment in general music: An overview. *The Orff Echo, 28*(2), 10–12.

Shuler, S. C. (2011). The three artistic processes: Paths to lifelong 21st-century skills through music. *Music Educators Journal, 97*(4), 9–13.

Singer, A. (2014). *SCALE and edTPA fire back: Methinks they doth protest too much*. Retrieved from http://www.huffingtonpost.com/alan-singer/scale-and-edtpa-fire-back_b_5506351.html

Smith, B. P., & Barnes, G. V. (2007). Development and validation of an orchestra performance rating scale. *Journal of Research in Music Education, 55*(3), 81–100.

Smith, B. P., & Hoffman, A. R. (2011). *Unintended outcomes: Sociodemographic diversity, within-school stratification, and access to middle level arts curricula*. Paper presented at the Annual Meeting of the American Educational Research Association, New Orleans, LA.

Stanford Center for Assessment, Learning, and Equity. (2015). *edTPA*. Retrieved from https://scale.stanford.edu/teaching/edtpa

State Education Agency Directors of Arts Education (SEADAE). (2014). *National Core Arts Standards*. Retrieved from https://nationalartsstandards.org/

State Normal School at Los Angeles. (1900). *Eighteenth annual catalog of the State Normal School at Los Angeles for the school year ending June 30, 1900, and circular for 1900–1901*. Retrieved from http://www.registrar.ucla.edu/archive/catalog/1900-01catalog.pdf

Student Success Act, H.R. 5, 114th Congress. (2015–2016).

TIMMS and PIRLS International Study Center. (2015). *TIMMS and PIRLS*. Retrieved from http://timssandpirls.bc.edu

Tucker, A. (1992). *Saving America 2000: Can the Bush administration retake the initiative on education reform?* Retrieved from http://www.heritage.org/research/reports/1992/05/saving-america-2000-can-the-bush-administration-retake-the-initiative-on-education-reform

Tuttle, L. (2018). *Music education and final state ESSA plans.* Retrieved from https://nafme.org/musiced-final-state-essa-plans/

Urban, W. J., & Wagoner, J. L., Jr. (2009). *American education: A history* (4th ed.). New York, NY: Routledge.

US Department of Education. (2006). *Improving teacher quality state grants: ESEA Title II, Part A: Non-regulatory guidance.* Retrieved from https://www2.ed.gov/programs/teacher-qual/guidance.pdf

US Department of Education. (2009). *No Child Left Behind: A toolkit for teachers.* Retrieved from http://www2.ed.gov/teachers/nclbguide/toolkit_pg10.html

US Department of Education. (2012). *ESEA flexibility: Frequently asked questions.* Retrieved from https://www2.ed.gov/policy/eseaflex/esea-flexibility-faqs.doc

US Department of Education. (2016a). *Accreditation in the United States.* Retrieved from http://www2.ed.gov/admins/finaid/accred/accreditation_pg13.html

US Department of Education. (2016b). *ESEA flexibility.* Retrieved from http://www2.ed.gov/policy/elsec/guid/esea-flexibility/index.html

US Department of Education. (2016c). *Improving basic programs operated by local educational agencies (Title I, Part A).* Retrieved from http://www2.ed.gov/programs/titleiparta/index.html

US Department of Health and Human Services. (2016). *Head Start timeline.* Retrieved from https://eclkc.ohs.acf.hhs.gov/about-us/news/head-start-timeline

Vu, P. (2008). *Do state tests make the grade?* Retrieved from http://www.pewtrusts.org/en/research-and-analysis/reports/2008/01/17/do-state-tests-make-the-grade

Williams, R. (2009). State of the art: ASTA roundtable finds alternative styles education moving a step ahead—slowly. *Strings, 170,* 26–27.

PART II

MEASUREMENT
THEORETICAL FOUNDATIONS

CHAPTER 19

PSYCHOMETRIC CONSIDERATIONS FOR MUSIC PERFORMANCE ASSESSMENTS

SUZANNE LANE AND YA ZHANG

INTRODUCTION

Assessment in the Era of Accountability

ASSESSMENT of what students know and can do typically serves two main purposes for state or national assessment systems: accountability and improving instruction and student learning. There is an inherent paradox in the use of assessments for both accountability purposes and for improving instruction and learning. Accountability requires the relevant entity (e.g., student, teacher, school, district, and state) to demonstrate competency according to an established standard, however, the same assessments used for accountability serve as tools for monitoring student learning and providing information to improve instruction.

Psychometrics provides us with tools and strategies to design quality assessments, although constraints will arise that will lead to trade-offs in achieving the different goals of assessment and accountability systems (Lane & DePascale, 2016). In general, for both accountability and monitoring purposes, some level of comparability across students, schools, districts, and states as well as over time is needed to help ensure valid and fair score interpretations and uses. Comparability of scores across students and time may be achieved by standardizing content, administration, and scoring, however, standardization may result in fairness issues as well as instructional value issues. To make informed decisions about assessment design and to better understand the inherent constraints, the competing purposes and uses of the assessments and different psychometric considerations for these purposes (e.g., reliability, generalizability, comparability) and uses should be delineated. Careful consideration must be given to both the design criteria (e.g., content representation) and psychometric criteria to ensure valid score interpretations and uses. Psychometrics can help inform many assessment design decisions to help ensure valid and fair score interpretations and uses.

Performance Assessments

Performance assessments have the capability of providing rich information to inform instruction, although there are significant psychometric challenges that need to be considered in their design, scoring, administration, and psychometric modeling as well as practical and logistical challenges (Gorin & Mislevy, 2013; Lane & DePascale, 2016). Performance assessments inherently may be less standardized, more multidimensional, and involve more complex thinking as compared to other assessment formats. A single score may not be adequate in capturing the exhibited performance due to the multidimensionality and complexity of the construct being assessed. When performance assessment scores are combined with scores from other formats of assessment, weighting the performance assessment scores is most likely needed so that the contribution from performance assessments is not diminished (Davey et al., 2015). Attention to validity, fairness, reliability, comparability, and generalizability should also be carefully integrated into the design of performance assessments to ensure the psychometric soundness of the assessment for accountability purposes and for monitoring and informing instruction and learning.

In addition to careful attention to the psychometric specifications, the design and validation of performance assessments should ensure that students are eliciting the targeted knowledge, skills, and abilities (KSA), and not irrelevant KSA, and that coherency among curriculum, instruction, and assessment is achieved. Available time, money, professional expertise, and technical support needs to be considered to ensure the practicality, affordability, and feasibility of using performance assessments in schools. These challenges in using performance assessments for dual purposes as well as additional challenges that are specific to the use of music assessments, including availability of existing music assessments and scoring rubrics, time required to demonstrate KSA in music, and opportunity to learn due to limited music instructional time, are discussed by Shuler, Brophy, Sabol, McGreevy-Nichols, and Schuttler (2016).

This chapter begins with an overview of music assessments in the United States at the national and state level as well as a discussion of student learning objectives (SLOs) that are used for accountability and monitoring student progress. The next section addresses design and scoring features that affect the psychometric properties of performance assessments. Following this is a discussion on the need for an argument-based approach to validity and a principled approach to test design to support score interpretations and uses. The last section addresses psychometric considerations in the design of performance assessments, including comparability, generalizability, rater effects, and decision accuracy. The chapter ends with some brief comments.

MUSIC PERFORMANCE ASSESSMENT

Music education was first introduced in elementary schools in the 18th century, and by the mid-19th century, music education had spread across all grades in K-12 (Keene, 2010). In the beginning of the 20th century, the launch of a series of music education projects, symposiums, and federal funding facilitated defining the scope and quality of music education. During the 1990s, standards in music education that exemplified innovation and reform and defined what a student should know and be able to do in music as a result of instruction were introduced.

The assessment of students' achievement and progress in music has long been recognized as a central challenge for music educators, and largely depended on subjective information, which often did not provide an accurate assessment of students' development in music (Boyle & Radocy, 1987). With the publication of the National Standards of Music Education in 1994, music assessments began to focus on objectively measuring acquired knowledge and skills over time as well as identifying future learning experiences that may be used to facilitate learning (Asmus, 1999). The development of national, state, and local music standards highlighted the importance of assessment, and provided a foundation for assessing students' achievement and learning in music.

The National Association for Music Education (NAfME) delineated the main goals of assessment in music education (National Association for Music Education, 2009). First, given the demand for teacher accountability, reliable and valid assessment results should provide meaningful information on what students are learning and mastering and signal what adjustments are needed to instructional strategies to enhance students' development in music. Second, standards-based instruction and assessment should encourage student progress and facilitate communication with parents about music education and student learning. Standards-based instruction and assessment provides concrete and observable criteria that students need to meet, holds students accountable for meeting these standards, and ultimately motivates student learning. Lastly, using assessments to document student progress in a systematic way over time helps demonstrate to the public that musical learning is taking place in the K-12 schools. The assessment of music therefore helps demonstrate the value of music education, provides a means for music accountability in public school education, and attracts public support for school music programs.

Performance assessments are well suited to assessing students' KSA in music in that they have high fidelity for the goals of music instruction, providing direct evidence of what students know and can do. Further, the use of portfolios that require students to collect their work over time makes students accountable for documenting their own growth in musical skills (Nierman, 2001).

NAEP Music Assessment

In 1971, the National Assessment of Educational Progress (NAEP) administered its first music assessment to determine what students knew and could do in music, including the assessment of students' ability to respond to existing works of music as well as students' original work in creating and performing music ("A National Assessment," 1971). The second NAEP music assessment administered in 1978, however, only measured students' skills in responding to existing works of music (Oliver, 2007). Therefore monitoring of student progress at the national level could only be achieved in the domain of responding to existing works. The narrower focus of the 1978 NAEP music assessment was counter to the original objective of measuring the processes of creating and performing music, and was criticized for not including performance tasks (Colwell, 1999).

The 1997 NAEP music assessment was administered to 8th-grade students and consisted of tasks that required students to respond to recordings, musical notation, and other stimuli, as well as performance tasks to measure students' abilities in creating and performing music (Vanneman, Shuler, & Sandene, 1998; White & Vanneman, 1999). Although NAEP included performance tasks in this assessment several concerns were raised, including reporting subscores without sufficient measurement of the skills, the amount of time it took to record full-length performances (Schneider, 2005), and the overall usefulness of the reports in supporting and guiding curricular changes and promoting music learning in instruction (Colwell, 1999). Although there was strong support for the use of music performance tasks in NAEP, these findings highlight several issues when using such tasks, including the amount of time needed to create a performance for an assessment and the number of tasks needed to provide reliable subscores and valid score interpretations and uses.

Unfortunately, due to budget constraints, the fourth NAEP 8th-grade music assessment conducted in 2008 did not make necessary changes based on what was learned from the previous assessment and was composed of responding tasks only (Shuler, 2009). According to music educators, the findings of the NAEP music assessments were limited in providing instructional guidance, improving students' ability in performing and creating, and evaluating the sufficiency of resources allotted to music education. Although the current arts assessment framework includes creating and performing music, the 2016 NAEP music assessment only assessed students' skills in describing, observing, analyzing, and evaluating existing works of music. The history of NAEP's music assessment highlights some of the concerns in the assessment of music, including the amount of time and resources that are needed for performance tasks and the practice of narrowing the targeted construct to the KSAs that are more easily assessed.

State Music Assessments

States began developing and administering arts assessments in the early 1990s. In 1993, Kentucky was the first state to develop and implement arts assessments statewide.

The music portion of the assessment included eight multiple-choice items and two open-response tasks, which placed an emphasis on student's ability in describing, analyzing, evaluating, and explaining musical work rather than demonstrating their musical skills. By 2001, approximately one-third of the states had either a mandatory or voluntary statewide arts assessment (Herpin, Washington, & Li, 2012).

A number of states were funded to create prototype performance assessment items in dance, music, theater, and visual arts beginning in 1994. The State Collaborative on Assessment and Student Standards (SCASS) developed training materials to facilitate the development of performance tasks as well as example performance tasks in music, dance, theater, and visual arts (Herpin et al., 2012). Since 1995 The Arts Education Partnership (AEP), a part of the Council of Chief State School Officers (CCSSO), has been monitoring state policies for arts education in the 50 states and the District of Columbia. According to AEP, by 2016 26 states defined the arts as a "core" or "academic" subject in state policy, indicating that the arts should have equal footing with other core subjects for support and assistance. In addition, 17 states reported a state-mandated assessment in the arts during this time frame.

Beginning in the 2008–2009 school year, the state of Washington required all school districts to assess students' progress in arts using the state-developed arts Classroom-Based Performance Assessments (CBPAs) to ensure that students are able to apply core arts concepts in at least one art form, including music. Districts are held accountable for this practice in that they need to submit an annual implementation report to the Office of the Superintendent of Public Instruction (OSPI) (Washington State Arts Commission, 2006). Washington's CBPAs are arts activities designed to be integrated into the curriculum as an integral part of a unit of study. The performance assessments require students to create, perform, and respond, using the creative processes of the arts, and were designed to provide evidence of instruction and learning in the arts that are aligned to the state Essential Academic Learning Requirements (EALRs) in the arts (Office of Superintendent of Public Instruction, 2006). Because the performance-based tasks are integral to the instructional unit, the students receive classroom instruction in the knowledge and skills being assessed prior to the administration of the assessment, and are provided with class time to develop their own work leading up to their performances for the assessment. An assessment guide is provided on the OSPI website for the teachers, which provides an overview of the art assessment selected, the script used to explain the assessment task to students, and the standards-based criteria by which the students' work will be evaluated. As an example, for an 8th-grade task the students are told that they are auditioning for a place in an all-state band, and each of them will need to sight-sing a line of music. Students are allowed to choose the pitch they feel comfortable with, and are given time to practice. They must then perform without stopping, and their performances are evaluated in terms of their rhythm as well as their performance of intervals and keys using a 5-level scoring rubric (OSPI, 2015).

Connecticut's Common Arts Assessment statewide initiative includes performance assessments in music for voluntary use at the district and school levels (Connecticut Department of Education, 2014). Performance tasks, which assess creating, performing, and responding, were designed as units embedded in instruction and are administered locally. In New Hampshire, all students in public schools must demonstrate mastery of course-level competencies, including the arts, to graduate from high school (New Hampshire Department of Education, 2006). Local schools have the responsibility of assessing music learning outcomes through the use of local assessments that are aligned with the state and district content and performance standards, and performance tasks are recommended in addition to more traditional item formats. The Rhode Island K-12 Grade Span Expectations in Music specifies the skills and concepts to be taught in the music classroom, and the format of musical performing is clearly defined in the state assessment target (Rhode Island Department of Education, 2010). The Colorado Department of Education requires only district-level assessments in music, which follow a generalist or performance track to meet the basic needs of all students and the advanced needs of those pursuing careers in music, respectively. In both tracks, students' ability to perform music accurately and expressively are important features in the assessment.

The South Carolina Arts Assessment Program (SCAAP) is a Web-based large-scale arts assessment. The SCAAP music assessment includes two 45-item multiple-choice test forms and two performance tasks (Stites & Malin, 2008; Yap, Lewis, & Feldon, 2007). The SCAAP 4th-grade music assessment was implemented in schools statewide beginning in 2004, while the SCAAP middle school music assessment was field-tested in 2007. The use of the SCAAP music assessments has been restricted to schools and districts that received state arts grants. By 2014, a total of 34 schools from South Carolina participated in the SCAAP 4th-grade entry-level assessments, and 2,535 students completed the music assessment (Office of Program Evaluation, 2014). The performance tasks require students to demonstrate their singing and rhythm improvisation skills, which are in line with the 2010 South Carolina Academic Standards for the Visual and Performing Art for grade 4. The tasks are scored by Web-based trained raters using analytic scoring rubrics, resulting in multiple scores. Approximately 20% of the music assessments are double-scored allowing for examining interrater consistency. A person-by-rater generalizability study resulted in dependability coefficients ranging from .68 to .94, although no evidence is provided for the comparability of the performance tasks. Additional examples of state music assessments are provided by Shuler et al. (2016).

The future holds promise for state music assessments, and these examples provide a clear indication of exemplary work by states in the design and use of performance assessments to measure student achievement and learning in music. The success of these assessment efforts depends on the ability to account for both psychometric and practical constraints while ensuring fidelity in measuring the targeted construct. To be sustainable, evidence is needed to ensure that these assessments are meeting both accountability and instructional goals given the many conflicting constraints. Documentation of the issues that arise in meeting both of these goals will assist others in the design and use of music performance assessments.

Student Learning Objectives

Student learning objectives are a tool that incorporates measures of student growth for both tested- and nontested grades and academic subjects (NTGS) in school evaluation systems. According to the Reform Support Network (n.d)), the SLO process is "a participatory method of setting measurable goals, or objectives, based on the specific assignment or class, such as the students taught, the subject matter taught, the baseline performance of the students, and the measurable gain in student performance during the course of instruction" (p. 1). Thus, SLOs are specific learning goals and assessments of student achievement and growth and are used to track progress toward those goals. More specifically, SLOs should be measurable, based on student growth and achievement, aligned with state or local standards, based on prior student achievement and learning data, able to measure teachers' impact on student learning, and aligned with course content (Lacireno-Paquet, Morgan, & Mello, 2014; Lane & DePascale, 2016).

The SLOs not only are used to monitor student progress but also serve as a tool for improving instructional practice. Their development is typically a collaborative process, where teachers, principals, and other administrators are involved in their design and use, with each having a different focus. In general, the development of SLOs follows several key steps such as identifying the student population, specifying the timeline within which students will reach an academic goal, prioritizing the learning content in terms of standards and previous data, establishing accurate baselines, selecting or developing appropriate assessments to measure progress, specifying rigorous and realistic expectations of student growth, and providing a rationale for the expected target (US Department of Education, 2012). At the heart of an SLO is the measurement of student progress toward the objective. The assessment developed or selected for measuring student progress must be sensitive to instruction and learning and provide valid score interpretations for both achievement and growth. According to a review of 50 states and the District of Columbia (Lacireno-Paquet et al., 2014), 25 states have established SLOs and included SLOs as part of their teacher evaluation systems. Progress and student growth toward meeting SLOs are evaluated through a variety of measures, including statewide assessments, district-developed assessments, school-based assessments, and classroom assessments, including performance-based assessments.

Ohio uses SLOs as a comprehensive framework for determining students' learning growth in grades and disciplines that are not involved in statewide testing, such as the arts (Ohio Arts Assessment Collaborative, 2015). Music students are measured with both written and performance-based music pre- and post-assessments. As specified in the Illinois Administrative Code Part 50, school districts are required to develop comprehensive teacher evaluation plans that include data and measures of student growth (Illinois State Board of Education, 2013). The Illinois Performance Evaluation Model requires that school districts use multiple measures of student growth as a significant factor in teachers' summative performance evaluations. To implement this model, SLOs are recommended as an approach for measuring growth. Teachers follow established procedures for using performance assessments, including presentations, projects, tasks, and portfolios of student work, in conjunction with SLOs. South Dakota's Commission on Teaching and Learning (SDCTL, 2015) developed a model system for teacher evaluation with a focus on professional practices and student growth measured by SLOs. Multiple forms of assessment are encouraged to be used to help assess achievement and learning, and performance assessment is recommended in the state SLO handbook as an alternative tool to evaluate growth. The South Dakota Education Association also developed an SLO process guide for different grades and subjects including 8th-grade music and elementary music.

Performance assessments in music in conjunction with the SLOs have the capability of capturing and monitoring the complex set of skills and processes inherent in the domain. To ensure the validity of the interpretations and uses of the assessment data, evidence is needed to demonstrate the design and psychometric characteristics of the assessment. The performance assessment needs to be aligned to the SLOs and corresponding grade-level music standards. Assessment conditions and instructions should be standardized across students and classes to help ensure comparability of results. Teachers need to be trained in scoring the assessments with rubrics that clearly articulate the criteria, and consistency in teacher ratings should be established. An audit process is recommended to ensure teachers are adhering to the guidelines for administration and scoring and produce accurate ratings.

DESIGN AND SCORING FEATURES THAT AFFECT PSYCHOMETRIC PROPERTIES OF MUSIC ASSESSMENTS

Psychometric considerations should be integral to the design of music performance assessments that are used for accountability purposes and for monitoring student achievement and progress. The unique characteristics of performance assessments will affect the decisions made in the design phase, since they bear on issues related to validity, reliability, comparability, and fairness.

Argument-Based Approach to Validity

The argument-based approach to validity (Kane, 2006, 2013) provides a foundation for assessment design considerations that can enhance the psychometric quality of performance assessments. It entails both an interpretative and use (IU) argument and a validity argument. The IU argument explicitly links the inferences from performance to conclusions, decisions, and actions, and the validity argument provides a structure for evaluating the IU argument, requiring both theoretical and empirical support for the appropriateness of claims (Kane, 2006). Each inference in the validity argument is based on a claim that requires support. The validity argument entails an overall evaluation of the plausibility of the proposed claims by providing a coherent analysis of the evidence for and against the proposed inferences and uses (American Educational Research Association [AERA], American Psychological Association, & National Council on Measurement in Education, 2014; Kane, 2006, Messick, 1989). The intended score inferences and uses inform the design of performance assessments, and the choices made in the design phase have implications for the psychometric quality of the assessment and the validity and fairness of the score inferences and uses.

Two sources of potential threats to the validity of score inferences are construct underrepresentation and construct-irrelevant variance (AERA et al., 2014; Messick, 1989). The *Standards for Educational and Psychological Testing* indicate, "both the tested and the target domains should be described in sufficient detail for their relationships to be evaluated.... Analyses should make explicit those aspects of the target domain that the test represents, as well as those aspects the test fails to represent" (AERA et al., 2014, p. 196). For performance assessments this is essential to ensure the fidelity in measuring the construct.

Construct-irrelevant variance occurs when, in addition to assessing the intended constructs, one or more unintended constructs is being assessed, resulting in artificially inflated or deflated scores and, as a result, hindering the validity of score inferences. Sources of construct-irrelevant variance for performance assessments can include features associated with tasks, scoring rubrics, raters, student characteristics and their responses, administration conditions, and the interaction of these facets (Lane & Iwatani, 2016; Lane & Stone, 2006). Clearly articulated scoring rubrics and effective training of raters can help minimize construct-irrelevant variance due to these sources. Student characteristics, such as student motivation, can be a source of construct-irrelevant variance. Perceived or actual stakes attached to performing well on an assessment may create differences in the level of motivation among students and interfere with their performance (Lane & DePascale, 2016). Departing from standardized test administration procedures, such as providing additional guidance to some students, can artificially raise the score of these students and affect the validity and fairness of score inferences.

Principled Approach to Music Assessment Design

Principled approaches to the design of music assessments, such as evidence-centered design (ECD; Mislevy, Steinberg, & Almond, 2003), allow for the explicit delineation of the knowledge and skills to be assessed as well as their progression, and provide guidance on what types of tasks, ancillary materials, rubrics, and administration procedures, to name a few, are needed to provide evidence for claims about student achievement and learning. The premise of ECD is that evidence observed in student performances on tasks that have clearly articulated cognitive demands can be used to make claims about student achievement and learning (Mislevy et al., 2003). The design of both task models and scoring models, which are fundamental features of ECD, allow for the design of multiple tasks that are intended to assess the same KSAs and be scored in the same manner by trained raters.

The design of task models is guided by the claims and the evidence that is needed to warrant the claims. Each task model that is associated with a claim and evidence allows for the generation of multiple tasks, providing a means for controlling the KSAs assessed by tasks. A task model in conjunction with performance-level descriptors can also be designed to target the assessment at a point along the score scale. A scoring rubric can then be designed and used for the tasks generated by the task model, promoting consistency of scoring across tasks with the same knowledge and skill specifications. The set of task and scoring rubric models serves as a concrete illustration of the test specifications and the construct being assessed (Lane & Iwatani, 2016).

In the design of scoring rubrics, scoring criteria need to reflect the KSAs that the tasks are intended to measure. The design of scoring rubrics requires the specification of the criteria for judging the quality of performances, the choice of a scoring rubric (e.g., analytic or holistic), procedures for developing criteria, and procedures used to apply criteria (Clauser, 2000). Scoring criteria and procedures should be clearly specified to help ensure the accuracy and consistency of scoring (AERA et al., 2014). The scoring criteria specified at each score level should reflect the KSAs being assessed and are guided by a number of factors including the cognitive demands of the tasks, the degree of structure or openness expected in the responses, the examinee population, the purposes of the assessment, and the intended score claims and inferences (Lane & Stone, 2006). The number of score levels depends on the extent to which the criteria across the score levels can distinguish among various levels of students' performances. In other words, the KSAs reflected at each score level should differ distinctly from those at other score levels, and raters should be able to reliably make these distinctions.

It should be noted that the use of predefined criteria for assessing complex works has been criticized in some settings. Instead it has been argued that a more integrated, holistic approach to evaluating work is needed. The practice of having students examine products and then develop their own evaluative criteria to analyze their own and their peer's work is a valuable instructional activity. For assessments with high stakes associated with them, it is imperative, however, to have validated standardized scoring procedures and rubrics that allow for comparable and fair assessment of students. A consensus approach is typically used for setting criteria, in that experts within the content domain agree on the criteria at each score level. Rubrics are then pilot tested by applying them to actual student performances. This may require several iterations in both the design of the tasks and scoring rubrics to ensure the intended construct is being assessed in both breadth and depth and sources of construct irrelevance are minimized (Lane & Stone, 2006).

Well-developed and -implemented scoring rubrics and rater training materials and procedures can help minimize construct-irrelevant variance due to raters. The use of benchmarks or anchors of student performance promotes a shared understanding of the expectations at each score level and will enhance the reliability of scores and validity of score inferences and uses.

Psychometric Considerations in the Design of Music Performance Assessments

Psychometrics has an essential role in ensuring valid score interpretations derived from performance assessments for state assessment and accountability systems. The assessment of performances, processes, and creative behaviors is complex, and therefore careful consideration of the psychometric requirements of assessments is needed from the initial design stages and through the entire process of collecting evidence to support the validity of score inferences and uses.

Comparability

The comparability of scores derived from performance assessments can be compromised by the many positive features of performance assessments, including their capability of measuring complex performances that are aligned to important instructional goals. When data collection procedures differ for different students or for the same students at different time points, comparing students with one another or monitoring students' progress over time often raises concerns about comparability (Lane & DePascale, 2016; Mislevy, Wilson, Ercikan, & Chudowsky, 2003). The use of music performance assessments for high-stakes decisions for evaluating student achievement, monitoring changes in student performance over time, and evaluating teacher effectiveness requires some level of standardization of the KSAs to be assessed, the administration of the assessment, and the scoring of performances within an administration occasion and across years (Lane & DePascale, 2016). The complexity of the task, extended time periods, and the use of raters may challenge the standardization of music performance assessments. Inferences drawn about the performance would be jeopardized when scores across students, forms, conditions, administrations, or time lack a level of comparability.

Decisions need to be made about what features need to be standardized and what features can be changed so as to meet the goals of instruction and to reach the desired level of comparability (Lane & DePascale, 2016). When making such decisions, similarity of the knowledge and skills that are to be assessed and the nature of the claims about student performance need to be considered. The level of comparability will differ if claims are about status performance or progress over time. If claims are about progress as compared to status performance, comparability across the score scale is needed. Further opportunity to learn is an important fairness consideration. If students do not have the same access to music instruction, then comparability and fairness in score interpretations and uses will be jeopardized.

It is important to design performance assessments and forms with comparability at the forefront because typical equating designs are generally not applicable (Lane & DePascale, 2016). The use of ECD can help promote comparability of test scores by clearly articulating the cognitive and skill demands of the tasks and the necessary knowledge and skills that provide evidence of student achievement and learning. The design of both task models and scoring models can help ensure the assessment is assessing the targeted construct and minimize the assessment of irrelevant constructs as well as help achieve the level of standardization that is needed to compare scores across forms, administrations, and years (Lane & DePascale, 2016). As indicated in the Standards for Educational and Psychological Testing (AERA et al., 2014, p. 77), "Specifications for more complex item formats should describe the domain from which the items or tasks are sampled, components of the domain to be assessed by the tasks or items, and critical features of the items that should be replicated in creating items for alternate forms." The use of the same scoring rubrics, rater training procedures and materials, and psychometric checks and analyses for accuracy and consistency help ensure that scores are comparable over students, forms, administrations, and years.

As an example, to implement performance-based music assessments to measure student growth and compare students' performances across school districts, the Ohio Arts Assessment Collaborative (OOAC, 2015) developed comprehensive administration materials, including administration and scoring guidelines and data collection forms. The Tennessee Fine Arts Growth Measures System provides teachers with an evidence collection guide, and teachers are asked to use a purposeful sample for measuring student growth, and are asked to provide student growth evidence collections that are standards-based in the assessment of music learning (US Department of Education, 2011). Scoring guides that clearly describe in detail the steps for teachers to follow when assessing student work are provided. Such procedures increase the comparability of student performances within an administration occasion and across time.

The threat to comparability due to tasks (i.e., the number of tasks, the context of tasks, etc.) used in music performance-based assessments is of concern. It is fairly common that in state and district music performance assessments only a small number of tasks are included, a performing task (i.e., singing or playing a musical passage) and/or a composition/improvisation task (i.e., Connecticut, South Carolina, New York, etc.). When using only a few tasks in a performance assessment, the interaction of student and task as well as the interaction of student, task, and occasion can jeopardize comparability across performance tasks and occasions (Shavelson, Ruiz-Primo, & Wiley, 1999). Occasion is an important facet that needs to be considered in assessing music performance, because directions and guidance by teachers may alter from occasion to occasion and strategies used by students may change from occasion to occasion To help alleviate concerns regarding the occasion facet, clear guidelines for teachers regarding their interactions and support for students should be delineated. In addition, the use of multiple tasks across occasions could be collected in a portfolio approach to assessment. The use of a portfolio approach, however, needs to be considered in light of time constraints and available resources for evaluating multiple works. Alternatively, performances can be assessed on a number of occasions with the best work being selected for submission for evaluation. Regardless of the assessment approach, the task–occasion interaction should be taken into account as a source of construct-irrelevant variance.

The use of multiple forms of assessments, with each form consisting of different tasks, to determine students' progress in music may result in comparability issues because different features may be assessed and task-specific rubrics may be used. As discussed previously, the use of a principled approach to assessment design, including task and scoring models, will help alleviate some of the concerns regarding comparability. In addition, if relative weights are being assigned to different tasks to help ensure comparability, these weights should be consistent across students and over time (Baldwin, Fowles, & Livingston, 2005). Although there is no universal formula for assigning weights, the general rule is to make the weight reflective of the importance of a particular task. The other rule is to weight the tasks in proportion to the time they require. More complex tasks would have a greater weight than simpler tasks, as they require more time to complete and have more fidelity to the targeted construct.

Another aspect to consider regarding the comparability of music performances is the interference of construct-irrelevant sources of variance. For example, Web-based performance music tasks may introduce some irrelevant features of the assessment such as student's computer skills or comfort level with various computer features needed for the assessment. Studies have found that the stress of preparing and delivering musical performance often creates high levels of anxiety (Cox & Kenardy, 1993), resulting in an inaccurate assessment of students' musical knowledge and skills. Motivation may be another source of construct-irrelevant variance in that student motivation may differ across classes and schools if there is variation in the use of assessment results in the grading process. To improve comparability it is critical to minimize the skills or knowledge that are irrelevant to the intended construct being assessed by the task.

In summary, comparability needs to be considered with respect to tasks, occasions, student populations, scoring performances, and administration conditions within and across sites and years. It is apparent that comparability issues should be addressed in all stages of assessment design, implementation, and analyses.

Generalizability of Scores

It is important to consider the generalizability of scores to the broader domain, especially since performance assessments consist of a small number of tasks and may be more susceptible to underrepresenting the construct than other forms of assessments, despite their fidelity. Generalizability theory provides both a conceptual and a statistical framework to examine the extent to which scores derived from an assessment can be generalized to the larger domain of interest (Brennan, 2001; Cronbach, Gleser, Nanda, & Rajaratnam, 1972). Generalizability theory can inform the design of an assessment to ensure the validity of score inferences and uses. It can provide information on the number of tasks, raters, and administration occasions that are needed to maximize the generalizability of scores. It is particularly relevant in the design of performance assessments because it examines multiple sources of errors such as raters, tasks, occasions, and potentially scoring methods that can limit the generalizability of scores. Error due to tasks occurs because there are only a small number of tasks typically included in a performance assessment. Error due to raters occurs because raters may differ in their evaluation of the quality of students' performances in a particular performance task and across performance tasks. Raters can differ in their stringency, resulting in rater mean differences, and they can differ in their judgments about whether one student's response is better than another student's response, resulting in an interaction between the student and rater facets. Occasion is an important hidden source of error, because performance assessments typically are only given on one occasion and occasion is generally not considered in generalizability studies (Cronbach, Linn, Brennan, & Haertel, 1997). Error due to occasion can occur because students respond differently across occasions (resulting in an interaction between student and occasion) and students respond differently on each task from occasion to occasion (resulting in a student by task by occasion interaction). Thus, generalizability studies that treat occasion as a studied facet are needed. To investigate the effectiveness of different types of scoring rubrics, a student × (rater: rubric) design can be used, where rubric may be an analytic versus a holistic rubric.

Generalizability studies in mathematics and science (Lane, Liu, Ankenmann, & Stone, 1996; Shavelson, Baxter, & Gao, 1993; Shavelson et al., 1999) have shown that the person × task interaction and person × task × occasion interaction accounted for a large proportion of total score variability, indicating that students responded to tasks differently due to task specificity, and students adapted their strategies to each task across testing occasions. In regard to the assessment of music, a generalizability study investigating the impact of person, rater, occasion, and sequence on music performance assessment showed that rater was a major source of measurement error, as would be expected given the complexity of assessing music (Bergee, 2007). A performer × occasion × rater design and a performer × (occasion × [rater: sequence]) design were used. Performers were eight high school woodwind and brass instrumentalists, occasions were three recordings of their solo performance, and 10 raters were randomly assigned to one of the five performance sequences. Sequence was the order of how the performances were recorded for evaluation. It was found that performer, rater, and performer × rater accounted for the most variability of scores. In addition, performer × occasion × rater explained a large share of variability in the ratings. Whereas the variance produced by sequence, performer × sequence, occasion × sequence, performer × occasion × sequence, and occasion × [rater: sequence] were negligible, suggesting that occasion and sequence produced little measurement error and it made little difference which sequence the raters evaluated. A minimum of five raters were necessary to reach a generalizability coefficient of .80 for relative decisions, indicating that the number of raters is an important facet to consider to obtain sufficient generalizability of scores.

Attention is needed to ensure quality rating materials and quality training of raters. As an example, the music performance assessment in SCAAP adopted a Web-based rater training and monitoring system, where raters were trained with anchor items, provided with a 10-item Web-based practice test after training, and were required to pass a 15-item randomly generated qualifying test before becoming eligible to rate student responses (Petrulis et al., 2010). Analytic rubrics were developed to produce scores in three domains for a singing task (rhythm, vocal, and tonal) and two domains for an improvisation task (rhythm, improvisation). Based on two person × rater designs, one for each task, the generalizability coefficients using two raters for the singing task were .68, .86, .94 (rhythm, vocal, and tonal, respectively) and for the improvisation task were .90 and .88 (rhythm, improvisation), suggesting that carefully designed scoring rubrics and the use of rater training helped minimize the effects of error due to raters. Because task was not considered a facet, the scores cannot be generalized beyond the task presented to the students.

Other sources of variance that are not explicitly represented in the design may also underestimate or overestimate the generalizability of music performance (Webb et al., 2006). For example, if students are given the option of selecting a musical piece to demonstrate their proficiency, the object of measurement (such as persons) may be confounded with some hidden facet (such as musical selection), making it hard to disentangle the effect of students' proficiency and the difficulty of selecting a particular musical piece (see Brennan, 2001). Although music performance assessment usually contains a very small number of tasks, in state assessments it is commonly used in conjunction with other item formats (i.e., multiple-choice items or constructed-response items), which may help improve construct representation and the generalizability of the domain. It is important, however, that the KSAs being assessed by these other item formats are parts of the intended targeted construct.

Rater Effects

Raters play a critical role in linking between students' performances and the scores these performances are awarded. Performance assessments are considered to be "rater-mediated," since they do not provide direct information about the domain of interest, but rather mediated information through raters' interpretations (Engelhard, 2002). Raters bring a variety of potential sources of construct-irrelevant variance to the rating process that may not be controlled for completely in the design of the rubrics, training materials, and training procedures. Potential sources of construct-irrelevant variance that are introduced in the rating process by the raters include differential interpretation of score scales, differential assignment of ratings to subgroups, halo effects, and bias in rater interpretation of task difficulty (Engelhard, 2002).

Rater effects, such as rater severity, rater accuracy, and rater centrality (tendency to assign scores in the middle of the score scale) have been studied using the multifaceted Rasch model (e.g., Engelhard, 2002, 2013; Wolfe, 2004; Wolfe & McVay, 2012) as well as multilevel modeling (e.g., Leckie & Barid, 2011). Using the many-facet Rasch partial credit measurement model (MFR-PC), Wesolowski, Wind, and Engelhard (2015) investigated the rater facet for a large group music performance assessment. The MFR-PC allows for modeling multiple facets of measurement that may contribute to measurement error, and can be used to study the systematic variability of raters and items, where the items are scored using more than 2 score levels. Facets included in this study were ensemble performances, items, raters, and school level. The interaction of rater severity and school level was also included in the model to examine whether raters' severity was invariant across school levels. It was found that raters demonstrated significant differences in severity when rating ensembles across different school levels. For example, raters as a group behaved more severe to high school ensemble performances compared to middle school ensemble performances. Based on the results, the authors indicated that comparability and fairness issues in rating these large group music performance assessments need to be addressed. They suggested improved rater training, use of exemplars to accompany the scale, and a clear benchmarking procedure to be implemented to produce more reliable ratings, thus leading to more valid and equitable assessment of music performances.

Classification Accuracy and Consistency

Tasks in music performance assessment are typically scored polytomously (i.e., more than 2 score levels). To facilitate score interpretation, raw scores are usually converted to a small number of ordered performance levels such as advanced, proficient, basic, and below basic. Because performance-level categorizations based on test scores are subject to measurement error, it is an important psychometric consideration to report the probabilities of accurate and consistent classification of students, which provides an alternative way of quantifying the precision of scores from the assessment. Both classification accuracy and classification consistency provide information on the appropriateness of classification of students into different performance levels.

Classification accuracy refers to the extent to which the classification of students based on their test scores agrees with the classification based on their "true" scores (i.e., the expected performance on all possible forms of the assessment; Traub & Rowley, 1980). Another associated concept, classification consistency, refers to the extent to which the performance classifications of students agree given two independent administrations of the same test or two parallel test formats on a different occasion. The precision (or reliability) of the scores affects classification accuracy, and students who have scores closest to the cut scores are more likely to be misclassified. Classification accuracy is also dependent on the number of proficiency levels and the higher the number of proficiency levels, the higher the probability that students will be misclassified (Ercikan & Julian, 2002). To estimate single-administration classification accuracy and consistency, various methodologies have been proposed in the literature including item response theory (IRT) models, the Livingston-Lewis procedure, and the compound multinomial model (Lee, 2005, 2010; Livingston & Lewis, 1995).

Conclusion

To help ensure the psychometric quality of music performance assessments and valid score interpretations and uses, the design phase should begin with an IU argument and validity argument that delineates the claims one wants to make about instructional guidance and student, teachers, and/or school accountability as well as the evidence that is required to support such claims. The claims will provide a foundation for addressing issues related to the instructional sensitivity of the assessment; construct representation; potential sources of construct-irrelevant variance; comparability needs across tasks, raters, forms, and time; and generalizability, reliability, and classification accuracy. In the design and implementation of music performance assessment and accountability systems standardization should not be considered as a threat to validity but instead a support to validity (Lane & DePascale, 2016), therefore decisions need to be made regarding the nature and level of standardization required to support the validity of score inferences and uses. Carefully designed studies should be integral to the development of music assessment and accountability systems, and psychometrics should serve as a tool in their design, development, and evaluation. To ensure a viable system a balance will need to be reached between design and psychometric considerations and more practical issues such as local resources.

References

A national assessment of achievement in music education. (1971). *Music Educators Journal, 58*(3), 73–78, 101–109.

American Educational Research Association (AERA), American Psychological Association, National Council on Measurement in Education. (2014). *Standards for educational and psychological testing.* Washington, DC: American Educational Research Association.

Asmus, E. P. (1999). Music assessment concepts. *Music Educators Journal, 86*(2), 19–24.

Baldwin, D., Fowles, M., & Livingston, S. (2005). *Guidelines for constructed-response and other performance assessments.* Princeton, NJ: Educational Testing Service.

Bergee, M. J. (2007). Performer, rater, occasion, and sequence as sources of variability in music performance assessment. *Journal of Research in Music Education, 55,* (4), 344–358.

Boyle, J. D., & Radocy, R. E. (1987). *Measurement and evaluation of musical experiences.* New York, NY: Schirmer.

Brennan, R. L. (2001). *Generalizability theory.* New York, NY: Springer-Verlag.

Clauser, B. E. (2000). Recurrent issues and recent advances in scoring performance assessments. *Applied Psychological Measurement, 24,* 310–324.

Colwell, R. (1999). The 1997 assessment in music: Red flags in the sunset. *Arts Education Policy Review, 100*(6), 33–38.

Connecticut Department of Education. (2014). *Common arts assessment initiative.* Retrieved from http://www.sde.ct.gov/sde/lib/sde/pdf/curriculum/VisualArts/CT_Common_Arts_Assessment_Initiative.pdf

Cox, W. J., & Kenardy, J. (1993). Performance anxiety, social phobia, and setting effects in instrumental music students. *Journal of Anxiety Disorders, 7*(1), 49–60.

Cronbach, L. J., Gleser, G. C., Nanda, H., & Rajaratnam, N. (1972). *The dependability of behavioral measurements: Theory of generalizability of scores and profiles.* New York, NY: John Wiley.

Cronbach, L. J., Linn, R. L., Brennan, R. L., & Haertel, E. H. (1997). Generalizability analysis for performance assessments of student achievement or school effectiveness. *Educational and Psychological Measurement, 57,* 373–399.

Davey, T., Ferrara, S., Shavelson, R., Holland, P., Webb, N., & Wise, L. (2015). *Psychometric considerations for the next generation of performance assessment.* Princeton, NJ: Educational Testing Service.

Engelhard, G. (2002). Monitoring raters in performance assessments. In G. Tindal & T. M. Haladyna (Eds.), *Large-scale assessment programs for all students: Validity, technical adequacy and implementation* (pp. 261–287). Mahwah, NJ: Erlbaum.

Engelhard, G. (2013). *Invariant measurement: Using Rasch models in the social, behavioral, and health sciences.* New York, NY: Routledge.

Ercikan, K., & Julian, M. (2002). Classification accuracy of assigning student performance to proficiency levels: Guidelines for assessment design. *Applied Measurement in Education, 15,* 269–294.

Gorin, J., & Mislevy, R. J. (2013, September). *Inherent measurement challenges in the next generation science standards for both formative and summative assessment.* Paper presented at Invitational Research Symposium on Science Assessment, Washington, DC.

Herpin, S. A., Washington, A. Q., & Li, J. (2012). *Improving the assessment of student learning in the arts: State of the field and recommendations.* Washington, DC: National Endowment for the Arts.

Illinois State Board of Education. (2013). *Guidebook on student learning objectives for type III assessments.* Retrieved from http://www.isbe.net/peac/pdf/guidance/13-4-te-guidebook-slo.pdf

Kane, M. T. (2006). Validation. In B. Brennan (Ed.), *Educational measurement.* Westport, CT: American Council on Education & Praeger.

Kane, M. T. (2013). Validating the interpretations and uses of test scores. *Journal of Educational Measurement, 50*(1), 1–73.

Keene, J. A. (2010). *A history of music education in the United States.* Centennial, CO: Glenbridge.

Lacireno-Paquet, N., Morgan, C., & Mello, D. (2014). *How states use student learning objectives in teacher evaluation systems: A review of state websites.* Washington, DC: US Department of Education, Institute of Education Sciences.

Lane, S., & DePascale, C. A. (2016). Psychometric considerations for alternative forms of assessments and student learning objectives. In H. Braun (Ed.), *Meeting the challenges to measurement in an era of accountability* (pp. 77–106). New York, NY: Routledge.

Lane, S., & Iwatani, E. (2016). Design of performance assessments in education. In S. Lane, M. R. Raymond, & T. M. Haladyna (Eds.), *Handbook of test development* (2nd ed., pp. 274–293). New York, NY: Routledge.

Lane, S., Liu, M., Ankenmann, R. D., & Stone, C. A. (1996). Generalizability and validity of a mathematics performance assessment. *Journal of Educational Measurement, 33*(1), 71–92.

Lane, S., & Stone, C. A. (2006). Performance assessments. In B. Brennan (Ed.), *Educational measurement* (pp. 387–432). New York, NY: American Council on Education & Praeger.

Leckie, G., & Baird, J. (2011). Rater effects on essay scoring: A multilevel analysis of severity drift, central tendency, and rater experience. *Journal of Educational Measurement, 48,* 399–418. doi: 10.1111/j.1745-3984.2011.00152.x

Lee, W. C. (2005). *Classification consistency under the compound multinomial model (CASMA Research Report No. 13)*. Iowa City, IA: Center for Advanced Studies in Measurement and Assessment, The University of Iowa.

Lee, W. C. (2010). Classification consistency and accuracy for complex assessments using item response theory. *Journal of Educational Measurement, 47*(1), 1–17.

Livingston, S. A., & Lewis, C. (1995). Estimating the consistency and accuracy of classifications based on test scores. *Journal of Educational Measurement, 32*, 179–197.

Messick, S. (1989). Validity. In R. L. Linn (Ed.), *Educational measurement* (3rd ed., pp. 13–104). New York, NY: American Council on Education and Macmillan.

Mislevy, R. J., Steinberg, L. S., & Almond, R. G. (2003). On the structure of educational assessments. *Measurement: Interdisciplinary Research and Perspectives, 1*(1), 3–62.

Mislevy, R. J., Wilson, M. R., Ercikan, K., & Chudowsky, N. (2003). Psychometric principles in student assessment. In T. Kellaghan, D. Stufflebeam, & L. Wingate (Eds.), *International handbook of education evaluation—Part 1* (pp. 489–531). Netherlands: Springer.

National Association for Music Education. (2009). *Assessment—The how, what, and why—Part 2*. Retrieved from http://www.nafme.org/assessment-the-how-what-and-why-part-2.

New Hampshire Department of Education. (2006). *Arts assessment handbook*. Retrieved from http://education.nh.gov/instruction/curriculum/arts/documents/handbook.pdf

Nierman, G. E. (2001). Can portfolios be practical for performance assessment. In *Spotlight on assessment in music education* (pp. 49–51). Reston, VA: MENC—The National Association for Music Education.

Office of Program Evaluation. (2014). *South Carolina Arts Assessment Program 2014 technical report prepared for the South Carolina Department of Education*. Retrieved from https://scaap.ed.sc.edu/documents/SCAAPTechnicalReport2014Final.pdf

Office of Superintendent of Public Instruction. (2006). *The arts classroom-based performance assessments (CBPAs)*. Retrieved from http://www.americansforthearts.org/sites/default/files/CBPA-Arts%20for%20WA%20State_0.pdf

Office of Superintendent of Public Instruction. (2015). *Music: All-state all-stars Grade 8 OSPI- developed performance assessment*. Retrieved from http://www.k12.wa.us/Arts/PerformanceAssessments/

Ohio Arts Assessment Collaborative (OAAC). (2015). *Measuring student growth in the arts for K-12 students*. Retrieved from http://www.oaae.net/en/resources/2016-04-19-18-28-32/ohio-arts-assessment-collaborative-measuring-student-growth-in-the-arts

Oliver, T. (2007). Establishing continuity of the NAEP Arts Education Assessments: Implications of the NAEP 1978 music assessment. *Journal of Historical Research in Music Education, 29*(1), 12–25.

Petrulis, R., Zhu, M., Zhang, X., & Lewis, A. (2010). *Technical documentation for the South Carolina Art Assessment Program (SCAAP): Entry-level music and visual arts assessment 2010*. Retrieved from https://scaap.ed.sc.edu/documents/SCAAP0910TechnicalReport.pdf

Reform Support Network. (n.d.). *Measuring student growth for teachers in non-tested grades and subjects: A primer*. Retrieved from https://www2.ed.gov/about/inits/ed/implementation-support-unit/tech-assist/measuring-student-growth-teachers.pdf

Rhode Island Department of Education. (2010). *Rhode Island K-12 grade span expectations in the arts—Music*. Retrieved from http://www.ride.ri.gov/Portals/0/Uploads/Documents/Instruction-and-Assessment-World-Class-Standards/Other-Subjects/Music-RI-GSEs.pdf

Schneider, C. (2005). Measuring student achievement in the future based on lessons from the past: The NAEP arts assessment. *Music Educators Journal, 92*(2), 56–61.

Shavelson, R. J., Baxter, G. P., & Gao, X. (1993). Sampling variability of performance assessments. *Journal of Educational Measurement, 30,* 215–232.

Shavelson, R. J., Ruiz-Primo, M. A., & Wiley, E. W. (1999). Note on sources of sampling variability in science performance assessments. *Journal of Educational Measurement, 36*(1), 61–71.

Shuler, S. C. (2009). Music assessment and the Nation's Report Card: MENC's response to the 2008 NAEP and recommendations for future NAEP in music. *Music Educators Journal, 96*(1), 12–13.

Shuler, S. C., Brophy, T. S., Sabol, F. R., McGreevy-Nichols, S., & Schuttler, M. J. (2016) Arts assessment in the age of accountability: Challenges and opportunities in implementation, design, and measurement. In H. Braun (Ed.), *Meeting the challenges to measurement in an era of accountability* (pp. 183–216). New York, NY: Routledge.

South Dakota Commission on Teaching and Learning. (2015). *South Dakota teacher effectiveness handbook.* Retrieved from http://doe.sd.gov/teachereffectiveness/documents/Handbook.pdf

Stites, R., & Malin, H. (2008). *An unfinished canvas: A review of large-scale assessment in K-12 arts education.* Menlo Park, CA: SRI International.

Traub, R. E., & Rowley, G. L. (1980). Reliability of test scores and decisions. *Applied Psychological Measurement, 4,* 517–545.

US Department of Education. (2011). *Tennessee arts growth measures system.* Retrieved from https://www2.ed.gov/programs/racetothetop/communities/tle2-tn-arts-system.pdf

US Department of Education. (2012). *Targeting growth: Using student learning objectives as a measure of educator effectiveness.* Retrieved from https://www2.ed.gov/about/inits/ed/implementation-support-unit/tech-assist/targeting-growth.pdf

Vanneman, A., Shuler, S., & Sandene, B. (1998). NAEP and music: Framework, field test, and assessment. *Focus on NAEP, 3*(2), 1–6.

Washington State Arts Commission. (2006). *Arts for every student: Arts education resources initiative.* Retrieved from http://www.arts.wa.gov/media/dynamic/docs/Arts-Education-Resources-Initative-Booklet.pdf

Webb, N. M., Shavelson, R. J., & Haertel, E. H. (2006). Reliability coefficients and generalizability theory. *Handbook of Statistics, 26*(4), 81–124.

Wesolowski, B. C., Wind, S. A., & Engelhard, G. (2015). Rater fairness in music performance assessment: Evaluating model-data fit and differential rater functioning. *Musicae Scientiae, 19,* 147–170.

White, S., & Vanneman, A. (1999). Student musical activities and achievement in music: NAEP 1997 arts assessment. *NAEP Facts, 4*(1), n1.

Wolfe, E. W. (2004). Identifying rater effects using latent trait models. *Psychology Science, 46,* 35–51.

Wolfe, E. W., & McVay, A. (2012). Application of latent trait models to identifying substantively interesting raters. *Educational Measurement: Issues and Practice, 31*(3), 31–37.

Yap, C. C., Lewis, A., & Feldon, D. (2007). *Efficacy of a web-based training and monitoring procedure in scoring performance tasks.* Paper presented at the Annual Meeting of the American Educational Research Association, Chicago, IL.

CHAPTER 20

....

VALIDITY, RELIABILITY, AND FAIRNESS IN MUSIC TESTING

....

BRIAN C. WESOLOWSKI AND
STEFANIE A. WIND

THE focus of this chapter is on validity, reliability, and fairness in music testing. A test can be defined simply as any procedure whereby data is collected. In the context of music, a test can be described more specifically as the collection and interpretation of data representing a particular musical behavior using a systematic and uniform procedure. As such, a test in music can encompass the evaluation of any number of musical behaviors and the collection of data using any number of techniques. Examples may include a multiple choice test to measure musical aptitude, a checklist to measure a musical procedure, a performance assessment to measure music performance achievement, an essay or oral exam to measure a student's ability to discuss steps they took to solve a musical problem, or a systematic observation to measure a student's ability on a particular musical task. With any test, the collection of data needs to be valid, reliable, and fair in order to ensure quality and provide defensibility of the assessment. With any assessment, test users need to ensure that quality inferences are made from a test (i.e., validity), be confident that students with similar knowledge, skills, and abilities will receive similar scores across repeated administrations (i.e., reliability), and certify that the test is accessible and appropriate for all students, regardless of any subgroup affiliation such as race, ethnicity, gender, socioeconomic status, and so forth (i.e., fairness). This chapter is designed to help music educators better understand validity, reliability, and fairness within the framework of measurement and evaluation and to help contextualize it in the field of music education.

VALIDITY

General Considerations and Definitions

The recent revision of the *Standards for Educational and Psychological Testing* (AERA, APA, & NCME, 2014) defines validity as follows:

> Validity refers to the degree to which evidence and theory support the interpretations of the test scores for proposed uses of tests. Validity is, therefore, the most fundamental consideration in developing tests and evaluating tests. The process of validation involves accumulating relevant evidence to provide a sound scientific basis for the proposed score interpretations.   (p. 11)

Tests are developed with specific objectives in mind. These objectives may include the measurement of how well a student performs at a given point in time in a particular content area, to forecast or estimate a student's future standing based on a related criterion, or to infer the degree to which a student possesses a particular latent quality that can be reflected by a testing outcome. Each of these objectives can be supported by specific validation methods. These may include the statistical demonstration that a particular set of items supports a particular content area, the correlation between a test and a criterion variable, or statistical support of how well particular items fit a latent construct. According to the *Standards*, multiple findings must be taken into account in order to assess the validity of a test for a particular interpretation and use.

The validation process includes the gathering of specific evidence that supports a test's outcomes in relation to the context in which it was used. Therefore, it is not the test itself that is validated, but the inferences one makes from the measure based on the context of its use. As Vernon (1960) argues, a test is always valid for some purpose, and therefore can be considered on a continuum of more valid or less valid depending on the circumstance for which it is being implemented.

History and Definitions of Validity Theory

Historically, "validation" is a catchall term for the procedures that determine the usefulness of a measure. Based on classic definitions of validity, a test is considered to be valid if it measures what it purports to measure. Over the years, however, philosophical shifts have occurred in the paradigms and frameworks of validity theory. Most notably, this shift is evidenced through the focus of the classification of multiple types of validity of the test itself to a unified approach of validity evidence in the context in which the test is being used. Broadly, the first half of the 20th century was led by the singular concept of a criterion-based (and closely associated content-based) model of validity; in the 1950s and 1960s, the concept shifted toward the construct-based model of validity. Starting in the 1980s, the concept began to shift toward a more unified, consequential-based model of validity that included expanded discussions of the moral foundations to testing and measurement (see Angoff, 1988; Hubley & Zumbo, 1996; Jonson & Plake, 1998; Kane, 2001, for detailed histories of validity theory).

The Criterion-Based Model of Validity

The earliest writings on validity include sophisticated summaries of how to calibrate values of an attribute of interest and correlate them to a preexisting, established criterion value (Cronbach & Gleser, 1965). Validity, from this perspective, is the accuracy in which the estimated values match the criterion values. As Cureton (1950) notes:

> A more direct method of investigation, which is always preferred wherever feasible, is to give the test to a representative sample of the group with whom it is to be used, observe and score performances of the actual task by the members of this sample, and see how well the test performances agree with the task performances.   (p. 623)

As an example, if a new music aptitude measure were to be constructed, the data gathered from the new measure could be correlated with data gathered from a previously existing music aptitude measure (i.e., criterion scores) to gather validity evidence of the new measure. In this case, each measure purports to measure musical aptitude and therefore, if the correlations are high and positive, evidence of criterion validity exists. According to the criterion-based model, there are four particular types of validity: (1) *predictive validity* (how well a score on a test predicts a measurable criterion); (2) *concurrent validity* (how well a test score corresponds to previously established measures of the same construct); (3) *convergent validity* (how well a test score converges, or is similar to tests that should theoretically have high correlations), and (4) *discriminant validity* (how well a test score diverges, or is dissimilar to tests that should theoretically have low correlations).

    Criterion-based models are useful in contexts where an appropriate criterion exists. However, a disadvantage to the criterion-based model is the availability and/or validity of the criterion measure itself.

The Content-Based Model of Validity

The disadvantage of criterion validity is accessibility to a high-quality criterion measure in the criterion-based model. This led to a content-based model of validity. The content-based model posits the establishment of a measure based on a desired outcome with content expert interpretation of the scores. As an example, intrinsic validity of a measure is accepted if a music performance achievement measure can appropriately discriminate between high and low achieving performances based on music content experts' opinions. Here, the measure itself is the criterion for performance achievement, as opposed to correlating it to another criterion measures. Messick (1989) describes content validity as "the domain of relevance and representativeness of the test instrument" (p. 17). Content validity arguments include two key components. First, items must adequately represent the domain of interest. The items ideally represent an adequate sample of a particular dimension of interest. Second, the measure should be constructed sensibly. Specifically, detail should be given to features such as clarity in instruction, appropriateness of language, and overall appearance of the measure itself. Although this model is acceptable in contexts such as auditions, placements, or other achievement-based assessments, it often comes with a confirmatory bias and subjectivity of content expert opinion.

The Construct-Based Model of Validity

The previous descriptions make clear that criterion- and content-based validity models are of limited value for the evaluation of constructs common to the field of music (as well as many other psychological and behavioral fields). For example, the constructs of musical aptitude, performance achievement, and musical intelligence are theoretical constructs that are not directly observable. Therefore, inferences must be made based on operationalizations set forth in the testing context and measurement instruments.

Cronbach and Meehl's (1955) construct-based model of validity was based on an adaptation of a hypotheticodeductive (HD) model of theory (Popper, 1959, 1962). The HD model is a scientific method of inquiry where hypotheses can be validated or falsified based on tests of observable data. The model is based on a set of axiomatic theorems connected by sets of empirical laws used to validate the observable data in order to infer evidence of an unobserved, latent trait. According to the 1966 *Standards* (APA, AERA, & NCME, 1966), construct validity "is ordinarily studied when the tester wishes to increase his understanding of the psychological qualities being measured in by the test.... Construct validity is relevant when the tester accepts no existing measure as a definitive criterion" (p. 13).

Construct validation is based on theories of unobservable (i.e., latent) traits that are inferred through secondary, observable variables:

> A psychological construct is an idea developed or "constructed" as a work of informed, scientific imagination; that is, it is a theoretical idea developed to explain and to organize some aspects of existing knowledge...the construct is much more than a label; it is a dimension understood or inferred from its network of interrelationships.   (APA, AERA, & NCME, 1974, p. 29)

The validation process is underscored by four distinct processes: (1) the development of a theory, (2) the development of a measure to both directly and indirectly reflect the theory, (3) the development of a hypothesis to reflect the theory, and (4) the testing of the hypothesis against the theory. As a result, the content validation process comprises three methodological principles: (1) a broader theoretical conceptualization of validation principles, (2) the explicit statement of a proposed hypothesis and related interpretation, and (3) the explicit statement of alternative hypotheses.

A Unified Model of Validity

Construct validation processes provided the foundation for broader and more current perspectives in the concept of validation. Messick (1989, 1996a, 1996b) provided early discussions of a unified view to the validity argument under the umbrella of construct validity, where heavier emphasis is placed on how the test scores are used and what context they are used in. According to Messick (1989), "validity is an integrated evaluative judgment of the degree to which empirical evidence and theoretical rationales support the *adequacy* and *appropriateness* of *inferences* and *actions* based on test scores or other modes of assessment" (p. 13, emphasis in original).

Messick (1996b) provides six key types of validity criteria that should function as interdependent and complementary forms of evidence for all educational and psychological measurement: (1) *content* (i.e., the knowledge, skills, and other attributes to be revealed by the assessment task), (2) *substantive* (i.e., the verification of the domain processes to be revealed in assessment tasks), (3) *structure* (i.e., scoring consistency with what is known about the internal structure of the construct domain), (4) *generalizability* (i.e., representative coverage of the content and processes of the construct domain), (5) *external factors* (i.e., the extent that the assessment scores' relationship with other measures and nonassessment behaviors reflect the expected high, low, and interactive relations implicit in the specified construct), and (6) *consequential* (i.e., evidence and rationales for evaluating the intended and unintended consequences of score interpretation and use in both the short term and long term).

Most notable of Messick's (1989) validity argument is the notion of consequence. If a music performance achievement measure is to be constructed, there may be several different meanings and interpretations of the resulting scores. These may include the result of a particular instructional intervention for a student, placement in an ensemble, acceptance into a program of study, or an ensemble adjudication (e.g., in the United States, an all-state ranking). Lane and Stone (2002) outline several examples of both intended and unintended consequences of validity arguments. Examples of intended consequences may include:

Motivation of the measure;
Content and strategies underscoring the assessment protocol;
Format of the assessment;
Improved learning;
Professional development support;
Use and nature of test preparation activities; and/or
Beliefs and awareness of the assessment, assessment process, criteria for judging; and use of the results.

Examples of unintended consequences may include:

The narrowing of the instructional process or curriculum to focus on specific learning outcomes assessed;

Use of preparation materials closely associated with the assessment without direct changes to curriculum or instruction;

Use of unethical assessment preparation or related materials; and/or Inappropriate
test scores by administrators.

In these cases, the validation process can be supported by the processes of constructing,
investigating, and evaluating arguments for and against the intended interpretation and
application of the resulting test scores. Questions that guide the development of these
arguments may include:

What is the purpose of this assessment?
How will the results of the assessment be used?
Who are the stakeholders that require an explanation of the results?
What are the stakeholders' perceptions of the assessment?
What are the intended and unintended consequences of the assessment?
What benefits have the participants gained in participating in the assessment?
What is the direct influence of student achievement through participation in the
assessment?
To what extent do particular variables influence and/or predict assessment outcomes?
What is the intended impact of assessment outcomes on future teaching and learning?
To what extent are students and/or teachers included in the accountability process of
the assessment?

Messick (1989) argues, "Inferences are hypotheses and the validation of inferences is
hypothesis testing" (pp. 13–14). Kane (2001) further elaborates that these inferences are
based on a network, which leads "from the scores to the conclusions and decisions based
on the scores, as well as the assumptions supporting these inferences" (p. 56). Validity,
therefore, can be conceptualized as an evaluative *argument* based on scientific theory.
Because validity evidence is contextual, no single hypothesis can be confirmed or discon-
firmed, only supported through appropriate evidence.

Sources of Invalidity

Two plausible rival hypotheses that challenge the proposed interpretation of the results
of an assessment may be generated when encountered with unintended consequences:
construct underrepresentation (i.e., *construct deficiency*) and *construct-irrelevant variance*
(i.e., *construct contamination*). *Construct underrepresentation* "refers to the degree to
which a test fails to capture important aspects of the construct" (AERA et al., 2014, p. 12).
In other words, the task being measured fails to account for important dimensions of the
construct, yielding an outcome that fails to provide evidence of a student's true ability.
As an example, an assessment developed to measure individual student performance
achievement may underrepresent the achievement construct if the difficulty level of the
student's instrument is not accounted for; or, the assessment instrument only accounts
for auditory facets of the performance when psychomotor facets, such as body carriage
or instrument positioning, may influence the outcome.

Construct-irrelevant variance "refers to the degree to which test scores are affected by processes that are extraneous to the test's intended purpose (AERA et al., 2014, p. 12). In other words, the test measures too many variables that are not relevant to the assessment context, leading to a systematic over- or underestimation of a student's ability level. As an example, in a large group music performance assessment, a sight-reading piece may be overly difficult for an ensemble. This may lead to a case of *construct-irrelevant difficulty*. Another ensemble may have familiarity with the sight-reading piece. This may lead to a case of *construct-irrelevant easiness*. Studies of internal and external assessment structures can provide empirical evidence of systematic patterning (Wesolowski, Wind, & Engelhard, 2015). These studies include analyses of *differential item functioning* (DIF) (i.e., subgroups of test takers with similar status on the assessment criterion have systematically different responses to a particular item), *differential rater functioning* (DRF) (i.e., subgroups of test takers with similar status on a performance-based assessment criterion show have systematically different results due to differential severity/leniency of a rater), and *differential facet functioning* (DFF) (i.e., subgroups of test takers with similar status on the assessment criterion have systematically different responses to any facet of interest).

The *Standards* (AERA, APA, & NCME, 1999) deliberately state:

> Validation is the joint responsibility of the test developer and the test user. The test developer is responsible for furnishing relevant evidence and a rationale in support of the intended use. The test user is ultimately responsible for evaluating the evidence in the particular setting in which the test is to be used.   (p. 11)

Therefore, the joint endeavor of both test developer and test user toward the validation of an assessment context is fundamental to the unified model of validity.

The validity of a musical test is one of the most important considerations in musical assessments. As Asmus (2010) notes, "Gathering evidence of validity should be standard operating procedure for anyone developing a music assessment" (p. 143). If the validity of a test is not established, the resulting data and any inferences drawn from the testing context are meaningless. Therefore, with the administration of any musical test, it is paramount for the test user, whether a policymaker, music administrator, or music educator, to be clear in what the test purports to be measuring and whether the test results will specifically answer what is being asked.

RELIABILITY

General Considerations and Definitions

The recent revision of the *Standards for Educational and Psychological Testing* (AERA et al., 2014) defines reliability as follows:

> The general notion of reliability/precision is defined in terms of *consistency over replications* of the testing procedure. Reliability/precision is high if the scores for

each person are consistent over replications of the testing procedure and is low if the scores are not consistent over replications.   (p. 35, emphasis added)

This definition highlights an emphasis within the *Standards* on the notion of replications as central to the conceptualization of reliability, where replications are defined to reflect a particular interpretation and use of test scores. Brennan (2001) points out that replications can be specified that reflect the various sources of measurement error of interest or concern for a given testing procedure. For example, in a rater-mediated music performance assessment, replications could be defined as raters, such that consistency over raters provides evidence of reliability. Likewise, replications of a standardized college admissions examination could be defined as administrations, such that consistency of student scores across administrations provides evidence of reliability.

A major theme emphasized in the recent revision of the *Standards* is the need for reliability evidence to support each intended interpretation and use of test scores. A variety of reliability coefficients have been proposed that reflect different underlying conceptualizations of replications and the role of measurement error. In the next section, we describe reliability estimates based on classical test theory (CTT; i.e., true score theory), followed by a discussion of reliability estimation methods based on modern measurement theories.

True Score Reliability Estimates

The first set of reliability coefficients presented in this chapter are based on the CTT model. As noted by Wesolowski, Wind, and Engelhard (2015, 2016a, 2016b), much of the empirical work done in the field of music teaching and learning related to measurement is based on the CTT framework (see Boyle & Radocy, 1986; Asmus & Radocy, 1992). Developed in relation to early work on correlation coefficients (e.g., Spearman, 1904, 1910, 1913), the CTT model is defined as shown in Figure 20.1.

In Figure 20.1, X is the observed score, T is the true score, and E represents error. Within the framework of CTT, true scores are a theoretical concept defined as the mean observed score (i.e., expected value) across infinite replications of a measurement procedure. Error scores are the difference between the observed score and the true score. The CTT model is based on three major underlying assumptions that facilitate the calculation of reliability coefficients. First, the average value of error scores for a population of test takers is zero. Second, the correlation between true scores and error scores within a population of test takers is zero. Finally, the correlation between error scores for repeated testing procedures (unique tests or unique occasions) is expected to be zero (Crocker & Algina, 1986; Lord & Novick, 1968).

$$X = T + E$$

FIGURE 20.1 Classical test theory model.

$$\rho_{XT} = \frac{\sigma_T}{\sigma_X}$$

FIGURE 20.2 Classical test theory reliability index formula.

Based on these assumptions, reliability is defined as the correlation between true scores and observed scores, which can be expressed as the ratio of the standard deviation of true scores to the standard deviation of observed scores using the *reliability index*. This is shown in Figure 20.2.

Because true scores are unknown, it is necessary to approximate the reliability index using observed scores. Accordingly, the *reliability coefficient* (ρ_{xx}) is defined as the correlation between observed scores across replications. The reliability coefficient ranges between .00 and 1.00. A reliability of 1.00 indicates that the differences between observed scores are perfectly consistent with differences in true scores. A reliability of .00 indicates that the differences between observed scores are perfectly inconsistent with differences in true scores.

Differences in the definition of replications lead to different specifications of the reliability coefficient. In this section, we describe reliability coefficients that reflect three major specifications of replications: (1) Replications across administrations, or stability coefficients; (2) Replications across alternate forms, called equivalence coefficients; and (3) Replications across items, known as internal consistency coefficients.

Replications Across Administrations: Stability Reliability Coefficients

The first category of CTT reliability coefficients describes the consistency of observed scores across administrations. Coefficients in this category can be considered *stability reliability coefficients*, because they describe the degree to which the ordering of test takers in terms of total scores is stable across administrations. First, the *test-retest coefficient* is the correlation between observed scores obtained from separate administrations of the same test form, where there is some time interval between administrations. Values of the test-retest coefficient describe the degree to which differences in observed scores can be attributed to differences across administrations, such as administration procedures, scoring errors, guessing, or other changes in behavior. No single rule exists regarding the appropriate length of time between administrations when test-retest reliability is of interest. However, Crocker and Algina (1986) offer the following advice:

> The time period should be long enough to allow effects of memory or practice to fade but not so long as to allow maturational or historical changes to occur in the examinees' true scores. The purpose for which test scores are to be used should be taken into account when designating the waiting time.   (p. 133)

In addition to the repeated administration of a single test form, it is also possible to estimate reliability using two administrations of similar test forms. Specifically, the *test-retest with alternative forms* coefficient is calculated as the correlation between observed scores on two similar test forms. Values of this reliability coefficient describe the degree to which differences can be attributed to administrations *as well as* differences in the content included in each form. Various criteria exist for establishing the degree of acceptable similarity between test forms, with the strictest definition based on the concept of *parallel forms*. Parallel forms exist when students have equivalent true scores on each form, and error variance for each form is equal—such that the two test forms have equivalent means and variances of observed scores.

Replications Across Alternate Forms: Equivalence Coefficients

The second category of CTT reliability coefficients includes coefficients that describe the consistency or equivalence of observed scores on alternative forms of a test. The *alternative forms reliability* or *equivalence coefficient* is calculated as the correlation between observed scores on parallel or similar test forms. Unlike the test-retest coefficient, data collected for alternative forms reliability studies should only include a short time period between administrations to prevent test-taker fatigue. Further, in order to prevent ordering effects, the presentation of the two forms should be reversed in half the sample, such that one half of test takers receives Form A first, followed by Form B, while the second half receives Form B first, followed by Form A. Values of alternative forms reliability coefficients describe the degree to which observed scores are affected by differences related to the two forms.

Replications Across Items: Internal Consistency Coefficients

The third category of CTT reliability coefficients includes coefficients that describe the consistency of observed scores across items within a single test form. These coefficients are desirable in situations in which only one test form will be administered on only one occasion. Internal consistency coefficients reflect the correlation between observed scores across items or subsets of items within a single form. Values of *internal consistency coefficients* describe the degree to which individual items or item subsets reflect the same content domain. A variety of CTT internal consistency coefficients have been proposed and are commonly applied in practice, including split-half methods and methods based on item covariances. This section describes two commonly used internal consistency reliability coefficients that reflect these two major categories: Spearman-Brown reliability and Cronbach's alpha coefficient.

Split-Half Methods

The first major category of internal consistency reliability coefficients is based on creating two subsets of items within a test form (i.e., two halves of a test) that are parallel or approximately parallel forms. A variety of methods are used in practice to create test halves, including random assignment of items to halves, splitting items based on odd and even numbers, rank-ordering items by difficulty and assigning items with odd and even ranks to different halves, and splitting the items based on content. After test halves are established, the correlation between observed scores on each half is used as an estimate of reliability.

Because reliability coefficients calculated from split-halves do not reflect the full length of test forms, several correction procedures have been proposed that provide an estimate of the reliability coefficient that would have been obtained using the entire test form. The *Spearman-Brown Correction* (i.e., the Spearman-Brown prophecy formula) is one such correction that is calculated using two halves of a single test form (Brown, 1910; Spearman, 1910). Stated mathematically, the correction is shown in Figure 20.3, where ρ_{AB} is the observed correlation between half-tests A and B. When applying the Spearman-Brown correction, it is important to note that the degree to which the halves used to calculate ρ_{AB} are parallel will affect the corrected value of the reliability coefficient. Deviations from parallel forms will result in less-accurate reliability coefficients.

Methods Based on Item Covariances

The second major type of internal consistency reliability coefficient is calculated using observed scores on individual items. These reliability estimates reflect the consistency of test taker performance across individual items on a test, thus overcoming potential problems associated with different reliability coefficients resulting from different definitions of half-tests. Several reliability coefficients based on item covariances are commonly used in practice, including the Kuder-Richardson formulas (Kuder & Richardson, 1937), and Cronbach's alpha coefficient (Cronbach, 1951). Because the two formulas yield equivalent results, and because Cronbach's alpha coefficient can be applied to both dichotomous and polytomous items, we focus here on Cronbach's alpha.

Cronbach (1951) presented a reliability coefficient for a single test administration that is based on the view of the k individual items within a test form as k individual subtests that act as a type of replication of the measurement procedure. Using the covariances

$$\hat{\rho}_{XX'n} = \frac{2\rho_{AB}}{1 + \rho_{AB}}$$

FIGURE 20.3 Spearman-Brown prophecy formula.

$$\alpha = \frac{k}{k-1}\left(1 - \frac{\Sigma\sigma_i^2}{\sigma_X^2}\right)$$

FIGURE 20.4 Cronbach *Coefficient Alpha* formula.

among the k individual items, Cronbach presented *coefficient alpha* (see Figure 20.4) as an internal consistency reliability coefficient that is calculated as follows for dichotomous or polytomous items:

In Figure 20.4, k is the number of items, $\hat{\sigma}_i^2$ is the variance of item i, and $\hat{\sigma}_x^2$ is the variance of the total test score. Values of coefficient alpha reflect an estimate of the proportion of variance that can be attributed to the true score, where higher values reflect higher levels of consistency across items.

Alpha-if-Deleted Statistics

Item analysis procedures based on CTT often include the use of item-level statistics that describe the change in internal consistency reliability that would occur if the item of interest was not included in the reliability estimate. For individual items, these *alpha-if-deleted statistics* are calculated using the equation in Figure 20.4 on the remaining k items. These statistics provide a valuable diagnostic tool for identifying items that are not homogeneous with the other items in a measurement procedure by comparing the observed alpha-if-deleted statistic to the value of coefficient alpha calculated from the entire set of items.

Modern Measurement Theory reliability coefficients

In addition to reliability coefficients based on CTT, additional methods for evaluating reliability have been proposed based on modern measurement theory frameworks. This section provides an overview of generalizability theory as a measurement framework that focuses on issues related to reliability, followed by a brief description of reliability analyses within the context of item response theory (IRT).

Reliability Estimates Based on Generalizability Theory

Generalizability theory (G theory) is a framework for considering a variety of reliability issues based on a combination of principles from CTT and analysis of variance (ANOVA; Fisher, 1925). The advent of G theory is marked by Cronbach and his colleagues' (Cronbach, Gleser, Nanda, & Rajaratnam, 1972) recognition that typical reliability coefficients are limited in that they do not provide a method for distinguishing among multiple sources of error in measurement procedures. Drawing on the statistical tools provided by ANOVA, Cronbach et al. (1972) applied ANOVA methods to the context of educational and psychological testing in order to systematically explore sources of error variance. In particular, they observed that researchers can "learn far more by allocating variation to facets than by carrying the conventional reliability analysis" (p. 2).

Specifically, G theory allows researchers to define reliability coefficients that reflect the unique combination of variables in a given measurement procedure, such as items, raters, or occasions, in order to identify the most efficient sample sizes and combinations of facets for future administrations. G theory analyses include two major steps. First, *generalizability studies* are conducted in order to estimate reliability using the observed set of facets. Second, *decision studies* are conducted in order to calculate the predicted changes in reliability coefficients that would occur with different sample sizes and subsets of the facets included in the generalizability study. While it is beyond the scope of the current chapter to explore methods for calculating reliability coefficients based on G theory in depth, there are useful introductory texts on G theory by Shavelson and Webb (1991) and Brennan (2010).

Reliability Estimates Based on Item Response Theory

Within the context of IRT (see Volume 1, Chapter 22, of this handbook), reliability analyses focus primarily on the concept of *targeting* between items, test takers, and other facets in a measurement procedure, where the magnitude of measurement error varies depending on the "appropriateness" of items for persons. Because IRT models allow for the estimation of items, test takers, and other facets on a common scale, it is possible to make direct comparisons between the two in order to examine targeting. Targeting can be maximized in order to yield optimal levels of "information" or precision in the estimation of achievement levels (Embretson & Reise, 2000). Additional details regarding the consideration of reliability issues within the context of IRT can be found in Hambleton and Swaminathan (1985) and Embretson and Reise (2000).

High reliability of a test is essential for a test to be valid. Therefore, it is important to ensure high reliability of all tests in music. Testing, however, is never without error. A misconception often demonstrated by practitioners is that a test itself has high reliability and/or high validity. Regardless of how well a test has been developed or how high of a reliability is cited for a test or measure, practitioners should understand that reliability changes from testing context to testing context, sample to sample. Therefore, estimates of reliability should be considered properties of the scores of the examinees of within the testing context, not the properties of the test itself. Because the estimates of reliability are sample-dependent, how can a practitioner ensure reliability of a measure within their classroom? According to Brookhart (2003), the goal of having a reliable assessment in the classroom is achieved by collecting "stable information about the gap between students' work and 'ideal' work (as defined in students' and teachers' learning objectives" (p. 9). Therefore, in the context of music assessment, teachers need to communicate clear learning objectives for their students, specifically how the students will be measured for each objective, and have an open communication between where the students' current ability is and what the standard for achievement is.

Fairness

This section describes the concept of fairness as it applies to educational and psychological testing in general.

General Considerations and Definitions

Essentially, fairness is a validity issue concerned with the degree to which measurement procedures result in accurate estimates of student achievement in terms of a construct. The 2014 revision of the *Standards* (AERA et al.) is the first version to include a standalone chapter on fairness as a separate foundational area for evaluating the psychometric quality of educational and psychological tests. In the standards, fairness is defined as "responsiveness to individual characteristics and testing contexts so that test scores will yield valid interpretations for intended uses" (p. 50).

The discussion of fairness in the *Standards* emphasizes the need to maximize test takers' opportunity to demonstrate their standing on the construct of interest in order to ensure fair testing procedures. Accordingly, test developers and test users are called to consider potential obstacles to these opportunities for individual and groups of test takers. These threats to fairness include a variety of aspects of the testing procedure that result in systematic patterns of observed scores within subgroups that lead to inappropriate interpretations and uses of test scores.

Threats to Fairness in Testing

A variety of factors can act as threats to fairness in a testing situation. The *Standards* (AERA et al., 2014) identify four major categories of threats to fairness: (1) test content; (2) test context; (3) test response; and (4) opportunity to learn. Minimizing these threats is key to ensuring fair testing procedures.

Threats to fairness related to *test content* result in systematic variation in test scores that are not related to the construct of interest (i.e., construct-irrelevant variance) and can be attributed to item content that systematically favors or disadvantages some groups over others based on prior knowledge, experiences, level of interest or motivation, or other variables. Such test content confounds the interpretation of test scores. Next, threats to fairness related to *test context* include aspects of the testing environment that systematically affect performance in a construct-irrelevant way. For example, a testing environment might introduce construct-irrelevant variance through the clarity or degree of specificity used in the test instructions, the complexity of vocabulary within the test items or tasks, and the language in which the test is administered.

The third major threat to fairness discussed in the *Standards* is related to the *response types* elicited by assessment tasks. Specifically, it is possible for fairness issues to arise when the type of response required for an assessment task results in different score interpretations across individual and groups of test takers. For example, writing or speaking tasks may result in differences in responses that are unrelated to the construct due to cultural views related to wordiness or rate of speech, and survey items may result in differences in responses due to perceptions of social desirability. Finally, threats to fairness can result from differences among test takers related to *opportunity-to-learn*. The *Standards* define opportunity-to-learn as "the extent to which individuals have had exposure to instruction or knowledge that affords them the opportunity to learn the content and skills targeted by the test" (AERA et al., 2014, p. 56). Different opportunities to learn across test takers can result in construct-irrelevant differences in test scores that threaten the validity of test score interpretations, particularly for high-stakes decisions.

Clarity in Operational Definitions

When considering issues related to fairness in testing, it is important to note the distinction between operational definitions of several key terms. Although the terms "differential facet functioning," "bias," and "fairness" are often used interchangeably, these terms have distinct definitions within the field of psychometrics. A brief description of these concepts is provided below.

Differential Facet Functioning

The terms "differential item functioning" (DIF), "differential person functioning" (DPF), and other forms of "differential facet functioning" (DFF) are frequently used in discussions related to testing to describe a lack of fairness that can be attributed to various facets in a measurement procedure, including items and persons. Broadly, the concept of DFF refers to differences in the probability for a correct or positive response between individual or subgroups of test takers with equivalent levels on the construct (i.e., the same ability level). A variety of methods exist for detecting DFF related to both CTT and IRT (see IRT, Volume 1, Chapter 22, of this handbook); across both approaches, DFF analyses focus on identifying interactions between response probabilities (i.e., item difficulties) and subgroup membership (e.g., race/ethnicity, gender, or socioeconomic status). It is important to note that the finding of DFF does not necessarily imply a threat to fairness. Rather, DFF analyses are used to identify subgroup differences for which qualitative evidence is needed to determine whether threats to fairness are observed (Millsap, 2011).

Bias

Whereas DFF refers to statistical evidence of interactions between a facet of interest and characteristics of test takers, *bias* in testing refers to qualitative evidence that these interactions result in meaningful patterns that suggest threats to fairness. Accordingly, statistical evidence of DFF is not sufficient to identify bias in a testing procedure; these patterns must be explored qualitatively in order to detect potential threats to fairness.

It is important to note that, although DFF provides a starting point for mixed-methods investigations of bias, statistical evidence of DFF does not always suggest the presence of bias.

Maximizing Fairness Through Changes to the Testing Procedure

As discussed previously, fairness is a broad concept that describes the degree to which test score interpretations are free from construct-irrelevant variance that results from differences in test takers' opportunities to demonstrate their standing on a construct (AERA et al., 2014). A variety of sources of evidence are needed in order to ensure fair testing practices for all test takers. The *Standards* summarize the requirements for ensuring fairness as follows:

> Fairness is a fundamental issue for valid test score interpretation, and it should therefore be the goal for all testing applications. Fairness is the responsibility of all parties involved in test development, administration, and score interpretation for the intended purposes of the test.   (AERA et al., 2014, p. 62)

According to the *Standards* (AERA et al., 2014), test design should be approached from the perspective of *universal design*, such that tests are designed to be as "usable as possible for all test takers" (AERA et al., 2014, p. 56). However, design principles are not always sufficient to ensure fair testing practices for all test takers. As a result, fairness efforts often result in adaptations to testing procedures in order to overcome threats to fairness and maximize access to the construct being measured for individuals or groups of test takers. These adaptations vary in terms of the degree to which the resulting test scores remain comparable with those obtained from the original procedure. Specifically, *accommodations* are relatively minimal changes to the testing procedure that maintain the intended construct, such as changes to the presentation, format, or response procedures. On the other hand, *modifications* are more substantial in terms of the construct; test scores obtained from modified testing procedures do not maintain the same interpretation in terms of the construct.

On the other hand, changes to testing procedures may result from test security considerations that result in the need for alternative forms of a test for use across administrations. When different forms of the same test are used, it is necessary to perform statistical procedures to arrive at a common scale for the two (or more) sets of scores obtained from different forms. A range of *scale linking* methods have been proposed based on CTT and IRT that aim to provide a common score scale across test forms. One commonly used form of scale linking is *test equating*, which is a statistical process used to identify exchangeable scores across different tests or test forms that measure the same construct and that are built to reflect the same content specifications.

Wolfe (2004) identified three major requirements for equating: (1) symmetry, (2) group invariance, and (3) equity. First, *symmetry* requires that student achievement measures be comparable in both directions (Form A can be equated to Form B and vice versa). *Group invariance* requires that the results from equating be independent of the particular group of students used to conduct the equating. Finally, *equity* requires that test takers will be indifferent to which of the equated test forms is used to obtain measures of their achievement (Cook & Eignor, 1991; Hambleton & Swaminathan, 1985; Lord, 1980).[1]

Fairness Considerations in Rater-Mediated Assessments

In the context of rater-mediated assessments, it is essential that fairness efforts include explicit consideration of sources of construct-irrelevant variance that can be attributed to the raters whose judgmental processes are used to evaluate test-taker performances. Concerns with the quality of ratings are prevalent across research on rater-mediated assessments in a variety of domains, including music assessment. As a result, numerous methods have been proposed for detecting patterns of ratings that may suggest threats to fairness, including rater errors and differential rater functioning. Framed from a fairness perspective, threats to fairness that can be attributed to raters suggest construct-irrelevant differences in rater interpretation of performances across individual or groups of test takers.

Several authors have proposed classification schemes for patterns of ratings that suggest threats to fairness. These patterns are often described as *rater errors*, and classifications of rater errors attempt to describe systematic scoring patterns that can be attributed to construct-irrelevant influences on a rater's judgmental process. For example, Saal, Downey, and Lahey (1980) conducted a review of research on methods for evaluating rating quality in research on educational and psychological testing and concluded that there is a general lack of consistency in the terms, definitions, and methods used to detect rater errors. However, these authors noted that the most common rater errors could be classified in four broad categories: (1) leniency/severity; (2) halo; (3) response sets; and (4) score range restriction. In general, these classifications are used to describe systematic deviations from expected rating patterns that are used to "flag" raters during training or operational scoring procedures for remediation in order to improve the quality of ratings.

Leniency/severity errors include the tendency for a rater to systematically assign lower or higher ratings than are warranted by the quality of performances. These errors are identified by comparing rater severity estimates based on observed average ratings or rater calibrations from an IRT model to the overall average ratings or calibrations for a group of raters. On the other hand, *halo* errors describe the tendency for a rater to judge performances holistically, rather than distinguishing between distinct aspects of performances. Murphy and Cleveland (1991) and Saal et al. (1980) identified several methods for identifying halo error in practice. Specifically, evidence for a halo effect may be obtained through examination of correlations among ratings assigned to distinct aspects of a performance (e.g., domain ratings on an analytic rubric), where high correlations suggest a lack of discrimination among domains. Other methods for detecting halo focus on standard deviations across domains and interaction effects in a rater-by-student-by-domain ANOVA. Methods based on IRT focus on patterns of residuals that suggest less variation than expected across domains (see IRT, Volume 1, Chapter 22, in this handbook).

The third category of rater errors is *response sets*. Response set errors occur when raters interpret and use rating scale categories in an idiosyncratic or unintended fashion. Several classifications have been proposed for rater response sets. For example, within the context of IRT, Engelhard (2013) distinguishes between "noisy" raters, who provide extreme unexpected responses, and "muted" raters, who demonstrate less variation in their rating patterns than expected. A type of response set, the final category of rater errors is *range restriction*. This class of rater errors refers to a rater's tendency to assign ratings that cluster around a particular rating scale category; this category may be located anywhere on the rating scale. Essentially, the definition of this rater error reflects a view that the true scores in a population are distributed across the score range, such that a uniform or tightly clustered rating distribution would be incorrect. Indices of range restriction that are used in practice include small standard deviations for individual raters across students within domains, kurtosis of a rating distribution, and the lack of a significant student main effect in a rater-by-student-by-domain ANOVA (Murphy & Cleveland, 1991; Saal et al., 1980).

When considering fairness issues for rater-mediated assessments, it is important to note that the differences between DFF and bias in testing in general also apply to raters. Specifically, analyses used to detect DFF can be extended to raters, where interactions between rater severity and construct-irrelevant characteristics of test takers suggest the presence of differential rater functioning (Engelhard, 2008). Further investigation using qualitative methods is needed in order to establish evidence for rater bias that may compromise the interpretation of ratings for certain test takers.

Thinking Holistically About Validity, Reliability, and Fairness in Music Assessment

Data-driven educational reform plans have required all stakeholders to standardize, centralize, and provide test-based accountability procedures in our school systems. As a result, assessment as a means for academic (i.e., teaching- and learning-based) improvement and assessment as a means for accountability (i.e., policy- and program-based) evidence have become increasingly intertwined for music educators (Wesolowski, 2014). Decision-making processes underscore assessment practices in both the accountability and academic assessment paradigms. As demonstrated in Table 20.1, decisions based on music assessment results can be made at local, district, state, and national levels by a variety of individuals, including music teachers, music specialists, and administrators.

Table 20.1 Summary of Music Assessment Decisions

Type of decision	Who makes the decision?	Type of assessment used to make the decision	Example
Instructional Decision	Music Educator	Educator-constructed	Music educator uses the assessment results to determine the pace, content, and focus of their class.
Grading Decision	Music Educator	Educator-constructed	Music educator uses the assessment results to assign a grade in their class.
Diagnostic Decision	Music Educator	Educator-constructed	Music educator uses the assessment results to understand student's strengths and weaknesses.
Placement Decisions	Music Educator	Educator-constructed or Standardized	Music educator or music specialist uses the assessment results to place students in chairs or ensembles within the school program or outside of the school program (e.g., district-, state-, or national-level opportunities).
Selection Decisions	Music Educator	Standardized	Music educator uses the assessment results to select students for program-, or institutional-level admissions decisions.
Guidance Decisions	Music Educator	Standardized	Music educator uses the assessment results to guide students toward specific majors and careers that best match the student's achievement level.
Program and Curriculum Decisions	Music Educator or Administrator	Standardized	Music educator or administrator use assessment results to determine success of a program or curriculum and to determine whether a program should be implemented or eliminated.
Administrative Policy Decisions	Administrator	Standardized	Administrator use assessment results to determine how money should be spent and what programs should receive money.

Source: Adapted from Thorndike, Cunningham, Thorndike, and Hagan (1991).

Each of these individuals is a part of the assessment process and therefore can be considered a test user, as they can be involved in the development, administration, scoring, interpretation, and/or application of the assessment measure. As a result, each individual needs to be trained and informed on the appropriate use and application of such assessments. If those involved in the assessment process are not properly trained, unintended consequences to test takers can be substantial.

Kane (2013) (as cited in Caines, Bridglall, & Chatterji, 2014) provides three perspectives on assessment that should be considered by all test users in order to support the validity of measures, reliability of scoring, and fairness of the testing context to all test takers:

> A *measurement perspective*, reflecting the typical mindset of test developers and measurement researchers in standardized testing programs, describing how this group tends to approach the tasks of test development and validation;

> A *contest perspective*, reflecting the typical mindset of test takers, who view passing a high stakes test as being similar to winning a contest to help them reach their goals.

> A *pragmatic perspective*, or the mindset of typical decision makers, who count on a test to be cost-efficient, objective, fair and dependable for taking necessary actions from an institutional perspective, without adverse or untoward repercussions. (p. 9)

The *measurement perspective* concerns itself with the interpretation, precision, and accuracy of the assessment outcomes. In music assessment contexts, it is of great concern that assessments estimate the "true" measure of the individual student, ensemble, or program's achievement as consistently and reliably as possible. The *contest perspective* concerns itself with a student, ensemble, or program receiving the highest possible outcome of an assessment. In music assessment contexts, it is of great concern that the assessment is fair in providing student, ensemble, or program the same opportunity to succeed. The *pragmatic perspective* concerns itself with the concrete and public perception of validity, reliability, and fairness from a policy-driven perspective. In music assessment contexts, inferences drawn from music assessment contexts can provide grounds for important decisions regarding program longevity and related funding. The current data-driven educational climate has left music students, music educators, music specialists, and administrators in need of valid, reliable, and fair assessment measures. Most importantly, the various contexts in which the assessment of musical experiences is conducted must meet the demands of all three of Kane's (2013) perspectives in order for the measurement and evaluation processes to be considered effective.

FINAL THOUGHTS

The psychometric theories of validity, reliability, and fairness discussed in this chapter are most often considered in the context of high-stakes, large-scale assessment. So what do the considerations brought forth in this chapter mean for the music classroom and music educator? The most clear and direct information students, teachers, and parents receive about achievement in the music classroom come from classroom assessments. The way in which classroom assessments are conducted differs from the way large-scale assessments are conducted. If the psychometric principles of validity, reliability, and fairness and the related development of development and implementation of classical test theory (CTT; see Volume 1, Chapter 21, in this handbook) and item response theory (see IRT, Volume 1, Chapter 22, in this handbook) are rooted in this tradition, how can a connection be made? We propose that in the context of classroom assessments, rather than considering the individual applications of validity, reliability, and fairness in terms of psychometric theory, these concepts should be considered holistically in order to develop and implement a "high quality music classroom assessment system." By considering all types of validity evidence in the assessment building process, a music educator may gain more accurate insight into the congruency between the intentions of the assessment and what is actually being measured. Furthermore, ensuring that there is a clear and open communication between teacher and student in terms of expectations set forth by the measurement instrument and student awareness of how their performance aligns with the teacher's expectations is foundational for the validity of the assessment process. Reliability within the assessment system can be achieved by ensuring consistency in the assessment process. More specifically, regularly evaluating student performances and communicating the level of performance achievement for all students can provide stability, and more importantly, reliability, in the assessment process. Lastly, providing multiple opportunities for students to demonstrate their knowledge, skills, and abilities across different assessment-types can provide more equitability of student assessment.

Validity, reliability, and fairness are all complex issues engrained within the music assessment paradigm. As conversations continue with regard to these constructs in the context of music assessment, it is important that all test users deeply consider the philosophical aspects of music assessment and continue to refine their technical knowledge and abilities related to measurement and evaluation.

Note

1. Additional details about scale linking and equating within the context of CTT are provided by Kolen and Brennan (2014), and within the context of IRT are provided by von Davier (2011).

References

American Educational Research Association (AERA), American Psychological Association (APA), & National Council on Measurement in Education (NCME). (1999). *Standards for educational and psychological testing*. Washington, DC: AERA.

American Educational Research Association (AERA), American Psychological Association (APA), & National Council on Measurement in Education (NCME). (2014). *Standards for educational and psychological testing*. Washington, DC: AERA.

American Psychological Association (APA), American Educational Research Association (AERA), & National Council on Measurement in Education (NCME) (1966). *Standards for educational and psychological tests and manuals*. Washington, DC: American Psychological Association.

American Psychological Association (APA), American Educational Research Association (AERA), & National Council on Measurement in Education (NCME) (1974). *Standards for educational and psychological tests and manuals*. Washington, DC: American Psychological Association.

Angoff, W. H. (1988). Validity: An evolving concept. In H. Wainer & H.nI. Braun (Eds.), *Test validity*. Hillsdale, NJ: Erlbaum.

Asmus, E. P. (2010). Assuring the validity of teacher-made assessments. In T. S. Brophy (Ed.), *The practice of assessment in music education: Frameworks, models, and designs* (pp. 131–144). Chicago: GIA Publications.

Asmus, E. P., & Radocy, R. E. (1992). Quantitative analysis. In R. Colwell (Ed.), *Handbook of research on music teaching and learning* (pp. 141–183). New York, NY: Schirmer Books.

Brennan, R. L. (2001). An essay on the history and future of reliability from the perspective of replications. *Journal of Educational Measurement, 38*, 295–317. doi: 10.1111/j.1745-3984.2001.tb01129.x

Brennan, R. L. (2010). *Generalizability theory*. New York, NY: Springer-Verlag.

Brookhart, S. M. (2003). Developing measurement theory for classroom assessment purposes and uses. *Educational Measurement: Issues and Practices, 22*(4), 5–12.

Boyle, J. D., & Radocy, E. E. (1986). *Measurement and evaluation of musical experiences*. New York: Schirmer Books.

Brown, W. (1910). Some experimental results in the correlation of mental abilities. *British Journal of Psychology, 3*, 296–322. doi: 10.1111/j.2044-8295.1910.tb00207.x

Caines, J., Bridglall, B. L., & Chatterji, M. (2014). Understanding validity and fairness issues in high-stakes individual testing situations. *Quality Assurance in Education, 22*(1), 5–18.

Cook, L. L., & Eignor, D. L. (1991). IRT equating methods. *Educational Measurement: Issues and Practice, 10*(3), 37–45.

Crocker, L., & Algina, J. (1986). *Introduction to classical and modern test theory*. New York, NY: Holt, Rinehart and Winston.

Cronbach, L. J. (1951). Coefficient alpha and the internal structure of tests. *Psychometrika, 16*, 297–334. doi: 10.1007/BF02310555

Cronbach, L. J., & Gleser, G. C. (1965). *Psychological tests and personnel decisions*. Urbana: University of Illinois Press.

Cronbach, L. J., Gleser, G. C., Nanda, H., & Rajaratnam, N. (1972). *The dependability of behavioral measurements: Theory of generalizability for scores and profiles*. New York, NY: John Wiley.

Cronbach, L. J., & Meehl, P. E. (1955). Construct validity in psychological tests. *Psychological Bulletin, 52*, 281–302.

Cureton, E. E. (1950). Validity. In E. F. Lingquist (Ed.), *Educational measurement*. Washington, DC: American Council on Education.

Embretson, S. E., & Reise, S. P. (2000). *Item response theory for psychologists*. Mahwah, NJ: Erlbaum.

Engelhard, G. (2008). Differential rater functioning. *Rasch Measurement Transactions, 21*, 1124.

Engelhard, G. (2013). *Invariant measurement: Using Rasch Models in the social, behavioral, and health sciences*. New York, NY: Routledge.

Fisher, R. A. (1925). *Statistical methods for research workers*. Edinburgh, UK: Oliver & Boyd.

Hambleton, R. K., & Swaminathan, H. (1985). *Item response theory: Principles and applications*. Boston, MA: Kluwer.

Hubley, A. M., & Zumbo, B. D. (1996). A dialectic on validity: Where we have been and where we are going. *Journal of General Psychology, 123*, 207–215. doi: 10.1080/00221309.1996.9921273

Jonson, J. L., & Plake, B. S. (1998). A historical comparison of validity standards and validity practices. *Educational and Psychological Measurement, 58*, 736–753. doi: 10.1177/0013164498058005002

Kane, M. (2001). Current concerns in validity theory. *Journal of Educational Measurement, 38*, 319–342. doi: 10.1111/j.1745-3984.2001.tb01130.x

Kane, M. (2013). Validity and fairness in the testing of individuals. In Chatterji, M. (Ed.), *Validity and test use: An international dialogue on educational assessment, accountability and equity*. Bingley, UK: Emerald Group.

Kolen, M. J., & Brennan, R. L. (2014). *Test equating, scaling, and linking: Methods and practices* (3rd ed.). New York, NY: Springer.

Kuder, G. F., & Richardson, M. W. (1937). The theory of the estimation of test reliability. *Psychometrika, 2*, 151–160. doi: 10.1007/BF02288391

Lane, S., & Stone, C. A. (2002). Strategies for examining the consequences of assessment and accountability programs. *Educational Measurement: Issues and Practice, 21*(1), 23–30. doi: 10.1111/j.1745-3992.2002.tb00082.x

Lord, F. M. (1980). *Applications of item response theory to practical testing problems*. Hillsdale, NJ: Erlbaum.

Lord, F. M., & Novick, M. R. (1968). *Statistical theories of mental test scores*. Reading, MA: Addison-Wesley.

Messick, S. (1989). Validity. In R. L. Linn (Ed.), *Educational measurement* (pp. 13–103). Washington, DC: American Council on Education and National Council on Measurement in Education.

Messick, S. (1996a). Standards-based score interpretation: Establishing valid grounds for valid inferences. *Proceedings of the joint conference on standard setting for large scale assessments, sponsored by National Assessment Governing Board and The National Center for Education Statistics*. Washington, DC: Government Printing Office.

Messick, S. (1996b). Validity of performance assessment. In Philips, G. (1996). *Technical issues in large-scale performance assessment*. Washington, DC: National Center for Educational Statistics.

Millsap, R. E. (2011). *Statistical approaches to measurement invariance*. New York, NY: Routledge.

Murphy, K. R., & Cleveland, J. M. (1991). *Performance appraisal: An organizational perspective*. Boston, MA: Allyn and Bacon.

Popper, K. R. (1959). *The logic of scientific discovery*. New York: Basic Books.

Popper, K. R. (1962). *Conjectures and refutations: The growth of scientific knowledge*. New York, NY: Basic Books.

Saal, F. E., Downey, R. G., & Lahey, M. A. (1980). Rating the ratings: Assessing the psychometric quality of rating data. *Psychological Bulletin, 88*, 413–428. doi: 10.1037/0033-2909.88.2.413

Shavelson, R. J., & Webb, N. M. (1991). *Generalizability theory: A primer*. Thousand Oaks, CA: Sage.

Spearman, C. (1904). The proof and measurement of association between two things. *American Journal of Psychology, 15,* 72–101.

Spearman, C. (1910). Correlation calculated from faulty data. *British Journal of Psychology, 3,* 271–295. doi: 10.1111/j.2044-8295.1910.tb00206.x

Spearman, C. (1913). Correlations of sums and differences. *British Journal of Psychology, 5,* 417–426. doi: 10.1111/j.2044-8295.1913.tb00072.x

Thorndike, R. M., Cunningham, G., Thorndike, R. L., & Hagen, G. (1991). *Measurement and evaluation in psychology and education.* New York, NY: Macmillan.

Vernon, P. E. (1960). *Intelligence and attainment tests.* London, UK: University of London Press.

von Davier, A. A. (Ed.). (2011). *Statistical models for test equating, scaling, and linking.* New York, NY: Springer.

Wesolowski, B. C. (2014). Documenting student learning in music performance: A framework. *Music Educators Journal, 101*(1), 77–85.

Wesolowski, B. C., Wind, S. A., & Engelhard, G. (2015). Rater fairness in music performance assessment: Evaluating model-data fit and differential rater functioning. *Musicae Scientiae, 19,* 147–170.

Wesolowski, B. C., Wind, S. A., & Engelhard, G. (2016a). Rater analyses in music performance assessment: Application of the Many Facet Rasch Model. In *Connecting practice, measurement, and evaluation: Selected papers from the 5th International Symposium on Assessment in Music Education* (pp. 335–356). Chicago, IL: GIA Publications.

Wesolowski, B. C., Wind, S. A., & Engelhard, G. (2016b). Examining rater precision in music performance assessment: An analysis of rating scale structure using the multifaceted Rasch partial credit model. *Music Perception, 5,* 662–678.

Wolfe, E. W. (2004). Equating and item banking with the Rasch model. In E. V. Smith & R. M. Smith (Eds.), *Introduction to Rasch measurement.* Maple Grove, MN: JAM Press.

CHAPTER 21

··

CLASSICAL TEST THEORY AND MUSIC TESTING

··

JAMES R. AUSTIN

ORIGINS OF CLASSICAL TEST THEORY

CLASSICAL test theory (CTT) is rooted in the work of psychologists and psychometricians from the late 19th and early 20th centuries (Traub, 1997). During this period, measurement was viewed as a mechanism by which human traits could be identified and individuals compared. Sir Francis Galton (1822–1911) introduced the expression "psychometry" in recognition of psychologists' efforts to measure and quantify operations of the mind (Kerr, 2008). Classical test theory evolved as early psychometricians developed techniques for measuring human traits, statistically analyzing the data that were produced, accounting for measurement error, and estimating test reliability and validity. Major contributors to these developments included Alfred Binet (1857–1911), James Cattell (1860–1944), Charles Spearman (1863–1945), Edward Thorndike (1874–1949), and L. L. Thurstone (1887–1955).

The ontological perspective adopted by classical test theorists is that human traits are real, even if they cannot be absolutely or perfectly known (Osterlind, 2010). Many traits of interest to psychologists (latent traits or mental constructs that encompass a range of cognitive processes and abilities) are not directly observable or measurable. Through the application of psychometric methods, psychologists seek to determine whether purported traits are real or imagined, and if real, what the essential nature of a given trait may be. The end goal is to measure cognition, mental processes, and other human traits as accurately and completely as possible.

At the heart of CTT is the notion that error is endemic to measurement. Measurement error is conceived of as the difference between a hypothesized true attribute score and an observed score. Over multiple measures of a specific trait or attribute, observed scores will distribute randomly around the true score. Hence, the concept of random or accidental measurement error. By the beginning of the 20th century, the concept of measurement error was well recognized, and psychometricians focused their efforts on estimating and accounting for error. Charles Spearman, for example, discovered that independent measures of a person's mental ability varied randomly from one trial to another, and argued that the correlation between measures should be corrected for attenuation due to measurement error (Traub, 1997). Formulas for estimating the index of reliability and standard error of measurement subsequently were conceived and implemented.

Classical test theory is predominant in the history of measurement and testing specific to music aptitude or musical intelligence (Grashel, 2008). Beginning with publication of Carl Seashore's *Measures of Musical Talents* by the Psychological Corporation in 1919, and continuing for over 50 years, psychologists and musicians isolated and measured specific facets of aural perception and discrimination as key indicators of musical ability. Over time, more holistic and authentic approaches to music aptitude testing evolved, as did the measurement of music achievement. But throughout, CTT provided the framework for test design, psychometric calculations, and interpretations of musical potential and accomplishment among school-age children.

A preoccupation with intelligence and other mental measures during the 20th century eventually gave way to more broad conceptions of psychometrics. Today, psychometricians work in disciplines within and outside of psychology, and psychometrics are used to produce data related to a range of human attributes, including cognitive perceptions, beliefs and attitudes, as well as behaviors, emotions, and physical characteristics. As Osterlind (2010) notes, "In the broadest sense, the greatest contribution of psychometrics as a science is to inform the grand question of all psychology: What is the nature of humankind?" (p. 7).

PRINCIPLES AND ASSUMPTIONS OF CLASSICAL TEST THEORY

Classical test theory, sometimes referred to as *true score theory*, is deemed "classical" because it represents the earliest use of mathematics to characterize the relationship between true and observed scores (Steyer, 2001; Wang & Osterlind, 2013). In CTT, an observed measure or score (X) consists of two constituent parts—the true score (T) and measurement error (E):

$$X = T + E$$

The true score is an unobservable, theoretical value that would be obtained in an ideal measurement context, or if an individual were tested an infinite number of times such that measurement error would be continuously reduced and the observed score would approach the true score. Because it is not practical to test an individual an infinite number of times, let alone multiple times, using a single measure, psychometricians eventually proved that the relationship between true and observed scores holds when there is a single administration of a measure to a group of individuals (Kline, 2005). This was an important development because it allowed for a more logical and comprehensible way of thinking about measurement error. If, for example, a single test is administered to every member of some defined population, scores obtained from population members will vary around the average or arithmetic mean. This variation in scores will be due, in part, to genuine or true differences in the trait being measured. Measurement error, however, also will account for a certain portion of score variance.

According to CTT, measurement error arises because mental processes are idiosyncratic and in a state of change such that individuals are incapable of performing optimally on a single test or performance task. Moreover, it is impossible to produce error-free measurement of human traits given the ambiguous nature of latent variables and the inherent limitations of instruments designed to measure them. There are two main forms of measurement error: random error and systematic error. Random error is part of each observed score, though the source and magnitude may vary from person to person. In the aggregate, random errors for a group of individuals are assumed to equal zero, with positive errors offsetting negative errors. To the extent that random error may be controlled or minimized, individual observed scores will more accurately reflect hypothetical true scores (Kline, 2005).

In contrast to random error, systematic error involves a consistent bias in the measurement process (typically negative in nature) that affects all individuals in a predictable manner. Systematic error often arises when the measurement process, as applied to all individuals, is poorly calibrated or unduly influenced by environmental factors. If the source of systematic error can be identified, it can usually be minimized or eliminated. Classical test theory does not address systematic error very effectively, but does account for random error through the calculation of the *standard error of measurement*.

The standard error of measurement (SEM) represents the average of the total random error for all individuals in a specific measurement context. The SEM serves as an index of score accuracy, allows for the creation of confidence intervals (bands within which the true score may lie) around the mean or other values within a score distribution, and is inversely related to test reliability (the smaller the SEM, the more reliable the test scores). The SEM is a measure of intrapersonal variation; just as the standard deviation represents the spread of observed scores for a group of individuals, SEM represents the spread of observed scores for a single individual if that person were tested multiple times. The SEM may be calculated, if the standard deviation (S) and reliability (r) for a set of test scores are known, using the following formula:

$$SEM = S\sqrt{1-r}$$

If you have a test with a standard deviation of 5 and a reliability estimate of .85, for example, the SEM would be calculated as follows:

$$SEM = 5\sqrt{.15} = 5(.39) = 1.95$$

Once the SEM is known, it is possible to establish a confidence interval within which future scores might fall should an individual complete the test additional times. Imagine a high-stakes testing situation in which students must exceed a cut score of 50 to pass. A certain student receives a score of 48, which is below the cut point and considered a failure. That score, however, is an imperfect measure of the student's true ability. Given an SEM of 1.95 (as illustrated above), a test administrator would be 95 percent confident that the student's true score lies within two SEMs of the observed score (48 +/− 3.9, or between 44.1 and 51.9). Because the upper end of this confidence interval exceeds the cut score standard of 50, the student either should be given an additional opportunity to take the test or additional information should be used in making a final evaluative decision. This is an important, practical application of SEM to test score interpretation contexts, be they large-scale or at the classroom level.

While the SEM is based on test results for one sample, it may be generalized to other individuals within the sample population, thereby allowing for test norms to be established. The fact that the SEM associated with a given measure is applied consistently to all population members is both a distinguishing feature of CTT and a limitation—a limitation in the sense that persons of varying ability who score at different points along a distribution might be expected to manifest random error to varying degrees, unless the testing process is highly reliable and produces scores that are normally distributed and tightly clustered around the mean. Modern test theories address this limitation, including generalizability theory and item response theory (IRT; see Wesolowski, Chapter 22, in this handbook).

Several assumptions underlie the classical true score model (Kline, 2005; Osterlind, 2010). The first is that measurement error for a population of test takers forms a normal distribution with a mean of zero; over multiple administrations, individual test scores may be higher or lower depending on the nature and impact of measurement error. A second assumption is that the correlation between true scores and error scores for a population is zero. That is, there is no systematic relationship between a true score and the likelihood that a person's observed score will reflect positive or negative measurement error. Third, the correlation between error scores from two independent but parallel measures is zero, such that there is no systematic pattern in how scores may fluctuate from one time to the next, or one measure to the next. These assumptions pose important implications for test design and score interpretation within a CTT framework—a framework that is focused on analyzing individual differences in test performance, improving the reliability and validity of measurement tools, and generalizing findings for samples to larger populations.

RELIABILITY AND VALIDITY

Reliability and validity are the cornerstones of all test theory (Wang & Osterlind, 2013), but are central to CTT given how estimation methods originated and evolved during the early 20th century (De Gruijter & van der Kamp, 2008). Reliability and validity also are related concepts in the sense that measurement must be reliable before it can be considered valid, but reliability alone does not guarantee valid measurement. While many educators continue to associate the terms "reliability" and "validity" with tests (e.g., a certain test may be reliable but is lacking in validity), an often overlooked subtly of CTT is that measurement instruments themselves are not considered reliable or valid; rather, the scores and inferences produced by the instrument are reliable or valid for a particular context or use.

Reliability

Reliability is commonly defined in terms of testing precision (less measurement error results in greater accuracy or precision) or the consistency of scores produced by a measure. Reliability may be assessed by comparing scores across time, across test forms or testing contexts, across items within a given test or subtest, and across judges or raters in the case of performance assessment (American Educational Research Association, American Psychological Association, & National Council on Measurement in Education, 2014). Temporal stability, or test-retest reliability, is estimated by correlating test scores for the same group of individuals at two points in time (anywhere from a few days to a few weeks apart). With a minimal amount of time between test administrations, scores should be more similar than not if the test is to be considered reliable. Test equivalence, sometimes referred to as parallel or alternate forms reliability, reflects the degree to which scores on one test form are correlated with scores on an alternate test form (for the same individuals or an equivalent group).

Internal consistency is the reliability estimate of interest when considering whether responses to a series of items within a given test are equivalent to each other. There are two methods used to determine internal consistency. Following the simple split-half method, scale items are systematically (odd-even) or randomly divided into two equivalent sections, with scores for a group of test takers on the first section correlated with their scores on the second section. If the test has strong internal consistency, scores on both halves should be similar for each individual. Because splitting the test in half reduces the number of items being correlated in estimating the reliability, and because tests with fewer items tend to be less reliable, a split-half reliability estimate must be corrected using the Spearman-Brown prophecy formula (described later in this section). More robust estimates of internal consistency that account for the average correlation between all possible pairs of items (reflecting the proportion of test takers passing the item) may be obtained through the Kuder-Richardson formulas (KR-21, which assumes all items are of equal difficulty, and KR-20, which does not). For psychological scales where there may not be one correct answer, Cronbach's coefficient alpha serves as the estimate of internal consistency. Coefficient alpha accounts for the pattern of correlations among responses to all scale items. At one point in time, psychometricians would calculate bivariate correlations, KR-20, KR-21, and Cronbach's coefficient alpha by hand. Calculations of reliability estimates, however, are now readily obtained through spreadsheet software (e.g., Excel), statistical programs (e.g., SPSS), and online calculators.

In the measurement of performance tasks, psychometricians may be interested in estimating interrater reliability—the consistency of assigned ratings or scores across multiple judges (Kline, 2005). The most straightforward method for determining inter-rater reliability is to tally the percentage of times that two or more raters reach agreement; agreement may be defined more restrictively as perfect agreement (exact same rating) or more liberally as adjacent agreement (ratings within one scale point in either direction). If 10 performances are evaluated, for example, and two judges agree when scoring seven of the performances, the interrater reliability coefficient would be .70. To account for the fact that some amount of agreement may be due to chance, the kappa *n* statistic is commonly employed to adjust (downward) interrater reliability estimates obtained through the percentage of agreement method.

When the performance adjudication process results in ratings across a wider evaluative spectrum, as with a 100-point scale, then it is more appropriate to calculate simple bivariate correlations for the judges' ratings, and average the correlations across pairs of judges to produce a composite estimate of interrater reliability. Averaging bivariate correlations, however, does not necessarily provide an accurate picture of the extent to which the magnitude of judges' ratings agree beyond the ordering of ratings. One judge, for example, could rate three performances as meriting scores of 95, 87, and 79, while a second judge could award scores of 88, 75, and 70 for those same three performances. While the ordering of these ratings match, the ratings themselves clearly reflect different internal evaluative standards and/or impressions of the performances. The intraclass correlation coefficient (ICC) provides a more comprehensive estimate of reliability when multiple judges are rating performances. The term "intraclass" is used because in most performance evaluation contexts judges are viewed as constituting representative but indistinguishable members of a specific class or group of judges. The ICC estimates of reliability account for the effects of performers, judges, and their interaction. Alternative methods of estimating interrater reliability should be used when judges are placing performances into nominal categories (Cohen's kappa coefficient, κ) or rank ordering a series of performances (Kendall's coefficient of concordance, W).

Regardless of the method of reliability estimation that one uses, a coefficient of .70 or higher is considered evidence of adequate reliability, though this standard will depend to some extent on the characteristic or construct being measured as well as the age or developmental level of the individuals being measured. Data obtained from children (as opposed to adults) or for more complex psychological phenomena (as opposed to discrete physical tasks) tend to yield smaller reliability coefficients. Coefficient alpha (internal consistency) represents the upper limit of reliability for a given measure; interrater, alternate forms, and test-retest reliability coefficients typically will be smaller but also vary to some degree on how similar judges are in experience and expertise, how comparable alternate forms are in item content and length, and how much time elapses between test administrations.

In certain measurement situations, attenuation may affect the estimation of reliability. For example, score response restrictions (e.g., ceiling effect) and homogeneity of population samples may reduce the variability of scores otherwise obtained, thereby constraining reliability estimation. Shorter tests, which may not provide a broad or complete sampling of a construct, typically yield smaller reliability coefficients than longer tests (up to a point at which test-taker fatigue may increase error and reduce reliability). To account for attenuation, psychometricians have developed various mathematical formulas. Arguably, the most commonly implemented of these is the Spearman-Brown prophecy formula.

$$\frac{2(r)}{1+r}$$

This correction is employed when estimating reliability after a test is randomly split into halves, thereby reducing the overall length of the test. The Spearman-Brown correction assumes that data distributions corresponding to the halves are comparable in variability to the original, full-length measure, and boosts the reliability coefficient to account for reduced test length. For example, if the initial split-halves reliability coefficient is .65 (below the minimum standard of .70), the adjusted reliability coefficient $\left(\frac{2(.65)}{1+.65}\right)$ becomes .79—reflecting adequate reliability for many testing situations.

Validity

As important as reliability is to ensuring that measurement has adequate precision and minimal error, validity is considered the sine qua non for CTT. In the *Standards for Educational and Psychological Testing* (American Educational Research Association, American Psychological Association, & National Council on Measurement in Education, 2014), validity is defined as "the degree to which evidence and theory support the interpretations of test scores for proposed uses of the test" (p. 11). More simply, a valid test is one that provides "truth in measurement." As with reliability, validity is evaluated and interpreted along a continuum (low to high) and is bound to a specific measurement context or population. A variety of evidence sources may be used as part of test validation, but psychometricians have traditionally considered three main types of evidence to be paramount: test content (content validity), internal structure (construct validity), and relations to other variables (criterion-related validity).

Content validity is the degree to which a test aligns with, adequately samples, and is representative of a psychological domain, performance domain, or domain of learning. Using logic, a test developer seeking to establish content validity would define and describe the domain being measured, articulate procedures used to develop and adapt test items or tasks, and provide some overarching blueprint of the test's scale and scope. This is a much more detailed and elaborate process than so-called face validity, which typically involves only a cursory inspection of the measurement instrument. Content validity is of paramount concern in school achievement testing, where test content is expected to mirror instruction and learning to a suitable extent. When measuring psychological traits or latent variables, however, psychometricians typically are more concerned with criterion validity and construct validity.

Construct validity is the degree to which the internal structure of a test corresponds appropriately to the psychological construct of interest that it purports to measure. In test design and scale construction, construct validity is often represented by the proportion of test or scale score variance that explains a hypothetical construct. A factor analytic approach to exploring construct validity involves extracting one or more factors from the correlation matrix for a set of scale responses, exploring relations among factors, and then determining how much cumulative variance is explained by the set of factors. If the model includes more than one factor, the underlying scale is considered multidimensional in nature and, for clarity of interpretation, may be divided into separate subscales or subtests. Convergent-discriminant validity (a specific extension of construct validity derived from the multitrait-multimatrix method) involves a careful examination of the pattern of correlations between scores representing the construct and other measured variables thought to be related to or distinct from the construct. Convergent validity is the degree to which the construct is positively related to other measures of the same construct or similar ones. Discriminant validity evidence arises when scores representing the construct are not strongly related to constructs for which there is no known or anticipated connection. Construct validity for a measure of music self-concept, for example, could be established by demonstrating that music self-concept scores are strongly correlated with scores on a measure of artistic self-concept, but not clearly related to math or science self-concept.

Criterion validity is the degree to which scores on a test or psychological measure are correlated with a criterion to which the test or measure is thought to be logically related. For example, scores on a music aptitude test should be positively correlated with music performance ratings. Criterion validity may be concurrent (test scores are correlated with a criterion measured at the same time) or predictive (test scores are correlated with a criterion measured in the future) in nature. To fairly assess criterion-related validity is it important that the criterion variable exhibit adequate reliability; a criterion that produces less than reliable scores will attenuate the validity coefficient. In fact, the maximum possible validity coefficient may be defined in terms of the square root of the product of the test reliability and the criterion reliability.

The interpretation of validity coefficients is not as straightforward as with reliability coefficients (Furr & Bacharach, 2013. One of the most common methods is to square the validity coefficient and interpret that figure (coefficient of determination, R^2) as the percentage of variance in the criterion variable that is explained by the test variable (Allen & Yen, 2002). If the correlation between scores on a music aptitude test and performance task ratings is .50, for example, music aptitude could be interpreted as accounting for 25% of the variability in performance task ratings. The "variance explained" approach, however, tends to produce conservative interpretations of test validity. Alternatively, psychometricians might consider classification accuracy as an indicator of test validity (Gruijter & van der Kamp, 2008). For example, the use of a music aptitude test with a validity coefficient of .30 might allow for more accurate classification of a group of students as high performers than relying on an alternative measure or no predictor at all. Tests of statistical significance also might guide the interpretation of validity coefficients, though larger samples tend to increase the likelihood of a modest validity coefficient being statistically significant.

In the field of psychological measurement, validity coefficients seldom exceed .50. For tests designed to measure more complex variables, which are then correlated with a criterion variable of marginal reliability, a validity coefficient of .30 or larger might be considered noteworthy. Overall, the stronger the evidence of criterion-related validity, the more confident test developers may be in predictions based on test scores, while recognizing that no single test will ever perfectly predict a related outcome.

APPLICATIONS OF CLASSICAL TEST THEORY TO K-12 MUSIC EDUCATION ASSESSMENT

Classical test theory had a direct and immediate impact on the development of standardized music aptitude and achievement tests that occurred throughout most of the 20th century. From the seminal work of Carl Seashore and Jacob Kwalwasser in the 1920s through that of Richard Colwell and Edwin Gordon in the 1960s and 1970s, standardized music tests embodied many of the principles and concepts central to CTT (Boyle & Radocy, 1987; Colwell, 1970; George, 1980; Gordon, 1987; Lehman, 1968; Whybrew, 1962). Test manuals from this era routinely included detailed information about reliability, validity, SEMs, test norms, and transformed or scaled scores. Aptitude and achievement constructs were defined in terms of varied musical tasks including: aural discrimination of rhythm, pitch, loudness, timbre, and texture; memory of rhythmic, melodic/tonal, and harmonic elements; sensitivity to tonality and musical style; comparison of notated and performed rhythms and melodies (aural-visual discrimination); notating of rhythmic and melodic aural examples; timbre preference; and eye–hand coordination. Over the years, some music supervisors and educators within US school districts made use of standardized music test data to place students in appropriate learning contexts, diagnose underlying learning difficulties, and gauge individual achievements in relation to national norms.

Since the 1980s most standardized music tests have gone out of print due to apathy or antipathy among K-12 music teachers toward standardized testing of all forms. The fact that music test developers were slow in adapting to changing sensibilities about test validity (e.g., ecological validity or consequential validity), test score interpretation and use (e.g., norm-referenced vs. criterion-referenced interpretations; evaluative decisions based on single, high-stakes tests vs. multiple measures), and test administration format (paper vs. computerized) likely did not help. While music achievement has been assessed as part of the National Assessment for Educational Progress (NAEP) at regular intervals since 1997 and most recently in 2016, and while large-scale music achievement tests have been developed in a handful of states during the past decade (e.g., Florida Performing Fine Arts Assessments, South Carolina Arts Assessment Program, Washington Performance Assessments for the Arts), most efforts within the field have turned to improving music teacher application of CTT principles and concepts to assessment at the classroom level. Among the CTT principles and concepts most germane to the work of K-12 music teachers are level of measurement, reliability and validity enhancement, and item analysis (Frey, 2015; McMillan, 2001, 2013).

Level of Measurement

Test scores and performance task ratings provide differing amounts of information depending on the level and precision of measurement. Following choir auditions, for example, vocalists might be categorized as sopranos, altos, tenors, or basses. The coding of these voice types (1 = soprano, 2 = alto, 3 = tenor, 4 = bass) serves as a name or label, but the numbers themselves do not represent specific quantities or a distinct hierarchy of performance. This is an example of nominal level measurement. At the next highest level of sophistication is ordinal measurement, whereby students might be ranked (1st, 2nd, 3rd, and so on) as to how quickly they perform scales or how many music notation problems they complete in 30 minutes. In such instances, the distance between ranks does not necessarily translate to equivalent performance differentials. Someone ranked 1st might have performed just slightly better than someone ranked second, while the person ranked second may be considered twice as proficient as the individual ranked third.

Interval level measurement occurs when student performance is associated with an underlying continuum or scale, and the distance or interval between adjacent score scale points represents equal gradations of performance. Under these conditions, differences in the quality of performance exhibited by students receiving ratings of 18, 15, and 12 (on a 20-point scale) would be considered equivalent. Ratio-level measurement also entails the use of equal score intervals, but there is a true zero scale point. In education, ratio level measurement is typically considered unattainable because students who receive scores of zero on a written test or performance task are not actually devoid of knowledge or skill. Moreover, tests or performance tasks may lack the calibration and sensitivity necessary to measure learning for students representing a broad spectrum of ability or achievement.

At the classroom level, educators should strive to assess students in ways that reflect interval level measurement. When developing written tests, for example, items that measure lower levels of knowledge or understanding (true-false, matching, fill-in-the-blank) should receive less weight and account for fewer points in the overall assessment than items that require more nuanced discrimination among ideas (multiple choice), interpretation of audio or visual prompts prior to deriving an answer (interpretive), or constructed responses that reflect application of knowledge or a more sophisticated ability to analyze, synthesize, and evaluate information (essays). The more complex the learning that is being assessed, the greater the need for item types and scoring approaches that can accurately depict student knowledge along an equal interval continuum of performance.

Music teachers commonly employ three types of performance assessment tools in their classrooms: checklists, rating scales, and rubrics. Checklists represent a nominal level of measurement in the sense that students either demonstrate a desired behavior or they do not. These "yes-no" decisions provide for efficient assessment, but they do not capture a continuum or range of performance. Rating scales allow for more precise measurement and evaluation, but many times the anchors underlying specific scale points are ambiguous (poor, fair, good, fine, excellent) such that performances end up being compared and ranked more so than independently scored in relation to specific criteria or standards. Rubrics provide interval level measurement when they include appropriately detailed benchmarks and descriptors that reflect an underlying equal interval scale. Rubrics also may be customized for various facets of performance. A tone quality rubric, for example, may address issues of color, support, or consistency across registers, while a phrasing rubric may focus on length, shape, and style.

Reliability and Validity Enhancement

To optimize the reliability of testing within music classroom contexts, teachers must make deliberate efforts to reduce the risk of measurement error. Measurement error can arise from a variety of sources including the testing environment, test takers, test scorers, and the test itself. When creating tests, music teachers must ensure that instructions are clear rather than confusing, and that item formats are free of common flaws (e.g., grammatical cues, response options that lack plausibility, double negatives, lengthy or ambiguous item stems) that might direct students toward or away from correct answers irrespective of actual knowledge. Including items of varied types and difficulty also is desirable. Some students might do very well in responding to multiple choice items, for example, while others may prefer interpretive tasks or extended essay formats. When students lack experience responding to certain types of items, it may advisable to provide practice as part of the test or in advance of the testing period. Including too many easy items may not allow the teacher to differentiate among learners (a high proportion of correct answers results in less score variability) while a preponderance of difficult items can lead to excessive guessing, second-guessing of correct responses, and anxiety. Available testing time must be commensurate to test length, so that students are not forced to guess, shorten responses, or skip questions. In general, it is preferable to base overall assessments of student learning on several shorter quizzes or tests rather than a single, lengthy exam.

Beyond test characteristics, music teachers need to be mindful of testing conditions and whether those conditions allow students to adequately demonstrate what they have learned. A room that is quiet, has adequate lighting, a comfortable temperature, and appropriate writing surfaces will yield more reliable testing results than one that is loud, dimly lit, too cold or hot, and without desks or tables. Student characteristics, such as their motivation, mood, study/practice habits, and test-taking skills might introduce random or systematic error to the testing process. Students who are excessively anxious or who cheat will reduce test reliability. Testing motivation can be enhanced and testing anxiety minimized by preparing study guides and conducting study sessions in advance of major assessments, and by helping students to pace themselves through a longer testing period—allocating time and effort to answering questions and rechecking answers based on the weight of various test items and sections. To discourage cheating, teachers can create parallel tests (same items presented in a unique order, different items addressing the same learning content/objectives), leave adequate space between students, roam the room, and remove any test-related information, answers, or clues from classroom boards.

Test scoring and performance adjudication procedures can introduce bias that reduces reliability. Testing bias can be minimized and objective scoring enhanced in several ways. Students can identify themselves by identification numbers/codes rather than by name (with teachers linking IDs and names only after all scores have been finalized). Teachers can refer to scoring keys, scoring guidelines (e.g., how partially correct or novel answers are handled), and exemplar responses in determining how tests and performances are to be scored and doing so consistently across all students. The use of detailed and well-constructed rubrics (analytic or holistic) also will minimize the risk of bias and increase reliability for both constructed response written test formats and performance assessment formats by promoting more credible differentiation of scores in relation to specific indicators and standards. Finally, the use of recordings with specific scoring protocols and multiple judges may be necessary when performance assessments are more prone to personal bias or contribute to high-stakes decisions. As compared to live performance assessment, the assessment of recorded performances allows for multiple evaluative passes and better scoring precision, and blinds evaluators to student identity (minimizing the risk of systematic bias).

When tests pose important consequences for students, teachers may wish to estimate test reliability. If students are pretested and posttested on opposite ends of an instructional unit, for example, test–retest reliability can be calculated by correlating pretest and posttest scores using simple bivariate (Pearson r) formula functions on Excel or some other spreadsheet/grading application. For a single test administration, teachers can randomly or systematically split the test into equivalent halves and correlate student performance between halves (while using the Spearman-Brown formula to adjust the reliability estimate upward).

To maximize test validity, it is important that test content reflect and align with course objectives, curriculum, and actual instruction. When constructing a test, music teachers should consider how well the test content samples instructional content and aligns with instructional priorities. Some experts recommend a minimum of five items to adequately measure a specific area of knowledge or skill. Objectives and topics that are considered more important or given greater emphasis as part of daily instruction should be given more emphasis or weight in the test, as opposed to those objectives and topics that are addressed minimally. Similarly, performance tasks should emphasize procedural knowledge and skills represented within method books, ensemble repertoire, or other performance materials, and that are thoroughly addressed through practice, lessons, or rehearsal instruction.

In constructing major tests of musical knowledge or substantial performance assessments, music teachers may consider developing a table of specifications, sometimes called a test blueprint or validity table. Within a test validity table, the teacher *specifies* which learning objectives are included in a unit of study, which learning standards are represented by those objectives, which pages, measures, or materials are linked to the objectives, the amount of instructional importance or emphasis ascribed to each objective, how much weight will be given to items assessing each objective, and which type of items will be used to assess each objective. By going through this very deliberate planning process prior to constructing the actual test, teachers will more reasonably ensure that students are tested on what has been taught and emphasized within class, and that an adequate number and variety of items are used to sample a breadth of learning across a representative spectrum of the cognitive or psychomotor domains.

In addition to test validity, music teachers also should consider whether a test is fair and not unduly influenced by factors (gender, race, age, disability) unrelated to the type and level of learning being measured. A biased test may result in some students receiving lower scores than appropriate (negative bias) or higher scores than appropriate (positive bias). Fairness also implies that test results are used in an ethical manner rather than in a capricious manner, as when a single test score is used to label students, force students into certain tracks, or prevent students from graduating from one level of schooling to the next. Fairness, as a corollary of consequential validity, is becoming an issue of increasing concern that can be challenging to address. Some basic steps that may be taken to enhance test fairness include: (1) making sure all students are aware of testing objectives, test formats, and scoring procedures in advance of test administration; (2) providing all students with equal opportunity to learn as reflected in access to teacher expertise, learning supports, and instructional resources; and (3) avoiding test items and formats that clearly favor students of certain backgrounds over others, or that differentially predict future outcomes for one group of students as compared to another.

Item Analysis

After administering a major test to a group of students, music teachers might be interested in knowing, on the basis of student responses, which items functioned as intended and provided accurate depictions of student learning. Item analysis statistics, including the difficulty index, discrimination index, and item-total correlations, may be used to identify quality test items as well as problematic test items that warrant being modified or even discarded (Kline, 2005). The difficulty index reflects the proportion of test takers who answer an item correctly or completely (total number of correct responses/total number of responses). Items that are of moderate difficulty (difficulty index ranging from .30 to .70) provide the highest level of discrimination between individuals in a testing situation. In most classroom contexts, however, teachers will also include a few easier items (difficulty index = .70 to .90) near the beginning of the test, and perhaps introduce more difficult items (difficulty index = .10 to .30) in the middle to later sections of the test. This approach tends to moderate testing anxiety and improve test performance motivation, while still allowing for adequate differentiation of test scores across students.

The item discrimination index reflects the difference between the proportion of students who scored highest overall on the test (top 25%–35%) and who answered the item correctly to the proportion of students who scored lowest overall on the test (bottom 25%–35%) and got the item correct. For example, if 80% of the top group answered an item correctly, while only 20% of the bottom did so, the item discrimination index would be .60. By contrast, if only 40% of the top group answered an item correctly while correct answers were provided by 35% of the bottom group, the discrimination index would be .05. For most test items, a discrimination index of .40 or higher is desirable. When test items have weak or negative discrimination indices, the pattern of incorrect or incomplete responses might be examined to determine why some top performing students did poorly on the item. This analysis could reveal, for example, that two answers were equally plausible or a particular foil misled/confused certain students. Beyond calculating item difficulty and discrimination indices, scores on individual items can be correlated with scores on the total test (item-total correlations). Test items that produce small or negative correlations with total test scores should be carefully reviewed to determine whether an inordinate number of students guessed correctly, were confused by item wording, selected incorrect but plausible response options (foils), or cheated.

When the item analysis process reveals that certain items are of marginal or questionable quality (very easy or very difficult, poor discrimination among highest and lowest test scorers overall, weak relationship between item and total test performance), then a teacher may wish to consider modifying the test scoring process by either throwing out marginal/weak items and reducing the number of items and total points possible for the test, or by awarding partial or full credit for any such items, thereby "curving" the test score distribution upward. At a minimum, music teachers should carefully consider item analysis statistics and make appropriate modifications to test items or discard test items altogether before administering the major test again at some subsequent point in time when teaching that same unit of study.

Strengths, Limitations, and Extensions of Classical Test Theory

For the first half of the 20th century, CTT exerted primary influence on testing and measurement practices within psychology and education. There are some practical reasons for this (DeVellis, 2006). Classical test theory draws on mathematical concepts that are well established and commonly understood within the psychological and educational measurement communities. With its emphasis on matrices, correlations, and covariances, CTT has spawned many sophisticated statistical techniques in common use today, including factor analysis, cluster analysis, path analysis, and structural equation modeling. Moreover, the statistical packages necessary to perform these statistical analyses are readily available and relatively easy or intuitive to use. Classical test theory also has wide applicability to the social sciences and education in contexts where multi-item scales are commonly used to measure variables of importance or interest.

Despite these advantages, modern test theory—including generalizability theory and IRT—emerged in response to perceived limitations of CTT (Gulliksen, 1950; Lord & Novick, 1968). For example, CTT provides in-depth analysis of item characteristics, while IRT methods are focused on understanding individual test scores and generalizing data to the level of the individual. Whereas CTT seeks to fit a model to a unique data set (inductive approach), IRT seeks to obtain data that fit a given model (deductive approach). Within IRT, a good test includes items that provide maximum information across a range of abilities, with the probability of a correct response being dependent on a test taker's estimated ability level. Classical test theory also is limited in the sense that test performance variability among students is rigorously assessed while within-subjects variability is assumed to be constant, thereby ignoring or underestimating how growth curves may reveal test performance changes for individuals across time. Classical test theory also estimates reliability as an average across all individuals, while IRT may be used to produce unique reliability estimates across different ranges of ability or performance and different SEMs for each observed score. Further, IRT measures are not dependent on results obtained from a single sample, so they provide greater flexibility in utilizing measures at different times, with different samples, in varied forms or contexts. Item response theory has spawned an era of test customization, with computerized adaptive testing formats producing unique sets of items for individuals based on their prior item performance, and achieving adequate reliability with far fewer items than would be possible within traditional CTT testing frameworks.

Over time, modern test theories have made it possible to solve many practical problems that were not adequately addressed by CTT, including constructing tests for optimum performance in specific applications, utilization of adaptive testing approaches to enhance psychometric quality while reducing testing time, and the use of large-scale assessments to evaluate programs and monitor trends for populations over time (Mislevy, 1996). Despite the progress that has been made, many experts view modern theories of measurement as complementing CTT vis-à-vis the adoption of a unique philosophical perspective on measurement and the use of alternative statistical methods (Hambleton & Jones, 1993; McDonald, 1999; Wang & Osterlind, 2013). And CTT remains salient and influential as a measurement theory. In considering the psychometric advances represented by modern test theories, Osterlind (2010) cautions, "one should realize that they are not in opposition to CTT, nor do they supersede CTT. In fact, their roots are firmly grounded in CTT. A more accurate view of modern theories is that they extend CTT; they do not replace it" (p. 60).

REFERENCES

Allen, M. J., & Yen, W. M. (2002). *Introduction to measurement theory*. Long Grove, IL: Waveland Press.

American Educational Research Association, American Psychological Association, & National Council on Measurement in Education. (2014). *Standards for educational and psychological testing*. Washington, DC: American Educational Research Association.

Boyle, J. D., & Radocy, R. E. (1987). *Measurement and evaluation of musical experiences*. New York, NY: Schirmer Books.

Colwell, R. (1970). *The evaluation of music teaching and learning*. Englewood Cliffs, NJ: Prentice Hall.

De Gruijter, D. N. M., & van der Kamp, L. J. T. (2008). *Statistical test theory for the behavioral sciences*. Boca Raton, FL: Taylor and Francis.

DeVellis, R. F. (2006). Classical test theory. *Medical Care, 44*(11), 50–59.

Fredericksen, N., Mislevy, R. J., & Bejar, I. I. (Eds.). (1993). *Test theory for a new generation of tests*. Mahwah, NJ: Erlbaum.

Frey, B. B. (2015). *100 questions (and answers) about tests and measurement*. Thousand Oaks, CA: Sage.

Furr, R. M., & Bacharach, V. R. (2013). Psychometrics: An introduction (2nd ed.). Thousand Oaks, CA: Sage.

George, W. E. (1980). Measurement and evaluation of musical behavior. In D. A. Hodges (Ed.), *Handbook of music psychology* (pp. 291–392). Lawrence, KS: National Association for Music Therapy.

Gordon, E. E. (1987). *The nature, description, measurement, and evaluation of music aptitudes*. Chicago, IL: GIA.

Grashel, J. (2008). The measurement of musical aptitude in 20th century United States: A brief history. *Bulletin of the Council for Research in Music Education, 176*, 45–49.

Gulliksen, H. (1950). *Theory of mental tests*. New York, NY: Wiley.

Hambleton R. K., & Jones, R. W. (1993). Comparison of classical test theory and item response theory and their applications to test development. *Educational Measurement: Issues and Practice, 12*(3), 38–47.

Kerr, M. S. (2008). Psychometrics. In S. F. Davis & W. Buskit (Eds.), *21st century psychology: A reference handbook* (Vol. 1, pp. 374–382). Thousand Oaks, CA: Sage.

Kline, T. J. B. (2005). *Psychology testing: A practical approach to design and evaluation*. Thousand Oaks, CA: Sage.

Lehman, P. R. (1968). *Tests and measurements in music*. Englewood Cliffs, NJ: Prentice-Hall.

Lord, F. M., & Novick, M. R. (1968). *Statistical theories of mental test scores*. Reading, MA: Addison-Wesley.

McDonald, R. P. (1999). *Test theory: A unified treatment*. Mahwah, NJ: Erlbaum.

McMillan, J. H. (2001). *Essential assessment concepts for teachers and administrators*. Thousand Oaks, CA: Corwin-Press, Inc.

McMillan, J. H. (Ed.). (2013). *Sage handbook of research on classroom assessment*. Thousand Oaks, CA: Sage.

Mislevy, R. J. (1996). Test theory reconceived. *Journal of Educational Measurement, 33*, 379–416.

Osterlind, S. J. (2010). *Modern measurement: Theory, principles and applications of mental appraisal*. Boston, MA: Allyn & Bacon/Pearson.

Steyer, R. (2001). Classical (psychometric) test theory. In N. J. Smelser & P. B. Bates (Eds.), *International encyclopedia of the social and behavioral sciences* (Vol. 14, pp. 1955–1962). Atlanta, GA: Elsevier Science.

Traub, R. E. (1997). Classical test theory in historical perspective. *Educational Measurement: Issues and Practice, 16*(4), 8–14.

Wang, Z., & Osterlind, S. J. (2013). Classical test theory. In T. Teo (Ed.), *Handbook of quantitative methods for educational research* (pp. 31–44). Rotterdam, Netherlands: Sense Publishers.

Wasserman, J. D., & Bracken, B. A. (2012). Psychometric characteristics of assessment procedures. In I. B. Weiner, J. R. Graham & J. A. Naglieri (Eds.), *Handbook of psychology: Assessment psychology* (Vol. 10, pp. 43–70). New York, NY: Wiley.

Whybrew, W. E. (1962). *Measurement and evaluation in music*. Dubuque, IA: W.C. Brown.

....

CHAPTER 22

ITEM RESPONSE THEORY
AND MUSIC TESTING

....

BRIAN C. WESOLOWSKI

THIS chapter presents an introductory overview of concepts that underscore the general framework of item response theory (IRT).

LATENT MEASUREMENT

....

Traits, abilities, and attitudes (i.e., constructs) in music teaching and learning are not directly measurable. Examples of these constructs include but are not limited to musical aptitude, music performance achievement, musical preference, self-efficacy, affective response to music, musical expectancy, and so forth. These constructs can be easily explained by descriptive criteria and qualitative attributes; however, they cannot be *directly measured*. The measurement of these constructs can only be inferred *indirectly* through the measurement of secondary behaviors that are considered to be theoretically representative of the construct. Any construct that cannot be directly measured but rather inferred through the measurement of secondary behaviors is considered to be *latent*.

In order to infer a latent construct from a secondary behavior, an apparatus must be constructed with the intent to collect data that specifically gathers empirical evidence of these secondary behaviors. Items must be carefully constructed with the explicit intent to provoke persons' responses that directly reflect the latent construct. The data collected from the interaction between each person's observed response and each item provide observable, empirical evidence that can serve as a starting point to establish inferences. A mere ordering of observed responses by persons who answered the least correct of items to persons who answered the most correct of items is not measurement, however. Similarly, an ordering of observed responses of items that were answered the least correct to items that were answered the most correct is not measurement. These are simply examples of ordinal rankings based on proportion-correct observed responses. This data answers the question of "how many" but not "how much" In order to answer the question of "how much," the implementation of a measurement model is necessary. Measurement models provide a mechanism for transforming observed responses into estimated measures of person ability and item difficulty. It is only with the implementation of a measurement model that persons and items can be validly, reliably, and fairly compared. Furthermore, it is only with the implementation of a measurement model that inferences can be drawn as to how well the items empirically define the intended construct being measured. The implementation of measurement models into steps of the scientific method, therefore, is necessary for meaningfully connecting the substantive theory of a latent construct with the measurement of persons and items.

"Item response theory," or latent trait theory, is broad umbrella term used to describe a family of mathematical measurement models that considers observed test scores to be a function of latent, unobservable traits (Birnbaum, 1957, 1958a, 1958b, 1967; Lazarsfeld, 1950; Lord & Novick, 1968). Item response theory uses probabilistic distributions of responses as a logistic function of person and item parameters in order to define a latent construct. In other words, IRT models provide methods of data analysis that use the latent characterizations of objects of measurement (i.e., persons) and latent characterizations of agents of measurement (i.e., items) as predictors of observed responses in order to empirically define a latent construct. Figure 22.1 represents a conceptual operationalization of a unidimensional latent construct.

The construct represented in Figure 22.1 has several notable characteristics:

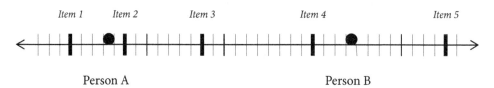

FIGURE 22.1 Operational definition of a unidimensional latent construct with calibrations of persons and items.

1. The latent construct is represented by a unidimensional, continuous line;
2. The line, acting as a scale of measurement (i.e. a "ruler"), is marked off in equal, interval-level units;
3. The items are calibrated to the line with a relative positioning that reflects each item's difficulty level; and
4. The persons are calibrated to the line with a relative positioning that reflects how much or how little of the construct each person possesses.

Items calibrated to the line from left to right represent less difficult items to more difficult items. Another way to conceptualize an item calibration is the item's rank ordering based on its discriminatory ability to best distinguish between persons at various locations on the continuum. This is discussed later under the section titled "Item Information Function." As demonstrated in Figure 22.1, item 1 is the least difficult item and item 5 the most difficult item. Similarly, persons calibrated on the line from left to right represent persons with less possession of the latent construct (e.g., lower ability or lower achievement) to persons with more possession of the latent construct (e.g., higher ability or higher achievement). In the example presented in Figure 22.1, Person B has a higher ability than Person A.

One important premise of IRT is to ascertain a *conceptual measurement* of a person's ability using a *conceptual ruler* the same way one would ascertain a *physical measurement* of one's height using a *physical ruler*. As a substantive example, assume a measurement apparatus was constructed in order to measure musical aptitude. A person's musical aptitude is not directly observable in the same way that the measurement of a person's height is. Therefore, the amount of musical aptitude one possesses can only be inferred based on a person's responses to test items that theoretically represent the construct of musical aptitude. In this case, the continuous line would represent the unidimensional construct of musical aptitude. The line acts as a conceptual "ruler" that is marked off in equal interval-level log odds (i.e., logit) units. Logits are discussed later in the section titled "Constructing Interval Units on the Continuum: Log Odds Units." Items are developed to represent the construct based on the test constructor's theory of specific observable tasks that represent musical aptitude. Each person would then interact with (i.e., respond to) each item, resulting in a collection of observed responses. Assuming the items called for dichotomous (i.e., correct/incorrect) scoring, each correct response would be marked with a score of "1" and each incorrect response would be marked with a score of "0." Once all of the observed responses are collected and dichotomously scored, both items and persons could be rank ordered based on their observed proportion-correct responses. Then, the implementation of an appropriate IRT measurement model would transform the observed responses into estimated linear measures. These estimated measures supply information that indicates: (1) which items appropriately define the latent construct of musical aptitude; (2) how well the items define the latent construct of musical aptitude; (3) how well the items discriminate between persons at various ability levels; (4) which persons were appropriately measured; and (5) how much musical aptitude those persons possess.

It is important to note that a measurement apparatus is a conceptual representation, or operational definition, of the developer's definition of the latent construct. Although the content of the apparatus is driven by theoretical, research-based principles and understandings, the unique collection of items is only one possible operationalization of the construct. Item response theory is the mechanism that provides an empirical rationale for the developer's definition of the operationalization.

Item Response Functions and Item Characteristic Curves

The example of musical aptitude provides one instance of a music assessment context where multiple persons respond to multiple items. This can be more specifically characterized by a single person's response (s) to a single item (i) resulting in an individual interaction (X_{is}). For a dichotomous item, only two possible *observed* outcomes for each interaction can be achieved: (1) a correct response ($X_{is}=1$); and (b2) an incorrect response ($X_{is}=0$). In order to model the *probability* of these responses as a distribution of the persons on a latent continuum, the ability of the person ($\theta \in (\infty,+\infty)$) must be parameterized as a logistic function of the item's difficulty ($b_i \in (-\infty,+\infty)$). An *item response function* (IRF) is the function of a person's ability (θ_s) to an item's difficulty (b_i). In other words, the IRF is a mathematical function that relates the latent construct to the probability of a single person answering a single item correctly. The probability of a correct response is denoted as $P(x_{is}=1)$, and the probability of an incorrect response is denoted as $P(x_{is}=0)$. The IRF is a logistic function, meaning that the probability of a correct response $P(x_{is}=1)$ increases with respect to the increasing position of a person's ability (θ_s) on the unidimensional continuum. Conversely, the probability of an incorrect response ($P(x_{is}=0)$) increases with respect to the decreasing position of a person's ability (θ_s) on the unidimensional continuum.

Each IRF can be characterized by a monotonically increasing function called an item characteristic curve (ICC). Figure 22.2 is a graphical depiction of an ICC.

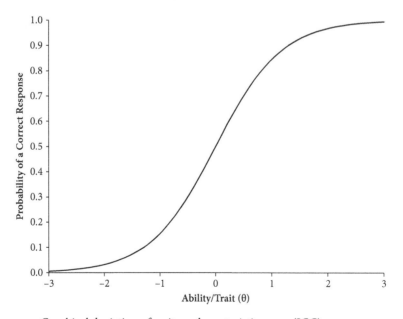

FIGURE 22.2 Graphical depiction of an item characteristic curve (ICC).

The abscissa (i.e., horizontal axis) represents person ability on the latent construct ($\theta \in (-\infty, +\infty)$), and the ordinate (i.e., vertical axis) represents the probability of a correct response in the range between 0 (0% chance of a correct response) and 1 (100% chance of a correct response). The S-shaped curve (i.e., ogive) is a graphical representation that provides a full illustration for items at all ability levels on the latent continuum.

The ICC is defined by the following mathematical expression that connects a person's probability of success on an item to their ability on the latent continuum:

$$P(x_{is} = 1) = \frac{\exp(b_i - \theta_s)}{1 + \exp(b_i - \theta_s)},$$

where:

$P(x_{is} = 1)$ = the probability that person s answers item i correctly;
b_i = a threshold parameter for the difficulty of item i;
θ_s = a threshold parameter for the ability of person s.

An important characteristic of the ICC is its inflection point. For most IRT models, the inflection point represents the intersecting point at which the probability of answering an item correct is .50. This can also be described as the threshold for where a person's odds change from a 50% chance of answering an item incorrectly to a 50% chance of answering an item correctly. The item parameters control the location of the IRFs. Therefore, this function indicates that a person possessing more of the latent trait should have a higher chance of correctly answering a more difficult item than a person possessing less of the latent trait. As discussed later in the chapter, this intersection point is of importance because this is the point at which there is the most item information. More specifically, the inflection point is the point at which the item maximally discriminates persons.

CONSTRUCTING INTERVAL UNITS ON THE CONTINUUM: LOG ODDS UNITS

In the same way that inches or centimeters are equal divisions of a physical ruler used to measure height, log odds units (i.e., logits) are equal divisions of a conceptual ruler used to measure items and persons on a latent construct. If we are interested in measuring musical aptitude, we may ask each person to respond to four items (i_1, i_2, i_3, i_4). If person 1 (θ_1) answers i_1 and i_2 correctly and i_3 and i_4 incorrectly, they would receive an observed sum score of 2. If θ_2 answers i_1 and i_2 incorrectly and i_3 and i_4 correctly, they would also receive an observed sum score of 2. However, let us suppose that items i_3 and i_4 were more difficult than items i_1 and i_2. Do θ_1 and θ_2 deserve to have the same observed sum score? If we assume for this example that the items and persons are functioning according to the expectations of the model, the answer is no. The next logical questions would then be "How much do the items differ?" and "How much do the persons differ?" In order to answer these two questions, there must be a mechanism in place to compare how much the questions differ in difficulty and how much the persons differ in ability. Therefore, a nonlinear transformation of proportion scores for both items and persons must be made to interval-level units. A logistic transformation of the nonlinear proportion correct scores of θ_1 and θ_2 and the proportion correct scores of i_1, i_2, i_3, and i_4 provides the mechanism needed to answer the "How much?" question. The transformation assigns both the persons and items an estimated interval-level measure (i.e., calibration of items and persons on the latent continuum) in logits.

This logit scale is developed independently of both the particular items included in the test as well as the particular persons being measured due to the assumption of parameter invariance. Wright (1993) notes:

> when any pair of logit measurements have been made with respect to the same origin on the same scale, the difference between them is obtained merely by subtraction... the logit scale is unaffected in variations in the distribution of measures that have been previously made, or which items... may have been used to construct and calibrate the scale. The logit scale can be made entirely independent of the particular group of items that happen to be included in a test... or the particular samplings of persons that happen to have been used to calibrate the items.   (p. 288)

The transformation produces values that theoretically fall between $-\infty$ and ∞. The example figures provided in this chapter limit those values to a more practical range of -3.0 to 3.0. A logistic transformation is defined as:

$$\Psi[x] = \ln\left[\frac{x}{1-x}\right],$$

where:
$\Psi[x]$ = logit transformation for x;
$\ln$ = natural logarithm;
$[x / x{-}1]$ = proportion correct responses.

Engelhard (2013) clearly delineates between the logistic transformations of persons versus the logistic transformations of items. Person logits are defined by:

$$\Psi[p] = \ln\left[\frac{p}{1-p}\right],$$

where:
p = number of correct items/total number of items for x.

Item logits are defined by:

$$\Psi[(p-value)] = \ln\left[\frac{(p-value)}{-(p-value)}\right],$$

where:
$(p\text{-}value)$ = number of correct responses/total number of persons responding to the item.

The logit units allow for the comparison of items and persons in a meaningful way that answers the question of "how much."

ASSUMPTIONS OF ITEM RESPONSE THEORY

The following section describes the assumptions of item response theory, including parameter invariance, unidimensionality, and local independence.

Parameter Invariance

Parameter invariance indicates an equality of item and person parameters from different person populations or measurement conditions. In other words, person and item parameters are sample independent. Item parameters are independent of (i.e., invariant across) the ability levels of persons responding to them. Likewise, person parameters are independent of (i.e., invariant across) the items measuring the ability of the persons.

The importance of parameter invariance comes in the form of providing inferences of generalizability between person ability and item difficulty. In order for generalizations to be valid, measurement models must be used that provide measurement conditions where parameters are invariant. Measurement models that do not maintain properties of parameter invariance succumb to the variability attributed to the sample. In other words, estimations of item difficulty and person ability are based on the observed interactions of the sample within each individual assessment context. Parameter invariance is estimated for unidimensional IRT models when θ is normally distributed with $M = 0$ and $SD = 1$. As a result, any variation in item or person estimates across different samples from the same population is considered to be a result only of measurement error. Perfect parameter invariance, however, is considered to be a measurement ideal that can never be achieved (Engelhard, 2013). Therefore, perfect model data fit is never expected.

Unidimensionality

Unidimensionality implies that persons and items can be described by a single latent construct. From a psychological perspective, unidimensionality refers to the specific construct that influences a person's performance (McNamara, 1996). Unidimensionality is possible when the items collectively measure the same weighted composite of ability. More specifically, the psychometric assumption of unidimensionality is met when: (1) all of the items used in the measurement apparatus measure the same construct; and (2) persons only use their ability on the construct to respond to the test items.

Wright and Linacre (1989) indicate that the empirical analysis of dimensionality can be addressed in three steps:

1. Analyze the relevant data according to a unidimensional measurement model;
2. Find out how well and in what parts these data do conform to our intentions to measure; and
3. Study carefully those parts of the data, which do not conform, and hence cannot be used for measuring, to see if we can learn from them how to improve our observations and so better achieve our intentions.

When the assumption of unidimensionality is true, local independence may be obtained (Lord, 1980; Lord and Novick, 1968).

Local Independence

The graphical representation of the ICC in Figure 22.2 represents one ICC. In other words, it represents only one probable outcome $P(x_{is}=1)$ resulting from the interaction between an item difficulty (b_i) and a person ability (θ_s). Multiple items, however, are necessary to operationalize latent constructs. Each item maintains its own representative ICC, and the likelihood of a person's success on an item is a represented by a function of only their ability related to the latent trait and the characteristic of that item. Parameters are therefore considered to be conditionally independent when each item response is independent given each examinee's position on the latent continuum. This means that after controlling for θ_s the item responses should be uncorrelated. Local independence provides statistically independent probabilities of item responses and can be characterized by the following function:

$$P(X_{is1} = x_1, X_{is2} = x_2 \mid \theta_s) = P(X_{is1}=1 \mid \theta)P(X_{is2}=1 \mid \theta).$$

The assumption of local independence posits that only the characteristics of the test items and person's ability relate to the construct being measured. As an example, if a test item somehow aids the test taker in correctly responding to another item, the assumption of local independence is violated.

Although Lord (1980) considered local independence to be met if the underlying assumption of unidimensionality was met, Hambleton, Swaminathan, and Jane Rogers (1991) argue that local independence and unidimensionality are distinct qualities: "local independence will be obtained whenever the complete latent space has been taken into account" (p. 11). It is argued that the results of item dependency present potential implications of biased parameter estimation, inflated reliability estimates, false estimations of measure precision, and artificially small estimates of standard error. Each of these implications has potential to affect the overall dimensionality of the measure, thereby making unidimensionality and local independence separate issues of concern.

COMMON ITEM RESPONSE THEORY MODELS

There are over 100 IRT models that can be classified into six basic categories: (1) models for items with binary-scored and/or polytomously-scored response categories, (2) nonparametric models, (3) models for response time or multiple attempts, (4) models for multiple abilities or multiple cognitive components, (5) models for nonmonotone items, and (6) models with special assumptions about response models (van der Linden & Hambleton, 1997). In this chapter I examine three of the more common models for binary response (dichotomous) items: one-, two-, and three-parameter logistic models and two of the more common models for ordered response (polytomous) response items: the partial credit (PC) model and the rating scale (RS) model.

One-Parameter Logistic Model

The one-parameter logistic (1-PL) model (Rasch, 1960) predicts the probability of a correct response from an interaction between a person's ability and one parameter: the item difficulty parameter. In other words, a person's chance of answering an item correctly is based on the relationship between the person's ability and how difficult the item is. The 1-PL model is mathematically specified as follows:

$$P(X_{is}=1|\theta_s,b_i)=\frac{\exp[a(\theta_s-b_i)]}{1+\exp[a(\theta_s-b_i)]},$$

where:
  θ_s = ability of person s;
  b_i = difficulty of item i;
  a = common discrimination parameter.

If persons s's ability is greater than the difficulty of item i, than θ_s will be greater than .00 logits and the probability of answering the question correctly will be greater than 50%. Conversely, if a person s's ability is less than the less than the difficulty of item i, than θ_s will be less than .00 logits and the probability of answering the question correctly will be less than 50%. The item difficulty parameter (b_i) represents an index of item difficulty that corresponds to the value of θ_s at the ICC's inflection points of the curve.

A unique characteristic of the 1-PL model is that there is a common discrimination parameter (a). The discrimination parameter provides information on how related the item is to the latent trait. More specifically, it is the slope of the curve as it crosses the probability of .50. A result of holding this parameter constant is that the items do not cross, meaning they are all equally discriminating. This indicates that the measures produced by the 1-PL model are sample-free for the agents of measurement (i.e., items) and test-free for the objects (i.e., persons). This sample/item-free characteristic is a property of measurement referred to as *specified objectivity*, and only occurs in the 1-PL

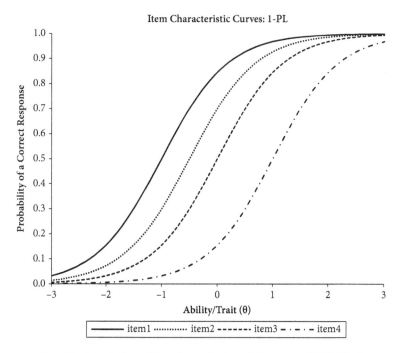

FIGURE 22.3 Graphical depiction of four item characteristic curves (ICCs) in the context of a one-parameter logistic model (1-PL): i_1 ($a_1 = 1.00$; $b_1 = -1.00$; $c_1 = 0.00$), i_2 ($a_2 = 1.00$; $b_2 = -0.50$; $c_1 = 0.00$), i_3 ($a_3 = 1.00$; $b_3 = 0.00$; $c_1 = 0.00$), i_4 ($a_4 = 1.00$; $b_4 = 1.00$; $c_1 = 0.00$).

model. The implication of employing only the item difficulty parameter is the displacement of the ICC from left to right. In all other aspects, the ICCs are identical. Figure 22.3 demonstrates four items with varying difficulty levels.

Each of the item ICCs run parallel to each other and do not cross because they have a common discrimination parameter that results in the same slope. As a result, each item is equally discriminating. The differences in the items are their difficulty, or the location (left to right) on the latent trait. The difficulty level is indicated by where the point of inflection occurs across the horizontal axis. Item 1 (i_1) has a difficulty level of -1.00 logits, i_2 has a difficulty level of $-.50$ logits, i_3 has a difficulty level of $.00$ logits, and i_4 has a difficulty level of 1.00 logits. Therefore, person s (θ_s) with a value of -1.00 has a 50% chance of correctly answering i_1 correctly, person s (θ_s) with a value of $-.50$ has a 50% chance of correctly answering i_2 correctly, and so forth.

Two-Parameter Logistic Model

The two-parameter logistic (2-PL) model (Birnbaum, 1957, 1958a, 1968) predicts the probability of a correct response to a test item based on two parameters: item difficulty (b_i) and item discrimination (a_i). The 2-PL model is mathematically specified as follows:

$$P(X_{is}=1|\theta_s,b_i,a_i)=\frac{\exp[a_i(\theta_s-b_i)]}{1+\exp[a_i(\theta_s-b_i)]},$$

where:

θ_s = ability of person s;

b_i = difficulty of item i;

a_i = item i's discrimination parameter.

In the equation represented by the 1-PL model, the common discrimination parameter was represented by a. In the equation representing the 2-PL model, a_i represents an item discrimination parameter that is freed to vary by item. The item discrimination parameter in the 2-PL model, therefore, describes the unique relationship of each item to the latent trait.

Figure 22.4 graphically depicts four items. Items i_1 and i_2 have the same difficulty level (b_1 = −1.00; b_2 = −1.00). Note the crossing of the ICCs at the intersection of .50 probability of a correct response and −1.00 logits. However, they differ in their discrimination slope (a_1= .50; a_2 = 1.00). Note the flatter slope of i_1 compared to the steeper slope of i_2. The same is true for items i_3 and i_4. Items i_3 and i_4 have the same difficulty level (b_3 = .00; b_4 = .00). Note the crossing of the ICCs at the intersection of .50 probability of a correct

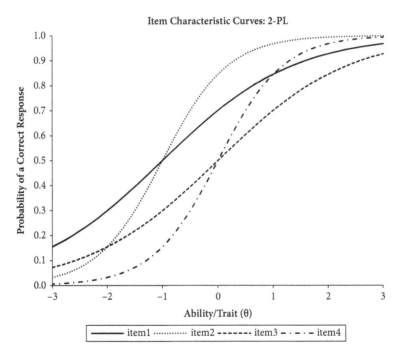

Item Characteristic Curves: 2-PL

item1 ··········· item2 ------- item3 − · − · − item4

FIGURE 22.4 Graphical depiction of four item characteristic curves (ICCs) in the context of a two-parameter logistic model (2-PL): i_1 (a_1 = 0.50; b_1 = −1.00; c_1 = 0.00), i_2 (a_2 = 1.00; b_2 = −1.00; c_2 = 0.00), i_3 (a_3 = 0.50; b_3 = 0.00; c_3 = 0.00), i_4 (a_4 = 1.00; b_4 = 0.00; c_4 = 0.00).

response and .00 logits. However, they differ in their discrimination slope (a_3 = .50; a_4 = 1.00). Note the flatter slope of item i_3 compared to the steeper slope of item i_4. The discrimination is an index represented by the steepness of the ICC at its inflection point. Parameters with larger a_i values will demonstrate steeper ICCs, and parameters with smaller a_i values demonstrate flatter ICCs. Substantively, this means that items i_2 and i_4 are stronger items, as they have stronger discriminating power. However, from a visual perspective, both pairs of ICCs cross at their inflection point, changing the ordering of persons and items. For a person where (θ_s) = −1.00, items i_3 and i_4 are more difficult. However, for a person where (θ_s) = 2.00, item i_1 is more difficult than item i_4. As opposed to the 1-PL model, the 2-PL model violates the measurement characteristic of specified objectivity, where the ordering of the persons and the ordering of the items does not remain constant across the continuum of theta values.

Three-Parameter Logistic Model

The three-parameter logistic (3-PL) model (Birnbaum, 1957, 1958a, 1968) describes the relationship between person ability and the probability of a correct response using three parameters: difficulty, discrimination, and guessing. The 3-PL model is mathematically specified as follows:

$$P(X_{is}=1|\theta_s,b_i,a_i,c_i)=c_i+(1-c_i)\frac{\exp[a_i(\theta_s-b_i)]}{1+\exp[a_i(\theta_s-b_i)]},$$

where:
  θ_s = ability of person s;
  b_i = difficulty of item i;
  a_i = discrimination parameter for item I;
  c_i = lower asymptote for item i.

The difference between the 3-PL model and the 2-PL and 1-PL models is found in the following portion of the equation: $c_i + (1-c_i)$. The parameter c_i represents the item lower asymptote, or the lower bound of probability that is independent of theta. This is often referred to as the "guessing" parameter. Because the probability is independent of the item difficulty and item discrimination parameters, the probability of answering a question correctly starts with the estimation of c_i ($c_i > 0$) then becomes dependent on θ_s, a_i, and b_i. Figure 22.5 demonstrates four items.

The items represented in Figure 22.5 have the same difficulty values and discrimination values as demonstrated in the 2-PL model example. In this example, however, the lower asymptote varies by item. Item i_1 has a lower asymptote value of .20, item i_2 has a lower asymptote value of .40, item i_3 has a lower asymptote value of .10, item i_4 has a lower asymptote value of .15. These values can be interpreted as the probability of a correct response as a result of guessing. In comparing Figure 22.5 to Figure 22.4, the compression of the ICCs as a result of adding the new parameter causes the slope to

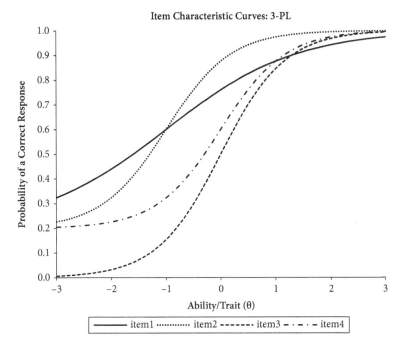

FIGURE 22.5 Graphical depiction of four item characteristic curves (ICCs) in the context of a three-parameter logistic model (3-PL): i_1 ($a_1 = 0.50$; $b_1 = -1.00$; $c_1 = .20$), i_2 ($a_2 = 1.00$; $b_2 = -1.00$; $c_1 = .30$), i_3 ($a_3 = 0.50$; $b_3 = 0.00$; $c_1 = .10$), i_4 ($a_4 = 1.00$; $b_4 = 0.00$; $c_1 = .15$).

decrease, or become more flat. Because the values have been compressed between c_i and 1.00, the discriminatory power of the item is reduced. Therefore, the larger the c value for an item, the less it can discriminate between persons, and the less item information it provides.

The 3-PL model is most popular in high-stakes educational settings and is most appropriately used when persons possessing low ability level answer difficult items correctly. The drawback, however, is that c_i is often difficult to estimate because very often there are few individuals with low θ values that provide helpful item responses to estimate c_i. The implication is that large sample sizes are needed to estimate the values with adequate precision.

The Rasch Model

Historical debates over "which model is better" inundate the psychometric and educational assessment literature. Most notable is the debate between Benjamin Wright and Ronald Hambelton (Wright, 1992) in the context of the model selection for the measurement of academic achievement. These debates are plentiful and too great to cover in this short chapter. However, there is one important distinction worth noting: the relationship between the Rasch model and the 1-PL model.

The Rasch model (Rasch, 1960) is often considered a pseudonym for the 1-PL model. However, the Rasch model is a specialized model with philosophical and developmental underpinnings that contrast with the 1-PL model or any other IRT models. The most important philosophical difference is the notion of "model-data fit" versus "data-model fit." The IRT paradigm argues that the rationale for the choice of one model over another is that the chosen model accounts better for the observed data. In this paradigm, most texts compare and contrast the models as 1-PL versus 2-PL versus 3-PL, and so forth. The Rasch perspective, however, focuses on the compatibility of measurement with properties of invariance and the quantitative laws of fundamental measurement. Andrich (2004) notes:

> the main challenge in the traditional paradigm is to those with expertise in statistics or data analysis to identify a model that accounts better for the given data, notwithstanding that they may find other problems in the data; the main challenge in the Rasch paradigm is for those with expertise in the substantive field of the construct to understand the statistical misfits as substantive anomalies and, if possible or necessary, to generate new data that better conform to the model while enhancing substantive validity of the variable.   (p. I–15)

ITEM INFORMATION FUNCTION

In IRT, item information refers to the value of the ability parameter. More specifically, it is an index that represents the item's ability to discriminate between persons. Fisher (1925) defined information as the reciprocal of the precision with which a parameter could be estimated. In IRT, precision is the standard error of measurement, or more broadly, the variance of the latent trait. Information, then, is the reciprocal of variance, and can therefore be connected to reliability. Under the CTT paradigm, reliability is equal to true variance divided by the added sum of true variance and error variance. Therefore, reliability is equal to information divided by the sum of information plus 1. The more information, the more precise the estimate of a person's ability. The less information, the less precise the estimate of a person's ability.

As an example, Figure 22.6 provides a visual representation of four item characteristic curves (ICCs) and item information functions (IIFs) for the 1-PL, 2-PL, and 3-PL models.

For the 2-PL model, items i_2 and i_4 have steeper slopes, indicating more discriminating power. However, more discriminating power does not equate to more information. The nonlinearity of the slopes at the extremes indicates less information. For persons with theta values between –1.00 and .00, items i_2 and i_4 are informative. However, for persons with theta values between 1.00 and 2.00, the items have less information. Additionally, because the discrimination varies freely by item, information is different for each item. If persons have a theta value between .00 and 1.00, item i_3 has more information than items i_1 and i_2. In this example then, the question of "how much information" is affected by both the theta value and the item. Information is maximized

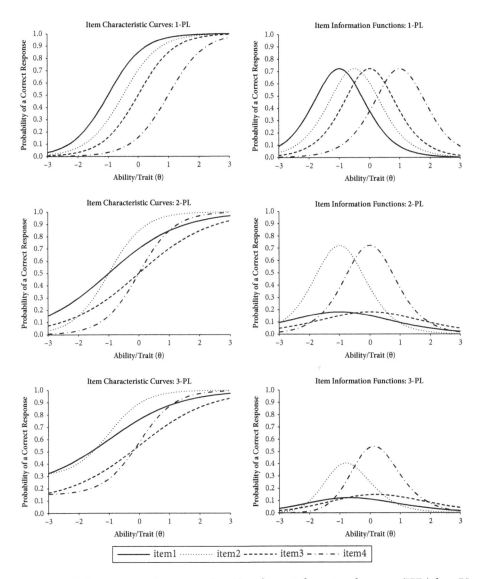

FIGURE 22.6 Item characteristic curves (ICCs) and item information functions (IFFs) for 1-PL, 2-PL, and 3-PL models.

at each ICC's inflection point and decreases as the ability level approaches the extremes of the IIF. Evaluation of the IIF for item i_2 in the 2-PL model demonstrates that the maximum amount of information is at the theta value of –1.00. In other words, the item best discriminates persons with an ability level of –1.00. In models other than the 1-PL where each item discriminates similarly, items can differ in both discrimination and difficulty, each affecting the item information. Therefore, both parameters play a role in selecting *how* good an item is, *where* the item is good, and *for whom* the item is good.

TEST INFORMATION FUNCTION AND STANDARD ERROR OF MEASUREMENT

Figure 22.7 provides a graphical depiction of test information functions (TIFs) and their reciprocal standard errors of measurement (SEMs) for the 1-Pl, 2-PL, and 3-PL models.

Item information, because it is on an interval-level scale, has additive properties. Therefore, test information can be computed through the sum of each item response functions over all the items on the test. Test information provides the information, or reliability, of a test at any given ability level. The test information function is defined as follows:

$$I(\theta) = \sum_{i=1}^{N} I_i(\theta),$$

where:
  I = test information at a given ability level (θ);
  I_i = the amount of information for item i at ability level θ;
  N = total number of items.

Test information is valuable, as it provides detailed levels of precision at all ability levels across the latent continuum. This information then provides insight into how the test functions in relation to the latent trait and provides diagnostic information in terms of particular areas to be targeted in adding or removing items. The range of a test information function is 0 to the number of items. The TIF approaches 0 as ability approaches ∞ and approaches the most information as ability approaches +∞. Therefore, a TIF is an increasingly monotonic function of ability.

Standard error of measurement is the reciprocal of test information, and is useful in building confidence intervals around an ability estimate. The lower the SEM, the higher the information. Conversely, the higher the SEM, the lower the information. The SEM function is defined as follows:

$$SEM(\theta) = \frac{1}{\sqrt{I(\theta)}} = \frac{1}{\sqrt{test\ information}}.$$

PROCEDURES FOR ESTIMATING ABILITY

Unlike the classical test theory paradigm, where persons are scored by summing the correct responses to items and converting the observed sum score to a standardized score, person measures in IRT are estimated based on persons' corresponding probabilistic

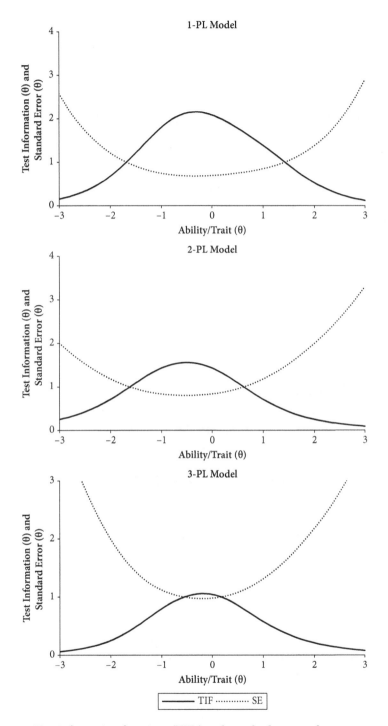

FIGURE 22.7 Test information functions (TIFs) and standard errors of measurement (SEMs) for the 1-Pl, 2-PL, and 3-PL models.

response pattern to a set of items. As an example, assume a person with high ability on the latent construct answers difficult items correctly. This is a likely scenario, as a person with a high ability has a higher probability of answering more difficult items correctly. Similarly, assume a person with low ability on the latent trait answers difficult items incorrectly. This, too, is a likely scenario, as a person with a low ability has a higher probability of answering more difficult items incorrectly. If a person with a low ability on the latent construct answers a more difficult question correctly, a less probable scenario is created. In this case, the IIF to this question would violate the probabilistic patterning.

In estimating the ability of a person, then, a value of θ is sought to maximize the highest likelihood for the predicted item response pattern based on the proposed measurement model. As discussed earlier, the assumption of local independence posits that each item information function is an autonomous reference to the underlying trait (see Figure 22.7). If item information functions serve as a referent, than the converse (the probability of an incorrect response) can be expressed as:

$$Q_i = 1 - P(X_i \mid \theta),$$

IRT models only express the possibility of a correct response. Therefore, in order to express joint probability of both answering items correctly and incorrectly, a likelihood function must be employed.

Under the umbrella of IRT, there are many procedures for estimation and many rationales for choosing among them, each with its own strengths and weaknesses. Due to the space limitation of this chapter, one of the more conventional approaches to ability estimation, *maximum likelihood estimation* (MLE), is discussed.

Likelihood Function

In an assessment context where items are restricted to binary response options, the response pattern (i.e., the number of possible outcomes) is represented by 2^k. If an assessment has four items, the total amount of distinct response patterns is 16. Joint probability of item responses is possible due to the assumption of local independence. Persons' responses to individual items are conditionally independent functions of their theta value. Therefore, they can be multiplied to obtain the probability of the pattern. A likelihood function is the expression of joint probability: the probability of both answering items correctly and incorrectly. As an example, the raw likelihood function of one item is expressed as follows:

$$L(u_{s1}, u_{s2} \ldots, u_{sI} \mid \theta_s) = \prod_{i=1}^{I} P_i(\theta_s)^{u_{si}} Q_i(\theta_s)^{1-u_{si}}.$$

This equation expresses the likelihood of a person's correct or incorrect response to an item and each successive item (in difficulty) through the last item. As an example, suppose a person takes a four-item exam. If each of the four items is ranked by difficulty and the person answers questions 1 and 2 correctly and 3 and 4 incorrectly, it could be expressed as $x_1 = 1$, $x_2 = 1$, $x_3 = 0$, and $x_4 = 0$. Within the context the equation, this can be expressed as:

$$L(x_{s1}, x_{s2} \dots, x_{sI} \mid \theta_s) = (P_1^1 Q_1^0)(P_2^1 Q_2^0)(P_3^0 Q_3^1)(P_4^0 Q_4^1).$$

With consideration to last two equations, the scores lie in the range of 0 to 1. Therefore, when joint probabilities are calculated, their quotient becomes increasingly small as test items increase. Therefore, the raw likelihood function is transformed to a log-likelihood function by calculating the natural logarithm of each IRC. The log-likelihood function is expressed as follows:

$$-\log L(u_{s1}, u_{s2} \dots, u_{sI} \mid \theta_s) = \sum_{i=1}^{I} u_{si} \log[P_i(\theta)] + (1 - u_{si}) \log[Q_i(\theta)].$$

Although the likelihood functions provide a brief overview of the conceptual idea behind estimation, this process is not necessarily convenient for large datasets consisting of many persons and many items.

The MLE function provides one of the more conventional and efficient methods for locating the exact maximum of the log likelihood in a pattern of person responses. The MLE function is an iterative method of estimation for obtaining item and person locations. More specifically, the Newton-Raphson method is a popular procedure for converging on an MLE in a manner that successively improves the estimation. The MLE procedure is a complex mathematical procedure that includes many steps to converge on an estimate. Full details and examples can be found in Embretson and Reise (2000).

COMMON MODELS FOR POLYTOMOUS RESPONSE ITEMS

Due to the responsive nature of music assessment contexts, student performances cannot always be appropriately measured in binary (right/wrong) terms. Music assessment and music psychology contexts often require more compelling evaluation experiences in order to more clearly define the latent construct. Therefore, many music assessment contexts necessitate the need for items requiring ordered responses, such as Likert-type items, semantic differential items, or other ordered-category items. Polytomous IRT models are extensions of binary models that examine the interaction between person response and ordered response categories. The principles of IRT in the context of binary responses can be extended to contexts where polytomous, ordered responses are more appropriate. These contexts, however, are much more complex. Therefore, I provide a brief overview of two common models that may be most relevant to the field of music from an introductory perspective: the partial credit (PC) model and the rating scale (RS) model.

For all polytomous IRT models, item information can be represented at both the item level and the category level. Category information can be represented as the log of the category response probability:

$$I_{ik}(\theta) = -\frac{\partial^2}{\partial\theta^2}\log P_{ik}(\theta),$$

where:

$I_{ik}(\theta)$ = information for category k of item i across the ability range of θ;
$P_{ik}(\theta)$ = probability of responding to in category k of item i.

The category information can then be summed to produce item information:

$$I_i(\theta) = \sum_k^m I_{ik} P_{ik}.$$

The Partial Credit Model

The partial credit (PC) model (Masters, 1982) is an extension of the 1-PL model that allows for the assignment of "partial credit" to a series of steps within a technical problem. As an example, if an item prompts person s to visually identify a chord in a written example of a sonata, this may include four distinct tasks: (1) identification of the root; (2) identification of the chord type; (3) identification of the inversion; and (4) proper figured bass labeling of the chord. For this particular item, four categories exist, each with a distinct probability for answering correctly and each with an independent difficulty threshold. This model is ideal for testing the assumption of the particular ordering. The PC model is mathematically specified as follows:

$$P_{ik}(\theta_s) = \frac{\exp\sum_{j=0}^k(\theta_s - \delta_{ik})}{\sum_{i=0}^{m-1}\exp\sum_{j=0}^k(\theta_s - \delta_{ik})},$$

where:

$P_{ik}(\theta)$ = probability of person s responding in category k for item i;
δ_{ik} = difficulty (i.e., location) of the category threshold parameter for item i.

Item information for the PC model is specified as follows:

$$I_i(\theta) = \sum_k k_i^2 P_{ik} - \left(\sum_k k_i P_{ik}\right)^2,$$

where:

$I_i(\theta)$ = information evaluated across the range of θ across item i summed across k categories ($k = 0, 1, \ldots, m$);
$P_{ik}(\theta_s)$ = probability of person s responding in category k of item i.

The δ_{ik} term is often referred to as a "step difficulty" of moving from category k to the adjacent category (k-1). For an item that has four distinct categories, three difficulty thresholds exist. If we assume that a monotonic relationship between categories exists where category b is more difficult than category a, category c is more difficult than category b, and category d is more difficult than category c, than three category thresholds exists: (1) the difficulty of moving from category a to category b (δ_{1i}); (2) the difficulty of moving from category b to category c (δ_{2i}); and (3) the difficulty of moving from category c to category d (δ_{3i}). Figure 22.8 illustrates an example of category response curves for a polytomous item with four response categories.

Each of the category thresholds is defined by where each of the category response curves intersect. For the exemplar item in Figure 22.8, the threshold parameters are $\delta_{1i} = -2.00$, $\delta_{2i} = -0.50$, $\delta_{3i} = 0.50$. At these intersection points, each step to the next category becomes probabilistically more likely to move to the next step as θ increases. The important conceptual idea to consider in applying the PC model is that categories are most often not equal in difficulty. Therefore, summed category responses in a polytomous item are equally as problematic as summed binary responses in a dichotomous item and warrant a similarly important empirical investigation.

The Rating Scale Model

The rating scale (RS) model (Andrich, 1978) allows for the analysis of polytomous items where the ordered response format is the same across all items. An example may include a Likert-type scale where the response categories are identical for each item (strongly

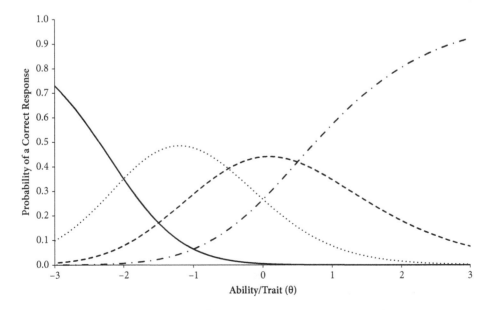

FIGURE 22.8 Category response curves for a four-category polytomous item.

agree, agree, disagree, strongly disagree). Each item is described by having a single scale location parameter (λ_i) that reflects the difficulty of the item. In the RS model, a category threshold measure (δ_j) is similarly described for all items in the measure. In other words, the RS model specifies that all of the items within the measure share the same rating scale structure. The RS model is mathematically specified as follows:

$$P_{ik}(\theta_s) = \frac{\exp \sum_{j=0}^{k}(\theta_s-(\delta_i+\tau_k))}{\sum_{i=0}^{m-1} \exp \sum_{j=0}^{i}(\theta_s-(\delta_i+\tau_k))},$$

where:

$P_{ik}(\theta_s)$ = the probability of person s responding in category k $(k = 0, 1, \ldots, m)$ of item I;
δ_i = the location (i.e., difficulty) of the item parameter;
τ_k = the common category threshold (i.e., boundary) for all items.

Item information for the PC model is specified as follows:

$$I_i(\theta) = \sum_k k_i^2 P_{ik} - \left(\sum_k k_i P_{ik}\right)^2,$$

where:

$I_i(\theta)$ = information evaluated across the range of θ across item i summed across k categories $(k = 0, 1, \ldots, m)$;
$P_{ik}(\theta)$ = probability of responding to in category k of item i.

Note that the model specification of item information for both the RS and PC models is the same. Both the PC and RS models as presented here adhere to the requirement of specified objectivity as in the 1-PL model. As a result, the item discriminations are both held constant and the model is in the same metric. However, $P_{ik}(\theta)$ will yield different results across the same dataset, thereby providing an overall difference in the analysis between the two models.

Linacre (2000, p. 768) provides nine important detailed considerations in deciding between a PC model and a RS model: (1) design of the items, (2) communication with the audience, (3) size of the dataset, (4) construct and predictive validity, (5) fit considerations, (6) constructing new items, (7) unobserved categories, (8) statistical information, and (9) antifragility (the simpler the better).

Multidimensionality

In contrast to unidimensional models, where only one parameter represents a person, multidimensional item response theory (MIRT) models include two or more parameters to represent persons (Reckase, 2009). Although unidimensional models are more sensible in educational contexts where most tests purport to assess one specific construct, arguments have been made that unidimensional models do not sufficiently model complex domains often associated with many psychological areas where multiple latent ability dimensions are manifested simultaneously or nested within a more broad construct as either compensatory (i.e., latent ability scores for multiple dimensions are assumed to be independent and combine additively to influence the probability of a correct response) or noncompensatory (latent ability scores for multiple dimensions are assumed to be confounded and combine multiplicatively to influence the probability of responding to an item correctly) factors. Where the probability of a correct response is dependent on a single estimate of ability (θ) for unidimensional IRT models, MIRT models posit that the probability of a correct response is dependent on a vector θ on K-dimensional, continuous latent ability dimension (θ_k).

There are a wide variety of MIRT models for a multitude of data types that are too exhaustive for this chapter (see Reckase, 2009). Therefore, only the basic multidimensional extensions of the 1-PL, 2-PL, and 3-PL models are outlined.

The multidimensional extension of the 1-PL model can be expressed as:

$$P(X_{is}=1|\theta_s,d_j)=\frac{\exp(\sum_m \theta_{sm}+d_i)}{1+\exp(\sum_m \theta_{sm}+d_i)},$$

where:

x_{is}= response of person s to item i;
θ_{sm} = ability for person s on dimension m;
d_i = easiness intercept for item i.

The multidimensional extension of the 2-PL model can be expressed as:

$$P(X_{is}=1|\theta_s,d_i,a_i)=\frac{\exp(\sum_m a_{im}\theta_{sm}+d_i)}{1+\exp(\sum_m a_{im}\theta_{sm}+d_i)},$$

where:

x_{is}= response of person s to item i;
θ_{sm} = ability for person s on dimension m;
d_i = easiness intercept for item i;
a_{im} = discrimination for item i on dimension m.

The multidimensional extension of the 3-PL model can be expressed as:

$$P(X_{is}=1|\theta_s,d_i,a_i,c_i)=c_i +(1-c_i)\frac{\exp(\sum_m a_{im}\theta_{sm}+d_i)}{1+\exp(\sum_m a_{im}\theta_{sm}+d_i)},$$

where:

x_{is}= response of person s to item i;
θ_{sm} = ability for person s on dimension m;
d_i = easiness intercept for item i;
a_{im} = discrimination for item i on dimension m;
c_i = lower asymptote for item i.

Substantive Implications for Measurement and Evaluation in Music

In an educational climate that is becoming increasingly data-driven, the field of music is at a clear pivot point where the "subjectivity" of music making is becoming progressively interconnected with the "objectivity" of measuring student achievement and program accountability. The field can no longer ignore the demands of having to provide empirical data that validly, reliably, and fairly reflect both students' growth in the classroom and program effectiveness. Furthermore, the field can no longer withstand minimal approaches to collecting, analyzing, interpreting, and disseminating such data, as there have never been higher consequences for the implications of its interpretation and use. It is the field's ethical responsibility to provide sound empirical data and robust assessment processes that reflect true student learning in meaningful ways. In order to do so in a valid, reliable, and fair manner, the field must (1) recognize the complex nature of measuring and evaluating musical constructs, (2) spend considerable time and energy gaining a more grounded and fundamental understanding of psychometric theories, and (3) provide better mechanisms and opportunities for training researchers and practitioners in appropriate selection and implementation of psychometric theories.

Item response theory is a viable option for music researchers who want to enhance the data analysis and measurement instrument construction processes. As the field of music becomes more familiar with the theories and applications of IRT, important music assessment issues may continue to be addressed and reexamined from new, interesting, and informative perspectives.

References

Andrich, D. (1978). A rating formulation for ordered response categories. *Psychometrika*, *43*, 561–573. doi: 10.1007/BF02293814

Andrich, D. (2004). Controversy and the Rasch model: A characteristic of incompatible paradigms? *Applications of Rasch Analysis in Health Care*, *42*(1), I7–I16.

Birnbaum, A. (1957). *Efficient design and use of tests of a mental ability for various decision-making problems* (Series Rep. No. 58–16, Project No. 7755-23). Randolph Air Force Base, TX: USAF School of Aviation Medicine.

Birnbaum, A. (1958a). *On the estimation of mental ability* (Series Rep. No. 15, Project No. 7755-23). Randolph Air Force Base, TX USAF School of Aviation Medicine.

Birnbaum, A. (1958b). *Further considerations of efficiency in tests of a mental ability* (Tech. Rep. No. 17, Project No. 7755-23). Randolph Air Force Base, TX: USAF School of Aviation Medicine.

Birnbaum, A. (1967). *Statistical theory for logistic mental test models with a prior distribution of ability* (Research Bulletin No. 67-12). Princeton, NJ: Educational Testing Service.

Birnbaum, A. (1968). Some latent trait models and their use in inferring an examinee's ability. In F. M. Lord & M. R. Novik (Eds.), *Statistical theories of mental test scores* (Chapters 17–20). Reading, MA: Addison-Wesley.

Embretson, S. E., & Reise, S. P. (2000). *Item response theory for psychologists*. Mahwah, NJ: Routledge.

Engelhard, Jr., G. E. (2013). *Invariant measurement: Using Rasch models in the social, behavioral, and health sciences*. New York, NY: Psychology Press.

Fisher, R. A. (1925). Theory of statistical estimation. *Proceedings of the Cambridge Philosophical Society, 22*, 700–725. doi: 10.1017/S0305004100009580

Hambleton, R. K., Swaminathan, H., & Jane Rogers, H. (1991). Fundamentals of Item Response Theory. Newberry Park, CA: SAGE.

Lazarsfeld, P. F. (1950). The logical and mathematical foundation of latent structure analysis. In S. A. Stouffer, L. Guttman, E. A. Suchman, P. F. Lazarsfeld, S. A. Star, & J. A. Clausen (Eds.), *Measurement and prediction* (pp. 362–412). Princeton, NJ: Princeton University Press.

Linacre, J. M. (2000). Model selection: Rating scale model (RSM) or partial credit model (PCM)? *Rasch Measurement Transactions, 12*, 641–642.

Lord, F. M. (1980). *Applications of item response theory to practical testing problems*. Hillsdale, NJ: Erlbaum.

Lord, F. M., & Novick, M. R. (1968). *Statistical theories of mental test scores* (with contributions by A. Birnbaum). Reading, MA: Addison-Wesley.

Masters, G. (1982). A Rasch model for partial credit scoring. *Applied Measurement in Education, 1*, 279–298.

McNamara, T. F. (1996). Measuring second language performance. New York, NY: Longman.

Rasch, G. (1960). *Probabilistic models for some intelligence and attainment tests*. Chicago, IL: University of Chicago Press.

Reckase, M. D. (2009). *Multidimensional item response theory*. New York, NY: Springer.

Van der Linden, W. J., & Hambleton, R. K. (Eds.) (1997). *Handbook of modern item response theory*. New York, NY: Springer.

Wright, B. (1992). *IRT in the 1990s: Which Models Work Best? 3PL or Rasch?* Ben Wright's opening remarks in his invited debate with Ron Hambleton, Session 11.05, AERA Annual Meeting 1992.

Wright, B. D. (1993). Logits? *Rasch Measurement Transactions, 7*, 288.

Wright, B. D., & Linacre, J. M. (1989). Observations are always ordinal; measurements, however, must be interval. *Archives of Physical Medicine and Rehabilitation, 70*, 857–860.

CHAPTER 23

THEORIES AND PRACTICES OF SEQUENTIAL CURRICULUM ALIGNMENT

Curriculum Design and Assessment for a 21st-Century Education Through Music

DEMARIS HANSEN

INTRODUCTION

As educators respond to the demands of the 21st century, the challenges of developing curriculum will continue to increase in complexity. The mechanics of curricular alignment in terms of design have not changed significantly in decades, but 21st-century workplace demands require an effectively functioning curriculum that is dramatically expanded in all educational environments. And, without careful curricular alignment, the most exquisitely designed assessment will not yield accurate information about student learning.

In this chapter, I first describe historically common procedures for designing and aligning a curriculum, and conclude with a discussion of the revised "The Alignment Loop," a construct I first designed in 2001. For each of the eight components of The Alignment Loop an in-depth discussion of the implications for teaching, learning, and assessing is offered, including: the necessity for curricular goals and the influence of the national standards in the United States; establishing curricular needs; professional development, instructional strategies; assessments; teacher and student evaluations;

and reflective practice. This is followed by a description and comparison of the results of a brief international survey of curricular practices. The chapter concludes with commentary directed at the need for developing a systemic and thoughtfully designed and aligned music curriculum that reflects the need for purposeful assessments and projects forward the profound workplace demands of the new century.

PHILOSOPHICAL FRAMEWORKS OF CURRICULUM DEVELOPMENT: A HISTORICAL OVERVIEW

The term "curriculum" is understood through varying perspectives. For some, it encompasses a general organizational plan for what should be learned. For others, the term represents a set of procedures, concepts, and processes to be carefully constructed in relation to a particular educational setting. Curricular standards, on the other hand, represent criteria and benchmarks for the skills and knowledge required of an educational content area. In many countries these are written by government officials, teachers, and/or education leaders. In the United States, national music standards serve as a framework for the development of curriculum at the state and local levels. Compliance with the standards is voluntary, often adopted by states and then subsequently school districts, as a framework for district curricula, scope and sequence, and potentially teacher evaluation.

Early attempts to define the construct of curricula were influenced by emerging industries. In his book *The Curriculum*, Bobbitt (1912) wrote that the purpose of education was to prepare the workforce. In his utilitarian view, he believed that people did not need to be educated in those areas they would not use for work, and that studies in conventional school subjects should be eliminated. His work was strongly influenced by industrialization of the time and behavioral psychology. Linked to this, but with a different purpose, Thorndike (1922), most noted for his application of psychometrics and learning theory to education, furthered a scientific approach to teaching and testing which became a catalyst for later behaviorist researchers including B. F. Skinner.

Alternatives to the "scientific" or "utilitarian" approaches to curriculum development ran concurrently to Bobbitt and Thorndike's work. Most notable was John Dewey's progressive education movement. He strongly believed that authentic, real-life experiences were the best teachers. Dewey wrote that educational practices that only delivered predetermined knowledge and skills did not provide the basis for students to become valued, equal, and responsible members of society (Dewey, 1916). Though the progressive education movement did not formally continue later in the 20th century, the concept of authentic learning continues to find its way into specialized schools and 21st-century teaching and learning practices. Today, a juxtaposition of traditional scientific and nontraditional progressive curriculum could not be more pronounced. Standardized testing, student assessments based on specific learning objectives or indicators of growth seemingly conflict with the call for authenticity in learning and student-centered instruction. Later in this chapter we also reflect on aesthetic and praxial approaches to curriculum development.

BLOOM'S TAXONOMY OF EDUCATIONAL OBJECTIVES: THE COGNITIVE AND AFFECTIVE DOMAINS

In the 1950s and 1960s Benjamin Bloom and associates gathered together to develop a set of taxonomies for measuring cognitive, affective, and psychomotor development. Bloom's taxonomy of the cognitive domain became immersed in our educational systems as a coherent means of measuring knowledge acquisition. While the taxonomy was not intended to be a curriculum, Bloom wrote, "Curriculum builders should find the taxonomy helps them to specify objectives so that it becomes easier to plan learning experiences and prepare evaluation devices. The term 'cognitive' is used to include activities such as remembering, recalling knowledge, thinking, problem solving, [and] creating" (Bloom, 1956/1984, p. 2). Bloom's taxonomy and the revisions that ensued still strongly impact teaching and assessing in the United States in all curricular areas.

The taxonomy of the affective domain was published in 1964 after fervent and challenging attempts to capture levels of affective development. The authors believed that affective objectives emphasized a "feeling tone, an emotion, or a degree of acceptance or rejection" (Krathwohl, Bloom, & Masia, 1964, p. 7). Gleaned through life experiences, affective growth progresses hand-in-hand with cognitive development. The affective domain included five categories that corresponded to various levels of meaning. Table 23.1 shows the five levels of affect, the corresponding levels of meaning, and

Table 23.1 Affective and Cognitive Domains: Conceptual Relationships

Affective domain categories and range of meanings	Relational cognitive domain categories
1. *Receiving*: Interest	Knowledge: Recall and Recognition
2. *Responding*: Interest and Appreciation	Comprehension: Understanding the knowledge
3. *Valuing*: Abstract or symbolic thinking, beginning to generalize and form judgments	Application of the knowledge
4. *Organization*: Determines interrelationships, begins to internalize	Analysis and Synthesis of the knowledge
5. *Characterization* by a complex value: Integration of beliefs, ideas, and attitudes into a personal philosophy or worldview	Evaluation: Judging the value of the knowledge

the relationships between the affective and cognitive domains. It should be noted that the affective categories overlap from one to the other.

The authors of the taxonomies realized through their investigations that the acquisition of "a goal or objective of one domain is viewed as the means to the attainment of a goal or objective in the other" (Krathwohl et al., 1964, p. 54). Krathwohl graphically described this phenomenon in this statement:

> In some instances the joint seeking of affective and cognitive goals results in curricula which use one domain as the means to the other on a closely-knit alternating basis. Thus a cognitive skill is built and then used in rewarding situations so that affective interest in the task is built up to permit the next cognitive task to be achieved, and so on. Perhaps it is analogous to a man scaling a wall using two step ladders side by side, each with rungs too wide apart to be conveniently reached in a single step. One ladder represents the cognitive behaviors and objectives; the other ladder represents the affective. The ladders are so constructed that the rungs of one ladder fall between the rungs of the other. The attainment of some complex goal is made possible by alternately climbing a rung on one ladder, which brings the next rung of the other ladder within reach. Thus alternating between affective and cognitive domains, one may seek a cognitive goal using the attainment of a cognitive goal to raise interest (an affective goal).   (Krathwohl et al., 1964, p. 60)

At this time, motivation theory was just beginning to germinate. Krathwohl et al. (1964) and their colleagues' visionary work in the early 1960s provided the theoretical foundation for our understanding of the interactions between life's cognitive learning experiences, our emotional responses, and motivational drives. For educators in arts and music, these relationships are real and observable. In music classes listening, moving, and performing music attracts our students' attention, to which they respond either because they are asked to, or because they wish to respond. As they experience music and learn about its conceptual and technical intricacies, we hope that they begin to place value on it and make it part of their value system and eventually part of their character. Acknowledging the circular interrelationships between knowledge acquisition and emotional response is conceptually significant to curriculum design. What appear to be conflicting educational practices between traditional or practical curriculum was an interweaving of both to the writers of the taxonomy of educational objectives.

COMPONENTS OF CURRICULUM DESIGN

The work discussed thus far focuses on early philosophical and organizational education principles. Designing a curriculum or standards is a process, regardless of whether it is from the national, state, district, or local and classroom levels. While many models of curricular design exist, models may be centrally focused on the subject-matter or skills to be acquired, the needs and interest of the students, or the expertise of the teacher. These broad categories often share similar components, but the way in which the instructors deliver the curriculum through classroom learning activities determines whether it is subject-skill based, student-centered, teacher-centered, a combination, or a hybrid.

Subject/Skill-Centered Curricular Design

Influenced by the "scientific" approach, subject/skill-centered design is driven by a pre-specified set of learning objectives. These curricula focus on the content of a specific curricular content, skill development, or interdisciplinary content. The development of the curriculum is sometimes based on a text or texts and discreet skills needed to complete a task. This particular design may be ideal if the text or literature from which the curriculum is built is of high quality and contains transferable concepts that relate to other learning. A skillful teacher will inherently understand how to make personal connections with students' prior knowledge or interests, but a subject-centered curriculum does not necessarily account for learner or situational diversity in its design.

In his book *Basic Principles of Curriculum and Instruction* (1949), Ralph W. Tyler formalized this scientific approach by promoting the development of educational objectives as the organizing principle of curriculum development known as the Tyler Rationale (Tyler, 1949/1969, p. vii). Tyler, however, recognized that objectives must be created in context with local philosophies, beliefs, and cultural norms. He also believed that curriculum should be created by administrators and then implemented by teachers. Tyler framed his ideas about curriculum development through four questions:

1. What educational purposes should the school seek to attain?
2. What educational experiences can be provided that are likely to attain these purposes?
3. How can these educational experiences be effectively organized?
4. How can we determine whether these purposes are being attained? (pp. 1–2)

A subject/skill-centered curricular design would have at its heart a desired set of knowledge or skills, then clearly defined linear and sequential steps that would lead to the acquisition of the subject matter or task. If the educational philosophy of the institution or governing body responsible for creating the curriculum advocates an approach primarily behavioral in nature, the components of this linear curriculum design process would most likely include in order: a needs analysis, formulating learning objectives, selecting and organizing content, selecting and organizing courses/texts/learning experiences that address the perceived needs, assessment and evaluation, revisions if necessary, and syllabus formulation. The evaluation process would be reliant on the students' ability to perform according to predetermined goals or standards and objectives. Figure 23.1 provides a visual for this category of curricular design. In this figure and those that follow, the asterisk indicates the starting point of the process.

Tyler claims to have originated the term "evaluation" as it applies to education (1949/1969, p. xi). He believed that objectives should be squarely tied to the assessment

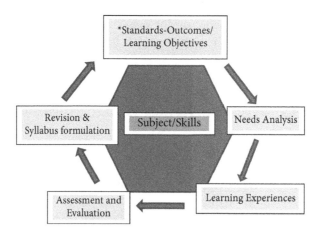

FIGURE 23.1 A linear subject/skill-centered curricular design.

of a student's learning. While Tyler did not believe in or promote standardized testing, some would argue that when objectives began to be tied to assessment the doors opened for this to occur. National and state standards and district curricula present a set list of what students should be able to know and do at the macro and micro level. The standards and the resulting objectives or growth indicators are the basis for assessment and for teacher evaluation in the United States.

Learner- or Student-Centered Curricular Design

A curriculum is considered student- or learner-centered when the needs and interests of the student are at the center of the curriculum design. Johann Heinrich Pestalozzi (1746–1827), and John Dewey (1859–1952), among many others, were the progenitors of this approach, each with their own unique interpretation. Pestalozzi strongly influenced Dewey and other progressive educators. To Pestalozzi, the organizing principle for curriculum was framed by nature, from the simple to the complex. He promoted the concept of self-realization: to strengthen one's ability to make correct judgments about moral questions. Pestalozzi believed that the purpose of education was to prepare individuals for their life's work and endeavors. "He advocated education reform that would permit pupils to relate life activities to education, thus making it more pragmatic" (Mark & Gary, 2007, p. 124).

John Dewey's writing reflected this philosophy as he compared his vision for a new, progressive education to older practices. Dewey believed that teachers should help motivate learners and allow them to have choice and direct their own learning at times. The music education philosopher Abraham Schwadron reflected on this practice:

> The real problems in contemporary music education which are daily concerns and considerable are to a certain extent value-centered. We are coming to realize that a new or alternate approach is needed for the construction of value-oriented curriculum

designs. The context of this merging curriculum will focus on issues related to the nature of music and to the lives of the students. It will lead students to ask fundamental questions, to engaging in intriguing musical activities, and to seek answers based on personal reflection, inquiry, discover, and research; it will help them formulate their values of music on both logical and introspective levels.... It seems very odd that the why of music has been investigated by those like Dewey, Mursell, Langer, and Meyer and yet categorically avoided by those directly responsible for daily musical instruction.   (Schwadron, 1967, p. 26)

Pestalozzi and Dewey viewed education as critical for preparing the workforce, but their viewpoint expanded greatly on the perspectives of Bobbitt and Thorndike. In the 21st century, we have returned to the belief that learner-centered learning in authentic, real-world situations best prepares students for their future life and professions.

In a learner-centered model of curricular design, the teacher serves as a facilitator of learning rather than a distributor of knowledge based on the text or learning objectives. When placed on a continuum of active student involvement, one end of the continuum represents little or some student involvement versus the opposing end that represents mostly student-driven learning. In other words, if the beliefs, theories, or perspectives of the instructor or governing bodies perceive that the student is at the center of the learning experience then those factors will serve as the center of how the curriculum is developed. In this model, subject matter/skills, learning objectives, learning experiences, and assessment-evaluation are still components in the process, but the curricular design process is interactive, revolving around the student's interests, prior knowledge and experiences, and personal needs at the center (Figure 23.2).

Two-Dimensional Curricular Design

Hilda Taba (1902–1967) is recognized in general education for her valuable contributions to curriculum development. She described similar curriculum attributes as Tyler's,

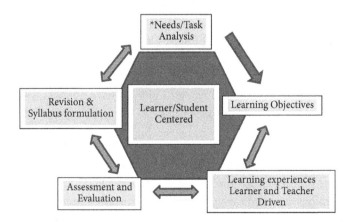

FIGURE 23.2 Learner-centered curricular design.

but noted that curricular development involved interaction between the components of the model rather than a linear approach. Taba believed that the needs of students should be at the forefront. In her landmark book, *Curriculum Development: Theory and Practice* (Taba, 1962), she wrote,

> Whether we want to produce scientists and mathematicians or simply responsible human beings and enlightened citizens for democracy, the curriculum needs to be child centered in the sense that a productive learning sequence cannot be constructed apart from starting where the child is and proceed developmentally.   (p. 420)

Taba realized that the curriculum design process involved multiple layers of development, beginning with a macro level that includes the aims and objectives of the school, the content and learning experiences built by the teachers, and the evaluation processes. The finer details of a curriculum revolve around what she called the scope (what content is covered, or what should be learned) and sequence (the order in which the material should be presented). Taba promoted a two-dimensional approach to curriculum design that integrated the growth of intellectual development and skills (student-centered learning) and the scope and sequence of content (subject-centered). With this organization, it is possible "to examine more precisely both the sequence of content that is being employed and the sequence in the powers and capacities that are developed in the successive levels of the curriculum" (Taba, 1962, p. 429).

Taba's holistic approach to curriculum design also called for the foundation of instruction to be based on ideas and concepts, rather than narrowly determined knowledge and skills. She describes big ideas or concepts through generalized statements such as, "People do things in different ways today than long ago, and differently in different cultures" (Taba, 1962, p. 430). Applied as an organizational tool for curriculum development, this statement has been central to the "backward design" principles used today.

Interestingly, Taba did not refer to Bloom's taxonomy of the cognitive domain (Bloom, 1956/1984) though it had been published 6 years prior to her book. She did, however, write persuasively about the need for teachers to advance students' levels of complex thinking as a consideration in the curriculum. While the taxonomy of the affective domain would not be published for another 2 years, she also clearly understood the need to address human emotion and internal values. She eloquently expressed this by writing, "It will also be possible to determine whether there is an increment in such powers as the capacity to analyze data, to organize ideas, to respond to feelings and values, to appreciate aesthetic qualities, or to express feelings and ideas" (Taba, 1962, p. 430). Taba's two-dimensional model for curriculum development might be represented like what is shown in Figure 23.3.

Taba's perspectives on curricular development and Bloom and Krathwohl's writings, all occurring at nearly the same time, seem remarkably illuminated and far-sighted. These foundations of design for the national, state, and local standards in the United States were germinated in the early- to mid-20th century and are very much present today. The processes transcend specific curricular disciplines. Thus, we now focus on philosophies of music education curricular design.

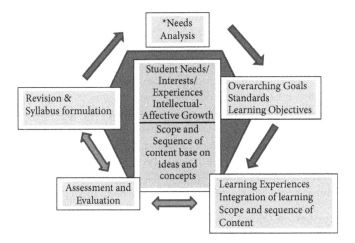

FIGURE 23.3 Taba's two-dimensional curricular design.

PHILOSOPHICAL INFLUENCES ON CURRICULAR DESIGN

Aesthetic Music Education

Through the centuries many philosophies have been expounded on the approach to and the need for music education. Philosophy may not constitute a curricular design, but certainly these beliefs are influential in curriculum development.

Bennett Reimer wrote eloquently for decades about the need to place aesthetic sensitivity to music at the heart of musical learning. Theoretically, a curriculum based on aesthetics would imply a learner-centered approach, but aesthetic sensitivity also involves the development of perceptions and reactions to music, an essential factor in all music learning experiences according to Reimer. In his influential book *A Philosophy of Music Education* (1970), Reimer referred to developmental stages of learning based on Piaget and Bruner to describe sequential growth of musical sensitivity. He emphasized that talented performers should be nurtured in music education, but that a wide variety of arts experiences should also be offered so that all students have the opportunity to explore and understand human feeling through music. Reimer suggested that the way in which a composer uses artistic elements should be at the heart of learning in an aesthetic experience. He described a sequence of activities, led by the teacher, but with a goal of the child developing their own perception and emotional reactions to musical beauty and craftsmanship:

> The children are asked to clap (produce) a succession of quarter notes. They are then asked to clap (produce) again, adding accents to some of the notes. The children notice (perceive) the interest (react) created by the added accents. They discuss (conceptualize) their finding and hypothesize (conceptualize) about why the accents

add music interest. They explore (produce, perceive, react) different accent patterns and decide (conceptualize, evaluate) which they think are most interesting (evaluated, value). They are then asked to consider (conceptualize, evaluate) how they might notate (analyze, conceptualize) the best examples so they can be performed again at some later time. The children discover (perceive) the difficulties involved in translating musical ideas into notational equivalents, and discuss (conceptualize) skills of notation as one kind of craftsmanship a composer must have. They then listen (perceive, react) to a complex, rhythmic excerpt from a piece by Stravinsky. A score of the music is examined (analyze, perceive) as an instance of just how much skill is involved in notating complex music. The children discuss (conceptualize) the craftsmanship Stravinsky exhibits (evaluate, value) and hypothesize (conceptualize) about how all composers' music have similar craftsmanship.   (Reimer, 1970, p. 159)

Reimer (1970) further described what we might characterize as a learning experience similar to Taba's double sequence. In it, children are guided to understand music in a comprehensive, high-level manner (pp. 159–160).

Clearly, this line of instruction encourages children to think about the qualities inherent in creating works of art. This approach is conceptual and student-centered, and driven by the personal aesthetic growth of the student rather than adherence to strict standards and objectives. A visual for the components of Reimer's aesthetic music education may thus appear as in Figure 23.4:

Practical or Praxial Approaches to Music Education

In David Elliott's *Mind Matters* (1995), practical or "praxial" teaching values the professional judgments of individual teachers in their specific educational environments. Elliott writes:

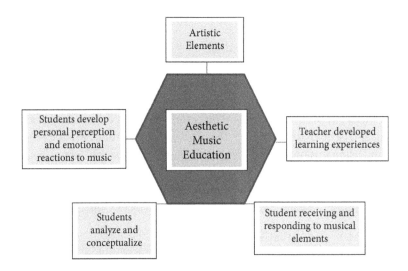

FIGURE 23.4 Basic components of an aesthetic music education.

The interests of practical curriculum making lie in shifting away from the technical-rational notion of teachers as curriculum retailers or interpreters to teachers as reflective practitioners; away from the specification of acontextual objectives to the organization of situated knowledge; away from highly specific verbal concepts and scripts to situated preparations and plans; and away from measurement and testing to assessment and evaluation. In sum, and in opposition to curriculum doctrine, practical curriculum making places the teacher-as-reflective-practitioner at the center of curriculum development.   (1995, p. 254)

Elliott's praxial education suggests similar components to the subject-skill and student-centered models. However, Elliott strongly resisted highly articulated lesson objectives and predetermined standards. He argued, "teaching is a reflective practice; excellent teaching is evidenced by the educational effectives of a teacher's actions, interactions, and transactions with students" (Elliott, 1995, p. 257). Elliott urged musical performance (musicking), creativity, and listening as central to a comprehensive music education. He also rejected philosophies related to aesthetic education. Developing a curriculum based on a purely aesthetic approach to music learning is flawed, according to Elliott. He wrote that aesthetic perception,

> begins with the implausible claim that music is a collation of objects. It then proceeds to narrow our musical understandings and experiences even further by insisting that listeners always listen aesthetically—with exclusive attention to the formal designs of musical works (in the nineteenth-century sense).   (1995, p. 33)

A visual interpretation of the components of a praxial music education is shown in Figure 23.5.

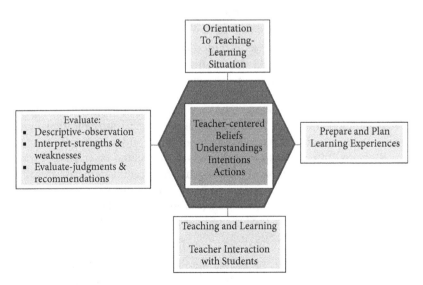

FIGURE 23.5 Components of a practical or praxial music education.

THE DEVELOPMENT OF NATIONAL
MUSIC STANDARDS

The ongoing tensions between subject-skill-centered, learner-centered, teacher-centered, and hybrid curricula remain with us today. In 1994, when the National Standards for the Arts (National Association for Music Education/MENC, 1994) were released (the first of the curricular disciplines, followed by mathematics, science, language arts, and others), the curriculum alignment processes in the United States changed. Instead of having the option to define outcomes based on local demographics and cultural character, the design of school curriculum would now be guided by standards developed at the national level. The curricular autonomy of the local school and district acquiesced to national standards that were adopted by states as the framework for curriculum at the local levels. For the years that have ensued, the standards-based curriculum overcame the student-centered approach in an attempt to make more educational continuity within and between states. Measurable learning objectives provided the basis for extensive testing that was locally developed and standardized. Standardized test data revealed whether students (and through a variety of inferential statistical methodologies, their schools) were, according to the state's definition, succeeding or failing.

Music educators designed similarly linear standards, objectives, and assessments. The 1994 National Standards for Music presented concrete areas of musical study through nine content standards. The standards represented decades of discourse between music educators who eventually came to consensus regarding their beliefs about what content, skills, and knowledge music education should include. The standards provided a foundation for a breadth, depth, and diverse nature of music study. While Western music remains in the center of music education in the United States, the standards also provided a means for valuing local culture and societal norms through standards 8 and 9. Though state and local curricula were framed by the standards, music educators still had the freedom to create day-to-day instruction and local curriculum relevant to their local culture. Marie McCarthy elegantly described this:

> The shift from a teacher-centered, high-art focus to a more egalitarian, student-centered orientation highlights several issues about musical and educational values. In the past, musical values were typically rooted in the widespread music conservatory system, and the music curriculum was implemented by classically trained music teachers. In the context of early twenty-first century education, musical values in education are increasingly motivated by multiple sources—political democracy, cultural policies, mass media, arts advocacy, social justice campaigns, school communities, and not least the individual musical preferences of teachers and students.   (McCarthy, 2009, p. 31)

In McCarthy's description of a student-centered curriculum is somewhat similar to that of Taba. Taba believed that a students' ethnic and cultural background should be considered as curriculum content was created. We see then that a combination of standards-driven and student-centered approaches is possible in the development of curriculum with subject matter at the center. I revisit this concept in the section devoted to instructional design.

CURRENT CURRICULAR DESIGN MODELS

Understanding by Design

Through the 1990s and into the early 21st century, curriculum design processes that recognized both subject matter content and the needs and interests of students continued to persist. Perhaps the most widely accepted approach to curricular and instructional design in the United States today is the process called *Understanding by Design* (UBD) (Wiggins & McTighe, 1998). Wiggins and McTighe drew from numerous educators and educational leaders to create a conceptual framework and template, and design process for curriculum development. The goal of UBD is to deepen students' understanding of stated curricular goals. Wiggins and McTighe refer to Ralph Tyler's rationale as an early model for their design:

> Educational objectives become the criteria by which materials are selected, content is outlined, instructional procedures are developed, and tests and examinations are prepared. The purpose of a statement of objectives is to indicate the kinds of changes in the student to be brought about so that instructional activities can be planned and developed in a way likely to attain these objectives.
>   (Tyler, 1949/1969, pp. 1, 45, as cited in Wiggins & McTighe, 1998, p. 8)

Understanding by Design is based on a "backward approach" to curriculum development. Rather than randomly choose activities for a given music class on a given day, the UBD starting point is to begin at the end—determine the goals, established standards, and curricular expectations. The next step is to determine how students will demonstrate that they have achieved the goals, standards, or curricular expectations. Wiggins and McTighe encourage teachers to "think like an assessor" (1998, p. 12) as they consider how to collect evidence of student work. Contrary to common practice, they encourage teachers to consider what assessments would yield the best evidence of goal or standards acquisition prior to designing specific units and lessons. The final step in the process is to plan the learning experiences and instruction. A visual representation of backward design is shown in Figure 23.6.

Step 1: Identify Goals, Standards and Curricular Expectations

Backward design, as defined through UBD, is a framework for creating curriculum and is an effective process on many levels, including national, state, and district as well

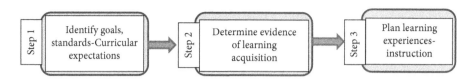

FIGURE 23.6 Backward design process.

as in the classroom. The design allows for flexibility within each of the steps. While it is a linear process, one of the most important aspects is the identification of enduring understandings and essential questions. For Step 1, the standards or curriculum writers must identify the most important concepts or skills that students may retain for a lifetime. These "big ideas" are at the heart of the design. When creating enduring understandings it is important to ask questions about the significance of existing or potential learning outcomes or objects, such as: "Why is this important?" "Of what lifelong benefit will this knowledge and/or skill be to the learner?" Writing enduring understandings requires serious thought from the beginning of curriculum development about what will be taught. Often, they are written simultaneously with "essential questions," which are designed to lead students to uncover the important curricular content and make learning more cohesive. This helps refine and delimit what could potentially be vast amounts of content and skills. For example, in the National Core Music Standards (Ensembles: Common Anchor #5, Rehearse, Evaluate and Refine) the Enduring Understanding reads: "To express their musical ideas, musicians analyze, evaluate, and refine their performance over time through openness to new ideas, persistence, and the application of appropriate criteria." The corresponding Essential Question is: "How do musicians improve the quality of their performance?" (National Core Arts Standards, 2014). The performance standard statements for each level (novice, intermediate, proficient, accomplished, and advanced) do not identify the criteria for specific musical concepts, techniques, or performance practices. Rather, the standard addresses the students' approach to addressing these very sophisticated learning goals. Teachers must foster active and collaborative learning processes, including self- and peer-evaluation, peer feedback, and development of strategies to address technical, expressive, and rehearsal strategies. The technical musical skills are assumed and the personal/social/behavioral skills are emphasized.

Once the most important concepts and skills have been identified through the enduring understandings and essential questions, it is necessary to further refine the identified desired results. As part of Step 1, the next question is "What must students be able to know and do?" And finally, "What should students be familiar with as it relates to the concept or skills?" In this way, writers establish priorities for the development of the standard, learning outcomes or objectives, or instructional units as well as the subsequent formative or summative assessments that determine the degree to which the learning priorities have been met.

Establishing these priorities may be guided by national or state standards, or they may be directly related to a local educational program. In either case, this approach helps teachers resist the temptation to create curriculum based on a basal music book series, the upcoming concert season, or an instructor's most favorite musical activities. Instead, it requires careful thought about the value of sequential learning and what students may retain for a lifetime.

Step 2: Determine Evidence of Learning Acquisition

Music educators have at their disposal many options for evaluating and assessing their students. Traditionally, we have gauged the success of our music programs by the quality of the performances. Musical performance is at the heart of our art form; yet, if we engage in the UBD process, the performance itself may not be the enduring understanding. An essential question to ask is, "What will my students learn about the performance practice, cultural influence, technical qualities, and/or personal interpretations of the music and musical experience?" In order to find out whether any of these particular curricular aims have been met, either a formative or summative assessment would be embedded in the learning experience.

For Step 2 of the UBD process, the nature and type of assessment and evaluation would be selected in relation to the predetermined goals, standards, or curricular expectations.

Music and arts educators predominantly assess their students using formative or informal types of assessments. The National Core Music Standards (NCMS) (National Core Arts Standards, 2014), as discussed earlier in the Step 1 example, suggest that students as well as teachers will actively participate in ongoing assessments. This implies three types of approaches: teachers assessing students, students assessing students, students assessing themselves. Students must have developmentally appropriate factual and conceptual knowledge and musical skills in order to assess their peers and themselves. This engagement of students in the assessment process provides a multipronged approach to determining whether students are reaching artistic literacy as illustrated in Figure 23.7.

Formative or informal assessments are essential, if not crucial, in a music classroom. These types of assessments should interact fluidly with instructional approaches, and should not be considered a "standalone" or disembodied activity (Hansen, 2013). In reality,

FIGURE 23.7 Reaching artistic literacy through assessment.

though, the assessments, standards, learning outcomes, or objectives themselves may not have much effect unless the actual classroom instruction is well planned and executed.

Step 3: Instructional Design

Despite a prescribed curriculum from a school district or standards from the state and national level, what happens in the classroom is the true determinant of how the curriculum unfolds in a classroom. At this level, the term "instructional design" is used to describe the instructional approaches within a class. As with curriculum design, it falls on a continuum between mostly teacher directed and mostly learner driven. The differences in a classroom between a subject-skill-centered instructional design and a learner-driven instructional design could be captured in the following essential questions a teacher might ask, as shown in Table 23.2.

In reality, a teacher's planning may rotate between these two instructional design approaches. With a focus on student learning, the emphasis is not to cover the required material or musical literature, but to construct learning goals that reflect what the students will learn and what they think about their own learning. The 2014 NCMS are based on the UBD model. The standards themselves are intended to serve as a framework for states, school districts, and teachers. In contrast to the 1994 National Standards for Music, which promoted knowledge and skill development through content and achievement standard statements, the intent of the 2014 standards is to focus on artistic processes that engage students in authentic musical experiences. The standards are framed by the concept of artistic literacy, defined in the NCAS Conceptual Framework as "the knowledge and understanding required to participate authentically in the arts." The statement in the Framework goes on to say:

> Fluency in the language(s) of the arts is the ability to create, perform/produce/present, respond, and connect though symbolic and metaphoric forms that are unique to the arts. It is embodied in specific philosophical foundations and lifelong goals that

Table 23.2 Contrasting Essential Questions for Instructional Design

Teacher questions from divergent instructional design models

Subject-Skill Teacher-Centered Instructional Design	Learner-Centered Instructional Design
What music activities will I have my students do today?	How can my students demonstrate their creativity in music today?
Can my students name the lines and spaces on the treble and bass staffs?	Can my students transfer their music literacy knowledge and skills to other music making?
What music should I choose for my concerts and performances that are scheduled this year?	How can I help my students select music for their concerts and performances?
Will my students do well on their district assessments?	Can my students effectively self-assess and peer-assess their music learning by the end of the year?

enable an artistically literate person to transfer arts knowledge, skills, and capacities to other subjects, settings, and contexts.

(National Coalition for Core Arts Standards, 2014, Section 2, p. 17)

In a sense, the conceptual focus on artistic literacy through authentic participation represents an implied shift to a learner-centered curricular design from a subject-skill-centered design. While the 1994 standards are sequenced in terms of student ability, the language of the 2014 performance standards describes the release of exclusively teacher-driven instruction in order to encourage students to learn to reflect and act on their own musical development.

Instructional approaches ranging from teacher-directed to student-led approaches guide students to demonstrate various types of learning. In Anderson and Krathwohl's revision of *Bloom's Taxonomy* (Anderson & Krathwohl, 2001), the authors described the following three classifications of student learning; and in parentheses, I added ways that the categories relate to music learning and potential teacher direction.

1. What Students Know: Knowledge-Facts and Concepts (music vocabulary and concepts: teacher directed)
2. What Students Can Do: Procedural Skills (executive skills and performance practices: teacher directed),
3. What Students Think About Their Learning: Artful Thinking (students becoming independent musicians: student led). (p. 85)

Fisher and Frey (2007, p. 41) described a model for the gradual release of responsibility for learning from teacher direction to student direction. The stages are: focused instruction, guided instruction, collaborative learning, and independent learning. This model described a sequence of instruction beginning with teacher modeling, moving to guided practice, and ending with individual performance of a skill. In *Leaders of Their Own learning*, Berger, Rugen, and Woodfin (2014) described extensive examples of actively involved student learning. They defined the qualities of the engaged learner as one who demonstrates mastery of content and skill-based standards, who explores pathways of learning based on interest and individual choice, and who is supported through challenging tasks and innovative instruction. The goal is to develop the student's ownership of their learning so that it is valued and internalized for a lifetime.

Together, these are approaches to active student learning in which the teacher constructs classroom and ensemble activities that are directly linked to previously agreed on standards and objectives. As with any academic discipline, the foundation of high-order or exemplary level practice is with basic factual and concept knowledge and skills. The initial learning then, is teacher directed so that the fundamentals of music learning are clearly communicated. With guidance, students are guided through various types of modeling and instruction that allow them to practice the expected skills and content knowledge. As the students elevate their confidence and ability they may collaborate to interactively create, perform, and respond to musical stimuli and become increasingly independent, artful, thinking musicians. A visual organizer that demonstrates these relationships is shown in Figure 23.8.

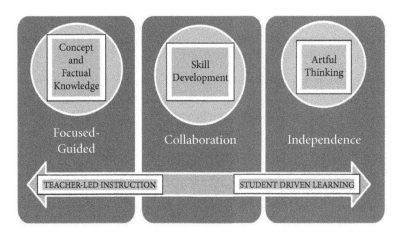

FIGURE 23.8 A continuum of learning experiences.

Learning Theory and Pedagogy

A variety of instructional approaches are needed when implementing the four stages of the Fisher and Frey model. In focused or direct instruction a teacher delivers specific knowledge and skills to the student. Students are informed of the proper vocabulary and its meaning, and given specific instructions for behaviors and approaches to skills. Students are reinforced, positively or negatively, for correct or incorrect responses. Behavioral techniques are used to manage students in large groups, and, if necessary, to maintain control.

As students begin to master the foundational skills and knowledge, teachers are able to relinquish control and provide more guidance through teacher and peer modeling, allowing students to engage in some experimentation and decision-making. For the cognitive learning theorist, pedagogy encourages students to think about their learning but not necessarily engage with others to enhance their understanding. The learning interactions at this stage are still primarily between teachers and students.

As students move toward more independence, they encounter more interaction with one another. In a collaborative learning environment students, now armed with foundational skills and knowledge, are able to peer evaluate (with guidance), self-reflect, discuss choices in music literature selection, and direct other learning experiences. In the *social* cognitivist approach, learning is considered to be enhanced through interactions with peers. Many techniques are associated with this type of teaching including think-pair-share, turn and talk, collaborative projects, consensus building, and others. Constructivism is sometimes considered a type of social cognitivist approach to learning. In it, students' needs, backgrounds, and active involvement are central to the learning environment. These approaches are representative of active learning classrooms. Wiliam and Thompson (2007) described strategies that would activate students as owners of their own learning or self-regulated learners. They suggested five key strategies:

1. Clarify, share, and understand learning intentions and criteria for success.
2. Engineer effective classroom discussions, questions, and tasks that elicit evidence of learning.
3. Provide feedback that moves learners forward.
4. Activate students as instructional resources for one another.
5. Activate students as the owners of their own learning (Wiliam & Thompson, 2007, p. 31).

In these social cognitive and constructivist approaches to teaching, teachers will rely heavily on formative assessments as they provide feedback and guide students toward independently motivated learning.

21st-Century Skills

The independent, self-regulated student may be described as a "21st-century learner." In the 1990s, a significant group of US teachers, education experts, and business leaders gathered to envision the knowledge and skills that students would need to succeed in the rapidly changing workplace of the 21st century. This group created a list of learning and innovation skills that included creativity and innovation, critical thinking and problem-solving, communication, and collaboration. When paired with life and career skills that included flexibility and adaptability, initiative and self-direction, productivity and accountability, and leadership and responsibility, these skills challenge educators to address a paradigm shift in how music and all other curricular disciplines are taught. Certainly, this view of the responsibility of educators to teach 21st-century skills alongside content areas is a much different approach to curriculum than the utilitarian approach promoted by Bobbitt a century earlier.

Most music educators view the list of 21st-century learning and innovation skills and life and career skills as clearly observable goals and outcomes of quality musical experiences. When students achieve excellent performances and musical understanding they inherently practice these skills. The examples that follow demonstrate some typical student-centered music classroom practices and the corresponding 21st-century skills needed to acquire the learning at hand.

- *Student-led rehearsals*: critical thinking, communication, responsibility, accountability
- *Self-peer evaluation*: analysis, communication, self-direction, problem-solving
- *Classroom-ensemble goal setting*: responsibility, initiative, self-direction, collaboration

It is common for teachers to feel uncomfortable with the idea of releasing control of a classroom. Certainly, in a music classroom, maintaining attention to musical tasks is challenging with potentially noisy instruments and movement. The skills students need to be collaborative and independent must be taught. Small steps with very clear directions and objectives with positive reinforcement help students gain these life skills. The paradigm shift with the NCMS is to focus the standards on what students do and how teachers will at first direct the instruction, then adjust their teaching from direct instruction to student-centered learning with fluency.

Implications for Professional Development

Professional development for all teachers must always be rich in the content area. Teachers must keep current with pedagogical techniques and research in music learning and share best practices with one another. However, techniques for fostering 21st-century skills may be generalized for all content areas.

PROCESSES FOR DESIGNING A CURRICULUM

The models that have been described so far describe processes and/or frameworks for constructing curriculum. Each step in the process is important; yet, on the practical side, actual implementation of standards or curriculum should include many other factors. There is a general consensus for establishing either linear or interactive components in a curriculum, including a needs analysis, standards, learning goals and/or objectives, learning experiences, assessment and evaluation, and construction of syllabi. The process of backward design is an alternative approach to the sequential steps of the design. Finally, some curricula are centered on a subject/skills formula while others may be student centered. I believe that it is possible to address all of these entities in a sequential yet interactive learner-centered model guided by strong standards frameworks and learning goals.

The Alignment Loop

Missing in most curricular designs is the mechanism for genuine implementation. What needs to happen to ensure that the standards or curriculum actually are established as the framework for teaching and learning? The alignment of curriculum development processes is incomplete when professional development and resources are not part of the formula. With this in mind, and considering the value of past models of curriculum development including my own (Hansen, 2008 p. 60), I offer a curriculum design process that incorporates attributes of previous models but looks to a holistic and well-balanced future for music education in Figure 23.9.

The Alignment Loop is a visual organizer for the components needed to create and implement an effective music program. The model follows the backward design process, but with added elements that are necessary for proper implementation of a curriculum. This model is interactive, allowing for a flexible interchange between the elements. A completely linear design may inhibit the realities of educational processes. At the center are active music learners who create, perform, respond, and connect their musicianship in authentic musical environments. This model reflects the many possible ways

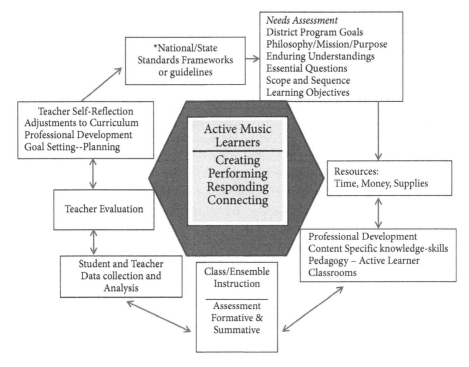

FIGURE 23.9 The alignment loop: A comprehensive design for curriculum.

that a comprehensive local curriculum may actually unfold. Regardless of the process, the components of the curriculum should align or correspond directly from one to the next. The model is named "Alignment Loop" to indicate that there should be a continual interaction of processes that has at its core an active learning environment for students and opportunities to teach comprehensive and meaningful content and skills.

Components of the Alignment Loop

COMPONENT 1: STANDARDS

This curriculum process follows backward design principles. At the beginning of the planning process are the national and/or state standards, or the end goals of the curriculum. In most countries, including the United States, music standards are voluntary. They provide a framework and consistent curriculum focus and implementation. The national standards directly influence state and/or local curricula. These curricula are most often designed by local administrators and teachers, and usually reflect the intent of the national standards and accommodate local social and cultural influences. If no national standards or curriculum framework exists, a curriculum might first reflect local expectations or perspectives.

COMPONENT 2: NEEDS ASSESSMENT

As local educators design their curricula, they should develop a viable philosophy and mission statement for music education. A philosophy statement declares core beliefs about why music education is vital for human culture, for preparation for future work, and for why teaching musical skills and knowledge is important. A mission statement may be generated from the philosophy and is a statement of what the music program will provide for music students in the future. From these statements, overarching and topical enduring understanding statements may be crafted. These statements, different from objectives, summarize the big ideas and important concepts addressed in instructional units, threads, or sequences. With them, teachers establish the reason for why particular musical activities are important for the students' growth and development. These statements might also be a reflection of essential questions: What are the musical activities and why are they important from the student's point of view?

Finally, any locally developed curriculum should include a statement of the purpose of the document. With this, local officials, parents, and students may have a clear understanding of how the program is constructed and executed. The scope and sequence or curriculum maps provide the guide for when concepts and skills should be taught. These may be organized by month, by concept or skill, by ensemble or music class, or in a way that makes sense for the sequential development of the student's knowledge, skills, and engagement. Learning objectives are usually developed at the classroom level and provide the most direct language for implementation of the curriculum in the classroom or ensemble.

COMPONENT 3: RESOURCES

Resources, including time and fiscal support, are imperative for effective implementation of a curriculum. Sadly, this component of the design is often the weakest link. Budget restrictions, lack of adequate planning time, and instructional supplies often inhibit opportunities for teachers to acquire proper training and instructional materials that help them set up a robust curriculum.

COMPONENT 4: PROFESSIONAL DEVELOPMENT

Ideally, professional development should be offered prior to initiating new instructional strategies and assessments. Particularly important are opportunities for teachers to regularly share their ideas and successes in the classroom. The practice of releasing teacher control in order to provide a collaborative and independent learning environment requires training. As musicians, we tend to teach the way we were taught, relying solely on direct instruction and behavioral approaches. It is important for administrators and teachers to advocate for the appropriate and adequate resources in order to truly prepare for active learning instruction.

COMPONENT 5: CLASS AND ENSEMBLE INSTRUCTION AND ASSESSMENT,
FORMATIVE AND SUMMATIVE

For this component of the loop, the second two stages of backward design are merged. It is critical to prioritize learning sequences so that a focus on the standards and enduring understandings is not lost in everyday activities. The instructional approach, learning activities, and the types of assessment to be administered needs to be flexibly determined so that teachers can adjust for particular learning needs in the classroom. For instance, if an ensemble experience calls for having to peer assess using a rubric, but the teacher discovers during the instruction that a checklist or rating scale may be more effi-cient and better understood by the students, the teacher may need to modify the assessment tool or the task. The tool itself, whether rubric, checklist, rating scale, or a combination of performance assessment types, must measure the targeted skills and knowledge identified by the learning goals and objectives in the curriculum (Step 1 of the backward design process). Formative and summative assessment and instruction are dynamic and necessarily adjustable, given the many variables that a teacher may encounter from day to day in the classroom. Formative assessment is ongoing, occurring constantly through music class and results in adjustments in instruction by the teacher and in learning approaches by the students. Formative assessment provides feedback for the students in their quest to learn and also for the teacher to adjust instructional direc-tion or content. Summative assessment provides the evidence of learning acquisition that is measured by a standard or grade (Popham, 2008). However, without a sequentially aligned curriculum, the assessment itself will not properly measure the learning at hand. The evidence of validity and reliability will be weakened.

COMPONENT 6: DATA COLLECTION AND ANALYSIS

In the United States teachers in all curricular disciplines are being asked to assess student growth in designated skills and knowledge. These indicators of growth are often evaluated by pre- and post-measures. The music teacher generally selects a particular skill, such as rhythmic accuracy or students' ability to sight-read a line of music. The instruction that follows then focuses on the selected skill, though it will only be a part of the actual music class. At the end of the instructional sequence, the teacher administers the test again to determine the degree to which the students have improved their perfor-mance of the tested skill. The resulting data from these summative assessments are a component of a teacher's evaluation in some school districts. Again, the assessment must be tightly linked to the learning goals and designated curriculum.

COMPONENT 7: TEACHER EVALUATION

Encouraging students to be responsible for their own learning through a release of teacher direction to student self-direction is becoming a more frequent expectation for teacher evaluation. However, teacher evaluation in the United States is inconsistent, ranging from minimal expectations to complex and stringent ones. In some states and school districts music educators are lumped into an overall evaluation of teacher effectiveness based on test scores in mathematics or language arts. The expectation in these schools is that all teachers participate in "core subject" teaching (core subjects are those that are traditionally tested in American schools, such as reading and math-ematics). In some school districts in the United States, accountability of student learn-ing in music is minimalized and reflects a lack of respect for its contribution to the overall education of their students. In sharp contrast are the states and school districts in which music educators are evaluated as are their peers in "core" subject areas.

One of the most frequently used teacher evaluation frameworks was created by Charlotte Danielson (2007). The Framework includes six criteria: (1) centering instruction on high expectations for student achievement; (2) demonstrating effective teaching practices; (3) recognizing individual student learning needs and developing strategies to address those needs; (4) providing clear and intentional focus on subject matter content and curriculum; (5) fostering and managing a safe, positive learning environment; and (6) using multiple student data elements to modify instruction and improve student learning. The six criteria are compartmentalized by four domains, as shown in Table 23.3.

Some state departments of education require or suggest that a teacher's evaluation be based on several elements, including: teacher practice (observations of teachers in the classroom and a review of how well they have reached their instructional goals), student learning outcomes (whether students demonstrated growth in their assessed skill or knowledge area), stakeholder feedback (sometimes parents and communities evaluate the teacher's effectiveness), and whole school performance (how well the entire school performs in selected measures overall). An increasing number of schools in the United States are also evaluating 21st-century skill development of the teacher and students. Indicators such as active learning community, collaboration, relationships, challenging expectations, and professional responsibility are part of the overall evaluation. This type of evaluation is a true departure from traditional practices.

COMPONENT 8: TEACHER SELF-REFLECTION

In the final component of the Alignment Loop the teacher assesses the work of the students, their own strengths and weaknesses, their lesson planning, and the viability of the curriculum that provides the instructional framework. This process is flexible, perhaps reviewed frequently in a given school year. The reflection provides an opportunity to adjust in-class procedures or instructional goals and objectives. It is a critical component in curriculum development.

Table 23.3 Domains of Teacher Evaluation

Domain 1: Planning and Preparation	Domain 3: Instruction
1a Demonstrating Knowledge of Content and Pedagogy	3a Communicating with Students
1b Demonstrating Knowledge of Students	3b Using Questioning and Discussion Techniques
1c Setting Instructional Outcomes	3c Engaging Students in Learning
1d Demonstrating Knowledge of Resources	3d Using Assessment in Instruction
1e Designing Coherent Instruction	3e Demonstrating Flexibility and Responsiveness
1f Designing Student Assessments	
Domain 2: Classroom Environment	**Domain 4: Professional Responsibilities**
2a Creating an Environment of Respect and Rapport	4a Reflecting on Teaching
2b Establishing a Culture for Learning	4b Maintaining Accurate Records
2c Managing Classroom Procedures	4c Communicating with Families
2d Managing Student Behavior	4d Participating in a Professional Community
2e Organizing Physical Space	4e Growing and Developing Professionally
	4f Showing Professionalism

Source: Danielson (2007).

National and International Standards and Curriculum

In December of 2015, I invited music education leaders from 14 selected countries to complete a brief survey regarding their curriculum development processes. Nine surveys were submitted and six of those responded to all questions with added comments. It is my hope that this initial sampling of curricular practices will be interesting and useful to music educators internationally and result in a much more robust collection of information and data. In this segment of the chapter in Table 23.4, I present the survey responses and then share the open-ended comments.

Table 23.4 International Education Survey Results

Question 1: Do you have a national, regional, or local curriculum?

Brazil	England	Germany	Italy	Russia	Singapore	Taiwan	Turkey	US
No	Yes	Yes	Yes	Yes	Yes	No	Yes	Yes

Question 2: How are the goals, outcomes, or standards developed?

England	Germany	Italy	Russia	Turkey	US
By government officials	By government officials, education leaders	By education leaders	By government officials	By teachers, government officials, education leaders	By teachers, government officials, education leaders

Question 3: What factors guide the development of the curriculum?

England	Germany	Italy	Russia	Turkey	US
Other	Cultural	National	Cultural National	Cultural National, Other	Cultural National

Question 4: What guidance does your curriculum provide?

England	Germany	Italy	Russia	Turkey	US
Other	Musical knowledge-performance skills, musical thinking (analysis, synthesis, evaluation)	Musical knowledge-performance skills, musical thinking (analysis, synthesis, evaluation)	Musical knowledge-musical-performance skills, musical thinking (analysis, synthesis, evaluation), creativity	Musical knowledge-musical performance skills, collaboration, creativity, and communication	Musical knowledge-musical or performance skills, musical thinking (analysis, synthesis, evaluation), creativity

(continued)

Table 23.4 Continued

Question 5: Do you have a curriculum review process?

England	Germany	Italy	Russia	Singapore	US
Yes	Yes	No	Yes	N/A	Yes

Question 6: Is your curriculum required for all schools or is it considered voluntary?

England	Germany	Italy	Russia	Turkey	US
Other	Required	Required	Required	Required	Required

Question 7: About how often is the curriculum written or revised?

England	Germany	Italy	Russia	Turkey	US
Varied	6–10 years	Rarely	2–5 years	Primary schools 1994–2006; secondary 1991, 2007	6–10 years

Question 8: Are the assessments of your curriculum included or expected?

England	Germany	Italy	Russia	Turkey	US
No	Yes	Yes	Yes	Yes	Yes

Question 9: Are teachers evaluated based on your curriculum?

England	Germany	Italy	Russia	Turkey	US
Other	No	No	No	No	Yes

Question 10: Is your professional development expected and/or provided either nationally or locally to help teachers use your curriculum?

England	Germany	Italy	Russia	Turkey	US
Other	No	No	No	No	Yes

Summary of Respondents' Commentary

Respondents from England, Germany, Russia, Turkey, and the United States indicated that government officials were integral to the curriculum development process. In Russia, the Ministry of Education and Science of the Russian Federation approves national and state requirements regarding the curriculum and basic general education programs. This curriculum is required and revised every 2–5 years. In contrast, education leaders in Italy prepare a national curriculum that is required though rarely reviewed or revised. In Brazil, there is no national curriculum, but guidelines, which are not required, are offered by the Ministry of Education. The revision process is undertaken centrally by government officials and expert curriculum advisory panels. Brazil is currently discussing a document called Common National Basis for the curriculum and music.

In Turkey, the curriculum is created by government officials, curriculum specialists, selected music teachers, and selected music education professors. The curriculum is required for primary (elementary and middle) school levels, but is voluntary for the high school level. The latest two curricula were written in 2004 and 2006. Similarly, development of the US national standards involves a large group of writers and stakeholders. These standards were crafted by over 200 teachers and education leaders from all over the country. In the United States, however, the revised National Standards (2014) are voluntary. These standards are not a curriculum, but they will become the framework for most state music standards (as were the 1994 standards).

A wide variety of practices were found in regard to teacher evaluation and professional development. In Turkey, a constructivist approach to teaching is encouraged in order to promote creative thinking. With this approach students participate in active and self-directed musical experiences. The learning environment is socially interactive and performance based. Most teachers, however, had not experienced this type of instruction in their own music education. In her 2010 study, Dilek Göktürk reported that while some teachers observed positive results from constructivism, most believed that more training and amenable classroom environments were needed to successfully implement the instructional approach. Teachers are not evaluated in Turkey based on the curriculum (Göktürk, 2010, pp. 3075–3079).

In the United States, Russia, and Germany assessments linked to the curriculum (or standards) are expected. In the United States the achievement of curricular goals is an important part of the accreditation process in all curricular disciplines and for institutions in most states. Increasingly, school districts are establishing a link between students' performance on assessments and the evaluation of teacher effectiveness. Professional development varies widely among the states, as many local districts often lack the means and/or resolve to meet the needs of music educators. However, teachers who are members of professional music organizations do have access to quality professional development. In Russia and Germany, teachers are included and expected, and are mandatory for secondary schools in Germany.

Summary: Implications for Visionary, Strongly Aligned Curriculum and Assessment

This chapter offers a wide-ranging discussion of curriculum development and the alignment of its components. Effective assessment is dependent on a purposeful and direct alignment to all of the constituents of the curriculum. Today's educational practices are complex, interactive, and multifaceted. Given rapidly changing workplace demands, our students must possess strong social, cognitive, and affective skills in addition to their content knowledge and skills. Involvement in music learning is a natural, engaging, and humanly satisfying means of obtaining those skills. To achieve this, however, a curriculum is needed that promotes contemporary educational expectations as well as teacher practice that skillfully moves students from focused instruction to independent learning. Assessment provides the pathway for determining whether our students have reached these goals. All components of a curriculum must be aligned and interactive to honor these practices. John Dewey (1938) prophetically envisioned such a curricular design, and his words ring true today. He wrote:

> There are certain common principles in the new education: from imposition from above to expression and cultivation of individuality, from external discipline to free activity, from learning from texts and teachers, to learning from experience, from acquisition of isolated skills and techniques by drill to acquisition as means of attaining ends which make direct vital appeal, from preparation for a more or less remote future to making the most of the opportunities of present life, from static aims and materials to acquaintance with a changing world.   (p. 19)

References

Anderson, L. W., & Krathwohl, D. R. (2001). *A taxonomy for learning, teaching, and assessing: A revision of Bloom's taxonomy of educational objectives.* New York, NY: Longman.

Berger, R., Rugen, L., & Woodfin, L. (2014). *Leaders of their own learning.* San Francisco, CA: Jossey-Bass.

Bloom, B. S. (Ed). (1956/1984). *Taxonomy of education objectives, Handbook I: Cognitive domain.* New York, NY: Longman.

Bobbitt, F. (1912). The elimination of waste in education. *Elementary School Teacher, 12,* 259–271. doi: 10.1086/454122

Danielson, C. (2007). *Enhancing professional practice: A framework for teaching.* Alexandria, VA: Association for Supervision and Curriculum Development.

Dewey, J. (1916). *Democracy and education.* New York, NY: Macmillan.

Dewey, J. (1938). *Experience and education.* New York, NY: Touchstone/Kappa Delta Phi.

Elliott, D. (1995). *Music matters.* New York, NY: Oxford University Press.

Fisher, D., & Frey, N. (2007). *Checking for understanding: Formative techniques for your Classroom.* Alexandria, VA: Association for Supervision and Curriculum Development.

Göktürk, D., (2010). The role of constructivist approach on creativity in primary school music curriculum in the Republic of Turkey. *Procedia: Social and Behavioral Sciences, 2,* 3075–3079. doi: 10.1016/j.sbspro.2010.03.468

Hansen, D. (2008). The alignment loop: A curriculum planning sequence and critical inquiry as catalysts for sound assessments. In T. Brophy & A. Wermser-Lehmann (Eds.), *Assessment in music education: Integrating curriculum, theory, and practice. Proceedings of the 2007 Symposium on Assessment in Music Education* (pp. 59–70). Oxford, UK: GIA Publications.

Hansen, D. (2013). Assessment for learning: Motivating music learning through formative assessment and thoughtful planning. In T. Brophy & A. Wermser-Lehmann (Eds.), *Music assessment across cultures and continents: The culture of shared practice. Proceedings of the 3rd international symposium on assessment in music education.* Oxford, UK: GIA Publications.

Krathwohl, D. R., Bloom, B. S., & Masia, B. B. (1964). *Taxonomy of educational objectives: The classification of educational goals. Handbook II: Affective domain.* New York, NY: David McKay.

Mark, M. L., & Gary, C. L. (2007). *A history of American music education* (3rd ed.) New York, NY: Rowman and Littlefield.

McCarthy, M. (2009). Re-thinking "music" in the context of education. In T. A. Regelski & J. T. Gates (Eds.), *Music education for changing times: Guiding visions for practice* (pp. 29–38). New York, NY: Springer.

National Association for Music Education (NAfME). (1994). *National standards for arts education: What every young American should know and be able to do in the arts.* Reston, VA: Author. (Original work published by MENC).

National Coalition for Core Arts Standards. (2014, June). *National core arts standards: A conceptual framework for arts learning.* Retrieved from: http://www.NationalArtsStandards.org

Popham, J. (2008). *Transformative assessment.* Alexandria, VA. ASCD.

Reimer, B. (1970). *A philosophy of music education.* Upper Saddle River, NJ: Prentice-Hall, Inc.

Schwadron, A. (1967). *Aesthetics: Dimensions for music education.* Reston, VA: MENC.

Taba, H. (1962). *Curriculum development: Theory and practice.* New York, NY: Harcourt, Brace, and World.

Thorndike, E. L. (1922). *The psychology of arithmetic.* New York, NY: Macmillan.

Tyler, R. W. (1949/1969). *Basic principles of curriculum and instruction.* Chicago, IL: University of Chicago Press.

Wiggins, G., & McTighe, J. (1998). *Understanding by design.* Alexandria, VA: Association for Supervision and Curriculum Development.

Wiliam, D., & Thompson, M. (2007). Integrating assessment with instruction: What will it take to make it work? In C. A. Dwyer (Ed.), *The future of assessment: Shaping teaching and learning* (pp. 53–82). Mahwah, NJ: Erlbaum.

TEST DEVELOPMENT

CHAPTER 24

AN OVERVIEW OF MUSIC TESTS AND THEIR USES

RICHARD COLWELL

IN some circles, the word "test" is pejorative, and in others, tests provide hope. Most negative descriptions of tests seem to originate with issues in education. The education historian Diane Ravitch (2016) states (slightly abridged but her exact words):

> Our national leaders have turned our most important domestic duty into a quest of higher scores on standardized tests. The heavy reliance on tests began with George W. Bush's No Child Left Behind. The punishments for not achieving higher test scores every year were increasingly onerous. After Bush left office and was replaced by Barack Obama, the obsession with testing grew even more intense. States, to qualify for money, had to evaluate teachers in relation to the rise or fall of the test scores of their students.   (p. 34)

These tests, thus, are high-stakes tests. The purpose in testing has not abated with the Every Student Succeeds Act (S. 1177, 114 Cong., 2015)—only the responsibility. As of- 2015, as many as 27 states required administration of at least one end-of-course test (Domaleski, 2011); 13 states required students to pass a test in order to graduate; 44 states and the District of Columbia (DC) require classroom observations to be incorporated in teacher evaluations (Ruzek, Hafen, Hamre, & Pianta, 2014); DC and 18 states have evaluation designs on how to measure student achievement in nontested grades. In addition, 35 states and DC required student achievement as a significant or the most significant factor in teacher evaluations, a policy that can be changed under Every Student Succeeds Act (Doherty & Jacobs, 2013; Ferrara & Way, 2016; Penuel & Shepard, 2016). The influential criteria for teacher and student tests are: higher-order cognitive skills, high-fidelity assessment of critical abilities, real-world assessments that are internationally benchmarked, use of items that are instructionally sensitive and educationally valuable (not reflecting students' out-of-school experiences), and assessments that are valid, reliable, and fair (Darling-Hammond et al., 2014.) These criteria seem unreasonable for music education; we can only keep them in mind. The purposes (and assessment) of music education may change with new or different standards. In visual arts, Elliot Eisner (2001) raised such an issue when visual culture replaced discipline-based arts education, and David Burton (2016) has written about the disconnect between the 2014 standards and opportunity to learn (reported in the 2008 National Assessment of Educational Progress). Tests, whether used in formative or summative assessment, provide data more valuable to teachers than to school administrators and politicians; music tests are no exception. Industry, medicine, and most research areas rely on tests as indicators of progress and failure. Positive results indicate that "something" is working satisfactorily. Failure of a test is important when safety issues are involved and may indicate that it is time to think anew—maybe even about learning. This chapter focuses on tests related to education and music education and, secondarily, tests used with music as an indicator for a range of outcomes in other professions. What are important about all tests are the purpose and the context in which they are used and the knowledge gained from interpreting the results.

Music has been used in ceremonies, theater, and in the reciting of epic poetry since the time of the Greeks and before. Plato was supposedly concerned about the impact of "new" music on youth, while other Greeks were investigating overtones as well as consonance and dissonance. Observation is the most common "test," and data from observations the most troublesome to interpret. The music critic comments on the performance of the musicians, of the conductor, of the music and of the programming. The critic often makes comparisons of the musician's growth over time and, occasionally, with other soloists and ensembles. The reviews in national media are important and can be considered "high stakes" for the performers. Observing a music teacher may be comparable, as it has become "high stakes," and interpreting the results of observation can range from dismissal to rewards. The accuracy of the critical test of observation has a large margin of error; thus, its use has been questioned. The Bill and Melinda Gates Foundation has invested 45 million US dollars to improve observation as a test (discussed later in this chapter) as part of a $335 million investment in improving teaching and learning (Bill and Melinda Gates Foundation, 2013, January; Kane, Kerr, & Pianta (2014).

The history and use of tests in music teaching and learning can inform us of the expected curriculum goals, and of priorities for teaching and for student learning of knowledge and skills. Commercially published tests have been selected for this chapter. Published materials should be instructionally sensitive and provide evidence of the importance of musical outcomes tested. Categories of tests include the following: aptitude, achievement, appreciation, psychological, creativity, teacher evaluation, and "interesting uses." Music teachers frequently create tests—these usually provide only a rough and incomplete estimate of student learning and should not be used for high-stakes purposes. Are music grades high-stakes? Certainly, for some teachers and students. We know that many tests designed for formative evaluation are used to justify music grades. If one's philosophy is that music learning is primarily a process without a product, most, if not all, summative assessments are inappropriate.

In the years after the American Civil War, music was used primarily for dancing and entertainment. With community-sponsored contests (tests) among instrumental soloists, and with the founding of symphony orchestras, auditions became a type of test. Teacher certification tests at the beginning of the 20th century required candidates to know the fundamentals of music notation and have reasonable competence in singing. The emphasis on notation and singing was a continuation of the rationale for music begun by Lowell Mason and his colleagues. Students, of course, were expected to learn to sing and were tested.

At the beginning of the 20th century, music followed education's interest in the role of talent (aptitude) in the schools. William Wundt had established an experimental laboratory to conduct research on human abilities in 1879. The philosopher Carl Stumpf became interested in psychology as he observed the experimental work in aesthetics by Gustav Fechner; with Stumpf publishing a music test in 1883 (Stumpf, 1883/1890), which used data on consonance and dissonance as well as tone color. In addition to testing for degrees of pleasantness, Stumpf asked subjects to sing a note that he played on the piano. He also asked subjects to judge the higher of two notes. By the end of the century, psychologists were developing sensory tests such as those used in the Binet-Simon scale to determine the role of inheritance. The laboratory experimentation was reasonably scientific (IQ testing, begun at that time, has had a lengthy shelf life, as has music aptitude). Measures for identifying music talent exist in all countries, and new aptitude tests continue to be developed.

TESTS OF TALENT AND APTITUDE

Carl Seashore (1932, 1936, 1938, 1946) believed that pure tasks from music stimuli matched the pure tasks in intelligence testing. This was wise, as the concern for the influence of culture (race and socioeconomic status [SES]) that marred other music talent tests as well as IQ testing is not an issue with discrimination competence. This interest in ability, aptitude, talent, or musicality dominated testing for more than half a century and continues to be present in new formats. It remains important, as does Seashore's foundational research. McPherson and Hallam (2009) suggest that the types of musical talent are performing, improvising, composing, arranging, analyzing, appraising, conducting, and music teaching, but these would not change Seashore's concepts, recognized or taught. Sound waves would be a necessary component of music ability, either native or acquired, a competence that James Mursell (1937) also accepted. Others with an interest in musical ability, like Géza Révész (1925/1999), were studying expert musicians and concluding that intuition, identifying notes in a chord and notes played on the piano, musical memory (singing back a melody), and imagery were factors in this ability. Sir Francis Galton (1869, 1883, 1889) had included music in his work with human competence, likely influencing Seashore to concentrate on using pure tasks that could be manipulated scientifically. Seashore states, "where there is no experiment there can be no science" (1946, p. 44). Seashore was a serious psychologist and experimented for some 20 years prior to publishing his list of tasks in 1919. His tasks, based on sound waves, were pitch, intensity, rhythm (added in 1925), time, consonance, and tonal memory. Intensity was later replaced by loudness and consonance, and these were replaced in 1939 with timbre. Seashore labeled his tasks as *Measures of Musical Talent* (1915) and cautioned that they were an incomplete test of music aptitude. Seashore gave his tasks to a wide variety of subjects, checking on any influence of gender, race, age, and experience. He found a wide variance in competence on the individual tasks as well as on the total test, data that he believed teachers could not ignore. This variance in competence for individual music tasks informed him that his tasks were not equal in difficulty and could not be weighted to obtain a total aptitude score. One could have a low score on one task and still be musical. The tasks are all tasks of discrimination, louder-softer; higher-lower, and so forth—skills that convinced him that the more talented individuals could make finer discriminations. Thus, he developed and published in 1939 a second test, part B, which required finer discrimination of intervals and patterns. For laboratory assessment, he developed but did not publish part C for research on perception competence. Seashore believed that music draws on math, physics, physiology, anatomy, genetics, anthropology, and general psychology (1946). The sound waves he investigated continue to be important in music psychology (Lahdelma & Eerola, 2016). A complex of pure tones, sine waves like a piano tone, can also have partials, each with its own frequency, amplitude, and phase. Complex tones with different spectral contents are perceived as having different sound qualities, tone colors, or timbres. Harmonic overtones also affect the degree of sensory consonance and dissonance of tone combinations presented simultaneously. Tone combinations with fundamental frequencies that are not related to each other such as the minor second 16:15 lead to sensory dissonance—important ideas in listening (Thompson & Schellenberg, 2006). There is ongoing research on pure tones, as harmonic overtones are not perceived as individual pitches. Complex tones with different spectral contents are perceived as having different sound qualities, tones, colors, or timbres.

James Mursell and Carl Seashore are seen as having opposite beliefs. This is only partially true; perception of sound is critical for both. Mursell's interest was in the application of sound. He argued the art of music is a creation of the mind of man with everything depending on the action of the mind. For Mursell, the essential function of music is to express and objectify emotion. The aural experience is related to behavior and to mental life different in important respects from visual or tactile experience. This is a biological and psychological fact (Mursell, 1937, p. 19). Musicality does not depend directly on sensory abilities but on a complex of psychological functions that exist in *varying degrees and relationships*. The art of music depends on some of the most foundational and universal human characteristics. Mursell's reaction to aptitude testing was to ascertain whether those who score high on a test display high musical behaviors like sight-singing, playing the piano, and doing well in music theory, all teachable. Mursell and Seashore had 30 consecutive articles on the psychology of music during the 1930s in the *Music Educators Journal*, an indication of the importance of these ideas. They agreed on the importance of four capacities: loudness, sense of pitch, sense of time, and sense of timbre. Mursell (Mursell & Glenn, 1931, 1938), suggested the results of psychological investigations in the field of music "can be of utmost value for the working music teacher, and can further the cause of music education in America" (p. iii). For Seashore, "psychology allows us to record, preserve, and interpret music in all forms of historical interest" (Seashore, 1946, p. 14). He believed,

> We should think in orderly, specific, describable, repeatable, and verifiable terms, as the musician can see in the score an astonishing number of features of which he otherwise would not be aware.   (p. 11)

> If music is to keep up with other subjects, we have to adopt the scientific point of view.   (p. 49)

> All kinds of sounds have musical value; one only needs training and talent.   (p. 184)

> Students being assessed should be able to give reasons for their responses.   (p. 191)

> All genuine musicians have superior auditory imagery that can recall a tone so realistically and objectively that it can be scrutinized in all its detail just as in actual hearing.   (p. 211)

> If the public school instructor has a clear conception of the role of tonal imagery and can evaluate it to some degree, he can understand in large part the success or failure, and the likes and dislikes, of the students, and he can guide them more successfully.
> (p. 198)

> Music is the life of feeling. One plays upon feeling to appreciate and create the beautiful in the tonal realm.   (p. 204)

Seashore intended to establish the importance of his measures in the public schools. Abraham Flexner (a well-known educational reformer of the time), however, suggested that any research results would be more convincing if conducted at the Eastman School of Music. George Eastman and Howard Hanson became strong supporters of the validity of the measures. Seashore's assistant, Hazel Stanton, worked at Eastman from at least 1921 to 1935 evaluating the measures.

Why such support? The public and the music education profession believed that knowing a student's musical aptitude could avoid frustration and a waste of taxpayers' money. To identify the most talented individuals and provide them with the necessary education would be more important than any attempt to educate the masses in areas for which they had limited talent. A similar belief exists today. Jose Abreu, the founder of the El Sistema program, believes that "if a thousand must be sacrificed so that four make it, the sacrifice is well worth it" (Baker, 2014, p. 203). Public school educators continue to express concern for the number of "dropouts" from the music programs on offer. A pleiad of music educators cite the low percentage of students enrolled in music in secondary schools as evidence of a problem. Music conservatories are talent-selective and there seems to be a concern for ignoring latent talent among the disadvantaged. "I'm not very musical" is a more common expression in America than "I'm not intelligent." Belief is strong.

The Eastman validity study (Stanton, 1935) was based on more than 2,000 music students. Test results provided a basis for dividing the study body into five categories and to use graduation as the dependent variable. Sixty percent of the top fifth of the class graduated; but only 17% of the lowest fifth did. The faculty voted to drop any student identified as deficient in talent, perhaps influenced by a study by W. W. Larson (1938) that found a correlation of .59 between scores on the original Seashore test and music theory grades. Stanton was unable to use faculty ratings of student potential, as Eastman faculty did not discriminate among their students, and estimates of individual competence changed little over the 4 years of study. The consonance-dissonance test did not discriminate among Eastman students but remains valued in research by music psychologists and early education researchers. The original consonance test was scored by psychologists who determined the better of two sets of tones based on smoothness, blending, and purity.

Seashore objected to his published test being the sole measure of musicality. Stanton (1935) created an accompanying test of tonal imagery, an ability that Seashore argued was required for retention, recall, recognition, and anticipation of musical facts. In his *Psychology of Music*, Seashore states that one creates music by hearing it in one's "minds ear"; "if one removes the aural image from the musical mind, one takes out the very essence of musicality" (1938/1967, p. 6). Surprisingly, Seashore believed that mental imagery could be developed to a marked degree, as music is essentially a play on "feeling with feeling." (Some of these early beliefs/statements may remind the reader of the ideas of Bennett Reimer and Edwin Gordon.) Seashore describes two aspects of feeling, one aesthetic and the other creative, stating, "music can be appreciated only through active feeling" (1938/1967, p. 9). Stanton's (1935) test of tonal imagery was scored on a six-point scale based on musical sensitivity, musical action, musical memory and imagination, musical intellect, and musical feeling. As the test was subjectively scored, suggestions were made to substitute either appreciation tests, attitude measures, or intelligence tests for tonal imagery. The Iowa Comprehension Test was selected, as it correlated with success. Stanton also used rating scales of musical environment, musical training and education, musical activity, musical feeling, and musical interests. These variables were scored in five ranks: safe, probably, possible, doubtful, and discouraged. She followed up with 10 discouraged students and found only 3 had graduated; the one graduate remaining in music became a public-school music supervisor in a small town (Stanton, 1935).

The importance of testing for talent is pervasive. The Seashore measures required about an hour to administer; many of the tests using similar tasks can be found in shorter or slightly modified tests including: *Musical Talent Test*, F.E. Olds & Sons, n.d.; *Selmer Music Guidance Survey*, n.d.; *What Instrument Should I Play (WISIP)*, n.d.; *Myers Music Aptitude Test*, n.d.; *Moyer Music Tests*, n.d.; *King Musical Instrument Appraisal Test*, n.d.; C. L. McCreery *Elementary Rhythm and Pitch Test*, 1937; *Conrad Instrument Talent Test*, 1941; *Tilson-Gretsch Musical Aptitude Tests*, 1941; *Pan American Music Aptitude Test*, 1951; *Kwalwasser Music Talent Test*, 1953; *Biondo Music Aptitude Test*, 1957; *Conn Music Aptitude Test*, 1976; the *Gordon Instrument Timbre Preference Tests*, 1984; plus some unpublished and teacher-constructed tests (University of Maryland Libraries, 2005).

Some tests have recordings; others require a teacher to administer the task. Discrimination tasks include pitch, time, intensity, consonance, chords, melodies, and counting the number of times a tone appears. The Gordon Timbre Preference Test is a preference test of 7 timbres (woodwind and brass) organized into 42 recorded test items. The independent Kwalwasser test took only 10 minutes to administer and was very popular. The test had two forms, grades 4–6, and 7 and above, and consisted of short melodic patterns with the task being to decide if the second pattern differed in pitch, time, rhythm, or loudness from the first.

Interest in developing better, more holistic, and substantive measures of musical talent than the Seashore tests continued until at least 1989. Seashore's student Jacob Kwalwasser (1926) could not resist the value of aptitude, but, likely influenced by James Mursell, labeled his melodic and harmonic sensitivity tests as aptitude. One judges the "better" of two-measure melodic progressions. In the harmonic sensitivity test, the task is to judge the better of three chords in conventional four-part harmonization. In 1930, Kwalwasser was joined by the music educator Peter Dykema in publishing a test that continued to use items from Seashore plus the addition of taste (e.g., Wing and Gordon) for tonal movement, melodic taste, pitch, and rhythm imagery. In a journal article in 1926, Lowery suggested that comparing cadences in various positions, same and different phrases, and musical memory for statements that contained irrelevant items was a more musical way of assessing musicality. Raleigh Drake's (1957) interest in the role of memory began in 1934 and was last published in 1957 (University of Maryland Libraries, 2005, series 6.2, box 43, folder 10; also in the Talbot Library, Westminster Choir College). In this test one had to compare from two to seven melodies with the original, indicating whether any perceived change was in key, time values, or notes. The addition of each melody clearly was a more difficult memory task, allowing Walter Vispoel (1987) to use the test in computer adaptive testing.

Madison's (1942) idea was that interval discrimination was the true aptitude test. The student compared four harmonic intervals to determine which one was different. James Froseth (1982, 1983) developed an ear-to-hand coordination test; the test was simplified by Mark Dickey (1991) for use in the public schools. The student is given a melodic pattern and required to match it on his or her instrument.

A Test of Musicality by E. Thayer Gaston appeared in 1942 and reached its fourth edition in 1957 (Gaston, 1942/1957). Instrumental teachers believed it to measure potential even though it contains notation. Students responded to whether a given note was in a chord, detected differences between sound and notation, and determined whether the final note of a phrase should be higher or lower; tonal memory was also tested, namely, identifying changes in pitch or rhythm. Herbert Wing's (Wing, 1958) *Standardized Tests of Musical Intelligence* followed a year later and consisted of seven tests. In Wing's test, the student is to identify the number of notes in a chord, detect a change of pitch between two chords played successively, identify the note changed in a short melody. In addition, four tests that measure taste and/or perception, were adopted 7 years later by Edwin Gordon; these four tasks were preferences for rhythmic accent, harmony, dynamic relationships, and phrasing. Bentley's (1966) *Measures of Musical Abilities*, designed for ages 7–12, comprised four tests: pitch discrimination, tonal memory, chord analysis, and rhythmic memory. Scores improved only 3% on a second testing, thus providing data for the argument that the test measured talent. Edwin Gordon (1965), whose *Musical Aptitude Profile* was published a year earlier, also found that scores improved only from 3% to 4% after a semester of instruction. Gordon's test is 115 minutes in length, an indication of the importance of aptitude and the difficulty in measuring it. Tonal, melody, and harmony imagery are assessed in part 1, with the respondent determining whether an embellished melody is the same, whether the harmony is changed by varying the lowest note, and, with rhythm, whether the tempo stays the same. In part 2 the task is to determine whether the metrical structure is the same or different. Three tasks are presented in part 3: select better phrasing, better ending, and better style. Gordon uses original music to reduce influence from the culture. In a 3-year study, Gordon (1967) obtained reliabilities of .17 to .56 with a composite from .35 to .71. Shorter Gordon aptitude tests are available for younger students but without the preference/perception tests and the supporting validity research. Gordon's (1979) *Primary Measures of Music Aptitude* has a tonal and a rhythm test. Tonal items differ due to a change of one or more tones. Meter differs due to grouping of tones within one meter. In 1982, an Intermediate Measure (Gordon, 1982) was published for students scoring above the 80th percentile on the Primary Measures. The main difference in the tests is a greater use of the minor mode in the tonal section. In 1989, the *Advanced Measures of Music Audiation* (Gordon, 1989) for college students was published. Although a short test, Gordon (1997) argues that it is not an achievement test. Two short, original, musical statements are given with the task being to indicate whether the second is the same as or different from the first; changes are either tonal or rhythmic. In Sweden, Holmstrom (1963) and Gabrielsson (1995) advanced the idea that musicality consisted of pitch, chord analysis, tonal memory, and rhythm. When he factor-analyzed his work, he found that musicality consisted of two factors, pitch perception and musical experience.

A different approach to aptitude has been taken by Kai Karma (1974, 1975, 1979, 1995), who defines music aptitude as the ability to hear temporal structure in sound material. He argues that temporal patterns (from the point of human psychology) are more essential than sound. Thus, there could be music without sound and musical ability without hearing. The argument is similar to visual temporal patterns. In his aptitude test, the task is to find the repeated pattern in a sound sequence and compare it with a single (not repeated) pattern, which may be similar or structurally changed. The structures are formed by varying either the pitches, intensities, or durations of the sounds. The Japanese researchers Umemoto, Mikuno, and Murase (1989), published an aptitude test that focused on pitch deviation of 50 hz up or down on a diatonic scale using tonal and atonal sequences of four, five, and six tones. Gembris (2002, 2006) reports that meter recognition is thought to not develop until the age of 7, and to stabilize at 9. Five-year-olds, however, can maintain a given meter (p. 124).

Many of the aptitude tests were well researched by the authors and important to music educators if the skills measured are truly aptitude or very difficult to teach. One thread in music aptitude is the importance of musical memory. Discrimination is also important. One learns to hear. This half century of interest in aptitude testing established that students do differ greatly on these tasks; whether teachers are using this knowledge to improve their curricula is unknown. The human cognitive apparatus can discern the organization behind the music with comparative ease.

MUSIC ACHIEVEMENT TESTS

Published achievement tests should be an indicator of what has been or is being taught—a sort of curricular priorities checklist. If there is a sight-reading test as part of a music contest, the hint is that sight-reading should be part of the curriculum. With achievement tests, the curriculum and the measure must be aligned and the test sensitive to the instruction. In American music education there is little agreement on a graded curriculum; the music curriculum is influenced by the texts/materials used in general music and instruction books in instrumental music. In the United States, it is surprising that the National Assessment of Educational Progress (NAEP) specified 8th grade as a benchmark. Grade level tests are possible only with a standardized curriculum like those that exist in mathematics and language arts. National and state summative reports at the end of music study are infeasible, as are grade and grouped-grade levels, due to differences in opportunity to learn. Formative assessment is viable but difficult. The point of testing is to articulate any common knowledge and skills that should be known. Music achievement results from the intelligent and persistent use of capacities (Davidson & Scripp, 1992). As we write, there is interest in incorporating character skills, social-emotional skills, self-management skills, psychological skills, behavioral skills, interpersonal and intrapersonal skills (soft skills), and skills selected from a list of 21st-century skills, into all of instruction. Rating scales would be used in these noncognitive skills such as anchoring of vignettes, forced choice, rank, and preference methods, and situational judgment tests. Other measures include observation, questioning, written work, informal and formal testing, and self- and peer evaluations. There is always a danger of attainment's taking precedence over progress.

In 1921, the Music Supervisors National Conference published a course of study for graded schools partially based on data from achievement tests. The interest was in "grading" the school (not the student) as being either average or good. Competence in singing was expected. National objectives were possible in tasks related to knowledge of notation. Fewer than 50% of 6th-grade students could recognize the national anthem from notation. Symbols, terms, and key and time signatures were poorly learned (Kwalwasser, 1927), with an appreciable loss of knowledge as students advanced in grade level. Professional educational organizations have no enforcement mechanism like the Food and Drug Administration or the Environmental Protection Agency, making for a loose alignment between what is taught and what is tested.

The early tests often contained items that had been established as aptitude. Which is aptitude and which is achievement is a decision for professionals. For example, the *Beach Music Test* of 1920 and 1930 and reprinted in 1938 (Beach, 1921) not only tested knowledge of music symbols but also had an aural component that required identification of duple, triple, or quadruple meter, ascending or descending melodies, similarity of phrases, identification of the highest or lowest note, identifying aural stimuli by syllable names, judging whether the notation is correct, and selecting from several written melodies from the ones heard. The student also had to match composers and artists. This eight-part test assumed a rigorous music curriculum and tasks that were accepted as important considering its more than two decades of shelf life. The *Kwalwasser-Ruch Test of Music Accomplishment* (Kwalwasser & Ruch, 1927) was similar, with more emphasis on knowledge of syllables. Alignment with the curriculum was supported by a high correlation with music grades for students in grades 6–12. Other 1920 achievement tests by Hutchinson and Pressey (1927), Gildersleeve and Soper (1921), Strouse (1937), and Torgerson and Fahnestock (1927/1930) required dictation skills; detecting changes in pitch, meter, and key signatures; ands recognition of song titles from notation.

Knuth's (1936/1966) *Achievement Tests in Music* gave the notation for two measures of four played on the piano, with the student having to select the last two measures from four choices. In 1964, Marilyn Pflederer-Zimmerman investigated whether Piaget's conservation stages applied to music (Pflederer, 1964). She continued the study with Lee Sechrest in 1968 under a federal grant, and later with Webster (1983). The deformations used were changes in instrument, tempo, harmony, mode, rhythm, contour, or interval of the phrases. Conservation of tonal patterns seems to appear earlier than that for rhythmic patterns, and alterations of instrumentation tempo and harmony are recognized earlier than those of mode, contour, and rhythm (Pflederer & Sechrest, 1968). Swinchoski's (1965) middle school test was standardized in 1965.

The Colwell *Music Achievement Tests* 1–4 (1965/1970) were a deliberate attempt to align testing with the curriculum. Colwell analyzed contemporary teaching materials, and convened a national teacher conference to verify that the objectives were being taught in most classrooms. In the following year, a similar alignment procedure was used to develop the first NAEP in music. The Colwell tests are structured similar to the Aliferis college-level tests (1947/1954, 1962), with an initial basic task followed by the same competency presented in a more musical version. These tests assess pitch discrimination, melody moving by steps or leaps, meter discrimination, major-minor discrimination, feeling for tonal center, and auditory-visual discrimination (pitch and rhythm), the last part requiring a comparison of the aural stimulus with notation. Test 3 has three parts: tonal memory, melody recognition, and pitch and instrument recognition. Test 4 has four parts: musical style, auditory-visual discrimination, chord recognition, and cadence recognition. The Colwell tests are the only music tests where item difficulty and item discrimination are reported for each item on the four tests based on a standardization sample of 20,000 students for Tests 1 and 2 and nearly 10,000 students for tests 3 and 4.

The *Farnum Music Notation Test* (1953/1969) consists of 40 printed melodic phrases with one of the four bars of each melody containing an error (compared to the aural stimulus) in either pitch or rhythm. The student marks the measure containing the error; most errors are in pitch. In the same year, Farnum (1969b) published a multiple part *Music Test* with the first part his notation test. Part 2 is a cadence test of 30 items where the last tone is missing and the task is to decide whether this tone should ascend or descend. To test for musical memory, patterns of four or five tones are performed twice with the task to identify which note has been changed in the second performance. In what is marketed as an eye-hand coordination test, part four has nine notes indicated by a unique pattern of dots. The student is to match the dot pattern with traditional notation within 2 minutes.

The Gordon *Iowa Tests of Musical Literacy* (Gordon, 1970/1991) comprises six levels, each of which has two divisions and each of which is basically measuring the same competencies. The two divisions, like all Gordon tests, are tonal concepts and rhythm concepts, each with three subtests: aural perception, reading recognition, and notational understanding. Aural perception at levels 1 and 2 consists of 22 items in either major or minor. To test reading recognition, students identify whether the notation is same or different from the performed melody. For the notational understanding items, students are presented with a written melody that is missing some notes; next, they listen to the complete melody performed three times, and then write in the missing notes. The rhythmic concepts task requires the student to identify duple or triple meter, and the reading recognition items require students to determine whether the written notation matches the aural stimulus. Level 3 uses melodies in a usual or an unusual mode (unusual being Dorian, Phrygian, Lydian, Mixolydian, Aeolian, and Locrian tonalities) with the student distinguishing among the modes in listening and reading. The rhythm concepts part has tasks of usual meter or mixed meter. The tests are aligned with Edwin Gordon's research; some specialized vocabulary is required.

The first NAEP (National Center for Education Statistics, 2018) in music was conducted in 1971–1972 and is the most complete of the three subsequent national assessments. The alignment remains exemplary for NAEP tests. One hundred fifty (150) exercises were developed in 1965 by music professionals, based on four age levels (9, 13, 17, and young adult [26–35]). A booklet of the objectives (Norris & Bowes, 1970) was printed and widely distributed, as well as the offering of pretest information sessions at national conferences. Approximately 24,000 school-age students were sampled at each age level, and about 5,000 young adults provided data, for a total of 80,000 individuals. The assessment covered five areas. Performance required singing familiar songs, repeating unfamiliar musical material, improvising, performing from notation, and, on a second day, performing a prepared piece. Notation and terminology included vocabulary, basic notation, and score reading. Instrumental and vocal media tested aural recognition, visual recognition, and performance practices (recognizing instruments from sound). Students were also asked how sound on the various instruments was produced. Music history and literature required some knowledge of periods in music history, musical genres and styles, and music literature. The fifth part was not scored; it asked about student attitudes. A tape of student performances on the test was provided with examples of the scoring standards of what was considered good, acceptable, and poor. This format continues to be appropriate for 2016.

The NAEP assessment was repeated in 1978–1979 with many of the same tasks but without the performance or adult participation components. The omission was due to a lack of support from the US National Assessment Governing Board (NAGB) and not because performance had a lower instructional priority. The third NAEP assessment took place in 1997 (the voluntary national standards replacing the curriculum align-ment stage) and again in 2008 and 2016, but with the same questions as on the 1997 and 2008 versions. Only 8th-grade students were tested due to budget constraints, and the reporting lacked the aural thoroughness of the original assessment.

Colwell (1979) published criterion-referenced tests marketed as the *Silver Burdett Music Competency Tests*. These were aligned with the Silver-Burdett Music Series text-books, and although criterion referenced, norms were provided due to teacher demand for comparisons and the availability of item discrimination. The tasks require the students to discriminate what they heard in a musical work: beat or no beat (or in doubt); fast or slow tempo; loud or soft dynamics; high or low pitch; whether the form is ABA, AB, or just A; and same or different style. Many of the same tasks are repeated at each grade level but in a more difficult format for a higher grade level. Other "what-to listen-for" tasks include hearing for accents, same or different rhythm patterns, ascending or descending melodies, tone color, tonality, style, and harmony–no harmony. At the higher grade levels, melody, duration, range, form, and tone color are combined to assess comprehensively what the student has learned to hear. As a caveat, the interpreta-tion of achievement tests comes with the knowledge that tests that can be given in groups miss important individual objectives.

College-level achievement tests have been common for most of the 20th and continue into the 21st century, focusing on music theory tasks that include taking dictation, per-forming, writing a four-part accompaniment for a folk tune, writing excerpts of a rock/ pop song in lead sheet format, and knowing the vocabulary and basic harmonization rules. The 1947 *Aliferis Music Achievement Test—College Entrance Level* (Aliferis, 1947/1954) was the first published and standardized test at this level. The test was endorsed by the National Association of Schools of Music (NASM), which facilitated procurement of a normative sample of some 1,700 cases. Part 1 requires the student to match one of four written intervals with the interval played on the piano. Melodic patterns are performed in the more musical task with the student, again, selecting from four choices. The variable is the last note of the pattern. Section two is chord recognition, with the student selecting the chord notation sounded from four choices. In the more musical section, a three-chord sequence is offered and the student selects from three possibilities. In section 3, a rhythmic figure is defined as the rhythm within one beat duration. The figure is repeated three times in a C major scale and the student selects from four rhythm notations. The more musical version contains two rhythmic elements.

James Aliferis was joined by John Stecklein, a measurement specialist, in 1962 in the release of the *Aliferis-Stecklein Music Achievement Test—College Midpoint Level* (Aliferis & Stecklein, 1962). The test was designed to verify student music theory competence after 2 years of study in a college or university program. The melodic interval test con-sists of 34 items that each present 4 printed notes. The listener hears the pattern, and then identifies the fourth note in the pattern from a four-choice response set. The chord test consists of 26 items, each presenting a four-voice chord in notation. The student hears the chord, and then compares the aural presentation of the chord with the chord notated in the test booklet. One tone in the chord is different and students identify the chord that is different. There are 19 items that present 6-beat rhythmic patterns in notation and played on one tone. The test taker then compares the notated pattern with the pattern played, and identifies the beat where the pattern played differs from the notation. Although norms are provided, there is scant evidence that the test was widely used. A graduation level test was constructed but not published.

The *Australian Test for Advanced Music Studies* (Bridges & Rechter, 1974) is designed for grades 13–16 (ages 19–22). The test, in three parts, measures aural imagery and memory, score reading, and aural/visual discrimination, comprehension, and application of learned musical formats. The aural stimuli are selected from vocal and instrumental music common in Australia using a wide range of timbre and textures. Classical, folk, ethnic, jazz, and pop music are used. The student must be able to audiate the sounds represented by visual symbols through recognizing intervals, tonality, triads, and styles of particular composers. Dr. Bridges likens the test to the American Advanced Placement (AP) theory test, a test that is revised annually, sponsored by the College Board (based in the United States), and designed to assess the traditional content of the first year of college music theory course. The AP test also has objective questions on discrimination and perception. Students take dictation, realize a figured bass, compose, sight-sing, and demonstrate an understanding of the cultural issues in college music theory.

The *Graduate Record Examination: Advanced Tests* (Educational Testing Service, 1951/2001) was designed for college seniors in music, and focuses on music history and literature with sections on instrumentation and orchestration, and on music fundamentals. An aural part was added in 1965. This advanced test was discontinued in 2001. The former National Teacher Examination consisted of 125 multiple choice items and covered all phases of music education: vocal, instrumental, elementary school, and senior high school.

Computer achievement tests such as *SmartMusic, Music Prodigy*, and *IPas* are not standardized learning systems that incorporate assessment. Researchers have established reliability data for *SmartMusic*.

A few states including Michigan, Minnesota, Illinois, Kentucky, Tennessee, Washington, New York, and Connecticut have attempted, since the 1970s, to develop their own competency test or item bank with mixed results and usually without important psychometric data. These tests have insufficient data to be inspiring.

MUSIC APPRECIATION AND PREFERENCE

Preference is of interest to music sociologists and music psychologists, and most of the tests in this area were designed to discriminate, to test one's knowledge, perhaps to encourage listening to better music, or to connect the school with the concert hall. They may measure emotion or nonmusic outcomes. Appreciation tests are subjective, relate minimally to instruction, and are usually culturally biased. A few ask the student to justify why specific works were preferred. Sociologists also review programming over time by major ensembles (for an example, see the sample programs in Farnsworth [1969, p. 114]). Sociologists and psychologists use data from perception and appreciation of music to portray the image of a musician, and make the argument that music preference is an integral parts of adolescents' social identity. Such study leads to the identification of typicality in personality studies. At an instructional level of music appreciation, thinking in music is one form of music intellect and is involved in responding to music. Brophy (2000) suggests that responding uses critical thinking skills and acquired musical knowledge that are required for one to make reasonable and informed judgments about music and personal values with respect to music. Responding (intelligently) to music is an expectation of universal outcomes from music instruction (Juslin, Liljestrom, Vastfjall, Barradas, & Silva, 2008; Juslin, Liljestrom, Vastfjall, & Lundqvist, 2010). Emotion is only one part of responding; how one responds depends on multiple factors, thus making standardized testing difficult. One's cultural background is important.

As early as 1910, C. Valentine discerned that students preferred the major third, then the minor third, followed by the octave (Valentine, 1913). Keston's preference test first appeared in 1913 with a simplified version appearing as a 176-page textbook in 1953 (Keston & Pinto, 1913/1955). The test consisted of 30 questions with the student indicating which of four works was preferred. Authors of tests include Courtis, Schultz, Gernet, Bower, Adler, Mohler, Trabue, Schoen, Fisher, Kwalwasser, Crickmore, Simons, and Long. Kate Hevner's (1936) descriptive adjective circle is the best-known list of adjective descriptors; it has been revised frequently, most recently by Asmus (1979). Hevner began her work as early as 1934, asking students to choose between an original and a distorted version (Hevner, 1935). Her published test is the *University of Oregon Musical Discrimination Test* (Hevner & Landsbury, 1935). With the additional assistance of R. Seashore, Hevner and Landsbury published five measures as the *Oregon Music Tests.* Like Carl Seashore, she used music psychologists to distort the music on rhythm, harmony, melody, and form. Newell Long (1965) obtained a federal grant to update and publish Hevner's work using string quartets, woodwind quintets, and organ music from the Baroque to contemporary in addition to the earlier piano selections. A 4,000-student standardization of the test was completed in 1967 and a shorter version for younger students in 1970 (Long, 1978).

Aesthetic Judgment and Taste

Kyme's (1954) doctoral dissertation was designed to measure aesthetic judgment and required content knowledge to justify answers. He used student solo performances, which were judged on the basis of intonation, tone quality, phrasing, interpretation, tempo, rhythm, and dynamics. Vocal and chamber music examples introduced factors of balance, diction, and blend. Orchestra performances were judged on tone quality, rhythm, balance, and so forth. Popular music items presented altered harmony, melody, and rhythm. Folksong examples were altered by tempo and style; one had to judge cadences on their finality; and a section on classical music required the listener to select a descriptive adjective such as "mischievous," "exciting," and "happy," to describe the music. The interest in this area continues (Tan & Spackman, 2005).

Interest in taste seems universal. In Stockholm, Wedin (1972) investigated emotional expression in music by tying musical structure to emotional expression in music. In the USSR, Bochkarev (1989) aligned composers' works with themes of melancholy, despair, delight, grief, and contemplation. He evaluated sensory and imagery characteristics of music as primary factors in psychological and operational sense. In France, Arlette Zenatti (1991) reported on her career research of aesthetic judgment and musical cognition. Mateos-Moreno (2015) developed a latent dimension structural model to measure attitudes toward contemporary music. The three constructs identified were "perceived complexity and stridency," "desire to discover," and "aesthetic respect."

Tests of Emotion Stimulated by Music

Related to music appreciation are tests of emotion stimulated by music. Most assessment is based on observation of behavior, verbal reports, self-report data, and performance on teacher-made assessments. (Self-reports are common, but little is known about their validity). Berger and Karabenick (2016) found that with 7th-grade students in math, validity concerns included memory failure, attention control, difficulty in understanding, and a lack of knowledge about strategies. Self-reports, however, are essential if how long one listens to a radio TV station or CD before changing to a different stimulus is the datum of interest. Self-reports measure an aesthetic response, or a temporary feeling. Teacher-made instruments are usually questionnaires asking "What were you thinking when you listened?" or "How did the music make you feel?" "Think-Alouds" have been successful. Bundra (1994) examined verbal reports and identified 17 categories of behaviors, descriptions, comparisons, and attitudes. Concept maps have been used. The German scholar Behne (1997), using a five-point questionnaire, identified listening styles as concentrated, emotional, and sentimental. Veronica Cohen (1997) developed "musical mirrors," where movements by children when seated were standardized to indicate what was heard.

A verbal report on the listening experience can indicate one's sensitivity (or what one hears) that results in tension, feelings, ideas, and desires. Hickey (1991) used this approach in teacher education. The semantic differential provides quantitative data similar to a rating scale or a type of paired comparison. Cell phones and logs can record feelings and reactions over time, and can be randomly stimulated. The "time-series" is a tool that records feelings and emotions over time and events; it can include a variety of responses such as tears and shivers. The time series has been used to evaluate skin conductance during movement in piano improvisation. The Continuous Response Digital Interface is a tool (not a test) that has been used to measure responses to music, but it may not differentiate between hearing and listening, or the context and purpose of the stimulus. *The Handbook of Music and Emotion: Theory, Research and Applications* (Juslin & Sloboda, 2010) has an entire section of five chapters on assessment measures.

The Measurement of Emotional Response to Music

The physiological and subjective measures of emotion and affect represent music test development in the 21st century. A large number of "tests" assess the human impact of the elements of music identified by Carl Seashore and others in the 20th century. Electroencephalograms (EEG), magnetoencephalography (MEG), superconducting quantum interference devices (SQUID), event related potential (ERP), magnetic resonance imaging (MRI), computer tomography (CT) and positron emission tomography (PET) allow for data collection that define tests focused on human response to music. The factors measured include amplitude, articulation, harmony, intervals, loudness, pitch, mode, and timbre. There are measures of the effects of music by biochemicals such as growth hormones, beta endorphins, blood glucose, dopamine, and more (Hodges, 2010). The assessment work follows Seashore's prognostication about scientific aesthetics and allows insight into how music affects our mental and bodily responses so strongly.

Berlyne's (1971, 1974) books on aesthetics and psychobiology initiated today's scientific definition of the aesthetic response. The theoretical postulates of Meyer (1956, 1967) inspired music educators to think about assessing music "appreciation." The psychologist Howard Gardner suggested musical development was more continuous than that of Piaget's four stages, and he also introduced the idea of music intelligence (Davidson, McKernan, & Gardner, 1981; Gardner, 2006). A recent study (Norman-Haignere, Kanwisher, & McDermott, 2015) using voxel decomposition, revealed that music and speech have separate cortical pathways, possibly confirming music intelligence. Variables may be sound-music-noise-silence (sound waves) sensation, perception, cognition, or a Gestalt approach that organizes stimuli for coherence. The tests are brain waves. From this research, music psychologists determined that the area of the somatosensory cortex representing the fingers of the left-fingering hand in violinists was larger than that in the contralateral hemisphere representing the right bow hand, and also larger than the area in nonmusicians. A continuing question is whether listening, performing, and composing are best understood in terms of neurons and networks or in terms of mental schemata and prototypes. Does emotion generated by music have a role in memory, reasoning, and problem-solving? Heiner Gembris (2006) suggests five areas for research by music psychologists: fetal learning and infant learning after birth, neurobiological research, expertise research, life-span development of musical abilities, and the emergence of developmental theories. Music psychologists suggest, as did Seashore a century earlier, that empirical findings can advise us to how and when to teach so that mind, memory, perception, and cognition can be developed most effectively—a new discipline of "neurodidactics."

Advances in qualitative research that support the use of self-report instruments like Likert scales, adjective checklists, visual analogue scales, continuous response versions of self-report instruments, nonverbal evaluation tasks, experience sampling methods, diaries, and portfolios along with the controls on narratives as a research tool opened the possibility of investigating the importance of questions about musical meaning.

Test development and research also found a home in curriculum changes in music education with emphases on music of all cultures, of responsibility for community music, and lifelong music experiences, and the incorporation of precepts from sociology into outcome discussions. This increased interest in the affective domain restored it to its rightful place in the hierarchy of music education. Cognition had reigned. Prominent music educators added their expertise to the interests of psychologists investigating music as critical to a meaningful life—taking an exception to Steven Pinker (1997), who argued that music was not part of the evolution of many and was only auditory cheesecake. Among the music educators whose names appear in psychology handbooks are Harold Abeles (Abeles & Chung, 1999), John Sloboda (2010), Donald Hodges (2010), David Hargreaves and Adrian North (2010), Susan Hallam (2016) Tia DeNora (2011), Gary McPherson (McPherson & Hallam, 2009), and Robert Woody (Woody & McPherson, 2010). Lucy Green at the University of London Institute of Education and Jeanne Bamberger at MIT suggest that music education should be more informal (the opposite of in-school music). Green's influence comes from her privately funded Musical Futures research with student outcomes of improved student motivation, enjoyment, and attitude. These three outcomes are assessed by teacher opinion of change in each (Green, 2008). A second assessment has been by student opinionnaire. Jeanne Bamberger (1978) agrees that school music promotes formal at the expense of intuitive understanding.

Harold Abeles with coauthor Jin Won Chung contributed to the change by documenting how responses to music related to the taxonomy of the affective domain (Krathwohl, Bloom, & Masia, 1964). Abeles cites 1974 research by Roderer, who provided two neurophysiological explanations of how music evokes meaningful and emotional responses. One neurological study clearly supports Meyers's expectation theory that predications are based on past experiences. A second study indicated that that limbic system is probably engaged during music processing (Roderer, 1974). Abeles and Chung (1999) provide a thorough description of tests designed to measure affective responses, mood, preferences, tastes, and attitudes. With a focus on music education, the use of the semantic differential, paired comparisons, rating scales, categorical judgements, and behavioral measures are analyzed to discern the confusion in terminology leading to different results from similar studies. In-depth test results are provided for specific mood-emotion responses such as anxiety and arousal. Abeles and Chung provide examples that have used the sophisticated bodily measures as well as the subjective tools that measure emotion and issues related to preference.

With the affective domain of equal importance to the cognitive domain, this new and different type of data collection is important, and only a brief description of its quality is given in this chapter (we do not suggest that affect exists apart from thought). The change in test development to music uses has been accompanied by changes in the curriculum. Music appreciation long had its objective to broaden taste, to hear the subtleties in the classics, and respond to the tonal qualities that were thought to lead to a love for exemplary performances in music's historical periods. Responding to music with this orientation was an important outcome, but vague and subjective. Tests were based on "What did you hear?" Today, responding by the body and the brain is accurately measured by laboratory tests. Accompanying subjective measures have often been well researched.

Research on response to music in daily life is a new objective. Hargreaves and North (2010) monitor music listening preferences not only by questionnaires, interviews, ranking, experience sampling, and observations but also with cell phones and similar devices. Multiple authors have amassed reliable preference scales by age, class, and country. Ratings are analyzed by multivariate techniques, factor analysis, cluster analysis, multidimensional scaling, or correspondence analysis to find a limited number of fundamental dimensions in this domain. Teachers want to know as much as possible about the impact of music and have confidence in the results of qualitative research. The National Assessment has attempted, since the first assessment, to obtain a general idea of student attitude, interest, and preference. Statements were along a continuum. Self-reports are necessary, as one cannot identify a specific emotion from physiological measures. Self-report instruments include Likert scales, adjective checklists, visual analogue scales, continuous response, nonverbal evaluation tasks (according to similarity without the verbal), experience sampling method (ongoing activities related to emotion and causes), diary study, free report, and narrative method. Emotion in music is a scientific construct that includes feelings, behaviors, and reactions in all of life (Zentner & Eerola, 2010).

The Geneva Emotional Music Scales are constructed each year on the basis of around 800 questionnaires. Confirmatory factor analysis found emotions of wonder, transcendence, tenderness, nostalgia, peacefulness, power, joyful activation, tension, and sadness (Zentner, Grandjean, & Scherer, 2008). A factor analysis was conducted in 2011 on genre-free cross-culture music preferences that results in five factors: (1) mellow, comprising smooth and relaxing styles; (2) urban, defined by rhythmic and percussive music; (3) sophisticated, which includes classical and jazz; (4) intense, defined by forceful and energetic music; and (5) campestral, a variety of music such as found in country and singer-songwriter genres (Rentfrow, Goldberg, & Levitin, 2011).

Changes in sociology and the sociology of music provide a rich resource for new measures. It has changed the emphasis from music production to how music is consumed and what it does in social life (WHOQOL, 1998). Sociology encompasses the production of culture, knowledge, institutions, organizations, and their conventions (Denora, 2010, 2011). Denora's own research was based on 50 in-depth interviews seeking to understand music's role in relation to the achieved character of feeling. The sociological approach stresses understanding of meaning as a result of experiences in music. In 1965, E. L. Rainbow conducted a pilot study to establish that a student's socioeconomic status was a significant predictor or musical aptitude (Rainbow, 1965). Most tests in the sociology of music today were developed to investigate how music is used in consumer societies and how social influences combine to shape musical tastes. These tests were built on the earlier adjective work of Hevner and Farnsworth (1954), often using semantic differentials. The belief seemed to suggest that the physical setting and social dynamics were more important than the music itself. Building on the ideas of

Csikszentmihalyi and Csikszentmihalyi (1988), Custodero (2002) found that musical flow experiences in early childhood tend to occur with active multisensory involvement presented in a socially playful or game-like context. Group flow exists with jazz structure and improvisation. Measurement occurs by eye contact and bodily gesture. In 1993, Madsen, Brittin, and Capperell-Sheldon reported on the development of a two-dimensional empirical-method for measuring an emotional response, the CRDI or continuous response digital interface. It is not clear whether the CRDI measures feeling or judgment (Madsen, Brittin, & Capperella-Sheldon, 1993). The idea for the CRDI is based on the operant music listening recorder and a practice of simply squeezing. Robert Woody and Gary McPherson (2010) connect emotion with motivation, partially based on Woody's research on learning to feel the music, where college students learned to feel the music by manipulating elements like tempo and dynamics.

Sociology of music includes research on folk music including that on Alan Lomax and how folksong styles in most cultures reflect economic and social conditions and attitudes. Sociology of music requires a definition of talents that are more extensive than those often championed. These were mentioned earlier and include performing, improvising, composing, arranging, analyzing, appraising, conducting, and teaching music, each requiring tests or test-like devises drawn from sociology and other related disciplines (McPherson & Hallam, 2009). The Department of Psychology at Uppsala University maintains a center, Appraisal in Music and Emotion (AMUSE), to describe and explain people's responses to music using multiple measures (Gabrielsson, 1995). The use of music, of context, and of students' ranges as an outcome from student to national identity is better. In 2005, US support for the war in Iraq was beginning to wane. The National Association for Music Education obtained the support from more than a dozen corporations and launched the National Anthem Project, a 3-year campaign trumpeted as "restoring America's voice through music education." Students and others were to learn to sing the national anthem (Garofalo, 2010; Quigley, 2004).The test of the project was traditional and subjective; the public judged the quality of the performance at the 21st world's largest concert.

Personality and attitude are also impacted by listening to music. The IPAT Music Preferences Test of Personality (Catell & Anderson, 1953; Cattell, Eber, & Anderson, 1954; Cattell & Saunders, 1954) is based on the assumption that personality types should prefer a definite type of music. The scale provides 11 factors that might be used in a clinical situation. Cameron, Duffy, and Glenwright (2015a) studied personality types of student musicians. They used the Myers-Briggs Type Indicator (Meyers-Briggs, 1944/1975) and found that singers were extraverted and used that knowledge in planning lessons and activities. Also in 2015, Singers Take Center Stage (Cameron, Duffy, & Glenwright, 2015b), a similar study, was published in *Psychology of Music*.

Emotion is only one part of responding: How one responds depends on multiple factors, thus making standardized testing difficult. One's cultural background is important. Personality test and music experiences are commonly investigated. In their most recent study at the time of this writing, Cameron et al. (2015a) again used the Myers-Briggs Type Indicator.

Attitude seems to have three components: feeling, beliefs, and values. Researchers use Likert scales, semantic differential, Guttman scalograms, Q methodology, double-digit analysis, and some multidimensional scaling (Kemp, 1981, 1996). The personality characteristics of musicians by instrument and section have been investigated by John Davies (1978) through interviews that included how the brass section is viewed by string players. Kenny, Driscoll, and Ackermann (2014) report on the psychological well-being of professional orchestral musicians in eight Australian orchestras, using the State-Trait-Anxiety Inventory, the Social Phobia Inventory, and the Anxiety and Depression detector. Kenny and Ackermann (2015) investigated performance anxiety and depression in orchestral players.

Performance

Probably no other component of teaching and learning is more important than performance, and observation is the primary "test" for gathering information. Hallam and Prince (2003) asked a sample of musicians, student musicians, educators, and the general public to define "musical ability." Seventy-one percent (71%) viewed musical ability as being able to play a musical instrument or sing. The new Every Student Succeeds Act (S. 1177, 114th Cong., 2015) in the United States delegates curricular responsibilities to localities and states; this change will shift teaching priorities. One can observe the technical proficiency of a performance or one can "enjoy" a performance. One observes music performances in the classroom, and the music critic observes in the concert hall. Any large-scale assessment must have a performance component in order to fairly represent teaching and learning in music. The first NAEP in 1971–1972 (National Center for Education Statistics, 2018) required students to sing familiar songs, repeat unfamiliar musical material, improvise, perform from notation, and demonstrate proficiency by performing music that had been "learned." "Testing" performance must usually be done one student at a time.

Sight-Singing

Although critically important, few formal tests for performance have been published. Hillbrand's sight-singing test was published by the World Book Company in 1923 (Hillbrand, 1923). It consisted of a four-page folder of six original songs and a list of criteria: notes wrongly pitched, transpositions, times flatted, times sharped, notes omitted, errors in time, extra notes, repetitions, and hesitations. Teachers today would probably use a similar list in testing for sight-reading. In 1925, Raymond Mosher published a group method of measuring sight-singing in *Teachers College Contributions to Teacher Education, 194* (Mosher, 1925) that applied a set of common criteria in a group method. Otterstein and Mosher (1932) published their sight-singing test of 28 exercises in both major and minor modes, plus a few more difficult intervals in 1932. Lists of sight-singing materials (which could be considered or used as tests) continue to be published with multiple editions. Zhukov, Viney, Riddle, Teniswood-Harvey, and Fujimura (2016) reported on strategies to improve sight-reading of advanced pianists. The available materials indicate that sight-singing remains an important competency for many teachers (Kopiez, Weihs, Ligges, & Lee, 2006). Gutsch (1965) conducted a federally funded study on the ability to sight-read rhythm on an instrument.

Instrumental Performance

John Watkins (1941) developed an objective measurement of instrumental performance (trumpet) which was adapted for all band instruments by Stephen Farnum (1954). It was designed to cover 6 years of learning and consisted of 14 "sight-reading" exercises graded in difficulty. The objective grading system was primarily on pitch and rhythm, but included observation of tempo, expression, and slur markings as well as the repeat sign. Fifteen years later, Farnum (1969a) released a string performance scale designed for grades 7–12. Farnum based the difficulty of 14 of the 17 string exercises on the performance competence of about 50 violinists but suggested that the test would be difficult to standardize. The Oregon State Department (1977) published a self-evaluation checklist for orchestra grades 4–12. Their argument was that students should check their own progress on concrete elements of orchestra performance. Gary McPherson and John McCormick have investigated the contribution of motivational factors to an instrumental performance examination (McPherson & McCormick, 2000; McCormick & McPherson, 2003). Self-efficacy was measured by obtaining strength of beliefs about self-performance competence on an 11-point scale. Using questionnaires on cognitive strategy use, anxiety/confidence, intrinsic value, and self-regulation, the authors conclude that how students think about themselves, the task, and their performance is just as important as the time they devote to practicing. Evans and McPherson (2015) in a 10-year study, asked questions about the students' perception of their future in music. Those with a long-term view demonstrated higher achievement and more practicing than students with a shorter view of the role of music in their lives.

Choral Music

Choral music tests are primarily based on observation and a nonstandardized checklist. Phillips and Doneski (2011) report that the 1997 NAEP test found that only 25% of 8th-grade students could sing "Twinkle Twinkle Little Star" at the adequate level or above. They state that this fact should have been a wake-up call for testing performance competence. Joanne Rutkowski (1990) has developed an unpublished but respected Singing Voice Development Measure to assess singing progress. It has nine levels from presinger to singer. The fourth level is termed "inconsistent limited range singer," where the student wavers between speaking and singing and uses a limited range, usually D3 to F3. The use of nine testing levels indicates that learning to sing could be a lengthy process.

Surprisingly, there are few attitude studies about choral music. Phillips and Doneski (2011) report only eight studies of children's attitude toward vocal music prior to 1990 and fewer since that time. Only 16 of the 42 common song repertoire list of NAfME are found on any other vocal list or songbook (McGuire 2000).

At the secondary level, Henry (2001, 2004) developed a vocal sight-reading inventory and tested it with about 180 students. Little additional information is available. Use of the spectrograph has been tried to measure individual and group performances but is unreliable for testing due to mike placement and room acoustics.

State Music Contests in the United States

Performance testing, individual and group, occurs at state music contests, both instrumental and choral. The process is open-ended, although in some states music must be performed from an approved list and difficulty levels assigned. Usually three judges use a standard checklist to arrive at a final rating. The checklist may have weighted items. Judges are often experienced but not formally trained. A number of research projects have proposed rating scales, but none are used for these state contests. The rating of "overall effect" seems to take precedence over individual performance items.

Other Tests of Performance

There is limited research that combines performance research results; Jennifer Mishra (2014) conducted a meta-analysis of 92 studies on sight-reading. Eighty-one percent of the studies found no impact in the intervention that tried to improve sight-reading. The interventions that helped were focused on aural training, controlled reading (eye movement), creative activities, and singing/solfège (p. 143). Although significant, the differences were small.

The Associated Boards of the Royal Schools of Music (ABRSM, http://us.abrsm.org) initiated a performance examination for piano, which has since been expanded to include all instruments. The ABRSM has seven practical tests for eight grades (these are grades of competence, not grade levels in school). Examiners are trained and some 700 examiners are based in 90 countries. Examiners use standardized rubrics for performance and for competence in scales, arpeggios, sight-reading, and aural tests. Jazz competence by instrument is assessed in addition to music theory. There are rubrics for ensembles and choirs, and diplomas in both teaching and conducting.

A few colleges have promoted tests of competency rather than course work to meet any requirements including graduation. New Hampshire allows competency tests in its public schools, including music. Performance may be the primary criterion at present. A student well versed in jazz can inform the school music teacher how his or her competence meets standards (Marion & Leather, 2015).

CREATIVITY

Developing tests for the assessment of creativity in music has been difficult. The first such test may have been Moorhead and Pond (1941). Assessment of creative work is based generally on the tests developed by Torrance (1974) in general creative thinking, fluency, flexibility, elaboration, and originality. Vaughan (1973) suggested measures of fluency, rhythmic security, ideation, and synthesis. The dependent variable was an "interesting response." Gorder (1980) developed creative tasks for an instrumentalist. Gorder's three tasks are straightforward divergent thinking tasks using musical materials. The student composes or improvises on simple melodies according to stimuli of various complexity rendered on percussion instruments. Students can respond by singing, whistling, or playing a familiar instrument. There is also a musical staff with space for recording the task, and an opportunity to demonstrate the task with a contour line. Peter Webster (1987/1992) continues to work on developing measures of creativity. He has developed composition tasks like composing a phrase for a triangle, a stimulating one to think about variations on a phrase and creating an extended composition, along with analysis of a melody and a duet. The student is to improvise rhythms on claves and melodies on bells, and to reproduce a melody on bells that are scored. He suggests (1987) the measurement is one of musical extensiveness, musical flexibility, musical originality, and musical syntax. Kodály expert Zoltan Laczo (1995), investigated musical abilities, especially the relationship between intelligence and vocal improvisation. Teresa Amabile (1996) has replaced Torrance as the leader in creativity. In testing, she equates reliability with validity. Her position is that creativity is easily recognized and, if so, consensual technique is all that is needed for assessment. Stefanic and Randles (2014) have developed consensual materials in music. Amabile's work is heuristic rather than algorithmic, requiring the student to have some factual knowledge, technical skills, and musical talent to engage in creating. Student personality and motivation are more influential than cognitive competence. Like other tasks, long hours of practice from an early age, belief in self, perseverance, unwillingness to accept the first solution, exposure to other composers, existence of mentors, and critics are possible ways to measure creative potential.

TESTS USED FOR TEACHER EVALUATION

Observation is used to test novice and experienced teachers. The observation of student teachers is "high stakes," as one can fail student teaching if the observer so deems. It is also subject to great error, as can be proven by varying stories of individuals who observe firsthand an accident but report important details incorrectly, or of subjects who mistakenly identify suspects in a line-up. Observation has become high-stakes in teacher evaluation. The interest of the US-based Bill and Melinda Gates Foundation in teaching resulted in a multiple-year study (Bill and Melinda Gates Foundation, 2013), mentioned earlier, on the validity of observation at a cost of at least 45 million dollars. The research on observation was conducted in mathematics (grades 6–8) and language arts (grades 4–6) accompanied by a student questionnaire (Tripod) developed by Ronald Ferguson (2012). The focus of the observation in the Gates's research was limited to its use in evaluating teachers. Several different observation "tests" or strategies were used: the Classroom Assessment Scoring System (CLASS), the Framework for Teaching (FfT), the Protocol for Language Arts Teaching Observations (PLATO), the Mathematical Quality of Instruction (MQI), and the Quality of Science Teaching (QST); the primary one being the Danielson (FfT), which is also fundamental to the National Board for Teacher Proficiency Test, Praxis III. Despite considerable training in observation, observers did not discern differences between score points on a rubric. The FfT framework was recently revised to clarify the rubrics used with Danielson's four phases of planning and preparation, classroom environment, instruction (including use of assessment), and professional responsibilities. Observation scores do differ by grade level but not by teacher characteristics, experience, education, demographics, classroom composition, or potential rater bias. Most observational scales focus on planning and preparation, classroom environment, instruction, and professional responsibilities. The MET study involved 3,000 volunteer teachers in six states and in urban situations (Bill and Melinda Gates Foundation, 2013).

What can music educators learn from this major study with a focus on two disciplines? Professional educators have accepted that there is a commonality to teaching. The Gates's research, however, should raise a cautionary flag for assessment based on observation. Principal ratings were lower for middle school than for elementary. With the need to have a cut-score in all meaningful assessments, judgment of where to place the cut score is important. Even after training, observers had difficulty discerning differences between score points even with the use of exemplars on the borders of score points (Bell et al., 2014). Public school music teachers recognize the importance of also being objective about parent and possibly administrative opinion. Observers were better at assessing classroom organization and environment than on instructional and emotional aspects of classrooms. Student–teacher interaction and instruction of complex topics were the most difficult to assess. With all observation systems studied, the first 30 minutes of the class were adequate to obtain enough information for assessment, as long as observers focused on a small set of complementary traits.

TEACHER CERTIFICATION TESTS

Many states have a subject matter examination (high stakes) as part of teacher certification using the ETS *Praxis* (Educational Testing Service, 2015). These may be local (some cities can certify teachers) or the state may contract with a professional organization like Pearson Education to construct and administer the test. The 2015 California subject matter test in music (California Educator Credentialing Examinations, 2015) is typical, requiring functional keyboard proficiency, vocal/instrumental proficiency, including proficiency on a required number on one's major instrument, knowledge of conducting, score reading, including recognition of be-bop from a score, applied music theory, orchestration, music history, and a relationship between music and dance, with a few questions on relationships such as acoustics and community relations. In addition, certification may require that competence be established for preservice music teachers (students in tertiary music education teacher preparation programs) by passing the edTPA, a portfolio evaluation that contains a video segment of the students' teaching. There is an accompanying list of questions that asks the student why they did what they did, what changes they would make the next time, and to reflect on their work. The statements are designed to have the student justify planning, teaching, and assessment decisions. The idea is to establish competence in curriculum goals, instructional strategies, assessment, use of research, rapport building, and fairness. The rubrics used to assess the teaching are those of the revised Danielson Framework (Ferguson & Danielson, 2014). In other states, different observation matrices similar to those listed earlier are used. Based on the philosophy that "teaching is teaching," the music student must carefully select those music teaching tasks that best fit what is to be assessed. edTPA is an incomplete, and perhaps unsatisfactory test, of the basics that a music teacher must know and be able to do (Jordan & Hawley, 2016; Wilkerson, 2015). One assumes that a job analysis has been conducted as is common with government employees or fire and police personnel, and that rating scales describe work responsibilities as well as knowledge that applies to the arts. The visual arts have made an excellent case that critical thinking does not apply to the teaching of painting—critical thinking is an important tool for the art critic but not the artist. One senses this possible disconnect in some proposed standards for music education. The work of Smith and Wuttke (2016) is encouraging.

OTHER USES OF MUSIC RELATED TESTS

Researchers who study intelligence, emotion, personality, physical, behavioral, and psychological reaction have used music and/or music tests. Space allows for only a few examples. David Healey (2016) investigated the impact of marching band membership on engagement of college students with diversity, personal social responsibility, reflective learning, and other concepts based on George Kuh's National Survey of Student Engagement (NSSE; Kuh, 2012). Zdzinski (2013) developed a test to measure parental involvement and home environment in music. That test, paired with Fortney's 1992 music attitude scales that measured attitudes of students in high school instrumental programs, was used on a national scale with more than a thousand students. Zdzinski's later research (Zdzinski et al., 2014–2015) was supported by National Association of

Music Merchants (NAMM), the Grammy Foundation, and the US Department of Education through a FIPSE grant. The finding was that parenting style was significantly related to all outcome variables in music as well as success in school. Martin-Santana, Muela-Molina, and Reinares-Iara (2015) reported on music in radio advertising and the effects on the spokesperson's credibility and advertising effectiveness. Athletes purposely use music to manage their emotional state and music listening may facilitate their subsequent reactive performance measured with an fMRI (Bishop, Karageorghis, & Kinrade, 2009; Bishop, Karageorghis, & Liouzu, 2007; Bishop, Wright, & Karageorghis, 2014). Tempo and intensity of pretask music modulate neural activity during reactive task performance based on the fMRI. The same authors (2007) investigated the effects of musically induced emotions on choice reaction time performance. They used grounded theory to assess young tennis players' use of music to manipulate their emotional state. Anxiety in music interested Osborne & Kenny (2005, 2008) and Sarbescu & Dorgo (2014).

Perhaps the most interesting test is the effect of a music instrument in obtaining a female's phone number. Three hundred females (ages 18–22) exiting a Paris underground station were approached by a handsome male of the same age who asked for her phone number, posing with a sports bag, no bag, or a guitar. Thirty-one percent responded positively to the male when he had the guitar; 14% with no bag, and 9% with the sports bag (Gueguen, Meineri, & Fischer-Lokou, 2014). Human judgment remains the ultimate test in music.

Rating scales are common in noncognitive assessment, but methods for moderating rating responses such as anchoring vignettes, forced choice, rank and preference methods, situational judgment tests, and performance measures are also used. Schellenberg (2016) identified more than 160 studies that related music to nonmusical abilities. Many of these investigated the relationship of music to intelligence. Others focused on language, speech, emotion, preferences, and memory. The measures used were reliable tests in each field as well as observation.

Conclusion

An exhaustive search of published and unpublished tests indicates that their value to teaching and learning has been underused for over 100 years. Many are not aware of what tests have to offer. Achievement tests have been developed for doctoral dissertations, an indicator of interest and importance, but few were influential or found a use in the stable of teaching/learning aids. One problem lies in defining what is meant by musicality and what aspects of musicality can be successfully taught and validly tested. Creating, performing, and responding are listed as three artistic processes that presumably could or should be taught. Process, however, is just that—a process, and incompatible with formative and summative tests. These three processes are too broad to provide guidance for a taxonomy of learning objectives.

A second problem is the lack of a felt need to test either talent or achievement. Music theory and music history are taught and evaluated in every school of music with no known demand for standardized and validated tests. Most of the colleges have an entrance/aptitude examination consisting of a one-shot performance that appears to satisfy any need. The aptitude tests developed in the 20th century identified the elements of sound and established that individuals differed in their ability to discriminate among these elements. There is agreement that artistry/musicality requires a good ear but that is insufficient; acute discrimination plus a vision of appropriateness or fitness is basic to musical interpretation. Improvisation and interpretation are creative musical processes that are not sufficiently generalizable for testing. Fitness requires explicit and implicit contextual knowledge along with the means to communicate. There is both a physical and mental component to fitness. These and other competencies are long-term goals requiring practice, which lacks instructional sensitivity.

Twenty-first-century psychologists are using tests to investigate brain and bodily activity resulting from human reaction to the musical elements identified by aptitude test developers. The work is exciting and interesting. Both James Mursell and Carl Seashore believed that aptitude was more holistic than simple measurement of the elements of sound. Mursell believed that an emotional reaction was necessary for sound to become music. Seashore (1947) believed that music was the language of emotion and as a means of communication it acquired its social value.

A third problem is the rise of qualitative thinking and the sociology of music in how music teaching should be conducted, and that any assessment should not be limited to the classroom. Bowman and Frega (2012) argue that it is more important to "do" music than to explore troubling and distracting questions about how it might be done more effectively. Elliott and Silverman (2015) pick up on John Dewey's philosophy that educational objectives are not prespecifications of learning but rather the outcomes of teacher-learning interactions. This idea would certainly complicate achievement testing. They argue against separating community and school music and believe that curriculum is established by teachers reflecting on subject matter knowledge, resources and materials, students' abilities, lesson aims and goals, teaching strategies, and evaluation procedures making teaching idiosyncratic. They also argue against the artificial mind-body split, and oppose standards suggesting that assessment is an interaction among students, teachers, and particular content. Penuel and Shepard (2016) also suggest that teaching is interactive and adaptive, suggesting that interim assessments do not have an extensive research base and were introduced only for No Child Left Behind as they lack the connection of embedded assessment. Riconscente, Mislevy, and Corrigan (2016) believe that assessment is a broad set of processes and instruments by which we arrive at inferences about learner proficiency. Behaviors and/or performances should reveal the constructs of the theory that facilitates communication, coherence, and efficiency in assessment. Fautley (2010), in a text on music assessment, states that it is difficult to write criteria for aesthetic quality and one should negotiate quality with the students. He also agrees with Bennett Reimer that understanding is a process, and one makes judgments along a continuum. Keith Swanwick (Swanwick, 1999) criticizes present assessment practices in developing tests in the United States for standards. Difficulty is assessed by quantity, not quality. A performance rated difficult has more things, more key signatures, more sharps and flats, more variety of rhythm patterns, and more notes.

Assessment and the curriculum must be compatible, even matched but difficult at best with a sociological orientation and music outcomes linked to community music. Describing student outcomes rather than providing comparison data has been encouraged by our most ardent supporters, including Robert Stake, Liora Bresler, and Elliot Eisner. Curriculum researchers admit the paucity of assessment instruments and hope the teacher understands and can build teaching/learning on the best available evidence. A careful reading of the material in this chapter indicates what is known, and what is known is the basis for better assessments.

REFERENCES

Abeles, H. F., & Chung, J. W. (1999). Responses to music. In D. A. Hodges (Ed.), *Handbook of music psychology* (2nd ed., pp. 285–342). San Antonio, TX: IMR Press.

Aliferis, J. (1947/1954). *Aliferis music achievement test-College entrance level.* Minneapolis: University of Minnesota Press.

Aliferis, J., & Stecklein, J. (1962). *Aliferis-Stecklein music achievement test—College midpoint level.* Minneapolis: University of Minnesota Press.

Amabile, T. (1996). *Creativity in context.* Boulder, CO: Westview Press.

Asmus, E., Jr. (1979). *The operational characteristics of adjectives as descriptors of musical affect* (Unpublished doctoral dissertation). University of Kansas, Lawrence, KS.

Baker, G. (2014). *El Sistema: Orchestrating Venezuela's youth:* New York, NY: Oxford University Press.

Bamberger, J. (1978). Intuitive and formal musical knowing: Parables of cognitive dissonance. In S. Madeja (Ed.), *The arts, cognition, and basic skills* (pp. 173–209). St. Louis, MO: CEMREL.

Beach, F. A. (1921). *Beach standardized music test.* (2nd ed.) Emporia, KS: Bureau of Educational Measurements and Standards.

Behne, K. (1997). The development of "Musikerleben" in adolescence: How and why young people listen to music. In I. Deliege, & J. Sloboda (Eds.), *Perception and cognition of music* (pp. 143–160). Hove, UK: Psychology Press.

Bell, C., Qi, Y., Croft, A., Leusner, D., McCaffrey, D., Gitomer, D., & Pianata, R. (2014). Improving observational score quality: Challenges in observer thinking. In T. Kane, K. Kerr, & R. Pianta (Eds.), *Designing teacher evaluation systems: New guidance from the Measures of Effective Teaching Project.* (pp. 50–97). San Francisco, CA: Jossey-Bass.

Bentley, A. (1966). *Musical ability in children and its measurement.* London, UK: Harrap.

Berger, J., & Karabenick, S. (2016). Construct validity of self-reported metacognitive learning strategies. *Educational Assessment, 21*(1), 19–33.

Berlyne, D. E. (1971). *Aesthetics and psychobiology.* New York: Appleton-Century-Crofts.

Berlyne, E. D. (Ed). (1974). *Studies in the new experimental aesthetics: Steps toward an objective psychology of aesthetic appreciation.* New York, NY: Halsted Press.

Bill and Melinda Gates Foundation. (2013, January). *Ensuring fair and reliable measures of effective teaching: Culminating findings from the MET Project's three-year study.* Retrieved from http://www.metproject.org/downloads/MET_Ensuring_Fair_and_Reliable_Measures_ Practitioner_Brief.pdf

Bishop, D., Karageorghis, C., & Kinrade, N. (2009). Effects of musically-induced emotions on choice reaction time performance. *The Sport Psychologist, 23*, 59–76.

Bishop, D., Karageorghis C., & Loizou, G. (2007). A grounded theory of young tennis players' use of music to manipulate emotional state. *Journal of Sport and Exercise Psychology, 29*, 585–607.

Bishop, D., Wright, M., & Karageorghis, C. (2014). Tempo and intensity of pre-task music modulate neural activity during reactive task performance. *Psychology of Music, 42*, 714–727. doi: 10.3389/fnhum.2015.00508

Bochkarev, L. (1989). *Psikhologicheskie mekhanizmy muzykal'nogo perezhivaniia.* [Psychological mechanisms of musical experience]. (Doctoral dissertation). Kyiv, Ukraine: Tara Shevchenko National University.

Bowman, W., & Frega, A. L. (2012). What should the music education profession expect of philosophy? In W. Bowman, & A. L. Frega, (Eds.). *The Oxford handbook of philosophy in music education* (pp. 17–36). Oxford, UK: Oxford University Press.

Bridges, D., & Rechter, B. (1974/1978). *Australian test for advanced music studies.* Hawthorn, Australia: Australian Council for Education Research.

Brophy, T. (2000). *Assessing the developing child musician: A guide for general music teachers,* Chicago, IL: GIA Publications.

Bundra, J. (1994). *A study of the music listening processes through verbal reports of school-aged children* (Unpublished doctoral dissertation). Northwestern University, Evanston, IL.

Burton, D. (2016). A quartile analysis of selected variables from the 2008 NAEP visual arts report. *Studies in Art Education 57*(2), 165–178.

California Educator Credentialing Examinations. (2015). *California Subject Examinations for Teachers (CSET): Music.* Retrieved from http://www.ctcexams.nesinc.com/TestView. aspx?f=HTML_FRAG/CA_CSET136_TestPage.html

Cameron, J. Duffy, M., & Glenwright, B. (2015a). Personality types of student musicians: A guide for music educators. *Canadian Music Educator, 56*(4), 13–17.

Cameron, J., Duffy, M., & Glenwright, B. (2015b). Singers take center stage! Personality traits and stereotypes of popular musicians. *Psychology of Music, 43*, 818–830. doi: 10.1177/ 0305735614543217

Cattell, R., & Anderson, J. (1953). The measurement of personality and behavior disorders by the IPAT Music Preference Tests. *Journal of Applied Psychology, 37*, 446–454.

Cattell, R., Eber, H., & Anderson, J. (1954). *The IPAT Music Preference Test of Personality (The MPT).* Champaign, IL: The Institute for Personality and Ability Testing.

Cattell, R., & Saunders, D. (1954). Music preferences and personality diagnosis: A factorization of 120 themes. *Journal of Social Psychology, 39*, 3–24.

Cohen, V. (1997). Exploration of kinesthetic analogues for musical schemes. *Bulletin of the Council for Research in Music education, 131*, 1–13.

Colwell, R. (1965/1970). *Music achievement tests, 1–4.* Chicago, IL: Follett.

Colwell, R. (1979). *Silver Burdett music competency tests.* Morristown, NJ: Silver Burdett.

Csikszentmihalyi, M., & Csikszentmihalyi, I. (Eds.). (1988). *Optimal experience: Psychological studies of flow in consciousness.* Cambridge, UK: Cambridge University Press.

Custodero, L. A. (2002). Seeking challenge, finding skill: Flow experience and music education. *Arts Education Policy Review, 103*, 3–9.

Darling-Hammond, L., Herman, J., Pelligrino, J., Abedi, J., Aber, J. L., Baker, E.,…Steele, C. (2014). *Criteria for high quality assessment.* Stanford Center for Opportunity Policy in

Education: Stanford University; Center for Research on Student Standards and Testing, University of California at Los Angeles; Learning and Science Research Institute, University of Illinois at Chicago.

Davidson, L., McKernan, P., & Gardner, H. (1981). The acquisition of song: A developmental approach. In *Documentary report of the Ann Arbor Symposium* (pp. 301–315). Reston, VA: Music Educators National Conference.

Davidson, L., & Scripp, L. (1992). Surveying the coordinates of cognitive skills in music. In Colwell, R. (Ed.), *Handbook of research on music teaching and learning* (pp. 392–413). New York: Schirmer Books.

Davies, J. (1978). *The psychology of music*. Stanford, CA: Stanford University Press.

Denora, T. (2010). Emotion as social emergence: Perspectives from music sociology. In P. N. Juslin, & J. A. Sloboda (Eds.), *Handbook of music and emotions: Theory, research, and applications* (pp. 159–183). Oxford, UK: Oxford University Press.

Denora, T. (2011). Emotion as social emergence: Perspectives from music psychology. In Julsin, P., & Sloboda, J. (Eds.), *Handbook of music and emotion: Theory, research, applications* (pp. 159–186). Oxford, UK: Oxford University Press. doi: 10.1093/acprof:oso/9780199230143.003.0007

Dickey, M. (1991). A comparison of verbal instruction and nonverbal teacher-student modeling in instrumental ensembles. *Journal of Research in Music Education, 39*, 132–142. doi: 10.2307/3344693

Doherty, K. M., & Jacobs, S. (2013). *Connect the dots: Using evaluations of teacher effectiveness to inform policy and practice (State of the states 2013)*. Washington, DC: National Council on Teacher Quality (NCTQ).

Domaleski, C. (2011) *State end of course testing program: A policy brief*. Retrieved from http://www.wyoleg.gov/InterimCommittee/2011/SelectAccountability/State%20End%20of%20Course%20Test%20Programs%2091511.pdf.

Drake, R. (1957). *Manual for the Drake Musical Aptitude Tests*. Chicago, IL: Science Research Associates.

Educational Testing Service. (1951/2001). *Graduate record examinations advanced tests: Music*. Princeton, NJ: Author.

Educational Testing Service. (2015). *Praxis performance assessment for teachers*. Princeton, NJ: Author.

Eisner, E. (2001). Should we create new aims for art education? *Art Education, 54*(5), 6–10. doi: 10.1080/00043125.2001.11653461

Elliott, D., & Silverman, M. (2015). *Music matters* (2nd ed.). New York: Oxford University Press.

Evans, P., & McPherson G. (2015). Identity and practice: The motivational benefits of a long-term musical identity. *Psychology of Music, 43*, 407–422. doi: 10.1177/0305735613514471

Farnsworth, P. R. (1954). A study of the Hevner adjective circle. *Journal of Aesthetics and Art Criticism, 13*, 97–103.

Farnsworth, P. R. (1969). *The social psychology of music*. Ames: Iowa State University Press.

Farnum, S. (1953/1969). *Farnum music notation test*. New York, NY: Psychological Corporation.

Farnum, S. (1954). *The Watkins-Farnum performance scale*. Winona, MN: Hal Leonard Music.

Farnum, S. (1969a). *The Farnum string scale*. Milwaukee, WI: Hal Leonard Music.

Farnum, S. (1969b). *Farnum music test*. New York, NY: Psychological Corporation.

Fautley, M. (2010). *Assessment in music education*. London, UK: Oxford University Press.

Ferguson, R. (2012). Can student surveys measure teacher quality? *Phi Delta Kappan, 94*(3), 24–28. doi: 10.1177/003172171209400306

Ferguson, R., & Danielson, C. (2014). How framework for teaching and tripod 7Cs evidence distinguish key components of effective teaching. In T. Kane, K. Kerri, & R. Pianta (Eds.), *Designing teacher evaluation systems: New guidance from the measures of effective teaching project* (pp. 98–143). San Francisco, CA: Jossey-Bass.

Ferrara, S., & Way, D. (2016). Design and development of end-of-course tests for student assessment and teacher evaluation. In H. Braun (Ed.), *Measuring the challenges to measurement in an era of accountability* (pp. 11–48). New York, NY: Routledge.

Fortney, P. (1992). The construction and validation of an instrument to measure attitudes of students in high school instrumental programs. *Contributions to Music Education, 19*, 32–45.

Froseth, J. (1982). *Test of melodic ear to hand coordination* (Unpublished doctoral dissertation). University of Michigan, Ann Arbor, MI.

Froseth, J. (1983). *Ear-hand coordination test*. Chicago, IL: GIA Publications.

Gabrielsson, A. (1995). Music psychology in Sweden. In M. Manturewska, K. Miklaszewski, & A. Biatkowski (Eds.), *Psychology of music today*. Warsaw, Poland: Fryderyk Chopin Academy of Music.

Galton, F. (1869). *Hereditary genius: An inquiry into its laws and consequences*. (reissued in 1892). London, UK: MacMillan Books.

Galton, F. (1883). *Inquiries into human faculty and its development*. London, UK: J.M. Dent.

Galton, F. (1889). *Natural inheritance*. London, UK: Macmillan/McGraw-Hill.

Gardner, H. (2006). *Multiple intelligences: New horizons*. New York, NY: Basic Books.

Garofalo, R. (2010). Politics, meditation, social context, and public use. In P. Juslin, & J. Sloboda (Eds.), *Handbook of music and emotions: Theory, research, and applications* (pp. 725–754). Oxford, UK: Oxford University Press.

Gaston, E. T. (1942/1957). *A test of musicality*. Lawrence, KS: Odell's Instrumental Service.

Gembris, H. (2002). The development of musical abilities. In R. Colwell, & C. Richardson (Eds.), *The new handbook of research on music teaching and learning* (pp. 487–508). New York, NY: Oxford University Press.

Gembris, H. (2006). The development of musical abilities. In R. Colwell (Ed.), *MENC handbook of musical cognition and development* (pp. 124–164). New York, NY: Oxford University Press.

Gildersleeve, G., & Soper, W. (1921). *Musical achievement test*. New York: Columbia Teachers College Press. (Also listed as 1929 or n.d. in some sources.)

Gorder, W. (1980). Divergent production abilities as constructs of musical creativity. *Journal of Research in Music Education, 28*(1), 34–42. doi: 10.2307/3345051

Gordon, E. (1965). *Musical aptitude profile*. Boston, MA: Houghton Mifflin.

Gordon, E. (1967). *A three-year longitudinal predictive validity study of the Musical Aptitude Profile*. Iowa City: University of Iowa Press.

Gordon, E. (1970/1991). *Iowa tests of musical literacy*. Iowa City, IA: Bureau of Educational Research and Service.

Gordon, E. (1979). *Primary measures of music audiation*. Chicago, IL: GIA.

Gordon, E. (1982). *Intermediate measures of music audiation*. Chicago, IL: GIA.

Gordon, E. (1989). *Advanced measures of music audiation*. Chicago, IL: GIA.

Gordon, E. (1997). Taking another look at the established procedure for scoring the advanced measures of music audiation. *GIML Monograph Series #2*. Narberth, PA: Gordon Institute for Music Learning.

Green, L. (2008). *Music, informal learning and the school: A new classroom pedagogy*. Surry, UK: Ashgate.

Gueguen, N., Meineri, S., & Fischer-Lokou, J. (2014). Men's music ability and attractiveness to women in a real-life courtship context. *Psychology of Music, 42,* 545–549. doi: 10.1177/0305735613482025

Gutsch, K. (1965). Evaluation in instrumental performance: An individual approach. *Music Educators Journal, 51*(3), 2–5.

Hallam, S. (2016). Motivation to learn. In S. Hallam. I. Cross, & M. Thaut, *The Oxford handbook of music psychology* (pp. 463–478). Oxford, UK: Oxford University Press.

Hallam, S., & Prince, V. (2003). Conceptions of musical ability. *Research Studies in Music Education, 20,* 2–22. doi: 10.1177/1321103X030200010101

Hargreaves, D. J., & North, A. C. (2010). Experimental aesthetics and liking for music. In P. N. Juslin, & J. A. Sloboda (Eds.), *Handbook of music and emotions: Theory, research, and applications* (pp. 515–546). Oxford, UK: Oxford University Press.

Healey, D. (2016). *E pluribus unum: An evaluation of student engagement and learning in the college marching band* (Unpublished doctoral dissertation). Boston College, Boston, MA.

Henry, M. (2001). The development of a vocal sight-reading inventory. *Bulletin of the Council for Research in Music Education, 150,* 21–35.

Henry, M. (2004). The use of targeted pitch skills for sight-singing instruction in the choral rehearsal. *Journal of Research in Music Education, 52,* 206–217. doi: 10.2307/3345855

Hevner, K. (1935). Expression in music: A discussion of experimental studies and theories. *Psychological Review 42,* 187–204.

Hevner, K. (1936). Experimental studies of the elements of expression in music. *American Journal of Psychology, 48,* 246–268. doi: 10.2307/1415746

Hevner, K., & Landsbury, J. (1935). *Oregon musical discrimination tests,* Chicago, IL: C.H. Stoelting.

Hickey, M. (1991). A comparison of verbal instruction and nonverbal teacher-student modeling in instrumental ensembles. *Journal of Research in Music Education, 39,* 132–142. doi: 10.2307/3344693

Hillbrand, E. (1923). *Hillbrand sight-singing Test.* New York, NY: World Book Company.

Hodges, D. A. (2010). Psychophysiological measures. In P. N. Juslin, & J. A. Sloboda (Eds.), *Handbook of music and emotion: Theory, research, applications* (pp. 279–311). New York, NY: Oxford University Press.

Holmstrom, L. G. (1963). *Musicality and prognosis.* SvenskaBokforlaget/Norstedts Publication #17. Stockholm, Sweden: Royal Swedish Academy of Music.

Hutchinson, H., & Pressey, L. C. (1927) *Hutchinson music tests.* Bloomington, IL: Public School Publishing Company.

Jordan, A., & Hawley, T. (2016, February 16). By the elite, for the vulnerable: The edTPA, academic oppression, and the battle to define good teaching. *Teachers College Record.* [ID Number 19461]. Retrieved from http://www.tcrecord.org.

Juslin, P. N., Liljestrom, S., Vastfjall, D. Barradas, G., & Silva, A. (2008). An experience sampling study of emotional reactions to music: Listener, music, and situation. *Emotion, 8,* 668–683. doi: 10.1037/a0013505

Juslin, P. N., Liljestrom, S. Vastfjall, D., & Lundqvist, L. (2010). How does music evoke emotions? Exploring underlying mechanisms. In P. Juslin, & J. Sloboda (2010). (Eds.), *The handbook of music and emotion: Theory, research and applications* (pp. 605–642). Oxford, UK: University of Oxford Press.

Juslin, P. N., & Sloboda, J. A. (Eds.). (2010). *The handbook of theory and emotion: Theory, research, and applications.* New York, NY: Oxford University Press.

Kane, T., & Kerr, K., & Pianta, R. (Eds.). (2014). *Designing teacher evaluation systems. New guidance from the measures of effective teacher project.* San Francisco, CA: Jossey-Bass.

Karma, K. (1974, 1979, 1995). Auditory and visual temporal structuring. In M. Manturzewska, K. Miklaszewsik., & A. Bialkowski (Eds.), *Psychology of music today*. Warsaw, Poland: Chopin Academy.

Karma, K. (1975). Selecting students for music instruction. *Bulletin of the Council for Research in Music Education 75*, 23–32.

Kemp, A. (1981). Personality differences between the players of string, woodwind, brass, and keyboard instruments, and singers. *Bulletin of the Council for Research in Music Education, 66–67*, 33–38.

Kemp, A. (1996). *The musical temperament: Psychology and personality of musicians*. Oxford, UK: Oxford University Press.

Kenny, D., & Ackermann, B. (2015). Performance-related musculoskeletal pain, depression and music performance anxiety in professional orchestral musicians: A population study. *Psychology of Music, 43*(1), 43–60. doi: 10.1177/0305735613493953

Kenny, D., Driscoll, T., & Ackermann B. (2014). Psychological well-being in professional orchestral musicians in Australia: A descriptive population study. *Psychology of Music, 42*, 210–232. doi: 10.1177/0305735612463950

Keston, M., & Pinto, I. (1913/1955). Possible factors influencing musical preference. *Journal of Genetic Psychology, 86*, 101–113.

Knuth, W. (1936/1966). *Knuth achievement tests in music*. San Francisco, CA: Creative Arts Research Associates.

Kopiez, R. Weihs, C. Ligges, U., & Lee, J. (2006). Classification of high and low achievers in a music sight-reading task. *Psychology of Music, 34*(1), 5–26.

Krathwohl, D. R., Bloom, M. S., & Masia, B. B. (1964). *Taxonomy of education objectives, handbook II: Affective domain*. New York, NY: David McKay Company.

Kwalwasser, J. (1926). *Melodic and harmonic sensitivity tests*. Iowa City, IA: Bureau of Educational Research and Service.

Kwalwasser, J. (1927). *Tests and measurements in music*. Boston, MA: C.C. Birchard.

Kwalwasser, J., & Ruch, G. (1927). *Kwalwasser-Ruch test of musical accomplishment*. Iowa City, IA: Bureau of Educational Research and Service.

Kyme, G. (1954). *The value of aesthetic judgments in the assessment of musical capacity* (Unpublished doctoral dissertation). University of California, Berkeley, CA.

Laczo, Z. (1995). Psychology of music in Hungary. In M. Manturzewska, K. Miklaszewsik, & A. Bialkowski (Eds.), *Psychology of music today* (pp. 50–51). Warsaw, Poland: Chopin Academy.

Lahdelma, I., & Eerola, T. (2016). Single chords convey distinct emotional qualities to both naïve and expert listeners. *Psychology of Music, 44*(1), 37–54. doi: 10.1177/0305735614552006

Larson, W. (1938). Practical experience with music tests. *Music Educators Journal, 24*(3), 70–84.

Long, N. (1965). *A revision of the university of Oregon music discrimination test* (Unpublished doctoral dissertation). University of Indiana, Bloomington, IN.

Long, N. (1978). *Indiana-Oregon music discrimination test*. Bloomington, IN: Mid-West Tests.

Madison, T. H. (1942). Interval discrimination as a measure of musical aptitude. *Archives of Psychology*, no. 268, (entire issue).

Madsen, C., Brittin, R., & Capperella-Sheldon, D. (1993). An empirical method for measuring the aesthetic experience to music. *Journal of Research in Music Education, 41*, 57–69.

Marion, S., & Leather, P. (2015). Assessment and accountability to support meaningful learning: New Hampshire's effort to move to competency education of PACE. *Education Policy Analysis Archives, 23*(9). doi: 10.14507/epaa.v23.1984

Martin-Santana, J., Reinares-Iara, E., & Muela-Molina, C. (2015). Music in radio advertising: Effects on radio spokesperson credibility and advertising effectiveness. *Psychology of Music* 43(6), 763–778.

Mateos-Moreno, D. (2015). Latent dimensions of attitudes towards contemporary music: A structural model. *Psychology of Music* 43(4), 545–562.

McCormick, J., & McPherson, G. (2003). The role of self-efficacy in a musical performance examination. An exploratory structural equation analysis. *Psychology of Music, 31*(1), 37–51. doi: 10.1177/0305735603031001322

McGuire, K. (2000). Common songs of the cultural heritage of the United States: A compilation of songs that most people "know" and "should know." *Journal of Research in Music Education, 48*, 310–322. doi: 10.2307/3345366

McPherson, G., & Hallam, S. (2009). Musical potential. In S, Hallam, I. Cross, & M. Thaut (Eds.), *The Oxford handbook of music psychology* (pp. 255–264). Oxford, UK: Oxford University Press.

McPherson, G., & McCormick, J. (2000). The contribution of motivational factors to instrumental performance in a music examination. *Research Studies in Music Education, 15*(1), 31–39. doi: 10.1177/1321103X0001500105

McPherson, G., & McCormick J. (2006). Self-efficacy and music performance. *Psychology of Music, 34*, 325–339. doi: 10.1177/0305735606064841

Meyer, L. B. (1956). *Emotion and meaning in music.* Chicago, IL: University of Chicago Press.

Meyer, L. B. (1967). *Music the arts and ideas.* Chicago, IL: University of Chicago Press.

Mishra, J. (2014). Improving sightreading accuracy: A meta-analysis. *Psychology of Music, 42*, 131–156. doi: 10.1177/0305735612463770

Moorhead, G., & Pond, D. (1941). *Music of young children: A three volume report.* Santa Barbara, CA: Pillsbury Foundation for the Advancement of Music Education.

Mosher, R. (1925). A study of group method of measurement of sight-singing. *Contributions to Education, 194* (entire issue). New York, NY: Teachers College, Columbia University.

Mursell, J. (1937). *The psychology of music.* New York, NY: Norton.

Mursell, J., & Glenn, M. (1931). *The psychology of school music teaching.* New York, NY: Silver Burdett.

Myers-Briggs, I. (1944/1975). *The Myers-Briggs Type Indicator.* Princeton: ETS, 1962; Gainesville, FL: Myers-Briggs Foundation, 1975.

National Center for Education Statistics. (2018). *National Assessment of Educational Progress (NAEP) (1974/1978/1997/2008).* Retrieved from https://nces.ed.gov/nationsreportcard/

Norman-Haignere, S., Kanwisher, N., & McDermott, J. (2015). Distinct cortical pathways for music and speech revealed by hypothesis-free voxel decomposition, *Neuron, 88*, 1281–1296. doi: 10.1016/j.neuron.2015.11.035

Norris, E. L., & Bowes, J. E. (Eds.). (1970). *National Assessment of Educational Progress: Music objectives.* Education Commission of the States, Denver, CO. Retrieved from ERIC database (ED063197).

Oregon State Department of Education (1977). *Self-evaluation checklist for orchestra, grades 4-12.* Salem, OR: Author. Retrieved from ERIC database (ED152662).

Osborne M., & Kenny, D. (2005). Development and validation of a music performance anxiety inventory for gifted adolescent musicians. *Journal of Anxiety Disorders, 19*, 725–751. doi: 10.1016/j.janxdis.2004.09.002

Osborne, M., & Kenny, D. (2008). The role of sensitizing experiences in MPA in adolescent musicians. *Psychology of Music, 36*, 447–462.

Otterstein, A., & Mosher, R. (1932). *O-M Sight-Singing Test*. Stanford, CA: Stanford University Press.

Penuel, W., & Shepard, L. (2016). Assessment and teaching. In D. Gitomer, & C. Bell (Eds.), *Handbook of research on teaching* (5th ed., pp. 787–850). Washington, DC: AERA.

Pflederer, M. (1964). *The responses of children to musical tasks embodying Piaget's principles of conservation* (Unpublished doctoral dissertation). University of Illinois, Urbana, IL.

Pflederer, M., & Secrest, L. (1968). How children conceptually organize musical sounds. *Council for Research in Music Education, 13*, 19–36.

Phillips, K., & Doneski, S. (2011). Research on elementary and secondary school singing. In R. Colwell, & P. Webster (Eds.), *MENC handbook on research on music learning* (Vol. 2, pp. 176–232). New York, NY: Oxford University Press.

Pinker, S. (1997). *How the mind works*. New York, NY: W.W. Norton.

Quigley, S. L. (2004). *Project to rekindle singing of the national anthem*. American Forces Press Service. Retrieved from http://www.defenselink.mil/news/newsarticle.aspx?id=24915

Rainbow, E. L. (1965). A pilot study to investigate the constructs of musical aptitude. *Journal of Research in Music Education, 13*(1), 3–14.

Ravitch, D. (2016). *The New York Review of Books*, 34–36.

Rentfrow, P., Goldberg, L., & Levitin, D. (2011). The structure of musical preferences: A five-factor model. *Journal of Personality and Social Psychology, 100*, 1139–1157. doi: 10.1037/a0022406

Révész, G. (1999). *The psychology of a musical prodigy*. (Trans. unknown). London, UK: Routledge. (Original work published 1925.)

Riconscente, R. M., Mislevy, R. J., & Corrigan, S. (2016). Evidence-centered design. In S. Lane, M. Raymond, & T. Haladnya (Eds.), *Handbook of test development* (2nd ed., pp. 40–63). New York, NY: Routledge.

Roderer, J. G. (1974). The psychophysics of music perception. *Music Educators Journal, 60*(6), 20–30.

Rutkowski, J. (1990). The measurement and evaluation of children's singing voice development. *The Quarterly, 1*(1–2), 81–95.

Ruzek, E., Hafen, C., Hamre, B., & Pianta, R. (2014). Combining classroom observations and value added for the evaluation and professional development of teachers. In T. Kane, K. Kerri, & R. Pianta, (Eds.), *Designing teacher evaluation systems: New guidance from the measures of effective teaching project* (pp. 205–233). San Francisco, CA: Jossey-Bass.

S. 1177, 114th Cong. (2015, December 10). *Every Student Succeeds Act*, Public Law 114-95. Washington, DC: US Government Printing Office. Retrieved from https://www.congress.gov/bill/114th-congress/senate-bill/1177/text?overview=closed

Sarbescu P., & Dorgo, M. (2014). Frightened by the stage or by the public? Exploring the multidimensionality of music performance anxiety. *Psychology of Music, 42*, 568–579. doi: 10.1177/0305735613483669

Schellenberg, G. (2016). Music and nonmusical abilities. In G. Mcpherson (Ed.), *The child as musician: A handbook of musical development* (2nd ed., pp. 149–176). New York, NY: Oxford University Press.

Seashore, C. (1915). *The measurement of musical talent*. New York, NY: Schirmer.

Seashore, C. (1932). The vibrato. *University of Iowa studies in psychology of music* (Vol. 1). Iowa City, IA: University Press.

Seashore, C. (1936). The vibrato. *University of Iowa studies in psychology of music* (Vol. 3). Iowa City, IA: University Press.

Seashore, C. (1938). *Psychology of music*. New York, NY: McGraw Hill.

Seashore, C. (1946). *In search of beauty in music: A scientific approach to musical esthetics*. (reprint). New York, NY: The Ronald Press Co.

Seashore, C. (1947). *In search of beauty in music: A scientific approach to musical esthetics*. New York, NY: Ronald Press.

Sloboda, J. A. (2010). Music in everyday life: The role of emotions. In P. N. Juslin, & J. A. Sloboda (Eds.), *Handbook of music and emotions: Theory, research, and applications* (pp. 493–514). Oxford, UK: Oxford University Press.

Smith, W., & Wuttke, B. (2016). Developing a model of the effective first-year secondary music teacher: Musical and teaching skills. In T. Brophy, J. Marlatt, & Ritcher, G. (Eds.), *Connecting practice, measurement, and evaluation* (pp. 177–192). Chicago, IL: GIA Publications.

Stanton, H. (1935). *Measurement of musical talent: The Eastman experiment*. Studies in the Psychology of Music, 2. Iowa City, IA: University of Iowa Press.

Stefanic, N., & Randles, C. (2014). Examining the reliability of scores from the consensual assessment technique in the measurement of individual and small group creativity. *Music Education Research, 17*, 278–295. doi: 10.1080/14613808.2014.909398

Stumpf, C. (1883/1890). *Tonpsychologie*. Leipzig, Germany: Hirzel.

Strouse, C. (1937). *Strouse music test*. Emporia: Kansas State Teachers' College, Bureau of Educational Measurements.

Swanwick, K. (1999). *Teaching music musically*. London, UK: Routledge.

Swinchoski, A. (1965). A standardized music achievement test batter for the intermediate grades. *Journal of Research in Music Education, 13*, 159–168. doi: 10.2307/3343670

Tan, Siu-Lan., & Spackman, M. (2005). Listeners' judgments of the musical unity of structurally altered and intact musical compositions. *Psychology of Music, 33*, 133–153. doi: 10.1177/0305735605050648

Thompson, W., & Schellenberg, G. (2006). Listening to music. In R. Colwell (Ed.), *MENC handbook of musical cognition and development* (pp. 72–113). New York, NY: Oxford University Press.

Torgerson, R. L., & Fahnestock, E. (1927/1930). *Torgerson-Fahnestock music test*. Bloomington, IL: Public School Publishing Company.

Torrance, E. P. (1974). *Torrance tests of creative thinking*. Berensville, IL: Scholastic Testing Service.

Umemoto, T., Mikuno, M., & Murase, A. (1989). Development of tonal sense: A new test of cognition of pitch deviation. *Human Developmental Research, 5*, 155–174.

University of Maryland Libraries. (2005, July). *Music tests*. Paul Lehman Papers, Special Collections, Series 6 (processed by T. McKay). Retrieved from http://hdl.handle.net/1903.1/19477

Valentine, C. (1913). The aesthetic appreciation of musical intervals among school children and adults. *British Journal of Psychology, 6*, 190–216.

Vaughan, M. (1973). Cultivating creative behavior: Energy levels in the process of creativity. *Music Educators Journal, 59*(8), 35–37. doi: 10.2307/3394272

Vispoel, W. (1987). *An adaptive test of musical memory: An application of item response theory to the assessment of musical ability* (Unpublished doctoral dissertation). University of Illinois, Urbana, IL.

Watkins, J. (1941). *Objective measurement of instrumental performance*. New York, NY: Columbia University Press.

Webster, P. (1987/1992). Research on creative thinking in music: The assessment literature. In R. Colwell (Ed.), *Handbook of research on music teaching and learning* (pp. 266–280). New York, NY: Schirmer Books.

Wedin, L. (1972). Multidimensional scaling of emotional expression in music. *Swedish Journal of Musicology, 54,* 115–131.

WHOQOL Group. (1998). Development of the WHOQOL.BREG Quality of life assessment. *Psychological Medicine, 28,* 551–558.

Wilkerson, J. (2015). Examining the interval structure evidence for the performance assessment for California teachers. *Journal of Teacher Education, 66,* 184–192.

Wing, H. (1958). *Standardized tests of musical intelligence.* Windsor, UK: National Foundation Education Research.

Woody, R. H. (2000). Learning expressivity in music performance: An exploratory study. *Research Studies in Music Education, 14,* 14–23.

Woody, R. H., & McPherson, G. E. (2010). Emotion and motivation in the lives of performers. In P. N. Juslin, & J. A. Sloboda (Eds.), *Handbook of music and emotions: Theory, research, and applications* (pp. 401–424). Oxford, UK: Oxford University Press.

Zdzinski, S. (2013). The underlying structure of parental involvement-home environment in music. *Bulletin of the Council for Research in Music Education, 198,* 69–88.

Zdzinski, S., Dell, C., Gumm, A., Rinnert, N., Orzolek, D., Yap, C. C., Cooper, S., . . . Russell, B. (2014–2015). Musical home environment, family background, and parenting style on success in school music and in school. *Contributions to Music Education, 40*(1), 71–90.

Zenatti, A. (1991). A comparative study in sample of French and British children and adults. *Psychology of Music, 19,* 63–73.

Zentner, M., & Eerola, T. (2010). Self-report measures and models. In P. N. Juslin, & J. A. Sloboda (Eds.), *Handbook of music and emotions: Theory, research, and applications* (pp. 187–221). Oxford, UK: Oxford University Press.

Zentner, M., Grandjean, D., & Scherer, K. (2008). Emotions evoked by the sound of music: Characterization, classification, and measurement. *Emotion, 8,* 494–521. doi: 10.1037/1528-3542.8.4.494

Zhukov, K., Viney, L., Riddle, G., Teniswood-Harvey, A., & Fujimura, K. (2016). Improving sight-reading skills in advanced pianists: A hybrid approach. *Psychology of Music, 44,* 155–167. doi: 10.1177/0305735614550229

CHAPTER 25

DEVELOPING TESTS OF MUSIC PERFORMANCE IMPROVISATION

GARY E. McPHERSON

INTRODUCTION

THIS focus of this chapter is on research aimed at developing and validating measures to assess instrumentalists' abilities to improvise music. The evidence discussed comes from my own teaching and research involving beginning, intermediate, and advanced level instrumentalists. Over a number of decades, my research interests have sought to clarify interrelationships among visual (i.e., perform rehearsed music, sight-read), aural (i.e., perform music from memory, play by ear), and creative (i.e., improvise) forms of musical performance (see Figure 25.1).

Given the dearth of information on creative forms of music performance, my explanation is meant to provide a personal perspective on assessing improvisational abilities of instrumentalists and vocalists who are learning in the types of instrumental programs we see in Western schools throughout the world. The basic technique could be applied to the assessment of improvisational abilities of students who are specializing in jazz and popular forms of music, but it is important to note from the outset that most of my research has been applied to students who are learning in traditional formal programs that emphasize learning notation and classical styles of performance.

It is therefore important to begin with a caveat. I am aware that every teaching situation is different, so the development of appropriate ways to assess students' abilities to improvise needs to begin with a thorough understanding of the context and the educational needs of the students. The development of appropriate music learning tasks that challenge students and that they find interesting and motivating is essential in situations where teachers intend to assess growth and achievement in this area. Consequently, the examples

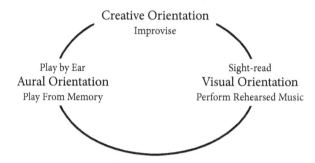

FIGURE 25.1 Visual, aural, and creative forms of music performance.

I advocate may be entirely inappropriate in other situations. It is my hope, however, that some of the techniques and the theory that underpins my ideas may prove beneficial for extending research and the improvement of teaching practice. Thus, to make best use of the techniques suggested in this chapter, music educators are encouraged to construct examples such as those identified in this chapter, but keeping in mind the age, instrument, and abilities of their students. This point is especially important given that much of the literature to date has focused on everyday practice rather than being grounded in theoretical frameworks that attempt to define the creative process more holistically.

This chapter describes the types of tasks that have been commonly used in research measures to assess improvisational abilities. This includes information on the types of evaluative criteria that are appropriate for the assessment of improvisation in research studies and the types of criteria used by the author in studies that have investigated stylistically conceived and freely conceived improvisation tasks. Included also is information on the reliability and validity of the author's Test of Ability to Improvise (TAI) and examples of responses from studies with high school instrumentalists (see McPherson, 1993, for a copy of the complete measure). The final section of the chapter discusses implications of the research for conceptions of musical development and the types of practical applications that arise from work within this area of research.

TEST OF ABILITY TO IMPROVISE (TAI)

In the process of designing appropriate tasks to assess young musicians' improvisational abilities, I consulted a number of prominent music educators, music education researchers, composers, and jazz improvisers, and reviewed available literature. I also pilot tested a number of techniques that I thought might be relevant to improvisation assessment with school-aged instrumentalists who were learning in formal school and community performance programs, where learning to perform by reading notation dominated instruction.

(A)

improvise closing phrase

(B)

improvise closing phrase

FIGURE 25.2A, B Two improvised closing phrase tasks.

Seven types of tasks were explored. The first, *Improvisation of a Closing Phrase*, appears in various forms in classroom teaching, jazz instruction, and traditional forms of organ/keyboard instruction, and in some forms of external evaluation of performance ability, such as those used by the Associated Board of the Royal Schools of Music (see: http://au.abrsm.org/en/about-abrsm/), which require candidates to improvise an answering phrase to a given opening phrase. Measures of musical creativity have also included a task that asks students to supply a closing phrase (see Figures 25.2a, 25.2b). This type of task is found in some of the earliest forms of creativity testing, such as Vaughan's (1971) Musical Creativity Test, designed for young musically untrained children, where students were asked to improvise an "answering" rhythm and "answering" closing phrase using tom tom and bells, respectively.

I decided to incorporate two short opening phrases in the TAI, which asked students to perform and continue a given phrase in a way that would provide a well-balanced melody comprising two phrases (i.e., antecedent–consequent structure). The task therefore, was to improvise a closing phrase that stylistically complemented the opening phrase, and that sounded finished. In this sense the stylistic requirements are set by the opening phrase, which finishes on the dominant and imposes a tonic to dominant–dominant to tonic structure for the two-phrase melody. To create a suitable response, the student would need to "feel" the shape and flow of the opening phrase in order to generate an appropriate closing phrase. There are numerous ways in which this could be achieved. For example, unity can be achieved by adopting a similar rhythmic pattern for the closing phrase; an ascending opening phrase might be mirrored by a descending answer; or repetition of sections of the opening phrase may form the basis from which a closing phrase is generated.

The second type of task, *Improvisation on a Rhythmic Pattern*, has been used to develop improvisational ability (Baker, 1969; Berkowitz, 1975; Campbell, 1990, 1991; Chase, 1988; Dean, 1989; Dickinson, 1964a, 1964b, 1964c; Frazee, 1987; Harvey, 1988; Hunt, 1968; Moore, 1990; Rowley, 1955; Schlieder, 1927; Simpson, 1963; Stubington, 1940; Texter, 1979; Thackray, 1978). As for the first task, the basis for a simple, well-balanced melody is predetermined by the rhythmic pattern, which students use to construct their own melody (see Figure 25.3). Of interest in this activity is the students' ability to shape their response by manipulating pitch in such a way as to fulfill the stylistic requirements of the task that will provide a musically interesting improvisation that finishes on the

FIGURE 25.3 Improvisation on a rhythmic pattern.

FIGURE 25.4 Two improvisation on a motif tasks.

tonic in an assigned key. Of most concern was the ability of the students to orient themselves to the key, and to provide an interesting solution.

The third task, *Improvisation on a Motif*, was designed to examine how young instrumentalists could generate a balanced melody of at least eight measures in length after being provided with a short introductory opening (see Figures 25.4a and 25.4b). Again, this form of exercise is common in the literature (Baker, 1969; Berkowitz, 1975; Chase, 1988; Coker, 1964; Dale, Jacob, & Anson, 1940; Dean, 1989; Department of Education and Science, 1990; Dickinson, 1964a; Frackenpohl, 1985; Frazee, 1987; Froseth & Blaser, 1980; Hunt, 1968; Judy, 1990; Kratus, 1990; Nicholls & Tobins, 1937; Rowley, 1955; Sawyer, 1923; Schlieder, 1927; Stubington, 1940; Thackray, 1968, 1978; Wittlich & Martin, 1989; Wunsch, 1972). Once again, we also see this type of task in early creativity measures such as Gorder's (1976, 1980) Measures of Musical Divergent Production. In the items chosen for use in the TAI, stylistic requirements of the melody are predetermined by the shape and rhythmic feel of the opening motif, which can be modified and adapted using a variety of musical techniques. For example, the motif could be repeated, inverted, transposed, varied by augmentation or diminution, or developed by fragmentation or elaboration. The taped instructions and sample performance that I devised for this task alerted the student to techniques (i.e., repetition, variation, and development) commonly used by performers while improvising on a motif.

The fourth type of improvised response, *Improvisation to an Accompaniment*, is the basis from which most jazz and popular music is improvised (Baker, 1969; Coker, 1964; Dean, 1989). In addition, traditional forms of improvisation (Berkowitz, 1975; Chase, 1988; Dickinson, 1964c; Rosfeld, 1989; Rowley, 1955; Sawyer, 1923; Stubington, 1940; Thackray, 1978) and classroom/instrumental music instruction abound with examples of this form of improvisation (see Figure 25.5). Likewise, early creativity measures such as Vaughan's (1971) measure adopted this technique by asking students to improvise a melody over an ostinato accompaniment. For the purpose of the TAI, students were asked to complement the style of the accompanying passage in order to create their own improvisation. Students were therefore free to choose their own rhythm, but encouraged to restrict their playing to diatonic notes of the C major scale.

FIGURE 25.5 Improvisation to an accompaniment.

The final part of the measure was devised to investigate student ability to improvise in a "freely conceived" style. The development of this section was influenced by previous work by Gorder (1976, 1980), Flohr (1979), Priest (1985, 1988, 1989), Swanwick and Tillman (1986), and Webster (1977, 1979). Discussions with expert musicians and music educators suggested the need for this type of exercise as the most challenging component of the measure.

The first four TAI sections were labeled "stylistically conceived" because these tasks provided models in the form of set criteria that dominated the range of possible solutions available. For these tasks, the instrumentalists responded to externally generated restrictions.

In the final task the instrumentalist were challenged to provide their own "freely conceived" response by formulating their own set of internally generated parameters. The directions included the following statement:

> For this task you are asked to perform an extended improvisation in any style or mood that you choose. You are free to play anything you like so let your musical imagination roam free. Your improvisation doesn't have to be in any particular key or conform to any set criteria. Just play your most interesting musical ideas.
>
> Before you begin take time to think of interesting ideas that you could use as the basis of your improvisation.
>
> Remember, you are completely free to do whatever you like—you may play for as long as you want!

The directions allowed scope for the component of creative thinking together with the opportunity to examine more closely facets of ability to improvise in a "freely conceived" format. Incorporating this final item also allowed differences between "stylistically conceived" and "freely conceived" styles of improvising to be explored and investigated.

Administering the TAI

The TAI, as used in my research studies, includes carefully constructed musical examples and vocal directions to enable the test to be efficiently administered within a standardized format. Before commencing the tape, which included voice directions and taped performances on clarinet (or trumpet), students read an introductory statement aimed at familiarizing them with what was to follow. Instrumentalists are also asked if they understood the directions or if they had any questions before commencing each task. Practice activities for the first three items were in the form of musical examples and a discussion of what is required for each of the test items. These introductory examples and taped directions aimed to familiarize each player with the form of each task. In the first two items, involving question-answer phrases, students were given an opportunity to perform improvisations according to well-defined guidelines. The tasks were sequenced to allow for longer and more involved improvisations as the performer moves to each successive item (McPherson, 1993).

In my research, I typically asked students to perform a second improvisation for all but the final more extensive "freely conceived" task. However, this is not necessarily needed when working with students in an educational setting.

Scoring the TAI

The scoring procedure I developed for the TAI was based on a literature review and discussions with academics, music educators, and expert improvisers. At the time, no measures were available that specifically examined high school instrumentalists' ability to improvise in a "stylistically conceived," traditional setting, so a new method of scoring had to be devised, one that incorporated aspects of measurement of creativity in music as well as the skills thought essential by authors and experts in the area of improvisation.

My first task was to adequately differentiate improvisational ability with that of creative thinking in music, and to ensure that the criteria used for improvisation assessment were consistent with how practitioners and researchers viewed this form of performance. Here, my thinking was influenced by Gordon (1989):

> it is easier to create than to improvise, creativity is a readiness for improvisation. Creativity is easier than improvisation, because there are more restrictions on a performer when he improvises than when he creates. For example, when a performer knows that he is to perform two tonal patterns in major tonality without any restrictions, he can be creative. When a performer knows that he is to perform two tonal patterns in major tonality and also that the first pattern is to be a tonic function and the second a dominant function, then he must improvise. Other restrictions may be in keyality, form, and style. When a student is creating he imposes restrictions upon himself. When he improvises, he is student to externally imposed restrictions. (pp. 71–72)

This view is consistent with methods researchers have adopted for the assessment of creativity and improvisation in music. It also contrasts measures of creative thinking, in which young untrained children are encourage to respond to open-ended tasks, with more "stylistically conceived" measures of improvisational performance. For example, the original form of Webster's (1989) Measures of Creative Thinking in Music, devised for young untrained children, involved evaluations using both objective and subjective techniques. Scoring was according to four factors:

1. *Musical Extensiveness*: the amount of clock time involved in the creative tasks.
2. *Musical Flexibility*: the extent to which the musical parameters of "high"/"low" (pitch); "fast"/"slow" (tempo) and "loud"/"soft" (dynamics) are manipulated.
3. *Musical Originality*: the extent to which the response is unusual or unique in musical terms and in the manner of performance.
4. *Musical Syntax*: the extent to which the response is inherently logical and makes "musical sense" (p. 3).

Vaughan's (1971) Musical Creativity Test involves six activities, with each task evaluated for fluency, rhythmic security, and ideation. Vaughan defines ideation as "the quality of variety and suitability within the given framework" (p. 65); for example, the manner in which a child improvises over an accompanying ostinato.

Gorder's (1976, 1980) Measures of Musical Divergent Production involves four short musical passages, which are scored using a procedure influenced by Guilford and Hoepfner (1971). These are:

1. *Musical Fluency*: the number of phrases produced.
2. *Musical Flexibility*: the number of phrases that used different kinds of musical content.
3. *Musical Elaboration*: the extent of content character over that necessary to produce a varied phrase.
4. *Musical Originality*: the rarity of usage of specific types of content.
5. *Musical Appeal*: the overall quality of the improvisation (global indication) (Gorder, 1980, p. 36).

In this scoring technique Gorder (1976, 1980) deviates from the four basic divergent production abilities as explained by Guilford and Hoepfner (1971) by including a fifth factor (i.e., *Musical Appeal*), which he believes adds "a global musical ability that was in contrast to the specific divergent production abilities, and that enabled further profiling capability" (Gorder, 1980, p. 35).

Webster (1979) provided an important contribution to the measurement of improvisational ability. His improvisation measure, administered to high school students involved in school music groups, involved four tasks. Activity one was a warm-up, while activity two involved free responses to a rhythmic and then melodic stimulus. Activity three asked students to perform *Twinkle, Twinkle, Little Star* and to then perform three variations on this melody. Activity four required students to improvise on an original melody, to create a transition from this improvisation to *Twinkle, Twinkle, Little Star*, and to conclude by again returning to an improvisation on the original melody. Like Gorder, (1976, 1980), Vaughan (1971), and Webster (1983a, 1983b), evaluative criteria were influenced by the theoretical literature of Guilford (1967) and Torrance (1966). In Webster's (1979) study improvisation was scored for fluency, flexibility, elaboration, and originality. However, each activity was scored for combinations of these factors, with no single task being designed to measure any one isolated factor (p. 232).

At the time I first started to devise assessment procedures for use in evaluating improvisational ability, a number of studies on jazz improvisation were also reviewed and considered (Aitken, 1975; Briscuso, 1972; Burnsed, 1978; Damron, 1973; McDaniel, 1974; Partchey, 1973; Pfenninger, 1990; Schilling, 1989). However, none of these techniques were considered relevant because of the distinctly different ways in which improvisations were performed, the low reliability estimates of some of the measures, the lack of information for some measures concerning the construction of the assessment criteria, or the tedious nature in which improvisational ability was assessed.

Establishing the Assessment Criteria

Figure 25.6 shows the flow chart that acted as the basis from which directions were formulated to evaluate each of the six "stylistically conceived" items on the TAI.

Instrumental Fluency

Instrumental fluency was defined as the ability to execute musical ideas clearly and accurately by responding freely, spontaneously, and with technical skill and musical expression. Improvisers demonstrate fluency through their ability to perform in a spontaneous manner, such as by moving easily from one musical idea to another.

Musical Syntax

Musical syntax (consistency of style) refers to the ability to organize musical material by adapting to the prevailing style and complementing set criteria. Musical syntax is demonstrated by the way the improvisation demonstrates rhythmic feel, melodic sense,

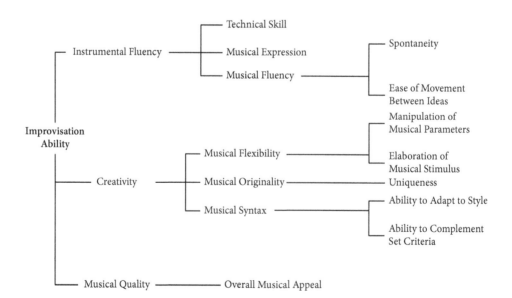

FIGURE 25.6 Assessment criteria TAI "stylistically conceived" items.

tonal organization, and shape (i.e., phrasing and form), and is able to provide a response that is inherently logical and that makes sense musically.

Creativity

Creativity is the ability to think divergently, as demonstrated in an original and imaginative product. This is evaluated through:

1. *Musical Flexibility*: the extent to which the improviser can manipulate musical elements (e.g., pitch, rhythm, articulation) through an elaboration of the musical stimulus (i.e., phrase, rhythm, motif, accompaniment).
2. *Musical Originality*: the extent to which the improviser can provide a musically unique or unusual response.

A unique or unusual response results from the manipulation and/or elaboration of pitch (e.g., use of sequence, diminution, inversion) or rhythm (e.g., augmentation, diminution, dotted versus nondotted, metric versus syncopated), or other musical elements (e.g., timbre, articulation, dynamics).

Musical Quality

Musical quality (overall musical appeal) is the ability of the improviser to perform fluently creatively conceived material that complements existing musical criteria or constraints. This global rating can be used to provide an indication of the overall musical appeal of the improvisation and the extent to which the performance was committed, played expressively, and in a musically meaningful and creative manner. Figure 25.7 shows the flow chart that acted as the basis from which directions were formulated to evaluate the final "freely conceived" item on the *TAI*.

For the "freely conceived" item the directions for the instrumental fluency dimension were identical to that used for the "stylistically conceived" items. The dimensions of musical syntax, creativity, and musical quality differed from those of the "stylistically conceived" items as indicated in what follows.

Musical Syntax

The improviser provides a response that is inherently logical and that makes musical sense. Musical syntax is demonstrated in the degree to which the improvisation demonstrates rhythmic feel, melodic sense, tonal organization, and shape (i.e., phrasing and form).

Creativity

This can be evaluated through an analysis of:

1. *Musical Flexibility*: the extent to which the improviser can generate differing musical ideas and manipulate/elaborate these ideas during the course of the improvisation.
2. *Musical Originality*: the extent to which the improviser can provide a musically unique or unusual response.

A unique or unusual response can result from the manipulation and/or elaboration of pitch (e.g., use of sequence, diminution, inversion) or rhythm (e.g., diminution,

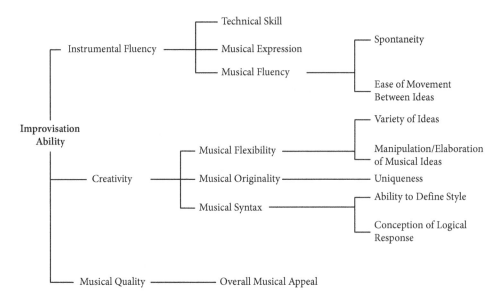

FIGURE 25.7 Assessment criteria TAI "freely conceived" items.

augmentation, dotted versus nondotted, metric versus syncopated), or other musical elements (e.g., timbre, articulation, dynamics).

Musical Quality

This global rating was used to indicate the overall musical appeal of the improvisation and the extent to which it was played expressively and in a musically meaningful and creative manner.

Final Scoring Method

In my original research studies, I used a five-point rating scale to assess each of the essential criteria on all seven items of the TAI, but for teaching contexts and added discrimination I would now recommend that this be expanded to a 10-point scale or even a percentage so that the four dimensions can be summed for a total improvisation score for each task (see Table 25.1).

Reliability and Validity

I analyzed data using the multitrait-multimethod (MTMM) approach formalized by Campbell and Fiske (1959) to find evidence of convergent and discriminant validity for each of the performance measures, and to determine the extent to which the attributes measured by the three judges predicted the specific trait in question (i.e., each individual item on the test). A separate matrix was computed for each of the measures according to scores for each of the three independent judges on each of the test items. Results for each

Table 25.1 Improvisation Rating Scale

	Hesitant & Laboured					Spontaneous & Confident				
Instrumental Fluency	1	2	3	4	5	6	7	8	9	10
	Illogical									Logical
Musical Syntax	1	2	3	4	5	6	7	8	9	10
	No Uniqueness								Marked Uniqueness	
Creativity	1	2	3	4	5	6	7	8	9	10
	Unappealing									Appealing
Musical Quality	1	2	3	4	5	6	7	8	9	10

of the measures showed a consistent pattern that satisfied the four criteria established by Campbell and Fiske (McPherson, 1993, 1995, 2005).

In addition, since few measures have been developed to assess improvisational ability, particularly with high school–age instrumentalists, it was necessary to establish the validity of the four evaluative criteria (i.e., instrumental fluency, musical syntax, creativity, and musical quality) used in the TAI. Using the MTMM, indications of convergent validity were obtained to gauge the level of agreement between each of the four separate criteria used to evaluate the seven items on the TAI, and the three separate evaluations by the judges for each of these criteria. Discriminant validity estimates were obtained to assess the level of correlation between each of the four criteria with the other three. Results showed a consistent pattern of correlations when analyzed according to each of the seven test items. As would be expected, the global evaluative dimension of musical quality tended to be more highly correlated with the other three evaluative criteria than correlation patterns between the other three dimensions (McPherson, 1993, 1995).

The interjudge correlations for the three judges who scored the TAI range from .71 to .94 for the four separate item assessments, and from .89 to .97 for the composite marks for each individual task on the measure. The Cronbach alpha indication of internal consistency was .90 (.90 standardized item alpha).

Original Study Sample

In the original study (McPherson, 1993), average scores for the TAI when used with students who had between 2 and 6 years of instrumental learning, revealed a good spread of marks from about 5% to 95% on the total measure. The sample was split into two groups. Group 1 included clarinet and trumpet students who had studied these instruments for 2 to 4 years and were undertaking Australian Music Examination Board (AMEB) externally assessed examinations at Grade 3 and 4 level of the AMEB syllabus. They were in school years 7 to 9 (ages 11.5 to 15). Group 2 included clarinet and trumpet students who had studied these instruments for 4 to 6 years and were undertaking AMEB examinations at Grade 5 and 6 of the same syllabus. These students were in school years 10–12 (ages 14.5 to 18.5). As would be expected, the more experienced musicians in AMEB grades 5 and 6 provided more sophisticated responses than their younger, less experienced counterparts. Inter-item correlation coefficients for the TAI were all significant ($p < .01$) and ranged between .46 and .68.

TEST OF ABILITY TO IMPROVISE

This section presents a discussion of the Test of Ability to Improvise and the studies pertaining to this test.

Repeated Attempts on the TAI

During the administration of the TAI students were given an opportunity to perform a second improvisation for each of the six "stylistically conceived" items on the test. A second attempt was not allocated for the "freely conceived" item, as this would have been too time consuming, considering the time limitations of the sessions and the concentration span of the students.

To assess whether these second attempts were significantly better than the first attempt, the second responses for 46 students participating in the study were combined with the first 101 performances of the combined population. During the analysis period, judges assessed a total of 147 improvisations for each of the six "stylistically conceived" TAI items, without any knowledge of the student, or whether it was their first or second attempt.

Analysis using the Scheffé multiple comparisons procedure revealed no statistically significant differences between the first and second responses for each of the six "stylistically conceived" improvisational tasks. The means for the first and second attempts of each item were very similar. However, the item that showed the greatest improvement for the second attempt was the rhythm item. In this item students were shown a rhythmic pattern and asked to improvise a melody to complement the notation (see McPherson, 1993, 1995).

Analysis of Transcriptions of Student Responses

This section presents a discussion of the results of the TAI and what the analyses of these results revealed.

Closing Phrase 1 and 2

The improvisations required for the two *Closing Phrase* items were the shortest tasks on the TAI. In these items students were asked to improvise a short closing phrase that complemented the given opening phrase. Because this task requires only a four-measure response, the resulting improvisations were somewhat pattern bound. The performer was restricted to a four-measure closing phrase in F major that ends on F. This stimulus therefore allows little scope for an improvisation to deviate far from the norm.

At the time of constructing the TAI it was considered important to include these items, so that a full range of improvisation, from the simplest and most restricted, to those that were more challenging and freely conceived, could be analyzed. I hoped that restricting the possibilities for response on the first two items of the test might allow the researcher to analyze essential performance characteristics that may be more difficult to observe in longer, more complex improvisations. In addition, the short period of 15 to 20 seconds allocated for each student to contemplate the requirements before commencing offered an opportunity to investigate how more gifted students prepared their response and thereby were able to plan their improvisation. From the outset it was assumed that a good improviser would provide an interesting and creative response no matter what the restrictions.

The most important question considered in the analysis of the closing phrase responses concerned the ability of students to provide a response that complemented the opening figure. The best responses came from students who had mentally prepared at least part of their response before commencing to play, although it could be argued that this is more "composition" than "improvisation." However, as experienced improvisers understand, improvisation often involves some form of planning prior to the performance because the process of improvising includes the ability to translate a preconceived idea into the movements necessary to perform correctly this intention on a musical instrument. A study by Hargreaves, Cork, and Setton (1990) confirmed these observations by highlighting the different strategy used by novice and expert jazz pianists. A distinguishing characteristic of expert improvisers in this study was their ability to start their performance with an overall strategy or plan.

The range of improvised closing phrases for the first two items on the TAI was extensive. They ranged from incomplete, hesitant statements of a couple of notes, to well-shaped, innovative phrases that adequately complemented the opening phrases. The lowest-scoring improvisers were characterized by a lack of ability to adhere to a four-measure statement, poor control of rhythm and pitch, and a dearth of ideas. Close observation of the players during the sessions followed by careful listening to the taped performances indicated a serious lack of ability by these students to coordinate ear and hand. Many of these improvisations appeared to be "accidental" in that the instrumentalists seemed unable to prepare an improvisation in any "holistic" sense, and to thereby show evidence of an ability to "think in sound." It was as if these performers had prepared the opening note or group of notes, but were unable to maintain the flow of ideas throughout the four measures. They tended to play what instinctively had been ingrained, rather than anything they had prepared mentally beforehand. Because the lowest-scoring improvisations showed a distinct lack of ability by the performer to audiate sounds as they were being played, they fit into the category described by Kratus (1990) as "exploration." These improvisers worked at a conscious level, not yet having assimilated the technical, aural, kinesthetic, and theoretical aspects of their playing.

The majority of improvised responses showed evidence of the players' intentions, however unsuccessful. It was clear that most of the players could provide a four-measure closing phrase, perform in correct tempo and key, and pick up the essential characteristics of the opening phrase by providing a well-shaped response that incorporated a similar rhythm and/or pitch pattern to the opening. Many of the better improvisers (1) performed confidently and spontaneously; (2) were capable of using the exact rhythm of the opening phrase, or subtle variations of it; (3) displayed a good sense of direction and overall phrase shape; (4) used appropriate articulations; (5) maintained the flow of their ideas; (6) easily conformed to the prescribed criteria; and (7) provided a musically satisfying response.

The highest-scoring responses displayed one further characteristic. These improvisations displayed not only technical control and theoretical understanding of the requirements but also originality as evidenced in their ability to stretch out and take risks. It was as if these improvisers had assimilated the technical, theoretical, aural, and kinesthetic aspects of their playing into one, and were thereby able to reach out beyond the norm to provide something unique or novel. Examples of "stretching out" were observed in (1) the wider choice of starting notes (one student started on the high A of the trumpet), (2) the more sophisticated sense of shaping (i.e., use of sequences, inversion of opening figures, rhythmic disruption through use of dotted rhythm and eighth notes, and wider range), (3) greater use of expression and tone color, and (4) an intuitive feel for the harmonic implications of the closing phrase. These techniques helped make the improvisation more interesting for the listener.

Rhythm

The *Rhythm* item allowed the study of a different dimension of an ability to improvise. Unlike the other items, where the improviser translates an aural conception into the physical movements necessary to perform this conception on a musical instrument, this item required the performer to process music visually at the same time as improvising a response based on this rhythmic pattern. Essentially, the task required the student to translate the rhythmic pattern (comprising familiar rhythmic patterns in $\frac{4}{4}$ time) into an interesting six-measure melodic response. For this to be possible, the performer must first be able to read and aurally comprehend the rhythmic pattern. The improviser must also be able to integrate this aural image with appropriate pitches to construct an interesting solution.

The highest-scoring improvisers were able to continue their response and perform the rhythm pattern correctly. These improvisers were clearly able to bring meaning to the notation and to conceive of the pattern holistically (rather than in individual notes or small patterns). They were more likely to (1) start on a note other than F, (2) use more leaps in their melody, (3) provide a strong sense of key by outlining the tonic triad in the first measure, and (4) provide a strong feeling of finality (e.g., by approaching the tonic from above and below). The ability of these improvisers to audiate the rhythmic pattern enhanced their skill to organize the music into logically conceived patterns. Because these improvisers could comprehend the rhythm on which to improvise they could work with a more definite aural orientation. Because of these features, high-scoring improvisers demonstrated the most sophisticated working styles. In summary, they seemed more capable of working at a more global level, of working in larger rhythmic units, and of maintaining the flow of their ideas throughout their improvisation.

The lowest-scoring improvisers were plainly not as efficient processors of the rhythm as their older more experienced colleagues. They were more likely to make errors in pitch (e.g., B natural instead of B flat), and to provide a less key-oriented response. This was evident in the stepwise motion of the opening measures and the weaker sense of finality (as evident in those responses that approached the tonic by stepwise movement, repetition, or inappropriate leap).

Analysis of the tapes and transcriptions also showed that many of the performers were not able to improvise an interesting melody using the assigned rhythmic pattern. It was as if the visual orientation involved when processing the notation made it difficult for the improviser to think aurally. Many of the improvisations used stepwise movement and repeated pitches, and many were poorly shaped. This gave the impression that many students improvised by focusing their attention on the individual notes within the notation. These improvisers lacked an ability to comprehend the pattern as a whole, or to anticipate the flow of the rhythm as they performed their response.

In many cases the process of translating the visual notation into an aural image clearly impeded fluency and spontaneity. Low-scoring improvisations were characterized by a dearth of ideas that were often unconnected. It was as if these students were trying to force the rhythmic pattern to fit their own conception rather than complement the existing framework. Above all, the improvisers worked at a conscious level and the resultant products largely centered around the physical and theoretical aspects of playing (e.g., scalewise movement, repetition). There was little evidence that they were able to respond to the demands of divergent thinking to explore the range of possibilities that existed for providing an interesting solution, or worked far enough ahead to ensure fluency and an interesting response. An ability to think divergently was therefore stifled as these students tried to adjust to the requirements. Many of these students performed B naturals and other incorrect notes in F major. They were also more likely to hesitate, stop, or restart their performance.

The lowest-scoring improvisers were incapable of performing the rhythm fluently and used repetition or stepwise movement throughout. In addition, they made numerous pitch errors. Also evident was a weak sense of key and a poor sense of the harmonic implications of their response. For these improvisers, processing the visual information and then coordinating the aural conception with the physical movement necessary to perform the improvisation on an instrument was a major problem. This was the least efficient working style.

The findings presented here parallel observations by jazz educators (Baker, 1979), who suggest that improvisation by sight stifles creativity and instrumental fluency. Improvisers who rely on "reading" the chord progression as they improvise are often hampered in their ability to feel the flow of the accompaniment. They are also more likely to think and work in small units rather than "holistically." This type of improvisation can lead to a disjointed approach without a clear sense of organization. It can also lead to a rigid focus on only one element (i.e., pitch or rhythm) without an ability to remain open to other ideas or to work with other players. Improvisers who have not memorized the chord progression and therefore need to read the changes by sight are often more restricted in what they play compared to those of similar ability who have memorized the changes and improvise without the music (Baker, 1979). In this sense, improvisation by sight as opposed to improvisation by ear can have a stifling influence on the ability of the performer to create an effective and well-shaped improvisation. Clearly evident in the performances on this task was the impression that spontaneity and creativity was impeded for each performer who was unable to fully audiate the rhythmic pattern.

Motif 1 and 2

For both *Motif 1* and *Motif 2* students were asked to use the prescribed opening melodic figures as the basis of an improvised performance of at least eight measures in length. Similar to the preceding items, there was a wide range of responses showing a diversity of skill and ability levels. The lowest-scoring responses were typically short statements of less than eight measures. These improvisations tended to use a restricted range with mostly stepwise movement and occasional leaps of thirds and fourths. Clearly, these improvisers were unable to manipulate, elaborate, or extend the given opening figure. Consequently, the improvisations also displayed a poor sense of phrase balance and were performed in a hesitant manner, leaving the impression that the player was unable to maintain a flow of ideas. These improvisations also tended to be unimaginative, random-like melodies that lacked musical logic and were stylistically inconsistent with the requirements expected. The improvisers were also unable to construct a string of ongoing two- or four-measure phrases, and to improvise a suitable second phrase, preferring instead to repeat ideas expressed in the first phrase. When breakdowns occurred, they typically gravitated back to the opening figure, with meaningless repetition, not knowing how to move beyond their opening ideas. Consequently, for these students, an ability to think divergently and creatively was lacking; they seemed oblivious to the possibilities that existed for providing an interesting solution. These features can be seen in the responses for *Motif 2*, shown in Figures 25.8 and 25.9.

In contrast, high-scoring students were able to provide an intelligent and musical response. An essential difference between students, as determined by length of time spent learning their instruments, was that the older more experienced musicians typically provided a longer and more interesting solution.

Figures 25.10, 25.11, and 25.12 are examples of some of the responses. High-scoring students (1) easily maintained a steady pulse; (2) seemed to have an intuitive feel for four

FIGURE 25.8 Group 1 low scoring response (*motif 2*).

FIGURE 25.9 Group 2 low scoring response (*motif 2*).

two-measure phrases, and an eight-measure response; (3) were capable of using the exact rhythm of the opening phrase or employing subtle variations of it; (4) used range to enhance the shape of their response; (5) moved easily within the key displaying a strong kinesthetic feel for G major; (6) provided a strong sense of cadence; (7) finished on the tonic; (8) mirrored patterns of the opening phrase or constructed logical sequences; (9) used inversion and repetition; (10) constructed logical balanced phrases using antecedent–consequent phrase relationships to enhance structure; (11) varied, manipulated, and elaborated the opening motif; (12) maintained the flow of ideas; (13) sustained the response throughout the entire improvisation; and (14) dealt with melody, phrase, and rhythm in a spontaneous and confident manner. It was obvious that these elements had been assimilated technically, aurally, and kinesthetically. Examples of these improvisations are given in Figures 25.10, 25.11, and 25.12.

FIGURE 25.10 Group 1 high scoring response (*motif 1*).

FIGURE 25.11 Group 1 high scoring response (*motif 2*).

FIGURE 25.12 Group 2 high scoring response (*motif 1*).

Interestingly, analysis of transcriptions shows that the majority of performances for both items in this section were exactly eight measures in length. Discussions with students after their performance revealed that many were not consciously trying to perform an eight-measure response. Most were unaware of the length of their improvisation, frequently expressing surprise that their performance had been exactly eight measures. For these students an eight-measure response resulted from the four two-measure phrases they had used to structure their improvisation. This aspect had been felt intuitively and was not consciously preplanned.

Accompaniment

An accompaniment figure was performed using an electronic keyboard and copied onto a recording device that could be used with the students (see Figure 25.5). Students were asked to improvise an interesting melody using only notes of the C major scale that captures the style of this accompaniment (i.e., based on chords I–ii–V).

Many of the poorest responses on this item showed a surprising lack of ability by the musicians to coordinate their playing with the accompaniment. These students tended to force their ideas to fit the existing framework with the result that their improvisation

FIGURE 25.13 Group 1 low scoring response (*accompaniment*).

FIGURE 25.14 Group 1 low scoring response (*accompaniment*).

seemed totally at odds with the chordal progression with which they were performing. Low-scoring responses also displayed a limited repertoire of rhythmic devices, often repeating the first idea over and over again. They tended to use mostly stepwise movement, with occasional leaps of thirds and fourths. These responses also lacked a sense of key, despite being in the key of C major, and were typically rambling, disjointed melodies often without a logical formation. The majority of these improvisers were unable to use sequences, rhythmic changes, or other devices to shape and enhance their response. Often they were unable to improvise a suitable second phrase, preferring instead to repeat ideas expressed in their first phrase, restrict their performance to the middle register, and perform unimaginative improvisations with little insight about what the accompaniment was "suggesting." These students displayed a lack of coordination between ear and hand, as if their improvisation was "accidental" rather than intuitive. Typical examples of these responses are shown in Figures 25.13 and 25.14.

The finest improvisations from both groups showed mature playing from innovative, skilled musicians. Many of these responses were musically very satisfying, and displayed a strong sense of personal involvement in the performance. There was also evidence of a strong kinesthetic feel for the instrument and an ability to make sense of the ideas and requirements. These students were also capable of sustaining their response throughout the entire phrase and of providing an improvisation with delicate expression (see Figures 25.15, 25.16, and 25.17).

Freely Conceived

Unlike the first six "stylistically conceived" items, the final task on the TAI asked students to perform an extended improvisation in any style or mood they chose. Of interest in this item was the ability of students to define their own style and to construct an improvisation that was both tastefully and logically conceived.

Analysis of transcriptions and master tapes revealed that many of the characteristics identified for the preceding items were also pertinent for this item. However, since this

FIGURE 25.15 Group 2 high scoring response (*accompaniment*).

FIGURE 25.16 Group 2 high scoring response (*accompaniment*).

FIGURE 25.17 Group 1 high scoring response (*accompaniment*).

item allowed more freedom for response, and typically involved a much longer improvised performance, there are a number of additional comments that can be made.

The poorest responses displayed an almost total lack of ability by the performer to start with an appropriately conceived opening motif that could be used as the basis for an interesting improvised performance. Figure 25.18 shows the transcription of one performer, who, devoid of ideas, was unable to elaborate or extend his opening figure and to use it as the basis for his improvisation. For this performer, a lack of coordination between ear and hand was evident in his playing. It was as though this player's improvisation centered on the technical and physical aspects of producing a response that was a secure part of his repertoire. Because of the stepwise movement and lack of elaboration and manipulation of musical parameters there is a feeling that the student's fingers were "walking" between notes without a clear impression that he had really planned what to do. Above all, this improvisation lacks a suitable preconceived idea that could provide the basis or "spark" to ignite the imagination and provide coherence to the rest of the improvisation.

At a slightly higher level of performance were improvisers who were more capable of moving beyond their opening phrase, and who displayed some sense of phrasing and shape. Figure 25.19 is an example of this type of response. Unfortunately, however, these students were limited in their ability to sustain their response throughout the entire improvisation and to extend or elaborate their ideas. Improvisation for these students was limited to a short, predictable response with few distinguishing characteristics or sparks of imagination or inventiveness.

Low-scoring improvisers who provided a longer response than the ones shown previously were typically unable to respond with a clearly defined and shaped performance. These improvisations were often disjointed and fragmented, and lacked a coherent conception. Low-scoring students displayed a limited repertoire of rhythmic devices,

FIGURE 25.18 Low scoring response (*freely*).

FIGURE 25.19 Group 2 low scoring response (*freely*).

tending to repeat the same rhythm over and over again. They were also more prone to use a restricted range, and where leaps occurred, they were often illogical and typically at points where the response broke down or where the student hesitated. In addition, these improvisers often performed rambling and disjointed pieces and tended to limit their response to a repetition of their first basic idea. They were also unable to control their performance, as seen in the number of notes performed outside the key or tonal center in which they were improvising.

In contrast to the limited improvisational ability of some of the students, many of the improvisations were musically satisfying and noteworthy. Economy of means was a characteristic of the better improvisations, especially for less experienced players. Many performers did not employ an extensive range of rhythmic devices but nevertheless performed an effective and original improvisation. Of prime importance to an effective performance was the ability of the improviser to sustain the flow of ideas, to connect ideas, and to end their performance effectively and musically.

A distinguishing characteristic of the best improvisations was the quality of the first basic idea chosen for performance. It was often the case that the better the quality of the opening statement the better the overall performance. Some students opened with an idea that was more technically than musically conceived. These improvisers chose a scale-like run, a tongued (or slurred) passage in thirds, or some other figure that had limited use as an opening motif for an extended improvisation. The best improvisers were those students who chose an interesting opening figure that allowed development and extension, and that acted as a "spark" to ignite their musical imagination.

Another characteristic of the better improvisations was the degree to which the performer displayed an intuitive feel for improvising in a freely conceived idiom. This was observed in a number of ways. First, there was the degree to which the performer had control of the instrument, and the quality of the ear-to-hand coordination. This was indicated in how well the player could finger the notes they were thinking, without making errors in accidentals or hesitating during their performance. It was also evident in the way in which an improviser restricted their options. The best improvisers were those students who manipulated, elaborated, and extended a few basic ideas, without "overplaying" or trying to do too much during their improvisation. These improvisers performed coherent improvisations that displayed an intelligent sense of shape.

Overall, these performances were rarely rushed. The performance moved naturally and effectively from one idea to another only when the music demanded a change of direction. The best performers were also the musicians who made themselves aware of the possibilities before commencing their performance. These characteristics have been cited in other discussions (e.g., Hargreaves et al., 1990; Pressing, 1988) as essential for a well-conceived and presented improvisation. Pressing argues that competent improvisation is a decision-making process in which an improviser begins with a musical idea that is then extended or elaborated using features inherent in the opening conception. This was clearly evident in one of the better improvisations (see Figure 25.20), where a female trumpeter extends and elaborates her opening motif in G minor and uses this to provide coherence and to shape her whole improvisation.

FIGURE 25.20 Group 2 trumpet high scoring female response (*freely*).

In general, the shorter improvisations displayed a clearer sense of shape than did the longer responses. Many of the longer responses for Group 1 students were described by one evaluator as "rambling soundscapes." Shorter responses from both groups were more likely to exhibit a clearer sense of form and overall shape.

When the three evaluators met approximately eight months after the initial evaluative period to discuss the performances on tape, they showed an uncanny ability to tell whether the improvisation they were listening to was performed by a male or female student. This was especially true of the most experienced musicians. Although no significant difference was found for gender in terms of the scores given for each section of the test, there were qualitative difference in the responses that were evident in many, but not all, of the improvised performances for the "freely conceived" section of the TAI, especially for students in Group 2. Female students tended to play expressive improvisations that were often slower and had more space and rests. Some were free in style, displaying a sophisticated sense of phrasing and time. Consequently, they were less "busy" with their choice of notes, and the ways in which they expressed their ideas. For Group 2, 22 of the sample of 25 female students had elected school classroom music (in comparison to 14 of the 23 male students). The "freely conceived" improvisations of female students in Group 2 typically demonstrated the influence of prior exposure and experience of composing in elective music classes.

Male students of Group 2, on the other hand, tended to provide more outgoing, faster, and busier improvisations than females. Many of these performances used a jazz or pop idiom and were more like the improvisations one would expect in a stage ensemble performance of a jazz or rock arrangement. However, these characteristics did not result from an increased exposure by males to jazz/pop ensembles. On the contrary, for the sample chosen for this study there were identical numbers of Group 2 males and females (i.e., eight) who were performing with jazz ensembles on a regular basis.

Figures 25.20 and 25.21 show two examples of high-scoring responses in this section of the battery. The first is by a female and the second by a male.

There were other aspects between groups that were also worthy of mention. First, an analysis of starting notes in the *freely conceived* item revealed only a slight difference in the choice of starting notes according to musical experience, with more than 50% of the students starting their improvisation on C. Analysis of the tonal center used for the improvisations was also unremarkable. Almost three-quarters of the improvisations used a tonal center of C, with far fewer adopting G and E and a very small percentage (around 3%) displaying a total lack of tonal center.

Although not as obvious, there were subtle differences between instruments in the extent of idiomatic devices that the soloist used. Clarinetists were more likely to use a wider range, employ wide leaps, and use other idiomatic devices typical of performance on this instrument. Likewise, trumpeters compensated for the difficulty in playing in the upper register by using idiomatic devices such as glissandi, trills, flutter-tonguing, and double and triple tonguing.

Finally, although some of the finest performances by less experienced musicians were similar in standard to the better responses of the more advanced musicians, there was

FIGURE 25.21 Group 2 trumpet high scoring male response (*freely*).

one further dimension that was mentioned by all evaluators. More experienced students were more likely to "stretch out" during their performance, to take chances and to attempt things that may not have been possible by their less experienced counterparts. The best performances were more "catchy" and memorable, and consequently, there was a feeling that the older, more mature students had a richer vein of prior experiences from which to tap during their performance. It was only the highest-scoring students who were able to reach out beyond the notes and to perform with expression and the highest technical control. It was as if these performers had fully assimilated the technical, aesthetic, theoretical, and kinesthetic dimensions of their playing into one.

Conclusions

The main points discussed in this chapter can be summarized as follows.

1. Second performances on the six "stylistically conceived" items of the TAI were not statistically significantly better than first attempts.
2. For the shorter improvised tasks (i.e., *Closing Phrase 1* & *Closing Phrase 2*) the best responses came from students who had mentally prepared their response before commencing to improvise. In this way, the better improvisers were characterized by their ability to commence a performance with an overall strategy or plan.
3. The less sophisticated improvisers worked at a conscious level, not yet having assimilated the technical, aural, kinesthetic, and theoretical aspects of their playing.
4. Better improvisers performed with technical control and theoretical understanding of the requirements of the task. However, a distinguishing characteristic of the very finest improvisers was their ability to reach out beyond the norm to provide a response that was unique or novel. Examples of "stretching out" can be seen in the wider choice of starting notes, the more sophisticated sense of shaping, greater use of expression and tone color, and an intuitive feel for the harmonic implications of their response. The integration of each of these aspects helped to make these responses unique.
5. There was evidence in the *rhythm* item that translating the visual notation into an auditory image clearly impeded fluency and spontaneity. This is similar to observations by jazz educators (e.g., Baker, 1979), who comment that improvisation by sight stifles creativity and instrumental fluency.
6. The best responses for the *freely conceived* item came from students whose first idea provided the basis or "spark" to ignite their imagination and provide coherence to the rest of the improvisation. Typically the better the quality of opening statement the better the overall performance. Also of critical importance to an effective performance was the ability of the improviser to sustain the flow of ideas, to connect ideas, and to end their performance musically and with a sense of finality.
7. Some gender differences were evident in the responses on the *freely conceived* item, especially for the more proficient students. Typically, female students tended to play moody, atmospheric improvisations that were often slower and had more space and rests. Some were free in style, displaying a sophisticated sense of phrasing and time. Some of these responses suggest the influence of prior exposure to

composition experiences in classroom elective music classes. Male students on the other hand, were likely to provide more outgoing, faster, and busier improvisations than females. Many of these performances used a jazz or pop idiom and were more like the improvisations one would expect in a stage ensemble performance of a jazz or rock arrangement.

8. Differences were also observed between the instruments studied in this investigation. Clarinetists were more likely to use a wider range, employ larger leaps, and use other idiomatic devices typical of performance on this instrument. Likewise, trumpeters compensated for the difficulty in playing in the upper register by using such idiomatic devices as glissandi, trills, flutter-tonguing, and double and triple tonguing.

In all of my work across the past 25 years, I have argued that a "balanced" approach to the development of "musicianship" on a musical instrument can be defined by the ability of a musician to perform music visually (sight-reading, performing rehearsed repertoire), aurally (by ear and from memory), and creatively (improvising).

These orientations are depicted in Figure 25.22, which shows multiple ways in which a teacher can introduce new material and approach the teaching of a range of performance skills. Such an approach is bound to be quite different from normal "traditional" styles of training, and is used here to describe some alternative strategies that could form the basis of teaching at all levels of instruction. For example, moving around the cycle anticlockwise a teacher could introduce a new melody by ear, ask students to improvise their own version of the melody by embellishing and varying it, and then teach them how to read the original melody or their own version using musical notation. After class the student could use the notation as the basis from which to transpose the melody to other keys. The sequence of activities suggested here would be visual to aural to creative and (with the out-of-class activity) visual to aural.

Examples of moving clockwise around the cycle would be activities such as the following. As a warm-up activity at the beginning of a lesson a teacher could start with a rhythmic pattern that is introduced using notation. Students would be encouraged to improvise in a specified key using only the durations of the rhythm pattern, to teach their own version to their classmates, and then to notate their own improvised composition using notation. Likewise, a short melodic motif can be introduced using notation, used as the basis from which to improvise an appropriate melody (by extending, elaborating, and embellishing the motif), and then refined into a final replicable composition,

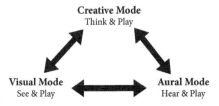

FIGURE 25.22 Orientations for music performance and learning.

which could be notated during the students' daily "music time" and transposed to different pitch levels. There are an infinite variety of ways in which the cycle shown in Figure 25.22 could be used to construct enjoyable and educationally valuable activities. Most of all, these activities would help strengthen a range of skills and foster musically independent instrumentalists. Fundamentally, these activities would also encourage students to "think in sound" before comparing their reproduced version with their internalized model (Schleuter, 1984; p. 26). The sound, therefore, precedes the symbol.

Of course, in any teaching there will be lessons in which students work predominantly from notation, but as suggested here, there should always be opportunities for aural and creative activities at some point in a lesson. These strategies are clearly of more benefit than teaching that stresses only one type of performance, and in which a student's progression is governed by what the next tune in the book happens to be. In this way, improvisation is a key skill for all musicians to learn and experience (McPherson, Davidson, & Faulkner, 2012).

In my opinion, an important goal for teaching students musical instruments is to nurture their talent so that they are capable of reaching their full potential and thus better equipped to cope with the demands of music making in a wider sense. The human need to improvise and learn by creating music, rather than just reproducing music, is a powerful force that can be used to drive and motivate musicians during all stages of their development.

References

Aitken, A. E. (1975). *A self-instructional audio-imitation method designed to teach trumpet students jazz improvisation in the major mode* (Doctoral dissertation). Retrieved from University Microfilms International. (76-15018).

Baker, D. N. (1969). *Jazz improvisation*. Chicago, IL: Maher Publications.

Baker, D. N. (1979). *Advanced improvisation*. Chicago, IL: Music Workshops Publications.

Berkowitz, S. (1975). *Improvisation through keyboard harmony*. Englewood Cliffs, NJ: Prentice-Hall.

Briscuso, J. J. (1972). *A study of ability in spontaneous and prepared jazz improvisation among students who posses different levels of musical aptitude* (Unpublished doctoral dissertation). University of Iowa, Iowa City, IA.

Burnsed, C. V. (1978). *The development and evaluation of an introductory jazz improvisation sequence for intermediate band students* (Doctoral dissertation). Retrieved from Dissertation Abstracts International. (79-1, 829).

Campbell, P. S. (1990). Crosscultural perspectives of musical creativity. *Music Educators Journal, 76*(9), 43–46. doi: 10.2307/3401077

Campbell, P. S. (1991). Unveiling the mysteries of musical spontaneity. *Music Educators Journal, 78*(4), 21–24.

Campbell, D. T., & Fiske, D. W. (1959). Convergent and discriminant validation by the multitrait-multimethod matrix. *Psychological Bulletin, 56*(2), 81–105.

Chase, M. P. (1988). *Improvisation: Music from the inside out*. Berkeley, CA: Creative Arts Book Company. doi: 10.2307/3398332

Coker, J. (1964). *Improvising jazz*. Englewood Cliffs, NJ: Prentice-Hall.

Dale, B. J., Jacob, G., & Anson, H. V. (1940). *Harmony, counterpoint, improvisation: Book II.* London, UK: Novello and Company.

Damron, B. L. (1973). *Developing and evaluating a self-instructed sequence in jazz improvisation* (Doctoral dissertation). Retrieved from Dissertation Abstracts International (35, 1141A).

Dean, R. (1989). *Creative improvisation: Jazz, contemporary music and beyond.* Milton Keynes, UK: Open University Press.

Department of Education and Science. (1990). *Music from 5 to 16: Curriculum matters 4.* London, UK: Her Majesty's Stationery Office.

Dickinson, P. (1964b). Improvisation 2: Interval and melodic pattern. *Musical Times, 105,* 377–378.

Dickinson, P. (1964a). Improvisation 3: Simple accompaniments and chords. *Musical Times, 105,* 538–539.

Dickinson, P. (1964b). Improvisation 5: Design. *Musical Times, 105,* 688–690.

Dickinson, P. (1964c). Improvisation 4: Rhythm and texture. *Musical Times, 105,* 612–614.

Flohr, J. W. (1979). *Musical improvisation behavior of young children* (Unpublished doctoral dissertation). University of Illinois, Urbana-Champaign, IL.

Frackenpohl, A. (1985). *Harmonization at the piano* (5th ed.). Dubuque, IA: Wm. C. Brown.

Frazee, J. (1987). *Discovering Orff: A curriculum for music teachers.* New York, NY: Schott.

Froseth, J., & Blaser, A. (1980). *Studies in creative musicianship: Ear training for musical improvisation: Levels 1 & 2.* Chicago, IL: GIA Publications.

Gorder, W. D. (1976). *An investigation of divergent production abilities as constructs of musical creativity* (Unpublished doctoral dissertation). University of Illinois, Urbana-Champaign, IL.

Gorder, W. D. (1980). Divergent production abilities as constructs of musical creativity. *Journal of Research in Music Education, 28*(1), 34–42. doi: 10.2307/3345051

Gordon, E. E. (1989). *Learning sequences in music.* Chicago, IL: GIA Publications.

Guilford, J. P. (1967). *The nature of human intelligence.* New York, NY: McGraw-Hill.

Guilford, J. P., & Hoepfner, R. (1971). *The analysis of intelligence.* New York, NY: McGraw-Hill.

Hargreaves, D. J., Cork, C. A., & Setton, T. (1990). Cognitive strategies in jazz improvisation: An exploratory study. *Canadian Music Educator: Research Edition, Special ISME Research Edition, 33,* 47–54.

Harvey, E. (1988). *Jazz in the classroom: Practical sessions in jazz and improvisation.* London, UK: Boosey & Hawkes.

Hunt, R. (1968). *Extemporization for music students.* London, UK: Oxford University Press.

Judy, S. (1990). Making music for the joy of it: Enhancing creativity, skills, and musical confidence. Los Angeles, CA: Jeremy P. Tarcher, Inc.

Kratus, J. (1990). Structuring the music curriculum for creative learning. *Music Educators Journal, 76*(9), 33–37. doi: 10.2307/3401075

McDaniel, W. T. (1974). *Differences in music achievement, musical experience, and background between jazz improvising musicians and non-improvising musicians at the freshman and sophomore college levels* (Doctoral dissertation). Retrieved from University Microfilms International. (75-13794).

McPherson, G. E. (1993). *Factors and abilities influencing the development of visual, aural and creative performance skills in music and their educational implications* (Doctoral dissertation). Retrieved from Dissertation Abstracts International. (54/04-A, 1277).

McPherson, G. E. (1995). The assessment of musical performance: Development and validation of five new measures. *Psychology of Music, 23,* 142–161. doi: 10.1177/0305735695232003

McPherson, G. E. (2005). From child to musician: Skill development during the beginning stages of learning an instrument. *Psychology of Music, 33*(1), 5–35. doi: 10.1177/0305735605048012

McPherson, G. E., Davidson, J., & Faulkner, R. (2012). *Music in our lives: Rethinking musical ability, development and identity.* Oxford, UK: Oxford University Press.

Moore, J. L. S. (1990). Strategies for fostering creative thinking. *Music Educators Journal, 76*(9), 38–42. doi: 10.2307/3401076

Nicholls, F., & Tobin, J. R. (1937). *Adventures in improvisation.* London, UK: Joseph Williams.

Partchey, K. C. (1973). *The effects of feedback, models, and repetition on the ability to improvise melodies* (Unpublished doctoral dissertation). Pennsylvania State University, State College, PA.

Pfenninger, R. C. (1990). *The development and validation of three rating scales for the objective measurement of jazz improvisation achievement* (Unpublished doctoral dissertation). Temple University, Philadelphia, PA.

Pressing, J. (1988). Improvisation: Methods and models. In J. Sloboda (Ed.), *Generative processes in music* (pp. 128–178). New York, NY: Oxford University Press.

Priest, P. (1985, March). Playing by ear. *Music Teacher, 64*(3), 10–11.

Priest, P. (1988). *Playing by ear: An investigation of the phenomenon and of its potential for instrumental learning as part of music education* (Unpublished masters thesis). University of London, London, UK.

Priest, P. (1989). Playing by ear: Its nature and application to instrumental learning. *British Journal of Music Education, 6,* 173–191.

Rosfeld, M. D. (1989). *The development of a series of instructional units for teaching improvisational principles to pianists* (Unpublished doctoral dissertation). University of Oklahoma, Norman, OK.

Rowley, A. (1955). *Extemporization: A treatise for organists.* New York, NY: Mills Music.

Sawyer, F. J., (1923). *Extemporization.* London, UK: Novello.

Schilling, R. (1989). *The construction and validation of rating scales for the objective measurement of jazz improvisation achievement.* Pennsylvania Music Educators Association, May.

Schleuter, S. L. (1984). A sound approach to teaching instrumentalists: Application of content and learning sequences. Kent, OH: The Kent State University Press.

Schlieder, F. (1927). *Lyric composition through improvisation.* Boston, MA: C.C. Birchard.

Simpson, K. (1963). *Keyboard harmony and improvisation.* London, UK: Alfred Lengnick.

Stubington, H. (1940). *Practical extemporization.* London, UK: The Epworth Press.

Swanwick, K., & Tillman, J. (1986). A sequence of musical development: A study of children's compositions. *British Journal of Music Education, 3,* 305–339.

Texter, M. (1979). *Musicianship in the beginning instrumental class.* Reston, VA: Music Educators National Conference.

Thackray, R. M. (1968). *Creative music in education.* London, UK: Novello.

Thackray, R. M. (1978). *Aural awakening.* Perth, Western Australia: University of Western Australia Press.

Torrance, E. (1966). *Norms-technical manual: Torrance tests of creative thinking.* Bensenville, IL: Scholastic Testing Service.

Vaughan, M. M. (1971). *Music as model and metaphor in the cultivation and measurement of creative behavior in children* (Unpublished doctoral dissertation). University of Georgia, Athens, GA.

Webster, P. R. (1977). *A factor of intellect approach to creative thinking in music* (Unpublished doctoral dissertation). University of Rochester, Rochester, NY.

Webster, P. R. (1979). Relationship between creative behavior in music and selected variables as measured in high school students. *Journal of Research in Music Education, 27*, 227–242. doi: 10.2307/3344710

Webster, P. R. (1983a). *Refinement of a measure of musical imagination in young children and a comparison to aspects of musical aptitude.* Paper presented at the Armington Symposium, Case Western Reserve University, Cleveland, OH.

Webster, P. R. (1983b). An assessment of musical imagination in young children. In P. Thomas Tallirico (Ed.), *Contributions to the symposium 83: The Bowling Green State University symposium on teaching and research.* Bowling Green, OH: Bowling Green State University.

Webster, P. R. (1989). Creative thinking in music: The assessment question. In J. W. Richmond (Ed.), *The proceedings of the Suncoast Music Education Forum on Creativity* (pp. 40–74). Tampa, FL: University of South Florida.

Whittlich, G. E., & Martin, D. S. (1989). *Tonal harmony for the keyboard.* New York, NY: Schirmer Books.

Wunsch, I. G. (1972, June/July). Improvisation...how? *The American Music Teacher 21*(6), 22–23.

CHAPTER 26

ASSESSMENT OF CREATIVE POTENTIAL IN MUSIC

PETER R. WEBSTER

> Creativity is inventing, experimenting, growing, taking risks, breaking rules, making mistakes and having fun.
>
> —May Lou Cook, Peace Activist

Millions of words have been written about creativity in the professional and popular literature over the years. Its importance for our well-being—our very core as humans—seems undeniable, and its positive effect on a more peaceful, equitable, and productive future can hardly be questioned for the global stage. Equally compelling to many is the importance of creative work as part of the educational experience of our children, as was noted by Gardner over 20 years ago (1991) and most recently by Robinson (Robinson, 2011; Robinson & Aronica, 2016).

Assuming that there are multiple ways of knowing (Eisner, 1987), it follows that strong arts programs in schools provide important opportunities to celebrate creative thinking somewhat differently than other curricular domains such as science, technology, engineering, and mathematics (STEM disciplines). There is no denying that STEM-focused activity requires its own kind of creative work in education, but it is the arts and certainly music that should provide rich experiences distinctly human and deeply meaningful for today's youth.

But an important question is how well music educators understand student creativeness in music, its potential and its various forms of achievement. In her keynote address to a recent symposium on assessment, Hickey noted the current awareness of creativity's importance in and outside of schooling, but pointed toward a lack of imaginative music teaching that can lead to poor assessment of creative work (2013). For example, the inclusion of teacher-centered composition and improvisation activities that are designed more as music theory exercises and less as opportunities for growth in personal or group creative thinking in sound is problematic. Understanding students' creative potential and how to encourage comprehensive creative growth in multiple music experiences (performance, composition, listening) are important goals for excellent teaching practice. This is difficult and complicated work, but doable given our emerging understanding of creative thinking in general and in music specifically.

This chapter begins with an overview of important concepts from both the general scholarship and from music studies. The intent is to help clarify important aspects that influence the assessment question in order to create a platform for future research and practice. This is followed by a summary of the work devoted to the development of assessment tools that identify creative music potential in younger children and then ends with some recommendations for future work. The chapter does not attempt a comprehensive summary of all assessment approaches to creative work in music; other chapters in this Handbook may be combined with this one to provide a complete overview.

Important Concepts in the General Literature and in Music

It is natural for a Handbook such as this one to concern itself with the assessment of creative potential in music—to wonder about matters of definition, techniques for identification, and acceptable ways to record student growth.[1]

What do we really know about both the topic of creative potential in general and more specifically in music? Despite the complexity of this topic and attending controversies and disagreements, we know a great deal. A credible literature—particularly in psychology, sociology, neurology, and the arts—has been developing since the mid-20th century that helps to explain creative work and to demystify what was once seen as inexplicable.[2] Study of creativeness in the music literature is no exception to this trend and has grown steadily in both number and quality in the last decades. Happily, some of the most compelling literature about the assessment of creative work in music has come from music education scholars (Barbot & Webster, 2018 also see reviews by; Burnard, 2012; Hickey, 2002; Rowher, 1997; Running, 2008; and Webster, 1992).

Questions of Definition: "Creativity" and "Creative Potential"

Creativity

Before much progress can be made in the assessment of creative potential, especially in the context of music teaching and learning, some understanding of what is being measured is essential. Most agree that the term "creativity" is an abstract construct whose definition is complicated by circumstance and social context. Many working definitions consider it an ability to produce ideas or objects that demonstrate a combination of novelty and appropriateness or purposefulness. One attractive approach to definition has been offered by Plunker, Beghetto, and Dow (2004). After noting many myths about creativity and its study and after a careful analysis of past work that attempted to define the construct, Plunker and his colleagues have suggested that creativity "is the interaction among aptitude, process, and environment by which an individual or group produces a perceptible product that is both novel and useful as defined within a social context" (p. 90).

There are many parts to this definition that hold special promise for research in music teaching and learning. The first is the notion of *aptitude*, which the authors felt is influenced in part by ability (either learned or innate), attitude, and motivation. For them, aptitude is not static but dynamic and influenced by experience. Much of the assessment work in music with more naïve subjects (described later) has this as a conceptual base.

Process is stressed because much of the literature argues for personal traits (aptitude[s] and personality factors) that provide an affordance for approaching problem-solving and finding, and other process-centered dynamics. This is developed more completely in this chapter.

Environment is featured in the Plunker, Beghetto, and Dow definition because of the mounting evidence that the creative act is influenced by social context, including influences of gender, peers, family, and many other variables that relate to the setting around the creator. A careful reading of other authors in this *Handbook* that speak to the importance of environment and social context will testify to this.[3]

Endorsement of the *interaction* between (1) aptitude (as broadly defined), (2) process that celebrates aptitudes and personality factors, and (3) environment helps to debunk many of the myths about creativity as unteachable, static (one either has it or not), or too mysterious to be studied. This provides a powerful basis for much of the research on both creative potential and achievement in music. It also helps to ground the idea of "creative thinking" (Webster, 1990), since the sum total of this interaction leads actively to the creation of a product.

The stress placed in the definition on a *perceptible product* produced by an *individual or group* places the emphasis on the need for a *result* that can be assessed in one way or another. Musical creativity cannot be truly understood without a tangible product (Webster, 1987b, 1990). This works well for creative work in music performance (both music of others and improvisation) and composition but is more difficult (but not impossible) for music listening. Happily, the work relating to the new National Core Arts Standards (Schuler, Norgaard, & Blakeslee, 2014) welcomes creative teaching strategies and products that can be evaluated in different ways.[4]

Novelty (or some prefer "originality") is widely used in most definitions in the literature. As noted below, however, novelty takes on different contexts given the creator's level of creative development.

Finally, the notion of *useful* (some prefer "appropriate") in a social context is perhaps more troublesome to some and also depends greatly on the experience level of the creator and the field of accomplishments. The notion of usefulness and appropriateness in social context is grounded in Csikszentmihalyi's systems approach (1988) that features the person in context with a domain and a field. This tends to work especially well with the study of eminent creators; but even in well-defined domains with field experts doing the assessment, a novel product may be considered bizarre at one point in time but may become ground-breaking later as history unfolds.[5] Despite these complexities, it remains possible to use the notions of novelty and usefulness as a frame for specified approaches to assessment with expert judges.

Creative Potential

Efforts to study creativeness in music are sometimes confused by the goals of assessment and the roles they play in research and practice. For example, researchers and teachers interested in monitoring the growth of creative ability in composition may ask experts to evaluate compositions consensually to determine the level of the creative product. Improvisations may be evaluated by a series of rubrics or checklists to determine the quality of the creative playing or singing. As part of portfolio work, performances of notated music might be compared for differences over time for growth in creative interpretation. Retrospective verbal descriptions of one's listening evaluations or the study of graphic or movement representations during listening might be compared for growth in creative thinking during listening. Each of these uses of assessment is an important example of work that focuses on the *achievement* of student work and is likely to be contextually related to experiments or descriptions of teaching practice.

Approaches to the assessment of creative *potential* or aptitude are somewhat different. The intent is to identify the likelihood of overall creative capacity in general. Such work may well include listening, composition, or performance tasks, but the purpose is not to function as an indicator of comparative achievement per se. Barbot, Besançon, and Lubart (2015) provide the following as further description of creative potential based on research and theory to date:

> it is increasingly acknowledged that creative potential represents simultaneously a domain-general ability (set of resources that is involved in the creative work across domains, regardless of the specific nature of the task), a set of domain-specific abilities (domain-relevant resources that are needed across creative tasks within a particular domain), and a set of task-relevant abilities (resources that are uniquely associated with a given creative outlet of interest.)   (p. 3)

It should be noted that such a focus on the personal characteristics of individuals is important for the understanding of personal creativeness and is a strong partner to the more current focus on the role of social context that dominates much of the literature in music education today.

Naïve Versus Expert

In addition to clarity of definition, a second concept of importance that is not always addressed adequately in the music teaching literature is the matter of creative experience level of individuals. Clapham (2011) noted:

> The conceptual definition of creativity must be operationalized, or expressed in observable terms, in order to develop creativity assessment techniques. Both the purpose of assessment and the theoretical perspective of the researcher affect how a construct is operationalized. Assessing creative potential in children, for example, requires a different measurement approach than evaluating the creative contributions of eminent historical figures. Because of the multitude of purposes for which creativity assessment might be used, a wide array of measurement techniques have been developed. (p. 459)

As in much of education discourse on adult/child difference, acknowledgment of the distinction between more naïve creative work versus work by expert creators is of critical concern for assessment. The often-referenced "Big-C/Little-C" comparison, attributed by Merrotsy (2013) to Stein (1987), has been refined by Kaufman and Beghetto (2009) to include a least two other levels: Mini-C and Pro-C. Big-C is well represented in the literature, with studies, for example, by Simonton (1994) and Gardner (1993). However, placing all other levels of creative work that might lead to this kind of eminence into only one Little-C category seems counterproductive, especially in terms of pedagogy and assessment.

According to Kaufman and Beghetto and to other researchers in the general literature, it might be wiser to consider a more nuanced approach to levels. Designating a base level of creative work, such as Mini-C, that might lead to more refined and highly practiced levels such as Little-C and Pro-C; thus, problems of definition and educational practice might be improved. For example, Mini-C creative work in music may be more correctly associated with elementary and some secondary school endeavors—the kind of creativity of most interest to a number of professionals reading this Handbook. According to Kaufman and Beghetto, "including [M]ini-[C] in conceptions of creativity helps bring a level of specificity necessary to ensure that the creative potential of children is nurtured (rather than overlooked)." (p. 3)

To be more specific in terms of music composition and improvisation,[6] a student experimenting with creative gestures while crafting a music product may demonstrate significant Mini-C ability, which can be studied more formally. Examples of assessment for these students might be researcher- or teacher-designed tasks in the form of a more standardized battery that could be studied by experts in the field. More qualitative work that features microgenetic techniques (Flynn, Pine, & Lewis, 2006) such as video and audio data analyses and self-reporting (immediate or retrospective) data to capture more subtle developmental changes could also play an important role. Judgments such as these about levels of Mini-C creativeness could play a critical role in the early identification of creative potential, especially in music.

Further, an older student, perhaps in high school, might have advanced to more sophisticated work with acoustic or computer-based technology—demonstrating a more developed level of craftsmanship and aesthetic sensitivity while also exhibiting novelty and usefulness. This person might be considered more at the Little-C level. Such work might have gone well beyond Mini-C, but still be relatively naïve when compared to professionals. Examples of assessment with this level of creativity might include researcher- or teacher-designed tasks and include peer-based assessment or self-assessment and include the use of rating scales and rubrics. Again, studies that are based on a more qualitative observation of processes might be appropriate. Judgments such as these about levels of Little-C creativeness may be considered more as indicators of achievement as well as potential, since older students would have had more time to develop more sophisticated skills and knowledge about music. It is during this developmental level that the distinction between aptitude and achievement becomes blurred.

Still more creative achievement might come later in life as an accomplished composer or performer as an adult—achieving at a creative level akin to what might be considered Pro-C. This level would be appropriate if considering the creative accomplishment of the many adult composers or improvisers engaged in creative work today. Big-C, then, would be appropriately reserved for those composers or improvisers whose work is widely regarded by the field as eminent. Often the decision of eminence is based on the body of work as significantly advancing a field of study. Assessment strategies for both Pro-C and Big-C are almost exclusively accomplished by experts in the field, although some methodologies that are based on historiometrics apply (Simonton, 1994).

Interestingly, progress has been made within the music education literature in assessment of composition and improvisation with Mini-C and Little-C but less so with Pro-C. As noted in the conclusion of this chapter, continued work across all levels of creative development is needed not only for music composition and improvisation but also for the performance of others' music and for music listening.

Product, Process, Person, and Place

In more general terms, a third concept of the study of creativity that has great implications for assessment is focus on *what* is being studied. The classic four P's categorization of research approach, attributed to Rhodes (1961), is noted consistently in one way or another in the major general texts about creativity (Amabile, 1996; Csikszentmihalyi, 1996; Davis, 1993; Gardner, 1993; Sawyer, 2012; Simonton, 1994; Weisberg, 1993).

Similar foci of effort can be noted in the music teaching and learning literature in the last several decades. The vast majority of work has centered on *products* such as compositions and improvisations and on the *processes* that creators follow in creative work. In terms of products, exemplary studies from the music literature abound and include the work of Madura (1996), Eisenberg and Thompson (2003), and Smith (2009) for jazz improvisation; McPherson (see this volume) for general improvisation; Dunn (1997) for music listening; and Hickey (1999), Priest (2001), Leung, Wan, and Lee (2009), Mellor (2008), and Menard (2015) for music composition. Carefully constructed rating scales, checklists, rubrics, and portfolios have been used effectively. Consensual assessment techniques popularized by Amabile (1982, 1996) and used by many researchers to study the achievement of creative work have been shown to be especially effective (see Hickey, 2001, for important work in composition assessment).

For the *process* focus, works by Auh and Walker (1999), Barrett (1996), Bennett (1976), Folkestad, Hargreaves, and Lindström (1998), Hennessey (1994), Kennedy (2002), Kratus (1989, 1994), Mills (2009), and Seddon and O'Neill (2003) are all noteworthy. Process studies such as those reported by Stauffer (2001, 2002) that are qualitative and developmental in nature are exemplary examples of microgenetic approaches.

Still other work on product and process, particularly with older subjects, include Clarke's work (2005) on musical performance creativeness, Hickey's work on free improvisation (Hickey 2009, 2015), Norgaard's studies (2011, 2016) of improvisational thinking with jazz performers, and very recent neuroscience work on improvisation (Beaty, 2015). These studies are intriguing and may be harbingers for future discovery.

The consideration of *place*, or the surrounding environment of the creator including broad issues of sociocultural context, has grown steadily in recent years. Work by Burnard (this volume, 2012) and Wiggins (2015) are noteworthy.

The study of *person* in terms of music and cognitive abilities has centered on the development of aptitude-like measures of music creative potential and is reviewed in some depth in the second section of this chapter. Interestingly, personality characteristics—an important part of the general creativity for the person—has not been the focus of extensive work in music education scholarship.

Measures of Creativity and Divergent Thinking Tests

Finally, an important part of the modern history of general creativity study, at least since the 1950s, has been the focus on individual difference and the prediction of creative potential within people using assessment measures (see Hocevar & Bachelor, 1989, for one review). Approaches have varied from various kinds of self-reports and lists of personal characteristics and achievements to measures of remote association between words that share characteristics. Runco and Prizker (2013) offer a summary of these approaches and provide a useful summary table of available measures that are more commonly encountered in the literature.

Of the measures in this listing, the most pervasive in practice for prediction of future creative work are those that use the concept of divergent thinking—tasks that seek multiple possible solutions to given problem. This is opposed to more convergent tasks that tend to commonly be found in achievement and intelligence testing.

The history of the use of divergent test items was enriched conceptually by the work of J. Paul Guilford. Guilford is known not only for his famous presidential keynote address (1950) to the American Psychological Association that is credited with a new energy among psychologists to study creativity, but also for his structure of intellect model (Guilford, 1967) that proposed expanding notions of "intelligence" to include a wider number of factors that were a function of cognitive operations (cognition, memory, *divergent* production, *convergent* production, evaluation), content fields (behavioral, semantic, symbolic, auditory, visual) and resultant products (units, classes, relations, systems, transformations, and implications).[7]

Guilford experimented with various forms of divergent and convergent testing based on his model, but it was E. Paul Torrance that authored the famous paper and pencil measures titled the Torrance Tests of Creative Thinking (1974, 2008), which are still in use today. Various versions are available, including one using word responses (verbal) and one with drawing content (figural). The measures are paper and pencil tests that are timed and are administered in a standardized format. The verbal version asks subjects of various ages to consider questions about an image, suggest causes and consequences of a pictured action, provide unusual uses of objects, and other types of prompts that elicit written responses. Results are scored—on defined factors of fluency (number of responses), flexibility (responses in different categories), originality, and elaboration—by an experienced rater guided by a manual. The figural version asks for figure completion and other drawing tasks. Most recent versions of the measures with slightly altered scoring criteria are available from the Scholastic Testing Service (STS),[8] which offers professional scoring services.

This classic approach to divergent thinking tasks, and others like it, were conceived as a way to index potential creative thinking ability not consistently measured by other tools such as intelligence test batteries. Scholarly reviews of the Torrance measures are mixed despite acceptable psychometric properties for aggregate samples. Some scholars agree that there is usefulness to the measures (Barron & Harrington, 1981), especially if used in conjunction with other evidence for identifying creative potential for younger subjects, however the consensus is that divergent thinking tests of this sort used alone are likely not effective in predicting long-term creative achievement in adults. Sawyer (2012) and other scholars advise caution in using these tests as a primary predictor. As Sawyer states, "Creative achievement requires a complex combination of DT, convergent thinking, critical evaluation, and other abilities, and creative people are good at switching back and forth at different points in the creative process" (2012, p. 53).

When applied to music, divergent tasks that employ music content (e.g., composition and improvisation activities) and that use some of the same type of factors for scoring have been an attractive approach. Often, more convergent-like factors for scoring of musical quality are used together with divergent factors.

APPROACHES TO THE ASSESSMENT OF CREATIVE POTENTIAL IN MUSIC WITH YOUNGER CHILDREN

With the review of these important assessment concepts as a foundation, we now consider more focused work on music aptitude. Notions that center on definition, level of creative work, focus on what is being measured, and the long history of divergent and convergent thinking research should set the context for what follows.

Early Approaches

Tarratus (1964), in a study with college music students, hypothesized that creative ability in music might be best studied with Guilford-like measures of divergent thinking (similar to Torrance's work described previously) with nonmusical tasks. Although some relationships were found between these measures and musical achievement in graduate students in jazz and composition, generally the non-music-based creative thinking measures did not correlate in a statistically significant way with music achievement. Roderick (1965) and Simpson (1969) also reported projects using nonmusic tests of creative thinking and music students and found similar low correlations.[9] A need clearly existed for a music-based measure of creative thinking.

As noted earlier, much if not all of the early work on the development of creativity assessment in music has been done by music education scholars and influenced by much of the general creativity assessment work done in psychology in the second half of the 20th century. Webster (1992) summarized this work in some detail, but highlights are included here.

In a series of studies from 1971 to 1977, Vaughan was among the first to create a measure of creative thinking in music using musical tasks based on general creativity testing principles at the time. The best description of the measure can be found in the author's dissertation (Vaughan, 1971, 1977). Subjects (elementary-aged children) were asked to improvise (1) rhythm patterns as a response to a given stimulus, (2) melody patterns in a similar manner, and (3) a piece showing how the subject felt during a thunderstorm. Instruments used were simple bells and percussion instruments. A panel of judges used a scoring scheme to evaluate factors of musical fluency, rhythmic security, and ideation. Data on interrater reliability and factor analytic properties of the measure were reported.

Also working with younger children, Baltzer published two studies (1988, 1990) that used the Wang Measures of Creativity in Sound and Music (MCSM). The measures consist of four activities that provide data on musical fluency and imagination. In the first activity children are asked to produce as many different examples of steady beat as possible using plastic containers with lids. Rhythm instruments are then used to imitate sounds related to events like a thunderstorm, a giant walking, a horse in motion, and others. A third activity asks children to demonstrate ostinatos, and a final set of tasks ask the children to move in appropriate ways to six selections of recorded music. Interrater reliability was high, and factor analytic data revealed underlying factors of fluency and imagination. Concurrent validity found by correlations with teacher's ratings of creative thinking in music were low, but this may been caused by teachers' inability to assess creativeness as a construct at the time of testing.

Both Webster (1979) and Gorder (1980) completed studies assessing high school–aged students using measurement approaches based on early divergent thinking approaches. Both studies did not have the construction of a measure of creative thinking potential in music as the main objective, but both researchers followed procedures for validation, and both measures are reported in detail in their respective dissertations for use by others.

Webster (1979) worked with 77 high school students to complete three sets of tasks related to improvisation, composition, and music analysis. The improvisation set included live (and recorded for later study) performances with tone bells that featured improvisations on a simple folk tune followed by the creation of an original song with the bells. The composition work was a take-home set of skeletal notation guides that presented subjects with an outline of a short musical phrase for triangle and some other instrument or voice parts. Reference points in the phrase were indicated by note heads, and subjects could use traditional or invented musical notation to complete the phrase. A number of these phrases were included and ranged from more specific reference points to more free structures. The analysis tasks (also designed for take-home work) asked the subjects to make as many imaginative and original observations as possible about the structure and design of a 14-measure melody extracted from Volume 1 of Bartok's *Mikrokosmos*. Other tasks in the set included duets by Bartok and Babbit. The Babbit work was a 12-tone composition constructed from two hexachords with a number of permutations and text written as a retrograde that makes sense when read in either direction. Scoring was based on notions of musical fluency, flexibility, originality, and elaboration. Interrater reliability was acceptable, and content validity was established by a panel of experts.

Gorder's instrument, Measures of Musical Divergent Production (MMDP), was improvisation-based. Working with 81 junior and senior high school students drawn at random from a pool of 542 potential subjects, participants were asked to improvise in four tasks either using their own instruments or by whistling or singing. Similar to Webster's work, the music base was represented by skeletal music notation and subjects were asked to improvise using the motives, note heads, or contour markings as guides. The approach taken for evaluation used a music content checklist related to melody, rhythm, tempo, style, dynamics, timbre, expressive devices, and form. Tasks were scored for fluency (number of phrases), flexibility (shifts of content character), elaboration (content beyond minimal expected), originality (unusual content), and quality (musical appeal). A panel of experts validated the measure, and interrater reliability for a sample of the data were found to be acceptable. Factor analysis also helped to establish construct validity.

Both Webster and Gorder, working independently without the knowledge of the others' work, demonstrated that the study of musically based tasks using creative thinking skills was possible. Both studies used the measures' scores to study relationship to other variables of interest. Correlations of creative thinking scores in music with traditional music aptitude and general intelligence measures were low and not generally statistically significant—a finding that has been shown repeatedly in research on creative thinking in music and in the general literature.

More Recent Developments

Measure of Creative Thinking in Music, Version II (MCTM-II).

Webster's Measure of Creative Thinking in Music (MCTM-II) (1994) is perhaps the most widely used measure of its type among scholars working in music education. It is freely distributed and actively supported. It grows out of a desire to provide a music-based assessment tool for potential creative ability in music. Developed over a period of 12 years (1982–1994), the measure has seen two versions and is now being revised a third time with more varied approaches to visual stimuli and sound production (forthcoming). The first published description (Webster, 1983) was supported in part by a grant from the Charles Rieley Armington Research Program on Values in Children at Case Western Reserve University in Cleveland. It was refined in its current version 4 years later (Webster, 1987a) and made available for free distribution in 1994.

It differs somewhat from earlier work in the following ways:

- It is designed for children, ages 6–10, with no expectation for formal musical experience and was meant to function as an aptitude instrument and not necessarily a measure of creative achievement.[10]
- Although inspired by the divergent thinking research in the general literature, it uses scoring factors that reflect both divergent and convergent thinking in the construction of quasi-improvised products.
- Video recording of improvised performances are rated both by a single researcher (flexibility and extensiveness) and a panel of judges (originality and syntax).
- Unlike typical consensual assessment approaches, the panel of judges is offered guidelines in the assessment of factors and asked to provide short explanations of why very high rankings are made. Also judges are encouraged to view all the subjects' creative work once before submitting ratings in order to calibrate judgments for the sample.
- Scoring factors are converted to standard scores and summed for a cumulative score.
- Subjects use three easily-played, informal sound sources of differing timbre that are capable of creating sounds that are capable of ranges from high to low, fast to slow, loud to soft. Voice is one of the sound sources.
- To begin the measure, a set of exploratory tasks is used that familiarize the subject with the sound sources and how they are played.
- Tasks start with very short time requirements and then progress to the creation of quasi-improvisatory compositions that are longer and allow more complex use of sound sources.
- Subjects are given time to "think about" their quasi-improvisatory compositions before performing them.
- Subjects are offered graphic depictions as prompts, which researchers can alter for their purposes.

A complete description of MCTM-II is available from several published sources (Webster, 1987b, 1992, 1994). The 1994 online distribution (available from http://www.peterrwebster.com/) contains a complete set of administration guidelines, supportive papers on validation, and a sample video clip.

There are 10 scored tasks, divided into three parts. Certain tasks have subjects enter into a question and answer dialogue with a set of five temple blocks, while other activities involve the creation of sound pieces with a round, soft ball and the piano or with the voice using a slightly amplified (echo-enhanced) microphone and speaker. As the measure progresses, subjects are invited to combine sound sources in multiple ways. Final tasks are more demanding and invite subjects to create a whole piece with a beginning, middle, and end. Time is always given to the subject to think about their music before they create and they are always encouraged to use sounds that are high and low, fast and slow, and loud and soft. Subjects are not given any time limits for creative work; however, a typical length of time for the full set of tasks is 30 minutes.

The scoring of the video recordings involves both objective and subjective techniques. The four scoring factors that are used across the tasks in different ways include (1) musical extensiveness—the amount of clock time in seconds; (2) musical flexibility—the use of the full ranges of high/low, loud/soft, and fast/slow; (3) musical originality—the extent to which the response is unusual or unique in musical terms and in the manner of performance; and (4) musical syntax—the extent to which the response is inherently logical and makes musical sense. Extensiveness and flexibility are measured objectively (guidelines given) and originality and syntax are more subjectively evaluated by a panel of judges.

Test-retest reliability and internal reliability are reported in two unpublished papers presented at professional conferences in 1988 and 1990. These papers are included in the test materials for download. Results were encouraging, with correlations in the .60 and .70 range. Also studied were the performance of two matched sets of students with no formal music background and some formal background in the form of Suzuki and Dalcroze instruction. Interestingly, students with music background did significantly less well with the originality factor while other factors seemed similar. No effects by gender were noted in total scores; but as expected, effects by grade level were noted with combined data sets from multiple studies, with older subjects improving with age. Factor analytic results supported two strong factors, one for extensiveness/flexibility and one for originality and syntax.

Independent Research Studies Using MCTM-II

The reference section of this chapter contains a listing of those research studies that have used MCTM-II as part of research work. It is not possible here to review each of these studies in detail, but this section offers a short description of how the MCTM-II was used and what populations have been studied and summarizes general findings. Table 26.1 provides a summary of the independent use of the measure since 1985.

Of the 17 published studies identified since 1985, seven used MCTM-II as part of correlation studies, seven used the measure as some sort of dependent variable in experimental work, and others used it more descriptively or in the study of reliability. The vast majority of work has centered on subjects younger that 14 years of age, including some preschool subjects. In many of the studies, internal reliability and interrater reliability were examined and shown to be good to excellent.

External validity in the form of comparisons to rated process and product scores on creative work is mixed; the most encouraging findings are for improvisatory evidence of various kinds and less so for compositional products. No studies were identified that

Table 26.1 Use of MCTM-II in Independent Research Studies

Study Author	MCTM-II use in design	Subjects	Major variables of interest in addition to creative thinking in music
Swanner (1985)	Correlation	N = 69, 3rd graders	Personality, gender, music aptitude, intelligence
Schmidt/Sinor (1986)	Correlation	N = 47, 2nd graders	Cognitive style, music aptitude, gender
Baltzer (1990)	Correlation	N = 90, 1st, 2nd, 3rd graders	Age, gender, music achievement, academic achievement
Wolfe/Linden (1991)	Correlation	N = 40, 3rd grade	Intrinsic motivation, music aptitude
Racana (1991)	Pre-post Test	4th graders	Effect of computer-based music lessons
Amchin (1995)	Pre-post Test	N = 129, 4th, 5th graders	Student and teacher interactions
Hickey (1995)	Correlation	N = 21, 4th, 5th graders	Compositional process, teacher ratings, musical composition quality
Hagedorn (1997)	Descriptive	N = 20, 1st, 2nd, 4th, 5th graders	Hearing-challenged vs. hearing students, family environment, gender
Fung (1997)	Post test	N = 66, 1st, 2nd graders	Effect on exposure to sound exploration program
Boehm (1999)	Pre-post test	N = 39, 1st graders	Effect of compositional teaching approach (invented notation), test of visual contours, music aptitude, music background, music achievement
Dingle (2006)	Correlation	N = 90, 7th, 8th graders	Music aptitude
Koutsoupidou (2008, 2009)	Post test	N = 25, 1st graders (6-year-olds)	Effect of teaching style that included music improvisation in teaching
Baek (2009)	Pre-post test	N = 39, 4- and 5-year-olds	Effect of picture books with creative music activities, music aptitude, reading ability
Yannon (2011)		N = 75, 5th graders	Instructional style (algorithmic/heuristic) music aptitude, composition ratings
Dingle (2014)	Reliability assessment	N = 90, 7th, 8th graders	Grade level
Crawford (2016)	Post test	N = 48, 3rd, 5th graders	Effect of computer-mediated vs. acoustic composition experience, music aptitude, composition process ratings, grade, gender
Roman (2016)	Correlation	N = 30, college-level	Relationship between skills and enabling conditions in university students in visual arts

have considered the measure to relate to creative performance or music listening. No predictive validity studies have been identified.

Nearly all studies show positive but low (statistically nonsignificant) relationships between scores on MCTM-II and convergent music aptitude measures. This is an expected finding, since approaches to measuring music aptitude are often based on the accurate perception of tonal and/or rhythmic pattern comparisons. One would expect these skills to be part of any creative ability set, but far from functioning as adequate predictive tools for musical creativity. Most researchers have found no gender differences for total scores derived from MCTM-II, however some have noted differences in favor of males on certain subscores.

Music Expression Test

An additional measure for creative music potential has been developed in recent years by researchers in psychology. The Music Expression Test (MET) (Barbot & Lubart, 2012) uses a multimethod approach by combining divergent production skills as used in measures like MTCM-II with process and product analysis of music composition in ways similar to the music literature noted earlier. Conceptually, MET is designed using established models in music (e.g., Webster, 1990) and uses a framework based on domain-specific assessment of potential for creativity as developed by Lubart, Besançon, & Barbot, (2011) and Barbot, Besançon, & Lubart, (2016).[11]

Intended for children, adolescents, and adults with little previous music performance or composition experience, the measure is administered individually and is designed in four stages: free composition, mini-games, composition, and improvisation. Total time for administration is estimated to be 1 hour and is offered individually within a music workshop setting.

The MET uses percussion and melodic instruments of various types for the more divergent tasks and also uses computer-based sequencing software for the creation of music products. Scoring uses a complex system of rater evaluation, which researchers identify as *orientation, structure,* and *function.* Consensual assessment techniques and more defined rating scales are also used for music products in the final stages. Preliminary reliability and validity data are reported and are statistically encouraging. Several parallels between this data and that reported in the music teaching and learning literature are offered (Barbot & Lubart, 2012, pp. 236–240).

The structure and scoring of MET is described in detail by Barbot and Lubart (2012). The measure continues to be used in studies by Barbot and colleagues (B. Barbot, personal communication, July 2015). As MET continues to be developed and used in different studies, it has the potential to be a significant advance in the study of creative potential in music. It seems conceptually sound in its construction, can be administered to a wide age-group, and includes composition and improvisation tasks that use a variety of sound sources including computer-based technology. The MET has received little attention in the music teaching and learning literature to date, despite the fact that it is related to a large part of this work. It is a major advancement in assessment work of this type and deserves serious attention by music education specialists.

New Directions Needed

Some might argue that such care taken to assess creative potential in music is a waste of time. Because of so many ways that students can make music on their own inside and outside of school, why not just let the creativity roll and the geniuses of the music world will "out" themselves without a lot of direction from others? In fact the social context of music making with others makes all this fuss about assessment seem terribly old fashioned and out of step with progressive education. Creativeness is a social construction, and looking inward at individual difference is not that important. We already have far too many tests.

Although these points of view are understandable and perhaps defendable to a point, this line of thinking as the sole approach to the study of creativity assessment and practice is troublesome. Understanding the nature of the developing creative person through every approach possible is time well spent. Research on the assessment of creative potential such as the efforts outlined here needs to continue, and strong partnerships between scholars in music teaching and learning and those in psychology, sociology, and education can be fruitful in understanding the complexity of creative thinking in music. Teaching effectiveness begins with as complete an understanding of the learner as possible, and using diverse ways to gain this understanding seems obvious.

Here are a few closing ideas that might guide researchers and teachers in future directions as they pair the study of musical creativeness within the sociocultural context with studies of individual differences:

- continued trial and development of measures like MCTM-II and MET to embrace domain-specific and domain-general tasks;
- attention to domain-general tasks (Barbot, Besançon, & Lubart, 2015, p. 3) matched with domain-specific tasks in music;
- creation of modern, normative data using music-based measures to help teachers form appropriate instruction and place students in any number of special programs if warranted (see Barbot, Besançon, & Lubart, 2011, for comment on this need);
- pairing of results of this sort with other assessment techniques that evaluate product and process to develop a more nuanced picture;
- as the epigraph that starts this chapter suggests, consideration of personal characteristics of music students (and the teachers that teach them) to include such things as risk tolerance, imagination, cross-domain interests, collaboration skills, and willingness to fail;
- inclusion of multiple music experiences in creative assessment including music listening and the performance of others' music; and
- thinking developmentally from early childhood to the Pro-C/Big-C levels of the adult world, expanding consideration of musical creativeness across a wider range of creative levels and including the role of developing craftsmanship (skill and knowledge of music) and the subtleties of aesthetic awareness in determining patterns of this development.

These closing ideas set a rather ambition agenda for the 21st century and beyond. What is truly exciting about all of this is that such work is consistent with emerging views of contemporary music teaching and learning that expand notions of *why* we teach music, *what* we teach, *how* we teach, *who* we teach it to.

NOTES

1. Several other chapters in this Handbook, especially those by Burnard, Randles, and McPherson, offer still more perspective on this topic and focus more on the assessment of achievement especially for older students and adults.

2. Sawyer (2012) provides a useful review of much literature from fields in and outside of music and includes the names and major accomplishments of key figures from pre-1950 to the present who have contributed to our understanding of the topic.

3. Sawyer (2012) believes this so completely that much of his text is devoted to the explanation of the role of environment and social context in framing our understanding of creativity.

4. See also: http://www.nafme.org/my-classroom/standards/mcas-information-on-taking-part-in-the-field-testing/.

5. Perhaps the most famous example of this is the influential art work of Vincent Van Gogh, which was not valued by his contemporaries until later, long after his tragic suicide at the age of 37. Luckily, this is more the exception than the rule.

6. Examples here are based on the composition and improvisation music experiences, but similar examples could (and should) be drawn for all music experiences, including developing levels of sophisticated listening.

7. Guildford is one in a long line of theorists who have argued for a more nuanced understanding of the notion of intelligence, including Gardner (1983). However, it was the embedding of both convergent *and* divergent cognitive operations across multiple content fields resulting in different products that was meaningful for creativity theory. Most agree that creativity as a construct is separate from but inextricably related to general intelligence and that there is a case to be made for domain-general and domain-specific creativity abilities. For a reasonably clear overview of these matters, see Sawyer (2012, pp. 52–61).

8. http://www.ststesting.com/ngifted.html.

9. In light of current theory, domain-general characteristics might play a role in prediction for music creativeness, but not as a sole predictor. Further research with both domain-general and domain-specific tasks is warranted.

10. In subsequent research by others, MCTM-II has been adapted for older and younger subjects and used for subjects with special needs. Others have used MCTM-II as a dependent variable in research design. (see the Reference section for citations of studies that have used the measure in various ways.)

11. Part of the conceptual foundation for MET relates to the more general effort by Lubart and colleagues in the construction of Evaluation of Potential Creativity (EPoC), a measure designed for children and adolescents. It measures divergent-exploratory creative thinking and convergent-integrative creative thinking in several domains of creative activity and endorses conceptually the study both of general creative ability and of creative work in specific domains.

REFERENCES

Amabile, T. (1982). Social psychology of creativity: A consensual assessment technique. *Journal of Personality and Social Psychology, 43,* 997–1013. doi: 10 037/0022-3514.43.5.997

Amabile, T. (1996). *Creativity in context: Update to the social psychology of creativity.* Boulder, CO: Westview Press.

Auh, M., & Walker, R. (1999). Compositional strategies and musical creativity when composing with staff notations versus graphic notations among Korean students. *Bulletin of the Council for Research in Music Education, 141,* 2–9.

Baltzer, S. (1988). A validation study of a measure of musical creativity. *Journal of Research in Music Education, 36,* 232–249. doi: 10.2307/3344876

Baltzer, S. (1990). *A factor analytic study of musical creativity in children in the primary grades* (Order No. 9029114). Available from ProQuest Dissertations & Theses Global. (303867258).

Barbot, B., Besançon, M., & Lubart, T. (2011). Assessing creativity in the classroom. *The Open Education Journal, 1*(5), 58–66. doi: 10.2174/1874920801104010058

Barbot, B., Besançon, M., & Lubart, T. (2015). Creative potential in educational settings: Its nature, measure, and nurture. *Education 3–13, 43*(4), 1–10. doi: 10.1080/03004279.2015.1020643

Barbot, B., Besançon, M., & Lubart, T. I. (2016). The generality-specificity of creativity: Exploring the structure of creative potential with EPoC. *Learning and Individual Differences, 52,* 178–187. doi.org/10.1016/j.lindif.2016.06.005

Barbot, B., & Lubart, T. (2012). Creative thinking in music: Its nature and assessment through musical exploratory behaviors. *Psychology of Aesthetics, Creativity, and the Arts, 6,* 231–242. doi 10.1037/a0027307

Barbot, B., & Webster, P. R. (2018). Creative thinking in music. In T. Lubart (Ed.), *The creative process: Perspectives from multiple domains.* (pp. 255–273). London, UK: Palgrave Macmillan. doi: 10.1057/978-1-137-50563-7_10

Barrett, M. (1996). Children's aesthetic decision-making: An analysis of children's musical discourse as composers. *International Journal of Music Education, 28,* 37–62. doi: 10.1177/025576149602800104

Barron, F., & Harrington, D. (1981). Creativity, intelligence, and personality. *Annual Review of Psychology, 32,* 439–476.

Beaty, R. (2015). The neuroscience of musical improvisation. *Neuroscience and Biobehavioral Reviews, 15,* 108–117. doi: 10.1016/j.neubiorev.2015.01.004

Bennett, S. (1976). The process of musical creation: Interviews with eight composers. *Journal of Research in Music Education, 24,* 3–13. doi: 10.2307/3345061

Burnard, P. (2012). *Musical creativities in real world practice.* Oxford, UK: Oxford University Press.

Clapham, M. (2011). Testing/Measurement/Assessment, In M. Runco & S. Pritzker (eds.), *Encyclopedia of creativity* (2nd edition), (pp. 458–464) Cambridge, MA: Academic Press, doi: 10.1016/B978-0-12-375038-9.00220-X

Clarke, E. F. (2005). Creativity in performance. *Musicae Scientiae, 9,* 157–182. doi: 10.1177/102986490500900106

Csikszentmihalyi, M. (1988). Motivation and creativity: Toward a synthesis of structural and energistic approaches to cognition. *New Ideas in Psychology, 6,* 159–176.

Csikszentmihalyi, M. (1996). *Creativity: Flow and the psychology of discovery and invention.* New York, NY: HarperCollins.

Davis, G. (1993, 2004). *Creativity is forever* (5th ed.). Dubuque, IA: Kendall-Hunt.

Dunn, R. (1997). Creative thinking and music listening. *Research Studies in Music Education, 8*, 42–55. doi: 10.1177/1321103X9700800105

Eisenberg, J., & Thompson, W. F. (2003). A matter of taste: Evaluating improvised music. *Creativity Research Journal, 15*, 237–296. doi: 10.1080/10400419.2003.9651421

Eisner, E. W. (1987). The celebration of thinking. *Educational Horizons, 66*, 24–29.

Flynn, E., Pine, K., & Lewis, C. (2006). Microgenetic method—time for change? *Psychologist, 19*, 152–155.

Folkestad, G., Hargreaves, D., & Lindström, B. (1998). Compositional strategies in computer-based music-making. *British Journal of Music Education, 15*, 83–97. doi: 10.1017/S0265051700003788

Gardner, H. (1983). *Frames of mind: The theory of multiple intelligences.* New York, NY: Basic Books.

Gardner, H. (1991). *The unschooled mind: How children think and how schools should teach.* New York, NY: Basic Books.

Gardner, H. (1993). *Creating minds.* New York, NY: Basic Books.

Gorder, W. (1980). Divergent production abilities as constructs of musical creativity. *Journal of Research in Music Education, 28*, 34–42. doi: 10.2307/3345051

Guilford, J. P. (1950). Creativity. *The American Psychologist, 5*, 444–454. doi: 10.1037/h0063487

Guilford, J. P. (1967). *The nature of human intelligence.* New York, NY: McGraw-Hill.

Hennessey, B. A. (1994). The consensual assessment technique: An examination of the relationship between ratings of product and process creativity. *Creativity Research Journal, 7*, 193–208. doi: 10.1080/10400419409534524

Hickey, M. (1999). Assessment rubrics for music composition. *Music Educators Journal, 85*, 26–32. doi: 10.2307/3399530

Hickey, M. (2001). An application of Amabile's consensual assessment technique for rating the creativity of children's musical compositions. *Journal of Research in Music Education, 49*, 234–244. doi: 10.2307/3345709

Hickey, M. (2002). Creativity research in music, visual art, theatre, and dance. In R. Colwell & C. Richardson (Eds.), *The new handbook of research on music teaching and learning* (pp. 398–414). New York, NY: Oxford University Press.

Hickey, M. (2009). Can improvisation be "taught"? A call for free improvisation in our schools. *International Journal of Music Education, 27*, 285–299. doi: 10.1177/0255761409345442

Hickey, M. (2013). Standards, assessment, and creativity in American music education: Intersection of opportunities. In T. Brophy & A. Lehmann-Wermser (Eds.), *Proceedings of the 3rd International Symposium on Assessment in Music Education* (pp. 15–35). Chicago, IL: GIA Publications.

Hickey, M. (2015). Learning from the experts: A study of free-improvisation pedagogues in university settings. *Journal of Research in Music Education, 62*, 425–445. doi: 10.1177/0022429414556319

Hocevar, D., & Bachelor, P. (1989). A taxonomy and critique of measurements used in the study of creativity. In J. A. Glover, R. Ronning, & C. Reynolds (Eds.), *Handbook of creativity* (pp. 53–75). New York, NY: Plenum Press.

Kaufman, J., & Beghetto, R. (2009). Beyond big and little: The four C models of creativity, *Review of General Psychology, 13*(1), 1–12. doi: 10.1037/a0013688

Kennedy, M. (2002). Listening to the music: Compositional processes of high school composers. *Journal of Research in Music Education, 50*(2), 94–110. doi: 10.2307/3345815

Kratus, J. (1989). A time analysis of the compositional processes used by children ages 7 to 11. *Journal of Research in Music Education, 37*, 5–20. doi: 10.2307/3344949

Kratus, J. (1994). Relationships among children's music audiation and their compositional processes and products. *Journal of Research in Music Education, 42*, 115–130. doi: 10.2307/3345496

Leung, C., Wan, Y., & Lee, A. (2009). Assessment of undergraduate students' music compositions. *International Journal of Music Education, 27*, 250–268. doi: 10.1177/0255761409337275

Lubart, T. I., Besançon, M., & Barbot, B. (2011). Evaluation du potential créatif (EPoC) [Evaluation of potential for creativity]. Paris, France: Editions Hogrefe France.

Madura, P. D. (1996). Relationships among vocal jazz improvisation achievement, jazz theory, knowledge, imitative ability, musical experience, creativity and gender. *Journal of Research in Music Education, 44*, 252–267.

Mellor, L. (2008). Creativity, originality, identity: Investigating computer-based composition in the secondary school. *Music Education Research, 10*, 451–472. doi: 10.1080/14613800802547680

Menard, E. (2015). Music composition in the high school curriculum: A multiple case study. *Journal of Research in Music Education, 63*, 114–136. doi: 10.1177/0022429415574310

Merrotsy, P. (2013). A note on big-C creativity and little-c creativity. *Creativity Research Journal, 25*, 474–476. doi: 10.1080/10400419.2013.843921

Mills, M. (2009). Capturing student progress via portfolios in the music classroom. *Music Educators Journal, 96*(2), 32–38. doi: 10.1177/0027432109351463

Norgaard, M. (2011). Descriptions of improvisational thinking by artist-level jazz musicians. *Journal of Research in Music Education, 59*, 109–127. doi: 10.1177/002242941 1405669

Norgaard, M. (2016). Descriptions of improvisational thinking by developing jazz improvisers. *International Journal of Music Education, 35*(2), 1–13.

Plunker, J., Beghetto, R., & Dow, G. (2004). Why isn't creativity more important to educational psychologist? *Educational Psychologist, 39*(2). 83–95. doi: 10.1207/s15326985ep3902_1

Priest, T. (2001). Using creativity assessment experience to nurture and predict compositional creativity. *Journal of Research in Music Education, 49*, 245–257. doi: 10.2307/3345710

Rhodes, J. (1961). An analysis of creativity, *Phi Delta Kappa, 42*, 305–311.

Robinson, K. (2011). *Out of our minds: Learning to be creative* (2nd ed.). West Sussex, UK: Capstone.

Robinson, K., & Aronica, L. (2016). *Creative schools: The grassroots revolution that's transforming education.* New York, NY: Penguin Books.

Roderick, J. (1965). *An investigation of selected factors of the creativity thinking ability of music majors in a teacher training program* (Order No. 6507156). Available from ProQuest Dissertations & Theses Global. (302170571).

Rowher, D. (1997). The challenges of teaching and assessing creative activity. *Update: Applications of Research in Music Education, 15*, 8–12.

Running, D. (2008). Creativity research in music education: A review (1980–2005). *Update: Applications of Research in Music Education, Fall/Winter 2008, 27*(1), 41–49.

Sawyer, K. (2012). *Explaining creativity: The science of human innovation.* New York, NY: Oxford University Press.

Schuler, S., Norgaard, M., & Blakeslee, M. (2014). The new national standards for music educators. *Music Educators Journal, 101*(1), 41–19. doi: 10.1177/0027432114540120

Seddon, F. A., & O'Neill, S. A. (2003). Creative thinking processes in adolescent computer-based composition: An analysis of strategies adopted and the influence of instrumental music training. *Music Education Research, 5*, 125–137. doi: 10.1080/1461380032000085513

Simonton, D. (1994). *Greatness: Who makes history and why.* New York, NY: Guilford.

Simpson, D. (1969). *The effect of selected musical studies on growth in general creative potential.* (Order No. 6913081). Available from ProQuest Dissertations & Theses Global. (302494894).

Smith, D. (2009). Development and validation of a rating scale for wind jazz improvisation performance. *Journal of Research in Music Education, 57*, 217–235. doi: 10.1177/0022429409343549

Stauffer, S. (2001). Composing with computers: Meg makes music. *Bulletin of the Council for Research in Music Education, 150*, 1–20.

Stauffer, S. (2002). Connections between the musical and life experiences of young composers and their compositions. *Journal of Research in Music Education, 50*, 301–322. doi: 10.2307/3345357

Stein, M. I. (1987). Creativity research at the crossroads: A 1985 perspective. In S. G. Isaksen (Ed.), *Frontiers of creativity research: Beyond the basics* (pp. 417–427). Buffalo, NY: Bearly.

Tarratus, E. (1964). *Creative processes in music and the identification of creative music students.* (Order No. 6503927). Available from ProQuest Dissertations & Theses Global. (302119135).

Torrance, E. (1974). *Torrance tests of creative thinking: Norms-technical manual.* Princeton, NJ: Personnel Press/Ginn.

Torrance, E. (2008). *The Torrance Tests of creative thinking: Norms-technical manual.* Bensenville, IL: Scholastic Testing Service.

Vaughan, M. (1971). *Music as model and metaphor in the cultivation and measurement of creative behavior in children* (Order No. 7211056). Available from ProQuest Dissertations & Theses Global. (302458092). Retrieved from http://libproxy.usc.edu/login?url=http://search.proquest.com.libproxy2.usc.edu/docview/302458092?accountid=14749

Vaughan, M. (1977). Musical creativity: Its cultivation and measurement. *Bulletin of the Council for Research in Music Education, 50*, 72–77.

Webster, P. (1979). Relationship between creative behavior in music and selected variables as measured in high school students. *Journal of Research in Music Education, 27*, 227–242.

Webster, P. (1983). An assessment of musical imagination in young children. *Proceedings Report: 1983 Bowling Green Research Symposium,* (pp. 100–123). Bowling Green, OH: Bowling Green State University.

Webster, P. (1987a). Refinement of a measure of creative thinking in music. In C. Madsen & C. Prickett (Eds.), *Applications of research in music behavior* (pp. 257–271). Tuscaloosa: University of Alabama Press.

Webster, P. (1987b). Conceptual bases for creative thinking in music. In J. Peery, I. Peery, & T. Draper (Eds.), *Music and child development* (pp. 158–174). New York, NY: Springer-Verlag. doi: 10.1007/978-1-4613-8698-8_8

Webster, P. (1990). Creativity as creative thinking. *Music Educators Journal, 76*, 22–28. doi: 10.2307/3401073

Webster, P. (1992). Research on creative thinking in music: The assessment literature. In R. Colwell (Ed.), *Handbook of research on music teaching and learning* (pp. 266–279). New York, NY: Macmillan.

Webster, P. (1994). *Measure of creative thinking in music (MCTM). Administrative guidelines.* Northwestern University, Evanston, IL. Unpublished manuscript. Available from http://www.peterrwebster.com/

Weisberg, R. (1993). *Creativity: Beyond the myth of genius.* New York, NY: W. H. Freeman.

Wiggins, J. (2015). *Teaching for musical understanding* (3rd ed.). New York, NY: Oxford University Press.

INDEPENDENT RESEARCH USING MCTM-II

Amchin, R. (1995). *Creative musical response: The effects of teacher-student interaction on the improvisation abilities of fourth- and fifth-grade students* (Order No. 9542792). Available from ProQuest Dissertations & Theses Full Text; ProQuest Dissertations & Theses Global. (304226893).

Baek, J. (2009). *The effects of music instruction using picture books and creative activities on musical creativity, music aptitude, and reading ability of young children* (Order No. 3361830). Available from ProQuest Central; ProQuest Dissertations & Theses Full Text; ProQuest Dissertations & Theses Global; ProQuest Education Journals. (304843746).

Baltzer, S. (1990). *A factor analytic study of musical creativity in children in the primary grades* (Order No. 9029114). Available from ProQuest Dissertations & Theses Full Text; ProQuest Dissertations & Theses Global.

Boehm, P. (1999). *The effects of a compositional teaching approach using invented notation and a non-compositional teaching approach on scores of music achievement and scores of music creativity in first-grade children* (Order No. 9933060). Available from ProQuest Dissertations & Theses Full Text; ProQuest Dissertations & Theses Global. (304531223).

Crawford, L. (2016). Composing in groups: Creative processes of third and firth grade students. (Unpublished doctoral dissertation). University of Southern California, Los Angeles.

Dingle, R. (2006). *Relationships between adolescents' stabilized music aptitudes and creative thinking abilities in music* (Order No. 3224426). Available from ProQuest Dissertations & Theses Full Text; ProQuest Dissertations & Theses Global. (305278495).

Dingle, R. (2014). A reliability assessment of African American adolescents' creative music-thinking abilities. In *NAAAS Conference Proceedings* (p. 869). National Association of African American Studies.

Fung, C. (1997). Effect of a sound exploration program on children's creative thinking in music. *Research Studies in Music Education, 9,* 13–19.

Hagedorn, V. (1997). *An investigation into musical thinking of deaf children* (Order No. 9803880). Available from ProQuest Dissertations & Theses Full Text; ProQuest Dissertations & Theses Global. (304368649).

Hickey, M. (1995). *Qualitative and quantitative relationships between children's creative musical thinking processes and products* (Order No. 9614754). Available from ProQuest Dissertations & Theses Full Text; ProQuest Dissertations & Theses Global. (304224038).

Koutsoupidou, T. (2008). Effects of different teaching styles on the development of musical creativity: Insights from interviews with music specialists. *Musicae Scientiae, 12,* 311–335.

Koutsoupidou, T., & Hargreaves, D. J. (2009). An experimental study of the effects of improvisation on the development of children's creative thinking in music. *Psychology of Music, 37,* 251–278. doi: 10.1177/0305735608097246

Racana, A. (1991). *Creativity, computers, and music: Promoting creativity in the fourth and fifth grade students* (Unpublished masters thesis). San Francisco State University, San Francisco, California.

Roman, H. (2016). Relationship between skills and enabling conditions in university students of visual arts according to the Model of Creative Thinking of Peter Webster. (Unpublished doctoral dissertation). Pontificia Universidad Catolica de Puerto Rico, Ponce, Puerto Rico.

Schmidt, C., & Sinor, J. (1986). An investigation of the relationship among music audiation, musical creativity, and cognitive style. *Journal of Research in Music Education, 34,* 160–172.

Swanner, D. (1985). *Relationships between musical creativity and selected factors, including personality, motivation, musical aptitude, and cognitive intelligence as measured in third grade children* (Doctoral dissertation). Retrieved from ProQuest Dissertations & Theses Full Text; (Order No. 8601941).

Wolfe, E., & Linden, K. (1991). *Investigation of the relationship between intrinsic motivation and musical creativity.* (ERIC Document Reproduction Service No. ED351370).

Yannon, K. (2011). *The effects of music aptitude, creativity, and heuristic and algorithmic instruction on the compositions of fifth grade students* (Order No. 3468188).

··

CHAPTER 27

PERFORMANCE ASSESSMENT AND RUBRIC DESIGN

··

M. CHRISTINA SCHNEIDER,
JENNIFER S. MCDONEL, AND
CHARLES A. DEPASCALE

INTRODUCTION

··

PERFORMANCE-BASED assessments, also known as performance tasks, are measures of student learning that require authentic generation of student work and performance (Kuhs, Johnson, Agruso, & Monrad, 2001). In general, three main characteristics that define high-quality, performance-based assessments are detailed in this chapter:

- Students are required to use information or processes stored in their long-term memory as a central tool in responding to the task.
- The task elicits student thinking beyond recalling knowledge or following directions, requires the students to integrate knowledge and skills, and frequently requires students to analyze or interact with a stimulus in order to respond to the task.
- The task is presented using best-practice creation guidelines.

In the United States, national, public school standards such as the Common Core define what students *should* know and be able to do by the end of an academic year. State assessments, including those from the Smarter Balanced Assessment Consortium and Partnership for Assessment of Readiness for College and Career Readiness (PARCC), measure student achievement in relation to expected learning outcomes; likewise, policymakers for these assessments define the assessment evidence needed to determine the extent to which students have, or have not, met the standards. That is, content standards and assessments together define intended outcomes of student learning. In the context of music classes, assessments and the performance evidence collected from those assessments must be aligned not only to state standards but also to the stage of students' development, which may vary among individual students due to differences in richness of children's home music environment, the relative time spent in music classes compared to other subjects, and the degree to which the child innately pursues and practices music independently (Etopio, 2009; McDonel, 2015).

Assessments also are used to provide an estimate of the amount a student has learned after a year of instruction. Teacher effectiveness measures are based, in part, on estimates regarding the amount a teacher's students have learned within a year. Given the focus on quantifying how much students have learned, it is surprising that states do not typically require educators to be formally trained in assessment competencies (Popham, 2009; Stiggins & Herrick, 2007), especially because educators engage in some type of assessment for 20%–30% of their time with students (Barton & Coley, 1994).

All music educators need training regarding how to create high quality performance-based assessments to (1) measure student learning in the classroom, (2) compare and rank students in an audition context, and (3) respond to and support student learning. Music, as a discipline, is a performance art; alongside creating and responding, performing is one of three artistic processes outlined in the National Core Music Standards (National Coalition for Core Arts Standards, 2014). Thus, multiple-choice items are not suitable to measure a large proportion of music learning. To teach music and to measure student learning, music educators must be skilled in development of high-quality, performance-based assessments that serve both formative and summative assessment purposes.

Identifying Purposes of Assessment

When teachers collect and analyze evidence of student learning and use that information to adjust instruction or provide feedback to students, they are using assessment for a formative purpose (Brookhart, Moss, & Long, 2008). Wiliam, Lee, Harrison, and Black (2004) defined specific *formative assessment* practices: teacher questioning, comment-only feedback, sharing grading criteria with students, facilitating student self-assessment, and peer feedback. Educators typically use these techniques during the instructional sequence. Music educators frequently provide formative feedback to students during rehearsals and private lessons through coaching. In these situations, formative assessment practices are informal and perhaps spontaneously given, aligning with the range of formative practices described by Ruiz-Primo, Furtak, Ayala, Yin, and Shavelson (2010).

Summative assessment, or "end-of-instruction" assessment, occurs at the end of an instructional unit or time period. Auditions, graded performances in the classroom, and large-scale assessments are considered summative because their purpose is to quantify how much learning has occurred during a specific time period and to evaluate that learning against some standard such as a grading scale ranging from A to F. The actions based on these summative assessments can include decisions on whether or not to place students into more elite performing groups, to provide a grade that is used to inform a report card marking period, or to evaluate a program or teacher.

Brookhart (2010) described feedback for commingled formative and summative purposes. In this model, the teacher or other evaluator provides feedback on a summative assessment to help students better target the expected outcome on the next concert performance or in a subsequent piece of music. Performance situations such as solo and ensemble or concert festival are examples of assessment situations with commingled purposes. Moreover, in K-12 music education, many ostensibly summative, performance-assessment experiences are applicable to this commingled category, with feedback serving as an important feature of the assessment.

In all these examples, authentic student performances are the intended outcome of interest; thus, performance-based assessments are the best tool with which to measure student skill. Regardless of assessment purpose, it behooves teachers and professional assessment developers to use the same high-quality assessment practices to understand student skills (Schneider, Egan, & Julian, 2013).

Defining the Intended Inference

Because the goal of all assessments is to draw inferences about what students know and can do in a content area—and, conversely, what they do not know or are not yet able to do—it is important that those inferences be based on observable evidence and a common understanding of the skills being assessed; otherwise different constructs, not related to the music skill of interest, may unintentionally be measured. For this reason, the first step in creating any assessment is to give careful thought about and document the meaning of the intended inference (what does the score say about what the student knows and can do?) and how assessment scores will be used (i.e., the purpose or resulting action of those scores). Thinking deeply about the meaning and intended use(s) of the score helps to identify what should be measured, why it should be measured, and the context in which the skill should be measured.

PLANNING AND CREATING
PERFORMANCE-BASED ASSESSMENTS

In planning and creating performance-based assessments in music, whether for the classroom, an audition, or as part of a state assessment, teachers and assessment developers must align the design of the assessment with its intended purpose and use. These principles are fundamental to evidence-centered design (ECD)—a research-based framework for designing, implementing, and using educational assessments. Developed in the late 1990s (Mislevy, Steinberg, & Almond, 1999), ECD has been applied in development of a variety of assessments, including programs such as PARCC, Smarter Balanced, and the College Board Advanced Placement exams. Although the application of ECD can become quite complex in practice, conceptually the process is built on asking and answering three questions:

1. What knowledge, skills, or other attributes of student performance should be assessed?
2. What evidence will demonstrate those knowledge and skills?
3. What tasks will elicit those evidence pieces from students?

The basis for development of all assessments used to measure student achievement or inform instruction in the classroom lies in the attempt to answer those deceptively simple questions.

In the context of K-12 assessment, state or national standards often serve as the starting point for answering the first question. Those standards define the knowledge and skills that students *should* possess as they progress across grade levels. In some cases, state and national standards also define progressions of knowledge and skills within grade levels, but often those within-grade progressions must be developed at the local level. In the context of music classes, assessments must be aligned not only to state standards but also to the appropriate stage of students' music development within a particular part of the year, which may vary among individual students (Etopio, 2009; McDonel, 2015).

The answer to the second question also stems from an understanding of state and national standards. After determining the knowledge and/or skills to be assessed, educators must determine the type of evidence needed to demonstrate that knowledge and skills. This process requires developing descriptions of the type and quality of student performances that provide evidence to support desired inferences about student performance, including descriptions of the context and conditions under which the student can demonstrate that performance (e.g., one-on-one during a private lesson, performing a solo recital before a large audience, or one key as opposed to another). These descriptions will inform decisions about the number of tasks that must be developed to provide the required evidence and conditions under which students must be assessed.

Subsequently, understanding the knowledge and skills to be measured and evidence required to demonstrate the knowledge and skills informs answers to the third question, in which the type of tasks required to elicit observable evidence of knowledge and skills must be determined. The following sections of this chapter address issues to consider when developing those tasks.

Task Development

Stimulus Development

In reading texts, learning to read is the primary instructional focus in grades K–2 (ages 5–7). Beginning in grade 3 (age 8) the focus generally moves away from learning to read toward what is often coined "reading to learn." Thus, in creating performance-based assessments in grades 3 and above, the focus of measuring reading is no longer on verbal or silent retrieval of words or even basic comprehension skills (e.g., who, what, where, when, and why) but on the higher-order skills of text analysis and synthesis. The same type of progression can be applied to learning to read music, although students' place within the progression will be more closely related to their "musical age," or developmental age specific to music (Runfola & Etopio, 2010) rather than chronological age or grade level, because children often are scheduled for fewer sessions of music instruction than reading instruction in elementary schools across the nation.

Reading music while performing on an instrument relies heavily on muscle motor memory skills as well as lower level cognitive demand frameworks (see the Webb *depth of knowledge* cognitive demand framework; Webb, 2005); the work and years of time that are necessary to acquire these skills must not be devalued, especially in the early elementary grades (ages 5–10). The aural precursor skills that should be developed well in advance of notation in order for students to engage in higher order critical thinking skills (e.g., improvisation) frequently are approached alongside notation reading and muscle memory skills (Gordon, 2012). For complex performance-based assessments to meaningfully inform their intended purposes, it is essential to codify what evidence is *most* central to measure, especially during early years of music skill acquisition.

At lower levels of cognitive demand, performance-based tasks may require students to solve well-posed problems using rote knowledge and/or procedural applications (Herman, Buschang, & Matrundola, 2014; Webb, 2005). Tasks that prompt students to retrieve information from notation such as identifying key signatures or performing familiar notation are tasks of lower cognitive demand, because the students are decoding the notation into tonal, rhythm, and melodic patterns to perform the music that they have practiced frequently with instructional supports.

No doubt improvising solos during a jazz band performance, sight-reading music, and writing music are tasks at higher levels of cognitive demand frameworks. Higher levels of cognitive demand are tasks that require students to *independently* generate their own solutions to a task and that focus on student abilities to generalize to new contexts. Performance-based assessment task complexity depends on how constrained the task is, the degree to which transfer is required, and the amount of information that must be processed to *create a solution* (Herman et al., 2014). Performance assessments typically require students to respond to a stimulus and use that information to help shape a solution.

Herman et al. (2014) described the processing demands of a stimulus as a key component of task complexity. Task complexity is a central component of high-quality performance tasks. For example, if a student only needs to process music from a single section of a movement or from rhythm patterns in isolation as the task stimulus, the processing demands are relatively easy compared to a task in which a student needs to make connections across an entire piece of music or across multiple pieces of music (e.g., partner songs, sonata-allegro form, etc.). These latter examples require greater degrees of inferential thinking to create independent generalizations across larger forms, works, and style periods of music.

Task Directions

Kuhs et al. (2001) and Schneider, Johnson, and Gowan (2011) outlined the following best practices with regard to communicating task directions to students. Kuhs et al. noted that directions should (1) specify the task response format (e.g., write, play, improvise), (2) be linked to measured curriculum standards, (3) prompt students to use a cognitive strategy, and (4) share the criteria for evaluation. Schneider et al. specified that task directions should be written directly to the students. If students are being asked to notate or create a composition, the task presentation space should be clear and uncluttered. Both Kuhs et al. and Hess and Thompson (2012) also noted that the task should be presented so that students have sufficient space to respond, and it is essential that students have enough time to complete the task. If 5% of students or higher are unable to complete the task in the allotted time, the teachers or test developers should increase the time students have to perform the task.

When formatting the text for children in elementary school, 11- or 12-point font is not advisable, as it is too small for children to read easily. Thus, larger font sizes should be used, such as 14-point font. When asking students to perform, it must be determined whether responses should be recorded (recommended) and whether click tracks should be provided to assist students and raters. Schneider, Johnson, and Porchea (2004) found that raters had difficulty agreeing on whether children were maintaining a steady tempo when scoring an 8-measure performance.

Rubric Development

A rubric is a measurement tool used with a performance assessment that defines and describes, *with thorough narrative descriptions*, the specific performance criteria and indicators associated *with each score point* along the measurement scale for each criterion being measured (Mertler, 2001). Research supports use of scoring guides, which include rubrics, in maintaining consistent evaluation criteria across multiple judges at events such as solo and ensemble performances (Abeles, 1973), college juries (Bergee, 2003), and all-state band auditions (Saunders & Holahan, 1997). Several types of scoring guides have been developed that have helped adjudicators produce consistent evaluations of student performance (e.g., Azzara, 1993; Cooksey, 1977; Smith & Barnes, 2007; Zdzinski & Barnes, 2002). Although these research-based scoring guides each contain unique attributes, as denoted by their names (e.g., rating scales, criteria-specific rating scales, continuous rating scales, additive rating scales), they all describe the evidence needed from a student's performance to draw conclusions about the level of student knowledge and skills.

Types of Rubrics

When well developed, rubrics provide feedback about students' strengths and weaknesses, assistance in planning instruction, and information to students and parents (Gredler & Johnson, 2004). There are two main types of rubrics: analytic rubrics and holistic rubrics. While both of these rubric types describe varying levels of performance achievement (Gredler & Johnson, 2004), typically, they are suited for different assessment purposes.

Analytic rubrics often are used when the evaluator ("evaluator" is used from this point forward to encompass the classroom teacher, audition judge, or festival adjudicator) feels each element of a performance is best measured separately from other elements. Analytic rubrics are optimal when the evaluator wants to give a student feedback about his or her performance, needs to make fine distinctions about differences in students' performances, or both. In this type of rubric, a description is developed for each point of the scale within a particular dimension of performance. For example, Saunders and Holahan (1997) developed the following dimensions to rate auditions for an all-state band: tone, intonation, melodic accuracy, rhythmic accuracy, tempo, and interpretation. The descriptions developed by Saunders and Holahan are shown in Table 27.1. When this type of rich information is returned to a student, it communicates why a particular score point was given. Most importantly, descriptions associated with higher score points show the student what he or she needs to master next to improve the performance.

A holistic rubric summarizes a performance and is used when the adjudicator views the dimensions of the performance as interconnected and inseparable. When summarizing performances holistically, the descriptor that *best* describes the overall performance is used. Optimally, the rubric is written to the student, as in Table 27.2, so that it becomes a communication tool developed expressly to support student learning and next instructional steps. This type of rubric can be particularly informative when worded to describe what the student can do to improve rather than focusing solely on the detriments of the performance. A holistic rubric may be appropriate in solo and ensemble settings or when scoring performances of a scale, as in the example below, or when developing items for a large-scale music assessment. The primary focus of a holistic rubric is to provide a more global rating of a student's performance. Notice that the Saunders and Holahan (1997) descriptors are embedded and extended here into the levels of a holistic rubric as an example of how developers can draw from research literature in developing their own rubric performance descriptors that aid in effective, consistent scoring.

Steps for Developing a Rubric

Mertler (2001) provided seven essential steps in creating a rubric, which outline the processes for developing either an analytic or holistic rubric. When these seven steps are combined with Stiggins's (2008) recommendation to guide students in applying performance criteria to their own work multiple times (e.g., 10 to 12 occasions), eight general steps are suggested from the literature in creating a rubric for formative purposes and seven steps for summative purposes.

Step 1. Examine the expected performance outcomes that have been taught and that need to be measured.

In this example, the target of measure is Cr1.1.2a: "Improvise rhythmic and melodic patterns and musical ideas for a specific purpose." In this task, the goal is to elicit a

Table 27.1 Instrumental Performance Rubric

Criterion	LEVEL 1 2 points	LEVEL 2 4 points	LEVEL 3 6 points	LEVEL 4 8 points	LEVEL 5 10 points
TONE	Not a tone quality characteristic of the instrument	Several major flaws in basic production (i.e., consistently thin/unfocused sound, forced, breath not used efficiently)	Exhibits some flaws in production (i.e., a slightly thin or unfocused sound, somewhat forced, breath not always used efficiently, etc.)	Characteristic tone quality in most ranges, but distorts occasionally in some passages	Full, rich, and characteristic of the tone quality of the instrument in all ranges and registers
INTONATION	Not accurate. Student's performance is continuously out of tune	Exhibits a basic sense of intonation, yet has significant problems; student makes no apparent attempt at adjustment of problem pitches	Mostly accurate, but includes out-of-tune notes. The student does not adjust problem pitches to an acceptable standard of intonation	Accurate, but student fails to adjust on isolated pitches, yet demonstrates minimal intonation difficulties	Accurate throughout, in all ranges and registers
MELODIC ACCURACY	Inaccurate pitches/notes throughout the music, (i.e., missing key signatures, accidentals, etc.)	Numerous inaccurate pitches/notes	Many pitches/notes are accurate	Most pitches/notes are accurate	All pitches/notes are accurate
RHYTHMIC ACCURACY	Most rhythm patterns are incorrect	Many rhythm patterns are incorrect or inconsistent	Many rhythmic patterns are accurate, but some lack precision (approximation of rhythm patterns used)	Nearly accurate rhythms, but lacks precise interpretation of some rhythm patterns	Accurate rhythms throughout
TEMPO	Not accurate or consistent	Inconsistent (i.e., rushing, dragging, inaccurate tempo changes)	Different from the printed tempo marking(s), resulting in inappropriate tempo(s) for the selection, yet remains consistent	Approaches the printed tempo markings, yet the performed tempo does not detract significantly from the performance	Accurate and consistent with the printed tempo markings

Source: Saunders and Holahan (1997).

Table 27.2 Holistic Rubric for a Chromatic Scale

You displayed most of the characteristics found in Level

LEVEL 4	You performed with characteristic tone quality at all times. You had appropriate breath control and support in all ranges of your instrument and maintained a correct embouchure at all times. These supported your ability to maintain proper intonation in all ranges and registers. Your pitches were accurate, and you performed the scale with appropriate rhythm patterns played evenly ascending and descending. You maintained a consistent tempo at or faster than the required marking with appropriate, clean articulation. You performed the natural rise and fall of dynamics and gave a musical performance!
LEVEL 3	You performed with characteristic tone quality. You had appropriate breath control and support in most ranges of your instrument and maintained a correct embouchure nearly all the time. The few moments of lost breath support or embouchure slightly detracted from your ability to maintain good intonation in all ranges and registers. Your pitches were relatively accurate, and you performed the scale with appropriate rhythm patterns played evenly ascending and descending. You maintained a nearly consistent tempo at or perhaps faster than the required marking with appropriate, clean articulation. You performed the natural rise and fall of dynamics and gave a satisfactory performance.
LEVEL 2	You performed with near characteristic tone quality in the middle range of your instrument. Develop good breath control and support in the extreme ranges of your instrument so that your sound is not at times thin or unfocused. Work to keep a correct embouchure when you are in the extreme ranges to help maintain proper intonation in all ranges and registers. Work on learning how to adjust pitches on your instrument that are characteristically out of tune. Some of your pitches were accurate; work on proper chromatic fingerings/positions for your instrument. You performed the scale with rhythm patterns that were not always even. Work on performing consistently at the required tempo marking while maintaining clean articulation. Work on performing the natural rise and fall of dynamics, another important characteristic of a musical performance.
LEVEL 1	You performed with uncharacteristic tone quality in all ranges of your instrument. Develop good breath control and support in the middle and extreme ranges of your instrument. Work with your teacher to correct your embouchure to help maintain proper intonation in all ranges and registers. When you have done this, you can next learn how to adjust the pitches on your instrument that are characteristically out of tune. Your pitches were oftentimes inaccurate, and you performed the scale with rhythm patterns that were frequently uneven. Work on performing consistently a slower tempo than the required tempo marking while maintaining appropriate, clean articulation prior to working at the required tempo. Work on performing the natural rise and fall of dynamics, another important characteristic of a musical performance.

second grader's improvisation of a four-beat rhythmic pattern in duple meter with the same tempo and meter as the teacher-delivered pattern that uses similar patterns as the teacher.

The desired inference from a high score is that a student can improvise a four-beat pattern in duple meter in the same tempo and meter as the teacher-delivered pattern.

The teacher engages students in call-and-response in the classroom activity, creating the stimulus to which a student must respond. In a large-scale assessment such as the South Carolina Arts Assessment Project (see Volume 2, Chapter 12, in this handbook), such stimuli are delivered via recordings on a computer. The student demonstrates an improvised, short response to a well-posed music question that sets the context so the task would be considered of moderate cognitive demand for an elementary student. The task is well posed (call-and-response), short (four beats), uses rhythm patterns only, and requires some decision-making on the part of the student.

Step Two. Describe, in writing, the specific qualities of performance you want to hear. Avoid generic words such "bad" or "good" to describe the performance.

In this example, the goal is to elicit a student-improvised, four-beat rhythm pattern that is different from the teacher-delivered pattern that maintains the same context the teacher provided—the same tempo, meter, and types of rhythm patterns. Eighth notes, quarter notes, half notes, and a whole note are expected outcomes, but it might be possible that students with a rich music foundation may provide more sophisticated rhythm patterns. Responses without rhythm syllables are expected in this situation, but if provided, it would be an aural indicator that the student is providing a more advanced response.

Step Three. Brainstorm the types of performances that you expect to hear.

When developing an analytic rubric, developers should brainstorm desired attributes by individual performance dimensions; whereas for a holistic rubric, brainstorming should occur by global performance category. Investigating some of the scoring guides in the research literature can be helpful, and documentation of those sources can support validity claims. In the example, the following types of student performances are expected:

- Some students will chant a pattern in triple meter.
- Some students will simply repeat the teacher-delivered phrase with consistent tempo, and some will do so with inconsistent tempo.
- Some students will not feel the phrase and will chant fewer than or greater than four beats.
- Some students will chant a pattern with unrecognizable tempo and meter.

Step Four. Write a detailed, narrative description for an outstanding performance and a poor performance for each dimension for an analytic rubric or the summary for an outstanding performance and a poor performance for the holistic rubric.

A high response would have:

- a different four-beat pattern chanted at the same consistent tempo and meter as the teacher-delivered pattern.

A low response would have:

- the same four-beat pattern chanted with a different and inconsistent tempo and/or meter OR a different pattern is incomplete or extended and performed with a different and inconsistent tempo and/or meter.

A decision should be made regarding how to handle responses that may be one or two beats in length. Such responses may make it difficult to determine whether a student does not internalize the length of the pattern or if rests were intended. If responses that are short are considered incomplete or will be scored lower than responses that have a clear four-beat chanted pattern, then this information should be shared with the students as a component of the task directions.

Step Five. Finish the rubric by writing detailed descriptions for the other middle levels of performance.

Often, rubric designers have to consider what they believe the continuum of performance to be and consider that different types of performance may show similar levels of achievement, but in different ways (see the examples in Table 27.3). The rubric descriptions should represent important benchmarks along the continuum (scale) of learning. Documenting the frequency of the response categories from Step 3, as well as intermediate steps students demonstrate as they develop skills over time, best supports an understanding of students' progress in auditing and responding in duple meter.

Table 27.3 Sample Rhythm Improvisation Holistic Rubric

You performed most like a Level

LEVEL 4	A different pattern is performed in the same meter and at the same consistent tempo as the teacher-delivered pattern.
LEVEL 3	A different pattern is performed in the same meter and at a consistent tempo that is different from the teacher-delivered pattern, OR A different, incomplete, or extended pattern is performed in the same meter and at the same, consistent tempo and as the teacher-delivered pattern.
LEVEL 2	A different pattern is performed in the same meter, but rushes or slows the teacher tempo slightly.
LEVEL 1	A different pattern is performed with inconsistent tempo and/or meter OR A different, incomplete, or extended pattern is performed with inconsistent tempo and/or meter
LEVEL 0	No response The pattern performed is the same as the teacher-delivered pattern

Step Six. Informally try out your rubric prior to using it or use samples of student work from a previous year to see how well the rubric is working.

It is optimal to record student responses so the rubric may be adjusted as needed—especially in a classroom situation. In a large-scale assessment situation, adjusting the rubric during field-testing with small samples of student responses (typically referred to as range finding) is often optimal because of the expense of rescoring responses. In determining how well a rubric is working, the most important considerations are:

- Does the task elicit the types of student performance described in the rubric? A common flaw in the first draft of rubrics is that authors describe a performance either not asked for or not required to complete the performance task, or they describe a performance not likely to be elicited in student responses to the performance task.
- Does the rubric capture all anticipated student responses (i.e., performances) within the range of performance being assessed? Although it may be acceptable within a given context (e.g., an audition) for a rubric not to address a performance that is well above or well below the required cutoff, it is not acceptable for a rubric to miss variations on performance within the critical range considered sufficient evidence that the student possesses the required skills.
- Does the rubric contain an appropriate number of score categories? The appropriate number of score categories in a rubric is dependent on a combination of the real differences in performance that can elicited by a task (e.g., there are only so many ways to perform a four-beat pattern with quarter notes, eighth notes, half notes and whole notes) and the type of distinctions that need to be made among students for the particular purpose of the assessment. In some cases, it might be acceptable to say that all 100 assessed students met the required level of performance and their performances fall within the same rubric category. In another case, such as an audition for a chorus, it might be necessary to distinguish among the top 15 to 20 students, even though all students have met the standard, and the rubric must support the need to make finer distinctions between students. The number of categories in a rubric should not be based solely on convenience or tradition (e.g., we have always have four categories; all rubrics should have five points).
- Can the rubric be applied reliably (i.e., consistently)? A rubric is of little use if it cannot be applied consistently by different evaluators to the same student performance or by the same evaluator to two different student performances. Do two evaluators applying the rubric to the same student performance arrive at the same rating(s) on a consistent basis? If not, are there systematic differences in their ratings that can be explained by flaws in the rubric? One of the often-overlooked uses of a rubric is to help evaluators maintain consistent scoring standards over time and across scoring occasions. Applying the rubric to rescore a performance that has been scored previously is one way to determine whether evaluators' scoring standards have drifted higher or lower. In these situations it is important not only

to calculate correlations between scores but to also calculate the percentage of student responses that were given the same score, adjacent scores (within one score point), and discrepant scores (given score points that differ by two or more points).

- Do scores based on the rubric distinguish between performances that differ in quality? On a well-functioning rubric, higher quality performances will be rated higher than lower quality performances. In most cases, the rubric will be designed to *reflect* quality, not *determine* quality. When testing a rubric, one question to ask is: Does the rubric produce credible results based on what is known about student performance?

Before using a rubric in an actual assessment, informally reviewing the rubric with samples of student responses can reveal potential problems in each of the areas just described. Additional analyses, such as looking at the distribution of scores across score points for reasonability or comparing the mean score of students in a rubric category against the composite score across all tasks or domains of an analytic rubric to ensure that as rubric categories increase the mean score on the composite measure increase, after the assessment has been administered will also provide helpful information, not only about how well students are performing but also about how well the rubric is performing. Rubric development is often an iterative process in which the rubric is refined based on feedback from student performances.

Step Seven. Review the rubric with your students, and give them sample performances for each level.

Students need multiple opportunities to rate themselves and each other as a way to internalize teacher expectations embodied by the rubric. This is an essential aspect of formative assessment (Andrade, Du, & Wang, 2008), and it is a unique opportunity for assessments that are administered in the classroom. Optimally, performances from a previous year on a similar but different task can be collected and then evaluated by students in the current year to support students' ability to internalize task expectations. This can be a powerful way to allow students independently to become aware of responses that are too long or too short.

Step Eight. After the evaluation is complete, revise the rubric as necessary so that you have it ready for the next time you need it.

With constructed-response items, some rubrics will work well and others may need revision to reflect accurately the characteristics an evaluator is trying to measure. In general, responses that occur more frequently are considered easier responses. Additionally, when considering a progression of skill development, more frequently occurring responses may be indicative of a more common pathway of development.

Counting Errors

One common error in writing a rubric is to count student errors rather than describe a common performance characteristic. If a developer builds the rubric so that mistakes are being counted, he or she is actually building a checklist (in which the criterion is either correct or incorrect, present or absent) but has formatted the checklist into the layout of a rubric. In these cases, the developer is not describing the types of mistakes, the quality of work, the type of evidence, or the continuum of proficiency related to the learning goal. Little formative value is provided with such an assessment tool; likewise, content validity for inferences about student thinking in the content area is not well supported.

Thus, although one may feel that three pitch errors are much fewer than four pitch errors, it is often more important to note how quickly a student recovers from an error in a performance and the extent to which such an error detracts from the overall quality of performance. A comparison of a single dimension of an analytic rubric designed to measure correct notes of a scale is presented in Table 27.4. Notice that there are only four score points (0–3) used when describing the performance, rather than five (0–4) points used when counting errors.

Rubric Formatting

When an analytic rubric is presented in a table format, the scale optimally moves from left to right, correctly representing the mathematical properties of the scale as shown in Table 27.1. This convention shows a trajectory of proficiency that grows. Some educators, however, feel that the highest number should be placed on the left-hand side so the student sees the highest expectation first. This can be accommodated while still showing the mathematical properties of the scale by formatting the analytic rubric in a manner similar to the holistic rubric. In this situation, the scale is presented in the left-most column from high to low, and each dimension is presented in a separate column to the right (as shown in Table 27.4). In the example, Level 0 indicates students who imitated the teacher pattern, because the purpose of the task was to elicit improvisations rather than imitations of the pattern. If the goal is to explain to a parent or student why no credit was given for a response, error type coding allows a teacher or test developer to provide this type of feedback.

Table 27.4 Comparison of Counting Versus Describing

Score Point	Correct Notes	
	Counting	Describing
4	No note mistakes present	
3	One mistake present	Mistakes are not made
2	Two or three mistakes present	Minor mistakes are made but do *not* detract from the general quality of the scale
1	Four or five mistakes present	Mistakes are made that detract from the general quality of the scale
0	More than six mistakes	Major mistakes are made that significantly detract from the general quality of the scale

Some of the rubrics shown in this chapter have a zero point while others do not. In making this decision, both the intended inference of what the score represents and personal preference may be considered. Some developers award students a point for trying, whereas others prefer to score a zero for inaccurate attempts. Either approach may be defensible if the inference about students' abilities is based on the lowest descriptor rather than the point value of the rubric.

Considerations for Using Rubrics to Support Student Self-Evaluation

Well-developed rubrics describe progressions toward a clearly defined objective or goal central to the discipline. In addition to supporting trained raters in providing consistent scores across time and across different persons, rubrics can become powerful tools of instruction. Hewitt (2002) found that when students used rubrics to self-evaluate, their achievement improved, which is consistent with research in elementary writing and mathematics (Andrade & Boulay, 2003; Andrade et al., 2008; Ross, Hogaboam-Gray, & Rolheiser, 2002; Ross, Rolheiser, & Hogaboam-Gray, 1999). Writing and mathematics researchers have found that to raise achievement, students need to evaluate their own work over time, using rubrics on at least 10–12 occasions before effects are measurable.

When training students how to use and interpret a music performance rubric, it is important to provide an audio demonstration of the expectations for each score point. This can be accomplished with a range of previously recorded examples of student performances or live examples performed by the teacher. Students should perform mock evaluations, in which individuals score each other, so they begin to internalize the teacher's expectations.

When a teacher uses a rubric in this fashion, he or she is doing several things. First, the teacher is demonstrating for students how to be successful, because his or her expectations are known. Second, the teacher is helping students become evaluators of their own learning so that students may then self-assess as they prepare for an upcoming evaluation. Finally, the process of using rubrics in teacher modeling, student self-assessment, and peer-assessment can be effective ways of incorporating Common Anchor #5: "Rehearse, Evaluate, and Refine" from the Core Arts Standards (2014).

Considerations for Using Rubrics to Support Student Learning Objectives

Student learning objectives (SLOs) are content- and grade/course-specific student learning targets, measured across time, to document student learning during a course or year of instruction (National Center for the Improvement of Educational Assessment, 2013). Nationwide, SLOs are becoming both a foundational tool to measure student learning during the year and the student achievement component of educator evaluation systems. As of 2014, 50% of states incorporated SLOs into their teacher evaluation systems (Lacireno-Paquet, Morgan, & Mello, 2014) as a measure of a teacher's contribution to student achievement.

Teachers engage in an SLO (or goal-setting) process when they establish learning goals for students, collect baseline information on student achievement at the beginning of the year or course, and then monitor student attainment of those goals in a formalized, documented process specified by the state or district as a component of their evaluation process. This process is used by the many teachers (69%) who instruct students in a grade or content area for which no large-scale assessment growth data exist (Prince et al., 2009) and sometimes as an additional student achievement measure beyond growth data obtained from large-scale assessments (Hall, Gagnon, Thompson, Schneider, & Marion, 2014; Lacireno-Paquet et al., 2014).

Because music education researchers typically are interested in understanding how students build enduring understandings in music, examining the acquisition of music skills described in the music education research literature (e.g., Gordon, 2012) can be an effective starting point for music teachers attempting to define important performance criteria for SLO rubrics. Further, there are different methods of developing SLO rubrics. A common approach is the pretest–posttest model, in which the same rubric is used across time. The pretest and posttest may be the same or a different performance-based assessment, depending on state or teacher requirements. However, one performance task at the beginning of the year is not a reliable indicator of student skill.

To obtain a reliable measure of student skill using performance assessments, between 6 and 12 tasks or samples of student work are needed (Shavelson, Baxter, & Gao, 1993; Shavelson, Ruiz-Primo, & Wiley, 1999). In instrumental music classes, measures such as the Watkins-Farnum (1970) or multiple, short samples of performance (e.g., etudes or method book) may be used to provide efficient, stable estimates of a student's present level of performance. However, without standardized district- or state-level exemplars and rubric scoring training, teachers are unlikely to use the scale of rubrics the same way; neither are they likely to use the same descriptors for score points intended to measure common criteria. For example, when measuring intonation, equal scores across teachers in the district will not represent the same degree of student achievement across classrooms.

The complexities of uncommon rubrics and performance assessments can, to some extent, be ameliorated by common performance tasks across a district at a particular grade level. Interpretations of student growth on common performance tasks, however, are dependent on the difficulty of the tasks that students receive. State officials often are silent regarding how task difficulty should be embedded into the SLO process, yet this is central to measuring and interpreting student growth. For many students, but not all, growth interpretations can be facilitated when pretest to posttest tasks are of equal difficulty. In this context we expect students to improve from Time 1 to Time 2. If the first task is at a reduced level of difficulty compared to the second it can appear that students did not make gains when in fact they did. Conversely, it could appear that students have made gains when they have not. It is important to specify that the grade level of music either remain the same from pretest to posttest or that it increase from pretest to posttest. Marion, DePascale, Domaleski, Gong, and Diaz-Bilello (2012) have written extensively on these issues.

Marion et al. (2012) and Briggs et al. (2015) noted that one remedy for these complex technical issues is to create SLOs based on teacher-developed learning progressions. When using a progression-based SLO, rubrics for measuring SLOs will differ from rubrics designed to measure student learning at a single point in time. The SLO rubrics, or achievement level descriptors, describe the evidence needed to infer that a student meets the intended evidence and conclude she or he is located in a particular point in the progression. Because a progression of skill acquisition requires more evidence over time than a simple pretest–posttest model, more samples of student work must be collected. This should, in turn, make the process more reliable, especially if teachers are trained and calibrate work across a district and match the evidence to the progression. Evidence statements in the SLO rubrics (or SLO achievement level descriptors) should describe the content, cognitive level (or motor skill level, as appropriate), and context of the tasks that demonstrate higher stages of reasoning in the construct or higher levels of performance skill over time.

Contextual characteristics of skills are the conditions under which a student can demonstrate their music skills. Often, this information is central to understanding why a student is or is not able to respond or perform a task (Schneider & Egan, 2014); thus, in developing these evidence statements, it is important to discuss contextual characteristics that must be present in order for the student to demonstrate a given skill. For example, a student may be able to sight read a Level 2 etude, but only in Concert B<flat> or as long as no accidentals are present. Or, a student may be able to improvise rhythmically and melodically only in pentatonic—or tonally and rhythmically in major tonality when the chordal structure is constrained to tonic and dominant functions. Without such constraints, students may not be able to sight-read or improvise independently; thus, it is critical to understand the context in which a student can perform standard-defined content and to embed SLO evidence statements within rubrics used to measure student learning across time. An example is shown in Table 27.5 with Figure 27.1 matching to the beginning level of sight-reading and Figure 27.2 matching to the growing level.

CONCLUSION

We began our discussion of rubrics by describing them as simple measurement tools intended to facilitate consistent scoring of student performances and provide feedback to students about the quality of those performances. Through their use with SLOs and learning progressions, we have positioned rubrics as a central component, if not a driving force, in developing curriculum or instructional scope and sequence within one school year or across multiple school years. The progression from single task to entire

Table 27.5 SLO Achievement Level Descriptor

SLO Learning Goal	Grade 6 (age 11) band students will sight read music with characteristic tone quality while maintaining a steady beat.			
	Beginning	Growing	Meeting	Advancing
Sight Read	sight-reads, with rhythmic and melodic accuracy, musical examples that are eight measures in length that primarily move stepwise within a 5-note pattern in 4/4 time using quarter notes/rests, half notes and paired eighth notes (on the same pitch) while maintaining a steady beat at most points in the performance in Concert B<flat>.	sight-reads, with rhythmic and melodic accuracy, musical examples that are eight measures in length that move primarily stepwise with some skips within a 5-note pattern in 4/4 and 2/4 time using quarter notes/rests, half notes/rests and paired eighth notes, while maintaining a steady beat at some points in the performance in Concert B<flat> and F.	sight-reads, with rhythmic and melodic accuracy, musical examples in 4/4 and 2/4 time using quarter notes/rests, half notes/rests, dotted half notes, whole notes/rests and paired eighth notes within an octave while maintaining a steady beat at most points in the performance in Concert B<flat> and F.	sight-reads, with rhythmic and melodic accuracy, musical examples in 4/4, 2/4, and 3/4 time using quarter note/rest, half note/rest, dotted half notes, whole note/rest and grouped eighth notes within an octave and a half while maintaining a steady beat at most points in the performance in Concert B<flat>, F, and E<flat>.
Embouchure	flat chin, firm corners, sustaining embouchure for short periods of time (two measures) with good breath control in mid-range of instrument	flat chin, firm corners, sustaining embouchure for one-phrase intervals with good breath control in mid-range of instrument	flat chin, firm corners sustaining embouchure for longer periods of time while tonguing and coordinating finger movements (two-phrase pieces) with good breath control in mid-range of instrument	adjusts embouchure, breath control, slide positions, and fingerings in *second* octave of instrument with frequent supports (e.g., arrows on page; tuner) so pitches are in tune with other instruments

FIGURE 27.1 Beginning level sight-reading example.

FIGURE 27.2 Growing level sight-reading example.

course was intentional, because *coherence*—the essence of rubric, performance task, assessment, curriculum, and instruction development—flows from that progression. Within each assignment or activity, a focus on specific details of the task being performed is needed, while at the same time understanding how that individual task fits within the larger picture of attaining the learning goals of a course or mastering skills specified in state standards.

Whether developing rubrics for informal classroom assignments or performance tasks to be used as part of an SLO, teachers and assessment developers must determine the purpose for the assessment and the desired inferences regarding a student's understanding or skills as the first step in the assessment process. Upon determining the desired inference, teachers and assessment developers must return to the core questions posed at the beginning of the chapter.

1. What knowledge, skills, or other attributes of student performance should be assessed?
2. What evidence will demonstrate those knowledge and skills?
3. What tasks will elicit those evidence pieces from students?

A focus on these questions will guide teachers throughout the process of developing performance assessments and rubrics and providing feedback to students. The assessment administered at an audition to select students for all-state chorus or orchestra will not be the same one administered as the end-of-year assessment for an introductory performance course. The amount and type of feedback expected from an assessment also will vary based on the purpose and context of the assessment. Finally, the purpose and context of the assessment must be kept in the forefront to guide development of performance assessments and their rubrics.

REFERENCES

Abeles, H. F. (1973). A facet-factorial approach to the construction of rating scales to measure complex behaviors. *Journal of Educational Measurement, 10,* 145–151.

Andrade, H., & Boulay, B. (2003). The role of rubric-referenced self-assessment in learning to write. *Journal of Educational Research, 97*(1), 21–34.

Andrade, H., Du, Y., & Wang, X., (2008). Putting rubrics to the test: The effects of a model, criteria generation, and rubric referenced self-assessment on elementary students' writing. *Educational Measurement, Issues, and Practice, 27*(2), 3–13.

Azzara, C. D. (1993). Audiation-based improvisation techniques and elementary instrumental students' music achievement. *Journal of Research in Music Education, 41,* 328–342.

Barton, P., & Coley, R. (1994). *Testing in America's schools.* Princeton, NJ: Educational Testing Services.

Bergee, M. J. (2003). Faculty inter-judge reliability of music performance evaluation. *Journal of Research in Music Education, 51,* 137–150.

Briggs, D. C., Diaz-Bilello, E., Peck, F., Alzen, J., Chattergoon, R., & Johnson, R. (2015). *Using a learning progression framework to assess and evaluate student growth.* Center for Assessment, Design, Research and Evaluation (CADRE) and National Center for the Improvement of Educational Assessment. Retrieved from http://www.colorado.edu/education/sites/default/files/attached-files/CADRE.CFA-StudentGrowthReport-ExecSumm-Final.pdf

Brookhart, S. (2010). Mixing it up: Combining sources of classroom achievement information for formative and summative purposes. In H. Andrade & G. Cizek (Eds.), *Handbook of formative assessment* (pp. 279–296). New York, NY: Routledge.

Brookhart, S. M., Moss, C. M., & Long, B. A. (2008, March). *Professional development in formative assessment: Effects on teacher and student learning.* Paper presented at the meeting of the National Council on Measurement in Education, New York, NY.

Cooksey, J. M. (1977). A facet-factorial approach to rating high school choral music performance. *Journal of Research in Music Education, 25*(2), 100–114.

Etopio, E. (2009). *Characteristics of early music environments associated with preschool children's music skills.* (Doctoral dissertation). Available from Proquest Digital Dissertations database. (250868671).

Gordon, E. E. (2012). *Learning sequences in music: A contemporary music learning theory* (8th ed.). Chicago, IL: GIA.

Gredler, M. E., & Johnson, R. L. (2004). *Assessment in the literacy classroom.* Boston, MA: Pearson.

Hall, E., Gagnon. D., Thompson, J., Schneider, M. C., & Marion, S. (2014). *State practices related to the use of student achievement measures in the evaluation of teachers in non-tested subjects and grades.* Dover, NH: National Center for the Improvement of Educational Assessment. Retrieved from http://www.nciea.org/sites/default/files/publications/Gates_NTGS_Hall_082614.pdf

Herman, J., Buschang, R., & Matrundola, D. L. T. (2014). *An explanation of ELA and math cognitive complexity frameworks.* Los Angeles, CA: CRESST; University of California.

Hess, K., & Thompson, J. (2012). *High Quality Assessment Review Tool.* Dover, NH: Center for Assessment.

Hewitt, M. P. (2002). Self-evaluation accuracy among high school and middle school instrumentalists. *Journal of Research in Music Education, 50,* 215–226.

Kuhs, T., Johnson, R., Agruso, S., & Monrad, D. (2001). *Put to the test: Tools and techniques for classroom assessment.* Portsmouth, NH: Heinemann.

Lacireno-Paquet, N., Morgan, C., & Mello, D. (2014). *How states use student learning objectives in teacher evaluation systems: A review of state websites* (REL 2014–013). Washington, DC: US Department of Education, Institute of Education Sciences, National Center for Education Evaluation and Regional Assistance, Regional Educational Laboratory Northeast & Islands. Retrieved from http://ies.ed.gov/ncee/edlabs

Marion, S. F., DePascale, C. A., Domaleski, C., Gong, B., & Diaz-Bilello, E. (2012). *Considerations for analyzing educators' contributions to student learning in non-tested subjects and grades with a focus on student learning objectives.* Dover, NH: National Center for the Improvement of Educational Assessment. Retreived from https://www.nciea.org/sites/default/files/publications/Measurement%20Considerations%20for%20NTSG_052212%20v2.pdf

McDonel, J. S. (2015). Exploring learning connections between music and mathematics in early childhood. *Bulletin of the Council for Research in Music Education, 203,* 45–62.

Mertler, C. A. (2001). Designing scoring rubrics for your classroom. *Practical Assessment, Research and Evaluation, 7*(25), 1–8. Retrieved from http://www.pareonline.net/getvn.asp?v=7&n=25

Mislevy, R. J., Steinberg, L. S., & Almond, R. G. (1999). *Evidence-centered design.* Retrieved from the Educational Testing Service http://einstein.pslc.cs.cmu.edu/research/wiki/images/5/51/Evidence-Centered-Assessment-Design.pdf

National Center for the Improvement of Educational Assessment. (2013). *Instructional guide for developing student learning objectives.* Retrieved from http://www.nciea.org/sites/default/files/slo-tools/3_Instructional-Guide-for-Developing-Student-Learning-Objectives.pdf

National Coalition for Core Arts Standards. (2014). *Core music standards.* Retrieved from http://nccas.wikispaces.com

Popham, J. (2009). Assessment literacy for teachers: Faddish or fundamental? *Theory into Practice, 48*(1), 4–11.

Prince, C. D., Schuermann, P. J., Guthrie, J. W., Witham, P. J., Milanowski, A. T., & Thorn, C. A. (2009). *The other 69 percent: Fairly rewarding the performance of teachers of nontested subjects and grades.* Washington, DC: Center for Educator Compensation Reform. Retrieved from http://cecr.ed.gov/pdfs/guide/other69Percent.pdf

Ross, J. A., Hogaboam-Gray, A., & Rolheiser, C. (2002). Student self-evaluation in grade 5–6 mathematics effects on problem solving achievement. *Educational Assessment, 8*(1), 43–59.

Ross, J. A., Rolheiser, C., & Hogaboam-Gray, A. (1999). Effects of self-evaluation training on narrative writing. *Assessing Writing, 6*(1), 107–132.

Ruiz-Primo, M. A., Furtak, E., Yin, Y., Ayala, C., & Shavelson, R. J. (2010). On the impact of formative assessment on student science learning and motivation. In G. J. Cizek & P. Andrade (Eds.), *Handbook of formative assessment* (pp. 139–158). New York, NY: Routledge.

Runfola, M., & Etopio, E. (2010). The nature of performance-based criterion measures in early childhood education research, and related issues. In T. S. Brophy (Ed.), *The practice of assessment in music education; Frameworks, models and designs. Proceedings of the 2009 International Symposium on Assessment in Music Education* (pp. 395–406). Chicago, IL: GIA.

Saunders, T. C., & Holahan, J. M. (1997). Criteria-specific rating scales in the evaluation of high school instrumental performance. *Journal of Research in Music Education, 45,* 259–272.

Schneider, M. C., & Egan, K. (2014). *A handbook for creating range and target performance level descriptors.* The National Center for the Improvement of Educational Assessment. Retrieved from https://www.nciea.org/sites/default/files/publications/Handbook_091914.pdf

Schneider, M. C., Egan, K. L., & Julian, M. W. (2013). Classroom assessment in the context of high stakes assessment. In J. McMillian (Ed.), *Handbook of research in classroom assessment* (pp. 55–70). Los Angeles, CA: Sage.

Schneider, M. C., Johnson, R. L., & Gowan, P. (2011). *Creating assessments for student success.* Columbia: South Carolina Department of Education.

Schneider, M. C., Johnson, R., & Porchea, S. (2004). Factors that affect the measurement of rhythm achievement. *Visions of Research in Music Education, 5,* 6–15.

Shavelson, R. J., Baxter, G. P., & Gao, X. (1993). Sampling variability of performance assessments. *Journal of Educational Measurement, 30,* 215–232. doi: 10.1111/j.1745-3984.1993.tb00424.x

Shavelson, R. J., Ruiz-Primo, M. A., & Wiley, E. W. (1999), Note on sources of sampling variability in science performance assessments. *Journal of Educational Measurement, 36,* 61–71. doi: 10.1111/j.1745-3984.1999.tb00546.x

Smith, B. P., & Barnes, G. V. (2007). Development and validation of an orchestra performance rating scale. *Journal of Research in Music Education, 55,* 268–280.

Stiggins, R. (2008). *An introduction to student-involved assessment for learning.* Upper Saddle River, NJ: Pearson.

Stiggins, R. J., & Herrick, M. (2007). *A status report on teacher preparation in classroom assessment* (Unpublished research report). Portland, OR: Classroom Assessment Foundation.

Watkins, J. G., & Farnum, S. E. (1970). *Watkins-Farnum Performance Scale: Form A book.* Milwaukee, WI: Hal Leonard.

Webb, N. L. (2005). *Web Alignment Tool (WAT): Training manual. Draft Version 1.1.* Wisconsin Center for Education Research, Council of Chief State School Officers. Retrieved from http://wat.wceruw.org/Training%20Manual%202.1%20Draft%20091205.doc

Wiliam, D., Lee, C., Harrison, C., & Black, P. (2004). Teachers developing assessment for learning: Impact on student achievement. *Assessment in Education, 11*(1), 49–65.

Zdzinski, S. F., & Barnes, G. V. (2002). Development and validation of a string performance rating scale. *Journal of Research in Music Education, 50,* 245–255.

CHAPTER 28

THE DEVELOPMENT OF STANDARDS-BASED ASSESSMENTS IN MUSIC

FREDERICK BURRACK AND KELLY A. PARKES

THE PURPOSE OF STANDARDS IN MUSIC EDUCATION

ACADEMIC standards are public statements about what students should know and be able to do as a result of a formal learning experience. These concise, written descriptions act as guideposts that schools use to develop curriculum and assessment and to focus instruction. A standards movement, sometimes referred to as standard-based education reform, has been ongoing in the United States (Miyamoto, 2008) since the publication of *A Nation at Risk* (United States National Commission on Excellence in Education, 1983). The standards movement grew out of accusations that public schools demonstrated academic laxity under a fragmented curriculum, and led many to call for rigorous academic standards (Ravitch, 2000). In the United States, three congressional acts stimulated this movement. Standards were meant, in essence, to make tangible what the learning goals were for American students. More recently the National Coalition for Core Arts Standards, (State Education Agency Directors of Arts Education [SEADAE], 2014) stated:

> The central purposes of education standards are to identify the learning that we want for all of our students and to drive improvement in the system that delivers that learning. Standards...to ensure success for both educators and students in the real world of the school.   (p. 2)

According to Shuler (1995), standards promote the expectation for all students to achieve a level of competence in the skills and knowledge often attained by students in exemplary classrooms. The use of standards focuses efforts to bring all student learning up to the level of students in our best programs. Essentially, the primary purpose of standards and accompanying assessments can be seen to improve teaching and learning.

In music, there are often only two perceived categories of standards: content standards and performance standards. Content standards describe specific content areas of music learning. For example, students will be able to analyze the structure and context of varied musical works and their implications for performance. Performance standards describe the level of expectation for performance achievement at a specific point in time (usually by grade level). They help constituents define the types of evidences that demonstrate students having met the content standards and the level of expectation (Professional Learning Board, 2016). Both content and performance standards are intended to guide instruction and assessment. Achievement is often divided into levels (e.g., advanced, proficient, novice, and basic), frequently with examples of authentic student work to illustrate expected quality for each level (Educational Broadcasting Corporation, 2004).

Academic standards also serve to communicate disciplinary content and performance expectations to all relevant stakeholders. Standards that are publicly available allow parents, students, and teachers to discern what should be taught and the extent to which it should be learned. They are visible goals for all students to attain if they have the appropriate opportunity to learn in the discipline. Lehman (2014) proposed that standards and aligned assessments lead toward greater transparency in grading, providing an advantage for teachers to justify the score and making it easier for parents to understand. "There should no mystery about what is expected of the student, about how it will be assessed, and no mystery about how to interpret the results" (Lehman, 2014, p. 10).

Nierman (2012) suggests that one primary purpose of standards is to bridge the gap between curriculum expectations, classroom instruction, and student learning assessment, interdependent through the curriculum and instructional process. Clarifying expectations to guide curriculum development and instructional implementation is an important purpose of standards. When the learning intent is communicated to students by teachers, the standards can become an incentive for students who may not have recognized desired learning of their coursework. Standards can enhance initiative students take regarding their work and know how to aim for those goals without any guidance (Educational Broadcasting Corporation, 2004). Students can also know precisely what is expected, thus enabling them to take ownership of their learning. According to Biggs (1996), learning is optimized when instructional processes and assessment procedures aligned with defined standards are clearly communicated.

In countries where schools are not required to follow a national curriculum in music, such as in the United States, standards are accepted as voluntary. In the United States, the National Core Arts Standards for Music are often adopted or freely adapted by states, and in some communities the music programs develop their own. This may call into question the merits of national music standards for the purpose of defining music learning through aligned assessments. If national and state standards are not descriptors of expected achievement across an educational system, then standards-based assessments will only provide meaning on the local level (Colwell, 2010). To have meaning beyond the local context, Sung (2010) suggests that consensus for content and performance standards are necessary.

"Assessment in standards-based curriculum frameworks is a highly contested area of school education. Some say assessment narrows outcomes of schooling" (Farrell, 2014, p. 225). For the most part, this belief may be a result of high-stakes testing and using reported data for public accountability, comparisons of schoolwide achievement, and compliance of political policy. Cochran-Smith and Fries (2001) and Luke (2011) suggested that results from the high-stakes tests such as Program for International Student Assessment (PISA) and Trends in International Mathematics and Science Study (TIMSS) have affected national policy in many countries. Although some suggest that large-scale assessment is ideally used for the purpose of accountability with a standards-based K-12 curriculum (Herman, 2007; Pedersen, 2007), others contradict this proposal, confident that large-scale assessment may not be appropriate for use to support standards-based arts education (Mishook & Kornhaber, 2006; Schultz, 2002; Stiles & Malin, 2008).

Many feel that the primary purpose of standards and accompanying assessments is to improve teaching and learning. When assessment is assigned too much responsibility, testing can take over and drive the curriculum. Assessment in the form of testing is sometimes used to identify weak schools or weak teachers, resulting in some form of penalization instead of guiding improvement (Lehman, 2014). Identifying weakness is a first step toward improvement, but using discovered weakness against a program defeats the purpose of standards-based assessment for program improvement.

Shuler (1996) endorsed that in addition to adapting state and local curriculum frameworks to incorporate standards, "institutions that prepare, license (certify), and employ music teachers must use standards... to bring all teachers up to the level of those who currently lead our profession" (p. 2). He suggests an overall integration through teacher preparation, teacher licensing, and in-service professional development is vital to enhance student achievement in learning outlined by standards. Brophy (2003) focuses on making a concerted effort to help music teachers recognize a need for standards-based assessments and to support teachers in "developing informal and formal standards-based assessments" (p. 1). He suggests that teachers themselves can organize the skills and knowledge to be assessed, determine appropriate response modes from students, and select appropriate assessment materials. Convinced that teachers can develop assessment tasks and scoring guides based on standards, Brophy also suggests that teachers can examine their students' work to identify examples that represent basic, proficient, and advanced achievement levels. This gives teachers autonomy in determining the progress made by students in relation to the standards (state, local, or national). There are however, mitigating effects such as legislative and policy decisions that affect how teachers can examine and assess student learning in the context of standards.

Local (School and District) Policy Effects on Standards-Based Assessment

In the United States, local policy prescribes expected learning in schools, while many correspond with a set of state or national standards. The key to effective local policy is designing a system of music learning assessments through sequential, standards-based music instruction and alignment of internal (district level) and external (state and national level) accountability measures so that teachers are able to explain their student learning as part of their own professional development plans. Alignment of individual courses across a school's curriculum requires comprehensive standards for the entire program that allow for autonomy within each course to design high-quality and contextual assessments, through which students demonstrate the quality of learning in an applied setting.

To address local policies, many school districts design music curricula focused around defined sequence of content, concepts, and skills. Each grade level or course selects specific learning materials, learning tasks, and course-based assessments through which students demonstrate achievement, often tied to standards. It is typical that student achievement is assessed at various points throughout each course. Those schools with a thoroughly defined curriculum may also follow individual student achievement across the entire sequence of coursework. Increasingly, student-learning data collected from coursework are analyzed within each grade level or course to identify student achievement relative to the expectations of the standard agreed on by the program with the intent to identify areas of student learning that need further instruction. Assessment findings can be used to focus discussions to guide programmatic and instructional decisions. Longitudinal analysis of student achievement data and documentation of curricular adjustments implemented and reassessed to identify impact of learning provides accountability beyond musical performance of students.

When achievement standards and assessments align, they establish the foundation for developing a defined, long-range strategic plan for student learning in a standards-based curriculum for music programs (Stites & Malin, 2008). In contrast to documenting content taught as defined in a curriculum document or course syllabus (Darling-Hammond, 2004), "standards coupled with standards-based assessments can play important roles in supporting the alignment of individual and collective expectations within schools and thus foster the internal accountability that leads to increased opportunities to learn and improved learning outcomes" (Stites & Malin, 2008, p. 27).

Although music programs across schools in the United States define their own curriculum and often are reflective of state or national standards, states have strongly influenced local decisions with overarching policies (Colwell, 2008). Colwell points out that national and state standards provide a framework for the school to design curriculum. Teachers use them to focus learning goals for their students. When curriculum is aligned with comprehensive standards that define expected learning, quality and accountability of school music programs can be supported by assessments of student competencies (Hartenberger, 2008).

Rothstein, Jacobsen, and Wilder (2006) suggest that standards defining specific levels of competency can either present challenge to typical students and be unattainable to lower performing students or be attainable for all, but no standards can simultaneously do both. Hence, it is important to recognize that standards can be reflected in school curricula through a variety of instructional and assessment tasks. Students can demonstrate competency of standards in multiple ways, suggesting that accountability must begin with realistic goals that recognize variability of how students demonstrate competencies through standards-based assessment.

Overview of National Standards in the United States

The US Department of Education began initiating policy for academic standards during the President's Education Summit with the Governors in 1989 (Klein, 2014). The intention was to promote greater uniformity of learning achievement across the states so American students would be more competitive with their peers around the globe. The meeting resulted in a set of six National Education Goals that were later reflected in an education plan called Goals 2000: Educate America Act (Hamilton et al., 2008). In 1994, the National Education Standards and Improvement Council required that organizations write standards with three goals for the process: (1) that the standards reflected the best ideals in education, (2) that they reflected the best knowledge about teaching and learning, and (3) that they had been developed with a broad-based, open process. The standards themselves were to define what students should "be able to know and do." While the arts were not included as a core area in Goals 2000, they eventually were included in the legislation. Organizations such as the National Association for Music Educators (NAfME, then called Music Educators National Conference, MENC) received grant funds from the US Department of Education, the National Endowment for the Arts, and the National Endowment for the Humanities to move forward. To stimulate implementation of the plan, the Department of Education offered grants to enable states to conduct broad-based planning intended to result in adoption of a standards-based approach to achieve the national education goals (Herbert, 1995). In 1994, nine music content standards were created with established minimum competencies at grades 4, 8, and 12 of aligned achievement standards (MENC, 1994b, p. 3; MENC, 1996). The competencies were an attempt to describe how well students should perform at various age levels contingent that students had an equal opportunity to learn, also presented as standards. These national music standards were promoted as voluntary in reference to state involvement and did not include accompanying assessment measures. An equal opportunity to learn was based on the premise of a qualified teacher with a minimum of 90 minutes of instructional time per week in the elementary grades and at least 45 minutes every other day at both the middle and high school (Consortium of National Arts Education Associations, 1995).

Standards in the United States have never been a prescriptive set of governing rules, rather, they have served as an important guide to the development of curricula (SEADAE, 2014). The US constitution requires that education is the responsibility of the states, so the country effectively has 50 different educational systems. Within those states there are over 13,000 districts, each with varying degrees of autonomy over the education of the citizens within their purview. Because of this decentralized educational system of the United States, national standards are voluntary. This issue is further problematic with the introduction of the new education law, the Every Student Succeeds Act (US Department of Education, ESSA, 2016). States will attempt to ensure accountability across all districts by redirecting resources and empowering local decision-makers to develop their own systems for school improvement (White House Press Office, 2015). These strategies may not be equitable for all schools or between different content areas, and there is special concern for the arts in which standards are considered. As mentioned, some states require that state standards be used, whereas others allow teachers to have choice between local, state, or national standards. Consideration of the arts in national policy and core curricula was considered a triumph in 1994, but became short-lived when state and local policy failed to carry through (Herbert, 1995), largely due to the differences in how states view standards, and this remains the crux of the issue.

More than a decade after the 1994 National Standards were developed, a committee appointed by leaders at the National Association for Music Education met and concluded that the 1994 standards needed to be revised and updated, to include "specific grade-by-grade minimum competencies, at least in pre-school through grade 8 . . . and combine grades for music instruction in non-traditional groupings" (Lehman, 2008, p. 28). Nierman (2012) stated that this initiative required a political move to get professional organizations and societies (Orff, Kodaly, American Choral Directors, etc.) to come to agreement on what minimum competencies should be expected at each level, as well as developing corresponding assessment tasks (p. 104). Another goal of the initiative was to impact local policy and instructional practice, in order to help define learning expected for the 1-year fine-arts credit required in schools. If achievement indicators on associated assessments could describe 1-year high-school proficiency, then local practice could use these expectations to better define proficiency expectations for the credit requirement.

Interaction Between Standards and Curriculum

Standards in the arts must be specific enough to provide a basis for developing curricula, associated lesson plans, and assessments of student learning (Nierman, 2012). To guide instructional development, the standards must be sufficiently descriptive to provide a foundation for assessments that can differentiate levels of student achievement and/ or qualities of learning as defined by the standard. Overall, the field of music education is approaching a level of specificity that is beyond what has previously existed. "Schools are changing what they are doing by focusing on teaching and learning and aligning curriculum and instruction with standards" (Herman, 2007, p. 18). Alignment of assessment with the standards and curriculum planning is crucial. If mismatch exists between what is being taught and what is assessed, then assessment has little or no relationship to student learning. There is no doubt that assessment should be directly linked to curriculum. According to Gordon (2010), standards precipitate design and construction of a curriculum. Teachers should plan specific learning outcomes associated with standards, whether they come from national standards, state standards, or local curriculum standards, then align assessments to reflect student learning of standards (Parkes, 2010).

In curriculum, learning outcomes that clarify expected learning pathways for students should be used to design assessment and scoring devices. Assessments should yield appropriate evidence of the depth of growth of knowledge, understanding, and skills (Farrell, 2014). When standards-based assessment practices are implemented, students' awareness of the learning target increases (McVeigh, 2013). Standards coupled with standards-based assessments play an important role in alignment of learning expectations across grade levels, fostering an internal accountability that often leads to increased learning. While music teachers rely on a variety of assessment strategies to monitor student achievement, teachers who used standards-based assessment have been found to be more likely to use formal assessments to determine student achievement and assess students both formally and informally on a regular basis (McVeigh, 2013).

STANDARDS-BASED ASSESSMENTS IN THE UNITED STATES

Philosophical Changes

Beginning in the 1990s, there have been considerable changes in the United States with respect to developing standards-based assessments. Schools in the United States have increased expectations of students to become competent in prescribed standards. There has been a shift in the paradigm of standards-based assessment as a result of three education acts: the 1965 Elementary and Secondary Education Act (ESEA), which when reauthorized became known as the No Child Left Behind Act (NCLBA, 2002); the Goals 2000: Educate America Act (1994); and the most recent reauthorization of the ESEA, the Every Student Succeeds Act (ESSA, 2016). The education acts and initiatives illustrate the extent of their impact on assessment in music education in the United States. In providing federal education funds through these acts, the government holds states accountable for the education of all children. States therefore need to report, with data, how specific groups of students are performing. The act of reporting progress of groups of students from lower-income backgrounds was meant to ensure states could explain student achievement with standardized test results. The NCLB Act required that all students would reach proficient levels of achievement; however, states could determine the parameters to constitute "proficient." This meant that the rigor of standards became the focus in the United States, with considerable differences in observed levels of rigor.

The requirements for students to pass standardized tests in literacy (reading) and mathematics diverted funding and scheduled instructional time away from the arts in order to support and increase student performance on those specific tests. As early as 2011, it became clear that 100% of students were not proficient on the tests required to demonstrate access to continued ESEA funding. Waivers were then allowed permitting states to meet alternative requirements to illustrate they were still serving their students equitably. The accountability system put into place then used students' standardized test scores (purported measures of growth) as evaluation measures for teachers. That is, teachers were evaluated by how well their students performed on mathematics and literacy tests, even if they taught subjects such as music, art, physical education, and so forth. This essentially tied student achievement, as reported on standardized tests, with teaching effectiveness and/or teaching quality. With the ESSA (US DOE, 2016), another reauthorization of the original law, US states are afforded more choice about how to measure teacher effectiveness, and both teacher evaluations and student achievement must be determined with multiple measures, rather than restricted to standardized test scores in literacy and mathematics. This may allow teachers to have more agency in determining what they measure in their students' learning of both national and state standards, depending on how each state responds to ESSA regulations.

Past Assessment Projects and Initiatives

National Assessment of Educational Progress (NAEP)

In the United States, the National Assessment of Educational Progress (NAEP) is administered, on a periodic basis, in what are considered core disciplines. The NAEP assessment is required to be carried out by the US Department of Education, and policy for NAEP is set by the National Assessment Governing Board, appointed by the secretary of education but independent of the department. It is important to note that the NAEP was not designed to test students individually but to provide a national profile of achievement levels and skills. The NAEP was first administered to three age groups: 9-, 13-, and 17 year-olds, which were randomly sampled from schools across the United States. The purposes of the test were to determine what the music students knew and could do and their attitudes toward music education. "Results of the exercises were generally low, although attitudes toward music were positive" (Rivas, 1974, p. i). The arts, specifically visual art and music, were included in NAEP in the 1970s. "Throughout the 1980s, however, they were absent, and only the basics of mathematics, science, reading, writing, and, occasionally, history and geography were tested" (Herbert, 1995, 16). A recommendation of the National Endowment for the Arts (1988) *Toward Civilization* report was to put the arts back into NAEP. Because of a lack of funding and possibly a lowered focus on the arts, the next inclusion on the NAEP was not until 1997, missing two administrations. The political efforts of national arts education organizations were largely successful in the 1990s in regaining the awareness of policymakers through the creation of the national arts education standards as well as their strong advocacy initiatives. By means of funding from the National Endowment for the Arts and the Getty Education Institute, the assessment project was administered by the Council of Chief State School Officers (CCSSO; Lehman, 1999).

To enhance assessment of student achievement, the CCSSO in the spring of 1994 was awarded a contract from the Educational Testing Service (ETS) to develop items for the NAEP arts assessment. Through this award, 15 state education departments were funded to create prototype performance assessment items in dance, music, theater, and visual arts. In 1995, the CCSSO created the State Collaborative on Assessment and Student Standards Arts Education Consortium (SCASS/Arts) to assist states in developing arts standards and assessments (Stites & Malin, 2008). The 1997 NAEP and 2008 NAEP Arts were based on three artistic processes: responding, performing, and creating. Examples of these tasks included listening analytically to a work of music (responding), performing that work, and improvising (creating) over its chord progression (National Assessment Governing Board, 1994).

> Unfortunately, the roughly 45-minute time limit imposed on NAEP administration greatly limited the extent to which those assessments could authentically measure students' ability to carry out the processes of Performing and Creating, because those processes are authentically carried out over a more extended period of time.
> (Shuler, 2016, p. 67)

In 1999, SCASS/Arts published *Arts Assessment: Lessons Learned from Developing Performance Tasks*, a handbook that contained model assessment tasks. These were exercises that had been developed for the 1997 NAEP arts assessment and aligned with the national arts standards but had not been selected for use. The items were revised to reflect grade-level expectations for grades 4, 8, and 12 (Stites & Malin, 2008). Many questions also were raised about whether states could replicate an assessment process similar to the 1997 NAEP arts assessment for the purpose of accountability. "The NAEP Arts Assessment has served as a model for many state arts assessment initiatives" (p. 9).

Many concerns have been raised regarding the 1997 assessment, which include the validity of the results, contradictions within the report card, the overall usefulness of the reports, and the delay in reporting all of the results (Colwell, 1999a). The 2008 NAEP measured only 8th-grade students in responding to music, eliminating performing and creating music, which are two areas that are central to the 1994 national standards (Shuler, 2009). Past research suggests that score gains on low-stakes (nonaccountability) tests, such as the NAEP, show some increase in achievement when associated with state accountability policies, although it is difficult to know the size of the actual increase (Hamilton et al., 2008).

National Music Standards in PK-12 Education

The National Standards for the Arts were released in 1994 in the United States, but it soon became apparent that music teachers did not know how to measure the learning of their students with respect to these standards (Brophy, 1997; Fallis, 1999; Lehman 1997; Russell & Austin, 2010). The challenge that music teachers faced was that the standards did not reflect instructional practice as a whole. Lehmann (2008) observed, "the standards were never intended to reflect the status quo, but rather to provide a vision for the future. They set forth long-term goals for what music education ought to be in our society" (p. 38). Elliott (2006) was critical of the 1994 music standards and characterized the content standards as reducing the complexity of music making to a list of behaviors.

The recent 2014 National Coalition for Core Arts Standards (NCCAS) Conceptual Framework declared the 2014 Core Arts standards would "guide the continuous and systematic operations of instructional improvement by:

- Defining artistic literacy through a set of overarching Philosophical Foundations and Lifelong Goals that clarify long-term expectations for arts learning.
- Placing Artistic Processes and Anchor Standards at the forefront of the work.
- Identifying Creative Practices as the bridge for the application of the Artistic Processes across all learning.
- Specifying Enduring Understandings and Essential Questions that provide conceptual through-lines and articulate value and meaning within and across the arts discipline.
- Providing Model Cornerstone Assessments of student learning aligned to the Artistic Processes." (p. 6) (For more detail, see the next section in this chapter.)

In May 2010, the Common Core Standards for English Language Arts and Mathematics were about to be released, and the national Science and Social Studies organizations had begun a process of revising their national standards. This initiated the State Education Agency Directors of Arts Education (SEADAE) to hold a gathering of over 50 arts education organizations, researchers, and stakeholders at the offices of the CCSSO in Washington, DC, to design an arts framework for the Common Core. In this historic meeting the assembled group voted to pursue revising the 1994 national arts standards.

By spring 2011 the work had begun, guided by the newly created NCCAS, whose members included the American Alliance for Theatre and Education, the College Board (1993), the Educational Theatre Association, the National Art Education Association, the National Association for Music Education, the National Dance Education Organization, and the State Education Agency Directors of Arts Education. As time went by, new partners were to join the cause, including leadership members Young Audiences Arts for Learning and Americans for the Arts. Additional supporting members included the John F. Kennedy Center for the Performing Arts and the Lincoln Center Education department. Monthly and then weekly meetings built the coalition that would fund and guide the work. The NCCAS reached out to Jay and Daisy McTighe, who became consultants to the work, guiding the inclusion of Understanding by Design elements (Wiggins & McTighe, 2006) to foster an inquiry approach to higher-order thinking skills within arts education.

By January 2012, five discipline-specific writing teams were in place for dance, media arts, music, theater, and visual arts. The writing teams and NCCAS leadership spent much of the first year creating the framework and the underpinning philosophical foundations and lifelong goals that would articulate broad goals for learning and defining artistic literacy. Artistic processes and process components became the framework to guide the writing. Enduring understandings and essential questions were drafted to ensure a plan for deep transfer of learning tied to the performance standards, and grade-by-grade standards writing began. The NCCAS leadership authored a white paper titled *National Core Arts Standards—A Conceptual Framework for Arts Learning* (SEADAE, 2014).

In 2013, NCCAS began releasing draft copies of the standards for public review. During a series of three public reviews, the coalition received over 1.5 million comments from over 6,000 reviewers, all of which were meticulously studied by research teams, with results driving revisions and edits. Focus groups were convened by SEADAE, the National Guild for Community Arts Education, Young Audiences Arts for Learning, the League of American Orchestras, and the Kennedy Center, among others, to provide additional commentary. The NCCAS heard a clear message in the reviews of the early drafts: a call to simplify the standards, to reduce the number of standards materials, and a clear call for more unity among the disciplines. In response to the comments, writing teams returned to the drawing board and simplified the grade-by-grade standards, created large overarching anchor standards that crossed disciplines, and moved Understanding by Design elements into optional instructional support packages.

The 2014 Core Arts Music Standards were developed through a backward design approach (Wiggins & McTighe, 2006), beginning with artistic processes from which the standards emerged. They were designed by teams of music supervisors, curriculum experts, and teachers, soliciting feedback from public stakeholders at two points preceding the eventual publication of the standards in 2014. The standards for all the arts are organized by three artistic processes—*perform*, *create*, and *respond*, with *connecting* being seen as integrated within the three processes in music. For each artistic process, component parts essential in the processes have been identified resulting in a sequence of performance standards that recommend goals for students as they progress.

On June 4, 2014, the newly revised national arts standards were published in a cyber-launch with the opening of their interactive website home at www.nationalartsstandards.org for a summer of beta testing, prior to a full launch event in October. Unlike other sets of standards published in hard copy, the new national core arts standards exist only as an Internet-based tool, within an interactive website, which allows users to access, sort, and print the standards in ways that are most pertinent to their needs. This marked the end of the 3-year process of writing and revising the standards, resulting in a set of comprehensive grade-by-grade arts standards for the disciplines of dance, media arts, music, theater, and visual arts, and supported by six research studies, Model Cornerstone Assessments (MCAs), inclusion guides for all learners, and other instructional supports.

The philosophical and pragmatic shift from 1994 content standards that describe the content that students are to be learning to the 2014 performance standards that describe the level of work students are to demonstrate has not become obvious to many music teachers, despite the number of teachers involved in their development. Although the new sequence is designed for outcomes, (Shuler, Norgaard, & Blakeslee, 2014) it is not clear across the United States how many teachers have examined or use the 2014 standards, perhaps due to issues such as size and accessibility of the document. Lehman (2008) reminded us, "standards are useless if we don't know whether or not they're being met, and the only way we can know that is through assessment. One of the most important results of the standards movement is that it has made assessment both possible and necessary" (p. 21). The 2014 National Core Arts Standards include MCAs, which measure student learning of the artistic processes using instructionally embedded tasks. The MCAs are designed to provide evidence from student work embedded in their school's curriculum to illustrate levels of achievement that can assist teachers in designing further instruction and document learning. At the writing of this chapter, the MCAs are being tested in schools for applicability, utility, reliability, and validity as assessments. In contrast to traditional assessment models, these standards-based assessments are not designed to compare students' learning between programs or states, but are to be used by teachers to provide indicators as to the extent to which students are able to apply and demonstrate the artistic processes prescribed in the standards.

The Development of Current Standards-Based Assessments

Model Cornerstone Assessments

In education, what is chosen for assessment signals what is to be valued. The MCAs connected to the 2014 standards provide a template in which programs can infuse curricular content to assess student achievement of the standards. MCAs are an example of standards-based classroom assessments because teachers typically select the scope and sequence of standards taught. The MCAs are designed to provide strong alignment between assessment and the 2014 standards. The performance standards describe how students demonstrate the components of the artistic processes. Pre-K through grade 8 performance standards are written per grade level. Because students' selection of ensemble courses can occur at any grade, the new music ensemble and specialty course standards are presented in five levels of proficiency rather than by grade: novice, intermediate, proficient, accomplished, and advanced. They are flexible so to accommodate the varying degrees of achievement existing in middle and high school music programs.

Each MCA is designed to be used within instruction through a series of interconnected tasks focused on the process components of the associated artistic processes (create, perform, respond). Within each task, students demonstrate a level of attainment of at least one performance standard measured with a scoring device (rubric). The rubrics are designed to assess the standard, even if the curricular content (repertoire) is altered. This enables the assessment to be useful within multiple curricula. It also allows for equitable assessment for the varied ways students demonstrate achievement within each artistic process. A key aspect of the MCAs is the use of self-assessment and peer assessment, reflecting how musicians move through the process components in practice. Black and Wiliam (2004) remark, "peer assessment is uniquely valuable because students may accept criticisms of their work from one another that they would not take seriously if the remarks were offered by a teacher," and they "learn by taking on the roles of teachers and examiners of others" (p. 14). Illustrative examples (videos of students and student work samples) garnered via the pilot study are provided for teachers to reflect genuine demonstration of student achievement at each level. The intent is that the student work illustrates levels of achievement, offering relevant and reliable evidence of what students understand, know, and can do. The Model Cornerstone Assessments are not meant to be considered as aggregated benchmarks against which educational programs evaluate music student achievement of standards between classrooms, schools and districts (Burrack & Parkes, 2018).

STANDARDS-BASED MUSIC ASSESSMENTS IN GLOBAL CONTEXTS

International Baccalaureate Program

The International Baccalaureate (IB) was developed with a rigorous, standardized curriculum to meet the educational needs of geographically mobile students who required to have academic credentials accepted worldwide, such as children of diplomats, students living abroad, and native students returning from abroad (Poelzer & Feldhusen, 1997). The International Baccalaureate Organization (IBO), a chartered, private, nongovernmental foundation headquartered in Geneva, Switzerland, is recognized by the Council of Europe and holds consultative status with the United Nations Educational, Scientific, and Cultural Organization (Nugent & Karnes, 2002). As described by Stites and Malin (2008), the International Baccalaureate Program (IBP) program of study is in use in over 60 countries, with many programs in the United States. The curriculum for the IB Music course requires both aural and visual analytical skills, and suggests at least 1 year of harmony and ear training prior to enrolling. However, if this is not possible, many instructors will incorporate harmony and aural training into the IB class (Rufino, 2007). Students receive a good grounding in the history of Western European music and become acquainted with music of other cultures. In addition to an IB Music test, the course requires a project called the musical investigation, which is scored by an external evaluator, requiring the candidate to formulate a thesis statement comparing or contrasting two distinct musical cultures. With a required length between 1,200 and 2,000 words, the musical investigation must be in the form of a "media script" such as a television program, PowerPoint presentation, a debate, an

exchange of written letters, or a radio program (Stites & Malin, 2008, p. 50). The performance portion is conducted at individual schools rather than through the external
examinations (Stites & Malin, 2008).

Creativity, Activity, and Service (CAS) are a mandatory component of the IB program. It encourages students to be involved in sports, artistic pursuits, and community
service. Fifty hours of participation are required to fulfill CAS in each of the three areas,
for a total of 150 hours. Participation in marching band, an extracurricular chorus, jazz
band, orchestra, or the school musical, for example, may fulfill one portion of the CAS
activity or creativity requirement (Rufino, 2007, p. 51). These three CAS components
are not formally assessed but students do reflect on these experiences as part of their
diploma program.

Learning Metrics Task Force

The Learning Metrics Task Force (2013) consists of the UNESCO Institute for Statistics
and the Center for Universal Education at the Brookings Institution. The Task Force, a
multistakeholder group of 30 organizations, collected input over 18 months from three
technical working groups of 186 experts, with consultations with more than 1,700 individuals in 118 countries. The guiding questions to their work were: (1) What learning is
important globally? (2) How should it be measured? (3) How can measurement of learning improve education quality? Their focus was on the performance standards resulting
in a series of recommendations. Their first recommendation called for a global paradigm shift from universal access to access *plus* learning. The second was to suggest that
education systems should offer opportunities for youth and children to master competencies in seven domains of learning: culture and the arts, physical well-being, social
and emotional well-being, literacy and communication, learning approaches and cognition, numeracy and mathematics, and science and technology. Culture and the arts were
defined as:

> creative expression, including activities from the areas of music, theatre, dance, or
> creative movement, and the visual, media and literary arts. Also, cultural experi-
> ences in families school, community and country. The subdomain examples were
> creative arts, cultural knowledge, self- and community-knowledge, awareness of
> and respect for diversity.   (p. 21)

The third recommendation encouraged learning indicators to be tracked globally,
initially focused on access, completion, literacy, and numeracy. The fourth suggested
that countries be supported in strengthening their assessment systems and, ultimately,
in improving learning levels, and the fifth stated that measurement of learning must
include an explicit focus on equity, with particular attention to inequalities within
countries. The sixth supported the notion that measures for globally tracked indicators must be a public good, with tools, documentation, and data made freely available.

The final recommendation was that stakeholders must take action to ensure the right to learn for all children and youth.

The LMTF currently seeks to support the development of robust systems for assessing learning outcomes (global, national, local) and use resulting the data to improve learning. The United States is not identified as a collaborator with this project, however 15 countries from Latin America, sub-Saharan Africa, South Asia, the Middle East and Northern Africa, and North America (Canada) are working in what is called LMTF 2.0. These countries, designated as Learning Champions, collaborate through governmental agencies, assessment associations, and teacher organizations to advance effective assessment systems. The areas of measurement are (1) learning for all—where measures of completion and learning are combined into one measure (reading proficiency at the end of primary school); (2) age and education matter for learning—timely entry, progression, and completion of schooling is measured along with population-based indicators to capture those who do not enter school or leave school early; (3) reading—measuring foundational skills by grade 3 and proficiency at the end of primary school; (4) numeracy—measuring basic skills by end of primary and proficiency by lower secondary school; (5) ready to learn—measuring acceptable levels of early learning and development across a subset of domains by primary school entry; (6) citizen of the world—measuring the demonstration of values and skills necessary for success in communities, countries, and the world; and (7) breadth of learning opportunities—tracking the exposure to learning opportunities across all seven domains of learning.

Standards-Based Assessment in an Environment of Educational Accountability

There are continual efforts to develop effective measures that reflect desired student performance. Many advocate that standards should be uniform and apply to all students, with an understood contingency that there is uniform opportunity to learn. Although standards and the associated assessments should be challenging and expand educators' beliefs about what students can learn, they must also be attainable to students as a result of available instruction. Hamilton, Stecher, and Yuan (2008) suggest, the "goal of improving student performance is to lead to improvements in educational practices" (p. 38). Assessment of music programs should align with content taught in the program curriculum. Assessments designed around standards are excellent resources to guide standards-based instruction.

A study by McVeigh (2013) identified how standards-based assessment impacts instruction and student achievement and provides several important findings. Teachers who used standards-based assessment were more likely to use formal performance-based assessments to determine student achievement and assess students on a more frequent basis. Furthermore, students' awareness of the expected level of learning increased. They became less reliant on teacher feedback and they were more likely to believe that their grade actually reflected their achievement in class.

Performance assessment is constrained by limitations of time, and therefore is able to provide, ideally, a valid snapshot of music learning within a restricted set of objectives. Emphasis should be placed on standards-based assessments to provide information for improved instruction. Once results of standards-based assessments are analyzed, this information has potential value for improving teachers' day-to-day work and strategic planning (Hamilton et al., 2008). Any assessment is an indicator of learning and cannot represent all the possible ways that learning can occur or be demonstrated by a student.

Inequities in opportunity continue to plague the education system, but using standards to guide instruction with aligned assessments tied to curriculum can address some concerns of equity. In consideration of using standards-based assessments for accountability of student learning, it is necessary to acknowledge individual differences among students and acknowledge that we cannot eliminate variability in performance. If policymakers are concerned with improving student learning aligned with performance standards, then professional development and other support to encourage high-quality instruction are essential. "It takes professional development to use (assessment) tools and to change one's teaching practice to incorporate them. School leaders and policymakers need to be respectful of teachers given the fact that they're going to need time and support" (Rebora, 2014, para. 9).

References

Biggs, J. B. (1996). Enhancing teaching through constructive alignment. *Higher Education, 32*, 1–18.

Black, P., & Wiliam, D. (2004). *Inside the black box: Raising standards through classroom assessment*. London, UK: School of Education, King's College.

Brophy, T. S. (1997). Reporting progress with developmental profiles. *Music Educators Journal, 84*(1), 24–27.

Brophy, T. S. (2003). Developing and implementing standards-based assessments. In C. Lindemann (Ed), *Benchmarks in action* (pp. 1–16). Reston, VA: MENC.

Burrack, F., & Parkes, K. A. (2018). *Applying Model Cornerstone Assessments in K-12 Music: A research-supported approach*. Reston VA: Rowman & Littlefield.

Cochran-Smith, M., & Fries, M. (2001). Sticks, stones, and ideology: The discourse of reform in teacher education. *Educational Researcher, 30*, 332–342.

Colwell, R. (1999a). The 1997 assessment in music: Red flags in the sunset. *Arts Education Policy Review, 100*(6), 33–39.

Colwell, R., (2008). Music assessment in an increasingly politicized, accountability-driven educational environment. In T. Brophy (Ed.), *Assessment in music education: Integrating curriculum, theory, and practice, Proceedings of the Florida Symposium on Assessment in Music Education* (pp. 4–16). Chicago, IL: GIA Publications.

Colwell, R. (2010). Many voices, one goal: Practices of large-scale music assessment. In T. Brophy (Ed.), *The practice of assessment in music education: Frameworks, models, and designs. Proceedings of the 2nd international symposium on assessment in music education* (pp. 3–22). Chicago, IL: GIA Publications.

Consortium of National Arts Education Associations. (1995). *Opportunity-to-learn standards for arts education: Dance, music, theatre, visual arts*. Reston, VA: Music Educators National Conference.

Darling-Hammond, L. (2004). Standards, accountability, and school reform. *Teachers College Record, 106,* 1047–1085.

Educational Broadcasting Corporation. (2004). *Concept to classroom.* Retrieved from https://www.thirteen.org/edonline/concept2class/standards/index.html

Elliott, D. (2006). Music education and assessment: Issues and suggestions. In P. Taylor (Ed.), *Assessment in arts education* (pp. 41–56). Portsmouth, NH: Heinemann.

Fallis, T. (1999). Standards-based instruction in rehearsal. *Music Educators Journal, 85*(4), 18–50.

Farrell, H. (2014). The blind assessor: Are we constraining or enriching diversity of music development and learning? In T. S. Brophy, M.-L. Lai, & H.-F. Chen (Eds.), *Music assessment and global diversity: Practice, measurement, and policy, Proceedings of the 4th International Symposium on Assessment in Music Education* (pp. 211–231). Chicago, IL: GIA Publications.

Goals 2000: Educate America Act, 20 U.S.C §§ 5801 (1994).

Gordon, E. (2010). The crucial role of music aptitudes in music instruction. In T. Brophy (Ed.), *The practice of assessment in music education: Frameworks, models, and designs. Proceedings of the 2nd international symposium on assessment in music education* (pp. 211–215). Chicago, IL: GIA Publications.

Hamilton, L., Stecher, B., & Yuan, K. (2008). *Standards-based reform in the United States: History, research, and future directions.* Santa Monica, CA: RAND Corporation.

Hartenberger, A. (2008). Connecting assessment to standards through core conceptual competencies. In T. Brophy (Ed.), *Assessment in music education: Integrating curriculum, theory, and practice, Proceedings of the 2007 Florida Symposium on Assessment in Music Education* (pp. 71–107). Chicago, IL: GIA Publications.

Herbert, D. (1995). The national arts education landscape: Past, present, and future. *Arts Education Policy Review, 96*(6), 13–20.

Herman, J. (2007). *Accountability and assessment: Is public interest in K-12 education being served? CRESST Report 728.* Los Angeles, CA: National Center for Research on Evaluation, Standards, and Student Testing.

Klein, A. (2014). Historic summit fueled push for K-12 standards: Historic sit-down propelled national drive for standards-based accountability. *Education Week, 34*(5), 1.

Learning Metrics Task Force (LMTF). (2013). *Toward universal learning: Recommendations from the Learning Metrics Task Force.* Montreal and Washington, DC: UNESCO Institute for Statistics and Center for Universal Education at the Brookings Institution.

Lehman, P. R. (1997). Assessment and grading. *Teaching Music, 5*(3), 58–59.

Lehman, P. R. (1999). Introduction to the symposium on the "NAEP 1997 Arts Report Card." *Arts Education Policy Review, 100*(6), 12–15.

Lehman, P. R. (2008). A vision for the future: Looking at the standards. *Music Educators Journal, 94*(4), 28.

Lehman, P. R. (2014). How are we doing? In T. Brophy (Ed.), *Music assessment and global diversity: Practice, measurement, and policy. Proceedings of the 4th International Symposium on Assessment in Music Education* (pp. 3–17). Chicago, IL: GIA Publications.

Luke, A. (2011). Generalizing across borders: Policy and the limits of educational science. *Educational Researcher, 40,* 367–377.

McVeigh, M. S. (2013). *Standards-based performance assessment in the comprehensive music classroom* (Masters thesis). University of Wisconsin-Milwaukee, Milwaukee, WI. *Theses and Dissertations, 236.* Retrieved from https://dc.uwm.edu/etd/236/

MENC: The National Association for Music Education. (1996). *Performance standards for music: Strategies and benchmarks for assessing progress toward the national standards, grades pre-K–12.* Reston, VA: Author.

Mishook, J., & Kornhaber, M., (2006). Arts integration in the era of accountability. *Arts Education Policy Review, 107*(4), 3–11.

Miyamoto, K. (2008). The origins of the standards movement in the United States: Adoption of the written test and its influence on class work. *Educational Studies in Japan: International Yearbook, 3,* 27–40.

Music Educators National Conference. (1994b). *The school music program: A new vision.* Reston, VA: Author.

National Assessment Governing Board. (1994). *1997 arts education assessment framework.* Washington, DC: National Assessment Governing Board.

National Endowment for the Arts. (1988). *Toward civilization: A report on arts education.* Washington, DC: National Endowment for the Arts.

Nierman, G. (2012). Making a case for high-stakes assessment in music. In T. Brophy & Lehman-Wermser (Eds.), *Music Assessment across cultures and continents: The culture of shared practice, Proceedings of the 3rd International Symposium on Assessment in Music Education* (pp. 97–107). Chicago, IL: GIA Publications.

No Child Left Behind Act of 2001. (2002). P.L. 107–110, 20 U.S.C. § 6319.

Nugent, S., & Karnes, F. (2002). The Advanced Placement Program and the International Baccalaureate Programme: A history and update. *Gifted Child Today, 25*(1), 30–39.

Parkes, K., (2010). Assessing student learning in music performance class: What works, what doesn't, and what we can do about it. In T. Brophy (Ed.), *The practice of assessment in music education: Frameworks, models, and designs. Proceedings of the 2nd international symposium on assessment in music education* (pp. 351–364). Chicago, IL: GIA Publications.

Pedersen, P. (2007). What is measured is treasured: The impact of the No Child Left Behind Act on nonassessed subjects. *The Clearing House, 80,* 287–291.

Poelzer, G., & Feldhusen, J. (1997). The International Baccalaureate program: A program for gifted secondary students. *Roeper Review, 19,* 168–171.

Professional Learning Board. (2016). *What are the differences between content and achievement standards?* Retrieved from http://k12teacherstaffdevelopment.com/tlb/what-is-the-difference-between-content-standards-and-performance-standards/

Ravitch, D. (2000). *Left back: A century of battles over school reform.* Simon & Schuster: New York.

Rebora, A. (2014, March 5). *The coming age of instructionally integrated testing* [Interview with James Pellegrino]. Retrieved from https://www.edweek.org/tm/articles/2014/03/05/ndia_pellegrinoqa.html

Rivas, F. (1974). *The First Music Assessment: An Overview. National Assessment of Educational Progress.* Report No. 03–MU–00. Carnegie Foundation, Ford Foundation and National Center for Education Statistics: New York. ERIC # ED097275.

Rothstein, R., Jacobsen, R., & Wilder, T. (2006). Proficiency for all: An oxymoron. *Education Week, 26*(13), 32–44. Washington, DC. ERIC # ED097275.

Rufino, V. (2007). Understanding the music curriculum in the International Baccalaureate Program. *Music Educators Journal, 93*(4), 48–53.

Russell, J., & Austin, J. (2010). Assessment practices of secondary music teachers. *Journal of Research in Music Education, 58*(1), 37–54.

Schultz, R. A. (2002). Apples, oranges, and assessment. *Arts Education Policy Review, 103*(3), 11–16.

Shuler, S. (1995). The impact of national standards on the preparation, in-service professional development, and assessment of music teachers. *Arts Education Policy Review, 96*(3), 2.

Shuler, S. (1996). Why high school students should study the arts. *Music Educators Journal, 83*(1), 22–49.

Shuler, S. (2009). Music assessment and the nation's report card. *Music Educators Journal, 96*(1), 12–13.

Shuler, S. (2016). Model cornerstone assessments: Clarifying standards, extending capacity, and supporting learning. In T. Brophy & Lehman-Wermser (Eds.), *Arts classroom-based performance assessment in Washington State: The journey continues. Proceedings of the fifth international symposium on assessment in music education* (pp. 57–73). Chicago, IL: GIA Publications.

Shuler, S., Norgaard, M., & Blakeslee, M. (2014). The new national standards for music educators. *Music Educators Journal, 101*(1), 41–50.

State Education Agency Directors of Arts Education (SEADAE). (2014). *National Core Arts Standards: A conceptual framework for arts learning.* Retrieved from http://nccas.wikispaces. com/file/detail/Framework%2005%2022-14.pdf

Stites, R., & Malin, H. (2008). *An unfinished canvas: A review of large-scale assessment in K-12 arts education.* Menlo Park, CA: SRI International.

Sung, Y. (2010). Implementing standard-based assessment in music classrooms: Experiences from Taiwan. In T. Brophy (Ed.), *The practice of assessment in music education: Frameworks, models, and designs. Proceedings of the 2nd international symposium on assessment in music education* (pp. 3–22). Chicago, IL: GIA Publications.

The College Board. (1993). *International Arts Education Standards: A survey of standards, practices, and expectations in thirteen countries and regions.* New York, NY: Author.

US Department of Education (2016). *Every Student Succeeds Act.* Retrieved from https://www. ed.gov/news/press-releases/education-department-releases-final-regulations-promote-high-quality-well-rounded-education-and-support-all-students

US National Commission on Excellence in Education. (1983). *A nation at risk: The imperative for educational reform.* Retrieved from https://www.edreform.com/wp-content/uploads/ 2013/02/A_Nation_At_Risk_1983.pdf

White House Press Office. (2015, December 2). *Congress acts to fix No Child Left Behind.* [Press release]. Retrieved from https://obamawhitehouse.archives.gov/the-press-office/2015/12/03/ fact-sheet-congress-acts-fix-no-child-left-behind

Wiggins, G. P., & McTighe, J. (2006). *Understanding by design.* Upper Saddle River, NJ: Pearson.

CHAPTER 29

....

CROSS-CULTURAL AND STANDARDS-BASED ASSESSMENT OF THE AFRICAN MUSICAL ARTS

....

RENÉ HUMAN

INTRODUCTION: CROSS-CULTURAL UNDERSTANDING AND CROSS-CULTURAL DIALOGUE

THIS chapter focuses on assessment in cross-cultural music education, based on cross-cultural understanding and dialogue, and aims to accommodate diverse forms of thinking. It introduces a generic, standards-based evaluation system as a holistic and formative process, setting levels or standards-levels[1] for the assessment of African musical arts.[2] This evaluation system takes the form of a generic curriculum framework, which is necessarily implementable outside its culture of origin. It demonstrates the development of compatible assessment standards for African musical arts, and is able to accommodate Western forms of thinking, which tend to be given primacy in formal education, as well as African-ness,[3] and African forms of thinking, mostly represented as informal education. Both of these forms of thinking are elaborated on in this chapter.

In this section, I introduce the measurability of African musical arts (including music, dance, drama, poetry, and costume art as an integrated whole), and develop a generic evaluation system based on recontextualized authenticity, implementable outside its culture of origin, titled *The Generic Crosscultural Assessment Framework for African Musical Art*. This system illustrates that the cultural-educational chasm between indigenous and international (or formal) music educations can be bridged. It introduces a reliable, valid, and objective evaluation system for the assessment of African musical arts, which can be recognized internationally, to the satisfaction of both Western and African cultures.

The Effect of Globalism on Music Education

The effect of globalism on education, and specifically on music education, is profound, and the course music education takes will undeniably be heavily influenced by its effects. As a dynamic and ever-evolving process, globalism impacts communities, cultures, and economies as well as educational concepts such as cross-culturalism (Aubert, 2007; Dunbar-Hall, 2005; Schippers, 2005), genericism[4] (Bhabha, 1994; Mushira, 2012; Taylor, 1971), holism[5] (Bjørkvold, 1992; Mans, 2012; Smuts, 1926), and recontextualized authenticity[6] (Brannen, 2004; Campbell, 2004; Dunbar-Hall, 2005; Elliott, 2005; Reimer, 2003; Westerlund, 2003).

When reflecting on the transcultural and transnational effects of globalism on education, the importance of musical transmission processes between cultures comes to the fore. As transmission terminology, "multiculturalism" and "cross-culturalism" are most useful terms, given the objectives of this chapter. Both are founded on the concept of cultural diversity.[7] Multiculturalism makes provision for the teaching of different musical cultures simultaneously, with each culture still enjoying the status of a separate entity. Cross-culturalism presupposes interaction, integration, and the working together of different cultures (Schippers, 2008). Cross-culturalism is a form of communication that negotiates its own cultural boundaries as well as the borders of others (Schippers, 2010).

The sharing of music is a universal trait. All known cultures make music and have rules by which they organize their sound. These rules are applied within a specific cultural framework (Fiske, 2008). Although music is cognitively understood, it is culturally defined (Blacking, 1976; Campbell, 2004; Fiske, 2008; Kubik, 2010). Collaborative and transformative learning represents a strong cultural shift from merely understanding one's own culture toward appreciating, respecting, and practicing the music of another culture (Akuno, 2011; Heneghan, 2001). The ability to share, appreciate, evaluate, and teach the music of another culture lies in developing an understanding of the music of that culture, as well as a willingness to adapt. This research focuses on musical meaning-making, musical performance, and comprehensive musicianship in the form of conceptual musical understanding[8] (Blacking, 1976; Campbell, 2004; Fiske, 2008; Kubik, 2010). Musical understanding thus engages with cultural understanding of meaning-making (Fiske, 2008), it seeks to develop pathways to greater tolerance and appreciation across cultural divides (Volk, 2004). Educators should be prepared to shift cultural boundaries and adapt to the requirements of contemporary living.

MOTIVATING AN INTERNATIONAL GENERIC STRUCTURED FRAMEWORK

The similarities, differences, and compatibilities between formal and informal music education have been addressed and theorized within both Western and African thought. Formal music education prioritizes formalized, analytical, theory-based, and individualistic learning processes. An informal education comprises a more holistic, informal learning process and prioritizes the integration of active, performance-based musical experiences (Carver, 2002). In a cross-cultural approach, both similarities and differences between cultures are identified, and this can lead to a basis for mutual negotiation of arts assessment and its boundaries.

Although formal and informal music education are often considered to be opposed to one another, the new curriculum framework seeks to accommodate both approaches. The most important characteristics, needs, and compatibilities of both formal and informal educations are identified and contextualized. Two essential cross-cultural educational needs, namely the structuring and formalization of African musical arts and the concept of integrated learning in contemporary education, are identified and addressed through the framework set out in this chapter.

First, African musical arts, as an indigenous art form that is based mostly on informal music education, need to be formalized, structured, and graded. The international recognition and credibility that this would lead to would be a valuable development for the art form. The framework aims to structure, grade, and provide measures for assessment that are reliable, valid, and objective.

Second, formal education needs to address the requirements of contemporary living. By this is meant that such education needs to nurture the ability of the learner to function in an interactional and everyday environment. The concept of integrative teaching, learning, and assessment, and the holistic education of the whole learner, are strongly linked with the philosophy of holism, which underpins informal/indigenous musics. The concept of holism is recontextualized in the framework as inclusive and collaborative learning. Moreover, holism in its modern context is interlinked with formative education and notions of recontextualization and recontextualized authenticity.

The Structure of the Evaluation System

For the purpose of clarity, the framework/evaluation system is divided into two units: (1) the design, with an organization and grading function, and (2) the standards (the four strands of music-cultural knowledge), which describe and accommodate knowledge/outcomes for an accomplished African practitioner. This chapter focuses particularly on the first section, namely the structural aspect of the curriculum framework, clarifying the implementation of achievement standards as basis for the framework. The objective of the evaluation system/framework is to describe: (1) the African-ness of African musical arts, illustrating the contemporary educational concept as contextualized in holism; (2) the formal and systematic structuring of the music; (3) the grading of the music into levels, and (4) adherence to its generic aim, by constantly adapting to these needs ands the requirements and standardization found in contemporary music education (Human, 2013).

Cross-cultural assessment implies that music travels over cultural boundaries and outside of its culture of origin, and as a result, the issue of recontextualization comes to the fore. Recontextualization, cross-cultural assessment, and meaning-making are inevitably linked to the authentic presentation of music in new settings.

Authentic Recontextualization

Dunbar-Hall (2005) discusses the influence of globalism on the ways music is performed, taught, and thought about as it moves from one cultural milieu to another. Each new milieu requires a new approach and a new way of thinking, whether the music is positioned in the original culture or in the host culture. Both cultures experience the dilemma of recontextualization (Gupta, 2010).

Hall agrees that whatever one teaches or assesses implies how one is positioned (Hall, 1994). The meaning of music may shift due to its function, its locality, and the different contexts in which it is practiced. The original purpose of a piece of music, for example as social activity or cultural artifact, may be negated in a new setting. Works can even be given new aesthetic positions derived from their roles as pedagogic examples (Dunbar-Hall, 2005). Therefore, due to the influence of globalism, the "recognition of 'musics in culture' carries with it a need to value cultural context, meaning and social significance" (Kwami, 1998, p. 84). Assessment within cultural context is one of the aims of the framework.

A recontextualized approach in cross-cultural music education implies that music travels outside of its culture of origin and interacts with new musics within the parameters of other cultural boundaries. I would contend that transplanting cultural products such as African musical arts from one cultural context to another will always present challenges. Some of these challenges involve the sending and receiving of messages and the impossibility of ensuring transmission of intended meaning within the context of new cultures (Brannen, 2004; Wodak & Fairclough, 2010). Cognizance is taken of the relevance of recontextualization and the authenticity discourse to this research, where recontextualization may result in a hybrid and not an authentic concept.

Authenticity in cross-cultural music education is understood as the performance of the music that remains as close as possible to its cultural roots, while adapting to meaning-making of the host culture. Adopting a mix of the traditions of teaching, learning, and assessing—while possibly adding new elements and new ways of thinking—is part of understanding and meaning-making of a new culture. Immersion in the music of the different culture takes place through the development of knowledge and practice of the music in its original form. The recreation process aims to stay authentic and within the style of the original music by representing it as truthfully and accurately as possible (Campbell, 2004). Recontextualized authenticity, then, upholds the culturally autonomic meanings of the music as practiced in the original culture, while understanding the culturally autonomic meanings of the host culture and the discrepancies that may arise in the translation process (Campbell, 2004; Dunbar-Hall, 2005).

Recontextualized authenticity entails change, and also involves acknowledging that both the donor and host culture's positions are of equal importance. Authenticity should be considered in both the culture of origin and the host culture and is not only found in the original setting in which the music was created but also needs to accommodate the process of meaning-making of the host culture. Culture and music form an ongoing and ever-changing practice that not only interacts with a changing society but also reflects it.

According to Schippers (2005, p. 30), "authenticity in music is rarely a comprehensive reconstruction of an original; it is marked by subjective choices and conjecture" in the process of meaning-making. Recontextualized authenticity forms the philosophical basis for the generic cross-cultural and standards-based approach of the framework and is proposed as a solution to the challenges of cross-cultural assessment in music education.

METHODOLOGY AND APPROACHES

When positioning the assessment of African musical arts, contrasting perspectives from within critical musicology (which constitutes an interdisciplinary field of knowledge) must be taken into account. As a holistic and formative concept, critical musicology addresses ethnographic research, comparative analysis, theory development, evaluative research, deconstruction theory, and social studies.

The research design of the methodology of this chapter combines documentary study, deconstruction theory, comparative research, cultural studies, and comparative analysis in an attempt to investigate the development of generic cross-cultural assessment standards. Documentary research in the form of a comparative literature review was conducted to provide a conceptual framework (Notar & Cole, 2010). Contemporary music education assessment is placed within the framework of cultural studies, and I acknowledge both art as a cultural system (Geertz, 1976) and that the teaching, learning, and assessment of art are invariably culturally embedded. Cultural studies clarify the relationship between music education and culture and form an essential aspect of this chapter (Blacking, 1976; Carver, 2002; Dunbar-Hall, 2005).

As evaluative research design, comparative musicology compares formal and informal education systems and assessment frameworks as well as teaching, learning, and assessment situations for differences, similarities, and inventive and resourceful contributions. The results of these comparisons were most useful when developing the framework.

Deconstruction theory "takes apart" and then "puts together" accepted and acknowledged lines of thought on a specific subject or in a specific field. The term denotes a particular kind of practice in reading, criticism, and analytical inquiry (Cuddon, 1991; Johnson, 1980). The techniques of critical thinking and analytical inquiry are ideally suited for the understanding and analysis of African musical arts. Some of the concepts that were examined include process-oriented and functional musics, and these were approached from within a cultural perspective (Akuno, 2011; Mushira, 2010), and recontextualization and the concept of hybridity were taken into account (Kilduff & Mehra, 1997).

I was ideally situated to contribute toward the internationalization of African musical arts, through the advantages of location as well as culture (being educated within a Western framework but based in Africa). I was able to establish meaningful contact with scholars at the forefront of this debate. These scholars include Akuno (2011, 2012) and Mushira (2012, 2010) in Kenya, Mans in Namibia (2012), and Nzewi in South Africa (2007).

The most significant aspect of African musical arts education, in my opinion, lies in its functionality or process-oriented approach:[9] how the music is used, when it is used, how it is communicated, how it engages the community, and so on. Functionality is an essential aesthetic in African musical arts (Akuno, 2011; Mushira 2010). It accommodates the interaction of the learner with the music, through these musical processes, and a cultural transformation of the learner ensues (Akuno, 2011). Based on their functionality, these processes can then be assessed in a valid, reliable, and fair manner.

Cross-culturalism challenges educators and scholars with a traditionally hegemonic Western perspective on music to reflect on alternative music educational approaches. Reimer proposes that a universal philosophy comprising generally accepted values of teaching, learning, and assessment in music education is both desirable and possible (Reimer, 2009). This is echoed in the framework through notions of inclusivity, adaptability, and generic abilities. The differing perspectives of Reimer (1993) and Elliott (1995), who are exponents of aesthetic (formal music education) and praxial (informal music education) philosophies of music education respectively, form the basis of the framework. Although these two philosophies tend to be considered as opposed to one another, the focus with reference to this research is not on the aesthetic-praxial debate as such, but in the inclusion of differing philosophical concepts (Bowman, 1993; Elliott, 1995; Reimer, 1993; Westerlund, 2003). The inclusion of these differing philosophies clarifies and accommodates diverse cultural thinking, values, and meaning-making applicable to recontextualized settings.

Outcomes- and standards-based education is founded on an assessment-driven approach, which has important consequences for curriculum development. Backward design forms an integral part of assessment-driven education. It facilitates the visualization of the end product, planning with a definite outcome in mind. Backward design has been employed in order to plan the structure and content of the framework, and to enable the writing of a curriculum for African musical arts. The inclusive approach of backward design aids in the arrangement of learning experience and determining of suitable content (Popham, 2011).

POSITIONING STANDARDS AND STANDARDS LEVELS IN A GENERIC CROSS-CULTURAL FRAMEWORK

The assessment reform debate (Heneghan, 2001; Lehman, 2002; Sadler, 2010; Watson, 2012), and debates regarding the adaptability of standards, are considered in this section, engaging in an investigation of what standards are. Present practice is analyzed and knowledge, skills, and performance levels are explored.

The term "standards" encompasses what the aim of this chapter is, namely the formalization of indigenous musics on an international level through the development of a generic crosscultural assessment framework. The general compatibility, acceptability, and accessibility of standards between formal and informal music education and between different education systems should be noted. Standards are autonomous and self-reliant and are neither philosophically bound nor methodologically constrained. Because they underwrite modern trends, they do not constitute any specific format and are, by implication, outcomes, and provide a basis for goal-specific efforts. They facilitate a stable form of reference to enable objective evaluation of development and quality of performance (Human, 2013; Lehman, 2002). Standards provide a structured basis, and a common language within which educations can align descriptions of teaching, learning, and assessment practice. They are ideally suited to determine and contextualize general music outcomes for future curriculum development.

Qualification or achievement standards were selected as an appropriate structuring basis for the framework. They are a planned combination of learning outcomes that have a defined purpose or purposes. Their aim is to provide qualifying learners with applied competence and a basis for further learning (Keevy, 2012). Because achievement standards are based on core and specific competencies, use learning outcomes, and inform qualification design, they are a suitable basis for learning programs and curriculum (Keevy, 2012). The achievement standards also consist of three components that underlie the structuring of the framework, namely: (1) learning outcomes, which are the end products of the learning process; (2) benchmarks, which describe these outcomes, competencies, and the learning process; and (3) applied competencies or skills (Hattingh & Killen, 2003).

The conceptualization of the grading and ranking of the standards-based framework is guided by level descriptors, which are based on core and specific competencies and which apply to learning outcomes (Keevy, 2012). The standards levels are divided into three tiers of competence, namely, novice, proficient, and master. The levels are based on international understandings of levels of achievement and on research on compatibility between African musical arts and contemporary music education (Akuno, 2005; Mushira, 2010). To illustrate what these levels of competence signify, the novice level may be compared to primary school level, the proficient to secondary school level, and master to senior secondary and/or tertiary level. However, in keeping with the concept of lifelong learning, levels should not be restricted to a chronological institutional order. Ability and competence should always be assessed, and these do not necessarily correlate with the age of a student. The largely Western concept of chronological time and chronological learning has limited relevance to the learning process found in African musical arts. Learning is a lifelong process in African culture. The framework does not employ the concept of a chronological time span, but rather one of chronological ability.

When determining how the standards should be developed, it was essential to examine the nature and value of music education and the contextualization of what musical understanding is (Elliott, 2009). In accordance with the University of Florida's Institutional Assessment Department, the three guiding principles, namely recency,[10] relevance,[11] and rigor[12] (Brophy, 2012), were constantly considered during the development of the standards. All four standards for African musical arts assessment are relevant to contemporary and modern-day educational needs and requirements, as well as to the aspect of holistic and vocational training (Brophy, 2012).

At this stage, it needs to be mentioned that the framework does adhere to Western structural requirements to a certain extent. In organizing the standards however, the purpose was not to conform to Western structures but to develop something "new," which would nevertheless be relevant and acceptable for both formal and informal music educations.

Achievement standards provide a common reference point to contextualize knowledge, understanding, performance, aim, and structure for generic standards development (Hayes, 2006). Such achievement standards are usually written as a series of domains grouped around issues of professional knowledge, practice, engagement, attributes, or variations of these. Therefore, it is essential that the development of standards for African musical arts should be developed by experts in their specific fields, to inform qualification design and form the basis for learning programs and syllabi (Keevy, 2012).

Presenting the Proposed Standards

The four strands of music-cultural knowledge and expertise that were identified depict the essence of African-ness in African musical arts, and are condensed as achievement standards. The most important characteristics that were incorporated into the assessment standards were (1) holism, as an integrated form of education; (2) communalism, as communal form of education; (3) interrelatedness, making teaching, learning, and assessment part of everyday living; and (4) praxialism, giving music its meaning. These concepts address the aspects mentioned in the discussion of standards and standards levels.

The four standards are:

Standard 1: Understand and conceptualize holism
Standard 2: Understand, know, and engage in communalism
Standard 3: Understand and know interrelatedness and interconnections
Standard 4: Understand, know, and engage in praxialism. (Human, 2013)

Standard 1 describes holism as an inclusive music educational approach, where subject and object, mind and body, self and the world, become one. It is considered to be central to cross-cultural arts education because it emphasizes the interrelatedness that characterizes African musical arts (Bjørkvold, 1992; Mans, 2004). Holism in arts education is recognized as an alternative form of education (Mans, 1997), and is recontextualized into a modern context as inclusive and formative education.

Standard 2 describes the artistic and social concerns founded in communalism: "to understand and know life as art and arts as life" (Chernoff, 1979, p. 87). The aesthetic of communalism lies in sociocultural knowledge, understanding, and participation of the music practitioner. It takes the form of humanistic responsibility, communicative leadership, and performance skills. Communalism is practiced within the context of a communal activity and collaborative learning (Mans, 1997).

Standard 3 illustrates the concept of interrelatedness in arts and music. Art is not divided against itself, but is an integral technique that is found in the interaction between the community, the musician, life, and arts. Assessment is part of intereducative connections. All these spheres are dependent on one another and are illustrated through meaning-making, practical orality, and verbal expression (Omolo-Ongati, 2005).

Standard 4 engages in praxialism as the simultaneous development of practical musicianship and creativity. It focuses on a nonverbal and skills-based context (Human, 2013). Praxialism represents a process-oriented approach and is the activity that gives music its meaning. The aspects of orality, kinesthetics, and memory retention are identified as part of aesthetics of praxialism (Cushner, McClelland, & Safford, 2006; Elliott, 2009; Scott, 2004; Westerlund, 2003).

Setting Standards Levels: Processes and Procedures

Standards-based assessment facilitates dialogue between the teaching, learning, and assessment processes in a cross-cultural context. One of the strongest assets of African musical arts is its functionality, which represents a praxial and process-oriented form of education. These processes are located in the music itself (Akuno, 2011; Elliott, 2005; Kwami, 1998; Mushira, 2012), and can be used as a step-by-step description of the route of cultural change and integration. Levels of enculturation and progression can be indicated and levels of competence can be assessed (Lindström, 2006; Popham, 2011).

The value of these African transmission processes for modern-day education lie in their generic abilities and their measurability as a reliable, valid, and objective process. They can be identified in the music and can then be contextualized in both formal and informal education, aiding in the development of standards and curricula. Cross-cultural music communication centers on how music information is exchanged, developed, and clarified in the process of understanding differing musical cultures. Praxial theories, specifically as advocated by Elliott (2005, 2009) in contemporary education, correlate very well with the practically informed learning and teaching methods of African musical arts. Process-oriented education therefore provides a means to contextualize a music-cultural development route that indicates specific levels of enculturation and progression, along a continuum.

Process-oriented education implies lifelong learning. As I intimated previously, ability and competence should always be assessed independently, and cannot be understood as merely age-related. The level of novice in African music education, for instance, can never be based on a concept of "not knowing," as is often the case in Western education. The interactional environment of the African musician, even from pre-birth, already makes music a part of their surroundings. If one takes lifelong learning into account, it becomes clear that such accumulative learning cannot be restricted to a chronological institutional order. The framework therefore, as mentioned before, is not based on a chronological time span, but on chronological ability.

All four standards for African musical arts assessment meet with contemporary/modern-day music educational requirements. The three guiding principles for the development of the standards, namely recency, relevance, and rigor, were constantly adhered to (Brophy, 2012).

The Generic Cross-Cultural
Assessment Framework for
African Musical Arts

After referring to international educational frameworks within which to organize the standards (Australian, American, Eastern, European, South African), a framework was developed that would suit both formal and informal music educations. The framework presented here is situated within the African, Eastern, and Western educational frames, and therefore accommodates alternative thinking.

I value the contribution of Coles (2006), whose understanding of an achievement framework is that it is an instrument applied for development, classification, and grading according to a set of level descriptors/benchmarks, to determine levels of learning achieved. The sorting of learning targets as found in Bloom's revised taxonomy (Anderson et al., 2001) is a widely accepted description of the dimensions of knowledge and cognitive skills that can be used to formulate educational objectives and develop measurable student learning outcomes (Brophy, 2012). Based on these notions, of the formulation of objectives and the development of measurable outcomes, the framework identifies expected outcomes and assesses the extent to which these outcomes are achievable through the benchmarks provided (Anderson et al., 2001; Brookhart, 2010; Brophy, 2012). The benchmarks can be employed to describe this process of cultural development along an intercultural continuum.

Student learning outcomes are organized into three broad categories: knowledge, skills, and values. In the framework, the learning outcomes are developed through a process of verbalizing and grading knowledge, skills, and/or competencies as benchmarks. These predefined benchmarks specify learning methods and expectations, while the grading categorizes levels of development. The framework contextualizes cross-cultural development through increasing stages of difficulty, measured along a continuum.

The framework should be read as:

- A guideline for cross-cultural assessment.
- A developmental approach that still has to be expanded further.
- An all-inclusive umbrella concept from which to develop specific assessment outcomes.
- An interdependent structure that does not organize the standards and standards levels in any specific hierarchical order. Due to the interrelatedness of African musical arts, the four standards are interconnected and interdependent, overlap, and cannot be ordered hierarchically.
- Recontextualized authenticity, which was found to be the appropriate space in which the generic cross-cultural standards could fulfill the purpose of this research.

It is generally acknowledged that the assessment of musical arts takes place within three domains, namely the cognitive domain (knowledge, which infers intellectual awareness), the metacognitive or psychomotor domain (skills, which infer knowledge regarding one's own functioning and self-regulation), and the affective domain (attitudes, which infer emotions and convictions) (Chomsky, 1965; Sercu, 2004; Yip, 2008). The holistic and praxial character of African musical arts implies the recognition of the interrelationships among these three educational domains. This complicates the grouping of standards into the three separate and acknowledged educational domains. Similarly, standards should be understood as interrelated, engaging in a demonstration of Hayes's assertion that "one 'standard' inevitably brings in a demonstration of others" (2006, p. 15). Therefore, the four standards are inclusive of all three educational domains (Robbins & Howard, 2007; Thames Valley University London, 2009–2012). For practical reasons, the domains naturally developed into the following:

- Domain 1—Knowledge: Musical/cultural knowledge (synthesis of theoretical and contextual knowledge)
- Domain 2—Skills: Technical skills accomplishment (cross-cultural communication through effective control of the voice or instrument or dance movements)
- Domain 3—Attitude: Musicality and humanity (ability to make sensitive and musical performance decisions).

An example of the structuring of the framework is given in Figure 29.1, with an illustration of Standard 2 (2.1 and 2.1.1). It is one of the shortest examples of the deconstructions of a standard, but is still able to exemplify its purpose. The third line (novice, proficient, master) does not tally with the final figure, but is added to provide a clarification of how the final table should be read.

The Generic Crosscultural Assessment Framework for African Musical Arts is presented in full in Appendix 29.1.

CONCLUSION: THE WAY FORWARD

There is a lack of mutual understanding between cross-cultural educational research, policymakers, and practitioners in the field of cross-cultural music education. The impact of globalism on contemporary music education needs to be acknowledged and accepted. One cannot close one's eyes to its impact and the consequential interchange and cross-pollination between music education cultures.

This chapter was written from a generic perspective, and the notion of genericism, in the sense of "generally true" or compatible within different cultural contexts, was explored. In conclusion, it is my contention that we need to move toward greater levels of specificity in achievement and recommendations in music education. The generic

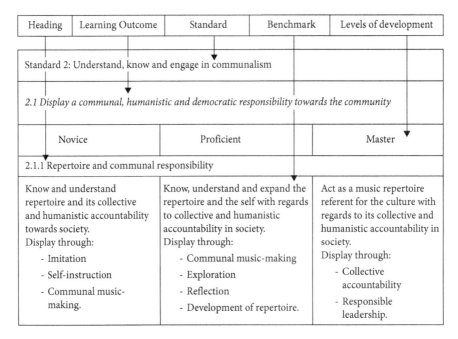

FIGURE 29.1 Illustration of Standard 2 (2.1 and 2.1.1).

function of the framework enables it to be applied by scholars, educators, and students alike. Although the framework and standards were developed to present the holistic and praxial worldview of the African musical arts practitioner, its compatibility with different education systems should be noted. The framework can be implemented as reference for the development of similar generic frameworks to bridge voids between other indigenous and formal music educations worldwide (Robbins, 2012).

This framework may be developed as a basis for an African musical arts curriculum. Expansion and refinement of the four standards may form a basis for the development of an African musical arts curriculum at an international level. African musical arts is well structured through its processes and procedures embedded in the standards. Facilitating the structuring and grading of the achievement levels will not only assist in the evaluation of competency across cultures but also solidify the international perception of the assessment of African musical arts as a reliable, valid, and objective process. The four standards and their descriptors are recommended for further research toward the writing of a curriculum for African musical arts.

The globalized reality of today requires a multicultural educational approach, encompassing diverse musical traditions within different social, historical, and cultural contexts. There is a need to understand and come to know "other" cultures and musics. To share and influence one another can only enrich lives and give a better perspective on one's own situation. Educators are not only responsible for and bound to their own students, communities, and countries, but also can be unified internationally and for a common cause, where shared objectives enable them to transcend cultural differences.

The impact of globalism on contemporary music education needs to be acknowledged and accepted. Educators should be prepared to shift cultural boundaries of understanding and adaptability, because globalism has already interacted with these boundaries. An open mind and heart, an inclusive approach, and respect and empathy for difference should inform our future actions.

APPENDIX 29.1

THE GENERIC CROSS-CULTURAL ASSESSMENT FRAMEWORK FOR AFRICAN MUSICAL ARTS

Standard 1: Conceptualize holism in African Musical Arts		
Novice	*Proficient*	*Master*
1.1 Think and perform inclusively as part of the transformational development of the whole person through the process of enculturation (enduring understanding)		
1.1.1 Culture and inclusivity		
Know and understand the self in the original culture. Display through: Participation Imitation Self-instruction Acknowledge and appreciate differences between people of different cultures. Display through: Recognition Acknowledgment Appreciation of difference.	Know and understand the self in the original culture and demonstrate an ever widening perspective of understanding differences between people of diverse cultures. Display (to make understanding visible) through: - Recognition - Awareness - Appreciation - Respect Analysis and synthesis of the concepts of holism, communalism, interrelationships, and praxialism Involvement Attitude (unprejudiced and positive) Practice (of appropriate skills).	Know, understand, and appreciate the fundamental unity of all humans as potentially fully integrated African musical arts practitioners. Display through: Immersion Involvement Mediation Fostering Recognition of music knowledge as constructed by the context of every-day life.
1.1.2 Philosophical concepts/Artistic values and inclusivity		
Know and understand artistic values of holism, communalism, interrelationships and praxialism of African musical arts.	Know, understand, and interact with artistic values of holism, communalism, interrelationships, and praxialism of African musical arts.	Know, understand, integrate, and communicate the artistic values of holism, communalism, interrelationships, and praxialism of African musical arts.

(continued)

Continued

Display through: Participation Identification Imitation.	Display through: Creative participation Analysis Synthesis.	Display through: Taking ownership Endorsement of recognition of prior learning (RPL) as a lifelong learning process.

1.1.3 Context and inclusivity

Know, understand, and engage with basic contexts such as repertoire, meaning-making, sounds, movements, etc., situated in historical, geographical, language, political, and religious contexts. Display through: Participation Imitation Self-instruction.	Know and understand contexts such as repertoire, meaning-making, sounds, and movements, which are situated in historical, geographical, language, political, and religious contexts. Display through: Investigative work Inventiveness Ability to use models Self-assessment	Know, understand, explore, exploit, and engage inclusively with contexts such as repertoire, ideas, values/meaning-making, sounds, movements etc., situated in historical, geographical, language, political, and religious contexts. Display through: Creative processes (investigative work, inventiveness, ability to use models, capacity for self-assessment) Guidance of the community Interaction in new and original ways.

1.2 Engage in collective thought processes as part of the transformational development of the whole person through the process of enculturation (enduring understanding)

Know, understand, and engage, on a tacit and practical level, in multiple thought processes of collective communication (such as appreciation and evaluation). Display through: Imitation Active music-making Becoming culturally adept.	Know, understand, and engage, on a tacit and practical level, in multiple thought processes of collective communication (such as appreciation and evaluation), collective performance, and creative processes. Display through: Active music-making/Performance Developing cultural adaptability Reflection Critical evaluation Synthesis Creative processes.	Know, understand, communicate, and integrate collective thought processes, such as collective communication, performance, and creative processes for betterment of society, on a tacit and practical level. Display through: Creative performance Facilitation of colleagues and students Representation Evaluation of tacit knowledge processes.

Standard 2: Understand, know, and engage in communalism		
2.1 Display a communal humanistic and democratic responsibility toward the community (enduring social responsibility)		
2.1.1 Repertoire and communal responsibility		
Know and understand repertoire and its collective and humanistic accountability toward society. Display through: Imitation Self-instruction Communal music-making Recognition of humanistically accountable aptitudes and capabilities.	Know, understand, and expand the repertoire and the self with regard to collective and humanistic accountability in society. Display through: Communal music-making Synthesis of humanistically accountable aptitudes and capabilities Exploration Reflection Development of repertoire.	Act as a music repertoire referent for the culture with regard to its collective and humanistic accountability in society. Display through: Developing and extending past, present, and future (new) repertoire to address communal needs Collective and humanistic accountability Responsible leadership Representation.
2.1.2 Mass musical cognition and human conscience/responsibility		
Know, understand, and participate in mass musical cognition to contribute to the well-being of society. Display through: Active music-making Communication Imitation.	Know, understand, participate, and interact with mass musical cognition to contribute to the well-being of society. Display through: Active music-making Communication Exploration Identification and addressing of communal necessities Creative development of the musical arts.	Know, understand, and develop mass musical cognition with regard to communal, humanistic, and democratic well-being of society. Display through: Excellence in leadership Addressing communal necessities Effective and influential communication Identification, interaction, and manipulation of the music for the well-being of society.
2.2 Display merging within a "community of practice" through the arts (enduring social responsibility)		
2.2.1 Communal communication		
Understand the importance of, and respond to the communicative value of, the music, especially through improvisation and creativity.	Increasingly understand the importance of and respond to the communicative value of the music. This takes place through interpretation, initiation, and development of especially improvisation and creativity.	Guide and support colleagues and students toward the understanding and practice of excellence in communication through music.

(continued)

Continued

Display through:	Display through:	Display through:
Participation	Communal music-making	Enjoyment
Imitation	Communicative abilities	Vitality
Clarification.	Creative improvisation	Effective communicative
	through communication	abilities (e.g., constant control
	Enjoyment	in/of the group)
	Clarification	An honest attitude
	Initiation.	Authentic presentation
		Integration with the music.

2.2.2 Communal creativity

| Understand and participate in the creative process of communal music-making. This takes place as interaction between the original composer, if known (individual or group), group members, and communal input (audience) through music.
Display through:
Participation
Imitation. | Understand and collaborate in the creative process of communal music-making. This takes place as interaction between the original composer (individual or group), group members and communal input (audience).
Display through:
Cooperative working
Adaptability to the group
Effective communication
Appreciation and evaluation
Composition and/or improvisation. | Sustain and support the creative process between the original composer, group members, and communal energy. This should take place within the context of improving performance of the whole group.
Display through:
Leadership
Cooperative working as director
Excellence in balance
Clarity of purpose
Precision
Originality
Integration with the music cohesion and merging of the audience, performers, and group members. |

2.2.3 Communal meaning-making

| Know, understand and comply with communal meaning-making reflected in behaviors, morals, and values (tangible and intangible) of the "community of practice."
Display through:
Participation
Imitation
Recognition. | Know, understand, and develop communal meaning-making, reflected in behaviors, morals, and values (tangible and intangible) of the "community of practice." Develop necessary communal capabilities for meaning-making. This is reflected in behaviors, morals, and values (tangible and intangible) of the "community of practice."
Display through:
Participation
Recognition
Synthesis
Socialization in group communication, group performance, and group interaction. | Know, understand, and work toward perfection in capabilities and relationships integral to communal meaning-making. This is reflected in initiating and nurturing behaviors, morals, and values (tangible and intangible) of the "community of practice."
Display through:
Socialization in group communication, group performance, and group interaction
Collaborative learning[13]
Creative performance
Facilitation
Evaluation. |

2.3 Display communal leadership

2.3.1 Musical roles and community

Know and understand the integrated roles of a musician as composer, performer, and musical director in the community. Display through: Active music-making Identification Imitation Self-instruction.

Know, understand, and unify the roles of a musician as composer, performer, and musical director in the community. Display through: Experiential music-making Reflection Synthesis of roles Merging of roles and the musical arts.

Know, understand, and *represent* excellence in the integrated presentation of the roles of musician as composer, performer, and musical director in the community. Display through: Technical skills Aptitude Composition Performance.

2.3.2 Leadership and community

Know, understand, and respect the most important characteristics of leadership in the community as: contributor, educator, musician, performer, and improviser. Display through: Active music-making Identification Imitation Self-instruction.

Know, understand, and develop the most essential characteristics of leadership in the community. Characteristics such as communal contribution; educational inputs; independent musicianship; skilled and experienced performance and improvisation, as well as being a referent for repertoire, are valued by the community. Display through: Performance Communication Music-cultural knowledge Education Synthesis.

Lead and contribute to the wider community and to the music profession as a fully integrated musical arts practitioner. This takes place through interactive and communal contribution; educational inputs; skilled and experienced performance and improvisation; being a music-cultural referent; negotiator and promoter of relationships. A leader in the community must be endorsed and acknowledged by the community. Display through: Performance Communication Being a cultural referent Education Negotiation Sustainment of cultural values.

Standard 3: Understand and know interrelatedness and interconnections

3.1 Engage in the interrelatedness of arts and life

3.1.1 Interconnections in arts

Know and understand the interconnections between the arts as aesthetic. The interconnections are found in the:

Know, understand, and engage with the interconnections between the arts as aesthetic. The interconnections are found in the:

Initiate collaborative activities to integrate and appreciate the inter-arts connections as an aesthetic. The interconnections are found in the:

(continued)

Continued

Practical domain. Between types of arts (dance/drama/costume/ drumming). Social domain. Between types of arts expression (spiritualism, move- ment, sound, morality). Educative domain. Between teaching, learning, and assessment. Display through: Participation Imitation Identification Experiential learning.	Practical domain. Between types of arts (dance/drama/costume/ drumming). Social domain. Between types of arts expression (spiritualism, movement, sound, morality). Educative domain. Between teaching, learning, and assessment. Display through: Active music-making Exploration Synthesis.	Practical domain. Between types of arts (dance/drama/costume/ drumming). Social domain. Between types of arts expression (spiritualism, movement, sound, morality). Educative domain. Between teaching, learning, and assessment. Display through: Interactive music-making Exploration Appreciation.

3.1.2 Interconnections between arts and life

Understand and know the aesthetic of the interconnections between arts, and arts and life (make an art of everyday life experiences). Display through: Participation Imitation Identification Experiential learning.	Understand, know, and engage with the aesthetic of the interconnections between arts, and arts and life (make an art of everyday life experiences). Display through: Identification Appreciation Reflection Creative exploration Synthesis	Understand, represent, and guide colleagues and students in the aesthetic of inter-arts experience, integrating all artistic and social concerns into a single unified concept. Display through: Communication Fostering Facilitation Integrative performance.

3.2 Engage in the intercommunal connections as an inclusive experience

3.2.1 Intercommunality and inclusivity

Understand, know, and engage with intercom- munal connections as an inclusive aesthetic experience. This takes place through collabora- tive learning, communal innovation, and interaction, between musicians/audience, musicians/musicians, and the musicians/ audience/music.	Understand, know, and engage on an increasing level with intercommunal connections as an inclusive aesthetic experience. This takes place through collaborative learning, communal innovation and interaction between musicians and audience, musicians and musicians, and the musicians, audience, and the music.	Collaborate, initiate, and guide colleagues and students in the aesthetic of intercommunal connections. Integrate all role players into a single unified/inclusive concept.

Display through: Participation Imitation Self-instruction.	Display through: Innovation Interaction Collaborative performance Communal creativity	Display through: Communication Guidance Facilitation Integrative performance.

3.2.2 Orality[14] and inclusivity

Understand and know the unifying and practical function of orality as aesthetic experience. Orality, as verbal expression, is demonstrated on a practical and intercommunal level for clarity. Display through: Participation Imitation Listening.	Understand, know, and develop the unifying and practical function of orality as aesthetic experience. Orality, as verbal expression, is demonstrated on a practical and intercommunal level for clarity. Display through: Listening Musicianship Composition Arrangement Improvisation Myths/stories.	Represent and guide the community to understand and demonstrate orality as unifying and aesthetic experience in intercommunal connections. Display though: Listening Creative musicianship Myths/stories Verbal expression on a practical level Interaction.

Standard 4: Understand, know, and engage in praxialism

4.1 Engage in kinesthetic mediation as an active meaning-making system in everyday life

4.1.1 Kinesthetics[15] and meaning-making

Understand, practice, and experience meaning-making in a culture through kinesthetic mediation. Display through: Mediation skills of sound Movement Vision Touch Imitation Repetition Memory retention.	Understand, practice, and experience meaning-making as an art form through kinesthetic mediation. This activity that gives music its meaning should correlate with the purpose of the music and the context in which it is taking place. Display through: Mediation skills Memory retention Synthesis Transmission Communal involvement Exploration.	Understand, practice, and experience on an increasing level with meaning-making as an art form through kinesthetic mediation. This activity that gives music its meaning should correlate with the purpose of the music and the context in which it is taking place. Display through: Mediation skills Communal involvement Adaptations Making/remaking of culture.

4.1.2 Tangible mediation[16]

Understand, practice, and experience kinesthetic mediation and mediation skills as interpretative performance.	Understand, practice, and experiment with kinesthetic mediation and mediation skills in interpretive performance by responding to communal needs and necessities.	Guide the community to understand and experience the value of kinesthetic/perceptible/tangible mediation as meaning-making through interpretative performance. This involves the act, construction, and appraisal of performance itself through social and individual input.

(continued)

Continued		
Display through:	Display through:	Display through:
Sound	Sound	Creative performance
Movement	Movement	Evaluation
Vision	Vision	Addressing necessity in the
Touch.	Touch.	community.
4.2 Address communal necessity as active meaning-making system of everyday-life		
Understand, know, and experience the process of meaning-making of relevant aspects of everyday-life; addressing communal necessity through communal participation involving performance, authentic recontextual-ization,[17] and relevancy. Display through: Participation Imitation Identification.	Understand, know, and experience on an increasing level with the process of meaning-making of relevant aspects of everyday life; addressing communal necessity through communal participation involving performance, authentic recontextualization, and relevancy. Display through: Identification Reflection Participation Exploration Adaption Creation Appraisal.	Further understand, know, and experience the process of meaning-making of relevant aspects of everyday life; addressing communal necessity through communal participation involving performance, authentic recontextualization, and relevancy. Display through: Producing new knowledge Cooperative music learning and problem-solving Interaction Joint musical products Appraisal Recreation Achieving what the music was created for in a specific setting.

NOTES

1. "Standardization" means agreed arrangement of fixed same levels of educational competence and quality attached to whole education and training systems (SADC, 1997, p. 2). Standards-levels/Achievement levels structure the development process of the learner into measurable stages or clearly defined steps. They describe at which level of understanding or development the learner is. Standards-levels for this research describe the different stages of becoming culturally adept in the knowledge, understanding and performance of African musical arts.
2. This is a product of the aims of my doctoral study (Human, 2013).
3. The "ness" in African-ness from our point of view, illustrates the concept of "being": being African, and contextualizes the characteristics of African musical arts.
4. The notion of genericism means in the sense of "generally true" or compatible within different cultural contexts.
5. Functionalism of/in the music is central to African musical arts practice. The concept of inclusivity/holism is founded in functionalism of African musical arts and considered an essential aesthetic.
6. Recontextualization is a process by which the consumer or translator makes sense of the artifact, practice, or service which is relocated from abroad into his or her own culture (Brannen, 2004).

7. This is the "neutral term referring to the representation of more than one culture" (Schippers, 2008), and presupposes respect for "the other."
8. "Musical understanding is demonstrated in the ability to communicate to an audience as performer, to listen to musical work and appreciate it, and to compose or improvise" music (Parai, 2002, p. 231).
9. Functionality in music or a process-oriented approach, is the activity that gives music its meaning. It is also strongly associated with the concept of praxialism.
10. "Recency has to do with the degree to which the outcome reflects current knowledge and practice in the discipline" (Brophy 2012).
11. "Relevance is the degree to which the outcome relates logically and significantly to the discipline" (Brophy, 2012).
12. "Rigor has to do with the degree of academic precision and thoroughness required for the outcome to be met successfully" (http://assessment.aa.ufl.edu/slo-resources).
13. Collaborative learning: encouragement, criticism, and support of individual performers through group participation and group response and commentary.
14. Orality is thought and verbal expression. It is a reliance on spoken, rather than written language for communication, where the fact or quality is communicated orally. Orality also stimulates demonstration of the verbal expression on a practical level through inter- action. Therefore it is inclusive and unifies the community, which is also approached as an aesthetic experience.
15. Everyone has a learning style. People usually fall largely into one of three categories: kin- esthetic, auditory, or visual. Kinesthetic learning (also known as tactile learning) is a learning style in which learning takes place by the student carrying out a physical activ- ity, rather than listening to a lecture or watching a demonstration. People with a kines- thetic learning style are also commonly known as "do-ers." The Fleming VAK/VARK model (one of the most common and widely used categorizations of the various types of learning styles) classified learning styles as follows:
    Visual learners
    Auditory learners
    Reading- or writing-preference learners
    Kinesthetic learners (Kinesthetic learning: https://en.wikipedia.org/wiki/Kinesthetic_ learning/).
16. Tangible mediation is the interpretative aspects of music as performing and improvising art.
17. Appraise the recreation of the performance context so that it approximates the original context, meaning, and values and whether it answers to what the music was created for in a specific setting. Understand and know that, although a recontextualized setting is not the original situation, the practice of the music should be kept as near as possible to the original.

References

Akuno, E. A. (2005). The role of research in music education. *East African Journal of Music, 1,* 64–77.

Akuno, E. A. (2011). Personal correspondence with Akuno. July 2011.

Akuno, E. A. (2012). Perceptions and reflections of music teacher education in Kenya. *International Journal of Music Education, 30,* 272–291.

Anderson, L. W., Krathwohl, D. R., Airasian, P. W., Cruikshank, K. A., Mayer, R. E., & Pintrich, P. R. (2001). *A taxonomy for learning, teaching, and assessing—A revision of Bloom's taxonomy of educational objectives*. New York, NY: Addison Wesley Longman.

Aubert, L. (2007). *The music of the other: New challenges for ethnomusicology in a global age*. Hampshire, UK: Ashgate.

Bhabha, H. (1994). *The location of culture*. London, UK: Routledge.

Bjørkvold, J. R. (1992). *The muse within: Creativity and communication, song and play from childhood through maturity*. (H. Halverson, Trans.). New York, NY: Harper Collins.

Blacking, J. (1976). *How musical is man?* London, UK: Faber and Faber.

Bowman, W. (1993). The problem of aesthetics and multiculturalism in music education. *Canadian Music Educator, 34*(5), 23–30.

Brannen, M. (2004). When Mickey loses face: Recontextualisation, semantic fit and semiotics of forgiveness. *Academy of Management Review, 29,* 593–616.

Brookhart, S. (2010). *How to assess higher-order thinking skills in your classroom*. Alexandria, VA: ASCD (Association for Supervision and Curriculum Development).

Brophy, T. 2017. *Developing Program Goals and Student Learning Outcomes*. University of Florida. Retrieved from https://assessment.aa.ufl.edu/media/assessmentaaufledu/academic-assessment/2017-18-University-of-Florida-guide-for-developing-program-goals-and-student-learning-outcomes.pdf

Campbell, P. (2004). *Teaching music globally: Experiencing music, expressing culture*. New York, NY: Oxford University Press.

Carver, A. (2002). *Unit standards for African musics in South Africa* (Unpublished master's dissertation). University of Pretoria, Pretoria, South Africa.

Chernoff, J. M. (1979). *African rhythm and African sensibility: Aesthetics and social action in African musical idioms*. London, UK: University of Chicago Press.

Chomsky, N. (1965). *Aspects of the theory of syntax*. Cambridge, MA: MIT Press.

Coles, M. (2006). *A review of international and national developments in the use of qualifications frameworks*. Torino, Italy: ETF.

Cuddon, J. A. (1991). *Dictionary of literary terms and literary theory* (3rd ed.). London, UK: Penguin.

Cushner, K., McClelland, A., & Safford, P. (2006). *Human diversity in education: An integrative approach*. Sydney, Australia: McGraw-Hill.

Dunbar-Hall, P. (2005). Training, community and systemic music education: The aesthetics of Balinese music in different pedagogic settings. In P. Campbell & J. Drummond (Eds.), *Cultural diversity in music education: Directions and challenges for the 21st century* (pp. 125–132). Brisbane, Australia: Australian Academic Press.

Elliott, D. J. (1995). *Music matters: A new philosophy of music education*. Oxford, UK: Oxford University Press.

Elliott, D. J. (Ed.). (2005). *Praxial music education: Reflection and dialogues*. New York, NY: Oxford University Press.

Elliott, D. J. (Ed.). (2009). *Praxial music education: Reflection and dialogues*. New York, NY: Oxford University Press.

Fiske, H. (2008). *Understanding musical understanding: The philosophy, psychology and sociology of the musical experience*. New York, NY: Edwin Mellen Press.

Geertz, C. (1976). Art as a cultural system. *MLN, 91,* 1473–1499.

Gupta, S. (2010). An interview, a story and three poems: *Muse India: A literary e-journal,* 31, May–June 2010. Retrieved from http://www.museindia.com/viewarticle.asp?myr=2005&issid

Hall, S. (1994). Cultural identity and diaspora. In P. Williams & L. Chrisnian (Eds.), *Colonial discourse and post-colonial theory* (pp. 392–403). New York, NY: Columbia University Press.

Hattingh, A., & Killen, R. (2003). The promise of problem-based learning for training pre-service technology teachers. *South African Journal of Higher Education, 17*(1), 39–45.

Hayes, T. (2006). *Professional teaching associations and professional standards: Embedding standards in the "discourse of the profession."* Acton, ACT: Teaching Australia.

Heneghan, F. (2001). *A review of music education in Ireland: Incorporating the final report of the music education national debate.* Dublin, Ireland: Dublin Institute of Technology.

Human, R. (2013). *Towards generic crosscultural standards in the assessment of African musical arts* (Unpublished doctoral thesis). University of Pretoria, Pretoria, South Africa.

Johnson, B. (1980). *The critical difference.* Baltimore, MD: Johns Hopkins University Press.

Keevy, J. (2012, July). *Overall conceptualisation and relationships.* A slideshow as part of a presentation in West Africa, June 25, 2012. Retrieved from personal correspondence with Keevy, Pretoria.

Kilduff, M., & A. Mehra. (1997, April). Postmodernism and Organizational Research. *The Academy of Management Review. 22*(2), 453–481.

Kubik, G. (2010). *Theory of African music* (Vol. 2). Chicago, IL: University of Chicago.

Kwami, R. (1998). Non-Western musics in education: Problems and possibilities. *British Journal of Music Education, 15*, 161–170.

Lehman, P. (2002). A personal perspective. *Music Educators Journal, 88*(5), 47–51.

Lindström, L. (2006). Creativity: What is it? Can you assess it? Can it be taught? *International Journal of Art and Design Education, 25*(1), 53–66.

Mans, M. (1997). *Namibian music and dance as ngoma in arts education* (Unpublished doctoral thesis). University of Natal, Pietermaritzburg, South Africa.

Mans, M. (2004). Learning aesthetic values in African musical worlds. In L. Bresler (Ed.), *International handbook of research in arts education* (pp. 803–824). New York, NY: Springer.

Mans, M. (2012). Personal correspondence with Mans. September 2012.

Mushira, E. (2010). *A critical analysis of indigenous Kenyan music processes for the development of a teaching model for secondary schools in Kenya* (Unpublished doctoral thesis). Kenyatta University, Nairobi, Kenya.

Mushira, E. (2012). Personal correspondence with Mushira. August 2012.

Notar, C. E., & Cole, V. (2010). Literature review organizer. *International Journal of Education, 2*(2), 1–17.

Nzewi, M. (2007). *A contemporary study of musical arts informed by African indigenous knowledge systems* (Vols. 1–3). Cape Town, South Africa: African Minds.

Omolo-Ongati, R. (2005). Prospects and challenges of teaching and learning musics of the world's cultures: An African perspective. In Campbell, P., Drummond, J., Dunbar-Hall, P., Howard, K., Schippers, H., & T. Wiggins (Eds.), *Cultural diversity in music education: Directions and challenges for the 21st century* (pp. 59–68). Brisbane, Australia: Australian Academic Press Limited.

Parai, P. (2002). Nurturing musical understanding: Thinking like an assessor. In B. Hanley & T. Goolsby (Eds.), *Musical understanding: Perspectives in theory and practice* (pp. 229–246). Edmonton, Alberta: Canadian Music Educators Association.

Popham, W. J. (2011). *Classroom assessment: What teachers need to know.* Boston, MA: Pearson.

Reimer, B. (1993). Music education in our multimusical culture. *Music Educators Journal, 79*(7), 21–26.

Reimer, B. (2003). *A philosophy of music education: Advancing the vision* (3rd ed.). Upper Saddle River, NJ: Prentice Hall.

Reimer, B. (2009). Choosing art for education: Criteria for quality. *Seeking the significance of music education: Essays and reflections.* Lanham, MD: Rowman and Littlefield.

Robbins, J., & Howard, J. (2007). *Whose performance is it anyway? Reflections on examining music, meanings, standards, and reliability in an international context.* Papers presented at the 33rd Annual (International Association for Educational Assessment) Conference, Baku. September 2007.

Robbins, J. (2012). To sit and value together: Assessments, examinations, results, uncertainties and the need for change. *International Graded Qualifications, Occasional paper.*

SADC (Southern African Development Community). (1997). *Protocol on education and training.* Retrieved from http://www.sadc.int/english/protocols/p_education_and_training.html

Sadler, D. R. (2010). Beyond feedback: Developing student capability in complex appraisal. *Assessment & Evaluation in Higher Education, 35,* 535–550.

Schippers, H. (2005). Taking distance and getting up close: The seven-continuum transmission model (SCTM). In P. S. Campbell (Ed.), *Cultural diversity in music education: Directions and challenges for the 21st century* (pp. 29–34). Brisbane, Australia: Australian Academic Press.

Schippers, H. (2008). *Facing the music: Shaping music education from a global perspective.* New York, NY: Oxford University Press. Pre-published copy: Draft 1.

Schippers, H. (2010). *Facing the music: Shaping music education from a global perspective.* New York, NY: Oxford University Press.

Scott, S. (2004, Winter). Evaluating tasks for performance based assessments: Advice for music teachers. *General Music Today. 17*(2), 17–27. New York: MENC.

Sercu, L. (2004). Assessing intercultural competence: A framework for systematic test development in foreign language education and beyond. *Intercultural Education, 15*(1), 74–89.

Smuts, J. (1926). *Holism and evolution.* New York: Macmillan, Compass/Viking Press.

Taylor, C. (1971). Interpretation and the sciences of man. *Review of Metaphysics, 25,* 3–51.

Thames Valley University London College of Music Examinations. (2009–1012). *Syllabus for step, graded, leisure play, ensemble and performance diploma examinations in Irish and Scottish traditional music 2009-2012.* London, UK: LCM Examinations, Thames Valley University. Retrieved from http://www.uwl.ac.uk/files/LCM/lcm_exams/syllabuses/irish_scott_trad_mus_grades_diplomas.pdf

Volk, T. (2004). *Music, education, and multiculturalism: Foundations and principles.* New York: Oxford University Press.

Watson, S. (2012). Developing teaching efficacy for inquiry-based learning. In *The Fibonacci Project European conference: Inquiry based sciences and mathematics education—Bridging the gap between education research and practice.* Leicester, UK: University of Leicester.

Westerlund, H. (2003). Reconsidering aesthetic experience in praxial music education. *Philosophy of Music Education Review, 11*(1), 45–62.

Wodak, R., & Fairclough, N. (2010). Recontextualising European higher education policies: The cases of Austria and Romania. *Critical Discourse Studies, 7*(1), 19–40.

Yip, L. (2008). Establishing standards-based assessment in music performance. In C. Leung, L. Yip, & T. Imada (Eds.), *Music education policy and implementation: International perspectives.* Hirosaki, Japan: Hirosaki University Press.

PART III

ASSESSMENT IN HIGHER MUSIC EDUCATION

CHAPTER 30

MUSIC ASSESSMENT IN HIGHER EDUCATION

FREDERICK BURRACK

THE ASSESSMENT OF MUSIC LEARNING IN HIGHER EDUCATION: A PHILOSOPHICAL VIEW

ASSESSMENT is central to the teaching and learning process in higher education. As Lebler (2015b) states, "It is one of the most significant influences on students' experience of higher education and all that they gain from it" (p. 1). What is assessed reflects what is considered important learning for students in higher education institutions. Near the end of the 20th century, Hodsoll (1988) recognized a lack of clarity in what the arts stated as its purpose in higher education, and this lack of clarity was reflected in assessment practice: "the arts are in triple jeopardy: they are not viewed as serious [disciplines], [their] knowledge itself is not viewed as a prime educational objective; and those who determine school curricula do not agree on what arts education is" (p. 19). However, as formalized planning for and implementation of programmatic assessment of student learning has become part of higher education in many countries, expectations for music faculty to document what students should learn and the extent to which it has been learned have become ubiquitous.

Elliott (2010) states, "Aristotle, John Stuart Mill, John Dewey, Nel Noddings, Jane Roland Martin and many others argue persuasively that the purpose of education is to nurture personal growth by igniting students' critical and creative thinking in classrooms and community situations" (p. 367). A similar philosophic stance considers the primary purpose of learning music as developing the knowledge and skills to solve musical problems through performing, creating, and responding to music. Contemporary learning theorists have suggested that providing experiences through which students engage with musical problems is considered a prime means for students to learn (Hanson &

Saunders, 2010). The teacher provides musical opportunities for students to actively seek knowledge, skills, and ideas from multiple sources, including the teacher (Scott & McCallum, 2010) and facilitates learning by providing prompts and feedback, thereby motivating students to solve the given musical situation. The student develops constructs within the discipline of music that eventually enable musical independence.

According to Orzolek (2010), students make meaning of knowledge and skills of musical experience through critical reflection. Developing the ability to "think about thinking" in music (Boardman, 2002, p. 18) is an essential skill to be assessed for music learning. Integrating assessment into the instructional process is enabled when professors have clearly defined intended student learning expectations in a course and across a program. Too often assessment is perceived as a separate process that follows instruction. This notion of assessment as a separate entity from instruction often disconnects knowledge and skills from meaningful application in the student's learning experience (Chiodo, 2010). On the contrary, learning objectives and their assessment should be integrated with musical experiences through which students demonstrate achievement of learning at each level of the learning process. When assessment is integrated into instruction and clearly communicated in the process of learning, students have a better chance of knowing what they are supposed to learn. Instruction guided by this philosophy transforms into "shared goals through mutual efforts; joint products lead to learning from and with others" (Elliot, 2010, p. 370). Professors and students participate in assessment through instruction resulting in assessments that are formative, summative, and transformative (Mezirow, 2000).

Other Considerations for Assessment of Music Learning

In higher education, the opportunity for students to demonstrate affective learning often occurs though experience within the student's cultural environment. Baxter-Magolda (1992) suggests that "life outside the classroom is an important venue that provides ample opportunities to synthesize and integrate material introduced in the formal academic program, to test the value and worth of these ideas and skills, and to develop more sophisticated, thoughtful views on personal, academic, and other matters" (p. 296). Bruffee (1993) concluded that the most important thing any faculty member can do is to create environments in which students learn the course content through their interactions with others, especially other students. Music faculty often use out-of-class learning environments such as student-led ensembles and sectionals, recitals and concerts, attendance at events, and community service experiences to enhance music learning. These experiences become a resource through which students achieve and demonstrate learning expectations (Williams, 1999). Astin (1993) suggests that student–student interaction in out-of-class activities is positively associated with educational attainment of learning outcomes. Kuh (1995) adds, "Among the more powerful out-of-class experiences are those that demand sustained effort and require that students interact with peers" (p. 145).

HISTORICAL VIEWS OF ASSESSING
LEARNING IN HIGHER EDUCATION

Into the 21st century, societal progress is increasingly "driven by developing and sustaining a skilled workforce, maintaining a globally competitive research base, and improving the dissemination of knowledge for the benefit of society at large" (Tremblay, Lalancette, & Roseveare, 2012, p. 16). Higher education plays a central role in the development and success of the future workforce (Dill & Van Vught, 2010). An interest in higher education outcomes and quality appears to be universal. Ewell (2010) proposes there is evidence of effects of this focus on institutions of higher education, but is skeptical as to the impact of quality assurance on teaching and learning. A paradigm shift from input-based conceptions (number of classes taken, study time, and student workload) toward outcome-based (student learning) considerations of higher education is part of the focus in the United States.

The United States

In the United States, society expects students graduating from higher education institutions to "be able to think critically, solve complex problems, act in a principled manner, be dependable, read, write and speak effectively, have respect for others, be able to adapt to change and engage in life-long learning" (Gardiner, 1998, p. 71). Student learning assessment has become a central focus of higher education since 2000, driven largely by increased public and political demand for accountability, which often focuses on improving efficiency and effectiveness (Pellegrino, 1999).

In the early part of the 20th century, higher education scholars focused on developing and implementing standards and standardization (Shavelson, 2007). From 1933 to 1947 institutions developed both general education and general colleges within universities. Standardized entrance examinations such as the Graduate Record Examination (GRE) emerged along with a national testing agency, which eventually became the Educational Testing Service (ETS). The original GRE was a comprehensive and objective test focused largely on content knowledge and reasoning to infer students' preparedness for graduate study (Savage, 1953). In 1954, ETS began to shift toward general reasoning by replacing content-focused tests with general area tests, which were used to assess broad outcomes for the liberal arts (ETS, 1966). In the 1960s and 1970s, ETS introduced the Undergraduate Assessment Program, which incorporated the GRE and ACT's College Outcomes Measures Project (COMP). However, higher education faculty members near the end of the 1970s were not happy with multiple-choice tests as a sole means to predict student success in higher education or measure outcomes.

As a result, test developers began to shift their foci to the assessment of broad abilities such as communication, analytical thinking, and problem-solving. As Orzolek (2010) confirmed, "Higher education has sought to improve critical thinking and reflective skills in its students as well—primarily though inquiry-based instruction" (p. 419). By the end of the 1970s, there were rumblings of discontent and worries about the state of American education that led to the appointment of the National Commission on Excellence in Education, which in time produced its report *A Nation at Risk* (United States. National Commission on Excellence in Education, 1983). Political pressures emerged to hold higher education institutions accountable for student learning through assessments. In response, a small number of states (i.e., Florida and Tennessee) incorporated some form of mandatory standardized testing in higher education during the 1980s, the American Association for Higher Education hosted fora that brought together some of the foremost thinkers from across the United States to discuss accountability concerns.

The limitations of traditional standardized testing quickly emerged when assessment results were seen as having little relevance to instruction and how students demonstrate learning in higher education. It was impossible to account for student effort because achievement on the tests was not tied to instruction, coursework, student interests, or grades.

Educators, business leaders, and policymakers in the United States have questioned whether the design of assessments in higher education were too focused on measuring students' recall of discrete facts and not on a student's engagement in complex thinking and problem-solving tasks. Ridgeway, McCusker, and Pead (2004) posited that narrowly focused high-stakes assessments produce, at best, deceptive student gains. Shavelson (2007) additionally noted that external standardized tests—those that are outside the regular curriculum and not developed by faculty—can do little to address needed improvements in teaching, learning, and curriculum: "Tests can, perhaps, signal a problem, but the test scores themselves do not necessarily point to where or why the problem exists or offer particulars as to solutions" (p. 40).

Following the wave of state mandates for assessment in the mid- and late 1980s and new accreditation requirements in the 1990s, institutional administrators and faculty began to organize their own responses. Higher education assessment began to move away from standardized campus-wide assessment to course-based demonstrations of proficiency. In the 21st century, educators, colleges, and universities are beginning to "take up the challenge to figure out and clearly articulate what they want their students to know and be able to do: the core task of assessment" (Shavelson, 2007, p. vii).

The Total Quality Management/Continuous Quality Improvement framework was initiated by accrediting agencies in the early 2000s. From 2000 to 2010, accreditors adopted standards that favored the documentation of student learning and deemphasized of the importance of operational metrics (e.g., courses offered, grades submitted, books in the library). One reason for this is that colleges and university faculty and staff have been able to access and use a variety of technologies that allow faculty to link classroom-based assessments such as lab work, projects, and portfolios to programmatic outcomes, and use these tools to collect and manage student learning achievement data obtained from student work.

The Ongoing Challenge

In the United States, a recent development is the Liberal Education and America's Promise (LEAP) initiative launched by the Association of American Colleges and Universities (AACU). The LEAP initiative established essential learning outcomes for tertiary students to master in both general education and the major (Loris, 2010). Colwell (2008) suggests that all institutions teaching music, including higher education institutions, need to be more curious about policies affecting music education (p. 4). While expectations of ongoing assessment activities pervade American colleges and universities, only a few institutions have realized assessment's potential to produce significant gains in learning. In a review of literature on the assessment of learning in higher education, Orzolek (2010) notes that the development of assessments is a challenging and rigorous activity that must be undertaken alongside and during lesson development. While the use of student learning assessments and assessment results to support learning and instruction in higher education has progressed, continued efforts are necessary to realize the potential that documentation of the student learning has for program improvement. Teachers use information about student achievement over a period of time to extend their knowledge of each student's strengths and weaknesses, gain insight into the educational experiences that will enhance the students' learning, and adjust their role as teachers to meet the needs of students. As Orzolek (2010) clarified, "The more teachers can determine about how their students' learn, the more effective they can be in their classrooms" (p. 416).

ASSESSMENT OF MUSIC IN HIGHER EDUCATION

Music Assessment in the United States

In higher education, there are few standardized tests in music, and those are primarily used as diagnostic measures, for qualification to enter a program, or to obtain advanced college credit. The GRE initially included music tests but was dropped in 2001 (Burton & Wong, 2005). Examinations for high school students designed to yield college course credit, such as the Advanced Placement (AP) tests, originally included theory and music listening. The AP Music Listening Test was dropped because in-depth music listening was not specifically being taught in American high schools, even though listening remained a priority in the 1997 and 2008 music National Assessment of Educational Progress (Colwell, 2010). Only the AP theory test remains, although music theory is not consistently taught in most American high schools. The theory test is still offered because music theory is a requirement in university music studies. In teacher education programs, ETS's Praxis Series: Music Content Knowledge test (ETS Praxis, 2016) includes theory and history components. Other forms of testing were developed by Pearson (2018) that are "evaluation systems group matched to specific state standards" (D'Agostino & Powers, 2009, p. 147).

Regional and Disciplinary Accreditation as an Assessment Driver

In response to calls for public accountability and for the higher education community to strengthen and improve quality, regional accreditors have increased expectations for institutional assessment and effectiveness practices in the United States. Although most decisions are made locally, education issues have advanced up the governmental hierarchy to state and federal levels (McDermott, 2007, p. 77). Quality assurance is a fundamental component for institutional eligibility for federal funding set forth in the Higher Education Act (H. Res. 9567, 1965; American Council on Education, 2016). The US Department of Education (2018) oversees regional accreditation, a highly regulated process that ensures that institutions of higher education meet federally determined acceptable levels of quality. Institutional assessment processes, data, and results are reported as part of accreditation expectations. Although program assessment is not necessarily done specifically for compliance with accreditation standards, it is likely that most music program faculty would not review and report assessment data in the absence of accreditation expectations. In response to these requirements, music program faculty develop academic program assessment plans that are framed within institutional assessment expectations. These plans fulfill a regional accreditation expectation, and when implemented with fidelity, yield valuable information for faculty about student learning and can guide program improvement.

The National Association of Schools of Music (NASM, 2018a) is the disciplinary accrediting body for music programs in the United States. In the assessment planning process, music faculty work to align with the NASM expectations with institutional assessment processes to provide evidence of student learning. Member institutions of NASM are reviewed for continuation as accredited members on a 10-year cycle. As a part of this accreditation process, institutions complete self-study documents that describe programmatic review of student learning assessment processes and effectiveness for learning. Program-specific student learning outcomes and measures are determined by the faculty but must be consistent with the goals of curricular expectations outlined in the NASM handbook (NASM, 2018b). As Ward, Wagoner, and Copland state:

> The intersection between the NASM self-study process and the assessment of student learning outcomes is through expectations from the United States Department of Education, which requires institutions to report the assessment of student learning. Regional accreditation standards have shifted from a focus on teaching to one of student learning.   (2015, p.132)

Higher education leaders pursue this endeavor to meet accreditation standards and to demonstrate excellence in response to public and government pressure for accountability (Ewell, 2002). The NASM handbook suggests that evaluation of coursework, projects, and performances take place throughout the undergraduate and graduate programs with summary evaluations as comprehensive reviews (NASM, 2018b). "In order to close the loop, institutions also need to examine the impact of the action on student learning" (Ward, 2014, p. 288). "Closing the loop" refers to the analysis of student learning results and the use of the results to modify and improve student learning in the program.

Based on self-study and analysis of assessment results for accreditation review, music faculty address the improvement of student learning in their programs. To evidence accountability and transparency, institutions are expected to communicate assessment results to all stakeholders: administrators, faculty, students, alumni, community leaders, and employers. American accreditation agencies have influenced significantly the development of program and student learning assessment in higher education.

Institutions Outside the United States

"Political influences on the world's educational systems have begun to require the embedding of assessment into the on-going classroom activities of the world's teachers" (Asmus, 2016, p. 559). This has been evident in Europe, where the Bologna Declaration established a key objective related to learning outcomes for all higher education programs (Tremblay et al., 2012). Many countries outside the Bologna Process are aligning their higher education systems to be Bologna-compatible to "facilitate description of qualifications, mutual recognition of degrees, and student mobility" (Kennedy, 2008, p. 387). Institutional and political efforts have increased globally to improve assessment of student learning. Zhukov (2015) found that music programs in many higher education institutions around the world rely on performance examinations as means of assessing music learning. Swanwick (1999) warns that it is "unwise to base curriculum more or less exclusively on performing" (p. 87). Burnard (2012) calls for assessing a "multiplicity of musical creativities" (p. 219) that enable musical engagement in the variety of ways that music is experiences and created. Assessment in music studios is influenced by the Innovative Conservatoire, an international collaboration to stimulate knowledge exchange, innovation, and reflective practice in conservatories across the world (ICON—Innovative Conservatoire, 2014). The ICON project supports participating universities in hosting international seminars with assessment exercises using a variety of holistic assessment built on predetermined criteria. These methods encourage music teachers in higher education to focus more deeply on content and skills of their particular area.

Higher music educators intentionally engage a range of assessment methods due to the varieties of ways students demonstrate learning. The future of assessment is in the hands of higher music education faculty, which will need to respond to various pressures, including increasing interest in comparability of standards between countries and institutions (Lebler, 2015b).

International Perspectives of Assessment in Music in Higher Education

Brazil

Assessment in Brazilian education is under the responsibility of the Ministry of Education (MEC), encompassing early-childhood through undergraduate and postgraduate university programs. "Brazilian educational administrators have been working in recent years to build not only instruments, but assessment systems in order to develop more accurate diagnoses of school education, at different levels and stages" (Figueiredo & Del-Ben, this volume, p. 334). National guidelines for all undergraduate courses were produced by the MEC and represent the basis of the exam. The undergraduate curriculum of all Brazilian universities must follow these national guidelines, which represent a common curricular orientation that allows the organization of a national exam (Figueiredo, 2012; Figueiredo & Del-Ben, this volume). An exam is used to discover the extent to which undergraduate students learn in the areas of knowledge, skills, and competencies. All university areas of study have a specific exam, which is developed by a faculty committee responsible for the topics to be included in the exam. The intent of this procedure is to examine the initial and final level of student performance. As described by Figueiredo and Del-Ben (this volume), the students' performance assessment includes a written exam for each specific knowledge area and a performance assessment measured against defined performance expectations. After several years of implementation, "its utility is still questioned. For many the test is performed because it is mandatory, and not necessarily because it would be a tool to contribute to the improvement of the courses" (p. 326). Each edition of the exam is updated to reflect issues, content, and analytical skills, but not all of the important components of the area of music learning are covered. "Music is absent from the evaluation of basic education, at least at the time this chapter was written" (p. 335).

Australia

The Australian Higher Education Standards Panel (HESP) ensures that higher education institutions clearly identify program learning outcomes for students to achieve and demonstrate a clear relationship of outcomes between component courses across the bachelors and masters programs. Lebler, Holmes, Harrison, Carey, and Cain state, the

> HESP will clearly have a significant impact for the higher education sector insofar as it implies that all graduates must meet the nationally applied standard and individual institutions must be able to provide the evidence that graduates have achieved these goals.   (2015, p. 41)

The approach defines a student learning outcome as what a learner is expected to know, understand, and be able to demonstrate after completion of a process of learning with an emphasis on verifiable achievement demonstrated, "whether it be at the end of an individual unit, or a discipline major, or at the point of graduation from a degree" (p. 42).

Hughes and Keith (2015) describe the Australian Qualification Framework as a set of defining standards to be benchmarked against similar accredited courses of study offered by a broad range of higher education providers. The intent in mapping music-specific capabilities with national and international standards is to provide guidance for uniform quality in assessment. The Creative and Performing Arts (CAPA) Threshold Learning Outcomes (TLOs) provide a national perspective of minimum graduate achievements in Australia. Hughes and Keith (2015) report, "the 2013 music specific capabilities were developed during an ongoing review of the music discipline" (p. 180). Assessment by juries or panels of experts is the dominant method for assessing skills. Students' self-assessment of their personal work while they are developing it is also considered important because "students themselves need to develop the capacity to make judgements about both their own work and that of others in order to become effective continuing learners and practitioners" (Boud & Associates, 2010, p. 1). The Australian Qualifications Framework (AQF) infuses self-assessment and peer assessment by requiring graduates to be able to demonstrate "cognitive and creative skills to exercise critical thinking and judgement in identifying and solving problems with intellectual independence" (Australian Qualifications Framework Council, 2013, p. 47). The use of external examiners is common for graduation or postgraduate performance assessment as a means by which achievement expectations can be commonly understood between institutions (Lebler, 2015a).

To facilitate the alignment of assessment methods with threshold learning outcomes in the creative and performing arts, the Assessment in Music (AiM, n.d.) project addresses issues related to academic standards and the assessment of creative works in Australian higher music education. The project focuses primarily on the alignment between assessment and learning outcomes statements at the bachelor degree program levels. This has taken place across a range of programs and musical subdisciplines (Lebler et al., 2015). A standards-based approach is used to communicate clearly to students the expectations of learning outcomes and qualities of expected achievement expected. The standards are designed to guide teachers as they lead students to focus on content and skills unlikely to have been addressed prior to entering university studies. It also acts as the structure that guides professors to identify qualities of student achievement in their assessment practice. Scoring rubrics outline expectations of student achievement and are aligned to learning outcomes (Blom, Stevenson, & Encarnacao, 2015).

Institutions are responsible to design their own assessment processes that comply with the regulations set out by Tertiary Education Quality and Standards Agency (TEQSA), and to employ processes to ensure valid and reliable assessment of musical performances (Lebler, this volume). "While there is no requirement for external examiners, the use of external examiners for such assessments as recital performances is not uncommon" (p. 201). In Australia, a national network of representative from higher education institutions has been established to facilitate interinstitutional collaboration to review comparability of assessment standards and practices (Lebler, this volume). The foundational consideration for music assessments in Australian higher education is to design assessment tasks that are "realistic and authentic representations of what musicians are likely to do in their professional lives after graduation, students' learning will benefit directly from the completion of the assessment tasks" (p. 204).

Europe

The European Association for Conservatories (AEC) works to connect institutions of higher education of music in Europe (Lennon, 2015). This organization connects member institutions with others in and beyond Europe (Association Européenne des Conservatoires, 2013). Conlon and Rogers (2010) reported that a movement began in 2002 by the United Kingdom's Quality Assurance Agency for Higher Education (QAAHE) to support disciplinary comparability. The effort expanded though the European Credit Transfer and Accumulation System (ECTS), making it a responsibility of universities and conservatories to assess learning and allocate credits. The ECTS system has led to international conformity and validation of qualifications to support student mobility and the possibility of joint course credit for students who intend to study music across multiple universities and conservatories in Europe (Rossi, Bordin, & De Cicco, 2014).

At the time this chapter was written, 50 European countries participated in the Bologna Process with the intent to unify achievement indicators across universities. The Bologna Process (Reinalda & Kulesza, 2006) was designed to (1) strengthen the competitiveness and attractiveness of the European higher education; (2) foster mobility for students, graduates, and educators; (3) increase employability in Europe; and (4) increase the opportunity for students and educators to contribute to the exchange and development of cultural practices and ideals (Conlon & Rogers, 2010). This is accomplished through a quality assurance framework with an emphasis on learning outcomes for undergraduate and postgraduate studies.

In music, the Erasmus Network for Music "Polifonia" (Polifonia, 2016) was established in 2004, aiming to implement, monitor, and further develop tools and approaches for learning outcomes in music, program comparability, and quality assurance relevant to the Bologna Process. A working group from Polifonia on assessment and standards works to (1) strengthen shared understanding of assessment methods, procedures, and standards in European higher music education; (2) highlight innovative examples of assessment and processes for competence-based learning; and (3) explore how external examiners might be used to enhance objectivity. The assessment process is designed around the establishment of an external evaluation body for higher music education institutions and programs. Curriculum design and assessment strategies have been a focus of the Polifonia Tunings Project, which identified learning outcomes and achievement thresholds for bachelor of music study (Polifonia, 2016). The threshold statements for learning outcomes identify the characteristics of learning expected of all students by the conclusion of the study cycle "without impinging upon an individual institution's autonomy to manage the myriad of structural, cultural, and contextual demands of a program" (Monkhouse, 2015, p. 77). The AEC instructs that when students receive basic pedagogical training they should have demonstrated satisfactorily the following theory and skills outcomes:

a) apply the interrelationships between their theoretical and practical studies,
b) implement knowledge for personal artistic development, and
c) demonstrate thorough application of pedagogical theory. (Rossi et al., 2014, p. 5)

Rossi et al. (2014) describe how the curriculum of musical studies in conservatories across Europe was profoundly restructured by standardizing courses previously divided into in homogeneous groups. Student achievement is documented with academic credits awarded following the passing of specialized exams and by recognition of activities according to the Bologna Process. In their review of assessments, Rossi et al. (2014) reported that technical skills are considered most important in examinations, followed by expressiveness and precision in performance.

In reference to accreditation, MusiQuE (2016) Music Quality Enhancement was created in The Hague, the Netherlands, in 2014 and offers accreditation with quality enhancement and advisory services to assist higher music education institutions. They provide guidance and associated training for benchmarking to be used as a learning and quality enhancement tool. Criteria from benchmarking have progressed into three new sets of standards for the review of higher music education institutions and programs: Standards for Institutional Review, Standards for Program Review, and Standards for Joint Programs Review. As an external contributor, the National Association of Schools of Music (NASM) was chosen as project partner in view of its expertise in accreditation of higher music education programs in the United States. The NASM chief executive contributed a substantial amount of information about how the NASM model functions.

The United Kingdom

There are four nations that make up the United Kingdom, and, although they are all governed by a common parliament, Scotland, Wales, and Northern Ireland have their own assemblies with some degree of independence from London. Education is controlled to a large extent by semiautonomous education departments in these countries (meNet, n.d.). Assessment in UK higher education involves "decentralized, subject-specific decision-making processes of quality assurance involving national agencies and review systems, external examining and local moderation" (Bloxham, Boyd, & Orr, 2011, p. 655). Contemporary developments in higher music education align with the Bologna Process through the Polifina project. Benchmarking processes take into account that an individual may perform significantly better than the threshold benchmark, or an institution may be operating at a higher level than others in its sector. Although higher music education requires assessors to be consistent in judgment and benchmark against widely acknowledged standards, Cox (2010) states, " the possibility of encountering individual manifestations of excellence that challenge or re-define those notions" may happen, and that "benchmark referencing against widely recognised standards promotes a broad understanding of achievement levels" (p. 3). To confirm consistency and fairness of the assessment process, external benchmarking or moderation is used for quality assurance. This is embedded in UK practice and carried out by internal colleagues, sometimes with an external perspective. If an external moderator is used, a written report is used to provide commentary.

Conceptual Considerations for Guiding Music Assessment in Higher Education

One consideration for assessing learning is focused on expectations of achievement to be demonstrated by students. Faculty-established assessment criteria provide the framework for determining the quality of student work and student achievement. Criteria are often prescribed and disseminated to students in advance to relay expectations of quality, enable objectivity of judgment, and provide efficiency of assessment processes. These criteria frame the assessment tasks, scoring methods, and the structure of feedback provided to students. Researchers have illustrated that the assessments of musical performance are formal in jury or recital settings. Parkes (this volume) found that studio teachers "have used categories illustrating various specific dimensions of music performance such as pitch, rhythm, intonation, tone, and musicality/expression" (p. 772).

Assessments should help the students understand learning goals and ways to achieve the desired expectations of achievement (Sadler, 1989). Another consideration focuses on a holistic approach to assessment. Since "quality often requires all-things-considered holistic judgements in which multiple criteria are attended to simultaneously in interlaced ways" (Sadler, 2010, p. 544), Sadler suggests an approach to the measurement of student learning that accommodates individual variability instead of complying with specific predetermined criteria. Consensus moderation can be a process used to determine quality in assessment while allowing for individual variability in applying known constructs of learning and ensuring that judgments of students' performance are consistent. This often consists of a peer-review process to reach agreement throughout the entire assessment process (Assessment Matters, n.d.). Sadler (2015) summarizes the framework as artifact-based, assessed by multiple reviewers with no predetermined criteria who must rationalize their appraisal. Criteria used for appraisal will emerge from the performance, rather than defined in advance. This framework suggests that standards of achievement are determined by consensus of student work, assigned a grade, and provided a justification of the assigned grade. He suggests students must learn to monitor and control the quality of their own performance to empower them to become self-regulated learners. Scott (2012) also suggests that assessment needs to intentionally engage students in the assessment process by having them assess model work, and that "by so doing, they gain an understanding of how the assessment criteria are used to describe musical performances and learn how their own performances will be compared to the levels of performance" (p. 33).

Newsome (2015) recommends that an assessment be designed to include a balance between the holistic assessment and criterion-based assessment to allow for an assessment process that addresses technical, musical, and aesthetic aspects of learning within the context of each education situation. Assessments should support students' continued learning and document the extent to which learning has occurred at any point in time. Whichever consideration is adopted, effective assessment allows students to demonstrate the extent to which they have learned with a valid and fair means to distinguish achievement qualities.

ALIGNING ASSESSMENT WITH INSTRUCTION TO ENHANCE STUDENT LEARNING

Methods of Assessment

"Higher education institutions throughout the world vary in how they communicate quality and results of student learning" (Ward, this volume, p. 748). With respect to higher education music programs, assessment has often been considered in terms of assigning a grade (Bauer, 2008). As Bauer (2010) asserts, assessments have purposes beyond assigning grades:

> (a) identifying what students need to learn; (b) evaluating whether students have accomplished a learning task and are ready to move on or if further instruction is needed; (c) deciding if students have mastered specific concepts and/or skills; and (d) assigning grades to students.   (p. 428)

Music assessment in higher education in the United States is an ongoing process used to determine the quality and depth of student learning at any particular point in time. Student achievement data attained from assessment should be used to inform students of learning needs and guide further instruction (Wiggins, 2001). Music faculty at institutions of higher learning in the United States are given considerable autonomy in the selection of the specific methods used to assess student learning and the definition of levels of achievement, bearing in mind they must provide evidence of student learning and continuous program improvement to meet accreditation expectations. Orzolek (2010) suggests that assessment of music in higher education should be both formal and informal using methods and tools such as rubrics, performances, oral interview, questioning, and portfolios. Parkes (2010) found that higher education studio teachers in the United States implement five primary measures of student achievement for a summative evaluation grade: jury scores, recital scores, attendance, effort, and progress. Newsome (2015) suggests that professional instruction typically targets artistic and technical mastery that are assessed by expert examiners. That is in contrast to the music classroom, where faculty focus on student knowledge acquisition and application in areas such as history and theory. Recent approaches include alternative forms of assessment to document students' performance, creation, and understanding of music (Bauer, 2010). New and emerging technologies "allow us to more efficiently and effectively develop assessment instruments, and in some cases enable new types of assessment approaches" (p. 431). Mobile technology used by college students (smartphones, laptop computers, and tablets) opens new opportunities in music for teaching, learning, and assessment.

Programmatic Assessment Plans

Program assessment is an ongoing process aimed at understanding and improving student learning (University of Hawai'i at Mānoa, 2011, p. 1) that reflects a program's mission. Yorke (1998) argues that there are three broad conditions that need to be satisfied if the management of programmatic assessment is to be effective: (1) a clear definition of the purpose and who is to be served; (2) a strategy designed to lead to the fulfillment of programmatic purpose(s) that involves all faculty in either data collection or resulting discussions; and (3) an operationalization plan that can be efficiently enacted within the teaching and learning processes of the university's music curriculum (p. 101). Included in program assessment are student learning outcomes that define what students should know and be able to do as a result of completing the program's curriculum.

Lebler (2015b) proposes that it is critical that student learning outcomes reflect the curricular learning sequences through the coursework in the program. Many programs have found a curriculum map useful in visualizing student learning across a course of study. On a curriculum map, program faculty identify the points in the program (usually specific courses) where the program outcomes are introduced, developed or reinforced, and assessed. Some curriculum maps indicate mastery at the senior (exit) level to provide a complete picture of the scope in terms of depth, breadth, and the sequence of the curriculum. Curriculum mapping is most valuable when faculty collaborate to discuss the development of student learning throughout the program and determine the best points in the curriculum sequence to assess student learning outcome achievement.

When faculty discuss the mapping of learning and assessment opportunities, one important consideration is if and when student are provided opportunities to think about and assess their own learning. Lebler (2015b) suggests that it is important for students to develop the ability to assess their own work in the process of becoming effective learners and practitioners. The practice of self-assessment is commonplace for music students, who do much of their work alone in a practice room, listening lab, or composition studio (Daniel & Parkes, 2015). They are expected to monitor their own progress toward goals set by themselves or their teachers by analyzing their strengths and weaknesses of work in progress (Monkhouse, 2015). Formal instruction in effective processes of self-assessment and peer-assessment, although uncommon in higher music education (Lebler, 2015b) may be an important component of both instruction and learning assessment.

Assessment of student learning throughout a curriculum provides valuable information for music faculty in courses and across the program to consider opportunities for program improvement. As a result of analyzing student achievement data, faculty can discover competencies that are not being addressed with sufficient depth and can develop and implement action plans that lead to program improvement and student learning. Although studies of curriculum mapping processes are present in the literature, there is little scholarship of curriculum mapping in relation to schools of music and NASM competencies (Ward et al., 2016).

Albert (2008) suggests that care must be taken that an assessment plan leads to the collection of student achievement data that can expose both student success and areas of learning needs so to guide programmatic decisions. Serafini (2002) identified three primary goals of an assessment process: to enhance curriculum and instruction, to enhance student learning, and to document student achievement over time. It is important that a measure of student learning provide data that validly and authentically represents the expected learning outcome. Lebler (2015b) supports customizing criteria in response to the work submitted for assessment with appropriate weight given to those aspects of student performance that are particularly noteworthy, reflecting a holistic consideration of assessment as described by Sadler (2009, 2010, 2015). Hughes and Keith (2015) suggest cohesiveness within a program's assessment plan, course-based assessments, and learning expectations aligned to program learning outcomes, which define "discipline-specific benchmarks, and graduate capabilities" (p. 175). Blom et al. (2015) add that desired outcomes must be made clear as possible to students through the "adoption of descriptive rubrics with criteria and standards of performance" (p. 125). Even though outcomes that essentially demonstrate credentialing expectations of a degree program are of primary importance in curriculum, when possible, program outcomes should also reflect institutional learning goals. Institutional learning goals (outcomes) are knowledge, skills, and attitudes that students are expected to develop as a result of their overall educational experiences at an institution of higher learning regardless of the discipline. These institutional learning goals often are specifically reflected within individual program student learning outcomes. If aligned, measures of student learning within a program's assessment process can simultaneously address course, program, and institutional outcomes. When implemented with fidelity, assessment plans yield student learning data that faculty analyze and review to reveal areas where curricular modification is needed to strengthen student learning.

Challenges to Assessment

The primary direct assessment of student learning used by faculty in American higher education is a course assignment. Faculty select specific assignments within their courses that directly measure their program learning outcomes. Ward (2014) asserts, "there continues to be disconnect between teaching and learning and assessment" (p. 288). Ewell (2002) suggests that this disconnect occurs most often when assessment is treated as an activity that is implemented after or separate from teaching instead of as a core component of the teaching and learning process. If assessment of student learning in a program is embedded in the curriculum, the efficiency of the process addresses the challenge of time to administer assessment, which is one of the most commonly cited challenges that Ward identifies.

An integrated process for university music program assessment addresses systematic review of assessment data, another challenge identified in Ward's (2014) study. Ward's results reveal that only 41% of respondents use assessment data in making course delivery decisions and 39% examine ongoing effectiveness of instructional adjustments ($N = 208$). If an assessment process is effectively integrated into curriculum through the teaching and learning process, faculty are enabled to review assessment data to modify and improve the program and student learning.

Gray (2002) claims that faculty ownership of assessment is the key to success because the primary purpose of assessment is instructional enhancement to improve the quality of learning in essential learning outcomes. Another identified challenge for American higher education music faculty is a limited understanding or expertise in assessment (Ward, 2014). Researchers may want to examine the attitudes and training of higher education music professors related to their understanding and skills of assessment. Sadler (2009) calls for faculty discussion to determine whether criteria for student learning achievement are to define outcomes, or whether criteria appropriate for an outcome are used to rationalize an assessor's judgment.

In Ward's (2014) survey of American music education professors, only 17% of respondents identify faculty involvement in the outcomes assessment process. Over half of the respondents noted that the program's assessment process is the responsibility of a single person. Outcomes assessment will be viewed as a duty of someone outside of their classroom and not incorporated into an assessment-informed instructional design (Ward & High, 2010, p. 506).

THE FUTURE OF MUSIC ASSESSMENT IN HIGHER EDUCATION

This chapter has presented varying contexts within which institutions define expected learning outcomes and identify useful methods of assessment in response to calls for greater accountability from various constituencies. As suggested by the Association of American Colleges and Universities (AACU, 2007), it is clear that standards for students' expected level of achievement must focus on the quality of the students' knowledge attained, mastery of key skills in the discipline, attentiveness to issues of ethical and social responsibility, and facility in integrating learning into a variety of applied situations. Shavelson (2007) raises the concern that if higher education learning outcomes for music education are narrowly measured because of cost, capacity, and convenience, there is a risk of narrowing the mission and diversity of music learning in higher education. Lebler (2015b) agrees by arguing that the challenge for the future of assessment is the need to demonstrate rigor, reliability, and validity as well as a degree of comparability of standards within and between institutions.

Assessment that is integral to the process of learning and teaching can significantly impact student achievement, but only if it becomes the focus of academic programs. In other words, this kind of assessment must become an essential part of the design and enactment of contemporary learning environments (Pellegrino, 1999). Although higher education faculty have been engaging in outcomes assessment, music units are still "developing mature assessment plans and cycles" (Ward, 2014, p. 308). To engage faculty in this process, leaders must view outcomes assessment as integral to teaching and learning and give faculty the time and resources to effectively assess the learning of their students. In the higher education learning environment, decontextualized assessments have minimal validity as indices of educational attainments. As Pellegrino (Rebora, 2014) suggests, devices used to measure what individuals know and can do should coalesce in the design and the administration of assessment in higher educational practice:

> A lot of what we want to know about student learning could be gleaned from information that could come out of the classroom.... In a world where much of the work that we do is mediated by technology and is done in technology-rich environments and learning systems, we could glean a lot of information spontaneously that would help us to track important things. We could embed into those environments periodic assessments that students take to demonstrate their competence.... There are times when we want and need to monitor progress and collect evidence of learning to see if students have mastered important knowledge and skills... ways for students to show they have mastered important standards in the context of their ongoing work.   (para. 11)

Angelo (2002) recommends that assessment "become part of routine practice" in higher education (p. 199). For faculty pursuing tenure, involvement in the outcomes assessment process should manifest into research productivity. Scholarship focusing on outcomes assessment is emerging, and many issues need to be explored. Ward (2014) suggests that experienced faculty members should mentor new faculty on how to use outcomes assessment to improve the teaching. If formalized as action research, these projects can lead to needed pedagogical studies in their area of teaching.

Learning assessment in higher education of young musicians should include not only demonstration of performance achievements but also how the student competently applies knowledge, integrity, and problem-solving requisite to enter a musical occupation. Expanding on Parkes, Doerksen, and Richter (2014), despite the good intentions of higher education faculty to prepare students for musical success in performance skills, very few instructional models exist for professional expectations beyond skills in those that complete degree programs in music. A framework that addresses the development of learning is necessary for a variety of applied musical environments. Student completion of a series of courses does not fully correspond to development of a student's artistic and professional learning. Assessments need to be considered and developed for curricular and extracurricular student learning experiences. However, student learning is not guaranteed by the efficacy of an assessment process. A balance of instruction and applied assessments can contribute to bringing out and developing enhanced student learning.

Music educators in higher education must create assessments that are appropriate for the variety of music learning essential for professional success. This requires learning outcomes that define what it means to be musical. Well-defined outcomes with appropriate measures provide information about student achievement that enables faculty to make curricular modifications and inform instructional planning. Musical and nonmusical criteria should be developed when creating assessment tasks and scoring tools used to measure student learning. These criteria should also enable students to develop the capacity to make judgments about their own work. Student understanding and competence with self-assessment has the "potential to facilitate our students' journeys toward lifelong involvement in music making" (Scott, 2012, p. 35).

Lebler (2015b) suggests that assessment of music learning, both academic and performance, will need to respond to a number of accountability pressures. With increasing interest in comparability of standards between countries and institutions, exploring various institutional and national structures for assessment of music programs in higher education may guide enhanced practice. "To serve our future students well, their experience of assessment should include a range of methods and practices in which they can justifiably have confidence, and it certainly should include the development of self- and peer assessment abilities" (p. 7).

In the United States, the National Institute for Learning Outcomes Assessment (NILOA, n.d.), established in 2008, provides valuable information for designing assessment plans, identifying appropriate measures, and disseminating ways that academic programs and institutions can productively use assessment data to inform and strengthen undergraduate education. Another valuable resource is the Association for the Assessment of Learning in Higher Education (AALHE), formed in 2009 to serve the needs of those in higher education interested in using effective assessment practice to document and improve student learning. Whether through national organizations or intercollegiate collaborations, guidance in the development and implementation of assessment processes is essential for music program faculty in higher education. As Ward (this volume) suggests, institutions must use assessments as a means to "manage themselves and how their students are achieving" (p. 762), taking into account an ever-changing landscape of needs and academic goals.

References

Albert, S. (2008). A cluster evaluation approach to the assessment of e-portfolios in music teacher education. In T. Brophy (Ed.) *Assessment in music education: Integrating curriculum, theory, and practice. Proceedings of the Florida Symposium on Assessment in Music Education* (pp. 351–362). Chicago, IL: GIA Publications.

American Council on Education. (2016). Higher Education Act. Retrieved from http://www.acenet.edu/advocacy-news/Pages/Higher-Education-Act.aspx

Asmus, E. (2016). Embedding assessment seamlessly into existing music teacher training courses. In T. Brophy (Ed.) *Connecting practice, measurement, and evaluation. Proceedings of the 5th International Symposium on Assessment in Music Education* (pp. 559–571). Chicago, IL: GIA Publications.

Assessment in Music (AiM). (n.d.). Retrieved from http://assessmentinmusic.com.au/

Assessment Matters. (n.d.). Griffith University. *Definition and explanation of terms.* Retrieved 2018 from http://app.griffith.edu.au/assessment-matters/docs/consensus-moderation/definition

Association of American Colleges and Universities (AACU). (2007). *College learning for the new global century: A report from the National Leadership Council for Liberal Education and America's Promise. Washington, DC.* Retrieved from https://www.aacu.org/sites/default/files/files/LEAP/GlobalCentury_final.pdf

Association Europeenne des Conservatoires. (2013). *Mission statement.* Retrieved from https://www.aec-music.eu/about-aec/mission-statement

Astin, A. (1993). *What matters in college: Four critical years revisited.* San Francisco, CA: Jossey-Bass.

Australian Qualifications Framework Council. (2013). *Australian Qualifications Framework* (2nd ed.). Retrieved from https://www.aqf.edu.au/sites/aqf/files/aqf_issuance_jan2013.pdf

Bauer, W. (2008). The teacher work sample methodology: A tool to develop pre-service music teachers' understanding of assessment. In T. Brophy (Ed.), *Assessment in music education: Integrating curriculum, theory, and practice. Proceedings of the Florida Symposium on Assessment in Music Education* (pp. 363–377). Chicago, IL: GIA Publications.

Bauer, W. (2010). Technological pedagogical and content knowledge, music, and assessment. In T. Brophy (Ed.) *The practice of assessment in music education: Frameworks, models, and designs. Proceedings of the 2nd International Symposium on Assessment in Music Education* (pp. 427–436). Chicago, IL: GIA Publications.

Baxter Magolda, M. (1992). *Knowing and reasoning in college.* San Francisco, CA: Jossey-Bass.

Blom, D., Stevenson, I., & Encarnacao, J. (2015). Assessing music performance process and outcome through a rubric: Ways and means. In D. Lebler, G. Carey, & S. Harrison (Eds.). *Assessment in music education: From policy to practice* (pp. 1–7). Cham, Switzerland: Springer International.

Bloxham, S., Boyd, P., & Orr, S. (2011). Mark my words: The role of assessment criteria in UK higher education grading practices. *Studies In Higher Education, 36,* 655–670.

Boardman, E. (Ed.). (2002). *Dimensions of music learning and teaching: A different kind of classroom.* Reston, VA: MENC.

Boud, D., & Associates (2010). *Assessment 2020: Seven propositions for assessment reform in higher education.* Sydney: Australian Learning and Teaching Council.

Bruffee, K. (1993). *Collaborative learning: Higher education, interdependence, and the authority of knowledge.* Baltimore, MD: Johns Hopkins University Press.

Burnard, P. (2012). *Musical creativities in practice.* Oxford, UK: Oxford University Press.

Burton, N., & Wong, M. (2005). *Predicting long-term success in graduate school: A collaborative validity study report.* Princeton, NJ: Educational Testing Service.

Chiodo, P. (2010). Designing assessment: The selection and construction of instructional objectives. In T. Brophy (Ed.), *The practice of assessment in music education: Frameworks, models, and designs. Proceedings of the 2nd International Symposium on Assessment in Music Education* (pp. 443–454). Chicago, IL: GIA Publications.

Colwell, R. (2008). Music assessment in an increasingly politicized, accountability-driven educational environment. In T. Brophy (Ed.), *Assessment in music education: Integrating curriculum, theory, and practice. Proceedings of the Florida Symposium on Assessment in Music Education* (pp. 4–16). Chicago, IL: GIA Publications.

Colwell, R. (2010). Many voices, one goal: Practices of large-scale music assessment. In T. Brophy (Ed.), *The practice of assessment in music education: Frameworks, models, and designs. Proceedings of the 2nd International Symposium on Assessment in Music Education* (pp. 3–22). Chicago, IL: GIA Publications.

Conlon, F., & Rogers, L. (2010). Music in further education colleges. In S. Hallam & A. Creech (Eds.), *Music education in the 21st century in the United Kingdom* (pp. 245–259). London, UK: Institute of Education.

Cox, J. (2010). *Admission and assessment in higher education.* Association Europeenne des Conservatoires Academies de Musique et Musikhochschulen: Erasmus network for music. Stockholm, Sweden: Polifonia. Retrieved from http://www.aec-music.eu/userfiles/File/en2a-aec-handbook-admissions-and-assessment-in-higher-music-education.pdf

D'Agostino, J., & Powers, S. (2009). Predicting teacher performance with test scores and grade point average: A meta-analysis. *American Educational Research Journal, 46,* 146–182.

Daniel, R., & Parkes, K. A. (2015). The apprentice to master journey: Exploring tertiary music instrument teachers' reflections on their experiences as learner. *Journal of Arts and Humanities, 4*(3), 52–63.

Dill, D., & Vught, F. (2010). *National innovation and the academic research enterprise: Public policy in global perspective.* Baltimore, MD: Johns Hopkins University Press.

Educational Testing Service (ETS). (1966). *The Graduate Record Examinations: Area tests.* Princeton, NJ: Educational Testing Service.

Elliott, D. (2010). Assessing the concept of assessment: Some philosophical reflections. In T. Brophy (Ed.), *The practice of assessment in music education: Frameworks, models, and designs. Proceedings of the 2nd International Symposium on Assessment in Music Education* (pp. 367–379). Chicago, IL: GIA Publications.

ETS Praxis. (2016). *Preparation materials.* Ewing New Jersey: Educational Testing Service. Retrieved from https://www.ets.org/praxis/prepare/materials/5113/.

Ewell, P. T. (2002). An emerging scholarship: A brief history of assessment. In T. Banta (Ed.), *Building a scholarship of assessment* (pp. 3–25). San Francisco, CA: Jossey-Bass.

Ewell, P. (2010). Twenty Years of Quality Assurance in Higher Education: What's Happened and What's Different? *Quality in Higher Education, 16*(2), 173.

Figueiredo, S. (2012). Perspectives and challenges for music assessment in Brazilian universities. In T. Brophy & A. Lehman-Wermser (Eds.), *Music assessment across cultures and continents: The culture of shared practice. Proceedings of the 3rd International Symposium on Assessment in Music Education* (pp. 59–68). Chicago, IL: GIA Publications.

Gardiner, L. (1998). Why we must change: The research evidence. *NEA Higher Education Journal, 14*(1), 71–88.

Gray, P. (2002). The roots of assessment: Tensions, solutions, and research directions. In T. W. Banta (Ed.), *Building a scholarship of assessment* (pp. 49–66). San Francisco, CA: Jossey-Bass.

H. Res. 9567, 89th Cong., Pub. L. 89–329, Nov. 8, 1965, 79 Stat. 1219 (20 U.S.C. 1001 et seq., 42 U.S.C. 2751 et seq.) (1965, November 8). (enacted).

Hanson, D., & Saunders, C. (2010). Expanding higher-order thinking in the music classroom: Suggestions for effective and efficient assessment. In T. Brophy (Ed.) *The practice of assessment in music education: Frameworks, models, and designs. Proceedings of the 2nd International Symposium on Assessment in Music Education* (pp. 253–265). Chicago, IL: GIA Publications.

Hodsoll, F. (1988). *Toward civilization: A report on arts education.* Washington, DC: National Endowment for the Arts.

Hughes, D., & Keith, S. (2015). Linking assessment practices, unit-level outcomes and discipline-specific capabilities in contemporary music studies. In D. Lebler, G. Carey, & S. Harrison (Eds.). *Assessment in music education: From policy to practice* (pp. 171–193). Cham, Switzerland: Springer International.

ICON—Innovative Conservatoire. (2014). *Welcome to the Innovative Conservatoire.* Innovative Conservatoire. Retrieved from http://www.innovativeconservatoire.com

Kennedy, D. (2008). Linking learning outcomes and assessment of learning of student science teachers. *Science Education International, 19,* 387–397.

Kuh, G. D. (1995). The other curriculum: Out-of-class experiences associated with student learning and personal development. *Journal of Higher Education, 66,* 123.

Lebler, D. (2015a). The BoPMAT: Bachelor of music popular music program. In C. Lebler, G. Carey, & S. Harrison (Eds.), *Assessment in music education: From policy to practice* (pp. 221–235). Cham, Switzerland: Springer International.

Lebler, D. (2015b). Future directions for assessment in music. In C. Lebler, G. Carey, & S. Harrison (Eds.), *Assessment in music education: From policy to practice* (pp. 1–7). Cham, Switzerland: Springer International.

Lebler, D., Holmes, J., Harrison, S., Carey, G., & Cain, M. (2015). Assessment in music in the Australian context: The AiM Project. In C. Lebler, G. Carey, & S. Harrison (Eds.), *Assessment in music education: From policy to practice* (pp. 39–54). Cham, Switzerland: Springer International.

Lennon, M. (2015). Assessment in music in the European context: The Polifonia project. In C. Lebler, G. Carey, & S. Harrison (Eds.), *Assessment in music education: From policy to practice* (pp. 21–33). Cham, Switzerland: Springer International.

Loris, M. (2010). The human journey: Embracing the essential learning outcomes. *Liberal Education, 96*(1), 44–49.

McDermott, K. (2007). Expanding the moral community or Blaming the victim? The politics of state education accountability policy. *American Educational Research Journal, 44*(1), 77–111.

meNet. (n.d.). *Music education network.* Retrieved from http://menet.mdw.ac.at/menetsite/english/t_content3_1_1_uk.html

Mezirow, J. (2000). *Learning as transformation: Critical perspectives on a theory in progress.* San Francisco, CA: Wiley & Sons.

Monkhouse, H. (2015). Bachelor of music: Purpose, desires, and requirements. In D. Lebler, G. Carey, & S. Harrison (Eds.), *Assessment in music education: From policy to practice* (pp. 71–86). Cham, Switzerland: Springer International.

MusiQuE. (2016). *Music quality enhancement.* Reston, VA: National Association of School of Music. Retrieved from http://www.musique-qe.eu/home

National Association of Schools of Music (NASM). (2018a). *Home page.* Reston, VA: National Association of Schools of Music. Retrieved from https://nasm.arts-accredit.org/

National Association of Schools of Music (NASM). Reston, VA (2018b). *National Association of Schools of Music Handbook 2017–18.* Reston, VA: National Association of Schools of Music. Retrieved from https://nasm.arts-accredit.org/accreditation/standards-guidelines/handbook/

National Institute for Learning Outcomes Assessment (NILOA). (n.d.). Retrieved from http://www.learningoutcomesassessment.org

Newsome, E. (2015). A search for balance: The development of a performance assessment form for classical instrumental music in the tertiary context. In D. Lebler, G. Carey, &

S. Harrison (Eds.), *Assessment in music education: From policy to practice* (pp. 153–170). Cham, Switzerland: Springer International.

Orzolek, D. (2010). In search of models for the assessment of thinking in music education. In T. Brophy (Ed.), *The practice of assessment in music education: Frameworks, models, and designs. Proceedings of the 2nd International Symposium on Assessment in Music Education* (pp. 415–426). Chicago, IL: GIA Publications.

Parkes, K. (2010). Measuring sense of efficacy in higher education applied music performance teachers. *Research Perspectives in Music Education, 14,* 21–32.

Parkes, K., Doerksen, P, & Ritcher, G. (2014). Measuring professional dispositions in pre-service music teachers in the United States. In T. Brophy (Ed.) *Music assessment and global diversity: Practice, measurement, and policy. Proceedings of the 4th International Symposium on Assessment in Music Education* (pp. 351–386). Chicago, IL: GIA Publications.

Pearson (2018). *Higher education.* Retrieved from https://www.pearson.com/us/higher-education.html

Pellegrino, J. (1999). *The evolution of educational assessment: Considering the past and imaging the future.* Princeton, NJ: Educational Testing Service.

Polifonia (2016). *Erasmus network for music "Polifonia."* Retrieved from https://www.aec-music.eu/polifonia

Reinalda, B., & Kulesza, E. (2006). *The Bologna process: Harmonizing Europe's higher education, including the essential original texts* (2nd rev. ed.). Farmington Hills, MI: Budrich.

Rebora, A. (2014). *The coming age of instructionally integrated testing.* [Interview with James Pellegrino]. Retrieved from http://www.edweek.org/tm/articles/2014/03/05/ndia_pellegrinoqa.html

Ridgeway, J., McCusker, S., & Pead, D. (2004). *Literature review on e-assessment.* Briston, UK: Futurelab.

Rossi, T., Bordin, A. M., & De Cicco, D. (2014). Assessment and professors' competence in Italian higher music education between tradition and new goals. *Creative Education, 5,* 1341–1352.

Sadler, R. (1989). Formative assessment and the design of instructional systems. *Instructional Science, 18,* 119–144.

Sadler, R. (2009). Indeterminancy in the use of preset criteria for assessment and grading. *Assessment and Evaluation in Higher Education, 34,* 159–179.

Sadler, R. (2010). Beyond feedback: Developing student capability in complex appraisal. *Assessment and Evaluation in Higher Education, 35,* 535–550.

Sadler, D. R. (2015, August 27). Consensus moderation, backwards assessment, and calibration. In D. Lebler (Chair), *Assessment in Music Symposium.* Queensland Conservatorium, Brisbane, Australia. Retrieved from http://assessmentinmusic.com.au/wp-content/uploads/2012/06/Royce-Sadlers-speaking-notes.docx

Savage, H. J. (1953). *Fruit of an impulse: Forty-five years of the Carnegie Foundation.* New York, NY: Harcourt, Brace, and Company.

Scott, S. (2012). Rethinking the roles of assessment in music education. *Music Educators Journal, 98*(3), 31–35.

Scott, S., & McCallum, W. (2010). Constructivist perspectives of instruction and assessment within instrumental music education. In T. Brophy (Ed.), *The practice of assessment in music education: Frameworks, models, and designs. Proceedings of the 2nd International Symposium on Assessment in Music Education* (pp. 253–485). Chicago, IL: GIA Publications.

Serafini, F. (2002). Dismantling the factory model of assessment. *Reading and Writing Quarterly, 18*, 67–86.

Shavelson, R. (2007). *A brief history of student learning assessment: How we got where we are and a proposal for where to go next.* Washington, DC: Association of American Colleges and Universities.

Swanwick, K. (1999). *Teaching music musically.* London, UK: Routledge.

Tremblay, K., Lalancette, D., & Roseveare, D. (2012). *Assessment of higher education learning outcomes: Feasibility study report.* The Organization for Economic Co-operation and Development (OECD). Retrieved from http://www.oecd.org/education/skills-beyond-school/AHELOFSReportVolume1.pdf

University of Hawai'i in Mānoa. (2011). *Program assessment defined.* Hawaii: University of Hawaii. Retrieved from https://manoa.hawaii.edu/ovcaa/policies/pdf/M5.110.pdf.

United States. National Commission on Excellence in Education. (1983). *A nation at risk: The imperative for educational reform: A report to the Nation and the Secretary of Education,* United States Department of Education. Washington, D.C.: The Commission: [Supt. of Docs., U.S. G.P.O. distributor]

US Department of Education. (2018). *College accreditation in the United States.* Retrieved from http://www2.ed.gov/admins/finaid/accred/accreditation.html

Ward, J. (2014). An examination of practices, faculty and administrative involvement, and resources and barriers in higher education music outcomes assessment. In T. Brophy, & A. Lehmann-Wermser (Eds.), *Music assessment across cultures and continents: The culture of shared practice. Proceedings of the 3rd International Symposium on Assessment in Music Education* (pp. 287–310). Chicago, IL: GIA Publications.

Ward, J., & High. L. (2010). Theory into practice: Teaching assessment strategies to preservice teachers through a third-through-fifth-grade vocal music laboratory. In T. S. Brophy (Ed.). *The practice of assessment in music education: Frameworks, models, and designs proceedings of the 2009 Florida Symposium on Assessment in Music Education* (pp. 499–512). Chicago, IL: GIA Publications.

Ward, J., Wagoner, C., & Copeland, R. (2016). Intersections of accreditation: An examination of a school of music curriculum mapping process to relate specialized accreditation and regional accreditation standards. In T. Brophy, J. Marlatt, & G. Ritcher (Eds.), *Connecting practice, measurement, and evaluation. Proceedings of the 5th International Symposium on Assessment in Music Education* (pp. 119–134). Chicago, IL: GIA Publications.

Wiggins, J. (2001). *Teaching for musical understanding.* New York, NY: McGraw-Hill.

Williams, D. (1999). Using out of class time in educationally purposeful ways. *Journal of Music Teacher Education, 9*, 1824. Retrieved from http://search.proquest.com.er.lib.kstate.edu/docview/195796482?accountid=11789

Yorke, M. (1998). The management of assessment in higher education. *Assessment and Evaluation in Higher Education, 23*, 101–116.

Zhukov, K. (2015). Challenging approaches to assessment of instrumental learning. In D. Lebler, G. Carey, & S. Harrison (Eds.), *Assessment in music education: From policy to practice* (pp. 55–70). Cham, Switzerland: Springer International.

CHAPTER 31

ASSESSMENT OF PRESERVICE MUSIC EDUCATORS

DAVID C. EDMUND AND JIAN-JUN CHEN-EDMUND

Emily is a music student teacher in a US public school, who delivers lessons while being observed by her supervising professor. After providing detailed lesson plans and a preobservation reflection document, she teaches three 40-minute general music classes with kindergarteners, second graders, and fifth graders. The supervisor types running commentary throughout each lesson, noting a tendency of the student teacher to modify instructional techniques in response to individual and group needs. Each instructional modification is appropriate for the musical and social situation. For example, upon noting reluctance from fifth graders to improvise individual solos on soprano recorder, the student teacher opts to divide children into groups of four and engages them in group call-and-response. This modification results in a greater degree of comfort for children and constitutes a form of scaffolding toward the development of individual musical creativity. This and other instructional modifications are directly in line with feedback commentary provided by the supervising professor.

Consider another scenario:

Sarah is a junior music education major participating in a site-based secondary choral field experience. She teaches two "micro lessons" while being observed by her cooperating teacher. Her lesson plans reflect a reasonable amount of detail, but there are questions about links between standards, objectives, and procedures. The cooperating teacher observes two 20-minute lessons and composes detailed observation commentary, noting many areas for improvement. For example, Sarah fails to detect inaccurate pitches sung by the altos in concert choir. When the alto sectional leader requests assistance with the phrase, Sarah responds by explaining that they should have learned it when addressed earlier. The alto section

> *responds by tuning out Sarah, opting to chat and make jokes throughout the*
> *class period. The situation escalates to the extent that the apprentice becomes*
> *flustered and exhibits a sarcastically negative attitude. Further, when the*
> *cooperating teacher inquires about the episode during observation reflection,*
> *the apprentice deflects blame toward the students for having poor attitudes.*

WHAT do these seemingly disparate observation experiences tell us about teacher readiness? Does Emily's near flawless performance indicate that she will be a long-time, successful teaching career professional? Is Sarah unfit for the music education profession? While these questions constitute critical considerations, especially for those who direct Emily and Sarah's clinical field experiences, any answers must be based on more comprehensive assessment evidence.

Undergraduate music education curricula are widely considered to be complex and rigorous (Asmus, 2016; Maranzano, 2000; Porter, 2010; Schuler, 2012). That curricular complexity is due not only to the multifaceted nature of music teaching positions in K-12 schools but also to the movement toward standards (district, state, and national) and accountability (Edmund & Chen-Edmund, 2014). Maranzano (2000) describes many of the teaching situations encountered by American K-12 music educators including elementary general, music theory, string ensembles, marching, concert and jazz band, concert choir, madrigal ensemble, and vocal jazz ensembles.

In addition to complexity, there is the notion of variability within music teacher education programs. Porter (2010) cites several variables, from musical competencies to variable certification structures, state regulations, credit hour limitations, and testing requirements among the factors affecting the variety of music teacher education programs. The age of accountability has made teacher evaluation a priority (Schuler, 2012; Ledwell & Oyler, 2016) for teachers, administrators, and policymakers.

The complex nature of music teacher education and uniqueness among state teacher standards results in variable music teacher preparation programs throughout the United States. There are, however, many similarities and common factors among preservice teacher assessments. Common assessment factors include portfolio assessments, evaluation of discreet musical competencies, field experience observations, assessment of preservice teacher dispositions, self- and peer assessments, and assessment via reflection (see Table 31.1). This chapter comprises examinations of selected assessment practices in particular states, with the identification of common themes among those practices.

States' attempts to Race to the Top (US Department of Education, 2009) offer one indicator of standardization and the high-stakes nature of teacher evaluation. With so many entities joining the rush to evaluate teachers, music education program coordinators have much to consider. Music teacher educators (MTEs) naturally need to prepare their candidates for the profession. The increasing prioritization of teacher evaluation may be an important consideration for the assessment of preservice teachers. If this is indeed the case, MTEs will need to consider the necessity, extent, and nature of restructuring within teacher preparation programs. These considerations will include examining similarities and differences between teacher evaluations and preservice teacher assessment (for example, the nature of standardization within teacher evaluations).

Given the federal, state, and local focus in the United States for assessment and teacher evaluation, there appear to be many more questions than answers. In this chapter we consider trending assessment practices in music teacher education. Several key questions are addressed, which include: What are the primary concerns involving the assessment of preservice music educators? What assessment strategies are administered in field experiences and student teaching? Which teacher characteristics may be considered artistic in nature? Can teacher artistry be learned, and if so, in what contexts?

With these questions in consideration, the purposes of this chapter are to

- share themes identified within the literature involving preservice teacher assessment,
- delineate critical issues in teacher evaluation and compare them with trends in preservice teacher assessment,
- consider criteria for preservice teacher assessment,
- share current research in preservice teacher assessment, and
- discuss artistry-based characteristics involved with teaching music.

Comparisons among benchmarks and gateways in select music teacher preparation programs (see Table 31.1), as well as standardized exams and performance assessments required for licensure (see Table 31.2) are provided. For the purpose of this chapter, the moniker "preservice teacher" refers to any music education student in a license-granting program (baccalaureate, postbaccalaureate, or graduate degree with licensure). The term "candidate" is substituted interchangeably.

Themes

A review of selected literature uncovered five primary themes concerning the assessment of preservice music teachers. Themes were determined at the authors' discretion and based on (1) the number of appearances within selected literature, (2) perceived significance, and (3) the knowledge and experience of the authors as MTEs. In-service teacher evaluation was a secondary theme, because it is beyond the principal scope of this chapter. Primary themes for this chapter are as follows.

- Benchmarks and gateways in preservice music teacher preparation
- Preservice teacher performance assessment
- Musician/teacher identity
- Dispositional assessment
- The artistry of teaching music

Teacher artistry constitutes a culminating and focal topic for this chapter. Scholars (Carillo, Baguley, & Vilar, 2015; Hope & Wait, 2013; Jorgensen, 2008; Miksza, 2014; National Association of Schools of Music, 2017) have suggested that teaching involves processes and skills that transcend technique. This may involve creating, crafting, communicating, engaging, and inspiring, and so forth. Such processes and skills may be difficult to assess, but are worthy of consideration. The teacher artistry section of this chapter consists of a rationale, comparisons between teaching and musical interpretation, a list of teacher artistry characteristics and the description of a survey beta test to determine music education professionals' attitudes regarding the relative importance of the characteristics.

Benchmarks and Gateways

The complex nature of teaching music has necessarily resulted in teacher preparation programs comprising intricate systems of assessment. These systems are referred here to as benchmarks and gateways. They comprise key indicators of teacher readiness, such as musicianship examinations (i.e., juries), field experiences, and teacher performance assessments. While music teacher education programs (MTEPs) differ in structure and focus (Marlatt, 2014), there are several common categories and themes associated with assessing preservice music teachers. Categories may be more technical (musical and pedagogical knowledge and skill) in nature, or more specifically construct-related (identity, disposition, etc.). In addition, there are the more external communicative factors associated with teaching music. Carillo et al. (2015) explain that there are technical aspects of teaching, but also "engagement with students as unique individuals" (p. 456). Goldie (2016) warns, "As teacher educators, we may need to examine what assessment practices we currently use that serve to further reinforce the identity of a person as a student, and not as a teacher" (p. 440). We note that while earlier candidate assessments tend to be more technical in nature, later forms of assessment (ex. student teaching) stray from technique and trend more toward aesthetics and nuance. Hope and Wait (2013) further note that MTEP assessments typically increase in measurement difficulty through time.

In addition to being complex, the development of music teaching competence is comprehensive, encompassing skills that involve many forms of judgment, from musical, to pedagogical, to personal and professional/ethical. Undergraduate music education assessments include auditions, course examinations, project assignments, juries, master classes, field experiences, self- and peer evaluations, and student teaching. Parkes, Doerksen, and Ritcher (2014) explain that the variability among state-level policies has resulted in the lack of "a uniform national approach for the structure of Music Teacher Education programs" (p. 352). Variability among state policies may stem from the complexity of the K-12 music teaching profession. In addition to content preparation, there is the matter of practice; and when it comes to teaching, there is not one, but many best practices. Carillo et al. (2015) claim, "a good teacher cannot be described in terms of

Table 31.1 Comparison of Assessment Categories for Preservice Music Educators

NASM Standards (2017)	Porter (2010)	Marlatt (2014)	Edmund & Edmund (2014)
Personal and professional attributes	Program entry indicators	Admissions	Admissions
Music competencies: Leadership, arranging, performance, analysis	Course work and academic measures	Sophomore screening	Course work
Specialization competencies: General, vocal, instrumental	Professional education exams	Music performance	Instrumental and Keyboard Proficiency
Teaching competencies	Student teaching assessments	Admission to student teaching	Field Experience
		Student teaching	Admission to Education Program
		Licensure	Student Teaching Teacher Licensure Exams

Note: Porter's (2010) program entry indicators include GPA, college preparations exam scores, and auditions.

isolated competencies, as this approach ignores aspects of the person of the teacher that are required for effective teaching" (p. 456).

Existing models for preservice music teacher assessment are categorized below (see Table 31.1). Categorical models were selected among MTEPs located in the literature and from the National Association of Schools of Music (NASM). The NASM (2017) is the primary accrediting agency for higher education music programs in the United States. It provides broad guidelines for music teacher attributes and competencies. Music competencies consist of leadership/conducting, situational repertoire arranging, instrumental/vocal/keyboard performance skill, and analytical/historical/literature knowledge. In addition, NASM identifies specialization competencies for grade level(s) and musical subject matter, including general, vocal, instrumental, and specialized music fields (ex. guitar, jazz, and computer music).

Collins (1996) details many of the music teacher education benchmarks required by NASM. Requirements include passing a piano proficiency exam, juries each semester on one's principal instrument or voice, and meeting GPA requirements for music classes. The NASM (2017) also outlines seven attributes, competencies, and procedures desired of preservice music educators:

- Commitment to music and students' artistic development, as well as the capability to demonstrate those commitments independently
- Direct students' understanding of music's communicative, intellectual, and cultural properties
- Cultivate students' imagination and their aspiration for musical knowledge and experience

- Advocate for music in education
- Work cohesively within diverse teaching situations
- Appraise arts policies and their impact on students
- Monitor and maintain currency with music education developments, evaluating their relevance and effectiveness for teaching and learning music

The NASM-recommended teaching competencies comprise varied ensemble leadership ability, class and rehearsal management, understanding of students' developmental growth, specified assessment abilities, specialized methodology/materials/repertoire, situational adaptations of methodology, and the ability to apply assessment/evaluation systems in examining the progress of students and curricula. Hope and Wait (2013) refer to the NASM standards as "frameworks, not blueprints, at least at the national level" (p. 5). Institutional goals, on the other hand, are necessarily more specific.

Burrack and Payne (2016) list nine Kansas teacher standards:

- The teacher of music has skills in teaching and evaluation techniques.
- The teacher of music has skills in improvising melodies, variations, and accompaniments.
- The teacher of music has skills in composing and arranging music.
- The teacher of music has skills in reading and writing music.
- The teacher of music has skills in listening to, analyzing, and describing music.
- The teacher of music has skills in evaluating music and music performances.
- The teacher of music has an understanding of music in relation to various historical periods and cultures.
- The teacher of music has skills in establishing effective music-learning environments.
- The teacher of music advocates for the school music program in the community at large. (p. 112)

Smith and Wuttke (2016) developed a model of traits, musical abilities, and teaching competencies for the successful secondary music teacher:

Traits

- Musical competencies
- Teaching competencies
- Professional dispositions
- Interpersonal skills
- Personality traits
- Teacher efficacy

Musical abilities

- Aural skills
- Sight singing/reading

- Musical modeling
- Musical analysis
- Conducting skills
- Accompanying skills

Teaching Competencies

- Methodology
- Planning
- Communication
- Classroom Management
- Use of Materials
- Professionalism (p. 179)

Smith and Wuttke (2016) found that among the traits, abilities, and competencies, music educators ranked classroom management highest, with communication second, and aural skills third, followed by professionalism, planning, and methodology. Notably, five of the top six characteristics related directly to teaching.

Given the competencies just listed, educational delivery may be considered a critical aspect of teaching music. Napoles (2013) examined the influences of teacher delivery and student progress on preservice perceptions of teaching effectiveness noting, "Although previous studies have indicated that teacher delivery has a strong influence on participants' perceptions, student progress has not been examined as a factor affecting perceptions of effective teaching" (p. 251). Student progress is another essential consideration for preservice teachers, due to the recent trend of evaluating teachers based on individual and group student gains. Napoles found teacher intensity to be another important variable, explaining, "Teacher intensity has been operationally defined as the sustained control of the student-teacher interaction, with efficient, accurate presentation of subject matter combined with enthusiastic affect and pacing" (p. 253).

Napoles (2013) examined 75 preservice music teachers' evaluations of six in-service music teachers. Results indicated "that teacher delivery was the best predictor of perceptions of overall teaching effectiveness, followed closely by student progress" (p. 249). Given such results, MTEs and developers of preservice teacher performance assessments must equally consider ways to effectively measure music teacher delivery *in addition to* student gains.

Collins (1996) cites the need for teacher development workshops that provide skills and content knowledge that were not included in the preparatory program. The MTEs and their candidates must also understand that no matter how robust a teacher preparation program is, not every musical and social situation will be adequately addressed during a 4-year undergraduate degree program. Certain skills, however, are indispensable for music teachers. We suggest that teacher delivery, the connection of musical skills to teaching, and teacher artistry (discussed later) be considered carefully in MTEPs.

RESEARCH IN PRESERVICE
TEACHER ASSESSMENT

While there appears to be a wealth of research and scholarship devoted to preservice teacher preparation and teacher evaluation, the research dedicated specifically to the assessment of preservice music teachers is relatively sparse. Scholars in the field of music teacher preparation have examined electronic portfolios (Bauer, 2010; Burrack & Payne, 2016), performance assessment (Edmund & Chen-Edmund, 2014), musician/teacher identity (Goldie, 2016; Marlatt, 2014), self-assessment (Hope & Wait, 2013; Powell, 2016), and assessment of dispositions (Holcomb, 2014; Nierman, 2014; Parkes et al., 2014).

Self-assessment and reflection are primary considerations when assessing music teacher readiness (Danielson, 2011; Elliott, 2010; Goldie, 2016; Hope & Wait, 2013; Porter, 2010; Powell, 2016; Smith & Wuttke, 2016). Danielson (2011) explains:

> a thoughtful approach to teacher evaluation—one that engages teachers in reflection and self-assessment—yields benefits far beyond the important goal of quality assurance. Such an approach provides the vehicle for teacher growth and development by providing opportunities for professional conversation around agreed-on standards of practice.   (p. 39)

Powell (2016) examined concerns of preservice teachers before and after video feedback. Candidates were engaged in 12-minute peer-teaching episodes 1 week before field teaching. This included reflection after teaching and reflection after viewing teaching videos. Instructor and peer feedback were given after a 24-hour period. Powell and a colleague coded data, using an intercoder agreement process. Results indicated that a majority of peer teaching concerns were task-related (55.5%), then self-related (39.9%), followed by student-related (4.7%). Candidates in field teaching, however, exhibited more student-related concerns (14%), with similar levels of concern for task-related (53%) and self-related (33%) items.

Powell reported the importance of video and self-reflection, explaining that video reflections were naturally more detailed, as candidates had more time to critique. Since peer-teaching episodes reflected lesser student-related concerns, the impact on student learning was reduced. Peer teaching, however, provides the advantage of increased focus on planning, content, and delivery. Powell found that group reflection offers the opportunity for candidates to fulfill the roles of teacher and critic. In essence, Powell (2016) suggested that METs "balance authentic experience with a low-risk, experimental environment" (p. 503).

LEGISLATION AND POLICY

Assessment is a primary consideration for policymakers and other decision makers concerned with the improvement of teaching and learning in the United States. Education reform has been manifested in numerous political events, from the launch of *Sputnik*, to the publication of *A Nation at Risk* (US National Commission on Excellence in Education, 1983) and more recently, the drive to privatize American schools (Ravitch, 2013). In 2009, President Barack Obama passed the American Recovery and Reinvestment Act (US Department of Education, 2009), which included Race to the Top, an act of legislation that has deeply impacted in-service teacher evaluation.

While state and federal policy continue to shape the evolution of educational practices, Colwell (2006a) notes that music teacher education has changed very little since the inception of the first 4-year curricula during the 1920s. While little may have changed from a curricular standpoint, assessment of preservice music teachers has become more thorough, complex, and standardized. Porter (2010) recognizes that certification practices have become increasingly centralized, though with the caveat that accountability trends have resulted in the "hope that teachers enter the workforce as omniscient, all knowing, miracle workers" (p. 460).

Music teacher education programs are obligated to comply with NASM and state standards for teacher preparation. Teacher licenses, however, are typically granted through institutional departments of education, which often have their own accreditation agencies; for example, the National Council on Accreditation of Teacher Education (NCATE). The MTEs will continue to be tasked with delivering quality programs with a degree of efficiency, while complying with NASM requirements and state teacher preparation standards.

The National Association for Music Education (NAfME), formerly MENC, is the primary professional organization for PreK through postsecondary music educators. In 1988 MENC piloted a professional certification program with the purpose of recognizing effective teachers and improving music education through the development of a national music-teaching certificate (Collins, 1996). The program helped to account for unique factors involved in teaching music and the qualities embodied by effective music educators. MENC's professional certification program was disbanded in 1994, due to cost and the pending implementation of National Board Certification. Until 1982, when the Society for Music Teacher Education (SMTE) was founded, MTEs had no professional organization devoted exclusively to the preparation of music teachers.

Race to the Top (RTT) encouraged state departments of education to develop evaluations of American teachers. McGuinn (2012) noted how RTT generated unprecedented efforts for teacher evaluation and compared implementation in six states (Colorado, Delaware, New Jersey, Pennsylvania, Rhode Island, and Tennessee). Several issues emerged from those comparisons:

- Time limitations for RTT grant requests
- Limited state resources for implementation
- Lack of clarity regarding the evaluation of teacher evaluators
- Disconnect between districts' need for flexibility of teacher ratings and states' ability to support such flexibility

Race to the Top and its various manifestations of teacher evaluation have resulted in considerable concerns, even fears, regarding the future of arts education. Hope and Wait

(2013) provide a list of five potential symptoms of adhering to current teacher evaluation structures:

- Placing arts educators in foreign evaluation environments, compromising the validity of arts education goals.
- Evaluation compliance will require valuable time, reducing productivity of more central endeavors.
- The illusion that assessment expertise (not subject matter expertise) would be adequate for evaluating arts educators.
- The loss of curricular and pedagogical autonomy for arts educators.
- Concern that the abandonment of artistic principles will further reduce productivity.

Ravitch (2013) states a concern that RTT suggests winners or losers and, further, that education reformers wish to opt for deselection, rather than hiring more qualified teachers, or training existing teachers toward improvement. Ravitch (2013) explains that America needs teachers who inspire, motivate, encourage creativity, that its teachers should be evaluated by their peers, and that "there is no statistical method today that can accurately predict or identify which teachers are 'great' teachers" (p. 113).

STANDARDIZED MEASURES OF PRESERVICE TEACHING

The preparation and assessment of preservice teachers has historically been relegated to teacher training programs within institutions for higher learning. Institutions are bound by standards administered by state governments (i.e., departments of education) and accreditation agencies. National accreditation agencies, commercial testing companies, and professional organizations have influenced assessment in MTEPs. The NCATE, NASM, and Educational Testing Service (ETS), in particular, have influenced the development of standards in music teacher education.

Acquisition of a music teacher license is dependent on passing standardized tests in multiple domains, often basic skills (reading, writing, and mathematics), pedagogy, and music content. Pearson Education and the ETS administer a majority of the tests, while others are maintained within states (e.g., Texas and California). State-contained tests are accompanied by agency-developed tests in other domains. For example, California combines its own test of basic skills with the ETS Music Praxis (Praxis II), which consists of musicianship, music learning/curriculum, and teaching practice. Collins (1996) explains that many of the Praxis II items incorporate listening examples and constructed-response items. Praxis II Music was designed to consist of three modules: Music Education (select-response), Concepts and Processes (constructed-response), and Analysis (constructed-response). Constructed-response items encompass

Table 31.2 edTPA Implementation Phases of Each State

Full implementation	Taking steps toward implementation	Considering implementation	Not participating
AR	AL	AZ	AK
CA	OH	CO	KS
DC		CT	KY
DE		FL	MA
GA		ID	ME
HI		IN	MO
IA		LA	MT
IL		MD	ND
MN		MI	NH
NC		MS	NM
NJ		NE	NV
NY		OK	SD
OR		PA	
TN		RI	
WA		SC	
WI		TX	
WV		UT	
		VA	
		VT	
		WY	

Source: Pearson Education (2017b).

instrumental or choral performance strategies, general music, critique/error detection, and score analysis (Collins, 1996). Test administration classifications among states are illustrated in Table 31.2.

Researchers have developed assessment tools and models specifically for preservice music teachers (Edmund & Chen-Edmund, 2014; Goldie, 2016; Marlatt, 2014; Melago, 2016; Parkes, et al., 2014; Smith & Wuttke, 2016). The task of assessing preservice teacher readiness, however, is often performed using standardized measures. Danielson's Framework for Teaching (FFT) is one of the most commonly used models (The Danielson Group, 2013).

The FFT, originally published in 1996, stemmed from the developmental stages of the Praxis III, a standardized measure of in-service teacher performance. Subsequent editions of the FFT were published in 2007, 2011, and 2013. The framework consists of four broad domains: Planning and Preparation, Classroom Environment, Instruction, and Professional Responsibilities (The Danielson Group, 2013). Each domain is divided into five or six components (e.g., teacher reflection within domain four), elements (e.g., pedagogical content knowledge in domain one), and indicators (e.g., taking advantage of teachable moments in domain three). There are a total of 22 components; each evaluated using a four-level rubric, from unsatisfactory, to basic, to proficient, and distinguished. Achievement indicators are provided for all levels.

The 2013 edition of the FFT was aligned with InTASC standards and grounded in constructivist theory. Each of the 10 InTASC standards is aligned with one or more domains, including specified components. For example, InTASC standard 6, Assessment, aligns with domains one (Planning and Preparation) and three (Instruction) of the FFT.

Porter (2010) cites the requirement for teacher training programs to deliver data-driven programs, explaining, "The central tenet of outcome-driven teacher education is that the training process must produce teachers who can ensure pupils' achievement, and this achievement has largely come to be measured by testing alone" (p. 463). Porter examined five candidates in Ohio taking the Praxis III, required for first-year teachers. The Praxis III consists primarily of observation and pre- and postobservation interviews. The study included admission requirements, academic measures during the degree, student teaching assessments (cooperating teacher/supervising professor), first-year teaching assessment data (Praxis III, self-evaluations, mentorship), and focus group discussion reflections as dependent variables. It was determined that Praxis III had no (.00) correlation with Praxis II Music and a negative correlation (-.20) with Praxis II Principles of Learning and Teaching (PLT). While there appeared to be no relationship between the teacher performance examination and standardized tests for licensure, the limited sample size suggests that further research should be conducted.

Porter (2010) claims, "The problem with Praxis III assessment is that it does not provide a real picture of music teaching" (p. 468). Porter further notes the disparity between knowing about and knowing how, citing the following issues: (1) Praxis III is not content specific. It may produce a good general evaluation, but does not reflect quality of the students' music-making (i.e., Does their choir sound good?) and (2) Praxis III is a one-shot observation assessment.

Standardization in the evaluation of preservice/in-service music teachers may dissuade innovation. Bartell, Dunn, and Richmond (2016) claim standardization makes it "far too easy to lose sight of the ways that teaching and learning are affected by knowledge, skills, and practices that may not be measured by these standards" (p. 102). They further state:

> We see the influence of neoliberal accountability regimes in teacher preparation in the form of the edTPA and other standardized assessments that are often linked to for-profit companies, value-added models that seek to link program impact with the test scores of program graduates' students, and national reviews by partisan groups such as the National Council on Teacher Quality.   (p. 103)

A balance should be stricken between standardization and accountability. Teacher preparation programs need to be rich and flexible. Edmund and Chen-Edmund (2014) state, "The complex nature of educational processes complicates the issue of standardized teacher performance assessment" (p. 322). Critical issues for the assessment and preparation of preservice music teachers will be considered among the remaining themes shared in this chapter.

Preservice Teacher
Performance Assessment

Performance assessment is an emerging trend in preservice teacher assessment and in-service teacher evaluation. The most widely used standardized performance tests are the edTPA (Pearson Education, 2017a), administered by Pearson Education, and the Praxis Performance Assessment for Teachers (Educational Testing Service, 2017), administered by ETS. Because the edTPA is required for teacher candidates in our state, we have chosen to emphasize it in this chapter. The edTPA is administered to varying degrees in 37 states (see Table 31.2). Each evaluation instrument requires that the pre-service/in-service teacher gather and submit teaching artifacts, to include lesson-planning materials, assessment evidence, assessment feedback, and teaching videos. Darling-Hammond, Amrein-Beardsley, Haertel, and Rothstein (2012) explain that effective standards-based measures are integrated, including evidence of student work, teacher videos, observations, and student feedback. Third-party individuals evaluate candidates' edTPA artifacts. Without firsthand knowledge of the teaching setting and student population, evaluator training is crucial.

edTPA

Ledwell and Oyler (2016) examined the edTPA's role as gatekeeper to the teaching profession and catalyst for curricular change in teacher preparation programs. They found that while the edTPA affected the student teaching seminar, it did not serve as an effective gatekeeper and it lacked formative feedback. Ledwell and Oyler considered the edTPA to be an "impotent gatekeeper in our context and a powerful curriculum change agent in only some programs" (p. 130).

Ledwell and Oyler (2016) cite the "dangers of outsourcing teacher evaluation" (p. 122), further noting, "Although teacher educators were quick to point out that their gatekeeping practices had not altered as a result of the edTPA, some did report that the edTPA was serving as a disincentive for candidates to apply to New York State for certification" (p. 126). They cite two major concerns: focus on one learner and focus on two goals (i.e., it provides a limited snapshot of teacher effectiveness). "Many teacher educators stated that the primary demand of the edTPA was learning how to 'follow directions' or 'jump through hoops'" (Ledwell & Oyler, 2016, p. 129).

While the edTPA is a standardized measure, we note that many gatekeeping practices among programs are NOT standardized. This may be an issue—using a one-size-fits-all approach among differing disciplines. Administration of the edTPA as a requirement for teacher licensure raises practical and ethical questions. For example, how much reading and written commentary is too much to expect from a teacher candidate during student teaching? Preservice music teachers who are required to complete the edTPA will be provided with a more-than-50-page *K-12 Performing Arts Assessment Handbook* and an over-30-page *Making Good Choices* document. In addition to the lesson planning, video, and assessment artifacts noted earlier, candidates submit as many as 29 pages of documentation for the edTPA. Associated costs raise ethical questions. Teacher candidates currently face increased tuition rates, higher student loan debt, fees for state licensing exams, and an additional cost associated with Pearson's edTPA ($300–$350, as of January 2017) (Au, 2013). Is the corporate nature of standardized assessments beneficial for students and preservice teachers? How many state licensing examinations does Pearson Education administer? Is such a monopoly "right" for education? We suggest the following: (1) Corporate financial interests constitute a threat to the teaching profession. Increasingly burdensome performance assessments and their associated costs diminish the enthusiasm of preservice teachers and early career professionals. (2) Pearson Education administrates an unhealthy proportion of state teacher licensing exams and teacher performance assessments. Decisions regarding the specific tests that are required and the corporations that administer the tests, are made by state government agencies, with little or no input from college teacher education faculty. (3) These issues may easily result in corporate monopolies, with less and less consideration for the needs of preservice teachers.

The Musician/Teacher

An identity formation process occurs when preservice music teachers progress through the undergraduate degree program. Candidates self-identify as musicians, but the development of teacher identity may be more situational. Some MTEs illustrate the importance of musicianship, while others suggest that a more-balanced identity be developed (if not skewed more distinctly toward teacher identity). The NASM guidelines suggest that no less than 50% of the undergraduate music education curriculum consist of musicianship and performance, with 15%–20% devoted to professional education. Colwell (2006b) noted the uniqueness of music content for teaching and indicated minimal correlation between NASM characteristics and the beliefs espoused by teacher preparation (nonmusic) programs.

Goldie (2016) sought to develop music teacher identity through a series of assessments. The aim was to develop occupational identity through three practices: (1) omposition of a personal "Music Educator's Creed" (p. 435) for an induction ceremony at the end of the Introduction to Music Education class, (2) participation in professional learning communities (PLCs), and (3) "Peer Evaluative Input" (p. 435) as secondary methods assessments. Skills/techniques classes involved teaching recitals and the development of instructional videos.

Marlatt (2014), on the other hand, described a conservatory approach, stressing the "identity of the musician teacher" (p. 342). Preservice music teachers completed a sophomore screening interview to continue in music education, as well as a sophomore screening jury for advanced applied lessons. Marlatt proposed a total immersion approach, with the prioritization of musicianship.

Smith and Wuttke (2016) developed a model of traits for successful first-year teaching, consisting of musical competencies, teaching competencies, professional dispositions, interpersonal skills, personality traits, and teacher efficacy. They found that five of the top six competencies were teaching (not musical) related and that "music teacher education programs should focus more on teaching skills than on musical skills" (p. 183). This suggests the importance of earlier field experiences, a strategy also promoted by NASM (2017).

Melago (2016) considered candidates' retention of knowledge and skills from the freshman to upperclassman years, with emphasis on musical performance. This occurred through the development of Music Methods Competency Examinations, claimed to be "the most significant musical benchmark examinations in the course of the music education program" (p. 273). The exams covered elementary, secondary, and instrumental skills. Criteria were rated on three achievement levels (unsatisfactory/proficient/distinguished). The elementary-level exam involved sight-singing, keyboard skills, and a guitar-teaching demonstration. Choral examinations involved playing, singing, and leading choral warm-ups; playing voice parts from a score on piano; playing a choral accompaniment; audiating parts; and conducting a choral selection. Instrumental methods involved conducting, transposition, and playing a secondary instrument. Competencies had to be passed in order to earn a grade in music methods courses. Melago discovered that students considered competencies as more than mere course requirements. The involvement of skills/techniques course competencies resulted in improved teaching in those courses, which are typically not led by music education faculty.

The notion of musician/teacher is not exclusive to the United States. Wang (2016) details teacher preparation assessments at a university in China, examining teacher musical preparation and the effects of portfolio assessment at the University of Macau. Wang's study involved peer examinations of microteaching, with peer and self-evaluation of six criteria on a five-point scale, from "fail" to "excellent." Teaching criteria were:

- Teaching approach
- Communication skills
- Introduction of rhythm
- Introduction of music theory
- Introduction of singing/sight-reading
- Piano accompaniment: rhythm, note, fluency (p. 226)

ASSESSMENT OF DISPOSITIONS

Researchers and scholars (Nierman, 2014; Parkes et al., 2014) cite the prevalence of NCATE (now Council for the Accreditation of Educator Preparation, or CAEP) standards in teacher preparation, specifically the attention to candidates' dispositions. Nierman (2014) claims, "while teacher knowledge and skills are important components of any teacher evaluation system, the affective nature of teacher dispositions contributes just as importantly to student achievement and therefore should be a component of assessment in any teacher evaluation system" (p. 399).

Parkes et al. (2014) explain that MTEs consider disposition a primary factor, especially prior to student teaching. They determined that responsibility and dependability were the most essential dispositions. Parkes et al. found that MTE faculty ranked "Musicianship, Professional Dispositions, and Methods Grades" (p. 356) among the most predictive factors for professional success. They noted that subjectivity involved with assessing dispositions is not cause for avoidance and examined five categories:

- Attitudes and Behaviors
- Beliefs and Character
- Communication
- Instruction
- Reflection (pp. 357–358)

Parkes et al. (2016) conducted a follow-up investigation seeking to determine the extent of validation for statements regarding dispositions. Their method involved surveys of MTEs, as well as analyses of model exemplars. The intent was to develop measures that address three dispositional categories: reflective, caring, and responsible. Coding of survey responses resulted in the development of twenty statements regarding reflection that implement the terms "accept," "seek" and "apply feedback." Statements pertaining to caring were categorized by relationships, empathy, nurture, respect, kindness, and classroom environment. For example, it was suggested that candidates "seek to understand how others experience the world, are sensitive to how students feel about their experiences and 'come alongside' to share other's experiences" (p. 320).

The 16 statements pertaining to responsibility included "are self-efficacious—*That is believing oneself to be competent*" (p. 323). This statement notably revealed the lowest extent to which MTEs agreed ($M = 3.93$ on a five-point scale) with 26% selecting "completely agree." There was more agreement for responsibility, followed by caring, and finally reflection, which may indicate that reflection is the least well-defined trait.

Nierman (2014) provided another list of dispositions: "intellectual curiosity, sensitivity to diversity, personal diplomacy, and empathy" (p. 400), reminding us, however, about the ambiguity of such constructs. Nierman (2014) also notes that many dispositional behaviors are nonverbal, conflating the difficulty of assessing.

THE ARTISTRY OF TEACHING

The most effective teachers we work with and learn from exemplify particular characteristics. They have a unique ability to captivate students and/or communicate meaningfully. They share their enthusiasm for music. They are able to adapt instruction in the moment, constituting a form of instructional improvisation. They are reflective and adept at developing lesson content, experiences, and procedures. Teachers who possess these characteristics illustrate what we refer to as teacher artistry.

Miksza (2014) stipulates, "artistry most often implies something extraordinary... something heavily soaked in personal meaning... and a mode of doing that can lead to transcendent experiences" (para. 5). Jorgensen (2008) suggests students long "for the spiritual and the sacred, for a sense of wholeness, wonder, and awe in the face of things that transcend the ordinary" (p. 21). Music educators who exhibit teacher artistry yield student outcomes, including a passion for music, student satisfaction in the moment, attitude, effort, and motivation. Elliott (2010) notes teachers can recognize such outcomes, if not measure them directly. Like musical artistry, teacher artistry produces extraordinary or aesthetic experiences for and within students.

The artistry of teaching bears similarities to the art of musical interpretation. Like musical interpreters, music educators establish priorities, goals, and objectives. They develop detailed strategies and procedures for executing their craft and sharing music. They establish techniques for successful teaching performance. They respond to their sonic environment, forming instantaneous judgments and making apt adjustments. As with musical performance, understanding goals is essential to successful assessment of music and teaching (Hope & Wait, 2013).

Assessing the artistry of teaching may be considered subjective in similar ways to the assessment of classroom musical outcomes. For example, assessing a teacher's communicative expression might be as subjective as assessing the expressive component in a student's improvised solo. One of the purposes of this section is to identify particular characteristics of teacher artistry and to help reduce the ambiguity associated with the classification or assessment of those characteristics.

The previously cited NASM (2017) attributes stipulate music educators' ability to develop students' artistry. It is further recommended that music educators be communicative, cultivate imagination, work cohesively, and appraise arts policies. These attributes contributed to the development of a list of seven teacher artistry characteristics. Characteristics were included in the list based on four guiding principles:

- Involves some form of creation (improvising, crafting, planning, revising)
- Is difficult or impossible to measure
- Is process-oriented
- Relates/aligns in one or more ways with NASM (2017) attributes

"Reflection and revision over time" is among the seven characteristics. Revision requires crafting and planning, is process-oriented, poses measurement challenges, and relates to the NASM attribute of remaining current with musical and pedagogical developments. Another characteristic is "captivation of student interest and imagination." This may involve instructional (i.e., delivery-based) improvising, may be impossible to measure, is process-oriented, and directly aligns with one or more of the NASM attributes. Jorgensen (2008) proposes, "the nature of musical imagination and how to cultivate it is of the greatest importance in music education" (p. 253). Our list of seven teaching artistry characteristics is as follows:

- Captivation of student interest and imagination
- Communicative delivery (oral and gestural expressiveness)
- Educational improvisation: flexibility and response in the moment
- Sharing of enthusiasm and the love of music
- Reflection and revision over time
- Novelty of lesson content
- Novelty of lesson procedures (i.e., strategies for student accomplishment)

Survey Beta Test

We conducted a survey beta test, with the purpose of eliciting music education professionals' perceptions of the relative importance among the characteristics and their thoughts about the extent to which each characteristic may be developed in different settings. A survey consisting of two primary items was administered. The first item (see Table 31.3) requested that participants rank the seven artistic categories in order of importance. The second item (see Table 31.4) requested that participants rate the extent to which they believe each characteristic:

- may be taught in teacher preparation courses
- may be developed through professional experience
- is intrinsic (or natural)
- is developed from another source (participants were asked to identify other sources)

The survey was administered at a major international music education conference. Though this chapter is dedicated primarily to the assessment of preservice teachers in the United States, we consider teacher artistry characteristics to be human traits that are not exclusive to particular nations or global regions, rendering the data useful. Survey responses were obtained from individuals ($N = 13$) in five different nations, including the United States ($n = 4$), Denmark ($n = 1$), Germany ($n = 1$), Brazil ($n = 1$), Australia ($n = 1$), and the United Kingdom ($n = 3$). Two individuals did not disclose their nationality. Nine participants cited "higher education" as their primary teaching setting; two participants cited secondary; and two did not indicate their teaching setting. Item one (priority rankings of the characteristics) yielded six complete responses, four partial responses, and three responses indicating no rankings. Item two (extent to which each characteristic may be developed in different settings) yielded eight complete responses and five partial responses. All participants were encouraged to provide comments regarding the survey and its contents, with nine participants complying. Christensen and Johnson (2014) suggest the generation of inductive codes for direct analysis of participant responses. Our coding process yielded four primary themes, described below.

Survey participants were recruited purposively, as data were gathered during an international music education conference. The session constituted a sharing of themes regarding the assessment of preservice music educators. Upon sharing the themes, we focused on teacher artistry, gathered survey responses, and guided discussion on the topic.

Survey responses from Item one (see Table 31.3) reflected elements of agreement and disagreement regarding the rank order of importance for each characteristic. Means of the rankings were calculated, which provided an indicator of participants' prioritization of each characteristic. Disagreement was partially reflected by the number of participants who completed full rankings ($n = 6$), those who provided partial rankings ($n = 4$), and those who did not rank the characteristics ($n = 4$) at all. In some cases, qualitative data provided indicators of participants' refusal to rank (see explanations and implications later). Agreement was reflected by the rankings of the highest and lowest priority characteristics. On a scale from one to seven, "Sharing of enthusiasm and the love of music" received the highest priority rank ($m = 1.78$). Six of the 10 complete and partial responses indicated this characteristic to be most important. "Novelty of lesson procedures" ranked lowest ($m = 6.33$). Eight participants ranked "Captivation of student interest and imagination" either second or third most important ($m = 2.4$).

Item two (see Table 31.4) of the survey addressed participants' beliefs about the extent to which each of the seven artistry characteristics may be taught in teacher preparation courses, may be developed through professional experience, are intrinsic (or natural), or are developed from another source. Each characteristic was considered across indicators and assigned a three if developed to a great extent for the particular indicator, a two if developed to a moderate extent, a one if developed to a small extent, and a zero if developed to no extent. Data for item two were considered complete if the participant assigned indicators for each of the first three columns. Most participants ($n = 8$) provided complete data sets, while all others ($n = 5$) provided partial data.

Response means for item two ranged from 1.1 (indicating that the characteristic may be developed to a small extent under the given circumstance) to 2.77 (indicating that the characteristic may be developed to a moderate/great extent under the given circumstance). Nine individuals provided comments referencing other sources of development

Table 31.3 Artistry–Based Characteristics of Music Educators

Characteristics	M	SD
Captivation of student interest and imagination	2.4	0
Communicative delivery	3.5	1.41
Educational improvisation	4.0	1.41
Sharing of enthusiasm and the love of music	1.8	2.12
Reflection and revision	3.5	0
Novelty/originality of lesson content	4.7	3.5
Novelty of lesson procedures	6.3	0.7

Table 31.4 Development of the Characteristics

Characteristic	Extent to which the characteristic is... 0 = to no extent 1 = to a small extent 2 = to a moderate extent 3 = to a great extent			
	taught in teacher preparation courses	developed through professional experience	intrinsic or natural	developed from another source (identify any additional sources)
Captivation of student interest and imagination	1.82	2.58	2.36	
Communicative delivery	2.33	2.58	2.1	
Educational improvisation	1.54	2.77	1.8	
Sharing of enthusiasm and the love of music	1.31	1.91	2.55	
Reflection and revision	2.54	2.23	1.7	
Novelty/originality of lesson content	2.08	2.58	1.1	
Novelty of lesson procedures	2.31	2.23	1.1	

Note: Means indicate average ranks, where 1 = highest and 7 = lowest.

and/or general comments. For example, one participant wished to operationally define "intrinsic" as having been "developed before/earlier in their life." Another participant questioned the notion of novelty and wondered if "risk taking" might be an additional descriptor for each of the two novelty characteristics.

Responses for the "intrinsic or natural" (see Table 31.4) column tended to be lower than the others. Both novelty characteristic means (m = 1.1) indicated that those characteristics are intrinsic to a small extent. The highest response was reflected by "educational improvisation" being developed through professional experience (m = 2.77). This indicated participants' feeling that educational improvisation is developed to a moderate/great extent through teaching experience. "Sharing of enthusiasm and the love for music," while considered the most important characteristic, notably ranked highest in the intrinsic column (m = 2.55), lower in the professional experience column (m = 1.91), and lowest in the teacher preparation courses column (m = 1.31). This may indicate that some of the most important teaching abilities are second nature, as opposed to being developed or nurtured.

Beta Test Outcomes

Results from the survey on artistry-based characteristics of music educators provided baseline data reflective of music education professionals' perspectives about the relative importance of each characteristic and the nature of characteristic development. While

Item one (see Table 31.3) reflected degrees of agreement and disagreement, certain patterns emerged. For example, half of the responses revealed a 2-3-5-1 or 2-3-4-1 ranking pattern among the first four characteristics. The "Sharing of enthusiasm and the love of music" were deemed most important by those who responded. The "Captivation of student interest and imagination" was deemed second most important. The fact that multiple participants chose not to complete the rankings may suggest that such a ranking system is not practical. Participants provided comments offering further insight regarding the relative importance and clarity of definition among the characteristics.

Qualitative data in the form of comments were independently analyzed and classified by each author, employing inductive codes. Inductive codes of the two authors reflected 100% agreement, offering a degree of intercoder reliability. After coding the data, each author detected four primary themes:

- An inclination to redefine "novelty," especially with regard to content
- Connection of musical skills to teaching
- Continued professional development
- Development through reading and research

Four participants attached the term "relevance" to characteristic six (novelty of content). This suggests that relevance be considered in association with content novelty. The data collection instrument will be modified to include this suggestion. Five participants commented on the importance of connecting musical skills to teaching. These comments were made in the context of both survey items. Consideration will be granted to ways in which musical skills are embodied within the list of characteristics and the connection of those skills to teaching. This consideration will help guide further revision of the survey instrument.

Two additional themes were professional development, from reading/research and as a continuous exercise. Both themes emerged from the second survey item, in which participants suggested professional development as an additional source for realizing teacher artistry. Because professional development typically takes place independently from the act of teaching, these considerations will be added to the survey instrument.

Qualitative analyses and the resulting themes provided a method for enhancing content validity of the survey instrument. A revision process will be undertaken as a result of input from music teacher professionals who attended a major international music education conference and participated in assessment sessions. After revising the survey instrument, data will be obtained from a larger sample size within the United States. In addition to the participation of higher education professionals, in-service teachers will be invited to respond. Another consideration may be to include preservice music educators and compare results among the various demographics. The purpose will be to produce outcomes that inform MTEs about how they may or may not assist with the development of teacher artistry characteristics. The question of whether or not the characteristics should be assessed must be considered. If yes, might those assessments resemble existing dispositional assessments? If results suggest that teacher artistry characteristics should not be assessed, how might the results otherwise inform the community of MTEs?

Implications and Future Considerations

This chapter presented themes involved with the assessment of preservice music teachers. Themes emerged through existing literature, the authors' MTE experience, and from research regarding the artistry of teaching. Emergent themes served to illustrate some of the ways preservice teacher readiness is assessed in MTEPs. Preparation of highly quali-fied in-service professionals is the fundamental purpose of MTEs. Ravitch (2013) insists, "The greatest imperative we face as a nation with regard to teacher quality is not to find and fire teachers but to find and develop a highly skilled professional teacher corps" (p. 132).

The artistry of teaching was a central theme within this chapter. Survey beta test results contributed to the revision of a data collection instrument, which will be shared in a more broad-scale investigation of artistry-based teacher characteristics. Future research results will be shared among MTEs through literature, conference sessions, and among professional organizations, including the SMTE.

Elliott (2010) reminds music educators about the importance of critical thinking, creativity, problem-solving, and valuing "mutual discussion, expression, intrinsic moti-vation, and self-efficacy" (p. 369). The MTEs should be in the business of *empowering* preservice teachers, not merely testing them in a narrow fashion. Teaching music is an immersive social and community engagement endeavor. Teacher delivery, identity, enthusiasm, and connection of musical skills should be prioritized in preparing preservice music teachers for the profession.

Let us revisit the opening scenarios from this chapter. Both candidates were observed in field experience contexts, Emily by her supervising professor during student teach-ing, and Sarah by her cooperating teacher during a secondary field experience. Emily demonstrated the ability to modify content within a given lesson. This resulted in greater student comfort, producing positive results. Her modifications represented a form of educational improvisation; an indicator that Emily exemplifies one characteristic of what we consider teacher artistry. Sarah struggled with the connection between stan-dards, objectives, and teaching procedures. Her ability to detect incorrect pitches was lacking, revealing a certain lack of connecting musical skills in teaching. Sarah also dis-played a negative attitude, which compromised her ability to captivate student interest and share enthusiasm.

We posed the question of whether these scenarios provide indicators of future success in the music teaching profession. The complicated reality is that neither scenario pro-vides definitive evidence about Emily or Sarah's future success as teachers. Let us remember the importance of context with preservice teacher assessment. Maturity may be a factor for Sarah, who may develop greater teacher abilities with increased experience and opportunities for reflection and revision.

Responses to a survey beta test on teacher artistry characteristics indicated that sharing enthusiasm and the love of music is primarily intrinsic in nature. This may provide a "red flag" for Sarah and her viability as a music teacher. However, these scenarios are mere snapshots of teacher ability. Musical, educational, and social factors may impact Sarah to the extent that she develops outstanding music teaching skills. The opposite could happen in Emily's case. These scenarios and their implications illustrate the complex nature of assessing preservice music teachers' readiness for the profession. As previously suggested, the assessment of preservice teachers requires comprehensive systems of evaluation. Such systems should address musical, scholarly, dispositional, delivery-based, and teacher artistry skills.

In addition to the development and administration of comprehensive candidate assessment systems, it is vital that MTEs account for the situational nature of each assessment. How do the extent of preparation, teaching environment, student population, nature of mentorship, and classroom events affect the candidate's success in a given situation? Was the candidate provided ample opportunities for success? Do individual assessment outcomes accurately reflect the pre-service music teachers' ability? These questions and considerations will be indispensable for future developments in preservice music teacher assessment. Thoughtful research on MTEP contents, programs of delivery, assessment systems, preservice teacher dispositions, musician/teacher identity, and music teacher artistry will serve to inform music teacher education programs and their curricula in the 21st century.

REFERENCES

Asmus, E. P. (2016). Embedding assessment seamlessly into existing music teacher training courses. In T. S. Brophy, J. Marlatt, & G. Ritcher (Eds.), *Connecting practice, measurement, and evaluation* (pp. 559–571). Chicago, IL: GIA Publications.

Au, W. (2013). What's a nice test like you doing in a place like this? The edTPA and corporate education reform. *Rethinking Schools, 27*(4), 22–27.

Bartell, T., Dunn, A. H., & Richmond, G. (2016). Beyond "tinkering": Enacting the imperative for change in teacher education in a climate of standards and accountability. *Journal of Teacher Education, 67*(2), 102–104. doi: 10.1177/0022487116628837

Bauer, W. (2010). Technological, pedagogical, and content knowledge, music, and assessment. In, T. S. Brophy (Ed.), *The practice of assessment in music education: Frameworks, models, and designs* (pp. 425–434). Chicago, IL: GIA Publications.

Burrack, F., & Payne, P. (2016). Validity of documenting students' individual progress associated with professional teaching standards through web-based portfolios. In T. S. Brophy, J. Marlatt, & G. Ritcher (Eds.), *Connecting practice, measurement, and evaluation* (pp. 99–118). Chicago, IL: GIA Publications.

Carillo, C., Baguley, M., & Vilar, M. (2015). The influence of professional identity on teaching practice: Experiences of four music educators. *International Journal of Music Education: Research and Practice, 33*(4), 451–462.

Christensen, R., & Johnson, L. (2014). *Education research: Quantitative, qualitative, and mixed approaches* (5th ed.). Thousand Oaks, CA: Sage Publications.

Collins, I. (1996). Assessment and evaluation in music teacher education. *Arts Education Policy Review, 98* (1), 16–21.

Colwell, R. (2006a). Music teacher education in this century: Part I. *Arts Education Policy Review, 108*(1), 15–27.

Colwell, R. (2006b). Music teacher education in this century: Part II. *Arts Education Policy Review, 108*(2), 17–29.

Council of Chief State School Officers. (2013). *Interstate Teacher Assessment and Support Consortium InTASC model core teaching standards and learning progressions for teachers 1.0: A resource for ongoing teacher development.* Retrieved from https://www.ccsso.org/resource-library/intasc-model-core-teaching-standards-and-learning-progressions-teachers-10

Danielson, C. (2011). Evaluations that help teachers learn. *The Effective Educator, 68*(4), 35–39.

Darling-Hammond, L., Amrein-Beardsley, A., Haertel, E., & Rothstein, J. (2012). Evaluating teacher evaluation. *Phi Delta Kappan, 93*(6), 8–15.

Edmund, D., & Chen-Edmund, J. (2014). Performance assessment in music teacher education: Models for implementation. In T. S. Brophy, M. Lai, & H. F. Chen (Eds.), *Music assessment and global diversity: Practice, measurement and policy* (pp. 321–340). Chicago, IL: GIA Publications.

Educational Testing Service. (2017). *The PPAT assessment from ETS.* Retrieved from https://www.ets.org/ppa/test-takers/teachers/about

Elliott, D. (2010). Assessing the concept of assessment: Some philosophical reflections. In, T. S. Brophy (Ed.), *The practice of assessment in music education: Frameworks, models, and designs* (pp. 367–379). Chicago, IL: GIA Publications.

Goldie, S. B. (2016). Fostering music teacher identity development through creative assessment practices in undergraduate music teacher education. In T. S. Brophy, J. Marlatt, & G. Ritcher (Eds.), *Connecting practice, measurement, and evaluation* (pp. 435–445). Chicago, IL: GIA Publications.

Holcomb, A. (2014). An investigation into the development of assessment dispositions of pre-service music teachers. In T. S. Brophy M. Lai, & H. Chen (Eds.), *Music assessment and global diversity: Practice, measurement and policy* (pp. 387–395). Chicago, IL: GIA Publications.

Hope, S., & Wait, M. (2013). Assessment on our own terms. *Arts Education Policy Review, 114*(1), 2–12.

Jorgensen, E. R. (2008). *The art of teaching music.* Bloomington: Indiana University Press.

Ledwell, K., & Oyler, C. (2016). Unstandardized responses to a "standardized" test: The edTPA as gatekeeper and curriculum change agent. *Journal of Teacher Education, 67*(2), 120–134.

Maranzano, C. (2000). Music teacher performance evaluation: A call for more inclusive models. *Journal of Personnel Evaluation in Education, 14*(3), 267–274.

Marlatt, J. (2014). Benchmarks and milestones: Assessing the undergraduate musician teacher. In T. S. Brophy M. Lai, & H. Chen (Eds.), *Music assessment and global diversity: Practice, measurement and policy* (pp. 341–349). Chicago, IL: GIA Publications.

McGuinn, P. (2012, November 13). *The state of teacher evaluation reform.* Retrieved from https://www.americanprogress.org/issues/education/report/2012/11/13/44494/the-state-of-teacher-evaluation-reform/

Melago, K. A. (2016). The music methods competency examination: A benchmark assessment for teacher candidates. In T. S. Brophy, J. Marlatt, & G. Ritcher (Eds.), *Connecting practice, measurement, and evaluation* (pp. 273–287). Chicago, IL: GIA Publications.

Miksza, P. (2014, September 8). *Artistry and music education.* Retrieved from petermiksza. com/2014/09/08/artistry-and-music-education

Napoles, J. (2013). The influences of teacher delivery and student progress on preservice perceptions of teaching effectiveness. *Journal of Research in Music Education, 61*(3), 249–261.

National Association of Schools of Music. (2017). *National Association of Schools of Music handbook 2017–18.* Retrieved from https://nasm.arts-accredit.org/wp-content/uploads/sites/2/2017/12/M-Handbook-2017-2018.pdf

Nierman, G. E. (2014). Music teacher evaluation: Don't forget the affective side of the house. In T. S. Brophy M. Lai, & H. Chen (Eds.), *Music assessment and global diversity: Practice, measurement and policy* (pp. 397–406). Chicago, IL: GIA Publications.

Parkes, K. A., Doerksen, P. F., & Ritcher, G. (2014). Measuring professional dispositions in pre-service music teachers in the United States. In T. S. Brophy M. Lai, & H. Chen (Eds.), *Music assessment and global diversity: Practice, measurement and policy* (pp. 351–386). Chicago, IL: GIA Publications.

Parkes, K. A., Doerksen, P. F., & Ritcher, G. (2016). A Validation process towards measuring dispositions in pre-service music educators. In T. S. Brophy, J. Marlatt, & G. Ritcher (Eds.), *Connecting practice, measurement, and evaluation* (pp. 315–326). Chicago, IL: GIA Publications.

Pearson Education. (2017a). *edTPA.* Pearson Education Incorporated. Retrieved from https://www.edtpa.com

Pearson Education. (2017b). *edTPA Participation map.* Pearson Education Incorporated. Retrieved from http://edtpa.aacte.org/state-policy

Porter, A. (2010). The problem with "No Problem": Music teacher assessment. In T. Brophy (Ed.), *The practice of assessment in music education: Frameworks, models, and designs* (pp. 459–471). Chicago, IL: GIA Publications.

Powell, S. R. (2016). The Influence of video reflection on preservice music teachers' concerns in peer- and field-teaching. *Journal of Research in Music Education, 63*(4), 487–507.

Ravitch, D. (2013). *Reign of error: The hoax of the privatization movement and the danger to America's public school.* New York, NY: Knopf.

Schuler, S. (2012). Music education for life: Music assessment, part 2-instructional improvement and teacher evaluation. *Music Educators Journal, 98*(3), 7–10.

Smith, T. W., & Wuttke, B. C. (2016). Developing a model of the effective first-year secondary music teacher: Musical and teaching skills. In T. S. Brophy, J. Marlatt, & G. Ritcher (Eds.), *Connecting practice, measurement, and evaluation* (pp. 177–192). Chicago, IL: GIA Publications.

The Danielson Group. (2013). *Framework for teaching.* Retrieved from https://www.danielsongroup.org/framework/

US Department of Education. (2009, November). *Race to the Top executive summary.* Retrieved from https://www2.ed.gov/programs/racetothetop/executive-summary.pdf

US National Commission on Excellence in Education. (1983). *A nation at risk: The imperative for educational reform.* Washington, DC: US Department of Education.

Wang, D. P. (2016). Assessing the influence of music courses on pre-service teachers' teaching competency. In T. S. Brophy, J. Marlatt, & G. Ritcher (Eds.), *Connecting practice, measurement, and evaluation* (pp. 217–231). Chicago, IL: GIA Publications.

CHAPTER 32

USING ACCOUNTABILITY TO IMPROVE STUDENT LEARNING IN HIGHER EDUCATION MUSIC PROGRAMS

JEFFREY WARD

THROUGHOUT the world, faculty in institutions of higher education are redefining teaching and learning, demonstrating student learning through valid and reliable assessment, and using assessment data to meet programmatic goals and improve the quality of their programs. This shift has intensified over the past 20 years, as institutions of higher education respond to increasing calls for accountability. Stakeholders, varying from governments to accreditation institutions, are closely examining what occurs in higher education and the benefits to students. Increased accountability of institutions of higher education is a result of growing concern among governments and their citizens that institutions of higher education are not providing adequate return on investment. Bernhard (2010) writes, the "United Kingdom shifted their governance from a more liberal orientation towards a stronger state regulation which affected funding as well as quality assurance matters. This happened in line with increased accountability, efficiency and a loss of trust towards higher education institutions from the state" (p. 42). While this scrutiny may on the surface seem threatening, it is an opportunity for institutions of higher education to examine their practices and find new ways to meet the needs of 21st-century students.

Meeting the call for accountability requires higher education administration and faculty to create procedures to assess student learning outcomes as an instructional and curricular task for the faculty and a documentation task for administration. Ward (2014) found that limited time and the burden of assessment documentation were the largest barriers to music faculty in institutions of higher education in the United States engaging in systematic assessment of student learning outcomes. Additionally, assessment was not viewed as a teaching responsibility but as a service responsibility, and only 15% of surveyed higher education music programs used faculty involvement in the outcomes assessment process as a factor in faculty evaluations for tenure and promotion. When faculty view assessment as a task outside of teaching and learning, assessment data is not used to improve instruction; however, when faculty and administration work together to systematically document assessment results, analyze those results, and create actions plans as a result of this analysis, teaching and learning and higher education programs improve overall.

In this chapter, the author examines accountability of higher education in select education systems throughout the world, specifically in terms of oversight, regulations, and accreditation of institutions of higher education by governments and peer institutions that make up accreditation agencies. Additionally, the author offers recommendations as to how accreditation standards and procedures can guide higher education administration and faculty to use assessment of student learning, required in accreditation standards and other forms of accountability, to improve educational programs in general and music programs specifically. A variety of best practices are offered in how to engage higher education music faculty in the assessment process to meet the needs of music program improvement.

Government Oversight and Accreditation

Higher education institutions throughout the world vary in how they communicate quality and results of student learning. Local, provincial, and national governments in some countries are heavily involved in influencing this communication. In other countries, however, peer and professional institutions, as empowered by their respective governments, guide higher education institutions in communicating program quality. Significant investment of faculty and administrative time and financial support is necessary to communicate program quality in a meaningful way.

Central and South America

Many countries in Central and South America have national ministries of education, which use national assessments for institutions of higher education. Institutions in Mexico voluntarily participate in the national assessment, the Examen General para el Egreso de la Licenciatura (EGEL) (General Exams for Bachelor's Degrees), to assess competencies in 39 disciplines upon graduation from a bachelor's program (Zlatikin-Troitschanskaia, Shavelson, & Kuhn, 2015). There are three divisions of the exams: Life Sciences and Behavior; Design, Engineering and Architecture; and Social Sciences and Humanities. The Social Sciences and Humanities division does not include music or other art disciplines, but instead assesses such disciplines as communication, business, law, education, social work, and tourism, among others (Ceneval, 2016). Additionally, higher education institutions in Mexico may participate in the Examen Nacional de Ingreso al Posgrado (EXANI-III) (National Postgraduate Entrance Examination), which assesses general student learning outcomes among students applying for postgraduate study. Content knowledge in 36 disciplines in technical universities are assessed using the Exámenes Generales para el Egreso del Técnico Superior Universitario (EGETSU) (General Exam for the Exit of Higher Technical University) (Zlatikin-Troitschanskaia et al., 2015).

Similar nationwide assessments are used in countries in South America as well. Columbia and Chile measure student achievement growth related to higher education experiences through the assessment of quantitative reasoning and critical reading at the beginning and end of higher education studies (Zlatikin-Troitschanskaia et al., 2015). Students in Brazilian higher education institutions are required to complete the Exame Nacional de Cursos (ENC) (National Graduation Course Test) to assess competencies in 24 disciplines (Zlatikin-Troitschanskaia et al., 2015). Additionally, the Brazilian Ministry of Education (MEC) administers the ENADE—Exame Nacional de Descepenho dos Estudantes (Students' Performance National Exam) to all undergraduate students (Figueiredo, 2013). This exam assesses content, skills, and competencies, and consists of specific assessments for each area of university study, including music. Exam results are used not only to examine student performance but also to assess the effectiveness of the institution and program area. According to Figueiredo, the ENADE does not appear to impact curriculum development, as "many university teachers do not know about" the exam (2013, p. 67). The music exam is entirely written, without "audible sounds in the exam rooms" (Figueiredo, 2013, p. 67) and is administered to all students regardless of their specific music curriculum.

Europe

According to Frank, Kurth, and Mironowicz (2012), an increase in European higher education enrollment has led to a focus on quality assurance of student learning. Institutions have responded through a variety of formal quality assurance procedures, causing governments to ease centralized regulations and allow evolving evaluations by external bodies (Bernhard, 2010). This shift was formalized with the Bologna Declaration in 1999, where 31 signatories agreed on "the promotion of European cooperation in quality assurance with a view to developing comparable criteria and methodologies" (p. 4), creating the European Higher Education Area (European Ministers of Education, 1999). The objective of the Bologna Declaration signatories was the recognition of degrees across signatory countries with relatable standards of accreditation and quality assurance (Frank et al., 2012). Through the Berlin Communiqué in 2003, the European Association for Quality Assurance in Higher Education (ENQA) was charged with exploring "ways of ensuring an adequate peer review system for quality assurance and/or accreditation agencies or bodies" (European Ministers of Education, 2003, p. 3). Through the 2005 Bergen Communiqué, 45 European signatories developed a framework for national qualifications in the European Higher Education Area (European Ministers of Education, 2005). European ministers met again in 2009, recommending "ongoing curricular reform geared toward the development of learning outcomes" in the Leuven and Louvain-la-Neurve Communiqué (European Ministers of Education, 2009, p. 3).

Prior to the Bologna Declaration, there was no external evaluation of higher education in Germany, as this was the sole responsibility of the state education ministry in each of the 16 federal states (Bernhard, 2010; Frank et al., 2012). Reforms spurred by the Bologna Declaration included mandatory program accreditation by external agencies, leading to greater autonomy of universities from the state education ministry; however, state education ministries issued accreditation criteria and the process of program accreditation (Suchanek, Pietzonka, Künzel, & Futterer, 2012). Program accreditation for the 370 (as of 2010) state and state-approved institutions of higher education (including 55 colleges of art and music) in Germany (Bernhard, 2010) is completed by 10 independent accreditation agencies, which are accredited by the Accreditation Council (Akkreditierungsrat) (Foundation for the Accreditation of Study Programs in Germany, 2017). This council consists of representatives from business and industry, government, and higher education institutions (Bernhard, 2010).

To be accredited, German institutions of higher education develop a self-study report, which includes descriptions of the program and the curriculum. The self-study is examined by the accreditation agencies from standards developed by discipline-specific professionals. The self-studies, which are focused on institutional efforts and teacher input, do not contain any evidence of student learning, reaffirming de Rudder's 1994 description that German institutions consider student learning not necessarily the responsibility of the institution but the responsibility of the student (de Rudder, 1994).

Higher education institutions in the United Kingdom have a high degree of autonomy, but external accreditation is mandatory for such professional programs as health, social work, and architecture (Bernhard, 2010), giving professional associations "direct and immediate involvement in program accreditation" (Frank et al., 2012, p. 85). In 1997, 2 years before the Bologna Declaration, the four regional Higher Education Funding Councils (HEFCs), which, coupled with the Research Councils, provide public funding to institutions of higher education in the United Kingdom, established the Higher Education Quality Council (HEQC). Among other responsibilities, the HEQC was charged with evaluating quality assurance processes, including quality assessment and program improvement (Bernhard, 2010). This increase of state regulation of higher education was eased in 1997 with the formation of the Quality Assurance Agency for Higher Education (QAA), as accreditation was shifted more to peer institutions.

Frank et al. (2012) describe this new process as a "market-driven approach to higher education" (p. 87), where institutions of higher education are pressured to provide training demanded by employers, particularly in the professional programs of health, social work, and architecture. Disciplines outside these professional areas are given more flexibility as they receive annual reviews from external peer institutions of higher education. In these reviews, a peer examiner compares the quality of student work from the institution seeking accreditation with that of the examiner's own institution. Based on the comparison between student work at the different institutions, the peer examiner offers program improvement recommendations. Program evaluations by the QAA only occur if problems are identified through the peer examiner process.

Unlike the United Kingdom and Germany, the basis for evaluation of program quality in higher education institutions in Poland is centralized state control, modeled after the Soviet, post–World War II era (Frank et al., 2012). The State Accreditation Committee (SAC), financed by the Polish central government, oversees quality assurance issues, focusing on academic quality, which is measured by the quality of facilities and faculty and "fitness for purpose" (Frank et al., 2012, p. 82). Fitness for purpose is measured by the level of compliance with the state-defined curriculum. According to Frank et al. (2012), the Polish government, "through program guidelines, controls up to 50 percent of the content of subject-specific curricula" (p. 83). As a result, higher education in Poland seems to be misaligned with market needs, as professional bodies and association have no input into the accreditation process and state curricular guidelines.

In Poland, an institution of higher education submits a self-study report to SAC, which then sends a team of four to six visitors to the institution. The visitors are SAC-considered experts in the programs areas offered by the institution. The visitors submit a report of their findings, which is then open to comment by the institution. Institutional programs that are given a positive evaluation have up to an 8-year period before the next accreditation review; while institutional programs with conditional approval have 1 year to improve the quality of the program.

United States of America

Individual states, rather than the national government, are responsible for public education, per the US Constitution. Public colleges and universities are funded through state governments, and as such, state governments wield significant influence in maintaining educational standards within their state. To hold higher education institutions accountable and transparent to the public, many colleges and universities funded by state government communicate program goals, specific student learning outcomes, retention and graduation rates, and job placement rates upon graduation to state agencies and the public. For example, all 16 public universities that make up the University of North Carolina system are required to communicate student learning outcomes for every degree program offered (http://www.ecu.edu/learningoutcomes/).

Additionally, state governments grant teaching licenses for students successfully completing a higher education teacher preparation program, allowing them to teach in precollege public schools. Although states vary in their licensure requirements, states are increasingly turning away from documentation of institutional input and, instead, examining specific student evidences, not only to grant teaching licenses to teaching candidates but also to approve teacher preparation programs of higher education institutions. Many states are looking to such standardized evaluation tools as the edTPA, a portfolio-based assessment developed by Stanford University (California) faculty at the Stanford Center for Assessment, Learning, and Equity (SCALE) (edTPA, 2016). The "edTPA is a performance-based, subject-specific assessment and support system used by teacher preparation programs throughout the United States to emphasize, measure, and support the skills and knowledge that all teachers need from Day 1 in the classroom" (edTPA, 2016, para. 3). Through writing samples, candidate-developed teaching materials and assessments, evidence of student work, and teaching videos, candidates demonstrate a variety of teaching competencies. As more states have begun using the edTPA as a teacher licensure requirement, researchers and university faculty have questioned the instrument's reliability and validity (Hurley, Colprit, & Ward, 2013) and the potential financial conflict of interest on the part of Pearson, the edTPA distributor (Singer, 2016).

In addition to funding through state government, institutions of higher education receive significant national or federal funding in the form of federal student loans and research grants that make the US federal government an influential stakeholder. In the Higher Education Act (HEA) of 1965, the United States charged accreditation organizations with ensuring academic quality of institutions of higher education, tying federal student aid funds to accredited higher education institutions (H. Res. 9567, 1965). These accreditation organizations sanctioned by the federal government are of two types: institutional accreditors, which are regional or national accreditors that examine the overall quality of the institution; and specialized/programmatic accreditors, which examine a particular discipline within an institution (US Department of Education, 2015).

Typically, accreditation is based on peer-review, ensuring that accredited institutions are maintaining a broad spectrum of standards, including that the assessment of student learning is planned and reported for all degree programs in the institution. At the 2015 Council for Higher Education Accreditation Conference, Mary Ellen Patrisko presented that the Western Association of Colleges and Schools Senior College and University Commission, a regional institutional accreditor, requires that

> the institution employs a deliberate set of quality-assurance processes... including new curriculum and program approval processes, periodic program review, assessment of student learning, and other forms of ongoing evaluation... collecting, analyzing, and interpreting data; tracking learning results over time; using comparative data from external sources.   (Patrisko, 2015, Slide 12)

In 2012, the Southern Association of Colleges and Schools Commission on Colleges (SACSCOC), another regional institutional accreditor, stated in its accreditation standard 3.3.1.1 that an "institution identifies expected outcomes, assesses the extent to which it achieves these outcomes, and provides evidence of improvement based on analysis of the results in... educational programs, to include student learning outcomes" (Southern Association of College and Schools Commission on Colleges, 2012, p. 27).

Specialized Music Accreditation

Institutions of higher education that offer music programs in the United States are accredited primarily by a "specialized/programmatic" association, the National Association of Schools of Music (NASM), made up of 653 accredited intuitional members (NASM, 2016a). Member institutions are reviewed for continuation as accredited members on a 10-year cycle. As a part of this accreditation process, institutions complete self-study documents. The purpose of these self-study documents is to "have a profound impact on cohesion of purpose, common understanding of challenges and opportunities, strategic thinking, and operational planning" (NASM, 2013, p. IN-1). The Commission on Accreditation, made up of elected music executive peers, reviews the self-study document, a report submitted by visitors to the institution, and the institution's response to the visitors' report to determine whether the institution is clearly meeting the accreditation standards created and voted on by the NASM member institutions. Unlike state teaching licensure departments and institutional accreditors, which require student evidences of achieving learning outcomes, NASM, through its self-study format, requests that higher education institutions communicate how the music program meets the standards of the association in terms of management and delivery of curriculum. As a result, music programs report how they teach and what they do to assess student learning, but do not necessarily communicate the results of their instruction and how those results are analyzed to lead to program improvement.

Higher education music programs in the United States, whose graduates are eligible for certification as a music therapist, are members of the American Music Therapy Association (AMTA). Like NASM, AMTA member institutions submit a reaccreditation self-study every 10 years. In the self-study, institutions document, through instructional syllabi and other instructional materials, how they teach 116 professional competencies (American Music Therapy Association, 2013a) and standards of practice (American Music Therapy Association, 2013b), developed by AMTA, that are the basis of defining "the range of responsibilities of a fully qualified music therapy professional" (American Music Therapy Association and Certification Board for Music Therapists, 2015). Unlike NASM, which has a site visit, music therapy program directors meet with the AMTA commission to discuss the contents of the self-study and its alignment with AMTA competencies and standards at the annual meeting of the association. The AMTA self-study process is similar to that of NASM in asking for institutional materials and instructor input rather than student output.

ASSESSMENT AND DOCUMENTATION
BEST PRACTICES

As described in the previous sections of this chapter, stakeholders' demands for accountability have resulted in an emphasis on the part of institutions of higher education to communicate quality within their programs. In meeting institutional accreditor requirements, institutions of higher education are documenting quality through the assessment of student learning outcomes. Institutions of higher education must invest significant time and resources to this endeavor. If systematic assessment occurs only for accreditation purposes, however, the efforts become irrelevant to faculty and the investment in these efforts far outweigh the benefits (Murphy, 2006; Suchanek et al., 2012; Veiga, 2012; Ward, 2014). Institutions of higher education must find authentic and time- and cost-efficient means to assess, document, and communicate their program quality. Instead of viewing this work as an obstacle and administrative task, institutions of higher education need to see assessment of student learning as an opportunity to improve teaching and disciplinary programs by using a variety of assessment strategies.

Backward Design Curriculum

Grant Wiggins and Jay McTighe (2005) first introduced the concept of backward design curriculum in their book *Understanding by Design*. In this book, they identified three stages of backward design curriculum:

1. Identify Desired Results
2. Plan Evidences
3. Plan Experiences

When using this approach, music faculty, in the first stage, through the guidance of specialized accreditors such as NASM and AMTA, determine what skills and content knowledge students attain or what processes are experienced as a result of the instruction, unit, course, or degree program. Music faculty determine these results, focusing on "what a student looks like" at the end of instruction, rather than focusing on the strategies to help students achieve these ends.

In the second stage, instructors then plan evidences that reflect successful understanding, skills, and habits of mind. Through this paradigm, Wiggins and McTighe describe curriculum not just as a plan to teach content, but also as a specification as to how learners accomplish important tasks with content. "Curriculum is thus inseparable from the design of valid, recurring performance assessment tasks" (Wiggins & McTighe, 2007, p. 41). Performance juries are an example of student evidence of "comprehensive capabilities in the major performing medium including the ability to work independently to prepare performances at the highest level" (NASM, 2016b, p. 101).

In the third stage, instructors plan experiences so that students can achieve the desired result at the appropriate level of achievement. In the example of performance juries, music faculty, through private applied lessons and rehearsals, in addition to coursework in music history and literature, prepare students for the performance jury assessment.

Assessment Strategies

Assessment in higher education is challenging in that many music faculty are not trained in assessment strategies. Murphy (2006) writes that although institutions of higher education in the United Kingdom have required and voluntary training for university faculty in the area of pedagogical strategies and student learning, they have not reexamined "traditional forms of assessment" (p. 38) and should "become more professional in their use of assessment techniques (p. 42). Ward (2014) found that "limited understanding or expertise in assessment" (p. 303) was a leading barrier to the outcomes assessment process among higher education music programs in the United States. Furthermore, Ward found only 42% of higher education music units reported annual assessment training for faculty. Ward recommended that faculty receive training to design authentic, valid, and reliable assessment methods, develop methods of data collection and analysis, and use that analysis to improve the music program.

Authentic assessment is the "essence of 'doing' the subject with core content" (Wiggins & McTighe, 2007, p. 42). As "making" music is inherent in the discipline, developing opportunities for authentic assessment is not challenging for music faculty; however, music faculty need to discern which assessment tools are most valid to use in evaluating student learning outcomes so that they are actually evaluating their intended outcome. Scott (2012) categorizes roles of assessment based on its use in teaching and learning: (1) assessment of learning when assessment serves in a summative role; (2) assessment for learning when assessment serves in a formative role; and (3) assessment as learning when assessment serves in a self-reflective role. By determining the role of assessment for a particular assessment strategy and considering how the data will be analyzed and used, faculty can best create assessment strategies that align with the desired result.

Diagnostic and formative assessment are common roles in which music faculty use assessment data to inform students of their current level of achievement in a learning outcome or the progress achieved by a student over time. Through diagnostic assessment tasks, instructors can discover misconceptions or survey knowledge, skills, attitudes, learning styles, interests, and readiness levels. Music faculty often diagnose a student's level of readiness for collegiate music study through an admission audition process. In the audition, faculty diagnose the musical background of candidates and predict the success of students in the music curriculum.

If the audition is considered a baseline or starting point for a music's student level of achievement, formative assessment is used throughout the higher education music curriculum to communicate to the student and to the faculty of the progress that a student has made. Black and Wiliam (1998) assert that formative assessment facilitates the significant gains in student achievement. In music, formative feedback frequently occurs through class discussions, checks for understanding, and applied lesson and rehearsal feedback. Constant analysis of formative assessment should be the basis of instructional pacing. Wiggins and McTighe (2007) recommend that faculty build time into the instructional schedule to accommodate necessary adjustments based on analysis of formative assessment data, thus calling on teachers to "not overplan but plan to adjust" (p. 54). Formative assessment data is the evidence that institutional accreditors and other stakeholders are looking for institutions of higher education to communicate when demonstrating the quality of their programs. As formative assessment can often occur informally or embedded in music instruction, it is challenging for faculty to effectively document and communicate this data to accreditors and stakeholders.

Another assessment strategy that can be used in a formative role is the cornerstone performance assessment. Wiggins and McTighe (2007) write that this form of assessment prevents "curriculum drift" by focusing content instruction around important recurring performances that facilitate transfer. Perkins and Salomon (1992) write, "transfer of learning occurs when learning in one context or with one set of materials impacts on performance in another context or with other related materials" (p. 3). Music students in ensembles demonstrate transfer every time they exhibit a musical technique in one musical style and use the same technique in another musical selection of a different musical style. In 2014, researchers with the National Association for Music Education in the United States began piloting model cornerstone assessments of music standards developed by the National Coalition for Core Arts Standards (National Association for Music Education, 2016). These assessments focus on three artistic processes (creating, performing, and responding) for grades 2, 5, 8, and 9–12. Through varied musical content, students create, perform, and respond to music with increasing levels of sophistication in a variety of contexts.

In a subjective discipline, such as music, reliability is an important consideration in faculty-developed assessment tools. If assessment data is going to guide instructional decisions, "then those who use them need to be reassured that they can trust them" (Murphy, 2006, p. 41). One of the ways to increase reliability of evaluators is through the use of rubrics or scoring guides where faculty can more consistently apply criteria to student evidences. Norris and Borst (2007) found that although evaluators using a more descriptive rubric rated performances lower, the interevaluator reliability was higher.

When the purpose of the assessment is for faculty to provide formative feedback for musical performance to students, Bergee (2003) recommends criteria-specific rating scales to address specific aspects within a performance. Criteria-specific rating scales or rubrics are commonly used in music performance assessments throughout the United States in solo and small and large ensemble evaluations, primarily for middle and high school students; however, higher education music programs use these evaluation tools for auditions and performance juries.

Some music faculty, however, find that the use of criteria-specific rubrics constrains the evaluation of a performance by its criteria and does not allow for the unique qualities present in an individual performance (Brophy & Ward, 2016). As an alternative to criteria-specific rating scales or rubrics, faculty use a holistic rubric to evaluate the synthesis of a performance. As criteria within a performance is interdependent, this approach acknowledges this interdependence and allows the evaluator to describe the totality of the performance, making the use of holistic rubrics most appropriate in a summative performance assessment. Because of the interdependence of music performance criteria, Sadler (2009) asserts that preset criteria, as defined in a criteria-specific rating scale or rubric, are inadequate in providing qualitative judgments in complex disciplines such as the arts. He proposes the use of consensus moderation, an approach used widely in Australia, which relies on the professional judgment of performance evaluators. Evaluator reliability is achieved through discussion of the performance in which the evaluators form a consensus in qualitatively describing the performance.

Accreditation Standards for Program Improvement

Michael Johnson, who was then senior vice president and chief of staff of the Southern Association of Colleges and Schools Commission on Colleges (SACSCOC), said in a 2015 presentation that accreditation preparation "is a terrible waste of resources if you are doing all this work for SACSCOC only and not to improve the institution" (Johnson, 2015). In order to meet the demands of stakeholders, higher education music programs are investing significant time and resources through self-studies and documentation of student learning and the meeting of standards. Suchanek et al. (2012) found that higher education administrators in Germany felt that the top-down approach from accreditation agencies was not effective for program improvement, that it infringed on the autonomy of institutions of higher education, and that the costs in time and resources far outweighed the benefits. Frank et al. (2012) raise similar concerns regarding the accreditation model in the United Kingdom "around academic freedom versus the dictate of the profession" (p. 89). Ward (2014) and Ward, Wagoner, and Copeland (2016) found that faculty felt documentation of student learning should be completed by administration because it is not a curricular task, but an accountability task. Can higher education music programs leverage the required documentation of student learning to satisfy the increasing call for accountability in higher education and improve their academic programs?

The NASM in the US states that self-study documents should "have a profound impact on cohesion of purpose, common understanding of challenges and opportunities, strategic thinking, and operational planning" (NASM, 2013, p. IN-1). These documents should not solely be prepared so that higher education music programs can show external stakeholders that they are doing their job. In today's age of accountability in education, higher education institutions must dedicate significant resources to communicate the quality of their programs, but as Michael Johnson points out, institutions should take advantage of this process by examining how they can improve. Suchanek et al. (2012) assert,

> as long as time and energy expended on driving innovations and qualitative improvements in teaching and learning have no bearing on the success of either HEIs [Higher Education Institutions] or their academic personnel, qualitative profiling of the educational activities will not become an integral part of institutional and individual strategy.   (p. 27)

Although these authors write in support of external accreditation as necessary to ensure quality, they assert that unless faculty are engaged and incorporate new approaches to teaching and learning gleaned from the accreditation process, program improvement will not take place, thus wasting all the time and resources invested in the accreditation process. Zlatkin-Troitschanskaia et al. (2015) recommend that in developing assessment of student learning that can be reported in accreditation processes faculty should (1) define outcomes, (2) develop means of assessment, and (3) draw "valid inferences from the response data" (p. 403). Ward and High (2010) proposed a "Cycle of Assessment Informed Instructional Design" (p. 504), which adapted teaching to the needs of students as identified through analysis of assessment results. This adaptation of teaching will not happen in higher music education as long as assessment is viewed as an accreditation task to be accomplished by administrators.

Faculty Dialogue Through Curriculum Mapping

Gray (2002) asserts that assessment is only successful if faculty are involved and describes a link between assessment and teaching and learning. If music faculty, involved with curriculum development, will be more engaged in assessment and facilitate the analysis of assessment results with their music colleagues, assessment will align with faculty practices in the classroom. Ward et al. (2016) studied a curriculum mapping process as a means to engage higher education music faculty in student learning outcomes assessment and curriculum examination and revision. Through a survey of faculty, these researchers found that curriculum mapping was an effective tool to encourage faculty conversation, leading to curriculum development and fostering a "culture of assessment and reflection" (p. 133).

The curriculum map (see Figure 32.1) created by Ward, Wagoner, and Copeland was designed to examine the scope and sequence of competencies based on the standards of NASM. Through the curriculum map, music faculty determined at which level of sophistication the competencies were met (introduction, reinforcement, application, and mastery) and summatively assessed. Music faculty were able to discover competencies that were not being addressed with sufficient depth or redundant within courses throughout the curriculum. The curriculum map process also allowed new faculty to better understand the scope and sequence of the curriculum and veteran faculty to communicate institutional knowledge and history to their colleagues.

Wiggins and McTighe (2007) advocate the use of curriculum maps as a means to look at curriculum not as a linear but rather a recursive phenomenon that fosters a constant revisiting of key ideas and challenges that are never mastered in one attempt. According to Wiggins and McTighe (2005), curriculum maps are good visual realizations of the backward design model described earlier. These maps can be teacher- or student-centered and should be customized by faculty, as faculty examine the scope and sequence of the curriculum (Kalick, 2006; Lenz, Adams, Bulgren, Pouliot, & Laraux, 2002; Norstrom, 2006; Veltri, Webb, Matveev, & Zapatero, 2011; Ward et al., 2016).

In addition to focusing on the program as a whole, a curriculum map can be used to focus on student learning outcomes in an individual course. In the curriculum map

Common Curriculum-Bachelor of Music					
NASM Competencies					
General Studies (VIII, A, 6)					
Musicianship Skills and Analysis (VIII, B, 2)	Introduced	Reinforced	Applied	Mastered	Assessed
An understanding of the common elements and organizational patterns of music and their interaction, the ability to employ this understanding in aural, verbal, and visual analyses, and the ability to take aural dictation (VIII, B, 2, a).					
Sufficient understanding of and capability with musical forms, processes, and structures to use this knowledge and skill in compositional, performance, analytical, scholarly, and pedagogical applications according to the requisites of the specializations (VIII, B, 2, b).					
The ability to place music in historical, cultural, and stylistic contexts (VIII, B, 2, c).					
Composition/Improvisation (VIII, B, 3)					
Students must acquire and rudimentary capacity to create original or derivative music (VIII, B, 3).					
History and Repertory (VIII, B, 4)					
Students must acquire basic knowledge of music history and repertories through the present time, including study and experience of musical language and achievement in addition to that of the primary culture encompassing the area of specialization (VIII, B, 4)					

Common Curriculum Courses	
Foundations	
MUSC 1156	Basic Musicianship
MUSC 1166	Basic Musicianship Lab
MUSC 1176	Basic Musicianship
MUSC 1186	Basic Musicianship Lab
MUSC 2156	Basic Musicianship
MUSC 2166	Basic Musicianship Lab
MUSC 2176	Basic Musicianship
MUSC 2186	Basic Musicianship Lab
MUSC 3176	Basic Musicianship V
MUSC 1406	Music History and Lit (WI)
MUSC 2406	Music History and Lit (WI)
MUSC 2416	Music History and Lit (WI)
MUSC 2248	Music of the World's Peoples
MUSC 3156	Conducting
MUSC 3166	Conducting
Lower Level Applied	
Upper Level Applied	
Large Ens	
Small Ens	
MUSC 1105	Beginning Group Piano
MUSC 1115	Beginning Group Piano
Recital	

FIGURE 32.1 Curriculum map based on NASM standards. East Carolina University School of Music (2014). Reprinted with permission.

shown in Figure 32.2, developed by the Department of Hospitality Management at East Carolina University in North Carolina, learning outcomes in a course are categorized around the curricular themes of think, value, communicate, and lead (only the "think section" is given in Figure 32.2). Through this course-level curriculum map, faculty compare courses within the curriculum to ensure that these curricular themes are being addressed with appropriate depth.

Just as curriculum mapping is a tool to spur faculty conversation about the content of the curriculum (Ward et al., 2016), faculty working together to analyze student learning outcome results can lead to program improvement. In many cases in higher education, the burden of assessment of student learning outcomes is left to an assessment coordinator who may or may not be a faculty member or a course instructor who evaluates a particular means of assessment (Ward, 2014). This "course-based" assessment has the potential to limit the knowledge of assessment results and an analysis of those results to a few faculty members, hindering improvement in the overall music program. By using a tool such as a curriculum map to facilitate faculty dialogue, music faculty identify student learning outcomes and the level of sophistication at which instructors at various points throughout the curriculum address these learning outcomes, and determine valid and reliable means of assessment to evaluate student levels of achievement of these desired results. Faculty, then, analyze assessment results as a group, through a programmatic rather than course lens, allowing varying perspectives to view the data and create action plans that have a greater impact than if it is left to the individual course instructor. Through this group analysis, music faculty can:

Introduced (I): By conclusion of this course, students will understand the meaning, definition, or interpretation of a hospitality concept. Students will be able to recall and use this information.
Reinforce (R): Students will be exposed to a concept in differing hospitality contexts. Students will be required to a use a concept in a new situation by recalling and applying what was introduced previously.
Emphasize (E): Students are expected to understand a hospitality concept well enough to make judgements within a given setting, identify the appropriateness and applicability of a hospitality concept, and apply it in an appropriate manner to achieve a desired end. Students now have a "hospitality tool" and are able to use it in context.

ABOUT HOSPITALITY MANAGEMENT:

	1a. Human Resources		1b. Accounting/Financial Management		1c. Engineering & Property Management
I	Staffing	I	Financial statements		Energy management
	Training & Devlopment		Manage budget		Preventative management
I	Workforce relations	I	Controlling		Site selection
		I	Cost control	I	Facilities/equipment management
		I	Yield management		Crisis management

	1d. Marketing Sales Management		1e. Service Management		1f. Management & General Administration
	Market Analysis	I, R	Guest Relations	I	Leadership
I	Marketing Mix	I	Manage stakeholder relationships		Risk Management
I	Advertising/Promotion/PR	I	Understand world class service		Project Management
	Sales Planning	I	Hospitality etiquette		Strategic planning
				I	Business Communication
				I	Management functions

	1g. Food and Beverage Management		1h. Lodging Management		1i. Meeting or Event Design
I	Menu analysis & design	I	Operations management	I	Site Planning & Site Design
	Food knowledge & production		Revenue management	I	Program Planning & Design
	Sanitation & safety		Guest liability & safety		On-site management
	Beverage management		Forecasting		Measure value
	Inventory & purchasing				
	Banquet management				

VALUE...

ISSUES RELATED TO HOSPITALITY LEADERSHIIP

I, R	Ethics	I	Diversity	I	Globalization	I, R	Service	?	Inquiry

FIGURE 32.2 Course-level curriculum map based on curricular themes (Deale and Crawford, 2013). Reprinted with permission.

1. Coordinate the rotation of an instructor or multiple instructors teaching the same course or learning outcome. If a course is reassigned to a different instructor, the new instructor needs to be aware of previous student achievement in relation to course content. For a course with multiple instructors, it is important for instructors to learn from each other and to work toward achieving the same desired results, particularly when teaching in a sequential, spiral curriculum like music.

2. Examine student learning assessment data with a lens beyond an individual course. Through systematic assessment of student learning, faculty can identify weaknesses or misconceptions that students have, and can communicate these weaknesses to the rest of the music faculty to provide support and scaffolds for the student or students. Students may pass a course, for example, but are still inconsistent in demonstrating appropriate proficiency in specific skills. The faculty needs to discuss how those skills can be strengthened in the next semester, perhaps through revising the planned learning experiences in the next sequential course.

3. Communicate issues to all faculty. Through the analysis of assessment results, issues may arise of which some faculty may not be aware. For example, music education students are assigned to complete 12 K-12 school observations in the semester. Unknown to the music education faculty, these students consistently arrive late to a musicianship lab, where they miss important content. After the analysis revealed that music education students are struggling in sight-singing assessments, the musicianship lab instructor and the music education faculty realize possible reasons and create an action plan removing those scheduling obstacles.

4. Create a mutually supportive community of educators whose goal is to help students achieve. When assessment is only seen as an accountability task, instructors become fearful that assessment results will be used to evaluate the effectiveness of their teaching. Unfortunately, high-stakes testing in precollege public schools in the United States and the way in which those test results are tied to school funding and job performance have created a negative faculty perception of assessment. Music faculty will only view assessment as a positive tool if it is viewed as a means to support their colleagues in helping students achieve, rather than an opportunity to punish faculty for poor student performance.

SUMMARY AND CONCLUSIONS

As enrollment in colleges and universities in Europe and the United States increase (Frank et al., 2012; US Department of Education, 2016), governments that fund and students and their families who pay tuition are calling for increased accountability in the quality of the education provided by institutions of higher education. While this may appear face threatening, it is also an opportunity to examine our programs and align them with the needs of 21st-century music learners.

In this chapter, we have examined accreditation and accountability procedures and standards from education systems in different parts of the world. In Central and South America, national education ministries used standardized assessments to evaluate students and the institutions of higher education where they studied. As the assessments are inconsistently aligned with learning outcomes taught in higher education curriculum, as evidenced with national music assessments in Brazil, the assessments do not provide the data that faculty need to improve their programs. In order for assessments to be authentic and align with instructional practices, educational organizations cannot assess for the sole purpose of higher education accountability. Through the Wiggins and McTighe backward design curriculum, the desired results are considered first, and then assessment instruments are developed based on those results. By approaching assessment in this matter, higher education institutions can ensure a better curriculum-assessment alignment and have a better opportunity to examine and improve their program.

In Europe, several reforms in higher education were created to facilitate cooperation across European nations to develop quality assurance measures that were comparable across borders. The results of these efforts have been a move toward an easing of government involvement, as accreditation institutions made up of academic, professional, and government officials in some cases, have been empowered to evaluate the quality of education in institutions of higher education. The United Kingdom has taken a "market" approach to accreditation (Frank et al., 2012, p. 87), where content and quality of professional programs are highly scrutinized by employers. In contrast, the national government in Poland is highly influential in the content of curricula in institutions of higher education, and these institutions are accredited according to how they conform to government-mandated curricula.

In the United States, individual states within the country are highly influential in the management of institutions of higher education, as they are a significant source of funding. The federal government has empowered institutional accreditors and specialized/programmatic accreditors to examine the quality of education. These accreditation agencies, made up of peer academics, highly influence how institutions of higher education communicate their instructional and management practices. In music, the specialized accreditors, the NASM and AMTA focus on what music faculty do. In this faculty-input model, higher education music programs through self-studies and documentation of instructional materials demonstrate how they are meeting the standards of each association. This approach is more in line with Germany's approach to accreditation, where no evidences of student learning are offered as a part of the self-study. The faculty-input model differs, however, from the approaches of many state teaching licensure agencies and institutional accreditors in the United States, where student evidences, or at least a communication of how student assessment is systematically analyzed to demonstrate program improvement, is a required component of the accreditation process. This dual accreditation model (student evidences model for institutional accreditors and state teaching licensure agencies, and faculty input model for music specialized/programmatic accreditors) is challenging for higher education music faculty to address. They are forced to have multiple accreditation processes and must invest more time and resources as a result. Institutional and specialized/programmatic accreditors in the United States need to streamline their processes to ease this burden and allow the faculty to better focus on student learning and program improvement.

In the end, accreditation is not about accountability. It is a means for institutions of higher education to examine how they manage themselves and how their students are achieving. The needs and academic goals of students are constantly changing. Unless faculty are constantly examining how they are meeting these changing needs, they are not serving their students; therefore, faculty should take advantage of all of the investment of time and resources dedicated to the accreditation process to improve their programs and meet the educational needs of their students.

Using the Wiggins and McTighe backward curriculum design as a model, we examined strategies for faculty to develop valid, reliable, and fair assessment strategies to identify student strengths and weaknesses and design learning experiences accordingly. Through various curriculum map models, music faculty can work together to examine their curriculum and analyze, as a group, student learning outcomes assessment data. By following an accreditation procedure, faculty can blend the requirements of varying accreditors and government bodies, improve their programs, and efficiently document that improvement. Whether learning occurs in the studio, rehearsal hall, or classroom, faculty need to analyze assessment data and examine new ways to improve student learning. This will lead to serving the student through improved music programs.

References

American Music Therapy Association. (2013a). *AMTA Professional Competencies*. Retrieved from http://www.musictherapy.org/about/competencies/

American Music Therapy Association. (2013b). *AMTA Standards of Clinical Practice*. Retrieved from http://www.musictherapy.org/about/standards/

American Music Therapy Association and Certification Board for Music Therapists. (2015). *Scope of music therapy practice*. Retrieved from http://www.musictherapy.org/about/scope_of_music_therapy_practice/

Bergee, M. J. (2003). Faculty inter-judge reliability of music performance evaluation. *Journal of Research in Music Education, 51*, 137–150. doi: 10.2307/3345847

Bernhard, A. (2010). Two European responses to assure quality in higher education. *Problems of Education in the 21st Century, 20*, 36–43.

Black, P., & Wiliam, D. (1998). Assessment and classroom learning. *Assessment in Education: Principles, Policy and Practice, 5*(1), 7–74, doi: 10.1080/0969595980050102

Brophy, T. S., & Ward, J. (2016, July). *Consensus moderation as an assessment of music learning*. 32nd World Conference of the International Society for Music Education. Symposium conducted in Glasgow, Scotland, UK.

Ceneval. (2016). *Centro Nacional de Evalución para la Educación Superior, A.C.* Retrieved from http://www.ceneval.edu.mx/

de Rudder, H. (1994). The quality issue in German higher education policy. *European Higher Education Journal, 29*, 201–219.

East Carolina University. (2016). *Hospitality management program: Core learning matrix*. Retrieved from http://www.ecu.edu/samktg/acad/ipar/tvcl/communicate/HMGT%201350%20Matrix.pdf

East Carolina University School of Music. (2014). *NASM self-study report*. Unpublished report. Greenville, NC: Author.

edTPA. (2016). *About edTPA*. Retrieved from http://www.edtpa.com/PageView.aspx?f=GEN_AboutEdTPA.html

European Minsters of Education. (1999). *The Bologna declaration of 19 June 1999*. Retrieved from http://www.magna-charta.org/resources/files/text-of-the-bologna-declaration

European Minsters of Education. (2003). *Realising the European higher education area*. Retrieved from http://www.enqa.eu/wp-content/uploads/2013/03/BerlinCommunique1.pdf

European Minsters of Education. (2009). *The Bologna process 2020: The European higher education area in the new decade*. Retrieved from http://www.ond.vlaanderen.be/hogeronderwijs/bologna/conference/documents/leuven_louvain-la-neuve_communiqu%C3%A9_april_2009.pdf

Figueiredo, S. (2013). Perspectives and challenges for music assessment in Brazilian universities. In T. S. Brophy & A. Lehmann-Wermser (Eds.), *Music assessment across cultures and continents: The culture of shared practice* (pp. 59–68). Chicago, IL: GIA Publications.

Frank, A., Kurth, D., & Mionowicz, I. (2012). Accreditation and quality assurance for professional degree programmes: Comparing approaches in three European countries. *Quality in Higher Education, 18*(1), 75–95. doi: 10.1080/13538322.2012.669910

Gray, P. J. (2002). The roots of assessment: Tensions, solutions, and research directions. In T. W. Banta (Ed.), *Building a scholarship of assessment* (pp. 49–66). San Francisco, CA: Jossey-Bass.

H. Res. 9567, 89th Cong., Pub. L. 89–329, Nov. 8, 1965, 79 Stat. 1219 (20 U.SC 1001 et seq., 42 U.SC 2751 et seq.) (1965, November 8). (enacted).

Hurley, C. G., Colprit, E., & Ward, J. (2013, September). *The edTPA: Does it really reflect best practice?* Presented at the Symposium on Music Teacher Education, University of North Carolina Greensboro, Greensboro, NC.

Johnson, M. (2015, December). *Using accreditation to enhance institutional improvement.* 2015 SACSCOC Annual Meeting. Meeting conducted at the George R. Brown Convention Center, Houston, TX.

Kalick, K. T. (2006). *Curriculum mapping: A step-by-step guide for creating curriculum year overviews.* Thousand, Oaks, CA: Corwin Press.

Lenz, B. K., Adams, G., Bulgren, J. A., Pouliot, N., & Laraux, M. (2002). *The effects of curriculum maps and guiding questions on the test performance of adolescents with learning disabilities.* (ED 469 292). Washington, DC: United States Department of Education Office of Educational Research and Improvement.

Murphy, R. (2006). Evaluating new priorities for assessment in higher education. In C. Bryan, & K. Clegg (Eds.), *Innovative Assessment in Higher Education* (pp. 37–47). New York, NY: Routledge.

National Association for Music Education. (2016). *Student assessment using Model Cornerstone Assessment.* Reston, VA: National Association for Music Education.

National Association of Schools of Music. (2013). *Procedures for institutions.* Retrieved from http://nasm.arts-accredit.org/

National Association of Schools of Music. (2016a). *National Association of Schools of Music.* Retrieved from http://nasm.arts-accredit.org/

National Association of Schools of Music. (2016b). *Handbook 2015–16.* Retrieved from http://nasm.arts-accredit.org/

Norris, C., & Borst, J. (2007). An examination of the reliabilities of two choral festival adjudication forms. *Journal of Research in Music Education, 55,* 237–251. doi: 10.1177/002242940705500305

Norstrom, B. (2006). Mapping curriculum to Ed Tech and industry standards. *Learning and Leading with Technology, 33*(6), 14–17.

Patrisko, M. E. (2015, January). *Student learning outcomes assessment: Progress to date, remaining challenges.* Presented at the 2015 Council for Higher Education Accreditation Annual Conference, Capital Hilton Hotel, Washington, DC.

Perkins, D. N., & Salomon, G. (1992). Transfer of learning. In T. N. Postlethwaite & T. Husen (Eds.), *International encyclopedia of education.* Oxford, UK: Pergamon Press.

Sadler, D. R. (2009). Indeterminacy in the use of preset criteria for assessment and grading. *Assessment and Evaluation in Higher Education, 34,* 159–179. doi: 10.1080/02602930801956059

Scott, S. (2012). Rethinking the roles of assessment in music education. *Music Educators Journal, 98*(3), 31–35. doi: 10.1177/0027432111434742

Singer, A. (2016, February 4). Pearson rips off students with tests designed for failure. Retrieved from http://www.huffingtonpost.com/alan-singer/pearson-rips-off-students_b_9157066.html

Southern Association of College and Schools Commission on Colleges. (2012). *The principles of accreditation: Foundations for quality enhancement.* Decatur, GA: Southern Association of College and Schools Commission on Colleges. Retrieved from http://www.sacscoc.org/pdf/2012PrinciplesOfAcreditation.pdf

Suchanek, J., Pietzonka, M., Künzel, R. H. F., & Futterer, T. (2012). The impact of accreditation on the reform of study programmes in Germany. *Higher Education Management and Policy, 24*(1), 9–32.

US Department of Education. (2015). *Accreditation in the United States.* Retrieved from https://www2.ed.gov/admins/finaid/accred/index.html

US Department of Education. (2016). *Digest of education statistics: 2015.* Retrieved from https://nces.ed.gov/programs/digest/d15/index.asp

Veiga, A. (2012). Bologna 2010: The moment of truth? *European Journal of Education, 47,* 378–391. doi: 10.1111/j.1465-3435.2012.01532.x

Veltri, N. F., Webb, H. W., Matveev, A. G., & Zapatero, E. G. (2011). Curriculum mapping as a tool for continuous improvement of IS curriculum. *Journal of Information Systems Education, 22*(1), 31–42.

Ward, J. (2014). An examination of practices, faculty and administrative involvement, and resources and barriers in higher education music outcomes assessment. In T. S. Brophy, M. Lai, & H. Chen (Eds.), *Music assessment and global diversity: Practice measurement and policy* (pp. 285–308). Chicago, IL: GIA Publications.

Ward, J., & High, L. (2010). Theory into practice: Teaching assessment strategies to preservice teachers through a third-through-fifth-grade vocal music laboratory. In T. S. Brophy (Ed.), *The practice of assessment in music education: Frameworks, models, and designs proceedings of the 2009 Florida Symposium on Assessment in Music Education* (pp. 499–512). Chicago, IL: GIA Publications.

Ward, J., Wagoner, C. L., & Copeland, R. E. (2016). Intersections of accreditation: An examination of a school of music curriculum mapping process to relate specialized accreditation and regional accreditation standards. In T. S. Brophy, J. Marlatt, & G. K. Richter. *Connecting practice, measurement, and evaluation: Selected papers from the Fifth International Symposium on Assessment in Music Education* (pp. 119–134). Chicago, IL: GIA Publications.

Wiggins, G., & McTighe, J. (2005). *Understanding by design.* Upper Saddle River, NJ: Pearson.

Wiggins, G., & McTighe, J. (2007). *Schooling by design: Mission, action, and achievement.* Alexandria, VA: Association for Supervision and Curriculum Development.

Zlatikin-Troitschanskaia, O., Shavelson, R. J., & Kuhn, C. (2015). The international state of research on measurement of competency in higher education. *Studies in Higher Education, 40,* 393–411. doi: 10.1080/3075079.2015.1004241

CHAPTER 33

ASSESSMENT IN THE APPLIED STUDIO IN HIGHER EDUCATION

KELLY A. PARKES

OVERVIEW

THE applied setting is unique in many respects and the lexicon in this setting has been debated. The applied studio is often referred to as one-to-one teaching, dyadic teaching, studio teaching or instruction, private teaching, and the master–apprentice or expert–novice dyad (Daniel, 2008; Donald, 2012; Gaunt & Westerlund, 2013; Georgii-Hemming & Westvall, 2010; Haddon, 2009; Kennell, 2002; Wöllner & Ginsborg, 2011). The term is used differently between countries and there is often a struggle between terms, even within institutions, in the quest to label this kind of teaching. For example, it is not similar enough to the visual art studio model, yet has familiar tenets. Administrators of music departments in universities often may find it difficult to describe the nature of the teaching, the nature of learning, and in describing accurately what the student learning outcomes should, or could, be. Conservatories (conservatoires, or dedicated music schools), on the other hand, can reach back into institutional history easily to articulate what applied studio teaching is because they can depend on traditional long-held understandings of this type of teaching.

Private teaching conducted by individuals in studios at their home, rather than in a higher education or conservatoire setting, is under-researched and outside the purview of this chapter. In their research, Ester, Batchelor and Lopinski (2014) suggest a planning guide for singing teachers—a strong indicator that private teachers outside of higher education. This indicates (1) that they are in need of assistance, (2) that they could benefit from professional development, and (3) that researchers should undertake work in this area. The applied studio setting can be isolating given that it occurs in a closed studio (Daniel & Parkes, 2015) usually between only two individuals. However, applied studio instruction in higher education institutions is pervasive in music education (Schmidt, 1992) and has been the prominent method of Western art music pedagogy for hundreds of years (Lennon & Reed, 2012; Long, Creech, Gaunt, Hallam, & Robertson, 2012; Presland, 2005; Slawsky, 2011). Mills (2007) suggested that instances of research carried out by performer-teachers is relatively rare. In her work, *Studio-based instrumental learning*, Burwell (2016a) investigated the interactions between teacher and student in deep micro-analysis research, including a case study, of the collaborative behaviors and the incorporated contextualization at the higher education (tertiary) level. She notes that applied "teaching and learning is not always well-connected to research" (p. 62) and as a performer-teacher-researcher, her work is important in identifying the complex nature of the teaching and learning undertaken in the applied studio.

Schmidt (1992) reviewed the literature surrounding applied music instruction, and in 2002 Kennell overviewed the applied setting and summarized the major research efforts. Since then there have been numerous investigations into the applied studio setting; into teacher behaviors, student behaviors, teaching and learning behaviors, along with assessment of the learning taking place (as summarized in Parkes, 2009, 2010d, 2011). Kennell (2002) made the observation that the theory of studio instruction continued to evolve as various members of the music research community focused further attention on the practices of teaching performance in this setting. Kennell (2002) also pointed out that "studio instruction is a cultural system interlocking with other cultural systems, including school music instruction, university music training, and the world of professional performance" (p. 249). This reminds us that there are several essential components at play, each worthy of individual study. It is the interplay of these components that makes the study of the applied studio rich and complex, as we continue to understand the influence of these changing elements. Kennell (2002) signaled difficulties that needed to be addressed in the early part of the 21st century; these were "the paradigmatic conflict that exists between the research community... [where] practitioners in studio teaching simply do not trust or value knowledge generated from systematic research" (p. 253). Since this observation, there have been a multitude of systematic research endeavors to define, describe, explain, and understand the nature of the applied studio as well as to investigate the practitioners' reluctance to engage in research itself. Researchers have reconsidered and recognized that our knowledge of the applied studio is, as Kennell (2002) has already pointed out, socially structured. Much of the current research has moved in that direction, examining the influence of the community of musicians as a part of the applied learning setting (Gaunt & Westerlund, 2013).

In general, the term "master–apprentice" has been the characteristic description and label given to the applied studio: one master (the expert teacher) and one apprentice (the novice learner) as observed by several researchers (e.g., Burwell, 2012; Nerland, 2007; Westerlund, 2006). It is expected of the learner to emulate, to the highest degree possible, the performance level of the teacher by following all directions from the teacher/master. It is tacitly understood today that this is still the case, leaning on evidence initially provided by Abeles (1975), Gipson (1978), Helpler (1986), and Kostka (1984). However, the model is changing. The path for learners to become masters in their own right is becoming more learner-centered, more collaborative, more reflective, and is becoming less teacher-directed. This change is similar to the constructivist paradigm seen in classroom teaching and learning (Gaunt & Westerlund, 2013; Lebler, Carey, & Harrison, 2015). McPhail (2010) makes the case, citing action research, that concepts from music teaching in the classroom have potential links to the applied studio. A constructivist classroom conceptualization of teaching is now frequently used in higher education classroom teaching settings (see the work of Weimer, 2002; Doyle, 2008) and may make an impact on the current applied studio setting. However, the potential for impact is perhaps not yet fully defined nor operational.

Over the past three decades there has been an observable shift in how applied studios operate within higher education as we move into an era of accountability and quality assurance. Applied studio teachers still produce new masters to join the field prepared for high-level musical performances; however, the students are more likely to have experienced collaborative processes with their teacher over the course of their studies. In the early 1990s Kennell (1992) introduced his teacher scaffolding model, suggesting that a scaffolding strategy is determined both with the teachers' assessments and attributions of the students' performances. In other words, teachers assess why the students' performances are successful and engage in building on student strengths in a joint problem-solving initiatives that also lead to some independent problem-solving on the part of the student. In the dedicated issue of the *Quarterly Journal of Music Teaching and Learning* to the applied studio, Manny Brand (1992) reminded the field (particularly those in the United States) that the applied studio was worth examining, and describing the processes much more closely, as it moved away from the traditional closed-door secrets between teacher and student. Brand (1992) described a veil of mystery over the applied studio with the exception of a few notable early attempts to lift that veil, including Abeles (1973, 1975) and Fiske (1977). More recently we see the level of empirical investigation into the practices used in the applied studio burgeoning in the last decades of the 20th century and into the 21st century.

Philosophical and paradigmatic inquiry around the applied studio setting shifted in the early 21st century, perhaps more so outside the United States than within. For example, in Europe the Innovative Conservatoire (ICon) in 2006 initially brought together four conservatories to focus on reflective communities of practice. The research project eventually grew to involve 23 conservatories, and their teachers, who joined together to reflect and share practice and research (Gaunt, 2013, p. 52). The foci of the project included one-to-one teaching, small group teaching, musicians in society, assessment and feedback, and methodologies in practice-based research.

Christopherson (2013) writes about collaborative learning in higher education, noting the perception of collaboration also implies some notion of democratic education. This can be seen as an emerging reconceptualization of the applied studio setting in higher education. She provides a new perspective on the dynamics of power within collaborative learning for musicians and thoughtfully describes the ethical considerations we might take when evaluating student outcomes in collaborative settings. King (2008) shares a rich mixed-methods study whereby collaborative techniques were used in a drum music studio. Pairs of learners worked with technology to promote full collaboration in studio learning and activities. This suggests that some applied studio teachers may no longer subscribe to the hierarchical paradigm of one master and one apprentice. Christopherson cautions us regarding formal evaluation of students in this collaborative setting. She points out, "while students may be trusted to learn and teach in groups, they are rarely trusted to grade each other" (p. 83), and she laments that evaluation often remains the responsibility of the teacher. Latukefu and Verenikina (2013) pursue new directions and see the master–apprentice model as expanding. In their research, they focus on the ways that learners interact and collaborate with teachers and peers with a purposefully designed sociocultural learning environment, with outcomes encouraging self-directed learning in students. Likewise, Ilomäki (2013) suggests that students can learn from one another's musicianship and a shift in teachers' responsibility means students are able to clarify their musical goals and "acquire tools for independent learning" (Ilomäki, 2013 p. 128). In research that merges the traditional applied studio with collaborative learning activities in a brass studio, Luff and Lebler (2013) illustrate that students engage in self-direction and peer direction along with equal leadership from teachers and students. Carey and Grant (2014) also provide a transformative approach to the applied studio in their efforts to reform the education of professional musicians. Burwell (2015) addresses the dissonance found in the applied studio, in the instance that a student reports a teacher's approach as inappropriate with respect to development. Rakena, Airini, and Brown (2015) present the complex narratives of indigenous and minority student learning within the conservatory model. In exploring the culture of power, their findings suggest that cultural barriers may be overcome within the applied studio space and students' stories provided an effective tool for the education of future applied studio teachers. These studies (Burwell, 2015; Carey & Grant, 2014; Rakena et al., 2015) signal that the landscape for applied studio teaching is shifting away from traditional perceptions from what "has always been" to what "might become" and future research should actively continue along this trajectory.

Student and Teacher Perceptions and Behaviors

As the applied studio and the master–apprentice paradigm shifts into the 21st century, a growing body of researchers report student and teacher perceptions about teaching and learning in the applied studio. Select examples include Mills (2002), Mills and Smith (2003), Fredrickson (2007), Gaunt (2008, 2009, 2011), and Carey and Grant (2015). Likewise, there are many researchers who attempt to define or illustrate the characteristics of the applied studio and which behaviors are found within. These were first summarized by Schmidt (1992) and later by Duke (1999/2000). Schmidt (1992) suggested that systematic research within the applied studio took place in several key areas. The first was using an instrument to measure teaching behaviors, the second examined student characteristics as a variable along with teacher characteristics. Schmidt also reviewed instructional methods and curricular issues. Duke (1999/200) later provided a systematic review of published experimental and descriptive research involving the applied studio setting. He identified the following variables within the applied studio research: allocation of time; teacher verbalizations, gestures, and activities; effects of multiple components on teaching and student behavior; variables affecting evaluations by observers; and experimental attempts to improve teaching. Rosenthal (1984) found that modeling alone may be the most effective tool for helping instrumental students and teacher "talk" was the least effective in what was considered a landmark study (Burwell, 2016a).

Kennell (2002) has also described the systematic inquiries that have been conducted and groups them into three areas: (1) the roles of student and teacher, (2) their behaviors and interactions, and (3) evaluation. These summaries are recommended as detailed descriptions of earlier research outlining the behaviors and elements of the applied studio. Duke and Simmons (2006) described common elements in applied teaching settings with artist-teachers and in replicating the study, Parkes and Wexler (2012) also found similar results in terms of teacher and student behaviors. The applied studio research has significantly grown in the past several decades in Australia, the United Kingdom, and the United States. The parameters for the research body have expanded descriptions of the nature and behaviors of the setting. With greater understanding and a view toward moving toward new paradigms, some researchers (e.g., Carey, Grant, McWilliam, & Taylor, 2013) are developing specific protocols for the examination of the applied studio teaching setting and others are examining relevant contemporary issues such as gender (Zhukov, 2012) and the culture of power (Rakena et al., 2015). The following section of this chapter focuses on assessments used to measure student learning, or musical achievement, as an outcome of applied teaching and learning.

ASSESSMENT OF MUSICAL PERFORMANCE IN THE APPLIED STUDIO

Assessment of musical learning as an outcome of teaching in the applied studio setting has been described as "ongoing informal assessments" (Abeles, 2010, p. 167). Abeles views assessment in the studio as a process of "listening to students playing, assessing their strengths and weakness... determining what additional experiences may strengthen their performance and develop them into well-rounded, independent musicians." He suggests, "even the idea of developing into an 'independent musician' focuses on the issue of assessment" (Abeles, 2010, p. 167). Regular informal assessments seem integral to the work of applied studio teachers in general, and these assessments complete a natural cycle of teaching and learning. Kennell (2002) observed that in the applied studio setting, the occasions such as juries, auditions, and competitions are used to rate, compare, and rank students' efforts (p. 252), however Abeles points out, "effective studio teachers are likely to be good at assessing student performances" even within lessons (p. 168). Boyle and Radocy (1987) highlight the difficulty in measuring musical performance due to its subjective nature (p. 171) yet also make the case that there are differences between a what they term a "global" approach, where judges make an overall impression based on personal criteria, and an itemized specific approach, where a judge is given a checklist or rubric to use with specific elements to assess. Boyle and Radocy (1987, p. 185) suggested that magnitude estimation, although rare, may be used to assess musical performances when a global-type evaluation is needed by matching one sensory continuum to another; that is, matching stimuli to numbers. The more "musical" a performance is, the greater the number assigned, however they acknowledge that any measurement procedure that involves subjective judgments may be questioned. Conversely, the itemized specific approach lends itself to be more quantified with measurements such as Likert-type scales, semantic differentials, paired comparisons, successive intervals, and rank ordering, and it is these measures that researchers have used most often.

Holistic dimensions of applied studio teaching were initially measured and defined by Abeles, (1975), which opened a specific line of inquiry pursued by Gipson (1978) and Hepler (1986) about teacher and student behaviors. Gipson (1978) found that, in wind instrument lessons, musical behaviors were more frequently observed than verbal appraisal behaviors, and that teacher behaviors were more frequently observed than student behaviors. Hepler (1986) created an Observational System for Applied Music (OSAM) for piano, guitar, wind, and string teachers. Findings illustrated that verbal teacher behaviors and student performances were the most frequently observed. Kostka (1984) investigated the behaviors of piano studios and found that student performances and teacher talk were observed most frequently. While Benson and Fung (2005) found some differences in student–teacher behaviors between the United States and China, the findings of teacher verbal predominance reflect how the applied studio has been known to operate. These studies (e.g., Benson & Fung, 2005; Gipson, 1978; Helpler, 1986; Kostka, 1984) gave empirical evidence of teacher behaviors with evidence of reliability/ precision and validity with respect to teacher-directed instruction.

Researchers have illustrated that the assessments of musical performance in more formal, summative instances have almost exclusively been used for the purpose of research in jury or recital settings. They have used categories illustrating various specific dimensions of music performance such as pitch, rhythm, intonation, tone, and musicality/ expression. This research has been centered on musical instrument-specific assessments. Woodwinds (Ables, 1973; Bergee, 1989a), brass (Bergee, 1988, 1989b, 1993; Fiske, 1977), guitar (Horowitz, 1994; Russell, 2010), strings (Zdzinski & Barnes, 2002), percussion (Nichols, 1991), piano (Wapnick, Flowers, Alegant, & Jasinskas, 1993), and voice (Jones, 1986) have been investigated. Ciorba and Smith (2009) created an assessment rubric that reportedly assessed both vocal and instrumental performances and Smith (2009) crafted a rating scale for wind jazz improvisation performance. These specific measures are all reported to assess music performance with acceptable evidence of reliability/precision and validity.

Abeles (1973) reported six areas (interpretation, tone, rhythm/continuity, intonation, tempo, and articulation) with interjudge reliability at .90 in what was the first, and perhaps most comprehensive, instrument construction study in the area of music performance assessment when he developed the Clarinet Performance Rating Scale (CPRS). Bergee (1989a) used the Abeles CPRS to investigate interjudge reliability when the numbers of judges was reduced and found that the CPRS displayed acceptable reliability and ample evidence of criterion-related validity as an evaluative instrument for university single-reed juries. Bergee (1988, 1989b) also created a rating scale for brass juries and specifically one for euphonium and tuba. In his 1993 study, Bergee demonstrated that the overall Brass Performance Rating Scale (BPRS) had four main areas—interpretation/musical effect, tone quality/intonation, technique, and rhythm/tempo—using 27 items. When the BPRS was used by faculty and students in assessing recorded performances interjudge reliability was reported with alphas between .83 and .96.

The Vocal Performance Rating Scale (Jones, 1986) consists of 32 items that were grouped into five factors: suitability of the repertoire, technique, tone/musicianship, interpretation/musical effect, and diction. The interjudge reliability alpha was reported at .89 when used with high school vocal performances. When examining a scale for one specific musical instrument for example, the Snare Drum Rating Scale (Nichols, 1991), the assessment criteria seem to be similarly focused. Used with 43 judges to evaluate 129 recorded performances, the Snare Drum Rating Scale had 6 categories in 3 areas: technique/rhythm, interpretation, and tone quality. The interjudge reliability alpha was reported at .69, and tone quality seemed to be especially difficult for judges to discern ($\alpha = .47$). The assessment of jazz improvisation has been investigated by Smith (2009) for use at the university level. Smith created a Wind Jazz Improvisation Evaluation Scale (WJIES) and uncovered two factors: performance skills and creative development. With 63 judges, Smith calculated consistency with Cronbach's alpha ranging from .87 to .95. Smith obtained ample evidence of convergent validity and marginal evidence of criterion-related validity.

Russell (2010) developed an assessment tool specifically for guitar, the Guitar Performance Rating Scale (GPRS), which, like others, has five factors—interpretation/musical effect, tone, technique, rhythm/tempo, and intonation—with 32 items and an estimated alpha reliability of .96. Ciorba and Smith (2009) created their Multidimensional Rubric for brass, woodwinds, strings, voice, piano, guitar, and percussion, with only three areas: (1) musical elements, (2) command of instrument, and (3) presentation. They reported a considerably lower Cronbach's alpha, above .70, for each of the three areas when the instrument was used with 28 judges and 359 student jury performances. Bergee (2003) found stable reliability evidence when investigating the assessment of performance juries across various instrumental groups, so perhaps the Ciorba and Smith alpha does not generate cause for concern.

The research examining assessment of piano performances (Wapnick et al., 1993) illustrated consistency of scoring in 80 judges. They were asked to judge recordings of 21 piano performances with two performances of same piece. Some judges had musical scores and others had rating scales (1 = worse 7 = superb) and the scales focused on note accuracy, rhythmic control, tempo, phrasing, dynamics, tone quality, interpretation, and overall interpretation in the rating scale. Findings showed that neither the scores nor the rating scales improved the consistency with which the judges scored the recordings.

There are differences between the assessment instruments discussed here, as Zhukov (2015) notes, where the specific factors such as interpretation, articulation, tone, rhythm, tempo, and intonation are important for wind and brass assessments, however for piano, intonation is not considered. Rhythm is seen to be one of only three specific criteria (technique/rhythm, interpretation, tone quality) for the Nichols (1991) assessment. In the case of singing, the text and diction become important criteria, along with coordination with an accompanist (Jones, 1986). The specificity of the assessment tools no doubt contributes to the evidence of reliability/precision and validity.

In all of the previously discussed research studies, the key investigative focus has been scale construction and reliability/precision evidence, but not everyone agrees that music performance should be measured this way. Mills (1991) argued that music should not be assessed with such detailed criteria because "performance is more than a sum of skills and interpretation" (p. 175) and holistic assessment (assessment that focuses on the whole work rather than specific elements) is as reliable and valid as other forms of assessment. Swanwick (1999) also called for a holistic approach to evaluating performance with four areas: (1) materials (2) expression, (3) form, and (4) value, but the earlier tests of these four factors yielded inconsistent interjudge reliability evidence, between .60 and .94. Sadler (2015) gives us grounds to be wary about the criteria-specific approach, arguing that holistic appraisals leave a set of criteria open, so that a piece of musical work may be listened to as a whole (p. 14). He suggests that only once the holistic appraisals are made is it appropriate to examine individual elements or criteria. Beheshti (2009) suggests that the success of an applied studio teacher, a master teacher, "lies in the organization and application of information that is relayed to a student" (p. 108) and that the students' learning styles must be taking into account.

The extent to which the non-holistic criteria-specific assessment tools are consistent between judges, whether they are students or teachers, seems to be more than adequate, and the published findings and reliabilities should give applied studio faculty confidence in their use. It is assumed that applied studio teachers would use these in juries and end of semester recitals and exams, yet it is unclear to what extent these types of measures are actually used by applied studio teachers. L'Hommedieu (1992) reported, in his case study, that teachers determined grades for their students based primarily on jury performance but also considered progress and achievement over the term (p. 189), yet there was no description of criteria. L'Hommedieu summarized evaluation of student learning as "a straightforward process" (p. 197), as grades were assigned based on the jury. He also noted that most students "routinely received A" grades and that the ultimate summative evaluation was the degree recital, the final recital given at the end of the bachelor or graduate degree.

In asking applied studio teachers in the United States about their assessment procedures, Parkes (2010a) found that while applied teachers ($n = 246$) hold high levels of teaching efficacy, they reported low levels of efficacy with respect to assessment. These teachers also reported the following methods of assessing musical performance (1) jury performance, (2) recital performance, (3) attendance, (4) effort in lessons, and (5) overall progress, with the latter three (progress, effort, and attendance) being the most important.

The study was not completely clear in defining how juries and recitals were being assessed (holistically or with criteria-specific measures) but it was reported that only 25% of these teachers felt satisfied with the way they were assessing their students. Carefully crafted, extensively tested assessments, for which evidence of reliability/precision and validity has been established, are available but they are not being used by applied studio teachers. This fact gives us pause for a question: What measures or assessments are applied studio teachers and their colleagues using to determine musical growth and achievement in their students? In a follow-up study, Parkes (2015) uncovered other measures of student growth being used by music departments and schools (*n* = 412) in the United States as part of endeavors to rate the effectiveness of applied studio faculty. She found that over half of the music departments used direct measures such as standardized tests, pre- and post-tests, departmental examinations, grade distributions, informal measures, and other indirect types of measures, such as tracking of graduates, jury exam completion, graduation rates, performance awards, and competition and job placements as representations of student growth and progress. Parkes (2010b) had already made the observation that in applied studio settings there are instruments available to conduct reliable and valid performance assessments of musical performance. However, it still seems evident that music departments are continuing to use a variety of measures that simply meet professional, organizational, and institutional accountability requirements. There seems to be a reluctance to use criteria-specific rating scales for measuring music performance to give specific skill- and content-based feedback to students.

Self-Assessment

When teachers allow students to self-assess, there have been several reported benefits such as encouraging students to take more control of their own learning and prepare more realistically for their studies. Bergee and Cecconi-Roberts (2002) found that students can self-assess more accurately after initial peer-interaction however, self-evaluation did not correlate with the instructors' scores and moved closer to the peer-evaluation scores (which were higher) over time. Parkes (2010c) found that employing a weekly reflection after listening to a recording of the week's lesson promoted (1) positive perceptions about the rubric from both teacher and students, (2) an increase in student awareness and recognition of how improvements could be made after using the rubric to evaluate their own lesson performance, and (3) a clear understanding of what the applied studio teacher was requiring.

Daniel (2001) examined self-assessment issues in the applied studio specifically with learners. He shared the importance of skills in self-assessment and outlines two problems. One is the reliance of the student on the teacher and the second is the reliance of students on recordings rather than finding their own interpretations. Results reported that most students (*n* = 35) still relied on teacher comments but that they were mostly positive about the introduction of a new method of assessment, where students were asked to view a video of their performance and write a 300-word "self-critical reflection." Students addressed several issues, such as presentation, musical accuracies, style, overall impression, and progress, and were also asked what their plans for future direction might be. Daniel found that nearly half were fairly critical of themselves but that 80% felt the actual process of writing the reports increased their performance skills to some degree. Fifty-seven percent responded that it was highly valuable and a further 26% reported it was moderately valuable.

Peer Assessment

Peer assessment offers an alternative strategy to the students in the applied setting. Daniel (2004) studied students' perceptions about a process where structured peer assessments were used, ones that that did not impact on final summative assessments or grades. Each student completed four peer evaluations each week with criteria sheets, which included elements such as accuracy, dynamics, tone, technical control, fluency, stylistic interpretation, professionalism, and presentation. These criteria were agreed on by faculty and students, establishing content validity and usability for the tool. After one semester most students ($n = 34$) reported a preference for the detailed evaluation sheet, and similar results were found for the second semester. Students reported that their peers were not appropriately critical, indicating that the scores from peers were too high and, as such, the level of criticism reportedly became more accurate in the second semester. The open discussion process available after the performances seemed to be most valued by the students. Daniel (2006) found that technology, more specifically video analysis, was also a helpful tool in closing what he terms the "feedback loop" and in providing a form of assessment.

Daniel (2007) surveyed students ($n = 40$) to determine the nature of assessment comments provided by both faculty and peers, and to examine the differences of student comments between year levels and between faculty. He wanted to understand the students' perceptions in regard to validity and relevance of the assessments. The average number of comments increased as year level increased and first-year students gave mainly positive comments. Advice and direction was given to their peers, mainly from second- and third-year students. Faculty were more consistent with the content of their comments, distributing between positive, critical, and general advice. Faculty gave the performers almost double the amount of comments than the students, who gave half the amount of comments to their peers. Daniel reported that students still value the comments of faculty more than that of their peers, supporting the halo effect observed by Abeles, Goffi-Fynn, and Levasseur (1992). The senior students in Daniel's study (2007) were most accepting of critical evaluations from both peers and faculty.

Researchers have been establishing the factors present in music performance assessments in a growing body of literature and the reported reliability/precision evidence is generally strong (e.g., Abeles, 1973; Bergee, 1988, 1989b; Ciorba & Smith, 2009; Fiske, 1977; Jones, 1986; Latimer, Bergee, & Cohen, 2010; Nichols, 1991; Russell, 2010; Zdzinski &

Barnes, 2002). Parkes (2011) asked, "are these tools appropriate to be used widely? Should they be published and be made easily and publically available?" and suggests that music departments may certainly benefit if they were. She goes on to also address the unstandardized nature of higher education music programs, and by default, the varied expectations of teachers at a variety of institutions. Burwell (2016b) has made a similar comment in observing that the applied studio is largely unregulated. Parkes (2011) suggested that faculty need to work together to identify student learning outcomes and goals that are appropriate for their students, recognizing the need for institutions and departments to let go of long-held traditions and to embrace and assess a variety of student goals. There is a clear need to develop multiple measures, because no single scale or rubric will be appropriate. Perhaps faculty working collaboratively in departments (brass, string, voice, piano, percussion, woodwind, etc.) could agree on goals for students and measures could be created at baccalaureate and graduate levels, across a variety of formats. The prospect here is that performance-based measures could be developed, along with peer- and self-assessment protocols such as those tested by Daniel (2001, 2004, 2007). Gaunt (2016) reports that as part of a Transformative One-to-One grant, her project has initiated program leaders to introduce cross-departmental observations of assessment processes at the Guildhall School of Music and Dance. As part of a professional development opportunity, peers are observed in pairs in order to develop protocols used in assessing applied studio teaching, and this seems to be transforming their practices.

Suggestions for Moving Forward

Some faculty have reported to researchers that they feel the best, and sometimes only, way to evaluate applied teachers is through the success of their students (Abeles et al., 1992); but Zhukov (2015, pp. 67–68) makes the following recommendations for future directions in assessment with respect to the applied studio: (1) self-assessments of recorded performances and lessons, (2) peer assessments of solo and chamber performances, (3) short reports on aspects of technique, (4) reflective journals, (5) engaging students in developing assessment criteria, (6) using technology to develop recordings for self- and peer-assessments, and (7) assisting students to develop and maintaining entrepreneurial skills. She suggests that Australian higher education systems are moving away from rubric development for practical exams and toward some of the more progressive multiple measures. It seems that applied studio teachers feel pressure with respect to accountability, and that, as the "master," they should be directive of student learning at all times (Gaunt, 2016). This is not necessarily the case, so what remains absent from the evaluation of music performance in the applied studio setting for teachers? Perhaps an understanding in applied teachers that there is not only one method to be used in assessing student learning. An understanding that reliable measures of student skills might be used formatively with criteria in lessons (and in self-assessments) and again at the jury exam stage. A more holistic, authentic assessment model could be used at the time of the recital. An understanding that portfolios and reflective work completed by students may also reveal their cognitive understandings about their learning, music performance, musical context, and musical interpretation. These measures could be embraced by applied studio faculty, yet, as Abeles et al. (1992) pointed out, these also need to be included in the preparation of graduate music students who will move into higher education applied studio teaching positions. While there is evidence to suggest that applied teachers are learning effective tools to use in evaluating students' musical development and progress on the job (Attar, 2010; Pieffer, 2004) or as part of wider institutional requirements for data on student learning, perhaps there is room in graduate music programs to include some preparation and guidance. This guidance may serve to "nurture the development of applied teaching competencies" (Abeles et al., 1992) and to include the assessment of student growth, learning, skills, and achievements. Given that most higher education applied studio teachers are now evaluated on the quality of their teaching, it seems important that developed and successful applied studio teaching strategies, and assessments, be incorporated into the education of performers as they move into the field of applied studio teaching, as well as through professional development for applied studio teachers that remain in the applied studio setting.

ASSESSMENT OF APPLIED STUDIO TEACHING

Burwell (2016a) observes specifically "applied teaching is an unregulated profession compared with...larger areas of education that are characterized by formal teacher training" (p. 62). However countries in Europe, as well as Australia and the United States, have higher education systems pushing for student outcome data as we move further into the age of accountability and quality assurance. The Quality Indicators for Learning and Teaching (QILT) and Tertiary Education Quality and Standards Agency (TEQSA) in Australia, the Teaching Excellence Framework (TEF) in the United Kingdom, and the European Commission's Measuring and Comparing Achievements of Learning Outcomes in Higher Education in Europe (CALOHEE) project (offering multidimensional testing to achieve direct assessment of student learning outcomes), all serve to illustrate this new age in higher education. These frameworks and initiatives derive from a governmental need to illustrate the quality of teaching in higher education. This means that some institutions now replace authentic measures of applied teaching (observations of teaching in action, self-assessment, peer evaluation, etc.) with student learning outcome data (scores on standardized tests, common assessments, capstone assignments, or in some cases grades awarded through study). The American Educational Research Association (AERA, 2013) recommends that the focus of teaching evaluation should be on relevant student learning outcomes. The National Association for Schools of Music (NASM, 2009) in the United States also recommend that indictors of merit in regard to teaching need to be determined, usually by individual institutions. Teacher quality, teacher effectiveness, teacher characteristics, and a sense that students can have some agency in their own learning are all elements that impact what students will learn in the applied studio. A unique combination of these elements, based on the complex interactions over time between student and teacher, is what is most likely to result in student learning and skill improvement, rather than only one. In evaluating applied studio teachers in higher education, these elements are often overlooked.

For over 25 years the nature of evaluating faculty in higher education has remained static with two predominant features; (1) observations of teaching quality and (2) student perceptions of teaching (Kulik & McKeachie, 1975; Seldin, 1999). Observations are typically made in person by supervisors, colleagues, or by the teacher using a self-observation protocol with video. Student perceptions of teaching are typically given to large classes but can also be used in the evaluation of applied studio teachers. Parkes (2015) noted these teachers often give high grades to students in music performance lessons and there is a trend for high correlation between the grade a student receives and their level of satisfaction with their teacher (Rodin & Rodin, 1972). This calls into question the reasoning for using of students' perceptions of teaching. It has been disputed by Aleamoni (1987) who states the correlation studies provide mixed evidence at best but regardless of this observation, it can sometimes be the case that despite earning a good (even high) grade, and giving the teacher a good evaluation, the student did not learn a great deal and cannot illustrate the scope of their skills or their knowledge growth.

Several researchers have identified effective characteristics and behaviors used by teachers in the applied studio, as presented in the work of Sogin and Vallentine (1992) and L'Hommedieu (1992), as well as the processes involved in applied instruction. Albergo (1991) found applied piano teachers commonly agree on the desired qualities: patience, knowledge of music, humor, knowledge of teaching techniques, and enthusiasm. Sogin and Vallentine (1992) reported the types of activities found in applied lessons: (1) student performance, (2) modeling, (3) performance modeling, (4) teacher talk, and (5) student talk. They reported that student performance and teacher talk were the dominant activities. L'Hommedieu (1992) found that the majority of students studying with applied teachers did so because of the level of reputation of the teacher. Teacher caliber (quality) as a performer is tacitly assumed to be important, as a teacher characteristic, in the applied studio. Abeles et al. (1992) found evidence of the "halo" effect, whereby students generally evaluated their teachers consistently highly and may have been "unable to discriminate among the performing abilities of applied faculty" (Abeles et al., 1992, p. 21). L'Hommedieu (1992) reported that teachers spent foundational time (scales and etudes) along with deeper conceptual focus on musical aspects. He stated that the teachers in his study allowed students to choose their own repertoire (p. 195), which seemed to indicate that students have some level of autonomy in their learning.

Duke and Simmons (2006) identified 19 characteristic elements evident in the processes of artist-teachers within three broad areas: (1) goals and expectations, (2) effecting change, and (3) conveying information. Their rich descriptions illustrate the complexity and nuanced work of applied teaching artists who taught at highly selective institutions. Parkes and Wexler (2012) replicated the Duke and Simmons (2006) study at a slightly less selective music institution and found similarly occurring complex teaching, however they found additional teacher behaviors in each of the three categories. The additional teacher and student behavior process included student struggle, teachers accepting flaws in students' performances, shorter student performances, side-coaching from the teachers, teacher demonstration of correct fundamentals, gestural conveyance of information (beat), and teacher discussion/demonstration about practicing.

Abeles (1975) examined the students' perceptions characteristics of effective applied studio music instructors and created his Applied Faculty Student Evaluation Scale (AFSES) where five factors emerged: (1) rapport, (2), instructional systemization, (3) instructional skills, (4) musical knowledge, and (5) general instructional competence. Interjudge reliability was reported as .90, however, there was some disagreement between students and teachers as to what the criteria should be for good applied instruction (p. 153). Abeles et al. (1992) examined the development and use of instruments for evaluating applied music faculty and found that after factor-analysis, five factors were important to nonmusic major students: rapport, communication, pedagogical skill, instructional organization, and flexibility, with an alpha reliability coefficient reported at .89 for a 30-item scale. After factor analyzing the responses of music major students, they discovered four factors: rapport, instructional systemization, instructional skill, and musical knowledge, with an alpha reliability coefficient of .88 on a 30-item scale. These were thought to be effective qualities in applied music teachers as determined by music majors, however, the performance ability of the teacher was not a factor, and they cite the "halo" effect as a probable reason. Students in the applied studio are perhaps not able to reliably provide assessment of their teachers' levels of proficiency given this effect.

L'Hommedieu found that the teachers in his study had a remarkable effect on students and this is typically the most salient feature of the applied studio. In short, the master takes the novice learner and transforms them. The effect L'Hommedieu saw on student performance was perhaps due to the teacher's own musical technical and musical prowess, but in the case study, it was difficult to parse out data and draw definitive conclusions about what was the specific cause of such heightened student improvement. Zoanetti and Champion (2016) provide an alternative for mitigating the halo effect when training assessors to score, by using a meta-cognitive guidance protocol as part of the scoring process. Wesolowski, Wind, and Engelhard (2015) also conducted a study whereby the halo effect was specifically examined with differential rater functioning in the context of music performance. Although they used group music performances, analyzed with the Many-Facet Rasch Partial Credit Measurement Model, they demonstrated that some raters have systematic levels of severity or leniency in their scoring that were linked with at least one school level. In using this newer model to investigate rater behaviors they were able to focus on improving the fairness and equity of music performance assessments.

Siebenaler (1997) investigated teaching in the piano studio and found that more frequent teacher–student interaction contributed to teaching effectiveness. Kurkul (2007) examined nonverbal behaviors within the applied lesson and used the Music Lesson Evaluation Form (MLEF), by adjusting the Abeles et al. (1992) Applied Faculty Student Evaluation Scale for Non-music Majors (AFSESNM) to be reused in a single lesson.

Sixty university-level applied studio teachers and one student each were assessed with the MLEF and other measures for nonverbal behaviors. Internal reliability coefficients for composite evaluation scores were reported at .72 for teachers and .78 for students. None of the duration of teachers' nonverbal behaviors significantly correlated with estimations of teaching effectiveness. This study presents a potential area (nonverbal teaching behaviors) that should be reexamined in more detail with respect to establishing other criteria that are useful in determining teaching effectiveness.

The notion that students and teachers disagree about the criteria for effective applied teaching (Abeles, 1975) has not been satisfactorily resolved, and further research is needed. What are student expectations? What are effective teacher behaviors? How do students improve? What are the best ways to illustrate learning to administrators? The reliability of untrained and trained observers in the evaluation of applied music has been examined by Duke (1987) and Schmidt (1992), but in the majority of applied studios in higher education in the United States, teaching may be measured in a variety of ways that have little to do with the established characteristics as outlined within this chapter. Evaluating faculty in music departments is especially problematic because of the diversity between instructional techniques (Abeles, 1975, p. 147). Parkes (2015) reported the processes by which music faculty are evaluated. Her work showed that regular music faculty are evaluated primarily with student evaluations of teaching and instruction, with peer evaluations of teaching, and with self-evaluations of teaching. In the majority of cases examined, the reliability/precision and validity evidence in the student evaluation scores were examined with a variety of procedures conducted by institutional offices or accountability programs. These procedures included assessment, research, or evaluation with cross-checking, statistical methods, face validity checking with expert panels or committees, and national norming procedures. The types of measures used for observing instruction varied and those measures had not been examined for evidence of reliability/precision, or validity. Another finding (Parkes, 2015) illustrated that almost half of the respondents (52%) use the assessment of student progress as a measure of the teaching effectiveness of their faculty. Measures of student progress ranged from standardized tests, pre-post tests, departmental examination, grade distributions, informal measures, and other measures. The scope of the other measures was wide, including jury and recital performances, employment after graduation, admission to other graduate programs, tracking instructors' self-assessment of course objectives, and other reports given by teachers or administrators about the students' progress. The majority (93%) of those measures had not been examined for reliability/precision or validity evidence.

Parkes (2014) examined the ways in which applied studio music faculty ($n = 47$) are evaluated and noted that in some cases, music departments had made efforts to specifically design a tool for the evaluation of applied music faculty (p. 266). In most cases, these were developed by the Chair of the music department, the applied music faculty, or by department leadership teams. Only 19% reported examining reliability/precision or validity evidence with these tools. Student ratings were most often used (96% of cases), as well as peer evaluation (85%). The peer evaluations comprised evaluation forms; narrative reports based on observations, questionnaires, reference letters; and personal statements from peers. It was unclear what types of evaluation forms were used by peers in this instance. Applied teachers were afforded the option to self-evaluate in 85% of the schools studied and in these cases, teachers illustrated their teaching in videos, self-reflective narratives, student scores or measures of achievement, and other purported indicators of quality teaching such as syllabi, student learning objectives, student success, and the actions taken to improve pedagogy in response to student evaluations. Looking to measures of student achievement or success as an indicator of quality teaching for applied teachers, 62% of administrators in this study reported that they considered the following: standardized tests, pre-post tests, departmental examinations, grade distributions, informal indicators, and other types such as "tracking graduates of particular teachers, instructors' self-assessment of how well students met course objectives, lists of students' achievements, the levels to which students performed in ensembles, jury exams, graduate placements, and reports created by other head administrators" (Parkes, 2014, p. 269). The extent to which these measures counted toward teaching evaluation summaries was mixed, but there was a significant acknowledgment on the part of the participating administrators that evaluating applied studio music faculty should indeed be different—that the focus should be on the teaching of individuals, rather than groups.

Some administrators in the United States evaluate all music faculty (applied or otherwise) with the same assessment tools and criteria (Parkes, 2015, p. 123), and this leads us to question the generalized nature of the evaluation of applied studio teachers. Given the specificity and complexity of the applied studio, why would teaching evaluations used for groups, such as theoretical and history classes, be used? Administrators value teaching evaluations for the specific purpose of improving teaching effectiveness (Parkes, 2014, 2015), so it seems important for administrators to know and understand the specific behaviors that are known to be effective. Measures such as those described in this chapter are considered useful when used in a corroborative manner with peer evaluations/observations of teaching, student evaluations of teaching, *and* with student progress markers such as job placements. This may give applied studio teachers more specific information that would allow them to improve their teaching quality or effectiveness if it were found to be lacking across the three types of measures.

Abeles (1975) and Abeles et al. (1992) had available reliable/precise measures for which ample validity evidence had been obtained, yet as far as we can ascertain (Parkes, 2014, 2015), they are not widely used by institutions of higher education to evaluate the teaching of applied studio teachers. There is an obvious question here. Why not? Should we engage the views of Mills (1991), Sadler (2015), Beheshti (2009) and Swanwick (1999) more carefully in the midst of so many criteria-specific methods? What is missing from the evaluation of applied studio teachers' quality and effectiveness? The collaborative reflective model as explored by Gaunt (2013, 2016) reveals new and appealing methods of evaluating applied teaching in higher education, especially when employed as a professional development process. Kieg and Waggoner (1994) suggested that collaborative peer review would assist teachers in their professional growth, so perhaps it is not a matter of simply using observational forms but that teaching goals should be clarified and multiple assessment points should be used in evaluating applied studio teachers. The "variety among teachers approaches appears to be enormous" (Burwell, 2016a, p. 62), and as such we need to find more appropriate methods of assessing the culturally complex work undertaken in the applied studio.

Future Directions

In challenging the relentless push toward data for accreditation, it is time to look past an "either-or-approach" to assessment within the applied studio. It need not take a holistic *or* criteria-specific path, but perhaps it should use both approaches and include student self- and peer-assessment as well. The following are recommended strategies for assessment of applied teachers: self-assessment of video recorded lessons, peer assessment of video recorded lessons, reflective processes (meetings, discussions, journaling, blogging, video-logging or "vlogging") both with peers and individually, short summaries of aspects of pedagogical behaviors or interactions to focus on, and group/peer mentoring to engage in professional development in professional learning communities. This would assist current applied studio teachers with developing their teaching skills and improving as professional teachers.

It seems clear that more needs to be done in the preparation of new applied studio teachers. Abeles (2011) supports the notion that applied studio teaching experiences should be designed to be at least partially based on empirical studies (p. 26) and he suggests that a course, or series of courses, could be considered that would better help prepare new studio teachers; this could include readings about teaching and with perhaps video recordings for them to self-reflect about their teaching or to elicit peer feedback. We can acknowledge, at least in the United States, that universities are becoming more concerned with supporting new faculty members (Abeles, 2011) but the education, mentoring, and professional development that new higher education applied studio faculty receive is still overlooked. Attention needs to be given to developing ways to assist new (and current) applied studio teachers in engaging with authentic professional development, where they can connect within professional learning communities and discuss the craft of teaching in the applied studio with peers regularly.

This chapter has highlighted many of the existing research regarding measures for both student learning and applied studio teachers. At a meeting of applied studio researchers held in Brisbane Australia, 2016 (see http://www.transformative121.com/symposium), several issues emerged as being important to transforming teaching and learning in the applied studio. Ideally, the nexus of research and practice should be improved so that scholarship can underpin and inform one-to-one teaching and learning. The attending researchers provided meaningful methods whereby researchers and applied studio teachers opened up the issues surrounding the applied studio (Gaunt, 2016), investigated the practice of students (Jorgensen, 2016) and focused on new inter-institutional research studies (Carey, 2016) that serve to transform one-to-one learning and teaching in tertiary institutions with the use of reflective practices. These researchers noted that access into applied studio teaching settings continues to be difficult but that reflective processes undertaken by applied studio teachers seems to be helpful in developing, improving, and evaluating pedagogical strategies when offered to applied studio faculty as an option to consider, rather than a mandate toward accreditation. Burwell (2016b) explained that applied studio teachers held a healthy skepticism toward research until they were invited for biannual professional development days. During the provided professional development sessions, applied studio teachers were exposed to research ideas with more approachable dissemination tactics (concepts rather than entire empirical journal articles) and they were offered time together to discuss the ideas and develop their pedagogies through reflection and explanation. Gaunt (2016) explained that program leaders at the Guildhall School of Music and Dance wanted to avoid merely "judging teaching" but instead moved toward a model that asks questions and seeks understanding via reflective practice. Teachers were engaged in developing assessment criteria across discipline areas so that they would be able to express shared values and have clarity. They focused on learning outcomes, assessment tasks, and the assessment criteria, which enabled program leaders to observe assessment procedures and ask questions such as "What am I seeing?" or "What am I learning?" and these included all types of assessments being used (portfolios, recitals, juries, etc.) Carey (2016, May) shared that reflective practices are useful to students along with applied studio faculty and that workshops can act as a platform for collaborative and reflective activities. Prompts were carefully designed to encourage conversations between students and teachers about learning goals. Both applied studio teachers and students needed support with reflective skills; however, it seemed to reduce the sense of isolation in applied studio teachers, along with empowering individuals to scrutinize and question their own practices. This ultimately engaged applied studio teachers in their own development, especially after the feedback in student journals provided valuable information about learning from the student perspective.

Reflective practice experiences for applied studio teachers requires a commitment and support from institutions, along with time for shared spaces, for teachers to come together rather than be isolated in their studios. While the accountability era is most likely here to stay, it seems that researchers can view accreditation as an opportunity to grow and develop, through the sharing of teaching and learning practices. Making professional development opportunities available to applied studio teachers is viewed as essential, and the first step should be conversational rather than mandatory. Professional development for applied studio teachers was described at the 2016 Symposium as a "basic right" (Gaunt), which allows applied studio teachers to develop and grow as practitioners. Professional development seems to be an appropriate step forward in developing both assessment of student learning and of applied studio teaching. Research investigating the professional development of applied studio teachers must move in this direction also, and completed research must be made available to applied studio teachers, in their settings and with appropriate practitioner vocabulary alongside academic journal publications. The responsibility of making this research accessible to applied studio teachers will need to be embraced by researchers in this setting.

CONCLUSION

In each section of this chapter, several models of assessment have been reviewed. The methods by which music performance is assessed in the applied studio are both quantitative and qualitative in nature, with both criteria specific/analytic measures and also more holistic methods being used. There are many criteria-specific assessments that show evidence of reliability/precision and validity; however, we are not sure the extent to which they are used by applied studio teachers, or even to what degree they might be useful for giving feedback to students about their performances. The assessment of applied studio teaching quality and effectiveness seems to be driven currently by a quality assurance model, at least in the United Kingdom, Australia, and the United States. Applied studio teachers are assessed with a variety of methods that may, or may not, accurately illustrate the quality, or separately, the effectiveness of their teaching. For the benefit of the higher education sector, research in this area must still continue; researchers should focus on the ways in which both assessment of student learning and of applied teaching informs (and actually assists) both the learner and teacher, particularly with the use of reflective practices with a view to professional development, rather than simply using data for accountability purposes. Research must also focus on the preparation of applied studio teachers, to determine whether future applied studio teachers are ready to assess student learning in meaningful ways and that they are able to advocate and engage in authentic assessments and development of their own teaching. There is promise in reflective practice and in the professional development strategies suggested in this chapter for applied studio teachers. New research also needs to be made available and accessible to the administrators of, and teachers within, the applied music studio. The summary of the research and observations made in this chapter may be of benefit to studio teachers, and their administrators, in the preparation and professional development of applied studio teachers.

REFERENCES

Abeles, H. F. (1973). Development and validation of a clarinet performance adjudication rating scale. *Journal of Research in Music Education, 21*, 246–255.

Abeles, H. F. (1975). Student perceptions of characteristics of effective applied music instructors. *Journal of Research in Music Education, 23*, 147–154.

Abeles, H. F. (2010). Assessing music learning. In H. F. Abeles & L. A. Custodero (Eds.), *Critical issues in music education: Contemporary theory and practice* (pp. 167–193). New York, NY: Oxford University Press.

Abeles, H. F. (2011). Designing effective music studio instruction. In P. M. Ward-Steinman (Ed.), *Advances in social-psychology and music education research* (pp. 19–28). Burlington, VT: Ashgate.

Abeles, H., Goffi, J., & Levasseur, S. (1992). The components of effective applied instruction. *Quarterly Journal of Music Teaching and Learning, 3*(2), 17–23. Published by University of

Northern Colorado, School of Music. Retrieved from https://openmusiclibrary.org/journal/music-teaching-and-learning/

American Education Research Association (AERA). (2013). *Rethinking faculty evaluation: AERA report and recommendations on evaluating education research, scholarship, and teaching in postsecondary education.* Retrieved from http://www.aera.net/Portals/38/docs/Education_Research_and_Research_Policy/RethinkingFacultyEval_R4.pdf

Albergo, C. (1991). How would you describe a good piano teacher? *Keyboard Companion,* (Winter), 4–6. Retrieved from https://www.claviercompanion.com/clavier-companion-articles/keyboard-companion-issues

Aleamoni, L. M. (1987). Student rating myths versus research facts. *Journal of Personnel Evaluation in Education, 1,* 111–119.

Attar, H. L. (2010). *A handbook for collegiate studio teaching: Applying the seven principles for good practice in undergraduate education to music-centered instruction.* DAI-A 71/10, p. 100. (Unpublished doctoral dissertation). University of Cincinnati, Cincinnati, OH.

Beheshti, S. (2009). Improving student music teaching through understanding learning styles. *International Journal of Music Education, 27,* 107–115.

Benson, C., & Fung, C. F. (2005). Comparison of teacher and student behaviors in private piano lessons in China and the United states. *International Journal of Music Education, 23*(1), 63–72, doi: 10.1177/0255761405050931

Bergee, M. J. (1988). The use of an objectively constructed rating scale for the evaluation of brass juries: A criterion related study. *Missouri Journal of Research in Music Education, 5*(5), 6–25.

Bergee, M. J. (1989a). An investigation of the efficacy of using an objectively constructed rating scale for the evaluation of university-level single reed juries. *Missouri Journal of Research in Music Education, 26,* 74–91.

Bergee, M. J. (1989b). An objectively constructed rating scale for euphonium and tuba music performance. *Dialogue in Instrumental Music Education, 13,* 65–86.

Bergee, M. J. (1993). A comparison of faculty, peer, and self-evaluations of applied brass jury performances. *Journal of Research in Music Education, 41,* 19–27.

Bergee, M. J. (2003). Faculty interjudge reliability of music performance evaluation. *Journal of Research in Music Education, 51,* 137–149.

Bergee, M. J., & Cecconi-Roberts, L. (2002). Effects of small-group peer interaction on self-evaluation of music performance. *Journal of Research in Music Education, 50,* 256–268.

Boyle, J. D., & Radocy, R. E. (1987). Measuring musical performance. In *Measurement and evaluation of musical experiences* (pp. 171–194). New York, NY: Schirmer.

Brand, M. (1992). Voodoo and the applied music studio. *Quarterly Journal of Music Teaching and Learning, 3*(2), 3–4.

Burwell, K. (2012). Apprenticeship in music: A contextual study for instrumental teaching and learning. *International Journal of Music Education, 31,* 276–291.

Burwell, K. (2015). Dissonance in the studio: An exploration of tensions within the apprenticeship setting in higher education music. *International Journal of Music Education, 34,* 499–512. doi: 10.1177/0255761415574124.

Burwell, K. (2016a). *SEMPRE studies in the psychology of music: Studio-based instrumental learning.* Abingdon, UK: Routledge. Retrieved from ProQuest ebrary.

Burwell, K. (2016b, May). *Transforming one-to-one OLT project: What has been learned?* Research paper presented at the Transformative one-to-one Symposium, Brisbane, Australia.

Carey, G. (2016, May). *Transforming one-to-one OLT project: What has been learned?* Paper presented at the Transformative One-to-one Symposium, Brisbane, Australia.

Carey, G., & Grant, C. (2015). Teacher and student perspectives on one-to-one pedagogy: Practices and possibilities. *British Journal of Music Education, 32*(1), 5–22.

Carey, G., & Grant, C. (2014). Teachers of instruments, or teachers as instruments? From transfer to transformative approaches to one-to-one pedagogy. In G. Carruthers (Ed.), *Relevance and reform in the education of professional musicians, Proceedings of the 20th International Seminar of the ISME Commission on the Education of the Professional Musician.* Australia: International Society for Music Education. Retrieved from https://www.isme. org/sites/default/files/documents/proceedings/2014-CEPROM-Proceedings.pdf

Carey, G., Grant, C., McWilliam, & Tayor, P. (2013). One-to-one pedagogy: Developing a protocol for illuminating the nature of teaching in the conservatoire. *International Journal of Music Education, 31,* 148–159.

Christopherson, C. (2013). Perspectives on the dynamics of power within collaborative learning in higher music education. In H. Gaunt, & H. Westerlund (Eds.) *Collaborative learning in higher music education: Why, what and how?* (pp. 77–85). Surrey, UK: Ashgate.

Ciorba, C. R., & Smith, N. Y. (2009). Measurement of instrumental and vocal undergraduate performance juries using a multidimensional assessment rubric. *Journal of Research in Music Education, 57,* 5–15.

Daniel, R. (2001). Self-assessment in performance. *British Journal of Music Education, 18,* 215–226.

Daniel, R. (2004). Peer assessment in music performance: The development, trial and evaluation of a methodology for the Australian tertiary environment. *British Journal of Music Education, 21*(1), 89–110.

Daniel, R. (2006). Exploring music instrument teaching and learning environments: Video analysis as a means of elucidating process and learning outcomes. *Music Education Research, 8,* 161–215.

Daniel, R. J. (2007). *Closing the feedback loop: An investigation and analysis of student evaluations of peer and staff assessments in music performance.* In the Proceedings of the XXIXth Annual Conference. Music Education Research, Values and Initiatives, pp. 28–31. Retrieved from https://researchonline.jcu.edu.au/3036/

Daniel, R. (2008). *Group piano teaching.* Saarbrucken, Germany: VDM Verlag.

Daniel, R., & Parkes, K. A. (2015). The apprentice to master journey: Exploring tertiary music instrument teachers' reflections on their experiences as learner. *Journal of Arts and Humanities, 4*(3), 52–63.

Donald, E. (2012). Music performance students as future studio teachers: Are they prepared to teach? In J. Weller (Ed), *Educating professional musicians in a global context: Proceedings of the 19th international seminar of the commission for the education of the professional musician (CEPROM).* Australia: Published by the International Society for Music Education. Retrieved from https://www.isme.org/sites/default/files/documents/proceedings/2012%2 BCEPROM%2BProceedings.pdf

Doyle, T. (2008). *Helping students learn in a learner-centered environment: A guide to facilitating learning in higher education.* Sterling, VA: Stylus Publishing.

Duke, R. A. (1999/2000). Measures of instructional effectiveness in music research. *Bulletin of the Council of Research in Music Education, 143,* 1–48.

Duke, R. A. (1987). Observation of applied music instruction: The perceptions of trained and untrained observers. In C. K. Madsen & C. A. Prickett (Eds.), *Applications of research in music education* (pp. 115–124). Tuscaloosa: University of Alabama Press.

Duke, R. A., & Simmons, A. L. (2006). The nature of expertise: Narrative descriptions of 19 common elements observed in the lessons of three renowned artist-teachers. *Bulletin of the Council of Research in Music Education, 170,* 7–19.

Ester, A., Batchelor, D., & Lopinski, J. (2014). Building private music education: The journey continues and the year ahead in your studio: A teacher's guide to planning for success. *Journal of Singing, 70*, 465–469.

Fiske, H. E. (1977). Relationship of selected factors in trumpet performance adjudication reliability. *Journal of Research in Music Education, 25*, 256–263.

Fredrickson, W. (2007). Perceptions of college-level music performance majors teaching applied lessons to young students. *International Journal of Music Education, 25*(1), 71–80.

Gaunt, H. (2016, May). *Transforming one-to-one OLT project: What has been learned?* Research paper presented at the Transformative one-to-one Symposium, Brisbane, Australia.

Gaunt, H. (2009). One-to-one tuition in a conservatoire: The perceptions of instrumental and vocal students. *Psychology of Music, 38*, 178–208.

Gaunt, H. (2008). One-to-one tuition in a conservatoire: The perceptions of instrumental and vocal teachers. *Psychology of Music, 36*, 215–245.

Gaunt, H. (2011). Understanding the one to one relationship in instrumental/vocal tuition in higher education: Comparing student and teacher perceptions. *British Journal of Music Education, 28*, 159–179.

Gaunt, H. (2013). Promoting professional and paradigm reflection amongst conservatoire teachers in an international community. In H. Gaunt & H. Westerlund (Eds.), *Collaborative learning in higher music education: Why, what and how?* (pp. 49–62). Surrey, UK: Ashgate.

Gaunt, H., & Westerlund, H. (Eds.). (2013). *Collaborative learning in higher music education: Why, what and how?* Surrey, UK: Ashgate.

Georgii-Hemming, E., & Westvall, M. (2010). Teaching music in our time: Student music teachers' reflections on music education, teacher education and becoming a teacher. *Music Education Research, 12*, 353–367.

Gipson, R. C. (1978). *An observational analysis of wind instrument private lessons.* DAI- A 34/4 (p 2118). (Unpublished doctoral dissertation). Pennsylvania State University, State College, PA.

Haddon, E. (2009). Instrumental and vocal teaching: How do music students learn to teach? *British Journal of Music Education, 26*, 57–70.

Hepler, L. E. (1986). *The measurement of teacher/student interaction in private music lessons, and its relation to teacher field dependence/field independence* (Doctoral Dissertation). Retrieved from ProQuest Dissertations & Theses Global. (303478831)

Horowitz, R. A. (1994). *The development of a rating scale for jazz guitar improvisation performance.* (Doctoral dissertation). Retrieved from ProQuest Dissertations & Theses Global. (304102194)

Ilomäki, L. (2013). Learning from one another's musicianship: Exploring the potential for collaborative development of aural skills with pianists. In H. Gaunt & H. Westerlund (Eds.), *Collaborative learning in higher music education: Why, what, and how?* (pp. 123–133). Surrey, UK: Ashgate.

Jones, H. (1986). *An application of the facet-factorial approach to scale construction in the development of a rating scale for high school solo vocal performance.* (Doctoral dissertation). Retrieved from ProQuest Dissertations & Theses Global. (303512065)

Jørgensen, H. (2016). *Scholarship in one-to-one teaching: Case studies investigating teaching students to practice.* Research paper presented at the Transformative one-to-one symposium, Brisbane, Australia.

Kennell, R. (1992). Toward a theory of applied instruction. *Quarterly Journal of Music Teaching and Learning, 3*(2), 5–16.

Kennell, R. (2002). Systematic research in studio instruction in music. In R. Colwell & C. Richardson (Eds.), *The new handbook of research on music teaching and learning* (pp. 243–56). New York, NY: Oxford University Press.

Kieg, L. W., & Waggoner, M. D. (1994). *Collaborative peer review: The role of faculty in improving college teaching.* (ASHE/ERIC Higher Education Report, No. 2). Washington, DC: Association for the Study of Higher Education.

King, A. (2008). Collaborative learning in the music studio. *Music Education Research, 10,* 423–438. doi: 10.1080/14613800802280167

Kostka, M. (1984). An investigation of reinforcements, time use, and student attentiveness in piano lessons. *Journal of Research in Music Education, 32,* 113–122.

Kulik, J. A., & McKeachie, W. J. (1975). The evaluation of teachers in higher education. *Review of Research in Education, 3,* 210–40.

Kurkul, W. W. (2007). Non-verbal communication on one-to-one music performance instruction. *Psychology of Music, 35,* 327–362.

Latimer, M. E. J., Bergee, M. J., & Cohen, M. L. (2010). Reliability and perceived pedagogical utility of a weighted music performance assessment rubric. *Journal of Research in Music Education, 58,* 168–183.

Latukefu, L., & Verenikina, I. (2013). Expanding the master-apprentice model: Tool for orchestrating collaboration as a path to self-directed learning for singing students. In H. Gaunt & H. Westerlund (Eds.), *Collaborative learning in higher music education: Why, what, and how?* (pp. 101–109). Surrey, UK: Ashgate.

Lebler, D. Carey, G., & Harrison, S. (Eds.). (2015). *Assessment in music education: From policy to practice.* Switzerland: Springer International.

Lennon, M., & Reed, G. (2012). Instrumental and vocal teacher education: Competences, roles and curricula. *Music Education Research, 14,* 285–308.

L'Hommedieu, R. L. (1992). *The management of selected educational process variables by master studio teachers in music performance.* (Doctoral dissertation). Retrieved from ProQuest Dissertations & Theses Global. (304012404)

Long, M., Creech, A., Gaunt, H., Hallam, S., & Robertson, L. (2012). Blast from the past: Conservatoire students' experiences and perceptions of public master classes. *Musicae Scientiae, 16,* 286–306.

Luff, P., & Lebler, D. (2013). Striking a balance brass pedagogy: Collaborative learning complementing one-to-one tuition in the conservatoire curriculum. In H. Gaunt & H. Westerlund (Eds.), *Collaborative learning in higher music education: Why, what, and how?* (pp. 173–177). Surrey, UK: Ashgate.

McPhail, G. J. (2010). Crossing boundaries: Sharing concepts of music teaching from classroom to studio. *Music Education Research, 12*(1), 33–45.

Mills, J. (1991). Assessing music performance musically. *Educational Studies, 17,* 173–181.

Mills, J. (2002). Conservatoire students' perceptions of the characteristics of effective instrumental and vocal tuition. *Bulletin of the Council of Research in Music Education, 153*(4), 78–82.

Mills, J. (2007). *Instrumental teaching.* Oxford, UK: Oxford University Press.

Mills, J., & Smith, J. (2003). Teachers' beliefs about effective instrumental teaching in schools and higher education. *British Journal of Music Education, 20*(1), 5–27.

National Association of Schools of Music (NASM). (2009). *Local assessment of evaluation and rewards systems for arts faculties in higher education.* Retrieved from http://nasm.arts-accredit.org

Nerland, M. (2007). One-to-one teaching as cultural practice: Two case studies from an academy of music. *Music Education Research, 9,* 400–416.

Nichols, J. P. (1991). A factor analysis approach to the development of a rating scale for snare performance. *Dialogue in Instrumental Music Education, 15,* 11–31.

Parkes, K. A. (2009). Recent research in applied studio instruction. *Musical Perspectives' Journal of Research in Music Performance, 1*(1). Retrieved from http://ejournals.lib.vt.edu/JRMP/issue/view/27

Parkes, K. A. (2010a). Measuring sense of efficacy in higher-education applied-music-performance teachers. *Research Perspectives in Music Education, 14,* 21–32.

Parkes, K. A. (2010b). Performance assessment: Lessons from performers. *International Journal of Teaching and Learning in Higher Education, 22*(1), 98–106. Retrieved from http://www.isetl.org/ijtlhe/past2.cfm?v=22&i=1

Parkes, K. A. (2010c). The use of criteria-specific performance rubrics for student self-assessment: A case study. In T. Brophy (Ed.), *The practice of assessment in music education: Frameworks, models, and designs* (pp. 455–460). Chicago, IL: GIA Publications.

Parkes, K. A. (2010d). Recent research in applied studio instruction II—Practice time and strategies. *Musical Perspectives' Journal of Research in Music Performance, 1*(2). Retrieved from http://ejournals.lib.vt.edu/JRMP/issue/view/26. doi: 10.21061/jrmp.v0i0.730

Parkes, K. A. (2011). Recent research in applied studio instruction III—Assessment and evaluation. *Musical Perspectives' Journal of Research in Music Performance, 1*(3). Retrieved from http://ejournals.lib.vt.edu/JRMP/issue/view/28. doi: 10.21061/jrmp.v0i0.729

Parkes, K. A. (2014). Teacher evaluation of applied music performance faculty in music institutions of higher education: Is it related to music student progress? In T. Brophy (Ed.), *Music assessment, and global diversity: Practice, measurement and policy* (pp. 263–277). Chicago, IL: GIA Publications.

Parkes, K. A. (2015). The evaluation of music faculty in higher education: Current practices. *International Journal of Teaching and Learning in Higher Education, 27*(1), 119–129.

Parkes, K. A., & Wexler, M. (2012). The nature of applied music teaching experience: Common elements observed in the lessons of three applied teachers. *Bulletin of the Council for Research in Music Education, 193,* 45–62.

Pieffer, P. (2004). Forum focus: Independent music teachers, studio teacher assessment tools. *American Music Teacher, 54*(1), 88.

Presland, C. (2005). Conservatoire student and instrumental professor: The student perspective on a complex relationship. *British Journal of Music Education, 22,* 237–248.

Rakena, T. O., Airini, & Brown, D. (2015). Success for all: Eroding the culture of power in the one-to-one teaching and learning context. *International Journal of Music Education, 34*(3), 286–298. doi: 10.1177/0255761415590365

Rodin, M., & Rodin, B. (1972). Student evaluations of teachers. *Science, 177,* 1164–1166.

Rosenthal, R. K. (1984). The relative effects of guided model, model only, guide only, and practice only treatments on the accuracy of advanced instrumentalists' musical performance, *Journal of Research in Music Education, 32,* 265–73.

Russell, B. E. (2010). The development of a guitar performance rating scale using a facet-factorial approach. *Bulletin of the Council of Research in Music Education, 184,* 21–34.

Sadler, D. R. (2015). Backwards assessment explanations: Implication for teaching and assessment practice. In D. Lebler, G. Carey, & S. Harrison (Eds.), *Assessment in music education: From policy to practice* (pp. 9–19). Switzerland: Springer International.

Schmidt, C. P. (1992). Systematic research in applied music instruction: Review of the literature. *Quarterly Journal of Music Teaching and Teaching, 3*(2), 32–45.

Seldin, P. (1999). Current practices-good and bad-nationally. In P. Seldin & Associates (Eds.), *Changing practices in evaluating teaching: A practical guide to improved faculty performance and promotion/tenure decisions* (pp. 1–24). Bolton, MA: Anker.

Siebenaler, D. J. (1997). Analysis of teacher–student interactions in the piano lessons of adults and children. *Journal of Research in Music Education, 45*, 6–20.

Slawsky, M. (2011). *Transitioning from student to teacher in the master-apprentice model of piano pedagogy: An exploratory study of challenges, solutions, resources, reflections, and suggestions for the future* (Unpublished doctoral dissertation). University of South Florida, Tampa, FL.

Smith, D. T. (2009). Development and validation of a rating scale for wind jazz improvisation performance. *Journal of Research in Music Education, 57*, 217–235.

Sogin, D. W., & Vallentine, J. F. (1992). Use of instructional time and repertoire diversity in applied music lessons. *Quarterly Journal of Music Teaching and Learning, 3*(4), 32–42.

Swanwick, K. (1999). *Teaching music musically*. London, UK: Routledge.

Wapnick, J., Flowers, P., Alegant, M., & Jasinskas, L. (1993). Consistency in piano performance evaluation. *Journal of Research in Music Education, 41*, 282–292.

Weimer, M. (2002). *Learner-centered teaching: Five key changes to practice*. San Francisco, CA: Jossey-Bass.

Wesolowski, B., Wind, S. A., & Engelhard, G. (2015). Rater fairness in music performance assessment: Evaluating model-data fit and differential rater functioning. *Musicae Scientiae, 19*, 147–170.

Westerlund, H. (2006). Garage rock bands: A future model for developing musical expertise? *International Journal of Music Education, 24*, 119–125.

Wöllner, C., & Ginsborg, J. (2011). Team teaching in the conservatoire: The views of music performance staff and students. *British Journal of Music Education, 28*, 301–323.

Zdzinski, S. F., & Barnes, G. V. (2002). Development and validation of a string performance Rating scale. *Journal of Research in Music Education, 50*, 245–255.

Zhukov, K. (2012). Teaching strategies and gender in higher education instrumental studios. *International Journal of Music Education, 30*(1), 32–45.

Zhukov, K. (2015). Issues in assessing music performance in higher education. In D. Lebler, G. Carey, & S. Harrison (Eds.), *Assessment in music education: From policy to practice* (pp. 55–70). Cham, Switzerland: Springer International.

Zoanetti, N., & Champion, H. (2016). Mitigating the halo effect: Managing the wow factor in music performance assessment. *Journal of Research in Music Performance*, (Spring), 1–17. doi: 10.21061/jrmp.v0i0.738

PART IV

MUSIC TEACHER EVALUATION

CHAPTER 34

....

MUSIC TEACHER EVALUATION

An Overview

....

DOUGLAS C. ORZOLEK

INTRODUCTION

....

IN 1992, Donald K. Taebel wrote, "teacher evaluation is a hazardous and complex undertaking, perhaps because the concepts of teaching and evaluation are multifaceted and complex" (p. 310). Today, few educators, principals, supervisors, and policymakers would disagree. Those who have deeply considered the topic and searched for ideas and answers, have found that even navigating through the research, opinions, and models related to systematic evaluation of educators is arduous. Braun (2015) describes the complexity of studying the subject in this manner: "A proverbial ocean of ink has been spilled on the subject of accountability for schools and educators" (p. 127).

It will come as no surprise to readers that this overview of music teacher evaluation suffers from that same level of complication. In recent years, there has been plenty written and shared on the nature of accountability and teacher evaluation in today's educational system, and there is certainly an abundance of emergent themes by which stakeholders might develop their own conceptions of teacher evaluation. The listing of themes include ideas related to the following: the intent of teacher evaluation; the role of teacher evaluation; what an effective teacher is; the importance of multifaceted evaluation systems; the place of student learning in the evaluative process; the various forms of evidence used to evaluate educators; the fact that research and practice should be intertwined in developing evaluation systems; the role of testing; the degree to which observation and self-reflection should be involved in teacher evaluation; the importance of clear and concise goals for learners; and the impact that systems of evaluation will have on the educators, schools, students, and American education as a whole.

Many of these themes are considered in further detail throughout this chapter, but it is worth noting that the research and supportive materials for all of these themes is not only wide and varied but can also be quite contradictory. In fact, even the question of the amount of research literature on teacher evaluation is convoluted. While some suggest that there is an enormous amount of literature on evaluating teachers (Levin, 1979), others argue that the amount is limited (Marzano & Toth, 2013; Robinson, 2015). Some writers suggest, "the entire field of teacher evaluation has suffered from a surplus of opinion and a shortage of evidence" and the existing "research provides little support for current practices in teacher evaluation" (Braun, 2015, p. 244). Levin (1979) even opines, "most of the literature on evaluation in schools is not based on empirical research. It is parochial at best" (p. 249).

While it is quite likely that every single educator, administrator, parent, student, policymaker, and citizen in the United States of America is keenly aware of the challenges and complication of teacher evaluation in our schools and the need to examine and consider these ideas in an appropriate way (Darling-Hammond, 2013), it is also important to state that all of these stakeholders hold strong opinions about education, teacher effectiveness, and the evaluation of educators. The author of this chapter is no different and readily admits that some biases and beliefs will be shared, albeit in a muted tone—especially as they pertain to the evaluation of music educators. One bias, however, should be clearly stated here, as it forms the basis of this chapter. Regardless of the inherent complications related to the assessment of music learning and the evaluation of music educators, I believe that our profession has an obligation to overcome all of the challenges described and presented throughout this paper. As Tait and Haack (1984) explained, "Because music functions among other ways as an art form, we might attempt to excuse ourselves from evaluation with the rationale that ;artistic intangibles' cannot be evaluated. But even if that were true for music, it would not be true of music education and its effects" (p. 148).

THE AGE OF ACCOUNTABILITY AND THE MUSIC EDUCATOR

Accountability is and will remain as the most significant issue facing the field of education for many years to come. The call for answers as to what is happening in schools, how American students stack against their peers around the world, and why certain schools and students do not seem to be doing well in our existing systems is certainly ongoing and omnipresent. With those calls has come additional scrutiny on those who are perceived to be the most important factor in the growth and achievement of students. As a result, perhaps no area of policy and public concern has seen more transformation and discussion in the last few decades than the area of teacher evaluation (Doherty & Jacobs, 2015).

Context, Policy, and Politics

While discussion about teacher evaluation has been vibrant over the past decade, nothing seems to have been resolved or settled. As Darling-Hammond (2013) notes, "Virtually everyone agrees that teacher evaluation in the United States needs an overhaul. . . . evaluation in its current form often contributes little either to teacher learning or to accurate, timely information for personnel decisions" (p. 1).

Education's arrival at this point may be due in part to previously existing systems of evaluation in which 99% of teachers were rated as being satisfactory even though student achievement was not improving (Doherty & Jacobs, 2015). Further, many evaluation systems relied too heavily on peer or supervisor observations of classroom work—a system in which even supervisors and teachers recognized that there were teachers who should be dismissed even though they were rated highly (Overland, 2014). It appears, however, out of all of this discussion has come an arrival at a point "where teacher evaluations were meaningless bureaucratic exercises to the point where teacher evaluations have become tools with great potential for improving teaching and where student learning is understood to be a critical indicator of teacher effectiveness" (Doherty & Jacobs, 2015, p. 2).

Teacher evaluation has indeed become "serious business" in schools and school systems (Grissom & Youngs, 2016) due to policies traced directly to state and federal funding dedicated to education. As our society has placed more emphasis on learning and provided support for a "free" education for every student, taxpayers and policymakers have increased its demands and expectations for exceptional results (Colwell, 1970). And, since salaries for educators are the largest piece of the education budget, it is not surprising that the development of accountability measures aimed at teachers would constitute much of the policy initiatives related to schools. While everyone—including the educators—understands the need for policies, the changes have occurred quite quickly, often without any educators engaged in the development process. In addition, the "policies have occurred at a dizzying pace, outstripping researchers' ability to study the validity and fairness of the systems themselves and the individual components of the systems" (Goe & Holdheide, 2011, p. 21).

And therein lies the biggest concern about the teacher evaluation policy movement. Most, if not all, of these policies mandate the development of evaluation systems that intend to provide stakeholders with data or information that allows decisions to be made about the relative effectiveness of educators. And, as states and districts develop these policies, "teachers, administrators, researchers and policymakers are raising important questions about the measures these systems rely on, what uses of those measures are appropriate or inappropriate, and how new teacher evaluation systems are—and are not—changing teacher practice, school leaders' decision making, and the culture of schools" (Grissom & Youngs, 2016, pp. 1–2). Frankly, if the recent efforts in the field of teacher evaluation have proven anything, it would be that a perfect system does not exist and that revision, rethinking, and more changes will be required (Doherty & Jacobs, 2015).

Writers and thinkers have also given attention to the matter of teacher evaluation policy development as it relates to music educators. Perhaps their biggest criticism is that most policies and their resulting systems are not readily applicable to music educators and their work in their own classrooms (Aguilar & Richerme, 2014; Goe & Holdheide, 2011; Maranzano, 2000; Robinson, 2015; Shuler, 2012; Taebel, 1992). If the evaluation system does not take into consideration what music educators do and the goals that they have established for learning in their classrooms, then it is not possible for the evaluations to either provide for accountability nor serve as a means to improve teaching (Taebel, 1992). An additional criticism of current evaluation systems as it relates to music teaching and learning is the heavy reliance on business-related accountability models—those interested in the "bottom line"—as a means to develop measures for school systems (Shuler 2012, p. 8).

Music education researchers have also spent a considerable amount of time focusing on the data, evidence, and information used to evaluate music educators. Chief among their criticisms of these policies is the use of math, reading, or other non-music-related test scores to evaluate music educators—typically known as value-added measures (Robinson 2015, p. 13). Ultimately, as Aguilar and Richerme (2014) note, "arts teachers and policymakers tend to take action and advocate for "fair systems" of teacher evaluation. None of these authors suggested eliminating teacher evaluation; rather, they argued for the implementation of teacher evaluation processes that consider the complexity of teaching and evaluate teachers through a transparent and equitable process" (p. 116). Music educators, who are certainly used to sharing their work with students in public through performances and other presentations, are not at all opposed to accountability through evaluation (Colwell, 1970, p. 13; Robinson, 2015, p. 10), they are, however, fearful and mistrusting of irrelevant and erroneous data being used as a means to measure their effectiveness (Robinson, 2015, p. 11). And, given their comfort with being evaluated, music educators should eagerly offer their thoughts and ideas about appropriate systems of evaluation when called on to do so (Aguilar & Richerme, 2014, p. 118).

Overall, it is fair to say that teacher evaluation policies and their subsequent systems are still in the very early stages of development in most states and districts. Policymakers, teachers, researchers, and administrators should continue their efforts to find measures that are appropriate, fair, accurate, valid, reliable, and, most importantly, worthy of the high goals and aspirations we have established for our nation's educational system. In the opinion of the author, we should move toward accountability and evaluation systems that take into account *all* of the facets impacting teaching and learning in our schools. Any accountability system that relies on policy aimed at one aspect of teacher evaluation (test scores, for example) will not only fall short of improving teaching but also inadvertently impact many of the other facets of our educational system in ways we have yet to determine.

Issues, Criticisms, Concerns, and Questions

In addition to the variety of concerns related to teacher evaluation policies and their implementation, many other issues and questions are raised in the development of measures to determine the effectiveness of teachers. These concerns fall into several different categories, and they are both wide and varied. While the goal of this chapter is not to solve these issues, it is important to be aware of them as we consider the direction of music teacher evaluation in the future.

One of the major concerns is related to the purpose and role of teacher evaluation—in essence, is the purpose of the teacher evaluation system geared toward accountability aimed to make summative decisions, or is the purpose of the evaluation to inform and improve the effectiveness of educators? While it is likely that an appropriate and judicious system can handle both of those charges, in the opinion of the author, this question should be the first one considered as policy, evaluative measures, and assessments are being developed. Data being used for a variety of purposes—summative and formative assessments—also raises questions of reliability and validity for each measure used (Taebel, 1992; Grissom & Youngs, 2016). Also, related to this concern is that various stakeholders who are interested in teacher evaluation will certainly want different kinds of data and information to satisfy their queries (Orzolek, 2004; Raiber & Teachout, 2014). Can these evaluation systems meet that requirement as well?

Allsup (2015) points out, "education in the twenty-first century witnessed a profound shift in emphasis from the teacher to the learner, or from pedagogical inputs to learner outcomes" (Allsup, 2015, p. 5). If this theory of learning is indeed true for our times, then it seems to suggest that evidence of student learning should play an important role in our evaluation of teachers. This same sentiment—more focus on the learner—is supported by research that estimated that only about 7% to 10% of the overall variation in student achievement can be attributed to a student's individual achievement. The largest influences, typically accounting for about 60% of the variance, are socioeconomic factors associated with individual students and the collective composition of the classroom and school (Darling-Hammond, 2013). Do these accountability systems take into consideration the role of the learner and the many contextual factors that determine a student's aptitude and achievement?

There are many strong opinions and thoughts about teacher evaluation practices and how they pertain to those educators working in nontested grades and subjects. Overall, there seems to be no consensus about how to evaluate these teachers or, for that matter, how to measure student growth in these areas (Jiang, Sporte, & Luppescu, 2015, p. 114). Maranzano (2000) writes that there was no consensus among music educators as to the criteria that should be used to measure their effectiveness. So "music educators were often evaluated using school-wide measures other than those directly associated with music achievement, such as attendance, dropout figures, and graduation rates" (in Nierman, 2014b, p. 8). How should we be evaluating music educators? What are the appropriate criteria?

Many educators would argue that their biggest concern and reservation about any model is its applicability and appropriateness for the special nature of music learning—in essence, a "one size fits all" approach to teacher evaluation is not satisfactory for most music teachers (Maranzano, 2000, p. 268). For example, many observation instruments are not specific enough for use in a music setting. In addition, those completing the evaluation may not feel qualified or comfortable enough to evaluate the teaching and learning occurring in the music classroom. However, Maranzano notes, "music teachers have long been an ideal subject for researchers to study as models of effective teaching when researchers contemplate the role of student engagement in the teaching and learning process" (Maranzano, 2000, p. 268). Simply put, music teaching is multifaceted and must be measured using multiple tools and instruments. Can we develop policies and systems which meet that requirement?

On a similar line of thought, Maranzano worries, "many common evaluation systems actually hinder a creative teacher's risk-taking and self-reflecting behavior" (Maranzano, 2000, p. 270). He also suggests, "music teachers as a whole have demonstrated the ability and willingness to accept constructive criticism offered by other professionals, peers, parents, students, and have successfully integrated this type of constructive criticism into their own self-reflecting behaviors" (Maranzano, 2000, p. 272). It is the view of this author that creativity, self-reflection, and the acceptance of criticism are important dispositions for an effective teacher to hold. Do we want an evaluative system that stifles any of those traits?

In the opinion of the author, music educators have considerable experience in every stage of accountability. We have learned to describe our goals and objectives through national, state, and local standards, and we are able to adapt them for application in our classrooms. We are skilled at using technology and other tools as resources to improve our work in various settings. Over the past decade, our profession has developed and learned to implement myriad assessment tools that allow us to evaluate our students' work and improve our own. In spite of this, we have not yet established a suitable means of reporting the learning that happens in our classrooms. We must learn about teacher evaluation policy and take a proactive approach into the development of a system for the evaluation of our effectiveness.

EFFECTIVE MUSIC TEACHING

It goes without saying that there is not "one ideal profile for effective teachers" (Abeles, Hoffer, & Klotman, 1994, p. 333) and perhaps any definition is "too restrictive" (Brand, 1985, p. 8). At best, it may be possible to generalize the various competencies, dispositions, and skill sets that may be required of a strong educator, but those should really be considered only minimal expectations and only be applicable to beginning or "marginal" teachers (Taebel, 1992, p. 312). Many stakeholders already believe, "effective music teaching [is] based upon fuzzy concepts and educational folklore" (Brand, 1985, p. 8). Further complicating this fact is society's strong desire to develop a single or composite score for educators as a means to rate and compare them—a task that is simply impossible due to the complexity of educating students (Overland, 2014, p. 60).

When it comes to music education, some note, "successful teaching is often confused with quality teaching" (Allsup, 2015, p. 16). While a successful conductor's ensembles may be perennial winners of awards, their approach in the classroom may not align with the practices and competencies believed to be associated with effective teaching: that is that the teacher contributes to student learning in the music classroom (Taebel, 1992, p. 312). Some even suggest that the question "Are your students learning?" is far more important than the question of "Are you an effective teacher?" (Elpus, 2011, p. 186). These questions and many others are important for us to consider as we develop our definition of an effective music educator. While it is complex and complicated, the author would argue that is requisite to help educators and the profession to advance.

Definitions of an Effective Educator

The impetus to defining what is meant by an effective educator in recent years was brought about by the many policies, laws, and changes in education as a result of the accountability movement in the early 21st century. These policies—for example, Race to the Top (Goe & Holdheide, 2011)—rely heavily on standardized testing scores that provide a sense of achievement in the general areas of reading, literacy, mathematics, and sometimes science. With that in mind, many of the definitions of the effective teacher were based on gains in testing scores of an academic year (Goe & Holdheide, 2011, p. 5). Even to those not deeply engaged in the research related to teacher evaluation will share that this "concept of measuring teacher effectiveness is far too narrow" to provide a succinct definition (Little, Goe, & Bell, 2009, p. 1). Few would dispute that we need a much more comprehensive definition if we truly wish to evaluate educators based on their impact in the classroom.

There are certainly many ideas and conceptions of what it means to be an effective educator. As Duke (1999) remind us, "Implicit in the use of the word 'effective' to describe teaching is the notion that the effect of interest is a positive change in some aspect(s) of student behavior—what students know or are able to do" (p. 16). Darling-Hammond would agree, and suggests that "effective teaching" "refers to strong instruction that enables a wide range of students to learn. Such instruction meets the demands of the discipline, the goals of instruction and the needs of students in a particular context. Teaching quality is in part a function of teacher quality—teachers' knowledge, skills and dispositions—but it is also strongly influenced by the context of instruction, including factors aside from what the teacher knows and can do" (p. 12). Certainly other thinkers, writers, and researchers have their own thoughts about effectiveness, but all of them share some combination of dispositions, traits, competencies, skills, and knowledge to form their own definitions.

Researchers have concerns about generalizing the competencies of an effective educator (Overland, 2014, p. 57; Taebel, 1992, p. 312). Taebel (1992) warned that early iterations of teacher effectiveness measures were "generic competencies [that] were assumed not only to be 'right' for all teachers, but [these competencies] were also major contributors to student learning" (p. 312). In the end, Taebel reported these competencies could only be considered as "minimal expectations" and not enough to establish whether or not an educator was effecting student learning (Taebel, 1992). To conclude, Taebel shared, the "evaluation of any teacher in terms of demonstrated competencies without consideration of the teacher's purpose, the students or the situation represents an atrophied conception of teaching" (p. 313).

Several music educators have raised concerns that these generic definitions and measures do not translate to the work of music educators well (Overland, 2014, p. 57) and have worked to develop definitions that take into account the specialized nature of teaching in the arts. Brand (1985) provides the following: "An effective music teacher is one who is able to bring about intended music learning outcomes" (p. 6).

It is clear that a teacher's impact on music learning should be at the core of evaluating a music educator's effect on students, but others reveal that they believe the context and other factors related to music learning are far too prevalent to ignore. Campbell, Demorest and Morrison (2008) offer that while there may be many factors impacting music learning, "regardless of where they work and under what conditions, the ace music teachers are effective because of who they are musically and humanly, and as pedagogically astute practitioners of their art. They have the power to persuade, to model, to inform, to facilitate the learning of their students, and to change their lives" (p. 284).

While our definition may be related to student learning, it is worthwhile to look at the attributes, dispositions, and characteristics of effective teachers since a listing may help teachers to reflect on potential areas of growth, provide evaluators with a basis for comments and suggestions for areas of improvement, and provide music teacher educators with guidance for the preparation of future music educators. The next section addresses some of the lists found in the literature.

Dispositions, Traits and Characteristics of the Effective Music Educator

Several significant researchers and thinkers both in music education and the larger educational arena have considered the traits that effective educators seem to possess. Some of those are presented here as a means to outline potential areas of evaluation. As expected, the dispositions are wide and varied and nearly all of the literature on the topic speaks to the importance and influence of context (school environment, social condition, policies) in evaluating any aspect of education—especially the educators! The next section of this chapter is dedicated to listing some of these traits with special attention given to those who have thought about the characteristics required of effective music educators.

The best summary of the general teaching dispositions required of an effective teacher seems to be the summary provided by Linda Darling-Hammond (2013) in her book *Getting Teacher Evaluation Right*:

> Research on teacher effectiveness, based on teacher ratings and student achievement gains, has found the following qualities to be important:

- strong content knowledge related to what is to be taught;
- knowledge of how to teach others in that area (content pedagogy) and skill in implementing productive teaching practices;
- understanding of learners and their development, including how to support students who have learning differences or difficulties, and how to support the learning of language and content for those who are not already proficient in the language of instruction;
- general abilities to organize and explain ideas, as well as to observe and think diagnostically; and
- adaptive expertise that allows teachers to make judgments about what is likely to work in a given context in response to students' needs. (p. 11)

While these listings of traits for all teachers can be helpful, it is also important to consider the uniqueness of each discipline when establishing evaluation criteria (Shuler, 1996, p. 14). Music researchers have done some of that work (Brand, 1985; Brophy, 1993; Grant & Drafall, 1991; Nierman, 2014a; Overland, 2014; Shuler, 2012, but they have also considered and critiqued the existing lists as they apply to music educators. Grant and Drafall (1991), for example, created a similar listing of dispositions and traits found in effective music educators. Their inventory includes the following:

- [An effective music educator] is adept at human relationships;
- is independent thinking;
- possesses a strong need to accomplish tasks;
- has a creative teaching style;
- is able to adapt instruction to student needs;
- maintains an appropriate rehearsal atmosphere;
- balances rehearsal and teacher talk effectively;
- is thoroughly prepared for class; and
- uses high quality literature. (in Brophy, 1993, pp. 38–39)

Edgar (2012) provides another listing of characteristics, but his list was developed from studies based on administrators' expectations of effective music educators. His inventory includes (1) professional attitude and appearance; (2) adequate knowledge of the subject area; (3) excellent communication skills; (4) strong character, positive attitude, moral values, and an engaging personality; (5) the ability to interact with parents and the community; and (6) an established philosophy of education (Edgar, 2012, p. 138). There are certainly a number of similarities in these lists. The key elements could be outlined as content knowledge, pedagogical knowledge, an understanding of learning, personality-related dispositions, and an ability to be creative in all of their work with their students. Their listing also speaks to specific concerns required of educators within the music classroom such as high-quality literature and issues related to rehearsals. Examining these lists and inventories provides an opportunity to consider other unique attributes of the effective music educator.

The research literature also suggests that a few other teacher characteristics should be considered when evaluating music teachers. These include items such as the ability to articulate goals and objectives (Edgar, 2012); an awareness and attention to the "affective" nature of music and music teaching (Nierman, 2014b); a capacity to describe and explain student learning outcomes (Taebel, 1992, p. 314); an involvement in the life of the school and community (Taebel, 1992, p. 314); and evidence that the teacher understands that learning to teach is a long process (Shuler, 2012, p. 14).

Taebel (1992) examined these lists and teacher qualities as he considered the appropriate means to evaluate music teachers and their effectiveness. For example, on the widely held notion that teacher personality is one of the major factors in teacher effectiveness and student achievement, he suggested that there is not enough evidence to support this perception and that using this as a measure of effectiveness should be carefully considered before implementing any evaluation tool (Taebel, 1992, p. 314). He also stressed the importance of considering the classroom situation and environment as an important part, but not the sole determinant, of effectiveness.

Taebel (1992) also suggests that our theoretical conceptions of teaching effectiveness and our theoretical conceptions of learning are not always aligned and this could cause for difficulties in developing evaluative tools that might measure some of these dispositions (p. 313). In the opinion of this author, and in the spirit of the previous comments from Allsup (2015), that very point may be crucial for the current era in which we live. If our current theories of education place a strong emphasis on the learning process (meeting goals, objectives, and standards) over products (standardized tests), then our evaluation of educators should place greater emphasis on that component of effective teaching. In the opinion of the author, the complicated nature of evaluating educator in 2016 proves that Taebel's concerns and predictions are accurate.

ROLE OF EVALUATION

If we can accurately define the nature and traits of the effective music educator, then it also holds true that we must examine the role(s) that evaluation holds in the profession. As previously mentioned, this is an issue of great concern and importance. There are those who strongly believe that the major role of these evaluations is to provide a summative and definitive decision about an educator's effectiveness. On the other side, there are those who hold very strong opinions that the role of any evaluation is to support the growth and development of the educator and their work with their students. Others have offered other potential roles for evaluation as it relates to teaching and learning. This section of the chapter examines this idea with specific attention to the music classroom and outlines some of the inherent difficulties related to clarifying the issue.

Taebel (1992) points out, "one's conception of evaluation has a strong influence on the teacher evaluation process" (Taebel, 1992, p. 310). With that said, stakeholders should consider the purpose and role of evaluation before they decide on the measures they plan to implement (Little et al., 2009, p. 17)—and that is where things get complicated for the field of music education. Teacher evaluation has come to serve many roles, with purposes of evaluation related to improving teaching and student learning (Boyle, 1989; Little et al., 2009; Marzano & Toth, 2013; Nielsen, 2014; Orzolek, 2004; Shuler, 2012; Tait and Haack, 1984; Taebel, 1992) as well as advancing the curriculum and the overall music program (Boyle, 1989; Shuler, 2012; Tait and Haack). There is, however, wide acknowledgment of the need for a multifaceted approach to teacher evaluation in music education. Tait and Haack (1984) remind us:

> As music educators, we are directly responsible and accountable for the growth and development of human beings. Such accountability requires more than student evaluation; it requires teacher and program evaluation as well. It requires more than test scores and grade reports; it requires constant formal and informal observations, needs assessments, self and program analyses, behavior scales, performance critiques, attitude assessments, achievement measures, and a host of other creative and imaginative tools and techniques. It requires more than the summative evaluations needed to assessment general levels of goal attainment; it also requires formative evaluations to facilitate the fairly specific diagnoses that guide further instructional planning.   (p. 148)

If teacher development is one of the goals and main purposes of an evaluation system, then it holds true that measures that support that role should be implemented, analyzed, and valued in that light. As Goe and Holdheide (2011) suggest, "little attention has been paid to how the instruments and processes of teacher evaluation can inform professional growth opportunities" and goes on to suggest that a "feedback loop" needs to be engaged in order for the evaluation to serve in this way (p. 18). Tait and Haack (1984) also refer to the need for a feedback loop, but they go on to suggest that it come from "frequent evaluation via various forms of student assessment and feedback" due to the "unique, complex, and holistic nature of musical [learning]" (p. 156). In order for the evaluation to support music teacher development, it should be the result of a well-grounded and systematic approach developed by district leaders and educators (Darling-Hammond, 2013, p. 14).

As expected, the majority of evaluation for this purpose is done via observation of the educator in the classroom setting. While this role seems to be readily accepted and appreciated, Raiber and Teachout (2014) provide these important points of consideration when teacher evaluation serves this aim: "When the teacher evaluation process is pursued as a 'top-down' endeavor, it is plagued by (a) infrequent evaluations, (b) lack of evaluator knowledge about the content areas in which they evaluate teachers, and (c) the absence of high-quality feedback for teachers" (p. 11). The importance of peer-, mentor-, and self-evaluation are extremely important to the growth of educators and they are gaining more attention in the research community. As Parker (1998) reminds us, "The growth of any craft depends on shared practice and honest dialogue among people who do it" (p. 144).

If student learning is one of the main purposes of teacher evaluation, then other evaluation processes should be considered. Nielsen (2014) suggests that we consider these two questions to address this purpose: "(1) What are students learning? and (2) How do we know they have learned it?" (p. 63). Boyle (1989) as well as Tait and Haack

(1984) would agree but would suggest that we look to evaluate a "teacher's ability to diagnose musical concerns and to select teaching strategies appropriate to those concerns in the context of the stated goals for the students of a particular program" (Tait & Haack, 1984, p. 147). Much more will be shared on this approach to teacher evaluation later in the chapter.

If improving the school music program is to be one of the purposes of teacher evaluation, then it behooves educators to find and present evidence of accountability to that end (Boyle, 1989; Tait & Haack, 1984). This is also quite complicated for music education. As Boyle (1989) mentions, "What people are willing to accept as evidence of [program] accountability may vary from district to district and state to state, but it is clear that music educators must join other educators in providing objective evidence of accountability. At the very least this implies providing some evidence of quality control, productivity, and efficiency" (p. 24).

Shuler (2012) summarizes the many purposes of teacher evaluation in this way: "The best of the emerging teacher evaluation initiatives push us to do *better* what we should have been doing *all along*: To identify what is most important through clear, thoughtful, and specific outcomes (i.e., *curriculum*); to measure how well that curriculum is learned (i.e., to *assess* student achievement); and to figure out how to help more students achieve success (i.e., to *improve instruction*)" (in Hash, 2013, p. 10). Most music educators would support these claims and admit that all of these variables and factors are basic components and characteristics of an effective music educator working within an effective music education program. The interdependence of all of the many factors influencing music education should always be taken into consideration as teacher evaluation measures and developed and implemented.

Finally, in some of the earlier writings about music teacher evaluation, Taebel (1992), Boyle (1989), Tait and Haack (1984), and Colwell (1970) discuss teacher evaluation as a framework to making judgments about student learning, teachers, and the overall program. They each speak of this frame as a way to evaluate teachers, but also as a means to examine and connect the many factors that influence the effectiveness of a music education program. These ideas are considered in more depth in the next section and a framework of this sort is presented at the end of the chapter.

HISTORICAL PERSPECTIVES ON MUSIC TEACHER EVALUATION

All of the previously mentioned literature, thoughts, and issues point to a need to consider music teacher evaluation from every possible angle. It is with this knowledge that we may be able to establish some sense of what directions the profession of music education should consider as it solidifies its position on the proper approach to evaluating music educators and their work. This section of the chapter considers perspectives and viewpoints on the topic of music teacher evaluation from sources prior to 1992. This date is chosen since Donald Taebel's chapter titled "The Evaluation of Music Teachers and Teaching" was published in the *Handbook of Research on Music Teaching and Learning* in that year. Much can be derived from the examination of these historical perspectives, as they provide a sense of how the profession has evolved. At the same time, this section reveals that much that was valued about music educators in past years is still important in today's music classrooms.

Some of the earliest thoughts and comments related to music teacher evaluation stem from publications aimed at music supervisors and music administrators—typically, those who were responsible for the hiring, reviewing, and support of music educators. Authors from the early part of the 20th century recognized that the evaluation of music educators was highly subjective (Snyder, 1959, p. 114), required a multifaceted approach (Dykema & Gehrkens, 1941, p. 368), and required competent evaluators (Prescott, 1938, p. 259). Although her comments do not speak directly to teacher evaluation but rather to teacher training, McEachern (1937) prompts us to remember, "the education of school music teachers is primarily concerned with evoking the spirit of music. The mechanics of school music education are merely a means of controlling physical conditions whereby this end may be best accomplished" (p. 249). Certainly all of these comments and thoughts still hold true in the complicated era of educational accountability in which music education finds itself in 2016.

By the 1960s there was a strong recognition that "evaluation ought to involve looking critically at the process of gathering and weighing evidence that will reveal changes in terms of a desirable musical product" (Weyland, 1960, p. 295). However, this approach seemed to be cast aside with the Competency-Based Teacher Education (CBTE) movement that outlined a specific set of skills and dispositions that could define effectiveness (Boyle & Radocy, 1987, p. 16; Taebel, 1992, p. 311). These competencies were often identified by the states, districts, and professional organizations that tended to draw on generic teacher skills and philosophical criteria rather than those grounded in actual classroom practice (Boyle & Radocy, 1987, pp. 16–17; Taebel, 1992, p. 311). Out of necessity, of course, the number of competencies grew to account for the complex nature of teaching as well as the variety of specific traits required for certain disciplines. "Eventually the number of competencies became unwieldy," so that states and schools broadened the scope, ultimately creating a checklist of competencies primarily measured through observation (Taebel, 1992, p. 312). This meant that evaluation was moving from a competency-based approach to one more oriented toward the observation of classroom performance (Taebel, 1992, p. 312).

Taebel (1992) points out that while defining the specific competencies to be evaluated was challenging, it was the measurement and validation of these traits that was extremely difficult (p. 311). Further, it was also not possible to "demonstrate that a teacher who exhibited a competency was necessarily more effective than one who did not" (Taebel, 1992, p. 311). Thus, the move to a more observation-based system likely brought some respite to those involved with the evaluation of music teachers—although with an inherent cynicism due to the overt subjectivity involved in this type of process. Colwell

(1970) acknowledges that skepticism during this time period, but questions why music educators would be overly concerned, since "the performer is evaluated regularly" in every aspect of their work (Colwell, 1970, p. 13). Ultimately, the next two decades find writings that suggest the melding of competency-based and performance-based assessments that serve both summative and formative roles in determining the effectiveness of music educators.

While work in these two areas expands and continues, other thinkers outlined and developed evaluative measures that more closely align with music teaching and learning. House (1973) speaks to evaluation for diagnostic purposes and promotes and describes the importance of measuring a teacher's impact on student progress—specifically in the area of their developing musicianship (pp. 85–86). House speaks to the need for reviewing course and lesson plans and the periodic observation of instruction as well as student and peer evaluation as other sources of measurement. House also is among the first to recognize that one tool cannot "provide a completely reliable index to a teacher's impact upon his students. But taken altogether they begin to add up to a convincing profile" (House, 1973, pp. 86–87). And while he admits that this is approach is complicated, House believed that the attempt to develop this type of evaluation tool would be preferable to allowing others to influence how music educators would be evaluated (House, 1973, p. 87).

In 1979, Levin listed the various general approaches to teacher evaluation that were identified in his review of literature from this particular era. While they are not specific to music education, they do provide a snapshot of tools being used. Levin also points out that of these modes, observation was the most commonly used technique. The six approaches included:

1. The use of students; ratings of teaching through questionnaires and other survey instruments;
2. Evaluation based on observation by supervisors, such as principals;
3. Evaluation using an observation instrument or system, such as the Flanders Interaction Analysis System;
4. Self-evaluation by teachers;
5. Evaluation based on gains shown by students on various tests;
6. Evaluation through specially designed teaching tests. (Levin, 1979, p. 244)

By the 1980s, the acceptance of these approaches as well as the recognition that evaluation teaching and learning could not be reduced to a short, easy-to-manage listing of competencies provided opportunities for the profession of music education to evaluate its positions and thoughts about the roles and processes appropriate for measuring the effectiveness of music education. Tait and Haack (1984), for example, called for teacher evaluation to focus on the act of teaching rather than specific teacher competency. They also believed that there were a number of criteria that should be considered including the teacher's ability to diagnose music learning and adjust to support student growth, use appropriate vocabulary (verbal behaviors), use appropriate nonverbal behaviors in our modeling of music learning, adapt flexible teaching style, manage the event flow and character of the learning experiences, and help students create a linkage or relationship with our learners (Tait & Haack 1984, pp. 157–160). The Music Educators National Conference (MENC, 1987) also developed a listing of important traits for the profession to consider.

Finally, Boyle served as a guest editor for special issue of the *Music Educators Journal* that focused on evaluation in 1989. His perspective on the status of evaluation on music education included reminders about the significance and value of evaluation at all levels of music education, the need to use both subjective and objective information in decision-making about music teaching and learning, and the importance of applying tests and testing procedures in a careful manner in the music classroom (Boyle, 1989, p. 23). Boyle, for the first time, recognizes and describes effective evaluation for the profession as serving many roles—that is, teacher effectiveness, student learning, and the music program.

Taebel's Agenda for Music Teacher Evaluation

Taebel's landmark writings on music teacher evaluation have been referenced and cited throughout this chapter, and it is likely the most cited writing on the topic to this date. The chapter on music teacher evaluation in the *Handbook of Research on Music Teaching and Learning* not only summarizes the issues related to the topic but also puts a focus on two very important areas of music teacher evaluation that are still pertinent today. Those areas are the reliability and validity of any teacher evaluation instrument and—since there was an increased emphasis on the observation of teaching as a primary means to evaluate teachers—a listing of directions and needs for future research on observation techniques and their use in evaluating music teachers. Both of these areas are described in great detail, and, as anticipated, Taebel's conclusions suggest significant work be done in both areas (Taebel, 1992, p. 323). In addition, and more pertinent to this overview of music teacher evaluation, Taebel developed an "Agenda for Music Teacher Evaluation." It is shortened here but it provides a clear view of:

1. A school district should develop a framework for evaluation of its music teachers.... The framework should include broad goals of musical learning for all students. These goals may be thought of as the outcomes of effective teaching, but they should not be dictated by what can be easily measured....Procedures for evaluation should be described, and the purposes of evaluation music be clearly stated....A variety of data-gathering approaches should be available....Teachers having a record of successful teaching may be given an opportunity to select the evaluation tools that are most appropriate to their professional objectives.

2. [...] Members of the [evaluation] team should be trained to observe classroom events and make accurate, objective records. Videotape episodes of music teaching,

including both positive and negative exemplars, should be used for initial training.... Team members should be aware of the threats to reliability and validity of observation instruments and be sensitive to the context variables that may affect teacher behaviors....

3. The school district should develop a plan for professional development that meets the needs and interest of all teachers, including music teachers, at various stages of professional development.... A number of routes should be available such as peer tutoring, mentoring, self-study, special interest groups, and outside consultations.

4. Finally, the evaluation system itself must be subject to evaluation. The ultimate goal of the system must be to improve learning, which is the result of improved instruction. Evaluation systems that change neither teaching nor learning must be revised. (Taebel, 1992, pp. 323–324)

Twenty-five years later, those engaged with the music teacher evaluation process would likely agree with Taebel's listing. His perspective, and that of others who were considering the topic prior to the 21st century offered some useful and grounded thoughts about the roles, functions, and importance of evaluation of music educators. The next part of this chapter addresses several of the recent trends in the evaluation of educators.

Recent Trends in Teacher Evaluation

While it is clear from the historical perspective that music teacher evaluation was an ever-evolving process, the recent trends and writings on the topic seem to suggest that many questions and issues have yet to be resolved. This section of the chapter considers, in detail, the trends and facets of teacher evaluation that are currently in use. Various models and ideas are drawn from the literature from music education and that of the broader world of education. These ideas are presented to provide readers with a sense of the status of teacher evaluation in 2016. As Grissom and Youngs (2016) note:

> Teacher evaluation has become serious business.... Spurred by [policies], many states and districts have implemented evaluation systems that... produce more comprehensive measures of teacher performance than have ever been available before. (p. 1)

As described earlier in the chapter, the move to well-designed performance-based measures continues to be an important consideration in this new era of teacher accountability. That approach requires evaluations that are truly designed to help teachers improve their work in the classroom—in other words, they are not evaluations but, rather, assessments. In the opinion of this author, that is a major change in the direction of teacher evaluation and one that should be warmly welcomed by educators and administrators alike. Darling-Hammond (2013) and others have found that these types of evaluations can "capture teaching in action," where things like scaffolding, teacher feedback, and student revisions can be observed and considered; examine strategies for meeting the needs of particular students; provide an opportunity to review student work in relation to goals and objectives; and make use of rubrics to help consider the quality of work accomplished (p. 26). In this approach, we see the potential and possibilities of aligning evidence derived from student work as a means to evaluate/assess the work of an educator.

This "philosophy" of teacher evaluation—one that is much more about the existing "evidence of learning" derived from the actual classroom performance of teachers and students—comes with some additional concerns to consider. This type of evaluation is likely to be considered much more subjective than other forms, but, in the case of music educators, this is certainly nothing new—we have been using "evidence-based" assessment for many years in our programs (Raiber & Teachout, 2014, p. 52). And evidence-based system of evaluation also allows administrators and other evaluators to serve in the role of a mentor and support—something that all educators need (Silverberg & Jungwirth, 2014, p. 199). In turn, this approach builds trust between evaluators and educators that can only serve to help the profession evolve and change (Maranzano, 2000, p. 272).

Silverberg and Jungwirth (2014) agree with all of this and describe this recent thinking in teacher evaluation: "A huge cultural shift for many teachers and administrators is making the shift to an evaluation system built on reflection, self-assessment, accountability and collaborative goal setting. This new way of being is supported by dialogue, collaborative analysis of data, and coaching" (p. xvi). And perhaps, most importantly, this approach soundly engages educators in the process and allows them to help shape the evaluation process (Powers, 2012, p. 41). With all of this in mind, the next section of the chapter considers current thinking about the common forms of teacher evaluation with an evidence/performance-based approach in mind.

Student Test Scores and Value-Added Modeling

Perhaps the most controversial teacher evaluation approach in recent years has been the use of student test scores to measure how much "value" or growth a teacher has "added" to a student from one school year to the next—these are known as "value-added models" (VAMs). In this model, a teacher's effectiveness is dependent on student test scores as well as how those scores compare to other students in a similar grade through various statistical procedures. In the end, a teacher is rated and/or ranked through comparisons to local and/or state norms. The efficiency and objectivity of these measures make them attractive to stakeholders, but there are many questions related to their validity, reliability, and potential to support an educators' growth due to the lack of substantive feedback (Darling-Hammond, 2013, pp. 73–74) Teachers' distrust in high-stakes testing and a sense that other forms are more reliable measures also play a factor the status of VAMs in current evaluative practice (Harris & Herrington, 2015, p. 73).

Researchers and thinkers from arts education are very concerned about the application of VAM scores in the evaluation or arts educators. First, and most obvious, is that the standardized tests from which these scores are drawn come from the areas of mathematics, reading, and literacy. Using these types of test scores to develop VAM scores of arts educators is, at best, highly questionable and inappropriate. The National Association for Music Education (NAfME, 2013) and many other organizations have developed position statements related to this type of teacher evaluation and each question the validity of these scores as well as the careful consideration of what these scores mean in making decisions about teacher effectiveness. In the end, most of the writings on the topic raise important questions about these measurements and their use in evaluating educators—especially when they are used as the only source of teacher evaluation (Marzano & Toth, 2013, p. 40). Overall, music educators must understand and articulate our stance on the use and implications of statistical models (like VAMs) in the evaluation of our work.

Student Learning Outcomes and Evidence of Student Learning

Many states, schools, and organizations are recognizing that the evidence of student learning should be a key component of teacher evaluation—particularly for those disciplines in which there is no standardized testing. The use of student learning outcomes (SLOs) is becoming the norm in many state and district models. In general, this approach is considered flexible and directly tied to teacher practice, since teachers establish the goals set for each student. The literature also reminds us, "the arts rely primarily on individual evaluation rather than standardized testing" (Hope, 2013, p. 4), meaning that issues of time and numbers of students begin to play a factor in using student evidence in the evaluation of music educators.

This form of teacher evaluation is gaining support in both the research literature and policies. Darling-Hammond (2013) believes, "student learning evidence needs to be multifaceted and accompanied by an analysis of the teacher's students and teaching context. It must be integrated with evidence about teachers' practice, and its use should be focused on improving teaching" (p. 88). She and others (Doherty & Jacobs, 2015, p. 17; Emmert, Sheehan, & Deitz, 2013, p. 31; Goe & Holdheide, 2011, p. 13; Shaw, 2014, p. 105) speak to the importance of educators writing measureable objectives that are rigorous, yet realistic. These authors also remind us that the entire process—including how student learning evidence will be used in the evaluation process—should be clearly explained and defined prior to the outset of the evaluation period.

In order for SLOs to be impactful in the evaluation of music teachers, the following seem important and apparent: Music educators need to develop clear, concise and measurable outcomes/objectives for the learning occurring in our classrooms; music educators need experiences with a wide variety of assessment tools and various means of collecting the evidence of student learning in our classrooms; and they need to develop an efficient and clear means of reporting our findings with a variety of stakeholders others. As Rawlings and Shaw (2014) suggest, "the development of authentic assessments for arts subjects will be critical to the implementation and sustainability of an arts teacher evaluation system that incorporates arts student learning data" (p. 163). In the strong opinion of the author, assessment of student learning is the most important area of need in music teacher development.

Observation of Teaching and Performance

Parker (1998) believes this form of evaluation is the most vital to the teaching profession. He writes, "When we cannot observe each other's teaching, we get evaluation practices that are distanced, demoralizing, and even disreputable. Lacking firsthand information about each other's work, we allow the artifacts of the student survey to replace the facts that can be known only in person" (p. 142). Over the years, observation of professional practice is the most common form of teacher evaluation—teachers and evaluators are familiar with this process, as it has been an integral part of teacher preparation for many years (Garrett & Steinberg, 2015, p. 225). Further, since context and environment is a crucial piece of effectiveness, observing the educator in the classroom is highly desirable.

The various comments, opinions, and conjectures about evaluation of educators through observation are equally taxing to absorb, but there are some apparent themes for our consideration. Most agree that observers need to be carefully trained in order to provide fair and consistent feedback and, in general, the reliability of the observations increases when more than one observer is part of the process (Maranzano, 2000, p. 270). In addition, the use of domain-based observation tools (e.g., the Danielson or Marzano models) with multiple rating levels (at least four) seems to provide more substantive feedback that encourages teacher growth and development.

Some have shared their concerns about making these observation tools as music-education friendly as possible. The NAfME (2013) developed workbooks based on the Danielson model that can be readily used by evaluators who are similar with the model, but may have concerns about their ability to address music-related concerns. Further development of the NAfME workbook might be accomplished by ensuring that the dispositions exclusive to teaching music and all of the contextual pieces related to music classrooms are included and taken into consideration. There is some support for the use of student perception surveys in the observation process as well. Overall, it is important that music educators take an active role in the development and implementation of the observation process.

Self-Evaluation and Reflection

Self-reflection is typically done through a narrative or oral interview. Several authors suggest that this type of evaluation can be enhanced and more effective when teachers focus their reflections on the processes of student learning rather than that of their own teaching (Delaney, 2011; Girod, 2002; Ward, 2012). However, when teacher reflection is focused on the final products of student learning, the results often include changes in the teaching process to enhance learning. The process of reflecting on your teaching is very time consuming and can be quite difficult, but the advantages seem to outweigh the difficulties. As Danielson (2013) notes, "Abundant evidence...indicates that a thoughtful approach to teacher evaluation—one that engages teachers in reflection and self-assessment—yields benefits far beyond the important goal of quality assurance" (p. 39).

This type of reflective process has become a relatively consistent part of learning to teach, and many preservice teachers are entering the field with a means of making this happen. Some warn that there is not enough research to support the claim that self-reflection is directly linked to teacher effectiveness (Sanderson & Peasant, 2016, p. 593), but others are firm that reflection coupled with mentor coaching can foster growth in teachers (Shuler, 2012, p. 8). The ability for us to articulate and share these reflections with others may hold a key to helping our colleagues and administrators evaluate our work more effectively.

Other Approaches to Teacher Evaluation

There are other options for the measurement of teachers and their work in the classroom. Feedback from parents and/or students—typically done through some form of standardized survey—has been implemented in some schools as a means to address certain aspects of a teacher's effectiveness. Items such as rapport with students, general knowledge of the subject, organization, and communication skills are quite common (Abeles, 1975, p. 334). Teachers in secondary schools and in higher education are often "rated" through online systems (for example, ratemyteacher.com), although there appears to be no research that suggests that any of this type of feedback is used in a formal evaluative process. Certainly additional research is needed here, but its application in music education may be readily supported, as music teachers have long accepted and considered the criticism and ideas shared by their peers, parents, students, and others (Maranzano, 2000, p. 272).

Testing of teachers for general knowledge of content and teaching strategies has also been implemented in the evaluation of teachers, primarily, however, with those in the early portions of the careers. In recent years, the Teacher Performance Assessment (also known as the edTPA) has been implemented in some states as a high-stakes test to determine whether a preservice teacher will attain licensure. Proponents suggest that the edTPA is a multifaceted and holistic measurement of a teacher's experiences in presenting and reflecting on their teaching through an extensive portfolio of videos, narratives, and student evidence. This portfolio serves as a means for an external evaluator to provide feedback using specific scoring criteria established in rubrics. But when the edTPA and its rubrics are used to create a composite score of a teacher's effectiveness with established cutoff scores determining whether or not a teacher is acceptable for a licensure, it becomes a test that requires checks for validity and reliability. In the opinion of this author and others, that question is yet to be fully examined (Colwell, 2016, p. 26).

Multiple or Multifaceted Measures

Most of those involved with teacher evaluation understand that teaching is a highly complex and challenging thing to do. And, there is no doubt that the work of music educators requires a vast array of skills, knowledge, approaches, dispositions, and contextual understandings that do not neatly fit into one simple measurement tool (Hunter-Doniger, 2013; Garrett & Steinberg, 2015; Goe, 2010; Maranzano, 2000; Peterson, 1996; Polikoff & Porter, 2014; Shuler, 2012). Or, as Maranzano (2000) states, "traditional approaches to the evaluation of fine and performing arts personnel have to date failed to supply evaluators with enough comprehensive information needed to make important educational decisions about music teacher performance" (p. 268). As a result, there is a strong promotion of multiple-measures of teaching as the best means to evaluate music educators (Grisson & Youngs, 2016, p. 7).

By incorporating a balanced, multimeasure approach using information collected from some combination of student outcomes, observations, and narratives, we may get the best picture of a teacher's impact on student learning (Smith & Wuttke, 2016, p. 184). Of course, the question then falls to how we might define that "balance." While most recent research seems to be suggesting that an equitable distribution of the facets (testing/outcomes, observations, student evaluations) seems to be the most reliable, it also implies that the least effective model is one that is wholly based on the observation of student work. Music educators should carefully monitor the weighting of each piece of these types of evaluations and, in my opinion, be armed with a model that they feel would best support their growth and development needs.

Some researchers and writers suggest this type of evaluation might best be accomplished through a portfolio developed by the music educator (Hunter-Doniger, 2013, p. 176; Nielsen, 2014; Orzolek, 2004) that might include items such as evidence of student learning, various feedback pieces (student/parent/peer/administrator reviews or perhaps adjudicator comments), videos, self-reflection narratives, and other materials (including tests, certifications, or other objective items) that support the notion of teacher growth (Darling-Hammond 2015, p. 136; Orzolek, 2004). As with any form of evaluation, it is imperative that the criteria, requirements, and expectations of this type of portfolio be clearly articulated prior to its implementation as a means to evaluate teacher effectiveness.

While the multiple-measures approach to evaluating teachers seems to be an appropriate fit for music educators, there is a need for extensive research on how these measures perform (Goe & Holdheide, 2011, p. 16; Polikoff & Porter, 2014). There is a strong sense that these measures are more reliable (Garrett & Steinberg 2015, 225) provide a "better picture" of a teacher's effectiveness than any single measure (Peterson, 1996, p. 24).

Finally, while this approach can be highly complicated, there is strong evidence suggesting that using multiple measures helps to improve teaching and learning more than any other form of teacher evaluation (Goe, 2010, p. 1).

A FRAMEWORK FOR EVALUATING A MUSIC TEACHER EVALUATION SYSTEM

As the previous sections of this chapter have clearly indicated, there is much to be considered in the development of a music teacher evaluation system. It is clear that there is plenty of opinion on the topic of what constitutes an effective teacher and how we might measure that effectiveness, but there does not appear to be enough specific research to support a particular system that seems applicable to all disciplines. The call for a teacher evaluation system that can evaluate many different teachers from many different teachings situation in a fair, reliable, and valid way while answering the questions of a multitude of stakeholders will not dissipate until the profession can provide practice-driven, research-based models. That is a difficult challenge but one that must be resolved by the education profession if it hopes to improve teaching and learning across the country. Perhaps the place to start this work is with the establishment of criteria that can be used for the designing an effective music teacher evaluation system.

Summary of Existing Criteria for Effective Music Teacher Evaluation

Brophy (1993) points out that there is research that "seems to target areas relating to music teacher evaluation criteria, [even though] it has not yet tackled the actual problem of evaluation itself" (p. 14). The author of this chapter supports that notion, especially as we consider the time period prior to 1993. But the previous sections of this chapter seem to suggest that the profession has come a long way in considering teacher evaluation and its related issues over the past 20 years. This suggests that the time to consider current criteria would not only be appropriate from a research perspective, but it will also have the potential to serve the music education community quite well. Before presenting a new model, it is worthwhile to consider the criteria and suggestions that have been previously considered.

For the purposes of this paper, the thoughts of Colwell (1970), Taebel (1992), Brophy (1993), Little et al., (2009), NAfME (2011), Darling-Hammond (2012), the Partnership for Music Education Policy (2012), Marzano and Toth (2013), Orzolek (2013), Darling-Hammond (2013), and Robinson (2015) have been selected as a means to find common themes, since these authors specifically address the establishment of criteria for teacher evaluation models. While some of the criteria come from a broader perspective of teacher evaluation, many of these authors are music educators and their suggested criteria for evaluation speak directly to the field of music education. The reader is highly encouraged to deeply examine the criteria presented by these authors as they develop their own models.

Drawing from all of these criteria, the following themes emerge as being very important to the establishment of a system of music teacher evaluation:

- The main goal of the evaluation system should be to improve teaching and learning in the music classroom through meaningful feedback aimed at supporting the growth of the teacher, students, and program.
- The evaluation system should be based on standards of effective teacher practice that have been previously established by the state, district, or building. Each standard should reflect the nature and complexity of teaching music by drawing on the dispositions, knowledge, skills, and understandings required for effective music learning.
- The evaluation system should make use of multiple measures and multifaceted evidence of teacher practice as a means to determine a music educator's effect on student learning. The evidence and measures should strive to provide a comprehensive vision of the educator, learner, and program, since all three areas are impactful on one another.
- The evaluation system must take into account all of the contextual factors impacting the educator, students, school, and community and weigh them appropriately as it considers the evidence related to student learning.
- The evaluation system should not seek to provide a composite score. Music teaching and learning are far too complex and multifaceted to be represented by a single score or grade.

    The purposes, processes, and outcomes of the evaluation system should be clear and concise. It should include appropriate training for both the evaluators and educators. Specific concerns related to the effective teaching and learning of music should be addressed and defined.
- The evaluation system should make use of the most valid and reliable forms of measurement in every facet of the evaluation process. These measures must be used for their prescribed purposes, and the results must not be deemed appropriate for use in measuring other aspect of music teaching or learning.
- Music educators should be engaged throughout the development of the teacher evaluation system.
- The evaluation system should provide the resources throughout the process including the support necessary to allow for teacher development that will address any concerns or issues raised by the evaluations.
- The evaluation system must account for the unique nature of music teaching and learning by considering the deep and sincere connections that exist between music and human nature.

Clearly, these criteria are merely a starting point for states, districts, administrators, and educators to use as they consider the development of teacher evaluation measures and tools in their own settings. However, once those criteria are in place and agreed on, it is important that they also be measured and evaluated against a standard or norm to ensure that they are reliable and valid. This seems to be a major shortcoming in the teacher evaluation movement, and is likely the result of a lack of research or consideration. Colwell (1970) did note this concern and mentioned the CIPP (Context, Input, Process, Product) Model for Program Evaluation designed by Stufflebeam may hold some promise for this purpose (p. 19).

Context, Input, Process, Product Model

Daniel Stufflebeam originally developed the CIPP Model for Program Evaluation in 1966 as a means to evaluate decision-making. When considering the application of this model for use in educational accountability, Stufflebeam wrote:

> Not only does it provide post hoc information for accounting for past decisions and past actions, but also in a formative sense it provides information proactively to decision making so that decision makers can be more rational in their decisions in the first place. The system which provides such a powerful combination would, it seems to me, be a great improvement over social accounting and standardized test information systems which are typically found in schools, colleges of education, government education agencies, and other education agencies.
>
> (Stufflebeam, 1971, p. 20)

The CIPP model addresses four areas in its consideration of whether or not a decision supports its intended outcome—in this case, the evaluation of teachers. Those four areas are (1) "Context evaluation," which considers the goals of the evaluation, or "What should we do?"; (2) "Input evaluation," which looks at the plans of the evaluation, or "How should we do it?"; (3) "Process evaluation," which reviews the process of the evaluation, or "Did we do it as planned?"; and (4) "Product evaluation," which considers the impact of the outcomes of the evaluation, or "Did it work?" (Stufflebeam, 1971, p. 18).

In 1980s and 1990s, Stufflebeam, along with several colleagues, considered the many pervasive and difficult questions surrounding teacher evaluation previously addressed in this chapter (Shinkfield & Stufflebeam, 1995). His comments and thoughts seemed to align with the criteria previously listed and the sentiments described in most of the literature. This provides further support for the use of the CIPP model as a means to evaluate any potential teacher evaluation tool intended for music educators. Most importantly, it is clear that Stufflebeam supported our profession's belief that the goal of teacher evaluation as "improving the performance of teachers, students and the organization as a whole" (Shinkfield & Stufflebeam, 1995, p. 2).

A Framework for Evaluating Music Teacher Evaluation Criteria

Using Stufflebeam's CIPP model as its basis, the following framework for evaluation could be used to determine whether or not the criteria being used in a music teacher evaluation model are appropriate, effective, and meaningful. The framework is presented as a series of questions to provoke thought and reflection.

1. Context Evaluation: Do the criteria align with the overall goals and objectives of the policies and intents of the teacher evaluation system? Why were these criteria chosen, and do they support the particular learning environment for which they are intended? Are the criteria clearly defined so that they useful in developing an appropriate evaluation system? Can problems and issues in the criteria be identified and addressed before the evaluation system is implemented?

2. Input Evaluation: Do the criteria outline a plan for implementation? Do the criteria address who will need to be engaged with the process of developing a teacher evaluation system? Do the criteria suggest important research or supporting pieces that might offer direction for the process? Do the criteria outline strategies for implementing an appropriate evaluation system? Do the criteria outline specific concerns and issues that will impact the overall plan for implementation?

3. Process Evaluation: Did the criteria outline a particular process for teacher evaluation? Did the criteria make suggestions about the types of feedback that would stem from the teacher evaluation system? Did the criteria speak to way that would allow for the monitoring of the evaluation system while it was active? Did the criteria use research and best practice to support the choices related to implementing the system?

4. Product Evaluation: Did the criteria outline the desired outcomes of the teacher evaluation system? Did the criteria suggest ways to ensure that the system was adaptable and sustainable? Did the criteria provide for a review of the outcomes to ensure that needed changes and alterations could be made to the system?

While the CIPP model may hold promise for the purpose of evaluating criteria, it is likely that the model may serve other purposes in the work of developing teacher evaluations as well. Further consideration of this model and its applications in music education decision-making should be considered and researched.

CONCLUSION

While this chapter may have raised additional questions and issues related to music teacher evaluation, one thing has become clear—teacher evaluation is becoming an entrenched part of the profession alongside administration, testing, budgeting, and policymaking. It requires research, time, communication, investment, effort, collaboration, and more models if our desire is to use it as a means to impact music teaching and learning. Yes, as McEachern (1937) reminds us, the profession should primarily concern itself with evoking the spirit of music in our students, but it also must take the time to reflect on how it will continue to grow and improve in its work to meet that end. If music education does not embrace evaluation as a key component of its responsibility, then its status as a profession should be called into question.

REFERENCES

Abeles, H. F. (1975). Student perceptions of characteristics of effective applied instructors. *Journal of Research in Music Education, 23*, 147–154. doi: 10.2307/3345287

Abeles, H. F., Hoffer, C. R., & Klotman, R. H. (1994). *Foundations of music education*. New York, NY: Schirmer Books.

Aguilar, C. E., & Richerme, L. K. (2014). What is everyone saying about teacher evaluation? Framing the intended and inadvertent causes and consequences of Race to the Top. *Arts Education Policy Review, 115*, 110–120. doi: 10.1080/10632913.2014.947908

Allsup, R. (2015). Music teacher quality and the problem of routine expertise. *Philosophy of Music Education Review, 23*(1), 5–24.

Boyle, J. D. (1989). Perspective on evaluation. *Music Educators Journal, 76*(4), 22–25.

Boyle, J. D., & Radocy, R. E. (1987). *Measurement and evaluation of musical experiences*. London, UK: Macmillan.

Brand, M. (1985). Research in music teacher effectiveness. *Update: Applications of Research in Music Education, 3*(2), 13–16. doi: 10.1177/875512338500300204

Braun, H. (2015). The value in value-added depends on the ecology. *Educational Researcher, 44*, 127–131. doi: 10.3102/0013189X15576341

Brophy, T. (1993). *Evaluation of music teachers: Toward defining an appropriate instrument*. Unpublished paper. http://eric.ed.gov/PDFS/ED375029.pdf

Campbell, P. S., Demorest, S. M., & Morrison, S. J. (2008). *Musician and teacher: An orientation to music education*. New York, NY: W.W. Norton.

Colwell, R. (1970). *The evaluation of music teaching and learning*. Upper Saddle River, NJ: Prentice Hall.

Colwell, R. (2016). Tergiversation today: Interpreting validity. In T. Brophy, J. Marlatt, & G. Ritcher (Eds.), *Connecting practice, measurement, and evaluation: Selected papers from the Fifth International Symposium on Assessment in Music Education* (pp. 3–28). Chicago, IL: GIA Publications.

Darling-Hammond, L. (2012). *Creating a comprehensive system for evaluating and supporting effective teaching*. Stanford, CA: Stanford Center for Opportunity Policy in Education.

Darling-Hammond, L. (2013). *Getting teacher evaluation right*. New York, NY: Teachers College Press.

Darling-Hammond, L. (2015). Can value-added add value to teacher evaluation? *Educational Researcher, 44*(2), 132–137. doi: 10.3102/0013189X15575346

Delaney, D. W. (2011). Elementary general music teachers' reflections on instruction. *UPDATE: Applications of Research In Music Education, 29*(2), 41–49. doi: 10.1177/8755123310396193

Doherty, K., & Jacobs, S. (2015). *State of the states: Evaluating teaching and leading and learning*. National Council on Teacher Quality. ww.nctq.org/dmsStage/StateofStates2015

Duke, R. A. (1999). Measures of instructional effectiveness in music research. *Bulletin of the Council for Research in Music Education, 143*, 1–48.

Dykema, P., & Gehrkens, K. (1941). *Teaching and administration of high school music*. Boston, MA: Birchard and Co.

Edgar, S. (2012). Communication of expectations between principals and entry-year instrumental music teachers: Implications for music teacher assessment. *Arts Education Policy Review, 113*, 136–146. doi: 10.1080/10632913.2012.719426

Elpus, K. (2011). Merit pay and the music teacher. *Arts Education Policy Review, 112*, 180–190. doi: 10.1080/10632913.2011.592466

Garrett, R., & Steinberg, M. (2015). Examining teacher effectiveness using classroom observational scores: Evidence from the randomization of teachers to students. *Educational Evaluation and Policy Analysis, 37*, 224–242. doi: 10.3102/0162373714537551

Girod, G. R. (2002). *Connecting teaching and learning: A handbook for teacher educators on teacher work sample methodology*. Washington, DC: AACTE Publications.

Goe, L. (2010). *Evaluating teaching with multiple measures*. Washington, DC: American Federation of Teachers. Retrieved February, 21, 2012 from https://www.oregoned.org/images/uploads/pages/AFT_-_Laura_Goe_Evaluating_Teaching_wtih_Multiple_Measures.pdf

Grant, J., & Drafall, L. (1991). Teacher effectiveness research: A review and comparison. *Bulletin of the Council for Research in Music Education, 108*, 31–48.

Grissom, J., & Youngs, P. (2016). *Improving teacher evaluation systems: Making the most of multiple measures*. New York: Teachers College Press.

Hash, P. (2013). Large-group contest ratings and music teacher evaluation: Issues and recommendations. *Arts Education Policy Review, 114*, 163–169.

House, R. (1973). *Administration in music education*. Edgewood Cliffs, NJ: Prentice-Hall.

Hope, S. (2013). Assessment on our own terms. *Arts Education Policy Review, 114*(1), 2–12.

Hunter-Doniger, T. (2013). Contextual A.R.T. factors in the evaluation of visual art educators. *Arts Education Policy Review, 114*(4), 170–177.

Levin, B. (1979). Teacher evaluation—A review of research. *Educational Leadership, 37*, 240–245.

Maranzano, C. (2000). Music teacher performance evaluation: A call for more inclusive models. *Journal of Personnel Evaluation in Education, 14*(3), 267–274.

Marzano, R., & Toth, M. (2013). *Teacher evaluation that makes a difference*. Alexandria, VA: ASCD.

McEachern, E. (1937). A survey and evaluation of the education of school music teachers in the United States. *The Teachers College Record, 39*(3), 248–249.

McLaughlin, M. W. (1990). 24. Embracing contraries: Implementing and sustaining teacher evaluation. In Millman, J., & Darling-Hammond, L. (Eds.). (1991). *The new handbook of teacher evaluation: Assessing elementary and secondary school teachers* (p. 403). Newbury Park, CA: Corwin Press.

Music Educators National Conference (MENC). (1987). *Music teacher education: Partnership and process*. Reston, VA: Author.

National Association for Music Education (NAfME). (2011a). *NAfME recommendations for music teacher evaluation*. Reston, VA: Author. http://smte.us/teacher-evaluation/

National Association for Music Education (NAfME). (2013a). *Workbook for building and evaluating effective music education in general music*. Reston, VA: Author.

National Association for Music Education (NAfME). (2013b). *Workbook for building and evaluating effective music education in school ensembles*. Reston, VA: Author.

Nielsen, L. (2014). Teacher evaluation: Archiving teaching effectiveness. *Music Educators Journal, 101*(1), 63–69.

Nierman, G. (2014a). Music teacher evaluation: Don't forget the affective side of the house. In T. Brophy (Ed.), *Music assessment and global diversity: Practice measurement and policy* (pp. 397–413). Chicago, IL: GIA Publications.

Orzolek, D. (2004). Creating a voluntary accountability report. *Teaching Music, 11*(3), 34–39.

Orzolek, D. (2013). *Your role in music teacher evaluation.* http://musicassessment.cmswiki. wikispaces.net/file/view/Orzolek+State+Journal+Article.pdf

Overland, C. (2014). Teacher evaluation and music education. *Music Educators Journal, 101*(1), 56–62.

Partnership for Music Education Policy Development. (2012). *Position statement: Criteria for designing a viable music teacher evaluation tool.* Retrieved from http://pmepd.weebly.com/ uploads/4/9/2/4/4924314/evaluation_tool_position_statement_dec_2012.pdf

Polikoff, M., & Porter, A. (2014). Instructional alignment as a measure of teaching quality. *Educational Evaluation and Policy Analysis, 36,* 399–416.

Powers, K. (2012). All eyes on the music teacher. *Teaching Music, 20*(3), 38.

Prescott, G. (1938). *Getting results with school bands.* Minneapolis, MN: Schmitt Music.

Prince, C. D., Schuermann, P. J., Guthrie, J. W., Witham, P. J., Milanowski, A. T., & Thorn, C. A. (2009). The other 69 percent: Fairly rewarding the performance of teachers of nontested subjects and grades. *Washington, DC: Center for Educator Compensation Reform. Retrieved February, 18,* 2011.

Raiber, M., & Teachout, D. (2014). *The journey from music student to teacher: A professional approach.* London, UK: Routledge.

Rawlings, J., & Shaw, R. (2014). A Review of "Getting Teacher Evaluation Right: What Really Matters for Effectiveness and Improvement" Linda Darling-Hammond. 2013. New York: Teachers College Press. 192 pp. *Arts Education Policy Review, 115*(4), 159–165.

Robinson, M. (2015). The inchworm and the nightingale: On the (mis) use of data in music teacher evaluation. *Arts Education Policy Review, 116*(1), 9–21.

Shaw, R. D. (2014). An interview with Marcia McCaffrey about the core arts standards: Implications for arts teacher evaluation. *Arts Education Policy Review, 115*(3), 104–108.

Shinkfield, A. J., & Stufflebeam, D. L. (1995). *Teacher evaluation: Guide to effective practice.* Evaluation in Education and Human Services. Norwell: Kluwer Academic.

Shuler, S. C. (1996). Assessing teacher competence in the arts: Should Mr. Holland have gotten the gig? Introduction to the symposium on teacher evaluation. *Arts Education Policy Review, 98*(1), 11–15.

Shuler, S. C. (2012). Music assessment, Part 2—Instructional improvement and teacher evaluation. *Music Educators Journal, 98*(3), 7–10.

Silverberg, D., & Jungwirth, L. (2014). *10 models of teacher evaluation: The policies, the people, the potential.* New York: Rowman and Littlefield.

Smith, T., & Wuttke, B. (2016). Developing a model of the effective first-year secondary music teacher: Musical and teaching skills. In T. Brophy, J. Marlatt, & G. Ritcher (Eds.), *Connecting Practice, measurement, and evaluation* (pp. 177–192). Chicago, IL: GIA Publications.

Snyder, K. (1959). *School music administration and supervision.* Boston: Allyn and Bacon.

Stufflebeam, D. L. (1971). *The relevance of the CIPP evaluation model for educational accountability.* Paper read at the Annual Meeting of the American Association of School Administrators.

Taebel, D. K. (1992). The evaluation of music teachers and teaching. In *Handbook of research on music teaching and learning: A project of the Music Educators National Conference.* Reston, VA: MENC. 310–332.

Tait, M., & Haack, P. (1984). *Principles and processes of music education: New perspectives.* New York, NY: Teacher's College Press.

Ward, J. (2012). *Can reflection on teaching be meaningfully assessed?* Blog. http://www8. georgetown.edu/centers/cndls/applications/postertoolindex.cfm?fuseaction=poster. display&posterID=301

Weyland, R. H. (1960). *A guide to effective music supervision.* WC Brown Company.

Appendix—Bibliography of Additional Resources

American Educational Research Association. (2014). *Standards for educational and psychological testing.* Washington, DC: American Educational Research Association.

Baker, P. (1982). The development of music teacher checklists for use by administrators, music supervisors, and teachers in evaluating music teaching effectiveness. *Dissertation Abstracts International Section A: Humanities and Social Sciences,* 423489.

Ballou, D., & Springer, M. (2015). Using test scores to measure teacher performance: Some problems in the design and implementation of evaluation systems. *Educational Researcher, 44*(2), 77–86. doi: 10.3102/0013189X15574904

Barrett, J. (2011). Judging quality and fostering excellence in music teaching. *Journal of Music Teacher Education, 21*(1), 1–6. doi: 10.1177/1057083711415010

Barrett, J. (2012). Wicked problems and good work in music teacher education. *Journal of Music Teacher Education, 21*(2), 3–9. doi: 10.1177/1057083711434403

Bennett, K. (2014). Turning the tables on teacher evaluation. *Interval, 71*(1), 27–28.

Bowman, W. (2005). To what question(s) is music education advocacy the answer? *International Journal of Music Education, 23,* 125. doi: 10.1177/0255761405052406

Brand, M. (2009). Music teacher effectiveness: Selected historical and contemporary research approaches. *Australian Journal of Music Education, 1,* 13–18.

Brandt, R. (1978). On evaluation: An interview with Daniel L. Stufflebeam. *Educational Leadership, 35,* 249–254.

Brophy, T. (2011). *Research in assessment of music teacher education: A systems view.* Presentation notes from the Society for Music Teacher Education Symposium, Greensboro, NC, September 15, 2011.

Buckley, K., & Marion, S. (2011). A survey of approaches used to evaluate educators in non-tested grades and subjects. *National Center for the Improvement of Educational Assessment.* http:// smte.us/wp-content/uploads/2011/11/Marion-Buckley_Considerations-for-non-tested-grades_201111.pdf

Burling, K. (2012). *Evaluating teachers and principals: Developing fair, valid and reliable systems.* New York, NY: Pearson.

Clements, B. S. (1988). Effects of the reform movement on the evaluation of teachers: The Texas experience. *Design for Arts in Education, 89*(4), 28–34. doi: 10.1080/07320973.1988.9938155

Clements-Cortès, A. (2011). Designing an effective music teacher evaluation system (Part One). *Canadian Music Educator/Musicien Educateur au Canada, 53*(1), 13–18.

Collins, I. H. (1996). Assessment and evaluation in music teacher education. *Arts Education Policy Review, 98*(1), 16–22.

Colprit, E. J. (2000). Observation and analysis of Suzuki string teaching. *Journal of Research in Music Education, 48*(1), 206–221. doi: 10.2307/3345394

Colwell, R. (2003). The status of arts assessment: Examples from music. *Arts Education Policy Review, 105*(2), 11–18. doi: 10.1080/10632910309603457

Conkling, S. W. (2015). Renewing commitment to bold thinking and action. *Journal of Music Teacher Education, 25*(1), 3–6. doi: 10.1177/1057083715598771

Cowden, R., & Klotman, R. (1991). *Administration and supervision of music* (2nd ed.). New York, NY: Schirmer Books.

Danielson, C. (2001). New trends in teacher evaluation. *Educational Leadership, 58*(5), 12–15.

Danielson, C. (2013). Evaluations that help teachers learn. *The Effective Educator, 68*(4), 35–39.

Darling-Hammond, L. (2010). *Evaluating teacher effectiveness.* Center for American Progress.

Darling-Hammond, L., Amrein-Beardsley, A., Haertel, E., & Rothstein, J. (2012). Evaluating teacher evaluation. *Kappan, 93*(6), 8–15. doi: 10.1177/003172171209300603

Darling-Hammond, L., & Bransford, J. (2005). *Preparing teachers for a changing world: What teachers should learn and be able to do.* San Francisco, CA: Jossey-Bass.

Darling-Hammond, L., Wise, A. E., & Pease, S. R. (1983). Teacher evaluation in the organizational context: A review of the literature. *Review of Educational Research, 53*, 285–328. doi: 10.3102/00346543053003285

Davis, A. P. (1998). Performance achievement and analysis of teaching during choral rehearsals. *Journal of Research in Music Education, 46*, 496–509. doi: 10.2307/3345346

Derby, S. E. (2001). *Rehearsal of repertoire in elementary, middle, and high school choirs: How teachers effect change in student performance* (Unpublished doctoral dissertation). The University of Texas at Austin, Austin, TX.

Doerksen, D. P. (1990). *Guide to evaluating teachers of music performance groups.* Reston, VA: MENC, the National Association for Music Education.

Doherty, K., & Jacobs, S. (2015). *State of the states: Evaluating teaching and leading and learning.* National Council on Teacher Quality. ww.nctq.org/dmsStage/StateofStates2015

Duke, D., & Stiggins, R. (1990). Beyond minimum competence: Evaluation for professional development. In J. Millman & L. Darling-Hammond (Eds.), *The new handbook of teacher evaluation.* Newbury Park, CA: Sage.

Duke, R. A. (2005). *Intelligent music teaching: Essays on the core principles of effective instruction.* Austin, TX: Learning and Behavior Resources.

Ellett, C. D., & Teddlie, C. (2003). Teacher evaluation, teacher effectiveness and school effectiveness: Perspectives from the USA. *Journal of Personnel Evaluation in Education, 17*(1), 101–128. doi: 10.1023/A:1025083214622

Emmert, D., Sheehan, S., & Deitz, O. D. (2013). Music teacher evaluation in Pennsylvania. *Music Educators Journal, 100*(1), 30–31. doi: 10.1177/0027432113495796

Frase, L. E., & Streshly, W. (1994). Lack of accuracy, feedback, and commitment in teacher evaluation. *Journal of Personnel Evaluation in Education, 8*(1), 47–57. doi: 10.1007/BF00972709

Friedman, T., & Mandelbaum, M. (2011). *That used to be us: How America fell behind in the world it invented and how we can come back.* New York, NY: Farrar, Straus and Giroux.

Gallagher, H. A. (2004). Vaughn Elementary's innovative teacher evaluation system: Are teacher evaluation scores related to growth in student achievement? *Peabody Journal of Education, 79*(4), 79–107. doi: 10.1207/s15327930pje7904_5

Gerrity, K. W. (2013). Measuring music education: Teacher evaluation in Indiana. *Music Educators Journal, 99*(4), 17–19. doi: 10.1177/0027432113486414

Goldhaber, D. (2015). Exploring the potential of value-added performance measures to affect the quality of the teacher workforce. *Educational Researcher, 44*(2), 87–95. doi: 10.3102/0013189X15574905

Goldring, E., Grissom, J., Rubin, M., Neumerski, C. M., Cannata, M., Drake, T., & Schuermann, P. (2015). Make room value added: Principals' human capital decisions and the emergence of teacher observation data. *Educational Researcher, 44*(2), 96–104. doi: 10.3102/0013189X15575031

Goe, L. (2007). *The link between teacher quality and student outcomes: A research synthesis.* Washington, D.C: National Comprehensive Center for Teacher Quality.

Goe, L. (2008). Key issue: Using value-added models to identify and support highly effective teachers. *City,* 1–25.

Goe, L., Bell, C., & Little, O. (2008). *Approaches to evaluating teacher effectiveness: A research synthesis.* Washington, D.C.: National Comprehensive Center for Teacher Quality.

Goe, L., Biggers, K., & Croft, A. (2012). *Linking teacher evaluation to professional development: Focusing on improving teaching and learning. Research and policy brief.* Washington, D.C.: National Comprehensive Center for Teacher Quality.

Goe, L., & Croft, A. (2009). *Methods of evaluating teacher effectiveness. Research-to-practice brief.* Washington, D.C.: National Comprehensive Center for Teacher Quality.

Goe, L., & Holdheide, L. (2011). *Measuring teachers' contributions to student learning growth for nontested grades and subjects. Research and policy brief.* Washington, D.C.: National Comprehensive Center for Teacher Quality.

Hamann, D. L., Lineburgh, N., & Paul, S. (1998). Teaching effectiveness and social skill development. *Journal of Research in Music Education, 46*(1), 87–101.

Harris, D., & Herrington, C. (2015). The use of teacher value-added measures in schools: New evidence, unanswered questions and future prospects. *Educational Researcher, 44*(2), 71–76.

Hendel, C. (1995). Behavioral characteristics and instructional patterns of selected music teachers. *Journal of Research in Music Education, 43,* 182–203.

Iwanicki, E. F. (1989). 10. Teacher evaluation for school improvement. In Millman, J., & Darling-Hammond, L. (Eds.). (1989). *The new handbook of teacher evaluation: Assessing elementary and secondary school teachers.* Newbury Park, CA: Corwin Press. 158.

Jiang, J., Sporte, S., & Luppescu, S. (2015). Teacher perspective on evaluation reform: Chicago's REACH students. *Educational Researcher, 44,* 105–116.

Johnson, S. M. (2015). Will VAMS reinforce the walls of the egg crate school? *Educational Researcher, 44*(2), 117–126.

Jorgensen, E. R. (2008). *The art of teaching music.* Indiana University Press.

Kelly, S. N. (2013). *Teaching music in the American society: A social and cultural understanding of music education.* London, UK: Routledge.

Levin, B. (1979). Teacher evaluation—A review of research. *Educational Leadership, 37,* 240–245.

Lindeman, C. (1992). Toward more meaningful assessment of future music teachers: The California agenda. *Journal of Music Teacher Education, 1*(2), 17–21.

Little, O., Goe, L., & Bell, C. (2009). *A practical guide to evaluating teacher effectiveness.* Washington, D.C.: National Comprehensive Center for Teacher Quality.

Loup, K. S., Garland, J. S., Ellett, C. D., & Rugutt, J. K. (1996). Ten years later: Findings from a replication of a study of teacher evaluation practices in our 100 largest school districts. *Journal of Personnel Evaluation in Education, 10,* 203–226.

Lovingood, K. (2004). National certification: One teacher's experience. *Music Educators Journal, 91*(2), 19–23.

Madsen, C. K., & Geringer, J. M. (1989). The relationship of teacher "on-task" to intensity and effective music teaching. *Canadian Journal of Research in Music Education, 30*(1), 87–94.

Madsen, K., & Yarbrough, M. (1998). The evaluation of teaching in choral rehearsals. *Journal of Research In Music Education, 46*(4), 469–481.

Madsen, C. K., Standley, J. M., Byo, J. L., & Cassidy, J. W. (1992). Assessment of effective teaching by instrumental music student teachers and experts. *Update: Applications of Research in Music Education, 10*(1), 20–24.

Manning, R. C. (1988). *The teacher evaluation handbook.* Englewood Cliffs, NJ: Prentice-Hall.

Maranzano, C. (2002). Evaluating music teachers in Virginia: Practices and perceptions (EdD, College of William and Mary, 2002). *Dissertation Abstracts International Section A: Humanities and Social Sciences, 63448.*

Master, B. (2014). Staffing for success: Linking teacher evaluation and school personnel management in practice. *Educational Evaluation and Policy Analysis, 36,* 207–227.

McAllister, L. (2008). Evaluating teaching effectiveness in music. *American Music Teacher, 58*(3), 14–17.

McEachern, E. (1937). A survey and evaluation of the education of school music teachers in the United States. *The Teachers College Record, 39*(3), 248–249.

McCroskey, J. C., Richmond, V. P., Sallinen, A., Fayer, J. M., & Barraclough, R. A. (1995). A cross-cultural and multi-behavioral analysis of the relationship between nonverbal immediacy and teacher evaluation. *Communication Education, 44,* 281–291.

McGreal, T. L. (1983). *Successful teacher evaluation.* Publications, Association for Supervision and Curriculum Development, 225 North Washington Street, Alexandria, VA 22314 (Stock No. 611-833000).

McWhirter, J. (2011). Thoughts on music teacher evaluation. *Tennessee Musician, 64*(1), 42–43.

Mead, S., Rothergham, A., & Brown, R. (2012). *The hangover: Thinking about the unintended consequences of the nation's teacher evaluation binge.* Teacher Quality 2.0 from American Enterprise Institute. http://smte.us/wp-content/uploads/2011/11/The-Hangover-thinking-about-the-unintended-consequences-of-the-nations-teacher-evaluation-binge-AII-9-12_1440087869601.pdf

MET Project. (2011). *Working with teachers to develop fair and reliable measures of effective teaching.* Bill and Melinda Gates Foundation. http://www.edweek.org/media/17teach-met1.pdf

MET Project. (2013). *Ensuring fair and reliable measures of effective teaching.* Bill and Melinda Gates Foundation. http://www.edweek.org/media/17teach-met1.pdf

Miksza, P., Roeder, M., & Biggs, D. (2010). Surveying Colorado band directors' opinions of skills and characteristics important to successful music teaching. *Journal of Research in Music Education, 57,* 364–381.

Millman, J. (1981). Student achievement as a measure of teacher competence. *Handbook of Teacher Evaluation,* 146–166.

Millman, J. (Ed.). (1981). *Handbook of teacher evaluation.* Newbury Park, CA: Corwin.

Millman, J., & Darling-Hammond, L. (1989). *The new handbook of teacher evaluation: Assessing elementary and secondary school teachers.* Newbury Park, CA: Corwin Press.

Mosle, S. (2013). *Teachers and policy makers: Troubling disconnect.* http://opinionator.blogs.nytimes.com/category/schooling/

MTNA. (2010). *Assessment tools for the independent music teacher.* https://www.mtna.org/media/24958/assessment.pdf

Murray-Ward, M. (1998). Book review: "Teacher evaluation: A guide to effective practice." *American Journal of Evaluation, 19*(1), 153–155.

Music Educators National Conference (MENC). (1994). *Opportunity-to-learn standards for music instruction: Grades PreK-12.* Reston, VA: Author.

National Association for Music Education (NAfME). (2011). *NAfME recommendations for music teacher evaluation*. Reston, VA: Author. http://smte.us/teacher-evaluation/

National Association for Music Education (NAfME). (2011). *NAfME teacher evaluation position statement*. Reston, VA: Author. http://smte.us/teacher-evaluation/

National Education Association. (2012). *Promoting and implementing: The national education association policy statement on teacher evaluation and accountability*. NEA Toolkit. http://www.nea.org/assets/docs/2011NEA_Teacher_Eval_Toolkit.pdf

Natriello, G. (1990). Intended and unintended consequences: Purposes and effects of teacher evaluation. In Millman, J., & Darling-Hammond, L. (Eds.). (1990). *The new handbook of teacher evaluation: Assessing elementary and secondary school teachers* (pp. 35–45.). Newbury Park, CA: Corwin Press.

Nierman, G. (2016). NAfME's music teacher evaluation workbooks—Assessment to promote professional growth. In T. Brophy, J. Marlatt, & G. Ritcher, *Connecting practice, measurement, and evaluation* (pp. 135–144). Chicago, IL: GIA Publications.

OHAlliance for Arts Education. (2012). *Ohio's teaching evaluation system*. http://www.omea-ohio.org/Static_PDF/OTES/OTESOverviewforMusicTeachers.pdf

Orzolek, D. (2014). Measuring music education teacher evaluation in Minnesota. *Music Educators Journal, 100*(4), 22–24.

Peck, C., Gallucci, C., & Sloan, T. (2010). Negotiating implementation of high-stakes performance assessment policies in teacher education: From compliance to inquiry. *Journal of Teacher Education, 20*(10), 1–13.

Perrine, W. (2013). Music teacher assessment and race to the top. *Music Educators Journal, 100*(1), 39–44.

Pizer, R. (1990). *Evaluation programs for school bands and orchestras* (pp. 32–33). West Nyack, NY: Parker.

Radocy, R., & Smith, A. (1988). Critique: An evaluation of music teacher competencies identified by the Florida Music Educators Association and teacher assessment of undergraduate preparation to demonstrate those competencies. *Bulletin of the Council for Research in Music Education, 95*, 88–93.

Reimer, B. (2012). Another perspective: Struggling toward wholeness in music education. *Music Educators Journal, 99*(6), 25–29.

Reimer, B. (2015). Response to Randall Allsup, music teacher quality and expertise. *Philosophy of Music Education Review, 23*(1), 108–112.

Roberts, C. (2010). Are you a good teacher? Ask your students. *Strings, 25*(3), 33–34.

Robinson, M. (2005). The impact of beginning music teacher assessment on the assessors: Notes from experienced teachers. *Bulletin of the Council for Research in Music Education, 164*, 49–60.

Salazar, L. G. (1996). Act IV: Theatre teacher assessment and evaluation. *Arts Education Policy Review, 98*(1), 27–31.

Sanderson, S., & Peasant, J. (2016). Connecting practice, measurement, and evaluation: Key issues for assessment in music education. In T. Brophy, J. Marlatt, & G. Ritcher (Eds.), *Connecting practice, measurement, and evaluation* (pp. 589–595). Chicago, IL: GIA Publications.

Schmidt, C. P. (1992). Reliability of untrained observers' evaluations of applied music instruction. *Bulletin of the Council for Research in Music Education, 112*(1), 17–28.

Schmidt, M. (1998). Defining "good" music teaching: Four student teachers' beliefs and practices. *Bulletin of the Council for Research in Music Education, 1*, 19–46.

Schools, W. J. C. C. P. (1997). *Teacher evaluation handbook*. Williamsburg, VA: Author.

Schulman, L. S. (1986). Those who understand: Knowledge growth in teaching. *Educational Researcher, 15*(2), 4–14.

Sezer, C. (2001). Accountability and assessment in the music classroom. *Spotlight on Assessment in Music Education* (pp. 72–74). Reston, VA: MENC: The National Association for Music Education.

Shaw, R. D. (2014). An interview with Marcia McCaffrey about the core arts standards: Implications for arts teacher evaluation. *Arts Education Policy Review, 115*(3), 104–108.

Sheley, W. M. (1981). Evaluating teaching and service in the 1980's. *Proceedings of the Annual Meeting, National Association of Schools of Music, 69*, 129.

Snyder, D. W. (2011). Preparing for teaching through reflection. *Music Educators Journal, 97*(3), 56–60.

Snyder, K. (1959). *School music administration and supervision.* Boston: Allyn and Bacon.

South Carolina Music Educators Associate Task Force on Teacher Evaluation. (2013). *SC music educator evaluation: A value-added model for assessing standards-based growth.* http://advocacy.nafme.org/files/2013/05/SCMEATeacherEvaluationStatement.pdf

Steele, J., Hamilton, L., & Stecher, B. (2010). *Incorporating student performance measures into teacher evaluation systems.* Santa Monica, CA: Rand Corporation.

Stronge, J. H. (1997). Improving schools through teacher evaluation. In *Evaluating teaching: A guide to current thinking and best practice.* Newbury Park, CA: Corwin.

Stronge, J. H., & Tucker, P. D. (1999). The politics of teacher evaluation: A case study of new system design and implementation. *Journal of Personnel Evaluation in Education, 13*, 339–359.

Stronge, J. H., & Tucker, P. D. (2003). *Handbook on teacher evaluation: Assessing and improving performance.* Larchmont, NY: Eye on Education.

Stufflebeam, D. (2001). Evaluation models. *New Directions for Evaluation, 89*, 7–98.

Swanick, K. (2008). The "good-enough" music teacher. *British Journal of Music Education, 25*(1), 9–22.

Taebel, D. (1994). Changes in teaching and teachers: Effects of time and place. *Proceedings of the World Conference of the International Society for Music Educators*, 255–262.

Taebel, D. K. (1990a). An assessment of the classroom performance of music teachers. *Journal of Research in Music Education, 38*(1), 5–23.

Taebel, D. K. (1990b). Is evaluation fair to music educators? *Music Educators Journal, 76*(6), 50–54.

Taebel, D. K., & Coker, J. G. (1980). Teaching effectiveness in elementary classroom music: Relationships among competency measures, pupil product measures, and certain attribute variables. *Journal of Research in Music Education, 28*, 250–264.

Teachout, D. J. (2001). The relationship between personality and the teaching effectiveness of music student teachers. *Psychology of Music, 29*, 179–192.

Townsend, A. S. (2003). Stop! Look! Listen! for effective band rehearsals. *Teaching Music, 10*(4), 22–25.

Townsend, A. S. (2008). Driving music education: Who's at the wheel? *Teaching Music, 16*(1), 30–32.

Townsend, A. S. (2011). *Introduction to effective music teaching: Artistry and attitude.* Lanham, MD: Rowman & Littlefield.

Tucker, P., Stronge, J., & Gareis, C. (2013). *Handbook on teacher portfolios for evaluation and professional development.* London, UK: Routledge.

VMEA-SMTE. (2011). *Music teacher evaluation: Clarification and recommendations.* http://www.vamea.org/VASMTE%20Position%20Nov%2017-%20Statement%20Uniform%20Perf%20Standards%20Draft.pdf

Weiss, E. M., & Weiss, S. G. (1998). *New directions in teacher evaluation.* ERIC Digest.

Wesolowski, B. C. (2012). Understanding and developing rubrics for music performance assessment. *Music Educators Journal, 98*(3), 36–42.

Wiggins, J. (2014). *Teaching for musical understanding* (3rd ed.). New York: McGraw Hill.

Willingham, L. (2011). Designing an effective music teacher evaluation system (Part Two). *Canadian Music Educator/Musicien Educateur au Canada, 53*(2), 22–24.

Yarbrough, M. C. (1973). The effect of magnitude of conductor behavior on performance, attentiveness, and attitude of students in related mixed choruses. *Dissertation Abstracts International Section A: Humanities and Social Sciences,* 341960.

Younger, K. G. (1998). *Analysis of effective and ineffective instructional sequences in intermediate level band and orchestra rehearsals* (Unpublished doctoral dissertation). The University of Texas at Austin, Austin, TX.

Zirkel, P. A. (1996). *The law of teacher evaluation: A self-assessment handbook.* Bloomington, IN: Phi Delta Kappa.

CHAPTER 35

....

OBSERVATIONS OF MUSIC EDUCATORS FOR TEACHER EVALUATION

....

JOHANNA J. SIEBERT

THE purpose of this chapter is to provide both a general and music-specific overview of historical, current, and changing practices in teacher evaluation, with a focus on the central event of the lesson observation and its application to the professional practice of music teachers. Information has been gleaned from professional literature from the fields of general and music education, as well as recent research findings derived from a nationwide survey instrument administered by this author to practicing school music educators.

HISTORIC AND CURRENT PRACTICES IN TEACHER EVALUATION

There are multiple components in the overall teacher evaluation process. Traditionally, observations by supervising administration were the mainstay of the totality of a summative evaluative rating; these occurred with variable frequency, usually depending on the experience level of the teacher and school district collective bargaining agreements. Tenured faculty members are usually subject to fewer annual observations in comparison with new and inexperienced teachers, with such requirements based on state and/or district requirements for advancement, licensing, and job retention. Observations vary, from narrative accounts of what was observed to checklists of identified skills to numerical scores and overarching ratings.

A teacher's adherence to nonteaching tasks as described by the "duties of the teacher" may also be included in an evaluation (Scriven, 1988), albeit as a smaller contribution than more professional responsibilities. Activities common to all teaching staff include membership on school committees, attendance at district and school level faculty meetings, and holding parent conferences; special subject teachers may be held accountable for additional duties that can include, for music educators, a minimum level of ensemble festival ratings, fundraising, Booster Club management, recruitment of students, overnight trips, and uniform and equipment inventory oversight (National Association for Music Education [NAfME], 2014). While these responsibilities may or may not be a direct outcome of instructional planning, administration may still interpret successful management of all facets of an educator's employment to be a part of a teacher's effectiveness rating.

In recent years, teacher evaluation systems based on principal observation were felt to be ineffective at differentiating teaching quality (Weisberg, Sexton, Mulhern, & Keeling, 2009). Weisburg and colleagues administered a survey to 12 districts and more than 15,000 teachers in which participants described numerous problems of districts failing to distinguish among teachers' levels of effectiveness (rating most as proficient or highly proficient), and evaluations failing to identify any areas for professional growth. This lack of identification of ineffective teachers was acknowledged to be one of the major reasons for the poor performance of students on state tests, across the nation, and became part of the impetus for changes in teacher evaluation programs.

Twenty-First-Century Changes to Teacher Evaluation

The 2009 American Recovery and Reinvestment Act (ARRA) brought a new component to the teacher evaluation process. Designed as a stimulus "to encourage and reward states that are creating the conditions for education innovation and reform," the ARRA became the basis for competitive grants for states applying for and gaining dollars for President Obama's Race to the Top (RTTT) funds (Race to the Top Act, 2011). One important stipulation for this award was to provide evidence of a rated teacher evaluation system that included the use of common standards and assessments for measuring student achievement, and for that achievement rate to become part of the overall individual teacher evaluation score.

Forty-six states and the District of Columbia submitted plans for such inclusion, which carried with them the requisite changes in the use of assessment scores in computing teacher evaluation ratings. Summative evaluation in those states now carried a combination of differently weighted ingredients: formal and informal observations, student test scores, and domain-based compliance with aspects of teaching professionalism. Depending on different districts' and states' plans, standardized tests could account for all included student scores, up to a rate of 50% of the overall evaluation, even in nontested areas such as music; in other districts and states, music teachers designed assessments for such "nontested" content, and then those results were used in the evaluative computations (Siebert, 2015).

The National Education Association (NEA) found much to disagree with in this new model. It believed that evaluation is only one component of a comprehensive teacher growth and development system, and was concerned that an evaluation system whose aim was to measure teacher competence would differ from the ideal that fostered teacher learning and consistent improvement (NEA, 2012). In its efforts to support effective teachers and improve student learning, the NEA published a white paper that voiced the problem:

> Current policy discourse about teacher evaluation is mired in a rewards-and-punishment framework that too often aims to: 1) measure the effectiveness of each teacher, 2) categorize and rank teachers, 3) reward those at the top, and 4) fire those at the bottom. Such a simplistic approach not only ignores the complexity of teaching but also overlooks the real purpose of teacher assessment and evaluation. The core purpose of teacher assessment and evaluation should be to strengthen the knowledge, skills, dispositions, and classroom practices of professional educators. This goal serves to promote student growth and learning while also inspiring great teachers to remain in the classroom.   (p. 1)

The NAfME also found issue with the changes to evaluation. The inclusion of nonmusic assessment scores in the tabulation of a music teacher's evaluation was becoming an all-too-common practice in states and districts that had not developed music measures that demonstrated students' *musical* growth and achievement. In its position paper on teacher evaluation (NAfME, 2014), the organization advised reliance on assessment scores derived only from music measures, the use of multiple measures in determining a teacher's effectiveness, and the observation by an administrator with music content knowledge to provide critical feedback for appropriate professional growth.

Teacher Evaluation Models and a Growth Mindset

While components of teacher evaluation continued to change, however, it is important to understand that the role of the observation as situated within a teacher's annual evaluation remained, even while it grew more prescribed. The rated evaluation system introduced by RTTT (Race to the Top Act, 2011) ushered in additional guidelines for identifying specific skills used by educators within the classroom. Formal supervisory products were soon developed and offered by various companies to communicate teaching expectations to administrators and teachers alike; frequently used models include those by Danielson (2007), Marzano and Toth, (2013), Marshall (2009), and McREL International (McRel, 2014).

There are common focus areas among the leading models for teacher effectiveness. Danielson's "Framework for Teaching" has four domains (Planning and Preparation, The Classroom Environment, Instruction, and Professional Responsibilities), as does the Marzano evaluation model (Classroom Strategies and Behaviors, Preparing & Planning, Reflecting on Teaching, and Collegiality and Professionalism). The Marshall series of rubrics are organized around six domains of learning, which claim to cover all aspects of a teacher's job performance (Planning and Preparation for Learning; Classroom Management; Delivery of Instruction; Monitoring, Assessment, and Follow-Up; Family and Community Outreach; Professional Responsibilities). McRel's system of nine instructional categories contributes to teachers' efficacy in the four overarching frameworks of Content, Understanding (and Application), Environment, and Support (CUES); the CUES Framework rubrics are aligned and measure behaviors found in each of the framework components and underlying elements.

In addition to the domain areas listed, these products specify multiple, nested components to be observed in each teacher's practice. Three of the four of these supervisory models use rubrics with a four-level rating scale to gauge teacher effectiveness, generally categorized as Unsatisfactory, Need for Improvement, Effective, and Highly Effective. (McRel's instructional practices are aligned to five performance levels of Not Demonstrated, Developing, Proficient, Accomplished, and Distinguished.) Among other similarities, all models recommend that evaluations of teachers require not only multiple observations of teaching but also discussions and conferencing between teachers and administrators regarding planning, instructional proficiency, reflection on practice, and overall professionalism within the evaluation process.

Various states and districts investigated, recommended, and purchased these and other sources of rubrics-based products to provide identification of progressively delineated elements of successful teaching; scores from the rubrics were then combined with other components to yield an overarching rating of each teacher's effectiveness. Training for principals was recommended (and often required) to be effective evaluators (Doherty & Jacobs, 2015) in order to transition from their role as administrative leaders (with an emphasis on scheduling, budget, and discipline) to that of instructional leadership for their schools.

Professional Growth

Another desired outcome of the teacher evaluation movement that was supported by the commercial products was the ability to target individual needs for teachers' professional growth (Danielson, 2009; Marzano, 2012). Now that such delineation in professional practice was available and administrators were trained in their use, school districts had tools for differentiating between teachers with varying degrees of effectiveness (McKay, 2013). The lens through which the quality of teaching was judged had changed. Differing scores in each domain area helped to identify individual areas of strengths and needs that in turn pointed to areas for development. Danielson provided additional support by explaining that effective educators most often "visited" the distinguished level (2007), but that:

> It is highly probable that a teacher will be ranked *basic* in one aspect of his or her teaching and *proficient* in another. Highly effective teachers may reflect levels of *proficient* in different domain subsets while displaying levels of *distinguished* at various times during instruction.   (p. 83)

The notion that not all teachers were highly effective in all aspects of their professional work was not a popular one for many educators to embrace. The mindset that constructive criticism and feedback for teachers were healthy to the goal of increased student learning challenged those who were accustomed to consistently high ratings in their observation reports (McKay, 2013). Critical feedback and dialogue between educator and observer were now emphasized as central to the evaluation process (Danielson, 2007; Goe, 2013, Marshall, 2012; Marzano, 2012; McRel, 2014). Dweck's research (2008) on a growth mindset supported the importance of the educator being open to feedback; this reinforced the theme of "not needing to be bad to get better" (McKay, 2013). The growth ideal supported the individual professional development criteria now recommended in evaluative summaries, and often provided room for progression to a higher level of competence in an overall rating. Neff (2016) found that most administrators were comfortable in providing such feedback, both in and outside of their trained content areas (86%); it is such informed and effective feedback from the administrator combined with the teacher's response that contributes meaning and evidence to the reflective process (Darling-Hammond, 2010; Roussin & Zimmerman, 2014), one of the domains identified in each of the supervisory models presented.

These models helped school districts and administrations to grow progressively definitive in identifying aspects and expectations for "good teaching" (Doherty & Jacobs, 2015), albeit in ways more specific and helpful to general classroom subjects than music. Many administrators saw a change in the use of instructional practices by teachers, and felt teachers used the guidelines from the evaluation system for future planning and to "strive for distinguished," the highest rating in the Danielson model (Neff, 2016). Formal models provide multiple and specific teaching examples of each rubric level for different grade bands, but are sparse in their references to music instruction and their settings. The rubrics and process can still provide welcome points of discussion, however, for clarifying the alignment of musical practices in effective programs to what is well understood in more general subject areas (NAfME, 2016a, 2016b). These conversations are recommended strongly by the designers for pre- and postobservation conferencing, and for pair-scoring of the observation by administrator and teacher; when carried out in such a manner, these practices can provide the administrator with invaluable insights into teacher planning and effectiveness as well as into less familiar environments and content (such as music), and support discussions that are responsible and respectful, especially when one considers the use and impact of individual teacher observation scores (NAfME, 2016a, 2016b).

Variety in Observation Formats

Two types of observations are used in the collection of teaching evidence. The informal observation, often called a "walk-through," is an unannounced, impromptu visit to a classroom by the supervising administrator or observer to gain insights into the day-to-day practices of the teacher (McRel, 2014). Informal observations are usually for a predetermined length of time and yield evidence connected to domains selected by the district and/or state. These visits are not scheduled with the teacher, and may occur with different frequency depending on local requirements. Many evaluation experts recommend multiple observations of this type throughout the year as the optimal way to gain an objective and realistic view of teachers' effectiveness, as well as to maximize administrative time (Marzano, 2007; Marshall, 2012; Westerberg, 2013; McRel, 2014). Unless frequent and with familiar faculty, however, walk-throughs can cause a lack of clarity for the observer, since they lack the preparation and clarity provided by the teacher of the strategies and instructional goals being addressed (Danielson, 2011).

In contrast, the formal observations of teaching personnel are scheduled in advance by the supervising administrator, often in conjunction with the teacher to be observed (Doherty & Jacobs, 2015). The precise time and setting for the observation can depend on multiple conditions—cyclical supervision requirements, agreement in scheduling calendars, concern for a specific teaching area identified by the administrator, and/or a teacher's desire to share particular strategies and lesson material. Once the date, time, and duration of the observation have been set, formal supervision models strongly recommend a preobservation conference between the teacher and the observer (Danielson, 2007; Marzano & Toth, 2013). (This does not usually occur in informal observations due to the nature of the visit.) Many teacher evaluations combine the use of informal and formal observations, for the reasons shared here.

This issue involves trade-offs between conflicting purposes of teacher observation. On the one hand, an announced observation, for an entire lesson, gives teachers the opportunity to provide evidence of their skill in planning in a preobservation (planning) conference, and deliver a lesson that represents their best work. On the other hand, some teachers are tempted to do a "dog and pony show" for their announced observation, whereas when administrators conduct a number of shorter, unannounced observations, they can discern patterns in the teacher's practice. There are strengths in both approaches, which is why I advise the use of both formats (The Danielson Group, 2013, para. 2).

DIFFERENCES IN MUSIC OBSERVATIONS

Given the current state of music observations, it is helpful to identify the multiple and varied configurations and settings in which these occur. Evaluative discussions that take place between administrator and educator (ideally) as a result of planning, preparation, and implementation of instruction will also be addressed.

Variety in Teaching Settings

Music teaching in school settings is divided into two configurations of instructional sets—classroom and large ensemble. Classroom settings are common for classes in elementary, middle, and high school general music, keyboard, theory, music history, and other types of direct instruction and project-based learning; often there are enrollment limits per class that are comparable to other subject areas that satisfy contractual agreements for teacher load. Teaching in such settings includes many shared aims with other disciplines, such as classroom management techniques and guided student engagement that are detectable on close observation and student questioning. Most administrators can find common ground for shared aims from their personal backgrounds when supervising music teachers in these classrooms. A major difference, however, between music and general education classrooms is the goal of building students' aural literacy rather than linguistic. Sounds have particular meaning in the development of musicianship, and the simultaneity of rhythm, tonal, and expressive aspects carried out by multiple students can need translation for administrators with little content knowledge.

Large group ensemble settings are a phenomenon unique to the field of music education (Doerksen, 1990). Ensembles are composed of groups of students working together, performing different roles simultaneously on different instruments and voice parts, such as in band, chorus, orchestra, and other musical groups. These groups can range in size from approximately 30 to over 100 students, with up to 8 different instruments that are further subdivided into multiple parts and on multiple pieces. Within an ensemble rehearsal, the music teacher's instruction will combine warmups with the full group, practice on different repertoire, trouble-shooting individual and varied parts, critical feedback in-time to students' performances, opportunities for student input into performance decisions, and embedded classroom management techniques for maintaining the ensemble's focus during whole-part instruction to the group. At first glance, the engagement of all performers may not be easily discernable due to the repertoire's compositional design, sharing of musical parts, and focus for the specific lesson plan. Non-musically trained administrators can find informed observation to be even more difficult in this setting, considering the number of students, simultaneous and varied roles, and diverse levels of work assignments (Doerkson, 1990; Siskin, 2013).

There is yet another difference in teaching setting between the music teacher and the general education teacher. In contrast to their general content colleagues, music teachers often hold itinerant positions, or teaching responsibilities at multiple schools. Organizational accountability can be complex when one considers the need to work with multiple supervisors and multiple interpretations of effectiveness (Siskin, 2013). Each partner in the process needs to understand the goals of the curriculum and lesson, and what observation evidence is appropriate in determining a rating (NAfME, 2012). In the case of multiple observers, collaborative discussions and comparisons of practice need to occur among observers regarding the performance of a single teacher, and agreement reached on effectiveness ratings. Planning and preparing for a music observation by all is an important step in beginning this supervisory event (Marzano, 2000).

Pre- and Postobservation Conferences

Preobservation conferences are designed to allow the teacher to share specific goals, objectives, teaching strategies, and planned student outcomes for the lesson with the administrator/observer (Danielson, 2009). As discussed, this can be extremely helpful for observation in music classrooms, where the observer often does not have a strong command of the content. A lesson plan, curricular goals, information about individual students, and the specific content's place in the sequence of instruction are important points to be shared by the teacher in a preobservation conference, allowing ample opportunity for the administrator to ask questions and to comment on any concerns. Depending on the dialogue during this conference, the teacher may decide to revise portions of the lesson plan based on queries or advice from the administrator. These conferences can be extremely enlightening to administrators in their preparation to observe the performance tasks, management, and formative feedback inherent in ensemble and general music classrooms (NAfME, 2016a, 2016b).

Postobservation conferences for informal and formal observations are also advised in all supervisory models, and take on an added importance for music educators. It is during these follow-up meetings that the administrator can ask specific questions of the teacher with regard to the observed lesson's classroom procedures, management, content, student performance and engagement, and assessment of student understanding; such questions are helpful, as they allow the teacher the opportunity to clarify additional music management or instructional issues. The final report and scoring of the actual observation can occur during this time, and should be accomplished collaboratively between the teacher and observer (as in all content areas) as a contributing conversation to the professional growth process (The Danielson Group, 2013).

An Informed Observation

The importance of pre- and postobservation conferences has already been stated as key components to successful observations, both for the teacher and the administrator/ observer. Danielson's *Framework for Teaching* (2007) designates four domains of professional practice that occur in a repeating cycle, with the planning and reflection domains designated as "offstage" and classroom environment and instruction as "onstage" or observable practices. While planning lessons and reflecting on practice are fundamental to the successful preparation, implementation, and revising of instruction, they are carried out in isolation from the observer; it is classroom management and instructional techniques that are viewed. Pre- and postobservation conferences gain even more importance as documentation of the offstage preparation and consideration of the observed lesson, and especially as the opportunity to prepare the administrator for his/her evidence-taking and informed lesson feedback.

Effective music instruction comprises multiple teaching skills, content, and pedagogical strategies that should be detected by the administrator. It is the responsibility of the administrator to record evidence of these components in the observation notes, for knowledgeable documentation of what occurred during the lessons, and discussion, feedback, and scoring with the practicing teacher. This can be difficult for a nonmusic administrator to do without the preparation provided in a preobservation conference, as well as the clarification and reflection delivered after the observation

(NAfME, 2016a, 2016b). It behooves music educators to provide such background, to the point of requesting a conference even when one is not recognized as part of the supervisory process (Shuler, 2012).

A Resource for Music Teachers' Observations

Models frequently used in music supervision are also those of Charlotte Danielson (2007), Marzano and Toth (2013), Marshall (2009), and McRel (2014). While all employ extensive resources and progressive rubrics for rating teacher performance in and out of the classroom, they are lacking in recommendations for adapting these to less general education settings, most specifically to music teaching settings. This came to the attention of NAfME, which led the effort to provide supports to its members in the form of national advocacy and a supervisory guide for administration.

Music Teacher Evaluation Workbooks

The dearth of observation resources for music educators came to the attention of NAfME in 2011. The organization formed its first Teacher Evaluation Task Force to discuss and develop a unified focus on appropriate and defined components for overall evaluation of its teachers. The work of this task force produced a teacher evaluation position paper (NAfME, 2014) and the first series of teacher evaluation workbooks, the *Workbook for Building and Evaluating Effective Music Education in General Music* and *Workbook for Building and Evaluating Effective Music Education in Ensemble* (NAfME, 2013a, 2013b).

In a recent revision the workbooks (NAfME, 2016a, 2016b) were expanded to include attention to the 2014 National Core Music Standards (National Coalition for Core Arts Standards, 2014) and designing and incorporating student assessment resources. The section titled "Curricular Goals and Measures" provides recommendations for music teacher goal-setting based on recognized artistic processes and the use of results from music-based assessments as a component in music teacher evaluation. Another section ("Observation of Professional Practice") is most closely aligned to the Danielson model and includes multileveled instructionally based music rubrics, practices, and examples for the four most common professional teaching domains and components; these depict actual music settings and student outcomes for both general music and performance ensembles. The need for pre- and postobservation conferences continues to be stressed to promote collegial conversations between the music educator and supervising administrator that support informed observation and evaluation as they contribute to a professional growth mindset.

To address the major differences between general music instruction and that of ensemble work, the task force sought and included examples of leveled performance from each of those settings to match the ratings of the four-leveled rubric scale (NAfME, 2016a, 2016b). Similar to those found in general education models, the purpose of the application to music-specific concepts and groupings (e.g., notation reading, pitch-matching, ensemble performance, communication via playing and conducting gestures) was twofold: (1) to supply best practice ideals for music educators for reflection and assessment of the quality of their own teaching, and (2) to enlighten nonmusic administrators to the role and intricacies of the music teacher in specific teaching venues.

The Observation Experiences of Music Educators

Much has been written in recent years regarding music teacher evaluation, with most of the focus on the varied uses of student assessment data as a portion of the summative evaluation score (Shaw, 2013; 2016). Little has been researched, however, on the central, supervisory event of the formal music observation. While current and planned practices in general education and music teacher observation have been shared here, it is helpful to know what we have learned from research and professional literature regarding music teacher observation in response to RTTT requirements, with particular attention to what those educators are actually experiencing in their own observations.

Observations in Music Education

Generalization of exemplary teaching skills and effectiveness to all teachers by education administrators continues to take place, regardless of content area and grade level. Brophy (1993) addressed this situation in describing the absence of true, agreed-on evaluative music criteria, and made the case for a music observation instrument that included specialized attention to eight domains of personal characteristics, musical competence and performance skills, effective use of nonverbal strategies, classroom management, effective planning across a wide age span, objective assessment of teaching style, and appropriate professional development. He further recommended the investigation of deriving ratable components and the importance of observer training in the use of such an instrument, as well as the incorporation of the impending 1994 national music standards as recognized objectives that could unite the field in instructional practices.

In more recent years, our understanding about music observation has been gathered through research on the larger topic of music teacher evaluation in different states. Minnesota's administrators and music teachers were surveyed to examine the criteria used for evaluation and its alignment with music teachers' beliefs about how they should be evaluated (Berberick, Clementson, Hawkinson, & Roland, 2013). Respondents identified disagreement between administrator and teacher ratings of importance in the observed domains of student engagement, classroom management, assessment and grading, and musical performance.

Martin's survey (2014) to music educators questioned the processes and measures of performance used in evaluation. This topic included which stakeholders were involved in evaluative decision-making; teachers' beliefs about the fairness and value of the processes; and the outcomes of evaluation results. Participants shared their concerns about the amount of time devoted to the evaluation process, how applicable the process was to actual music teaching, and the lack of observer expertise in the content area. Teachers also indicated that they preferred evaluation systems that applied the results of observations to professional growth options rather than only a part of a summative outcome.

Additional solutions were offered in response to the whole-scale use of generic supervisory models and observation resources by administration. The Indiana Music Educators Association formed a task force to design a four-leveled observation rubric that could define and rate music teacher effectiveness (Gerrity, 2012). Much like the NAfME workbooks, the use of the "Music Teacher Effectiveness Rubric" by school districts is voluntary; it is designed to work in place of or in tandem with other observation assessment tools, and includes seven competencies in a content-specific measurement tool (Teaches Comprehensively; Engages Students in a Variety of Music Experiences; Differentiates Instruction; Provides for the Application of Musical Skills and Knowledge; Utilizes Musically Appropriate Assessments; Demonstrates a Commitment to Cross-Curricular Instruction; Provides a Model for Professionalism). Nielsen (2014) recommended music educators create a portfolio system to document all components of their evaluation process; using the Danielson framework as a model, he provided examples of adherence to "offstage" domains, school goals, and results of individual students' musical growth and achievement as evidenced by performance on appropriate music assessments.

What Music Teachers Think About Observations: Survey of K-12 Music Educators in the United States

In order to inform the current understanding of music observation practices, this author developed the Music Observation Survey to investigate in-service music teachers' observations as incorporated into their evaluation process. Resulting data from this research are described in the following sections.

Research Method

Using the membership roster and services of the NAfME, an electronic questionnaire was administered to active kindergarten through grade 12 music teachers ($n = 5,000$). The survey consisted of forced choice and open-response items that included district demographics, individual teaching experience, frequency and length of time of observations, scheduling input, use of selected supervision model, content expertise of the observer, presence and content of pre- and postobservation conferences, observer feedback, use of observation results, and teacher satisfaction with the specific observation process. Respondents also supplied comments and suggestions that could provide improved alignment with their content, desired student outcomes, and need for professional growth.

Demographics

A response rate of 18% was realized, with replies from 43 states and the District of Columbia; due to the large number of responses (n = 882) and widespread geographical representation it is believed that there is adequate representation to generalize much of the findings. Suburban and rural educators supplied the majority of the responses (48% and 36%, respectively), with urban teachers also represented (16%). There was an even distribution of teaching assignments across three levels of school populations, with 78% of the respondents holding 11 years of teaching experience or more.

Supervisory Models

Formal supervision models were used for observation by 79% of the respondents; of those, 30% used the Danielson Framework, 14% used the Marzano system, and 35% employed a combination of multiple sources that included other commercially available frameworks (McREL, 3%; Marshall, 2%), state-developed systems, and district-designed processes. Many reported that no formally recognized model was used in the observation process (21%).

Observation Types and Frequency

When questioned about the types of observations in their schools, 89% shared that formal observations were held, while 73% experienced informal (unscheduled) observations; comments revealed that many teachers experienced both types annually within their professional practice (55%). The number of required annual observations varied from one (23%) to two (36%) to three (41%), yet 44% reported being observed less than annually in the past 3 years due to district designs for summative evaluation cycles, and 5% reported no observations within that time span. The most common recommended lengths of time for a formal observation were 30 minutes (38%) and 45 minutes (35%), with 20% stating that it was the length of a class period.

Preobservation Conferences

While participants reported that approximately half (57%) experienced a preobservation conference before their formal observations, a larger majority (85%) shared their instructional goals with their observers before the lessons. Some respondents supplied additional comments to the question (n = 16 of 75 comments, or 21%) and offered that even without a formal meeting, they provided their instructional goals to their observers via submitted lesson plans and goals to increase understanding of their curricular goals. Half of the respondents (50%) selected collaboration with their observers in scheduling the observation, while 27% made suggestions for (and received) specific times and classes for the event. Most often the lesson content was left to the choice of the teachers (85%), and 90% included the curricular goals in their personal lesson planning.

Postobservation Conferences

Almost all teachers (90%) took part in postobservation conferences. The content of these conferences included feedback on the lesson implementation that was informed by either the observer's music content knowledge (25%); cursory information (19%); comments on instructional goals (45%); or nonconstructive (or no) feedback (11%). Observation scores or ratings (depending on the supervisory model followed) were provided for 68% of the respondents during this conference, with rubric-based scoring accounting for 73% of those ratings. Dialogue between the observer and music teacher during the conference contributed to the identified 10% of collaborative scoring, while scores assigned by the observer alone during this event accounted for 18% of scores.

Additional comments from some of the participants (n = 69) described various conversations with their observer at the postobservation conference. Many of those conversations included scripted accounts of the teaching aligned to specific references in the rubric language and level attained (28, or 25%); others commented that the observing administrators had little or no background in music to provide useful feedback to music educators (10, or 7%).

Informed Feedback

When asked who performed the formal observation, a great majority of the respondents (94%) shared that it was the building administrator, while others were observed by a district-wide administrator who at times was also a building level resource (12%), an out-of-district evaluator (1%), a peer music teacher (6%), a teacher out of their content area (8%), and other personnel (4%). "Other personnel" was individually identified by participants as graduate studies professor, practicum supervisor, student teacher, music mentor, school walk-through task force, and athletic director. The need for music content knowledge was an important qualification for the observers of teachers as noted frequently in the multiple comment sections throughout the survey, while only 15% of the observers were reported to possess this. Formal music supervisors accounted for 8% of the administrator observers.

Personal Satisfaction with the Observation Process and Suggestions for Changes

The categories of dissatisfied (20%) or highly dissatisfied (8%) described some individuals' levels of satisfaction with their observation experience while almost three-quarters of those surveyed were somewhat (52%) or very satisfied (20%) with their experience. A subsequent question asked respondents to provide comments for suggested changes to the observation practice that would cause them to be very satisfied with their experience. Of those 330 open-response comments, the need for changes in the following areas were cited: 42% described the need for a music supervisor or observer with music content knowledge; 11% detailed the need to improve the quality and frequency of constructive feedback; 10% felt that music teaching should be judged for its own discipline and not be required to "fit the mold" of other content areas; 6% identified the need for actual music-based scoring rubrics; and 4% would prefer that options for professional growth be addressed and impacted based on the individual observation evidence, and not just become the basis for the accumulation of scores for annual evaluations.

The final question asked respondents to provide any additional pertinent information about the observation process not already solicited through the survey. Once again a large percentage of responses (60 of the 172 comments, or 35%) identified the need for a music administrator to carry out "respectful observations" of music educators and content. Also stated was a "call to action" (3%) for national and state music organizations to design music teacher evaluation models and resources for use and training for nonmusic administrators and observers. At the same time, 7% commended both their districts' observation processes and supervising administrators for their attention to the pedagogical, instructional, and logistical differences inherent in music education.

Discussion

Music teachers identified the need for changes in the current observation process for music educators. As indicated by responses from survey participants, teachers experienced the observation process in varied ways, depending on their years of experience, school district protocols, and individual observing administrator. Not surprising, the lack of music content knowledge by those in charge of the supervision process of music educators is frequently mentioned.

Pre- and Postobservation Conferences

Almost all music teachers took part in postobservation conferences, while approximately half had scheduled preobservation discussions with their administrators. The frequency of informal observations can help to explain the lack of prior discussions of specific lessons, but in the case of formal observations, one-fifth of the teachers without preobservation conference meetings appeared concerned enough to provide their administrators with lesson plans before the scheduled observations, even though these were not required. All supervisory models described recommend preobservation discussions (in formal observations) to acquaint observers with the planned teaching through discussions and questioning, and are especially helpful for nonmusic administrators; survey responses demonstrate that music teachers work to ensure that understanding by supplying information even when not requested to do so.

Conferences following the observations were consistently held, for both formal and informal observations, yet informed feedback—a major tenet of teacher evaluation and individual personal growth—was sorely lacking, according to participants. This is explainable when considering that music administrators accounted for only 8 of the observers in music lessons, yet it is hardly an acceptable practice. Training for supervising observers has been offered through multiple organizations, but via more of a "one-size-fits-all" approach. Danielson admits this (2009), and that while there is not a separate framework for individual content areas, we need to recognize that the implementation of teaching in different subjects may look (or sound) different. Just as it behooves music teachers to coach their administration in the content and skills of their subject, administrators need to take the initiative to be competent in offering respectful understanding and discipline-specific guidance to all of their teachers.

Personal Satisfaction

Surprising in the responses was the percentage of music teachers satisfied with their observation process, when considering the lack of content-informed supervision. Although almost three-quarters of the teachers were somewhat or highly satisfied with their experiences, more than one-third cited the need for changes in the system. It does not appear that music teachers are receiving poor observations ratings due to nonmusic content supervision. Reasons for this satisfaction could be that many good observation ratings were achieved due to past practice when differentiating accurately among teachers' levels of quality was a systemic issue (Weisberg et al., 2009), or that a collegial relationship between the teacher and administrator had been cultivated over years of collaboration and trust.

Interestingly, administrators believe they can offer informed feedback outside of their own content certification area (Doherty & Jacobs, 2015; Neff, 2016), yet the need for a bona fide music supervisor was referenced repeatedly as a means to providing music educators with the informed feedback and respectful supervision being afforded to other members of the teaching profession. Many participants elaborated on their selected responses by commenting on the inadequacy of feedback when it was received, and the need to "fit the mold" of other subjects as well as the expertise of the observer. It is clear from participants' replies that current supervision practice is not meeting the needs of professional growth development for teachers in this population.

Toward More Meaningful Music Observation Practices

While multiple factors are considered in determining a teacher's competency, the formal teacher observation remains the mainstay of the supervisory process. Current thought recommends collaboration between educators and their administrators in planning, observing, discussing feedback, and scoring such observations for the ideals of increased teacher efficacy, personal growth, and ongoing student achievement. And while not as common as would be effective, this interaction is crucial for supervising administrators in areas of less familiar content such as music. The following actions are recommended in order to improve the current music observation experience for music educators.

Increasing Opportunities for Informed Feedback

Meaningful dialogue throughout all teachers' observation processes is essential in actualizing the benefits of a growth mindset (Danielson, 2007; Goe, 2013; Hill & Grossman, 2013; Marzano, 2012; McKay, 2013; McRel, 2014; NAfME, 2014; NEA, 2012; Neff, 2016; Roussin & Zimmerman, 2014; Scriven, 1988; Taebel, 1990; Westerberg, 2013). As admitted, this is challenging not only when the observing administrator lacks content expertise but also when he or she is accountable for numerous teachers' supervision (Doherty & Jacobs, 2015); making time for planned preobservation conferences, multiple observations, and follow-up feedback for just one teacher's evaluation process is difficult when compounded by 20 or more other teachers' needs. To help with administrators' time constraints, Marshall recommends only multiple, brief informal observations (10 or more) throughout the school year as a means to reduce more lengthy classroom visits, yet still advises early goal-setting conversations, short-term *and* informative feedback, and midyear touch-points for the monitoring of goals (2012). Increased yet abbreviated observations, when multiplied by the number of assigned faculty, is still an impressive time commitment to the evaluation process, and not necessarily a solution to the problem.

To assist with the time required to manage their evaluation system, some districts and states have adapted their evaluation cycles to differentiate between and among nontenured teachers, ineffective tenured teachers, and effective tenured teachers (Doherty & Jacobs, 2015). Those educators new to the profession and/or district and other teachers deemed ineffective receive annual evaluations based on multiple classroom observations (and other components); effective tenured staff are summatively evaluated over a longer period of time (typically 3 years), with fewer observations in nonsummative years. This practice of staggering evaluations is recommended to honor the multiple demands placed on the administrator; it can increase the availability of time needed to conference, observe, and provide the informed attention and feedback that respects the professional needs and practice of all educators who demonstrate a variety of levels of professional practice.

Attested to in the survey responses shared in this chapter (with strong agreement from the field of teacher evaluation) is the need for observers who are able and available to recognize a range of classroom examples of best practice, interpret that evidence against specific levels of performance, and engage teachers in productive conversations about their practice. Integrity in performing this function, whether in familiar or unfamiliar content areas, requires both the time and desire of supervising administrators to contribute to the professional growth of their individual faculty members. Attention to pre- and postobservation planning and discussion with music educators can help to ameliorate the lack of well-informed feedback from content experts, but when music teachers lack confidence in their observer's ability to capture meaningful evidence of their students' learning and to engage in insightful dialogue, the value of such supervision is questionable (Martin, 2015; Taebel, 1990). More is needed to increase the reliability in this process for the music education profession.

A More Meaningful Observation Instrument

One way to address the limitations of the current system is to increase the usability and availability of observation resources for music classrooms. Observation instruments can offer excellent potential for providing better feedback to all teachers on aspects of instruction when they are specific to each content area. According to responses in the Music Observation Survey, a number of participants identified a need for teacher evaluation models and resources aligned specifically to music education. The same demand is endorsed by Hill and Grossman (2013) whose focus on teacher observation instruments revealed, "if they are to achieve the goal of supporting teachers in improving instructional practice, (observation instruments) must be subject-specific, involve content experts in the process of observation, and provide information that is both accurate and useful for teachers" (p. 2). The type of feedback teachers receive is framed largely by the categories of the observation instruments. And since most instruments are generic, this increases the likelihood that feedback music teachers receive—overwhelmingly from observers with little music expertise—will also neglect discussion about the instructional differences inherent in their subject's teaching settings (Martin, 2015).

Broadening the general education observation expectations for use by school districts and administrators to include music-centered ideals and illustrative rubrics is an excellent way to accomplish this. Few music observation resources are available that attend to specific musical pedagogical, strategic, content, and management issues (Gerrity, 2012; NAfME, 2016a, 2016b); it befits the field of music education to use these, both in current settings and as examples for the development of additional supports.

Content Expertise Evaluators

There is an undeniable need for more informed music supervision. In tandem with established rubrics and expectations spelled out for music classrooms, the increased presence of competent music supervisors in school districts is key to improving the goals of music observations and evaluations. Evaluators must be able to assess teachers accurately so that teachers accept the judgments as valid and feel partners in a respectful and informed professional partnership; this is not happening for many music educators, however, in current evaluation systems. Multiple reasons can account for the lack of certified music supervisors in school districts—intense attention and funding devoted to tested subjects (and diverted from nontested disciplines), reduced music program size, smaller numbers of music teachers in schools than their general education peers, and a lack of music teachers going into the field of administration (Siskin, 2013). However real these impediments may be, districts need to find avenues for their solution.

There are multiple strategies for increasing this resource. Districts could identify observers from within existing personnel with personal music experience and assign those administrators as supervisors to music faculty. Small districts could collaborate to hire and share a music supervisor whose role would be to oversee all music departments' evaluation responsibilities. Music teachers could be trained to be observers and coaches by gaining waivers from contractual and state requirements. (This is already occurring in some districts and states, as reported in the survey responses.) Employing these approaches would increase the level of content knowledge among the supervisors of music teachers as well as an informed response to music observations, and go further in helping to realize the true goals of teacher evaluation for music educators.

Focus on All Students and All Teachers

Even as teachers continue to be held to stringent evaluation expectations, a change in education law has brought a renewed look at the importance of arts education. The Every Student Succeeds Act of 2015 (ESSA) replaced the No Child Left Behind legislation (2001) in its latest version of the Elementary and Secondary Education Act. No longer a listing of grade-level achievements for students in core academic subjects (narrowly defined as reading and mathematics), ESSA enjoins states in providing a "well-rounded education" to America's children, citing the subject of music as part of that education. Schools are now able to assess their ability to provide a well-rounded education (including music, specifically) and address any deficiencies using federal funds, and states must include multiple progress measures in assessing school performance that can include student engagement, parental engagement, and school culture/climate, already components of most formal supervisory models.

While too soon to judge if districts have experienced growth in their music programs as a result of this focus, it appears that the door has been opened to address the integral nature of the arts to student success. And if teacher effectiveness was deemed essential to student success in the eras of No Child Left Behind and Race to the Top, it makes ethical sense that those teacher evaluation resources and protocols need to be expanded to capture the content, pedagogy, and instructional settings that represent the current ideals of education.

Policies that aim to support student learning must also create systems for teacher learning. By focusing on informed observation, feedback, and collegiality that reflect the standards of individual subject areas, the core tenets of teacher evaluation—increased student achievement and individual teacher growth—can be supported for those teaching in the field of music education.

References

American Recovery and Reinvestment Act of 2009, S. 115, 111th Cong. (2009).

Berberick, D., Clementson, C., Hawkinson, J., & Rolandson, D. (2013). *Current practices and perceptions regarding music teacher evaluation in Minnesota.* Research presented at The Society for Music Education Symposium, UNC Greensboro, NC.

Brophy, T. (1993). *Evaluation of music educators: Toward defining an appropriate instrument.* Retrieved from: https://files.eric.ed.gov/fulltext/ED375029.pdf

Danielson, C. (2007). *Enhancing professional practice: A framework for teaching* (2nd ed.). Alexandria, VA: Association for Supervision and Curriculum Development.

Danielson, C. (2009). *Implementing the Framework for Teaching in Enhancing Professional Practice.* Alexandria, VA: ASCD.

Danielson, C. (2011). Evaluations that help teachers learn. *Educational Leadership, 68*(4), 35–9.

Darling-Hammond, L. (2010). *Evaluating teacher effectiveness: How teacher performance assessments can measure and improve teaching.* Center for American Progress. https://www.americanprogress.org/issues/education/report/2010/10/19/8502/evaluating-teacher-effectiveness

Doherty, K. M., & Jacobs, S. (2015). *State of the states: Evaluating teaching, leading, and learning.* National Council on Teacher Quality. Retrieved from https://www.nctq.org/publications/State-of-the-States-2015:-Evaluating-Teaching,-Leading-and-Learning

Doerksen, D. P. (1990). *Guide to evaluating teachers of music performance groups.* Reston, VA: NAfME.

Dweck, C. S. (2008). *Mindset: The new psychology of success.* New York: Ballantine Books.

Every Student Succeeds Act, S. 1177, 114th Cong. (2015).

Gerrity, K. W. (2012). Teacher evaluation, research, and the evolution of an assessment rubric. *Indiana Musicator, 68*(2), 24–26.

Goe, L. (2013). Can teacher evaluation improve teaching? *Principal Leadership, 13*(7), 24–29.

Hill, H. C., & Grossman, P. (2013). Learning from teacher observations. *Harvard Educational Review, 83*(2). Retrieved from http://hepg.org/her-home/issues/harvard-educational-review-volume-83-number-2/herarticle/challenges-and-opportunities-posed-by-new-teacher

Maranzano, C. (2000). Music teacher performance evaluation: A call for more inclusive models. *Journal of Personnel Evaluation in Education, 14*(3), 267–74.

Marshall, K. (2009). *Rethinking teacher supervision and Evaluation: How to work smart, build collaboration, and close the achievement gap.* Hoboken, NJ: Jossey-Bass.

Marshall, K. (2012). Fine-tuning teacher evaluation. *Educational Leadership, 70*(3), 50–53.

Martin, L. (2015). *An exploratory study of music teacher evaluation practices in multiple states with Race to the Top funding: K-12 music educators' experiences, perspectives, and recommendations.* Research presented at The 5th Annual Symposium on Assessment in Music Education, Williamsburg, VA.

Marzano, R. J. (2007). *The art and science of teaching.* Alexandria, VA: ASCD.

Marzano, R. J. (2012). The two purposes of teacher evaluation. *Educational Leadership, 70*(3), 14–19.

Marzano, R. J., & Toth, M. J. (2013). *Teacher evaluation that makes a difference.* Alexandria, VA: ASCD.

McKay, C. B. (2013). *You don't have to be bad to get better: A leader's guide to improving teacher quality.* Thousand Oaks, CA: Corwin.

McRel International. *McREL's teacher evaluation system.* (2014). Retrieved from http://www.mcrel.org

National Association for Music Education. (2012). *Recommendations for music teacher evaluation.* Retrieved from http://advocacy.nafme.org/files/2012/04/teacher_evaluation_ad_guide.pdf

National Association for Music Education. (2013a). *Workbook for building and evaluating effective music education in general music.* Reston, VA: Author.

National Association for Music Education. (2013b). *Workbook for building and evaluating effective music education in the school ensemble.* Reston, VA: Author.

National Association for Music Education. (2014). *Teacher evaluation: Position statement.* Retrieved from http://musiced.nafme.org/about/position-statements/teacher-evaluation

National Association for Music Education. (2016a). *Workbook for building and evaluating effective music education in general music* (2016 ed., revised). Reston, VA: Author.

National Association for Music Education. (2016b). *Workbook for building and evaluating effective music education in the school ensemble* (rev. ed.). Reston, VA: Author.

National Coalition for Core Arts Standards. (2012). *National core arts standards: A conceptual framework for arts learning.* Retrieved from https://www.nationalartsstandards.org/sites/default/files/Media%20arts_resources/NCCAS_%26_Media_Arts_7-28-12%20FINAL.pdf

National Education Association (NEA). (2012). *Teacher assessment and evaluation: White paper.* Washington, DC: Author.

Neff, J. L. (2016). *Administrators' perceptions of the impact of the Pennsylvania standards-based teacher evaluation model* (Unpublished doctoral dissertation), Immaculata College, PA.

Nielsen, L. D. (2014). Teacher evaluation: Archiving teacher effectiveness. *Music Educators Journal, 63*(9), 1–7.

No Child Left Behind, H. R. 6301, 20th Cong. (2001).

Race to the Top Act of 2011, H. R. 1532, 112th Cong. (2011).

Roussin, J. L., & Zimmerman, D. P. (2014). Inspire learning, not dread: Create a feedback culture that leads to improved practice. *Journal of Staff Development, 35*(6), 36–39.

Scriven, M. (1988). Evaluating teachers as professionals: The duties-based approach. In S. J. Stanley & W. J. Popham (Eds.), *Teacher evaluation: Six prescriptions for success* (pp. 110–42). Alexandria, VA: ASCD.

Shaw, R. (2013). *Music teacher evaluation in Michigan: A survey of practices and beliefs.* Presentation at the Society for Music Teacher Education Symposium, Greensboro, NC.

Shaw, R. (2016). Arts teacher evaluation: How did we get here? *Arts Education Policy Review, 117*(1), 1–12, doi: 10.1080/10632913.2014.992083

Shuler, S. (2012). Music education for life: Music assessment, part 2—Instructional improvement and teacher evaluation. *Music Educators Journal, 98*(7), 7–10.

Siebert, J. (2015). 21st century skills and the common core state standards. In C. Conway (Ed.), *Musicianship-focused curriculum and assessment* (pp. 113–130). Chicago, IL: GIA.

Siskin, L. S. (2013). Outside the core: Accountability in tested and untested subjects. In D. J. Flinders & S. J. Thornton (Eds.), *The curriculum studies reader* (4th ed., pp. 269–278). New York and London: Routledge.

Taebel, D. K. (1990). Is evaluation fair to music educators? *Music Educators Journal, 76*(6), 50–54.

The Danielson Group. (2013). Should observations be announced or unannounced? In *Questions about observations of classroom practice*, para. 2. Retrieved from https://www.danielsongroup.org/questions-about-observations-of-classroom-practice/

Weisberg, D., Sexton, S., Mulhern, J., & Keeling, D. (2009). *The widget effect: Our national failure to acknowledge and act on differences in teacher effectiveness.* Brooklyn, NY: The New Teacher Project.

Westerberg, T. R. (2013). Feedback for teachers: Focused, specific, and constructive. *Principal Leadership, 13*(7), 30–33.

CHAPTER 36

MUSIC TEACHER EVALUATION AND STUDENT GROWTH IN MUSIC

DRU DAVISON AND RYAN A. FISHER

As the landscape of public policy in education reform continuously evolves, it is imperative that music teachers discern which policy shifts will have the greatest impact on the field of music education. Beginning in 2009, several key elements of education policy reforms in the United States created urgency for considerations such as the use of student growth and achievement data as part of systems of teacher evaluation, recruitment, retention, and compensation. Policy changes can have the potential to increase equity of access for standards-based high-quality music education, but it is important to note that well-intended policy changes can potentially also have negative unintended consequences for music education. In order to minimize the unintended consequences that can result from well-intended policy changes at the federal, state, and local levels, music teachers should research the goals of the policy reforms in order to better have a voice in how policies are implemented. When contemplating the role of student growth in music teacher evaluation systems, it is important to consider the reasoning behind including student growth as a portion of a multiple-measures teacher evaluation system. Through a careful examination of the goals associated with the Race to the Top initiative (US Department of Education [USDOE], 2009 and the multiple-measures teacher evaluation systems, it is possible that some of the most challenging aspects of the reform efforts could possibly benefit the goals of standards-based music education.

In this chapter, we provide a brief overview of the Race to the Top legislation and the No Child Left Behind waivers (USDOE 2013) as they relate to the increased attention to the use of student growth and achievement data in teacher evaluation systems. We provide an overview of the multiple-measures evaluation systems with particular attention to the use of the student growth data portion of the multiple measures, and discuss the initial guidance from the USDOE regarding various approaches of incorporating student growth data in teacher evaluation systems. This chapter also presents an in-depth analysis of the development and implementation of an alternative student growth measures system specifically designed by arts educators to provide teachers with a fair, flexible, and rigorous method of demonstrating teacher effectiveness as part of a multiple measures teacher evaluation system. For purposes of this chapter, we will use the definition of student growth as included in the Race to the Top executive summary. Student growth means "the change in student achievement . . . for an individual student between two or more points in time" (USDOE, 2009, p. 14).

The Legislation

While the field of music education has been proactive in terms of documenting the role of assessment in teaching and learning music (Colwell, 2008; Fisher, 2008; Hoffer, 2008), there has not been an abundance of music education research (with the exception of Parkes, Rohwer, & Davison, 2015) devoted to the use of music assessments for the purpose of demonstrating teacher effectiveness for student growth.

A careful review of the American Recovery and Reinvestment Act (ARRA) of 2009 (H. R. 1, 111th Cong., 2009) clarifies why the use of assessment data was emerging for consideration as a part of restructured teacher evaluation systems. According to the USDOE Race to the Top executive summary:

> The ARRA lays the foundation for education reform by supporting investments in innovative strategies that are most likely to lead to improved results for students, long-term gains in school and school system capacity, and increased productivity and effectiveness. The ARRA provides $4.35 billion for the *Race to the Top* Fund, a competitive grant program designed to encourage and reward States that are creating the conditions for education innovation and reform; achieving significant improvement in student outcomes, including making substantial gains in student achievement, closing achievement gaps, improving high school graduation rates, and ensuring student preparation for success in college and careers; and implementing ambitious plans in four core education reform areas:
>
> • Adopting standards and assessments that prepare students to succeed in college and the workplace and to compete in the global economy;
> • Building data systems that measure student growth and success, and inform teachers and principals about how they can improve instruction;
> • Recruiting, developing, rewarding, and retaining effective teachers and principals, especially where they are needed most; and
> • Turning around our lowest-achieving schools. (USDOE, 2009, p. 2)

The four core education reform areas outlined in the *Race to the Top* legislation all have an impact on the field of music education in the United States, and it is important to note that each core area does not exist in a vacuum. Rather, each core reform area is interwoven. For example, it is difficult to recruit, develop, reward, and retain effective teachers and principals if you do not have systems in place to adequately measure the value that each teacher or principal contributes to student learning. This is an important concept if we are to understand how each component of a multiple-measures teacher evaluation system informs how we approach turning around our lowest-achieving schools, how we approach strategic teacher compensation and retention initiatives, and how we implement rigorous standards that prepare all students for college, career, and life readiness.

Multiple Measures Systems

Before discussing the components of a multiple measures evaluation system and how these components related to the overall goals of Race to the Top, it is important to recognize that *Race to the Top* was a competitive grant program, and not all states applied for the funding. The states that applied for the grant were required to articulate their plan to construct a new evaluation system as well as align their goals to the basic components of Race to the Top. Even so, there were still many states that either did not apply for funding or were not granted funding, and these states were under no obligation to adopt the core principles of the Race to the Top and therefore, each state had a different sense of urgency in regard to whether or not a student growth measures system would be implemented.

In addition to the student growth measures portion of the multiple-measures system stipulated in Race to the Top, states were also revising the observation of teacher behavior portion of teacher evaluation process. Generally, this is the portion of teacher evaluation that was most similar to previous evaluation systems. In this portion, a principal, principal's designee, or other district official observes the teacher delivering instruction and the teacher's actions would be evaluated using a rubric. The reforms for the observation area meant there would be more frequent observations than previously required, the rubrics would be more rigorous, and the scores would count significantly less than previous teacher evaluation systems.

Before addressing the specifics surrounding the various components of the multiple-measures systems that were being developed by the states involved in the Race to the Top initiative, it is important to recognize that concurrent efforts were underway from other states that sought waivers from certain provisions of No Child Left Behind (USDOE, 2013). Arne Duncan, US Secretary of Education from 2009 to 2016, stated:

> America's most sweeping education law—the Elementary and Secondary Education Act (ESEA), also known as No Child Left Behind—is outmoded and constrains state and district efforts for innovation and reform. The smartest way to fix that is through a reauthorized ESEA law, but Congress has not agreed on a responsible bill.

Therefore, the federal government has worked with states to develop waiver agreements that unleash local leaders' energy for change and ensure equity, protect the most vulnerable students, and encourage standards that keep America competitive.

(USDOE, 2013, para. 3)

In order for states to have flexibility with regard to the requirements of No Child Left Behind, they needed to demonstrate plans toward principles similar to the core areas of reform outlined in the Race to the Top competitive grant process. These included the adoption of college- and career-ready standards, differentiated accountability targeting the lowest-performing schools, and evaluation systems that take into account student growth (USDOE, 2013).

Considering the number of states involved in either the Race to the Top reform efforts or the 34 states that applied for and received No Child Left Behind waivers, music teachers in almost every one of the United States have experienced some variation of teacher evaluation reform efforts since 2009. Each state had a varied sense of urgency depending on the development/implementation timelines and/or the degree by which the evaluation outcomes would affect human resource decisions such as recruitment, tenure, retention, and compensation. Perhaps another factor that contributed to the varied urgency for music teachers related to each state's plan for developing the multiple measures that would contribute to the evaluation process. Many music teachers were most familiar with the direct observation portion of the multiple measures evaluation system. Even though the direct observation portion of evaluations are the most familiar to teachers, and now account for a smaller percentage of the total teacher effectiveness rating, stakeholders have paid considerable attention to the observation portion of the evaluation systems in relationship to other aspects such as student growth.

Common Components

To understand better the relationship between the various components of multiple-measures systems, consider the following common components. For most teachers, the measure that is most similar to previous teacher evaluation systems is the observation of teacher practice. Previously, a building or district level administrator would conduct a teaching observation annually or semiannually. In current practice it is more common for multiple administrators to conduct the teaching observations several times annually, and use rubrics that are aligned to standards for professional practice.

Another component of a multiple-measures teacher evaluation system is the qualitative documentation of teacher professionalism. The integration of quantitative measures such as Stakeholder Feedback Surveys is also common, and these might include student surveys, parent surveys, peer surveys, or surveys of other stakeholders. Other measures require considerable preparation to plan, implement, and operationalize are the measures of student growth and achievement.

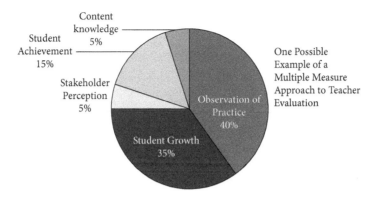

FIGURE 36.1 Example of multiple measures approach to teacher evaluation.

Before we discuss the methods of measuring student growth and achievement in traditionally nontested grades and subjects, we examine an example of a multiple-measures system and how each measure contributes to the overall teacher effectiveness score (see Figure 36.1). In the school district where the initial Fine Arts Portfolio pilot was conducted (Memphis City Schools) the multiple measures included Teacher Observations of Practice (40% of the overall weight), Teacher Content Knowledge (5% of the overall weight), Student Growth (35% of the overall weight), and Student Achievement (15% of the overall weight). Generally, in instances where the growth measure is higher than the achievement measure, the growth measure also counted for the achievement measures, which would total a 50% weighting. This means that the score from all growth measure could have more weight than any of the other measures, including the observation of teacher practice.

While the observation of teacher practice accounts for significantly less than before the implementation of multiple-measures systems, it still generally accounts for the largest weighting in many multiple-measures systems. While the other components of multiple-measures systems impact music teachers (and other teachers in traditionally nontested grades and subjects) in a number of ways, the one that impacts teachers of nontested grades and subjects most is that of implementing student growth data as a significant portion of the teacher evaluation. Teachers in subjects and grades that are traditionally tested with standardized measures might have a pathway toward populating their teacher effectiveness data that is less complicated than those educators without standardized measures. Having stated this, some stakeholders, including the authors of this chapter, would argue that the standardized measures being used in traditionally tested grades and subjects are not specifically designed to measure teacher effectiveness (see Goe & Brophy, this volume) and may not be the best tools for calculating teacher effectiveness data that could be used to influence human resources decisions such as recruitment, tenure, retention, and compensation.

The Construction of Multiple Measures Evaluation Systems

For teachers of subjects and grades traditionally tested with state-level, standardized measures, student growth data was more readily accessible than it was for teachers who taught in the nontested grades and subjects like music (and the arts). The USDOE, as part of its Reform Support Network (RSN, 2012) issued guidance to districts and states as they began to construct evaluations systems to include measures of student growth.

State Options for the Measurement of Student Growth

Initially, the USDOE issued options to states for measuring student growth for teachers in nontested subjects as part of its Reform Support Network (RSN, 2012). Their recommendations included the following options: (1) student learning objectives (SLOs), (2) "other assessments" (i.e., standardized assessments), and (3) measures of collective performance. Within the measures of collective performance were suggestions of "school-wide student growth measures, team-based collaborative achievement projects, and shared value-added scores for co-teaching situations" (RSN, 2012, p. 2).

Student Learning Objective Systems

Advantages stated in the USDOE report for using SLOs included the adaptability of SLOs to a variety of teaching assignments, the teacher's role in developing SLOs, and that SLOs permit a high degree of specialization for students and teachers. Some of the stated challenges for implementing SLOs included the lack of common assessments or common requirements for assessment, and the development of SLOs would require significant time from administrators/evaluators. For music teachers, SLOs were to be developed in consultation with a school administrator, typically the school principal. The primary responsibility for developing these SLOs would rest largely on the music teacher, and the teacher was responsible for providing evidence of SLO attainment. The principal, usually not an expert in music content, would then evaluate the degree to which the music teacher adequately met each of the previously agreed on SLOs. If a principal determines that s/he is unable to give the music teacher specific feedback necessary to support the student growth measure outcome, this can pressure principals to align teacher evaluation scores on one measure (i.e., teacher formal observations) with another measure (i.e., SLOs). This approach can compromise the intended goals of using SLOs.

Other Measures—Standardized Assessments

There are benefits to using "other assessments" according to the USDOE. These include (1) their comparability to other tested fields of study, (2) increased teacher "buy-in" (acceptance of the process as beneficial), and(3) some readily available assessments could be used (i.e., Advanced Placement [AP] or International Baccalaureate [IB] assessments). There are also challenges to the implementation of "other assessments": (1) the assessments may not cover all nontested subjects taken by students, (2) the development of these assessments could be extremely time consuming for teachers, and (3) the preexisting assessments (AP or IB) were not designed for measuring student growth or teacher effectiveness (a validity issue, mentioned earlier). There are also possible unintended consequences for using standardized tests in the music classroom, namely, the extensive class time spent preparing for, implementing, and scoring the standardized assessment. Developing a standardized test for music would also be cost prohibitive for states and districts, due to the labor-intensive and difficult nature of scoring musical performances and creative musical works. In addition, the expense of constructing logistics systems for the administration of teacher and scorer training, capturing assessment data, and integrating assessment results into frameworks that impact human resources decisions would be prohibitive for most states and districts.

School-wide Collective Measures of Performance

The advantages for measures of collective performance included collective school-wide effort focused on student achievement and common, agreed-on measures used by all teachers regardless of field. There are several challenges associated with this. First, these could be perceived as unfair, since teachers are held accountable for subject content in which they have limited impact, and could present a validity issue that Lehman refers to as "the case of the mysterious missing validity" (Lehman, 2014, p. 12)—where music teacher effectiveness is determined by an arbitrarily assigned percentage of student growth attributed to the music teacher from a test in a nonmusic subject. Additionally, these measures may give little information as to how individual teachers are performing in their classroom. In this approach, the music teacher is held responsible for performance of students with whom they may or may not have direct instruction or interaction. When principals are making personnel decisions, teachers who are specialists in music may not be perceived to be as advantageous to student advancing growth as teachers with a musical background who could provide more expertise in remediation in math or language arts. For underperforming schools, it may become difficult for school leaders to recruit and retain highly effective music teachers when it is likely that a significant portion of a teacher's evaluation score will be below expectation due to collective performance. It is relatively undisputed that assigning nontested teachers a school-wide score can lead to issues of equity, parity, and ownership. Teachers who receive a collective growth score are disincentivized to work in struggling schools because of the probability of receiving a low growth score, which is counterproductive to the goals of providing at-risk students with equity that result from having highly effective teachers. These teachers receive mixed messages about the value of their subject because a disproportionate emphasis is placed on the instructional time and resources that contribute directly to the tested subjects. Additionally, teachers without individual growth scores can lack a feeling of personal ownership of their own evaluation score.

An Alternative System Developed by Arts Educators: The Tennessee Fine Arts Portfolio Model

In 2015, the USDOE released a new report that outlined additional approaches for measuring student growth (RSN, 2015). Much of the report highlighted the use of portfolios of student growth, using those developed by music teachers in North Carolina and Tennessee as the primary examples. This section focuses on the background and development of the Tennessee Fine Arts Portfolio Model.

Background of the Portfolio Student Growth Measures System

In 2010, the Tennessee Department of Education (TDOE) convened a meeting with stakeholders representing nontested subject areas. This committee, the Fine Arts Growth Measures Committee (GMC) examined possible measures of student growth in their content areas. The GMC began with consultation from state and national associations for dance, music, theater, and visual art, the Tennessee Council of Visual and Performing Arts Supervisors, and other national consultants. After reviewing existing literature on arts assessment, the GMC developed and distributed a statewide teacher survey to solicit arts teachers' professional opinions about how student growth in the arts could be appropriately and authentically measured. Responses from the survey strongly favored: (1) the use of student performance/art work via artifacts in their evaluation of student growth, (2) ensemble performance should be included as a measure of student growth, (3) content-specific educators should be involved in the measurement of student growth in the arts, (4) arts teachers' evaluations should be tied to student growth in their specific content area, and (5) individual school districts should have input in evaluations. Davison (2011) includes the complete findings from the survey.

Results from the survey were presented to the TDOE in 2011, and a proposed budget for developing a portfolio assessment was presented. The GMC also advocated that (1) arts teachers should measure student growth, (2) state growth measures rubrics should be used to document the rate of student growth according to state standards, (3) measures should include multiple methods including both written work and performance samples (individual and group, when appropriate), and (4) subject-specific peer review teams should provide blind adjudication of each teacher's student growth evidence portfolio to substantiate and verify the teacher's reported student growth data. The TDOE collected the committee's recommendations and forwarded the report to the Teacher Evaluation Technical Advisory Committee.

Framework Development

Because the Portfolio of Student Growth Measures System was specifically designed to capture student growth data for the purpose of demonstrating teacher effectiveness, careful attention was given to make sure that the final results would be not only valid but also fair and defensible. Following the GMC committee recommendation to the TDOE, Memphis City Schools (MCS) sponsored the development of the Student Growth Rubric Development Committee composed of nine MCS music teachers to design a portfolio model based on the GMC survey results. The committee was tasked with thoroughly reviewing assessment resources, creating a student artifact evaluation rubric, establishing scoring criteria, and developing lists of possible student artifact examples. The committee also developed a questionnaire in which teachers could provide information on their teaching load, instructional time with each class, grade levels taught, and any other pertinent information a teacher wished to disclose. They also recommended that multiple student work samples be taken from each course for which the teacher was responsible. The work samples should also all four music domains (create, perform, respond, and connect) as required by the Tennessee Fine Arts Standards.

Once the framework was established, a small cohort of MCS choir directors was assembled to conduct a field test. All of the documents created by the Student Growth Rubric Development Committee were presented to the field test participants, and the proposed process for submitting evidence collections was explained. Participants of the field test expressed concern about submitting growth evidence for students in every course they taught. Based on their feedback, the number of evidence collections was reduced so that not every course required an evidence collection, and not as many students' individual work samples would be required.

In order to assess the reliability of the peer review process, a pilot study was conducted in 2011. Fifty-four Memphis City Schools elementary, middle school, and high school visual arts and music teachers volunteered to participate in the pilot study. Participants submitted up to eight collections of evidence that represented student growth in four domains: perform, create, respond, and connect. For each evidence collection, the participant used the scoring guide to determine the levels of growth represented. Though the specific details concerning the peer review process are discussed in detail later in this chapter, we felt it was important to document the reliability of the scoring process. While early scoring protocols of the Tennessee system called for two independent reviews, the system evolved to a consensus ratings process that ensured that each reviewer's expertise is leveraged most effectively. The self-score mean on a five-point scale was 3.45, while the peer review mean was 2.86 (each portfolio collection in the pilot was scored by two reviewers). Interrater reliability was calculated ($r = .97$) and the portfolio review was found to be highly reliable. In the pilot study and subsequent datasets, the effectiveness ratings distributions were found to resemble a normal distribution.

Following the pilot, the TDOE accepted the model as an approved choice for districts to implement for the evaluation of fine arts teachers, and three districts opted in the first year. As additional districts and subject areas adapted the portfolio model, it became increasingly important to develop and implement a peer review structure that focused on factors such as teacher fairness, peer reviewer training/certification, funding to pay peer reviewers, protected time for reviewers to score submissions, and constructing a logistics platform that could facilitate content-specific reviews that could follow specific parameters of the review process. A cloud-based technology platform, Growth in Learning Determination Information System (GLADIS), was built to allow continuous uploads of purposively sampled student evidence and allow teachers to construct a portfolio of student growth evidence that aligns with their self-reported growth objectives. When teachers submit their collected evidence, they self-reflect on the levels of growth they declare that the evidence supports. It is then peer reviewed. Though the pilot study used two independent peer reviews of each submission, it was determined that a consensus review process was desirable. For instance, if the primary peer review score aligns within one point (on a five-point scale) with the teacher self-reported score, that collection is finished with reviews and averaged with the remaining scores of the other collections. In the event that the score assigned by the primary peer reviewer is more than one point different from the teacher's self-score, an additional content-specific peer reviewer will conduct a secondary review of the collection and the score will become an average of the two reviews provided the independent reviews are within one point of agreement. If the difference between the two peer evaluators' scores is larger than one point, a third review (known as an executive review) provides conciliation. If consensus still cannot be reached depending on the complexity of a given situation, a fourth level of committee review is implemented to make sure every score a teacher receives as part of their evaluation is fair and rigorous. This process is programmed into the GLADIS platform so that if a discrepancy between the reviewer and the teacher's self-score exists, the collection is automatically navigated to the secondary reviewer, and so on. This is known as the GLADIS Consensus Score Protocol (GCSP). The GCSP also automatically routes separate collections submitted by one teacher to three different reviewer groups. For example, a music teacher who teaches a piano class, guitar class, and a string orchestra ensemble submits collections for each class; the GCSP would send the piano class evidence collection to a peer reviewer who teaches a piano class, the guitar class evidence to a peer review who teaches a guitar class, and so forth.

TEACHER SUBMISSION COMPONENTS

The Fine Arts Student Growth Measure System was designed to provide Fine Arts teachers with an authentic, individualized, and student-centered evaluation that contributes to professional learning and development. At its core, this system uses a peer review process to evaluate growth evidence in representative student work samples.

Teachers collect, self-score, and submit evidence collections in a portfolio using a purposive sampling process. These collections are then scored using a blind peer review process. The reviewers (trained, exemplary, content-specific teachers) conduct reviews of the student evidence collections to measure growth toward state standards using a scoring guide to determine a growth score for each evidence collection.

Within the online portfolio system, GLADIS, teachers complete an initial questionnaire about their teaching assignment that will provide their evaluators with proper context. In this section, teachers can inform the reviewer about their course load and any other information that the reviewer should consider to ensure a fair and equitable process.

The completed portfolio must include evidence from a representative sampling of students as determined by criteria that follow. The portfolio must:

- Contain four total evidence collections (each must contain evidence from two points in time within the year). One additional collection may be added if needed.
- Contain collections that represent three of the four Tennessee Fine Arts Standards domains (perform, create, and respond, connect). Each collection can only be scored for one of the domains.
- Be proportionally representative of the teacher's course load.
- Demonstrate evidence of the teacher's impact on student learning in diverse populations. At least two of four collections must contain evidence of growth for three levels of learners.

There are two types of evidence collections submitted in the portfolios. *Group evidence* collections represent growth from ensembles or groups of students without specific regard to individual learning levels. When considering purposeful sampling, it is important to show how *all* students have grown, not just the high or low achievers. *Differentiated collections* demonstrate growth for multiple learning levels (emerging, proficient, and advanced). To achieve this, at least two collections must identify students of three various learning levels and document how they have grown in the same skills/performance tasks.

Teachers receive technology guidelines that describe best practices and reduce the time teachers spend on technology-related concerns. Generally, reviewers prefer Adobe Portable Document Format (.pdf) documents, PowerPoint (.ppt) files with embedded images (but not embedded videos), audio recordings (2–3 minutes per file), and videos (2–3 minutes per file). Teachers are encouraged to upload files throughout the year to avoid waiting until the submission deadline, which is typically 6 weeks before the end of the academic school year.

Once the portfolio has been submitted, teachers then self-score using the Scoring Guide Framework, which is based on the Tennessee State Standards for Arts Education. The Scoring Guide Framework has four domains: perform, create, respond, and connect. The indicators in the scoring guide are meant to serve as a *guide* rather than a *formula* for rating evidence. Teachers are strongly encouraged to consult the scoring guide for clarity on which domain lessons are targeting to avoid submitting evidence that is self-scored in the incorrect domains.

Peer Review

A panel of stakeholders, including state department officials, school principals, and content supervisors, selects peer reviewers. Interested teachers apply for this responsibility, and applications are screened to make sure each potential reviewer has successful teaching experience, content expertise, and professional judgment. Training is required for all peer reviewers, and to ensure reviewers comply with the scoring guidelines, they must successfully complete a reviewer assessment and content norming following the mandatory training. Content norming is the process by which peer reviewers examine evidence collections, score the collections, and learn if their scores match consensus ratings that are predetermined by veteran reviewers. The process repeats until the reviewers' ratings are in agreement with the predetermined consensus ratings.

The inclusion of a student growth component in teacher evaluation, whether it is a value-added measure like the Tennessee Value-Added Assessment System (TVAAS) or a portfolio-based measure like the one presented here, relies on the premise that teacher effectiveness can be inferred from student growth. Specifically, effectiveness is understood as the amount of growth made by a teacher's students in one year compared to the growth they would be *expected* to make. If a group of students makes *more* than expected growth, we think of their teacher as *more* effective than average. If a group of students makes *less* than expected growth, we think of their teacher as *less* effective than average.

Scoring

The first step in the scoring process is to identify student achievement as presented in the portfolio. The Scoring Guide Framework provides indicators designed to reflect the grade/course level expectations from Tennessee state standards for music (TDOE, n.d.). These are meant to serve as a guide to rating artifacts. Because the domains (perform, create, respond, connect) contain Checks for Understanding/Student Performance Indicators (measureable student actions within the Tennessee State Standards that may be used to determine whether the standards are being met) from a combination of state standards, peer reviewers are informed this guide should not be understood as a *checklist* of indicators. Rather, a score is determined by assigning the performance level that fits the *preponderance of the evidence* and represents the *best fit*. Clarification of the qualifiers (masterfully, exceptionally, sufficiently, inconsistently, and insufficiently) is found in the "Checks for Understanding" and the "Student Performance Indicators" of the Tennessee state standards.

Peer reviewers then calculate student growth. Once artifacts have been rated for *achievement* using the scoring guidelines, student growth may be determined. This is essentially a calculation of the growth in *achievement* from the first to the second (or last) artifact. For example, if an early artifact from a student is judged to be a "3," while a later one is judged to be a "5," this would represent two levels of student growth. Note that evidence collections may include artifacts from multiple students or a group of students—the peer reviewer would determine the *typical* student growth across the entire collection.

Once the reviewer has calculated student growth, teacher effectiveness is determined.

The determination of teacher effectiveness results from a comparison of the *achieved* student growth to the *expected* student growth. The creators of the portfolio system define the expected growth for a student as one level per year as measured between two points in time. Based on the effectiveness levels defined by the state of Tennessee, each evidence collection would receive a score of 1 through 5, according to the following guidelines:

Level 1—*Significantly Below Expectations*—Students demonstrated, on average, little to no growth

Level 2—*Below Expectations*—Student demonstrated, on average, less than one level of growth

Level 3—*At Expectations*—Student demonstrated, on average, one level of student growth

Level 4—*Above Expectations*—Student demonstrated, on average, approximately two levels of student growth or one level plus evidence of student critical thinking (i.e., video of students discussing their thought processes around individual creative choices and the interaction of multiple artistic standards)

Level 5—*Significantly Above Expectations*—Students demonstrated, on average, three levels of student growth or two levels of student growth plus evidence of student critical thinking

For example, a seventh-grade student in choir was tested at the beginning of the school year on a specific performance indicator as listed in the state music standards. The student's performance on the test indicated the student was performing at a fourth-grade level. The student was tested again near the end of the academic year on the same performance indicator and was performing at a seventh-grade level. According to the scoring guideline above, the student demonstrated three levels of growth; therefore, the teacher would be scored as Level 5—Significantly Above Expectations for that evidence collection.

The Tennessee Department of Education oversees the portfolio process for districts who have chosen the model. This includes generating and publishing all of the training materials on their website, setting the portfolio submission deadlines, facilitating the peer review training, and overseeing the peer review scoring process. Once all of the portfolios have been scored, the state disseminates to districts the date in which the scores will be available to the teachers. Districts can then use the results to inform professional growth opportunities for teachers.

Reflections on the Tennessee Fine Arts Portfolio Model

Advocates of the portfolio growth measures system point to several factors that make the process appealing to educators and policymakers. Former US Secretary of Education, Arne Duncan (2012) used the Tennessee Fine Arts Portfolio model as an example of arts educators and state education department officials working together to create a fair system of measuring teacher effectiveness. Duncan also highlighted the blind peer review aspect of Tennessee's portfolio system, which remains a sole example of this type of review in the student growth measure options promoted by the USDOE. Laura Goe, a research scientist at the Educational Testing Service, praised the Tennessee portfolio model stating, "To me, it is a model for where we want to ultimately go, and where I think we will go in most subjects" (Robelen, 2013). This system allows teachers to be evaluated using authentic assessments they already implement in their classrooms. As the Memphis music teacher Jeff Chipman stated, "We wanted to be evaluated on how we help kids grow, but we don't want to turn the arts program into a testing machine" (Banchero, 2012). Parkes et al. (2015) also noted the benefit of embedded professional development associated with the teacher planning instruction, administering formative assessments throughout the year, and self-reflecting on the demonstrated growth as is required in the portfolio submission process.

While all student growth measures systems have potential benefits, it is also important to recognize their potential unintended consequences. While there are teachers, administrators, and policymakers who favor portfolios as valuable components of multiple-measures systems for teacher evaluations, there are also critics who point out the difficulties with the implementation of such systems with fidelity. Some of the potential unintended consequences include the amount of time spent in the preparation and submission of portfolios. While the system relies on the teacher to collect work samples from assessments they were already implementing, the collection, organization, and upload of these samples takes place typically after normal school hours. District administrators are responsible for professional development on effective portfolio construction as well as technology use. They also must administer policies on compliance and manage timelines for training sessions, support, peer reviewer selection, compensation, audits, and peer reviews. Additionally, both experienced and novice teachers can become frustrated when the evaluation paradigm shifts from one of accountability that focuses on group/ensemble achievement to accountability focused on individual student growth in music.

Adding components in teacher evaluation to include student growth does not remove the responsibilities that music teachers often feel in terms of demonstrating success at traditional large-scale music assessments (i.e., concert festivals, marching contests), as the results from these assessments are often used informally (and sometimes formally) by stakeholders such as principals and district supervisors. Additionally, district leadership must consider the expense not only in terms of time investment from multiple stakeholder groups but also in terms of compensating peer reviewers with stipends, professional leave, or differentiated compensation models. Another expense associated with the model is associated with the data storage and the logistics platform to house and manage the consensus review process. As stakeholders manage projects to include various components of multiple measures, specifically student growth, it is important to determine the long-term investment required in terms of logistic and financial support needed to implement a system with fidelity.

Summary

Assessment in music education is conducted for many reasons with many motivations from various stakeholders. As education policy evolves, music educators in the United States must remain vigilant to make sure the primary motivation for assessments in any classroom is to better inform teacher practice to strengthen all students' proficiency in the standards. In 2015, the USDOE released a press release warning too many states and districts are testing in excess, which has led to undue stress for educators and students and consumed too much instructional time (USDOE, 2015). As various stakeholder groups are formulating solutions to address issues of teacher accountability and student achievement, it is very important that music teachers take an active role in influencing policy at the local, state, and national level (Schmidt & Colwell, 2017). Music educators must recognize that there are multiple stakeholder groups inside and outside education that often need to be influenced, such as nonprofit foundations, educational policy "think tanks," and other well-intended voices in educational reform efforts. There are various ways of engaging such groups such as participating in surveys, roundtable discussions, maintaining guest blogs, proposing and conducting pilot programs that present solutions to perceived problems, and, most importantly, by keeping student interests and quality music education opportunities for all students at the center of each discussion. Many American states have embarked on this journey, and the framework of Tennessee's fine arts portfolio development has served as a guide for some.

Student Growth Portfolios beyond the Tennessee Fine Arts Model

The North Carolina Department of Public Instruction examined the Tennessee Fine Arts Portfolio as an option for value-added measures for teacher effectiveness determination and created a portfolio model called the Analysis of Student Work (ASW). According to Jennifer DeNeal, North Carolina Department of Public Instruction *Race to the Top* Project Coordinator for Teacher and Leader Effectiveness, there are multiple subject and grade levels using the ASW process. She stated:

> The North Carolina Analysis of Student Work (ASW) process is the student growth measure for select teachers in Arts Education, Advanced Placement, Healthful Living, International Baccalaureate, and World Languages. Participants in the ASW process create Evidence Collections of student work samples aligned to five learning objectives from the North Carolina Standard Course of Study, College Board Advanced Placement Standards, or International Baccalaureate Learning Objectives. Teachers may choose to collect student work in whole class or individual student formats. For individual student work samples, teachers upload the work of three students randomly selected for each objective. Evidence Collections are reviewed by

a minimum of two content area experts. The content area experts are currently licensed North Carolina educators with at least five years classroom experience in the area(s) they wish to review. If the first two reviewers disagree on the final rating, the Evidence Collection is sent to a third reviewer who decides between the two initially given ratings.

North Carolina school districts have the option to develop local processes for measuring student growth in lieu of using the state-developed ASW process. Many of the currently adopted local models closely resemble the state ASW process with one major difference: the review process is carried out by building principals instead of peer content experts. Annual student growth data is combined into a three-year rolling average for each teacher. Student growth data is not included as a formal standard in the North Carolina Educator Evaluation System but is a standardized artifact that evaluators may consider when completing an educator's summative evaluation.

(Jennifer DeNeal, personal communication, September 22, 2016)

According to Nathan L. Street (personal communication, April 22, 2016), arts education coordinator for Guilford County Schools, North Carolina, the ASW process was initially met with resistance among some educators. However, a number of benefits surfaced as a result of the preparation for implementation of the system. Conversations and discussions in professional development sessions began to center around implementation of teacher standards and objectives with fidelity. Street reported (personal communication, April 22, 2016) that perhaps the most encouraging conversation currently occurring is that of the authenticity of assessment as measured by the ASW. In the ASW process, teachers are not constrained to "teaching to the test." The teacher selects the representative student work by which he or she will be measured from the repertoire of the lessons s/he has taught throughout the year. Not only does this process empower the teacher but also it empowers the student to learn the whole curriculum rather than a version that is limited to only what is tested.

A group of music education researchers and music program leaders in Virginia also explored a portfolio model as an option to demonstrate student growth. Using the Tennessee portfolio development as an example, a group of music education leaders and scholars in Virginia surveyed arts educators and administrators to understand their preferences for value-added measures. Parkes et al. (2015) documented this process and the results of the pilot study in which this portfolio model was implemented. Overall findings suggested this assessment could be valid and reliable if teachers and reviewers were properly trained. The authors also noted that one of the most beneficial aspects of the portfolio model was its usefulness as a professional development tool. Because teachers collected data from their students that was aligned with standards and focused on individual growth, they were more reflective on their instruction and purposeful in choosing appropriate assessments that tracked student progress over time. Despite the positive findings of this study, the state did not adopt the portfolio model, and instead decided to have their nontested subject teachers use another growth measure option.

Physical education teachers in Tennessee also adopted a portfolio option for their student growth measures (TDOE, 2016). In 2012–2013, a group of world language teachers in MCS also developed and piloted a portfolio system (modeled after the Fine Arts Portfolio) in three school districts (Shelby County Schools [SCS], 2013). The model was submitted to the Tennessee State Board of Education and approved in the summer of 2013 as an alternate growth measure. In 2013–2014, Shelby County Schools K-8 world language teachers implemented the model (TDOE, 2016). The TDOE continues to allow districts to choose which student growth measure they wish to adopt for their nontested subject area teachers.

Teachers outside of traditionally "nontested" grades and subject areas have also explored the portfolio option as a measure of student growth. In 2014–2015, Pre-kindergarten and kindergarten teachers as well as administrators and academic coaches worked to develop a portfolio growth measure pilot using other portfolio measures like the Tennessee Fine Arts Portfolio as a model (TDOE, 2015). Three districts participated in the pilot, and the Tennessee Board of Education approved their portfolio measure as an option in 2015. As of 2016–2017, 1st-grade teachers in Tennessee could submit a student growth portfolio model (TDOE, 2016).

FINAL THOUGHTS

The Race to the Top legislation and other education reform efforts of the Obama administration have undoubtedly impacted the urgency with which educators address the role of assessment in all classrooms. When contemplating the role of assessment in music education classrooms, it is critical to consider several important principles, especially when the results of such assessments could impact teacher evaluation data or other important human resources decisions like differentiated compensation packages, tenure policies, or recruitment incentives. When designing systems for operationalizing assessments for the purpose of teacher evaluations, it is critical that assessments reflect authentic student work that is already happening in the classrooms. The assessments should value the curricular choices of the teacher and school leaders and be reflective of a variety of the artistic processes in the standards, with weighting options that reflect the major work of the course. Content-specific experts should score the assessments and growth evidence scores should be consensually arrived at by multiple reviewers when possible. Scoring should be based on standards-based rubrics, frameworks, and scoring guides. However, the professional judgment of the reviewers must be considered as a major factor in the final determination of teacher effectiveness and triangulated with rubric scores and other data. The overall process should empower teachers and capitalize on their professionalism and specific content knowledge. The process should remain consistent with the practice of professional growth and support, and we should avoid turning well-intended educational policies into meaningless adherence to bureaucratic exercises in compliance and paperwork.

As public policies continue to evolve, music educators and arts advocates should make sure their voices are heard. If there are to be policy solutions that are innovative, collaborative, creative, and logical, there is no better stakeholder group than music educators to find them, as these qualities are central to our art.

REFERENCES

Banchero, S. (2012, March 8). Teacher evaluations pose test for states. *Wall Street Journal*. Retrieved from http://www.wsj.com/articles/SB10001424052970203961204577267562780533458

Colwell, R. (2008). Music assessment in an increasingly politicized, accountability-driven educational environment. In T. S. Brophy (Ed.), *Assessment in music education: Integrating curriculum theory, and practice* (pp. 3–16). Chicago, IL: GIA Publications.

Davison, P. D. (2011). *Tennessee fine arts teacher evaluation pilot update and original recommendations*. Retrieved from http://smte.us/wp-content/uploads/2011/11/TN-Fine-Arts-Pilot-Update.pdf

Duncan, A. (2012, July 23). *The Tennessee story*. Huffington Post. Retrieved from http://www.huffingtonpost.com/arne-duncan/the-tennessee-story_b_1695467.html

Fisher, R. (2008, September). Debating assessment in music education. *Research and Issues in Music Education*, 6. Retrieved from http://www.stthomas.edu/rimeonline/vol6/fisher1.htm

H. R. 1, 111th Cong. (2009, February 17) (enacted). *American Recovery and Reinvestment Act*. Public Law 111–5, 123 Stat. 115. Retrieved from https://www.congress.gov/bill/111th-congress/house-bill/1

Hoffer, C. R. (2008). Issues in the assessment of K-12 music instruction. In T. S. Brophy (Ed.), *Assessment in music education: Integrating curriculum theory, and practice*, (pp. 29–36). Chicago, IL: GIA Publications.

Lehman, P. R. (2014). How are we doing? In T. Brophy, M.-L. Lai, & H.-F. Chen (Eds.), *Music assessment and global diversity: Practice, measurement, and policy* (pp. 3–18). Chicago, IL: GIA Publications.

Parkes, K. A., Rohwer, D. A., & Davison, P. D. (2015). Measuring student music growth with blind-reviewed portfolios: A pilot study. *Bulletin of the Council for Research in Music Education, 203*, 23–44. doi: 10.5406/bulcouresmusedu.203.0023

Reform Support Network (RSN). (2012, October). Washington, DC: United States Department of Education. *Measuring student growth for teachers in non-tested grades and subjects*. Retrieved from https://www2.ed.gov/about/inits/ed/implementation-support-unit/tech-assist/measuring-student-growth-teachers.pdf

Reform Support Network (RSN). (2015, August). *Emerging approaches to measuring student growth*. Washington, DC: United States Department of Education. Retrieved from https://www2.ed.gov/about/inits/ed/implementation-support-unit/tech-assist/emergapprotomeasurstudgrowth.pdf

Robelen, E. W. (2013, September 17). Classroom portfolios used as alternative teacher- evaluation measure. *Education Week*. Retrieved from http://www.edweek.org/ew/articles/2013/09/18/04arts_ep.h33.html

Schmidt, P., & Colwell, R. (2017). Introduction. In P. Schmidt & R. Colwell (Eds.), *Policy and the political life of music education* (pp. 1–7). Oxford, UK: Oxford University Press.

Tennessee Department of Education (TDOE). (2015). *Pre-K/Kindergarten*. Retrieved from http://team-tn.org/prekindergarten/

Tennessee Department of Education (TDOE). (2016). *Student growth portfolio model: First grade teacher guidebook*. Retrieved from http://team-tn.org/wp-content/uploads/2016/07/First-Grade-2016-17-Student-Growth-Portfolio-Model-Guidebook_Final.pdf

Tennessee Department of Education (TDOE). (2016). *World languages portfolio of performance-based practice.* Retrieved from http://team-tn.org/wp-content/uploads/2016/07/World-Language-Portfolio-Scoring-Guide-2016.pdf

Tennessee Department of Education (TDOE). (2017). *Student growth portfolio model– Physical Education (K-5) Teacher Guidebook 2016–17.* Nashville, TN: Author. Retrieved from http://team-tn.org/wp-content/uploads/2016/07/PE-2016-17-Student-Growth-Portfolio-Model-Guidebook.pdf

US Department of Education (USDOE). (2009, November). *Race to the Top program executive summary.* Retrieved from https://www2.ed.gov/programs/racetothetop/executive-summary.pdf

US Department of Education (USDOE). (2013, August 29). *States granted waivers from No Child Left Behind allowed to reapply for renewal for 2014 and 2015 school years* [Press release]. Retrieved from http://www.ed.gov/news/press-releases/states-granted-waivers-no-child-left-behind-allowed-reapply-renewal-2014-and-2015-school-years

US Department of Education (USDOE). (2015, October 24). *Fact sheet: Testing action plan* [Press release]. Retrieved from http://www.ed.gov/news/press-releases/fact-sheet-testing-action-plan

CHAPTER 37

MEASURING DISPOSITIONS IN PRESERVICE MUSIC EDUCATORS

KELLY A. PARKES, GARY K. RITCHER,
AND PAUL F. DOERKSEN

REVIEW OF INTEREST IN AND CONCEPTUALIZATIONS OF PROFESSIONAL DISPOSITIONS

Overview

Our research has been motivated by and taken place in the context of widespread professional interest in, and an evolving understanding of, the term "disposition." In the first part of our chapter we seek to situate our research by clarifying the present state of understanding within the American teacher education profession, expanding on our earlier discussion (Parkes, Doerksen, & Ritcher, 2014) and drawing on the work of numerous other researchers and policymakers. Smith recently asserted, "Today, there is little debate among educators about the value of dispositions" (2015, p.1). Whether educators agree about the meaning of the word "disposition" or what constitutes a meaningful set of dispositions would seem to be another matter. Raths (2007) states that if dispositions were paired with competencies, as some suggest, the result could be over a thousand dispositions. Wasicsko notes, "Today, there are almost as many different definitions of dispositions as there are institutions preparing teachers" (2007, p. 54). Books by Dietz and Raths (2007) and Murrell, Diez, Feiman-Nemser, and Schussler (2010) present examples of the wide range of ways in which institutions define and assess dispositions.

Knopp and Smith (2005) reviewed a large number of studies related to dispositions (Parkes et al., 2014). They found the studies employed a wide range of terms to define disposition, stating, "The lack of cohesive and consistent definition has muddied the discourse and complicated the application of research findings" (p. 2).

Influence of the Standards Movement

In 2005, Clark suggested several influences contributing to the profession's interest in dispositions. Of these the standards movement stands out. Freeman (2007a) has suggested it may be possible to draw a line from a seminal article by Katz and Raths (1985) to the work of such standards-related bodies as the Interstate New Teacher Assessment and Support Consortium (INTASC), National Council for the Accreditation of Teacher Education (NCATE), and Council for the Accreditation of Educator Preparation (CAEP). As he notes, linking these events involves a measure of conjecture, but is not unreasonable to suggest. Though earlier writings by Aristotle, Dewey, and Arnstine have been noted (Smith, 2013a), Katz and Raths launched, and in many ways framed, the current interest in and discussion about dispositions. Drawing on the work of Buss and Craik (1983), they described dispositions as attributions based on patterns of action. Raths subsequently served as a consultant for the writing of the 1986 document *Minnesota's Vision for Teacher Education: Stronger Standards, New Partnerships* (Task Force on Teacher Education) which promoted the use of dispositions and echoed the positions of Katz and Raths. This document, in turn, was included in a study done by Darling-Hammond and her colleagues for the RAND corporation (1990). Two years later, in 1992, Darling-Hammond chaired the writing of the INTASC standards, which famously enshrined the knowledge-skills-dispositions triumvirate as part of the standards movement (INTASC, 1992).

The INTASC standards had a direct influence on many state departments of education (Smith, 2013a). They were also highly influential in the writing of the 2000 NCATE standards, which echoed the INTASC formulation of knowledge, skills, and dispositions (Smith, 2003a). As the most important accrediting body for teacher education prior to the creation of the CAEP, NCATE had a strong influence on the shape of teacher education (Parkes et al., 2014). The appearance of dispositions in the language of the standards practically guaranteed dispositions would become part of the landscape at teacher education institutions. This is corroborated by the results of our 2010 survey (Doerksen et al.), which cited NCATE as an important source of dispositions. An earlier survey (Doerksen & Ritcher, 2007) revealed that the great majority of institutions responding were NCATE schools.

Lack of Clear Conception in Standards Documents

The NCATE, however, defined dispositions using such a variety of different terms (NCATE, 2008), that the confusion noted in Knopp and Smith's review of the literature

(2005) was perpetuated. The NCATE (2000) further complicated the picture by suggesting that dispositions published by professional organizations and state departments of education should be considered. The result was that identifying and assessing dispositions became a high-stakes expectation, but given the lack of a clearly articulated theoretical framework in the NCATE documents, the definition of "disposition" was left in doubt (Feiman-Nemser & Schussler, 2010; Freeman, 2007a; Parkes et al., 2014).

Dispositions appear in the standards of the CAEP, the accrediting body that supplanted NCATE and the Teacher Education Accreditation Council (TEAC) (CAEP, 2015). Standard 1 is titled "Candidate Knowledge, Skills and Professional Dispositions." Standard 1.1, in language similar to NCATE, calls for understanding of the INTASC standards as a basis for establishing candidate knowledge, skills and dispositions. Standard 3.3, "Additional Selectivity Factors," includes "attributes and dispositions beyond academic ability." Once again, however, the definition that appears in the CAEP glossary does little to clarify how teacher educators are to conceive of dispositions, stating: "Dispositions are the values, commitments, and professional ethics that influence behaviors towards students, families, colleagues, and communities that affect student learning, motivation, and development as well as the educator's own professional growth" (CAEP, 2013). Other than references to "caring educators" and respect for professional expectations including "codes of ethics," no specific dispositions are specified. Furthermore, CAEP continues the call for awareness of state and professional guidelines, specifically mentioning the National Association of Schools of Music as an example. The dilemma of high-stakes expectations regarding candidate dispositions paired with a conception of disposition that is lacking a focus and theoretical basis would seem to continue (Parkes et al., 2014).

Theoretical Frameworks as a Basis

In fairness to NCATE, the expectation that institutions will operate on the basis of a conceptual framework that they develop has always been a central feature of the NCATE standards. In this view, it is the responsibility of the program to articulate (among many other things) the particular theoretical perspective on dispositions they wish to follow. The notion of conceptual framework survives in CAEP. Formulating dispositions on this basis is something quite different from merely relying on common sense or trying to please NCATE or CAEP (Parkes et al., 2014). Indeed, the importance of proceeding from a conceptual framework is recommended as early as the article by Katz and Raths (1985) and appears as part of most descriptions of the process for developing dispositions (Feiman-Nemser & Schussler, 2010; Smith & Skarbek, 2013). The alternative is dubbed by Diez as the "compliance" model of developing dispositions—an approach that results in an all too common lost opportunity for meaningful growth (2007).

Fortunately, a number of theoretical frameworks have been advanced (Parkes et al., 2014). Interestingly, these tend to illuminate some of the influences described by Clark (2005) that go beyond the standards movement. For instance, in Hugh Sockett's *Teacher Dispositions: Building a Teacher Education Framework of Moral Standards* (2006), both the notion of teaching as a moral activity and the ethic of care can be seen, where Sockett suggests three possible frameworks—character, intellect, and care. He states,

> Dispositions as professional qualities of character imply such virtues as self-knowledge, courage, sincerity, and trustworthiness. Qualities of intellect imply such virtues as truthfulness, accuracy, fairness, and impartiality. Qualities of care imply such virtues as tolerance, tact, discretion, civility, and compassion. Institutions will determine their own emphases and commitments across these three broad categories, enriched by their own traditions, experiences, and orientations. (p. 23)

Diez and Raths (2007) present five possible theoretical frameworks:

- A social cognitive perspective adopted by Alverno College that emphasizes the importance of reflection in connecting beliefs about good practice with actual teaching practice;
- Wasicsko's use of a suite of instruments that measure teachers' perceptions in four areas (self, others, purpose, and frame of reference) as these correlate with effective teaching;
- Oja and Rieman's focus on development in three domains (conceptual/reflective judgment, ego maturity, and moral/ethical judgment and action);
- Freeman's emphasis on context and reasoned eclecticism as a meta-disposition in dealing with the complexity of teaching; and
- Hare's description of Palmer's emphasis on teacher formation and the understanding of self in the role of teacher.

Dottin, Miller, and O'Brien (2013) describe the development of the approach to dispositions taken at Florida International University, in which they stress the importance of establishing a conceptual framework. They describe teaching as a moral act because of its impact on individuals and society. They stress the importance of inquiry and reflection in dealing with complex problems and of having the disposition to wonder. They draw their list of 12 dispositions from Costa and Krallick (2000).

Wilkerson and Lang (2007) describe a process for the development of instruments for assessing dispositions. They take their frame of reference from a combination of the INTASC standards and the levels of the affective domain developed by Krathwohl, Bloom, and Masia (1964). Murrell et al. (2010) present descriptions by seven teacher education programs of their approaches to dispositions and offer a helpful summary of these programs. They take the stance that there is much to be learned from viewing actual practice. This has a good deal in common with the phase of our research, described later, in which we gathered exemplars, and the ways in which we have used data from programs in combination with theoretical approaches to understanding dispositions. In reviewing the seven programs presented in their book, the authors note differences—as would be expected from programs with differing conceptual frameworks—but also similarities. This seems a good and optimistic description of the current state of affairs. So long as programs are grounded in a reasoned set of beliefs and understandings, differences in the appearance of how dispositions are approached are to be expected, but do not rule out areas of agreement.

Issues in Defining the Term "Disposition"

There are a number of issues that challenge program faculty when they define dispositions. Among these are:

> Are dispositions fixed or malleable?
> Are they general aspects of personality or more specific to the profession?
> Are they subject specific?
> How sensitive are they to context? and,
> Are they entities or actions?

In the following section we discuss these questions.

Fixed or Variable?

The issue of malleability affects the decision of *when* it is most important to assess dispositions. If dispositions are fixed, assessing them prior to program admission becomes more important (Wasicsko, 2007). If they are malleable, strategies for developing dispositions come to the fore and formative assessment assumes equal importance with summative assessment (Diez & Murrell, 2010; Feiman-Nemser & Schussler, 2010). General aspects of personality may be seen as more difficult to change compared to dispositions more narrowly related to professional behavior (Diez, 2007).

The number of studies of subject-specific professional dispositions would suggest the prevailing notion is that the academic subject being taught is an important variable and that dispositions are not limited to or wholly dependent on global personal characteristics (Freeman, 2007b). Some authors have suggested that the most important disposition is the disposition to respect the complexity of instructional decisions and rely on a process of inquiry and reflection rather than conventional solutions (Dottin, Johnson, & Weiner, 2013). This, too, argues for a more flexible, context-specific, notion of disposition.

Cognition or Behavior?

A theoretical issue that appears unavoidable, the resolution of which is an important distinguishing feature of different models, is the question of whether dispositions should be thought of as "properties" or "occurrences" (Freeman, 2007a, p. 24). Katz and Raths (1985), drawing on Buss and Craik (1983), viewed dispositions as attributes ascribed to patterns of behavior. In their view, dispositions do not include an internal element that causes the observed pattern of behavior. Other approaches seem to focus more on the inner cognitive/emotional aspect. Freeman (2007a) mentions Palmer as an example from this end of the spectrum. Most writers posit some combination of the cognitive and behavioral realm, describing dispositions as, "who we are and how we behave"

(Feiman-Nemser & Schussler, 2010, p. 179) and "patterns of thoughts about issues of morals, ethics and diversity and the actions associated with these patterns" (Smith, 2013a, p. 7). Katz and Raths themselves promote the cognitive aspect of dispositions by their use of the phrase "habits of mind."

Katz and Raths (1985) also posit the existence of predispositions (internal inclinations) as an ancillary notion to dispositions (the resulting pattern of behavior). Smith, Knopp, Skarbek, and Rushton (2005) have proposed that these predispositions might be construed as beliefs. In their view, the construct of belief might be a more elegant choice than the previous array of possibilities (attitude, value, etc.). They also note there is a large body of research on the topic of beliefs (Parkes et al., 2014). In the following section we briefly survey the field of teacher beliefs and consider the feasibility of a definition that combines beliefs and associated patterns of action as a clearer and more researchable way to conceive of the idea of disposition.

Beliefs

As Fives and Gill note in their *International Handbook of Research on Teacher Beliefs* (2015), our understanding of teacher beliefs is informed by 50 years of scholarship, underscoring both the extent of the literature and the continuing interest of the profession. It is also an indication of the complexity of the construct and the multiple ways in which the term "belief" is understood. While acknowledging this variety, Skott (2015) notes some common features and offers this synthesis: "The term ['teacher belief'] is used to designate individual, subjectively true, value-laden mental constructs that are the relatively stable results of substantial social experiences and that have significant impact on one's interpretations of and contributions to classroom practice" (p. 19).

Early assumptions about the direct influence of beliefs on teachers' actions have undergone modification. The results of research about this connection have been mixed (Skott, 2015). Several mitigating factors have been suggested. Beliefs may serve different functions (as filters or to help frame problems as well as to guide actions) (Fives & Gill, 2015). Beliefs may be core or peripheral; they may be conscious or unconscious. Individuals may hold beliefs but lack the skills to execute them. The setting may be one in which it is challenging to act on one's beliefs (Skott, 2015). An example relevant to our interest in preservice professionals is the sometimes dampening effect of working with a cooperating teacher who does not share one's beliefs (Buehl & Beck, 2015). Above all, context may determine which of several, sometimes inconsistent beliefs are most salient.

Some beliefs, such as self-efficacy, have been thought of as meta-beliefs. Buehl and Beck (2015) state "the teacher must believe in his or her ability to implement a practice, view him or herself as responsible for students' learning, and believe that students are capable of learning for beliefs... to be implemented" (p. 75). In addition to self-efficacy, this suggests a central role for a sense of responsibility, one of the three dispositions we have been studying, and for the belief that all students can learn, one of the only dispositions that NCATE specifically mentioned. It has also been suggested that the connection between beliefs and actions is stronger for experienced than for less experienced teachers (Buehl & Beck, 2015).

Researchers offer a number of suggestions for assessing beliefs. Basing measures on a theoretical framework, using multiple measures, and taking steps to assure the reliability and validity of measures are among the recommendations. The use of vignettes and scenarios and the opportunity to reflect about the connection between one's beliefs and behaviors are seen as important supplements to traditional psychometrics and behavior scales (Bullough, 2015; Schraw & Olafson, 2015).

It is clear that research in teacher beliefs is addressing the connection between beliefs and behaviors. Our original definition of "disposition," put forward in 2014 (Parkes et al.), was "patterns of action based on professional beliefs." Though the connection may not be one of simple cause and effect, research in the area of beliefs is beginning to clarify the complex, reciprocal relationship that exists. This affirms our choice to include both beliefs and behaviors in our definition of disposition and suggests that our definition may evolve as more is learned about this connection. Also affirmed are some of our choices of dispositions to examine and the use of a variety of measures, including scenarios.

Assessment of Dispositions

Planning for the assessment of dispositions is a topic a number of researchers have addressed (Diez, 2007; Feiman-Nemser & Schussler, 2010; Smith & Skarbek, 2013; Wilkerson & Lang, 2007). An early step in the process of creating an assessment plan is to identify and define desirable dispositions. This should be done within the context of the program's conceptual framework, which incorporates their core beliefs and the research that supports these beliefs (Smith & Skarbek, 2013). A two-step process, in which experts generate dispositional statements that are then narrowed by a second panel, can help insure validity (Raths, 2007). This is a process we have employed in our work. The importance of reaching a manageable number of dispositions has been stressed. Smith and Skarbek (2013) recommend five to ten dispositions. Raths speaks in terms of finding an optimal conceptual size. He states that programs must "resign themselves to incompleteness" (2007, p. 159). Wasicsko speaks of a necessary parsimoniousness in the selection of dispositions (2007). As will be seen, this has been our approach in selecting a limited number of important dispositions to study.

A next step in the process is to design an evaluation system (Smith & Skarbek, 2013). The purpose of assessment is an important consideration. Is it to identify candidates who are not suited for teaching (Wasicsko, 2007), as a tool in the development of positive dispositions (Breese & Nawrocki-Chabin, 2007), for building a professional community (Diez & Murrell, 2010), for program improvement (Smith & Skarbek, 2013), or some combination of these? What kinds of measures to use and when to use them are some of the decisions that rest on this question of purpose. A recurring suggestion is to use multiple measures and multiple assessors (Diez & Raths, 2007; Smith & Skarbek, 2013). In addition to psychometric and observational tools there are numerous mentions of the use of recalling, creating, or responding to scenarios and vignettes as a way of gaining insight into an individual's dispositions and to avoid responses that are faked (Diez, 2007; Diez & Raths, 2007; Dottin, Johnson et al., 2013; Smith & Skarbek, 2013; Wasicsko, 2007). As will be seen, we have adopted this approach in our work.

Next, the measures themselves must be created. The validity and reliability of the measures are critical (Wilkerson & Lang, 2007). Diez (2007) decries the sometimes inadequate nature of psychometric scales created in some programs. Wasicsko (2007) speaks of the importance of training raters in the use of measurement instruments. While dispositions and the assessment plans that accompany them should be a coherent reflection of a program's beliefs, studying what other programs are doing is a way to broaden the range of possible dispositions and approaches to their assessment (Smith & Skarbek, 2013). This is the approach taken by Murrell et al. (2010) in examining seven programs and their strategies for defining, assessing, and developing dispositions. It is also the approach we have taken in collecting exemplars in the area of music teacher education.

Caring, Reflection, and Responsibility

Our research is currently focused on the dispositions related to caring, reflection, and responsibility. These emerged as significant areas of interest in our surveys (Doerksen, Parkes, & Ritcher, 2014). They also are frequently mentioned in the literature. Smith (2013b) and Smith and Emigh (2005) devote chapters to the disposition of caring. Sockett (2006) mentions caring as one of three possible frameworks for approaching dispositions. Caring appears as an important disposition in the writings of Breese and Nawrocki-Chabin (2007), Dottin, Miller et al. (2013), Oja and Reiman (2007), and Wasicsko (2007). It is the one disposition specifically mentioned in the CAEP standards (2015). Reflection likewise is a frequently mentioned disposition (Breese & Nawrocki-Chabin, 2007; Dottin, Johnson et al., 2013; Oja & Reiman, 2007; Skarbek & Williams, 2013; Wasicsko, 2007). Responsibility is sometimes narrowly defined in terms of attendance and completing work on time. As such, it may be an early program goal. It is also possible, however, that it relates to broader themes such as agency, taking responsibility for student success and self-efficacy. Finally, we note that reflection (Breese & Nawrocki-Chabin, 2007) and a sense of responsibility for student learning (Buehl & Beck, 2015) have been mentioned as facilitating the development and deployment of other dispositions.

SUMMARY

In summary, we have traced some of the influences that underlie the interest in dispositions and the way they are understood. We have established how the vague formulations found in NCATE and CAEP have contributed to confusion about the nature of dispositions. We have seen the importance of clearly drawn theoretical perspectives in advancing the discussion and development of dispositions. While these may not result in complete consensus, they may help us move beyond a culture of compliance on the one hand and a more locally conceived, but merely common-sense list of dispositions on the other.

We note that any definition of disposition needs to take into account both the internal (cognitive/emotional) and external (behavioral) dimension. We follow Smith, Knopp et al. in asserting that predispositions (the internal dimension) might be understood as beliefs (2005). We see in reviewing recent literature on teacher beliefs confirmation of this possibility. We conclude that conceiving of professional dispositions as "patterns of action based on professional beliefs" (Parkes et al., 2014) could serve as a helpful starting point in the process of understanding and assessing dispositions.

The second part of our chapter describes a line of research we have conducted in the area of teacher dispositions dating back to 2007. We have sought to understand and participate in the positive work being done by teacher education institutions, to identify certain dispositions that seem to be of common interest and to begin to develop measures with which to assess those dispositions.

Grounding Work and Rationale

Current Practices in Music Teacher Education Programs

The 2007 National Survey of Music Teacher Certification Programs (Doerksen & Ritcher, 2007) was an outgrowth of the 2005 Symposium on Music Teacher Education, sponsored by the Society for Music Teacher Education (SMTE) and held at the University of North Carolina at Greensboro in the United States. The symposium brought together members of the Music Educators National Conference (now the National Association for Music Education), the College Music Society, and the National Association of Schools of Music. Two events from the 2005 Symposium established a need and provided a working group for the survey: Ritcher (2005) presented research results about assessment in music teacher programs; and a new ASPA (one of 12 Areas for Strategic Planning and Action) was formed—Program Admission, Assessment, and Alignment.

Six parts composed the *2007 National Survey*: "Program Background"; "Audition Procedures for Entering Freshman Music Majors"; "Program Assessment, Decision Points, and Admission/Continuation Criteria"; "Assessment Related to Student Teaching and Program Completion"; "Predictive Quality of Assessments and Use in Program Improvements"; and "Professional Dispositions and Teaching Skills." Through the assistance of SMTE state and regional chairs, 790 institutions—each with a music teacher education (MTE) program, and a chair or coordinator who could complete the survey—were identified from across the United States and the District of Columbia. A total of 339 institutions participated in the survey over a 3-week period, providing a 43% response rate.

The overall intent of the *2007 National Survey* was to provide baseline data about MTE programs. Part Six—"Professional Dispositions and Teaching Skills"—focused specifically on six areas: Program assessment of dispositions, the predictive quality of dispositions for teaching success, satisfaction with disposition assessments, ways in which the objectivity and usefulness of disposition assessments could be improved, program settings where teaching skills were addressed, and ways in which the assessment of teaching skills could be improved. While 94% of respondents assessed dispositions (at all decision points, some decision points, or for only feedback), the levels of satisfaction with disposition assessments varied: very satisfied, 27%; somewhat satisfied, 60%; and not satisfied, 12%. Additional results from this survey section included 144 responses that identified ways in which the objectivity and usefulness of disposition assessments could be improved.

While composite results of the *2007 National Survey* provided useful information for faculty and administrators charged with music teacher preparation, the data gleaned from Part Six was considered to be of such significant interest to the Program Admission, Assessment, and Alignment ASPA's mission that a focused (national) study about the use of professional dispositions in MTE programs was undertaken for the 2009 SMTE Symposium: *The Assessment of Professional Dispositions in Music Teacher Certification Programs* (Doerksen & Ritcher, 2009). Adjusting the methodology for identifying MTE programs by using respective state Department of Education accrediting agency resources (compared to using the assistance of SMTE state and regional chairs from the

Table 37.1 Comparison of Select 2007 and 2009 Survey Data

	2007 Survey	2009 Survey
Student Enrollment		
Fewer Than 25 Students	27%	31%
25–49 Students	24%	18%
50–99 Students	25%	27%
100 or More Students	24%	24%
Assessment of Dispositions		
Yes, at all Decision Points (Admission, Retention, Completion)	42%	23%
Yes, at Some Decision Points	36%	62%
Yes, but Only for Student Feedback	16%	8%
No	6%	7%
Dispositions as Highly Predictive of Teaching Success		
Student Teaching	82%	90%
Upper-Level/Prior to Student Teaching	70%	73%
Sophomore Year	22%	18%
Freshman Year	6%	3%
Prior to Music Study/During Audition	6%	3%
Program Satisfaction with Disposition Assessments		
Very Satisfied	27%	30%
Somewhat Satisfied	60%	62%
Not Satisfied	12%	8%

earlier survey), a list of 816 institutions was created for the 2009 survey. Among those institutions, 471 MTE programs were randomly selected to participate; 193 completed the online survey. Five sections composed the survey: "Background" (similar to the *2007 National Survey*), "Using Professional Dispositions," "Applying Professional Dispositions," "Development and Ratings," and "Final Thoughts and Next Steps." See Table 37.1 for a comparison of select data between the two surveys.

Participants in the 2009 survey also evaluated a series of questions and statements about the application of dispositions, stages of development, the importance of use, strategies of assessment, and possible impediments. Themes and questions about professional dispositions emerged, as illustrated in Tables 37.2, 37.3, and 37.4.

Table 37.2 Select Results from the 2007 Survey—Response Percentages and Mean Ratings

	Percentage	Mean Rating
Essential Dispositional Statements (Highest Percentages)		
"Is Responsible and Dependable"	94%	1.06
"Displays Mature Judgment and Self-Control"	81%	1.20
"Is Punctual and Regular in Attendance"	79%	1.21
Essential Dispositional Statements (Lowest Percentages)		
"Demonstrates Commitment to Working With Parents and School Personnel"	48%	1.56
"Show Initiative"	47%	1.55
"Dresses Appropriately"	33%	1.84
Ratings of Disposition Statements: Strongly Agree Responses (Highest Percentages)		
"Having Positive Professional Dispositions is an Important Part of Overall Teaching Effectiveness"	80%	1.38
"It is Important to Gather Assessments From a Number of Different People"	58%	1.5
Ratings of Disposition Statements: Strongly Agree Responses (Lowest Percentages)		
"The Subjectivity of Disposition Assessment Makes Assessment of Dispositions Something to Avoid"	4%	3.92
"Disposition Statements Should be Subject-Specific (i.e., Related to Only Music)"	4%	3.68
Importance for Assessment ("1" High to "5" Low): Highest Percentages for "1"		
"Assessments Based on Actual Teaching"	81%	1.28
"Instructor-Rating Scales"	50%	1.67
"Interviews"	46%	1.80
Importance for Assessment ("1" High to "5" Low): Highest Percentages for "2"		
"Student Reflections"	43%	2.00
"Self-Rating Scales"	38%	2.40
"Student Philosophical Statements"	36%	2.5

Table 37.3 Select Results from the 2007 Survey—Response Percentages

	Percentage
Use of Disposition Assessment over the Previous Two Years	
"About the Same Use of Disposition Assessment as Two Years Ago"	58%
"More Use of Disposition Assessment as Two Years Ago"	41%
"Less Use of disposition Assessment Than Two Years Ago"	1%
Providing Dispositional Feedback to Students	
"Once or Twice During the Program"	45%
"At Least Once a Semester"	27%
"Every Year"	27%
"Never"	2%
Status of Dispositional Assessment	
"We Have Assessments for Dispositions, Though They Need Minor Revisions"	34%
"We Have Assessments for Dispositions That We Believe are Working Effectively"	27%
"Beginning to Develop Assessments for Dispositions"	17%
"We Have Assessments for Dispositions, but Feel That They Need Major Revisions"	16%
"No Plans to Assess Dispositions"	6%
Impediments to Dispositional Assessments	
"Time"	99%
"Large Classes"	29%
Sources for the Development of Professional Dispositions	
"Based on Our Experiences and Common Sense"	65%
"Based on NCATE Standards"	50%
"Uses a Common Form Developed by Our Teacher Education Unit"	45%
"Based on Empirical Evidence of How Dispositions Predict/Affect Teaching Success"	25%
"Based on Lists Used by Other Institutions"	25%
"Revised a Common Form for Our Program That was Developed by Our Teacher Education Unit"	24%

Table 37.4 Select Results from the 2007 Survey—Additional Response Percentages

	"1"	"2"
Highest Percentages for Input: Scale of "1" (High) to "5" (Low)		
"Input From Music Education Faculty"	80%	12%
"Input From K–12 Teachers"	57%	27%
"Input From Other Music Faculty"	33%	41%
"Input From Teacher-Education Faculty"	32%	36%

The final question from the 2009 survey asked about willingness to participate in a follow-up study. Fifty-three percent (53%) indicated "Yes," setting up *The 2010 Select Survey of Professional Dispositions* (Doerksen, Parkes, & Ritcher, 2010).

Emerging Applications of Disposition Statements

Volunteers from the 2009 survey ($N = 102$) were contacted to participate in the *2010 Select Survey*. To confirm their continuing interest to participate, the volunteers were provided an explanation about this latest stage of the ongoing research into dispositional use. Ninety invitations were extended for the new survey based on volunteer responses. (Note: The MTE programs of these volunteers had self-described procedures in place for the assessment of professional dispositions.) Fifty-eight participants started the survey; 55 completed it. The online survey grouped questions into three distinct areas: (1) questions about the development and use of dispositional goals (framed as statements); (2) questions—focused on satisfaction among department faculty members, involvement of stakeholders, and length of use—to help narrow the subsequent group size for future sample collection; and (3) questions leading to next steps, such as program demographics and willingness to share program examples of dispositional statements and assessment models. See Table 37.5 for select results.

Table 37.5 Select Results from the *2010 Select Survey*

	Response
Program Status: Highest Response Percentages	
Program Size (Student Enrollment)	50–99 Students (31%)
Assessment of Dispositions	"Yes, at Some Decision Points" (59%)
Levels of Agreement: Highest Response Percentage per Statement	
"Dispositions Are Best Evaluated Once Candidates Are Hired and Are Active in the Profession"	53% Strongly Disagreeing
"Dispositions Are Best Measured by Observable Behaviors"	59% Agreeing
"Dispositions Are Best Understood as Stable Personality Traits"	47% Disagreeing
"Disposition Assessments are Best Left out of the Teacher Preparation Program"	64% Strongly Disagreeing
"Dispositions Can be Modified by the Experiences Teacher Education Programs Provide"	68% Agreeing
"The Set of Desirable Dispositions May Vary With the Setting to Which They Apply"	55% Agreeing
"The Types of Dispositions That Should be Expected May Differ at Different Levels of the Program"	53% Agreeing
Sources for Disposition Statements: Top Three Ranked Responses	
"Formulated by the Teacher Education Unit"	72%
"Designed to Meet NCATE Standards"	51%
"Formulated by the Music Education Faculty"	47%
Satisfaction of Disposition Assessments	
"Very Satisfied"	26%
"Somewhat Satisfied"	64%
"Not Satisfied"	9%
Current Status of Disposition Assessments	
"We are Beginning to Develop Assessments for Dispositions"	18%
"We Have Assessments for Dispositions, but Believe That They Need Major Revisions"	16%
"We Have Assessments for Dispositions, Though They Need Minor Revisions"	29%

(continued)

Table 37.5 Continued

	Response
"We Have Assessments for Dispositions That we Believe are Working Effectively"	37%
Top Three Ranked Challenges in Developing and Assessing Disposition Statements	
Rank 1	"Creating Reliable Assessment Tools"
Rank 2	"Providing Students With Feedback About Their Dispositions"
Rank 3	"Formulating Disposition Statements"
Application of Disposition Assessment	
Denying Students Admission to Teacher Education or Music Teacher Education	79% "Yes"
Permission to Student Teach	68% "Yes"
Passing Student Teaching	60% "Yes"
Benefits of Disposition Assessments: Highest Response Rates for Very Important Benefit	
"Clarifying Program Expectations Regarding Dispositions for Students"	
"Helping Students who Lack Appropriate Dispositions to Develop Them"	
"Counseling Students who Lack Appropriate Dispositions out of Music Education"	

Results from the *2010 Select Survey* provided (1) further data for categories and samples of disposition definitions; (2) sample dispositional statements; (3) evidence for disposition assessments as predictive of teaching effectiveness; and (4) final thoughts, questions, and comments of the participants. Six categories emerged—based on survey responses—for the definition of dispositions: Personal/Nature (e.g., demeanor); Personal/ Features (e.g., characteristics); Mindful (e.g., attitude); Moral/Ethical (e.g., humane); Professional (e.g., teaching); and Behavior (e.g., skills). The single most-used term among respondents was "behavior." An ongoing question in the discussion of dispositions is whether the focus should be on values and beliefs, or actions. It is noted, though, that the term "behavior" was often paired with a more internal designation, such as "attitude." Three examples of disposition definitions (of many provided) are "Commitment to music education"; "Tendencies, habits of students in the teaching setting"; and "personal and academic characteristics appropriate for future educators." Respondents also provided numerous samples of disposition statements. These were later organized among five researcher-created categories (resulting from an extensive analysis and coding of all collected statements).

1. Attitudes, Behaviors, Collaboration, Conduct, Responsibility, and Work Ethics (e.g., "Arrives on time early" and "Is responsible and dependable");
2. Beliefs, Character, Ethics (not Work), Integrity (e.g., "Commitment to ongoing learning" and "Honest & Trustworthy");

3. Communication: Verbal and Written (e.g., "Able to communicate effectively in writing and verbally" and "Listens to others");

4. Instruction, Instructional Planning, and Classroom Behaviors (e.g., "Commitment to the learning of all children" and "Has compassion for students"); and

5. Reflection (e.g., "Demonstrates ability and willingness to self-assess" and "Makes choices after pondering ideas and experiences").

The question about applying disposition assessments as predictive tools for teaching effectiveness proved difficult on multiple levels. While a small number of programs identified future plans for collecting such evidence, many programs did not have current practices in place for this type of collection. Select MTE programs, though, did offer anecdotal evidence—while other programs provided more direct evidence. A reoccurring sentiment among respondents articulated caution about the usefulness of dispositions and the difficulty in defining teaching effectiveness. Anecdotal, informal, and indirect sources of evidence included (1) certifications sought, positions taken and kept; (2) colleagues and administrators that hire; (3) direct observations; (4) postgraduation practices; and (5) success of candidates who received warnings about their performances and went on to demonstrate improvement. Direct evidence included comparison of pre-student teaching evaluations and cooperating-teacher evaluations; course assignments; evaluations by supervisors, cooperating teachers, and principals; formative assessments; INTASC and NCATE research; and high grades and grade point averages (GPAs, a numerical mean of student grades translated to a quantitative scale—usually 0–4). The survey's final section invited final thoughts, questions, and comments from participants. Many responses supported the current research and its dissemination. Other comments spoke more to the notion of disposition use in music teacher preparation. One such comment:

> Dispositions ratings force us to consider student strengths and weakness early on in their careers. They force us to consider the big picture for each student. That said, it is a constant struggle to focus on ratings and to do the follow-up remediation. Transcripts are easier.

A second example:

> It's hard to explain to the modern student how important it is to be professional and what professional means. The students have been trained to focus on grades—which don't always help us discern their readiness for internships and student teaching.

The Analysis of Disposition Assessment in Eleven Exemplar Programs

Eleven MTE programs were ultimately designated as "exemplar" by 2012—from among self-identified programs of the *2010 Select Survey*, and other programs later peer-identified—that had current disposition assessments believed to be effective. A content analysis of assessment documents from the 11 programs determined 6 had assessment forms that were music-education specific. And all but 1 of the 11 programs had assessment forms or items that were in common with their respective Colleges of Education/Teacher

Education units. Evaluators who used the assessment forms included music faculty, music education faculty, cooperating teachers and university supervisors, and students (as self-evaluations). The timing of evaluations varied across programs. However, most programs had multiple points at which assessments of dispositions took place. Examples include prior to—and during—student teaching; prior to being officially admitted (during the sophomore year for many programs); all pre-clinical courses (such as methods) and student teaching; sophomore admission and every semester following—including student teaching; an introductory course, through methods, and into student teaching; and by all faculty teaching music-education courses. Perceptions of the values and benefits of disposition assessments among the exemplar MTE programs include "gate keeping," and the opportunities for conversations and necessary preparations they allowed; opportunities for multiple observations and multiple raters; authenticity—assessments based on student actions and behaviors; the ability for students to receive feedback from Colleges of Education/Teacher Education units; and (noted by many MTE programs), the clarity of professional expectations on the part of students.

Reliability and Validity

Reliability and validity of disposition assessments used by the 11 exemplar MTE programs were of interest. Two programs simply stated "No" to a question about assurances for reliability, while other programs had mixed responses. A consensus among most programs was that interrater reliability appeared to be good—faculty tended to agree with the results ("if one sees a problem, so will another"), with one program noting that agreement between raters was especially strong during the semester of student teaching. Still, as one program observed, consensus is usually reached—but nothing is calculated. Regarding validity, uniform agreement was evident across the MTE programs. Content validity seemed strongest in those programs where multiple faculty members used the assessment instruments—noting apparent agreement among faculty, and observing that instruments were viewed as authentic (e.g., measuring actions). Further, MTE programs offered anecdotal evidence of observed correlations between first-year dispositions and eventual teaching successes. Considering deficiency outcomes from disposition assessments, exemplar programs identified a wide spectrum of actions taken. These included student counseling and action plans for improvement (before and during student teaching); students not recommended to move forward in the program; less formal (i.e., lower stakes) conversations; and remedial plans that may include repeating professional courses. While work toward student improvement was a common theme among MTE programs, one program noted the difficulty among faculty members in determining consequences for, and follow-up to, remedial actions. Even though the majority of the exemplar programs did not express concerns with the use of their disposition assessments, four issues were identified: The uncertainty of what happens when results are provided outside of music education (i.e., to colleges of education/teacher education units); the desire for all involved faculty to take the assessment process seriously; making necessary time at the end of each semester to complete assessments, and to review results for needed discussions; and, finally, finding appropriate and effective consequences for less-than-desirable results.

Creating Categories and Validating Statements

American national accreditation requirements for teacher education and music-teacher education programs—current at the time this chapter was written—include language about professional dispositions. The INTASC, the National Association of Schools of Music, and the CAEP describe teacher qualities among their respective standards. Such examples include "the teacher takes responsibility for promoting learners' growth and development" (Critical Disposition 1(j): Council of Chief State School Officers, 2011, p. 10); "the ability and desire to remain current with developments in the art of music and in teaching" (Desirable Attribute 7: National Association of Schools of Music, 2015, p. 116); and "candidates use research and evidence to develop an understanding of the teaching profession and use both to measure their P-12 students' progress and their own professional practice" (Candidate Knowledge, Skills, and Professional Dispositions I.I: CAEP, 2016). However, while such language published in accreditation documents provides a focus on the application and assessment of dispositions, a consensus about core statements (and their reliability and validity) does not yet appear evident.

The *2010 Select Survey* provided a body of disposition statements and allowed for the subsequent collection of exemplar disposition assessments. Rather than attempt to define a potentially large number of disposition categories from this body of data—initial analysis of the *2010 Select Survey* results suggest up to 30 categories of dispositions—a decision was made to focus on a narrow range of dispositions. Three categories of dispositions emerged for exploration: reflection, caring, and responsible. In order to determine the importance of these specific disposition categories—and to explore the various ways in which the dispositions are understood and described—a content analysis was conducted of responses to, and exemplars from, the *2010 Select Survey*. Patterns were explored across these data using an inductive reasoning analysis. Statements describing a belief or pattern of action were coded as illustrating reflective, caring, or responsible beliefs or behaviors. Clusters of linked statements expressing similar meanings emerged. This approach was continued and replicated to ensure validity and consistency. Overall, content analysis of the three categories of disposition statements was achieved through independent reviews and through themes determined during two rounds of agreement discussions. A total of 73 statements were thus created: 20 for reflective dispositions (e.g., "Preservice music educators reflect about their growth over time"), 34 for caring dispositions (e.g., "Preservice music educators value individual differences"), and 19 for responsible dispositions (e.g., "Preservice music educators accept and assume responsibility").

An online survey was next created to validate the statements. Music teacher educators from 778 institutions across the United States (an updated list from the 2009 survey) were invited to participate; 127 colleagues responded and completed the entire survey. Mean responses for items from each of the three disposition categories were calculated. Most statements were found to be accurate reflections of associated dispositions, with more support indicated for the "responsible" dispositions statements, followed by "caring" statements and then "reflective" statements. Further analysis of survey results identified statements with high mean scores and small standard deviations that were fully supported by more than 50% of respondents. Items meeting these combined criteria (mean above 4.25 and SD below .90) resulted in 24 validated disposition statements: one for reflective, 13 for caring, and 10 for responsible. The selection and measurement of three specific disposition statements from this collection are discussed in the next part.

MEASUREMENT INSTRUMENTS

Researchers have made many efforts to measure dispositions, using a variety of definitions, in a variety of contexts, and across a range of constructs. This section examines measures being used in both wider educational settings and within music education, the selection of three specific dispositions relevant to music educators, the development of measures, the findings of using the measures, and the direction that measurement of dispositions might take.

Review of Psychometric Instruments

Educational psychologists and psychometricians have, in the past, been concerned with measuring specific domains in teachers' beliefs. Pajares (1992) gives a detailed overview of the beliefs of teachers, and how best to tackle this issue. He suggested that teachers' beliefs are a "messy construct" (Pajares, 1992, p. 307), yet that they should be the focus of educational research. He cites Fenstermacher (1979), who suggested that the study of beliefs would develop the focus for teacher effectiveness research, and Pintrich (1990), who also argued that beliefs would ultimately be the most valuable psychological construct to teacher education (Pajares, 1992, p. 308). Brandes and Cowson (2008) focused on beliefs about inclusion and students with disabilities and, using regression, were able to uncover predictors for prejudice against students with disabilities and opposition to inclusion. Dee and Henkin (2002) were concerned with attitudes about cultural diversity and, using regression, illustrated that students expressed problematic attitudes toward cultural diversity dependent on their comfort with assimilation and diversity. Woolley, Benjamin, and Woolley (2004) examined constructivist and traditional attitudes toward teaching with the development of a teacher beliefs survey, and Flowers (2006) found, using confirmatory factor analysis, a three-factor model that illustrated professionalism, teaching quality, and relationship with others.

Other researchers (e.g., Gay, 2010; Villegas, 2007) have been concerned with the obvious connection between behaviors and beliefs. Gay (2010) explored the need to prepare teachers for cultural diversity, to understand how beliefs about race, class, culture, ethnicity, and experience affect instructional behaviors. Villegas (2007) argued that the assessment of dispositions related to social justice beliefs and behaviors is reasonable and defensible. Some researchers (Johnston, Almerico, Hanriott, & Shapiro, 2011) focused on only their students, at the preservice level, and their field-experience behaviors to attempt to describe the dispositions that were most relevant for their particular contexts. Content-specific studies (e.g., Beverly, Santos, & Kyger, 2006; L'Allier, Elish-Piper, & Young, 2006) have focused on special education and advanced reading programs respectively.

In reviewing the work conducted by music educators, it becomes apparent that this area is under-researched. Miksza and Tan (2015) examined dispositions toward practicing and Hickey (2015) investigated the dispositions of ensemble leaders with respect to free-improvisation. However, these studies were not focused on the specific array of dispositions required of music education preservice teachers. Fredrickson and Madsen (2010) previously investigated how current and future music teachers perceived stress, in an effort to understand how the levels of emotional stress affect teachers' daily satisfaction in relationship to longer-term career goals. Abrahams (2009) observed the preservice practicum experience to explore connections and dispositions through multiple perspectives in a critical grounded theory. Woody, Laird, Gilbert, and Munderloh (2014) presented a promising pilot model comparing the dispositions of music education majors and non-music-education majors, and Hourigan (2006) promoted the case study as a method to promote reflective thinking in music education preservice students. McKoy (2013) has specifically considered cross-cultural competence, using three constructs: (1) readiness to teach in culturally diverse settings, (2) factors constraining readiness to teach in culturally diverse settings, and (3) education experiences related to multicultural education and music education. Shaw (2015) explored how culturally responsive teaching enacts with choral music educators' contextual knowledge, and in turn, their pedagogical practices. With the exception of McKoy's and Shaw's studies, the music education research community in the United States has yet to really examine the definition of what professional dispositions are in the music preservice teacher. Building from the work referenced within this chapter, we conducted an examination of key assumptions, and attempted to define and conceptualize the terminology and the conditions. We tested which are precise meanings about dispositions (in terms of statements) and which are those that are imprecise; we then created measures designed to capture caring dispositions of preservice music educators.

Specific Dispositions to Study in Music Preservice Educators

As described in the previous section, we worked for several years to determine what music teacher educators use to describe and measure dispositions. We asked them to identify their own descriptions of dispositions and we validated a series of statements that music teacher educators agreed on as important and relevant (Parkes, Doerksen, & Ritcher, 2016). We categorized them into three main areas: (1) caring, (2) reflection, and (3) responsibility. Instruments were then developed to measure the disposition of caring through three methods: (1) psychometric, (2) scenario, and (3) behavioral. In previous research (Parkes, Doerksen, & Ritcher, 2015a; 2016) we established acceptable face and content validity for a series of statements related to the dispositions of caring, responsibility, and reflection. Music teacher educators validated the appropriateness of these statements as expectations for preservice music educators. The disposition of "caring" was identified as the first construct to measure, and the internal subsets of relationships, nurturing, and empathy were selected. As previously reported in Parkes, Doerksen, and Ritcher (2015b), the following constructs were identified as the six for which to develop measures. The measures were designed to determine the extent to which preservice music teachers believe and act on the proposition that it is important:

1. to establish caring relationships with students,
2. to be compassionate,
3. to be concerned about all aspects of a child's well-being,
4. to affirm and encourage the best in others,
5. to be supportive, and
6. to be discrete and maintain confidentiality.

The first measure was a psychometric tool to be administered to preservice music educators. This instrument has 18 items and asked preservice music educators to rate the extent to which they agree or disagree with items in the instrument. An example of an item that measures the first construct is, "Establishing caring relationships with students is a high priority to me." Participants then selected from a six-point scale their level of agreement/disagreement with the statement.

The second measure was a projective prompt, also called a scenario prompt. This work was derived from the work of Woody et al. (2014). These six scenarios created a situation to which the preservice teacher participants responded. The students selected a response from three provided as to the most or least caring response.

The third measure was a behavioral rating scale to be completed by both preservice student teachers and their clinical or cooperating teachers. An example of an item on this scale for the first construct is "The student teacher makes an effort to develop positive relationships with students," followed by a frequency scale (1:Never–5:Always). Student teachers also completed this instrument about themselves.

Participants

Thirty-seven music teacher educators indicated in our 2014 study they would like to be further involved with ongoing research. Fourteen responded that they were willing to administer our three measures to their students and cooperating teachers. The participants were from the states of Texas, New Hampshire, Ohio, Kansas, North Carolina, West Virginia, California, Virginia, Pennsylvania, Minnesota, and Tennessee (with more than one institution participating from some states). Due to the differences in programs, not all students completed all three instruments.

Analyses

Psychometric item scores were entered into SPSS 22, and basic descriptive means for each student were calculated ($N = 286$) and four were removed because they were incomplete

(N = 282). Correlations were conducted and factor analyses completed with principal component analysis using a varimax rotation. For the projective prompts, central tendencies, frequency distributions, and standard deviations were calculated (n = 280). For the behavioral ratings (self, n = 69, and from the cooperating teacher, n = 37), mean scores and standard deviations were calculated. (Matched pairs of self-ratings and cooperating teacher ratings n = 19). Mean scores, standard deviations, and correlations were also calculated.

Examples of Items

Figures 37.1, 37.2, and 37.3 illustrate the items to measure the first example statement: "It is important to establish caring relationships with students."

Findings

For the psychometric scale, means clustered between 4.88 and 5.84 (lowest score was 1, highest was 6). All items were significantly correlated with each other at the 0.01 level (2-tailed). A factor analysis revealed four weak factors but did not load around the six statements as predicted. One factor was determined on a scree plot, eigenvalue of 1. The overall reliability, as determined with Cronbach's alpha, was 0.88. There were no

---

1. Establishing caring relationships with students is a high priority to me.
2. Having empathy for my students matters to me.
3. Developing trusting relationships with students is a high priority for me.

Strongly Disagree	Disagree	Sort of Disagree	Sort of Agree	Agree	Strongly Agree
1	2	3	4	5	6

FIGURE 37.1 Psychometric example.

Scenario:
Steve is a first-year teacher, recently hired to lead a middle school orchestra program. His summer graduation delayed his move, and it is now just three days from the start of the new school year. Steve received an e-mail from a rising senior, on behalf of a small group of string students. They are offering to meet with their new teacher, so that they can tell him of all the good things the orchestra did last year. What do you think Steve should do? (Choose one)

❏ Inform the students that he is already making plans for the new year and that he will see them on the first day of school.

❏ Thank the students and ask that they reply by e-mail with a few things that he could read when he has time.

❏ Offer to meet with the students the next day in the orchestra room.

FIGURE 37.2 Projective prompt (Scenario) example.

1. The student teacher makes an effort to develop positive relationships with students.
     Never   Rarely   Inconsistently   Often   Always
       1   2   3   4   5

2. The student teacher has caring relationships with students.
     Never   Rarely   Inconsistently   Often   Always
       1   2   3   4   5

1. I make efforts to develop positive relationships with students.
     Never   Rarely   Inconsistently   Often   Always
       1   2   3   4   5

2. I have caring relationships with students.
     Never   Rarely   Inconsistently   Often   Always
       1   2   3   4   5

FIGURE 37.3 Behavioral rating for Cooperating Teacher example.

differences between the means of class levels (e.g., freshmen, sophomores, juniors, and seniors). Graduate students ($n = 3$) had a much lower mean, but this was attributed to the low n size. While seemingly reliable, this instrument measures students' beliefs about the six statements together rather than as six separate caring constructs. The instrument did not adequately discriminate between low and high caring beliefs of preservice music education students.

For the projective prompt, all undergraduate class means clustered closely to overall means for each of six scenarios. Overall, the differences in means for each scenario among undergraduate classes were negligible. Freshman means were at—or slightly below—overall means and sophomore means were at—or slightly above—overall means. Ratings of "3" were a large majority of all ratings across the six scenarios. Ratings of "2" consistently had the second-largest response percentages across the six scenarios (often 15%–30%). Ratings of "1" consistently had the lowest response percentages across the six scenarios, ranging from .71% to 3.96%. Freshmen had somewhat lower response percentages for "3" ratings—and somewhat higher response percentages for "2" ratings—compared to other undergraduate classes. These findings indicate that the projective prompts did not adequately discriminate between low and high caring beliefs of preservice music education students.

Thirty-seven cooperating teachers and 69 student teachers completed the behavioral measures. Of these it was possible to identify 19 cooperating teacher–student teacher pairs. The correlation between the total score on the form completed by the cooperating teacher and the total score on the corresponding form completed by the student teacher was $r = .378$ ($p = .055$). The correlations for the individual items were mostly low and nonsignificant, due in part to lack of variability.

Behavioral ratings were high for both cooperating teachers and student teachers, but higher for student teachers. The mean cooperating teacher total score was 53.37 (out of a possible 60); the most common score was 60 (21.1%). The mean student teacher total score was 57.53 and the most common score was 60 (31.6%). Table 37.6 presents the results for the behavioral measure. Student teachers ranked higher on 11 of the 12 items.

Table 37.6 *Behavioral Measure* (*n* = 17):
Forms C (Cooperating Teachers) and D
(Student Teachers) (Pairs Only)

Item Number	Form C	Form D
	Mean (S.D.)	Mean (S.D.)
1	4.47(.61)	4.74 (.54)
2	4.26 (.65)	4.74 (.45)
3	4.16 (.77)	4.84 (.378)
4	4.42 (.69)	4.79 (.42)
5	4.37 (.60)	4.95 (.23)
6	4.37 (.60)	4.84 (.38)
7	4.37 (.60)	4.95 (.23)
8	4.47 (.50)	4.79 (.42)
9	4.68 (.48)	4.95 (.23)
10	4.68 (.48)	4.89 (.32)
11	4.47 (.77)	4.26 (.99)
12	4.74 (.56)	4.79 (.42)
Total	53.37 (5.24)	57.53 (2.67)

Note: Possible item score range: 1 to 5 with 5 being the highest rating. Possible total score range: 12 to 60.

FUTURE DIRECTIONS

It became obvious to us that Pajares (1992) was correct—not only are dispositions a "messy construct" (p. 307) but also they are difficult to measure, especially for MTEs. Based on our research, we offer the following considerations and suggestions for the field.

We anticipate that we may attempt to continue our work and examine responsibility and reflection dispositions. While the three types of measures we developed seem interesting, the lack of discrimination is problematic and unhelpful for the profession. We did find, anecdotally, that the conversation elicited in the scenario prompts during class seemed to engage students in critical thinking and thoughtful discussions, so rather than use the projective scenarios as an assessment, they could be used as a pedagogical tool by music teacher educators; this is supported in the work by Woody et al. (2014).

For those who develop measures for future use, there are two alternatives to consider. First is the model presented by Wilkerson and Lang (2007). This is a standards-based model with five steps toward valid measurements using the "Disposition Assessments Aligned with Teacher Standards" (DAATS) procedure. This is aligned with the disposition standards set out by the INTASC and focuses on adequate evidence and operational understanding of those standards. This model outlines their definition of dispositions, methods for assessing dispositions, types of assessment inputs, instrument development, data management, and continuous improvement.

The second approach to consider is the group interview technique, first developed by Shechtman (1992) and later promoted by Ingles (2016) as the dispositions attributes proficiencies (DAP) model. This involves a group interview, with trained observers, to examine the verbal/oral skills, human interaction skills, and leadership skills of incoming preservice teachers. Ingles suggests that this model can predict teaching success in student teaching—or at least her initial studies show a positive correlation with high scores on the DAP and in student teaching evaluations.

If music teacher educators and researchers are committed to developing independent measures, Kyllonen (2016) suggests several influential frameworks for measuring noncognitive skills such as personality, attitudes and values, social and emotional, and self-management skills in educational and workforce outcomes. Kyllonen notes the five-factor model of personality (conscientiousness, agreeableness, neuroticism/emotional stability, openness, extraversion), and it seems that some of these characteristics are helpful in the classroom. These constructs were criticized in the 1970s and 1980s for various reasons, but since the 1990s, psychologists have rediscovered this model.

Beyond these five constructs are attitudes, specifically cultural and social attitudes, along with values that have been studied by psychologists. The 21st-century skills framework (AACTE, 2010) offers the following that are part of teacher dispositions: (1) "ways of thinking"—critical thinking, problem-solving, decision-making; (2) "ways of working"—communication, collaboration; and (3) "skills for living"—personal responsibility. Other interrelated sets of affective and behavioral competencies such as self-awareness, self-management, social awareness, relationships skills, and responsible decision-making all seem to have relevance for preservice teachers. Kyllonen (2016) notes that large-scale assessments, such as the Program for International Student Assessment (PISA), are including noncognitive outcomes in their assessments such as attitudes, sense of belonging, interest, motivation, and cultural competence. If large-scale assessment developers are measuring these outcomes in students, it may be possible and appropriate to also measure these in preservice teachers. Kyllonen specifically suggests innovative methods such as self-rating, ratings by others, situational judgment tests, and interviews,—and offers the observation that noncognitive assessments generally show smaller or no differences in performance or passing rates between gender and race-ethnicity groups. He states that it is likely we will see more noncognitive tests being developed and implemented. This is a promising observation, and as we move forward with the measurement of dispositions in music education preservice teachers, we call for music education researchers to collaborate to investigate this area more fully.

REFERENCES

AACTE (2010). *21st century knowledge and skills in educator preparation*. American Association of Colleges of Teacher Education and The Partnership for 21st Century Skills (P21) White paper. Retrieved 2015, from http://www.p21.org/storage/documents/aacte_p21_whitepaper2010.pdf

Abrahams, F. (2009). Examining the preservice practicum experience of undergraduate music education majors: Exploring connections and dispositions through multiple perspectives, a critical grounded theory. *Journal of Music Teacher Education, 19*(1), 80–104. doi: 10.1177/1057083709347166

Beverly, C., Santos, K., & Kyger, M. (2006). Developing and integrating a professional disposition curriculum into a special education teacher preparation program. *Teacher Education and Special Education, 29*(1), 26–31. doi: 10.1177/088840640602900104

Brandes, J., & Crowson, M. (2008). Predicting dispositions towards inclusion of students with disabilities: The role of conservative ideology and discomfort with disability. *Social Psychology of Education, 12*, 271–289. doi: 10.1007/s11218-008-9077-8

Breese, L., & Nawrocki-Chabin, R. (2007). Social-cognitive perspective in dispositional development. In M. E. Diez, & J. Raths (Eds.), *Dispositions in teacher education* (pp. 31–52). Charlotte, NC: Information Age.

Buehl, M. M., & Beck, J. S., (2105). The relationship between teachers' beliefs and teachers' practices. In H. Fives, & M. G. Gill (Eds.), *International handbook of research on teacher beliefs* (pp. 66–84). New York, NY: Routledge.

Bullough, R. V. (2015). Methods for studying beliefs: Teacher writing, scenarios, and metaphor analysis. In H. Fives, & M. G. Gill (Eds.), *International handbook of research on teacher beliefs* (pp. 150–170). New York, NY: Routledge.

Buss, D. M., & Craik, K. H. (1983). The act frequency approach to personality. *Psychological Review, 90*, 105–26. doi: 10.1037/0033-295X.90.2.105

Clark, K. B. (2005). A contemporary rationale for dispositions in education. In R. L. Smith, D. Skarbek, & J. Hurst (Eds.), *The passion of teaching: Dispositions in the schools*. Lanham, MD: Scarecrow Education.

Costa, A., & Krallick, B. (2000). *Activating and engaging habits of mind*. Alexandria, VA: Association for Supervision and Curriculum Development.

Council for the Accreditation of Educator Preparation (CAEP). (2013). *CAEP glossary*. www.caepnet.org

Council for the Accreditation of Educator Preparation (CAEP). (2015). *CAEP accreditation Standards*. www.caepnet.org

Council for the Accreditation of Educator Preparation (CAEP). (2016, June). *2013 CAEP standards*. Retrieved from http://caepnet.org/standards/introduction

Council of Chief State School Officers. (2011, April). *Interstate teacher assessment and support consortium (InTASC) model core teaching standards: A resource for state dialogue*. Washington, DC: Author.

Darling-Hammond, L., Gendler, T., & Wise, A. E. (1990). *The teaching internship: Practical preparation for a licensed profession*. Santa Monica, CA: Rand.

Dee, J., & Henkin, A. (2002). Assessing dispositions toward cultural diversity. *Urban Education, 37*(1), 22–40. doi: 10.1177/0042085902371003

Diez, M. E. (2007). Assessing dispositions: Context and questions. In M. E. Diez, & J. Raths (Eds.), *Dispositions in teacher education* (pp. 183–201). Charlotte, NC: Information Age.

Diez, M. E., & Murrel, P. C. (2010). Dispositions in teacher education—starting points for consideration. In P. C. Murrell Jr., M. E. Diez, S. Feiman-Nemsler, & D. L. Schussler (Eds.), *Teaching as a moral practice: Defining, developing, and assessing professional dispositions in teacher education* (pp. 7–26). Cambridge, MA: Harvard Education Press.

Diez, M. E., & Raths, J. (2007). *Dispositions in teacher education*. Cambridge, MA: Harvard Education Press.

Doerksen, P. F., Parkes, K. A., & Ritcher, G. K. (2010, March). *The application of professional dispositions in music teacher certification programs.* The 2010 Biennial Music Educators National Conference: Special Focus on Research in Music Education and Music Teacher Education (MENC: The National Association for Music Education), Anaheim, CA.

Doerksen, P. F., Parkes, K. A., & Ritcher, G. K. (2014, April). *Pre-service music educators as reflective, caring, and responsible practitioners: An examination of three categories of professional dispositions.* Session presented at National Association for Music Education: The 2014 Music Research & Teacher Education National Conference, St. Louis, MO.

Doerksen, P. F., & Ritcher, G. K. (2007, September). *The 2007 national survey of music teacher certification programs.* The 2007 Symposium on Music Teacher Education: Collaborative Action for Change (The Society for Music Teacher Education), Greensboro, NC.

Doerksen, P. F., & Ritcher, G. K. (2009, September). *The assessment of professional dispositions in music teacher certification programs.* The 2009 Symposium on Music Teacher Education: Enacting Shared Visions (The Society for Music Teacher Education), Greensboro, NC.

Dottin, E. S., Johnson, B., & Weiner, M. (2013). Examining how pre-service teacher education students conceptualize and frame problems of professional practice in light of professional knowledge and habits of mind. In E. S. Dottin, L. D. Miller, & G. E. O'Brien (Eds.), *Structuring learning environments in teacher education to elicit dispositions as habits of mind* (pp. 1–26). Lanham, MD: University Press of America.

Dottin, E. S., Miller, L. D., & O'Brien, G. E. (Eds.). (2013). *Structuring learning environments in teacher education to elicit dispositions as habits of mind.* Lanham, MD: University Press of America.

Feiman-Nemser, S., & Schussler, D. L. (2010). Defining, developing, and assessing dispositions: A cross-case analysis. In P. C. Murrell Jr., M. E. Diez, S. Feiman-Nemser, & D. L. Schussler (Eds.), *Teaching as a moral practice: Defining, developing, and assessing professional dispositions in teacher education* (pp. 177–201). Cambridge, MA: Harvard Education Press.

Fenstermacher, G. D. (1979). A philosophical consideration of recent research on teacher effectiveness. In L. S. Shulman (Ed.), *Review of Research in Education* (Vol. 6., pp. 157–85). Itasca, IL: Peacock.

Fives, H., & Gill, M. G. (2015). *International handbook of research on teacher beliefs.* New York, NY: Routledge.

Flowers, C. (2006). Confirmatory factor analysis of scores on the clinical experience rubric: A measure of dispositions for preservice teachers, *Educational and Psychological Measurement, 66,* 478–488. doi: 10.1177/0013164405282458

Fredrickson, W., & Madsen, C. (2010) Emotional differences between early and late degree program music teacher education students using a concise emotional inventory. *Update: Applications of Research in Music Education, 29*(1), 33–39. doi: 10.1177/8755123310378452

Freeman, L. (2007a). An overview of dispositions in teacher education. In M. E. Diez, & J. Raths (Eds.), *Dispositions in teacher education* (pp. 3–29). Charlotte, NC: Information Age.

Freeman, L. (2007b). Teacher dispositions in context. In M. E. Diez, & J. Raths (Eds.), *Dispositions in teacher education* (pp. 117–38). Charlotte, NC: Information Age.

Gay, G. (2010). Acting on beliefs in teacher education for cultural diversity. *Journal of Teacher Education, 61*(1–2), 143–152. doi: 10.1177/0022487109347320.

Hickey, M. (2015). Learning from the experts: A study of free-improvisation pedagogues in university settings. *Journal of Research in Music Education, 62,* 425–445. doi: 10.1177/0022429414556319

Hourigan, R. (2006). The use of the case method to promote reflective thinking in music teacher education. *Update: Applications of Research in Music Education, 24*(33), 33–43.

Ingles, S. (2016). *Developing dispositions.* Dubuque, IA: Kendall Hunt.

Interstate New Teacher Assessment and Support Consortium (INTASC). (1992). *Model standards for beginning teacher licensing, assessment and development: A resource for state dialogue.* Washington, DC: Council of Chief State School Officers.

Johnston, P., Almerico, G. M., Henriott, D., & Shapiro, M. (2011). Descriptions of dispositions for assessment in pre-service teacher education field experiences. *Education, 132,* 391–401.

Katz, L. G., & Raths, J. K. (1985). Dispositions as goals for teacher education. *Teaching and Teacher Education, 1,* 301–307.

Knopp, T. Y., & Smith, R. L. (2005). A brief historical context for dispositions in teacher education. In R. L. Smith, D. Skarbek, & J. Hurst, *The passion of teaching: Dispositions in the schools.* Lanham, MD: Scarecrow Education.

Krathwohl, D. R., Bloom, B. S., & Masia, B. B. (1964). *Taxonomy of educational objectives. The classification of educational goals. Handbook II: Affective domain.* New York, NY: David McKay Co. Inc.

Kyllonen, P. C. (2016). Designing tests to measure personal attributes and noncognitive skills. In S. Lane, M. Raymond, & T. Haladyna (Eds.), *Handbook of test development.* New York, NY: Routledge, Taylor and Francis.

L'Allier, S., Elish-Piper, L., & Young, E. E. (2006). Evaluating candidate dispositions in advanced reading certification programs: The road ahead is here. *Reading Research and Instruction, 46*(2), 151–174. doi: 10.1080/19388070709558465

McKoy, C. (2013). Effects of selected demographic variables on music student teachers' self-reported cross-cultural competence. *Journal of Research in Music Education, 60,* 375–394. doi: 10.1177/0022429412463398

Miksza, P., & Tan, L. (2015). Predicting collegiate wind players' practice efficiency, flow, and self-efficacy for self-regulation: An exploratory study of relationships between teachers' instruction and students' practicing. *Journal of Research in Music Education, 63,* 162–179. doi: 10.1177/0022429415583474

Murrell, P. C., Diez, M. E., Feiman-Nemser, S., & Schussler, D. L. (2010). *Teaching as a moral practice: Defining, developing, and assessing professional dispositions in teacher education.* Cambridge, MA: Harvard Education Press.

National Association of Schools of Music. (2015). *Handbook 2015–16.* Reston VA: Author.

National Council for Accreditation of Teacher Education (NCATE). (2000). *Professional standards for the accreditation of schools, colleges, and departments of education.* Washington, DC: NCATE.

National Council for Accreditation of Teacher Education (NCATE). (2008). *Professional standards for the accreditation of teacher preparation institutions.* Washington, DC: NCATE.

Oja, S. N., & Reiman, A. J. (2007). A constructivist-developmental perspective. In M. E. Diez, & J. Raths (Eds.), *Dispositions in teacher education* (pp. 117–138). Charlotte, NC: Information Age.

Pajares, F. (1992). Teachers' beliefs and educational research: Cleaning up a messy construct. *Review of Educational Research, 62,* 307–332. doi: 10.3102/00346543062003307

Parkes, K. A., Doerksen, P. F., & Ritcher, G. (2014). Measuring professional dispositions in pre-service music teachers in the United States. In T. Brophy (Ed.), *Music assessment and global diversity: Practice, measurement, and policy* (pp. 351–386). Chicago, IL: GIA Publications.

Parkes, K. A., Doerksen, P., and Ritcher, G. (2015a, September). *Measuring pre-service music educators' dispositions of caring: A tri-fold investigation.* Poster presentation at the 2015 Symposium for Music Teacher Education. Greensboro, NC.

Parkes, K. A., Doerksen, P., & Ritcher, G. (2015b, February). *Validating dispositions in pre-service music educators.* Research presentation at the 5th International Symposium on Assessment in Music Education: Connecting Practice, Measurement, and Evaluation. Williamsburg, VA.

Parkes, K. A., Doerksen, P., & Ritcher, G. (2016). A validation process for measuring dispositions in pre-service music educators. In T. Brophy (Ed.), *Selected papers from the fifth international symposium on assessment in music education: Connecting practice, measurement, and evaluation* (pp. 315–326). Chicago, IL: GIA Publications.

Pintrich, P. R. (1990). Implications of psychological research on student learning and college teaching for teacher education. In W. R. Houston (Ed.), *Handbook of research on education* (pp. 826–857) New York, NY: Macmillan.

Raths, J. (2007). Experiences with dispositions in music education. In M. E. Diez, & J. Raths (Eds.), *Dispositions in teacher education* (pp. 153–163). Charlotte, NC: Information Age.

Ritcher, G. K. (2005, September). *Assessment systems used in undergraduate programs of music teacher education.* Research presentation at the Society for Music Teacher Education National Conference, Greensboro, NC.

Schraw, G., & Olafson, L. (2015). Assessing teachers' beliefs: Challenges and solutions. In H. Fives & M. G. Gill (Eds.), *International handbook of research on teacher beliefs* (pp. 87–105). New York, NY: Routledge.

Shaw, J. T. (2015). "Knowing their world": Urban choral music educators' knowledge of context. *Journal of Research in Music Education, 63,* 198–223. doi: 10.1177/0022429415584377

Shechtman, Z. (1992). A group-assessment procedure as a predictor of on-the-job teacher performance. *Journal of Applied Psychology, 77,* 383–387. doi: 10.1037/0021-9010.77.3.383

Skarbek, D., & Williams, E. (2013). Reflection. In R. L. Smith, & D. Skarbek (Eds.), *Professional teacher dispositions: Additions to the mainstream* (pp. 37–50). Lanham, MD: Rowman, & Littlefield Education.

Skott, J. (2015). The promises, problems, and prospects of research on teacher's beliefs. In H. Fives & M. G. Gill (Eds.), *International handbook of research on teacher beliefs* (pp. 12–30). New York, NY: Routledge.

Smith, R. L. (2013a). *A brief introduction to dispositions in education.* In R. L. Smith & D. Skarbek (Eds.), *Professional teacher dispositions: Additions to the mainstream* (pp. 1–11). Lanham, MD: Rowman & Littlefield Education.

Smith, R. L. (2013b). *Caring, empathy and love.* In R. L. Smith & D. Skarbek (Eds.), *Professional teacher dispositions: Additions to the mainstream* (pp. 13–24). Lanham, MD: Rowman & Littlefield Education.

Smith, R. L., & Emigh, L. (2005). A model for defining the construct of caring in teacher education. In R. L. Smith D. Skarbek, & J. Hurst (Eds.), *The passion of teaching: Dispositions in the schools* (pp. 211–222). Lanham, MD: Scarecrow Education.

Smith, R. L., Knopp, T. Y., Skarbek, D., & Rushton, S. (2005). Dispositions and teacher beliefs: A heuristic to inform efforts toward improving educational outcomes. In R. L. Smith, D. Skarbek, & J. Hurst (Eds.), *The passion of teaching: Dispositions in the schools.* Lanham, MD: Scarecrow Education.

Smith, R. L., & Skarbek, D. (2013). A model for evaluating dispositional behaviors in teacher education and schools. In R. L. Smith & D. Skarbek (Eds.), *Professional teacher dispositions: Additions to the mainstream* (pp. 141–139). Lanham, MD: Rowman & Littlefield Education.

Sockett, H. (2006). Character, rules and relations. In H. Sockett (Ed.), *Teacher dispositions: Building a teacher education framework of moral standards*. Washington, DC: AACTE Publications.

Task Force on Teacher Education. (1986). *Minnesota's vision for teacher education: Stronger standards, new partnerships*. St. Paul, MN: Task Force on Teacher Education, Minnesota Higher Education Coordinating Board and MBOT.

Villegas, A. M. (2007). Dispositions in teacher education: A look at social justice. *Journal of Teacher Education, 58,* 370–380. doi: 10.1177/0022487107308419

Wasicsko, M. M. (2007). The perceptual approach to teacher dispositions: The effective teacher as effective person. In M. E. Diez & J. Raths (Eds.), *Dispositions in teacher education* (pp. 53–89). Charlotte, NC: Information Age.

Wilkerson, J. R., & Lang, W. S. (2007). *Assessing teacher dispositions: Five standards-based steps to valid measurement using the DAATS model*. Thousand Oaks, CA: Corwin Press.

Woody, B., Laird, L., Gilbert, D., & Munderloh, R. (2014). *Music teacher dispositions: Self-appraisals and values of university music students*. Poster presented at the NAfME Music Research and Teacher Education National Conference, St. Louis, MO.

Woolley, S. L., Benjamin, W. J., & Woolley, A. W. (2004). Construct validity of a self-report measure of teacher beliefs related to constructivist and traditional approaches to teaching and learning. *Educational and Psychological Measurement, 64,* 319–331. doi: 10.1177/0013164403261189

CHAPTER 38

CHALLENGES TO RELIABILITY AND VALIDITY IN THE EVALUATION OF MUSIC TEACHING

LAURA GOE AND TIMOTHY S. BROPHY

VALIDITY in performance evaluation is a topic of great interest in many fields in which actual performance is deemed as or more important than results from other types of assessment. In K-12 education, the common practice of evaluating teachers on their performance in the classroom is subject to validity challenges, and teachers and those who employ them may reasonably question whether results from classroom performance evaluations are accurate and fair. Usually conducted with observations and often including a portfolio or review of documents related to teachers' practice, these evaluations typically have consequences that may impact employment status. In recent years, the inclusion of measures of teachers' contributions to student learning growth in most evaluation systems has added another layer of complexity to teacher evaluation, particularly for those teachers in the arts, in which assessments of growth in student performance as well as improvement in understanding of musical concepts may be more appropriate measures of growth than scores on a standardized multiple-choice test.

In this chapter, we first provide a brief overview of the key concepts of validity and reliability, followed by a general discussion of teacher evaluation and aspects of the validity and reliability of various measures and processes. We then turn to the validity challenges specific to the evaluation of music teachers. We then discuss areas in which more research is needed, and offer recommendations for the identification and management of validity challenges in the evaluation of teaching.

VALIDITY AND RELIABILITY

While many music educators understand validity to be the extent to which an assessment measures what it is supposed to measure, in its recent revision of the standards for educational and psychological testing, the American Educational Research Association, American Psychological Association, and the National Council for Measurement in Education (2014) describe validity as follows:

> Validity refers to the degree to which evidence and theory support the interpretations of test scores for proposed uses of tests... The process of validation involves accumulating relevant evidence to provide a sound scientific basis for the proposed score interpretations. It is the interpretations of the test scores for proposed uses that are evaluated, not the test itself. When test scores are used in more than one way (e.g., both to describe a test taker's current level of the attribute and to make a prediction of a future outcome), each intended interpretation must be validated.   (p. 11)

It is the use of scores or assessment results (and the inferences drawn from them) for more than one purpose that lies at the heart of the validity challenges for the evaluation of music teaching. Steele, Hamilton, and Stecher (2010) researched the validity issues associated with certain aspects of teacher evaluation and described validity as follows: "Validity applies to the inference drawn from assessment results rather than to the assessment itself. If one thinks of reliability broadly as the consistency or precision of a measure, then one might conceptualize validity as the accuracy of an inference drawn from a measure" (p. 6). This is a useful way of thinking about validity, since it is the *inferences* about teachers that are drawn from the teacher evaluation process that we are most concerned with, not the validity of the measures per se.

To further emphasize the point that it is the *inferences* drawn from the assessment, not the assessment itself, that makes it possible to define validity, we turn to the validity expert Michael Kane, who provided a concise description of the development of validity theory over the years (Kane, 2013a), followed by his recent theoretical contribution, the "interpretation/use argument" or IUA (Kane, 2013b). He states,

> To validate an interpretation or use of test scores is to evaluate the plausibility of the claims based on the scores. An argument-based approach to validation suggests that the claims based on the test scores be outlined as an argument that specifies the inferences and supporting assumptions needed to get from test responses to score-based interpretations and uses. Validation then can be thought of as an evaluation of the coherence and completeness of this interpretation/use argument and of the plausibility of its inferences and assumptions.   (p. 1)

In other words, validity is not inherent to an assessment, but must be considered in light of an argument that is convincing in its "coherence and completeness." While Kane discusses test scores in the article, the interpretation/use argument can be applied more generally to any type of assessment. We are most interested in its application to measures of teacher performance (teacher evaluation). Of particular note is that an interpretation/use argument containing "inferences and supporting assumptions" is needed that leads from the performance to "score-based interpretations and uses." As an example, the results of standardized tests in subjects such as reading and mathematics have been validated for assessing student performance in these subjects. However, the use of student test results has not been validated for determining teachers' performance in these subjects. For our purposes, this suggests that we must use caution in determining the validity of measures of teacher performance (particularly music teachers' performance) in light of a set of inferences and supporting assumptions. When these inferences or supporting assumptions are challenged by the actual messiness of measuring teacher performance, then we must continually revisit them and consider how to address these challenges. To clarify, the accumulated validity evidence (interpretation and use) for a particular assessment (such as a 4th-grade mathematics assessment) should not be "repurposed" to support the interpretation and use for the different purpose evaluating teaching or teacher effectiveness. We address this more fully later in the chapter.

In subsequent sections, we consider how the interpretation and use argument might be applied to two commonly used measures in American state and district teacher evaluation systems. These measures are: (1) formal observations using rubrics, and (2) teachers' contributions to student learning growth, represented by growth models such as value-added models (VAMs) and student growth percentiles (SGPs), and student learning objectives (SLOs).

Reliability has to do with the *consistency* of results across administrations of a measure—which means that findings (such as scores or ratings) are repeatable or replicable, given defined circumstances. For example, if multiple trained evaluators gather in a classroom to observe a teacher and score the teacher's practice with the same rubric, then resulting scores should be consistent with (or close to) each other, and the coefficient of agreement among these evaluators is referred to as *interrater reliability*. We consider the nature of teaching and reliability of measures in a subsequent section.

Teacher Evaluation

Purposes of Evaluation

Teacher evaluation serves multiple purposes in K-12 educational systems in the United States. In most systems, it serves to establish whether teachers are performing their professional duties at a level deemed satisfactory for the school, district, and state. A primary purpose of teacher evaluation is to ensure that classroom teachers have at least a minimal level of competence in teaching. A score may be determined, typically from multiple measures, and associated with a level descriptor such as "Basic" or "Distinguished." State and district practices vary widely in terms of the consequences and benefits associated with various levels of performance. Teachers who exhibit poor performance may be assigned a mentor or may be evaluated more frequently, and if performance does not improve, the teacher may be terminated. In some schools and districts, teachers who demonstrate exceptional performance may receive recognition or, less frequently, a bonus based on performance.

In addition to the assignment of performance levels for administrative actions, a second, and arguably more important, purpose for teacher evaluation is to impart information to teachers that can lead to improved teaching practice and increased student learning. Providing the teacher with feedback on what is being done well is essential, in addition to feedback on what needs to be improved. Moreover, the feedback should include both the *what* and the *how* of improvement.

Both formal and informal structures are in place in most American schools to provide teachers with opportunities to discuss their performance with their evaluators (usually an administrator such as a principal or assistant principal). Teachers generally receive written feedback from formal observations and may also receive verbal or written feedback from "walk-throughs" or "drop-ins" in which the principal comes into the classroom unannounced. Often, the "walk-throughs" are not scored but instead provide an opportunity for the principal to affirm positive teacher actions and provide direction for less-positive actions. Targeted feedback is assumed to lead to improved teaching practice, and the outcome of improved teaching practice should be observably more effective classroom instruction and improved opportunities for students to learn at high levels.

Evaluation Systems

Evaluation systems vary widely across the United States and are determined primarily by the state departments of education. However, in recent years, federal policies such as Race to the Top have contributed to changes in evaluation systems to bring them into alignment with federal priorities, such as the inclusion of measures of student learning growth. In addition, the Elementary and Secondary Education Act made specific demands on states to bring aspects of their K-12 education systems into alignment with federal priorities in order to obtain a "waiver" from requirements put in place through No Child Left Behind (Pennington, 2014).

At one end of the spectrum is a single statewide evaluation system that all districts are expected to use. At the other end are states that provide minimal or optional guidance to districts and allow them to determine how best to conduct teacher evaluation based on local contexts and preferences. Most states are somewhere between the two extremes. In these states, there are generally a set of "approved" evaluation systems, which include rubrics to guide scoring teachers' performance that districts select based on local preferences. The exception is that states that use student test scores as part of the evaluation process typically manage the data collection, analysis and reporting at the state level, providing districts with reports on individual teachers' contributions to student learning growth, which is discussed at greater length later.

A report on emerging state approaches to teacher evaluation expressed some concern about how state governments are overseeing the process:

> State review and approval of district evaluations may not be an adequate approach to ensuring quality and rigor. State approval sounds like a good idea in states that leave it to districts to design a performance-based teacher evaluation system. But it may not be realistic given state capacity. These states may do better to provide specific tools, models and detailed frameworks for conducting and scoring teacher evaluations. States that have left districts to their own devices without any oversight are even more worrisome. There is a good reason to be skeptical that all districts in such states will have the capacity and will to implement strong evaluation systems on their own.   (Lacireno-Paquet, Morgan, & Mello, 2014, p. iii)

In terms of validity challenges, school districts left on their own to design evaluation systems is worrisome, since the effort and resources needed to establish, oversee, and assess the validity of complex evaluation systems may be overwhelming to some districts, especially smaller ones with limited staff. Recall that the interpretation and use argument must affirm that the inferences from an assessment (teacher evaluation measures, in this case) are adequately and convincingly supported. In particular, a key challenge to validity is a lack of training (for both evaluators and the teachers who will be evaluated) in the tools, processes, and systems used for evaluation. Determining the validity of the evaluation system is a pervasive concern for music education. Several authors have noted not only the lack of training for music teacher evaluators but the lack of music specialists who are trained as evaluators (Colwell, 2016; Lehman, 2014; see Orzolek, this volume); one notable exception is the Tennessee Fine Arts Portfolio System, which uses trained, exemplary, content-specific teachers as evaluators (see Davison & Fisher, in this volume). At the 4th International Symposium on Assessment in Music Education, participants determined that one way to address this is to establish partnerships between classroom music teachers and researchers to (1) establish validity evidence of in-service teacher evaluation protocols and (2) prepare music specialists as evaluators (Goldie, 2014). Simply put, if the users of the system do not fully comprehend it, then this is a threat to validity.

State government–led research on their own evaluation systems has found that even though simple rubrics or checklists have been replaced with a multiple-measure, complex rubric-based, standards-aligned observation system combined with student learning growth, most teachers are still ranked as "effective or better" (Sawchuk, 2013). For example, Michigan's first year of their new evaluation system showed that 97% of their teachers were rated "effective" or "highly effective" (Keesler & Howe, 2012). Michigan is not alone—other states have reported very similar percentages for the combined category of "effective" and "highly effective" including New Jersey[1] (97%) and New York[2] (95%). These ratings of teacher performance would appear to show a disconnect with more recent data on student performance nationally, which shows that only 40% of 4th graders and 33% of 8th graders were proficient in mathematics, and 36% of 4th graders and 34% of 8th graders were proficient in reading. It seems reasonable to argue that reading and mathematics scores are low primarily because of the many factors that impact student learning other than teaching—factors that are beyond the control of teachers and schools. But the seeming disconnect may be at least partly due to inflation in teacher evaluation. If so, that raises a concern about validity, if we were to argue that a rating of "effective" or "highly effective" is an indicator of effective teaching that is associated with acceptable (or better) levels of student learning. This concern leads us back to the interpretation and use argument. How do states determine whether their highly rated teachers are in fact producing better outcomes for students, given the multiple factors that may contribute to student success or failure? Again, for the interpretation and use validity argument, we must consider the plausibility of its inferences and assumptions (Kane, 2013b). More research and validity studies will need to be done to establish whether the current implementations of evaluation systems are in fact differentiating among teachers at different levels of effectiveness through a combination of measures.

Virtually all evaluation systems require training for those being evaluated and those doing the evaluations (usually building administrators). As noted previously, student growth models are typically managed by the state. For the observation components common to all evaluation models, most states have selected or recommended to districts one of more of the commercially available observation-based evaluation systems (see what follows), and most offer specific training in the use of the systems. Evaluation systems available to schools, districts, and states typically include a set of specific tools, forms, and guidance documents. A rubric to be used in conducting classrooms observations almost always provides the primary focus of these systems. Forms for reflection and identifying professional growth opportunities may be included, as well as forms for giving feedback to teachers on their performance. Besides participating in training, both teachers and the administrators or evaluators are expected to study the rubrics and other materials so that they will be prepared for the evaluation process.

By using complex rubrics that categorize and describe most aspects of teachers' work such as Charlotte Danielson's framework for teaching,[3] Robert Marzano's teacher evaluation model,[4] James Stronge's teacher effectiveness performance evaluation system,[5] McRel's teacher evaluation system[6] and others, teachers are expected to internalize descriptors for the rubrics and aim for the highest performance levels ("Distinguished" in the Danielson framework and McRel system; "Innovating" in the Marzano model; and "Highly Effective" in the Stronge system). For each of these systems, the documentation provides a clear message that the evaluation results should be used to focus professional development efforts in specific areas identified through the evaluation process. School leaders are then expected to provide support and opportunities for teachers to tackle the areas in which growth is needed and thus improve their professional practice and performance ratings in coming year. The assumption made by this process is that through improved teaching practice, students will have increased opportunities to learn and student outcomes will also improve.

All of the evaluation systems listed here document the alignment of their systems with the Interstate New Teachers Assessment and Support Consortium (INTASC) Model Core Teaching Standards.[7] Because the INTASC Standards are seen as the "national" teaching standards in the United States, demonstrating alignment of an evaluation system with these standards lends credibility to the systems.

The INTASC standards and these evaluation systems were created primarily to assess teachers of academic subjects (mathematics, English/language arts, reading, social studies, science, and foreign language). For federal accountability purposes, the only two subjects that actually "count" are mathematics and reading. But teachers of the arts, technical education, and physical education have unique challenges related to how and what they teach, and have their own professional standards for teaching that are specific to their subjects. The same rubrics and systems offered by evaluation systems providers for content-area teachers are also used for specialized teachers (such as music teachers). In some respects, these rubrics do work because of a great deal of overlap with academic teaching expectations. For example, all teachers are expected to manage their classrooms, write lesson plans, engage students in worthwhile learning activities, and assess students' performance. But there are crucial differences in what music teachers do (as well as other specialized teachers), and to the extent that these differences are missing from the rubrics, the validity of evaluation results may be in question.

To underscore this issue, Lehman (2014) writes about the "case of the mysterious missing validity":

> In an astounding lapse of common sense one state is considering a program in which student growth would be based solely on scores in reading and math (Richerme, 2013). This means that every teacher in that state would be held hostage to student test scores in those two disciplines. I wonder what would be the reaction if math teachers and other teachers were evaluated solely on the basis of how well the school choir sang or the band played.   (p. 12)

We will compare what music teachers versus academic subject teachers do in an effort to identify the threats to validity that may result from one-size-fits all evaluation.

Validity of Observations

Is it true that principals know good teaching when they see it? An answer to that question may be found in a study by Jacob and Lefgren (2008), in which principals' ratings of teachers were compared with a measure of teachers' effectiveness (student learning growth as measured by VAMs—discussed later) and found that principals were "generally able to identify teachers who produce the largest and smallest standardized [student] achievement gains, but have far less ability to distinguish between teachers in the middle of the distribution" (p. 1). Since most teachers are not at the extremes of the distribution, it seems apparent that an approach that is more sensitive to variations in teaching practice that contributes to differences in student outcomes is needed.

In order to consider the validity of observations for teacher evaluation purposes, we must first separate observation into two parts: the observer and the observation protocol (often in the form of a rubric). Bell et al. (2012) used Kane's interpretation and use argument model to illustrate how a particular observation protocol would be validated using an interpretation and use argument. Lessons learned from this process include:

> One of the strengths of the approach is that it presses researchers to make explicit their conceptions of the relationships among constructs, instruments, and inferences. More clarity on such issues can only improve the quality of observational research. This approach also lays bare many of the "implementation" procedures that must be examined as a part of the validity argument. In the case of observations, detailed descriptions ranging from how observers are calibrated to the ways in which lessons are sampled over a school year could facilitate more careful use of observation protocols for consequential purposes. This is especially important given the newness of these high-stakes purposes.   (p. 84)

From Bell et al. (2012), we can conclude that it is possible, though not necessarily easy, to establish the validity of an observation instrument for the particular interpretation and use (as measure of teaching effectiveness). However, the instrument used in their interpretation and use argument study is not one that is commonly used in teacher evaluation, though it was used in the Measures of Effective Teaching study, along with the Charlotte Danielson Framework for Teaching. Both instruments were chosen by the Measuring Effective Teaching (MET) project researchers (Bill and Melinda Gates Foundation, 2013) because a research base already existed which provided some potential evidence for the validity of the rubrics, and in fact, the MET study found that scores on both instruments correlated with value-added scores.

Given the need to ensure appropriate levels of competence among teachers, observations should distinguish among teachers at all performance levels. Unfortunately, there is considerable evidence that observers (usually principals) tend to find almost all teachers "good or great," as evidenced in the "The Widget Effect" (Weisberg, Sexton, Mulhern, & Keeling, 2009). Furthermore, research has shown that even among well-trained observers, there are some who may not be able to accurately differentiate among teacher performance levels (Pratt, 2014).

It is not expected that the distribution of teacher effectiveness ratings based on observations should look like a normal curve. Given that teachers must complete a teacher preparation program or alternative certification program and pass subject-specific tests to become licensed to teach, it is likely that many teaching candidates who are *least* likely to be effective in the classroom have already decided on another career. One would expect that well-prepared teachers would perform competently. The problem arises when either the instruments themselves or the observers are unable to accurately differentiate among teachers who are truly effective and those who are not effective or only marginally effective and in need of additional professional development opportunities or other types of support and coaching to become effective. With only four score points in most observation rubrics, there can be a very wide range of performances that are deemed "effective," and those near the bottom end of the performance band may need additional support. This suggests that it may be worthwhile for state Departments of Education to recommend that schools and teacher evaluators within schools analyze more closely the actual data on which scores are based in order to identify specific areas in which support and professional development may be needed.

Aggregated data, as in domain-level scores, can hide considerable variance. As an example, the Danielson framework consists of 22 components organized into 4 domains. A teacher may achieve an overall rating of "Proficient" in a domain, but still have individual components that were scored on the low end ("Basic" or "Unsatisfactory"). If a school or district recorded data at the *component* level and identified areas in which more support for individual teachers or groups of teachers was needed, they could arrange for targeted, specific professional development, coaching, and so on. This targeted approach would allow teachers to concentrate on their areas of need and may also provide cost savings for districts and schools that can avoid providing professional development in areas in which there is little demonstrated need and instead spend those funds on the teachers who need the support, in just the practices where support is needed.

The primary assessment tool that observers use is an observation rubric. The validity of the assessment, via the interpretation and use argument, is determined by the knowledge and skills of the person conducting the observation (the observer) *and* how well the observation rubric differentiates among teachers at different skill levels. Even with a rubric that has been validated through an interpretation and use argument, the validity of the results from using a rubric is dependent on the ability of the observer using the rubric to accurately place the teacher's performance correctly on the rubric.

For example, if we want a valid measure of teachers' classroom performance, we may choose one of many rubrics, frameworks, and systems designed to be used by an observer to evaluate teachers' performance. But how do we know if the combination of a particular observer and a particular rubric or framework can actually measure what it is supposed to measure? Perhaps the observer can accurately determine a teacher's performance level when they are observing a mathematics teacher in a classroom setting. Would the observer also be able to accurately determine a teacher's performance level in a *music* classroom where the observer (let us say they know little about music) sees the teacher conducting a choral group? Or perhaps selected students are getting specific feedback from the teacher on fingering techniques for the violin, or the correct embouchure for the French horn, or transposing music, while other students do timed exercises to enhance their fluency in reading musical notation. Threats to validity as determined by the interpretation and use argument arise when either the rubric is not sufficient to the task or the observer lacks the appropriate knowledge or training to accurately interpret what they see, or both.

Reliability of Observations

How many observations are enough to accurately determine a teacher's level of proficiency? Teachers are typically observed two or three times over the course of the school year, though in some cases they may be observed only once, particularly if they are tenured or have already demonstrated that they are performing at levels deemed effective or highly effective. In some states, teachers get a "pass" on observations once they have demonstrated effectiveness. This frees up administrator time to conduct more frequent observations with new or struggling teachers.

The reliability of teacher proficiency estimation increases as the number of observations increases. This idea is not specific to teacher observations. The more times a person engaged in an activity is observed or measured, the narrower the error band around the resulting score. For example, if a teacher was observed every week during the school year, the resulting average of all those scores would provide a more reliable assessment of the "true" performance of the teacher than if the teacher was observed only once per semester. However, the resources involved (personnel time) in conducting multiple observations are considerable, which is why the number of observations is typically limited.

More observations are particularly important for reliably measuring teacher performance, given the likelihood of continuous or rapid change or growth that can occur, even day to day, particularly for teachers who are new to the profession, the school, the grade level, or a particular assignment within the school. Ideally, evaluating a teacher with a reliable instrument on multiple occasions would ensure that score changes are captured with minimal measurement error. However, error can be introduced into the process when the evaluation instrument (usually a rubric) is not thoroughly understood or consistently applied by the evaluator.

Recent studies that examined reliability using multiple observers and multiple observations were revealing. According to research from the Measures of Effective Teaching research project (Bill & Melinda Gates Foundation, 2013), "Adding a second observer increases reliability significantly more than having the same observer score an additional lesson" (p. 5). Hill, Charalambous, and Kraft (2012) provide a superb discussion and illustration of the increase in the reliability of observation scores when more raters are used and/or more observations are done. But they also point out that the number of observations and/or raters needed should be based on the intended purpose of the observations. If the goal of the evaluation system is simply to identify the lowest performing teachers in the "Unsatisfactory" range so that they can be provided with intensive support and/or removed from the classroom, then more observations will likely be unnecessary, unless the goal is to document improvements in the teachers' performance as they receive intensive support.

On the other hand, if high observation scores ("Distinguished") would result in monetary awards, there may be a need for ensuring fairness in the process, which might then include multiple observers and multiple observations. Furthermore, if observation results are seen as an opportunity to provide specific feedback to teachers and/or engage them in conversation about their teaching practice, then multiple observations might be conducted not for reliability purposes but to promote professional growth opportunities. This might be a particularly good practice with new teachers who would benefit most from feedback.

Fortunately, lessons learned from research and early implementation can assist in "getting observations right." Woods et al. (2014) provide a discussion of best practices, including action steps for states and districts, to move fledging or mature observation systems toward fulfilling their two main purposes: differentiating among teachers for evaluation purposes and improving teaching practice through targeted feedback.

MULTIPLE MEASURES IN
TEACHER EVALUATION

Shulman (1988) described teacher evaluation as a "union of insufficiencies," arguing that "A combination of methods—portfolios, direct observations, assessment centers, and better tests—can compensate for one another's shortcomings as well as reflect the richness and complexity of teaching" (p. 36). Searching for more rigorous methods to evaluate teaching performance led to increasingly complex systems for observation, such as those described earlier. But a perceived need to demonstrate that teachers were "effective," that is, that their classroom practice contributed to expected learning gains among students, led to a few states experimenting with measures designed to estimate teachers' contribution to student learning growth. Following the "union of insufficiencies" line of reasoning, Goe, Bell, and Little (2008) examined the research base on multiple measures of teacher performance, including observations, portfolios, classroom artifacts, student surveys, and value added. The authors confirmed that different measures provide distinct types of information about a teacher's performance and combining the information from multiple measures may come closer to ensuring that the information collected is accurate. Moreover, some measures, such as observations, are more likely to result in actionable information that can be used to support teachers' improvement. On the other hand, while student test results may identify a teacher whose students are performing poorly, there is little actionable information to be gleaned from this measure to help the teacher improve. Furthermore, measures that provide results over multiple points in time are more likely to allow both teachers and their students to document growth.

Two seminal papers contributed greatly to the interest in using teachers' contributions to student learning growth as a measure of teachers' performance. The first was Sanders and Rivers (1996), who described the Tennessee Value-Added Assessment System (TVAAS) as "an efficient and effective method for determining individual teachers' influence on the rate of academic growth for student populations" (p. 1). School administrators in Tennessee in the late 1990s received value-added rankings for each of their teachers of tested subjects, the first time value added was used as a "measure," even though it was an informal measure and not meant to be counted in a teacher's evaluation. Later, Tennessee became an early adopter of value added as a component of their evaluation system, and many states followed suit.

Hanushek, Kain, O'Brien, and Rivkin (2005) authored the second paper that greatly influenced the movement toward the use of VAMs. Using data from Texas teachers, they found "substantial variation in the quality of instruction, most of which occurs within rather than between schools" (p. 1). Their research has been widely cited as a justification for including teachers' contributions to student learning as a component of teacher evaluation.

Along with observations, most evaluation systems in the United States now include measures of teachers' contributions to student learning growth. Value-added measures are used in about half the states, while SGPs are used in the rest (Goe, 2015). A handful of states have not mandated inclusion of teachers' contributions to student growth in their evaluation systems. Both SGPs and VAMs allow teachers to be ranked within a system (either within the state or within a district) based on the estimated growth of their students on standardized tests compared to the students' expected growth (value added) or the students' growth relative to "academic peers" who have similar prior test scores (SGPs), within a margin of error that depends on the number of students (small number of students results in large error band, large number of students results in smaller error band). Estimated student growth (or lack of it) is then attributed to the teachers who taught the tested content. Both VAMs and SGPs have proponents and detractors, and there are numerous research studies and policy statements that champion or question the use of such measures in teacher evaluation (e.g., Braun, Chudowsky, & Koenig, 2010; Chin & Goldhaber, 2015; Everson, 2016; Harris, Ingle, & Rutledge, 2014; McCaffrey, Sass, & Lockwood, 2009; Milanowski, 2016). For music educators, Orzolek (this volume) cautions,

> While most recent research seems to be suggesting that an equitable distribution of the facets (testing/outcomes, observations, student evaluations) seems to be the most reliable, it also implies that the least effective model is one that is wholly based on the observation of student work.   (p. 815)

Evaluating Teachers in Nontested Subjects/Grades

Between 60% and 70% of teachers cannot be measured with VAMs or SGPs because they are in "nontested" subjects or grades. In order to use VAMS or SGPs, students must be assessed annually with a standardized test. In virtually all states, only reading and mathematics from 3rd grade up are tested. In order to be "fair" (meaning to hold all teachers accountable for their students' learning growth), most states adopted some version of "student learning objectives" (SLOs), which require teachers in the nontested subjects and grades to demonstrate their contribution to student learning growth through collecting information on students at the beginning of the year, setting learning goals, and then assessing their progress at the end of the year. Student learning objectives were originally implemented as part of a performance pay experiment in Denver, Colorado (Slotnick & Smith, 2004), but are now used primarily as a means of establishing teachers' contributions to student learning growth (Gill, Bruch, & Booker, 2013; Lacireno-Paquet et al., 2014; Morgan & Lacireno-Paquet, 2013). Music teachers, along with 2nd-grade teachers, foreign language teachers, and many others, are required to create SLOs each year and assess student progress. An online search for music SLOs reveals numerous examples for music teachers, but the quality and rigor of the objectives and measures varies considerably, which is also true of other subjects. Key to managing threats to validity are providing teachers with sufficient training and guidance in creating SLOs, choosing appropriate assessments, and analyzing data. Principals need training to be able to oversee the process and score the results accurately. Gill et al. (2013) note that more research is needed, noting, "SLOs have the potential to better distinguish teachers based on performance than traditional evaluation metrics do, but no studies have looked at SLO reliability" (p. ii).

The advent of SLOs as part of teacher evaluation appears to be an attempt to ensure that *all* teachers, not just those in tested subjects, are held accountable for student growth. Of course, all requirements in an evaluation system are likely to get attention from teachers, and in this case, teachers will focus on measurable student outcomes, which may benefit both students and teachers. However, there is limited research on the using SLOs in evaluation systems as measures of teachers' contributions to student learning growth, and the process has yet to be researched through an interpretation and use argument. In other words, research has not yet demonstrated that teachers who create and implement rigorous learning objectives, and whose students meet those objectives, are actually more competent teachers. Given the variability in states' requirements and processes for SLO development and scoring, and given differences in how teachers and principals are trained and supported in the creation and scoring of SLOs, it will be difficult to determine whether this approach as a whole is serving its intended purpose. At some point, it may be possible to determine which implementations of this approach are yielding valid results and replicate those processes.

EVALUATION OF MUSIC TEACHERS

Music Teacher Evaluation

Before discussing the evaluation of music teachers as a special case of teacher evaluation, we should consider what it is that music teachers are supposed to know and be able to do. The INTASC standards described previously are intended to describe good teaching practice without regard to subject matter. However, support of the validity of an interpretation and use argument for evaluation instruments and processes should include alignment with appropriate professional standards. One resource is *Music Teacher Preparation in California: Standards of Quality and Effectiveness for Subject Matter Programs* (Music Subject Matter Advisory Panel, 2010), which describes what music teacher candidates should know and be able to do, from the perspective of the preparation program. Another resource that can be used by music teachers as well as those who prepare them to teach and those who evaluate them are The National Board for Professional Teaching Standards Music Standards (National Board for Professional Teaching Standards, 2001).

The National Association for Music Education (NAFME) has created a thoughtful and thorough "workbook" for the purpose of evaluating music education (and educators) in schools (National Association for Music Education, 2013). The *Workbook for Building and Evaluating Effective Music Education in the School Ensemble* provides a framework/rubric that is similar in structure to Charlotte Danielson's framework. The authors of the *Workbook* also provide an alignment table showing how the NAFME framework aligns with three popular evaluation frameworks: Danielson, Marzano, and McRel. Most importantly, the *Workbook* provides excellent guidance for states, districts, and schools focused on the structures and implementation of systems for the evaluation of music teachers. Aligning evaluation systems with the best practices described in the *Workbook* should greatly contribute to improving music teacher evaluation.

For music as well as for other specialized subjects, there are validity challenges for measuring student growth and attributing that growth (or lack of growth) to the specialized teacher. Of key concern is the amount of contact time the teacher has with the student. In some large high schools, the music teacher may have one 15-minute meeting with a student per semester in which to assess their individual progress on their instrument and offer feedback and direction for improvement. Since the majority of progress in musical performance happens during practice outside of the school, or during group work (i.e., band, chorus, and orchestra) within the school, the teacher may have very limited opportunities for involvement in students' individual progress over the course of the year. Thus, holding teachers accountable for student progress in performance when they have limited contact with students is a threat to the validity of inferences about teachers' contributions to individual students' growth. In the interpretation and use argument (IUA), is it plausible to say that student learning gains in music, including knowledge, skills, and performance, are directly and solely (or even mostly) attributable to the music teachers' efforts? If not, are there aspects of students' music learning that are more likely to be under the influence of the teacher, and if so more reasonably attributed to the teachers' efforts? These types of questions should be guiding efforts to ensure validity in attributing student learning growth to music teachers.

Brophy and Colwell (2012) noted the following validity challenges to the evaluation of music teachers:

- Student achievement data used for music teacher evaluation must be from reliable music assessments, not an arbitrary attribution of the effect of the music teacher on scores for the "usual tested subjects" of mathematics, reading, science, and writing
- There must be ample validity evidence that supports the inferences derived from scores on measures of student music achievement
- Inferences made from scores on "other measures" used must be supported by validity evidence for their specified uses for music teacher evaluation
- Observations and evaluative tools must be implemented by trained personnel who are content experts in music education

Colwell (2014) remarks, "validity is probably the most important concept in music assessment and least understood" (p. 84). Shuler, Brophy, Sabol, McGreevy-Nichols, and Schuttler (2016) note:

> The development of validity arguments for arts assessments is a paramount concern for the field, especially when developing assessments for accountability purposes. We have documented that the field has increased arts assessment development in recent years, but validity arguments are often missing from the available materials.   (p. 208)

Threats to validity for student arts assessment are in fact the main threat to validity for music teacher evaluation. Without arts assessments of student achievement for which appropriate validity evidence has been established, attributing student learning in the arts to the effect of the teacher is compromised.

Student learning objectives maybe a reasonable option for music teachers, since they would be the ones to choose the learning objectives and how progress will be determined. For example, teachers are required to submit student learning objectives wherein they assess students' performance early in the year and then set measureable objectives for individuals or groups of students. Groups may include above average, average, or below average students in some set of knowledge or skills, based on appropriate content standards for that age group. Group membership would be identified by the teacher through collecting data on students' knowledge and skills. Data from an assessment of knowledge (perhaps a paper-and-pencil test) and skills (performing vocally or on an instrument) would be used to determine groupings for purposes of setting appropriate growth targets. The teacher is evaluated at the end of the year on whether students achieved their learning objectives. This seems like a reasonable approach if the music teacher has been provided with adequate training on the process of collecting data on students' knowledge and skills; sets measurable objectives that are rigorous but attainable; and identifies appropriate methods of assessing students' progress on objectives. Obviously, standardized assessments of students' knowledge and skills in music would provide useful results as well, but the dearth of such assessments means that alternatives must be found.

In contrast, some states have taken a very different approach to evaluating teachers' contributions to student learning growth in the nontested subjects and grades, which includes music. In these states, the music teacher and teachers in art, foreign languages, computers, technology, and other nontested subjects do not need to provide any evidence of their contributions to their student learning growth. Instead, the music teacher is "credited" with the schoolwide average of student learning growth in the tested subjects (as measured with VAMs or SGPs). So the 30%–40% (varies by state) of the music teacher's evaluation that is intended to reflect contributions to learning growth is based on mathematics and reading test scores and is not related to the music teacher's effort. We pointed out earlier that Lehman (2014) identified the validity issues related to the arbitrary attribution of a portion of the test scores from a nonmusic tested subject (such as mathematics and reading) to the effect of the music teacher:

> A teacher assessment based on only reading and math scores would be easy to implement but I don't think it will happen because judging the effectiveness of a teacher on the basis of data utterly irrelevant to that teacher's work would be an outrageous violation of the basic principle of test validity.   (p. 12)

This is not a critique of the tests themselves, but of the use/misuse of tests for purposes other than those which have been supported by validity studies. It would be difficult to imagine an IUA that would provide reasonable support for using assessments designed to measure students' current knowledge as a mechanism for evaluating teachers' performance, particularly given the multitude of factors that impact student performance that are unrelated to the classroom instruction students receive from an individual teacher. Some states have—with good intentions—inadvertently raised validity questions related to the use of arts assessments for teacher evaluation purposes (Colorado Department of Education, 2012, 2014a, 2014b; Colorado Professional Learning Community, 2013).

The Colorado Content Collaboratives identified a set of assessments that music teachers could use for the purposes of teacher evaluation, but Shuler et al. (2016) note:

> For example, in Colorado, a bank of existing assessments developed for a variety of purposes has been reviewed by trained groups of teachers and recommended for consideration for a variety of different uses, including possibly as instruments for the measurement of student growth for teacher evaluation. The inferences from scores and ratings from arts assessments developed for one purpose may not be appropriate for another purpose.   (p. 208)

While there are certainly validity challenges with using SLOs to allow music teachers to demonstrate their contributions to students' learning, there are few reasonable alternatives, and in states where teachers' contributions to student learning growth are required, they may be an alternative to "giving" music teachers the schoolwide average of their mathematics and reading colleagues' growth scores on the standardized tests in those subjects. Even if a good standardized written or multiple-choice assessment could be given in pre- and posttest form that would allow students to show learning growth in some aspects of music, such assessments would not capture students' growth in skills in performance. While "making music" is certainly not the sole focus of music education, it is certainly part of music education standards and is important and highly valued. Teachers' contributions to skills development in musical performance should not be ignored because it is difficult to "fit" into a standardized test. Instead, other methods of assessing students' growth in musical performance can be used. Asmus (1999) wisely noted, "For some music teachers, the very idea of objectifying music is to be shunned. Yet, there are substantive means for accurately evaluating the music learning of students without sacrificing the quality of their musical experiences" (p. 19). Asmus states, "Three factors are inherent in all music teaching and learning: (1) the music instruction content and process, (2) the ongoing assessment during instruction, and (3) the outcome of instruction" (p. 20).

Parkes, Doerksen, and Ritcher (2016) have taken initial steps in the developing a validity argument for music teacher dispositions, an area of growing interest in preservice music teacher evaluation. They presented music teacher educators with three sets of disposition statements, categorized as *reflective, caring,* and *responsible.* Their research revealed the most validity support for the "responsible" disposition items, followed by the "caring" disposition items, and then the "reflection" disposition items. The translation of this research to the evaluation of in-service music teachers has not been completed.

Even if measurement tools and practices are developed and IUAs support their role in teacher evaluation, there are still challenges in providing a fair evaluation for music teachers. These challenges are discussed here.

Opportunity to Learn: Widely Varying Responsibilities and Expectations Among Teachers Across and Within Schools and Districts

In his keynote address to the first International Symposium on Assessment in Music Education, Colwell (2008), stated that of the national standards for music, the "most important are the *opportunity to learn standards.* There is no point in getting excited about assessment if the student has not had an opportunity to learn the material" (p. 7). Shuler et al. (2016) point out that the variance in opportunity to learn music in schools—the differences in the number of minutes per week of instruction in music, teacher expertise, having access to a musical instrument at home (piano, for example), existence of quality curriculum and resources, and the numbers of students and classes that music teachers are assigned—all impact what students learn. For example, some teachers are assigned to a particular school and may teach all 300 students in the school. Another teacher in the same district may teach at a school with only 200 students. Does teaching 100 additional students have an adverse impact on performance? In general, will differences in numbers of students taught affect the validity of inferences that can be made from evaluation results?

Some music teachers are itinerant teachers, going from school to school, particularly in rural areas. How does the fact that they have limited and infrequent interactions with their students affect their evaluation, and how does it compare to a teacher who is able to interact with students daily or at least regularly? It seems reasonable to assume that the more limited the interactions between teacher and students, the more difficult it will be to make a measureable impact on students' knowledge and skills in music.

Differences in Socioeconomic Status and Advantages

Students with advantages such as private music lessons, access to music camps, participation in local youth orchestras or community choirs, opportunities to perform publicly, opportunities to attend concerts, and so on, may show greater interest and engagement in music learning and increase more rapidly in knowledge and skills. The teacher may receive the "credit" for students' success in the evaluation, but how much of the credit is deserved (due to excellent instruction) and how much is due to the good fortune of teaching students with the types of home and community advantages that promote success? If only teachers with similarly advantaged students were being evaluated, this would not be a threat to validity. But great disparities in family income and student access to music opportunities often exist in a single school district.

Students who are less advantaged may lack funds for music lessons, purchasing instruments, and attending concerts and summer music camps. This may slow their progress, which may result in poor learning outcomes that are then attributed to the teacher. Again, how much of the delay in progress in developing knowledge and skills is the "fault" of the music teacher and how much is attributable to teaching students with few advantages?

Evaluators' Limited Understanding of Music Performance, Music Standards (for Both Teachers and Students), and the Appropriate Roles of Music Teachers

Can an evaluator with no musical training or understanding of music teaching methods and practices evaluate a music teacher, distinguishing among levels of practice in order to determine an accurate score? Charlotte Danielson, whose framework for teaching is one of the most widely used evaluation instruments in the United States, responded to queries about lack of content knowledge among evaluators:

It is certainly true that many aspects of teaching (particularly those in domain 2) are generic, and can be observed in a class regardless of the subject being taught, and by an observer without content expertise. However, it is also true that in advanced subjects, or at the higher levels of performance in all subjects, that content and content-specific pedagogy matter; if observers do not have that expertise, it is difficult for them to be aware of the nuances in a teacher's practice (Danielson, 2016).

Danielson goes on to make recommendations about how someone without content knowledge should approach the evaluation process, including using content experts for reviewing planning documents to assess the accuracy of content and pedagogical approaches, and having a conversation with the teacher "designed to elicit evidence of expertise." However, as discussed in what follows, an even better solution is to have an expert music teacher involved in the evaluation of music teachers. Because there are rules in some districts that only administrators can conduct teacher evaluations, one solution would be to "co-observe." The administrator and expert music teacher would observe together, then discuss the performance. The administrator would be the official evaluator, but might receive valuable insights that would guide scoring and feedback.

Lack of Evaluation Instruments That Are Aligned with Music Teaching Standards

The majority of teacher evaluation instruments are focused primarily on evaluating teachers of English, mathematics, science, social studies, and so on, and do not reflect the different arrangements, structures, and methods that may be "normal" for a music classroom. General evaluation systems are almost all aligned with the INTASC standards (previously described), which are considered the national teaching standards and which have been widely adopted. While there are many areas of overlap with teacher practices, knowledge, and skills, there are many standards specific to music teaching that are not reflected in the INTASC standards.

RECOMMENDATIONS FOR IMPROVING VALIDITY OF MUSIC TEACHER EVALUATION

In their *Workbook for Building and Evaluating Effective Music Education in the School Ensemble*, NAFME provided a clear statement about how the evaluation of music teachers should be conducted, including this directive: "[Successful music teacher evaluation] [m]ust limit observation-based teacher evaluations to those conducted by individuals with adequate training in music as well as in evaluation" (National Association for Music Education, 2013, p. 4).

In a similar vein, Hill and Grossman (2013) discussed "challenges and opportunities" resulting from new evaluation systems and made important recommendations for improving teacher evaluation:

First, these [evaluation] systems must make available subject-specific observation instruments that provide concrete guidance on desirable teaching practices. Second, these new systems must draw content experts within districts into the process of teacher evaluation, both for the sake of improving coherence in the messages transmitted to teachers and in order to leverage existing expertise around the improvement of instruction. Finally, states and districts must design systems in which feedback from observations is both accurate and usable in the service of improving instruction." (p. 372)

Hill and Grossman were not speaking specifically about music teachers, but about *all* teachers, arguing that generalized rubrics are not sufficient. If validity in evaluation results is a primary goal, that is, correctly identifying teachers performing at different levels, then using evaluation instruments that are specific to the content and grade level being taught is likely to contribute substantially to the validity of evaluation results.

Furthermore, ensuring that content experts are conducting the evaluations should not only improve the accuracy of scores but also enable better targeting of professional growth opportunities, both of which are key purposes of evaluation. Surely an expert in music teaching will be better able to recognize the specific needs of another music teacher and provide appropriate guidance for improving practice. An additional benefit of having music teaching experts evaluating music teachers is that it may lead to a sustained community of practice that provides teachers with common interests with opportunities to share information and learn from each other in ways that will likely benefit teaching and ultimately, student learning.

Summary

To mitigate many of the challenges to validity described herein, processes and instruments, as well as trained observers with expertise in music, should be developed and used. Evaluation rubrics based on music teaching standards should be used to ensure validity of teachers' scores. In addition, when music teachers' contributions to student learning growth are a required part of evaluation, contributions to student learning should be measured with appropriate assessments, including rubrics for determining growth in student music performance skills. For states that require all teachers to show contributions to student learning growth, appropriate assessments need to be identified. Alternatively, SLOs based on appropriate K-12 music standards and incorporating performance assessments may be considered. Both of these alternatives would need to be viewed in the light of an interpretation and use argument in order to be able to make valid inferences. But either of these alternatives is superior to crediting music teachers with the schoolwide average of student growth in tested subjects like mathematics and reading.

Fortunately for the profession of music teaching, there are active and productive organizations that are promoting high quality and fairness in the evaluation of music teachers. Recognizing a clear need for better music teacher evaluation, they have already contributed greatly to the effort to guide states and others in the evaluation of music teachers (c.f., National Association for Music Education, 2013). Their development of an appropriate rubric for evaluating music teachers is laudable, as is their leadership in recommending processes for evaluation, including who should evaluate music teachers and how contributions to student learning growth should be measured.

Nearly three decades ago, Brophy (1993) noted,

> Solutions to the evaluation dilemma are as complex as the issue itself.... The evaluation of music teachers remains an area in need of relevant research, and the development of an appropriate evaluation and observation instrument must be urgently addressed. It is now the responsibility of the united music teaching profession, in tandem with active music education researchers, to address this challenge. (pp. 17, 19)

For music educators, a balanced combination of student outcomes, observations, and narratives collected over time in a portfolio may offer the "best picture of a teacher's impact on student learning" (see Orzolek, this volume, p. 815). While there has been considerable progress in the research on the validity and reliability of the evaluation of music teaching, as states, districts and schools continue to implement, research, and revisit their evaluation systems, instruments, and processes, we can hope that they will be guided toward continuous improvement by the collective wisdom of music professionals and associations. Any interpretation and use argument to be put forth in order to make valid inferences about music teachers' performance must be guided by these individual experts and associations.

NOTES

1. New Jersey teacher effectiveness report. http://www.nj.gov/education/AchieveNJ/resources/201314AchieveNJImplementationReport.pdf?1462031677332
2. New York teacher effectiveness report. http://data.nysed.gov/evaluation.php?year=2013&&report=appr
3. http://www.danielsongroup.org/charlotte-danielson/
4. http://www.marzanoevaluation.com/
5. http://www.mcvea.org/extras/StrongeBook.pdf
6. https://www.mcrel.org/personnel-evaluation/
7. https://www.ccsso.org/index.php/resource-library/intasc-model-core-teaching-standards

REFERENCES

Asmus, E. P. (1999). Music assessment concepts. *Music Educators Journal, 86*(2), 19–24. doi: 10.2307/3399585

Bell, C. A., Gitomer, D. H., McCaffrey, D. F., Hamre, B. K., Pianta, R. C., & Qi, Y. (2012). An argument approach to observation protocol validity. *Educational Assessment, 17*(2–3), 62–87. doi: 10.1080/10627197.2012.715014

Bill & Melinda Gates Foundation. (2013). *Ensuring fair and reliable measures of effective teaching: Culminating findings from the MET Project's three-year study*. Seattle, WA: Bill & Melinda Gates Foundation. Retrieved from https://eric.ed.gov/?id=ED540958

Braun, H., Chudowsky, N., & Koenig, J. A. (2010). *Getting value out of value-added: Report of a workshop*. Washington, DC: National Academies Press. Retrieved from https://www.nap.edu/catalog/12820/getting-value-out-of-value-added-report-of-a-workshop

Brophy, T. (1993). *Evaluation of music educators: Toward defining an appropriate instrument*. Retrieved from https://files.eric.ed.gov/fulltext/ED375029.pdf

Brophy, T., & Colwell, R. (2012, March 30). *Teacher evaluations: Issues of validity and reliability*. Presented at the biennial meeting of the Assessment Special Research Interest Group, National Association for Music Education National Conference, St. Louis, Missouri.

Chin, M., & Goldhaber, D. (2015). *Impacts of multidimensionality and error: Simulating explanations for weak correlations between measures of teacher quality*. Retrieved from https://eric.ed.gov/?id=ED562267

Colorado Department of Education. (2012, June 22). *Determining high quality assessments*. CDE Resource Bank. Retrieved from http://www.cde.state.co.us/EducatorEffectiveness/downloads/Implementation%20Resources/CC%20C-intro-review-tool.pdf

Colorado Department of Education. (2014a, August 18). *Assessment Review Tool*, RT-6-2-2014. CDE Resource Bank. Retrieved from http://www.coloradoplc.org/assessment/assessment-review-tool-0

Colorado Department of Education. (2014b, August 18). *Assessments*. CDE Resource Bank. Retrieved from http://www.coloradoplc.org/assessment

Colorado Professional Learning Community. (2013, September 16). *Performance assessment development process*. Colorado Professional Learning Community (eNetColorado). Retrieved from http://www.coloradoplc.org/node/12765.

Colwell, R. (2008). Music assessment in an increasingly policitized, accountability-driven educational environment. In T. Brophy (Ed.), *Assessment in music education: Integrating curriculum, theory, and practice* (pp. 3–16). Chicago, Illinois: GIA Publications.

Colwell, R. (2014). The Black Swans of summative assessment. In T. Brophy, M.-L. Lai, & H.-F. Chen (Eds.), *Music assessment and global diversity: Pracitce, measurement, and policy* (pp. 67–102) Chicago, IL: GIA Publications.

Colwell, R. (2016). Tergiversation today: Interpreting validity. In T. S. Brophy, J. Marlatt, & G. K. Ritcher (Eds.), *Connecting practice, measurement, and evaluation: Selected papers from the 5th International Symposum on Assessment in Music Education* (pp. 3–28). Chicago, Illinois: GIA Publications.

Courtney, A., Bell, D. H. G., McCaffrey, D. F., Hamre, B. K., Pianta, R. C., Qi, Y. (2012). An argument approach to observation protocol validity. *Educational Assessment, 17*(2–3), 62-87. doi: 10.1080/10627197.2012.715014

Danielson, C. (2016). Charlotte Danielson on rethinking teacher evaluation. *Education Week, 35*(28), 20–24.

Everson, K. C. (2017). Value-added modeling and educational accountability: Are we answering the real questions? *Review of Educational Research, 87*(1), 35–70. doi: 10.3102/0034654316637199

Gill, B., Bruch, J., & Booker, K. (2013). *Using alternative student growth measures for evaluating teacher performance: What the literature says*. Washington, DC: Department of Education, Institute of Education Sciences, National Center for Education Evaluation and Regional Assistance, Regional Educational Laboratory Mid-Atlantic.

Goe, L. (2015). *Comparison of state use of VAMs and SGPs*. Princeton, NJ, Educational Testing Service.

Goe, L., Bell, C., & Little, O. (2008). *Approaches to evaluating teacher effectiveness: A research synthesis.* Washington, DC: National Comprehensive Center for Teacher Quality.

Goldie, S. (2014). Key issues in assessment in music education. In T. S. Brophy (Ed.), *Music assessment and global diversity: Practice, measurement, and policy* (pp. 423–432). Chicago, IL: GIA Publications.

Hanushek, E. A., Kain, J. F., O'Brien, D. M., & Rivkin, S. G. (2005). *The market for teacher quality.* NBER Working Paper No. 11154. Cambridge, MA: National Bureau for Economic Research. Retrieved from http://www.nber.org/papers/w11154.

Harris, D. N., Ingle, W. K., & Rutledge, S. A. (2014). How teacher evaluation methods matter for accountability: A comparative analysis of teacher effectiveness ratings by principals and teacher value-added measures. *American Educational Research Journal, 51*(1), 73–112. doi: 10.3102/0002831213517130

Hill, H., & Grossman, P. (2013). Learning from teacher observations: Challenges and opportunities posed by new teacher evaluation systems. *Harvard Educational Review, 82,* 371–384. doi: 10.17763/haer.83.2.d11511403715u376

Hill, H. C., Charalambous, C. Y., & Kraft, M. A. (2012). When rater reliability is not enough: Teacher observation systems and a case for the generalizability study. *Educational Researcher, 41*(2), 56–64. doi: 10.3102/0013189X12437203

Jacob, B. A., & Lefgren, L. (2008). Can principals identify effective teachers? Evidence on subjective performance evaluation in education. *Journal of Labor Economics, 26,* 101–136. doi: 10.1086/522974

Kane, M. T. (2013a). The argument-based approach to validation. *School Psychology Review, 42,* 448–457.

Kane, M. T. (2013b). Validating the interpretations and uses of test scores. *Journal of Educational Measurement, 50*(1), 1–73. doi: 10.1111/jedm.12000

Keesler, V. A., & Howe, C. (2012). *Understanding educator evaluations in Michigan: Results from year 1 of implementation.* Lansing, MI: Michigan Department of Education.

Lacireno-Paquet, N., Morgan, C., & Mello, D. (2014). How states use student learning objectives in teacher evaluation systems: A review of state websites (REL 2014–013). Washington, DC: U.S. Department of Education, Institute of Education Sciences, National Center for Education Evaluation and Regional Assistance, Regional Educational Laboratory Northeast & Islands. Retrieved from http://ies.ed.gov/ncee/edlabs.

Lehman, P. (2014). How are we doing? In T. S. Brophy, M.-L. Lai, & H.-F. Chen (Eds.), *Music assessment and global diversity: Practice, measurement, and policy* (pp. 3–17). Chicago, IL: GIA Publications.

McCaffrey, D., Sass, T., & Lockwood, J. (2009). The intertemporal stability of teacher effect estimates. *Education Finance and Policy, 4,* 572–606. doi: 10.1162/edfp.2009.4.4.572

Milanowski, A. (2016). *Lower practice ratings for teachers of disadvantaged students: Bias or reflection of reality? (Or just murky waters?).* Paper presented at the 41st Annual Conference of the Association for Education Finance and Policy, Denver, CO.

Morgan, C., & Lacireno-Paquet, N. (2013). *Overview of student learning objectives (SLO): Review of the literature.* Waltham, MA: Northeast Educator Effectiveness Research Alliance, Regional Education Laboratory (REL Northeast and Islands).

Music Subject Matter Advisory Panel. (2010). Music teacher preparation in California: Standards of quality and effectiveness for subject matter programs (pp. 1–45). Sacramento, CA: California Commission on Teacher Credentialing.

National Association for Music Education. (2013). *Workbook for building and evaluating effective music education in the school ensemble.* Reston, VA: The National Association for Music Education.

National Board for Professional Teaching Standards. (2001). *Music standards for teachers of students ages 3–18+* [Press release]. Retrieved from http://boardcertifiedteachers.org/sites/default/files/ECYA-MUSIC.pdf

Parkes, K. A., Doerksen, P. F., Ritcher, G. K. (2016). A validation process towards measuring dispositions in pre-service music educators. In T. Brophy, J. Marlatt, & G. Richer (Eds.), *Connecting practice, measurement, and evaluation: Selected papers from the 5th International Symposium on Assessment in Music Education* (pp. 315–326). Chicago, IL: GIA Publications.

Pennington, K. (2014, May 7). *ESEA waivers and teacher-evaluation plans: State oversight of district-designed teacher-evaluation systems.* Retrieved from: https://www.americanprogress.org/issues/education-k-12/reports/2014/05/07/89121/esea-waivers-and-teacher-evaluation-plans/

Pratt, T. (2014). *Making every observation meaningful: Addressing lack of variation in teacher evaluation ratings* (Office of Research and Policy Brief). Nashville: Tennessee Department of Education.

Richerme, L. (2013). *Private survey of state music educators associations.* (Unpublished results).

Sanders, W. L., & Rivers, J. C. (1996). Cumulative and residual effects of teachers on future student academic achievement (pp. 1–12). Knoxville: University of Tennessee Value-Added Research and Assessment Center.

Sawchuk, S. (2013). Teachers' ratings still high despite new measures. *Education Week, 32*(20), 18–19.

Shuler, S. C., Brophy, T. S., Sabol, F. R., Mcgreevy-Nichols, S, & Schuttler, M. (2016). Arts assessment in an age of accountability. In H. Braun (Ed.), *Meeting the challenges of measurement in an era of accountability* (pp. 183–216). National Council for Measurement in Education Applications of Educational Measurement and Assessment Series. New York, NY: Routledge.

Shulman, L. S. (1988). A union of insufficiencies: Strategies for teacher assessment in a period of educational reform. *Educational Leadership, 46*(3), 36–41.

Slotnick, W. J., & Smith, M. D. (2004). *Catalyst for change: Pay for performance in Denver final report.* Boston, MA: Community Training and Assistance Center.

Steele, J. L., Hamilton, L. S., & Stecher, B. M. (2010). *Incorporating student performance measures into teacher evaluation systems.* Santa Monica, CA: Rand.

Weisberg, D., Sexton, S., Mulhern, J., & Keeling, D. (2009). The widget effect: Our national failure to acknowledge and act on differences in teacher effectiveness. Brooklyn, NY: The New Teacher Project.

Woods, J., Tocci, C., Joe, J., Holtzman, S., Cantrell, S., & Archer, J. (2014). *Building trust in observations: A blueprint for improving systems to support great teaching* (MET Project Policy and Practice Brief). Retrieved from http://k12education.gatesfoundation.org/wp-content/uploads/2015/12/MET_Observation_Blueprint.pdf/

INDEX

Note: Tables, figures, and boxes are indicated by an italic t, f, and b following the page number. Notes are indicated by n following the page number.